SPECIAL EDITION

# USING Adobe® Photoshop® CS and Illustrator® CS

*Peter Bauer*

800 East 96th Street
Indianapolis, Indiana 46240

# SPECIAL EDITION USING ADOBE PHOTOSHOP CS AND ILLUSTRATOR CS



International Standard Book Number: 0-7897-3041-3

Library of Congress Catalog Card Number: 2003106145

Printed in the United States of America

First Printing: March 2004

07 06 05 04 4 3

## Trademarks



## Warning and Disclaimer



## Bulk Sales

Pearson offers excellent discounts on this book when ordered in quantity for bulk purchases or special sales. For more information, please contact

**U.S. Corporate and Government Sales**
**1-800-382-3419**
**corpsales@pearsontechgroup.com**

For sales outside of the U.S., please contact

**International Sales**
**1-317-428-3341**
**international@pearsontechgroup.com**

**Acquisitions Editor**
Betsy Brown

**Development Editor**
Lorna Gentry

**Managing Editor**
Charlotte Clapp

**Project Editor**
Sheila Schroeder

**Copy Editor**
Bart Reed

**Indexer**
Heather McNeill

**Proofreader**
Jessica McCarty

**Technical Editor**
Doug Nelson
Andrew Shalat

**Publishing Coordinator**
Vanessa Evans

**Multimedia Developer**
Dan Scherf

**Interior Designer**
Anne Jones

**Cover Designer**
Anne Jones

# Contents at a Glance

# CONTENTS

## V Illustrator CS

# ABOUT THE AUTHORS

**Peter Bauer** is the help desk director for the National Association of Photoshop Professionals (NAPP), the largest graphics association of its kind. He is an Adobe Certified Expert in both Adobe Photoshop and Adobe Illustrator. A computer graphics consultant, he writes for PlanetPhotoshop.com and IllustratorWorld.com and is a contributing writer for *Photoshop User* and *Mac Design* magazines. He is also a member of the instructor "Dream Team" for Photoshop World.

Pete is the author of *Special Edition Using Adobe Photoshop 7* (with Jeff Foster), *Special Edition Using Adobe Illustrator 10*, *Sams Teach Yourself Adobe Illustrator 10 in 24 Hours* (with Mordy Golding), *Special Edition Using Adobe Illustrator 9*, and a contributing author for *Photoshop 6 Web Magic*. He has also served as technical editor on a number of computer graphics books. Pete writes software documentation and does software testing for a variety of Photoshop- and Illustrator-related products.

Pete and his wife, Professor Mary Ellen O'Connell of the Ohio State University Moritz College of Law, live in the historic German Village area of Columbus, Ohio.

Contributing author **Richard Romano** is a writer and analyst for TrendWatch Graphic Arts, a division of Reed Business Information, for which he writes market research reports on various aspects of the graphic arts, printing, and publishing industries. He is also a writer and editor for TrendWatch Inc., an independent company created by the original founders of TrendWatch Graphic Arts that surveys the visual effects and broadcast/television markets. In 2001, he helped launch, and was executive editor of, *CrossMedia* magazine, a periodical that covers issues of interest to creative professionals producing content for print, Web, wireless, and other media.

Romano is the co-editor, with his father Frank Romano, of *The GATF Encyclopedia of Graphic Communications*, a compendium of more than 10,000 graphic arts terms published in 1997 by the Graphic Arts Technical Foundation. As if that weren't enough, he is also the author of several books on graphics hardware and software, including *Sams Teach Yourself Adobe InDesign 1.5 in 24 Hours*, published by Sams Publishing, and *The Scanning Workshop*, published by Que Publishing. Richard was a contributor to *Special Edition Using Photoshop 7*, also published by Que. He also does free-lance graphic design and editorial work. A former resident of such disparate places as New York, Los Angeles, and Salem, New Hampshire, he now lives in Saratoga Springs, New York.

Contributing author **Daniel Giordan** is an artist and designer who works as the design director for AOL Web Properties, coordinating the publishing designs for online properties such as Netscape, CompuServe, Mapquest, AIM, ICQ, and others. In addition to this book, he has authored four other books on Photoshop, including *The Art of Photoshop*, *How to Use Photoshop CS*, *Using Photoshop*, and *Dynamic Photoshop*. He has written other books addressing subjects such as Dreamweaver, Kai's PowerTools, and general design subjects. Dan also writes a monthly column for *Photoshop User* magazine.

With a master's degree in fine arts, Dan paints and works with photography while indulging an excessive interest in capturing every moment of his son's life on film.

## Dedication

*For my parents, Gloria Mencotti Bauer, from whom I get my love for puzzles (including Photoshop), and the late Herbert J. Bauer, from whom I received my aptitude for solving those puzzles.*

# ACKNOWLEDGMENTS

First, I'd like to thank the contributing authors on this project. They provided their incredible expertise in order to ensure that you, the reader, get the highest quality coverage of the programs of the Adobe Creative Suite. Richard Romano and Dan Giordan are top-notch professionals and deserve a round of applause.

Also near the top of my acknowledgement list must certainly be the entire team at Que. Acquisitions editor Betsy Brown rode herd on the project with an unmatched professionalism. During a difficult period in the middle of the project, following the death of my father and a serious illness of my own, she showed the concern and understanding of a much-honored colleague. And, when necessary, she showed she can crack the whip with the best of 'em, too! Development editor Lorna Gentry worked tirelessly to ensure that every line of the book is not only error-free, but clear as a bell. ("When in doubt, add another figure!") Bart Reed not only worked diligently to exterminate typos, he provided another excellent eye on content. The entire group performed efficiently and diligently to ensure that the product is the best possible, and that it was available to you as expeditiously as possible.

Next, let me acknowledge the fine professionals at Adobe who produced the Creative Suite, as well as my colleagues who shared their expertise and knowledge during the production of these excellent programs. I'd also like to thank those individuals and companies that supplied the "goodies" you'll find on the CD: Stephanie Robey of PhotoSpin, the gang at nik multimedia, and Takashi Hayashi of CValley. (Many of the images used in the illustrations of this book are from PhotoSpin, too.)

A special thanks to those incredibly caring and generous folks at the National Association of Photoshop Professionals (NAPP). Scott and Kalebra Kelby, Jim Workman and Jean Kendra, Jeff Kelby, Dave Moser, Felix Nelson, Chris Main, and the whole gang are such wonderful people that I feel truly honored to call them colleagues. And I owe a huge debt to the membership of NAPP—if it weren't for their often-esoteric questions to the Help Desk, I doubt I'd know half of what I do about Photoshop and Illustrator.

I'd also like to take a brief moment to expand on the dedication of this book. I've always been fond of solving puzzles, a gift I credit to my mother. And from the beginning, I've looked at learning the intricacies of Photoshop, Illustrator, and the other programs and products with which I work as just that—puzzles. How does *this* do *that*? What can I do if I try *these* settings, followed by *those* settings? Why does this feature have *this* effect here, yet has *that* effect there? The methodical manner in which I generally approach such puzzles is likely the result of being the son of a German engineer. My father, the late Herb Bauer, had a rather amazing career. As a human factors engineer, he helped design tanks and automobiles. (Think of him when the seatbelt warning reminds you to buckle up.) As a psychology professor, he taught the first college classes ever offered for credit over television. Yet, I'll remember him most for his love for his wife and his children.

And, as always, I owe a tremendous debt to my own lovely wife, Professor Mary Ellen O'Connell, for her patience, understanding, support, and continued love during the preparation of this book.

# WE WANT TO HEAR FROM YOU!

As the reader of this book, *you* are our most important critic and commentator. We value your opinion and want to know what we're doing right, what we could do better, what areas you'd like to see us publish in, and any other words of wisdom you're willing to pass our way.

You can email or write me directly to let me know what you did or didn't like about this book—as well as what we can do to make our books stronger.

*Please note that I cannot help you with technical problems related to the topic of this book, and that due to the high volume of mail I receive, I might not be able to reply to every message.*

When you write, please be sure to include this book's title and author as well as your name and phone or email address. I will carefully review your comments and share them with the author and editors who worked on the book.

**Email:** feedback@quepublishing.com
**Mail:** Mark Taber
Associate Publisher
Que Publishing
800 East 96th Street
Indianapolis, IN 46240 USA

# READER SERVICES

For more information about this book or others from Que Publishing, visit our Web site at www.quepublishing.com. Type the ISBN (excluding hyphens) or the title of the book in the Search box to find the book you're looking for.

# INTRODUCTION

## WHO SHOULD READ THIS BOOK?

You didn't upgrade to Adobe Photoshop CS, you upgraded to the Adobe Creative Suite. You took advantage of the tremendous discount offered by Adobe and increased the power of your creative arsenal. You're good at what you do and you know the tools with which you've worked. But now you've got a whole new set of tools…

You've got the programs, and you want to know how to use them to meet your creative and productive needs. Photoshop CS, Illustrator CS, InDesign CS, GoLive CS—it's quite a lot of complex power. Perhaps you won't use all the programs regularly, but when you need them, there they are. And you need to know what to do with them. Few people are masters of all four programs. (In fact, this book is a collaboration among subject matter experts.) If you're not one of those few, this book is for you.

Perhaps your background is in Web design with GoLive, or vector art with Illustrator, or perhaps you're a page layout pro who has worked with InDesign since version 1, and now you've moved to the Adobe Creative Suite and you're going to learn Photoshop, too. Indeed, this book is for you, too. But in all honesty, if you're brand new to Photoshop, start with *Sams Teach Yourself Adobe Photoshop CS in 24 Hours*, by the incredible Carla Rose, and then immerse yourself in the full Creative Suite with this book.

# WHY YOU SHOULD USE THE ADOBE CREATIVE SUITE

The Adobe Creative Suite comes in two versions. The Premium Edition combines Photoshop CS, Illustrator CS, InDesign CS, GoLive CS, Adobe Acrobat 6.0 Professional, and the new Version Cue project management software. The Standard Edition includes Photoshop, Illustrator, InDesign, and Version Cue. With the exception of Version Cue, the Creative Suite programs are also available individually. Whether you own a pair of the programs or all six, you've got a lot of creative and productive power on your hard drive.

## Design and Create, Productively

Adobe Photoshop, the legendary image-editing program, becomes increasingly versatile in the Creative Suite. The long-awaited type-on-a-path capability, 16-bit editing with layers and type, a vastly improved File Browser and integrated Camera Raw plug-in, several new image-adjustment commands, and customizable keyboard shortcuts are just a few of the improvements. Photoshop's sidekick ImageReady adds a new dimension to your work with its new Flash (SWF) export capability.

Illustrator CS adds a number of features that can certainly improve your productivity. The new type engine features character and paragraph styles, enabling you to format text in a single click. Starting projects has never been easier—over 200 professionally designed templates are included (and, of course, you can save custom templates, too). Although you may not use them often, the new 3D Effect and Scribble effects/filters offer some interesting design possibilities.

InDesign CS brings to the Creative Suite a new Story Editor, a built-in word processor for text across multiple frames, and a Stroke Style Editor for customizing lines and paragraph rules. New palettes include Flattener Preview, Separation Preview, Control, and Info. In addition to these productivity enhancements, you'll also find that InDesign now supports EPS and PDF transparency better, Photoshop duotones, direct export of PDF, and mixed inks.

GoLive gets better and better at working with interactive media and advanced coding languages. Improvements include better XHTML support, QuickTime and RealOne Player authoring, new PDF capabilities, and more. The workspace gets better, too. The Toolbar can emulate Photoshop or appear in a more GoLive-native style. The new CSS Editor shows you the effects of your changes as you make them. The Source Code Editor is far more flexible, and GoLive now supports design templates (several dozen of which are supplied with the program).

## Even Greater Integration

The Smart Objects technology enables you to place Photoshop's PSD file format, Illustrator's AI files, and PDFs directly into InDesign and GoLive projects, edit those files in their own programs with a simple button click, and automatically update the graphics as necessary. InDesign now supports Photoshop duotones (and tritons and quadtones), too. However, the Smart Objects technology is just the tip of the iceberg. Integration among the CS programs enables you to maintain consistency throughout a project, from print to Web and then back again. Here are some of the other integration features that make the Creative Suite truly "sweet":

- Swap files back and forth between Photoshop and Illustrator, even those including type on a path.
- Package your InDesign layouts for GoLive, automatically creating Web-ready elements from your print-ready layout.
- Export GoLive Web sites to PDF, with all links, bookmarks, and graphics intact.
- Manage projects throughout the creative process with Version Cue, whether as a single user or as part of a workgroup.
- Take advantage of layered PDF files, in effect giving you multipage PDF support right in Photoshop and Illustrator.
- Take advantage of Suite-wide color management. Use the same settings in all the programs and be assured of consistent color throughout.
- Rely on enhanced across-the-board support for XMP metadata to provide information about virtually every file with which you work.

All this integration among products comes with an interface that feels comfortable and familiar as you move from program to program. What's more, the interface is customizable in ways that can greatly improve your productivity, including design-them-yourself keyboard shortcuts that help you maintain consistent work habits in Photoshop, InDesign, Illustrator, and GoLive.

### ...and Digital Video Support!

Although the Creative Suite itself doesn't include digital video (DV) editing, you'll find that DV is well supported, nonetheless. Photoshop offers native support for nonsquare pixels, including new document presets. Illustrator continues to support NTSC color, and GoLive has improved handling of both QuickTime and RealOne Player media.

## WINDOWS AND MACINTOSH

The Adobe Creative Suite runs on only three operating systems: Windows XP, Windows 2000, and Mac OS X. The capabilities of the Creative Suite and the individual programs are almost identical on all three operating systems.

In this book, we address both platforms. Because the modifier keys on the keyboard differ between Windows and Macintosh, we've used the following system of key identification:

- **(Command) [Ctrl]**—This identifies the Mac Command key and the Windows Ctrl key. The modifier key does nothing on its own and is always used in conjunction with another key and/or another modifier key.
- **(Option) [Alt]**—The Option key on Mac and the Alt key on Windows are also modifier keys that are used in conjunction with other keys.

- **(Control)-click, right-click**—Although Mac OS X supports multibutton mice and right-clicking, the tradition (Control)-click is still listed, indicating the user holds down the Mac's Control key and clicks the mouse button (the left button on multibutton mice). Windows users click the right-side mouse button.

You may see a couple modifier keys used with another key. For example, when we're discussing the default keyboard shortcut used for copying to a new layer in Photoshop, you will see this convention used:

(Command-Shift-J) [Ctrl+Shift+J]

# HOW THIS BOOK IS ORGANIZED

*Special Edition Using Adobe Photoshop CS* has five distinct parts, plus a color insert that shows key images in full color, and a CD containing some extra "goodies."

## Part I: Creative Suite Common Concepts

As tightly integrated as the Adobe Creative Suite is, many core technologies and basic concepts are used throughout it. Part I discusses and examines subjects such as Version Cue, file formats, color theory and color management, automation with Actions and scripting, the difference between raster and vector artwork, and how to select and set up your hardware.

## Part II: Fundamental Photoshop CS

Photoshop remains the focus of the Adobe Creative Suite for many users. The chapters in Part II examine, from both a technical and a practical point of view, the basic creative and productive power of Photoshop. From bringing images into Photoshop, to enhancing them with filters and styles, to working with Photoshop's vector capabilities (both shape layers and type), these chapters give you a solid foundation from which to master Photoshop. If you're new to Photoshop, purchasing the Creative Suite from an Illustrator, GoLive, or InDesign background, you'll find that you need a little background before you can swim with the Photoshop sharks. Again, let me recommend that you start with *Sams Teach Yourself Adobe Photoshop CS in 24 Hours* before you dive into this section of the book.

## Part III: Power Photoshop

Just as Part II addresses the basic skills needed to function competently in Photoshop, so does Part III address the advanced skills. With an eye toward the technical explanation of "how it works" so that you can apply the concepts to your own projects, these chapters take you a step further. Channels, color correction, the theory behind each of the blending modes, Photoshop's filters, and preparing an image for print are all topics discussed.

## Part IV: ImageReady

A powerful tool in its own right, ImageReady creates graphics for the Web—and not just graphics, but *graphics*! You can create rollovers, animations, and even export to Flash (SWF) format—all without losing sight of the GIF and JPEG files that make up the bulk of your Web graphics. The chapters in Part IV help you create lean graphics that do the job with the fastest possible downloads—whether they're static images or animations.

## Part V: Illustrator CS

Fifteen chapters look at every aspect of Illustrator, from the basics through the advanced features. This section of the book is written from an Illustrator perspective, providing the information necessary to work with Illustrator and what you need to know to integrate Illustrator into the Adobe Creative Suite.

# CREATIVE SUITE COMMON CONCEPTS

## IN THIS PART

# THE ADOBE CREATIVE SUITE WITH VERSION CUE

## IN THIS CHAPTER

The Adobe Creative Suite is more than just a package of related programs packed into a single box. Rather, it is a natural extension of the component programs' interoperability. Photoshop CS, Illustrator CS, InDesign CS, GoLive CS, and Adobe Acrobat 6 are all available as individual products but achieve new heights when purchased as the Adobe Creative Suite. Certainly the most significant difference between purchasing the Adobe Creative Suite and the individual programs is Version Cue—a file-management and version-tracking program that is not available as a standalone product.

In this chapter, we'll take a look at the thinking behind the Adobe Creative Suite, how the component programs work together, and the powerful new Version Cue program. We'll also take a look at some of the significant new features in each of the component programs of the Adobe Creative Suite.

# THE SUITE CONCEPT

Take world-class creative and productive software and make sure everything works together flawlessly. Not a bad idea, is it? Adobe has gone a step further—not only do the programs work together, they are largely based on a core technology—the Portable Document Format (PDF). PDF is most easily identified with Adobe Acrobat. However, Acrobat itself is not a content generator. The documents from which you create PDFs have to start somewhere, and that "somewhere" is now the Adobe Creative Suite.

## Creative Suite Versus Component Programs

Purchasing the Adobe Creative Suite rather than the individual programs has a number of advantages. In addition to saving money, you work with a single serial number. In fact, the Adobe Creative Suite is technically a single product. (Adobe will offer future versions of the Creative Suite as a single-product upgrade, although registered pre-CS software will still qualify for single-product upgrades in future releases.)

The most important difference between purchasing the Adobe Creative Suite and the individual component programs is, of course, Version Cue. The file management and coordination component of the Adobe Creative Suite is not available as a standalone product or as a separate purchase. It comes only as part of the Creative Suite (Premium or Standard Edition).

Another difference is the program documentation. Although the Creative Suite includes online Help and PDF versions of program manuals, the printed manuals are a separate purchase through the Adobe Store. When purchased individually, each component program comes with its printed manual.

## Installing, Registering, and Activating

Installation of the Adobe Creative Suite couldn't be easier! It is, in fact, a one-step installation process. The Creative Suite is installed as a single product, with a single serial number and a single installer. When you use the default installation option, Easy Install, the entire Creative Suite is installed into the location you select. When you opt for Custom Install, you can install the component programs individually (see Figure 1.1).

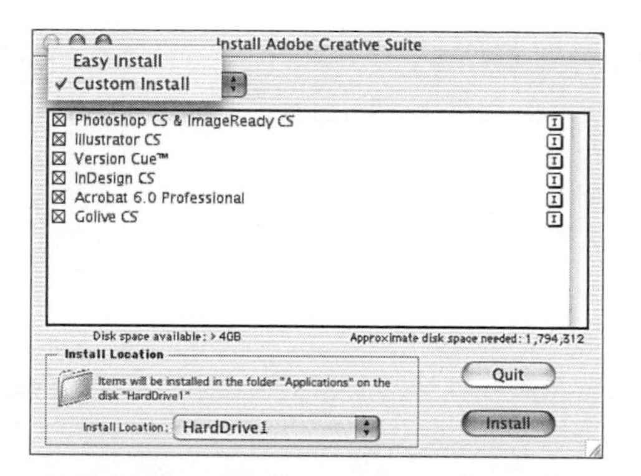


**Figure 1.1**
You cannot install individual parts of each program, just the programs in their entirety.



The Custom Install option does not give you control over part of the component programs. You cannot, for example, reinstall just Photoshop's EPS & PDF parsing module to alleviate a problem opening EPS files. However, a full Photoshop reinstall would certainly replace a damaged element of a component program.

> Because reinstalling involves replacing an entire program and all its files, it's even more important to make sure you save custom and third-party actions, styles, swatches, and other bits in a folder *outside* the program folder. Otherwise, you risk losing them when a problem occurs.

## Registering the Adobe Creative Suite

At the end of the installation process, you'll have the option of registering by any of a variety of methods or to skip the registration process (see Figure 1.2).

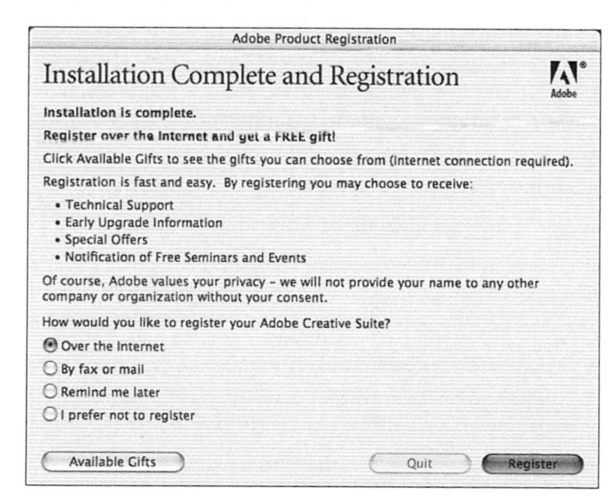


**Figure 1.2**
Registration is required for Adobe technical support. In addition, Adobe encourages registration by offering "gifts" such as stock art, free issues of *Step* magazine, an OpenType Pro font, or a code to unlock additional videos on the Total Training disc that ships with the Creative Suite.

For the easiest, most pain-free registration, make sure you can access your Internet connection before beginning the installation procedure. After installation, simply click the Register button and you'll be taken to the appropriate page of the Adobe Web site. You must register via the Internet to qualify for any of the available free gifts.

1

## Activation (Windows Only)

When using the Adobe Creative Suite (or the standalone version of Photoshop CS), Windows users must complete an activation process. Activation, designed to reduce incidents of piracy and stolen software, is separate from and in addition to registration. There are three ways to activate: Internet, interactive voice-response telephone call, and a telephone call to Adobe Customer Service.

> If, for some reason, you need to change computers more often than every six months, contact the Adobe Store for information on maintaining activation for the Creative Suite.

The Adobe Creative Suite will run for 30 days without activation (reminding you to activate each and every one of those days that you use it). Then it will stop working until activated. Once you have activated the Creative Suite, it remains activated, even through reinstallation.

Under the terms of the Adobe licensing agreement, a single user can install the Creative Suite on two computers, although only one of them can be running the programs of the Creative Suite at any given time. (The license agreement is designed to facilitate use of the programs on, for example, an office computer and a laptop or home computer.) If licensed for multiple users, the license will state the "permitted number" of users.

The activation mechanism is capable of identifying the difference between a reinstallation and installation on an additional computer. Minor hardware changes won't trigger an activation problem, but upgrading a motherboard and/or replacing the hard drive upon which you've installed the Creative Suite may. Moving the hard drive from one computer to another may also cause an activation problem. However, Adobe is rather liberal in such matters (when compared to other software companies that require activation of their products). You can change hardware every six months and reactivate without a problem.

# Interoperability Among the Component Programs

The great interoperability among Adobe products gets even better with the Adobe Creative Suite. In addition to smart objects, you now have coordinated color management, type engines that work together, and OpenType capabilities across the Creative Suite.

Adobe's smart objects technology enables you to place Photoshop and Illustrator files—in their native formats—into InDesign and GoLive documents. The page layouts and Web layouts use a merged-layer composite for display and output, while leaving the original image intact. You can also simply double-click the PSD or AI file in the layout to launch the originating program and edit the image. The placed image is then automatically updated.

Color management is improved in the Creative Suite with Adobe's common color architecture. Use the same settings in each program and get consistent color, all day, every day, regardless of which component program you're using.

*For more on color management in the Adobe Creative Suite, see Chapter 6, "Color Management in the Adobe Creative Suite," p. 189.*

PDF helps unify the latest releases of InDesign, Illustrator, and Photoshop. All three programs can output PDF files that can then be optimized, output, or repurposed in Acrobat 6 Professional Edition. GoLive can import InDesign layouts and export HTML-based pages as PDF, with links and bookmarks intact. However, the PDF print workflow is certainly facilitated with the Creative Suite. Adobe Acrobat 6 now includes preflighting capabilities that ensure your compact PDF is complete—a single file for delivery. Layered PDF files also enable designers to maintain a greater level of editability of PDF files.

You'll also see advances in the way type is handled in the primary programs of the Creative Suite. Illustrator now supports character and paragraph styles, similar to those found in InDesign. Illustrator also now offers a font menu that can, if you desire, show you the font name in the font itself. Perhaps just as welcome is Photoshop's new "type on a path" capability.

When you install the Adobe Creative Suite or component programs, fonts are added to your hard drive. In fact, installing the full Adobe Creative Suite Premium Edition installs OpenType fonts that would cost hundreds of dollars if purchased separately.



The programs of the Adobe Creative Suite are also capable of working with metadata through enhanced support for Extensible Metadata Platform (XMP), which captures and preserves metadata throughout the workflow. Also, File Info is quite a powerful beast now (see Figure 1.3).

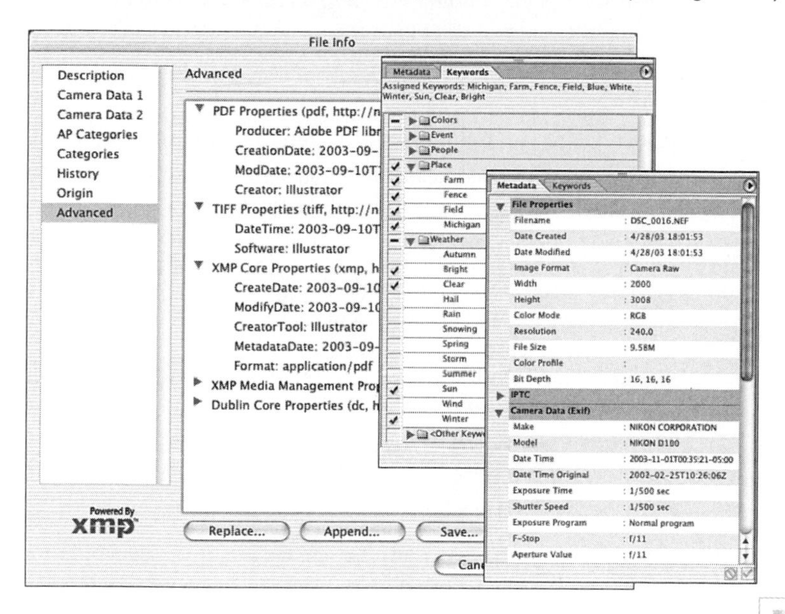


Figure 1.3
The File Info dialog box (behind) contains a great deal more information than before. On the right, you can see a few of the entries that Photoshop's File Browser can use.

# AN INTRODUCTION TO VERSION CUE

Version Cue is a file management and version-tracking program that's not only great for workgroups, it's also an excellent resource for one-person operations. Whether you're part of a team that's sharing the load on a project (or projects) or are going solo on a creative or production job, Version Cue can be a great aid in tracking your work.

Only one computer in a workgroup needs to have Version Cue installed. All others using component programs of the Adobe Creative Suite will be able to take advantage of the technology, whether they have the full Creative Suite installed or have just updated a single program. However, pre-CS versions of the Adobe programs will not be able to access Version Cue.

Have you ever found yourself in one of these situations?

- You've prepared a number of variations of a single project, and the client tells you which one to use, but can't remember the filename. (Version Cue can work with a file's metadata. You can Save keywords, categories, notes, and comments about a file and then search using Version Cue. The client might, for example, say "It's one of the versions with a blue background, and I think the logo was in red." If you added those words to a description or comment, your search is a breeze—the proper variation can be quickly identified and located.)
- Like you've been trained to do, you've saved early and often...and overwritten a version of the project that you'd desperately like to have back. (With Version Cue, you create a new *version* when you save the file back to the project folder. Meanwhile, the file from which you started remains a separate version, unchanged and intact.)
- You're part of a workgroup and have spent a lot of time perfecting an image, only to find out that someone else was working on another copy of the file at the same time—and the two sets of changes are not compatible. (Versions Cue lets other know that the file is in use by changing its status from Available to In Use.)
- You need to get some work done on a shared project, but someone else has locked the file, preventing you from accessing it. (As long as the Version Cue workspace is available, you can access the files and make new versions.)
- Your workgroup has a tight deadline, and it can be met, but only if two or more people can be doing different things to the project file at the same time. (Version Cue allows multiple copies of a file to be open at the same time, and it guides the users to minimize conflict in their changes.)

Version Cue uses workspaces, projects, and versions to track and manage jobs at various levels (see Figure 1.4).

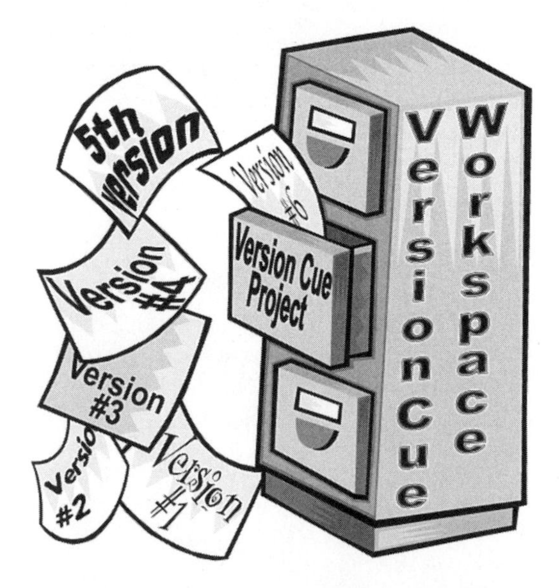


Figure 1.4
The Version Cue workspace can contain a number of different projects. Each project includes multiple files, and each file can exist in a multitude of versions.

Rather than thinking of the Version Cue workspace as a directory or folder on the hard drive, consider it to be a framework within Version Cue through which administration of projects is handled.

# ENABLING VERSION CUE

Once the Adobe Creative Suite is installed, you'll find folders for each component program in the location specified during the install. On Windows, that's the Program Files\Adobe folder by default. The default install location for Macintosh is the Applications folder. Before you can use Version Cue, the Creative Suite programs must be prepared and Version Cue itself must be enabled. Here's how to set up each of the Creative Suite component programs to use Version Cue:

- **Photoshop CS**—Start Photoshop. In Preferences, File Handling, check the box Enable Version Cue Workgroup File Management. Close the Preferences dialog box and quit Photoshop.
- **Illustrator CS**—Start Illustrator. In Preferences, File Handling & Clipboard, check the box Enable Version Cue. (And while you're there, if you'll be using Illustrator with Photoshop, also check the AICB check box in the lower part of the dialog box so that the two programs can transfer artwork smoothly.) Close the Preferences dialog box and quit Illustrator.
- **InDesign**—Start InDesign. In Preferences, File Handling, check the box labeled Enable Version Cue. Close the Preferences dialog box and quit InDesign. (You need to restart this program for Version Cue to be enabled.)
- **GoLive**—Version Cue is enabled by default in GoLive.
- **Adobe Acrobat 6.0**—Acrobat 6.0 does not use Version Cue.

In a workgroup environment, you'll also need to set up the Prefs for all other copies of Photoshop, Illustrator, and InDesign that will be working with Version Cue.

Version Cue is not started like a normal program. Rather, you use the Windows Control Panel or the Macintosh System Preferences for Version Cue. (Version Cue is added to the Control Panel or the System Preferences during installation.)

Version Cue doesn't start by default (until you set that option). Rather, you use the Control Panel (Windows) or the System Preferences (Mac) to enable Version Cue. The first time you run Version Cue, immediately after it starts, click the Advanced Administration button, which will launch your default Web browser, allowing you to configure Version Cue (see Figure 1.5).

The very next step should be changing the System Administrator password. In the Web browser window, you can change the username as well as the password (see Figure 1.6). However, note that the login remains "system," regardless of what you enter in place of System

> In addition to the programs of the Creative Suite, Adobe InCopy is Version Cue capable.

> Remember that all copies of the CS programs can work with Version Cue, regardless of whether they were purchased as part of the Adobe Creative Suite or individually. Only one computer actually needs to have Version Cue installed and running, but the other computers must be able to access that computer's Version Cue workspace.

Administrator. Adding a telephone number and an email address enables others using your Version Cue workspace to contact you with problems.

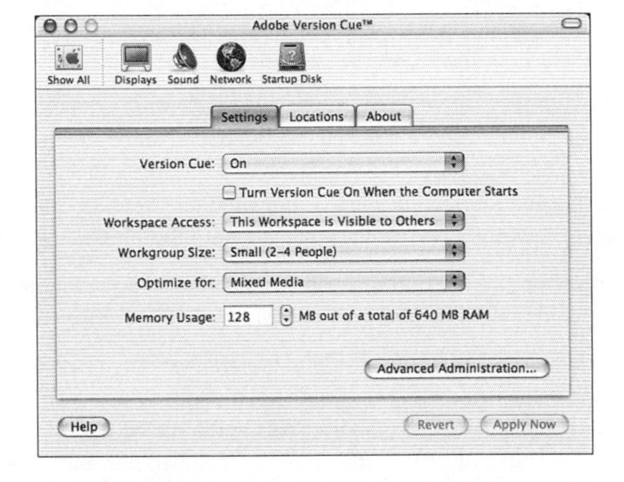


**Figure 1.5**
The Advanced Administration button remains grayed out until you start Version Cue. Your Web browser will launch to proceed.

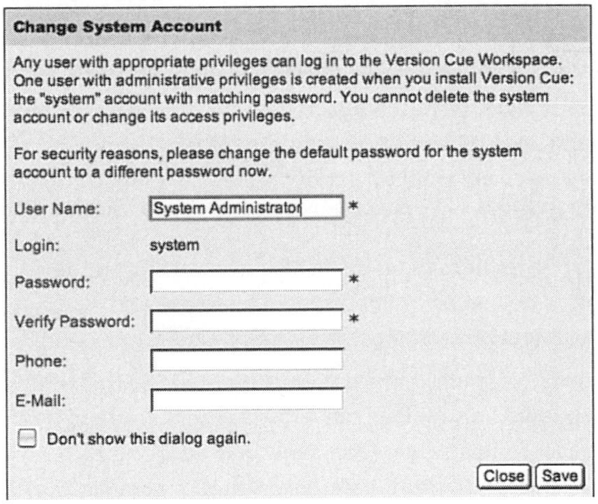

**Figure 1.6**
If you'll be the only one using Version Cue, you may find it unnecessary to access the Advanced Administration options right away.

Change System Account

Any user with appropriate privileges can log in to the Version Cue Workspace. One user with administrative privileges is created when you install Version Cue: the "system" account with matching password. You cannot delete the system account or change its access privileges.

For security reasons, please change the default password for the system account to a different password now.

User Name: System Administrator *
Login: system
Password: *
Verify Password: *
Phone:
E-Mail:
Don't show this dialog again.
Close Save

After changing the System Administrator password, you can continue with the advanced administration setup of Version Cue. Once you've logged in as the System Administrator, you'll be able to create new users for your workspace, edit existing users, start new projects, and more (see Figure 1.7).

*Having trouble logging in to Version Cue's Workspace Administration after changing the password? See "New Password, Same Login" in the "Mastering the Adobe Creative Suite" section at the end of this chapter.*

Suppressing pop-up windows may suppress the Version Cue window used to change the default system username and password on first startup. If you don't see the pop-up window, log in to Version Cue Workspace Administration using "system" as both the username and the password.

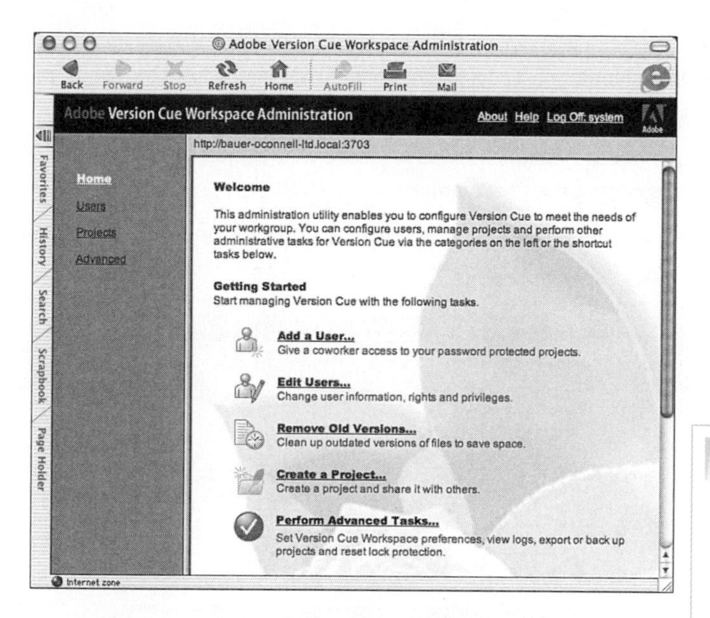


Figure 1.7
Upon starting Version Cue for the first time, you'll likely need only establish a user (or users) and perhaps create a new project.



## Version Cue at Work: Setting Up Users

As the System Administrator, you have access to all projects in your workspace. However, you'll probably want to set up an additional identity through which you actually *work* on the projects. To create a user identity for yourself or for another user, you need to access the Advanced Administration control for the Version Cue workspace and follow these steps:

1. In the Control Panel (Windows) or System Preferences (Mac), click Adobe Version Cue.
2. In the Settings panel, click Advanced Administration.
3. Once your Web browser launches, log in as the System Administrator (using the login "system" and your password) and then click Add a User.
4. Determine what level of *privileges* the new user will have (see Figure 1.8), as detailed in the following list (these options can be changed later by the administrator):
   - **None**—This privilege is not nearly as restrictive as it sounds—the user can open, edit, and save files within projects; however, the user cannot access the Version Cue administration utility.
   - **User**—This privilege enables the individual to not only work on projects, but also to access reports on

> Adobe recommends that the Version Cue workspace be restarted once per week. (There's no need to restart the computer, just the workspace.) Version Cue is also self-repairing under most circumstances. It examines its data regularly and notifies you when it finds a problem. You'll have the option to attempt recovery (which, generally, you should indeed attempt). If Version Cue can't repair the problem, elect to export your projects, reinstall Version Cue, and then import the projects again.

> Anyone who has access to the Version Cue workspace (via your subnetwork or the IP or DNS address) can work on projects with his or her Creative Suite programs. A login will automatically be created, without a password, when the individual first accesses a project. The System Administrator can restrict access to projects or restrict the projects to which a specific user has access.

projects and review information about projects to which the user is not assigned. (User-level privileges can also be expanded on a project-by-project basis to include basic administrator authority to back up, export, and delete projects.)

- **Project Creator**—This privilege enables a user to create new projects and to export, delete, back up, and otherwise control the user's projects.
- **System Administrator**—This privilege includes the power to create and administer user IDs, as well as to restore and delete project backups and workspace data.

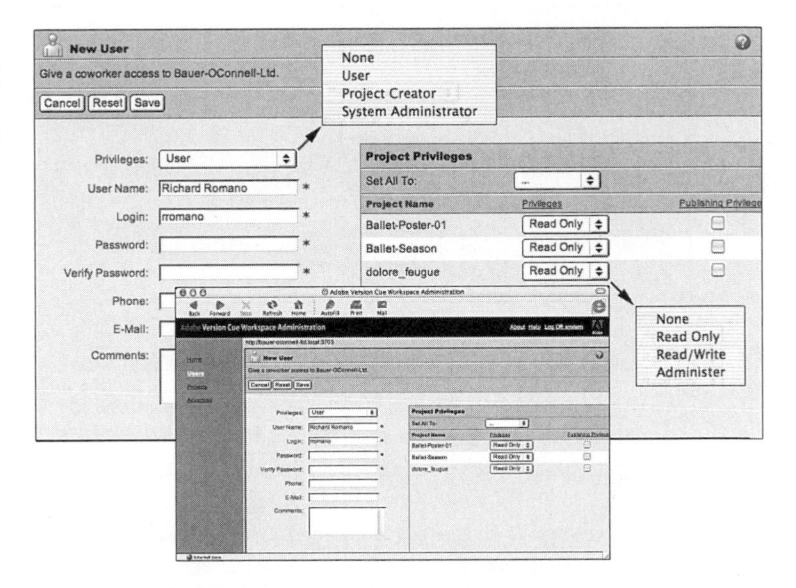


**Figure 1.8**
The two pop-up menus are shown separately. In the foreground, at the bottom, is a view of the entire browser window.

5. Fill in the User Name, Login, and Password fields. (The user will be able to change the password later.) Note that the username and the login are distinct and need not be the same. Consider, for example, the difference between *Pete Bauer* as a username, which appears in comment fields and version info, and *peterbauer*, which is used only to gain access to the Version Cue workspace. You can also add such information as email address and telephone number, although those fields can remain empty.

6. To the right of the window, you assign the user's privileges for each existing project. In Figure 1.8, the new user will have Project Creator as the overall level of privileges and will be an Administrator for two existing projects, but will have only Read/Write authorization for a third project.

   When the Privileges pop-up menu to the left is set to None, the pop-up menus for specific projects offer the choice of None, Read Only, and Read/Write. When User or Project Creator is selected to the left, the pop-up menus on the right also offer Administrator for each project. When the user is created as a System Administrator, on the right you'll see Administrator for each of the existing projects.

> It's a good idea to have a second user with System Administrator privileges, to prepare for vacation, illness, or an accident. However, having *every* user as a System Administrator defeats the purpose of Version Cue.

7. To the right in the window is a check box for each project. The Publish Privileges check box, when selected, authorizes the user to publish the project to an FTP or WebDAV server.
8. After you've established the parameters for the new user, click the Save button. The user will be added to the workspace's list, which will be displayed in the browser window (see Figure 1.9).

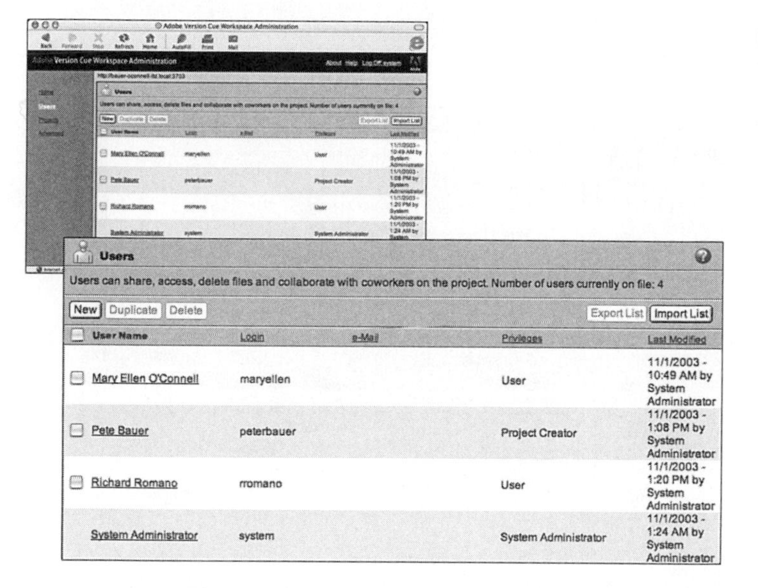


**Figure 1.9**
The full window is shown in the background. In the foreground, you can see what information is displayed for each user.

## Creating Projects as the System Administrator

A new project can be created by the System Administrator using the Version Cue Advanced Administration feature in the Control Panel (Windows) or the System Preferences (Mac). Projects can also be created "on the fly" as you work. With Version Cue enabled and running, you can create projects right from the Save As, Open, or Place dialog box in Photoshop, Illustrator, and InDesign, or through GoLive's New Site command. (Creating projects as you work is discussed in the following section.)

As System Administrator, you add new projects to the workspace through the Version Cue panel of the Control Panel (Windows) or the System Preferences (Mac) by clicking the Advanced Administration button (shown earlier in Figure 1.5). After using the login "system" and your password, you simply click Create a Project in the Version Cue Workspace Administration window (shown earlier in Figure 1.7).

You can create a new blank project, use the contents of an existing folder as the basis for a project, or import an existing project from an FTP or WebDAV server (see Figure 1.10).

In the following windows, the choices you make depend on the source of the project. If you're creating a blank project (as shown in Figure 1.11), you'll assign a name, decide whether other users will have access to the project (and, if so, whether they will need to log in first), and whether you want to enable lock protection for the project. (Lock protection prevents multiple users from editing the project at the same time. When a file is open, it will be labeled In Use and unavailable to other users.) You can also add project comments in this window.

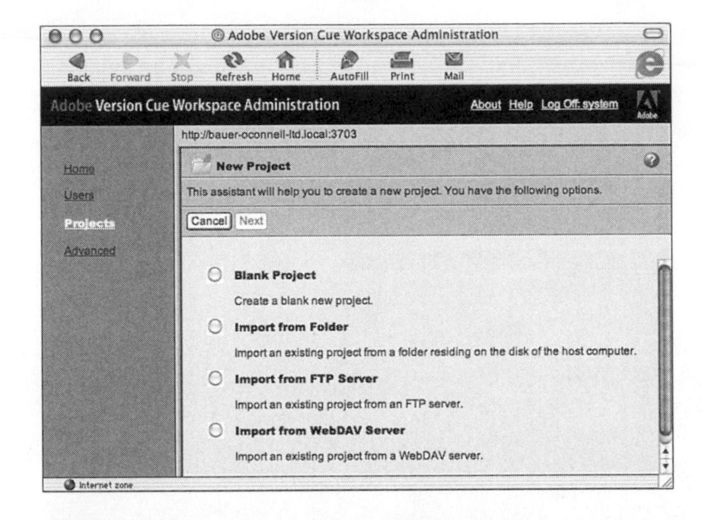


**Figure 1.10**
The lower two options are used to import existing Version Cue projects from workspaces on other computers.

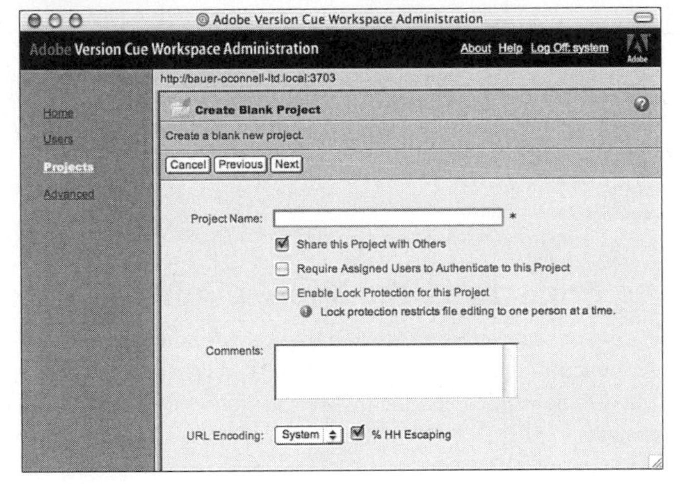


**Figure 1.11**
These basic options appear whether you're creating a blank project or importing an existing project from a folder or server.

When importing a project, you have the options just listed and you also need to identify the source of the project. When importing from a folder, you use the Browse button to locate the folder and then you click one file within that folder. When importing from a server, whether FTP or WebDAV, you need to identify the server and the directory you're importing, choose whether to import the directory as a Web site, and supply a valid username and password for the directory.

In each situation, you'll also see an option to decide how to handle the project's URL. You can choose System or UTF-8, the latter of which is the default encoding for XML and is necessary if non-standard characters are to be used.

The option "% HH Escaping" replaces non-safe characters in a URL with the percent symbol and a two-digit number. In a Web browser's address field you might see the following, for example:

```
http://Applications/Adobe%20Version%20Cue/Help/help.html
```

In this case, the characters `%20` represent a space in a filename.

*Trying to import a folder to create a new Version Cue project but the Open button remains grayed out? Check "Projects from Folders" in the "Mastering the Adobe Creative Suite" section at the end of this chapter.*

Version Cue must be enabled from within the program preferences for Photoshop, Illustrator, and InDesign before the capabilities are available. You must restart InDesign after you enable Version Cue, but Photoshop and Illustrator are set to go as soon as you close the Preferences dialog box.



# ACCESSING VERSION CUE FEATURES IN THE CREATIVE SUITE PROGRAMS

Once Version Cue is up and running, you work with it from within Photoshop, Illustrator, InDesign, and GoLive. (Adobe InCopy, which is not part of the Creative Suite, is also Version Cue capable.) Version Cue capabilities are accessed through the Version Cue button in dialog boxes for Photoshop, Illustrator, and InDesign.

Photoshop provides Version Cue buttons in the Open, Save As, and Save a Version dialog boxes. Illustrator allows access to the Version Cue workspace from the Open, Save, New From Template, Save a Copy, Save As Template, and Place dialog boxes. When you're using InDesign, Version Cue is available in the New Book and New Library dialog boxes (but not New Document), as well as the Save As, Save a Copy, Place, Import XML, Export, and Package Publication for GoLive dialog boxes. An example of the Macintosh version of the button is shown in Figure 1.12.

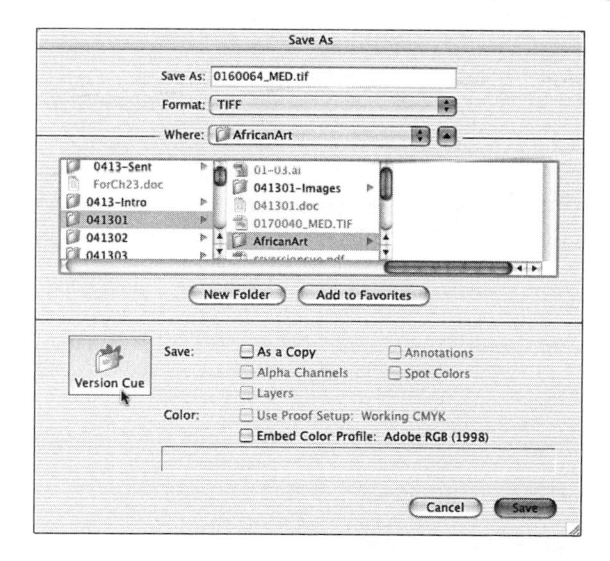


Figure 1.12
**Shown is Photoshop's Save As dialog box. The Version Cue button is visible only when Version Cue is enabled in the program's preferences.**

After you click the Version Cue button, the dialog box is replaced by the Version Cue variation (see Figure 1.13). You'll have access to the Project Tools, from which you can create a new project or work within the current project. (You must have the proper Version Cue privileges to create a new project.)

When you're working on the computer that hosts the Version Cue workspace, or when you're logged in to a project, the available project folder will be shown. Otherwise, use the Project Tools command Connect To in order to contact the Version Cue workspace and access the projects for which you have appropriate privileges.

After you create a new project, the Project Tools menu will include the command Synchronize. Synchronizing the new project with the Version Cue workspace early can avoid coordination and communication problems later.

**Figure 1.13**
The Version Cue Save As dialog box from Photoshop is visible. Note the Local Files button, which returns you to the Photoshop Save As dialog box.

GoLive handles Version Cue in a more integrated manner. When creating a new site, you can choose to create a new Version Cue project or work within an existing project (see Figure 1.14).

When opening files through Version Cue, you have access to an incredible amount of information. In the Open dialog box for Photoshop, Illustrator, or InDesign, click the Version Cue button and then select the server and project from which you'll open a file. In the Documents folder of the project, you'll find the available files, as well as the files' status, size, version number, comments, and more (see Figure 1.15).

A file's status can be any one of the following:

- **Available**—You can open and edit the file.
- **In Use By Me**—You've already opened the file.
- **In Use By Me Elsewhere**—You've opened the file on another computer.
- **In Use By [username]**—Somebody else has opened the file.
- **Offline**—You're no longer connected to the Version Cue workspace.

- **Ready for Download**—The file is available and you can download it to your local hard drive for editing.
- **Ready for Use**—You've downloaded the file to your local hard drive and can open it for editing.

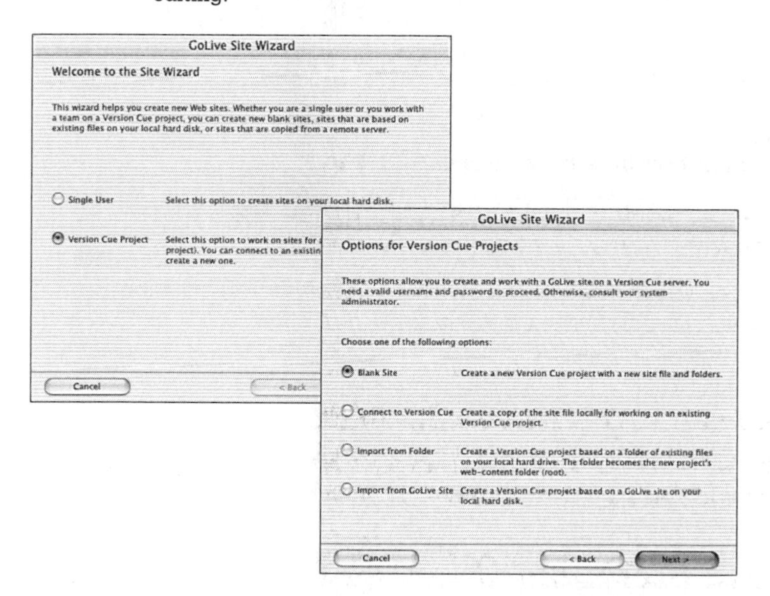


Figure 1.14
After electing to create a Version Cue project, you click Next, select a Version Cue server, and then log in.

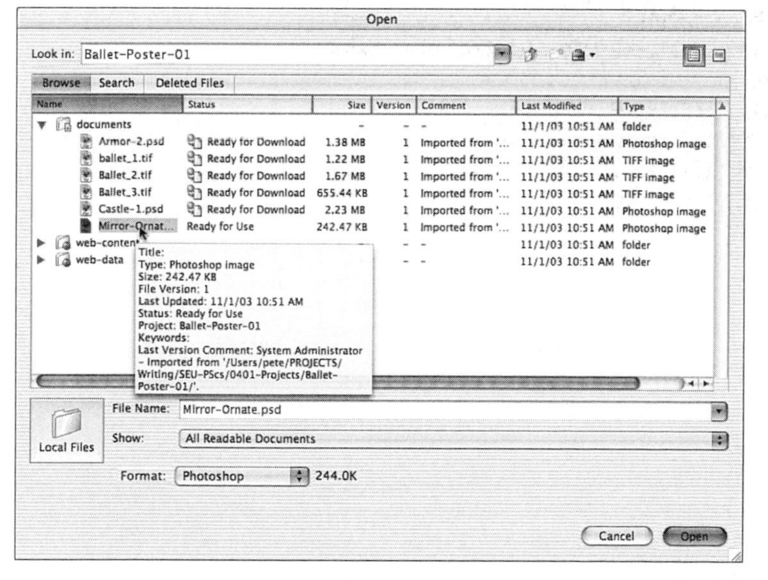


Figure 1.15
The button in the upper-right corner of the dialog box switches to the Thumbnails view. Using thumbnails in conjunction with the ToolTips gives you a look at the image as well as its information.

Also note in Figure 1.15 the Search and Deleted Files buttons to the right of Browse. Search enables you to look into the XMP data saved with a file, including the comments saved with a version (discussed in the next section) to find a specific document or version. Deleted Files shows versions no longer part of the project but not yet eliminated completely. You can use the Restore command from the Project Tools menu to revive any file listed in the Deleted Files tab. Afterward, you can return to the Browse tab and use the Project Tools command Refresh.

> **Caution**
>
> Unlike the operating systems on which it works, Version Cue sees filenames as case sensitive—it recognizes <Logo.eps> and <logo.eps> as two different files. Although this opens the door for a variety of naming schemes when using Save As, it can create conflicts on your hard drive or other media. If you're using Save As to distinguish the document as a separate file, you should alter more than the capitalization of the filename.

## Saving Versions in Version Cue

Version Cue revolves around "versions." You create a file, creating Version 1. Later, you make some changes to graphics in the file and use the command Save a Version, creating Version 2 and leaving Version 1 intact. Someone else opens Version 2 and begins working on the text. You also reopen Version 2 and start making additional changes to the graphics. Your co-worker saves, creating Version 3. You save, creating Version 4. Reconciling Version 3 and Version 4 may consist of opening both versions, copying the text changes from Version 3 to Version 4, and then saving as Version 5.

The key to saving and working with versions in Version Cue is providing adequate information in the version's Comments field. The comments let you and other users know what makes that particular version unique. You enter comments when you use the Save a Version command, and you can review the comments for all available versions with the File, Versions command (see Figure 1.16). Remember, too, that the comments you save with a file are the most effective way of identifying a version when using the Search feature.

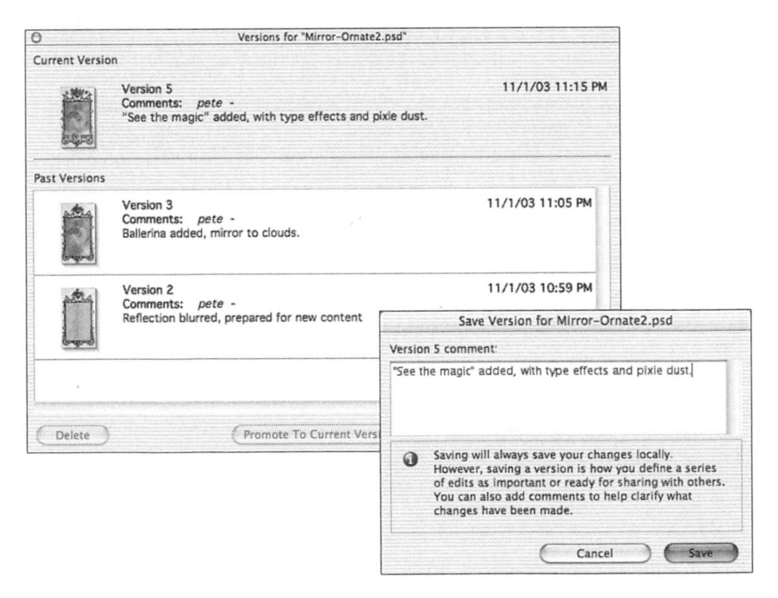


**Figure 1.16**
The comments you enter after selecting the command Save a Version are used to identify the specific file. The Versions dialog box, available when a version of a managed document is open, enables you to reopen (or *promote*) an earlier version and to delete unnecessary versions.

You can also use the Save As command from Photoshop, Illustrator, and InDesign to establish a new file within the project. Just as when you're working with the Save As command outside of Version Cue, a new file is generated from the current state of the document, the new name is applied, and the document you originally opened is closed as it was last saved. With Version Cue, the new document starts as Version 1.



## Working Offline and Synchronizing Versions

What happens if you lose your network connection while working remotely with Version Cue? What do you do if you need to take managed files home or on the road so that you can continue to work on them while you're away from the office? Version Cue lets you *synchronize* your edited files with the workspace, creating new versions as necessary. You can synchronize individual files, folders of files, or entire projects.

If you're preparing to work offline, simply log in to the Version Cue workspace and open the files or projects you need, downloading them to your hard drive, and then close the files. They'll be available to you locally in these folders:

- **Windows**—My Documents\Version Cue\[project name]\Documents
- **Macintosh**—[hard drive]>Users>[username]>Documents>Version Cue> [project name]> documents

If you lose your network connection while working remotely with Version Cue, you'll get a warning message such as the one shown in Figure 1.17.

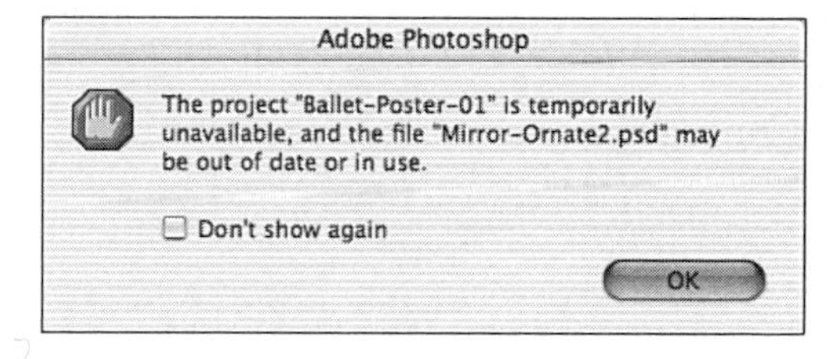


Figure 1.17
If the Version Cue connection breaks, your local version should stIll be safe in My Documents\Version Cue (Windows) or Documents>Version Cue (Mac).

When you're reconnected with the Version Cue workspace, you synchronize the files on your hard drive and those in the workspace's project file through the Open dialog box of Photoshop, Illustrator, or InDesign. Choose File, Open and then click the Version Cue button. Navigate to and select the project folder. If you want to synchronize the entire project, select Synchronize from the Project Tools menu (see Figure 1.18). If you need to synchronize only a folder or a file, open the project, navigate to the proper element, select it, and then choose the Synchronize command from Project Tools.

> You can locate a Version Cue file on your hard drive by using the Open command, clicking the Version Cue button, and selecting the file and using the Project Tools command Show in Finder (Mac) or Show in Explorer (Windows).

If a newer version of a file exists in the workspace, you'll see the File Conflict dialog box, which offers two choices. To save your work to the project folder, choose Save a Version. To retain the version already in the folder as the latest version, select Skip This File.

*Having trouble getting your Macs to talk to each other through Version Cue? See "Opening a Version Cue Connection" in the "Mastering the Adobe Creative Suite" section at the end of this chapter.*

Sometimes the fastest and easiest way to add multiple files to an existing project is with Synchronize. Copy the files to the project's documents folder in your local hard drive's My Documents\Version Cue folder (Windows) or Documents>Version Cue (Mac) folder and then synchronize with the project in the Version Cue workspace.

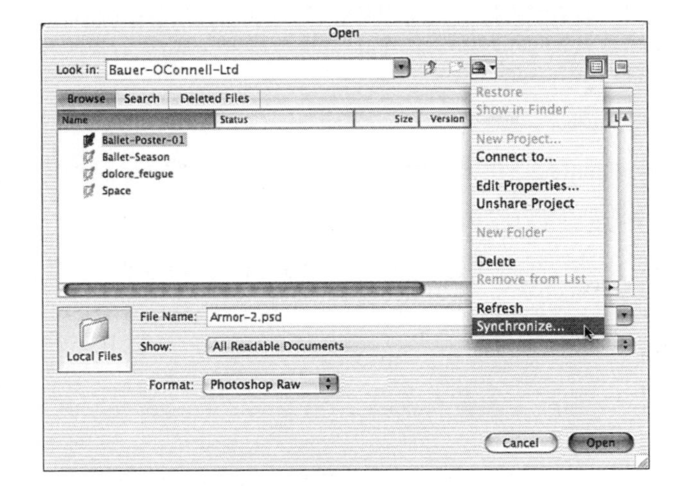


**Figure 1.18**
You can and should synchronize the content of your local project folder and the content in the workspace any time you've been disconnected from the workspace while working on a project.

# TOP NEW FEATURES IN THE CREATIVE SUITE PROGRAMS

Although Version Cue is without doubt the biggest new thing in the Adobe Creative Suite, each of the component programs has been given a set of fresh, new features and capabilities. Many are answers to long-standing customer requests, such as Illustrator's font menu that shows the font name in the actual font and Photoshop's type on a path. Others are addition through subtraction, such as streamlining the ImageReady toolbox and discontinuing support for multiple master fonts. This section gives you a brief look at many of the most important new features. You'll find additional information on these and other new features throughout the following chapters.

## New in Photoshop CS

The list of new features in Photoshop CS is rather extensive. Many of them are relatively minor tweaks, whereas others are radical changes. Here are some of each:

- The File Browser, when introduced with Photoshop 7, was hailed as a breakthrough and perhaps even as the death of the Open command. However, many Photoshop users quickly found themselves thinking "Wouldn't it be great if the File Browser could...." Or "I wish the File Browser could...." Or even "Why in the heck didn't those folks at Adobe make the File browser do...?" Most of those wishes have come true in this new, extremely powerful version of the File Browser. Favorites. Rotate without opening in Photoshop. Edit expanded metadata and keywords. Custom sorting. Search within the File Browser. You name it, it has likely been added.
- Photoshop CS finally makes it feasible to do truly creative work with 16-bit images. You can copy/paste, add layers, even use type in 16-bit images. And most of the adjustments and filters are now available, too.
- Speaking of filters, Photoshop CS makes it easy to use filters in combination with the new Filter Gallery. Most of the creative filters are available in a single dialog box, with a unified preview, so that you can see how your image will look with multiple filters applied. You can add and subtract filters at will, changing settings and balancing their effects before applying the combined filters. (Note, however, that filters in Photoshop are not yet "live." Once you apply the filter, it cannot be reopened and the settings changed.)
- Type on a path makes it to Photoshop! Rather than relying on the Warp Type feature, you can now place editable type along any path in Photoshop—and exchange type on a path with Illustrator CS, too.
- Another recent addition to the Photoshop family of products scored big with many digital camera users. The Photoshop Camera Raw plug-in enabled photographers to open and manipulate Raw images from a variety of high-end cameras. That capability has been integrated into Photoshop CS and expanded as well.
- Image adjustments in Photoshop itself also claim new capabilities. Under the Adjustments menu, you'll find new commands such as Shadow/Highlight (adjust the far ends of the tonal range independently), Photo Filter (simulate the effect of lens filters, including cooling and warming filters), and Match Color (use the color range of one selection or image to adjust one or more additional images). The histogram gets a huge promotion, too. It's now a palette rather than a rarely used adjustment window. And what a palette it is! Expand to show all channels at once, with or without statistics. Show the channels in their own colors. Even preview how an adjustment will affect the distribution of pixels in the histogram.
- Layer comps enable you to save variations of an image in a single file, quickly and easily. And, perhaps more importantly, you can show those variations to clients with just a click or two. Change the order, position, and visibility of layers, as well as the layer style, and save as a layer comp. Rearrange the Layers palette and produce another layer comp. Switch between them in the Layer Comp palette in a flash.
- No more recording Actions and assigning them to F-key combinations just to open the Image Size or Gaussian Blur dialog box. Photoshop CS now has customizable keyboard shortcuts. Assign your own shortcuts to virtually any tool, palette, or command, including many palette commands.

Other new features and improvements include Photomerge (panorama creation), automated PDF presentation and multipage PDF creation, History Log (track changes to an image as metadata or in a text file), interactive Web Photo Galleries, editable Picture Package layouts, Color Replacement tool, maximum image size of 300,000×300,000 pixels and 56 channels, nonsquare pixel support for digital video, and much more.

## New in ImageReady CS

ImageReady got some new features of its own, too, with the release of the Creative Suite:

- Export to Flash (SWF) format. Export frames of an animation as individual files. Export layers of an image as individual files.
- With the new Conditional Actions feature, you can program the Action to look for one or more characteristics and then do (or don't do) something else in the Action. "If the image aspect ratio is Landscape, run the following three steps of the Action. However, if the image is Portrait, skip those steps." Conditional Actions can be triggered by a number of characteristics. Some examples are aspect ratio, height and/or width greater than or less than a certain number of pixels, this many layers or that many layers, and a certain something in the layer or document name. This is one feature we can hope to see (in a vastly expanded form) in other programs of the Creative Suite.
- A consolidated Web Content palette that enables you to work with ImageReady's multiple slice sets and remote rollovers much more intuitively. And it has point-and-shoot targeting.
- Leaner, more compatible HTML, which is easier to edit and has new controls for nested tables and support for XHTML.
- Select multiple objects in the image window and work with them all at once. Instantly group selected objects and have nested groups up to five layers deep.
- Automatic smart guides to assist you visually with precise alignment of objects.
- Data-driven graphics. Create variables and data sets and then let the Web site virtually update itself.

And that doesn't come close to addressing all the new features. Don't forget ImageReady's new Web-focused Toolbox or the streamlined "jump back and forth to Photoshop" feature.

## New in Illustrator CS

When looking at new features in Illustrator CS, Adobe's premiere vector graphics software, it's easy to be mesmerized by the whiz-bang 3D Effect and the new Scribble filter, and perhaps overlook the new capabilities that will be of use on a daily basis. Here are some of the *other* features new to Illustrator CS that make this a very powerful upgrade indeed:

- The new type engine supports character styles and paragraph styles. Not only do styles enable you to quickly format type objects, they ensure consistency from object to object, document to document, project to project. They also translate well into InDesign.

- Advanced support for OpenType fonts, including the new OpenType palette.
- Layered PDF support, suitable for preparing multiple layout variations in a single document.
- Over 200 professionally designed templates. No more trying to manage customized "Startup_CMYK" and "Startup_RGB" files. Instead, use the File, New from Template command.
- Optional WYSIWYG font menu. Select this feature in the Preferences dialog box and the font menu gives you "what you see is what you get," with font names displayed in their own typeface.
- Improved text linking. Link type containers and type on a path, in any sequence.
- Linked EPS and PDF files with transparency intact. And EPS duotones, too!
- A new Print Options dialog box, offering you marks and bleed control, color management, graphic output, and output control, all in one dialog box. This dialog box includes an interactive preview window as well.

Other notable improvements include better integration with Microsoft Office, support for SVG primitives, a lock button on the Transform palette to constrain proportions while scaling, the ability to load libraries right from their respective palettes, and much more.

## New in InDesign CS

InDesign, Adobe's professional page layout program, continues to pull ahead of the competition with the release of the Creative Suite. Here are just a few of the new enhancements:

- Style and edit text in the new Story Editor. Think of it as a built-in word processor, perfect for working with text that fills multiple frames.
- Support for placed PSD files that include spot colors, as well as PSD duotones, tritones, and quadtones.
- Nested styles enable you to ensure consistency—and speed formatting—by including character styles within paragraph styles.
- A new Stroke Style Editor enables you to save and apply dashed, dotted, even striped lines and paragraph rules.
- Customized document presets enable you to quickly get rolling on projects with a common layout.
- Table headers and footers that span multiple linked text frames.

InDesign CS includes numerous other improvements, both evident and subtle. You'll also find yourself taking advantage of the new Control and Info palettes, as well as the Separation Preview and Flattener Preview palettes. You'll be able to automatically style imported XML documents, easily export to GoLive CS, and save custom workspaces. Pathfinder commands, improved text wrapping, mixed-ink support, direct export of PDF (including "rich" PDF), and the new Measure tool are some of the additional benefits of InDesign CS.

## New in GoLive CS

GoLive's new features concentrate on helping you produce better Web sites, faster, more easily, and with cutting-edge features. Here are some of those enhancements:

- Build and save queries to find errors, site assets, and even HTML elements. Nested queries can perform extremely complex searches, and a number of predefined queries handle simpler tasks.
- A new Cascading Style Sheets editor lets you see what happens when you restructure styles. Re-sort style elements, apply existing styles, create new styles, and see it all happen, right before your eyes.
- The design templates, nearly 60 in all, make basic layout a breeze.
- The new Source Code Editor gives you far more capability—and flexibility—to select HTML elements, auto-complete code, and even customize your syntax coloring.
- A transformable Object Toolbar lets you work in "Photoshop style" or "GoLive style."
- A rich authoring environment for both QuickTime and RealOne Player media lets you create interactive content like never before.
- Among the most powerful new features is GoLive's capability to export to PDF format—with links, formatting, and bookmarks intact!

GoLive is well integrated into the Creative Suite, too. It shares the Adobe-standard color engine, works with Photoshop and Illustrator smart objects, and accepts InDesign layouts (through InDesign's Package for GoLive command). These are just some of the features you can use to ensure your "presence" matches from medium to medium.

GoLive co-author mode lets you share the work. With the separately licensed Co-Author interface, you can establish content that contributors can update on their own, while still restricting access to the remainder of the site.

# MASTERING THE ADOBE CREATIVE SUITE

## New Password, Same Login

*I changed the System Administrator password, as suggested, but now I can't log in to the Advanced Administration pages. Did I misspell my own name when I changed the username?*

The problem isn't spelling but rather what you're typing. You don't log in to the Workspace Administration area with the username and password but rather with the unchangeable "system" as the login and your new password. You can change the name of the System Administrator, and you can change the password for the System Administrator, but the System Administrator will always enter the login "system." (Take a look at Figure 1.6 earlier in this chapter. You'll see that the word *system* is unchangeable.)

## Projects from Folders

*I'm trying to create a new Version Cue project from an existing folder of work, but the Open button remains grayed out. What's the problem?*

Although it seems natural to click the folder to select it while browsing in Version Cue, you actually need to select a file *inside* the folder. The folder, rather than the file selected, will be added to the Directory listing in the window.

## Opening a Version Cue Connection

*We've got a very simple network among our office Macs, linking through an Ethernet hub. What do we need to do to reestablish a connection to the Version Cue workspace?*

Several things need to be set up properly to get the computers to talk to each other:

- On the computer that hosts the Version Cue workspace, you must go to the System Preferences, Sharing and then enable sharing.
- Also on the host computer, open Version Cue through the System Preferences and make sure it's on.
- On each of the other computers connected to your network, in the Finder, open the Go, Connect to Server dialog box. Select the host computer from the list and log on as a guest or a registered user.
- The last piece of the puzzle is to actually connect to the Version Cue workspace. From a Creative Suite program, use the File, Open command (or any of the other commands that enable access to Version Cue) and click the Version Cue button, if it's visible. (If you see the Local Files button, you're already there.) From the Project Tools menu, near the upper-right corner of the dialog box, choose Connect To. You'll need to know the name of the host computer and add the suffix **`:3703`**. For example, around my office, the Version Cue workspace is hosted on a computer named Bauer-OConnell-LTD. So here's how to access the Version Cue workspace I connect to:

  ```
  http://bauer-oconnell-ltd.local:3703
  ```

  You can also use the host computer's IP address (which can be found in that computer's System Preferences, Network dialog box).

Once sharing is enabled and Version Cue is on, connecting to the Version Cue workspace is simply a matter of hooking up with the right computer and connecting to Version Cue.

2

# CHOOSING HARDWARE AND SETTING UP YOUR SOFTWARE

## IN THIS CHAPTER

Photoshop and the other programs of the Adobe Creative Suite are rather sophisticated pieces of software. As such, they won't run on just any old computer. There are certain minimum requirements for both the computer's hardware and the operating system. In this chapter, in addition to the hardware and operating system requirements for the Adobe Creative Suite, you'll find information on customizable keyboard shortcuts and an item-by-item look at the preferences for Photoshop, ImageReady, and Illustrator.

Of special importance in this chapter is the section "Quick Fix—Replacing the Preferences." When a program starts misbehaving or things aren't working correctly, replacing the "Prefs" is usually the place to start your repairs.



*You'll find "Quick Fix—Replacing the Preferences" starting on p. 76.*

# THE ADOBE CREATIVE SUITE: MINIMUM REQUIREMENTS

Which program of the Adobe Creative Suite drives your hardware and OS requirements depends upon the type of work you do. Book-length projects in InDesign can be demanding, as can cartography in Illustrator. Working with huge Web sites in GoLive might be your biggest strain. Or perhaps your projects involve 16-bit, multilayered Photoshop files.

When considering your hardware requirements, think about the work you typically do, the occasional extra-heavy-duty project, and whether or not you run multiple programs at the same time. If, for example, you switch back and forth among InDesign, Illustrator, and Photoshop during the course of a work session, you'll likely need more than the minimum amount of RAM. (Even with the memory allocation capabilities of modern operating systems, you'll probably want to add far more than the minimum requirements of RAM.)

## Windows Requirements

Photoshop CS and Illustrator CS require a whole lot more in terms of hardware than did their predecessors, Photoshop 7 and Illustrator 10. The biggest change is perhaps the minimum amount of screen space required to run Photoshop. Photoshop CS can't be used with monitors at resolutions below 1,024×768 pixels. (Photoshop 7's monitor requirement was 800×600 pixels, although the Palette Well wasn't available at that setting.)

Adobe recommends running Photoshop and Illustrator on Intel Pentium III or Pentium 4 processors, but it can function properly with comparable CPUs from other manufacturers. (Intel's Celeron and M-class processors, available in early-to-mid 2003, can be considered to be Pentium 4 chips.) The minimum RAM requirement for each program is now a hefty 192MB, with 256MB recommended. Keep in mind that the operating system and any other programs running in the background also require memory. For smooth operation, your computer should have no less than 512MB of RAM installed. Installation will also take up 280MB of hard drive space for Photoshop and 470MB of drive space for Illustrator. Also, installation requires a drive that can read CD-ROM discs, which includes most DVD drives.

Also notable is the OS requirement for Photoshop and Illustrator. Windows XP and Windows 2000 (Service Pack 3 for Photoshop, Service Pack 2 for Illustrator) are the only supported versions of Windows. No more Windows NT, no more Windows 98.

Photoshop CS for Windows also requires an Internet connection or a telephone call to verify your ownership. For more information, see the Sidebar "What Is Activation?"

Installing the entire Adobe Creative Suite? The Premium edition requires 1.55GB of hard drive space; the Standard edition requires 1.105GB of drive space.

InDesign CS requires a Pentium II or later processor, 128MB of RAM, 185MB of hard drive space, 1,024×768 monitor resolution, and Windows 2000 (Service Pack 2) or Windows XP.

GoLive CS needs a Pentium III or 4 processor, Windows 2000 (Service Pack 2) or Windows XP, 128MB of RAM (192MB recommended), and 200MB of free hard drive space.



**What Is Activation?**

In an effort to cut down on piracy, the illegal duplication and distribution of software, Adobe is implementing new security procedures. After installation, activation is a simple matter of contacting Adobe via the Internet, an automated telephone procedure, or a call to Customer Service to verify your purchase.

Although the process of activation is simple, the restrictions that the system places on additional installations or reinstallation can be a bit confusing. Here are the basics:

- You can use the serial number and activation to install the program on two computers. Under the terms of the standard Adobe licensing agreement, that's two different computers for one user—the two versions should not be running at the same time. (The theory is that you can buy the program once and use it at the office and at home or on the road, as long as you don't have two people using two copies of the program with the same serial number at the same time.)
- Each of the two installations "rolls over" every six months. If you replace your computer, you can activate on the new hardware.
- You can uninstall and reinstall the same version of the program on the same computer as often as necessary. Erasing or reformatting the hard drive will require reactivation. Replacing the motherboard could also require reactivation.

And if you don't activate? Each time you start the program during the first 30 days, you'll get a reminder. After 30 days, the software refuses to run until you proceed with activation.

## Macintosh Requirements

Photoshop CS and Illustrator CS both require a PowerPC processor (G3 or later) and Mac OS X, version 10.2.4 or later. (Neither program operates in OS 9 or in Classic mode.) Both require a minimum of 192MB of RAM, with 256MB recommended. Photoshop CS needs 320MB of hard drive space, whereas Illustrator occupies 450MB of drive space. Photoshop CS runs only on monitors set to a resolution of at least 1,024×768. Both ship on CD-ROM, so an appropriate drive is required for installation.

InDesign CS and GoLive CS have minimum requirements that are comparable. They will run on Mac OS 10.2 or later. InDesign needs a minimum of 128MB of RAM and 250MB of hard drive space, whereas GoLive CS requires 128MB of RAM (92MB recommended) and 200MB of drive space.

A full installation of the Adobe Creative Suite Premium edition requires 1.775GB of hard drive space, whereas the Standard edition requires 1.17GB of drive space.

# CUSTOMIZABLE KEYBOARD SHORTCUTS: EFFICIENCY AT HAND

Photoshop CS joins Illustrator in offering customizable keyboard shortcuts. (GoLive CS also offers customizable shortcuts, whereas InDesign offers a number of preconfigured sets of shortcuts, including shortcuts for Quark users.) Tool activation, menu commands, and palette menus can all be assigned keyboard shortcuts in Photoshop. Illustrator CS offers customization of shortcuts for tools and menu commands.

## Saving Time, Saving Tendons

With the introduction of graphical user interfaces (GUIs) almost two decades ago, we started to say good-bye to keyboards for anything other than text entry. Mouse clicks replaced keystroke-based coding and commands. Since then, such issues as repetitive motion injuries, monitor size, and just plain speed have taken us away from the mouse. Sending a cursor from the lower-right corner of a 21-inch monitor to the upper-left corner just to save a document is far more time consuming and much more inconvenient than pressing a modifier key and S on the keyboard.

Power users have long written Actions to execute repetitive or often-used commands. Assigning keyboard shortcuts can simplify things even a bit more. For example, the creation of a manuscript with illustrations requires that crop marks be prepared for every image in Illustrator. Rather than use the mouse to activate the menu command Object, Crop Marks, you can record an Action that invokes this command and assign it to one of the 12 or 15 function keys. The number of function keys available is limited, but the wealth of modifier key combinations for shortcuts removes any realistic limitation. In addition, you can assign keyboard shortcuts that are easier to remember. To continue this example, you might find it easier to remember using (Command-Option-C) [Ctrl+Alt+C] to make crop marks than F5.

In Photoshop, many of the most common commands have no assigned keyboard shortcut. Image, Image Size, for example, is used regularly, yet requires a mouse movement unless a function key (F-key) combination assigned to an Action is used.

*For information on creating and using Actions, see Chapter 7, "Working Smarter with Scripting and Actions," p. 217.*

Although it's certainly possible to save different sets of keyboard shortcuts for different purposes, it's generally better to have one set of custom shortcuts. Assigning different shortcuts to one tool or command, or assigning one shortcut to multiple tools or commands, can be counterproductive and lead to confusion.

Photoshop and Illustrator both can be set up to save you time and wear-and-tear on your mousing hand. Using custom keyboard shortcuts can speed production as well. Remember, too, that different sets of shortcuts can be saved for different users on one machine.

## Photoshop at Work: Creating Custom Keyboard Shortcuts



The process of creating sets of customized keyboard shortcuts is similar in Photoshop and Illustrator. Because this capability is new in Photoshop and has been around since version 9 of Illustrator, we'll demonstrate it in Photoshop. To create custom keyboard shortcuts in Photoshop, follow these steps:

1. Open Photoshop.
2. Use the menu command Edit, Keyboard Shortcuts or the (default) keyboard shortcut (Shift-Option-Command-K) [Shift+Alt+Ctrl+K].
3. In the Shortcuts For pop-up menu, make sure Application Menus is selected.
4. Click the triangle to the left of Image to expand that group of menu commands and then scroll down to Image Size.
5. Click to the right of Image Size, under the Shortcut column. A small highlighted field will appear (see Figure 2.1).
6. Hold down (Shift-Option-Command) [Shift+Alt+Ctrl] and press 9 on the keyboard. Photoshop will warn you that this particular shortcut cannot be assigned because it's one of the reserved shortcuts for the Channels palette. (Some shortcuts cannot be overridden or reassigned.)
7. With the shortcut field still selected, hold down (Option-Command) [Alt+Ctrl] and press the I key. Photoshop will warn you that this particular keystroke combination is already assigned to the File, File Info command. This warning enables the Accept and Go To Conflict button and the Undo Changes button (see Figure 2.1).

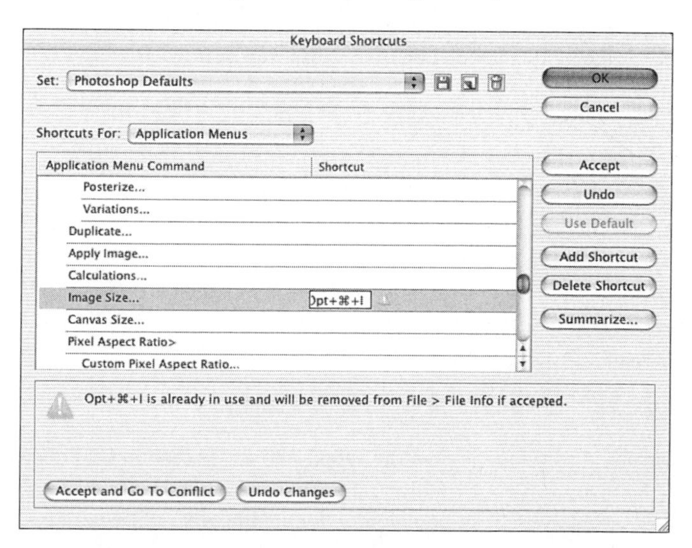


**Figure 2.1**
If you attempt to assign a keyboard shortcut that's already in use, Photoshop and Illustrator will let you override, resolve, or avoid the conflict. You can resolve a conflict by assigning a different shortcut to one of the conflicting items.

8. With the warning still visible and the Shortcut field still active, press (Shift-Option-Command-I) [Shift+Alt+Ctrl+I]. This combination is not assigned by default and, therefore, is available for Image Size.
9. Click the OK button.
10. Click the Summarize button. In the resulting dialog box, choose a location and save the file. If it doesn't open automatically in your Web browser, open the browser, use the File, Open command, and open the HTM file just created. You'll see a handy list of all currently assigned keyboard shortcuts.
11. To continue assigning keyboard shortcuts, switch back to Photoshop's still-open Keyboard Shortcuts dialog box.
12. At the top of the dialog box, to the left of the OK button, click the middle of three buttons to create a new set of keyboard shortcuts.



At this point, you can continue assigning shortcuts, if you like. After you've finished, make sure to click the Save button to the left of the OK button. The custom shortcuts can be saved in the Presets, Keyboard Shortcuts folder inside the Photoshop CS folder.

Note that Photoshop offers a number of buttons below the OK and Cancel buttons:

- **Accept**—This button simply confirms the change you've made.
- **Undo**—Use this button to reverse the most recent change. It comes in handy when conflicts arise. It becomes the *Redo* button after you undo a change.
- **Use Default**—Should you change the shortcut of a tool or command for which Photoshop has a default setting, this button restores the original shortcut. (You must select a command with a default shortcut first.)
- **Add Shortcut**—Use this button to assign multiple shortcuts to a single tool or command.
- **Delete Shortcut**—You can remove an assigned shortcut with this button.
- **Summarize**—As you've seen, this button generates an HTM list of all shortcuts that can be viewed in a Web browser.

Illustrator's Keyboard Shortcuts dialog box is a bit simpler than the one you've seen for Photoshop. You assign shortcuts in the same way, and you can assign a symbol to appear in the menu next to a command. While assigning shortcuts, you have available the buttons Undo, Clear, and Go To (to resolve conflicts). For managing your shortcut sets, Illustrator offers the straightforward buttons OK, Cancel, Save, Delete, and Export Text (to create a list of shortcuts).

## SETTING PHOTOSHOP'S PREFERENCES

Much of how Photoshop looks and acts depends on a file called Adobe Photoshop CS Prefs. This file contains such information as how you last arranged the palettes, the dimensions and color mode of the most-recent new document, what style of cursors you prefer, and how you like to name files when saving them.

Photoshop organizes the preferences into nine groups, each of which is displayed and changed in a separate pane of the Preferences dialog box. Windows users can open Preferences by using the menu command Edit, Preferences. Mac OS X users will find Preferences under the Photoshop menu. The first pane of the dialog box, General, can be opened with the keyboard shortcut (Command-K) [Ctrl+K]. Once the Preferences dialog box is open, you can switch among panes using the pop-up menu at the top or with the (Command) [Ctrl] key and the number keys 1 through 9. You can also move among the nine panes by using the Next and Prev buttons, which appear in all nine panes.

Photoshop preferences are updated and the file rewritten every time you quit the program. Because this file is rewritten so often, it is subject to corruption. Fixing problems that stem from a bad Prefs file is discussed later in this chapter in the section "Quick Fix—Replacing the Preferences."



## Preferences, General

The General preferences include a variety of settings that affect the way Photoshop operates. The General preferences are shown with their default settings in Figure 2.2.

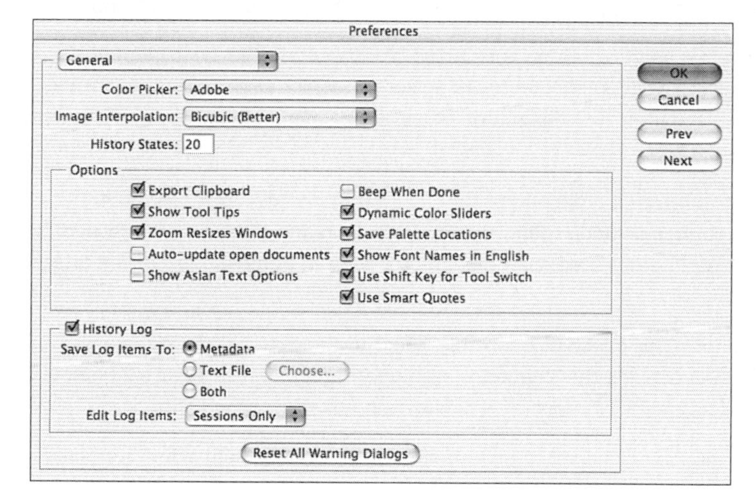


**Figure 2.2**
In Windows, the General preferences are comparable to those shown.

Here are the options available in the General preferences:

- **Color Picker**—You have the choice of using Adobe's Color Picker, the Photoshop standard, or the color picker supplied by your operating system.

- **Interpolation**—Photoshop CS has two new variations of bicubic interpolation. When you transform a selection, Photoshop must add or subtract pixels to make the new size conform to the image's resolution. *Bicubic* interpolation looks at a range of surrounding pixel color values to determine what color to make new pixels. This option produces the highest quality for photographic and continuous-tone images. Photoshop CS adds Bicubic Smoother and Bicubic Sharper to the choices. Think of the first Bicubic choice as "Bicubic-between-Smoother-and-Sharper" or simply as the basic Bicubic choice. *Bilinear* interpolation compares the adjacent pixels. It is faster than bicubic interpolation, but it generally produces less satisfactory results for photographs and images with gradients. It can, however, be an excellent choice when you're resizing artwork with areas of solid color and vertical or horizontal lines, such as interface elements. *Nearest neighbor* interpolation is the fastest of the three, but it should be avoided for photographic images. On the other hand, the Nearest Neighbor option is most appropriate for images that have large areas of solid color, especially in linear and rectangular shapes.



- **History States**—The history states, available through the Undo/Redo commands and the History palette, are saved in the memory allocated to Photoshop. Having more history states gives you increased flexibility and more "undos." Having fewer history states frees up memory for other Photoshop tasks.
- **Export Clipboard**—If you'll need to use something you copied from Photoshop in another program after exiting Photoshop, leave this option selected. If you deselect it, the contents of the Clipboard will not be available when you switch programs, nor will it be saved upon quitting Photoshop (and Photoshop will shut down somewhat faster).
- **Show ToolTips**—When on, ToolTips show you the name of any tool or button—simply leave the cursor over the tool icon or button for a second or two. You'll also find a variety of helpful tips throughout Photoshop. If you find these little reminders annoying, deselect this option.
- **Zoom Resizes Windows**—When this option is selected, zooming with keyboard shortcuts resizes the image window. If you use the keyboard to zoom out, the image window shrinks. If you zoom in, the window expands (to a maximum of the space available onscreen). The window resizes so that the image fills it.
- **Auto-Update Open Documents**—If a document that is open in Photoshop is also open in another program and a change is made there, this option allows the Photoshop version to be updated. When this option is deselected, changes are not seen in Photoshop until the image is closed and reopened.
- **Show Asian Text Options**—This check box controls whether the options for Chinese, Japanese, and Korean (CJK) text are visible in the Character and Paragraph palettes. Figure 2.3 shows the difference. If you don't work with CJK fonts, there's no need to show these options.
- **Beep When Done**—Photoshop can be set to give an audible announcement when it finishes a task. If Photoshop runs slowly on your system or if you work with extremely large files, this option may be of use (especially if you do other things while waiting for Photoshop). If the program runs on your system quickly and efficiently, however, the beeps might be an annoyance.
- **Dynamic Color Sliders**—This option allows the color bars above the sliders in the Color palette to be updated as you drag. Without this option, the color bars retain their basic color, no matter how the sliders are arranged. Dynamic sliders, the default, enable you to see how changes to a component color will affect the overall color.
- **Save Palette Locations**—When this option is selected, Photoshop writes the location and visibility of each palette to the Prefs file, which is updated every time you quit Photoshop. With this option selected, the palettes will be restored to their most recently recorded positions at Photoshop's next startup. When the option is not selected, the palettes automatically return to their default locations when Photoshop is reopened.

- **Show Font Names in English**—If you use non-roman fonts, this option shows their names in English in the Font menu. If this option is not selected, such fonts are listed only with their actual names. This preference is designed for use with the Chinese, Japanese, and Korean versions of Photoshop.

> With Photoshop's capability to save workspaces (Window, Workspace, Save Workspace), the Save Palette Locations option is not nearly as important as it once was. You can record multiple sets of palette locations and easily switch between them.

- **Use Shift Key for Tool Switch**—When this option is active, you can rotate among tools that share a keyboard shortcut by holding down the Shift key and typing the assigned letter shortcut. When this option is inactive, the Shift key is not required. For example, changing from the Lasso tool to the Magnetic Lasso tool by default requires pressing Shift+L twice. (The first keypress changes from the Lasso to the Polygon Lasso, and the second to the Magnetic Lasso.) With this preference box deselected, you need only press L twice.

- **Use Smart Quotes**—*Smart quotes* is the term used for quotation marks that differ at the beginning and end of the quoted material, pointing inward toward the quote (see Figure 2.4). You'll also find the term *curly quotes* used to describe them. When this option is not selected, Photoshop uses the same character for the quotation marks in both locations.

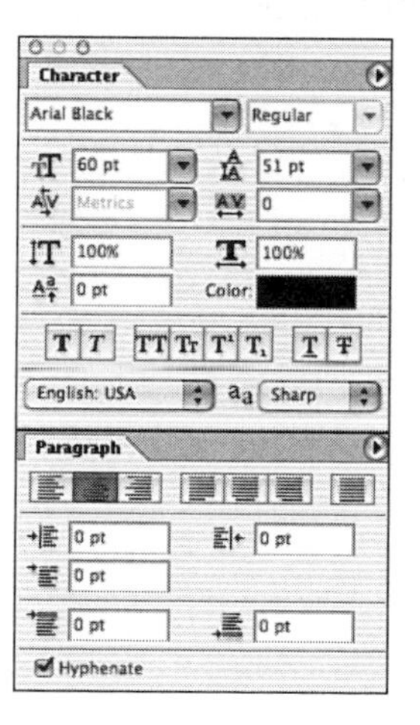


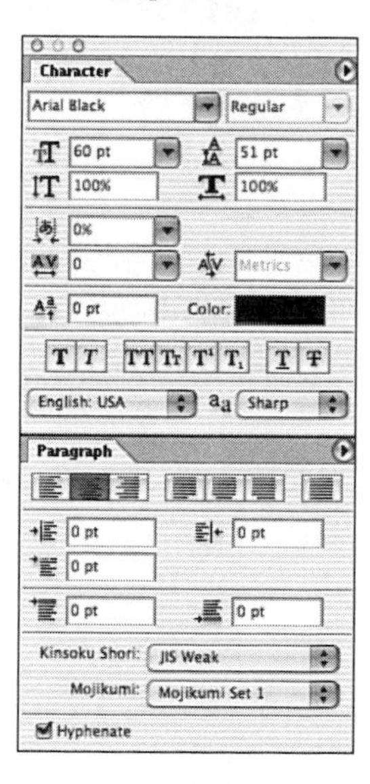


Figure 2.3
On the left are the palettes without the Asian options. On the right, the same palettes with the options visible.

- **History Log**—In answer to the requests for a savable, printable History palette, Photoshop now offers the history log. The log won't store the history states for "undo" changes in later editing sessions—when you close the file, the history is still lost—but you can store and print the log. The log can be added to the image's metadata, posted to a text file, or both. The history log can record data in one of three ways:

- **Sessions Only**—The first option creates a simple log of the date and time when Photoshop was started and stopped, along with which files were opened and closed (and when).

- **Concise**—The second option records Photoshop starting and stopping, as well as which files were open and what tools and commands were used.
- **Detailed**—The third option creates a very complete record of what was done to which images, including which commands and tools were used and what was done with them. When History Log is set to Detailed, the history log contains information even more specific than what is recorded in an Action.

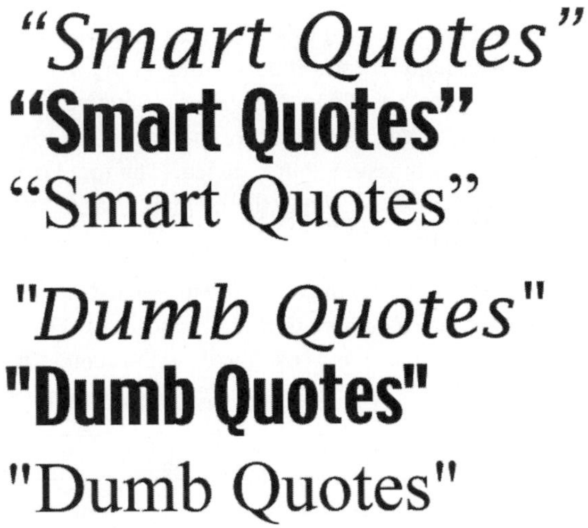

Figure 2.4
Changing the Use Smart Quotes preference does not affect type that has already been set.

*“Smart Quotes”*
**“Smart Quotes”**
“Smart Quotes”

*"Dumb Quotes"*
**"Dumb Quotes"**
"Dumb Quotes"

### Working with History Logs

Table 2.1 shows a comparison of the type of information recorded in the three types of History logs available in Photoshop. In all three cases, the only steps taken were these: Photoshop opens. The image is opened. The image is rotated. A Levels adjustment is made. The image is saved. The image is closed. Photoshop quits.

In the table, {dt} stands for date and time. In the history log, regardless of which option is selected, the date and time are recorded in the format YYYY-MM-DD HH:MM:SS. For example, Santa's arrival could be recorded as follows:

2003-12-25 03:25:37

**Table 2.1** Comparing History Logs

| Sessions Only | Concise | Detailed |
|---|---|---|
| {dt} Photoshop Launched | {dt} Photoshop launched | {dt} Photoshop launched |
| {dt} File 001.tif opened | {dt} File 001.tif opened | {dt} Reset Brushes of current application |
| {dt} File 001.tif closed | {dt} Rotate Canvas | {dt} Reset Tool Presets of current application |

**Table 2.1** Continued

| Sessions Only | Concise | Detailed |
|---|---|---|
| {dt} Photoshop quit | {dt} Levels | {dt} Get |
| | {dt} File 001.tif closed | False |
| | {dt} Photoshop quit | {dt} Get |
| | | <unknown> |
| | | 8 |
| | | 0 |
| | | 0 |
| | | {dt} File 001.tif opened |
| | | {dt} Open |
| | | c:\PeteDocuments\Vacation |
| | | {dt} Rotate Canvas |
| | | {dt} Rotate first document |
| | | Angle: 90° |
| | | {dt} Levels |
| | | {dt} Levels |
| | | Adjustment: levels adjustment list |
| | | Levels adjustment |
| | | Channel: composite channel |
| | | Input: 10, 245 |
| | | Gamma: 1.1 |
| | | {dt} Save |
| | | {dt} File 001.tif closed |
| | | {dt} Close |
| | | {dt} Photoshop quir |

As you can see in Table 2.1, the Detailed logs can get pretty long, even for the simplest of editing sessions. Recording such logs in the metadata of a file can increase the amount of time required to save a file and the file size—in some cases, substantially. Which option you choose depends on how much information you need to save.

When the history log is recorded to an image's metadata, it can be retrieved and edited within Photoshop or other programs that can access the information. In Photoshop's File Browser, you can use commands in the Edit menu to replace or add to a file's metadata using metadata templates.

- **Reset All Warning Dialogs**—Clicking this button in the General preferences resets all warnings. Photoshop offers you the opportunity to skip certain warning dialog boxes (see Figure 2.5). If you select the Don't Show Again check box in a warning, you don't have to see it again. However, you also don't get the reminder that you're making a substantial change, one that could affect your ability to edit or make changes to the image later. If you share a computer or are using Photoshop on a particular computer for the first time, resetting the warnings is a good idea.

Photoshop 7 had two preference items in the General pane that have disappeared. Rather than using Preferences to determine the Print versus Print with Preview and the Redo/Undo keys, you now use Keyboard Shortcuts, found under the Edit menu.



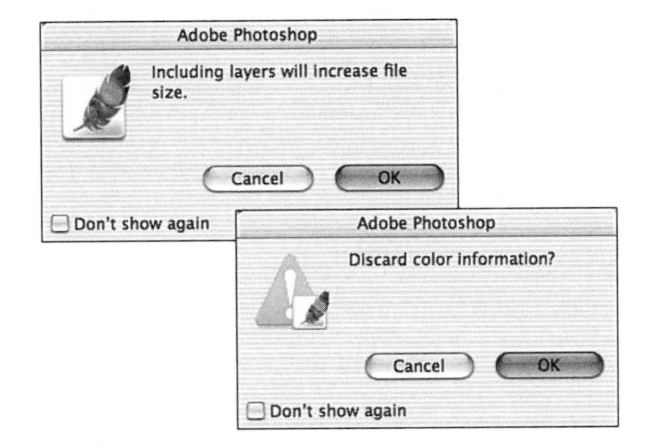


Figure 2.5
These are a couple of the warning messages that Photoshop allows you to turn off.

## Preferences, File Handling

Because of differences in the way that Windows and Macintosh handle previews, Photoshop offers several more options on the Mac for saving files (see Figure 2.6).

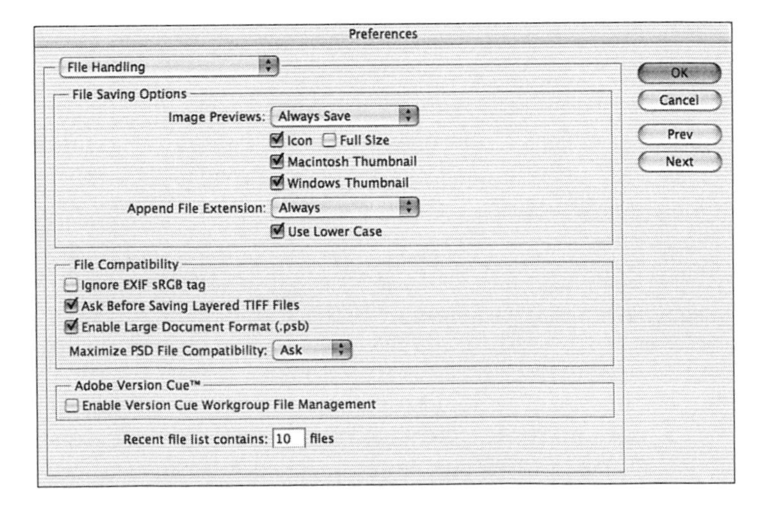


Figure 2.6
The upper portion of the Windows version of this pane has only the Image Previews pop-up menu and a choice of lowercase or uppercase letters for the file extension.

Although the Image Preview options differ, the bottom portion of the File Handling pane is the same for Macintosh and Windows:

- **Image Previews**—Windows users have the option of always saving previews, never saving previews, or making the decision at the time the image is saved (Ask When Saving). The difference is simply a check box in the Save dialog box. The Thumbnail check box will be deselected and grayed out (Never Save), selected and grayed out (Always Save), or available for you to select or deselect (Ask When Saving).

  Macintosh users, on the other hand, have a variety of options and choices available in Preferences.



### Image Previews

Full-sized previews are used by some page layout programs. The Macintosh and Windows previews are used in the Open dialog boxes (and sometimes elsewhere). Many programs can generate previews from the image file itself, depending on file format, instead of relying on the presence of an embedded preview.

The embedded previews can have an effect on the size of a file. Using the file Eagle.psd from the Photoshop CS Samples folder, the information in Table 2.2 was generated. (File size is listed in bytes.)

**Table 2.2** Sample File Sizes

| Icon | Full Size | Mac Thumbnail | Win Thumbnail | File Size in Bytes |
|---|---|---|---|---|
| O | O | O | O | 1,622,000 |
| X | O | O | O | 1,663,786 |
| O | X | O | O | 1,714,744 |
| O | O | X | O | 1,669,504 |
| O | O | O | X | 1,665,386 |
| X | X | O | O | 1,716,072 |
| X | O | X | O | 1,670,824 |
| X | O | O | X | 1,668,250 |
| O | X | X | O | 1,721,854 |
| O | X | O | X | 1,718,124 |
| O | O | X | X | 1,675,304 |
| X | O | X | X | 1,676,630 |
| O | X | X | X | 1,722,626 |
| X | X | X | X | 1,728,948 |

The difference between no previews and all optional previews is some 100KB in this instance. Keep in mind, however, that the size and complexity of the original image play a large part in how much the file size increases. The artwork for a simple Web button, 64×16 pixels, was saved without previews and with all previews. The file size increased from 35,556 bytes to 42,920 bytes.

Although embedded previews can increase a file's size, such factors as the file's format, compression (if any), and even the formatting of the disk can play far more important roles in file size.

- **File Extension (Append File Extension)**—This option also differs in Windows and Macintosh. Windows users have the option of including the file extension in lowercase or uppercase (but it must always be included). Macintosh users can choose among Always, Never, and Ask When Saving, and, if the extension is added, they have the option of lowercase or uppercase. For maximum file compatibility, you should append the file extension in lowercase.

At this time, only Photoshop takes advantage of the TIFF standard's more sophisticated capabilities. For that reason, there is little use for this option. If layers are important, save the file as PSD (Photoshop's native format) and skip layered TIFF.

- **Ignore EXIF sRGB Tag**—Some digital cameras embed information in an image's EXIF data saying that the photo was captured in the sRGB color space. For many cameras, this isn't quite accurate, because the image was actually captured in a larger color space. Ignoring the false sRGB tag prevents the image from accidentally being degraded through conversion to a real sRGB gamut. If your camera doesn't embed the sRGB tag, or if it actually captures in that small gamut (check the User Guide for the camera), this option is insignificant.
- **Ask Before Saving Layered TIFF Files**—The so-called Enhanced TIFF format (also known as Advanced TIFF) supports layers as well as annotations and transparency. If a layered TIFF file is open in a program that doesn't support Enhanced TIFF, a flattened version is used.

- **Enable Large Document Format (.psb)**—Previous versions of Photoshop had a maximum image size of 30,000×30,000 pixels. With this option enabled, files can be saved in the new PSB file format, which supports image dimensions up to 300,000×300,000 pixels. This file format can be used only within Photoshop CS (and, most certainly, subsequent versions of Photoshop).

*For more on the new PSB files, see "Large Document Format (.psb)" in Chapter 3, "Understanding and Choosing File Formats," p. 93.*

- **Maximize PSD File Compatibility**—When you save a file with maximum compatibility, a full-size, full-resolution version with all layers merged is saved along with the actual Photoshop (PSD) file. The flattened version ensures that other programs that can use the Photoshop format show the image properly. You have the option to save the merged version Never, Always, or Ask. The Ask option will prompt you when you save the image.

- **Enable Version Cue Workgroup File Management**—Version Cue is available only with the Adobe Creative Suite (you cannot purchase it separately or in conjunction with a single CS program). It serves as a file-management and organization tool, working with both the most current and historical versions of documents. With Version Cue enabled, you can preview and check the metadata of any version of a file saved using the system. In addition, workgroups can avoid conflicts—Version Cue monitors edits made simultaneously to the same version of a workgroup file. (Version Cue is discussed in more detail in Chapter 1, "The Adobe Creative Suite with Version Cue.")

- **Recent File List Contains __ Files**—You can specify a number from 0 to 30 for this list, and you can open the files by selecting them from the menu File, Open Recent. Tracking recent documents allows you to quickly locate and reopen an image on which you recently worked. However, making the list too long can reduce its usability.

## Preferences, Display & Cursors

The options in this pane of Photoshop's Preferences dialog box are identical for Windows and Macintosh. They are shown in Figure 2.7.

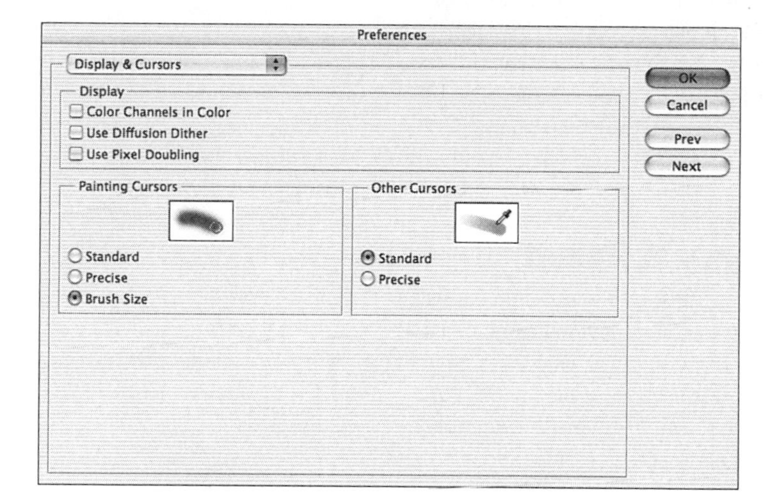


Figure 2.7
All tools that use brushes are considered painting tools for the purposes of this dialog box.



The choices you make in this pane can have a major impact on your interaction with Photoshop:

- **Color Channels in Color**—When this option is selected, Photoshop shows each of the color channels in its own color rather than as a grayscale image. Although this display option can ensure that the correct channel is being edited, particularly with RGB images, the lack of contrast in the Yellow and Cyan channels could be a problem. When showing multiple (but not all) color channels in the Channels palette, the image window will be in color, using the selected channels. The option includes spot channels but has no effect on alpha channels.
- **Use Diffusion Dither**—For use only with monitors showing 8-bit color (a total of 256 colors), diffusion dither allows Photoshop to simulate a higher color depth.
- **Use Pixel Doubling**—When you're dragging selected pixels onscreen, pixel doubling can speed screen redraw. By reducing the selection's resolution, this option reduces the amount of data required to refresh the screen. It can be of use with high-resolution images on low-power systems.
- **Painting Cursors**—Photoshop allows you to show the cursors for the painting tools in one of three ways: Standard, Precise, or Brush Size. Standard cursors show the tool's icon, which could be useful if you often change tools by using the keyboard shortcuts. Precise cursors use a crosshair to indicate the center of the tool's brush. Brush Size shows a circle that's the diameter of the selected brush for that tool.

When a hard, round brush is selected, the Brush Size option shows the cursor as a circle; the painting tool can affect pixels within that area. When a feathered (soft) brush is active, the affected area extends some distance beyond the circular cursor.

Remember, too, that noncircular cursors are included. When Brush Size is selected, you'll also see the cursor as irregularly shaped brushes.

- **Other Cursors**—Like the painting tool cursors, Photoshop's other tools can show either a tool's icon or a crosshair. (Because nonpainting tools don't use brushes, the third option—Brush Size—is not available.) The Caps Lock key toggles between the Standard and Precise options.

The Caps Lock key switches between Precise and Brush Size cursors. When either option is active, pressing Caps Lock swaps to the other. When Standard is selected, pressing Caps Lock switches between the tool icon and Precise cursors.

If keeping track of which tool is in use is critical to you, remember that the Status Bar can be set to Current Tool, leaving you free to use Precise (or Brush Size) for your cursors.

## Preferences, Transparency & Gamut

Think of transparency as being able to see through a layer to the layer(s) below. When an area of an image has no opaque pixels on one layer, you see through to the next layer below. If there are no opaque pixels on any layer, there's nothing to see in that area of the image. That's where the transparency grid comes into play. Photoshop arranges a pattern of squares below an image to indicate where there is nothing opaque in an image. The transparency grid is nonprinting and does not appear in any final artwork. With reduced opacity (partial transparency), the grid is partially visible. You can set both size and color for the grid (see Figure 2.8).

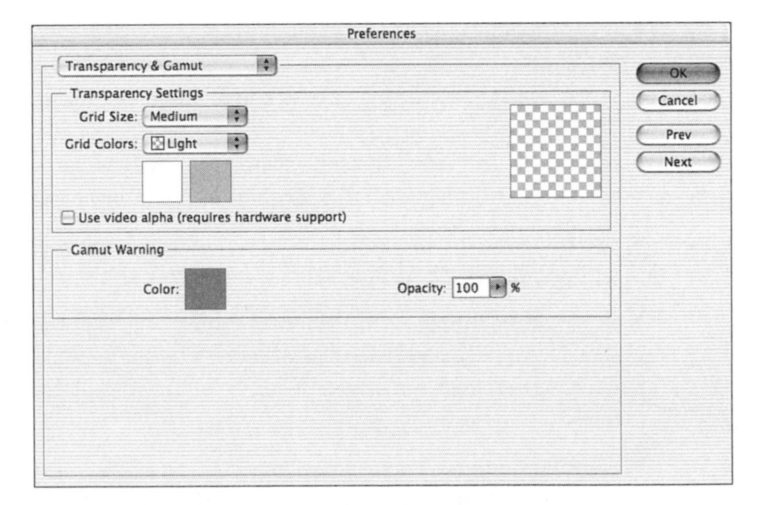


**Figure 2.8**
The default values, shown here, are the same for Macintosh and Windows.

The transparency grid can be customized through the following settings to make it most appropriate for the image with which you're working:

- **Grid Size**—The options are Small, Medium, Large, and None, which turns off the transparency grid.
- **Grid Colors**—This pop-up menu offers grids of light gray/white, medium gray/light gray, and dark gray/medium gray. If gray interferes with your work—for example, when working on a grayscale image—you can also choose grids of white with one of five other colors. In addition, you can use the Color Picker to select the two grid colors; simply click the swatches to open the Color Picker.

  When this pane of the Preferences dialog box is open, you can also change the colors of the transparency grid by clicking and (Option)-clicking [Alt]-clicking in any open image. Click to change the first transparency color and then (Option)-click [Alt]-click to change the second transparency color. Remember that the change affects all images, not just the one(s) in which you click.

*Transparency grid not visible? See "Transparency and Background Layers" in the "Mastering the Adobe Creative Suite" section at the end of this chapter.*

- **Use Video Alpha (Requires Hardware Support)**—If your computer includes a video board that supports chroma-key, such hardware allows the video board to overlay an image from Photoshop onto a live video signal.

Although gray transparency grids are the least likely to interfere with color perception, it can sometimes be difficult to judge partial opacity with them. In those situations, a colored grid may make more sense.

If you have two prominent colors in an image, you can maximize the transparency grid's contrast like this: Press (Command-I) [Ctrl+I] to invert the image's colors. Open the Transparency & Gamut Preferences. Click and then (Option)-click [Alt]-click to set the grid colors, and then click OK. Press (Command-I) [Ctrl+I] again. The resulting transparency grid will have extreme contrast with your image's principle colors.

- **Gamut Warning**—Click the color swatch to choose a color; drag the slider or type a percentage to set the opacity. The gamut warning is used to identify colors in an image that cannot be reproduced in the selected CMYK gamut. (It can, in fact, also be used with other color modes, but it is designed to prepare images for offset presses.) To toggle this option, use the menu command View, Gamut Warning.

## Preferences, Units & Rulers

This pane of the Preferences dialog box, shown in Figure 2.9, governs the units of measure used generally throughout Photoshop and for type.

In addition, several settings affect the dimensions of new documents:

- **Rulers**— In addition to Photoshop's rulers, this setting governs most units of measure, from dialog boxes to palettes to the Options Bar. The available options are Pixels, Inches, Centimeters, Millimeters, Points, Picas, and Percent. (When Percent is selected for rulers, absolute dimensions, such as those required when creating a new document, use inches.) You can also change this setting without opening the Preferences. (Control)-click right-click the ruler in any image and select the new unit of measure from the pop-up list.

- **Type**—Type in Photoshop is governed separately from other units of measure. Type can be measured in points, pixels, or millimeters. Points are the standard unit of measure for type in print.
- **Column Size**—Photoshop's New dialog box allows you to specify the dimensions of a new document. One of the options is Columns (see Figure 2.10), which uses the width established in this setting.

Remember that you can enter abbreviations for units of measure in most numeric fields. For example, enter **36 px** when the units are set to inches, and Photoshop recognizes it as 36 pixels.



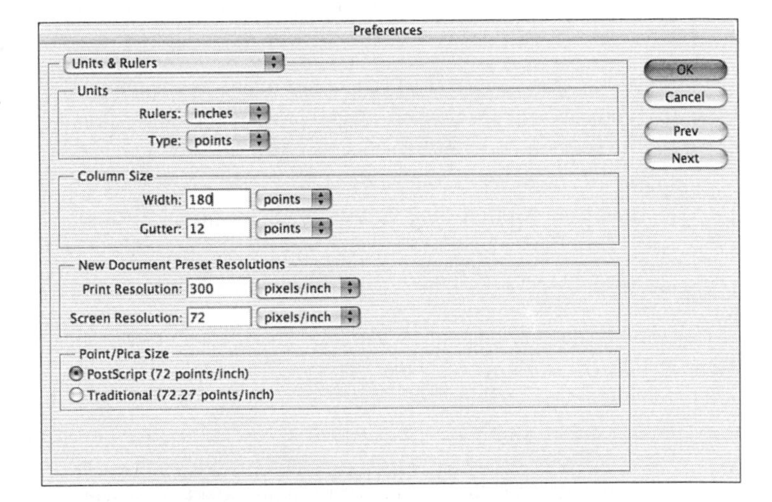


Figure 2.9
The default values of the Units & Rulers pane are all print oriented.

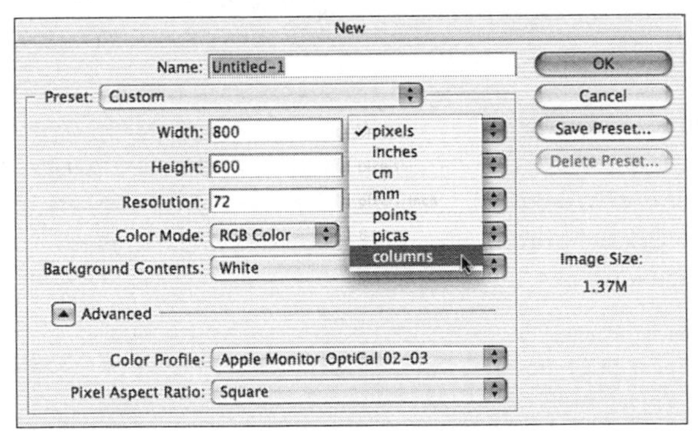


Figure 2.10
The width of a column is determined in the Units & Rulers preferences.

Columns can be used effectively when you're preparing an image to be placed into a multicolumn page layout. The New dialog box calculates the width of such a document by multiplying the specified number of columns by this Width value and adding the amount specified by the Gutter value between the columns.

- **New Document Preset Resolutions**—As shown in Figure 2.11, Photoshop's New dialog box offers over two dozen preset sizes (plus any custom sizes you create). Some are designed for print, and some for Web or video. This pair of preferences allows you to specify which resolution is associated with each of the presets. It is simply a convenience—the resolutions can still be changed in the New dialog box.

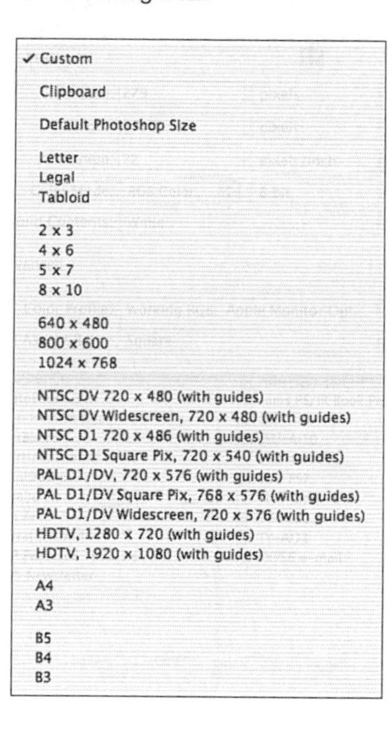


**Figure 2.11**
The Preset menu of the New dialog box shows the default presets, as well as any currently open images (which appear at the bottom of the list). Selecting an open document duplicates the file's specifications in the New dialog box.

- **Point/Pica Size**—With the advent of PostScript, the traditional measurement of a point was rounded down to 1/72 of an inch. In some press environments, it's important to maintain the conventional measurement by changing this preference to the Traditional option.

## Preferences, Guides, Grid & Slices

In addition to allowing you to set the style and color for guides and grids, Photoshop now allows you to specify the slice color globally. The preferences shown in Figure 2.12 affect only the onscreen appearance; guides, grid, and slice lines are nonprinting. All three can be shown and hidden through the View menu.

The default values might not be appropriate for the images with which you work. These settings allow you to choose colors that may be more visible or perhaps less distracting:

- **Guides**—A pop-up menu offers nine preset color values, or you can choose Custom. You can also open the Color Picker by clicking the swatch to the right. The Style menu allows you to set guides as lines or dashed lines.
- **Grid**—The grid can also be set to one of nine presets or to a custom color. In addition to lines and dashed lines, the grid can be shown as a series of dots. This pane of the Preferences dialog box also enables you to specify the grid's spacing. Both major grid lines and their subdivisions can be entered, using any of Photoshop's units of measure. The gridlines are thicker than the subdivisions to differentiate between the two onscreen.

- **Slices**—Used to define subdivisions of Web graphics, slices can be shown in only one of the nine preset colors. Photoshop does not offer custom colors for slices. You also have the option of hiding slice numbers while leaving the slice lines visible.



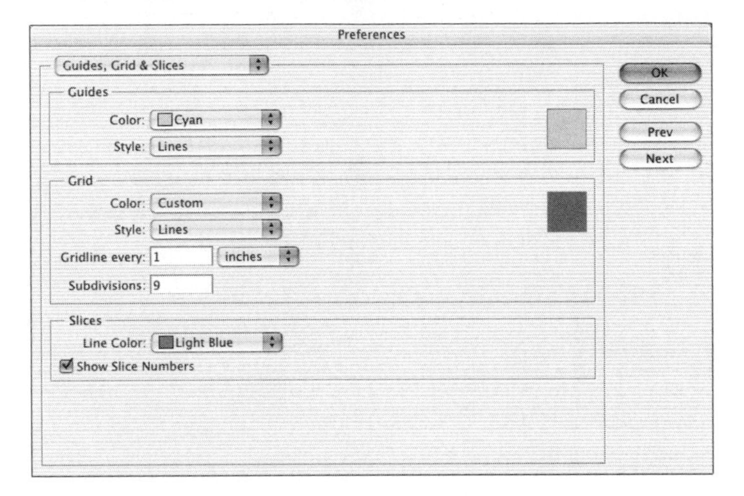


**Figure 2.12**
Photoshop's defaults no longer show both guides and slice lines as light blue. You can still customize one or the other (or both) to further minimize visual confusion.

## Preferences, Plug-Ins & Scratch Disks

*Plug-ins* are supplements to Photoshop's capabilities that you can run from within the program. *Scratch disks* are hard drive space used by Photoshop to supplement the allocated memory. The Plug-Ins & Scratch Disks pane of the Preferences dialog box, shown in Figure 2.13, allows you to regulate what folders Photoshop uses for plug-ins and what hard drives are used for scratch disks.

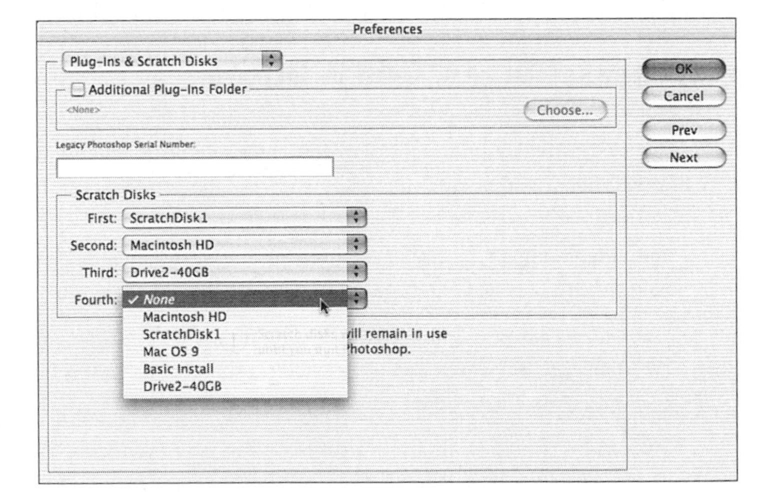


**Figure 2.13**
If you want Photoshop to load only the default plug-ins folder, leave the upper check box deselected. If you have only one hard drive, Startup is the appropriate scratch disk choice.

You can have several folders for plug-ins, but only one additional folder can be used at a time. Choose from these options to set the Plug-Ins & Scratch Disks preferences:

- **Additional Plug-Ins Folder**—If desired, you can have Photoshop load plug-ins from a second source when the program starts. Click the check box, click the Choose button, and then navigate to the target folder. Select the folder in the window, and click the (Choose) [OK] button. When Photoshop next starts, it will load plug-ins from the primary Plug-ins folder and the designated second Plug-ins folder (including any subfolders.)
- **Legacy Photoshop Serial Number**—Some plug-ins require a valid Photoshop serial number. Older plug-ins may not recognize Photoshop CS's serial number. If you're loading plug-ins that need a previous version of Photoshop's old-style serial number, enter that number in this field.
- **Scratch Disks**—Scratch disks are used to support Photoshop's memory. If there is more data than Photoshop can hold in memory, it writes some to the disk for later retrieval. When things are slow, Photoshop can write the entire contents of memory to the scratch disks.

  You can assign up to four different disks and partitions as scratch disks. When multiple hard drives are available, you might see an increase in performance if the primary scratch disk is a disk other than the startup disk. (Windows and Macintosh both use the startup disk to support memory. When the OS and Photoshop are both trying to write to the same disk, slowdowns are possible.) All available drives appear in each of the four pop-up menus. The First pop-up menu includes the option Startup, which is the default. This setting is not dependent on the hard drive's name. The Second, Third, and Fourth scratch disk pop-up menus won't offer Startup, but they do have the choice of None.

Changes to the scratch disk preferences don't take effect until the next time Photoshop is started. To save time, you can change them *while* starting Photoshop. Hold down the (Option-Command) [Alt+Ctrl] keys during Photoshop startup to select scratch disks.

**Caution**

Never use removable media, such as Zip or Jaz drives, as scratch disks. In addition to their being slow, the removable nature of such disks can lead to unexpected crashes and problems. In addition, network drives should never be assigned as scratch disks.

Remember the difference between a *partition* and a *drive*. A single hard drive can be partitioned into separate volumes, each of which your OS sees as a drive. Partitions are still physically part of the same drive, however, so the computer cannot write to multiple partitions of one drive at the same time, so assigning multiple partitions of the same hard drive as scratch disks is inefficient.

**Plug-Ins and Photoshop**

Plug-ins can greatly expand Photoshop's capabilities, but some care must be taken. Here are some notes on using plug-ins:

- Remember that plug-ins load with Photoshop when you start the program. An excessive number of plug-ins can drastically increase the time required to start the program.
- A number of other programs use Photoshop-compatible plug-ins. You can use the Additional Plug-Ins Folder preference to load plug-ins from Painter, After Effects, Illustrator, and other programs' plug-ins folders.
- If you hold down the (Shift-Command) [Shift+Ctrl] keys while Photoshop is starting up, you can choose an additional plug-ins folder to load. With this capability, you can have several additional plug-ins folders and load only the set you'll need for that work session. This speeds loading and reduces the memory overhead required to run Photoshop.
- Plug-ins folders can contain subfolders to keep plug-ins organized.

Hundreds of plug-ins from a variety of sources are available for Photoshop. Commercial third-party software companies generally provide high-quality products. However, some shareware and freeware plug-ins can cause stability problems or crashes. It's always a good idea to keep track of which plug-ins were installed when so that if problems develop, you can try to trace them to a specific plug-in. Likewise, it's a good idea to load new plug-ins singly, or in small groups, and test them immediately.

Check with the manufacturers of legacy plug-ins for Photoshop CS compatibility information.

# Preferences, Memory & Image Cache

The image cache stores low-resolution versions of an image that can be used to speed screen redraw. The increased monitor response can come at the price of accurate detail, however. Photoshop also enables you to manage how the cache is used.

Windows and Mac OS X dynamically allocate memory to active programs as they need it. You use the Preferences pane shown in Figure 2.14 to specify what percentage of the *available* memory should be allocated to Photoshop.

These settings have an impact on how Photoshop performs:

- **Cache Settings**—When set to the default of 4, Photoshop stores four low-resolution versions of a high-resolution image in memory. These four are at increasing zoom levels from 100%. When zoomed in, Photoshop uses the low-resolution images to redraw the image on the monitor more quickly. The cache, which uses memory allocated to Photoshop, can be set from 1 to 8.

  Using the cache for histograms allows Photoshop to more quickly generate the histogram for such operations as Levels. Although using the low-resolution cached version of the image produces a less accurate histogram, the differences are rarely significant. If you need to

If the cache is not set to 1, you should always return to 100% zoom before making critical decisions on high-resolution images—the low-resolution cached image might not be accurate.

check for posterization, it's best to use a histogram based on the entire image rather than a sampling. No matter what the cache setting is, you can view an accurate histogram by holding down the Shift key while selecting the menu command Image, Histogram.

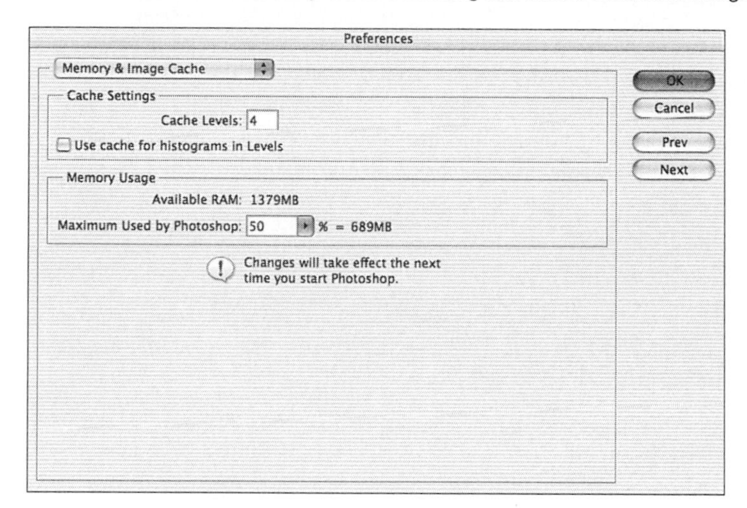


**Figure 2.14**
The available memory will not include that reserved by the computer's operating system.



- **Memory Usage**—This section of the Preferences dialog box shows you how much RAM is available and allows you to specify a preferred percentage. This setting, which can be changed by typing a value in the numeric field or by dragging the slider, puts a limit on the amount of memory you allow Photoshop to use. Changes are not put into effect until Photoshop is restarted.

## Preferences, File Browser

Photoshop CS's File Browser is a vast improvement over the initial implementation included in Photoshop 7. Along with the increased sophistication and power comes, of course, more complexity. The File Browser section of the Preferences dialog box, shown in Figure 2.15, helps control the operation of the File Browser.

- **Do Not Process File Larger Than ___ MB**—File Browser can slow to a crawl trying to extract or generate previews from huge files. This setting caps the size of a file for processing. The files will still appear in the File Browser with a generic icon or the word *Placeholder* in the area where a preview would be generated. Although the file's metadata isn't read by File Browser, the basic file information still appears (see Figure 2.16).
- **Display ___ Most Recently User Folders**—Located in the center of the File Browser window above the thumbnails and previews, the Locations pop-up menu includes recently visited folders at the bottom of the list. The number of folders there is set by this option.
- **Custom Thumbnail Size ___ px Wide**—File Browser's View menu has several choices for thumbnail size, including Custom. The values for this field can range from 128 pixels to 1,024 pixels.

- **Allow Background Processing**—When background processing is enabled, you can continue to work while File Browser generates previews and reads metadata for files.
- **Pre-generate High Quality Previews**—When this option is selected, File Browser doesn't wait until you click a file to generate the preview. Using this option and the preceding one, of course, requires some of your computer's attention, perhaps slowing things down somewhat.

If you work with small to moderately sized images, background processing and pregeneration of previews can be handy. If you work with very large images, you'll probably want to forego these options in most circumstances.



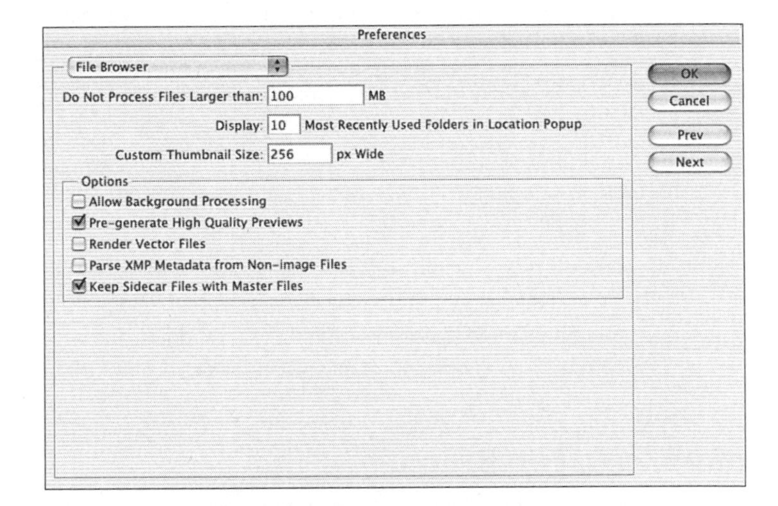


**Figure 2.15**
The preferences for the File Browser are generally aimed at improving performance.

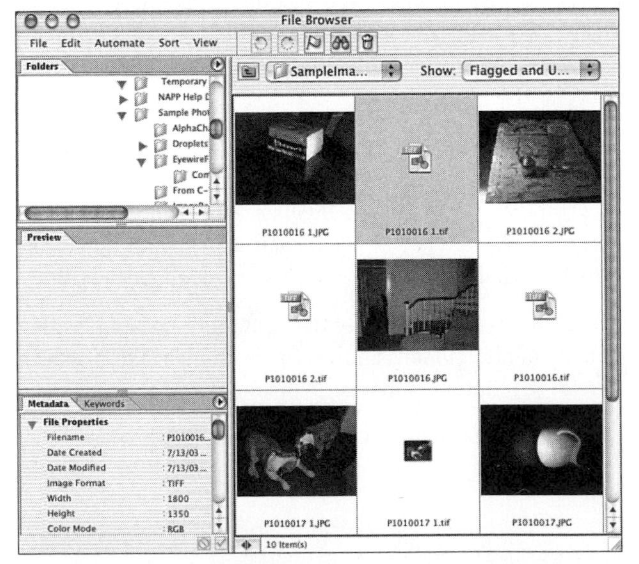


**Figure 2.16**
The selected file is too large for processing, so no preview is generated. Note, however, that the middle image in the bottom row was saved with a thumbnail, which appears despite the too-large-for-processing file size.

- **Render Vector Files**—Photoshop doesn't work with most vector file formats, such as WMF, EMF, and the AutoCAD DWG and DXF formats. It can, however, open formats such as EPS and PDF that may contain vector data. (Remember that EPS files are rasterized, including type, when opened in Photoshop.) This check box permits File Browser to attempt to generate previews of EPS and PDF files that do not contain thumbnails.
- **Parse XMP Metadata from Non-image Files**—When non-image files are included in a folder, File Brower generally ignores them. However, some file formats require additional files to store certain types of information outside the image file. You may need to peruse the metadata associated with an image file that's stored outside the image file itself. Use this option to enable that capability in File Browser.
- **Keep Sidecar Files with Master Files**—*Sidecar files* are files associated with an image file that contain information the image's own format can't retain. Examples include THM files containing thumbnails (hence the .thm extension) for some RAW files, and XMP files for formats that can't include that type of metadata. It's good practice to keep these files with the associated image file.



# SETTING IMAGEREADY'S PREFERENCES

ImageReady's preferences are independent of Photoshop's, but several of its options are comparable to options in Photoshop.

## Preferences, General

The General preferences for ImageReady have several choices that are identical to those in Photoshop's General preferences (see Figure 2.17). However, changing one program's option has no affect on the other program. Here are the available preferences:

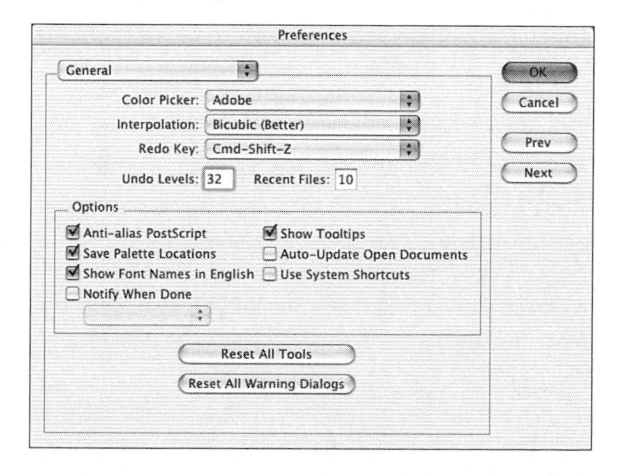


Figure 2.17
Windows doesn't offer the Use System Shortcuts option, but the General preferences are otherwise identical.

- **Color Picker**—Like Photoshop, ImageReady offers the option to use the system's color picker rather than the Adobe Color Picker.

- **Interpolation**—ImageReady CS offers the same five choices that are available in Photoshop CS, including the two new variations of bicubic interpolation. When you transform a selection, ImageReady must add or subtract pixels to make the new size conform to the image's resolution. *Bicubic* interpolation looks at a range of surrounding pixel color values to determine what color to make new pixels. This option produces the highest quality for photographic and continuous-tone images. ImageReady CS adds Bicubic Smoother and Bicubic Sharper to the choices. The first Bicubic option is somewhere between the Sharper and Smoother versions. *Bilinear* interpolation compares the adjacent pixels. It is faster than bicubic interpolation, but it generally produces less satisfactory results for photographs and artwork with gradients. Bilinear is an excellent choice when you're resizing artwork with areas or solid color and vertical or horizontal lines, such as interface elements. *Nearest neighbor* interpolation is the fastest of the three, but it should be avoided for photographic images. On the other hand, the Nearest Neighbor option is most appropriate for images that have large areas of solid color, especially in linear and rectangular shapes.

> Although more undo levels increases editing flexibility, it also increases the amount of memory used by ImageReady as you work. If RAM is not an issue, increase the Undo Levels setting. If memory is in short supply, keep the number small.

- **Redo Key**—ImageReady lacks Photoshop CS's new customizable keyboard shortcuts, so the Redo Key options take on somewhat more significance. The Undo shortcut remains (Command-Z) [Ctrl+Z], and this preference is where you select the opposite shortcut. The default, shown in Figure 2.17, simply adds the Shift key to the Undo shortcut. You also have the options of (Command-Y) [Ctrl+Y], which mirrors the Microsoft Office shortcut, and (Command-Z) [Ctrl+Z] to toggle between Undo and Redo.
- **Undo Levels**—ImageReady CS now has a History palette, similar to that in Photoshop. That feature makes the number of undo levels less important. How many levels are retained in memory is set by this option. The maximum value is 200.
- **Recent Files**—This field governs how many files will appear in the File, Open Recent list. The maximum is 50.
- **Anti-Alias PostScript**—When PostScript graphics are pasted into a raster image, they can be antialiased to smooth edges. Unchecking this box could lead to *jaggies* (that stair-step appearance) along curves and diagonal lines.
- **Save Palette Locations**—ImageReady CS's capability to save workspaces—arrangements of palettes—makes this option less important than in past versions. When this option is checked, the screen setup is saved when you quit. The next time that ImageReady is started, the palettes appear as last seen. When this option is unchecked, the palettes revert to their default locations every time the program opens.
- **Show Font Names in English**—Many non-English fonts have English-language equivalent names available. When this option is selected, the English name will appear in ImageReady's Font fields in the Options Bar (with the Type tool active) and the Character palette. If you don't work with foreign-language fonts, you can ignore this option.

- **Notify When Done**—If you'd like ImageReady to make an audible noise when it's finished with a long task, select this option. ImageReady for Windows will "beep" when the task is completed, whereas on the Macintosh side, you can be notified with the selected system alert sound or with a verbal warning using Text to Speech.

The preference Show Font Names in English has no effect on the appearance of symbol font names in the Font field. Such fonts as Zapf Dingbats and Wingdings will always be identified by the font name.

- **Show ToolTips**—*ToolTips* are the small message boxes that appear when the cursor is paused over an interface item. In ImageReady, ToolTips include the names of tools, naturally, as well as information about and tips for a variety of commands, palette buttons, and dialog check boxes (see Figure 2.18).

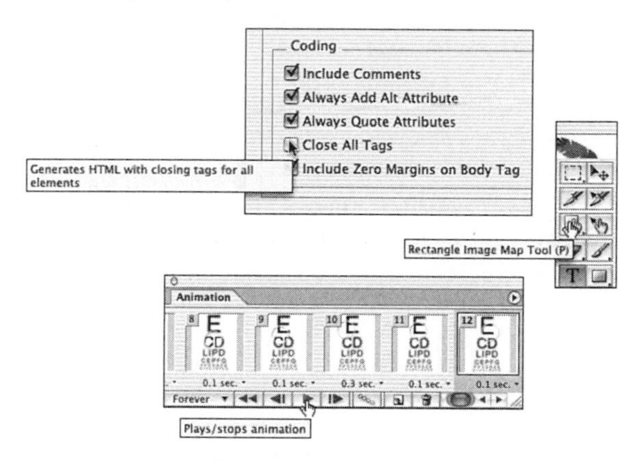


**Figure 2.18**
Although certainly not as "in depth" as the information in this book, ImageReady's ToolTips can provide valuable guidance.

- **Auto-Update Open Documents**—If a file is open in both ImageReady and another program and a change is made in the other program, this option determines whether that change will automatically be applied when you return to the ImageReady version of the artwork.

- **Use System Shortcuts (Mac only)**—Referring to the Mac OS keyboard shortcuts, this option offers you a chance to override ImageReady's shortcuts when they conflict with those of the OS. If you use OS X's shortcuts regularly, or have some special shortcuts, you can elect to have them retain their function while you're working in ImageReady. When this box is not checked, keyboard shortcuts will execute their ImageReady assignments while you're working in the program.

You don't need to worry about the Auto-Update option when switching between ImageReady and Photoshop. In the Creative Suite versions of the programs, only one copy of the file remains open when you switch back and forth between the two programs.

- **Reset All Tools**—Clicking this button restores the default behavior of all tools in ImageReady. This can also be done by (Control)-clicking right-clicking the tool icon at the left end of ImageReady's Options Bar (see Figure 2.19).

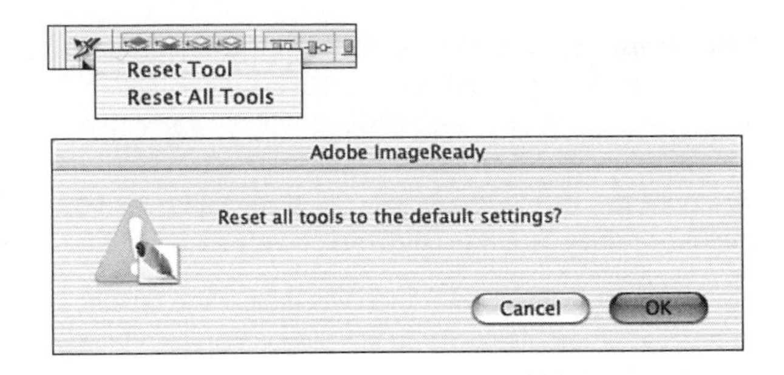


Figure 2.19
Unlike using the Reset All Tools button in the General preferences, resetting the tools from the Options Bar presents a verification dialog box.



- **Reset All Warning Dialogs**—If you've elected to check the Don't Show Again box in one or more warning dialog boxes, you can restore them to visibility by clicking this button.

## Preferences, Slices

The Slices options shown in Figure 2.20 do one thing and one thing only: They customize the appearance of slice lines onscreen. If you work with slices regularly and intensively, this customization can be quite handy. If you regularly work with color schemes that conflict with the default slice line colors, it makes sense to visit this Preferences panel. If you work with slices but let ImageReady do most of the work for you, perhaps you'll want to simplify the appearance of slice lines onscreen.

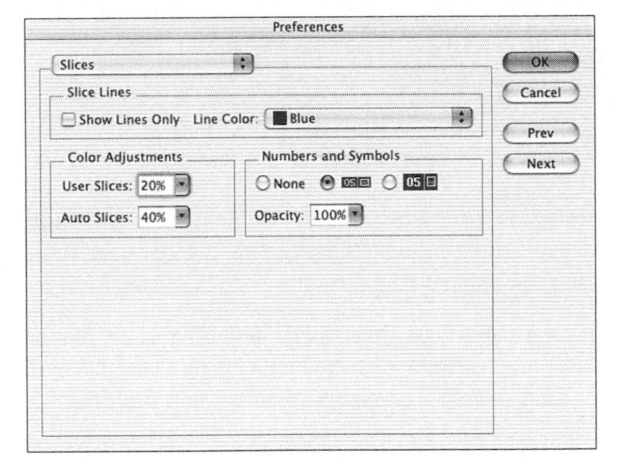


Figure 2.20
These options have no effect on how slices are created or recorded in HTML; they are for onscreen appearance only.

Here's a list of the Slices preferences:

- **Show Lines Only**—Checking this box simplifies the appearance of slices in ImageReady. You'll see only the slice lines themselves—no slice numbers and no differentiation between user slices and auto slices. You will, however, be able to identify a selected slice (see Figure 2.21). Checking this box disables the options in the dialog box, with the exception of Line Color.
- **Line Color**—ImageReady offers two dozen choices of the lines that show the boundaries of each slice. You have options ranging from blue, red, and green, to ochre, burgundy, and peach. There is no option for user-definable slice line color.

- **Color Adjustments**—As you can see in Figure 2.21, unselected slices are dimmed in the image window. The amount of dimming is determined by the options for the Color Adjustments preference. The User Slices field controls the dimming on unselected user slices, whereas Auto Slices handles the slices generated automatically by ImageReady. Using different values makes it easy to differentiate between the two types of slices.
- **Numbers and Symbols**—ImageReady offers the options of showing the slice number and symbol, in the upper-left corner of each slice, in two sizes, or not at all. In addition, you can adjust the transparency of the slice identifier.

Most of the time there's no need to see the slice symbol and slice numbers. You can select None in the Numbers and Symbols section of the Slices preferences. The slice number will still be visible in the Name field of the Slice palette.

Figure 2.21
To the left, Show Lines Only is selected in Preferences. On the right, you see the default slice appearance.

## Preferences, Image Maps

The appearance of image maps onscreen is controlled through the set of options shown in Figure 2.22 and detailed in the following list:

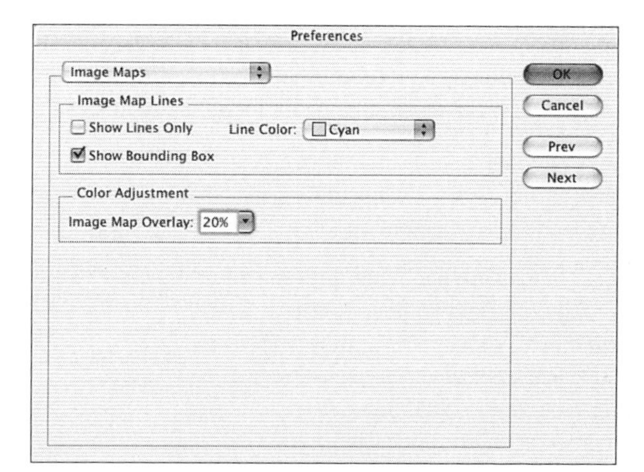


Figure 2.22
The Image Maps settings in this dialog box affect only the appearance of the image map on the monitor and have no impact on the final file.

- **Show Lines Only**—When this option is selected, the area enclosed by image maps will not be dimmed.
- **Line Color**—You have a selection of 24 colors from which to choose for image map outlines. The selected image map(s) will change to an automatically selected contrasting color.
- **Show Bounding Box**—This check box affects only circular image maps. When this option is selected, a square bounding box will indicate the extent of the image map. When this option is unselected, the anchor points of the bounding box will be visible, without connecting lines (see Figure 2.23).



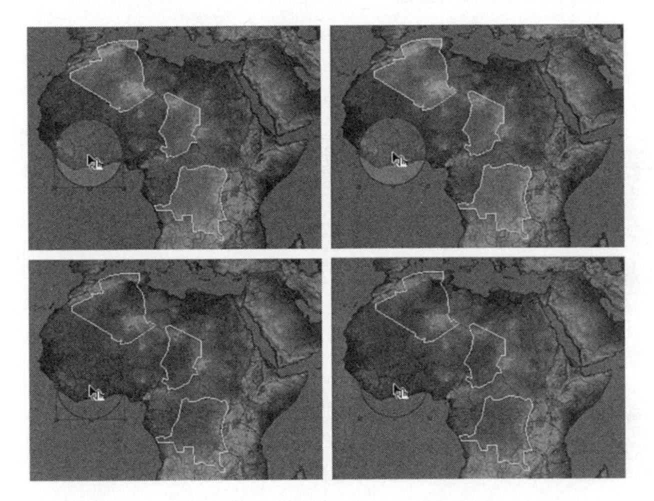

Figure 2.23
In the upper-left example, the bounding box is visible. In the upper-right example, the bounding box is hidden. In the lower-left example, Show Lines Only and Show Bounding Box are both selected. In the lower-right example, Show Lines Only is selected and the bounding box is hidden.

- **Image Map Overlay**—This option determines the opacity of each image map's white overlay. (The default, 20%, is shown in Figure 2.23.) At high values, the image within the image map is obscured by the overlay, whereas low values enable you to see the content.

## Preferences, Guides and Grid

The Guides and Grid options in ImageReady's Preferences dialog box are shown in Figure 2.24. There are a number of differences between these options in ImageReady and their Photoshop counterparts:

- **Guide Color**—ImageReady offers a list of 10 colors for guides. Unlike Photoshop, there is no Custom option.
- **Smart Guide Color**—*Smart guides* are lines that appear to indicate alignment among objects in an image. When you're dragging an image map, for example, a guide will appear to indicate that a corner or edge of the image map is aligned to another (see Figure 2.25). ImageReady offers 10 preset color choices for smart guides.

Remember that the keyboard shortcut (Command-H) [Ctrl+H] toggles the visibility of the items selected in View, Show Extras Options. By default, that includes image maps. You can use the shortcut to hide and show image maps as necessary.

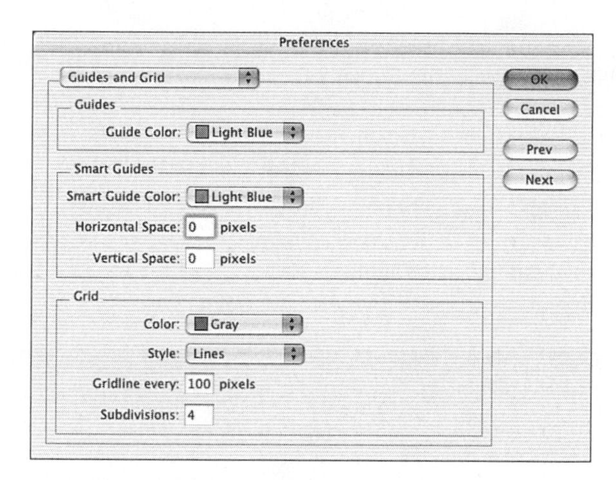


**Figure 2.24**
Unlike Photoshop, ImageReady does not offer dashed lines for guides.

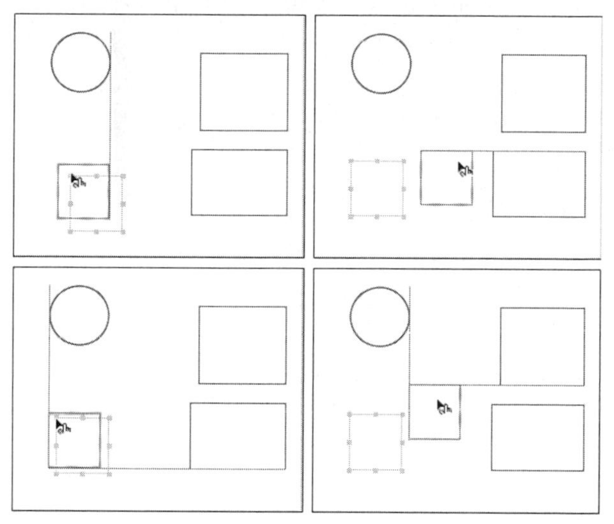

**Figure 2.25**
The smart guides are the horizontal and vertical lines that show alignment. (The image itself has been hidden to make the image maps and smart guides more apparent.)



In Figure 2.25, the smart guides indicate the alignment of the image map being dragged. (Note that the Smart Guides monitor all four edges of the object being moved, showing each edge's relationship, as appropriate.)

- **Upper left**—Aligned with the left edge of the circle.
- **Upper right**—Aligned with the top of the lower rectangle.
- **Lower left**—Aligned with the right edge of the circle and the lower edge of the lower rectangle.
- **Lower right**—Aligned with the right edge of the circle and the lower edge of the upper rectangle.

- **Horizontal and Vertical Space**—The Space fields give the smart guides two parameters for alignment. In addition to the actual edges of an object, you can specify a distance from the object, vertically or horizontally, to which the alignment will *also* be indicated. For example, if the Horizontal and Vertical Space fields are set to 10 pixels each, smart guides will appear when an object being moved is aligned with another object's edge *and* when the object being moved is aligned with an imaginary point 10 pixels outside the object. Distances up to 500 pixels can be specified. The fields also accept negative numbers for alignment to points within an object, such as the center point.

Although the Grid Subdivisions field allows you to input any value from 0 to 500, no subdivisions will appear unless the spacing is at least 4 pixels.

- **Grid Color**—Ten preset colors are available for the grid, but ImageReady doesn't offer the option of assigning a custom color.
- **Grid Style**—The grid can be shown onscreen as solid or dashed lines or as a series of dots.
- **Gridline Every ____ Pixels**—This field specifies the spacing of grid lines. Values can range up to 500 pixels.
- **Subdivisions**—This value determines the number of intermediate gridlines that will be visible. Subdivisions are rounded to the nearest whole pixel.

## Preferences, Optimization

The Optimization preferences determine the default values in the Optimize palette and the content of the panes in the 2-Up and 4-Up views:

- **Default Optimization**—Your choices for the default settings in the Optimize palette are Previous Settings (excellent when preparing a series of similar images or interface elements), Auto Select GIF or JPEG (great when you're working with a wide variety of images in one or more sessions), and Named Settings (perfect for use when 100% consistency must be maintained from image to image).
- **2-Up Settings**—When you're using ImageReady's 2-Up view, a pair of images are compared onscreen. By default, the left pane (or the top pane for short, wide images) shows the original image, whereas the second pane shows the current settings of the Optimize palette. When the first pane is set to Original, the second pane must show the value in the Optimize palette (Current in the pop-up menu). If the first pane is set to show the current palette values, the second pane can show how the image will appear with any of the preset values of the palette. (The list of values is shown in Figure 2.26.)
- **4-Up Settings**—The four panes of the 4-Up view can be set to a variety of behaviors. However, the first pane can show only the original image or the current settings of the Optimize palette. When the first pane is sent to Original, the second pane will show only Current. The third and fourth panes can show any of the values

If your work varies from day to day or session to session, remember that Default Optimization can easily be changed to fit your current needs. You don't even have to restart ImageReady after changing the preference.

shown in the pop-up menu in Figure 2.26. If you change the first pane to Current, all three of the other panes can show any value from the pop-up menu.

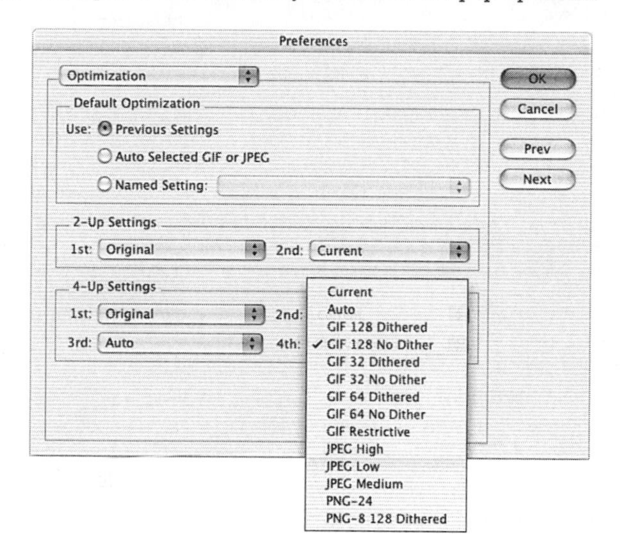


**Figure 2.26**
The Auto value calculates optimization settings based on the content of the image.

## Preferences, Cursors

Like Photoshop, ImageReady offers a choice of cursor appearance for the various tools. Painting tools can show the tool icon (Standard), the Precise cursor crosshairs, or the Brush Size cursor. For the nonpainting tools, you have the option of Standard or Precise. Certain tools have only the tool icon cursors, including the Move, Slice Select, Image Map Select, Hand, and Zoom tools.

Remember that the Caps Lock key toggles between cursors. If you've got the Brush Size and Standard cursors selected, the Caps Lock key will bring up the Precise cursor.

## Preferences, Transparency

The Transparency options affect only the appearance of the transparency grid, the onscreen pattern that indicates transparency in an image. Visible "behind" the image where pixels have reduced opacity, the default appearance is a gray-and-white checkerboard pattern. In the Transparency preferences, you can choose from three sizes of grid (or no grid) and the color of the grid squares. Select light, medium, or dark grays, or from white and one of five other colors. In addition, you can select Custom from the pop-up menu or click each of the sample swatches and assign colors from the Color Picker.

If you're having trouble seeing partial transparency or if the grid conflicts with your image, try changing the grid size and/or colors in Preferences.

## Preferences, Plug-Ins

On startup, ImageReady can load plug-ins from a second folder in addition to the default folder. You set the location of the second folder in the Preferences, Plug-ins pane. Keep in mind that the more plug-ins you load, the longer it takes for ImageReady to start. Also, the memory requirements for the program to operate are higher.

You can have as many plug-ins folders as you want, remembering that ImageReady will only load one additional set of plug-ins per session. You can create different folders with different sets of plug-ins for different purposes. If you have plug-ins that you use all the time and others that you need only for certain types of projects, you can add shortcuts of the "need-always" plug-ins to each folder.



# SETTING ILLUSTRATOR'S PREFERENCES

Illustrator has eight dialog box panels devoted to application preferences. You can access all of them by choosing Illustrator, Preferences for Mac OS X, or Edit, Preferences for Windows. Additionally, pressing (Command-K) [Ctrl+K] opens the first dialog box (Preferences, General), and you can assign keyboard shortcuts to each panel individually.

When Illustrator doesn' t want to work correctly, one of your first troubleshooting steps should be deleting the Preferences file. When Illustrator cannot find the appropriate file, a new set of preferences is generated with the factory-default settings. See the section "Quick Fix—Replacing the Preferences," later in this chapter.

## Preferences, General

The General preferences include the basic behavior and interface selections for Illustrator (Figure 2.27 shows this dialog box):

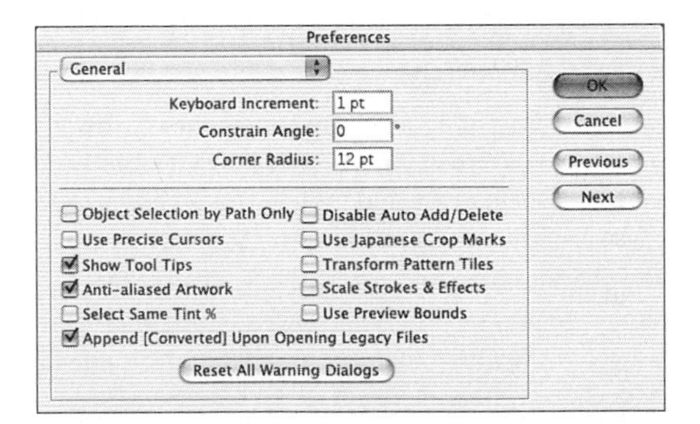


Figure 2.27
You can access the General preferences through the keyboard shortcut (Command-K) [Ctrl+K] or by choosing Edit, Preferences, General.

- **Keyboard Increment**—This field controls how far a selected object will move when an arrow key is pressed.
- **Constrain Angle**—The value entered here rotates the theoretical angle of the artboard and document. Objects that are created along the vertical or horizontal axis are affected, including patterns, text, and graphs. You also can drag with the Shift key and use the arrows keys with

the new angle. This feature can be handy for working with perspective. Existing objects and anything not angle dependent (blending, rotating, the Pencil tool, and so on) are not affected.

- **Corner Radius**—This option changes the default setting for the Rounded Rectangle tool. When you click the tool on the artboard and make an adjustment in the dialog box, the General preferences are also updated.
- **Object Selection by Path Only**—When this box is checked, you must click the stroke (path) of an object to select it. When the option is not selected, you can click an object's fill to select it as well as the path. Checking this option can be helpful when many objects overlap.
- **Use Precise Cursors**—The various tools' cursors change to their precision equivalents. Drawing tools, lassos, transform tools, and the like now appear on the artboard as crosshairs rather than their regular icons or brush sizes. The Caps Lock key toggles between the cursor options for many tools.
- **Show ToolTips**—This option enables you to see the names and shortcuts (if any) of various tools and information about various fields in many palettes. Pausing the cursor over an icon in the Tool palette brings up the little ToolTip message. When you're familiar with Illustrator's interface, these tips may be unnecessary.
- **Anti-Aliased Artwork**—Antialiasing smoothes the appearance of artwork onscreen. It softens edges by adding gray or colored pixels to help edges blend, avoiding the problem known as the jaggies. This option can, however, make thin curved lines and small text look blurry onscreen and can substantially slow screen redraw on less-powerful machines. This option has no effect on printed illustrations.
- **Select Same Tint %**—This option determines whether tints of a color will be added to a selection with the Select commands. When you choose Edit, Select, Same Fill Color and the related commands, Illustrator, by default, adds to the selection all objects with the same color, regardless of tint. Objects with a 20% tint of the color are selected along with objects having an 85% tint. When this box is checked, on the other hand, the Edit, Select commands treat each tint percentage as a separate color.
- **Append [Converted] Upon Opening Legacy Files**—When a file from an earlier version of Illustrator is opened in Illustrator CS, this check box gives you the option of identifying the file as such. The word *Converted*, in square brackets, will appear both in the image window's title bar and also in the filename in the Save As dialog box.
- **Disable Auto Add/Delete**—Checking this box prevents the Pen tool from changing to the Add Anchor Point tool or the Delete Anchor Point tool when over a path segment or anchor point. You can obtain this same effect by holding down the Shift key when starting a new path. (Note that you should press the Shift key, press the mouse button, release the Shift key, and then release the mouse button.)
- **Use Japanese Crop Marks**—These crop marks are substantially different from those considered standard in many other parts of the world. They produce pairs of marks in each corner, one set for vertical and one for horizontal, as well as centering marks on all four sides. When you get

accustomed to them, they can convey far more information. However, they remain nonstandard in much of the world.

- **Transform Pattern Tiles**—This option determines whether any pattern in a transformed object also gets transformed. When a box filled with a pattern is rotated, for example, the pattern remains vertical when this box is not checked.
- **Scale Strokes & Effects**—This choice is for use with the Transform commands. When this box is unchecked, the stroke and any effects applied to an object retain their original proportions when the object is scaled. When this box is checked, stroke weight and the size of the effects are scaled to preserve the relative appearance of an object.
- **Use Preview Bounds**—When this option is checked, a bounding box will include all of an object's effects. The bounding box expands to include the entire area covered by the object and applied effects. When this box is unchecked, the bounding box in Preview mode is the size of the selected object or objects. (Note that the bounding box always includes the area of filters applied to an object, whether or not this option is checked.)
- **Reset All Warning Dialogs**—Click this button to restore warning dialog boxes that have been checked for Don't Show This Warning Again. This button does not reverse the check mark for the preference Disable Warnings.



## Preferences, Type & Auto Tracing

The Type & Auto Tracing pane of the Preferences dialog box, shown in Figure 2.28, is divided into two sections. The top half pertains to type, text, and fonts, and the bottom portion involves only the performance of the Auto Trace tool.

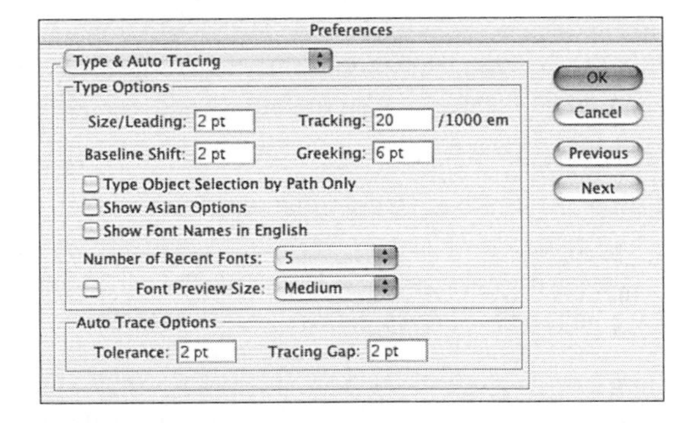


Figure 2.28
The two halves of this dialog box have nothing in common. They are grouped together for convenience.

You can choose from these settings for Type preferences:

- **Size/Leading**—This field determines the increment of change for keyboard adjustments of leading (vertical spacing between lines of type). (*Leading* is pronounced like the name of the metal rather than as a form of the verb *to lead*.) The keyboard shortcut for adjusting leading is (Option) [Alt] and the up or down arrow key.

- **Baseline Shift**—This value determines the increment of change for keyboard adjustments of the position of one or more selected characters. Baseline Shift can either be positive (superscript) or negative (subscript). To change the baseline of selected text using the keyboard, press (Shift-Option) [Shift+Alt) and the up or down arrow key.

- **Tracking**—You can adjust the increment for changing the space between a series of letters with this field. Tracking is applied to two or more letters, including entire words, lines, and paragraphs. Tracking is measured in thousandths of an *em*, whose size is equivalent to the current font size. For example, in a 12-point font, an em is equal to 12 points, and in a 24-point font, an em is equal to 24 points. Tracking by negative numbers moves letters closer together than is the norm for the particular font; positive tracking values spread the letters out. To adjust tracking, select one or more characters on the artboard and use (Option) [Alt] and the left or right arrow key. Adding the (Command) [Ctrl] key increases the adjustment by a factor of five.

> The Tracking field also controls the amount of change for keyboard kerning. To adjust tracking, you select one or more characters. To change kerning, click between two characters. The keyboard shortcuts are the same for tracking and kerning.

- **Greeking**—*Greeking* replaces type that is too small to read onscreen with a gray bar, which serves as a placeholder for the text. When this option is set at the default of 6 points, any text added to the artboard at 6 points or smaller appears as a bar. However, if the image is displayed at a zoom factor of 200%, that 6-point type becomes legible again because it is proportional to 12-point type at 100% zoom. Likewise with the default, 12-point type gets greeked when the zoom factor is at 50%. Greeking does not affect printed artwork; it serves only as an *onscreen* reminder/placeholder for text that is too small to read.

- **Type Object Selection by Path Only**—When checked, this option allows you to select a line or block of type only when you click the Direct Selection tool (or other selection tool) on the path (baseline) or a type object. When this option is unchecked, you can select type by clicking anywhere on the type object.

- **Show Asian Options**—When this box is checked, the Character and Paragraph palettes expand to show options specific to Asian fonts.

- **Show Font Names in English**—This option applies only to double-byte (2-byte) fonts, such as Chinese, Japanese, and Korean (CJK) typefaces. The font menu shows either the font's true name (with this option unchecked in Preferences) or its English equivalent (checked).

- **Number of Recent Fonts**—When the Type tool is active you can (Control)-click right-click to show the contextual menu and select from a list of recently used fonts (see Figure 2.29). This field determines how many fonts will be listed, up to a maximum of 15.

- **Font Preview Size**—Illustrator CS now shows fonts in their typefaces in the Font menu, if this option is selected. (When this option is unchecked, the name appears in the font in the standard interface appearance.) You can select Small, Medium, or Large for the preview. The larger the size, the better the view of the font, but the fewer fonts that can be displayed without scrolling the menu. Previewing fonts can also slow the appearance of the Font menu onscreen.

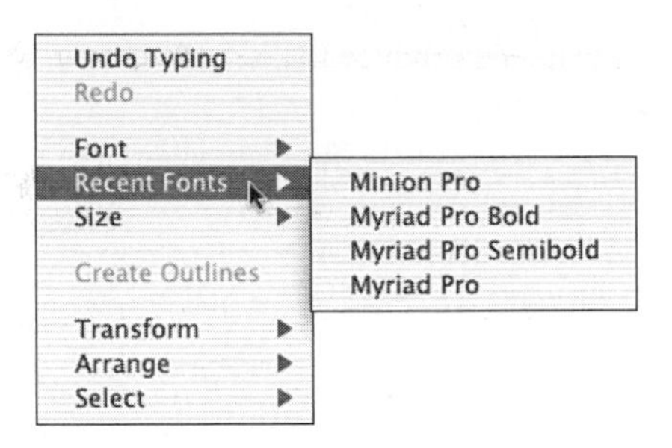


Figure 2.29
The contextual menu is a great way to speed font selection, especially when you're using only a few fonts.

The Auto Trace area of this Preferences pane offers these options:

- **Auto Trace Tolerance**—This field determines how closely a path produced by the Auto Trace tool will follow the original.
- **Tracing Gap**—Use this value to compensate for small breaks in artwork being traced with the Auto Trace tool.

## Preferences, Units & Display Performance

The two halves of the Units & Display Performance pane, shown in Figure 2.30, like a number of preference combinations, have little in common.

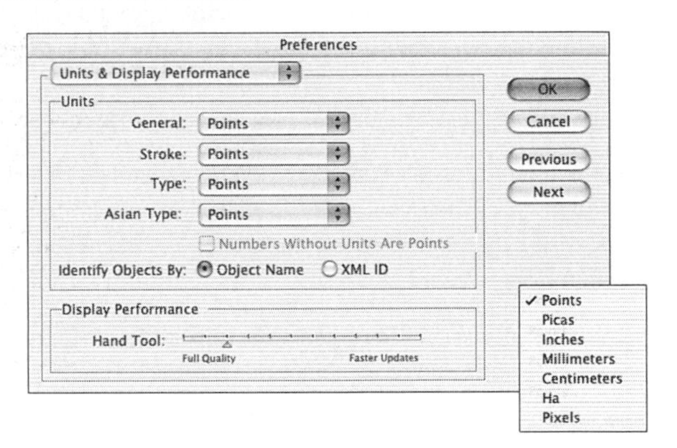


Figure 2.30
Several units of measure are available in Illustrator, as shown in the inset to the lower right.

These settings are available for Units preferences:

- **General**—This value represents the unit of measure of most Illustrator operations. In addition to the obvious application of the unit to the rulers, it also affects some of the Transform tools, the Info palette, moving objects, and guides and grid settings. This setting does not affect type or text. There are 72 points in 1 inch and 12 points in 1 pica. When you're preparing images for the Web, pixels are the most appropriate unit of measure.
- **Stroke**—Use this pop-up menu to set the unit of measure for lines and strokes of objects. The choices are the same as those shown in Figure 2.30 for General.

- **Type**—The Type pop-up menu determines the unit of measure for text. In addition to the standard points, Illustrator allows you to measure type in inches, millimeters, Q's (one-quarter of a millimeter), or pixels.
- **Asian Type**—This pop-up menu offers only points, inches, millimeters, Ha, or pixels. (100 Ha, abbreviation H, is equal to 2.5 centimeters or 0.984 inches.)
- **Numbers Without Units Are Points**—This check box is only available when the General unit of measure is set to picas.
- **Identify Objects By**—This option gives you the choice of identifying objects by name or by the Extensible Markup Language (XML) ID. The latter is used with some of Illustrator's advanced Web-related capabilities.

*You've set the units that you want to use, but the rulers don't agree with you. They don't seem to know which way is up. Check "Setting the Point of Origin" in the "Mastering the Adobe Creative Suite" section at the end of this chapter.*

The Display Performance area offers a single setting:

- **Hand Tool**—When you're zoomed in or working on a very large document, the Hand tool can be an easy and quick way to navigate. This slider determines whether onscreen appearance or the speed of screen redraw will take precedence.

## Preferences, Guides & Grid

In addition to starting with the same letter, the Guides & Grid preferences actually have much in common and are well suited to share a dialog box (see Figure 2.31). Both are used to align and regulate the position of artwork, both are nonprinting, and both can be shown or hidden through the View menu:

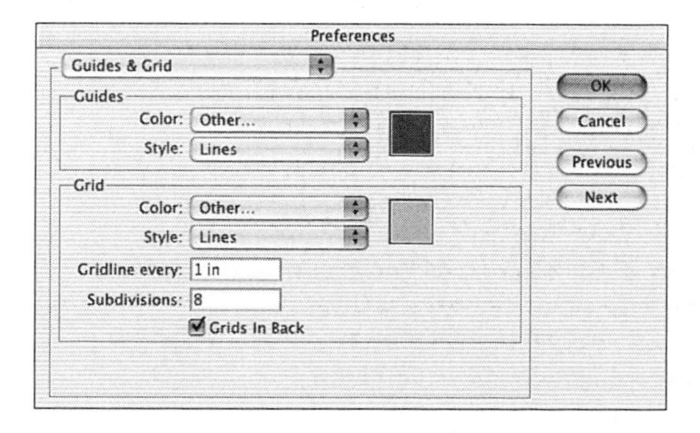


Figure 2.31
The guides and grid are both nonprinting, "snappable," alignment tools.

- **Guides**—Illustrator gives you a choice of nine presets as well as Other, which opens the Color Picker and a nearly infinite variety of colors for the guides. Although the default color is fine for most projects, an image that is blue itself may require guides of a different color. You also have a choice of lines or dots for the guides' appearance onscreen.

- **Grid**—Here, you've got the same nine presets as with Guides, as well as Other, as the color choices for the grid. Like guides, the grid can be composed of lines or dots. You use this panel of the Preferences dialog box to specify the spacing of the grid's lines as well as the number of minor divisions between those lines. When the Grids in Back box is checked, artwork appears on top. When this box is unchecked, the grid will show above the artwork.

## Preferences, Smart Guides & Slices

You can activate smart guides by choosing View, Smart Guides. These temporary guides conform to your current needs. They are governed by the choices made in the Smart Guides & Slices pane of the Preferences dialog box, shown in Figure 2.32:

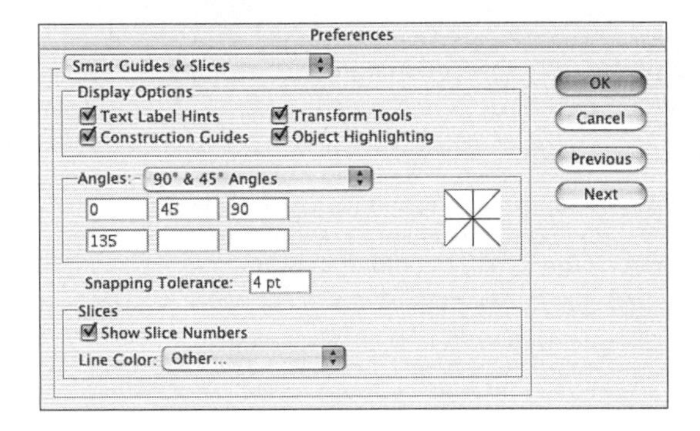


Figure 2.32
The Smart Guides preferences have no effect if smart guides are not activated through the View menu.

- **Text Label Hints**—These onscreen "hints" show you what the smart guide is using as a reference point.
- **Construction Guides**—When this option is selected, smart guides will include the intersection of guides as points from which they can take a bearing.
- **Transform Tools**—This option activates smart guides when you rotate, shear, or scale an object.
- **Object Highlighting**—When this box is checked, an unselected object underneath the cursor will be highlighted as a selected object is dragged over it.
- **Angles**—This pop-up menu offers you several options for the activation of smart guides: 90°, 45°, 90° & 45°, 60°, 60° & Horizontal, 30°, 90° & 15°, and Custom. The boxes below the pop-up menu and the thumbnail to the right are updated with the choice.
- **Snapping Tolerance**—Use this field to determine how close an object (and the cursor) must be to another object to snap to it. The unit of measure is that set for General in the Units & Undo preferences panel.
- **Show Slice Numbers**—When this box is checked, Illustrator shows a slice's number in the upper-left corner of the slice. Slices are used on the Web to break a

Smart guides are not available when Snap to Grid is active, even if the option is checked in the View menu.

single image into multiple parts for optimization and image mapping. Slices are visible only when that option is selected in the View menu.

- **Line Color**—You select the color used to identify the edges of slices (when visible) with this pop-up menu. You can choose from nine presets, or you can use Other to assign your own choice.

## Preferences, Hyphenation

As you can see in Figure 2.33, the Hyphenation pane of the Preferences dialog box is relatively straightforward:

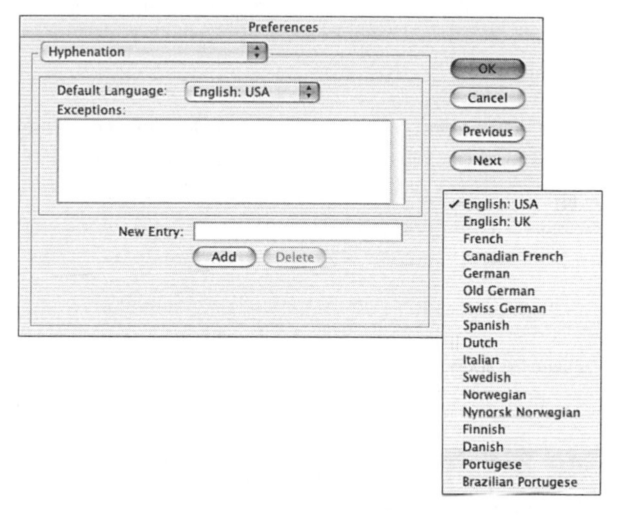


Figure 2.33
The hyphenation options, although simple, offer word-by-word control in a variety of languages.

- **Default Language**—Illustrator offers 17 choices, shown in the inset of Figure 2.33.
- **Exceptions**—This is a list of words that should be hyphenated as specified in the list rather than as specified in Illustrator's hyphenation files.
- **New Entry**—This field is used to add a word to the Exceptions list. To add a word, type it in the text entry field, inserting hyphens where you want the hyphenation points to be, and click Add. Likewise, use the Delete button to remove a custom entry.

If you work in only one language, you can delete the files for other languages. You can find them in a folder called Text Filters inside the Illustrator Plug-ins folder.

## Preferences, Plug-ins & Scratch Disk

*Plug-ins* are mini programs that work within Illustrator to accomplish certain tasks. In addition to the supplied plug-ins that work with filters, file formats, and tools, you can add third-party plug-ins. Figure 2.34 shows the dialog box for the Plug-ins & Scratch Disk preferences, which enables you to choose a folder of plug-ins.

Illustrator uses scratch disks to support the allocated memory. They are especially important when you're applying memory-intensive filters or effects to complex objects.

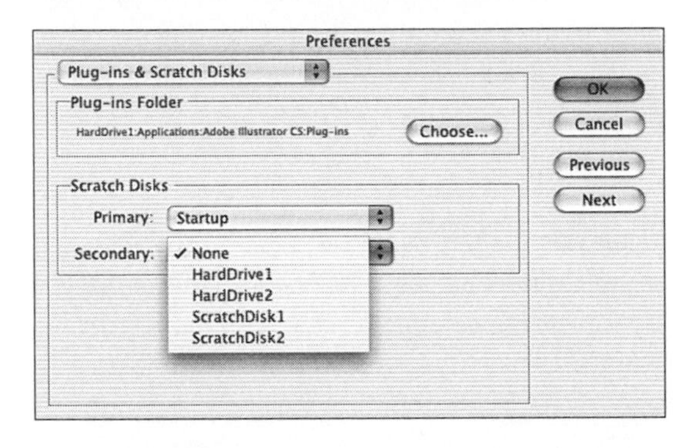


Figure 2.34
The two halves of this preferences dialog box are, again, unrelated.

Here are the options available in the Plug-ins & Scratch Disk pane of the Preferences dialog box:

- **Plug-ins Folder**—The Choose button enables you to select a folder of plug-ins. Note that Illustrator recognizes only one plug-ins folder at a time. Because plug-ins add to loading time, if you have many, you might want to split them into separate folders. If you do, make sure you copy key plug-ins to each folder. Such things as tools and file formats might be needed with all sets. You also might want to delete unnecessary plug-ins from the default folder.
- **Scratch Disks**—The Primary and Secondary pop-up menus let you assign scratch disks to Illustrator. The upper pop-up menu offers Startup and any additional drives available, whereas the second menu offers all drives and the option of None.

## Preferences, File Handling & Clipboard

The File Handling & Clipboard preferences, shown in Figure 2.35, involve saving files and exchanging information between programs:

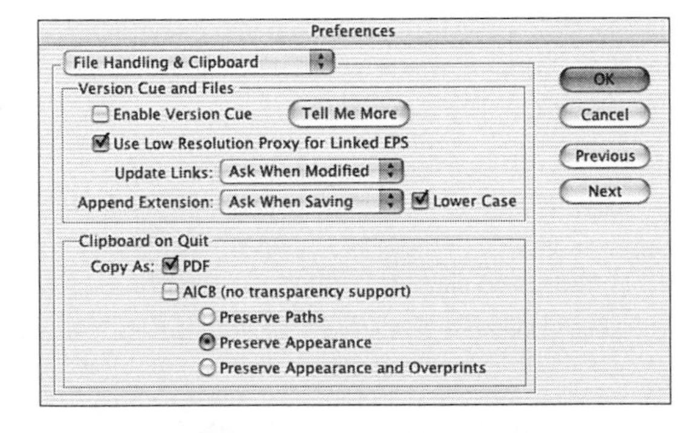


Figure 2.35
The Append Extension option doesn't appear in the Windows version of this dialog box. Appending the file extension is a requirement when you're preparing files that will be used on Windows machines.

In the Version Cue and Files section, choose from these settings options:

- **Enable Version Cue**—Version Cue is Adobe's latest workgroup file-management product. It enables multiple individuals to work on a single file without creating conflicts or overwriting each others' work. The Tell Me More button takes you to the appropriate entry in Illustrator's Help.

- **Use Low Resolution Proxy for Linked EPS**—When this option is selected, Illustrator will use a low-resolution image onscreen for any linked EPS file. The full-resolution image will output, but screen redraw may be faster (although less accurate).
- **Update Links**—The choices in this pop-up menu are Ask When Modified, Automatically, and Manually. The three choices are all designed to help you ensure that the correct version of a linked file is used. When Automatically is selected, Illustrator always uses the latest version of the linked file. If you choose Manually, it will be up to you to update the file. Ask When Modified monitors the linked file, and if there are chances from the version currently used in the Illustrator document, you'll be prompted to update the linked file.

There may be times when you *don't* want to update a linked file. Perhaps you've got the perfect version for your chart or illustration, but you know further changes will be made to the original. Having Update Links set to Manually ensures that your linked file won't be accidentally replaced by a more recent version. And when this is the situation, consider embedding rather than linking (if the file format can be embedded).

- **Append Extension (Mac only)**—Illustrator offers Macintosh users a choice of when to add the file format extension to a filename when saving. The choices are Never, Always, and Ask When Saving.
- **Lower Case**—This box ensures maximum filename compatibility when checked.

In the Clipboard on Quit area, you can choose between a couple ways to handle data copied to the Clipboard in Illustrator:

- **Copy As PDF**—Illustrator uses the Portable Document Format for the Clipboard, in addition to the PICT data. The internal Clipboard can be used among Adobe products or can transfer data to another program. Some programs, such as Adobe InDesign, require the PDF version of the data.
- **Copy As AICB**—This option adds a copy of the selection to the Clipboard as Adobe Illustrator Clipboard data. Similar to EPS, it simulates transparency. This is the preferred format for Adobe Photoshop.
- **Preserve Paths**—You can give priority to the integrity of the vector paths, allowing them to be edited.
- **Preserve Appearance**—This option forgoes paths to maintain the look of an object.
- **Preserve Appearance and Overprints**—If the image will be output on an offset press as CMYK, you may need to preserve the overprinting instructions.

# QUICK FIX—REPLACING THE PREFERENCES

Sometimes Photoshop doesn't seem to work quite right. Tools don't perform correctly, commands don't execute the way they should, the interface is mangled, Photoshop runs slowly or crashes often—these problems could all be signs of a corrupted Preferences file. Instead of reinstalling the entire Photoshop program, you can often simply replace the "Prefs."

## The Prefs: What They Are and How They Work

In addition to the options selected in the Preferences dialog box, the Prefs file stores such settings as the positions of the palettes, tool settings, guide and grid settings, scratch disk locations, and file-saving settings. It is updated every time you quit Photoshop. (It is not updated during a crash.) Because the file is rewritten so often, it is subject to corruption.

When Photoshop is started, it looks for the Prefs file and loads the last settings. If it cannot find a Prefs file, Photoshop loads the default settings.

*If you restarted Photoshop and your most recent settings weren' t loaded, see "Unwritten Preferences" in the "Mastering the Adobe Creative Suite" section at the end of this chapter.*

## Finding the Prefs

Photoshop's Prefs file is stored in different locations for different platforms. In the following list, folder names are separated by slashes. The notation [username] represents the name of your particular account on that computer. For example, in the Mac OS X hierarchy, [username] might be replaced by pbauer or jfoster. Here, then, is where the Prefs file is stored on these popular platforms:

- **Mac OS X**—Users\[username]\Library\Preferences\Adobe Photoshop CS Settings\Adobe Photoshop CS Prefs
- **Windows XP**—Documents and Settings\[username]\Application Data\Adobe\Photoshop\8.0 \Adobe Photoshop CS Settings\Adobe Photoshop CS Prefs (see Figure 2.36)

**Figure 2.36**
The path shown to the right is comparable for Windows 2000.

| Mac OS X | Windows |
|---|---|
| [hardrive] | C: |
| Users | Documents and Settings |
| [username] | [username] |
| Library | Application Data |
| Preferences | Adobe |
| Adobe Photoshop CS Settings | Photoshop |
| Adobe Photoshop CS Prefs.psp | 8.0 |
| | Adobe Photoshop CS Settings |
| | Adobe Photoshop CS Prefs.psp |

- **Windows 2000**—Documents and Settings\[username]\Application Data\Adobe\Photoshop\8.0 \Adobe Photoshop CS Settings\Adobe Photoshop CS Prefs

## Replacing the Prefs to Reset Photoshop

The easiest way to cure basic Photoshop ills is to replace a corrupted Prefs file. The easiest way to do that is simply to delete the file and let Photoshop generate a new one to replace it. To restore Photoshop to its default settings, hold down (Command-Option-Shift) [Ctrl+Alt+Shift] when starting the program.

One way to help prevent corruption of the Photoshop Prefs is to lock the file with one of these methods:

- In Mac OS X, locate the file in the Finder and press Command-I to open Get Info. Click once on the Locked check box.
- Windows users should find the Prefs file in My Computer and click it once to highlight it. From the File menu, select Properties (or right-click to pen the contextual menu). Select the Read-only check box and click OK.



## The Additional Preferences Files

In addition to the Prefs file, the Adobe Photoshop CS Settings folder holds a variety of other files. You'll find separate files for the Actions palette, brushes, styles, shapes, swatches, and more. That's also the location of a folder called Workspaces, which holds your custom work setups.

What you *won't* find in the Settings folder are preferences for Save for Web and ImageReady. On both Windows and Macintosh, Save for Web and ImageReady generate their own Preferences files. You'll find the folders in the same location as the Adobe Photoshop CS Settings folder.

## Photoshop at Work: Replacing the Prefs File

Replacing the Photoshop Prefs file is often the fastest and easiest way to cure problems with the program—it's certainly easier than suffering through a full reinstall of the program. There are some things that can make this process easier. For example, rather than restore to the factory defaults, you can replace a corrupt Preferences file with a copy that is preset to restore your preferred settings. Create a custom set of preferences and then copy that file as a backup. Use it to replace a corrupt file. Here's how to set it up:

1. Shut down Photoshop if it's running and then delete the existing Prefs file.
2. Start Photoshop and set up everything just the way you like it. Arrange palettes, select tool presets, and establish your preferred settings in the Preferences panes.
3. Immediately quit Photoshop.
4. Locate the new Prefs file.
5. Duplicate the file and put it someplace other than the Photoshop Settings folder.
6. When you need to replace a corrupt Prefs file, simply delete the bad file and copy the duplicate into the Settings folder (make sure that the name is exactly the same).

# MASTERING THE ADOBE CREATIVE SUITE

## Transparency and Background Layers

*No matter how I set the transparency grid, I can't see it. What's wrong?*



Open the Layers palette and look for a layer named Background. A background layer does not support transparency, so you won't see the grid "behind" it. To correct the problem, convert the background layer to a regular layer by renaming it. Double-click the word *Background* in the Layers palette and type the new name.

## Unwritten Preferences

*I set up all my palettes, tools, and settings just the way I wanted them and then immediately quit Photoshop. When I restarted the program, my custom settings weren't there, just the defaults. Any ideas?*

Check the Prefs file to see if it's locked. Photoshop won't warn you when it can't update the Prefs, assuming that you've locked the file to protect it.

## Setting the Point of Origin

*I like to use pixels as my "general" unit of measure, but it doesn't do me any good when the rulers seem to start in strange places. What can I do to fix things?*

Because your unit of choice is pixels, my guess would be that you work with the Web. Typically, a Web page begins measurement from the upper-left corner of the page. Print pages, on the other hand, default to the lower-left corner as the so-called "point of origin." Show the rulers by choosing View, Show Rulers or by pressing (Command-R) (Ctrl+R). Go to the upper-left corner of the screen, where the vertical and horizontal rulers come together. Click and drag from that point to the upper-left corner of the document and release. The rulers are then reset to that spot as the point of origin.

3

# UNDERSTANDING AND CHOOSING FILE FORMATS

## IN THIS CHAPTER

In this chapter, file formats are discussed, as are the various capabilities of each format and information on which format to select for which purpose. The information you learn here will help you determine an appropriate file format based on a file's final destination. You'll find a handy chart presenting the format capabilities and limitations of the major raster image formats. The chapter also offers an extensive discussion of how the JPEG file format compresses data, and the hazards of saving as JPEG multiple times.

Photoshop's new PSB file format for large images is presented here, as is the JPEG 2000 file format.

# CHOOSING A FILE FORMAT

Selecting the proper file format for your final artwork or project can mean the difference between having a usable document and a worthless collection of zeros and ones recorded to magnetic media. The file format should be determined by the image's final destination; for example, the Web has different requirements than do page layout programs. Even the Web design or page layout program you use can make a difference in what format to choose.



Within the broad categories of Web and print, additional choices need to be made. The file content will help you determine which format to choose.

## Basic Concepts

Different file formats have different capabilities. Photoshop's native PSD format supports all the program's features. Some formats restrict the number of colors that can be used in a file (GIF and PNG-8, for example), and many don't support the CMYK color mode. The capability of portraying transparency with clipping paths and/or alpha channels also varies among formats. Vector type and vector paths can be supported in only a few file formats. Illustrator, InDesign, and GoLive—the other programs of the Adobe Creative Suite—all have their own file formats. The choice of format may require that you consider such features.

Generally speaking, working in a program's native file format until your project is complete is a good idea. You can then make a copy of the original file, saving in the required format. In Photoshop, for example, saving the original, with all layers intact, in unrasterized type, and in PSD format, gives you the most flexibility for future editing or repurposing of a file. *Repurposing* can be considered making another copy of a file in a different format, size, or color mode for a different purpose. For example, an image prepared as part of a print advertising campaign can be repurposed as a Web graphic for the advertiser's site.

It's also important to understand that file formats differ in how they record information. You can't change a file's format simply by going to Windows Explorer or the Mac's Finder and changing the three-letter extension at the end of a file's name; instead, you must resave or re-export the file to change the format.

You might also find that several file formats are appropriate for your end use and image content. Which one you choose could depend on factors beyond your control. For example, your service bureau or print shop might have a preference, or perhaps the intended audience for your Web site cannot be expected to have the plug-in required to see a particular format. However, in some cases, there is no difference between formats, and you're free to choose as you will.

## Save, Save As, Save for Web, and Export

Generally speaking, the Save command updates a file on disk. The Save As, Save for Web, and Export commands are used to save the document in a file format other than its current format.

The primary methods of assigning file formats in Photoshop are the menu commands File, Save As and File, Save for Web. Illustrator relies heavily on the Export command to produce non-PostScript file formats. InDesign can create InDesign documents and templates with Save As, and it uses Export to generate PDF, EPS, and Web file formats (HTML, SVG, and XML). GoLive can export certain types of content as QuickTime movies, and you can export site diagrams as PDF or SVG files.

Illustrator CS uses the Export command to create so-called "legacy" files. If you need to save artwork as an Illustrator file that can be properly read by prior versions of Illustrator, use the Export command to generate an Illustrator legacy file. You can specify compatibility with Illustrator versions 10, 9, 8, 3, and the Japanese version of Illustrator 3. You can also use Export to create EPS files that can be used in the same earlier versions of Illustrator.



### Save

If you create a document in Photoshop using the command File, New, the menu command Save is not available until a file format has been assigned by using Save As. Afterward, using the Save command updates the file on disk, maintaining the same format, if possible. If you've added layers or have otherwise changed the file so that it can no longer be saved in the original format, using the Save command opens the Save As dialog box. You have the option of changing to the Photoshop file format or saving the file as a copy.

Photoshop's Save As dialog box tells you which features force the file to be saved as a copy—small warning triangles appear next to the check boxes of features in the image.

In Illustrator, the Save command is available immediately after opening a new document. It simply opens the Save As dialog box.

### Save As

Photoshop's Save As command can be used to create files in virtually any file format the program supports. Illustrator, in contrast, uses Save As to create only PostScript file formats and SVG. Illustrator's Export command generates other file formats supported by the program.

Photoshop uses As a Copy to prevent accidental loss of image features. If, for example, you have numerous layers in an image and attempt to save the image in a format that doesn't support layers, Photoshop will, by default, attempt to make a copy. This preserves the layers in the original for continued editing.

Any time you select a file format in the Save As dialog box that cannot support all the document's features, Photoshop defaults to saving a copy of the file. The As a Copy check box will be selected and grayed out to prevent deselection, the word *copy* will be appended to the filename (if the filename and format remain unchanged), and a warning message will appear at the bottom of the dialog box (see Figure 3.1).

Common triggers for the As a Copy warning are layers and transparency, which are supported by only a few file formats. When you see the warning, you have the option of saving the image as a copy or selecting a different file format from the Format pop-up menu. If you select a file format that does support the features of the image being saved, the warning disappears.

**Caution**

In addition to Photoshop's native PSD file format, layers are supported in TIFF, but at some cost. The so-called "advanced" or "enhanced" TIFF features create files that might not be compatible with your page layout program. InDesign 2.0 can place layered TIFF files.



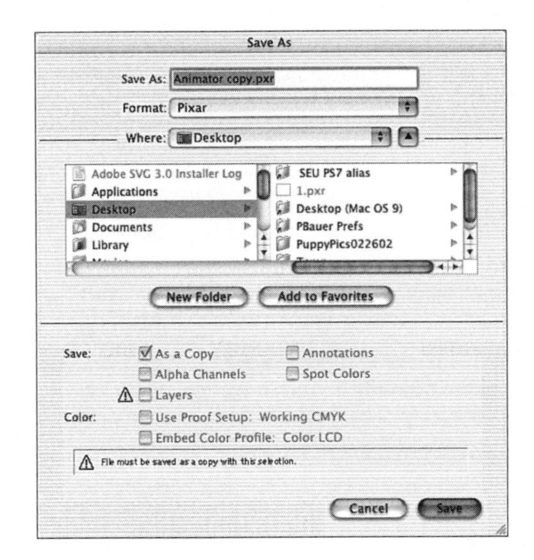


Figure 3.1
The image being saved contains layers, and the Pixar file format cannot support layers.

Photoshop's Save As command enables you to create files in a wide variety of file formats, suitable for a wide range of applications (see Figure 3.2).

## Save for Web

Photoshop and Illustrator both offer Save for Web, which is (as the name implies) a Web-oriented tool and, therefore, is restricted to the Web-related formats. (The difference between Web and print formats is explained in the section "Web Versus Print," later in this chapter.) Save As can also be used to convert a file to a variety of Web-friendly formats, including JPEG and GIF. You cannot create a WBMP file using Save As.

*For an in-depth look at Save for Web, see Chapter 22, "Save for Web and Image Optimization," p. 695.*

*For more information on using Photoshop to prepare images for commercial printing, see Chapter 21, "Preparing for Print," p. 671.*

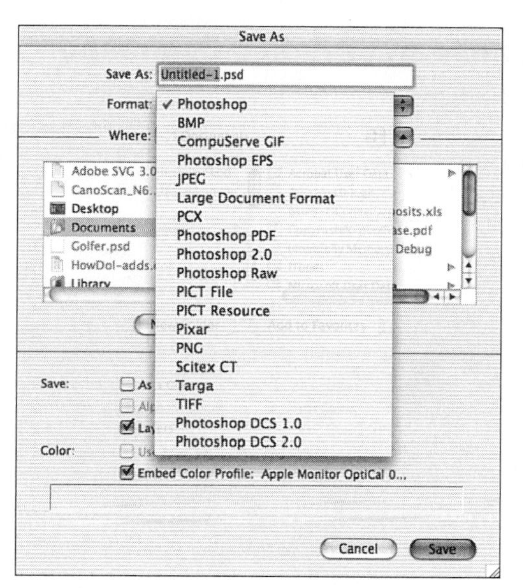


Figure 3.2
The Large Document Format option is not available in Save As unless that option is activated in Photoshop's File Handling preferences.

## Export

Photoshop's Export command can generate paths for use with Adobe Illustrator. Using this command creates an Illustrator format file (AI). When the file is opened in Illustrator, it contains only the unstroked, unfilled paths. The paths can be used to create objects or perhaps as clipping paths to identify visible areas of an image.

Export can also create ZoomView files. ZoomView, from Viewpoint Corporation, is a sophisticated Web presentation technology that allows for quick downloading of interactive graphics. The viewer can zoom and pan within the graphic without any additional hardware. For information on obtaining a license to broadcast ZoomView files over the Internet, contact Viewpoint (`www.viewpoint.com`).

Illustrator uses the Export command to create rasterized versions of artwork, in a variety of file formats, and vector-based artwork for use with Macromedia's Flash, Microsoft Office, and AutoCAD, as well as legacy Illustrator and EPS files (see Figure 3.3). You can also export type from an Illustrator document as plain text (TXT).

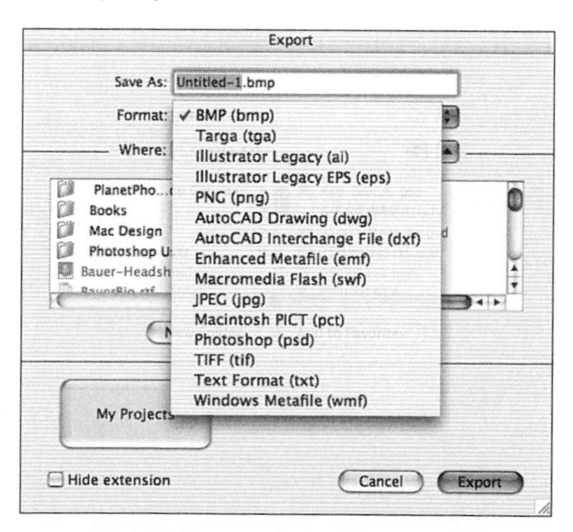


Figure 3.3
These and other file format choices are explained individually later in this chapter.

# Photoshop's Export Transparent Image Command

Another way Photoshop can assign a file format to an image is found under Photoshop's Help menu. The Export Transparent Image command walks you through the process of creating an image with a transparent background for use in a Web page or page layout document. You need answer only two questions, and an appropriate file is generated (see Figure 3.4).

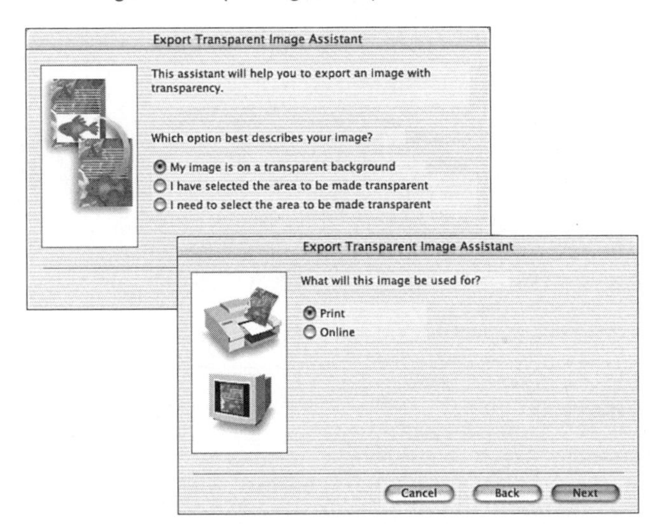


Figure 3.4
If you click the I Need to Select the Area to Be Made Transparent radio button, you will be instructed to make the selection before returning to the assistant.

If the image is not already on a transparent background, you should make a selection of the area before selecting the menu command. Depending on your needs, the automated assistant generates an EPS file with a clipping path (for print) or a transparent GIF or PNG (for Web). After the file is created, the Save As dialog box opens. Do not change the file format in the Save As dialog box. The final file will have transparency defined as a matte (GIF) or by a clipping path (EPS).

*Clear on the difference between transparency created with clipping paths or mattes and that generated with masks? If not, see "Hard and Variable Transparency" in the "Mastering the Adobe Creative Suite" section at the end of this chapter.*

After you've saved the file created by the assistant, you'll be presented with a final dialog box. After clicking Finish, you can close the Photoshop file generated during the process. There's no need to save the file.

# Photoshop's File-Handling Preferences

Several file-saving options can be set in Photoshop's Preferences dialog box. The top section of the File Handling pane, shown in Figure 3.5, enables you to determine what preview (if any) is saved with the file as well as whether the file extensions are added to the name automatically. (Windows requires the file extension and offers the choice of upper- or lowercase; Windows limits the Image Preview options to Always, Never, and Ask When Saving.)

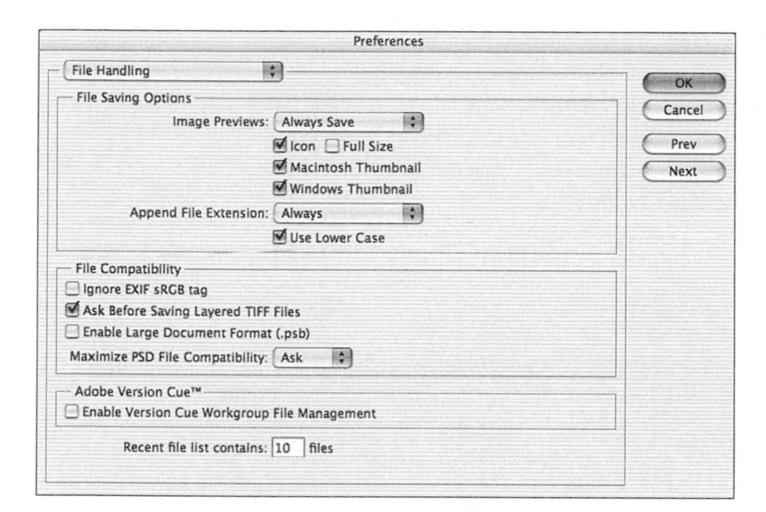


**Figure 3.5**
The file extension is required for Windows, suggested for Mac OS X, and optional for Mac OS 9. Remember that many programs in which you place or view files require file extensions.

The File Compatibility section of the File Handling pane contains important options for file sharing and compatibility. Many digital cameras list sRGB as their color space when they actually capture a much larger color gamut. This inaccurate color profile tag can cause an image to be converted to that working space when opened in Photoshop. Because sRGB is a small gamut, this can adversely affect the appearance of the photo. Ignoring the sRGB tag in the EXIF data prevents this problem and has no effect on digital camera shots with other embedded profiles. (If your camera embeds another color profile, you can ignore this option.)

Photoshop can create TIFF files that include layers, which might not be usable by other programs. To avoid compatibility problems, Photoshop offers the option of reminding you when saving a layered file as a TIFF.

In versions of Photoshop prior to Photoshop CS, the maximum image size was 30,000 pixels by 30,000 pixels. That limit still holds for the Photoshop (PSD) file format. However, you can now work with images much larger than that. The new maximum pixel dimensions are 300,000×300,000 pixels. Files over 30,000 pixels in either dimension can be saved as TIFF (up to 4GB, the maximum size the TIFF standard supports) or Photoshop Raw (not to be confused with Camera Raw). There is also the option of using the new PSB file format—effectively a large-image version of the Photoshop PSD format. You activate the PSB file format capability in the File Handling pane of the Photoshop Preferences dialog box by checking the box Enable Large Document Format (.psb).

*The PSB file format is discussed in greater depth later in this chapter. See "Large Document Format (.psb)," p. 93.*

Depending on compression, layered TIFFs can be somewhat smaller than layered Photoshop files. Otherwise, there is no real advantage to using layered TIFF files over layered PSD files.

**Caution**

The PSB file format is not compatible with earlier versions of Photoshop, nor with any other program. It can be used only within Photoshop CS. If you need to share an oversized image with someone who isn't working in Photoshop CS, use TIFF.

The option to maximize Photoshop compatibility adds a flattened composite of the image, which increases file size (often substantially). The composite is used by early versions of Photoshop (4.0 and before) and by some programs that can place Photoshop files. If this option is turned off, you'll get a reminder when saving unflattened files (see Figure 3.6).

Both InDesign and Illustrator can place and print PSD files that were saved without the Maximize PSD File Compatibility option. The onscreen preview may differ slightly, but the output should be identical.

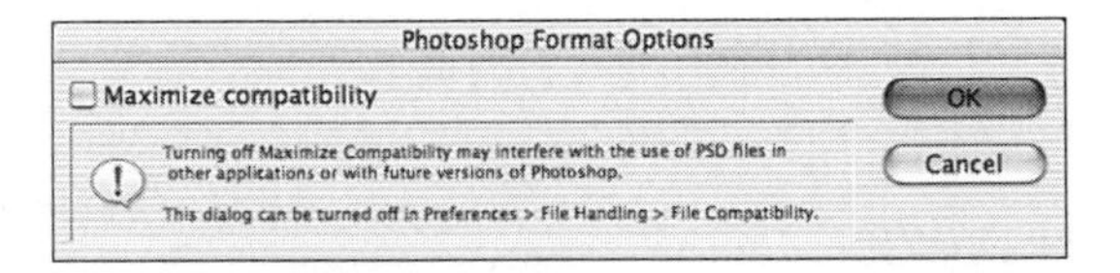


Figure 3.6
To turn off this warning, select Never in the Maximize PSD File Compatibility pop-up menu of the File Handling preferences.



## Illustrator's File-Handling Preferences

The Files & Clipboard pane of the Illustrator Preferences dialog box offers a few options that affect the way files are saved (see Figure 3.7). You can elect to include the file format extension never, always, or have Illustrator present a dialog box each time you save a new file. The file extension can be forced to lowercase (for improved compatibility) using the Lower Case check box. Placed files that are linked to the Illustrator document can be updated manually, automatically, or you can have Illustrator present you with an update option when the linked file is modified. Illustrator's Files & Clipboard pane also offers the option of using a low-resolution image for linked EPS files. This option can speed screen redraw, but the proxy image won't be as detailed as the high-resolution version.

*For more information on linked images, see Chapter 36, "Linking and Embedding Images and Fonts," p. 1071.*

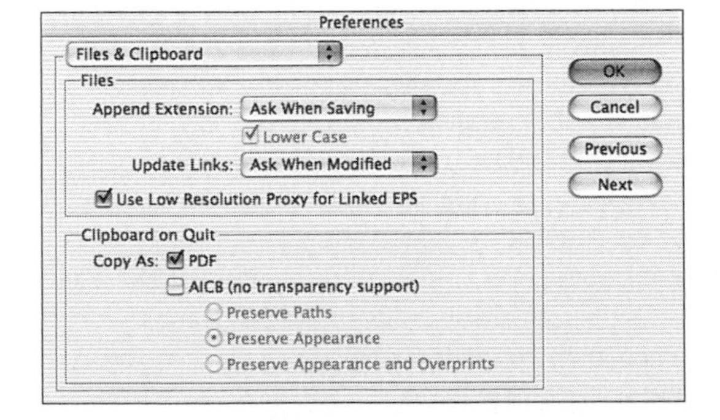


Figure 3.7
Guidelines for using file extensions with Illustrator are similar to those discussed for Photoshop earlier in this chapter.

## Additional Considerations: Platforms and Compression

Although all the Web file formats and the major print-oriented formats are *cross-platform* (they can be viewed on both Macintosh and Windows computers), a number of the less common formats are primarily for use on one system or the other. In addition, such factors as filenaming conventions and media format could affect your ability to move a file from one operating system to another.

Windows requires each file to have an appropriate *extension*—a dot (period) and two- or three-letter suffix at the end of the filename. Lowercase extensions maximize compatibility. This extension identifies the file format and tells the operating system which program to use to open the file. Mac OS X prefers a file extension, but if a file or file type has been associated with a particular program, the file can still be opened by double-clicking. When no program is associated with a file or file type, a warning dialog box appears, and you're asked to pick an application for opening the file (see Figure 3.8).

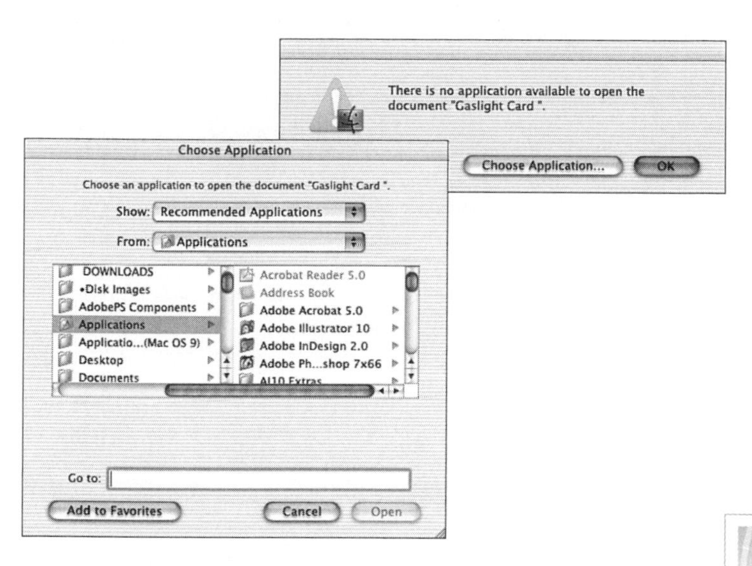


**Figure 3.8**
The Mac OS X warning message is shown in this example. When you click Choose Application, the dialog box is opened for you.

Mac OS 9 requires no file extension. However, using extensions is a good idea. Even if you never plan on sharing the file(s) with anyone using a different operating system, eventually you'll upgrade to Mac OS X and want the files to still be usable.

File compression can also be an issue. Compression schemes available in a file format are either *lossy* or *lossless*. Lossy compression reduces file size, in part, by discarding image data. When the file is reopened, the missing data is reconstructed from the surrounding image information. Lossless compression maintains all the original data. JPEG uses lossy compression, on a sliding scale, and PNG and GIF use lossless compression. Lossy compression can result in substantially smaller file sizes, but at the cost of some image quality.

The compression supplied by a file format should not be confused with that available through utilities. Compressed *archives* can be produced by such programs as StuffIt and from within Windows (see Figures 3.9 and 3.10).

When archiving files, consider using a compression utility rather than the JPEG file format. The size of Photoshop and TIFF files can be substantially reduced, without losing any image quality.

Compression utilities are especially handy when you're transferring image files via email. In addition to reducing the file size, which speeds transmission and helps avoid "over limit" message rejection, compression helps protect the files from corruption in transmission.

Zipped, stuffed, and other archived files must be uncompressed by the same or another utility before a program can open them. In the archive, the file retains the format with which it was saved. These types of file compression can be considered lossless—that is, they do not degrade the image quality.

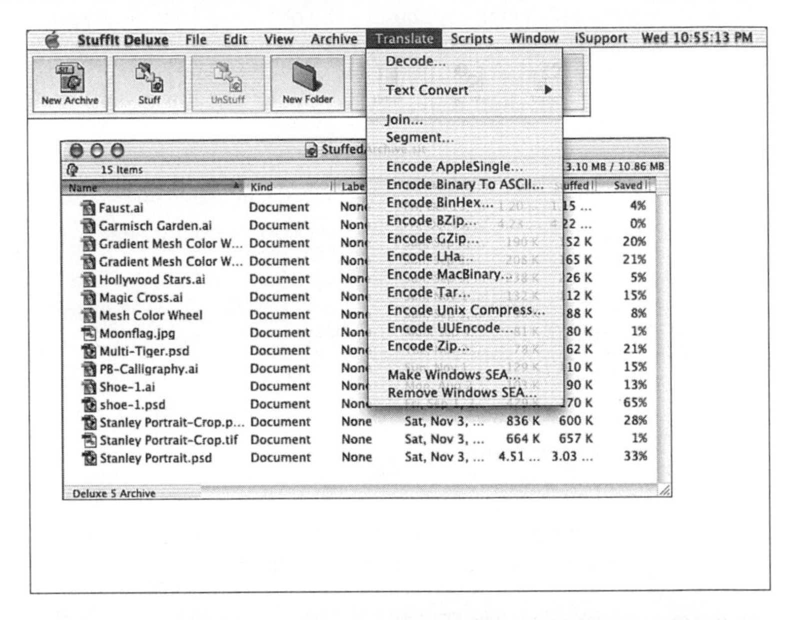


**Figure 3.9**
Utilities such as StuffIt can produce a variety of compressed files.

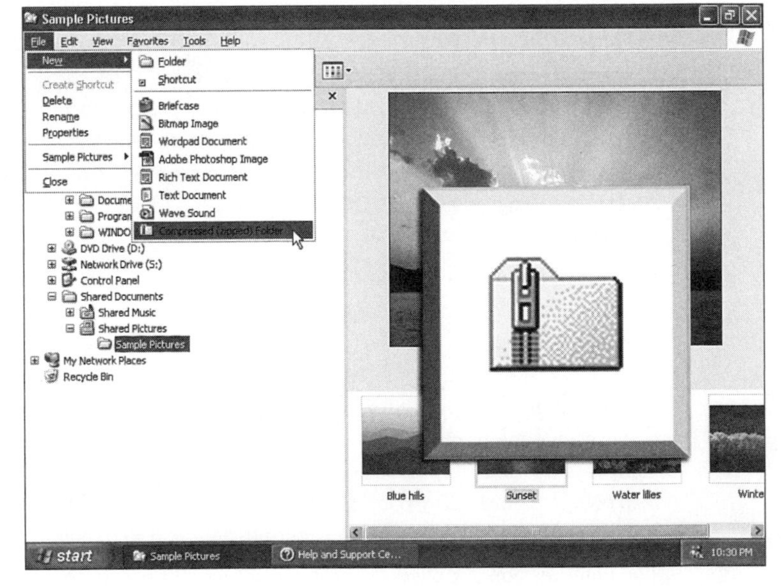


**Figure 3.10**
Windows XP can compress files, folders, and drives in a variety of ways. The inset shows the icon for a "zipped" folder.

## Filenaming Considerations

The following are some considerations when you're naming files:

- Windows filenames can be up to 256 characters long, and they are not case sensitive (upper- and lowercase letters are seen as the same letter). Several characters cannot be used in filenames: forward slashes (/), backslashes (\), colons (:), asterisks (*), question marks (?), quotation marks ("), left angle brackets (<), right angle brackets (>), and vertical slashes (|).
- Macintosh filenames through OS 9 can be up to 31 characters long and are not case sensitive. The only forbidden character is the colon (:).
- Under Mac OS X, you can have filenames as long as 255 characters, and the colon (:) is the only forbidden character.
- Unix filenames can be 256 characters long, cannot use the slash character (/), and are case sensitive.
- MS-DOS filenames can use only the 8.3 format and have the same character restrictions as Windows.
- ISO 9660 for CD-ROMs uses the 8.3 filename format and allows only the 26 letters, the numbers 0 through 9, and the underscore (_). These names are not case sensitive. (This standard is designed to allow a CD-ROM to be recognized by any computer.)

**Caution**

When you're preparing files for the Web, including the three-character filename extension is important. Although the platform and operating system (OS) may support filenames without extensions, Web browsers require them. Because of the peculiarities of the Web, my best advice to you is to be as conservative as possible. Unless you have direct knowledge of (and control over) the server on which your files will be stored, use the lowest common denominator for filenames:

- Use the 8.3 naming convention and never forget to add the filename extension.
- Stick with the 26 letters, the 10 numerals, and the underscore (_).
- Use only lowercase letters.



# THE FINAL DESTINATIONS

The vast majority of images created or prepared in Photoshop and Illustrator are destined for the World Wide Web or for print. The difference between the two is substantial, and you must consider the ultimate use of your image when selecting a file format.

Check the documentation for the program in which you'll be using the Photoshop artwork. You'll want to check for information on file formats that can be opened or placed in the program, color mode and bit depth requirements, limits on file sizes, applicability of alpha channels or clipping paths for transparency, and any other factors that could determine which file format is most appropriate.

## Web Versus Print

The World Wide Web uses certain standards in an attempt to ensure that everybody can see everything in a Web page, as long as the viewer has a decent computer and a relatively recent Web browser. These standards include certain types of file formats for graphics so that all browsers can display images from the Web.

Page layout programs accept certain file formats that allow for the best reproduction of the image with ink on paper. Illustration programs that you use with Photoshop are able to create graphics for both print and the Web.

Because the requirements are different, and even the color mode differs between the Web (RGB) and print (CMYK), the file format you choose should depend on the image's final destination.

Generally speaking, the print file formats are TIFF, EPS, and PDF. For Web, Photoshop/ImageReady and Illustrator can produce GIF, JPEG, PNG, and WBMP files. Illustrator can also generate SVG and SWF files for the Web. In addition, a variety of other file formats are available for different purposes.



## Commercial Printing Versus Inkjet Printers

Keep in mind that there's a huge difference between preparing an image for commercial printing and preparing an image for output to an inkjet printer. With the exception of those using a hardware or software RIP (raster image processor), inkjet printers require RGB color data. The overwhelming majority of inkjet printers are used with programs that do not support CMYK color. (CMYK color mode is available only in professional-grade graphics and layout programs.)

Another important difference is that images prepared in Photoshop that eventually are printed commercially are usually placed into a page layout program. Inkjet-destined images are typically printed directly from Photoshop. Additionally, inkjet printers can output virtually any file format created from Photoshop.

# PHOTOSHOP'S FILE FORMATS

Each file format that can be generated from Photoshop has its specific capabilities and intended purpose. Most offer one or more options as you save the file. Typically, a supplemental dialog box opens after you have selected a filename, format, and location in Save As.

## Format Capabilities: The Overview

Different file formats have various capabilities. Table 3.1 shows a summary of the features of the most important file formats, along with those of some less-common formats for comparison.

The primary formats are discussed individually in the sections that follow.

### Outputting to Film Recorders

Film recorders (sometimes referred to as *slide printers*) can be considered printers. However, instead of using paper, they print to photographic film. The most common recorders typically print to 35mm slide film. High-end professional models can print to negative as well as transparency film and can handle medium- and large-format film. Recorders designed for 35mm slide film often produce foggy images when photographic negative film is used. Images are often printed to slides for presentation purposes and printed to negative or positive for printing and archiving.

Graphic images to be output to film need to be measured a bit differently. Most film recorders measure resolution as a series of vertical lines across the film. The standard resolutions are 4,000; 8,000; and 16,000 lines. Note that these are not "lines per inch" but rather total lines. Each line represents a dot. The higher the number, the more information sent to the film.

The sharpness of the output can vary widely among film recorders of the same resolution. One recorder may use 4,000 lines on a cathode ray tube (CRT) measuring 4 inches wide. Another might place 4,000 lines on a 6-inch CRT. The actual size of the dots (measured in millimeters) can also vary from recorder to recorder. As the image is projected onto the CRT, each dot "blooms," or spreads. The more overlap, the softer the image. Typically (but not always), larger CRTs have less overlap. However, a smaller dot on a 4-inch CRT might produce a sharper image than a larger dot on a 6-inch CRT.

Another feature of film recorders is 33-bit or 36-bit color. This feature allows for a wider range of colors, often more than the source program can produce. Images being recorded to film almost always are RGB. The exceptions are usually CMYK images that are being archived or must be duplicated from film.

Depending on the film recorder's software, Photoshop can print directly to a film recorder, as it would to an imagesetter, laser printer, or inkjet printer. The film recorder is selected just as you would select a printer. The command File, Export is used with some film recorders. In other cases, the image must be prepared to be opened in or imported into a program that serves as the interface with the recorder. Among the most common file formats required are TIFF, EPS, BMP, PICT, and JPEG. PostScript is often an option on film recorders.

The documentation of many film recorders suggests appropriate sizes for images to be output in terms of file size. For example, the documentation may recommend that a 24-bit image be 5MB to fill a 35mm slide. If the image will occupy only part of a slide (in a presentation, for example), the file size can be reduced proportionally.

However, when you're preparing an image for a film recorder, it's better to know the actual *addressable* dimensions, in pixels. This is the number of pixels needed for an exact fit onto the film. A number of popular slide printers use the dimensions 4,096×2,732 pixels for 35mm film.

When you're working with film recorders to produce images that fill a frame, the aspect ratio is important. The ratio for 35mm film is 3:2. Film called 4×5 actually has an aspect ratio of 54:42, and 6×7 film is 11:9. (By convention, the larger number comes first when you're discussing aspect ratios. The names of the film sizes list width before height.)

If an image is not proportioned properly, you can resize it or add a border. When you're working with presentation slides, a border is often preferable to a blinding white reflection from the projection screen.

Some digital film recorders are designed to use 35mm or 16mm movie film. These cameras require aspect ratios appropriate for the film being used.

3

**Table 3.1** Capabilities of Key Raster File Formats

| Format | Clipping Paths | Alpha Channels | Spot Channels | Paths | Vector Type | Layers | Primary Use |
|---|---|---|---|---|---|---|---|
| PSD | Y | Y | Y | Y | Y | Y | General |
| PSB[1] | Y | Y | Y | Y | Y | Y | Oversized images |
| BMP | Y[2] | Y | N | Y | N | N | RGB |
| DCS 2.0 | Y | Y | Y | N | N | N | Print |
| EPS | Y | N | N | N | Y[3] | N | Print |
| GIF | N[4] | N | N | N | N | N | Web |
| JPEG | Y | N | N | Y | N | N | Web/archive |
| JPEG 2000 | Y | Y | Y | N | N | N | Print/archive |
| PCX | Y | N | N | Y | N | N | RGB |
| PDF | Y | Y | Y | Y | Y[3] | Y | (Various) |
| PICT | N | Y | N | Y | N | N | RGB |
| Pixar | Y | Y | N | Y | N | N | Video |
| PNG | Y | N | N | Y | N | N | Web |
| Raw[5] | Y | Y | Y | Y | N | N | Photo |
| SciTex | Y | N | N | Y | N | N | Scans |
| Targa | Y | N | N | Y | N | N | Video |
| TIFF | Y | Y | Y | Y | Y[6] | Y[6] | Print |
| WBMP | N | N | N | N | N | N | Web |

[1] In Photoshop, PSB is also referred to as Large Document Format.

[2] Clipping masks are stored but not used by most other programs. Adobe InDesign does read the clipping path.

[3] Type and shape layers are rasterized if the file is reopened in Photoshop.

[4] Transparent background can be maintained in GIF.

[5] Files are saved as Photoshop Raw, but Photoshop CS is capable of opening Camera Raw files from most digital cameras.

[6] TIFF advanced mode preserves layers.

Photoshop CS ships with optional plug-ins for a variety of file formats that are not needed by the vast majority of Photoshop users (see Figure 3.11). Should you need to work with one or more of these formats, drag the plug-in into the File Formats folder of Photoshop's Plug-ins folder. The next time you start Photoshop, the file format will be available.

## Photoshop (.psd)

Photoshop's native file format supports all the program's capabilities. Files in this format can be placed in the latest versions of InDesign and GoLive as smart objects and can be opened in Adobe Illustrator. This is the default file format. Most workflows (but not all) benefit from maintaining a file in Photoshop format until it's time to create a final TIFF, EPS, JPEG, or other file. It's also usually a good idea to maintain the original image, with editable type and layers, for future use.

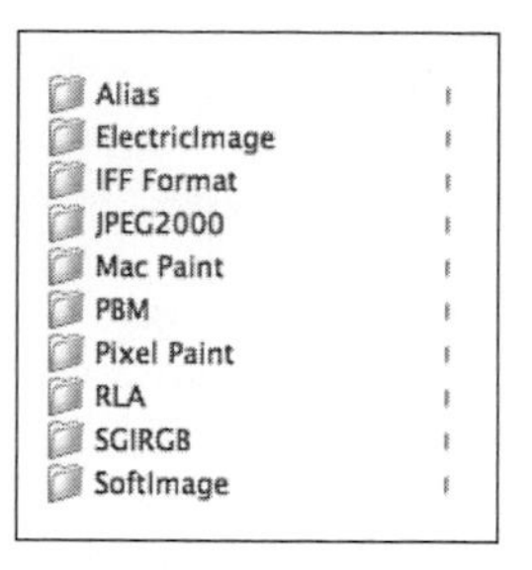


**Figure 3.11**
Look for these plug-ins in the Optional Plug-ins folder, inside the Goodies folder, on the Photoshop CD.

When saving in Photoshop format, you can see that the Save As dialog box indicates which features are used in the image (see Figure 3.12). If a check box is grayed out, that feature is unused. If you uncheck a box, the file is saved as a copy. If you disable a feature (layers, for example) and save the image as a copy, when the image is reopened, that feature is gone—no more layers.

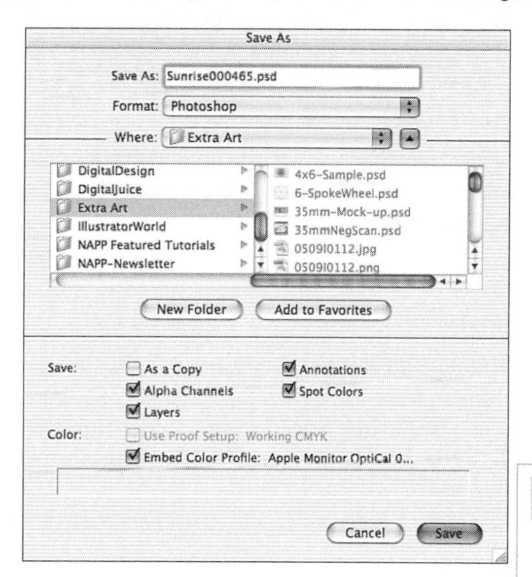


**Figure 3.12**
Selecting the As a Copy check box without changing other options simply appends the word *copy* to the original filename.

Remember that Photoshop's Large Document Format (PSB) is not available until you enable the feature in the File Handling pane of Photoshop's Preferences dialog box.

## Large Document Format (.psb)

New in Photoshop CS is the capability of saving truly huge images. In earlier versions of Photoshop, the maximum image size was 30,000 pixels by 30,000 pixels. The new PSB file format can handle images as large as 300,000×300,000 pixels. Other than the maximum image size, the PSB file format is functionally similar to the PSD (Photoshop standard) file format.

Photoshop will remind you that the PSB file format is compatible *only* with Photoshop CS (see Figure 3.13). Other programs and earlier versions of Photoshop will *not* recognize the format.

If you have a very large image that you need to use with a program other than Photoshop, use TIFF. TIFF supports the maximum image dimensions allowed by Photoshop and file sizes as large as 4GB.

Figure 3.13
Any file can be saved in the PSB format, but it won't be readable in any program other than Photoshop CS. That's another good reason to have this reminder.

## CompuServe GIF

GIF is a common Web file format, suitable for illustrations and other images with large areas of solid color and no or few gradients or blends. Many logos and cartoons, as well as Web navigation items, such as banners and buttons, are appropriate for GIF. This file format is not appropriate for most photographs and other continuous-tone images because it can record a maximum of only 256 distinct colors. (A photograph might have thousands or millions of individual colors.) Although very small and adequately detailed thumbnails of photographs can be created as GIFs, a continuous-tone image typically suffers from *posterization*. When areas of similar (but not identical) color are forced into a single tint, the image quality can suffer severely.

The color table (the list of specific colors included in the image) is controlled through the Indexed Color dialog box. This box opens after you select the CompuServe GIF file format, a name, and a location for the file and then click OK.

*For full information on the color options available for GIF files, see "Indexed Color," p. 173, in Chapter 5, "Color, in Theory and in Practice."*

Among GIF's capabilities are interlacing and animation. When a GIF image is interlaced, a Web browser displays every other line of pixels, first, and then fills in the balance of the image. This allows the Web page's visitor to see the image loading, giving the impression that progress is being made and that the image is loading faster. Animated GIFs are created in ImageReady.

*Animated GIFs are discussed in Part IV, "ImageReady." See Chapter 23, "Creating Rollovers and Adding Animation," p. 733.*

The GIF format supports transparency in a limited way: A specific pixel can be opaque or transparent. You cannot have any pixels that are partially transparent in a GIF image. If the image is on a transparent background, you need only select the Transparency check box in the Indexed Color dialog box (see Figure 3.14).

You can also specify a color to be made transparent by using the Matte options in the Indexed Color dialog box. All pixels of the specified color then become transparent, regardless of location in the image. Dithering allows an image in Indexed Color mode to simulate more colors than are actually contained in the color table by interspersing dots of two or more colors.

*GIFs can also be created with Save for Web. See Chapter 22, "Save for Web and Image Optimization," p. 695.*

The GIF standard is maintained by CompuServe, and software that creates or displays GIF images must be licensed by Unisys. (The licensing fee was paid by Adobe, and part of Photoshop's purchase price goes to the licensing.)

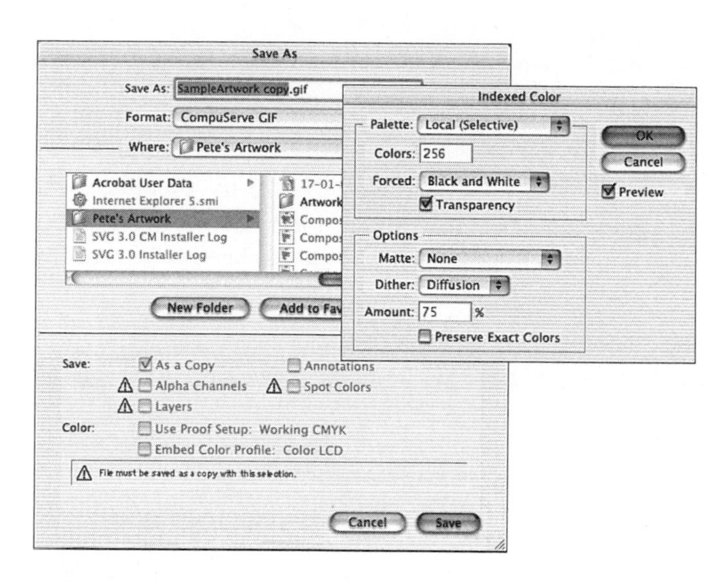


Figure 3.14
The Indexed Color dialog box opens automatically when you use Save As to create a GIF.



## Photoshop EPS

PostScript is a page description language developed by Adobe, and it was at the heart of the desktop publishing revolution of the 1990s. An *Encapsulated PostScript (EPS)* file can contain any combination of text, graphics, and images and is designed to be included (encapsulated) in a PostScript document. EPS files contain the description of a single page or an element of a page.

EPS is typically used for elements to be included in a page layout or PDF document. Because PDF files can be designed for onscreen display as well as print, EPS supports the RGB color mode in addition to the CMYK and Grayscale modes. EPS files cannot be displayed by Web browsers (although they can be incorporated into PDF files, which can be shown through a browser plug-in).

One of the greatest advantages of EPS as a file format is the capability of including both raster and vector data and artwork.

*To learn more about the difference between raster and vector images, see Chapter 4, "Pixels, Vectors, and Resolutions," p. 129.*

EPS supports all color modes, except Multichannel, and it does not support layers or alpha and spot channels. (The DCS variation of EPS supports both spot colors and masks and is discussed separately, later in this chapter.) The EPS Options dialog box, shown in Figure 3.15, offers several options.

The Preview option determines which image—if any—will be shown in the page layout program where you're placing the file. The preview doesn't normally have any effect on the printed image and is used for onscreen display only. Windows offers only None and TIFF as preview options. Here are the options offered by other platforms:

- **None**—No image preview is saved. Although Photoshop's File Browser can still generate a thumbnail, files placed into a page layout document may show on the screen as a box with diagonal lines.

- **TIFF (1 bit/pixel)**—A black-and-white (not grayscale) version of the image is shown in a page layout document.
- **TIFF (8 bits/pixel)**—A color version of the image is displayed onscreen in page layout programs. This option provides a reasonably accurate preview and is cross-platform.
- **Macintosh (1 bit/pixel)**—A black-and-white PICT preview is included with the EPS file. The PICT file format is designed for use on Macintosh systems but can be used for Windows programs as well.
- **Macintosh (8 bits/pixel)**—A color PICT preview is prepared.
- **Macintosh (JPEG)**—A JPEG preview is used, which can reduce the file size but also the compatibility.

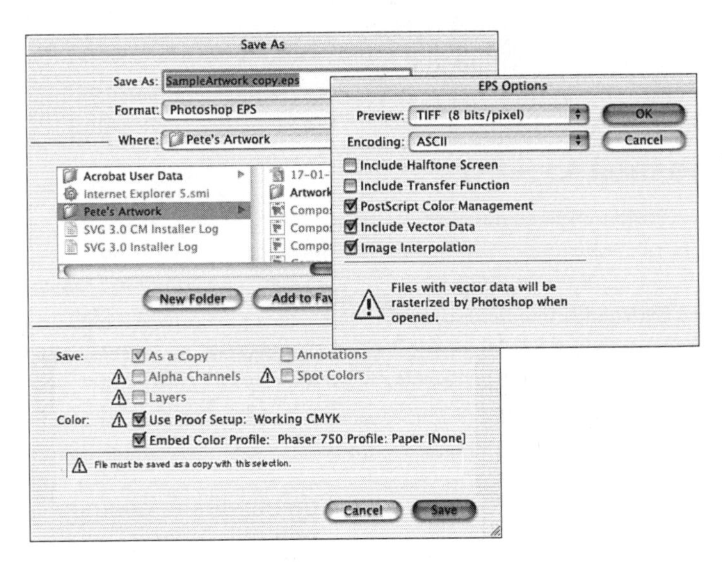


**Figure 3.15**
Note in the Save As dialog box that the warning triangles indicate which features are not supported by the EPS file format.

The Encoding options include ASCII, Binary, and JPEG. ASCII is cross-platform and compatible with virtually all page layout programs. Binary is a Macintosh encoding system, and it can produce smaller files. JPEG encoding produces comparatively tiny files but uses lossy compression (which can result in image degradation) and is not compatible with all page layout programs. In addition, JPEG encoding can prevent an image from properly separating to individual color plates. ASCII is certainly the safest choice when the image will be sent to a printer or service bureau.

Halftone screens and transfer functions are established through the Print Preview dialog box. Screen frequency, angle, and shape can be established for each ink. These criteria determine the distribution and appearance of the ink droplets applied to the paper. The transfer function compensates for a miscalibrated imagesetter.

Never change the halftone screen settings or transfer functions unless specifically instructed to do so by your printer or service bureau. Incorrect data can result in project delays and additional costs.

PostScript Color Management is available only for CMYK images outputting to devices with PostScript Level 3. This option should *not* be selected if the image will be placed into another document that itself will be color managed.

When the image contains unrasterized type and/or vector artwork or paths, select the Include Vector Data check box. When you're outputting to a PostScript device (such as a laser printer or imagesetter), the vector outlines will be preserved and the artwork will print more precisely. You need not include vector data when outputting to an inkjet printer.

The advantages of vector type and artwork are lost if an EPS file is reopened in Photoshop. Photoshop must rasterize an EPS file to work with it. If you've saved vector data, do *not* reopen the EPS file in Photoshop.

Checking Image Interpolation allows a low-resolution image to be *upsampled* (resampled to larger pixel dimensions) when printed to a PostScript Level 2 or 3 printer. Increasing the resolution during printing helps smooth edges and improve the general appearance of low-resolution images, but this could introduce a slight out-of-focus appearance. If the output device isn't PostScript Level 2 or higher, this option has no effect.

*For more information on upsampling, see "Two Types of Resampling," in Chapter 15, "Image Cropping, Resizing, and Sharpening," p. 481.*



## JPEG

Joint Photographic Experts Group (JPEG) is technically a file compression algorithm rather than a file format. The actual file format is JFIF (JPEG File Interchange Format), although JPEG is more commonly used. JPEG supports Grayscale, RGB, and CMYK color modes and can be used with files more than four times as large as Photoshop's 30,000×30,000 pixel maximum. JPEG does not support transparency, alpha channels, spot colors, and layers. Paths can be saved with a JPEG file, including clipping paths (although most programs can't use the clipping path, with the notable exception of InDesign). Type is rasterized when a file is saved as JPEG.

JPEG is commonly used on the Web for photographs and other continuous-tone images in which one color blends seamlessly into another. Because of its support for 24-bit color (in RGB mode), JPEG is far better than GIF for displaying the subtle shifts in color that occur in nature. (Rather than GIF's maximum of 256 distinct colors, JPEG files can include more than 16.7 million colors.) JPEG is the most common file format for digital cameras because of the outstanding file size reduction capabilities.

When you choose JPEG as the file format and click OK, Photoshop's Save As dialog box is replaced with the JPEG Options dialog box (see Figure 3.16). You can select a matte color, a level of compression, and one of three options for Web browser display.

*JPEG files can also be created with the Save for Web option. See Chapter 22, "Save for Web and Image Optimization," p. 695.*

It's important to keep in mind that JPEG is a *lossy* compression system. Image data is thrown away when the file is saved. When the image is reopened, the missing data is re-created by averaging the colors of surrounding pixels. For more information, see "Resaving JPEG Images," later in this chapter.

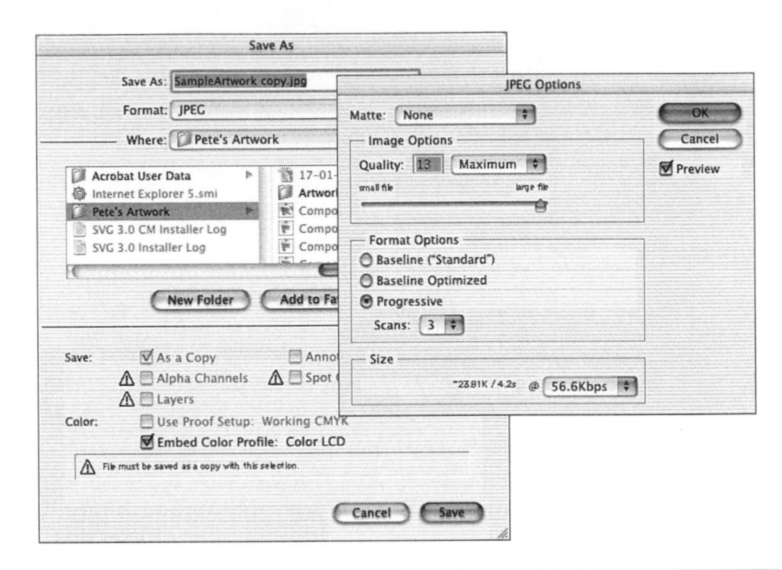


Figure 3.16
The bottom of the dialog box shows the estimate of the amount of time it will take, under optimal conditions, for the file to download at a given modem speed at the selected quality setting.

3

## Simulating Transparency in JPEG Files

Although JPEG does not support transparency, you can choose a matte color that will help simulate transparency in your image. From the Matte pop-up menu in the JPEG Options dialog box, choose a color that matches the background of the Web page into which the image will be placed. By replacing transparent areas of the image with the selected color (rather than just flattening to white), you cause those areas to match the Web page's background (see Figure 3.17).

> With the Preview check box selected in the JPEG Options dialog box, you'll see the matte applied to the image. If you're saving the image as a copy (which you will if the image has a transparent background), remember that the matte is applied only to the copy, not the original image.

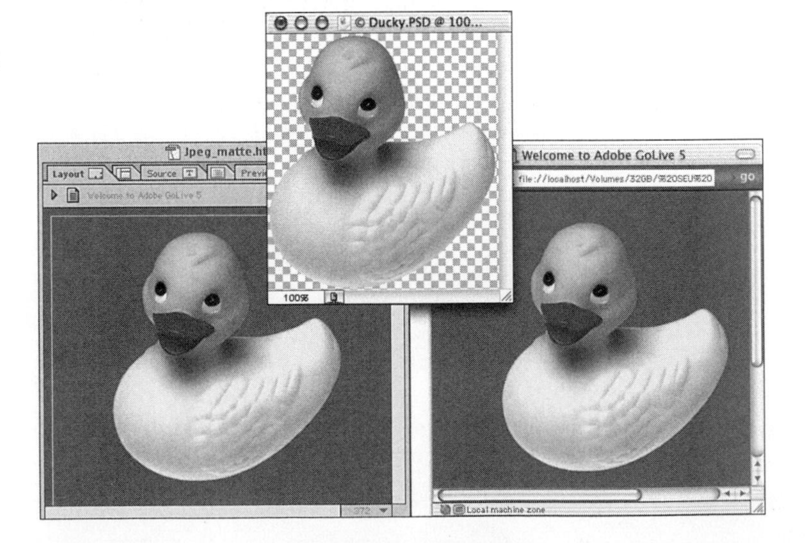


Figure 3.17
The Photoshop image is shown at the top. To the left, it has been saved as a JPEG with a red matte and placed into a GoLive document with a red background. On the right is the image as it appears in a Web browser—a JPEG duck surrounded by "transparency."

## Optimization Options

The cornerstone of the JPEG format is image optimization. The JPEG Options dialog box presents you with the tools to strike a compromise between file size and image quality. The Preview check box enables you to monitor changes to the image's appearance. The Image Options slider ranges from 0 (very small file, possibly substantial quality loss) to 12 (large file, very little—if any—damage due to file compression). The Quality pop-up menu offers Low (3), Medium (5), High (8), and Maximum (10) settings. Figure 3.18 shows a comparison of file sizes and file quality, using the duck image from the previous figure. The chart shows file format, compression type or level, and file size as reported by Mac OS X's Get Info command. (Different images might produce substantially different results.)

**Caution**

When preparing images for the Web, you should generally make final decisions based on the images' appearance at 100% zoom. With the exception of SVG images, Web browsers can display images only at 100%, so base your decisions on how the pictures will look to the Web page's visitor.

Different programs use differing JPEG quality/compression scales. Photoshop uses a 13-step scale (0–12), Illustrator uses 0–10, and Save for Web works with 0%–100%.

3

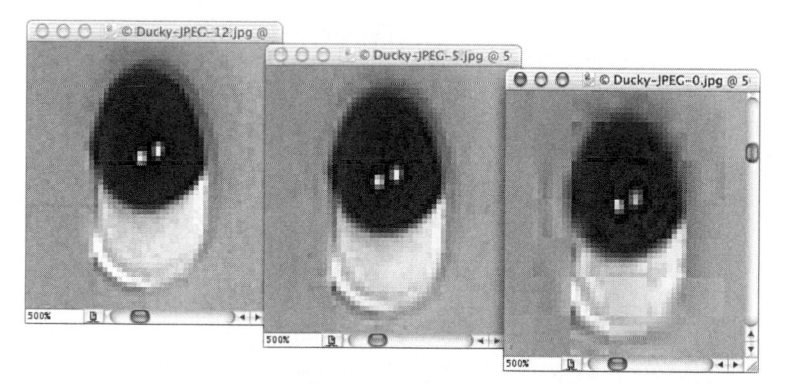


| Photoshop | Tiff | Tiff | JPEG | JPEG | JPEG | JPEG | JPEG | JPEG |
|---|---|---|---|---|---|---|---|---|
| uncompressed | uncompressed | LZW | 13 | 10 | 8 | 5 | 3 | 0 |
| 248 KB | 236 KB | 104 KB | 104 KB | 60 KB | 52 KB | 48 KB | 44 KB | 44 KB |

**Figure 3.18**
From left to right, the three images show JPEG quality settings of 12, 5, and 0. Note the substantial image quality degradation at the lowest quality setting.

## Format Options

The Format Options section offers three JPEG format versions from which to choose:

- **Baseline ("Standard")**—This is the most widely compatible version of JPEG, which can be displayed by all graphics-capable Web browsers. It's also the version to use for non-Web JPEG files.

- **Baseline Optimized**—Optimized JPEG can produce better color fidelity but is not compatible with all older Web browsers.
- **Progressive**—Like interlaced GIF files, progressive JPEG files appear in stages in a Web browser, providing visual feedback and the illusion of speed to the Web page's visitor. You can elect to have the image appear fully in three, four, or five passes. (Three passes is usually adequate.) Progressive JPEG files are typically (but not always) slightly larger than baseline (standard) versions of the same files.

At the bottom of the JPEG Options dialog box is an area that shows the size of the file that will be created with the selected options as well as how long such a file will take to download. The pop-up menu enables you to select modem speeds ranging from 14.4Kbps to 2MBps.

JPEG/JFIF became an ISO standard in 1990. Baseline JPEG is in the public domain, but many variations are patented and licensed. Variations of lossless and near-lossless JPEG are under development.



## Resaving JPEG Images

Because JPEG is a lossy compression scheme (some data is thrown away during compression), it's generally understood that files should be saved in the format only once (if at all). Resaving a JPEG file in JPEG format sends the image through the compression process again, possibly resulting in damage to the image's appearance because of the second round of data loss.

With the booming popularity of digital cameras, more and more images are being captured as JPEGs. Completely eliminating JPEG as a file format for resaving these images (and JPEGs created for the Web) after editing is unfeasible. To best understand how to avoid damaging an image when resaving it as a JPEG, you should know a little about *how* JPEG compresses.

Lossy compression, such as JPEG, can produce far smaller file sizes than lossless compression. That's because some image information is actually thrown away during the compression process. When the image is reopened, the existing data is averaged to re-create the missing pixels. However, the cost is image quality (see Figure 3.19).

To the left is the original. In the middle, saving at the highest quality produces little degradation. On the right, a JPEG Quality setting of 1 greatly reduces the quality of the image. Zooming in to 800% shows one key aspect of how JPEG works. In the low-quality version of the image, JPEG's distinctive 8×8 blocks of pixels are visible (see Figure 3.20). Colors can be averaged or patterns determined based on the content of the blocks.

Because JPEG uses blocks of pixels to compress an image, cropping becomes important. If you must crop an image that has already been substantially compressed with JPEG, any cropping from the top and left should be in increments of 8 pixels. Two copies were made of the image saved at JPEG Quality 1 (see Figure 3.21). One copy (left) was cropped exactly 8 pixels from the top and 8 pixels from the left. The second copy (right) had 4 pixels cropped from the top and left. Both copies were then resaved at JPEG Quality 1.

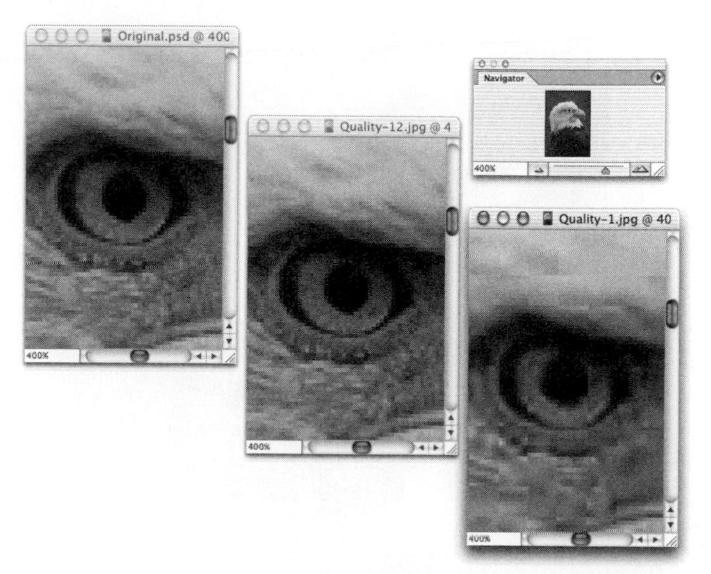


**Figure 3.19**
As you can see, the image on the right (saved at Quality 1) has a much degraded appearance compared to the original (left) and the image saved at Quality 12 (middle). However, the lower-quality image has a file size about one-third that of the higher-quality image.

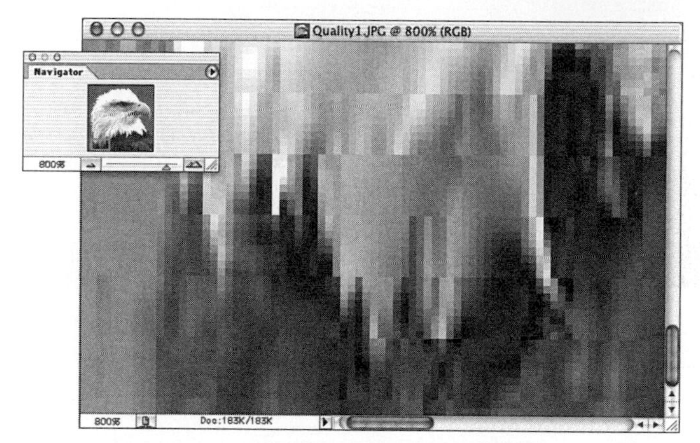


**Figure 3.20**
An image is broken down into these 8×8 pixel blocks, starting from the top-left corner.

Perhaps the most precise way to crop an image in increments of 8 pixels is to use the Canvas Size dialog box. It not only allows you to specify an exact pixel size, but the Relative check box even eliminates the need to do math—select the check box and enter a negative number to reduce the canvas size (see Figure 3.22).

Another technique for preserving image quality when resaving a JPEG file as a JPEG file is to use exactly the same compression setting as originally used. *If* the original quality/compression setting is known, and *if* the image is being recompressed in the same program, *then* this technique is valid. However, keep in mind that different programs use different "scales" of JPEG compression. Saving a JPEG file at Quality 4 in Photoshop is not the same as saving as Quality 4 in Illustrator, nor is it the same as using 40% in Save for Web. Also, there is no set formula to translate between compression settings from a digital camera and Photoshop.

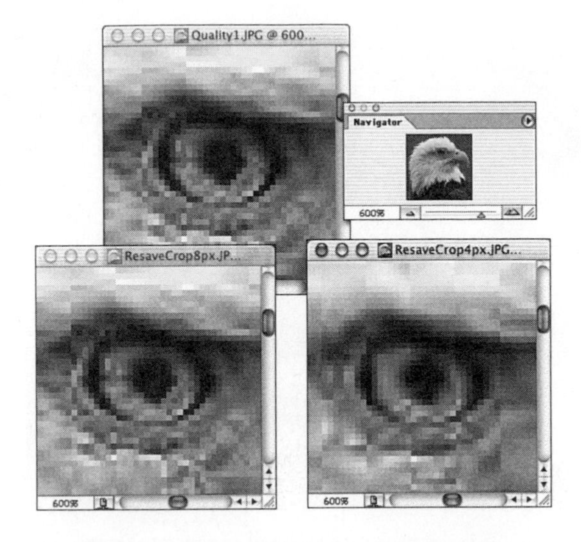


**Figure 3.21**
The image that was cropped in increments of 8 pixels (left) bears far more resemblance to the original (top). On the right, the image that was cropped in increments of 4 pixels looks much blurrier.

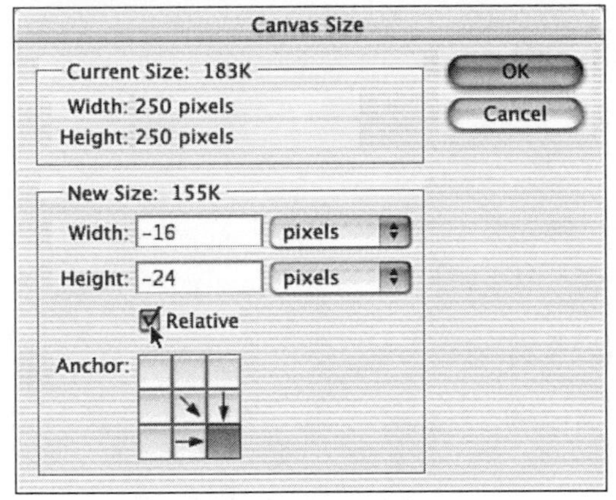


**Figure 3.22**
The grid, called the *proxy*, determines from where the canvas will be reduced or enlarged. If you're cropping from the center, remember to work in increments of 16 pixels (8 pixels for each edge).

When minimizing additional image degradation is important, consider resaving JPEG files at High or Maximum Quality, especially if the image has been cropped. The file size might be somewhat larger than the original JPEG, but quality will be maintained.

If you use a digital camera, a little experimentation can help you determine which quality setting you should use. In the example shown in Figure 3.23, the image in the upper right was taken at SQ (Standard Quality), which captures 640×480 pixels for this camera. To the left is the same scene, shot at HQ (High Quality), which produces an image 1,600×1,200 pixels, compressed at approximately the equivalent of using JPEG Quality 7 in Photoshop. The image in the lower right was shot at SHQ (Super High Quality), 1,600×1,200 pixels, minimal compression.

The two larger JPEG images are cropped to about 469KB when open in Photoshop. The original images as captured were 480KB (left) and 956KB (lower right). With the minimal difference in image quality and the substantial difference in file size between HQ and SHQ, for most purposes the more practical setting for this camera is HQ. Your camera may differ.

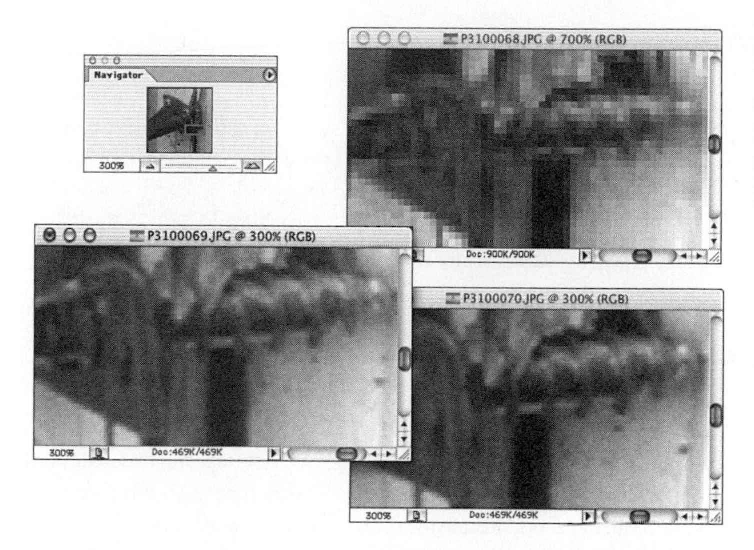


Figure 3.23
The two lower images are zoomed to 300%. The upper-right image, because of the smaller pixel dimensions, is zoomed to 700%.



## Photoshop at Work: Controlling JPEG Compression

JPEG is an important file format when you consider the number of such images on the Internet and those taken with digital cameras. The lossy compression algorithm that JPEG uses is worth exploring. To practice controlling JPEG compression, follow these steps:

1. Open an image, any image, in Photoshop.
2. Use the menu command File, Save As and then select JPEG as the file format.
3. Use an image quality value of 0 and save the file to your desktop.
4. Close the open file and use the menu command File, Open to open the file you just saved.
5. Click the leftmost button at the bottom of the History palette to create a copy of the open image.
6. Save this copy, appending "-1" to the name. Again, use JPEG quality 0. Close and reopen the –1 file.
7. Position the two windows next to each other and zoom in 500% on an area of detail. Compare the two. Although neither looks good, they should be nearly identical.
8. Use the menu command Image, Canvas Size. Click in the lower-right corner of the proxy (the 3×3 grid labeled Anchor). Switch the unit of measure to pixels and then input a height and width, each 4 pixels smaller than the original value. Click OK.
9. Save the file as JPEG again, using the lowest quality setting.
10. Close and reopen the image.
11. Zoom in 500% and compare this version to the original.

You should see that saving the same image at the same setting doesn't cause much harm, but using a low compression setting after cropping an image that has *already* been compressed with JPEG can cause severe quality reduction.

> To create a JP2-compatible file, you *must* check the box to include the document's color profile in the Save As dialog box. If you don't include the ICC profile, the JP2 Compatible box will be grayed out in the JPEG 2000 window.

# JPEG 2000 (.jpf)

JPEG 2000, an improved variation of the JPEG file format, is now supported in Photoshop. Although this format is used for both print and the Web, most Web browsers require a plug-in to display JPEG 2000 images. You'll need to install the JPEG 2000 plug-in from the Photoshop CS CD to use this format.

Photoshop opens files in the extended JPEG 2000 format (JPF), but it can also create JPF files that are compatible with the JP2 format for JPEG 2000. (The file extension remains .jpf, regardless of whether the file is JP2 compliant or not.) The JPF format is more flexible than JP2, but fewer Web browser plug-ins are available. JP2 files will be 1KB larger than their JPF counterparts.

Among the advantages of JPEG 2000 over the earlier version of JPEG are transparency and lossless compression. You also have some control over what metadata is included with the file and how the image will appear in a browser as it downloads.

The JPF format supports RGB, CMYK, and Grayscale color modes, in either 8-bit or 16-bit color. Alpha channels, spot color channels, and paths are retained. Layers are merged when saved as JPF.

To create a JPF file, select the file format in the Save As dialog box, name the file, and choose a location. If desired, check the boxes to include the document's ICC profile (mandatory if JP2 compatibility is required) and spot or alpha channels. Then click Save. The JPEG 2000 window will open (see Figure 3.24).

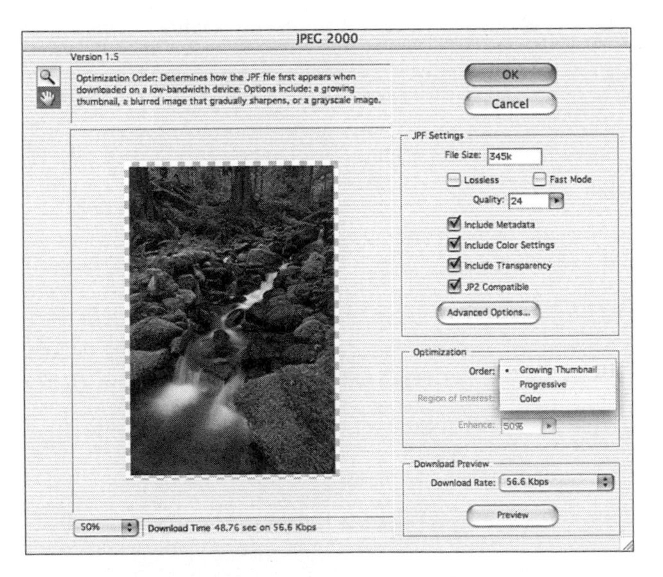


**Figure 3.24**
More than just a dialog box, the JPEG 2000 window is reminiscent of a less-complex Save for Web window. You can resize the window by dragging the lower-right corner.

The JPEG 2000 window consists primarily of a large preview area to the left and settings options to the right. Here are the principle features of the JPEG 2000 window:

- Standard Zoom and Hand tools are available in the upper-left corner.
- The lower-left corner offers a zoom pop-up menu, with 10 preset zoom factors, ranging from 3.125% to 1600%.
- The File Size field enables you to select a target size for the file. This option is not available if lossless compression is used.
- The Lossless option prevents degradation of the image caused by lossy compression. Selecting Lossless will produce larger file sizes.
- Fast Mode improves the speed of the JPF file encoding, without harming the image. The File Size option is grayed out when Fast Mode is selected, although the actual file size can still be changed using the Quality slider or entering a value in the field.
- The Quality slider is used to determine the amount of compression applied to the file. It is not available when the Lossless box is checked because it controls only the lossy compression scheme. Like Save for Web, the Quality slider's values range from 1 to 100.
- You can elect to include metadata with the file. Depending on the choices made in the Advanced Options, you can include the image's metadata as XML (JPEG 2000 specific), XMP (Photoshop's File Info format), and/or EXIF data (from a digital camera).
- The image's ICC profile will be included, provided all three of the following boxes are checked:
    - Embed Color Profile (in the Save As dialog box)
    - Include Color Settings (in the JPEG 2000 window)
    - ICC Profile (in the Advanced Options dialog box of the JPEG 2000 window)
- The Include Transparency option is only available when the image is on a transparent background. Layers will be merged upon saving, but the image will not be flattened.
- JP2 compatibility increases the file size by 1KB, but a wider variety of plug-ins will be able to open the file.
- The options accessed by clicking the Advanced Options button provide you with a choice of what types of devices you want the file to be compatible with (currently there is only one choice), the type of lossy compression "wavelet" you want to use, Integer (more consistent throughout the image) or Float (a bit sharper), the Tile Size setting (generally 1,024×1,024 is appropriate), the metadata format, and the type of ICC profile(s) to include (standard or the restricted profiles intended for cell phones and wireless devices). The Float compression scheme, available only for lossy compression, is useful for images with lots of fine detail, but it can create artifacts along edges. The tile size, which determines the areas of each "block" used for compression, is generally best left large. However, images for wireless Web access may benefit from a smaller tile size. Also, although the JPEG 2000 standard implies that a "restricted" ICC profile should be embedded in every JPF file, the devices for which the restricted profiles are intended (cell phones and PDAs) are not generally color managed...yet.

- As shown in Figure 3.24, you can specify how you want the image to display as it downloads using the Order pop-up menu. The options are Growing Thumbnail (a small image appears, then larger and larger versions of the image appear until the image is fully loaded), Progressive (the image starts fuzzy and then sharpens as it downloads), and Color (a grayscale version appears, which changes to color when the image is finished downloading).

Keep in mind that if your image is *not* intended for the Web, the only significant options are in the JPF Settings section of the window.

- If the file contains one or more alpha channels, a channel can be selected as the "region of interest." The alpha channel determines what areas of the image require the highest quality. Because the Region of Interest option doesn't increase file size, all improvements within the region of interest result in decreased quality outside the region.
- The Enhance slider determines how much priority is given to the region of influence. The higher the level, the greater the quality within the area designated by the alpha channel (and the lower the quality outside).
- The Download Rate pop-up menu enables you to choose an Internet connection speed that will be "previewed" in the window. You can see how long it will take your image (nominally) to download over a connection of that speed in the field to the left, below the preview area.
- The Preview button shows you how your selected optimization order looks. Click the button, and the image will appear in the preview area as it would load into a Web browser.



## Photoshop PDF

Adobe's Portable Document Format (PDF) is a cross-platform format that can be opened and viewed in the free Acrobat Reader, available for most computer operating systems. PDF is, at heart, a PostScript file format. Photoshop breaks PDF into two categories: Photoshop PDF and Generic PDF. Both can be opened, but only the former can be created.

Photoshop PDF supports all of Photoshop's color modes, transparency, vector type and artwork, spot and alpha channels, and compression (JPEG or ZIP, except for bitmap images, which use CCITT-4 compression).

The PDF Options dialog box, shown in Figure 3.25, offers a choice of compression schemes as well as several other choices.

ZIP compression is most effective for images with large areas of solid color, and it is also more reliable than JPEG for PDFs that are destined for process printing. (PDFs compressed with JPEG might not separate correctly.) JPEG, however, can produce substantially smaller files (at the cost of image quality).

Photoshop can produce only single-page PDF documents and can open only one PDF page at a time. However, the menu command File, Automate, Multi-Page PDF to PSD can be used to create a separate document from each page of a PDF file. In addition, Photoshop CS now offers the command File, Automate, PDF Presentation. Use this command to generate a multi-page PDF or a presentation in PDF format from several single-page PDF documents.

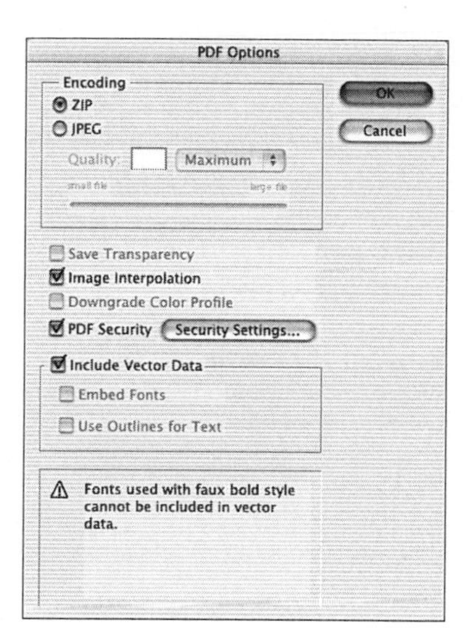


**Figure 3.25**
After you select a filename, location, and Photoshop PDF as the file format, clicking OK opens this dialog box.



Photoshop also enables you to use standard PDF security, such as that added to PDFs in Adobe Acrobat (see Figure 3.26). Passwords can be required for opening the document as well as for printing, selecting, changing, copying, or extracting the document's content.

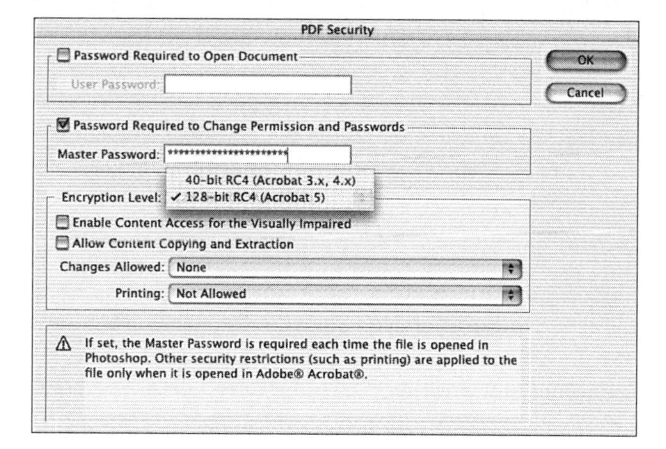


**Figure 3.26**
Other check boxes in the PDF Security dialog box are made available if they pertain to the file being saved.

## PNG

Developed as an alternative to GIF and JPEG for the Web, Portable Network Graphics (PNG) comes in both 8-bit (Indexed Color) and 24-bit (RGB) variations. JPEG's lossy compression and the licensing requirement associated with GIF's compression lead to the demand for an alternative. PNG-8 and PNG-24 are both now widely supported by Web browsers.

The Save As dialog box makes no distinction between PNG-8 and PNG-24, instead using the file's existing color mode. If the image is RGB, PNG-24 is automatically created. If the image is Indexed Color, PNG-8 is used. Grayscale is also 8-bit. (Save for Web allows you to specify whether you want to create an 8-bit or 24-bit PNG file.) Because PNG does not support CMYK, it is not appropriate for commercial printing applications.

Like interlaced GIF and progressive JPEG, PNG files can also be displayed incrementally in a Web browser. After you select the PNG format, name, and location and then click OK, the PNG Options dialog box enables you to make the selection (see Figure 3.27).

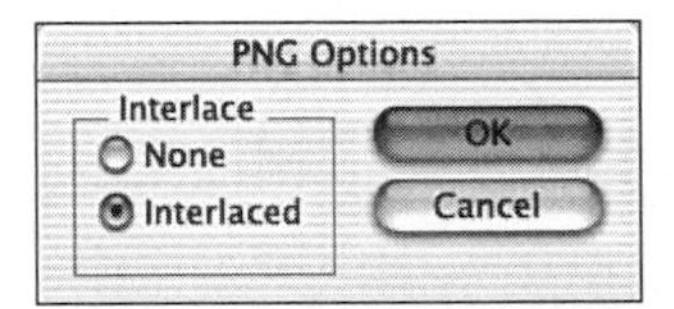


Figure 3.27
Interlacing can add slightly to the file's size. It's not necessary with small interface items but is often appropriate for larger images.

Images in Indexed Color mode are comparable in size and appearance when saved as GIF and as PNG-8. PNG-24 cannot match the file size reduction available in JPEG; however, the format does offer transparency (which is not available at all in JPEG) and uses a lossless compression algorithm, thus preserving image quality.



## Raw

In Photoshop, it's necessary to differentiate between Raw files saved from the program (Photoshop Raw) and digital camera files being opened in the program (Camera Raw). Many high-end cameras use proprietary versions of the Raw format. Previous releases of Photoshop could not natively open such files. The various camera manufacturers had their own software to open and process the files, from which you could save a TIFF file to open in Photoshop. In early 2003, Adobe released a Photoshop 7 plug-in called Camera Raw for use with the top cameras from Canon, Nikon, Minolta, Olympus, and FujiFilm. That plug-in has been incorporated into Photoshop CS and has some additional capabilities.

### Photoshop Raw

The Photoshop Raw file format records pixel color and very little else. Each pixel is described in binary format by color. Because the file doesn't record such basic information as file dimensions and color mode, coordination and communication are important. If incorrect data is entered into the Raw Options dialog box when an image is opened, an unrecognizable mess is likely to result (see Figure 3.28).

When saving an image in the Raw file format in Macintosh, you can specify the four-character file type, the four-character creator code, how many bytes of information appear in a header before the image data begins (if any), and in what order to save the color information (see Figure 3.29). When interleaved, color information is recorded sequentially for each pixel—the first pixel's red, green, and blue values are followed by those three values for the second pixel, and so on. The sequence is recorded as R,G,B, R,G,B, R,G,B.... Noninterleaved order records the red values for all the pixels, then the green values for the pixels, and then the blue values. The sequence is then R,R,R... G,G,G... B,B,B....

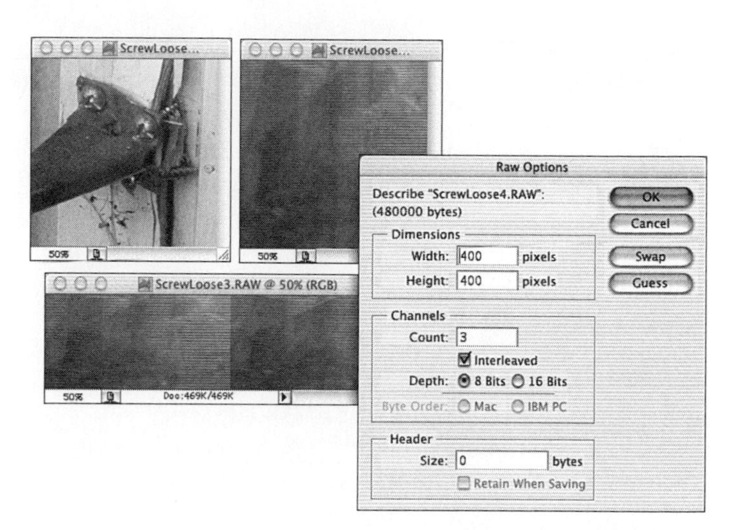


Figure 3.28
In the upper left, the image was opened properly. To the right, the Interleaved option wasn't selected. Below, the dimensions were incorrect. If the number of channels or the bit depth is wrong, you'll see a warning that the file size doesn't match.

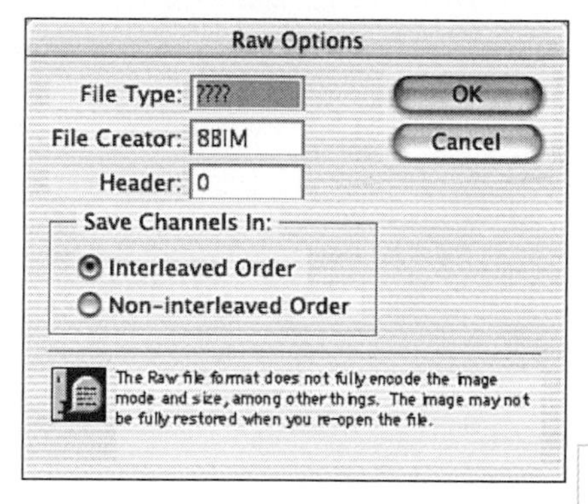


Figure 3.29
Before saving a file in the Raw format, make sure you know and understand the requirements for the program in which the file will be opened.

## Camera RAW

When you select and open an image from a high-end digital camera, Photoshop will, if necessary, launch the Camera Raw plug-in. (Some Raw files can be opened directly in Photoshop.) The Camera Raw plug-in offers very powerful image-adjustment capabilities. Global color and tonal adjustments, sharpening, noise and moiré reduction, and compensation for color fringing caused by chromatic aberration are some of the features of Camera Raw.

Camera Raw is only available for images in certain Raw format variations. Check Adobe.com for a list of supported cameras and updates to Camera Raw.

If you're comfortable working with the software that came with your camera, you may not want to use Camera Raw. However, if your camera's Raw images launch Camera Raw, take a look at the plug-in's powerful features. You may want to change your workflow.

# TIFF (.tif)

Tagged Image File Format (TIFF) and EPS are the two most widely accepted image formats for commercial printing. TIFF files can be produced directly by most desktop scanners and many digital cameras. The format supports CMYK, RGB, Lab, Indexed Color, Grayscale, and Bitmap color modes. In Bitmap mode, alpha channels are not supported, but they are available in all other color modes. Spot channels are supported, and clipping paths can also be saved with TIFF images to denote areas of transparency.

Photoshop offers a variety of TIFF options, some of which are not supported in other programs. Background transparency, layers, and JPEG compression are three. Additional TIFF options are found in the TIFF Options dialog box, which appears following the Save As dialog box (see Figure 3.30).

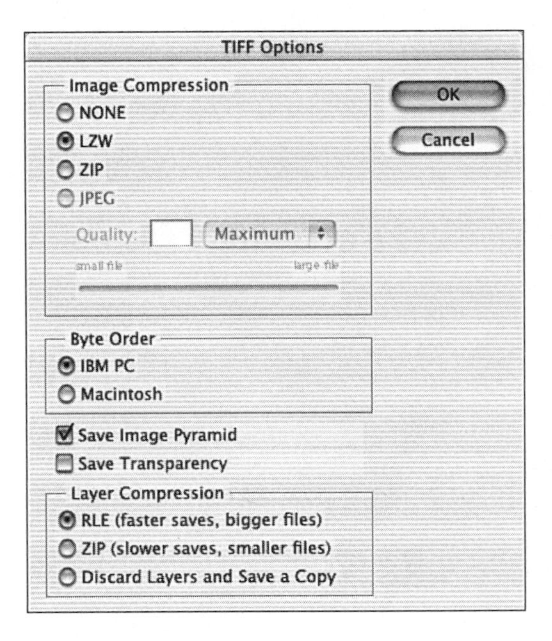


**Figure 3.30**
**Some options in this dialog box might be grayed out and unavailable, depending on the image's content.**



For maximum compatibility, choose LZW as the compression scheme. ZIP and JPEG are not supported by many programs that use TIFF files. JPEG offers the same 0–12 scale of quality available in the JPEG Options dialog box.

The Byte Order option determines compatibility with Macintosh or IBM PC computer systems. Because the Mac has no trouble reading the IBM version of TIFF files, that is the safest choice.

Although Photoshop itself doesn't read a TIFF file's image pyramid, the multiresolution data can be saved for other programs, such as InDesign. *Image pyramid* refers to multiple versions of the same image being stored in one file, each at a different resolution. Photoshop reads only the highest-resolution version of a TIFF file.

If the file contains background transparency, you can elect to save that transparency. As with other advanced TIFF features, the transparency option is not widely supported for TIFF files; however, it is supported by InDesign 2.0. (Remember that this transparency refers to the entire file, not layers above a background layer.)

When a file is saved with layers, you have the option of determining how those layers will be compressed. Because layers can greatly increase file size, ZIP may produce substantially smaller files. You can also choose at this point to disable layers in the TIFF file and save as a copy. In terms of the resulting file, there is no difference between discarding layers (flattening the image) with this option and unchecking the Layers check box in the Save As dialog box.

Because not all other programs can read a TIFF file's layers, Photoshop saves a flattened version of the image as well. Saving layers in TIFF file format triggers a warning message from Photoshop (see Figure 3.31). Because a flattened version of the image is also saved in the TIFF file, the warning can be ignored.

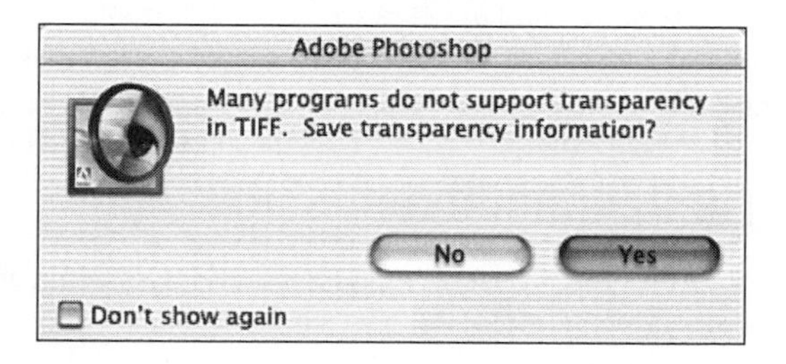


Figure 3.31
If your image is to be used in a program that doesn't support layered TIFF files, discarding the layers can greatly reduce file size with no loss of functionality.



# Photoshop DCS

Desktop Color Separations (DCS) is a version of EPS developed by Quark. (The file that's produced has the .eps extension.) The original DCS file format is now referred to as DCS 1.0, whereas an updated, more flexible version is called DCS 2.0.

## Photoshop DCS 1.0

Version 1.0 should be used only with older programs that don't read the DCS 2.0 standard. DCS 1.0 supports CMYK and Multichannel modes and creates a separate file for each color channel, plus an optional 8-bit color or grayscale composite. The DCS 1.0 Format dialog box appears after you click OK in the Save As dialog box (see Figure 3.32).

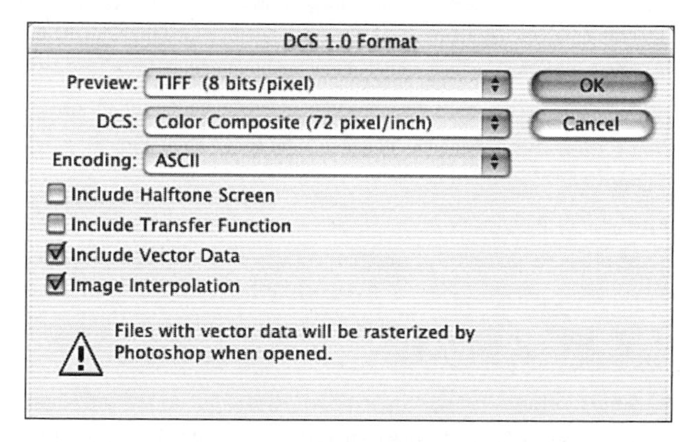


Figure 3.32
These options determine compatibility with page layout programs.

You can elect to save no preview, a 1- or 8-bit TIFF preview, and in Macintosh, a 1- or 8-bit Macintosh (PICT) preview or a JPEG preview. The 8-bit TIFF preview is the most widely supported. In addition to the preview, which is used primarily in dialog boxes, you have the option of including a grayscale or color composite image or no composite at all. The composite is used to show the image when a page layout document is viewed onscreen.

The encoding options include Binary, ASCII, and JPEG. As with EPS files, ASCII is used in Windows and can be read by Macintosh programs, Binary produces smaller files but is Mac specific, and JPEG reduces both file size and compatibility. In addition, JPEG encoding can prevent an image from properly separating to individual color plates. ASCII is certainly the safest choice when the image will be sent to a printer or service bureau.

The Print Preview dialog box offers access to halftone screens and transfer functions for the file. These criteria determine the distribution and appearance of the ink droplets applied to the paper. The transfer function compensates for a miscalibrated imagesetter. Do not make changes to the screens or include a transfer function without explicit guidance from your printer or service bureau.

## Photoshop DCS 2.0

DCS 2.0 is a more sophisticated version of Desktop Color Separations. The majority of its options are the same as those described for DCS 1.0. However, DCS 2.0 gives you several options when it comes to what file or files are actually produced (see Figure 3.33).



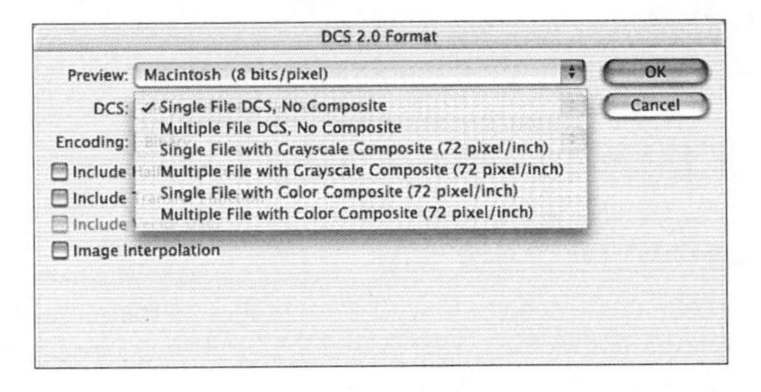


**Figure 3.33**
The six Preview options boil down to one file or one file for each channel and a choice of composite image.

If you choose any of the three Multiple File options (no composite, grayscale composite, color composite), one file is generated for each color channel. The four process channels (if present in the image) use the channel's letter for a file extension. Spot channel extensions are numbers, starting with 5. The composite, if generated, will have the .eps extension.

For example, the file "Target" with two spot channels could be saved as DCS 2.0, with multiple files and a color composite. The files generated would be Target.C, Target.M, Target.Y, Target.K, Target.5, Target.6, and Target.eps.

DCS 2.0 should be selected over DCS 1.0 in any circumstance where both are supported. The single file saves disk space and can simplify file exchange and handling.

# ILLUSTRATOR'S FILE FORMATS

Illustrator uses the Save As command to create AI (Illustrator), EPS, PDF, and SVG files. The Export command offers 15 additional file formats, including AI and EPS, compatible with earlier versions of Illustrator.

Illustrator CS can open files in more than two dozen formats, in more than 50 different versions. The full list is shown in Figure 3.34. (Keep in mind that not all features of all formats are preserved in Illustrator.) The default (All Readable Documents) shows all files Illustrator can open. Selecting a specific format can make it easier to find the file you need.

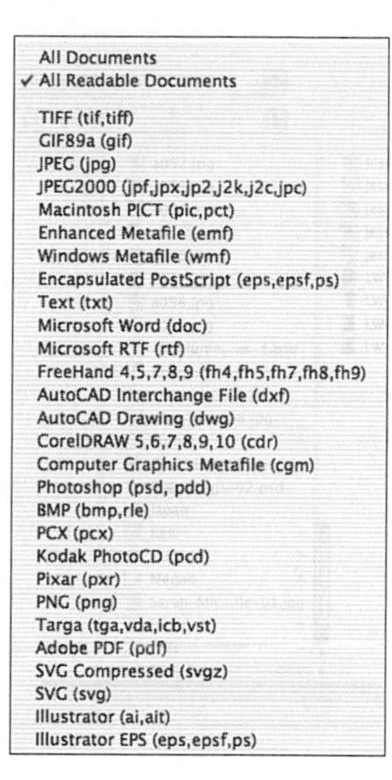


**Figure 3.34**
This is the Show pop-up menu from Illustrator CS's Open dialog box.



# Placing Files into Illustrator Documents

One of the two ways that you can place artwork in an Illustrator document from another file is *linking*. A linked image remains separate from the document to which it is linked. This is somewhat similar to a hyperlink for the Web; only a pointer is placed in your illustration, and the external image is loaded when your file is opened. Illustrator notifies you if any changes have been made to the original. Keep in mind, though, that your image must always be able to find the external artwork. If you were, for example, to send out your image on disk without including a copy of the linked file, the linked artwork would not be available to anyone opening your image from the disk—a warning dialog box would appear. The Save As command (and Save the first time it is used) allows you the option of including linked files.

*Embedding* is the other way to include artwork from another file in an Illustrator document. When you embed an image, a copy of the artwork is incorporated into your Illustrator document. You are not notified of any changes to the original artwork, and the only way to update the embedded image is to replace it. The advantage is that the placed artwork becomes part of your Illustrator document, and it doesn't have a link that can be accidentally broken. The Illustrator document's size increases by the size of the placed artwork.

Illustrator can place files of any format that it can open, with the exception of the Illustrator (AI) format. The formats in the following list, however, must be embedded rather than linked:

- CGM
- DOC
- DXF/DWG
- Freehand
- RTF

- SVG
- WMF

## File Formats Available Under Save As

The Save As dialog box offers six file formats from which to choose:

- **Adobe Illustrator Document (.ai)**—This is the native file format for Adobe Illustrator. It supports all the features of the program. However, earlier versions also use the .ai file extension and do not support all the features of Illustrator CS.

  Illustrator offers you several options when saving a file in its native format. You can see them in the dialog box shown in Figure 3.35.

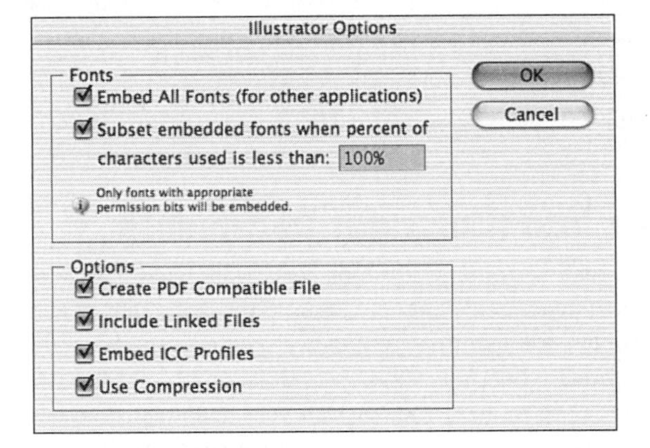


**Figure 3.35**
After you select a name and location for a file and click OK, this dialog box opens.

- **Illustrator EPS (.eps)**—PostScript is a page description language developed by Adobe. Encapsulated PostScript (EPS), like PDF, supports both vector and raster information. EPS is often used to put a graphic element into a page layout program. Typically, the EPS file is an image on a page, but it can be a complete page as well.

  EPS files can contain previews that are visible in a page layout program. When no preview is present, a placeholder (a box with two crossing diagonal lines) is shown on the page. Macintosh previews are available in PICT (Macintosh) or TIFF format, and either can be 1-bit (black and white) or 8-bit (color). Windows EPS files can have previews in TIFF or Windows Metafile (WMF) format.

  In addition to choosing the file format, you can opt to have transparency for TIFF previews in the EPS Format Options dialog box (see Figure 3.36).

> Remember that you use the Export command in Illustrator CS to create Illustrator documents compatible with earlier versions of the program.

> Because TIFF previews are compatible with both Windows and Macintosh, you should choose this option when saving as an EPS file. Also, although the 8-bit color preview will increase the file size slightly, you should choose it rather than the 1-bit black-and-white version.

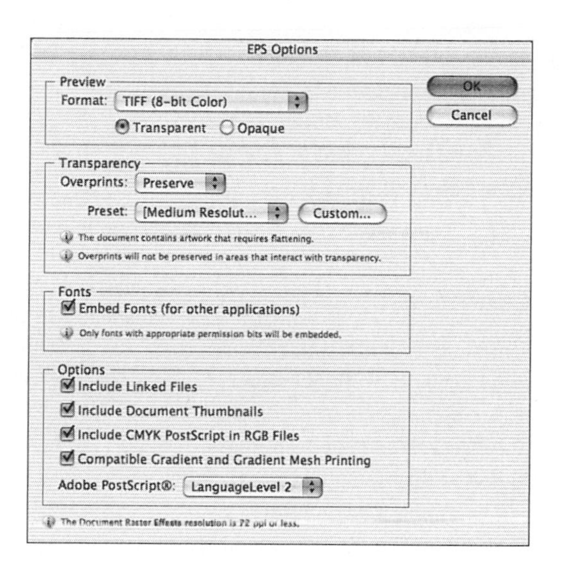


**Figure 3.36**
Illustrator CS gives you greater control over EPS images than did prior versions.

- **Illustrator Template (.ait)**—Templates can be created to give you a head start on recurring projects or layouts. Illustrator CS ships with over 200 ready-made templates (inside the Illustrator folder, in a folder named Templates). You can also create custom templates to fit your work. Open or create a document, set it up the way you want things to be when you start a similar document, and save it as an Illustrator template. When you open a template, you're creating a new, untitled Illustrator document. Think of templates as unlimited custom Startup files. Here are the customizable features of templates:
  - Artboard and document sizes and layouts.
  - The opening document view, including zoom, position of the artboard in the window, and ruler point of origin.
  - View menu options, including guides, rulers, and the various Show/Hide choices.
  - Palette contents. You can add (or delete) any swatches, symbols, brushes, styles, and Actions.
  - You can add any artwork to the artboard that you want to include in any project you start with this template—copyright information, the company logo, even artwork you'll use only sometimes. (After opening the template, you can delete any default artwork.)

Like the Illustrator file format, EPS files compatible with earlier versions of Illustrator are created with the Export command.

The Illustrator template format also generates two new commands in the File menu: Save as Template (which is the same as using the Save As command and selecting Illustrator Template as the file format) and New from Template (which is the same as using the Open command and selecting a template). These two commands are simple conveniences that can be very handy when working with templates.

- **Illustrator PDF (.pdf)**—The native format of Adobe Acrobat, PDF files are now very common. Acrobat Reader can be found on most modern computers and is freely available for others. Documents saved in PDF format can be viewed on almost any computer.

  PDF files support both vector and raster (bitmap) information. Although PDF pages are PostScript at heart, they can also contain annotations and notes and can be searched and hold hyperlinks.

  Illustrator CS's PDF Options dialog box offers five panels of options, most of which are comparable to Acrobat's options. You can select ODF security, image compression and downsampling, font embedding and subsetting, and ICC profile embedding. You can also specify printer's marks and bleeds. What's more, when Acrobat 6 compatibility is selected, you have the option of creating PDF layers from the top-level Illustrator layers.

Before saving complex illustrations as PDF files, you can take an extra step to help preserve the appearance of your image and ensure problem-free printing. Working on a copy of your original, open the Layers palette. From the palette menu (the little triangle in the upper-right corner of the palette), select Flatten Artwork. You can then save the file in PDF format with its original appearance intact.



- **SVG (.svg)**—Scalable Vector Graphics files are used on the World Wide Web. When saving in this format, you have the option of including part of a font or the entire font. Any placed images can be embedded or linked. You can retain the capability of editing the image in Illustrator if necessary. When you click the Advanced button, you'll see the additional options shown in Figure 3.37.

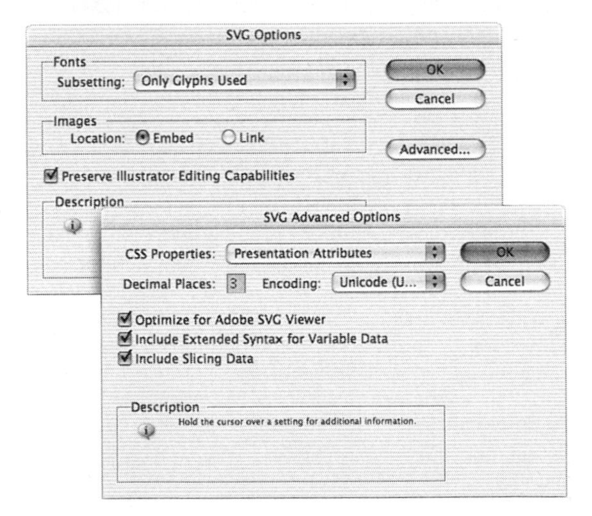


Figure 3.37
The SVG Options dialog box contains an Advanced button that opens the additional dialog box.

- **SVG Compressed (.svgz)**—The options for this file format are identical to those for the standard SVG format. The compressed version of the format is not supported by all SVG plug-ins.

# Export

In addition to the three primary file formats and SVG available in the Save As dialog box, Illustrator offers a variety of export formats. The default file formats that you can create with the Export command are shown in Figure 3.38.

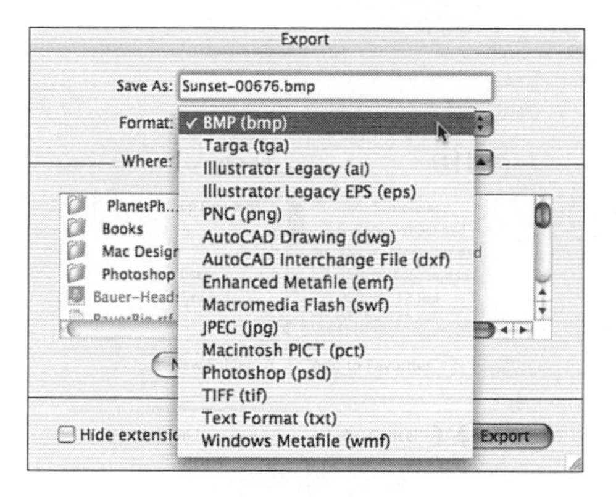


**Figure 3.38**
Any of these formats you are unlikely to ever need can be deleted from the Photoshop Formats folder, found within Illustrator's Plug-ins folder.

A number of Illustrator's export formats require rasterization (conversion to pixels) before you save the file. The Rasterize Options dialog box is shown in Figure 3.39.

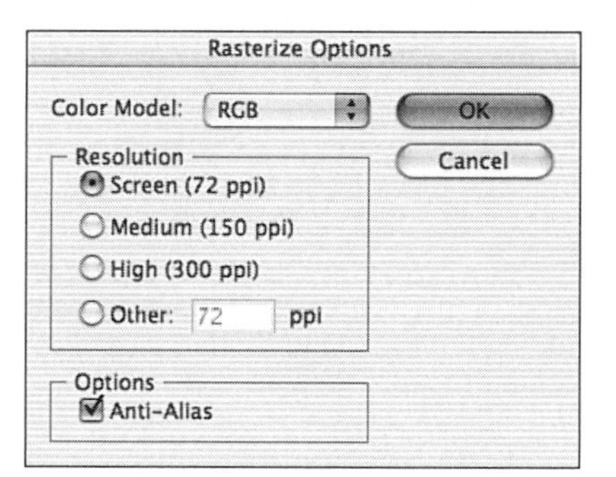


**Figure 3.39**
CMYK, RGB, Grayscale, and Bitmap color modes are supported, depending on the selected file format, as well as choices of resolution and antialiasing.

Here is a list of the formats, presented in alphabetical order:

- **AutoCAD Drawing (.dwg)**—AutoCAD is a premier architectural and engineering design tool. DWG is the program's standard vector file format. DWG (and its sister format, DXF) swaps white fills and strokes for black. The DXF/DWG Options dialog box is shown in Figure 3.40.
- **AutoCAD Interchange File (.dxf)**—This file format is used to exchange information between AutoCAD and programs that do not support the DWG format. From Illustrator, it can also be used to exchange information with those programs. When you're working directly with AutoCAD, however, DWG is usually a better choice. DXF is a tagged format. The dialog box is identical to the one shown in Figure 3.40.
- **Bitmap (.bmp)**—BMP requires that an image be rasterized before you save it. The Rasterize Options dialog box offers RGB, Grayscale, and Bitmap color modes. In addition, the BMP Options dialog box offers compatibility with Windows or IBM's OS/2 format, a choice of color depth, and (in some cases) compression (see Figure 3.41).

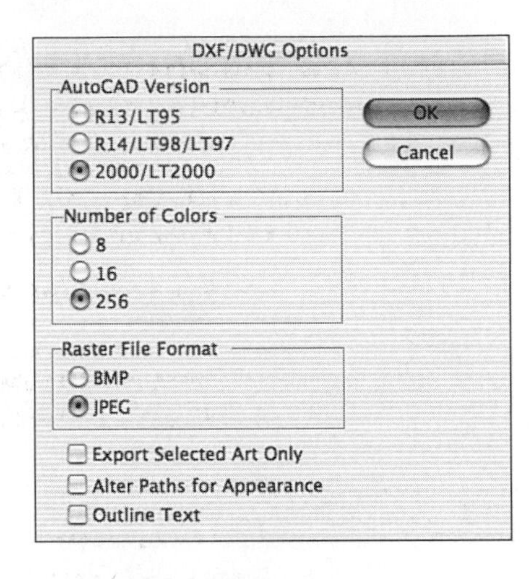


**Figure 3.40**
AutoCAD version, bit depth, and raster format for fills and textures are among the choices for the DWG format.

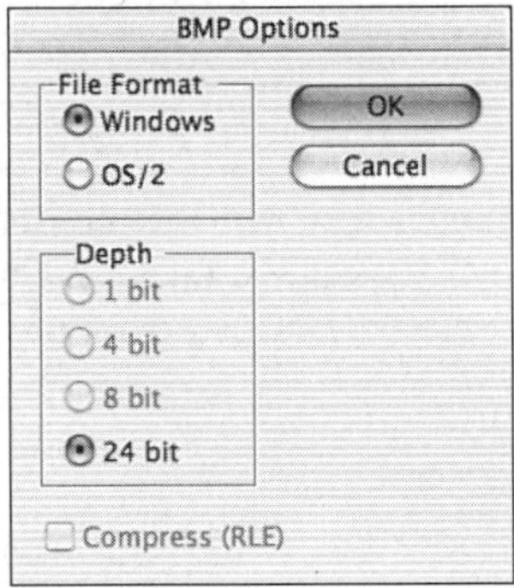


**Figure 3.41**
The Run Length Encoding (RLE) compression option is not always available.

- **Enhanced Metafile (.emf)**—An advanced version of Microsoft's Windows Metafile (.wmf) format, EMF is available only for 32-bit Windows. The export function has no user-defined options.
- **Illustrator Legacy (.ai)**—You can create AI files compatible with earlier version of Illustrator using the Export command. You can generate files suitable for Illustrator 10, 9, 8, and the English and Japanese versions of Illustrator 3. The options shown in Figure 3.42 will vary, depending on which version is selected in the pop-up menu at the top.
- **Illustrator Legacy EPS (.eps)**—Just as you use the Export command to generate Illustrator files compatible with earlier versions of the program, so, too, do you use Export to create legacy EPS files. The options are shown in Figure 3.43.
- **JPEG (.jpg)**—One of the two main file formats on the Web, JPEG is a 24-bit file format best suited for photographs and other continuous-tone images. In addition to Export, JPEG is available through Illustrator's Save for Web feature. The JPEG Options dialog box, shown in

> The term *bitmap* is used generically to refer to any raster image and can also be used to refer to the 1-bit color mode, in which every pixel is either black or white. To avoid confusion, the file format is generally referred to as "BMP."

Figure 3.44, offers choices of quality/file size, (using a scale of 1 to 10), baseline or progressive downloading, image resolution, antialiasing, ICC profile embedding, and image map management (for Internet links). More information is available in Chapter 37, "Illustrator and the Web."

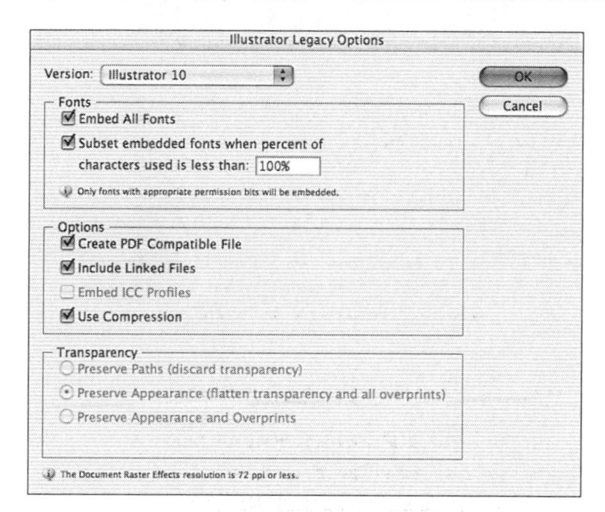


**Figure 3.42**
The Transparency section of the dialog box is used only for versions of Illustrator that do not support transparency natively.

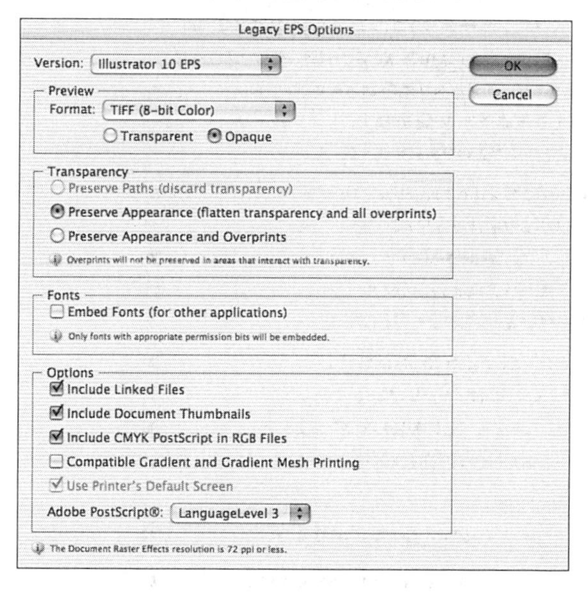


**Figure 3.43**
This dialog box is a hybrid of the EPS Options and the Illustrator Legacy Options dialog boxes.

- **Macintosh PICT (.pct)**—PICT supports both raster and vector artwork. However, should you reopen a PCT file in Illustrator, you may find that the vectors have not been preserved in the original format. Don't export to PICT if you intend to further edit the artwork later.
- **Macromedia Flash (.swf)**—Although not the native Flash format, SWF fulfills the need for a vector-based, interactive file format. SWF is actually the Shockwave file format. (Flash's FLA is a proprietary format controlled by Macromedia.) SWF is a Web format, but viewers must use a

browser equipped with the Flash plug-in. Figure 3.45 shows the dialog box for Flash (SWF) Format Options.

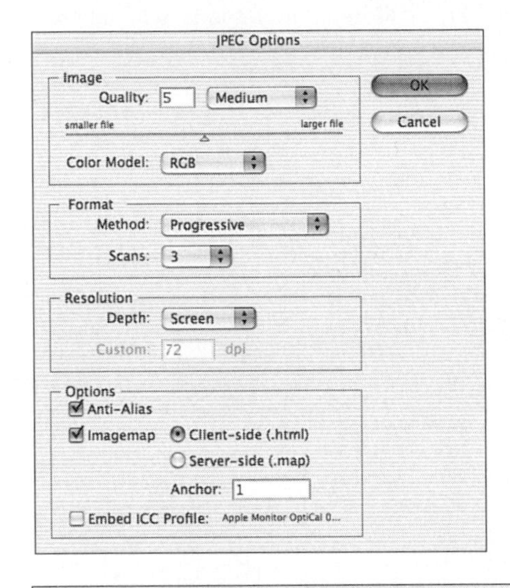


Figure 3.44
Download method and image map management are relevant only to images destined for the Web.



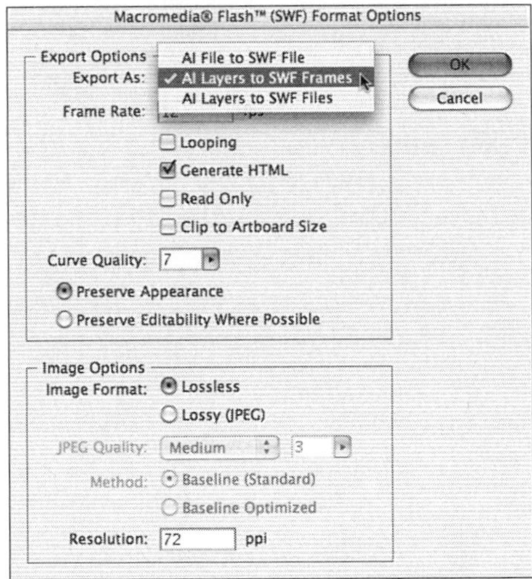


Figure 3.45
You can export the image as a single SWF file, a series of animation frames, or as a series of SWF files.

- **Photoshop (.psd)**—Layered Illustrator documents can be exported to Photoshop with layers intact. You can choose compatibility with recent versions of Photoshop, or you can export a file that can be read by Photoshop 5.5. You have the option of color mode (RGB, CMYK, or Grayscale), resolution, and whether to flatten layers or retain them. Figure 3.46 shows the Photoshop Export Options dialog box.
- **Portable Network Graphics (.png)**—The PNG file format is a raster image format used on the Web. It offers lossless compression to preserve image quality. When exporting a file as PNG from Illustrator CS, you can specify resolution and either a transparent background or a colored background (see Figure 3.47).

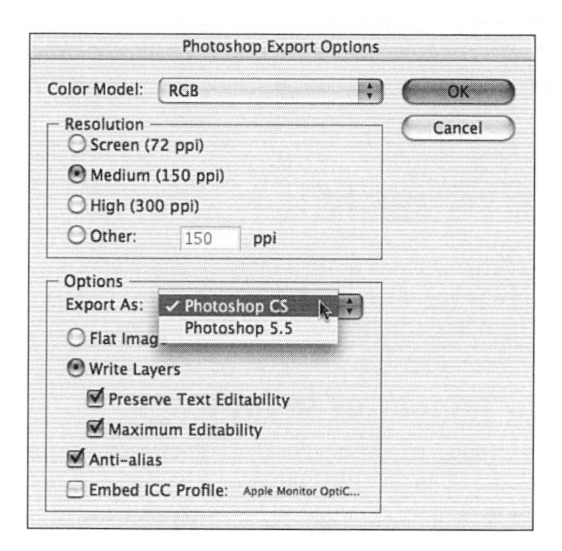


Figure 3.46
With layers and editability selected, "type on a path" can be edited in Photoshop CS (but not previous versions).

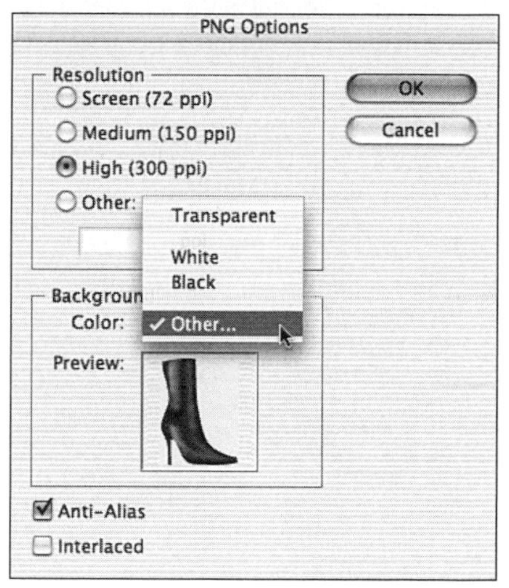


Figure 3.47
Selecting Other as a background color opens a small Color Picker that enables you to match the background of a Web page.

- **Targa (.tga)**—Targa files can be used with digital video programs, such as Adobe Premiere and AfterEffects. Artwork is automatically rasterized (refer to Figure 3.39) when saved as Targa. TGA supports RGB and Grayscale color modes.
- **Text (.txt)**—This "plain text" format is a most basic text format. It is a suitable choice when you need to move text to a word processor without fancy formatting. Such options as baseline shift and character scaling will be ignored.
- **Tagged Image File Format (.tif)**—TIFF (as the file format is known) is among the most common raster image formats. In addition to image-editing programs, many scanners produce TIFF files. This format is among the most common for placing rasterized images into page layout programs. In addition to the settings shown in the Rasterize Options dialog box (refer to Figure 3.39), the TIFF options include LZW compression settings and ICC profile embedding.

- **Windows Metafile (.wmf)**—The basic file format of clip art from Microsoft Office for Windows (among other programs), WMF is a vector format. There are no options for exporting to WMF format.

# FILE FORMATS FOR INDESIGN

When discussing file formats for use with InDesign, we need to consider three aspects of the program: What formats can be opened by InDesign? What types of files can be placed into an InDesign document? What file formats can be generated (output) by InDesign?

## Opening Documents and Templates in InDesign



InDesign, naturally, opens its own documents and templates. InDesign documents use the file extension .indd, templates use the extension .indt, and InDesign books have the file extension .indb.

The Open a File dialog box, shown in Figure 3.48, offers the option of Open Normal, Open Original, or Open Copy. Generally speaking, Open Normal is the appropriate choice. Open Original is used to edit a template, and Open Copy automatically creates a duplicate of the selected file, leaving the original unchanged. (To create a new document from a template, use Open Normal.)

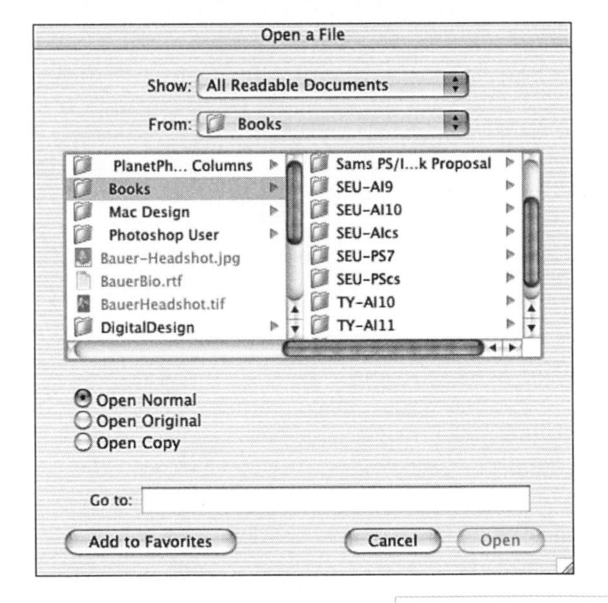


Figure 3.48
The Show pop-up menu offers the choice of All Readable Documents or All Documents.

In addition to InDesign's own documents and templates, you can open documents and templates from PageMaker (version 6.5 or later) and QuarkXPress (version 3.3 or later). Note that InDesign does not support Quark XTensions. Any graphic added with an XTension won't display or print properly.

> To make sure that linked files in a PageMaker or Quark document are available when the file is opened in InDesign, copy them to the save folder as the page layout document.

InDesign also uses the Open command to open Object Libraries. Object Libraries are collections of graphic elements, pages, text, guides and grids, and shapes. When opened, these elements appear in a palette, ready to be added to the open document. InDesign library files use the file extension .indl.

## Placing Files into InDesign Documents

Although it certainly is possible to copy/paste or drag/drop to add graphics to an InDesign document, the most reliable method is the File, Place command, which enables you to control resolution, color, and some format-specific characteristics of graphics. (You can also use Place to add a text file to your document.) Figure 3.49 shows a list of those file types generated by Photoshop and Illustrator that can be placed into an InDesign document. Note the Show Import Options box. This option, by default, is not selected, although it gives you greater control over the artwork being added to the document.

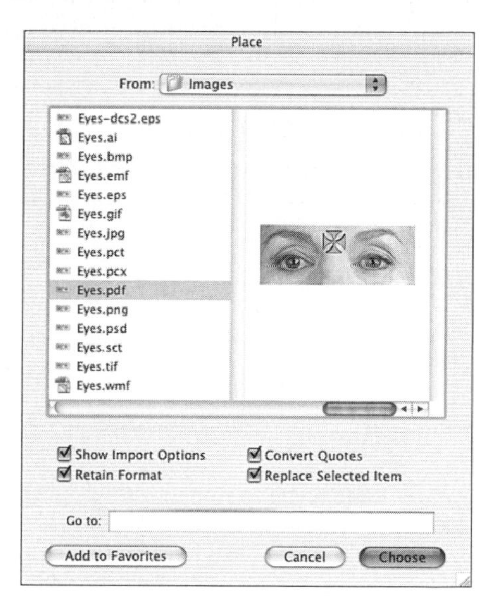


**Figure 3.49**
Among the file formats you cannot place into InDesign are JPEG 2000, Raw, and Photoshop's Large Document Format (PSB).



Of the file formats that you *can* place into an InDesign document, there are only a few that you *should* place. Such formats as PICT, PCX, and WMF may be suitable for output to low-resolution inkjet printers, but they are not acceptable for commercial printing presses. Here are some points to remember when placing files in an InDesign document:

- Photoshop, Illustrator, PDF, EPS (and the derivative format DCS 2.0), and TIFF should be the first choices.
- For documents that will eventually be posted on the Internet, JPEG, GIF, and PNG can be used.
- WMF and EMF files can be opened in Illustrator and saved as Illustrator, PDF, or EPS files.
- BMP, PCX, PICT, and SCT files can be opened in Photoshop and saved as Photoshop, PDF, EPS, or TIFF files. All except Scitex (SCT) can also be opened in Illustrator and saved or exported in a preferred format.

## Import Options for Placed Graphics Files

When the Show Import Options box is checked in the Place dialog box, placing Photoshop, TIFF, JPEG, GIF, BMP, PCX, and SCT files gives you the options shown in Figure 3.50. You can apply a clipping path (if one is embedded in the image) and elect how to color-manage the document (when ICC profiles are available).

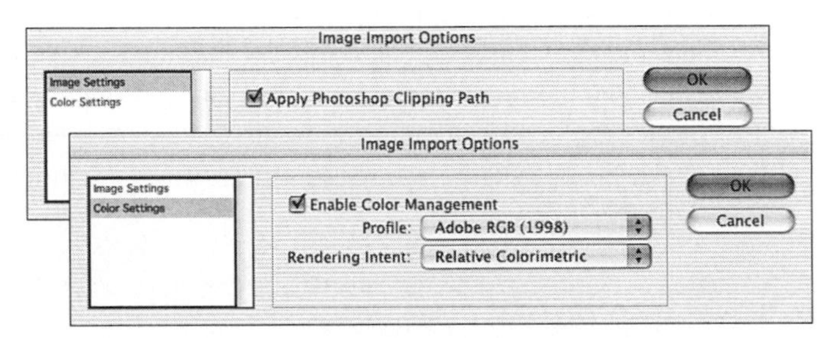


**Figure 3.50**
When no clipping path or ICC profile is available, the Image Import Options dialog box does not appear.



The PNG file format includes one additional set of options, shown in Figure 3.51. If transparency has been designated in the image with an alpha channel or a specified color, you can use that information in InDesign. Gamma correction can adjust the tonality of an image to match that of a non-PostScript printer.

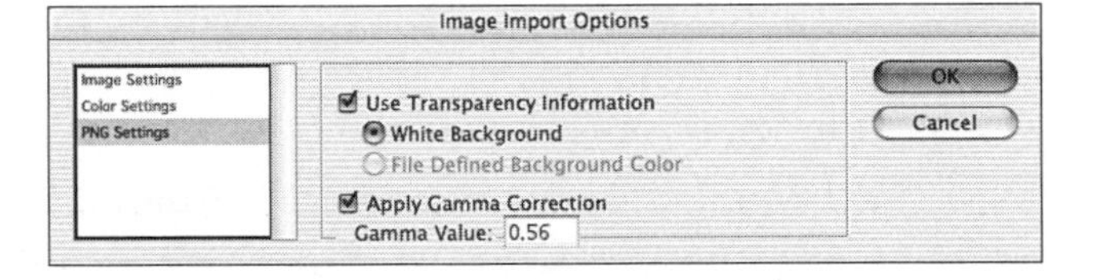


**Figure 3.51**
Remember that the PNG file format does not support CMYK color. PNG images will not separate.

The Illustrator and PDF file formats enable you to crop, preserve halftone screen information, and retain transparency in a placed image. The Place PDF Options dialog box is shown is Figure 3.52.

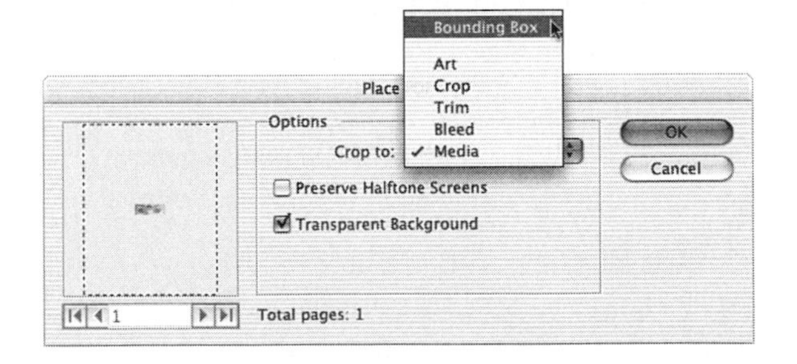


**Figure 3.52**
Because the Illustrator (AI) file format is based on PDF, it shares the Place PDF options.

If Show Import Options is selected when placing an EPS or DCS file, you'll see the dialog box in Figure 3.53. If a low-resolution proxy is embedded in the image, you can elect to use that for onscreen display by checking the Read Embedded OPI Image Links box. (Although a low-resolution version of the image will appear on the monitor, the actual high-resolution image will print.) If saved with the file, a clipping path can be used. You also have the choice of using an embedded TIFF or PICT preview or having InDesign generate a preview from the actual image data.

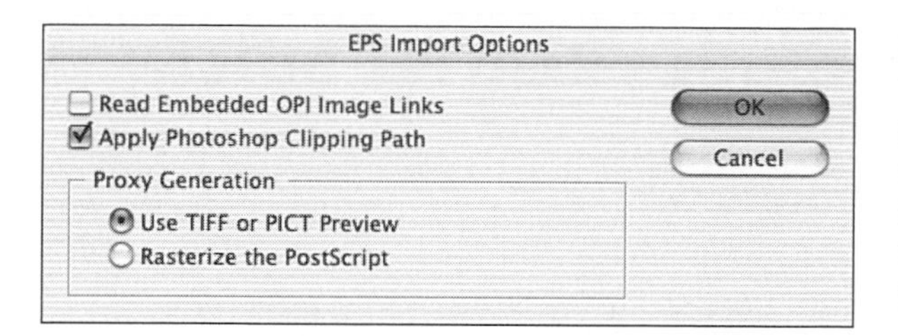


Figure 3.53
The proxy appearance has less to do with these options than it does with your choice of Optimized Display, Typical Display, or High Quality Display in InDesign's View menu.

When placing PICT, WMF, and EMF files, you have no Options dialog box.

## Saving and Exporting InDesign Documents

When you use the Save command, InDesign creates (the first time) or updates (during subsequent saves) an InDesign document. The Save As command offers the option of saving as a template. You can also use Save As to assign a new name to the file, thus creating a copy. The Save a Copy command makes a copy of the file, document, or template and appends "copy" to the name.

InDesign's Export command enables you to save the document in a variety of formats. PDF and EPS are available for print-related projects. PDF, HTML, SVG, and compressed SVG are available for Web projects. InDesign can also generate XML, which is handy for projects that require multiple destinations, such as print, the Web, and PDAs.



# GOLIVE AND FILE FORMATS

GoLive opens Web pages and Web sites created in GoLive, as well as HTML (and related) documents generated by other programs. It can work with text files and graphics in a variety of file formats. GoLive also takes advantage of Adobe's Smart Objects technology, which enables you to place artwork from Illustrator, Photoshop, or LiveMotion directly into the GoLive page. GoLive optimizes the file for the Web and stores the optimization information. Should the source file be changed, GoLive can quickly and easily update the Web page. You can double-click the image in GoLive to launch the parent application and edit the file.

Although the standard graphics formats for the Web are JPEG, GIF, and PNG, GoLive can work with a variety of other formats as smart objects. Photoshop (PSD), Illustrator (AI), LiveMotion (LIV), PDF, TIFF, and EPS files can all be used. In addition, less-common file formats are available, including Amiga IFF, BMP, PCX, PICT, Pixar, and Targa.

Scalable Vector Graphics (SVG) and Flash (SWF) files can also be used in GoLive. SVG files can be generated in Illustrator, and both Illustrator and LiveMotion can produce SWF files.

# MASTERING THE ADOBE CREATIVE SUITE

## Formats and Platforms

*What makes .tif or .psd files different in Macintosh and Windows?*

Actually, nothing. A file extension indicates a particular file type. File types are almost always standardized so that they work equally well on both Windows and Macintosh computers (assuming that the appropriate program is available). However, the file must be on a disk or drive that can be read by the computer. Macintosh computers can read and write Windows-formatted disks, but Windows computers can't read Mac-formatted disks without a utility.

Remember, too, that file formats can change with versions of the software. Just as a PSD file created by Photoshop can have features that cannot be used in Photoshop 4, so, too, do the most recent DOC files from Microsoft Word have features unavailable in Word 4.2.



## Hard and Variable Transparency

*I want a soft drop shadow around my image, but Export Transparent Image always seems to leave a white halo below the shadow.*

The transparency generated for EPS and GIF files is *hard-edged* transparency, in which a pixel is either completely transparent or completely opaque. Your drop shadow relies on *variable transparency*, in which pixels can be partially transparent.

Save for Web can now generate GIFs with dithered transparency, interspersing opaque pixels and transparent pixels. Print applications are a good bit trickier. InDesign 2.0 supports variable transparency, but other page layout programs do not. There are various techniques for simulating such effects as drop shadows, but generally it's easier to replicate the page's background in Photoshop.

## Lossy Compression

*I want to get my files really small for the Web, but it takes a long time. I save an image at one compression level and open it up to look at it. Then I have to go back and try a different compression level to get what I want. Isn't there a way to preview an image being saved as a JPEG?*

Use the menu command File, Save for Web. This feature allows you to compare up to four versions of the same image, all at the same time. You pick the versions that best meet your needs for quality and file size and then click OK.

## RGB for the Web

*I created JPEG files of a lot of the images my company used in its latest brochure so that I could post them on the Web, but they don't show up. I exported them as JPEGs, so what's the problem?*

For a brochure, eh? I'll bet those images were CMYK. Although that color mode is perfectly acceptable for JPEG, it's not acceptable on the Web. Your images need to be converted to RGB before they can be seen by a Web browser. Throw away the CMYK JPEGs and go back to the originals. Use Save for Web rather than Export, and the color mode will automatically be converted for you.

What's that? Why does JPEG accept CMYK if you can't see it on the Web? Well, JPEG does more than just Web graphics. It's also one of the major file formats used to compress images for storage or archiving—and many of those images are CMYK.

4

# PIXELS, VECTORS, AND RESOLUTIONS

## IN THIS CHAPTER

The two basic classifications of digital images are *vector* and *raster*. Vector image files, such as those native to Illustrator, contain descriptions of geometric objects. Photoshop's raster image files (also known as *bitmap images*) contain descriptions of colored pixels arranged in a grid or raster. InDesign works with both types of graphics. GoLive uses primarily raster artwork, with the exception of the vector-capable SVG and SWF formats. (This discussion will focus on the artwork-generating programs, Photoshop and Illustrator.)

The two types of artwork have their strong points and their weak points. They are designed for different jobs, and they do their jobs well. Determining when to use which image type, when you have a choice, depends on a variety of factors. Sometimes file format requirements dictate whether your illustration can remain vector or must be rasterized into a series of pixels. Sometimes you need to incorporate a raster image into an illustration, and such artwork needs to be in an appropriate format in order to be placed into the vector image. Likewise, vector shapes can be used in Photoshop artwork, and raster images can be converted to vector shapes.

This chapter looks at how raster and vector images are created and the advantages of each. It also gives you the background you'll need to make informed decisions when creating your artwork.

# DEFINING RASTER AND VECTOR ARTWORK



Vector art generally produces sharper images than raster when printed. Raster, however, can incorporate special effects and techniques that are impossible to reproduce in a vector art program, and it can reproduce fine variations in color. Illustrator is, at heart, a vector illustration tool. Photoshop is the premier raster program. With the releases of Illustrator CS and Photoshop CS, the line continues to blur between the programs. Each program, however, specializes in one type of artwork and has some capability with the other.

## What Is Raster Art?

The term *raster* refers to a grid. In the case of digital art, the grid consists of rows and columns of *pixels*. The pixel is the lowest common denominator in raster art. Each raster image is made of a series of squares, and each square can be exactly one color. These squares (pixels) cannot be subdivided. They are the smallest element in an image, and all images are made of them. Figure 4.1 shows a raster image and a close-up of the pixels used to display the image.

There are four key points to remember about pixels:

- Pixels are square or, for some digital video, rectangular. (Photoshop CS supports nonsquare pixels.)
- Each pixel can be exactly one color. Even when reproduced in grayscale, you can see in Figure 4.1 that each of the small squares is monotone; none blend from one shade to another. Some of the pixels are the same color or very close to those neighboring them, but there can also be very definite color differences between adjacent pixels.

Generally speaking, when you see the term *illustration*, think "vector." Photos are always raster. The terms *artwork* and *image* can be used with work that is vector, raster, or a combination of both.

- Every pixel in an image is exactly the same size. Although pixel size can vary from image to image, there can be no variation in a particular image. Likewise, the pixels must maintain their alignment within the image.
- Each pixel is independent. There are no "objects" in raster artwork. Although a series of pixels may show a building or a circle, the artwork is nothing more than a series of pixels.

**Figure 4.1**
The close-up is of the third pane in the left column of the original.

Because each pixel is square and can contain only a single color, each has distinct corners and edges. In Figure 4.1, the left image is shown at 100% zoom. The individual pixels are not visible. In the inset (400% zoom), however, each pixel is visible. Note that the "curve" to the right of the inset consists of pixels, each with distinct corners.



## What Is Vector Art?

Vector art is recorded in a file as a series of mathematical relationships. If you were to translate the file data into English, it might read something like this:

> Start an oval shape near the upper-left corner and go to the middle of the page. It should be almost round, but taller than wide. Make the line that draws the circle about one-twentieth as wide as the page and color it black.

The result would look the same, regardless of page size (see Figure 4.2). Of course, the computer file would be far more precise, never recording data as "near" or "almost" or "about."

Vector artwork uses paths to record shapes. A path can be a straight or curved line, a circle or square, or a more complex object (see Figure 4.3).

## Vector Paths, Lines, and Points

Vector paths are also known as *Bézier curves*, named for the French engineer Pierre Etienne Bézier (1910–1999), who pioneered their use in design. Each path segment is bordered by a pair of *anchor points*. Paths can consist of one or more path segments, with segments joined at their anchor points. The direction and shape of a curved path segment is determined by *direction lines* and *control points* at the anchor points. Control points can have one or two path segments connecting them, but no more than two. The anatomy of a Bézier curve is shown in Figure 4.4.

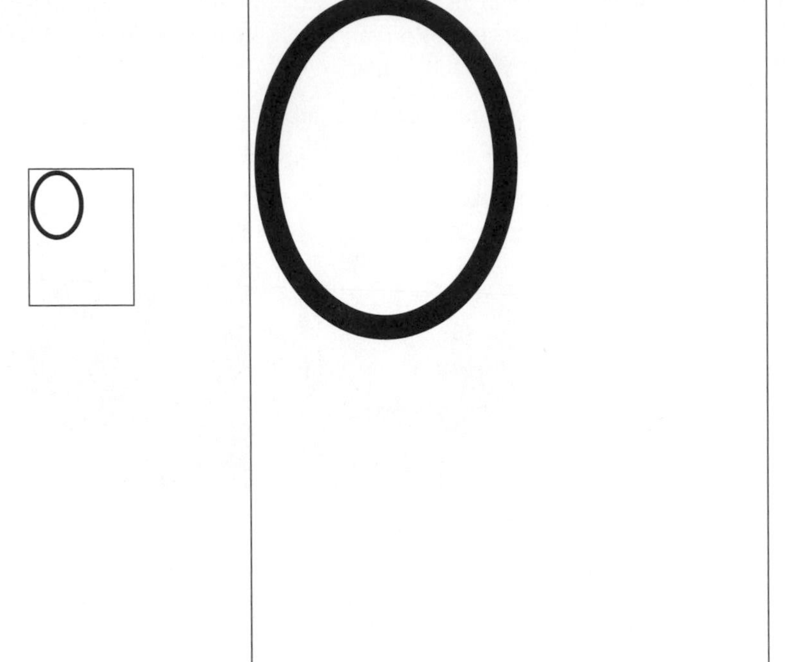

**Figure 4.2**
Regardless of page size, the relative terms produce an object that is relationally the same.

**Figure 4.3**
Each of these objects is a single path in Photoshop's Paths palette.

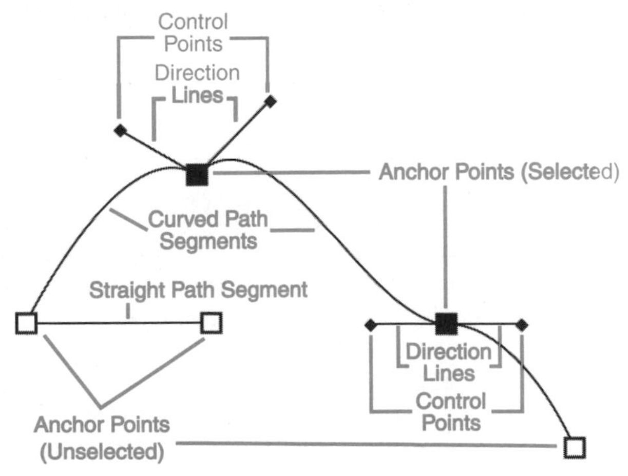


**Figure 4.4**
The control points and direction lines, like the path itself, are nonprinting. Only the stroke and/or fill applied to a path is printed.

Anchor points with diametrically opposed direction lines are referred to as *smooth points* because the path continues smoothly, without changing direction, as it passes through these points. Anchor points without direction lines or those that contain direction lines that are not 180° from each other are *corner points*. The distance and angle of the direction line from the anchor point determine how the path will be shaped from that point. When there are smooth anchor points at either end of a segment, the direction lines and control points influence each other to create the curve. Compare the two curves in Figure 4.5.

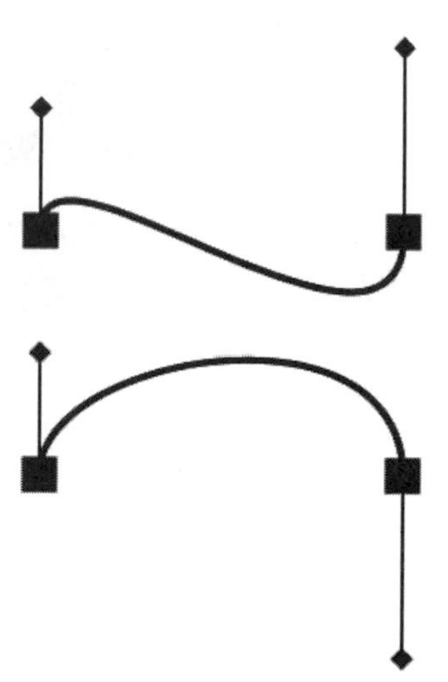

Figure 4.5
The left anchor points for the two paths are identical. Notice how the path changes according to the difference between the direction lines to the right.



A straight path segment has corner anchor points at each end. The points can have no direction lines or control points, or they can have one direction line (for a curved path segment bordering the straight segment). The straight path segment extends directly from one anchor point to the neighboring anchor point.

Paths can be *open* or *closed*. The anchor points at each end of an open path connect to only one path segment, but each anchor point in a closed path has a segment on either side. Consider the difference between a piece of string and a rubber band. The string has two distinct ends, whereas the rubber band (in most cases) forms a loop with no visible start or stop.

Each piece of artwork in Figure 4.6 consists of a single path. Paths can be *open*, with distinct endpoints, such as the paths on the left, or *closed*, continuous paths with no visible start or end, such as the paths on the right.

Whether open or closed, paths can be stroked and filled. The upper paths in Figure 4.7 were stroked (color was applied to the paths) but unfilled. The paths below are both stroked and filled. Note that the open paths are filled to an imaginary line that could be drawn between the endpoints. The closed paths are filled everywhere that these paths enclose.

Because vector artwork consists of path segments, you can manipulate an object in its entirety or change only a portion of it by manipulating path segments, anchor points, or direction lines.

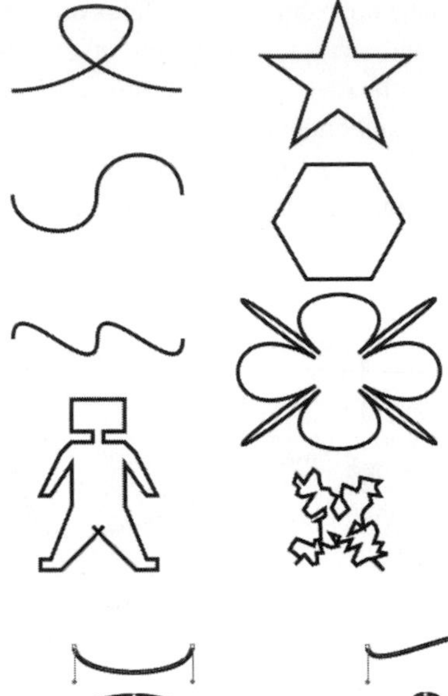

Figure 4.6
The top and bottom paths on the left are open paths, even though each path crosses over itself. Any path with endpoints is an open path.

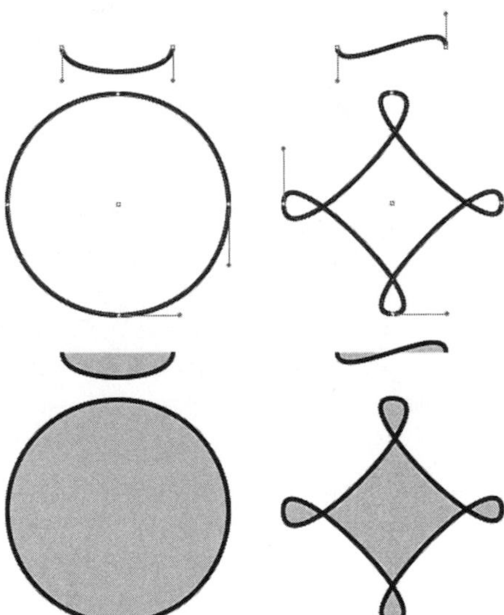

Figure 4.7
In the upper examples, the anchor points appear as white spots on the paths, and the direction lines extend out from them. At the end of the direction lines are the direction points.



## How Vector Art Is Resized

Mathematically defined vector objects enable you to control their characteristics when editing or printing. When changing the size of a vector object, called *scaling*, you can choose to have its appearance attributes change proportionally or remain static. For example, when scaling a circle that consists of a single black line, you can choose to have the line remain the same size (stroke width) or have it change proportionally to retain the overall look of the circle. The difference is shown in Figure 4.8.

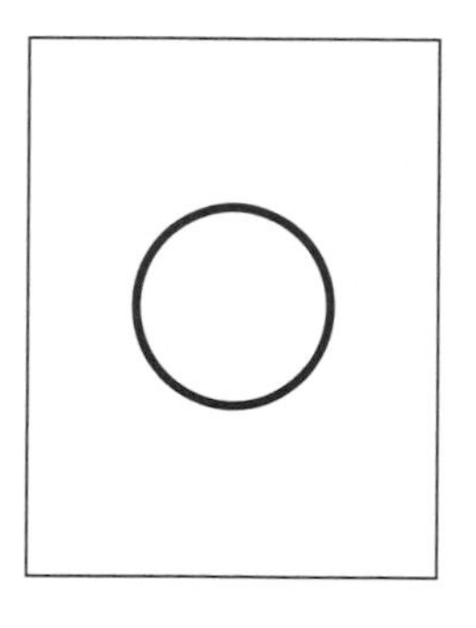
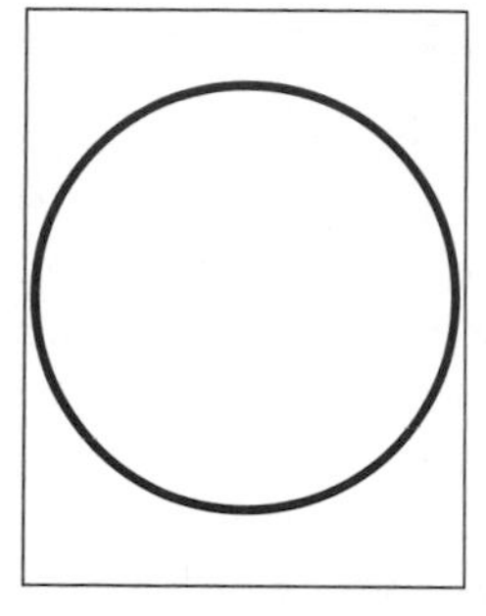
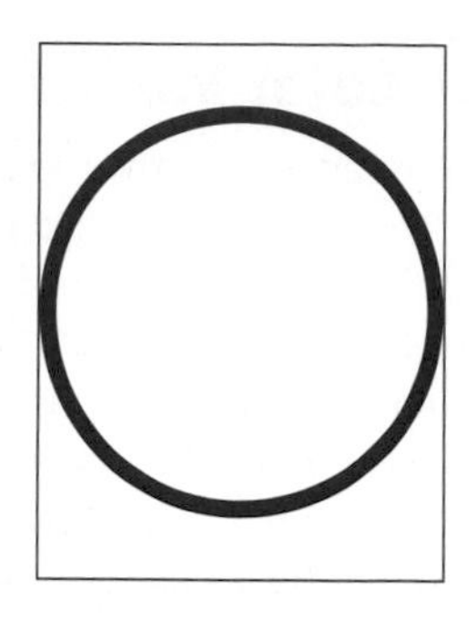

Figure 4.8
The original circle (left) is scaled without resizing the stroke (center) and with the stroke also scaled (right).

When you resize the stroke, the circle retains its appearance. The image on the right in Figure 4.8 is proportionally identical to the one on the left. It could be used, for example, as a "zoomed-in" look at the circle. The image in the center, on the other hand, could not be used in such a manner because the stroke size is smaller in relation to the diameter of the circle.

The capability to adjust the appearance of an image during scaling is just as important when you're reducing the size of an illustration. An example is shown in Figure 4.9.

Figure 4.9
The original is on the left, a copy scaled without resizing the strokes is in the center, and a scaled copy with the strokes also scaled is on the right.



As you can see, leaving the strokes at their original weights in an illustration one-half the size (center) can seriously degrade the integrity of the image. Rescaling the strokes (right) along with the image size maintains the appearance. Sometimes, however, it's better to leave the stroke unscaled when you change an image's size. In Figure 4.9, for example, the boxes that indicate page outlines for the second and third images are actually copies of the rectangle on the left. Leaving these strokes unscaled maintains the relationship between the two sizes of the rectangle.

## Comparing Vector and Raster

The greatest strength of raster artwork is its capability to reproduce photographic-quality images. It is certainly possible to produce vector illustrations that are photorealistic (the work of Bert Monroy immediately comes to mind). However, gradients in a vector-based illustration program, such as Adobe Illustrator, cannot easily reproduce the look of textures and surfaces in nature. That is one of the reasons why most photorealistic illustrators use Photoshop in conjunction with their illustration program.

## Displaying Subtle Color Variations

One of the advantages of raster artwork is the capability of displaying subtle variations in color. Although vector artwork in Illustrator can be filled with gradients or gradient meshes, only rasterized art can achieve the subtlety of pixel-by-pixel color variation. (Compare the relative smoothness of the tunnel walls in Figure 4.10 and Figure 4.11, later in this section.) Photographs, for example, cannot be stored in vector format. Photoshop's capability of producing extremely subtle color transitions from pixel to pixel enables it to produce extraordinarily realistic textures and shadows. Gradients, gradient mesh objects, and patterns can all be used to simulate surfaces and textures in a vector-based illustration program. However, it's almost impossible to match the realism achieved by scanning the surfaces and textures of actual objects into Photoshop.

*Want a little more information on why it's tough to make vector illustrations look perfect? See "Texture in Nature" in the "Mastering the Adobe Creative Suite" section at the end of this chapter.*

Despite the radical differences in the way that vector and raster art record data, they can coexist in a number of file formats. (See Chapter 3, "Understanding and Choosing File Formats.") Photoshop's native format (.psd), Illustrator's native format (.ai), DCS, EPS, and PDF are all examples of formats that can contain both types of artwork. Common raster file formats that cannot include vector imagery include BMP, GIF, JPEG, and PNG. (Do not confuse clipping paths with vector artwork.)

4

## Editing and Moving Image Elements

Although the contents of a photo consist of individual objects in reality, once captured on film or digitally, the contents of the image no longer exist as separate objects. You could not, for example, open a picture of a city in a vector art program and click a building to drag it to a new location. In a raster art program, however, you could select the pixels that represent the building and move *them* to a new location in the image.

On one hand, pixels can produce a perfect representation of the building (such as a photograph), whereas the vector artwork produces an illustration of a building. On the other hand, selecting an object or group of objects in a vector art illustration and dragging to a new spot on the artboard is far easier than selecting some of the pixels in a rasterized version of the image. In addition, in most raster image formats, moving pixels results in empty space or whitespace being left behind. (Most raster formats readable by Illustrator do not support layers.)

In Figure 4.10, a vector ring and its shadow have been grouped. They can easily be moved by dragging with the Selection tool.

In comparison, see Figure 4.11, which shows a rasterized version of the same image.

Attempting to move the ring and its shadow in the rasterized image causes several problems:

- Most obviously, the tunnel floor and walls are not behind the pixels that make up the ring and its shadow. Transparency (or white) is left behind when pixels are moved.
- Selecting the correct pixels can be difficult and time consuming.
- Selecting a drop shadow (or any of a number of other effects) cannot be done properly. Because a shadow or glow fades toward the edges, the background color shows through. Separating the shadow from the background color is impossible.

**Figure 4.10**
In vector art, the ring and its shadow remain objects that can be selected and moved, independent of the background or other objects.

**Figure 4.11**
The ring and its shadow are no longer objects; rather, they are represented by individual pixels. The checkerboard pattern represents transparency.

*Have a scan or other raster image that you need to turn into vector art? See "Vector-izing" in the "Mastering the Adobe Creative Suite" section at the end of this chapter.*

In Illustrator, many filters and effects are available for both raster and vector artwork. In Photoshop, a dedicated raster-imaging program, you have far more control over the appearance of a raster image. Sophisticated adjustments for color correction, color selection and replacement, and manipulation

> Photoshop has the capability to work with layers. Pixels on one layer can be moved without disturbing pixels on other layers. In Figure 4.11, if the ring was on a separate layer, it could be moved without affecting the tunnel.

(via commands such as Liquefy) are available. In addition, image-editing software has tools you can use to select and edit pixels.

## Type as Vector and Raster Artwork

One area where vector is almost always superior to raster is text. Type set at very small sizes and very large sizes almost always is sharper and clearer as vector text, as illustrated in Figure 4.12.

**Figure 4.12**
The lower word was rasterized at 72ppi, which is not horrible at full size. However, the inset shows a good comparison of vector and raster type at 400% zoom.



Font selection can make a difference when type will be rasterized. In Figure 4.13, you can see 20 different fonts and how they rasterize at a low resolution. The top row is vector type, and the second row has been rasterized at 72dpi with antialiasing selected (you learn about antialiasing in the next section of this chapter). Both rows are shown at 100% zoom. In the box, the rasterized letters are shown at 150% zoom.

**Figure 4.13**
The rasterized characters in the box are shown at 150% zoom. For most fonts, antialiasing does a good job of disguising the pixel edges at 100% zoom.

Note that when this text is viewed at 150% zoom, the rasterization becomes quite apparent. This gives an indication, too, of how the low-resolution raster text may appear on a printed page.

As you can see, fonts with straight vertical and horizontal lines suffer least from the *jaggies*, that stair-step appearance caused by visible pixel corners. Curly and angular fonts suffer most.

## Antialiasing Raster Type and Artwork

*Antialiasing* adds colored pixels to a raster image to soften the edges of curves. The added pixels blend between the color of the type or shape and the background color. For example, a black shape on a white background would have shades of gray added to antialias (or soften) the curves (see Figure 4.14).

Figure 4.14
On the left, the letter has no antialiasing. On the right, the curves appear smoother when viewed at 100% zoom (the frame at the top) because of the antialiasing. The bottom view is at 700% zoom.

Notice, too, that without antialiasing, the straight edges of the pixels form perfect horizontal and vertical lines.

A number of Photoshop's selection tools have antialiasing available in the Options Bar. The selections made with this option have a slight amount of antialiasing to avoid the jaggies. You learn how to use these antialiasing tools in Chapter 9, "Making Selections and Creating Masks."

# VECTORS IN PHOTOSHOP

Photoshop CS uses vector paths in a variety of ways. For example, vector clipping paths are used to designate part of an image as transparent for a page layout program. Vector paths are also used with Photoshop's shape layers. Type in Photoshop also uses vector paths.

*The following sections provide a brief overview of Photoshop's vector capabilities. For more in-depth discussions, see Chapter 11, "The Pen Tool and Shape Layers: Vectors in Photoshop," p. 363, and Chapter 12, "Adding Text: Photoshop's Type Capabilities," p. 389.*

## The Paths Palette

Photoshop's paths are nonprinting. They can be stroked and/or filled and can be used with shape layers to produce printable artwork, but the paths themselves do not print. In fact, unless selected in the Paths palette, paths are invisible in the image.

Photoshop uses the Paths palette, shown in Figure 4.15, to manage paths. Each path in an image is listed separately. To select a path and make it visible in the image, click it in the Paths palette. Only one path can be active at a time, but as you can see from the thumbnail of Path 2 in Figure 4.15, a single path can consist of multiple subpaths.

> Antialiasing can make small type and fine lines look fuzzy. Web graphics with small text, for example, should use sans serif, vertical fonts without antialiasing to maintain legibility.

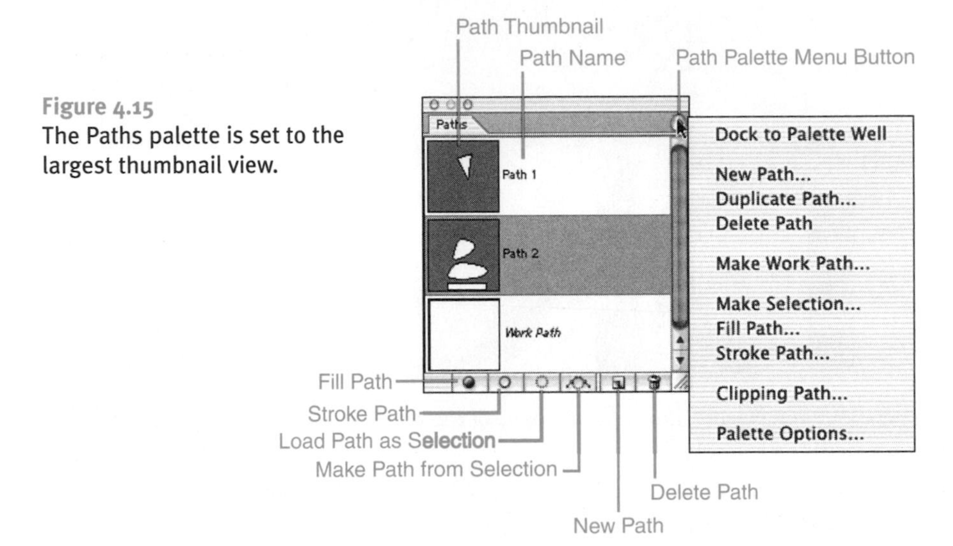


**Figure 4.15**
The Paths palette is set to the largest thumbnail view.

The term *Work Path*, which is italicized in the Paths palette in Figure 4.15, refers to a temporary path, currently being created or edited. Work paths are created with the Pen tool, Shape tools, or the Make Path from Selection button. An image can have only one work path—creating a new work path deletes any existing work path. You can save a work path as a regular path by renaming it. To do this, double-click a work path to open the Save Path dialog box (see Figure 4.16). By default, Photoshop suggests the name Path 1 or the next available number. Paths, however, can be given any unique name.

**Figure 4.16**
Naming a work path allows you to save it as a regular path.

Paths can be created in several ways:

- Make a selection and then click the Make Work Path from Selection button at the bottom of the Paths palette. A new work path is created, replacing (not supplementing) any existing work path.
- Use the Pen tool (with the Paths option selected in the Options Bar) to create a new work path.
- Click the New Path button at the bottom of the palette and then use the Pen tool to create the path.
- Create a shape layer by using one of Photoshop's Shape tools (see Figure 4.17).
- Set a Shape tool to create a work path using the appropriate button in the Options Bar.

Clipping paths are created by using the Paths palette menu command.

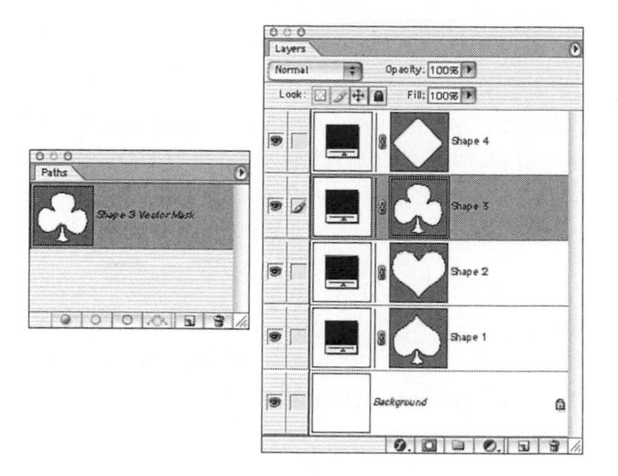


Figure 4.17
The Paths palette shows the path of the shape layer that's active in the Layers palette.

## The Pen Tools

Incredibly precise paths can be created with Photoshop's Pen tools, and with the click of a button, these paths become incredibly precise selections. The Pen tools can also be used to edit existing paths, including those created with Photoshop's Shape tools.

Photoshop CS offers several path-related tools, including two tools for creating paths and five for editing existing paths (see Figure 4.18).

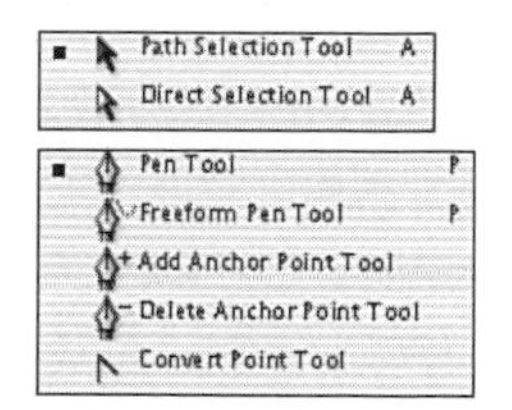


Figure 4.18
The tools are selected from fly-out palettes in Photoshop's Toolbox.



Each of the path-related tools has one or more functions:

- **Path Selection tool**—Identifiable by the black arrow icon, this tool is used to select and move paths. It can select only the path that is active in the Paths palette. When a path consists of multiple subpaths, each can be selected individually, or you can Shift-click to select more than one subpath. The Path Selection tool can be used to scale and otherwise transform a path when Show Bounding Box is selected in the Options Bar. The Options Bar also allows subpaths to be combined, intersected, excluded, and aligned.
- **Direct Selection tool**—Individual anchor points can be selected and manipulated with the Direct Selection tool. Moving an anchor point with the Direct Selection tool, of course, alters the shape of the path. In addition to dragging anchor points, the Direct Selection tool can be used to drag path segments. When you drag a segment bordered by two corner anchor points, the points are dragged with the segment. When one or more bordering anchor points have direction lines, the anchor point remains stationary and the direction line is adjusted to meet the path segment's new shape. After you click an anchor point to show the direction lines and control points, you can use the Direct Selection tool to drag the control points of smooth anchor points.

- **Pen tool**—The primary tool for creating paths in Photoshop is the Pen tool. You can place each anchor point individually with this tool by clicking. Dragging the Pen tool creates a curved path segment and a smooth anchor point. When Auto Add/Delete is selected in the Options Bar, the Pen tool automatically switches to the Add Anchor Point or Delete Anchor Point tool when positioned over a path segment or an anchor point. The Options Bar also enables you to conveniently switch to the Freeform Pen tool or any of Photoshop's Shape tools. You can also use it to combine subpaths.
- **Freeform Pen tool**—Instead of clicking or dragging to establish anchor points and path segments with the Pen tool, you can use the Freeform Pen tool to simply draw a path. Drag the Freeform Pen tool, and Photoshop automatically places anchor points.
- **Add Anchor Point tool**—When positioned over a path segment, this tool enables you to add corner anchor points (click) or smooth anchor points (drag) to the path. When positioned over an existing anchor point, the tool automatically switches to the Direct Selection tool.
- **Delete Anchor Point tool**—You can delete an existing anchor point by clicking it with this tool. When not positioned over an anchor point, the Delete Anchor Point tool functions as the Direct Selection tool.
- **Convert Point tool**—Use this tool to convert a smooth anchor point to a corner point (click) or to convert a corner anchor point to a smooth point (drag). When not over an anchor point, the tool functions as the Direct Selection tool.

## Shape Layers

Photoshop's shape layers simulate vector objects. Instead of being actual vector objects, each is a layer filled with a color, pattern, or gradient. In the Paths and Layers palettes, a shape layer is identifiable by the thumbnails of the filled layer (left) and the layer's vector mask (right) as well as by the default name "Shape" (see Figure 4.19).

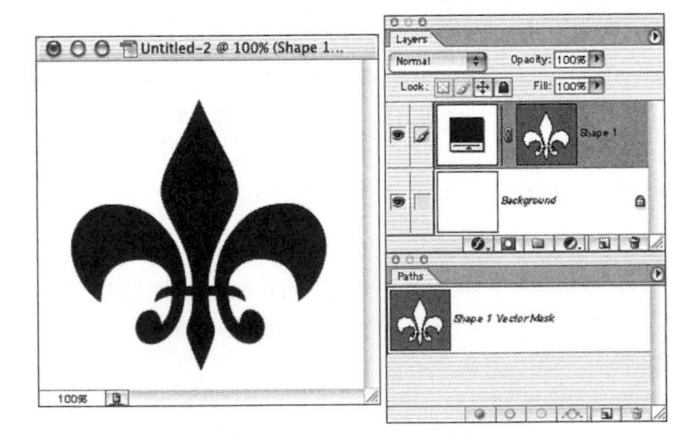


Figure 4.19
If the layer's name is changed in the Layers palette, the path name is automatically updated in the Paths palette.

In the Layers palette, the layer fill is visible in the thumbnail to the left, and the layer vector path is visible in the thumbnails of both the Layers and Paths palettes.

## Creating Shape Layers

The primary method of creating shape layers in Photoshop is using the Shape tools. However, the Pen tool can also be set (in the Options Bar) to create shape layers. When pasting an object from Illustrator, you'll also have the option of creating a shape layer. (Illustrator's AICB clipboard option must be activated in the program's Preferences.)

The "shape" is created with a vector path that selectively shows and hides areas of the layer. You can Shift-click the thumbnail of the layer vector mask in the Layers palette to disable it. With the mask disabled, you can see that there's a fill color throughout the layer (see Figure 4.20).

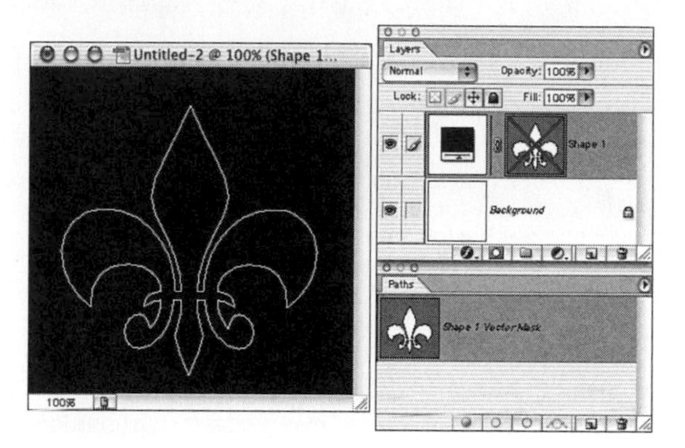


**Figure 4.20**
The layer vector mask can be enabled through the same shortcut—Shift-click the mask thumbnail in the Layers palette.

Whether enabled or disabled as a layer vector mask, the path can be selected in the Paths palette and edited with Photoshop selection and Pen tools.

Shape layers can have layer styles in the same way as regular layers. In addition, the menu command Layer, Change Layer Content allows you to use gradients and patterns in addition to solid colors. You can even convert shape layers to adjustment layers by using that command (see Figure 4.21). No matter the fill or type of layer, the layer mask remains a vector mask.



## Photoshop at Work: Editing Shape Layers

After you've created a shape layer, you can edit it to better fit your needs. Here's how:

1. Open a new document with the following specs: RGB, 800×600 pixels, filled with white, 72ppi.
2. Select the Custom Shape tool from the Toolbox.
3. In the Options Bar, open the Custom Shape palette and select any interesting shape.
4. Drag the tool in the window, creating a large shape.
5. Select the Direct Selection tool from the Toolbox. (It's the tool with the white arrow icon, found beneath the black-arrow icon, the Path Selection tool.) The keyboard shortcut, by default, is the A key. Because the two tools share the shortcut, A then Shift+A should bring it up.

(Control-clicking) [right-clicking] the mask thumbnail opens the contextual menu, through which you can also disable a mask. The contextual menu also enables you to delete a vector mask or to convert it to a pixel-based layer mask (using the Rasterize Vector Mask command).

6. Click once on the edge of the shape to select the path. (You can also make the path active by clicking Shape 1 Vector Mask in the Paths palette.)
7. Click any visible anchor point and drag away from the shape. Notice how the path is adjusted and more of the shape layer's fill is exposed.

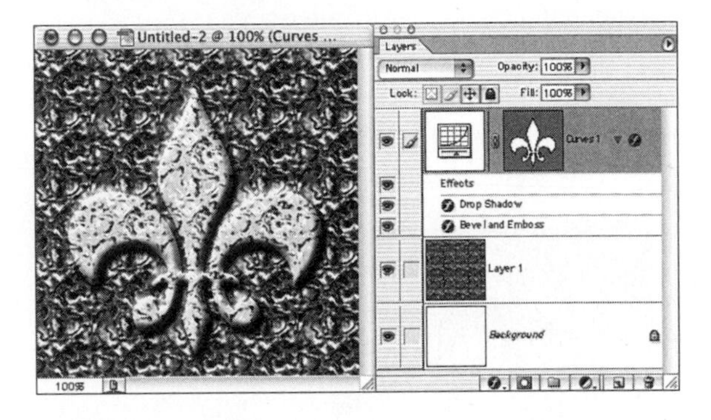


**Figure 4.21**
As you can see from the Layers palette, the shape layer is now a Curves adjustment layer, with layer effects applied.

## Vector Type

Using vector paths to create type outlines enables laser printers and other PostScript devices to produce sharp, clean-edged type that can be scaled. Because vector type (like vector artwork) uses mathematically defined outlines, even the printer itself can resize it, without losing quality. Bitmap type, on the other hand, is designed to be reproduced at a specific size. Although bitmap fonts often have multiple sizes, the type should not be scaled.

Remember, too, that Photoshop's Type tool allows you to create letter-shaped selections. When in Type Mask mode (see Figure 4.22), Photoshop is not creating vector type. Rather, it is making a mask in the shape of the type. The selection created from the mask can then be filled, used as a layer vector mask, or otherwise used in Photoshop, but it is not vector based.

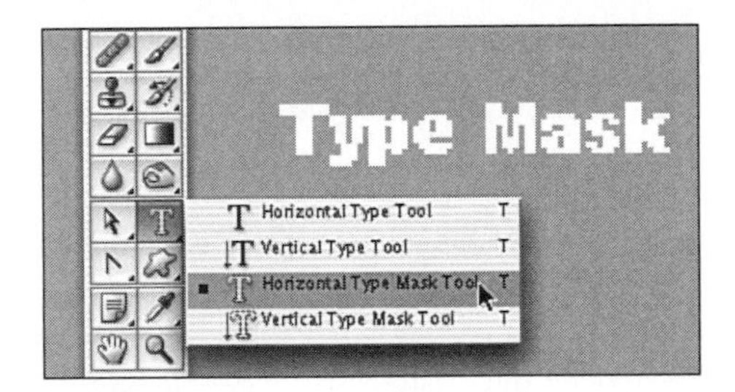


**Figure 4.22**
A red overlay, such as that used in Quick Mask mode, is created by a Type Mask tool. It is converted to a selection when you switch tools.

# RASTERIZING OBJECTS IN ILLUSTRATOR

Illustrator gives you two ways to rasterize an object: through the Object menu and through the Effect menu. When you're rasterizing as an effect, the appearance of the object or text is changed, but it remains vector artwork. You can reverse

> Bitmap fonts should not be used with Photoshop, and it's a good idea to delete them from your system. They are outdated and might cause problems for your system.

the rasterization by selecting the object and deleting the effect from the Appearance palette. Knowing when and why to rasterize and understanding the basic settings you use to do so are key to preserving the appearance of artwork in Illustrator. You learn these details of rasterizing in the following subsections.

> The command Object, Rasterize converts a vector object to pixels. Effect, Rasterize changes the *appearance* of the object, but the object remains vector. Raster effects are those effects created with pixels that are applied to an object, such as shadows and glows.

## The Rasterize and Raster Effects Settings Dialog Boxes

When you are rasterizing a selection, the dialog box offers you the choice of grayscale, bitmap (black and white), or the color mode of the document. (You cannot rasterize an object as CMYK in an RGB document, or vice versa. Illustrator does not allow objects of more than one color mode in the same document.) Figure 4.23 shows the Rasterize and Document Raster Effects Settings dialog boxes; you access these through the Effect menu.

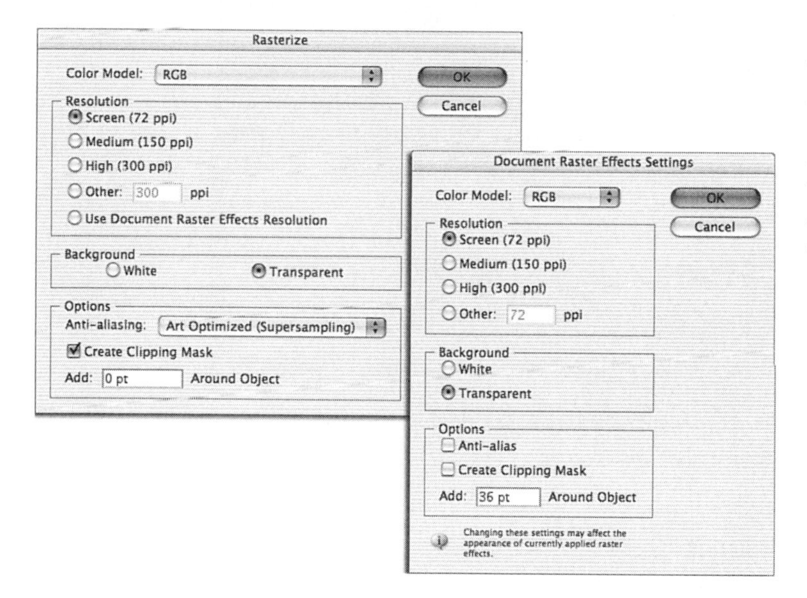


**Figure 4.23**
The options for rasterizing objects (rear dialog box) include more extensive control over antialiasing than is required for the rasterization of effects, such as drop shadows and glows (front dialog box).

4

*For more information about rasterizing effects, see Chapter 35, "Illustrator's Effects and Filters," p. 1029.*

The resolution of an object or text to be rasterized should depend on the final destination of the object (you learn more about resolution in "Image Resolution," later in this chapter). Images destined for the Web should be rasterized at low resolution to keep the pixel dimension comparable to those at which the element was designed. Images created for commercial printing should be of an appropriate resolution for the line screen frequency of the press.

You should select a transparent background if the rasterized object will be placed in front of or otherwise interact with another object. Figure 4.24 shows the difference between white and transparent backgrounds.

You use the settings in the Document Raster Effects Settings dialog box to rasterize drop shadows, glows, and other live effects when artwork is exported or printed. Objects that are rasterized when exported or printed use the settings located in the Printing & Export panel of the Document Info dialog box.

The Rasterize command also enables you to apply antialiasing and add background pixels around the object. This extra space is sometimes referred to as *padding*. In Figure 4.24, note that the lower text is clipped on the left side, despite being left-aligned. The Rasterize command uses the baseline of a type object, the imaginary line on which the type sits, to determine left and right edges. The upper example does not clip off the left side of the letter *j* because padding of 36 pixels was selected in the Document Raster Effects dialog box (refer to the bottom of the dialog box shown in Figure 4.23).

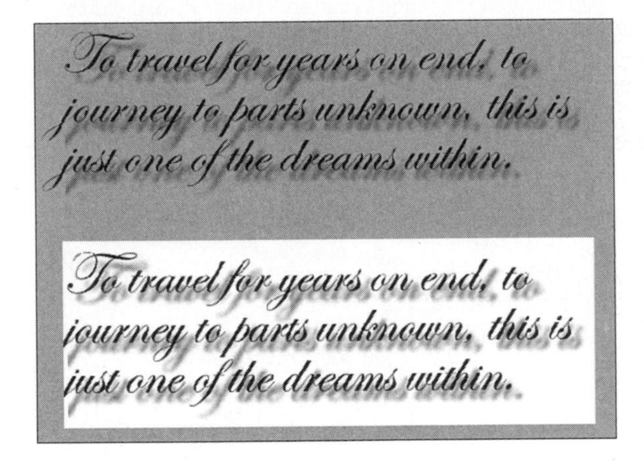


Figure 4.24
Rasterization produces a rectangular object. Both pieces of text are rasterized, but the upper example has a transparent background.

*Rasterized at the wrong settings? Can' t use Undo? See "Rerasterizing" in the "Mastering the Adobe Creative Suite" section at the end of this chapter.*

## Resolution and Antialiasing

The resolution (dpi/ppi) at which artwork is rasterized can make a large difference in its appearance. In Figure 4.25, four identical paths were created, each with a one-point black stroke and no fill. Three of the lines were rasterized at different settings, using the command Object, Rasterize.

*DPI (dots per inch) is properly used for artwork on paper, printed materials. PPI (pixels per inch) is used for images still digital in nature—existing only as pixels. For additional clarification, see "Image Resolution" later in this chapter.*

**Caution**

Remember that the Object, Rasterize command permanently changes the vector object to pixels. In contrast, the command Effect, Rasterize is "live," and you can reverse it by deleting it from the Appearance palette.

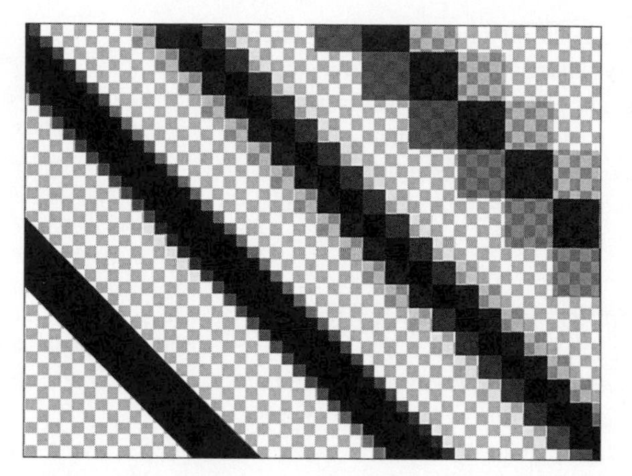

Figure 4.25
Zoomed to 4,800%, the three top lines are rasterized at the three basic settings, all with antialiasing selected.

The bottom line remains vector art, with sharp edges that ignore the pixel grid. The next three lines were rasterized at 300dpi, 150dpi, and 72dpi, respectively. Note that the top line, rasterized at 72dpi, does not conform to the 300ppi grid in the background. That grid, created separately, is visible only to show the pixels.

When rasterizing an object, in addition to choosing the resolution, you must select or forego antialiasing. As discussed earlier, *antialiasing* is a technique whereby the sharp, jagged edge of pixels is disguised. As you saw in Figure 4.25, rasterized curves are constructed of pixels, which have sharp corners. The antialiased lines soften those edges visually by adding in lightly colored pixels along the edges. Figure 4.26 shows the differences among lines rasterized at various resolutions, with and without antialiasing selected.

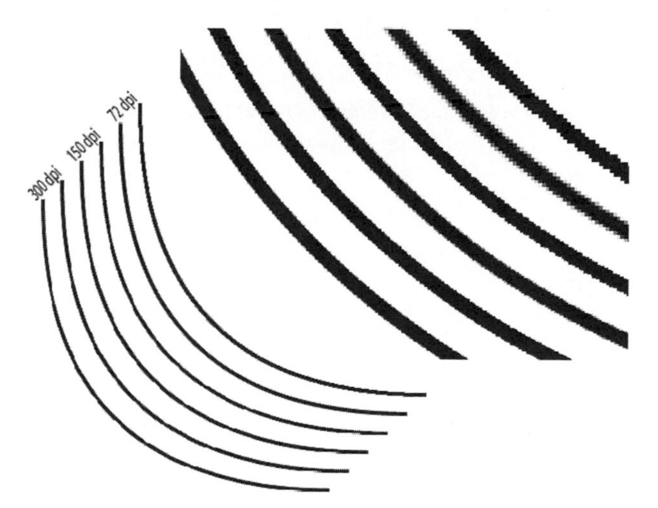


Figure 4.26
These identical lines were rasterized with and without antialiasing at 300, 150, and 72dpi. The close-up is at 500% zoom.

As you can see, the three antialiased lines, despite the difference in resolution, are very similar at 100% zoom. You can also see that antialiasing is far more important at lower resolutions than at high resolutions. At 100% zoom, antialiasing makes a substantial difference for the 72dpi lines. (As mentioned earlier in this chapter, the stair-step pattern of pixel edges visible along the edges of the non-antialiased curves is a problem called *jaggies*.) As you can see in the 100% zoom comparison, antialiasing is very effective in minimizing the appearance of jaggies.

You need to keep in mind a few points when considering rasterization for a vector object. Solid color objects that consist entirely of horizontal and vertical edges can be rasterized without antialiasing. Objects rasterized through the Object menu cannot be used in blends, but those rasterized using the Effect menu can be blended. A blend can be rasterized through the Effect menu or the Object menu.

Illustrator does an adequate job of rasterizing most artwork. However, when it comes to gradients and gradient meshes, you may experience *banding*. Banding occurs when similarly colored pixels are grouped together into a single color. The subtle variations within gradients can be lost, replaced by linear or ovoid stripes.

You can avoid this problem simply by saving the file as an Illustrator file and opening it in Photoshop. Photoshop rasterizes the artwork much more smoothly.

**Preparing Raster Images for Use in Illustrator**

When you're using an image-editing program to prepare raster artwork for inclusion in an Illustrator document, you need to keep three concepts in mind: dimensions, color mode, and file format.

Illustrator can accept raster artwork in any size and resolution and resize it to fit the allotted space. However, such resizing may degrade the quality of the image. It is preferable to prepare the artwork in the exact size and, if for print, resolution required. If the image must be resized, using a pixel-based program such as Photoshop, resampling yields better results. Remember that images that will end up on the Web should be measured in pixels, not inches or centimeters.

Preparing an image may require a change in color mode. Remember that Illustrator no longer allows RGB and CMYK objects in the same document. Let your raster image editor do the color conversion; you'll have more control over the process.

Lastly, the file must be in a format that Illustrator can read. Although you can open and place the majority of the most common bitmap (raster) image formats, some proprietary files are not readable. Those programs can usually allow you to save or export in a usable format. Deneba Canvas's native file format, for example, cannot be imported into Illustrator, but Canvas allows you to save in several formats that can be read.

## IMAGE RESOLUTION

*Resolution* is a term used for several different concepts. An image's resolution is the relationship between its size in pixels and its size on a printed page. Resolution determines how large or small a raster image appears in print and the relative fineness or coarseness of detail. Although raster images are recorded and stored as a series of square pixels, they are printed as a series of dots.

The term *resolution* is also used to identify the capabilities and characteristics of various devices, such as monitors and scanners.

## Displayed and Captured Resolutions

A computer monitor has a certain resolution, which refers to the number of pixels displayed on the screen. You might also hear the term *color resolution* when discussing monitors. That's actually the monitor's color bit depth—the number of different colors that the monitor is set to display. Figure 4.27 shows both Windows and Macintosh monitor resolution capabilities, which vary according to monitor and video card.

Resolution for a scanner or digital camera is the number of pixels per unit of measure that it can capture. For scanners, it is usually measured in pixels per inch (ppi). Digital cameras, on the other hand, are usually marketed by the overall number of pixels that can be acquired, which is measured in megapixels.

When discussing raster images and rasterizing vector artwork, you might find it easier to think of "resolution" slightly differently. Rather than the number of pixels in an inch on the printed page, consider resolution to be the *size* of the individual pixels. In an image at 300ppi, there are 300 pixel per inch. Therefore, each pixel is exactly 1/300th of an inch on paper. In a 72ppi image, each pixel is 1/72nd of an inch. And *that* explains why low-resolution images look so blocky!

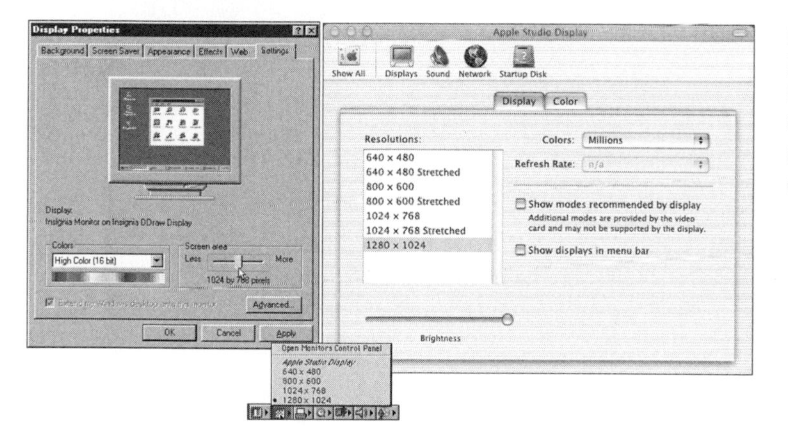


**Figure 4.27**
From the left, a Windows Display Properties dialog box, a Mac OS 9 Control Strip resolution menu, and a Mac OS X Display dialog box.



For scanning, the resolution determines the number of pixels captured for the image. The higher the resolution, the greater the number of pixels. Therefore, in a higher-resolution image, the same area of an image is reproduced with more pixels than in a low-resolution image. Because there are more pixels reproducing a given area, the individual pixels must be smaller, and when the pixels are smaller, the image's detail is finer (see Figure 4.28).

Inkjet and laser printers have resolution, too. Printers can place a certain number of dots per inch (dpi) on a sheet of paper. The output of commercial printing presses, however, usually depends on their *line screen frequency*, measured in lines per inch (lpi). The line screen frequency is a measure of the size of the halftone cells used to print the image.

The difference between the terms *dots per inch* and *pixels per inch* involves hardware. Use dots (dpi) when referring to physical output from a printer or an imagesetter, or when discussing the resolution of images that will be printed. Use pixels (ppi) when discussing digital data, such as images shown or stored on a computer, or captured by a digital camera or scanner. Other than that, there's no practical difference; both terms are used for that smallest building block of which raster images are constructed.

## Resolution with Raster and Vector

Resolution is critical to raster artwork. If the resolution is not appropriate, the project might not print correctly. Vector art, on the other hand, can be resolution independent when it's printed to a PostScript device. Because vector art is defined mathematically and can be scaled without losing quality, resolution can be insignificant to the artwork itself.

Figure 4.29 shows two versions of an image prepared to print at a size of 2 inches by 2 inches. On the left, the image is 300 dots per inch (dpi), appropriate for a glossy magazine. On the right is a version at 128dpi, a resolution you might use for newsprint.

The terms *ppi*, *dpi*, and *lpi* all refer to *linear* inches. Therefore, 200 pixels per inch is the number of pixels side by side, not in a square inch.

The difference in resolution for these two small images results in a large difference in quality. The high-resolution image contains far more pixels, each one much smaller than the low-resolution image's pixels. To be precise, the "hi-res" image contains 360,000 pixels. (That's 300 pixels per inch, times 2 inches wide, for a width of 600 pixels. The height is also 300 pixels times 2; therefore another 600 pixels. You calculate the total number of pixels by multiplying the number of pixels wide by the number of pixels high.) The "lo-res" image has 20,736 pixels (128ppi × 2 inches = 256 pixels; 256 × 256 = 65,536).

Keep in mind that non-PostScript printers and most file formats rasterize any vector artwork or type in a Photoshop image. If you're outputting to a non-PostScript printer (such as an inkjet) or using a file format that rasterizes your vectors, make sure the image's resolution is high enough to maintain the quality of the artwork.

Although the difference in resolution is a factor of a bit more than 2 ⅓ (300 divided by 128 equals 2.34), the difference in the number of pixels is a factor of 5 ½ (360,000 divided by 65,536 equals 5.49). The high-resolution image contains more than five times as many pixels in the same physical amount of space on the printed page; therefore, each printed dot is less than one-fifth as large and that much more difficult to see. And the harder it is to see the individual pixels, the finer the detail of the image. Figure 4.30 shows close-ups of how these two different resolutions might be printed by a four-color press. Notice the relative dot size.

Figure 4.28
On the left, an image scanned at 72ppi. On the right, the same image scanned at four times the resolution. The insets show the difference in detail.

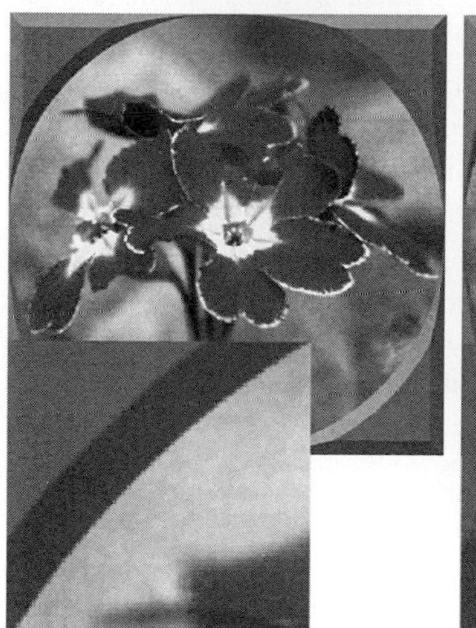

Figure 4.29
These images occupy the same space on the page, but one uses smaller (and more) pixels for finer detail.

*Confused by the math? See "Calculating Resolution for Print" in the "Mastering the Adobe Creative Suite" section at the end of this chapter.*

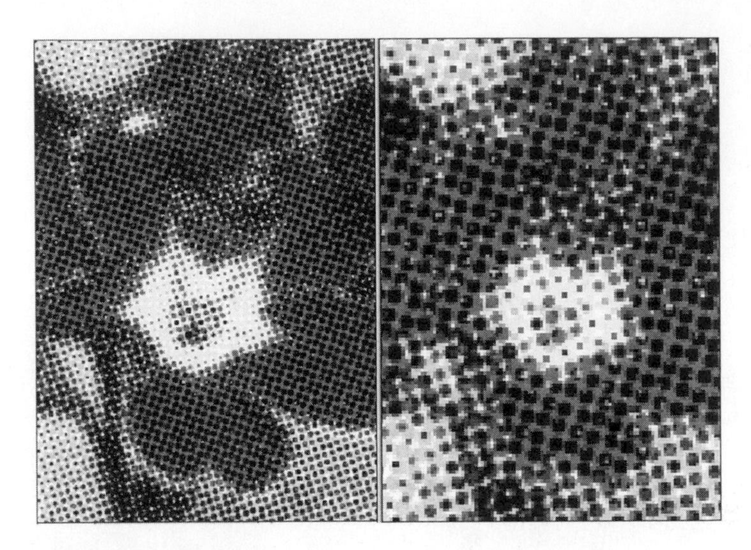

Figure 4.30
The image on the left represents printing at 150 lines per inch (lpi), whereas the image on the right might be produced by an 85lpi screen.

## Determining Resolution for Offset Presses

Because the difference in dot size can be so dramatic, why not save all images at the highest resolution the computer can support? Because there are limits to the capability of the printer.

The appropriate resolution for print is determined by the output device. Inkjet printers typically give maximum or near-maximum quality at 240dpi. Resolution for commercial printing presses is determined by the line screen frequency being used for the particular job, measured in lines per inch. Resolution should be 1.5 to 2 times the lpi.



Line screen frequencies are rather standard throughout the printing industry. For newsprint, you're likely to see 50, 85, or 100lpi. Uncoated paper can be printed at 110, 120, or 133lpi. Coated stock line screen values are often 120, 133, 150, or 175lpi. There are, however, often exceptions. Consult the print shop at the start of a project and have all images scanned or produced at the appropriate resolution.

## Image Resolution for Inkjets

There is a difference between the "resolution" of an inkjet printer and the appropriate image resolution. An inkjet's advertised 1,440×720 resolution, for example, refers to the ink droplets. It takes several droplets to replicate a colored pixel on a sheet of paper.

The image's resolution refers to the actual pixels in an image. To get the maximum quality from an inkjet printer, you should use an image resolution of one-third the printer's stated resolution. When two numbers are given, divide the smaller. In the example of 1,440×720 inkjet resolution, an image resolution of 240 is optimal.

Remember, too, that inkjet printers are rather limited in the file size they can handle. If your printer can produce 1,440×1,440 droplets per inch, the one-third rule would indicate an image resolution of 480dpi. Run a few tests, and you might find no visual difference between 240 and 480dpi for your printer. There could be, however, a huge difference in output time—or whether the image even prints at all.

## Photoshop at Work: Finding the Optimal Print Resolution

Although the general rule of thumb is that *most* inkjet printers reach maximum quality at 240dpi *most* of the time, you can find your own printer's best balance between quality and file size by following these steps:

1. Open a new Photoshop document. Make it RGB, filled with white, 6 inches wide, and 1 inch tall at 200ppi.
2. Select the Gradient tool from the Toolbox. In the Options Bar, choose Linear and the Spectrum gradient.
3. Drag from the upper-left corner of the document to the lower-right corner to create a diagonal gradient: red-magenta-blue-cyan-green-yellow-red.
4. In the Print with Preview dialog box, uncheck the Center Image box and input a top margin of 1 inch. Leave the left margin as it was set.
5. Print the gradient on glossy paper, using your printer's highest quality output settings.
6. Open another new Photoshop document, identical to the first but with a resolution of 240ppi.
7. Drag an identical gradient from the image's upper-left corner to the lower-right corner.
8. In the Print with Preview dialog box, again uncheck Center Image, but this time make the top margin 2 inches.
9. Reload the same sheet of glossy paper into the inkjet printer and print the second document. (Make sure the ink from the previous printing is completely dry before reloading into the printer.)
10. Create a third, new document at 300ppi and fill it with a gradient. Print the third gradient on the same sheet of paper, 3 inches from the top.
11. Print a fourth gradient, 400ppi, 4 inches from the top of that same sheet of paper. You should have a single sheet of paper with four near-identical gradients, as shown in Figure 4.31.

After the gradients are printed, use a magnifying glass or a loupe to examine the print quality. If you cannot see any improvement between the 240ppi and the 300ppi samples, there's never a reason to use the higher resolution. If you do see a difference, or if you can't see any difference between the 200ppi and the 240ppi samples, you might want to consider flipping the paper around 180° and printing some additional samples on the other end at some different sample resolutions.

## Resolution and the Web

It's common to hear that Web graphics should be 72ppi. The rationale is that computer monitors reproduce images at 72ppi. However, if you hold a ruler to the screen and measure one inch, it's improbable that you'll find exactly 72 pixels.

Figure 4.31
The gradients are identical, but the print quality can differ.

4

A typical 17-inch CRT monitor has a viewing area approximately 12.5 inches wide. (The 17-inch designation comes from the diagonal measurement.) If that monitor is set to show 1,024×768 pixels, there are about 82 pixels per linear inch (because 1,204 divided by 12.5 is just a bit under 82). If the same monitor is set to 800×600 pixels, there are 64 pixels per inch.

You can safely ignore resolution when creating raster images for the Web. Instead of thinking about a certain number of pixels per inch, consider only the pixels themselves. A Web page has certain dimensions, measured in pixels. Determine what part of the page should be occupied by the image, and size it to match those dimensions.

An image with print dimensions of 4 inches by 6 inches at 72dpi has pixel dimensions of 288 pixels by 432 pixels. It will occupy exactly 288×432 pixels in a Web page. If that image is resampled in Photoshop to 4×6 inches at 300dpi to improve print quality, the pixel dimensions change to 1,200×1,800 pixels. Instead of improving the image's appearance on the Web, the image simply occupies more space onscreen (see Figure 4.32).

You might need to consider resolution for Scalable Vector Graphics (SVGs). These files can be printed at resolutions higher than 72dpi from the Web. Photoshop does not work with SVG files, but they can be created in Illustrator.

**Figure 4.32**
Resampling an image in Photoshop changes the file's pixel dimensions, which affects the size of images on the Web.

# MASTERING THE ADOBE CREATIVE SUITE

## Layers and Objects

*You say that Photoshop doesn't recognize such things as circles and squares and other objects made from pixels. Yet I routinely drag a circle made from pixels around in an image. What's going on?*

If the pixels that form the "circle" are on a separate layer, you can treat them as a separate object. You're not dragging an object; you're repositioning a layer. This, by the way, is an important concept for moving artwork back and forth between Photoshop and Illustrator. Illustrator recognizes objects. When you open a Photoshop file in Illustrator, you can have each layer become a separate object. You can then manipulate the "objects" individually in Illustrator. (The artwork will still be rasterized, however.)

## Texture in Nature

*I've seen some truly wonderful photorealistic illustration by such artists as Bert Monroy and Felix Nelson, but why can't I achieve that level of perfection?*

That level of perfection comes from being less than perfect. The textures created and applied by computer often look *too* good. Textures, whether created manually or scanned, are typically applied to an area of an illustration from a sample, which can be quite small. For example, a wall in an image might be filled with a texture to simulate painted stucco. The actual texture that's applied could be only 100 pixels square to fill an area many times that size.

Because of the repeating pattern, the wall has a uniform look across its entire surface. In nature, walls have marks here and there, the paint possibly isn't applied uniformly, and the surface could be chipped. Top photorealistic illustrators take time to "personalize" their surfaces to make them look more realistic. Photoshop has a collection of tools that are great for this job. The Burn, Dodge, Desaturate, Blur, and Sharpen tools can all be used to make surfaces a little less regular.

## Calculating Resolution for Print

*The numbers are mind-boggling. What do I need to know to get the right resolution for my print job?*

You need to know the line screen frequency (in lines per inch, lpi) that will be used to print the job. Call the printer that will handle the actual production. Multiply the number you get by 1.5, and you have your minimum safe image resolution. You can also use two times the lpi for your image resolution, but use either 1.5 or 2 as the multiplier.

## Vector-izing

*Changing an image from vector to raster is called rasterizing, but is there a way to go backward? I need to make editable paths from some line art I scanned.*



Illustrator comes complete with the Auto Trace tool. It can follow the lines of the artwork and produce usable vectors. However, you'll get much better results with a dedicated program, such as Adobe's Streamline. Virtually any image can be converted to vector art for use in Illustrator, and line art is right at the top of the list. By the way, you'll want to scan your line art at very high resolution (at least 600ppi) in order to create good vector artwork.

## Rerasterizing

*I've made a mistake and need some help. In Illustrator, I rasterized an object at the wrong resolution. What can I do?*

The easiest thing, of course, is to use Undo. If that's not available because the file was closed and reopened, or because of intervening actions, you may still be okay. If you choose Effect, Rasterize, Rasterize, you can change the settings by selecting the object on the artboard or in the Layers palette and using the Attributes palette. Double-click the Rasterize entry, and the dialog box opens for you to make changes.

If you chose Object, Rasterize, the steps are a little different. If the object was rasterized with a white background, you're stuck with it. If you need to add a white background or change the resolution, simply rerasterize with the same command and different settings. Figure 4.33 shows an object that was rasterized at 72ppi and then again at 300ppi. The antialiasing tells the story.

Figure 4.33
The smaller pixels of the image on the right, which was rasterized at 300ppi, are visible in the antialiasing.

5

# COLOR, IN THEORY AND IN PRACTICE

## IN THIS CHAPTER

All the programs of the Adobe Creative Suite use color. One key to using color *correctly* is understanding how it works and how to control it digitally. Throughout this chapter you'll find references to Photoshop and Illustrator, with occasional mentions of ImageReady, InDesign, and GoLive. As you read, remember that GoLive and ImageReady are Web oriented. They work with RGB color and subsets of RGB in Indexed Color mode. InDesign is primarily a print tool, working with CMYK and spot colors.

It's important that you know a few things about color theory so that you can use it properly to communicate effectively with your audience. Color selection and combination are best left to the design school. Here, the discussion looks at the technical end of color use.

One very intriguing aspect of color theory is more important than ever with the release of Photoshop CS. Photoshop now supports most major editing and creative features in 16-bit color. Layers, cut and paste, and all the basic adjustments and filters are now available for 16-bit color. You'll find a description of the difference between 16-bit color and 8-bit color (used for most Photoshop and all Illustrator artwork) in this chapter.

# ARTWORK, IMAGERY, AND COLOR

An image in Photoshop *is* color. Whether the image is in bright, vivid colors, various shades of gray, or even just black and white, it doesn't exist without color. At its heart, Photoshop is about assigning the correct color to each pixel.

Color is equally critical in Illustrator images. Without color, Illustrator has only invisible paths. A *path* is an abstract concept, conveying no information to the viewer, until the application of a fill and/or a stroke of color. It's color that produces the image, attracts the attention, *and* conveys the message. Virtually everything done in Illustrator is about putting color in the correct places to create an image.

This section describes how Photoshop and Illustrator record color and the differences between the two types of color—additive and subtractive.

5

## How Photoshop and Illustrator Record Color

Photoshop works primarily with raster artwork, although it does have some sophisticated vector capabilities. Raster images, also known as *bitmap images*, consist of a rectangular pattern of pixels, with a single color assigned to each of the tiny squares. The differences in color among the pixels determine the appearance of the image.

*For more on the difference between raster and vector artwork, see "Defining Raster and Vector Artwork," in Chapter 4, "Pixels, Vectors, and Resolutions," p. 130.*

Be aware that the term *bitmap* can have two different meanings. First, it can be used as a synonym for *raster* (as in "That is not vector artwork; it's a bitmap image."). In this usage, it refers to an image consisting of pixels arranged in rows and columns. Second, when you're talking about color, *bitmap* refers to black-and-white images. In Bitmap color mode (also called 1-bit color), each pixel is either black or white. There are no shades of gray or other colors.

In simple terms, raster image file formats record image data pixel by pixel, keeping track of each pixel's location in the image and that particular pixel's color values. Theoretically, you could digitally re-create the *Mona Lisa* by assigning specific colors, one at a time, to each pixel. Remember that each pixel is a single color. The color can be changed, but a pixel can have only one color at any time (see Figure 5.1).

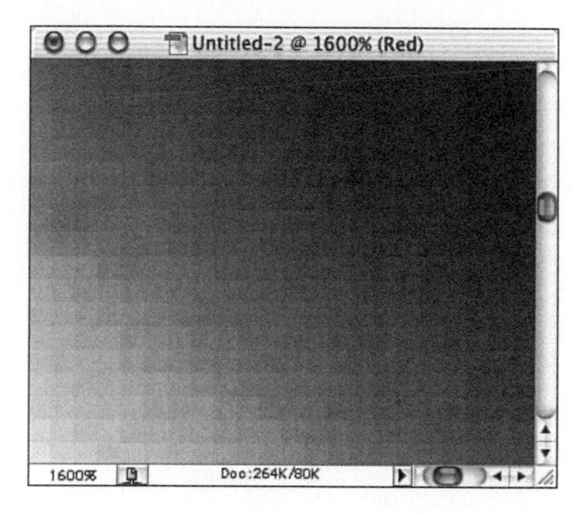


Figure 5.1
Even in a white-to-black gradient, each pixel has only one color.

Although Illustrator also handles raster imagery, it works primarily with vector artwork. In vector art, the individual objects have strokes applied to paths and fills within the paths. The color of the stroke and the color of the fill (or colors for gradient and pattern fills) are recorded.

## What Is a Color Model?

The actual recording of a pixel color or a vector object's assigned color depends on a couple factors. The file format you select determines, of course, how the actual data is recorded. (Photoshop handles that process transparently as the file is saved.) The document's *color mode* is assigned by the user and depends on the image's final destination and its content. This is the "color space" within which the document's colors are recorded. The most common color modes are RGB (for digital imaging and the Web) and CMYK (for commercial printing). This is in contrast to the term *color model,* which refers to the system within which you define specific colors. For example, in an RGB document, all colors are recorded in the RGB color mode, regardless of whether you defined the colors using the grayscale, HSB, Lab, or RGB color model. The color mode (with the color model) determines what *component colors* are used to create the specific colors in the image.

The RGB color mode, for example, records the entire range of color as proportions of the component colors red, green, and blue. CMYK, on the other hand, records each color as percentages of cyan, magenta, yellow, and black (the CMYK component colors). A grayscale image is composed of grays, measured as percentages of black. Each of the major color modes and color models is discussed individually in this chapter.

*Unsure about why the difference between color modes and color models? See "Modes Versus Models" in the "Mastering the Adobe Creative Suite" section at the end of this chapter.*

# THE TWO TYPES OF COLOR

Colors in Photoshop and Illustrator can be considered *additive* or *subtractive*. Additive colors produce white when all colors are combined (added) at full strength. Subtractive colors produce white by removing (subtracting) all component colors. Conversely, a lack of color in an additive model produces black, whereas combining all colors in a subtractive model black.

Consider spotlights in a theater. The more spotlights you train on a specific area of the stage, the more brightly lit that area is—this is additive color. You can aim spotlights of many colors at the same spot, but when you've added enough different lights, regardless of their color, the audience sees only white light.

Although there are lots of ways to classify color (for example, primary colors, warm and cool colors, earth tones, and pastels), for the Adobe Creative Suite the largest determining factor is how colors are reproduced. The resulting color can be similar, but the differences in how additive and subtractive colors are created result in different treatment in your artwork, page layouts, and Web pages.

Now consider preparing paint for a blank canvas. Without any paint, the canvas is white. As with subtractive color, when you start mixing various paints together, they get darker. (The result is more likely to be muddy brown than black, but the concept is the same.)

## Additive Colors

Additive color is produced from a light source that's typically filtered to present color. For example, a household light bulb (which emits "white" light) behind a blue lampshade gives you blue. Behind a yellow lampshade, the same bulb gives you yellow. A stage spotlight can be filtered with a gel, a translucent piece of colored gelatin or acetate, to produce colored light. Multiple gels can be combined to create a wide range of colors.

Televisions and computer monitors produce additive color. The light is viewed directly or near directly, preferably without interference from other light sources. The light is filtered into red, green, and blue components that, in combination, produce all the colors that can be created with that device. Many large front- and rear-projection TVs actually use three synchronized lights, one of each of these colors, to produce images onscreen. Televisions, computer cathode ray tube (CRT) monitors, and liquid crystal display (LCD) screens for computers, TVs, and other devices all use red, green, and blue light in combination to produce the colors of the spectrum.

When working in the Adobe Creative Suite, you should remember these key concepts about additive colors:

- The component colors (red, green, blue) combined at full intensity produce white.
- The complete lack of the component colors produces black.
- The light is seen directly, reaching the eye either from a colored source or from a source through a colored filter.

- In theory, by varying the amount of each component color (red, green, blue), you can reproduce virtually all colors of the visible spectrum. (In reality, not all colors can be reproduced because of limitations of the devices.)
- Because the component colors are red, green, and blue, additive color is referred to as *RGB* in Photoshop and other graphics programs.

## Subtractive Colors

Subtractive colors are, generally speaking, seen with reflected light. A white or colored light source reflects off a colored surface to the eye. The color that's visible to the eye is that part of the spectrum not absorbed by the colored surface. For example, if you shine a white light on a wall painted yellow, you see yellow because all other colors are absorbed by the paint, and yellow is reflected back to the eye. The wall itself is not a light source; rather, light bounces off the wall to the eye.

Like the wall's yellow paint, subtractive colors are applied to a surface. The visible color of the paint or ink is that part of the spectrum is reflected rather than absorbed. Subtractive color is used to design for print, where ink is applied to paper (or another substrate) to reproduce the artwork.

For Photoshop, Illustrator, and InDesign, subtractive color is reproduced by using cyan, magenta, yellow, and black inks. The color mode is called *CMYK*. Theoretically, the entire range of color can be produced with varying amounts of CMY inks, but it's necessary to add black to reach the darkest colors. (CMYK inks can be supplemented with other inks, called *spot colors*, to produce colors not available with just cyan, magenta, yellow, and black.)

Remember these key concepts about subtractive colors:

- The component colors (cyan, magenta, yellow) can theoretically be combined to produce the full visible spectrum. However, in reality, printing inks are limited in the range of color they can reproduce.
- The lack of component colors results in white (or whatever the color of the substrate upon which the ink is applied).
- Combined at full intensity, CMY should theoretically produce black. However, once again, there are limitations with real-world inks. Because mixing cyan, magenta, and yellow inks produces a dark brown rather than black, printers must add black ink (K) for CMYK printing.
- With subtractive colors, light is reflected rather than seen directly. The color perceived by the eye is that portion of the visible spectrum that the colored surface doesn't absorb. For example, when you're looking at a red wall, all parts of the spectrum *except* red are absorbed, and red is reflected to the eye.
- Printing on a press with CMYK inks is often referred to as *four-color process printing*, and the four inks are called the *process colors*.

> *K* is used for black to differentiate it from blue, represented by *B*. *K* can also be thought of as standing for *key color*, from the days when black was printed first to assist in registering the other colors.

5

- In printing, CMYK inks can be supplemented with additional inks, often called *spot colors*. Spot colors are usually predetermined, premixed inks of a specific color. They are typically applied to a specific area (spot) on the image. It is not unusual to use one or more spot colors in place of CMY inks to create two- or three-color images. Spot colors can add color that the CMYK inks cannot produce. Neon, metallic, and even white are examples of colors that can be printed only with spot inks.

One of the biggest differences between RGB and CMYK color modes is the number of channels. Each component color is recorded in a separate color channel. Because RGB has three component colors, it has three color channels (plus a composite channel). CMYK has four component colors, so there is one more color channel and a composite channel.

*Unsure about why the difference between additive and subtractive color is important? See "How Color Is Made" in the "Mastering the Adobe Creative Suite" section at the end of this chapter.*

# RGB, CMYK, AND SPOT COLORS

The vast majority of work in Photoshop (and all work in Illustrator) is done in RGB or CMYK color mode. Virtually all output is done in RGB, CMYK, or Grayscale mode, although Photoshop actually supports eight color modes. Illustrator can accept grayscale artwork into either RGB or CMYK documents, but each document can contain artwork of only its own color mode.

*For more on the additional color modes, see "Photoshop's Other Color Modes and Models," later in this chapter.*

5

## The Relationship Between RGB and CMY

Theoretically (but not in practice), all RGB colors could be replicated by using cyan, magenta, and yellow. Likewise (and also theoretically), all CMY colors could be reproduced by using red, green, and blue. (Black [K], remember, is added to CMY to compensate for impurities in the inks. It is not one of the theoretical component colors.) The relationship among the six component colors is shown in Figure 5.2.

The relationship is also shown in Table 5.1.

**Table 5.1** RGB and CMY Relationships

| Combine | And | To Create |
|---|---|---|
| Red | Green | Yellow |
| Red | Blue | Magenta |
| Green | Blue | Cyan |
| Cyan | Magenta | Blue |
| Cyan | Yellow | Green |
| Magenta | Yellow | Red |

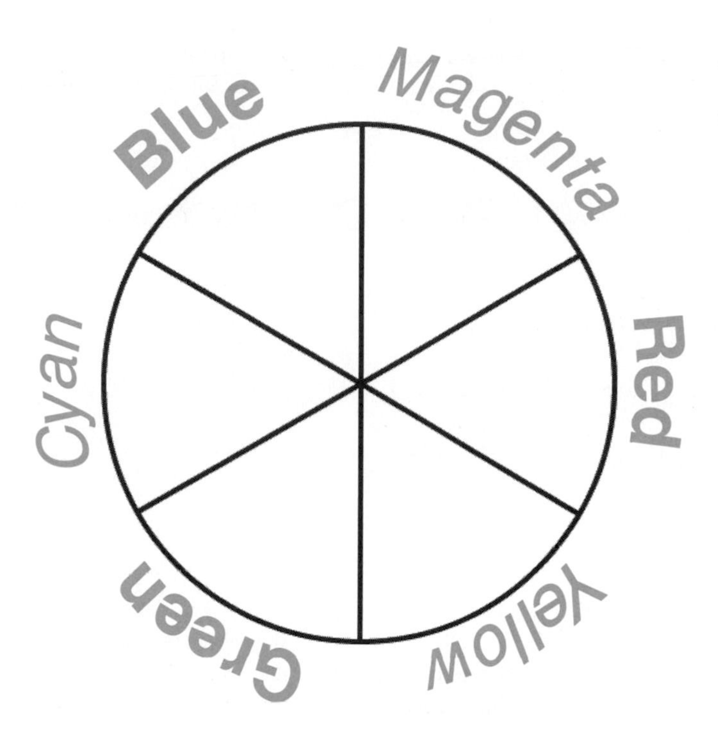


Figure 5.2
Notice that RGB and CMY alternate.

These relationships may not be the same as those you learned in preschool, or even art school, but they are the relationships among component colors in Photoshop and Illustrator (and other digital imaging and illustration programs).

When displayed in a *color wheel* (a circular arrangement of colors), the relationships among the component colors is clear. A color wheel, such as the one in Figure 5.3, shows the way that the component colors interact with each other. Red is at zero degrees, the "three o'clock" position on the circle.

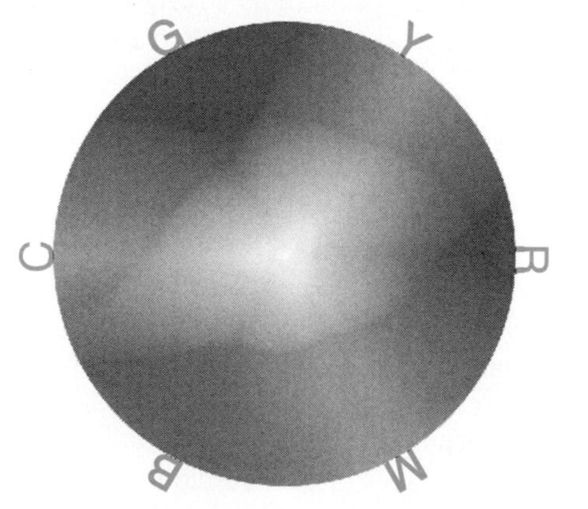


Figure 5.3
The 0° point is typically to the right of a color wheel.

In a color wheel, each of the RGB colors is opposite a CMY color. These opposites represent the *inverse relationship* among colors. The inverse colors are also easily summarized (see Table 5.2).

**Table 5.2** Inverse Relationships

| Color | Inverse |
|---|---|
| Red | Cyan |
| Green | Magenta |
| Blue | Yellow |
| Cyan | Red |
| Magenta | Green |
| Yellow | Blue |

## Choosing a Color Mode

An image's color mode should be dependent on the image's final destination. The two major color modes, RGB and CMYK, are intended for different applications. CMYK is for use with commercial four-color printing presses and those smaller printers specifically designed for the color mode. These devices include color laser printers, proofers (printers that simulate a printing press's output), and some high-end inkjet printers used for fine-art prints.

RGB is intended for use on the Internet, on monitors and kiosks, with film recorders, for broadcast and digital video, and with most inkjet printers. Virtually all Photoshop and Illustrator work not destined for a commercial printing press should be done in RGB mode.

In the following discussions, Photoshop's 8-bit color mode is assumed. Photoshop also permits you to work in 16-bit color. You'll find more information on that subject in the section "A Note on Color Bit Depth," later in this chapter.

> The inverse relationships among the component colors make color correction much simpler. For example, if an RGB image has a magenta cast to it, adding green is the same as subtracting magenta.

> **Caution**
>
> When using the terms *print*, *printing*, and *printer*, always keep in mind that there are differences between the inkjet printers likely to be found in studios, offices, and homes on one hand, and the commercial offset printing presses, color laser printers, high-end inkjet proofers, and fine-art printers on the other hand. When designing for home/office inkjets, remember to use RGB rather than CMYK. Although these printers actually use cyan, magenta, yellow, and black ink, the printers' software requires RGB image data.

## RGB Color Notation

RGB colors are designated as proportions of the three component colors: red, green, and blue. Each value can range from 0 to 255. These 256 possible values for each component color are a product of 8-bit color depth. The standard notation is (red value)/(green value)/(blue value). For example, 35/120/57 means that the red value is 35, green is 120, and blue is 57. Keep in mind that when all three component colors are 0, black results, and when all three are 255, you get pure white. When the component color values are equal and between 0 and 255, you get shades of gray.

The specific color for each pixel is broken down into the three component colors. Each component color value is recorded in the appropriate color channel. In practice, each color channel is a grayscale copy of the image, with only the component color values recorded in the channel.

Because each color channel can have 256 possible values, the total number of different colors that can be reproduced in 8-bit RGB is 16,777,216. That's 256×256×256. Consider, if you will, the sequence of colors 0/0/0, 0/0/1, 0/0/2, 0/0/3 through 135/87/42, 135/87/43, 135/87/44, 135/87/45 all the way to 255/255/252, 255/255/253, 255/255/254, and 255/255/255. The difference between 135/87/42 and 135/87/43 is too subtle for the human eye to see, even in two color swatches side by side. In fact, variations of as much as five in a single color component are difficult to detect in most circumstances. A variance of five in *two* color components can, on the other hand, be very noticeable.

## CMYK Color Notation

Like RGB colors, CMYK colors are recorded as proportions of the component colors. Unlike RGB, CMYK has four components. Therefore, the notation is a bit longer. If you have a green color recorded in RGB as 35/120/57, a comparable shade of green could be recorded as 85/29/100/17 in CMYK. (Depending on the color settings in use, there could be considerable variation in the specific values. Also note that several different combinations of CMYK colors could produce similar shades of green.)

Besides the additional component, CMYK notation differs from RGB notation in a very significant way: RGB values range from 0 to 255, but CMYK components are measured in percentages. Each of the four values can range from 0% to 100%. In practical terms, the percentage represents the ink density for that particular color. Values less than 100% can be thought of as "thinning the ink."

Although in theory a particular spot on the page could have 100% each of cyan, magenta, yellow, and black ink, in practice, that is not done. Depending on the paper used, maximum ink density is typically between 250% and 300%.

Like RGB color mode, CMYK records the component color value for each pixel in a separate color channel. CMYK images have one channel for each of the component colors, plus a composite channel.

> Both RGB and CMYK artwork can contain areas that appear to be grayscale. Even if (in a CMYK image) that area will be printed with only black ink, it is still technically part of a *color* image. In RGB notation, all three component colors will be represented and they will have equal values (50/50/50, 128/128/128, 225/225/225). In a CMYK image, there can be a considerable variation in the amount of each ink used to represent "grayscale."

## Identifying Spot Colors

Photoshop and Illustrator also enable you to specify a particular color using *spot colors.* These predesignated colors, chosen from a library of color, represent premixed inks for use in commercial printing. Spot colors are used in addition to, or in place of, CMYK inks. The color is identified by name in the image, and the press operator mixes the exact color, using a specific formula or a premixed ink.

Photoshop supports a variety of spot color collections. Most common in North America are the Pantone collections. These and other spot color collections can be accessed through Photoshop's Swatches palette menu (see Figure 5.4).

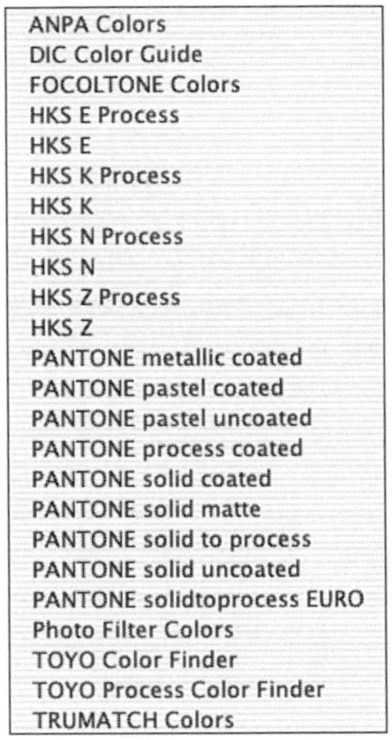

**Figure 5.4**
Photoshop's Swatches palette menu contains a wide variety of spot color libraries, often referred to as *books*.

ANPA Colors
DIC Color Guide
FOCOLTONE Colors
HKS E Process
HKS E
HKS K Process
HKS K
HKS N Process
HKS N
HKS Z Process
HKS Z
PANTONE metallic coated
PANTONE pastel coated
PANTONE pastel uncoated
PANTONE process coated
PANTONE solid coated
PANTONE solid matte
PANTONE solid to process
PANTONE solid uncoated
PANTONE solidtoprocess EURO
Photo Filter Colors
TOYO Color Finder
TOYO Process Color Finder
TRUMATCH Colors

One of the most common uses of spot colors is to ensure an exact color match. For example, the specific red of the Adobe logo can be specified in a print image as Pantone 485, Toyo 8096, or Dainippon 2497. This particular shade of red can also be reproduced by using CMYK 0/100/100/0.

Spot colors can also be used to supplement an image's tonal or color range. They can also provide a cost-effective printing method, using black ink and one spot color rather than all four process (CMYK) colors. Keep in mind that although most spot colors can be reproduced by using process colors, the premixed inks require only a single pass through the press, instead of three or four.

Some colors cannot be reproduced on a printing press using the CMYK inks, so other spot colors are added. Metallic and neon colors, for example, can be added to an image only through the use of spot colors. These inks cannot be duplicated with process inks.

Spot color names are assigned by the company that produces the inks. The notation varies from company to company (and within brands, to some extent). Pantone inks for use with uncoated paper have a three- or four-digit number, followed by the letter *U*. Inks for use with coated paper have the letter *C* following the number. A specific color has the same number, whether the ink is for use with coated or uncoated paper. Most other manufacturers also use numeric designations for their inks.

> In print, you might see *PANTONE*, in all capital letters, indicating a registered trade name.

> Although you could specify a spot color when working in RGB color mode, spot colors are designed for use with CMYK.

Here are descriptions of some of the spot color collections installed with Photoshop CS:

- **ANPA Colors**—These 300 colors are designed for use on newsprint. The name comes from the American Newspaper Publishers Association, now known as the Newspaper Association of America.
- **DIC Color Guide**—This is a collection of 1,280 CMYK spot colors that can be matched against the *DIC Color Guide* from Dainippon Ink & Chemicals. These spot colors are most commonly used in Japan.
- **FOCOLTONE Colors**—Focoltone colors are designed to be used with the parent company's charts showing overprint and absorbency characteristics with different stocks. Focoltone International, Ltd., of the United Kingdom, provides these 830 CMYK colors.
- **HKS E**—HKS-Farben is a German firm with four different collections of colors for use with inks from BASF or Hostmann-Steinberg. The "E" series (from the German *Endlospapiere*) is composed of the 88 colors designed for use with continuous forms papers.
- **HKS K**—The "K" (*Kunstdruckpapiere*) series is for use with gloss art papers. This set also has 88 colors.
- **HKS N**—These 86 colors are for uncoated paper (*Naturpapiere* in German).
- **HKS Z**—The *Z* stands for *die Zeitung* (German for *newspaper*), and this collection of 50 spot colors is for newsprint.
- **TOYO Colors**—These colors are as common in Japan as the Pantone colors are in the United States. There are 550 predesignated colors in this set.
- **TRUMATCH Colors**—Trumatch is a system for designating CMYK colors. The first digit of each color's name represents one of 50 hues. The next pair of digits represents the saturation (*a* through *h*) and the amount of gray (1 through 7).



# PHOTOSHOP'S OTHER COLOR MODES AND MODELS

Photoshop enables you to work in six color modes in addition to RGB and CMYK. The six are Grayscale, Bitmap, L*a*b (also seen as Lab), Indexed Color, Duotone, and Multichannel. Each of the color modes has specific characteristics and can be used for specific purposes. In this section, each of the color modes—and a pair of color models—are explained.

## Grayscale

Often referred to (incorrectly) as *black and white*, this color mode offers 256 shades of gray, including black and white. Grayscale mode uses one color channel. Although Grayscale is an 8-bit color mode (with 256 shades of gray), Photoshop measures each pixel's color as a percentage of black. Grayscale can be used in commercial printing, on the Web, or for output to other devices, such as inkjet printers and film recorders. Photoshop also permits you to work with 16-bit grayscale images (see "A Note on Color Bit Depth," later in this chapter).

When you convert color images to grayscale, all color information is lost. The image retains only the brightness value of each pixel, expressed in varying shades of gray. Converting a grayscale image to

RGB or CMYK mode does not add color to the image; rather, it adds color channels, allowing you to add color.

*When grayscale images are output to an inkjet printer, sometimes the output has a slight color tint, usually magenta or cyan. For advice on how to avoid this problem, see "Inkjet Grayscale" in the "Mastering the Adobe Creative Suite" section at the end of this chapter.*

> **Caution**
>
> Do not confuse "Bitmap color mode" with "bitmap image." Bitmap color mode refers to the possible colors of an image's pixels, and it's in contrast to terms such as RGB, CMYK, and Grayscale modes. Bitmap image, on the other hand, is the same as *raster image* and means that the image is made up of pixels. It is used in contrast to *vector art*, in which the image is constructed of mathematically defined objects. Bitmap images can be of any color mode. (For more on the difference between raster/bitmap and vector artwork, see Chapter 4.)

## Bitmap

Bitmap color mode is true black and white. Perhaps clearer would be the phrase "black *or* white." Each pixel in such an image is either black *or* white; there are no shades of gray and no colors.

As you can see in Figure 5.5, each pixel is either white or black. The Navigator palette indicates the area of the image that is shown in the document window. In addition, note that the Channels palette shows only a single channel (and the image is somewhat identifiable in the palette thumbnail).

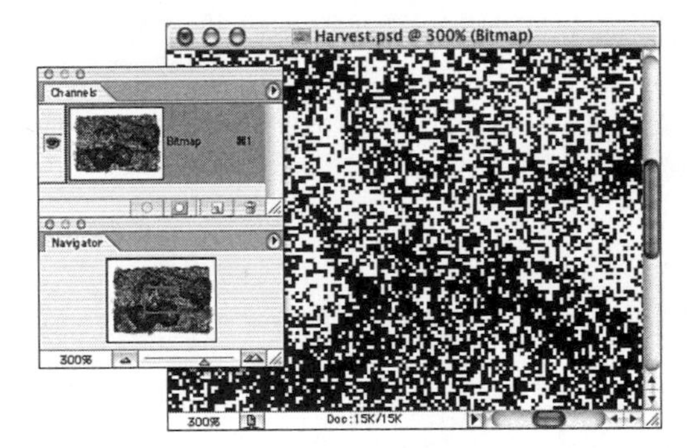


Figure 5.5
The image is shown at 300% zoom so that individual pixels are recognizable.

Bitmap color mode can be used effectively with certain line art and for special effects. Bitmap color mode greatly reduces file size but generally is not appropriate for most images. It is the color mode of the WBMP file format, designed for graphics viewed on some wireless devices and cell phones.

A file must be in Grayscale mode or Duotone mode to convert to bitmap. When converting from Grayscale to Bitmap mode, you have several options for how the gray pixels are converted to black or white (see Figure 5.6).

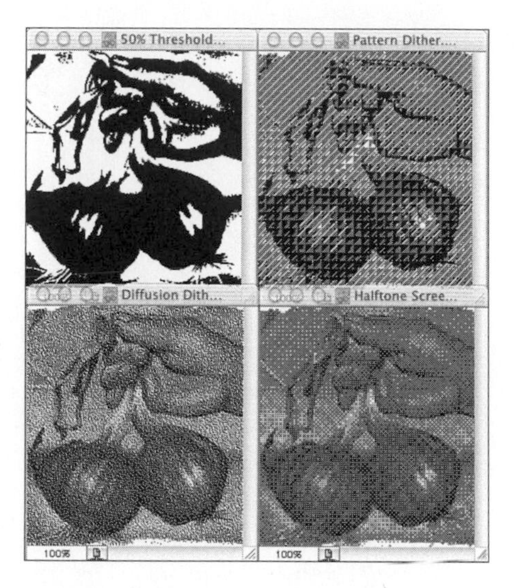


**Figure 5.6**
The results of four different bitmap conversions are shown.

Photoshop uses different criteria for the four types of bitmap conversion:

- **50% Threshold**—Pixels with gray values higher than 128 (50% gray) are converted to white. Pixels with gray values lower than middle gray are converted to black (refer to Figure 5.6, upper left).
- **Pattern Dither**—Geometric patterns of black and white dots are created to represent the image's general appearance (refer to Figure 5.6, upper right).
- **Diffusion Dither**—This technique bases the conversion on the color of the pixel in the upper-left corner of the image. Unless that pixel is pure white or pure black, the transformation to either white or black produces some margin of error. That error is transferred among the surrounding pixels, and thus "diffused" throughout the image (refer to Figure 5.6, lower left).
- **Halftone Screen**—By specifying a halftone screen, you create a bitmap image that simulates reproduction with halftone dots. You can specify the line screen frequency (up to 999 lines per inch, or *lpi*) and the dot shape. (Typically, newspapers are printed at 85lpi and magazines at 133 or 150lpi.) The example in Figure 5.6 at the lower right uses 133lpi and a diamond-shaped dot to convert a grayscale original at 72dpi.

5

A closer look at the results of the four bitmap conversions shows the different distributions of black and white pixels (see Figure 5.7).

In Photoshop, you can also specify custom screens when converting to Bitmap mode, but you must create a pattern first. If the pattern is smaller than the image, it is tiled. The Custom Pattern option simulates shades of gray by making the halftone pattern thicker and thinner.

**Caution**

After an image is converted from Grayscale to Bitmap, converting back to Grayscale does not restore the image to its prior appearance. Each pixel is still black or white, until editing the image changes the color value.

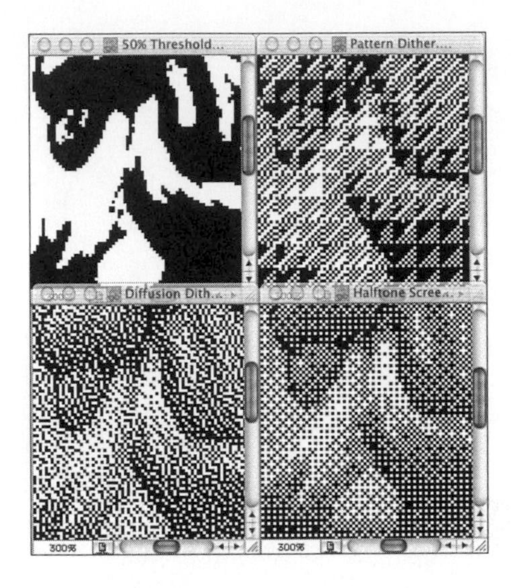


Figure 5.7
Here, each of the bitmap images shown in Figure 5.6 is zoomed to 300% at the center of the image.

## L*a*b

This color mode, often called simply *Lab*, uses three channels. Unlike RGB and CMYK modes, the channels do not contain component color information. Rather, one channel contains only the lightness value for each pixel (L), and the additional channels (a and b) split the color spectrum into two pieces (see Figure 5.8).

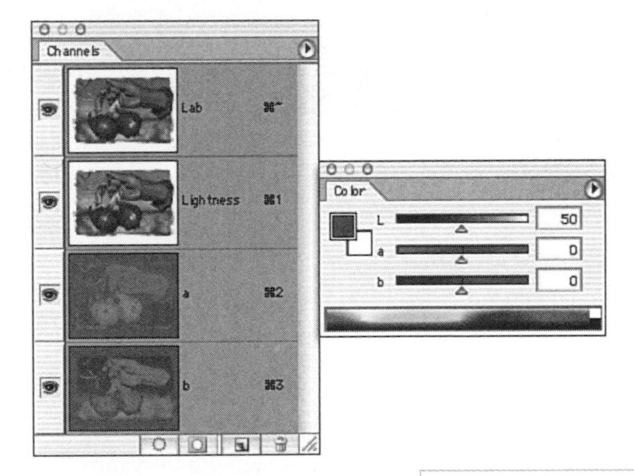


Figure 5.8
The top channel is the composite channel. Next is the Lightness channel (L), followed by the two color channels (a and b).

The *L* (Lightness) channel controls the brightness of a pixel, with a range of 0 to 100. The *a* channel contains the color value of the pixel along a red-green axis. The value normally ranges from –120 (green) to +120 (red). The *b* channel contains color information running along a blue-yellow axis. This value, also normally –120 (blue) to +120 (yellow), is combined with the *L* and *a* channels to produce the pixel's color.

In Figure 5.8, you can see that the L channel of a Lab image has a good grayscale likeness of the image as a whole. If converting from RGB or CMYK to Grayscale leaves your image looking flat, try converting to Lab and then deleting the a and b channels.

The Lab color gamut is wider than RGB or CMYK, containing a range of colors not otherwise reproducible. When Photoshop converts between RGB and CMYK, it uses Lab as an intermediate color model.

Lab images can be printed to many PostScript devices (Level 2 and 3 only) and can be used to edit Photo CD images. In addition, converting from RGB or CMYK to Lab enables you to work directly with the luminance values in the image.

> **Caution**
>
> Don't submit Lab images or place them into a page-layout document without prior approval from your service bureau or printer. If it can't work with the Lab color mode, you'll likely incur additional expenses.

## Indexed Color

Indexed Color mode is a subset of RGB. Rather than 8 bits of information for each of the color channels, files in Indexed Color mode contain only a total of 8 bits of color information for each pixel. For that reason, each image can contain a maximum of 256 different colors. They can be any RGB colors, even 256 different shades of blue or red or yellow, but there can be only 256 different colors.

> Many basic Photoshop capabilities are not available in Indexed Color mode. For example, the image is restricted to a single layer and most filters cannot be used.

Indexed Color mode is used with GIF and PNG-8 file formats, and it can be specified for some other formats. The advantage of 8-bit color is smaller file sizes, but that is often outweighed by the sometimes drastic degradation in image quality. Many photographic images cannot be accurately reproduced with such a limited palette.

*Can' t edit an image in Indexed Color mode? See "Index Editing" in the "Mastering the Adobe Creative Suite" section at the end of this chapter.*

An image in Indexed Color mode has a single color channel, called *Index*, in the Channels palette. Photoshop records the colors used in an Indexed Color mode image in a *color lookup table (CLUT)*. The color table is recorded with the file and might be unique to that file or a standardized color table. If you attempt to add a color to the image that isn't among the 256 available colors, it is converted to the nearest color.

Only RGB and Grayscale mode images can be converted to Indexed Color. Grayscale conversions happen automatically because there are a maximum of 256 shades of gray in an 8-bit grayscale image. When you're converting an RGB image, however, the Indexed Color dialog box appears (see Figure 5.9).

> **Caution**
>
> Images must be flattened before converted to Indexed Color mode. Make sure you don't have any necessary layers hidden at the time of conversion—they will be lost.

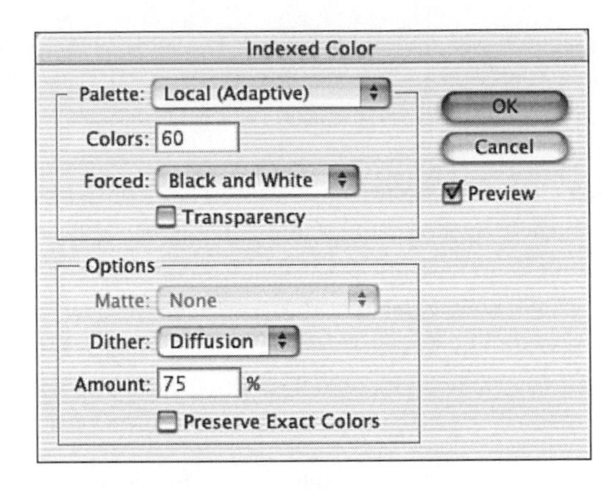


Figure 5.9
The Indexed Color dialog box offers some control over an image's reduction to 256 colors.

The Palette pop-up menu offers 13 conversion options:

- **Exact**—If the RGB image contains 256 or fewer colors before conversion, the Exact option lets you create a color table using those colors. The image's appearance is maintained.
- **System (Mac OS)**—The image's colors are converted to the Macintosh system's 8-bit palette.
- **System (Windows)**—The 8-bit palette standard for Windows is used to produce the color table.
- **Web**—The Web-safe palette of 216 colors common to both the Macintosh and Windows system palettes is used.
- **Uniform**—The color table is created by taking samples from the RGB spectrum. Six evenly spaced values for red, green, and blue are taken: 6×6×6 = 216. If the total number of colors is limited to fewer than 216 in the dialog box, the next smallest perfect cube (125, 64, 27, or 8) is used.
- **Perceptual**—The color table is created giving priority to those colors for which the human eye has greater sensitivity. (Local emphasizes colors within the image, and Master relies on the RGB gamut.)
- **Selective**—Large areas of consistent color are taken into account when creating the palette with this option. Otherwise, it generally follows the guidelines for Perceptual. Generally, this option does the best job of preserving an image's appearance.
- **Adaptive**—An adaptive palette is created by using the colors that appear most frequently in the image. If the color of a specific area of the image is most important, you can make a selection of that area before converting and choose Adaptive.
- **Custom**—This option enables you to edit the color table directly. It opens with the adaptive palette. You also have the option to load a previously saved palette.
- **Previous**—The most recently used custom palette is used to create the color table. This option enables you to convert numerous images using the same palette.

The difference between Local and Master for the Perceptual, Selective, and Adaptive options is most apparent when the color table is reduced from 256 to a smaller number of colors. Local emphasizes colors that exist in the image, whereas Master looks at the RGB gamut. Dithering can be critical when using the Master options.

You can enter a specific value in the Colors field to shrink the file size even more by choosing to retain fewer than 256 colors.

The Forced pop-up menu enables you to specify colors that must be maintained in or added to the image's color table. Forcing black and white adds those two colors to the table, regardless of whether they're used in the image. The Primaries option adds black, white, red, green, blue, cyan, magenta, and yellow. Web adds the 216 Web-safe colors (see the following section, "Web-Safe RGB," for more information on the Web-safe palette). If you select Forced: Custom, you can specify colors that must be added to the image's color table.

Selecting the Transparency check box maintains any areas of transparency that exist in the image. When this option is not selected, any existing transparent pixels are filled with the specified matte color or, if no matte color is selected, with white.

Selecting a matte color helps edges along a transparency blend with the designated color by using antialiasing. If, for example, the image will be placed on a Web page with a specific background color, using that color as the matte color helps the edges blend into the background. Choosing None in the Matte pop-up menu results in a hard-edged transparency or, if Transparency isn't selected, a white fill for transparent pixels.

You can also select the type and amount of dithering to apply. Dithering simulates colors missing from the color table. Pixels of colors that *are* in the color table are interspersed to simulate the missing color. Diffusion, Pattern, and Noise dithering are all available (as is the choice of None). Here's how they differ:

- **None**—Instead of attempting to simulate a color, this option substitutes the nearest color in the color table.
- **Diffusion**—An error-diffusion method of dithering is applied, which results in a less structured appearance than does Pattern dithering.
- **Pattern**—A pattern of dots similar to a halftone pattern is used to simulate colors that are not in the color table.
- **Noise**—Adding noise along edges helps break up potentially visible seams in sliced images. (Slices are used with Web graphics to control optimization and downloading.)

The option Preserve Exact Colors, which is available with Diffusion dithering, ensures that colors already existing in the color table are not dithered. It is helpful for preserving fine lines and type. Preserve Exact Colors is not available for Pattern dithering and is mandatory for Noise dithering.

An image's color table can be edited directly by using the menu command Image, Mode, Color Table. The resulting dialog box, shown in Figure 5.10, enables you to make changes to the individual colors saved with the file.

Figure 5.10
This color table shows the maximum 256 unique colors allowed for any image in Indexed Color mode.

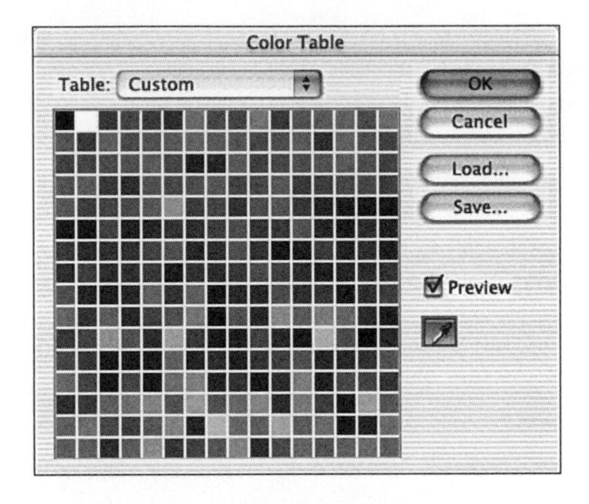


You have several options when editing a color table:

- Select the Preview check box to see the effect of your changes on the image.
- Select a standardized color table in the Table pop-up menu, if desired. Leave Table set to Custom to use the color table created during the color mode conversion.
- Click any color in the color table to select it and open the Color Picker. In the Color Picker, you can designate a new color to replace the selected color throughout the image.
- Drag the cursor through the table to select multiple colors. You can then use the Color Picker to assign a range of colors to replace those selected. When the Color Picker opens, select the first color. After you click OK, the Color Picker reopens so that you can pick the ending color. A gradient is then generated, with each step replacing one of the selected colors.
- (Command-click) [Ctrl-click] to delete a color from the table.
- (Option-click) [Alt-click] a color to designate that color for transparency. You can also click the Eyedropper tool in the dialog box and use it to designate the transparent color.
- Custom color tables can be saved and loaded. Color tables should be saved with the file extension .act. Tables can be loaded from ACT files or from GIF files.



## Web-Safe RGB

The color model *Web safe* is that subset of an 8-bit RGB gamut (Indexed Color) that is common to both the Macintosh and Windows system palettes. The two operating systems have built-in color palettes for use with 8-bit color (256 maximum colors, not 8 bits per channel). Color values are recorded in a single color channel. (Web-Safe RGB is a subset of the RGB color mode, but it should actually be considered a variation of the Indexed Color mode.)

Both the Macintosh and Windows system palettes contain 256 colors (the maximum allowed under 8-bit color), but only 216 of the colors are common to both palettes. These are the Web-safe colors.

HTML, the basic language used with the World Wide Web, records color as a base-16 (hexadecimal) value. Rather than 10 possible values for each digit (the numerals 0 through 9), hexadecimal notation permits 16 different values for each digit. In addition to the 10 numerals, the letters *A* through *F* are used.

### Hexadecimal Colors

For use with Hypertext Markup Language (HTML, the basic language of the Web), hexadecimal color notation is based on 16 possible values for each digit. (The more familiar decimal system, called base-10, allows for only 10 possible values for each digit: the values 0 through 9.) To work with this system and not have to invent another six numbers to replace what we call 10 through 15, letters are substituted.

Using 0 through 9 to represent themselves, hexadecimal adds the letters *A* through *F* as single-digit replacements for 10 through 15. In this system, therefore, the number 11 is represented by B, and 17 would be recorded as 11. Likewise, 0F is 15, and F1 would, in base-10, be 241.

Why this base-16 system? Each of the 256 possible values for red, green, and blue (0 to 255) needs to be represented by only two digits in HTML. Using base-10, the purest white would have to be recorded as 255255255 (R-255, G-255, B-255). In base-16, it is FFFFFF—a six-digit number rather than nine digits. (Higher values represent lighter colors; lower values are darker.) Base-16 can represent any of the 16.7 million possible RGB colors in a total of six digits ($16 \times 16 \times 16 \times 16 \times 16 \times 16 = 16{,}777{,}216$).

Although learning the translation from decimal to hexadecimal may have some value to Web designers and HTML coders, the majority of Illustrator users can rely on the Color Picker and Color palette to make adjustments. Simply choose your color and let the program determine its hexadecimal name. If you do need to be able to read or write hexadecimal, refer to the translation table shown in the following figure.

| Decimal | 0 | 1 | 2 | 3 | 4 | 5 | 6 | 7 | 8 | 9 | 10 | 11 | 12 | 13 | 14 | 15 |
|---|---|---|---|---|---|---|---|---|---|---|---|---|---|---|---|---|
| Hexadecimal | 00 | 01 | 02 | 03 | 04 | 05 | 06 | 07 | 08 | 09 | 0A | 0B | 0C | 0D | 0E | 0F |
| Decimal | 16 | 17 | 18 | 19 | 20 | 21 | 22 | 23 | 24 | 25 | 26 | 27 | 28 | 29 | 30 | 31 |
| Hexadecimal | 10 | 11 | 12 | 13 | 14 | 15 | 16 | 17 | 18 | 19 | 1A | 1B | 1C | 1D | 1E | 1F |
| Decimal | 32 | 33 | 34 | 35 | 36 | 37 | 38 | 39 | 40 | 41 | 42 | 43 | 44 | 45 | 46 | 47 |
| Hexadecimal | 20 | 21 | 22 | 23 | 24 | 25 | 26 | 27 | 28 | 29 | 2A | 2B | 2C | 2D | 2E | 2F |
| ... | | | | | | | | | | | | | | | | |
| Decimal | 95 | 96 | 97 | 98 | 99 | 100 | 101 | 102 | 103 | 104 | 105 | 106 | 107 | 108 | 109 | 110 |
| Hexadecimal | 5F | 60 | 61 | 62 | 63 | 64 | 65 | 66 | 67 | 68 | 69 | 6A | 6B | 6C | 6D | 6E |
| ... | | | | | | | | | | | | | | | | |
| Decimal | 240 | 241 | 242 | 243 | 244 | 245 | 246 | 247 | 248 | 249 | 250 | 251 | 252 | 253 | 254 | 255 |
| Hexadecimal | F0 | F1 | F2 | F3 | F4 | F5 | F6 | F7 | F8 | F9 | FA | FB | FC | FD | FE | FF |

Using letters to represent the numbers from 10 through 15, hexadecimal notation is a base-16 system.

A true hexadecimal system uses a single digit to represent the numbers 0 through 15 (as we represent 0 through 9 in the base-10 system). HTML, however, requires that each number be represented by two digits, thus the leading zero for the values in the top row of the chart. Also, note that following the final value in this table would be 100 (256 in base-10). This number is not used in HTML hexadecimal notation.

## Duotone

Duotone color mode in Photoshop actually refers to four different types of color images. *Monotones* use a single colored ink, much like printing a grayscale image with an ink other than black. *Duotones* use two inks, typically black and a color. *Tritones* use three inks, and *quadtones* use four. In practice, unless an ink's curve is edited, each image appears as a tinted grayscale image.

> The term *duotone* is used generically throughout this discussion to refer to monotones, duotones, tritones, and quadtones. When a point refers specifically to monotones, tritones, or quadtones, that term is used.

What sets these color modes apart is that the inks are used throughout the image, rather than placed in specific areas. Each of the inks is, by default, distributed according to the single color channel.

Duotones can be created only from grayscale images. To convert RGB, CYMK, or another color mode to Duotone, first use the menu command Image, Mode, Grayscale. The Duotone Options dialog box, shown in Figure 5.11, enables you to select mono-, duo-, tri-, or quadtone in the Type pop-up menu.

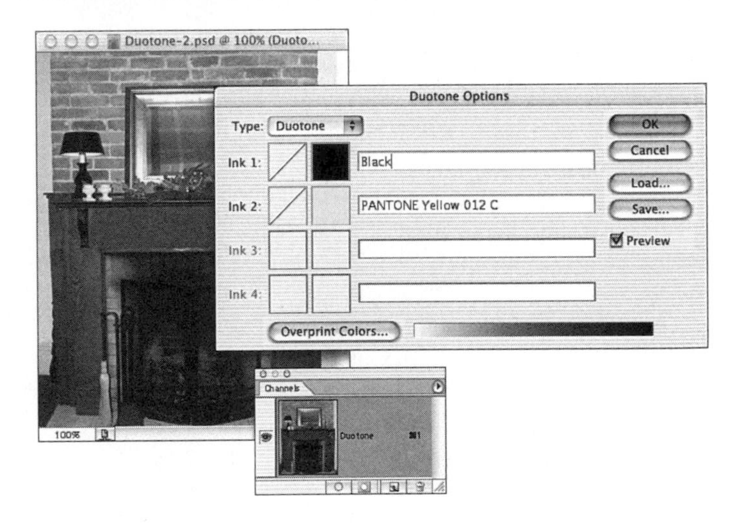


**Figure 5.11**
As you can see in the Channels palette, this image has already been converted to Duotone and the dialog box is reopened, enabling a change of color if necessary.

5

Clicking a color swatch to the left of a color name opens the Color Picker in Custom Color mode. A Pantone or other custom color can be selected.

Clicking the thumbnail in the left column, which by default has a diagonal line, opens the Duotone Curve dialog box for that ink. Adjusting the curve gives you control over the distribution of the ink in the image. By default, each ink is printed at the gray value of each pixel. For example, a 50% gray midtone pixel is printed at 50% tint of the ink, whereas a darker pixel in a shadow area is printed with a higher tint. The straight-line curve uses the pixel's brightness value as the tint percentage for each ink.

The curve can be modified to change the distribution of an ink. Reopen the Duotone Options dialog box by using the menu command Image, Mode, Duotone. In Figure 5.12, the curve has been changed to eliminate the yellow ink from the image's highlights and shadows, and to print yellow at a darker tint in the midtones. Note that both the curve thumbnail and the image preview are automatically updated.

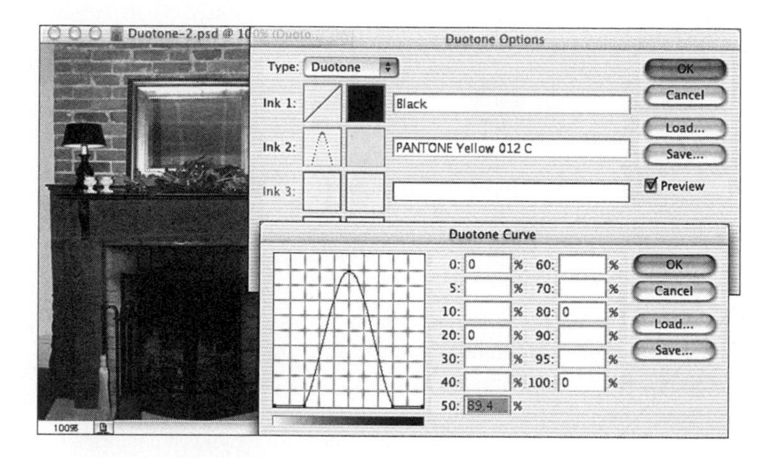


Figure 5.12
In this example, the yellow ink will be printed only in the image's midtones.

Note that custom curves can be saved and loaded in the Duotone Curves dialog box. The Duotone Options dialog box also has Load and Save buttons. Photoshop ships with a variety of predesigned duotones, tritones, and quadtones. You'll find them all in the Duotones folder, inside the Presets folder, within the Photoshop folder. The presets include a variety of duotones, tritones, and quadtones in shades of gray, with Pantone custom colors and with process (CMYK) inks.

The Overprint Colors button in the Duotone Options dialog box shows you how the inks will interact (see Figure 5.14). Clicking a color swatch in the Overprint Colors dialog box opens the Color Picker, allowing you to modify the overprint color.

> The Info palette will show you the "before" and "after" values while modifying a duotone curve. Move the cursor around the image to get the ink percentages at any point (see Figure 5.13).

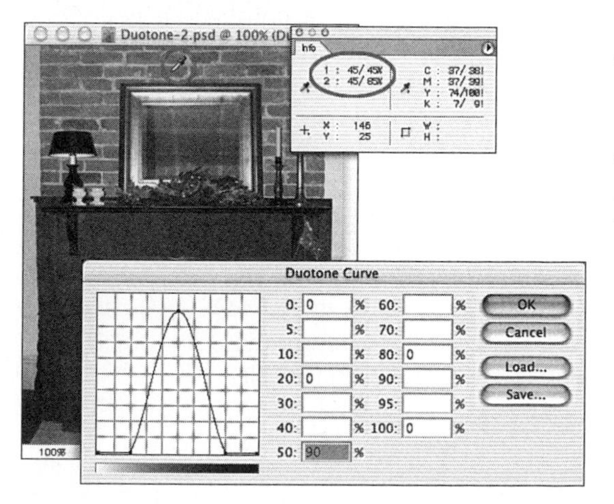


Figure 5.13
The cursor changes to the Eyedropper when moved in the image window. The Info palette tells you each ink's tint percentage before (left) and after (right) the new curve is applied.

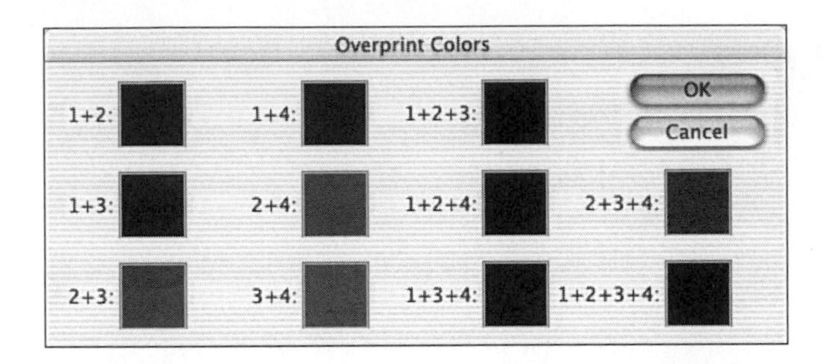


**Figure 5.14**
With a duotone, only 1+2 is available. With a tritone, 1+2, 1+3, 2+3, and 1+2+3 are available.

Images in Duotone color mode can be saved and printed in the Photoshop (PSD), EPS, PDF, and RAW file formats. In PSD format, all of Photoshop's capabilities are available, including spot channels, layers, and filters. Photoshop CS's new large Document Format (PSB) can be used to save extremely large images in Duotone mode. (PSB must be activated in Photoshop's file-handling preferences.)

> **Caution**
> Modifying an overprint color with the Color Picker can produce an unprintable image. If you select a color that cannot be reproduced with the designated colors, your preview will not match the printed result.

## Multichannel

Multichannel color mode uses a separate color channel for each of the image's component colors, just as the RGB and CMYK color modes do. However, Multichannel mode does not include a composite channel, so each color channel can be considered a spot color.

Multichannel mode is designed for use with some specialized image printing (such as some Scitex CT format images) and can be used to edit individual color channels. In Photoshop, it is typically used with images destined for commercial printing, including CMYK and duotone images.

Although most of Photoshop's capabilities are available for Multichannel mode images, they can be used on only one color channel at a time. Because there is no composite channel as there is in RGB or CMYK mode, the entire image cannot be manipulated at once.

Multichannel images can be created from CMYK, RGB, Lab, Duotone, and Grayscale files. Converting a CMYK image creates spot channels from each of the four color channels and deletes the composite channel. The four resulting channels are cyan, magenta, yellow, and black. There might be some color shift during the conversion. RGB images converted to Multichannel mode typically undergo a large color shift. During the conversion, the red, green, and blue channels are changed to cyan, magenta, and yellow.

> Some of Photoshop's filters produce unexpected results with duotones because of the lack of color channels. For example, the filter Pixelate, Color Halftone cannot produce four-color halftone dots without color channels with which to work.

> When working in Multichannel mode, you can't apply a filter to the entire image at once because there's no composite channel. Remember that a filter can be repeated on each channel individually with the keyboard shortcut (Command+F) [Ctrl+F]. Apply the filter to one channel and then switch to the next and use the keyboard shortcut to apply the same filter with the same settings. Repeat this for each channel.

Converting an image from Lab color mode to Multichannel creates three alpha channels rather than spot channels. Because a grayscale image starts with only one color channel, converting to Multichannel mode results in an image with only one channel. The channel's name is switched from Gray in Grayscale mode to Black in Multichannel mode, but it's otherwise identical.

A duotone image can be converted to Multichannel mode, creating one color channel for each of the inks. This allows direct editing of the color placement, which is not possible in Duotone mode.

An image converted from Duotone to Multichannel mode cannot be converted back to Duotone mode. It can be converted to Grayscale and then to Duotone. Doing so, however, eliminates any changes made to the color channels in Multichannel mode.

## HSB: The Non-Mode Color Model

Photoshop offers one additional way to define color, but it's not found under the Image, Mode menu. *HSB* stands for hue, saturation, brightness. Rather than a color mode, it is a *color model* used with the Color palette and the Color Picker. Images themselves are not recorded as HSB, but this color model can be used to define colors in the file in RGB, CMYK, Indexed Color, Lab, or Multichannel mode. (HSB is not available for images in Grayscale, Bitmap, or Duotone color mode.)

HSB is designed to replicate the way human eyes (and the brain) recognize color, breaking it down into color, purity, and brightness. Hue (color) is based on the color wheel and is measured in degrees. The six primary component colors (RGB and CMY) are found evenly spaced around the wheel (see Table 5.3 and Figure 5.15).

**Table 5.3** Hue Values for Photoshop's Primary Colors

| Color | Hue Value |
|---|---|
| Red | 0° |
| Green | 120° |
| Blue | 240° |
| Cyan | 180° |
| Magenta | 300° |
| Yellow | 60° |



Saturation determines the purity of the color, from gray (0%) to pure or fully saturated (100%). Brightness (also sometimes called *lightness*) is the relative darkness (0%) or lightness (100%) of the color. When brightness is at 0%, the hue and saturation are insignificant—black results. When brightness and saturation are both at 100%, the result is white, regardless of the hue.

Most Photoshop users employ HSB on a regular basis, perhaps without recognizing it. By default, Photoshop's Color Picker is set to Hue (see Figure 5.16).

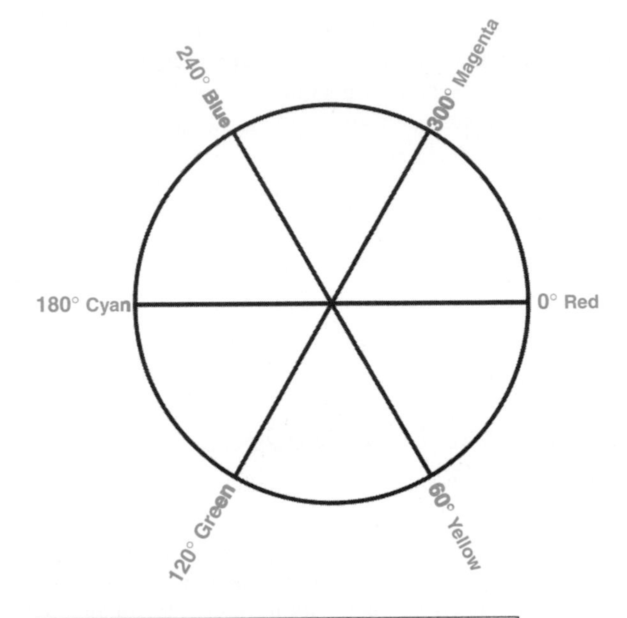


Figure 5.15
The hue values for the primary colors are typically measured from the three o'clock position on the color wheel.

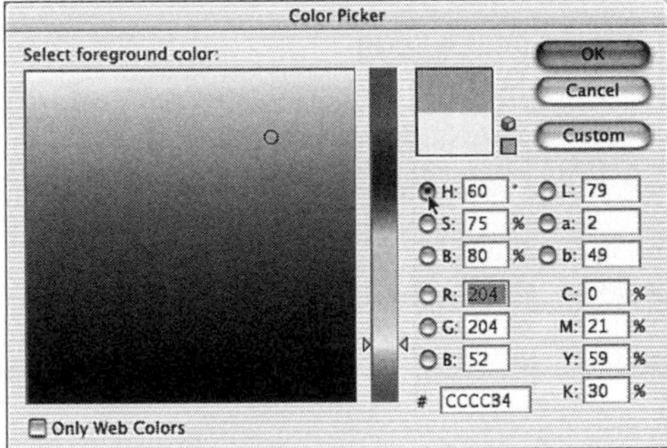


Figure 5.16
The H stands for *hue*. The Color Picker can also be set to use saturation (S), brightness (B), the RGB colors, or the Lab components as the basis for color selection. As you can tell from the lack of radio buttons, the CMYK colors cannot be used as a basis for color definition.



## Color Modes Compared

A number of Photoshop's capabilities cannot be used in certain color modes. Table 5.4 summarizes what features are and are not available for images in the various color modes.

**Table 5.4** Photoshop Features for the Color Modes

| Color Mode | Channels | Layers | Paint Tools | Filters | Composite Channel |
|---|---|---|---|---|---|
| RGB | 3 (R, G, B) | Yes | All | All | Yes |
| CMYK | 4 (C, M, Y, K) | Yes | All | Most | Yes |
| L*a*b | 3 (L, a, b) | Yes | All | Most | No |
| Indexed Color | 1 (Index) | No | Most | No | No |
| Grayscale | 1 (Gray) | Yes | All | Most | No |

| Color Mode | Channels | Layers | Paint Tools | Filters | Composite Channel |
|---|---|---|---|---|---|
| Bitmap | 1 (Bitmap) | No | Some | No | No |
| Duotone | 1 to 4 | Yes | All | Most | No |
| Multichannel | Varies | No | All | Most | No |

# A Note on Color Bit Depth

In addition to the various color modes, Photoshop permits you to work in 16-bit color for RGB, CMYK, Grayscale, Lab, and Multichannel modes. Rather than 256 possible values for each pixel in each color channel, 16-bit color theoretically has 65,536 possible values. With over 65,000 possible values for each of the three channels, the theoretical number of colors available is overwhelming.

Although most output devices can't handle the additional color information, or don't have the capability of reproducing such fine variations among similar colors, 16-bit mode can be printed. Some film recorders, especially with grayscale images, can show improved tonal range.

In previous versions of Photoshop, few editing options were available for an image in 16-bit color. There were no layers, you couldn't cut or paste, and most of the filters were grayed out. Photoshop CS has greatly expanded support for 16-bit images, making it feasible to edit images using most of Photoshop's capabilities.

# Bits, Bytes, and Color

The terms *8-bit color* and *16-bit color* refer to the actual amount of computer data recorded for each pixel's color. A *bit* is a single piece of digital information. Groups of eight bits of related data are called a *byte*. (A group of eight bits of unrelated data is better called an *octet*.) Think of bits as letters of the alphabet, bytes as words, and an entire computer file as a book.

Each bit can be either a zero or a one; it can have no other value. Computers are—for now, anyway—binary machines. Each bit can be either value and must be one or the other. Consider the difference between a standard household light switch and a dimmer switch. The typical light switch is either on or off, but the dimmer switch can be set to any of a variety of "on" positions. With binary systems, there are no dimmer switches, just the old-fashioned on/off.

In Photoshop, 8-bit color uses eight bits (one byte) for each component color of each pixel. A pixel in an RGB image has eight bits of information for each of the three colors. A CMYK pixel has eight bits of color information for each of four component colors. Grayscale images have only eight bits of information for each pixel's color. In 16-bit color, each component color can have 16 bits of color data, whether RGB, CMYK, or Grayscale.

How does this actually work? With 8-bit color, each of the bits can be a zero or a one, and the values work together. Because each of the eight bits can be only one of two possible values, you can calculate the number of possible combinations like this:

2×2×2×2×2×2×2×2 = 256

For example, let's create a fictional set of colors in Table 5.5.

Photoshop CS actually works in 15-bit color, with one additional color value. The 32,768 possible values are much easier to calculate than 65,536, and the results are indistinguishable.

**Table 5.5** A Simulated 8-Bit Color Notation

| 8-Bit Color | Color Name |
|---|---|
| 00000000 | White |
| 00000001 | 1/254 Gray |
| 00000010 | 2/254 Gray |
| 00000100 | 3/254 Gray |
| 00001000 | 4/254 Gray |
| 00010000 | 5/254 Gray |
| 00100000 | 6/254 Gray |
| 01000000 | 7/254 Gray |
| 10000000 | 8/254 Gray |
| 00000011 | 9/254 Gray |
| 00000101 | 10/254 Gray |
| 00001001 | 11/254 Gray |
| … | |
| 11101111 | 251/254 Gray |
| 11011111 | 252/254 Gray |
| 10111111 | 253/254 Gray |
| 01111111 | 254/254 Gray |
| 11111111 | Black |

Now if you consider an RGB pixel, the possible colors are based on combinations of eight bits of information for each of the three channels. For example, one pixel might be

00000000/00000000/00000000

whereas another pixel could have this combination:

11101111/00001001/10000000

The first, using the color notation from Table 5.5, would be RGB 255/255/255, or pure white. The second would be 4/244/247, which is a bright cyan.

Keep in mind that the terms *8-bit* and *16-bit* as used here to refer to the number of bits *per channel* in an image. In contrast, Indexed Color mode, like Grayscale mode, records a total of eight bits of information for each pixel, and that byte's worth of information can represent a totally different color from image to image. The eight-character string records a reference to a place in that particular image's color table, not a reference to an objective color mode.

# MASTERING THE ADOBE CREATIVE SUITE

## Modes Versus Models

*I'm not sure I understand the difference between a color mode and a color model. Which is which?*

Remember that *color mode* refers to the image as a whole, specifying how the colors are *recorded* in the actual file. (It can also be referred to as a *color space.*) A *color model*, on the other hand, is a system of *defining* color. The color model is used to assign the attributes or components of a specific color, perhaps to add that color to an image.

The difference is this: A file can be in the RGB color *mode*, intended eventually for the World Wide Web, but colors within the file can be defined during editing by the color *models* RGB, Grayscale, Lab, and HSB (Hue, Saturation, Brightness). Although the artwork can be defined as you work using several color *models*, the file itself actually is recorded with all colors in one color *mode*. You assign a color mode to an image with Photoshop's menu command Image, Mode. Color models are used when defining a particular color, specifically when using the Color palette or the Color Picker.

RGB, CMYK, Grayscale, and Lab are all *both* color modes and color models. Indexed Color, Bitmap, Duotone, and Multichannel are color modes, but not color models. Finally, HSB is a color model, but not a color mode, in Photoshop.

## How Color Is Made

*What is the big deal about additive and subtractive? How does it relate to RGB and CMYK?*

The key to both additive/subtractive and RGB/CMYK is how color is actually created. (You use RGB for the additive colors and CMYK for the subtractive colors.) Additive color is created by and viewed from an active light source. Computer monitors are active color sources, as are televisions, projectors, and candles. Subtractive color is seen "on the bounce." It is reflected light, coming from a painted or printed surface. The printed page of a book, the walls in a room, the computer's keyboard—all are seen because light reflects from them to the eye. They appear to have color because parts of the light are absorbed and parts are reflected. You see the reflected light.

When working with color modes in Photoshop, consider whether the colors will be seen directly from a light source, such as colors on a monitor, or whether they'll be seen on a surface, such as a sheet of paper. Remember, though, that inkjet printers are the exception. Although the end product is subtractive (CMYK), the print driver typically assumes RGB input and converts the colors for you automatically.

## Inkjet Grayscale

*When I'm printing to my inkjet printer, my grayscale images come out either magenta or cyan. How can I get them to print only in shades of gray?*

Your printer supplements black ink with a mix of CMY inks to maintain detail in shadows. This *rich black* (also called *process black*) enables the printer to produce a wider number of "blacks" in the darker areas of an image. To print with only black ink, check your Print dialog box. A sample dialog box, from an Epson printer, is shown in Figure 5.17.

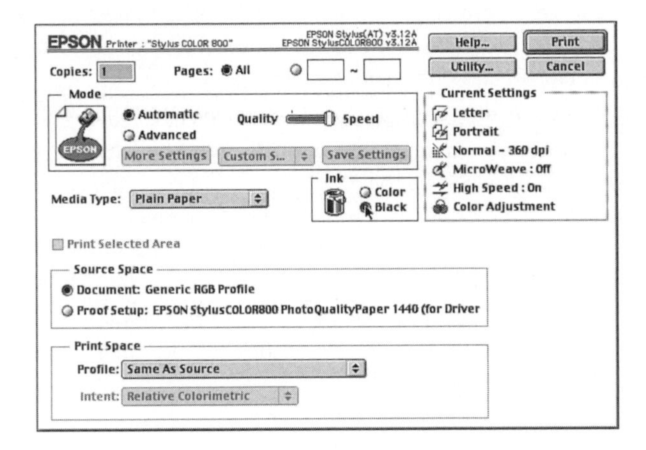


**Figure 5.17**
Your printer's dialog box might differ. Look for an option to print in black or color.

## Index Editing

*I can't use the Layers palette, filters aren't available, I can't even add text. What's going on?*

Check the image mode (using the Image, Mode command from the menu bar) and convert the image from Indexed Color mode to RGB. After editing the image, convert it back to Indexed Color. That color mode doesn't support the features you're trying to use because of the restricted color table.

## Legacy Illustrator Documents with RGB *and* CMYK Objects

*I opened one of my old Illustrator files and got a warning that the document contained objects of both CMYK and RGB color. The warning box wanted me to change them, but I was afraid of messing up my artwork, so I clicked Cancel. What should I do?*

The Convert Color Mode dialog box is, indeed, formidable. Illustrator now allows only one color mode per document. Here are the guidelines for choosing between RGB and CMYK: If the document is intended for a four-color process printing job, click CMYK and let Illustrator convert your RGB colors. Any colors that are outside the CMYK gamut (and would therefore not be reproduced accurately by the four-color process inks) are converted to the nearest CMYK color. If you don't plan to use the document in a four-color job, select RGB. Because virtually all CMYK colors fall within the RGB gamut, no conversion is necessary.

## Multiple Color Modes

*I'm preparing several illustrations that I would like to use both in print and on the Web. Considering the differences between RGB and CMYK, is this possible?*

Some images, including logos and other small art, are multipurpose. When you're preparing an image for both RGB (Web or monitor) and print (CMYK), consider the following:

- If the colors must match exactly for every employment of the image, ensure that your RGB version doesn't contain any out-of-gamut colors. One way to do so is to work in CMYK and then convert a copy to RGB when you're finished.
- If a piece of art is headed for both print and the Web, and the colors must match, consider working in the Web-safe RGB palette. Those 216 colors don't give you any out-of-gamut warnings.
- If color matching is not critical, take advantage of RGB's larger gamut by doing your work in that mode. At the end of the creation process, reduce a copy for your Web needs and convert a copy to CMYK for print. Maintain the original in the full RGB spectrum for later use.

6

*by Richard Romano*

# COLOR MANAGEMENT IN THE ADOBE CREATIVE SUITE

## IN THIS CHAPTER

Color management is a vast, complicated topic that goes to extraordinary lengths to deal with the age-old question, "Why doesn't what I print match what I see on my computer screen?" It's an easy question to answer ("because a monitor and a printer/printing press use different ways of producing color"), but a far from easy situation to resolve.

In this chapter, we'll touch on the basics of color management: why it is a problem and, more importantly, how the integration that is the hallmark of the Adobe Creative Suite can be used to ensure accurate color reproduction at all points in the workflow.

# WHAT IS COLOR MANAGEMENT?

In professional graphic arts, the attitude toward color management falls into, very generally, two categories: those who use elaborate hardware, software, and proofing technologies to ensure that color is produced accurately, and those who just eyeball an inkjet print or (increasingly) a screen-based PDF and say, "That's good to go." (Interestingly, in both these cases, everyone thinks that they're doing color management, which shows how vague the term can be, even to pros.)

It is precisely because of the advanced color-reproduction capabilities of applications such as Photoshop (and the Creative Suite applications in general) that the prevailing tendency toward color management is to "set it and forget it" (as Ron Popeil would say). In other words, you simply turn color management on in Photoshop, InDesign, and Illustrator, and not worry about it again.

## Color Perception

One of the primary reasons we need color management is that, despite the best efforts of scientists and engineers, color has always been very difficult to quantify objectively. For example, you can look at an orange and say, "It's orange." But the orangeness of the orange is as much a function of your own individual visual system as it is of the natural colorants found within the skin of the fruit.

Another issue is that the specific orangeness of that fruit will vary depending on the illumination of the environment. That is, if you take the orange outdoors on a sunny day, it will be one shade of orange. Carry it into a darkened movie theater, and it will appear to be a different shade of orange. Take the orange into a drug store or supermarket lit with fluorescent lighting, and it will appear to be yet another shade of orange. Take it to a softly lit restaurant, and it will appear to be yet another shade of orange.



And it's not just the illumination. The orangeness will vary from individual to individual. We're all peculiar (especially if we walk around town clutching an orange). The photoreceptors (cones) in your eyes will probably sense color somewhat differently from those of someone a lot younger, or older, or even the same age.

What's more, it's not just what the photoreceptors in the eye pick up; it's also how the brain interprets the data coming in from the optic nerve. Assume you need to communicate the color quality of a given orange to someone else, such as a print vendor. What you describe has been subject to not only a certain kind of lighting, but also to the peculiarities of your retinas; the information has been interpreted by your brain and then translated into a verbal description, or perhaps a numerical specification based on your comparison of the orange you see to a color swatch you also see (which adds additional layers of variability). Therefore, by the time a color you perceive is specified to someone else, it's like a fifth-, sixth-, seventh-, maybe even eighth-generation photocopy.

This gives you some idea of what we're all up against when we need to specify and reproduce colors accurately.

## A Question of Transmitted Versus Reflected Color

Color is light. White light can be separated into the constituent colors of the spectrum—red, orange, yellow, green, blue, indigo, and violet. Each color represents a different wavelength of light, from red, which has a wavelength between 610 and 780 nanometers (nm), to violet, which has a wavelength between 400nm and 450nm. When different wavelengths hit the human eye, they are perceived as different colors. Other animals perceive colors differently; bees, for example, can see into the ultraviolet, which creates all sorts of problems if you need to publish color documents for bees.

There are two basic types of color: *transmissive* or *additive* color and *reflected* or *subtractive* color. Transmissive color is produced by the direct transmission of light, such as the colors displayed on a computer monitor. The three primary colors—red, green, and blue—interact to produce all the colors of the spectrum. When all three primary colors are present in equal amounts, they form white light.

Reflected color is produced by light reflecting off a colored surface. When a beam of light strikes an orange, its surface absorbs all the wavelengths except orange, which is then reflected back to the eyes of the viewer as orange light. That's why this is called "subtractive" color; the color that is seen is what's left when all the other colors have been removed.

Additive/transmissive color is produced by the interaction of colored lights (for example, a computer monitor or television set), whereas subtractive/reflected color is produced by the interaction of colorants (for example, inks or toners). The three primary subtractive colors are cyan, yellow, and magenta. When all three of these colorants are present in equal amounts, the result is black.

## Color Space Is the Place

The two types of color—additive and subtractive—comprise two separate "color spaces": RGB (red, green, blue) and CMYK (cyan, magenta, yellow, and black).

RGB is the color space used by computer monitors, digital cameras, and scanners, whereas CMYK is the color space used by desktop printers and printing presses. In terms of media, RGB is the color space used when viewing Web pages, PDFs, and other onscreen documents, whereas CMYK is the color space used when something is printed.

Here's the crux of the matter: When you are scanning, editing a digital image in Photoshop, or working on an InDesign page, you are looking at it on your monitor. Regardless of whether you convert the colors in the document to CMYK, it won't matter until you output the document because you can't see the CMYK color space on a monitor. You can convert an image to CMYK in Photoshop or specify CMYK colors in InDesign and Illustrator, but the colors you see onscreen will be RGB simulations of CMYK colors. This is one of the big issues in color management: how best to simulate CMYK colors in the RGB color space.

> Black is given the initial *K* because in process-color printing, it is the "key" plate to which the others are printed in register.

One of the big problems with CMYK is that it is a much smaller color space; it isn't capable of reproducing as many different colors as RGB. This is another cause of trouble when professional graphic artists move from the computer screen to the printed page. A logo color, for example, may look great onscreen or on a Web page, but when it's printed, the specific color is out of the gamut of the CMYK color space.

## Reproducing Color

Think about all the elements in the digital imaging workflow. Say you've got a photograph of an orange. You place it on your scanner and scan it. The scanner detects color one way, which is a function of the scanner's CCD (the Charge Coupled Device, which is a light sensor system), the optics, and other mechanical aspects of the device. So the scanner generates a file in which the orange color of the fruit has certain color properties. Does that match the original photograph? At this stage, you don't know. You may never know. Sure, you can go to the Info palette in Photoshop and see that the orange is defined as R=251, G=174, B=24, but such information is, at this stage, purely academic.

Not all monitors display colors the same way, which is a function of the video card and of the tubes in the monitor itself. What's more, the same monitor may not even display colors the same way. A monitor will change how it displays color the longer it's left on; as the elements heat up, perceptible color shifts can occur. And let's not forget that the lighting in the room in which you are viewing the monitor will also change your perception of the colors displayed on it.

You can look at the original photo of the orange (or the orange itself) while holding it next to the display of the scanned image on your monitor and see that it doesn't match. You can try for best of three. You print the file to your color printer or proofer. You compare it to the monitor's display, and you compare it to the original photo. Doh! Now you've got three completely different versions of the same thing.

So you adjust the color in Photoshop. After a little tweaking, the image on the display matches the original photo. But so what? That just means you've made the image to match the monitor's display. You still have no idea whether the file was scanned properly. If your monitor is really screwy, the orange will look good only on it. And in fact, you could take your corrected file to another workstation and see something completely different.

To make a short story long, this is what we're all up against. (And doesn't this sound more than a little like the strictly visual problem of color perception we talked about earlier?)



## Enter Color Management

The need for color management has arisen because in today's graphic design workflows, all sorts of devices are being cannibalized into a single workflow: a scanner and/or a digital camera here, a monitor there, an inkjet printer over yonder—a situation referred to in the trade as *open loop color.*

To resolve these problems, color management was spawned. It can be defined as a set of hardware and software that tries to get all the various devices to reproduce color consistently.

Basically, color management has two components: color profiles, which are detailed descriptions of how specific devices replicate color, and a color management system (CMS), which coordinates all the profiles and keeps everything colorimetrically kosher.

## Color Profiles

A *color profile* is a file that stores information about how a device represents color. It includes information about what color gamuts and models the device supports. By using a standard test target having color patches whose color values have been scientifically determined in a lab, a color management application generates a profile by comparing how a scanner, monitor, printer, or other device displays or detects those color patches compared to the predetermined values.

The profile pretty much says, "This scanner takes *this* red and thinks it's *that* red." Any color-savvy program using that profile knows what the device's quirks are and adjusts the display (or "remaps the colors") accordingly.

But what if each profile were created differently? A fine kettle of fish that would be. After all, just as every device can display colors differently, so, too, can each device have its color characteristics described differently. It's like getting all the eyewitnesses at the scene of a traffic accident to describe the same thing. You'll get as many different accounts as there are people involved.

Enter the International Color Consortium (ICC). The ICC profile is a standard way of describing color characteristics. Any ICC-compliant color management system—which any self-respecting color management system should be—can use the profile in the same way, keeping all the devices on the same page, as it were.

## Color Management System

The *color management system (CMS)* coordinates all the profiles. For example, if you were working in a program that supports color management—such as Photoshop, Illustrator, or InDesign—the CMS would look at the colors you have defined in your document, compare them to the profiles for your monitor, and adjust them accordingly so that the monitor displays the colors as accurately as possible in comparison to the original image. Similarly, the CMS will look at the profile you have defined for your printer and attempt to keep the output on a par with what you are seeing onscreen. If the printer is unable to replicate a color that you see onscreen, the CMS will recalibrate it to its closest equivalent.

If you need to know more about color management, *The GATF Practical Guide to Color Management* (by Richard M. Adams II and Joshua B. Weisberg, published in 1998 by GATF Press) is a handy and easy-to-read resource. It's a few years old and could use an update (and out of print, according to Amazon, but can still be found in libraries, book stores, or via the GATF Web site), but the information it presents is still perfectly valid. *Real World Color Management*, by Bruce Fraser, Fred Bunting, and Chris Murphy, published in 2003 by Peachpit Press, is also a good reference.

# Sailing the Cs of Color Management

Three stages are involved in the color management process, which the authors of *The GATF Practical Guide to Color Management* refer to as the "three Cs":

- Calibration
- Characterization
- Conversion

## Calibration

This is the stage where all devices are put on the same page. A scanner is calibrated by adjusting the response of the sensors in the CCD so that specified values are always read the same way. Devices such as scanners are calibrated so that the input is always consistent.

## Characterization

Characterization is an interpretation of the way a device captures colors using a standard color target. The color target is scanned, and the various color squares are compared to a data file containing the "real" values of those color squares. Those "real" values were determined in a special lab where people are paid a lot of money to do things such as measure the values of little squares of color.

Monitors are calibrated and characterized by setting them to a standard white point (that is, RGB color balance) and contrast (or gamma). This is usually done by attaching a colorimeter or spectrophotometer (a device that has a suction cup and a sensor that sticks to the monitor screen, reminiscent of the face-hugging creature in the movie *Alien*) and measuring a series of colored squares. (There are also self-calibrating monitors.)

To calibrate and characterize a printer, you would print out a color target and then measure the output values with a colorimeter or spectrophotometer, which feeds those values to the color management software.

## Conversion

Finally, in the conversion stage, the color management system uses the characterization profiles to remap the colors of one device to match that of another.

It's all a lot more complex than that, but you get the general idea.

How profiles are created and managed—and how accurately this is done—is generally what distinguishes one solution from another. Another distinguishing feature is ease of use, as well as lack of reliance on color measuring equipment. (A good spectrophotometer will set you back a few grand.)

# Do I Really Need Color Management?



Well, it's a free country, after all, and no one will force you to color-manage your workflow. Not all graphic designers use color management—heck, all *printers* don't even use color management. You've probably gotten a sense already of how expensive, time consuming, and unwieldy a process it can be—and let's face it, you have to do it flawlessly; otherwise, you create more problems than you solve. Therefore, many firms have said, "Nope, let's not go there," whereas others have in fact gone there and have come back with arrows in their hats.

Not all workflows are created equal, and some graphic arts pros are content to simply color-correct visually—if at all. Many professionals who work in small shops have developed an intuitive sense of color management; in other words, they know how their monitor displays in relation to other output devices and can compensate accordingly "by feel." That sounds a bit esoteric, but in many cases it works.

The answer to the question "Do I really need color management?" is, in large part, a function of one more set of color "spaces": critical versus good enough.

### Critical Versus Good Enough Color

TrendWatch Graphic Arts is a company that, since 1995, has been conducting twice-yearly surveys of trends in the design (print and Internet), publishing, and printing industries, and has been tracking interest in and the need for color management. The company has defined two basic types of color reproduction:

- **Critical color**—This refers to jobs for customers in which color matching—from file to proof to print—has to be *exact.* These types of jobs can include high-quality catalogs (clothing or other items purchased by color), upscale magazines, print ads, brochures, marketing materials, corporate identity (especially corporate logos), and commercial photography.
- **Good enough or pleasing color**—This refers to jobs for clients in which color doesn't need to be exact, just "in the ballpark." For example, as long as skin tones are not green, the sky isn't a flaming red, and nothing else looks freakish and disturbing, the color is deemed fine. This category can include lower-quality catalogs in which color is less of a customer concern (such as computer products or plumbing supplies); news, business, B2B, and trade publications; stationery and letterhead; user guides and product documentation; and business reports.

So when we speak of color management, we're really only talking about folks who have critical color customers or needs.

Ah, but here's the rub: Much of the reason the second category exists at all is that the inherent color management of applications such as Photoshop and the other elements of the Creative Suite is getting better and more reliable. The easier it is to set up these applications to work with color consistently, the less need there is to fret about making third-party color management work.

## SETTING UP YOUR SYSTEM FOR COLOR MANAGEMENT

Before you can configure Photoshop or any of the other applications in the Creative Suite, you need to configure your system. Setting up a CMS will thus allow you to manage color profiles for scanners, digital cameras, monitors, printers, and so on.



### Color Management Systems

Each platform (Macintosh and Windows) has its own brand of color management built in. The Mac has ColorSync, whereas Windows uses ICM.

### Macintosh: ColorSync

One of the oldest and most popular color management systems is Apple's ColorSync, which has been an integral part of the Mac OS since System 7 days. In OS X, it is found in the System

Preferences. Selecting ColorSync opens a two-tabbed dialog box. The first tab contains the default profiles (see Figure 6.1).

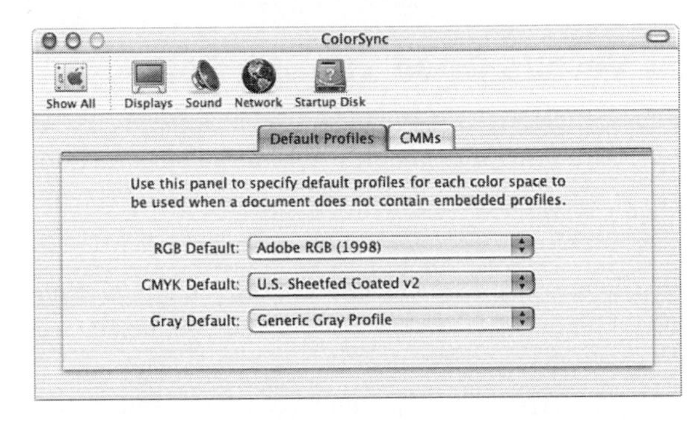


**Figure 6.1**
The Default Profiles tab in the ColorSync dialog box lets you specify default color profiles to use when working with documents.

The Default Profiles tab is where you select which color profile to use for which application:

- **RGB Default**—This setting specifies which color profile to use when working with documents that use the RGB color space.
- **CMYK Default**—This setting specifies which color profile to use when working with documents that use the CMYK color space.
- **Gray Default**—This setting specifies which color profile to use when working with documents that use the Grayscale color space.

The second tab is CMMs (Color Management Modules), which is where you select a color management system to use. Unless you have installed a third-party CMM, Automatic and Apple CMM will be the only options available here (see Figure 6.2). Automatic is the preferred choice.

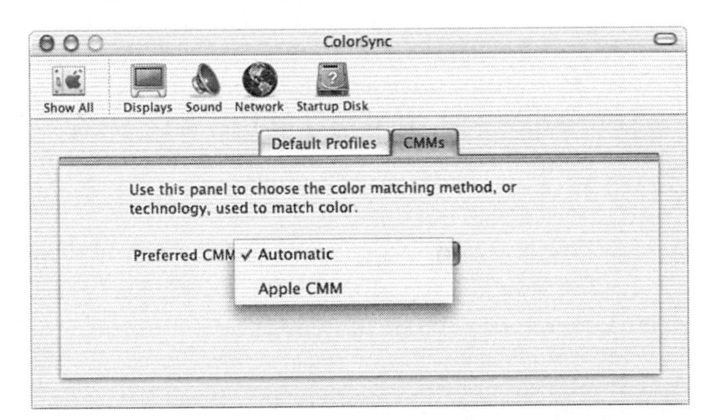


**Figure 6.2**
The CMMs tab in the ColorSync dialog box lets you specify which color management system to use to coordinate all the color profiles.

6

With the ColorSync utility, you can see what profiles are installed for which devices, and you can repair profiles. ColorSync is found in the Applications, Utilities folder in Mac OS X. This utility contains three panes. The Devices pane lets you see what profiles are installed for which class of device (see Figure 6.3).

> These default profiles are only used when a document contains no embedded profile.

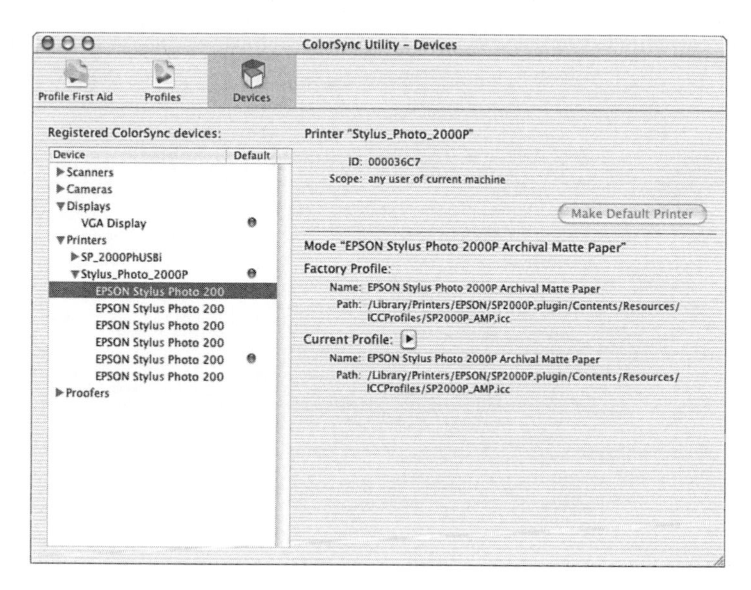


**Figure 6.3**
The Devices pane of the ColorSync utility tells you what profiles are installed for which devices. Clicking a profile gives you information about that profile.

Profiles don't need to be in any particular folder (some are in folders grouped with other files specific to a device), so the Profiles pane tells you where your profiles are located (see Figure 6.4).

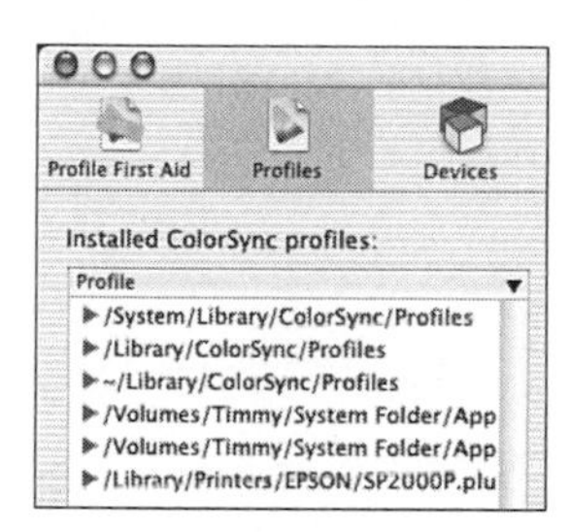


**Figure 6.4**
The Profiles pane tells you where all your device profiles are located.

The ColorSync utility also lets you repair any profiles that do not conform to ICC specifications. The Profile First Aid pane is reminiscent of the Disk First Aid utility (see Figure 6.5).

The best aspect of ColorSync is that you can generally "set it and forget it."

## Windows: Windows CMS

There was talk some years ago of porting ColorSync to the Windows platform, but because that would have simplified color management greatly (especially in cross-platform applications), it was abandoned.

Windows uses ICM (Image Color Management), a component of Windows designed to work with ICM-aware programs and devices to standardize color. ICM is not used directly from Photoshop. However, if you use other programs that are ICM aware, set them to use ICM. From the File menu in those programs, choose Color Management.

You can assign profiles to a Windows monitor by going to Settings, Control Panel, Display, clicking the Settings tab, clicking the Advanced button, and then clicking the Color Management tab in the resulting dialog box (yes, it's certainly out of the way, isn't it). This pane tells you what color profile is currently assigned to your monitor. If you have more than one profile, you can assign a new one here (see Figure 6.6).

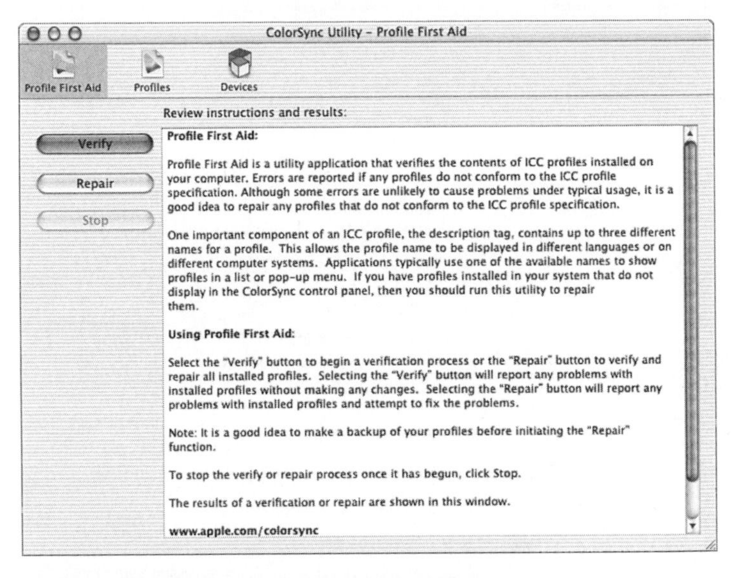


**Figure 6.5**
The Profile First Aid pane lets you repair profiles that do not conform to ICC specifications.

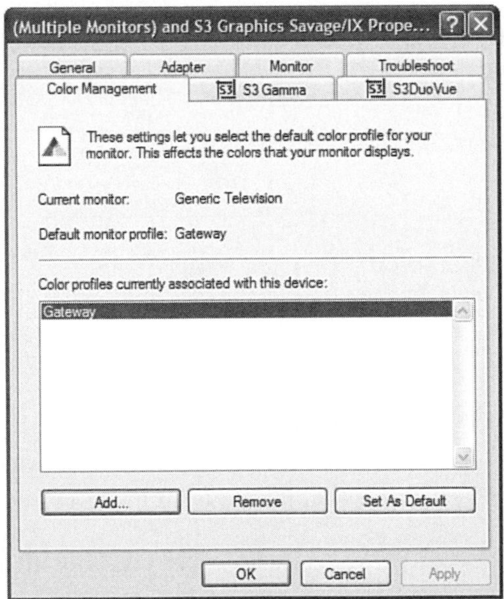


**Figure 6.6**
This well-hidden dialog box's Color Management tab is where you assign color profiles to Windows monitors.

To assign a profile to a printer, select Settings, Printers and Faxes to open a list of installed printers. Right-click the printer to which you would like to assign a profile and then select Properties from the contextual menu. Click the Color Management tab, and you'll see the default profile assigned to that printer. In this tab, you also can assign different profiles (see Figure 6.7).

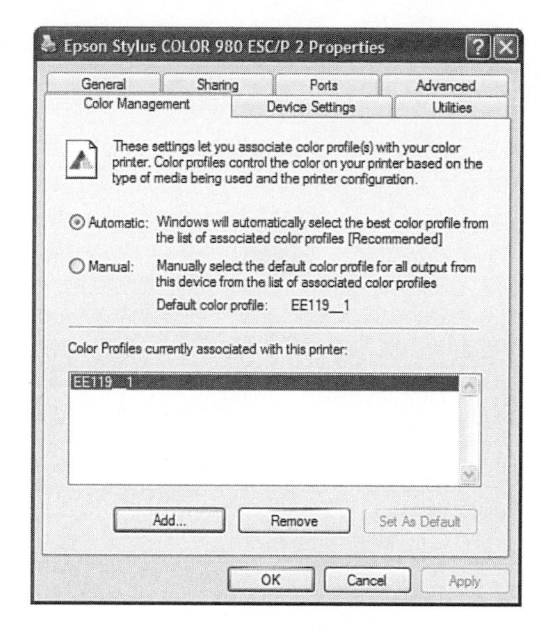


**Figure 6.7**
The Color Management tab of the Properties dialog box is where you assign profiles to Windows printers.

# Calibrating and Profiling Your Monitor

Accurately calibrating your monitor is the best first step to take in a color-managed workflow. Because the monitor is what you actually look at when you make color corrections, work with images, and put pages together, monitor calibration is your first line of defense against color inaccuracy.

There are two basic ways of calibrating your monitor: the hard way and the easy way. Naturally, the hard way is the most accurate, but the easy way yields very good results.

The hard way involves using calibration hardware from such companies as GretagMacbeth (`www.gretagmacbeth.com`), ColorVision (`www.colorpar.com`), and X-Rite (`www.xrite.com`). These companies manufacture hardware and software combinations that let you accurately adjust your monitor. Prepress professionals and other critical-color Photoshop users who rely on color accuracy should invest in hardware calibration equipment. If you merely output to a home/office inkjet printer or create images and documents designed for the Web, this type of investment may be overkill.

The easy way involves calibrating and profiling your monitor without needing external hardware. It's not going to be as accurate as using dedicated hardware and software, but it will go a long way toward ensuring reasonably accurate color.

## Macintosh Monitor Profiling

In OS 9 and earlier, a utility from Adobe called Adobe Gamma let you calibrate and profile your monitor. Adobe Gamma doesn't exist for OS X, but OS X has a built-in display calibrator called, cleverly enough, Display Calibrator. It's found in the Utilities folder in the OS X Applications folder. This is an assistant-based utility that walks you through the steps needed to calibrate and profile a monitor (see Figure 6.8).

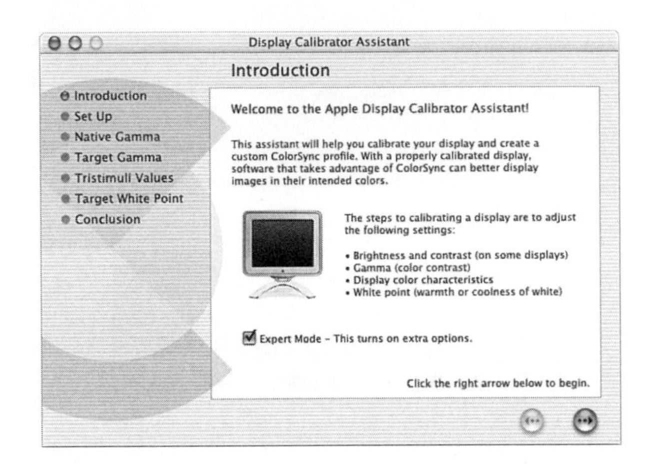


**Figure 6.8**
Apple's Display Calibrator Assistant walks you through the steps needed to calibrate and profile your monitor.

The Expert Mode check box on the opening screen provides additional options. Folks doing color graphics work should use the Expert Mode.

The six panes walk you through the process, which is self-explanatory. The final pane sums up your settings and asks you to name the profile (see Figure 6.9).

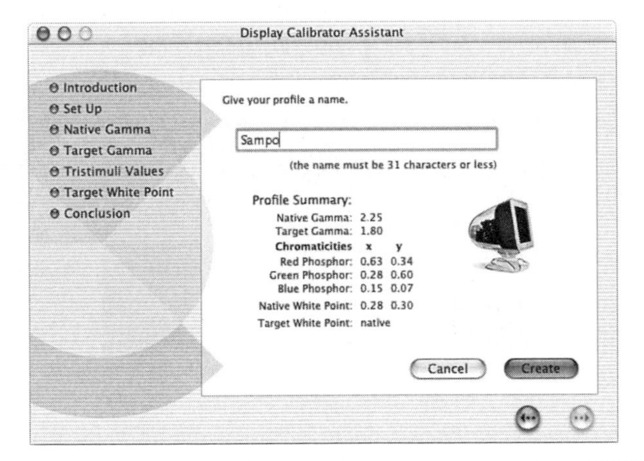


**Figure 6.9**
When you have wended your way through the steps of the calibration process, name your monitor profile and click Create.



If you now go to System Preferences, Display and then click the Color tab, you will be given a list of profiles. Select the one you just created (see Figure 6.10).

If you click the Calibrate button, you will open the Display Calibrator and can again go through the calibration and profiling steps. It may be a good idea to run the calibration utility every so often (every few weeks or months) to make sure your monitor is still behaving itself.

Back in the ColorSync dialog box, make sure that you select your profile as the RGB Default. In the next section, when we start looking at the specific color management settings in the Creative Suite applications, you'll be selecting this profile as your RGB color profile.

> The Expert Mode specifically adds additional panes for setting red, green, and blue values, as well as highly customizable white point corrections.

> For the most accurate results, let the monitor warm up for at least a half hour before calibrating it.

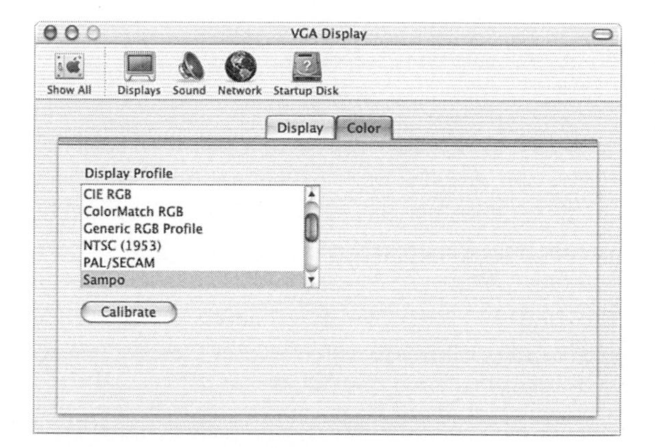


**Figure 6.10**
The Color tab of the Display preferences is where you can apply the profile you created.

## Windows Monitor Profiling

When you install the Creative Suite applications, the installer adds the Adobe Gamma control panel for Windows in the Control Panel, accessed through the Start menu. This functions not unlike the OS X Display Calibrator.

When you open Adobe Gamma, you'll be given the choice of working directly in the control panel or having the wizard walk you through the process, step by step. The wizard is easy and self-explanatory if you're a profiling newbie (see Figure 6.11).

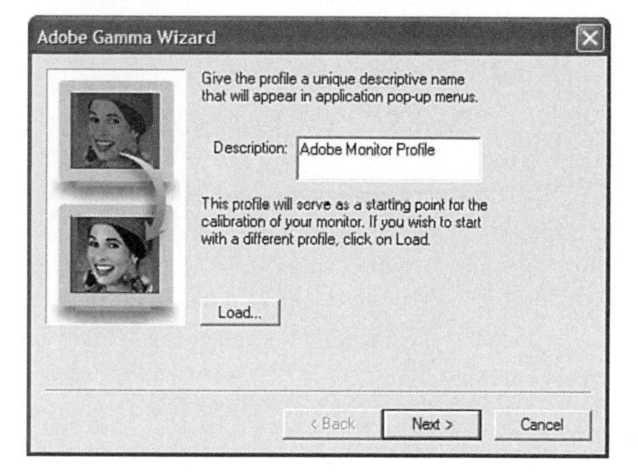


**Figure 6.11**
One of the first steps is to give a descriptive name to the profile that will be created. The name you select here will be what you choose in the Creative Suite's applications' Color Setting dialog boxes.

The wizard will then walk you through the process for setting up white point, gamma, and so on.

Those are the basics of setting up your system for color management. If you decide to use a third-party profiling, calibrating, or CMM system, the process will be roughly similar, but will naturally vary from application to application.

> **Caution**
>
> Do not use the Adobe Gamma control panel to profile an LCD monitor—it works only with CRTs. Third-party hardware calibration/profiling packages are available, and your LCD monitor's manufacturer may have included a utility.

### Environmental Protection

One of the most basic ways of ensuring accurate color is to work in an environment that is conducive to accurate color viewing. That involves carefully controlling the environment in which you are working.

Ambient light can cause problems. If you don't actually work in a hermetically sealed underground concrete bunker, light coming in through the windows not only can conflict with your monitor in general, but can conflict in different ways over the course of the day. As the sun changes position, the amount of light coming through the windows changes. Colors onscreen look differently in the morning than they do in the afternoon. If a day is overcast, colors onscreen will look different than on bright sunny days. Other light sources, such as ceiling lights and desk lamps, can affect the way you perceive colors on your monitor. (Remember the orange example earlier in this chapter?)

On the other hand, working in a completely dark office sealed off from daylight, bathed only in the glow of a monitor, may not be the best approach, unless you're given to vampirism. More practically, because colors tend to look more saturated and richer in a completely dark room, it also isn't the best environment in which to be evaluating color.

So what can be done? Control ambient lighting when doing color correction. Above all (or most) else, the work environment should be comfortable; you don't want a joyless, strictly utilitarian workspace. Your boss may want you to, but you certainly don't. (If you're seeing red all the time, that also isn't conducive to good color decisions!) But when doing color-critical work, you may have to compromise. Here are some issues you should consider when preparing an environment suitable for proper color management:

- The monitor can be shielded from ambient light using a hood. Although professional-quality color-correction hoods are available from graphic arts dealers, you really don't need anything that elaborate. Simply shield the top and sides of the monitor to a distance of at least 12 inches, and paint the inside of the hood matte black.
- Your computer's Desktop should be neutral gray. Avoid colorful family pictures and beautiful scenery. To keep your life from being one of joyless servitude to color management, you can create a temporary background in Photoshop simply by pressing the F key. Photoshop's Full Screen Mode with Menu Bar creates a gray background around your image. If you want to work in Standard Screen Mode, try this: Open a new document. Fill it with 50% gray. Press F to put that image into Full Screen Mode with Menu Bar. Zoom a couple times until the image fills the screen. Now open your work image(s). The Windows version of Photoshop always adds a gray background behind the working area, as long as the window is maximized.
- Objects on and around the monitor should be removed. Until such time as Post-It Notes come in neutral gray, they should not be stuck to the side of a monitor used for color correction.
- Walls within sight when looking at the monitor should also be free of colorful decoration and painted a neutral gray. Turn off any strobing disco lights you may have in your office, however entertaining you may find them.

How critical are these adaptations to the work environment? Only as critical as the accuracy of your color. The more important a color match, the more important the environment in which that match is made.

# COLOR MANAGEMENT IN PHOTOSHOP

The trick to color managing documents across the Creative Suite is to set up color management in each of the components. Most of the options are the same for each of the three primary applications—Photoshop, InDesign, and Illustrator—so we'll go through them once in detail in the Photoshop section that follows. In successive sections we'll look at specific issues in InDesign and Illustrator.

## Photoshop's Color Settings

The first time you launch Photoshop, you will have the opportunity to customize your color settings. However, if you don't avail yourself of the opportunity there and then, you can always change your color settings at any time.

Color settings are changed by going to (Photoshop CS) [Edit], Color Settings, which will bring up the Color Settings dialog box (see Figure 6.12).

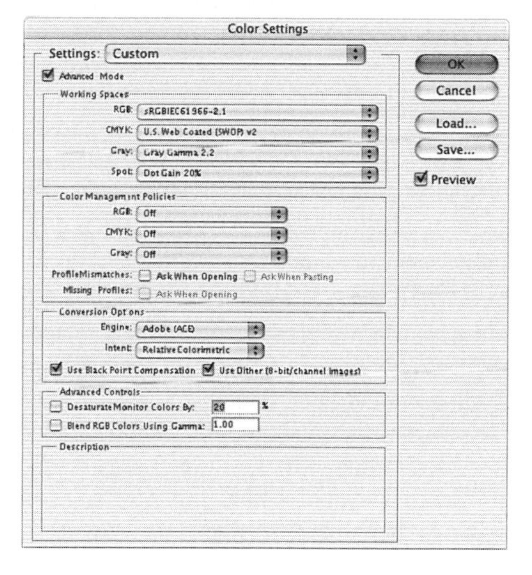


**Figure 6.12**
The Color Settings dialog box in Photoshop has an Advanced Mode, which is where power users (like you!) set up advanced color management.

The Color Settings dialog box—with the Advanced Mode check box selected—is divided into several sections.



## Settings

At the top of the Color Settings dialog box is the Settings menu. This menu contains a list of preset color settings, appropriate for general categories of work, such as European Prepress Defaults and Japan Color Prepress (see Figure 6.13).

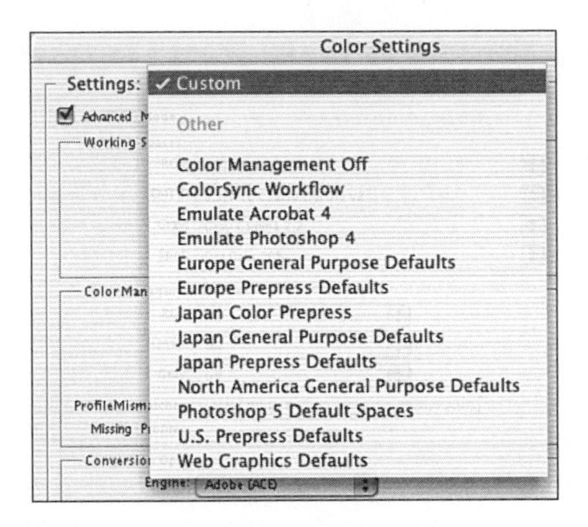


Figure 6.13
Selecting any of these choices will automatically configure the rest of the fields and values in the Color Settings dialog box.

Using these preset profiles is really worthwhile only in a workflow that is geared toward them. However, once you have configured the entire Color Settings dialog box, you can save custom settings—which is, as you shall see, the key to taking advantage of the Creative Suite's integrated color management.

## Working Spaces

The pop-up menus in the Working Spaces portion of the Color Settings dialog box is where you choose which default color profile to convert documents to.

The RGB working space menu is where you define your RGB working space. When you embed a color profile in an RGB image, the RGB working space is basically what you're including.

If you have a perfectly calibrated monitor (using hardware calibration) and work in a production environment with several other perfectly calibrated monitors, it might make sense for all systems to use Adobe RGB (or another large gamut) as the RGB profile. If you have Radius Pressview monitors, ColorMatch RGB should be the choice. Wide-gamut dye-sublimation printers and many photo-quality printer operations may benefit from ProPhoto RGB. If you send images to a service bureau or print shop as RGB files, it may prefer one gamut over another.

Photoshop users who don't send out RGB images (including Web professionals) will want to choose a device-independent profile—such as Adobe RGB or any custom profile designed to be the standard for all color reproduction—as the working space. Photoshop and the other Creative Suite applications use the working space as the *source* profile, or the indicator of what the file *really* looks like. When you calibrate your monitor using the custom monitor profile that was created with the OS X Display Calibrator utility or with Adobe Gamma, Photoshop considers that the *destination* profile. It studies the quirks of your display, compares them to the source values, and adjusts the display accordingly.

> You typically only send out RGB files to a service bureau or printer for one of two reasons: a) you or the service bureau/printer has specifically requested that it handle all RGB-to-CMYK conversion, or b) you like getting yelled at.

*How can you check the accuracy of your color profile? If you're a Mac OS X user, there is a little-known-but-very-cool utility that lets you do this. See "Meter Made" in the "Mastering Photoshop" section at the end of this chapter.*

To load custom RGB profiles, check the Advanced Mode box in the upper-left corner of the Color Settings dialog box. When this box is checked, Load RGB will be an option in the RGB pop-up menu. When the box is not checked, you cannot load custom profiles.

The CMYK working space is where you set the profile to use for CMYK images. Inkjet printers are an interesting anomaly. Although inkjet printers are actually CMYK devices at heart, they print using RGB data. Many inkjet printers install several different ICC profiles for various combinations of resolution and paper quality—counterintuitively, they are found in the RGB working space pop-up menu (and therefore the CMYK working space will be ignored). Indeed, if you are working in the CMYK color space, the inkjet printer will convert it to RGB before printing, even if it is using C, M, Y, and K colorants to print. Choose the one you normally use, and change the profile if you print to a different paper.

If you're preparing images for output to a specific printing press, contact your output service provider to see if there's a custom CMYK profile available. If not, or if you don't know (or haven't yet decided) which printer will be handling your job, choose the stock profile that best fits the specifications of your job—coated or uncoated paper or newsprint, webfed or sheetfed press. Most output providers don't care what profile you embed because they simply strip it out anyway and use their own.

When you know the specifications of a press, you can create a profile for it using the Custom CMYK selection from the menu. Talk with your print shop to get the correct values for each field (see Figure 6.14).

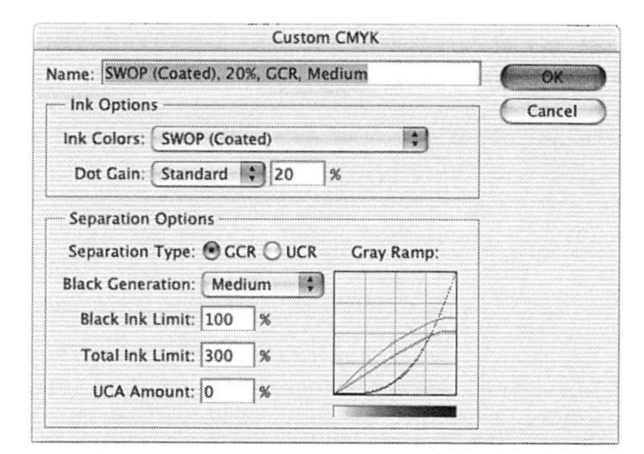


**Figure 6.14**
The Custom CMYK dialog box lets you add a profile for a specific printing press. Naturally, you don't want to make a guess about these values. Consult with your printer before setting one of these up.

The Gray working space affects only the onscreen appearance of a grayscale image. It enables you to see the effects of dot gain or gamma on an image. If you work in prepress, especially newspapers, use your standard dot gain. Web professionals, on both Mac and Windows, are best served by gamma 2.2 (the Windows setting), unless the primary audience for the graphic is Mac oriented. If you use a strict ColorSync workflow, choose that profile. (Web designers probably don't need to worry about dot gain, which is strictly a print-based phenomenon.) The Spot pop-up menu refers to spot colors. The dot gain for spot channels is typically that of the press in general, but dot gain can be a function of the paper type and the ink type—and is more of a problem for process inks. *Dot gain* refers to the fact that uncoated papers slurp up more ink than coated papers do, which causes halftone dots to spread out, thus making images muddy. Compensating for dot gain shrinks the dot so that when it expands upon printing, it will end up being about the size it should be. The default is 20%.

## Color Management Policies

The Color Management Policies section of the Color Settings dialog box is where you get the opportunity to decide how you want Photoshop to handle color profiles. The options for each of the three color spaces are Preserve Embedded Profiles (which means that Photoshop uses the profile embedded in the image without converting it), Convert to Working RGB/CMYK/Gray (which means Photoshop will use the profile you defined in the Working Spaces section), and Off (which means Photoshop will ignore color profiles).

These options aren't necessarily as clear-cut as they sound, and this section of the Color Settings dialog box can be a two-edged sword. Generally speaking, the following issues hold true:

- If your computer (that is to say, monitor) is not the last stop for an image before it gets sent out to a service provider, and you will be returning an image to a server or another workstation, do *not* convert to your working space, be it RGB or CMYK. Rather, use the command Image, Mode, Assign Profile to change the appearance onscreen while you review or work. (The Assign Profile command is discussed in the section "Changing Embedded Profiles," later in this chapter.) Converting an image and then converting back to another profile can cause needless color shifts and can clip the image's tonal range. Instead, assign your profile, review or edit, return the image, and let the receiver know that the original profile should be reassigned. If you have a device-independent profile set up as your working space, there is no need to noodle with profiles at all. You would only use the Assign Profile command to simulate CMYK on your screen, not to try to get the file to optimize itself for display on your monitor.

- If your computer *is* the last machine to handle the image and the final output will be prepared on your computer, convert to your working space.

- If you are doing high-quality grayscale work, color management can help maintain the gamma (or contrast) of a grayscale image. Otherwise, it's safe to turn off color management completely for grayscale images. Assigning profiles and converting images is unlikely to improve the appearance or output.

- Color management policies don't need to be an all-or-nothing affair. You can make decisions on a case-by-case basis by using the Profile Mismatches options (described in the next section).



If you're a prepress professional and you receive files from outside sources, you'll generally want to preserve the embedded CMYK profile until you have had a chance to evaluate it. If it's the correct profile, there's no need to strip it out and add it back later. (However, it is the policy of many production operations to automatically strip any CMYK profile from any image submitted.)

If you work with Web graphics, it's usually acceptable to convert to your working space. Digital photographers might notice that Photoshop CS reads the EXIF data embedded by many cameras. If you're confident that the embedded profile is correct, you may want to keep it when opening the image and later assign or convert to your working space. That gives you the luxury of the Undo command if you happen to notice color shifts or clipping.

Under the Color Management Policies pop-up menus is the Profile Mismatches check box. Checking Ask When Opening brings up a dialog box that tells you what profile is embedded in the image, and which profile is set up to be the working space (see Figure 6.15).

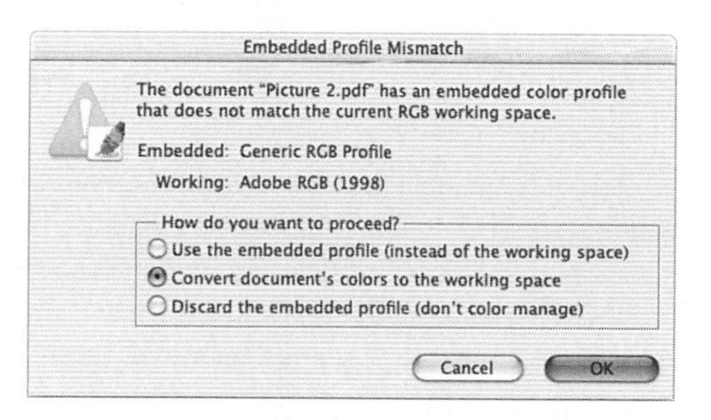


Figure 6.15
When you tell Photoshop to let you know when an image's embedded profile doesn't match the working space, it asks you what to do about it.

Most Photoshop users should turn on mismatch notification. It gives you the opportunity to evaluate the situation on an image-by-image basis and choose whether to save the embedded profile, convert to your working space, or discard the profile completely.

However, it can be helpful to uncheck the mismatch notification boxes in some situations:

- When you'll be opening a series of images that you know must be converted to your working space.
- When you need to strip incorrect profiles from a series of images.
- When you'll be batch processing a folder of images and you have decided that they all must be handled the same. Indeed, one of the options in the Batch dialog box (found under File, Batch) is Suppress Color Profile Warnings.

## Conversion Options

Checking the Advanced Mode option in the upper-left corner of the Color Settings dialog box presents some additional options.

In the Engine pop-up menu, all the available color engines do a good job of converting color from one profile to another. Adobe (ACE) is the usual choice. Macintosh users have the option of ColorSync or Apple CMM, whereas Windows offers the Windows ICM engine.

Your choice for Intent determines how the color engine deals with colors that fall outside the destination gamut. When converting from one profile to another, it's possible that your image will be going from a larger gamut to a smaller one. Or, perhaps, certain colors are possible in the fringe area of one gamut that cannot be achieved in the other gamut. In either case, the engine needs to have instruction. Here are the options:

- **Perceptual**—The result of the color conversion will be as close as possible to the original for the human eye. If the source gamut is larger than the destination gamut, all colors will be shifted. For example, the brightest red will remain the brightest red, the second brightest is the second brightest, and so on. If the first red is not reproducible in the new gamut, but the second is, they will both shift anyway (as will all the other reds in the image). Use Perceptual when you want to maintain the overall appearance of the image and don't need to retain any specific colors within the image.

- **Saturation**—Any colors that are out of the destination gamut retain their saturation values and are brought into gamut by adjusting the lightness and hue. Colors that are in the destination gamut are unchanged. Use Saturation for very richly saturated artwork, such as clip art, graphs, and logos.
- **Relative Colorimetric**—Colors reproducible in the destination gamut are unchanged. The colors that fall outside the new gamut are brought into gamut by adjusting hue and saturation. This preserves the overall tonality of the image. Use Relative Colorimetric for most images. Only those colors on the fringe of the gamut are affected, and they maintain their lightness value. The human eye is far more sensitive to tonal changes than to changes in hue.
- **Absolute Colorimetric**—The absolute Lab coordinates of the source colors are mapped to the destination gamut without regard for white point mapping. Some very unusual color shifts are possible. Use Absolute Colorimetric for one- or two-color logos or, in some situations, when preparing hard proofs. Absolute Colorimetric is not generally acceptable for conversion of continuous-tone images such as photographs.

Remember that Intent comes into play primarily when converting from a larger gamut to a smaller gamut. You are unlikely to see any color shift when converting from, for example, sRGB (a very small gamut) to Adobe RGB (one of the largest RGB gamuts). You are very likely to perceive color shifting when converting a bright and colorful image from Adobe RGB to any CMYK gamut.

When Use Black Point Compensation is checked, the darkest neutral pixels in the source gamut are mapped to the darkest neutral color in the target gamut. When this option is unchecked, the neutral shadow is mapped to black. When converting from RGB to CMYK, you'll normally want to have the option selected.

When Use Dither is checked, banding can be reduced. If too many related colors are mapped to too few colors in the destination gamut, visible stripes of colors (called *bands*) can appear in gradients and other areas of blended color. Dithering thus reduces the potential problem. Use Dither doesn't have any impact when converting 16-bit and Indexed Color images.

> Once you've evaluated your color management needs, selected your working spaces, and chosen your options, you can save the settings by clicking the Save button. Be sure to include the .csf (color settings file) file extension. You can also establish a number of different configurations, any of which can be selected with the Load button—often faster than navigating to find a custom CMYK profile and swapping options.



## Advanced Controls

Enabling Desaturate Monitor Colors enables you to see more detail in highlight areas of images in very large RGB spaces such as Adobe RGB. This option should be selected only when you're actually working in those highlight areas, and only if that part of the gamut is not being portrayed onscreen. If the Info palette shows that there are variations in the very lightest areas, but you can't see them onscreen, try checking this box. Remember to uncheck it afterward, because it skews all colors.

Blend RGB Colors Using Gamma is another option to be used only if your onscreen representation is obviously flawed, because changing the gamma can reduce artifacts along distinct edges in an image. By default, Photoshop uses the assigned monitor gamma to blend red, green, and blue onscreen. If you're zoomed in very close and the monitor shows artifacts that the Info palette tells you shouldn't be there, try this option. Increase or decrease the gamma to smooth the RGB blending. Remember to deselect the option before resuming your regular work.

Color settings are stored in a file called Color Settings in the Adobe Photoshop CS Settings folder, which is located in the Preferences Folder (Mac OS X). In Windows, you first need to go to Settings, Control Panel, Folder Options, click the View tab, and click the Show Hidden Files and Folders radio button. Then you can make the arduous trek to Documents and Settings, [username], Application Data, Adobe, Photoshop, 8.0. Deleting this file restores Photoshop to its default color settings.

## Changing Embedded Profiles

The color profile embedded in an image can be changed in a variety of ways. You can convert an image to your working space upon opening, you can change the color mode of the document, you can strip the profile from the image by selecting Discard the Embedded Profile when notified of a mismatch, and you can change the embedded profile or the profile and the image's color space. The following subsections discuss each of these methods in detail.

### Assign Profile

The Assign Profile command (accessed by choosing Image, Mode, Assign Profile) lets you strip the embedded profile from a document, tag the document with the working profile (RGB, CMYK, or Grayscale), or choose another profile of the appropriate color mode (see Figure 6.16).

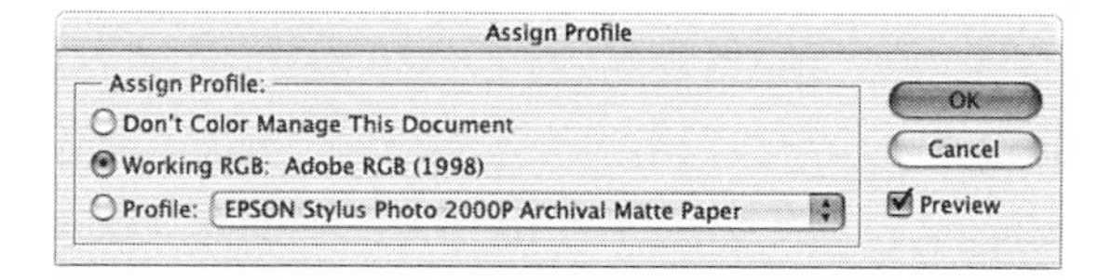


**Figure 6.16**
You can assign a profile to an image on the fly using Assign Profile.

Assigning a new working space does *not* change the color values in the image. Instead, it simply embeds a new profile in the document and shows you onscreen what the image will look like with that new gamut. The Preview option enables you to see what the new profile will look like without actually assigning it. If the preview looks unacceptable—or if you just want a quick peek at the possible conversion—click Cancel to retain the document's original embedded profile.

### Convert to Profile

To access the Convert to Profile options, choose Image, Mode, Convert to Profile. Unlike Assign Profile, Convert to Profile *does* change the color values in the image. The image's colors are mapped from the embedded profile to the profile you select in the Convert to Profile dialog box (see Figure 6.17).

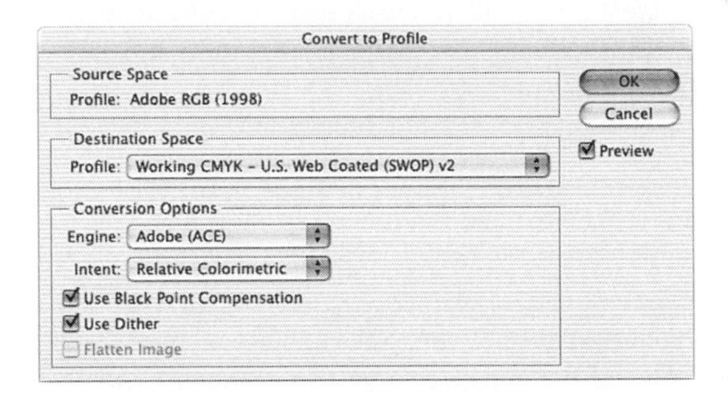


**Figure 6.17**
You can convert an image from one profile to another on the fly using Convert to Profile.

Convert to Profile attempts to maintain image appearance as closely as possible when remapping, using the engine and intent specified in the dialog box.

Color profiles can also be embedded in files during the Save As process. With Color Management turned on, Embed Color Profile is a check box in the Save As dialog box. The profile that will be saved will correspond to the working space specified for the color mode of the document.

# COLOR SETTINGS IN THE OTHER CREATIVE SUITE APPLICATIONS

All the applications in the Creative Suite have a Color Settings dialog box that is virtually identical to that in Photoshop, with the same options and same settings. Ideally, for a "closed-loop" workflow, simply ensure that all three applications use the same profiles and the same color settings, and you're done. You will never have any color-matching problems ever again.

Well, that probably won't be the case, but it's a good start. The following subsections discuss how to work with the color settings in the other Creative Suite applications, for all those cases that *don't* fall into the closed-loop ideal.

## Illustrator's Color Settings



Illustrator's color settings are found at Edit, Color Settings. These settings feature the same options as Photoshop's Color Settings dialog box. Likewise, there is an Edit, Assign Profile command that, like the corresponding command in Photoshop, lets you apply a color profile to the current document on the fly.

When you save an Illustrator document, you also get an option to save ICC profiles along with the document (see Figure 6.18).

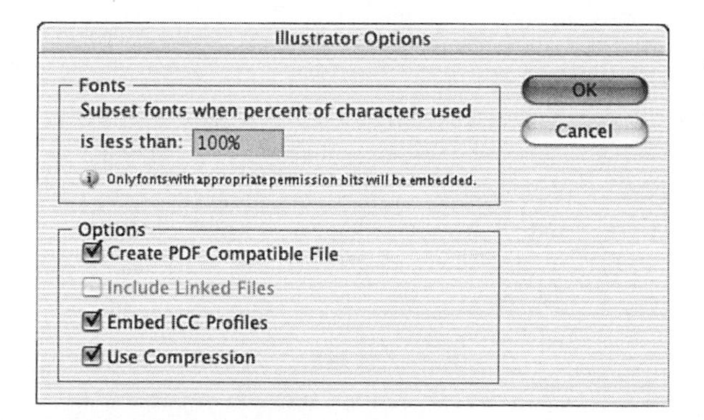


**Figure 6.18**
You can embed ICC profiles when saving an Illustrator file.

## Illustrator and Photoshop

If you open the Illustrator file in Photoshop, the color profile embedded in the image is available in the Mode pop-up menu in the Rasterize Generic PDF Format dialog box (see Figure 6.19).

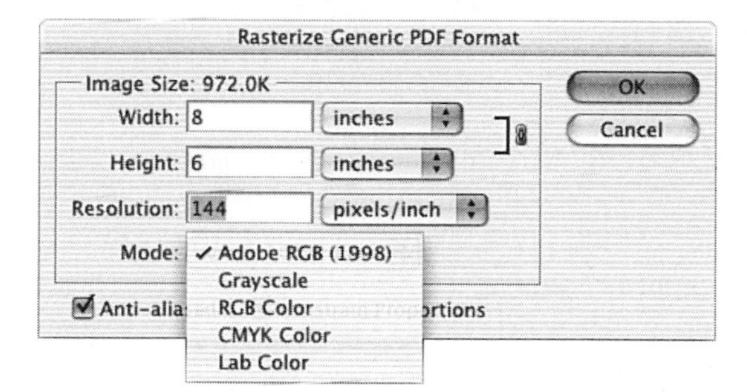


**Figure 6.19**
If you save an Illustrator file with an embedded profile, it is available in the Mode pop-up menu when rasterized in Photoshop.

To keep Photoshop from converting the file to the working RGB or CMYK space, you need to select Preserve Embedded Profile in the Color Management Policies section of the Color Settings dialog box. When rasterizing an Illustrator file, Photoshop doesn't ask you what to do.

When you import a Photoshop image into Illustrator, you will get a profile mismatch warning (if indeed the profiles are mismatched and you have the warnings turned on in the Illustrator Color Settings dialog box).

## InDesign

Like Illustrator's, InDesign's Color Settings dialog box is accessed via Edit, Color Settings.

Because InDesign is "command central" for the workflow—in other words, it is where vector art from Illustrator, raster art from Photoshop, and its own native objects are all combined—color management in InDesign has to encompass two aspects:

- Color managing the InDesign document itself
- Color managing linked objects

> **Caution**
> To open an Illustrator file in another Adobe application, you must have saved the file with the Make PDF Compatible option checked. Otherwise, when you open the image in Photoshop, instead of the image created in Illustrator, you'll get a paragraph of text telling you to resave the file with the PDF option!

You set up color management for the InDesign document itself the same way you do in Photoshop and Illustrator: Go to Edit, Color Settings and select the desired profiles, policies, and options.

To color-manage linked objects, you can set a profile and a profile mismatch policy when you import an image into InDesign via the Place command. When you select File, Place, make sure Show Import Options is checked. When you click the Choose button, you'll get a two-tabbed Image Import Options dialog box. The Color tab of this dialog box is shown in Figure 6.20.

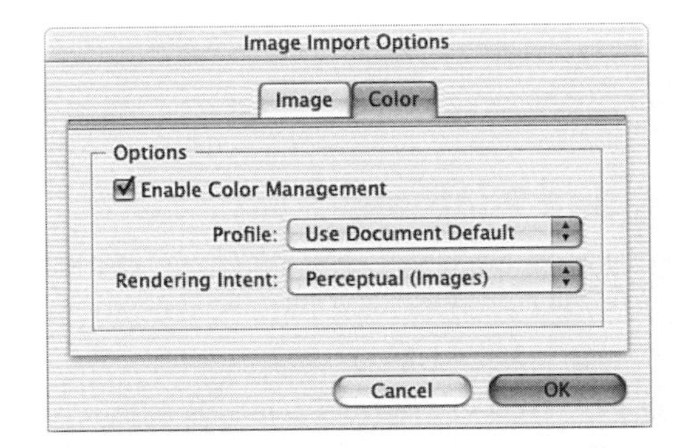


**Figure 6.20**
The Image Import Options dialog box includes color management policies regarding imported images.

Here, you can select whether to enable color management, which profile to apply, and what the rendering intent is. Selecting Use Document Default will apply the default working space set in the Color Settings dialog box for the image type in question (RGB, CMYK, or Grayscale).

When you assign a profile to a linked image in InDesign, the original Photoshop or Illustrator file is unchanged; only its appearance in InDesign is affected—as is any output from InDesign.

When you create page objects in InDesign, such as colored shapes, they will be created using the prevailing color profile set up for that image type (RGB versus CMYK). Changing a document profile using the Edit, Convert to Profile command will only apply that change of profile to native InDesign elements. Linked objects will be unaffected.

InDesign is also the only application in the Creative Suite that allows both RGB and CMYK objects in the same document. Therefore, the Assign Profile command will allow both RGB and CMYK profiles to be assigned, rather than simply the prevailing color mode's profile, as in the other two applications.



## Printing

When printing, you can assign a color profile to just the printed copy of a document. Both InDesign and Illustrator use the type of Print dialog box that has a separate Color Management pane (see Figure 6.21).

You can change the profile assigned to a linked image at any time by (Control)-clicking right-clicking an image and selecting Graphics, Image Color Settings from the contextual menu. This will open the Image Color Settings dialog box, and you can reassign a profile and/or rendering intent.

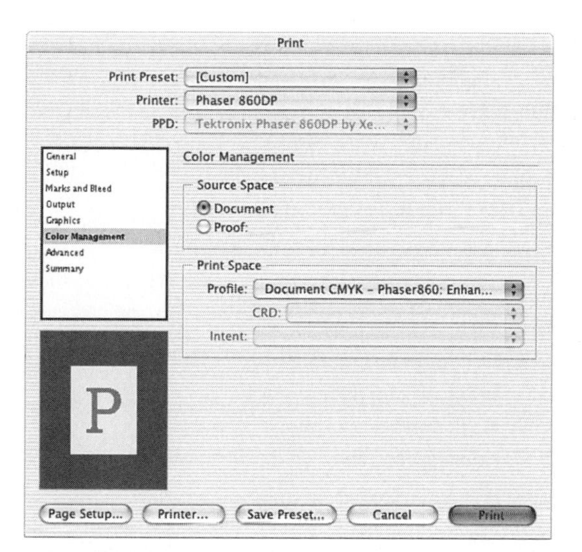


**Figure 6.21**
The InDesign Print dialog box has a Color Management pane in which you can choose which color profile to use while printing. This should match the device you're printing to. Illustrator's dialog box is virtually identical.

In the Color Management pane, you can select which color profile to use while printing.

In Photoshop, color management of output is handled through the Print with Preview dialog box (accessed via File, Print with Preview). Figure 6.22 shows this dialog box.

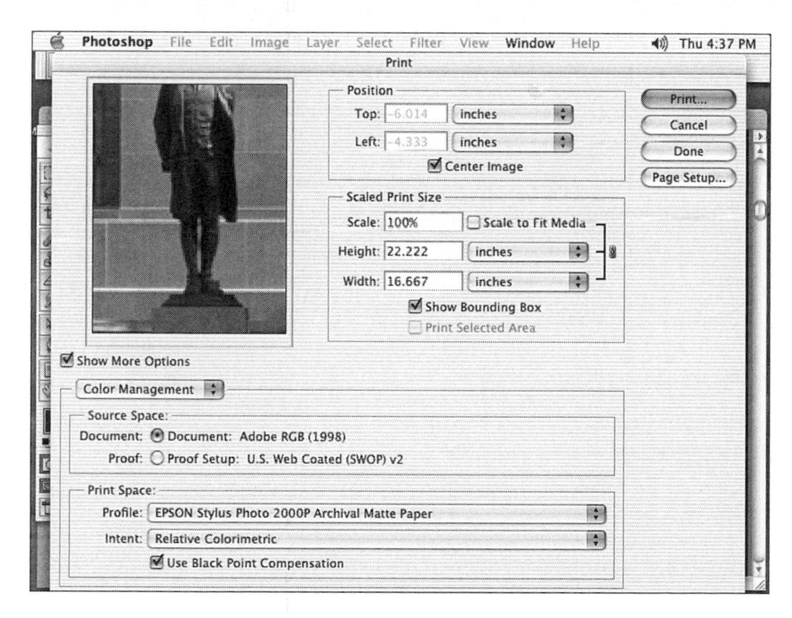


**Figure 6.22**
The Print with Preview dialog box in Photoshop is where you set the color profiles to use while printing.

Again, ideally, you'll select the Print Space profile that corresponds to your specific output device.

You can apply two levels of color simulation in InDesign and Photoshop. In both applications, View, Proof Setup lets you choose what color profile should be used for the ultimate print source (such as U.S. Web Coated [SWOP]). Because you're not actually going to print to a Web press, go to Print, Color Management (or to Print with Preview in the case of Photoshop) and, in the Source

Space section, click the Proof radio button. This will show the device you had selected in Proof Setup. If you then select the profile for your color printer/proofer from the Print Space pop-up menu, InDesign will attempt to simulate uncoated Web printing on the device to which you are outputting.

If your file is going to be output by a prepress shop or printer, it will likely have its own color management tools built in to its RIP (the device that processes the output to make plates, film, or images on the press directly). Therefore, any profiles you assign in the Print dialog box are for your own in-house proofers and printers.

## Exporting to PDF

In both Photoshop and Illustrator, documents are converted to PDF format via the Save As command. InDesign documents are converted to PDF via the File, Export command. If you are exporting a document to PDF, you can also apply a destination profile. In InDesign, this is handled via the Advanced pane of the Export PDF dialog box (see Figure 6.23).

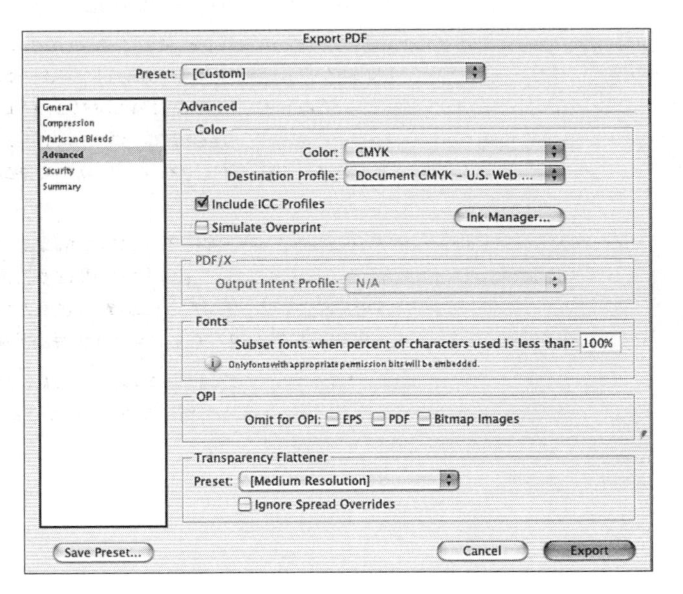


Figure 6.23
The Advanced pane of InDesign's Export PDF dialog box lets you set the destination color mode as well as what profile to apply to it.

6

# MASTERING PHOTOSHOP

## Meter Made

*How can I easily tell whether my monitor is producing color accurately?*

A little-known-but-very-cool Mac OS X utility called DigitalColor Meter can help you determine how accurately your monitor is producing color. To use it, follow these steps:

1. If you haven't already, profile your monitor using the Display Calibrator or another utility (as discussed earlier in this chapter).
2. In Photoshop, load your monitor profile as the RGB working space in the Color Settings dialog box.
3. Go to View, Swatches to open the Swatches palette. Move it to the center of the screen. Select the Swatches palette menu command Reset Swatches. Choose to replace (the OK button) rather than append.
4. Now open DigitalColor Meter (it's in the Utilities subfolder in OS X's Applications folder). Set the readout to RGB As Percentage and make sure that Aperture Size is set to one of the three leftmost settings. If it's not, press Command-Shift-H, change it, and then press Command-Shift-H again. Position the DigitalColor Meter window where it will be visible while you work.
5. Switch back to Photoshop and position the cursor over the upper-left swatch (it should be red). If your monitor is showing accurate color, it's calibrated correctly, and your RGB profile is good, DigitalColor Meter will read R:100, G:0, B:0. Try the other swatches. Make sure to include the grayscale swatches.
6. For comparison, in Photoshop's Color Settings, switch to Adobe RGB as the RGB profile. Measure the swatches again. There will likely be some variation, which can illustrate the danger (or the efficacy) of using your monitor profile as the default working profile (see Figure 6.24).

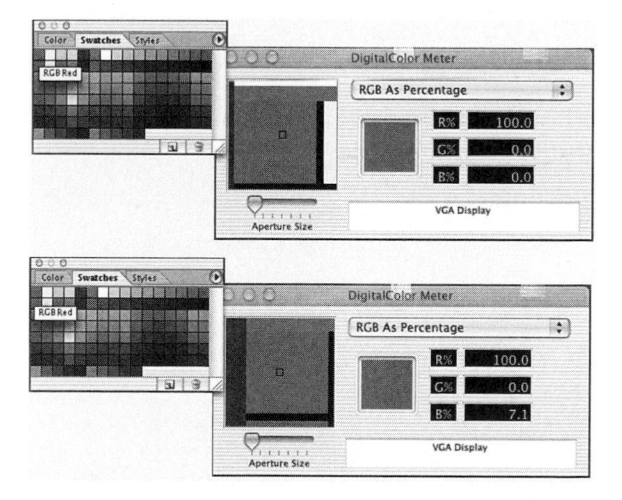


**Figure 6.24**
(Top) With the monitor profile assigned as the working space, the leftmost color swatch's values naturally read as R=100.0, G=0.0, and B=0.0. But when the device-independent Adobe RGB profile is assigned as the working space, the color values become R=100.0, G=0.0, and B=7.1. Comparing these readings (and those for the other swatches) lets you determine how the colors switch when you switch profiles.



The first six swatches should give the following readings: 100/0/0 (RGB Red), 100/100/0 (RGB Yellow), 0/100/0 (RGB Green), 0/100/100 (RGB Cyan), 0/0/100 (RGB Blue), and 100/0/100 (RGB Magenta). The gray swatches in the top and second rows should be close to the appropriate percentage, but more importantly, the amounts of each of the three component colors should be equal.

When you're using your custom monitor profile as the RGB setting, if your readings vary substantially or show a consistent discrepancy, it's a good reason to not use your monitor profile as the working space, because any image you assign your monitor's profile to will be inaccurate.

# WORKING SMARTER WITH SCRIPTING AND ACTIONS

## IN THIS CHAPTER

Both scripts and Actions are recorded series of commands that you can run or play back, respectively, to perform the same (or conditionally similar) steps on additional files. In addition to saving time and making standard production tasks simpler, automation with Actions and scripts can provide a level of precision that might not be possible otherwise—the same steps, with the same settings, performed in the same order, on each file. The two primary reasons for automating tasks in Photoshop, Illustrator, and InDesign are speed and precision.

> Although you'll see the terms *Action* and *script* both used in conjunction with GoLive, that program itself cannot be automated. Rather, you record Actions and write scripts that become part of your Web pages. Like GoLive, Adobe Acrobat 6 uses JavaScript for interactivity rather than automation.

Scripting and Actions help you automate tasks in the Adobe Creative Suite. Scripts are actual programs you write (or record) to perform tasks. Photoshop, Illustrator, and InDesign can use OLE-compatible scripting languages (such as Visual Basic) on Windows computers, AppleScript on Macintosh computers, and the less-powerful JavaScript on both. Scripts not only can perform tasks within a program, they can *call* or *invoke* other programs (accessing the second program and its features) and even work with hardware and the operating system itself.

Actions, in contrast to scripts, are merely a series of recorded steps within the program. They cannot talk to other programs. For example, although an Action can play back a program's Print command, it cannot make changes in the printer's dialog box, whereas a Visual Basic or AppleScript command can make changes to the printer's own settings.

Another important difference between Actions and scripts is logic. Scripts can contain if/then statements that enable the automation to perform different tasks (or the same task differently) if conditions change. Actions, with the exception of ImageReady's new conditional Actions, cannot differentiate among variable conditions—an Action does the same thing to each file upon which you play it, every time.

In this chapter, we'll take a brief look at what scripting can do in the Adobe Creative Suite, some of the resources provided with the Adobe Creative Suite, and additional resources that you can use to become proficient enough with scripting to improve your productivity and add a new level of precision to repetitive tasks.

The chapter also explores, in somewhat greater depth, Actions in Photoshop, ImageReady, and Illustrator. (InDesign uses only scripting, whereas GoLive is not automated.) Because Actions require only a knowledge of the program with which you're working and no knowledge of Visual Basic, AppleScript, or JavaScript, they are considerably more accessible (although far less powerful) than scripts. With Actions, you can automate the vast majority of the repetitive tasks you perform in these three programs.



## SCRIPTING THE ADOBE CREATIVE SUITE

Think of scripting as that studio assistant you can't afford to hire—the one who does all the little tasks, freeing you to be creative and dynamic. No, scripting won't make coffee (yet), but it *will* handle many of the small-but-important tasks that seem to eat up the work day. Create crop marks around the selected objects in InDesign; select each character in Illustrator text and incrementally decrease type size and baseline shift; resize, apply a saved Curves adjustment, sharpen, rotate if necessary, and print in Photoshop.

> ImageReady's conditional Actions are perhaps the next wave, the cross between Actions and scripting. Although they are Actions and, as such, can only work within the program itself, conditional Actions can make some basic decisions based on the specific situation within which they are run.

Scripting can also be used for those jobs not within the scope of Actions. Have you ever wanted to add the name of a file in, say, the lower-left corner, along with your copyright information? And you wanted to do this to an entire folder of images—without losing a night's sleep? What if the images are not the same size or orientation? An Action in Photoshop or Illustrator isn't capable of determining whether an image is portrait or landscape oriented. Scripts, on the other hand, can be written to handle such jobs. A script can get information, evaluate that information and perform calculations, and make decisions based on the information. Actions, on the other hand, are "dumb"—they can perform the same steps and settings with which they were recorded.

## Utilizing Scripting in the Adobe Creative Suite

Each of the scriptable members of the Adobe Creative Suite can be controlled with JavaScript, Visual Basic (Windows), or AppleScript (Mac). Once again, the purpose of this chapter is not to teach programming or scripting languages. Instead, this chapter introduces you to the possibilities and then provides you with resources that enable you to capitalize on those opportunities to improve efficiency and free more time for creativity.

Virtually every aspect of Photoshop, Illustrator, and InDesign can be controlled through scripting. Visual Basic and AppleScript can *call* programs outside of the program within which you're running the script. Running a script in Photoshop could, for example, open Illustrator, find a specific piece of artwork, copy it, switch back to Photoshop, paste the artwork, save the file in a format appropriate for print, open InDesign, add the Photoshop file to a document, save the document, and print the proof. In a nutshell, if *you* can do it using the keyboard and mouse, it can probably be recorded in Visual Basic or AppleScript. And don't overlook the fact that a script can play an Action within Photoshop or Illustrator.

You might consider scripting to be of value only for production environments. However, that's not the case. Any procedure you do more than once is a candidate for scripting. More advanced scripts can be written to handle extremely complex creative tasks as well. (If you use Actions at all, you are most certainly a candidate for scripting.)

## JavaScript, AppleScript, Visual Basic: Which One?

> Remember one key difference between using JavaScript and Visual Basic or AppleScript: JavaScript cannot call or invoke another program—it runs only within the host program.

JavaScript is cross-platform—meaning the same script will perform identically on both Windows and Macintosh versions of your programs. However, a JavaScript must be run from within the program and cannot call another program. AppleScript and Visual Basic are more powerful, can be run from outside a specific program, and can run multiple programs. However, they are both platform specific—an AppleScript cannot be used in Windows, and Visual Basic cannot run on a Macintosh.

Keep in mind that both AppleScripts and Visual Basic scripts can execute a JavaScript, but JavaScripts can't call the others.

Inside Photoshop CS's Scripting Guide folder, you'll also find the ScriptingListener plug-in. When installed, ScriptingListener records most of what you do in Photoshop as JavaScript code in a file at the root level of your hard drive. For Windows, it also creates VBScript code in a separate file. (AppleScripts call the JavaScript.) Install ScriptingListener in Photoshop's Plug-Ins folder *only* when you're actually using it to create scripts. Photoshop might run more slowly with the plug-in installed, and it generates a file on your hard drive that is otherwise not required.

## Scripting Resources Supplied with the Adobe Creative Suite

Each of the scriptable members of the Adobe Creative Suite (Photoshop, Illustrator, InDesign) has some scripts included with the program, as well as additional resources and information either on CD or available through Adobe.com:

- **Photoshop CS**—Under the File, Scripts menu, you'll find a few JavaScripts that can be very handy: Export Layers to Files, Layer Comps to Files, Layer Comps to PDF, and Layer Comps to WPG. Inside the Photoshop folder on your hard drive, you'll find the Scripting Guide folder. In PDF format, you'll see reference guides for scripting in general (105 pages), JavaScript (254 pages), AppleScript (63 pages), and Visual Basic (64 pages). In addition, the folder contains additional prerecorded scripts (23 JavaScript, 18 AppleScript, and 19 Visual Basic). An additional PDF file describes each of the sample scripts.
- **Illustrator CS**—By default, Illustrator CS installs five JavaScripts on your hard drive. The bulk of the scripting support for Illustrator is found on the program CD. Look in the Illustrator Extras, Scripting folder for a wealth of information, including hundreds of pages of reference material in PDF format and dozens of sample scripts and related files.
- **InDesign CS**—The InDesign CS Scripting Guide, found in PDF format on the InDesign CD, is almost 2,000 pages of reference material! This extremely comprehensive document examines the basics of scripting in InDesign, and it includes specific reference sections for JavaScript, AppleScript, and Visual Basic. You'll also find a couple dozen sample scripts on the CD, as well as a PDF guide to the sample scripts.

Remember, too, that resources are available to you at Adobe.com in the Experts Centers for each product. You'll also find assistance and information in the various scripting forums within the product forums of Adobe.com.



## To Learn More About Scripting...

Here are some online resources you can use to learn more about scripting:

- `www.javascript.com`
- `www.javascriptcity.com`

- http://javascript.internet.com/tutorials/
- www.apple.com/applescript/
- www.applescriptsourcebook.com
- www.macscripting.com
- www.scriptweb.com
- http://msdn.microsoft.com/vbasic/
- www.developer.com/net/vb/

The Internet is just one source of information on scripting. Especially if you're new to high-level automation, check out these additional resources:

- *Special Edition Using JavaScript*, Paul McFedries
- *JavaScript Goodies*, Joe Burns and Andree Growney
- *Sams Teach Yourself JavaScript in 24 Hours*, Michael Moncur
- *Sams Teach Yourself JavaScript in 21 Days*, Jonathan Watt, Andrew Watt, Jinjer Simon
- *Sams Teach Yourself Microsoft Visual Basic .NET 2003 in 24 Hours Complete Starter Kit*, James Foxall
- *Sams Teach Yourself Microsoft Visual Basic .NET 2003 in 21 Days*, Steve Holzner
- *Visual Basic .NET Primer Plus*, Jack Purdum

# PHOTOSHOP'S ACTIONS

Photoshop offers an extremely powerful, yet underused, feature for improving your efficiency. It's likely that there are numerous tasks you perform regularly in Photoshop. Automating those tasks with Actions not only saves time but ensures precision by applying the same steps every time.

*Actions* are simply prerecorded steps in Photoshop. You play an Action to repeat those steps on one or more images. Photoshop ships with dozens of Actions, and others are available at minimal cost or free on the Web. The true power of Actions, however, is in recording your own to automate your tasks.

Virtually anything you can do in Photoshop, an Action can do for you. Some Actions are completely automated and can be run while you're away from the computer; other Actions require you to enter specific values for certain procedures. Photoshop also enables you to specify whether to use the values originally recorded with an Action or to pause the Action for you to input new values.

You create, store, organize, and play back Actions by using the Actions palette. You can create *droplets*, which are mini-applications that run Actions when one or more files are dragged onto them. Droplets are available for both Photoshop and ImageReady. You can even run Actions on multiple files sequentially as a *batch*. Batch processing of a folder of files can include subfolders.

## How Actions Work

An Action consists of a series of steps in Photoshop. They are the same steps you normally would use to accomplish the same thing manually. For example, if you want to prepare an image for a page layout program, you might need to change the resolution, sharpen, and change the color mode to CMYK. In this case, here are the three steps you would take:

1. Image, Image Size
2. Filter, Sharpen, Unsharp Mask
3. Image, Mode, CMYK Color

When this process is recorded as an Action, the same three steps are taken when the Action runs.

An Action can record the same settings as those applied when the Action was recorded, or it can pause so that you can input different settings. Commands and paths can be inserted. The use of painting tools, which require dragging the cursor in the image, cannot be recorded, however.

Remember that painting tools can be applied along paths and that paths can be inserted into Actions. You can insert a path and apply a painting tool (or other brush-related tool) along that path.

## The Actions Palette

You use the Actions palette to record, play, and manage Actions. The palette contains three columns and a series of buttons across the bottom. Figure 7.1 shows the first Action of the Default Actions set, installed in the Actions palette when you installed Photoshop.

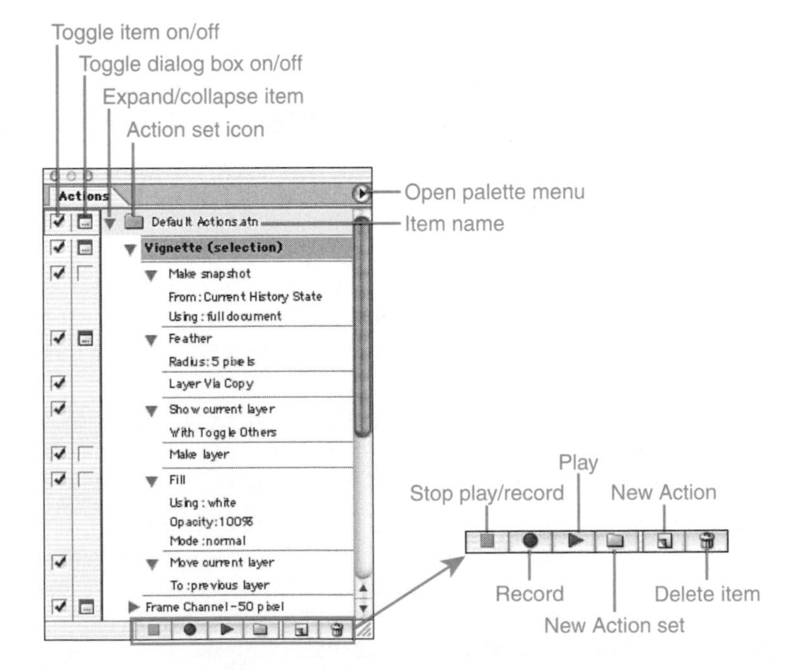


**Figure 7.1**
Click the triangles next to Action sets, Actions, and the individual steps of the Action to expand them, as shown here.

7

## The On/Off Column

You use the first column to toggle items on and off. When a check mark does not appear to the left of an Action set, none of the Actions in the set are available. When the check mark is black, all Actions and each step of each Action are checked. A red arrow indicates that some, but not all, of the Actions or steps are checked. A black check mark next to an Action shows that all of its steps will run when the Action is played. A red check mark lets you know that at least one step will be skipped. The individual steps of an Action either show a black check mark (the step will play) or are blank (the step will be skipped). Use this column primarily to select which steps of an Action to execute when the Action is played. The check marks next to the Actions and Action sets are there to warn you of steps that have been turned off.

## The Modal Control Column

The second column shows an icon of a dialog box, an empty box, or nothing next to each step, Action, or set. These are the *modal* indicators. An icon or an empty box shows that the step (or one or more steps within an Action or set) has user-definable parameters: a dialog box. The Action can play with the options used when the step was recorded (empty), or it can stop at the step and wait for you to change the dialog box and click OK (icon).

Like the first column, the second column is color coded. A black icon indicates that every step that has a dialog box is set to open its dialog box and wait for input. A red icon shows that one or more steps will play with the prerecorded values. An empty box tells you that *all* steps will play with prerecorded values. If there is no icon and no empty box, none of the steps within the Action (or set) are modal.

## The Palette Body

Examine the third column of the Actions palette shown in Figure 7.1:

- The top line is the Action set to which the Action belongs. Default Actions.atn is identifiable as a set by the folder icon. You can click the downward-pointing triangle to hide the contents of the set.
- The second line, indented slightly, is selected and therefore highlighted. It is the Action named "Vignette (selection)." Selection is part of the name (assigned by the person who prepared the Action) to indicate that a selection must be made before running the Action. Clicking the triangle to the left of the name hides or shows the Action's steps.
- Below the Action name are the steps of the Action, indented slightly. They are the actual commands that are executed when you run the Action. Some can be expanded and collapsed with triangles; some steps require a single line in the palette.

Check the color of the arrows and modal icons before playing an Action. They tell you whether the Action will play as originally recorded, with all steps set to run with the original parameters. If an arrow is red, one or more steps will be skipped. If a modal icon is red or black, one or more dialog boxes will open while the Action is playing.

- The last item visible in the Actions palette is another Action, named "Frame Channel-50 pixel." Note that it is aligned with the Action "Vignette (selection)," showing that it is also a member of the Default Actions set.

## The Actions Palette Buttons

Use the six buttons across the bottom of the Actions palette to create, record, play, and delete Actions. All these capabilities are duplicated by commands in the Actions palette menu:

- The leftmost button's icon is a simple square. This symbol has been used for "stop" buttons on tape recorders, VCRs, CD players, and other electronic devices for decades. When an Action is being recorded or played, click this icon to stop it.
- The Record button is also a replica of that used on various devices for a generation. Click the button to record or rerecord a step in the selected Action.
- The Play button, which should also look familiar, plays the selected Action on the active document. The Action will execute according to the check marks in the first two columns next to each step.
- Create new sets of Actions by using the button with the folder icon. You can move Actions from set to set by dragging them within the Actions palette.
- When you click the New Action button, a dialog box opens in which you can name the new Action and assign it to a function key for quick-and-easy play. Duplicate an Action set, an Action, or a step by dragging it to the button.
- Action sets, Actions, and individual steps can be deleted by using the button with the trash icon. You can select multiple items by Shift-clicking or (Command)-clicking) [Ctrl]-clicking them in the palette, and then you can delete them by clicking the button. Alternatively, you can drag items to the button to delete them.

# The Actions Palette Menu

The Actions palette's menu contains a variety of commands for creating, using, and managing Actions. Commands specific to recording and playing Actions are discussed in the appropriate sections of this chapter.

Several of the palette's menu commands can be considered "palette maintenance" commands. You can use the menu to remove all Action sets and Actions (Clear All Actions), return the palette to its default content (Reset Actions), add Action sets or Actions to the palette (Load Actions), exchange the current content for a different set of Actions (Replace Actions), and save a set of Actions so that it can be reloaded at a later time (Save Actions).

> Recording actions and creating Action sets in the palette doesn't preserve them. To ensure that you won't accidentally delete your custom Actions by resetting the palette, use the Save Actions command.

You can save Actions as text files and view or print them. Select a set of Actions, or create a new set and copy one or more Actions into it. Hold down the (Option-Command) [Alt+Ctrl] keys and select Save Actions from the Actions palette menu. A text file (.txt extension) will be generated. (Remember that you can only use the Save Actions command with sets of Actions, not individual Actions.)

## Button Mode

The Actions palette can also be displayed in Button Mode (see Figure 7.2). In this configuration, you play an Action by clicking it. Note that the palette shows no buttons for recording Actions—this mode is for playing Actions only. In fact, when in Button Mode, the Actions palette's menu commands related to creating, recording, and even playing are grayed out.

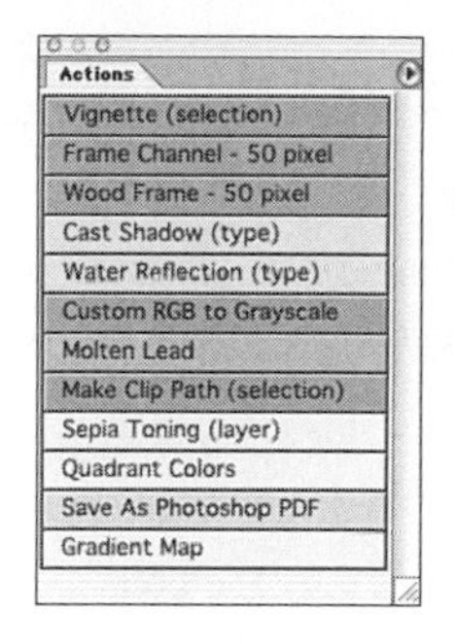


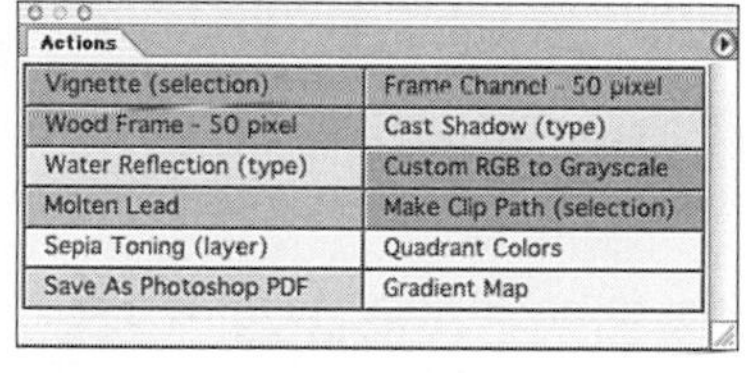


**Figure 7.2**
Depending on the size and shape of the palette, Button Mode can display Actions in one column or multiple columns.

Actions are sorted in the palette according to their order, not by assigned color. (An Action's color can be assigned when recorded or through the palette's menu command Action Options.) Actions sets are ignored in Button Mode.

*If you're running in Button Mode and the Actions are misbehaving, see "Double-Check" in the "Mastering the Adobe Creative Suite" section at the end of this chapter.*

Before switching to Button Mode, you can rearrange actions by dragging them up and down in the Actions palette.

# WORKING WITH ACTIONS IN PHOTOSHOP

An Action can be played on a selection, an image, or even a folder filled with images (using the Batch command). The Action can run while you're away from the computer—even at home, fast asleep—or you can sit at the keyboard and make changes to how the Action is applied to each image.

**Caution**

When you play an Action by clicking it in Button Mode, it plays as last configured. Steps that are unchecked do not play, and modal controls are shown or not shown as last set. Button Mode gives no indication if one or more steps of an Action will not play.

## Running an Action

In a nutshell, you select the Action in the Actions palette and click the Play button at the bottom of the palette. Some

Actions require that a selection be made first to identify a part of the image with which to work. Other Actions may require that a type layer be available or that an image meet minimum or maximum size requirements. Color mode can also be a factor, especially when an Action applies a filter or uses an Adjustment command.

The Actions palette menu includes the Playback Options command. You can choose from three "speeds" at which the Action can run:

> Because Actions typically execute a number of steps, taking a snapshot in the History palette beforehand is a great idea. Should the Action not produce the expected results, you've got a one-click Undo.

- **Accelerated**—This is the "normal" speed. The Action runs as fast as it can, moving through each step in sequence. It stops for modal dialog boxes and preprogrammed stops.
- **Step by Step**—After each step executes, the screen is completely redrawn, and then the Action continues. This option is somewhat slower, but it does give you the opportunity to stop the Action if something drastically unexpected appears.
- **Pause For**—You can have the Action play back in steps, pausing for a specified period, between 1 and 60 seconds, before executing the following step. The screen is updated after each step.

If an audio annotation has been recorded with the Action, you have the option of pausing until the message is completed or continuing with the Action while you listen.

An icon in the column immediately to the left of a step's name in the Actions palette indicates that it is modal, and a dialog box will open. Photoshop waits until you click OK before continuing with the Action. If you click Cancel, the Action stops at that step and waits for you to again click the Play button.

To play a single step of an Action, select that step in the palette and (Command)-click [Ctrl]-click the Play button. Alternatively, you can press (Command) [Ctrl] and double-click the step in the palette.

## Loading Actions

The Actions palette menu's bottom section shows a list of all Action sets in the Photoshop Actions folder. By default, Photoshop installs several sets of Actions. You can add your own sets to the list by placing them in the folder. You'll find the Photoshop Actions folder inside the Presets folder, within the Adobe Photoshop CS folder.

You can load sets of Actions not located in the Photoshop Actions folder into the palette by using the palette's menu command Load Actions. In the dialog box, navigate to the Actions, select them, and click Load. They will appear at the bottom of the Actions palette, ready to be played.

The palette menu also offers the commands Clear All Actions (which empties the palette), Reset Actions (which restores the palette to its default content), Replace Actions (which clears the current content and adds the selected set), and Save Actions (which saves the selected Actions set).

> Remember that you risk losing your custom Actions until you use the Save Actions command. If Photoshop needs to be reinstalled, or if you use the Clear Actions or Reset Actions command, any unsaved Action sets will be lost.

## Batching It

A folder full of files can have the same Action applied to it with one command. Using the command File, Automate, Batch opens the Batch dialog box shown in Figure 7.3.

You select a number of settings in the Batch dialog box:

- The set that is currently selected in the Actions palette appears; however, you can select another from the Set pop-up menu. If no selection is currently in the Actions palette, the first set in the palette is shown.
- The Action is the one currently selected. If no Action is currently selected, the first Action in the selected set is shown. Any other Action in that set can be selected from the Action pop-up menu.

> Keep a copy of your custom Action sets (as well as custom and third-party styles, tool presets, swatches, and so on) stored *outside* your Photoshop folder. That helps prevent accidental loss, should you ever need to reinstall Photoshop. Also, it's a good idea to back up your custom elements to CD or an external disk, too.

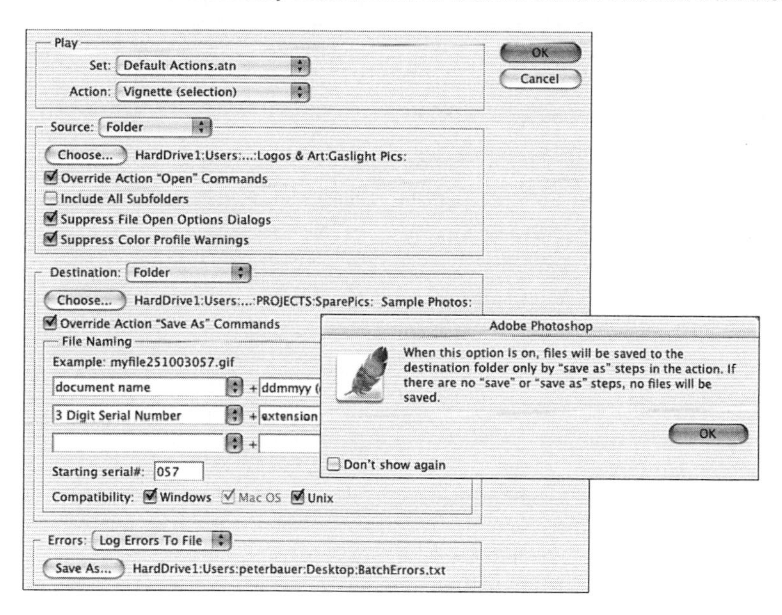


**Figure 7.3**
Shown to the right of the Batch dialog box is the message that appears when you check or uncheck the option Override Action "Save As" Commands.

- The Batch command needs to know which files are to be modified. You can make the selection by using the Choose button in the Source section. In the dialog box, navigate to and select the folder containing the images you want to modify.
- The Override Action "Open" Commands option ignores any commands within the Action that call for opening a file. When a folder is selected, the files inside are automatically opened by Batch.
- If the source folder includes subfolders, the Include All Subfolders option enables you to decide whether to include their contents.

- The Suppress File Open Options Dialogs option, new in Photoshop CS, is designed for use with images in the Raw format. The images will open with the default settings for the file rather than opening with the Camera Raw or Photoshop Raw Options dialog box. When the option is not selected, the Action will pause upon opening a Raw file, waiting until you click the OK button in the dialog box.
- The Suppress Color Profile Warnings option is especially useful if you'll be away from your computer when the Action is run. If your color management policies are set to notify you of profile mismatches, this option prevents those warnings from stopping the Batch command. When this option is not selected, any warning stays onscreen (and no work will get done) until you click OK. If your color management policies are *not* set to warn you of mismatches, this option is unnecessary. (The policies are set in the Color Settings dialog box.)
- The Destination pop-up menu offers three choices. None leaves the altered files open in Photoshop. Save and Close replaces the original files with the modified versions. Folder (refer to Figure 7.3) enables you to choose a location for the modified files. This way, you can avoid overwriting the originals.
- When you select Folder as the Destination option, you can choose to override any Save As commands that have been written into the Action. This option ensures that the file is saved to the folder specified in Batch, rather than that specified in the Action.
- The six File Naming fields can be used in combination to create unique names for files when Folder is selected in the Destination pop-up menu. The document's original name, a one-to-four-digit serial number, a serial letter, the date (in a variety of formats), and the file extension are all possibilities. The document name and extension can be in uppercase or lowercase letters, and the document name can have initial uppercase letters for each word.

You can also enter text into one or more fields for inclusion in the new files' names. Remember, however, that at least one of the fields must change from file to file, so you must include the original document name or a serial number or letter.

**Caution**

Be aware that *all* Open commands are overridden by the Override Action "Open" Commands option. If an Action requires that a second file be opened to complete its task, that command, too, is ignored. As an example, consider an Action designed to open one file, open a second file, select all and copy from the second file, return to the first, and then paste. If the Override Action "Open" Commands option is selected, this Action will fail because it cannot open the second file.

Aliases (Macintosh) or shortcuts (Windows) to other folders are considered subfolders by Batch. You can use them to process multiple folders with a single Batch command.

It's a good idea to select Folder for Destination whenever possible. After verifying that all went well with the Batch command, you can delete the original folder. But should the Batch operation not work the way you wanted it to, you'll still have the original images, undamaged.

- Another addition to the Batch dialog box in Photoshop CS is the Starting serial# field. When one of the naming fields is set to add a serial number, this field can be used to specify the first number. Rather than starting with 1, you could, for example, start with 57.

If an Action contains a Save As command that is not overridden and it is run on a folder as a Batch command, each file is saved with the name and location specified in the Action—in other words, each file overwrites the preceding file. When the Batch command is done, you'll have only one file.

- The Compatibility options ensure that the filename will be acceptable on the selected platform(s). If the original filename includes spaces or forbidden characters (characters not allowed in filenames in some operating systems), they are deleted or replaced with dashes or underscores. The Mac OS does not allow the colon (:) in filenames and is not case sensitive (uppercase and lowercase letters are seen as the same letter).

  Windows filenames can be up to 256 characters long, and they are not case sensitive. Several characters cannot be used in filenames: forward and back slashes, colons, asterisks, question marks, quotation marks, left and right angle brackets, and vertical slashes. In order, these characters are as follows:

  / \ : * ? " < > |

  Unix filenames can be 256 characters long, cannot use the slash character (/), and are case sensitive.

- Error messages can be handled in one of two ways: Photoshop can halt the batch processing until you've given it the okay to continue after an error, or you can create a text file with the details. If you choose the latter approach, you must select a name and location for the log file before you start the batch.

*Do you have an Action that stops partway through for no apparent reason? See "Unscheduled Halt" in the "Mastering the Adobe Creative Suite" section at the end of this chapter.*

## Using Batch to Change File Formats

The Batch command saves files in their original format, whether the Destination field is set to Save and Close or to Folder. To automate a change of file format, you must include three steps:

- When recording the Action, include a Save As command followed by a Close (Don't Save) command.
- In the Actions palette, check to make sure that the modal column is not checked next to the Save As command or the Close command.
- In the Batch dialog box, choose Folder in the Destination pop-up menu and then select the Override Action "Save As" Commands check box.

The end result will be copies of the original images in the file format specified in the Action. The original files will be unchanged.

Depending on the file format selected for the Save As command, you might need to flatten the file and delete alpha or spot channels. Record these steps in the Action before the Save As command.

## Actions as Droplets in Photoshop and ImageReady

Consider a *droplet* to be an Action packaged in an application. Instead of opening a document in Photoshop to play an Action on it, you can drag the file to the droplet's icon, and the Action is executed automatically. If Photoshop is not running, it is started so that the Action can run.

Not all Actions are appropriate for droplets. If, for example, an Action requires an active selection to run, it cannot be executed unless the file is already open in Photoshop. In such cases, simply playing the Action from the Actions palette is required.

You convert Actions to droplets by using Photoshop's menu command File, Automate, Create Droplet. The Create Droplet dialog box is shown in Figure 7.4.

Use the Save Droplet In section of the dialog box to name the droplet and choose a location. Select the Action from which the droplet will be created in the Play section. If the Action needs to open another file to execute a step—for example, to copy from one image and paste into another—do not override Open commands. You also have the option of including any subfolders when a droplet is played on a folder. If you'll be running the droplet while away from your computer, make sure you suppress color warnings; otherwise, you might return to find a warning showing onscreen and no files processed.

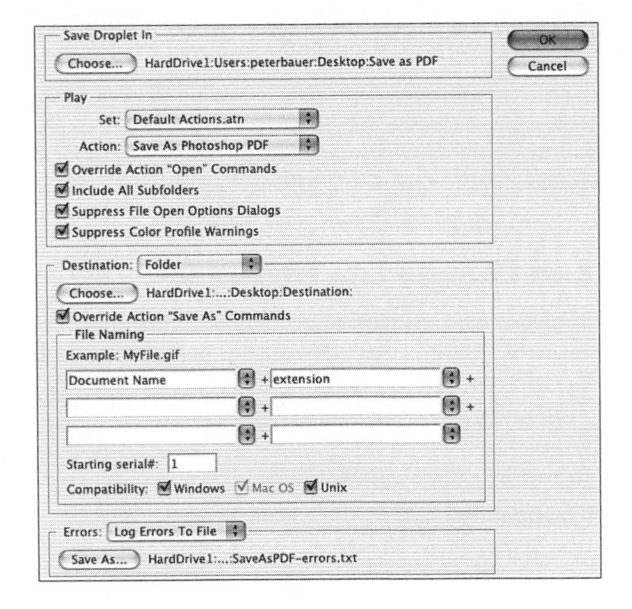


Figure 7.4
The Destination section of the dialog box looks familiar to anyone who uses the Batch command or the File Browser's Batch Rename command.

What Photoshop does with the files processed by the droplet is determined in the Destination section of the dialog box. You can elect to leave the files open (None), save the changes and close each file (Save and Close), or save the files to a new location (Folder). When Folder is selected, you have access to the options shown in Figure 7.4.

> If a droplet is created with the option to include subfolders, it plays its Action on all files in the folder and the subfolders. You can also include aliases or shortcuts to other folders.

You can also create droplets in ImageReady. Such droplets automatically run the Action and apply any recorded optimization settings to any files dragged onto them. You can also optimize folders of images by dragging them onto a droplet.

> If an ImageReady Action doesn't include a Set Optimization step, any droplet created from the Action uses whatever optimization settings are current in ImageReady when the droplet is used.

Creating a droplet from ImageReady can be as simple as dragging the Action from ImageReady's Actions palette to the desktop. Alternatively, you can choose the Actions palette menu command Create Droplet. The only options are location and name.

You can also create ImageReady droplets directly from the Optimization palette. Instead of executing an Action, such droplets only apply optimization settings. Set the optimization parameters and then either drag the Optimization palette's Droplet icon to the desktop or click the Droplet icon in the upper-right corner of the Optimization palette, shown in Figure 7.5.

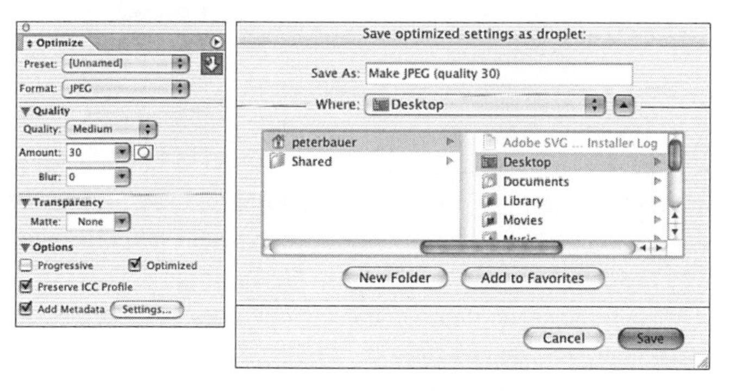


**Figure 7.5**
ImageReady suggests an appropriate name for the droplet based on the settings selected. You can, of course, choose a different name and specify a location.

# CREATING CUSTOM ACTIONS IN PHOTOSHOP

The true power of Actions comes through when you record them yourself. Because your custom Actions are tailored to your needs and your work, they are best suited to improving your productivity.

## Recording a New Action

An Action must belong to a set. Actions are not allowed to float free in the Actions palette. You can assign an Action to an existing set by clicking the set in the Actions palette. Alternatively, you can create a new set by using the Create New Set button at the bottom of the Actions palette or the

New Set command from the palette's menu. Both open the New Set dialog box (see Figure 7.6), in which you can give the set a name.

**Figure 7.6**
The only option available for Action sets is the name, which can also be changed by double-clicking it in the Actions palette.

Clicking the New Action button (or using the New Action command from the palette menu) opens the dialog box shown in Figure 7.7.

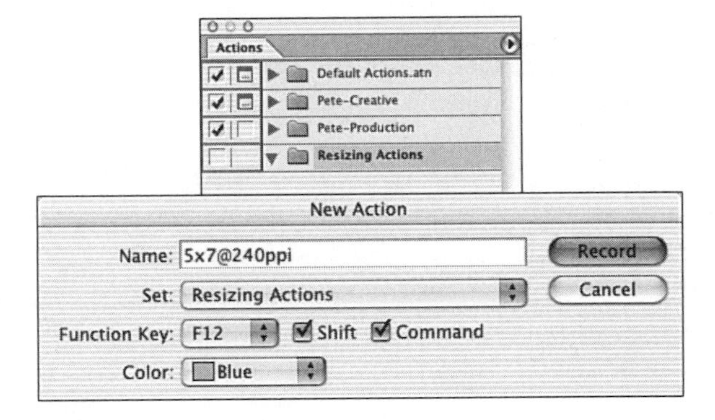


**Figure 7.7**
You can change your mind and assign the Action to a different set right in the dialog box.

In addition to giving the new Action a name, you can assign it to a function key, with or without modifier keys. Pressing the assigned key combination executes the Action, even if the palette is hidden. Any color assigned to the Action is used only in Button Mode.

After you click the Record button, virtually every move you make in Photoshop becomes part of the Action. You can pause the recording at any time by clicking the Stop button or using the Stop Recording command from the palette menu. To continue, click the Record button. The Record button gives a visual indicator when an Action is actually being created.

The New Action and New Set commands are not grayed out while recording an Action. You can, in fact, create new sets and Actions while recording an Action. You can even work in the Actions palette, deleting Actions and sets, while recording. These activities are not recorded as steps in the current Action.

> Remember that Photoshop executes commands while you're recording. For that reason, it's best to work on a copy of your file when recording an Action.

The actual steps that can be recorded in an Action fall into several categories: recordable commands and tools, non-recordable commands and tools, inserted paths, and stops. In addition, you can decide whether a command will use the settings with which it was recorded or pause while you enter new settings (modal commands).

After you've gone through all the steps you want in the Action, simply click the Stop button at the bottom of the palette or use the Stop Recording menu command. It is usually a good idea, especially with more complicated Actions, to make another copy of the original file and test the Action.

# What Can and Can't Be Recorded

Generally speaking, any tool that relies on cursor movement cannot be recorded in an Action, including the Move tool and the painting, toning, healing, and eraser tools. The Zoom and Hand tools cannot be recorded, nor can the pen tools. You can, however, record options for many tools, including brushes.

Photoshop's other tools are recordable, as are these palettes: Actions, Channels, Color, History, Layers, Paths, Styles, and Swatches.

## Recording Menu Commands

Most menu commands can be recorded in an Action. There are, however, two ways to do so. If, while recording, you select a menu command, enter values in any dialog box, and click OK, the Action is recorded with *those* values. You can record the Action without assigning any value (and without changing the current image while recording). From the palette's menu, choose Insert Menu Item. With the dialog box open (see Figure 7.8), move the cursor to select the desired command. After selecting the command, click OK to close the dialog box.

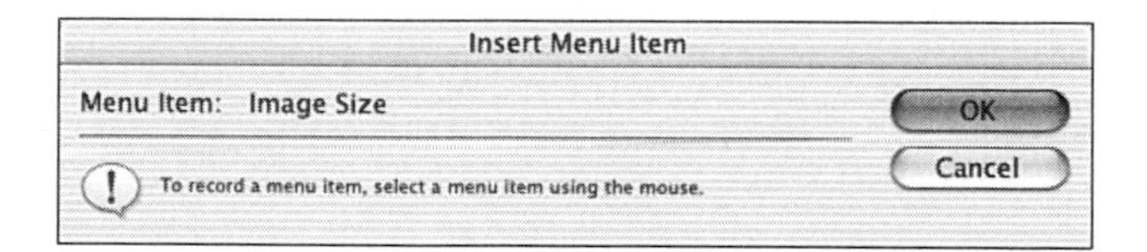


Figure 7.8
This dialog box remains open while you mouse to the command that you want to record in the Action.

When the Action is played back, nonmodal commands are executed immediately. If the command is modal, it doesn't execute until you approve the values in the dialog box by clicking OK. Remember that you cannot disable the modal control for an inserted command—when you play the Action, the dialog box *will* open and wait for you to click OK, whether you're sitting at your computer or not.

## Inserting Paths

Although the Pen tool cannot be recorded, the shape tools can, and you can save a custom shape to be added in an Action. You can also insert paths into an Action. The path must already be available in the Paths palette while the Action is recorded. Select the path in the Paths palette and then choose Insert Path from the Actions palette menu. When the Action is played back, the path is added as a work path. If you need to retain the path in the image, make sure to also record a Save Path command from the Paths palette menu.

In Figure 7.9, you can see how the Action records a rather simple path.

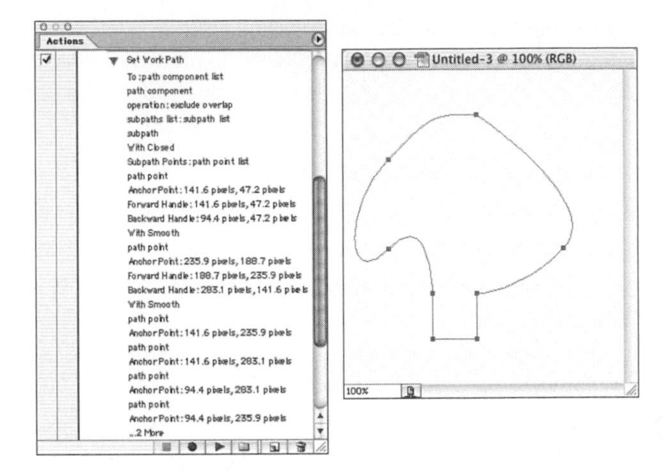


**Figure 7.9**
Only the first six anchor points (corner or smooth) are listed when a path is recorded in an Action, although all points are recorded. Coordinates for anchor points and direction points for smooth anchor points are specified from the upper-left corner of the image.

## Inserting a Pause for Playback

When an Action is played back, you can force it to stop and display a message. Use the Actions palette menu command Insert Stop at any point in the recording process. You type a message to be displayed in the Message window of the Record Stop dialog box (see Figure 7.10).

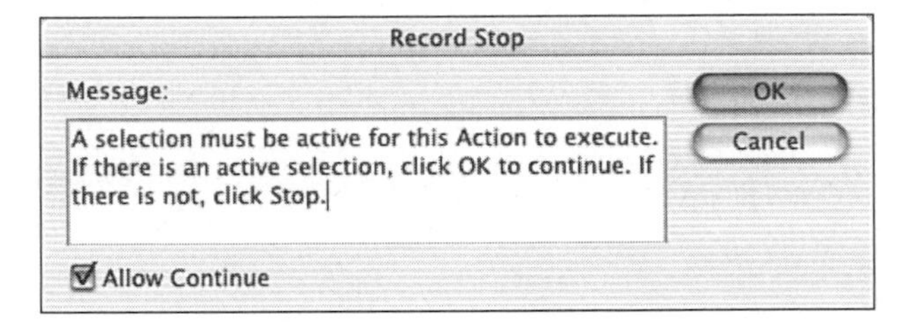


**Figure 7.10**
The message can be up to 255 characters (and spaces) long.

The Allow Continue option determines what buttons will be available in the message box when the Action is played. When Allow Continue is selected, the box contains two buttons: Stop and Continue (see Figure 7.11). When the option is not selected, only one button is available.

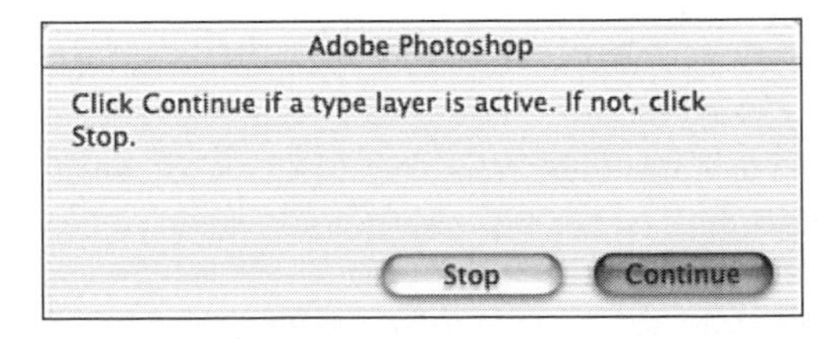


**Figure 7.11**
The best stops are recorded with explicit instructions.

*Does the Action seem to run right past your stop? See "Stop Sign" in the "Mastering the Adobe Creative Suite" section at the end of this chapter.*

**Caution**

Be aware that adding complex paths (whether a custom shape or a work path) to an Action can tax the memory assigned to Photoshop.

## Editing an Existing Action

You can perform seven basic types of editing on an existing Action:

- **Delete a step**—Select the step in the Actions palette and either drag it to the trash icon or click the icon.
- **Rerecord a step**—Double-click the step, perform the task as you want it, and then click Stop.
- **Add a step**—Click the step in the Action immediately above where you want the new step(s) and then click the Record button. When you've finished adding to the Action, click the Stop button.
- **Rearrange the order of steps**—Drag a step from one spot in the Action to another.
- **Duplicate a step**—(Option)-drag [Alt]-drag a step from one location to another in the Action, drag a step to the New Action button, or use the Actions palette menu command Duplicate.
- **Turn a step off (or on)**—Click in the left column of the Actions palette next to the step. When the check mark is visible, the step runs when the Action is played. If there is no check mark, that step is skipped when the Action is played.
- **Change the modal setting**—The second column of the Actions palette determines whether the dialog box for a modal command or tool shows when the Action is played. If the icon is visible next to a step, the Action stops at that step, shows the dialog box, and waits for you to change options and click OK. If there is an empty box in the column, the Action plays using the values recorded in the step. If the icon is grayed out, the step was added with the command Insert Menu Command, and the dialog box will always show. If there is neither an icon nor an empty box in that column, the step is nonmodal.

## Sources of Actions

In addition to the Default Actions set loaded in the Actions palette, six other Photoshop-standard Action sets are immediately available. You can load any of them by selecting the set from the bottom of the Actions palette menu. The new Actions are added to the bottom of the palette.

Actions are also available, commercially and free, from a wide variety of sources on the Internet. ActionFX (`www.actionfx.com`) is an excellent source of useful, practical, and fun Actions. You'll also find a wide variety of Actions and more at the Adobe Studio site (`www.studio.adobe.com`).

You can also save Action sets and exchange them with other Photoshop users. Make sure that you attach the .atn extension to the filename when saving. To save Actions, follow these steps:

1. Select the Action set in the Actions palette. Remember that only Action sets, not individual Actions or steps, can be saved. To save a single Action, create a new set, (Option)-drag [Alt]-drag the Action into the set to copy it, and then save the new set.

> You can drag a step from one Action to another. In fact, you can (Option)-drag [Alt]-drag to *copy* a step from one Action to another, and you can Shift-click to select multiple steps to copy, move, or delete.

2. With the set selected, choose Save Actions from the Actions palette menu. If the command is grayed out, it's likely that an Action or a step, rather than an Action set, is selected in the palette.
3. In the Save dialog box, specify a name and location for the saved Action set. Include the .atn file extension in the filename.

# PHOTOSHOP'S AUTOMATE COMMANDS

The commands found in the File, Automate submenu don't do anything that you can't do manually in Photoshop. They simply do it faster and more efficiently (although sometimes not as flexibly as you might like).

## Batch and Create Droplet

The Batch command is used to run an Action on a folder of images. Instead of opening each image individually and running the Action, you use the Batch command to streamline the process.

As you learned earlier, droplets are mini-applications that open Photoshop and run an Action. You activate a droplet by dragging a file or folder onto it.

## PDF Presentation

Photoshop CS includes a new feature that enables you to create a multipage PDF file or an onscreen presentation that can be played back in Adobe Reader 6 (or the earlier versions, called Acrobat Reader). You select a series of images in the PDF Presentation dialog box (see Figure 7.12), choose to create a presentation or a multipage PDF, and decide whether you want to open Acrobat (or Reader) and see the finished product right away. If you're creating a presentation, you specify how long you want each slide to appear (or uncheck the Advance Every box for manual slide switching), whether you want the slideshow to play once or repeat, and select a transition for moving from slide to slide.

When a presentation is opened in Reader or Acrobat, the program automatically goes into full-screen mode, hides the program interface, and surrounds each slide with a plain black background. Slides can be advanced manually with the (Return) [Enter] key, and a slideshow can be halted with the Esc key.

When saving a PDF presentation, choose JPEG as the compression method rather than ZIP to enable additional editing in Acrobat 6 or Adobe Reader (see Figure 7.13).

**Caution**

If a PDF presentation will (or may) be viewed in Acrobat Reader 5 or earlier, do *not* include 16-bit images. Although they can be shown in Adobe Reader 6, 16-bit images will generate an error message in the earlier versions.

**Caution**

PDF Presentation doesn't offer the option of suppressing color profile warnings. If you plan on creating a PDF presentation while away from your computer, first go to Color Settings and uncheck the profile mismatch warning options. Remember, too, that PDF Presentation will not suppress File Open option dialog boxes for Raw images.

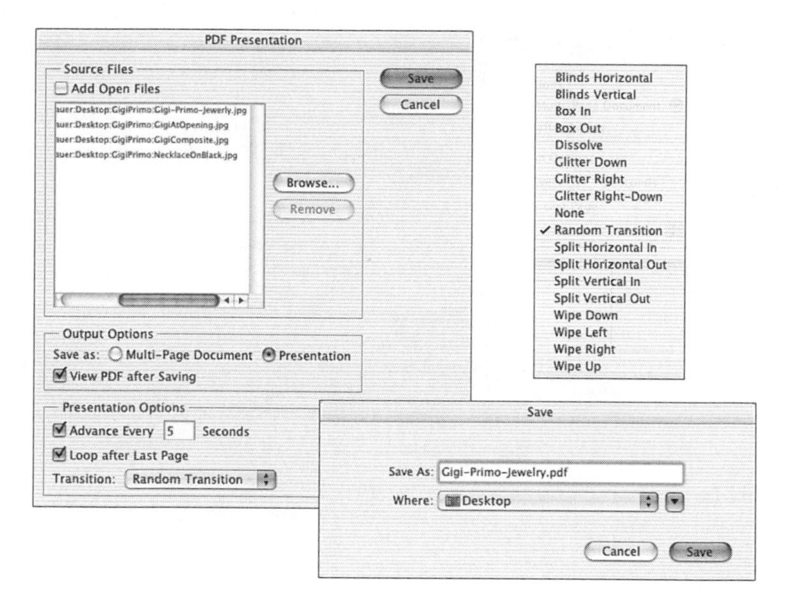


Figure 7.12
After clicking Save, you'll select a name and location for the presentation or multipage PDF document. The slide transitions available in PDF Presentation are shown to the upper right.

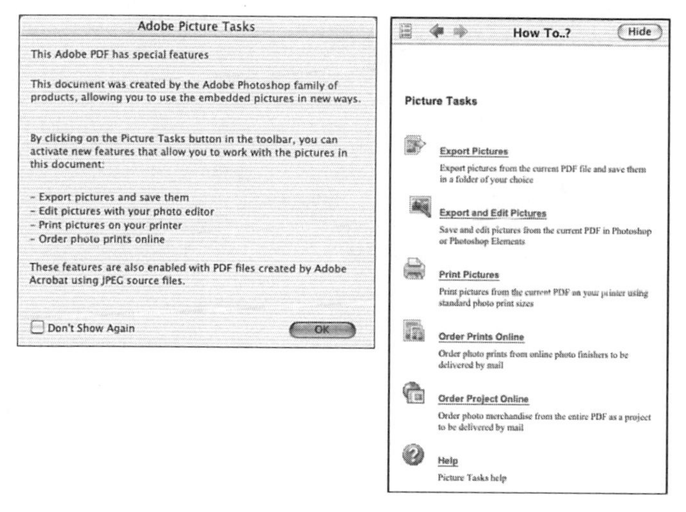


Figure 7.13
The message on the left and the How To palette are features of Adobe Acrobat 6. Acrobat's Picture Tasks are not available if you create the PDF presentation using ZIP compression.

Keep in mind that saving the presentation with PDF password security can prevent the presentation from being viewed (Password Required to Open Document) or can place restrictions on the Acrobat Picture Tasks (see Figure 7.14).

## Conditional Mode Change

This command is designed to be recorded in an Action to prevent error messages while using the Batch command. When an Action changes a color mode or contains a step that can be run only in certain color modes, Conditional Mode Change should be included. If, for example, you record an Action that relies on a specific channel and apply it to a folder of images that are not of the same color mode, an error message appears when the color channel isn't found (see Figure 7.15).

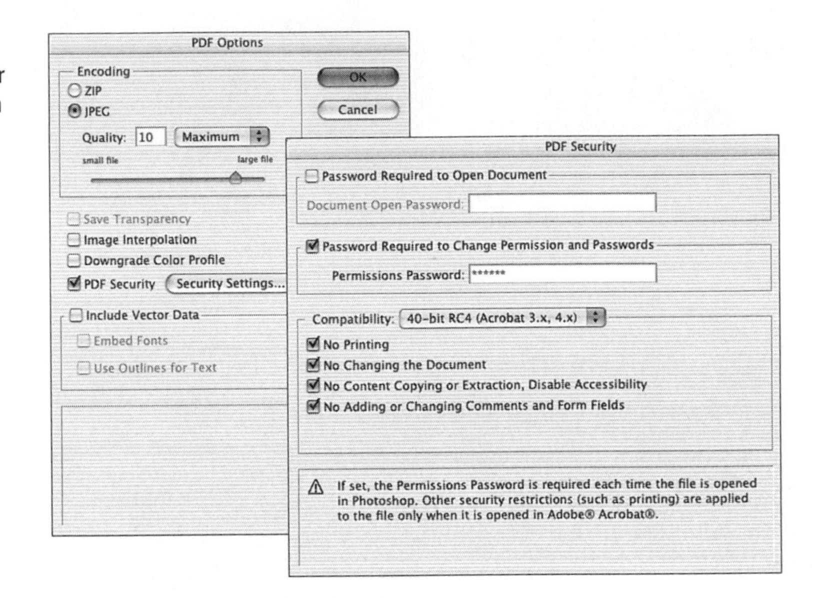


Figure 7.14
Remember that restrictions other than Password Required to Open Document apply only to Acrobat and Acrobat Reader. When the presentation is opened in Photoshop, printing and editing are available, regardless of PDF security settings.

Figure 7.15
The Action requires the presence of a channel named Blue, but the image is CMYK. An error message stops the Batch process.

By using the Conditional Mode Change command, you indicate that all images processed by the Action will be changed to the appropriate color mode. You select the color mode to which you want to convert the images, and you designate which color modes to convert *from* (see Figure 7.16).

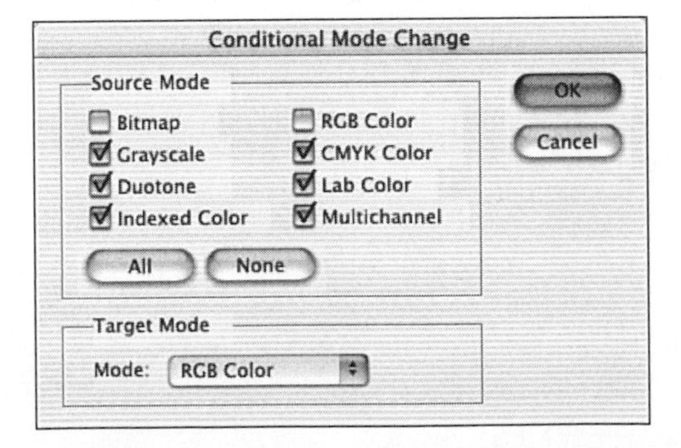


Figure 7.16
If this command had been recorded in the Action before the step shown in Figure 7.15, the image would have been converted to RGB mode and the Batch command would not have aborted.

## Contact Sheet II

You can create pages of thumbnail images with captions by using Contact Sheet II. Use the dialog box shown in Figure 7.17 to select the source folder of images, describe the page on which the thumbnails will be placed, specify the layout, and add captions from the filenames, if desired.

If you select the Include All Subfolders check box, you can place aliases of or shortcuts to additional folders in the designated source folder.

Contact Sheet II dynamically resizes the thumbnail dimensions to allow adequate space for captions, if that option is selected. As you increase the font size, the thumbnail size shrinks.

**Caution**

Converting from Bitmap to a color mode requires that Conditional Mode Change first convert the image to Grayscale and then to RGB. The conversion to Grayscale is modal and requires that you be at the computer to click OK, even if the modal icon is not visible next to the step in the Actions palette.

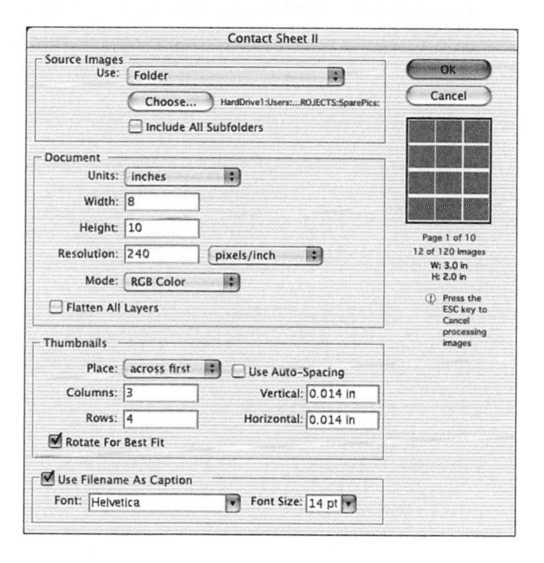


**Figure 7.17**
Remember that the document size should be the printable area of your page, not the paper size.

This command generates as many documents as needed to include all images in the designated folder and subfolders. The pages are not saved, nor are they automatically printed. However, Contact Sheet II can be recorded in an Action that saves and closes each page of thumbnails.

Photoshop CS adds a few new features to the Contact Sheet II dialog box. In the Thumbnails section, note the option Rotate for Best Fit. This option ensures that all images are oriented to either landscape or portrait, depending on the layout of the page. Although this gives you a better fit, it does mean that some images may be sideways on the page.

Also different in this release is the option to specify the vertical and horizontal spacing between images. Generally, you'll want to use auto-spacing, but you can tweak the spacing somewhat, changing the size of the images in the process (as long as you respect the selected document size).

Because Contact Sheet II must open each image, you can speed things up a bit by setting the number of History states very low (in the General preferences) and electing not to create an initial snapshot (in the History palette options).

Contact Sheet II now displays a summary to the right, showing how many images will be processed, how many pages will be created, and how large each image will be. Another welcome change is the ability to interrupt Contact Sheet II as it processes images. The Esc key shuts it down, preventing wasted time if you change your mind while the feature is running.

## Fit Image

The Fit Image command is comparable to using the Image, Image Size command to resample an image. Use the Fit Image command to quickly and easily make images fit a specific pixel dimension, especially for Web sites. The dialog box is extremely simple, offering only Width and Height fields. You enter the dimension within which the image must fit and click OK. Photoshop resamples the image (using the resampling algorithm specified in the Preferences), constraining proportions, to meet that specified dimension. For example, if an image is 3,000×2,000 pixels and you enter 150 pixels for the width, the Fit Image dialog box retains 2,000 pixels for the height, but when you click OK, the image is resized to 150×100 pixels. You can also upsample with Fit Image.

## Multi-Page PDF to PSD

Photoshop's Open command can handle only one PDF page at a time. The Multi-Page PDF to PSD command automatically creates a series of PSD files from a multipage PDF document. In the dialog box shown in Figure 7.18, you select the original document, determine which pages to translate, select the resolution and color mode for the resulting Photoshop files, and select a destination folder.

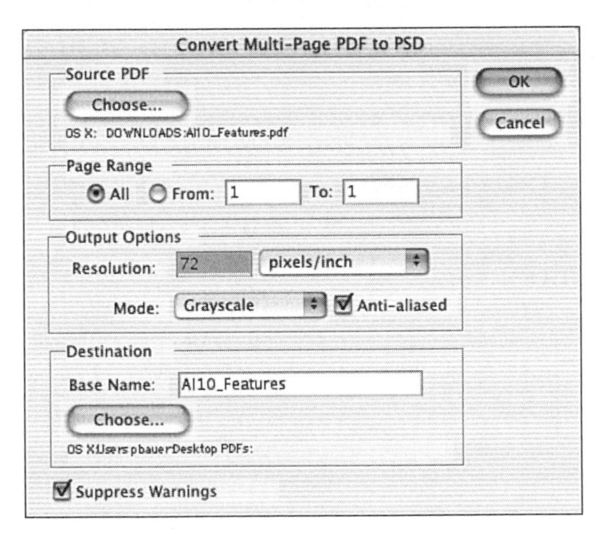


Figure 7.18
Use the Base Name field to create the filename for the resulting Photoshop files. A four-digit sequential number is added to the base name for each PSD file.

## Picture Package

Picture Package is improved again in Photoshop CS, and quite a bit more customizable. Use this command to place multiple images on a single sheet for printing. You can add multiple copies of a single image or copies of various images from a folder. The dialog box shown in Figure 7.19 gives you the choice of three paper sizes: 8×10, 10×16, and 11×17 inches. The resulting document can be of any resolution, and the color mode can be RGB, CMYK, Grayscale, or Lab. The document can also be flattened if desired.

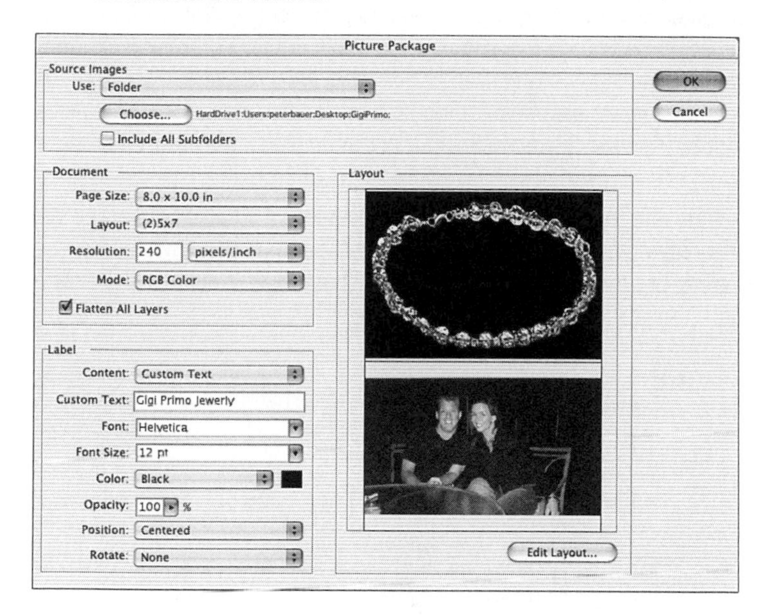


**Figure 7.19**
In the Use pop-up menu, choose Frontmost Document, File, or Folder for the source image or images.

Picture Package offers the option of adding text or a caption to the images, with a choice of position and rotation. You can enter custom text, use the filename, or have Photoshop access the File Info for the copyright, caption, credits, or title data saved with the image.

New to Picture Package is the Edit Layout button. Use the Picture Package Edit Layout window to create custom Picture Package layouts (see Figure 7.20).

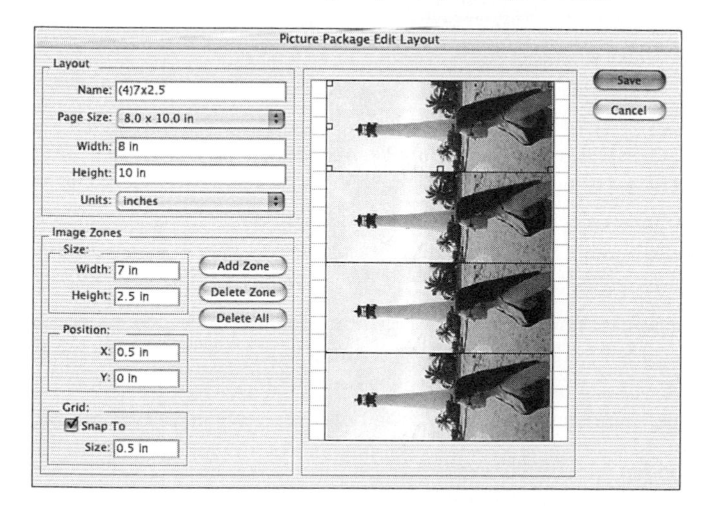


**Figure 7.20**
Use the bounding box handles (shown at top) or enter sizes numerically for each zone.

## Web Photo Gallery

Although Photoshop is an image-editing program, it does offer support for the Web. The primary examples are, of course, ImageReady and Save for Web. Both of these are also graphic-creation tools. Photoshop does offer one feature aimed at creating Web *pages*. Web Photo Gallery can create an entire Web site, ready for posting to your host server. Keep in mind, however, that this is a very basic capability, and you won't be creating any award-winning ecommerce sites with Web Photo Gallery.

Aimed at assisting photographers and digital artists in posting examples of their work on the Web, Web Photo Gallery takes folders filled with images and creates Web pages in which they are displayed. A simple dialog box gives you a number of variations, but limited control, over the final product (see Figure 7.21).

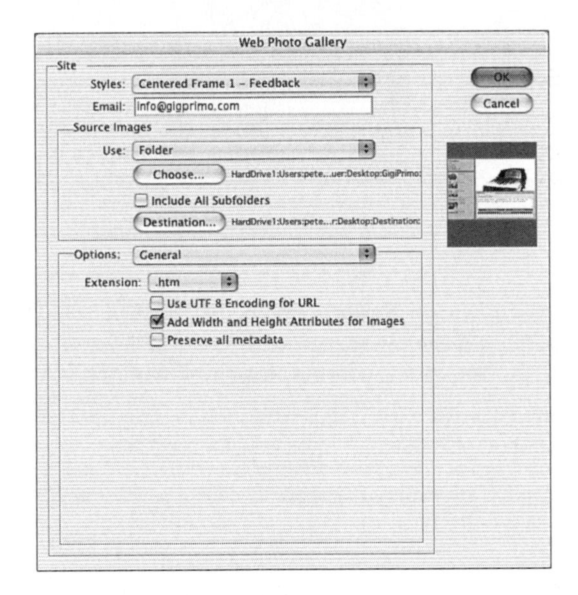


**Figure 7.21**
One dialog box is all Photoshop requires to build a Web site to display your artwork.

The Site section of the dialog box offers 11 different styles for the Web pages. As you change your selected layout, the preview to the right is updated to reflect the new look. You can include an email address for the pages, and you can elect whether to use the file extension .htm or .html for the generated pages. (Some Web servers require a three-character extension—check with your Web hosting service for information about its policy.)

Select both the source and destination folders in the Source Images section of the dialog box. The destination folder cannot be within the source folder. The Options pop-up menu in the middle of the dialog box leads to six sets of options for Web photo galleries (the first of which is shown in Figure 7.21). You select the large and thumbnail image sizes, the banner (if any), colors for the site, and a security message (if desired) that is displayed across the image. Not all options are available for all layouts. Figure 7.22 shows these additional options panes.

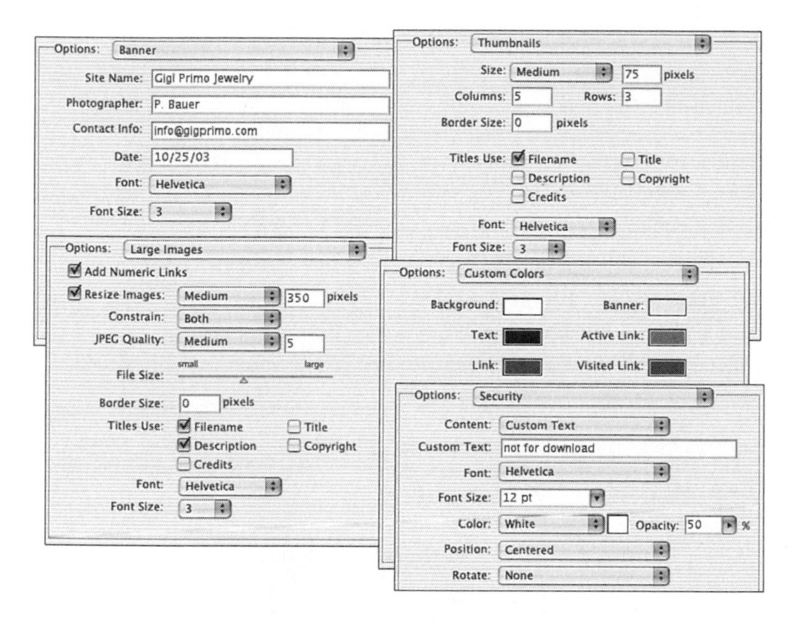


**Figure 7.22**
If the selected layout doesn't support an option, it will be grayed out and you'll see a message to the right reminding you that not all options are available.

Here are the options available in each pane:

- **Banner**—The site name, your name and contact information (one line only), and the date appear in various places, depending on the page style selected in the Site section. Your font choices are limited to Arial, Courier New, Helvetica, and Times New Roman. The font size (1–7) refers to HTML relative size rather than point size.
- **Large Images**—If you select the Resize Images check box, you can choose Small (250 pixels wide), Medium (350 pixels), or Large (450 pixels), or you can choose a custom size. Constraining both height and width prevents distortion of the image, but you can elect to constrain only one dimension. The images will be optimized as JPEGs to the quality you specify. You can select a border size from 0 (no border) to 99 pixels. The image title, if any, can be the filename or any of several items from the File Info fields, and you have the same font options as you have for the banner. You add File Info through the File menu for each image individually.
- **Thumbnails**—Thumbnails are clickable links to the full-size images. They can be Small (50 pixels wide), Medium (75 pixels), Large (100 pixels), or a custom size. For the Table and Simple layouts, you can choose the number of rows and columns. You have the same border and titling options that you have for the large images.
- **Custom Colors**—Custom colors are used with the Simple, Vertical Frame, and Horizontal Frame styles. You use the Color Picker to assign colors.
- **Security**—The term *security* in this situation refers to pasting some information on the images to reduce the chance that your artwork will be stolen. You can add custom text or information recorded with the file in File Info. The text, in your choice of five fonts (Times is available, in

addition to the four fonts mentioned for Banner), size, and color, can be positioned in the middle of the image or in any corner, and it can also be rotated.

Web Photo Gallery is no substitute for Adobe GoLive, but it can quickly and easily produce serviceable Web sites for displaying photos or other artwork. If you're handy with HTML, the code can be customized to suit your individual needs.

New with Photoshop CS's Web Photo Gallery are the "feedback" layouts. When you create a Web Photo Gallery using one of the feedback designs, clients can review the images online and email feedback directly to you (see Figure 7.23).

**Caution**

The fancier styles built in to Web Photo Gallery create *huge* Web pages. The pages need to be scrolled even on monitors set to 1,024×768 pixel resolution. Before investing time in creating a Web site with a lot of pictures, run some tests with a folder containing four or five images, just to make sure you'll like what you get.

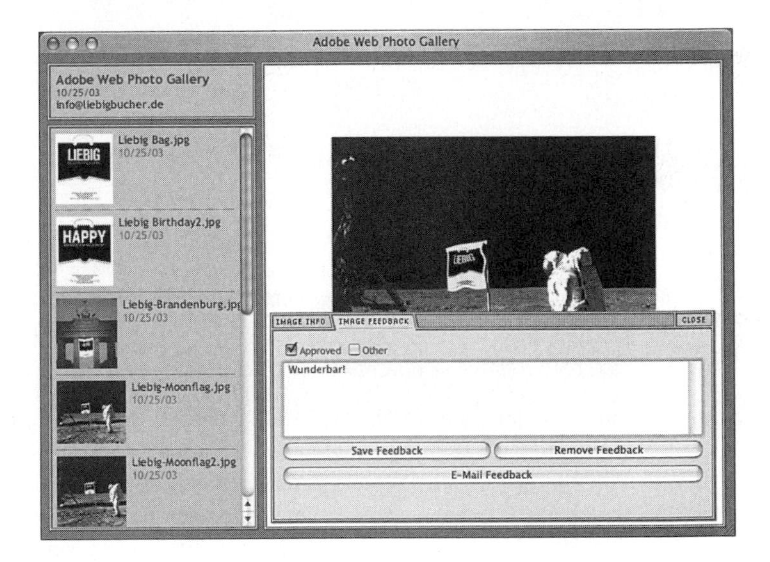


Figure 7.23
Feedback can be saved, emailed, and deleted right from the Web page. Clicking the E-Mail Feedback button launches your email program and starts a new message to the email address specified when the gallery was created.

## Photomerge

New in Photoshop CS is Photomerge, an automated panorama creator. You select two or more images in the Photomerge dialog box, tell Photomerge whether you want it to attempt to arrange the images automatically, and click OK (see Figure 7.24).

Once the images are identified and you click OK, the images will be opened into the Photomerge workspace. The dialog box shown in Figure 7.25 includes a "lightbox" at the top for images not currently being used, a large central work area for arranging and compositing, and several options and tools.

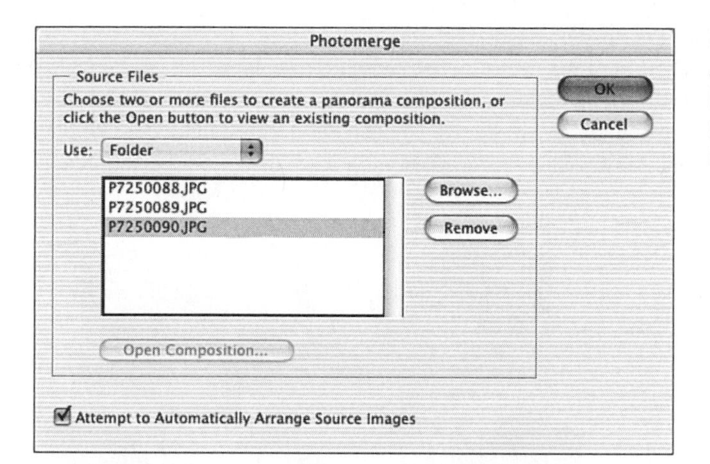


**Figure 7.24**
After a panorama (composition) has been saved, it can be reopened and edited in Photomerge.

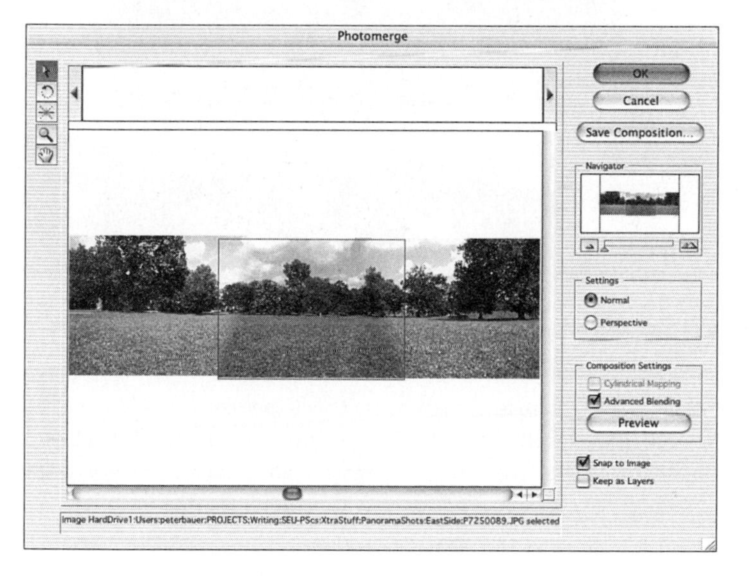


**Figure 7.25**
The Navigator section can be used in conjunction with or instead of the Zoom and Hand tools. Cylindrical mapping is available only with Perspective selected; Advanced Blending can be used with or without Perspective. Snap to Image lets Photomerge try to mate overlapping areas of images, and Keep as Layers prevents the flattening of the image after you click OK.

## Photomerge Tools

The Select Image tool is used to select and move images in the work area and can be used to drag them to and from the lightbox area. The Rotate Image tool is used with the selected image to compensate for irregularities that can creep in, even when using a tripod. The Vanishing Point tool identifies an image to use (with the Perspective option selected), and the Zoom and Hand tools perform their usual duties.

## Perspective in Photomerge

When the Perspective option is selected in the Settings area of the Photomerge dialog box, you can specify an image to use as the *vanishing point*, the most distant point of the panorama. Use the

Vanishing Point tool to click the specific image that contains the most distant point (for example, the corner of a room photographed from the center). Photomerge recalculates the relationship among the component images (which can take quite a long time). After the perspective is calculated and the image is redrawn in the Photomerge work area, you can check the Cylindrical Mapping option to compensate for the distance. The Preview button shows the result of cylindrical mapping. (See the comparison in Figure 7.26).

**Figure 7.26**
From the top: Set to Normal, set to Perspective, and previewing Cylindrical Mapping.

## Advanced Blending in Photomerge

When Advanced Blending is selected, Photomerge attempts to compensate for differences in exposure among the images in the panorama. In areas of reasonably consistent color and little detail, blending is applied over a larger area to smooth the transitions. In areas of fine detail, the blending change is more confined. Consider using Advanced Blending when compositing images with, for example, walls of rooms or buildings. It is often less effective with panoramas that include much detail, such as outdoor shots of wooded or grassy areas.

# Photoshop at Work: Using Actions and Automate Commands

To see how all the parts of this section come together, try this:

1. Create a folder called Source and add copies of eight of your favorite images.
2. Record an Action (name it Create Tiffs) that resizes an image to a maximum height or width of 500 pixels (use Fit Image rather than Image, Image Size), sharpens (Filter, Sharpen, Sharpen), and saves the file as a TIFF file in a folder named Originals.
3. Run the Action Create Tiffs as a batch on the Source folder. Create a folder named Destination in which to save the files.
4. Use Contact Sheet II to create a single page with thumbnails of your TIFF images.

5. Use Picture Package to create a single page of eight 2.5×3.5 images, one for each of your TIFFs.
6. Use Web Photo Gallery to create a Web site, in your choice of layout, to show off your images.

*If you ended up with copies of the files in both Originals and Destination, or if you couldn't get the Batch command to properly save the TIFFs at all, see "Using Batch to Change File Formats," earlier in this chapter.*

# IMAGEREADY'S CONDITIONAL ACTIONS

Generally speaking, ImageReady's Actions are similar to those in Photoshop. You record, play back, save, and load Actions in much the same way as you do in Photoshop. Batch application of an Action is available, and you can create droplets (both from the Actions palette menu).

There are, however, a couple significant differences between Photoshop and ImageReady Actions. ImageReady's Actions palette, for example, does not support Action sets. The most important difference is ImageReady's conditional Actions, a powerful feature that many hope will make its way to Photoshop and Illustrator soon.

## Working with If/Then Statements

When a conditional is added to an Action, the Action examines the image upon which it's being run and evaluates it in terms of a specific property. If the property meets the condition specified, the Action then performs the step or steps you select. If the property does not match the conditional, the step or steps are skipped.

For example, if you have a large number of images that are being batch processed, but some are landscape and some are portrait, a conditional can be inserted into the Action. The conditional can examine the orientation of the image currently being processed and rotate landscape images while leaving portrait images unrotated.

## Adding a Conditional

While recording (or later, when editing) an Action, you select Insert Conditional from ImageReady's Actions palette menu. In the dialog box that opens, you specify what you want the conditional to look for and what to do if it does/doesn't find that image characteristic. The Actions palette then shows a step named "Conditional" (see Figure 7.27).

If a conditional already exists in an Action, you can edit it by double-clicking the step in the Actions palette.

## Specifying the Condition

In the Conditional dialog box, you use the top section to specify when you want something to happen; you use the bottom portion of the dialog box to specify what you want to happen (see Figure 7.28).

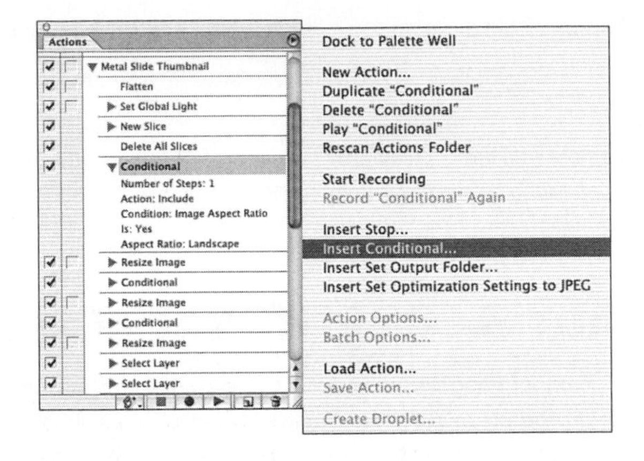


**Figure 7.27**
When the Conditional step is expanded in the Actions palette, you can see what will happen if the condition is met, as well as the condition itself.

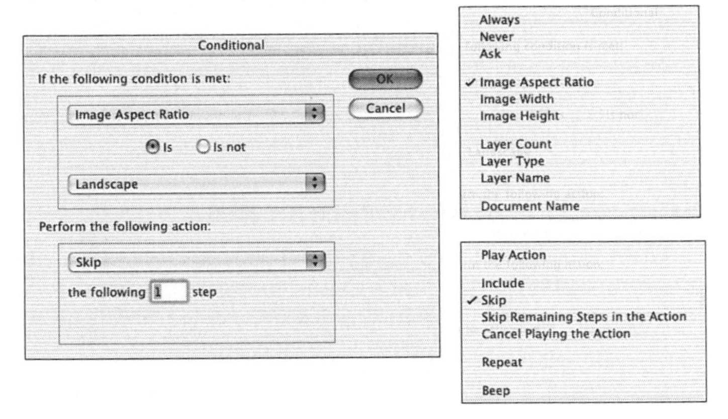


**Figure 7.28**
The content of the upper pop-up menu is shown to the upper left. The content of the middle pop-up menu is contingent on the selection above it. The content of the lower pop-up menu is shown to the lower right.

The first three options in the upper part of the Conditional dialog box are Always, Never, and Ask (see Figure 7.29). If Always is selected, whatever is specified in the lower part of the dialog box will execute, just as if the conditional were a regular step in the Action. With Never, the lower part of the dialog box is ignored. The Ask option has a field for text entry. When the Action is played, the text is displayed in a dialog box with buttons that allow you to continue executing the conditional (Yes), stop executing the conditional (No), and stop the Action in its entirety (Cancel). The phrasing of the Ask text must make sense in terms of the lower part of the dialog box. For example, with the question "Does the image require rotating?" the Action should execute a rotate command if the Yes button is clicked and skip the rotate step if No is clicked.

> Use Always and Never to temporarily change the behavior of an Action. For example, use Always when a batch command should execute the conditional's "Perform the follow action" on every image; use Never when you need to temporarily disable the conditional.

The next group of conditions are true conditionals—the image is evaluated for a specific characteristic, and if that characteristic is found, the conditional proceeds. They look at the physical dimensions of the image being processed by the Action. The options for Image Aspect Ratio, Image Width, and Image Height are shown in Figure 7.30.

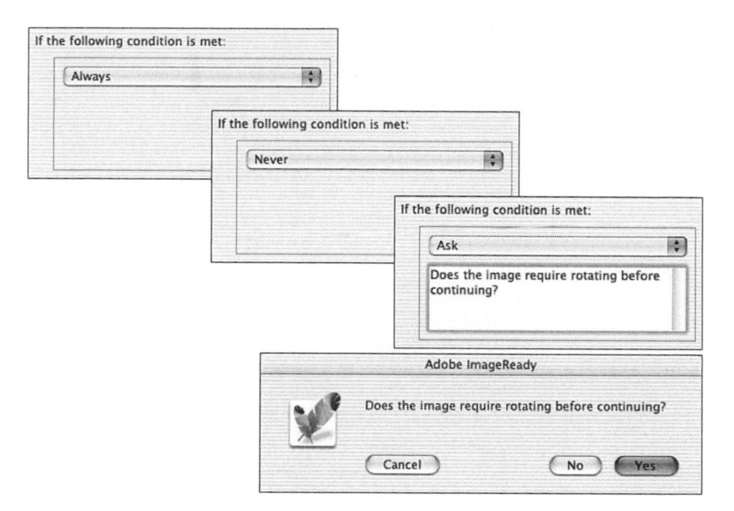


**Figure 7.29**
Note that Always and Never are not truly conditions, because the behavior is exactly the same each time when either is selected.

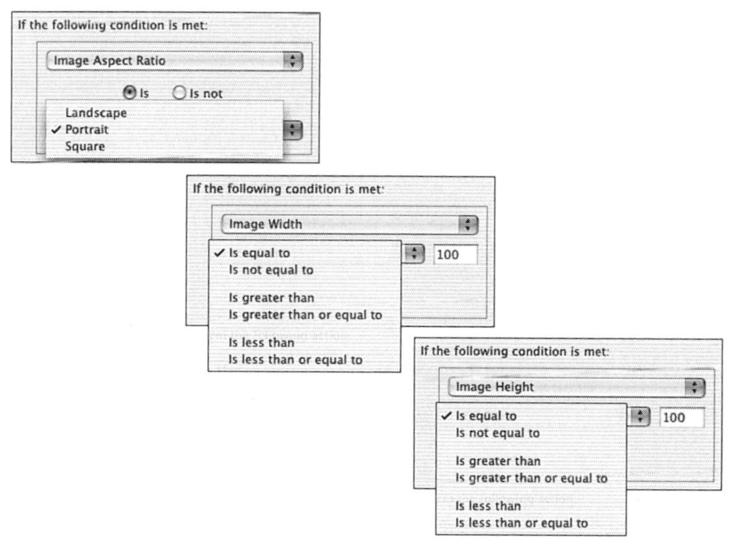


**Figure 7.30**
The unit of measure for the Image Width and Image Height conditionals is pixels.

Conditionals can also examine the content of the Layers palette and look at the currently active layer, as well as check the document's name (see Figure 7.31).

## Specifying the Result of the Conditional

The lower part of the Conditional dialog box is where you specify what happens if the condition in the upper part is met. As you can see in Figure 7.32, there are seven options.

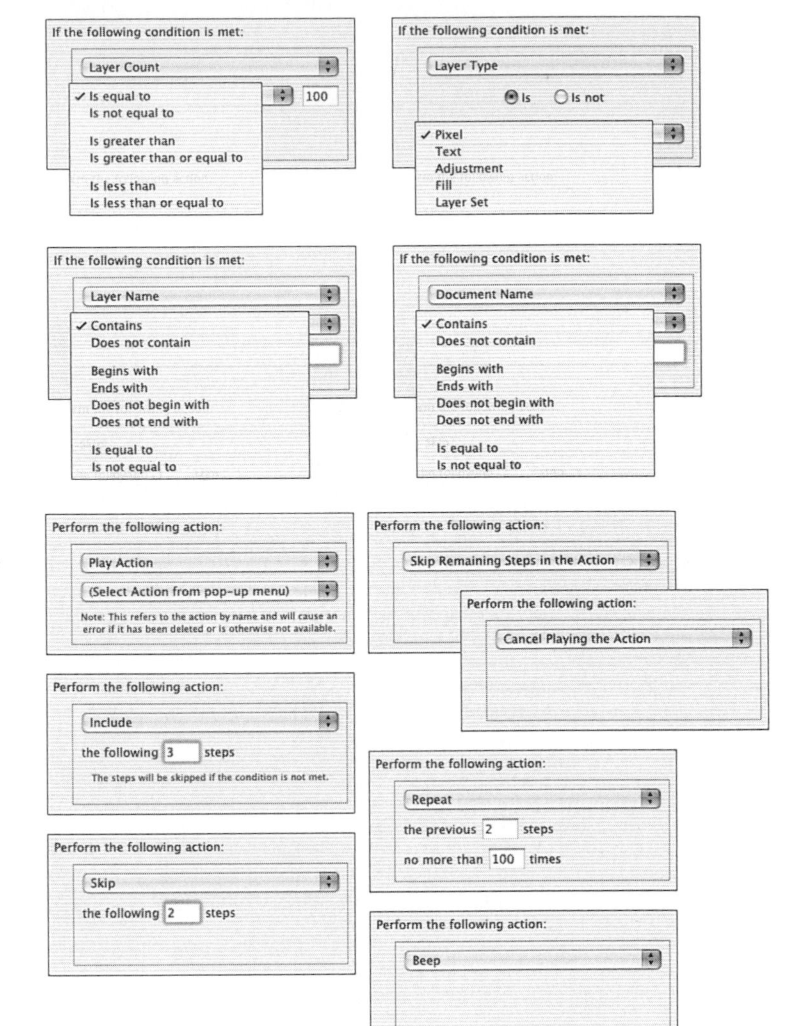


**Figure 7.31**
The Layer Name and Document Name conditions include fields for text entry (partially visible behind the pop-up menus).

**Figure 7.32**
The numeric fields accept values from 1 to 1000.

In practice, there's little difference between Skip Remaining Steps in the Action and Cancel Playing the Action. Likewise, you may find no practical difference between meeting a condition and including steps and not meeting the same condition and skipping steps. For example, consider the Actions shown in the two views of the Actions palette in Figure 7.33.

These four Actions all perform the same task on nonsquare images—they rotate landscape-oriented images but not portrait-oriented images. Each of the Actions includes the same Rotate command. The different conditionals establish when the Rotate step will be included and when it will be skipped. Consider the following:

- **Rotate Landscape**—If the image is landscape, then rotate.
- **Don't Rotate Non-Landscape**—If the image is *not* landscape, then do *not* rotate.
- **Don't Rotate Portrait**—If the image is Portrait, then do *not* rotate.
- **Rotate Non-Portrait**—If the image is *not* portrait, then rotate.

The key to effectively using conditionals in ImageReady's Actions is establishing a condition that effectively identifies the images you need to single out. The Action will then do *something* (specified in the Action) to those images or it will skip that *something* for those images, performing that step (or steps) only on the images that are not singled out by the condition.

ImageReady's conditional Actions look only at one condition. To simulate an "and" statement, forcing the Action to consider two characteristics of the image, include a conditional set to "Include the following two steps," followed immediately by a conditional set to "Include the following one step." The first conditional establishes one characteristic, the second establishes the second characteristic, and if the image being processed meets *both* requirements, the next step is executed.

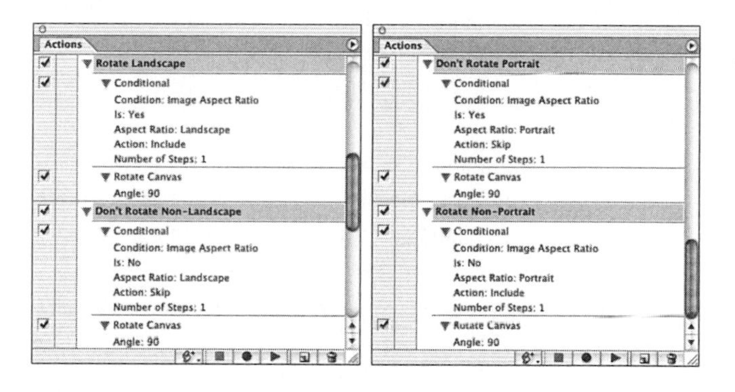


**Figure 7.33**
The names of the Actions are highlighted.

# ACTIONS IN ILLUSTRATOR

Actions are simply prerecorded steps. You can use them to perform a series of tasks with a single click. Illustrator installs, by default, two dozen Actions, and many more are available free or at minimal cost on the Web. However, the true power of Actions comes to the fore when you write your own custom Actions. You can even share your Actions with others and load their Actions for your own use and customization.

Virtually anything you can do in Illustrator, an Action can do for you. Some Actions are completely automated and can run without any input from a human operator; other Actions require you to enter specific values for certain procedures. Illustrator also enables you to specify whether to use the values originally recorded with an Action or to pause the Action for you to input new values.

You create, store, organize, and play back Actions by using the Actions palette. You can specify how Actions are played back and can even run them on multiple files sequentially as a *batch*. Batch processing of a folder of files can even include subfolders.

## What Is an Action?

To appreciate the power of Actions, you need to understand what they are and how they work. Figure 7.34 shows the steps recorded in a simple Action, one of those installed by default by Illustrator. (The Actions palette itself is explained in depth in the section "The Actions Palette," later in this chapter.)

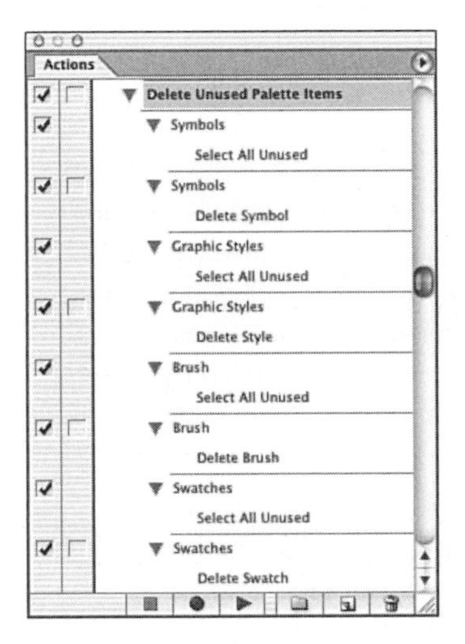


Figure 7.34
The Action shown, Delete Unused Palette Items, is part of the Default Actions set installed, by default, with Illustrator CS.

Cleaning up the palettes is a good way to minimize file size and confusion. Unused items are removed from the palettes, making it easier to find those that you need while you're working, and sometimes file size is reduced significantly. Using this Action makes cleaning up a simple matter rather than a time-consuming step that is likely to be skipped.

When the Action is run, eight commands are executed. First, all unused symbols are selected and deleted, then unused graphic styles are selected and deleted, then all unused brushes are selected and deleted, and finally all unused swatches are selected and deleted.

Performing this cleanup using the Action requires—at most—five basic steps involving between five and eight clicks:

1. Open the Actions palette (if it's not already visible).
2. Expand the Default Actions folder (if it's not already expanded).
3. Scroll to the Style/Brush/Swatch Cleanup Action (if it's not already showing) and select it.
4. Click the Play button.
5. Click OK to confirm each of the deletions. (You'll have to move the mouse just once. The three dialog boxes appear in exactly the same place, so you can simply click three times.)

This process takes about 10 seconds; 5 seconds if the Action set is organized properly. Cleaning up manually requires several more steps:

1. Open the Styles palette, if it's not already visible.
2. Open the palette's menu, scroll down to the command Select All Unused, and click it.
3. Open the palette's menu again, scroll down to the command Delete Style, and select it.
4. Confirm the deletions by clicking OK in the dialog box.
5. Click the tab to open the Brushes palette.
6. Open the palette's menu, scroll down to the command Select All Unused, and click it.
7. Open the palette's menu again, scroll down to the command Delete Brush, and select it.
8. Confirm the deletions by clicking OK in the dialog box.
9. Click the tab to open the Swatches palette.
10. Open the palette's menu, scroll down to the command Select All Unused, and click it.
11. Open the palette's menu again, scroll down to the command Delete Swatch, and select it.
12. Confirm the deletions by clicking OK in the dialog box.

This procedure takes approximately 30 seconds, so the time savings is not overwhelming. However, you will discover a tremendous advantage in both convenience (fast and easy) and accuracy (no steps skipped). The simple step of cleaning up an image's palettes is something you should do with every file. Yet, because of the inconvenience, it's an often-neglected step, even when it does come to mind. Using the Action makes it a realistic part of the workflow for every document.

As you can see, everything in this Action you can do manually. However, recording the steps is far more convenient. An Action is simply a series of Illustrator commands and tools recorded and stored for later playback.

## The Actions Palette

In Illustrator, you create, organize, and utilize Actions through the Actions palette (see Figure 7.35). It is, by default, docked with the Layers and Links palettes.

The Actions palette is simply and logically organized:

- The first column, shown with check marks, determines whether a specific step in an Action will run.
- The second column is for modal control. A *modal* tool or command is one that requires clicking OK or pressing (Return) [Enter] to apply the selected settings. Modal control allows you to specify settings for certain types of steps in an Action. (Modal steps will be discussed in the section "Using Actions," later in this chapter.)
- Actions are stored in *sets*, represented by folder icons, which you expand by clicking the triangle to the left. Notice that the sets can also be identified by a shaded bar in the palette.
- Actions are indented below the sets, with triangles to expand or hide the individual steps.

- The individual steps are indented below the Action's name. Most steps can be expanded to show their settings, but some have no settings. Simple commands, such as Paste in Front, appear in the palette as a single line entry below the Action.

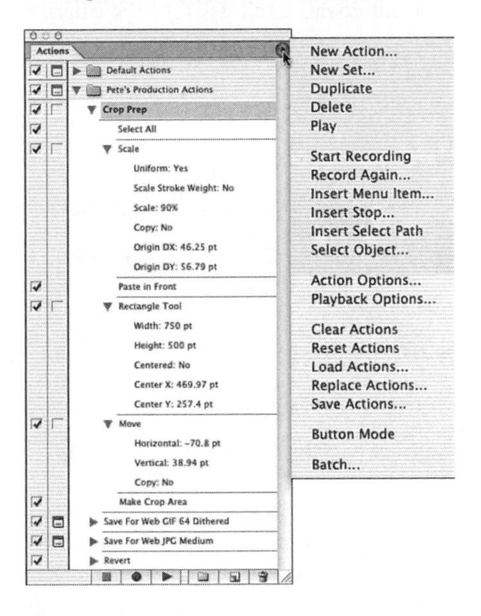


**Figure 7.35**
Triangles next to the folder and Action names indicate that they can be expanded.

Select All, the first step in Crop Prep (a custom Action, rather than one of Illustrator's default Actions), which is the third Action in the Actions palette shown in Figure 7.35, is a nonmodal step. Nothing appears in the second column, whereas modal steps show either the dialog box icon (next to Save for Web GIF 64 Dithered) or an empty box (next to Rectangle Tool).

The buttons across the bottom of the palette are, in order from left to right, Stop, Record, Play, Create New Set, Create New Action, and Delete Selection. You can use the Delete Selection button to remove a step from an Action or a set of Actions. These buttons are not available when the palette itself is in Button Mode (see Figure 7.36).

In Button Mode, you can visually identify and group Actions. A single click runs the Action as it is, with any unchecked steps omitted. When the Actions palette is in Standard Mode, you can double-click an Action to assign both a color and Function key and change the Action's name. You can assign these options when the Action is first recorded, or you can access the dialog box with the palette menu command Action Options.

Unlike styles, brushes, and swatches, new sets of Actions are loaded through the palette menu rather than through the Window menu.

> You can drag Actions in the Actions palette to rearrange their order. Similar Actions can be placed together or dragged into sets.
>
> In Standard Mode, the Actions palette enables you to sort Actions in different sets for various purposes. You can have multiple copies of the same Action in different sets. Simply drag an Action to the New Action button at the bottom of the palette to duplicate it. You need not give it a different name. You can then drag the Action copy to its new set.

**Figure 7.36**
When the Actions palette is in Button Mode, not all the menu's commands are available, nor are sets, although the buttons are listed in order by set.

# Using Actions

Although playing an Action is as simple as clicking its button in Button Mode or clicking the Play button when the palette is in Standard Mode, some options can make Actions even more powerful tools for you:

- As noted earlier, in one column in the Actions palette (Standard Mode only), you can deselect steps in an Action. Unchecking steps enables you to skip them during playback of an Action, which is an easy way to customize the procedure for specific purposes.
- The Actions palette also enables you to turn on and off the modal dialog boxes. (Modal controls will be discussed in greater depth in the section "Modal Controls," later in the chapter.) When the icon is missing, the step plays with the built-in settings. When the icon is visible, the dialog box opens for your input.
- Some Actions require that you make a selection before you run the Action.
- You can play an entire set of Actions at the same time by selecting the set and clicking the Play button.
- You can put an Action inside another Action, playing the first inside the second.
- You can play a single step of an Action. While pressing (Command) [Ctrl], double-click it in the Actions palette. You can also highlight the step and then (Command)-click [Ctrl]-click the Play button.
- The Actions palette's menu offers the Playback Options command. After you select this command, you can choose from three different speeds at which to play back Actions (see Figure 7.37).

Keeping in mind that you can duplicate Actions and that you can have multiple copies of the same Action in different sets, you can create sets of duplicate Actions for a specific purpose and run them as a group.

*You clicked the Actions palette's Play button, and the Action didn't do what it was supposed to do. See "Double-Check" in the "Mastering the Adobe Creative Suite" section at the end of this chapter.*

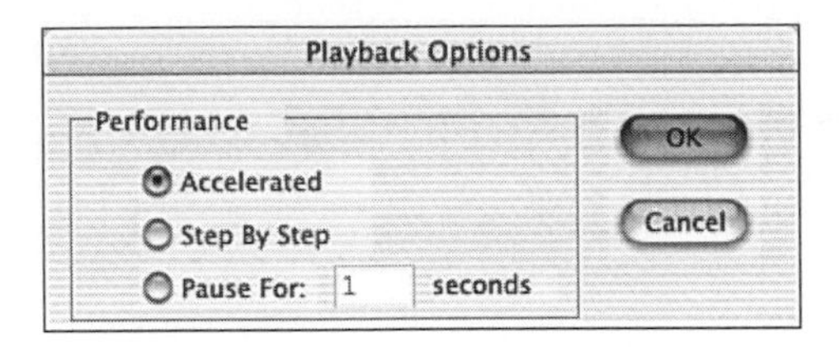


Figure 7.37
Accelerated plays the Action as quickly as possible, Step By Step slows the Action so that you can watch for problems, and Pause For enables you to set the delay.

## The Batch Command

A folder full of files can have the same Action applied to it with one command. Using the Batch command from the Actions palette menu opens the dialog box shown in Figure 7.38.

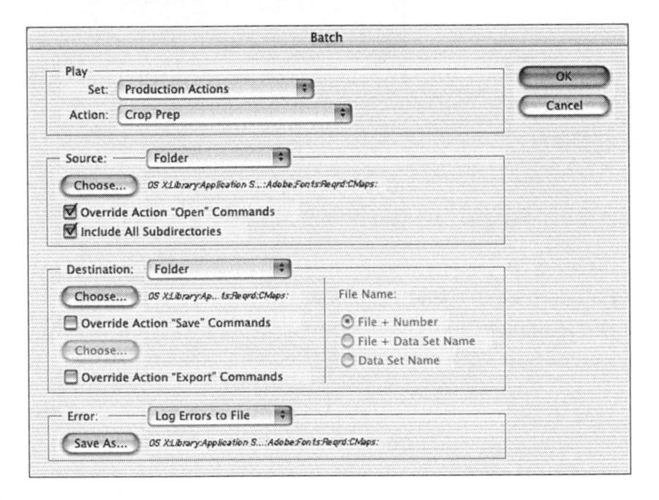


Figure 7.38
The Batch command applies the selected Action to all files in the folder that Illustrator can open. Some Actions, however, may not be appropriate for all files.

You can select a number of settings in the Batch dialog box:

- The set that is currently selected in the Actions palette appears; however, you can select another from the Set pop-up menu. If no selection is currently in the Actions palette, the first set is shown by default.
- The Action is the one currently selected. If no Action is currently selected, the first Action in the selected set is shown. Any other Action in that set can be selected from the pop-up menu.
- The Batch command needs to know which files are to be modified. You can make the selection by using the Choose button in the Source area. Figure 7.39 shows the resulting dialog box.
- The Override Action "Open" Commands option ignores any commands within the Action that call for opening a file. When a folder is selected, the files inside are automatically opened.

**Caution**

Be aware that all Open commands are overridden by the Override Action "Open" Commands option. If an Action requires that a second file be opened to complete its task, that command, too, is ignored. As an example, consider an Action that is designed to open one file, open a second file, select all and copy from the second file, return to the first, and then paste. If the Override Action "Open" Commands option is selected, this Action will fail because it cannot open the second file.

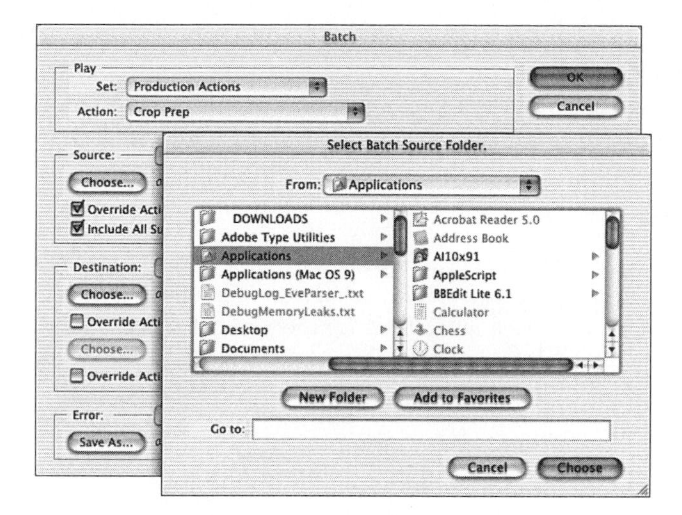


**Figure 7.39**
This dialog box is similar to a standard Open dialog box, with one exception: It allows you to choose only folders, never individual files.

- If the source folder includes subfolders, the Include All Subdirectories option enables you to decide whether to include their contents.
- The Destination pop-up menu offers three choices. None leaves the altered files open in Illustrator. Save and Close replaces the original files with the modified versions. Folder enables you to choose a location for the modified files. This way, you can avoid overwriting the originals.
- When you select Folder as the Destination option, you can choose to override any Save commands that have been written into the Action.
- Likewise, when Folder is the destination of choice, you can override Export commands. If you choose to override the Export commands, the files will still be exported, but you'll be prompted to select another folder for them to be exported into rather than the one specified in the Action.
- Error messages can be handled in one of two ways. Illustrator can halt the batch processing until you've given it the okay to continue after an error, or you can create a text file with the details. If you choose the latter approach, you have to select a name and location for the log file before you start the batch.

*Do you have an Action that stops partway through for no apparent reason? See "Unscheduled Halt" in the "Mastering the Adobe Creative Suite" section at the end of this chapter.*

# ILLUSTRATOR'S CUSTOM ACTIONS

The true power of Actions becomes apparent when you record your own. Most of the 22 Actions supplied with Illustrator are of no particular value (with the notable

> Subdirectories can include aliases for (Macintosh) or shortcuts to (Windows) other folders. You can use them to process multiple folders with a single Batch command.

exception of Delete Unused Palette Items). They replicate rather simple procedures that you can accomplish with a single click or two.

Before recording an Action, you should always make a copy of your original file. Because Illustrator executes the steps of an Action while it's being recorded, you should always work with a copy.

## Recording a New Action

An Action must belong to a set. Actions are not allowed to float loose in the Actions palette. You can assign an Action to an existing set or create a new set using either the Create New Set button at the bottom of the Actions palette (the icon looks like a folder) or the New Set command from the palette's menu. Both open the New Set dialog box (see Figure 7.40), in which you can give the set a name.

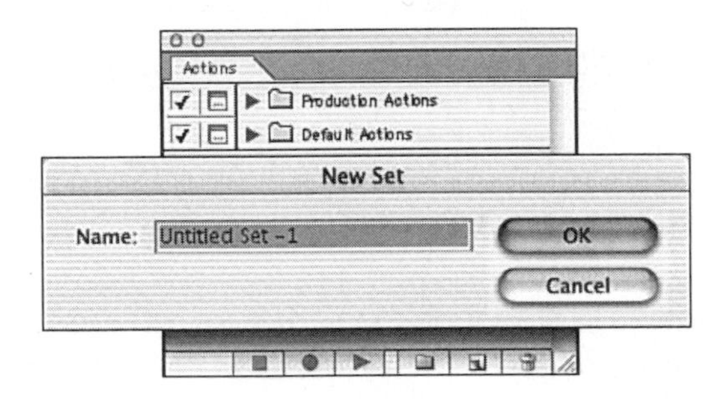


Figure 7.40
The only option for a new set of Actions is the name.

If the new Action will belong to an existing set, you need only click the Create New Action button at the bottom of the Actions palette (the icon is next to the trashcan) or use the New Action command from the palette's menu. Both open the New Action dialog box, shown in Figure 7.41.

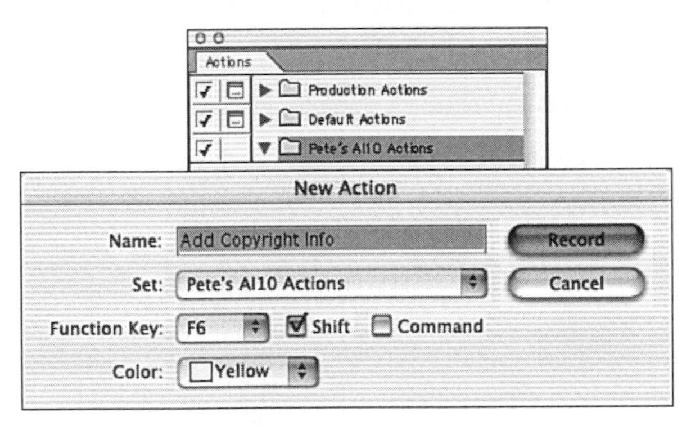


Figure 7.41
In the New Action dialog box, you can name the new Action, assign it to a set, assign a function key (with or without modifier keys), and color-code it for use in Button Mode.

After you click Record, you are actually in the process of creating the Action. You can pause the recording at almost any time by clicking the Stop button (far left at the bottom of the Actions palette) or using the Stop Recording menu command (see Figure 7.42).

Note that the New Action and New Set commands are not grayed out. You can, in fact, create new sets and Actions while recording an Action. You can even work in the Actions palette, deleting Actions and sets, while recording. These activities are not recorded as steps in the current Action.

7

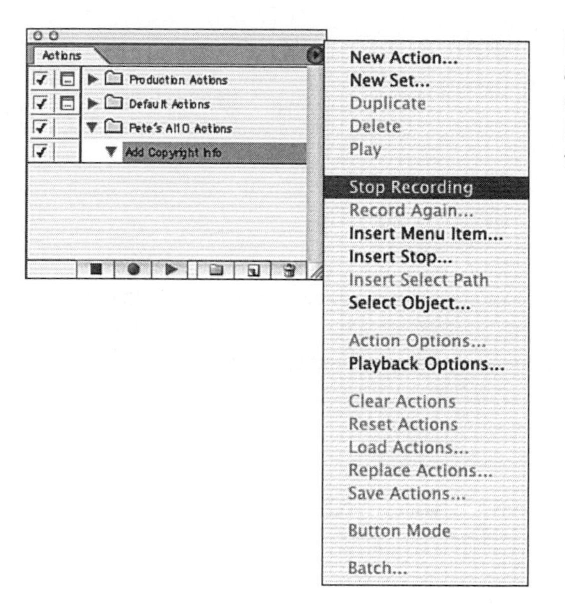


**Figure 7.42**
An Action is being recorded, as evidenced by the highlighted Record button at the bottom of the Actions palette.

The actual steps that can be recorded in an Action fall into several categories: recordable commands and tools, nonrecordable commands and tools, inserted paths, and stops. In addition, you can decide whether a command will use the settings with which it was recorded or pause while you enter new settings (modal commands).

After you've gone through all the steps you want in the Action, simply click the Stop button at the bottom of the palette or use the menu command Stop Recording. It is usually a good idea, especially with more complicated Actions, to make another copy of the original file and test the Action.

The following tools cannot be recorded in Illustrator:

- Selection tool
- Direct Selection tool
- Group Selection tool
- Lasso tool
- Direct Select Lasso tool
- Pen tools
- Type tools
- Paintbrush tool
- Pencil, Smooth, and Erase tools
- Symbolism tools
- Graph tools
- Gradient Mesh tool

- Gradient tool
- Eyedropper and Paint Bucket tools
- Scissors and Knife tools
- Hand, Page, and Measure tools
- Zoom tool

Despite the fact that these tools are nonrecordable, you can accomplish some of the things the tools do in other ways. For example, the Selection tool cannot be recorded because it relies on cursor position. You can make selections, however, by using the Actions palette menu command Select Object. You cannot create paths using the pen and pencil tools (they also rely on cursor position and movement), but you can use the Insert Select Path command. Both of these commands will be discussed in the section "Paths in Actions," later in this chapter.

## Inserting Nonrecordable Commands

In addition to the tools that cannot be recorded, various commands cannot be recorded. Illustrator, however, enables you to insert most of these commands by using the menu command Insert Menu Item. The Insert Menu Item dialog box is shown in Figure 7.43.

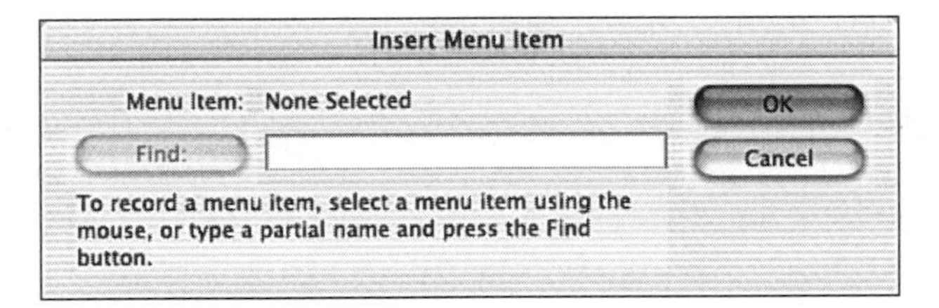


Figure 7.43
Inserting menu commands is one way to circumvent nonrecordable commands and tools.

Be aware that no commands are grayed out in any of Illustrator's menus, although not all can be inserted into an Action. After you select a command, look at the Actions palette to see whether it was actually inserted.

Some inserted commands, such as Select All, execute when an Action is played. However, those inserted menu commands that have dialog boxes do not execute automatically. Rather, the Action opens the command's dialog box and waits for you to insert the desired values and click OK. This topic will be discussed further in the section "Modal Controls," later in this chapter. Actions with such inserted commands, of course, cannot run unattended.

**Caution**

Inserting a menu command does not execute that command on the artboard. To properly observe the command's impact (and to make sure that following steps in the Action have the intended effects), you should use the command before inserting it. For example, if you want to apply the command Effect, Artistic, Colored Pencil to a selection, you should first apply the effect and then use the command Insert Menu Item.

7

## Paths in Actions

The Actions palette menu command Insert Select Path makes up for the lack of recordability for the pen and pencil tools.

Illustrator creates a record of the selected path and inserts it into any document when the Action is played. Like menu commands, paths can be inserted without the Action being in Record Mode.

To make a path part of an Action, follow the steps listed here (if you are recording an Action already, you should click the Stop button if you will be using a recordable tool to create the path or paths):

You don't have to click the Record button to insert a menu command. Simply click the step that should precede the menu command in the Actions palette and then use the palette menu command Insert Menu Item.

1. Draw the path that you want to be inserted into the Action. Illustrator can insert multiple paths.
2. Apply any desired transformation commands.
3. Make sure that the path is selected.
4. Either click the Action step that is to precede the insertion of the path or start recording a new path.
5. Use the Actions palette menu command Insert Select Path.
6. Continue to record the Action as necessary or click the Stop button if you're finished. (Remember that an Action need not be in Record Mode for you to use the Insert Select Path command.)

Here's what is recorded in the Action:

- The location of the path on the artboard in relationship to the zero-zero point of the rulers. (By default, this is the lower-left corner of the artboard.)
- The shape of the path, including any transformations that have been applied.
- The results of certain filters, including the Colors filters Convert To, Invert Colors, Overprint Black, and Saturate; the Distort filters; and the Round Corners filter.

Here's what is not recorded in the Action:

- The stroke color or pattern
- The fill color, gradient, or pattern
- Any effects
- Filters not in the preceding list

Several filters can make a path ineligible for the command Insert Select Path. Among them are the following:

- Crop Marks
- Add Arrowheads
- Drop Shadow

When you play the Action in a document, the path is reproduced using the then-current stroke and fill and placed at the top of the active layer. If effects have been applied to the active layer, the object created, naturally, has the effects applied.

## The Select Object Command

Using the Actions palette menu command Select Object, you can select a specific path or image in an Action. The command relies on the annotation feature of Illustrator's Attributes palette. It searches the notes attached to all objects for entries that match what you've typed in the command's dialog box (see Figure 7.44).

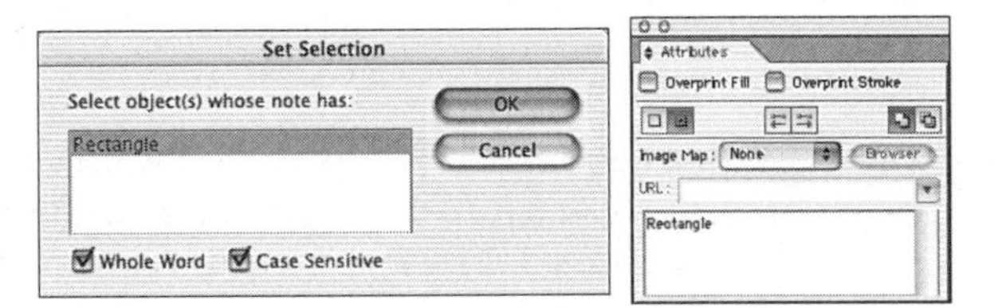


**Figure 7.44**
You access the Set Selection dialog box through the Actions palette menu command Select Object.

If Whole Word is selected, the entire entry must match exactly. If Case Sensitive is checked, uppercase and lowercase versions of each letter are considered separate characters. If more than one object has matching notes, they all are selected.

Depending on the planning with which you create annotations, the Select Object command can be a very powerful tool. For example, in Figure 7.45, the six objects have been annotated as Rectangle #1, Rectangle #2, Rectangle #3, Oval #1, Oval #2, and Oval #3. Using the command with the word *Oval* makes the selection as shown.

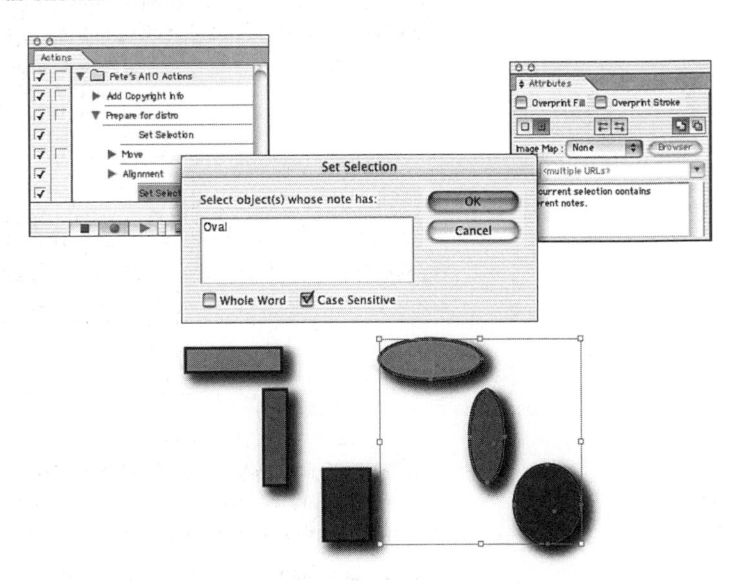


**Figure 7.45**
Only objects with the word *Oval* in their notes are selected.

On the other hand, if the Set Selection dialog box contains the entry #2, the selection is that shown in Figure 7.46.

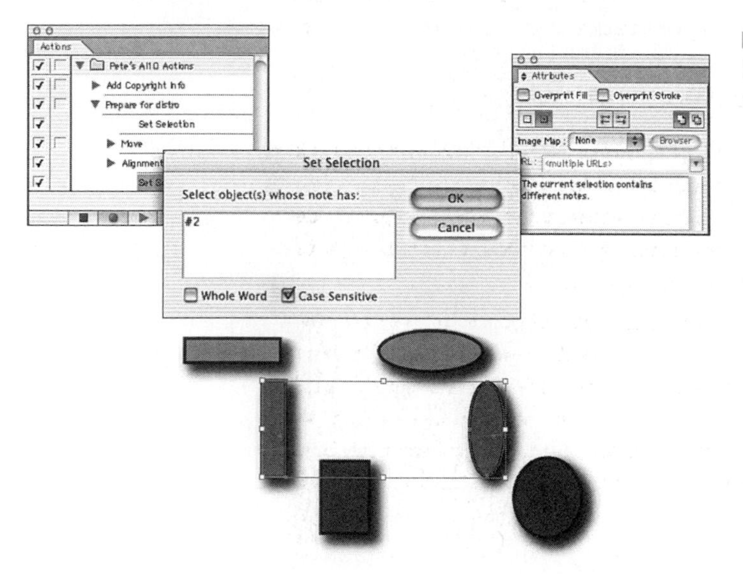


**Figure 7.46**
In this case, a different set of objects is selected.

The annotation field of the Attributes palette can contain up to 240 characters. To enter a note, select the object on the artboard or in the Layers palette, open the Attributes palette, and click in the rectangle at the bottom. When you're done, click elsewhere in a palette or on the artboard to continue working.

## Stops

You add a stop to an Action by using the Actions palette menu command Insert Stop. Stops halt the Action during playback and display a message of your choosing. The modal control column must show the icon for the stop message to be displayed. (Modal controls will be explained in the following section.) It is best if the message gives explicit instructions, such as those shown in Figure 7.47.

In the Record Stop dialog box, shown in Figure 7.48, you can enter the text of the message using up to 255 characters.

If the option Allow Continue is selected, the warning box has Continue and Stop buttons rather than a single OK button, as shown in Figure 7.49.

*Stop messages don't show? See "Stop Sign" in the "Mastering the Adobe Creative Suite" section at the end of this chapter.*

If you plan to enter the same note, or basically the same note, for multiple objects, select them all at once. Whatever you enter in the Attributes palette is added for all selected objects. (You can make changes to specific notes individually afterward.) In the examples shown in Figures 7.45 and 7.46, the three rectangles were selected together and the word *Rectangle* was annotated. They were then selected individually to add the #1, #2, and #3.

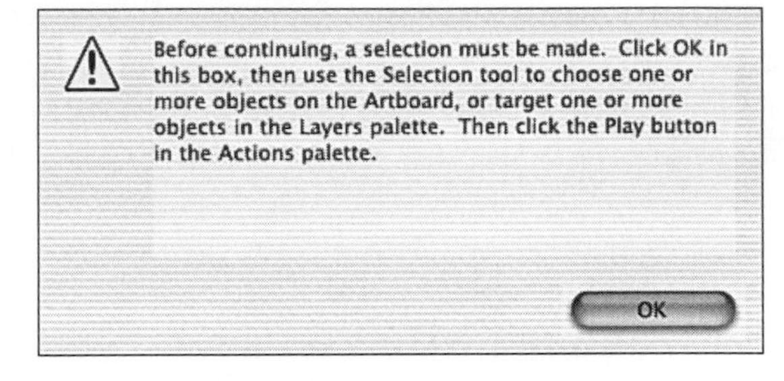


Figure 7.47
Especially if the Action is to be shared or distributed, give exact instructions in a message.

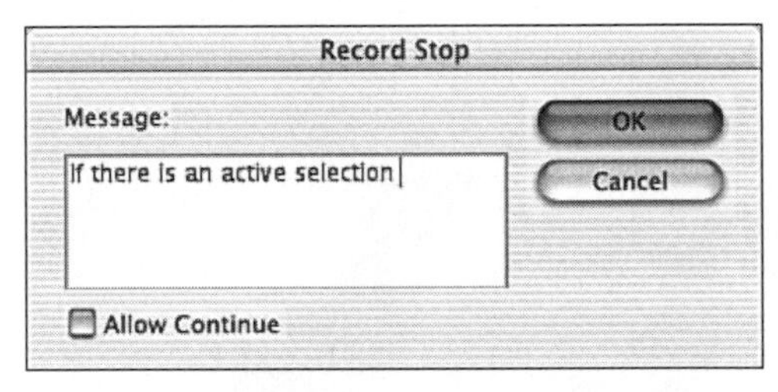


Figure 7.48
You open the Record Stop dialog box by using the Actions palette menu command Insert Stop.

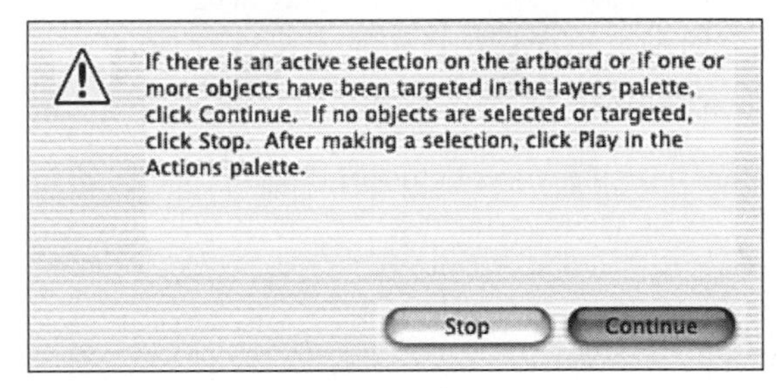


Figure 7.49
Notice that the instructions have been rephrased.

## Modal Controls

A modal control pauses an Action during playback to display a dialog box. Modal controls are available for modal commands and modal tools. Modal commands and tools have dialog boxes that require that the OK button be clicked or that (Return) [Enter] be pressed. While you're working with tools directly in Illustrator (rather than applying them through Actions), some tools can be both modal and not. You can drag the Rectangle tool, for example, on the artboard to create a rectangle. Pressing (Return) [Enter] is not required. However, clicking the same tool on the artboard opens a small dialog box. That dialog box does require that you press (Return) [Enter] or click the OK button to continue. In that mode, the Rectangle tool is modal.

If a modal tool or command in an Action has an icon visible in the Modal Control column, its dialog box opens. If the column has no icon, the step executes with the settings with which it was recorded. If the column has no place for an icon, the tool or command is not modal. Figure 7.50 shows several modal tools and commands.

> If an Action requires that a selection be made before running, you may want to start the Action with a message to that effect as a reminder. Insert a stop as the first item.

The icons immediately to the left of the three Action sets all have red icons in the Modal Control column. The red icons indicate that some, not all, of the modal steps within the sets open their dialog boxes. The Action named "Prepare for distro" also has a red icon because not all its modal commands open dialog boxes. The step Move has no icon and is therefore executed with the default values. The step Stop does have an icon and opens its dialog box. The Set Selection steps and the Alignment step have no place for an icon in the Modal Control column because these commands have no dialog box to open.

Figure 7.50
The Modal Control column is the second from left.

# Editing Actions

After you record an Action, you can go back and make changes at any time (except while it is running). Here's how:

- Move an Action from one set to another by dragging it in the Actions palette.
- Move a step within an Action by dragging it, similarly to rearranging the Layers palette.
- Delete sets, Actions, and steps by highlighting them and clicking the Delete Selection button at the bottom of the Actions palette. You can select multiple steps, Actions, or sets, but the Actions must be in the same set and the steps must be in the same Action. Click and then Shift-click to select two or more contiguous items; (Command)-click [Ctrl]-click to select noncontiguous items.
- Double-click an Action or set to change its name and, for Actions, its function key (if any) and color.
- Double-click a modal step to open its dialog box and change settings. You cannot change the name of a step.
- Drag an Action or set to the New Action button to duplicate it.
- Click any step in any Action and then click the Record button to insert one or more steps or commands.

# Consolidating Actions

Because you can duplicate steps and use the Actions palette to determine which steps will run and which will not, you can have one Action take the place of several. As an example, look at Save for Web (multi) in Figure 7.51.

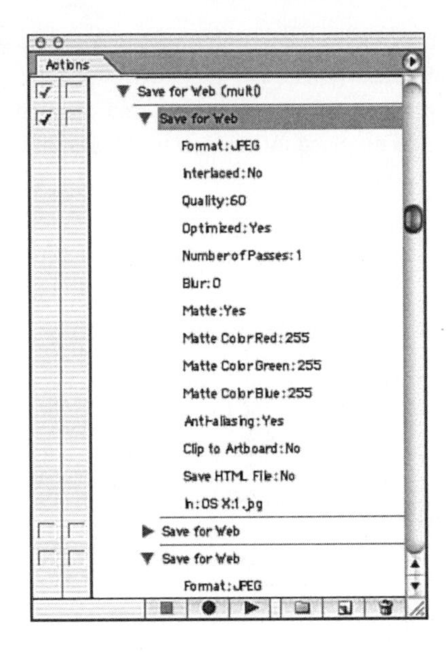


Figure 7.51
This Action has three steps, only one of which should be active at a time.

This Action replaces three Actions, each of which uses the Save for Web command. The first step, which you can see is selected to run (a check mark appears next to it in the first column), saves a file as JPEG at high (60%) quality. The second step, which is not expanded, has no check mark, so it does not run. (It is set to save files as JPEG medium quality.) The third step (also expanded), which is also not set to run, saves a file as JPEG low quality.

Before you run the Action, decide which quality is required, check the first column next to that step, and uncheck the boxes next to the other steps. That simply, you can consolidate all the JPEG Save for Web Actions into one easy-to-use Action.

## Saving and Sharing Action Sets

After you click the Stop button or use the Stop Recording command, the Action is ready to go in the Actions palette. However, if you want to make the Action available for use in other documents, you must save it separately.

The Actions palette menu command Save Actions opens the dialog box shown in Figure 7.52. If the command is grayed out (not available), an individual Action or step is selected in the Actions palette rather than a set. Only sets can be saved.

Illustrator Actions are cross-platform. However, to share Actions created on a Macintosh computer with the Windows version of Illustrator, you should add the extension .aia to the filename.

After you save a set of Actions with a new name, that name sticks with the file. The set appears in the Actions palette

> Remember that Actions must be in sets. If you want to save or share a single Action, make a new set and copy the individual Action into the set. You can duplicate the Action by dragging it to the New Action button at the bottom of the Action palette, or you can hold down (Option) [Alt] and drag the Action to a new set in the palette.

with the name assigned there, but every time you use the palette menu command Save Actions, the actual filename appears in the Save Set To dialog box.

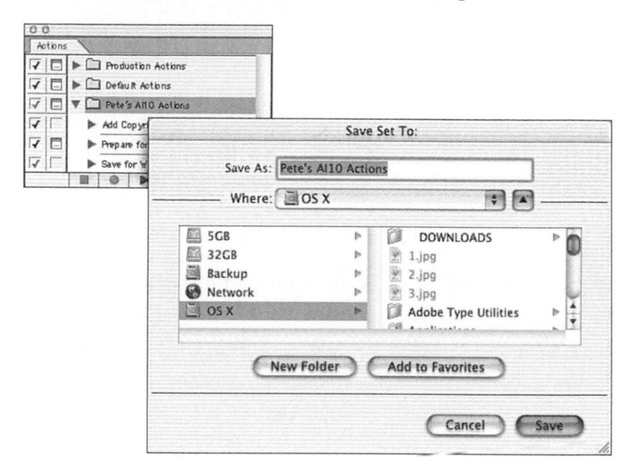


**Figure 7.52**
In the Save Set To dialog box, you can give the set a unique name. It does not have to be the same as the set's name in the Actions palette of the original document.

### Getting into the Action

Actions are actually text files. The following figure shows what an Action really looks like.

Production Actions
Last Saved: 10/09/01 04:22:01 PM
File Path: OS X:User...:Production Actions

```
/action-3 {
    /name (Crop Prep)
    /keyIndex 0
    /colorIndex 0
    /isOpen 1
    /eventCount 4
    /event-1 {
        /internalName (adobe_selectAll)
        /localizedName (Select All)
        /isOpen 0
        /isOn 1
        /hasDialog 0
        /parameterCount 0
    }
    /event-2 {
        /internalName (adobe_scale)
        /localizedName (Scale)
        /isOpen 1
        /isOn 1
        /hasDialog 1
        /showDialog 0
        /parameterCount 4
        /parameter-1 {
            /key 1970169453
            /type (boolean)
            /value 1
        }
        /parameter-2 {
            /key 1818848869
            /type (boolean)
            /value 0
        }
        /parameter-3 {
            /key 1935895653
            /type (unit real)
```

Actions are organized by number within a set. This set contains only one Action.

Any major word processor, such as Microsoft Word, or text editor, such as BBEdit (shown here), can open an Action. In the word processor's Open dialog box, select Show All Documents (or the equivalent command), select the Actions set, and click Open.

There is little practical use to opening an Action as a text file, but it can give you some insight into how various Illustrator tools and commands operate.

# MASTERING THE ADOBE CREATIVE SUITE

## Double-Check

*I've organized and color-coded all my Actions, and I'm using Button Mode to make things easier to find, but I seem to have messed up some of my Actions. They're not giving me the results I used to get.*

Step out of Button Mode for a moment and check the Actions that are giving you trouble. The most common source of this problem involves steps being skipped. When you're in Standard Mode, you can easily see whether all steps have the check mark next to them. In Button Mode, you have no such reminder; each Action plays according to the steps selected when you entered Button Mode.

## Unscheduled Halt

*I have an Action that stops in the middle, but no message appears. I have to click the Play button again to make it continue.*

Expand the Action in the Actions palette and look for a Stop at the point where the Action halts. Now look in the second column. An icon must be visible in the Modal Control column for the stop's warning box to appear.

## Stop Sign

*My Actions go right past my Stop messages sometimes, just not showing them at all. What can I do to fix this problem?*

Open the Actions palette, click the triangle next to the specific Action to expand it in the palette, and take a look at the first column. If you don't see a check mark, the step is skipped.

# FUNDAMENTAL PHOTOSHOP CS

## IN THIS PART

# 8

# BRINGING IMAGES INTO PHOTOSHOP

## IN THIS CHAPTER

Although some projects and artwork are created from scratch in Photoshop, the vast majority of work is done on existing images. (Even if an image is created from a blank document, the second time that file is opened in Photoshop, you're working with an "existing image.") Certain techniques and procedures can make working with existing images much simpler and easier, and improve the final product. In this chapter, you learn to start with good work habits when bringing pixels into Photoshop.

Digital photography has found its way into the home, workplace, and even studio. The differences between working with film and pixels are many, but some are of particular importance when working in Photoshop. Scanners are used regularly to bring photos and other artwork into Photoshop. As you learn in this chapter, understanding a few key points about scanner resolution and software can substantially reduce the amount of work you do *after* scanning. This chapter also takes a look at the world of stock photography, explaining some basic terms and some copyright concepts.

# DIGITAL CAMERA BASICS

One of the most common sources of images for Photoshop now is the digital camera. Once reserved for big-budget journalism operations, digital photography is within the reach of virtually all Photoshop users. Ranging in price from under $100 to well over $10,000, quite a selection of digital cameras is available. There is also a huge range of capabilities among digital cameras, involving such variables as the number of pixels captured, ISO simulation, lens range (and zooming), and even the hardware with which the image is actually captured.

## Digital Versus Film

Some high-end digital cameras capture enough data that they rival 35mm film cameras for detail. The majority of digital cameras, however, fall short of that level of precision. Some specialty digital backs for large-format cameras are even suitable for studio work.

The primary limitation for most digital cameras is the actual amount of detail that can be captured. The size of the individual pixels is determined by the number of pixels used to capture the image. If the number of pixels is low, each pixel must be large to capture the image. If, for example, the image is a landscape with power lines in the distance, extremely fine detail may be required to capture those power lines so they are displayed clearly in the image. If each pixel is larger than the width of the power line, there are not enough pixels to capture all the detail.

*Megapixels* is the measure of how much information a digital camera will capture. Instead of measuring pixels per inch (ppi) at a certain physical size (such as 4×6 inches at 200ppi), the megapixel number represents the millions of pixels captured, regardless of resolution or print size. (You'll see the abbreviation *MP* for megapixels.) Typical camera ratings range from 1.3 megapixels to over 6 megapixels. Table 8.1 explores the relationship among megapixels, pixel size, and print size.

**Caution**

Cramming too many pixels onto too small a CCD (the part of the digital camera that captures the image) is a bad idea. The pixels can be too small to record detail accurately. When shopping, you should compare both megapixels and CCD size.

**Table 8.1** Megapixels Versus Print Size

| Megapixel Rating | Pixel Dimensions | Print Size at 240dpi |
|---|---|---|
| 1.3 | 1,280×960 | 5.33×4.0 |
| 2.1 | 1,600×1,200 | 6.67×5.0 |
| 2.3 | 1,800×1,200 | 7.5×5.0 |
| 3.1 | 2,160×1,440 | 8.0×6.0 |
| 3.3 | 2,048×1,536 | 8.53×6.4 |
| 4.0 | 2,272×1,704 | 8.47×7.1 |
| 5.2 | 2,560×1,920 | 10.67×8.0 |

For the sample print resolution, 240dpi was selected because it's the resolution at which many inkjet printers reach maximum quality.

Keep in mind that these are maximum pixel dimensions. Numerous other factors may play a role in whether you have suitable resolution for your desired print size. For example, many cameras can capture images at multiple resolutions. The lower resolutions are designed to reduce file size and can be used when you need less resolution or when you want to capture more individual images on the camera's storage medium.

Another factor to consider is cropping. It's fine to say that a 5.2MP camera can capture enough data for an 8×10-inch inkjet glossy. However, if the picture is taken at the wrong distance or with an improper zoom, the digital photo might need to be substantially cropped to compose it properly. Figure 8.1 shows an example.

**Figure 8.1**
The original image is 2,560×1,920 pixels. When cropped to the desired image area, it measures only 1,440×1,152.

Cropping can reduce an image to pixel dimensions that are unsuitable for reproduction at 8×10 inches. In this example, the cropped image would output to 8×10 inches at 144 pixels per inch, which is less than optimal for inkjet output. (If an image is worth printing at such a size, it's worth having appropriate resolution.) You could, of course, use Photoshop to resample the image to a higher resolution, but that can introduce softness. Sharpening can reduce softness, but generally it's better to use an image's original pixels. Images properly captured on film, on the other hand, lose very little quality when enlarged to reasonable sizes.

*To learn more about determining the right resolution for inkjet and other output devices, see "Image Resolution" in Chapter 4, "Pixels, Vectors, and Resolutions," p. 148.*

## File Formats and Compression

Digital cameras often offer the choice of several compression levels and sometimes a choice of file formats. Suffice it to say that although compression helps reduce file size and enables you to capture more images on the same media, too much compression can seriously damage digital images.

*JPEG compression (and its effect on file quality) is discussed in Chapter 3, "Understanding and Choosing File Formats," p. 79.*

To maintain quality, keep compression to a minimum. Capturing images in TIFF and RAW file formats can maximize quality; however, many cameras cannot capture a large number of TIFF or RAW images on their storage media. Table 8.2 shows the storage capabilities of a sample 2.1MP camera.

**Table 8.2** Storage Capabilities for a 2.1MP Camera

| File Format | Pixel Dimensions | Images per 8MB Smartcard |
|---|---|---|
| TIFF | 1,600×1,200 | 1 |
| JPEG-SHQ | 1,600×1,200 | 7 |
| JPEG-HQ | 1,600×1,200 | 16 |
| JPEG-SQ | 1,024×768 | 38 |
| JPEG-SQ | 640×480 | 82 |

As the table demonstrates, the file format and pixel dimension options have a tremendous impact on the number of images that can be captured to a single card. (The numbers shown are for the Olympus C-700 Ultra Zoom.) Capabilities vary from camera to camera, so check the documentation for a specific camera (or the manufacturer's Web site). No matter the size of the images captured by your camera, make sure you have adequate storage media (and batteries) on hand for your shooting needs.

The figures shown in Table 8.2 are for comparison. Feel free to shoot in TIFF—just make sure you have enough storage media to handle your shoot. Also, don't forget that in many circumstances, you can download to a computer during a shoot. If you have a suitable laptop, you can even download in the field.

# COMMON PROBLEMS WITH DIGITAL CAMERA IMAGES

Two quite common problems with digital cameras are noise and color cast. *Noise* is viewed in the image as spots of blue, red, green, or gray scattered throughout the picture. These spots are called *artifacts*. Even in grayscale, some noise is evident to the left in Figure 8.2.

Figure 8.2
The irregular "grain" in the background is digital noise.

In properly exposed digital images, noise is most commonly seen as blue artifacts. Underexposed images and shadow areas often have noise in the Red channel. The Green channel is typically the least affected. In Figure 8.3, each of the channels is shown individually.

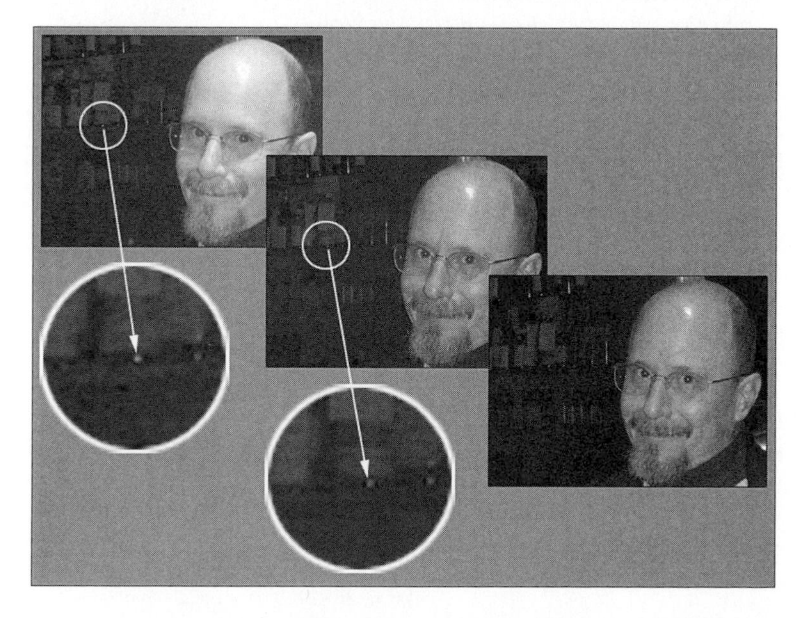

Figure 8.3
From the top, the channels are Red, Green, and Blue. The noise is most evident in the background area of the Red channel, especially when compared to the Green channel.

By using the Photoshop filter Blur, Gaussian Blur; Noise, Despeckle; or Noise, Median, you can minimize the artifacts in the damaged channel or channels, leaving the remaining color channel(s) untouched.

8

Photoshop also offers an easy fix for those unwanted tints known as *color casts*. When an image shows a distinct cast, you can use Image, Adjustments, Auto Color as an easy solution. By balancing the highlights, midtones, and shadows, and then extending that correction throughout the image, you can remove unwanted tinting with a single click.

*To learn more about color correction, see Chapter 17, "Manipulating Color and Tonality," p. 543.*

Should the Auto Color command not produce the result you want, remember that Curves and Levels can each be used on individual color channels. Just as blurring a single channel can remove unwanted artifacts, correcting a single channel can repair an overall color cast.

Rather than correct digital noise and color casts in Photoshop, you should avoid them in the first place. Make sure your digital camera is set to the proper white balance, the proper light source, and the proper ISO for the conditions. Check your camera's documentation and consider using autoexposure, if available.

# FROM CAMERA TO PHOTOSHOP

Moving images from a digital camera to Photoshop can take any of several forms. Your camera, its software, and your computer's operating system all can play a role. The various combinations of camera, software, and OS are many; this section presents some generalities, and it uses one camera as an example. Consult the documentation for your camera, software, and OS, and use the Internet to get the latest information and software updates for your configuration.

Depending on the media your camera uses to record and your camera's connection capability, you may be able to access the images directly from the camera. Alternatively, you might need to connect a media reader to your computer. Some cameras record directly to floppy disks or mini-CDs (Sony Mavica cameras, for example), which can be read directly by the computer.

## Using the Camera's Software

A huge variety of software is supplied with digital cameras. Some software is designed only to download images from the camera to the hard drive. Other software is often provided to help you work with those images. Many cameras come bundled with Adobe Photoshop Elements or another image-editing program. These programs do not necessarily allow you to access the images while in the camera.

Many cameras are considered "auto-connect" USB devices and require no software. The camera is seen as a hard drive and can be accessed as such (in a read-only configuration). Both Windows XP and Mac OS X have software built in to the operating system for downloading digital images from cameras.

Remember that *resolution* refers only to a printing instruction, telling the output device the size of the pixels and, therefore, how tightly to pack them on the page. At 72ppi,

You may find it easier to think of resolution as the size of each pixel on the printed page. At 72ppi, each printed pixel is 1/72 of an inch. At 300ppi, each pixel is 1/300 of an inch. The smaller the individual pixels, the finer the detail in the image.

each pixel is 1/72 of an inch square. If the same image is converted to 240ppi, each pixel is 1/240 of an inch. If the image isn't resampled, the same number of pixels fits into an area about 1/10 the size.

Consider an image that's 1,600×1,200 pixels in size. At 72ppi, printing that image would require a sheet of paper that's more than 22×16 inches, and the image would look pixilated because of the size of the individual pixels. Maintaining those same pixel dimensions (1,600×1,200 pixels) but printing at 240ppi yields an image that's 6.67×5 inches on paper, and the image's quality is greatly enhanced.

## Photoshop at Work: Resolution Adjustment

Many digital cameras capture and record pixels without regard to future use of the image. Photoshop opens these images and prepares them for viewing on the monitor, assuming a monitor resolution of 72ppi. Other cameras record a resolution of 300ppi in the file's EXIF data (EXIF stands for *Exchangeable Image Format*, as you learn in the next section of this chapter). It's likely that neither of these resolutions is optimal for all your projects.

To maintain the highest image quality possible, follow these steps to change an image's resolution:

1. Open the image in Photoshop.
2. Open the Image Size dialog box by using the menu command Image, Image Size.
3. Deselect the Resample Image check box. This locks the upper part of the dialog box and prevents changes to the image's actual pixel size (see Figure 8.4).

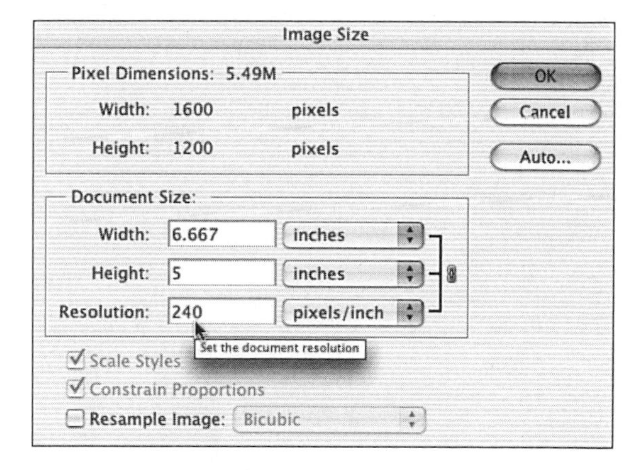


Figure 8.4
When Resample Image is unchecked, Image Size merely changes the resolution instruction for printing. It makes no change to the image's actual pixels, thus preserving the picture's original quality.

4. Enter the desired print resolution in the Resolution field, or enter the desired height or width and let Photoshop calculate the resolution.
5. Click OK.

By not resampling, you preserve the image's pixels exactly as captured. You can adjust the resolution and let Photoshop calculate the image's print dimensions, or you can enter the desired height and/or width and let the program determine the resolution.

*Not clear on resampling? See "Adding, Subtracting, and Preserving Pixels" in the "Mastering Photoshop" section at the end of this chapter.*

8

## EXIF Data

Exchangeable Image Format (EXIF) is actually the file format used by digital still cameras. Originally developed in the mid-1990s by the Japan Electronic Industry Development Association (JEIDA), this format now includes even audio format instructions. EXIF requires the use of JPEG for compressed image files and TIFF (version 6.0) for uncompressed files. Some versions of the RAW file format support EXIF data.

One benefit of using EXIF is the image information stored with the picture. Date, time, camera settings, image pixel dimensions and resolution, and even data from a global positioning system (GPS) device are among the dozens of pieces of information that can be recorded with the file. You can use Photoshop CS to access the EXIF information through the File Browser or with the menu command File, File Info.

# PHOTOSHOP'S IMPROVED FILE BROWSER

Introduced with Photoshop 7, the File Browser enables you to preview a folder of images at once, reviewing specific information about each, as well as ranking, renaming, and even relocating the images on your drive.

*File Browser has its own set of preferences in Photoshop CS. For information on these preferences, see "Preferences, File Browser," in Chapter 2, "Choosing Hardware and Setting Up Your Software," p. 55.*

Photoshop CS has a greatly improved File Browser, with all the features most requested by Photoshop users. In Photoshop CS, the File Browser has been promoted to a full-time window and no longer can be docked in the Palette Well. You can open the File Browser with the File, Browse command or the Window, File Browser command. In Figure 8.5, you can see the sections of the new File Browser identified.

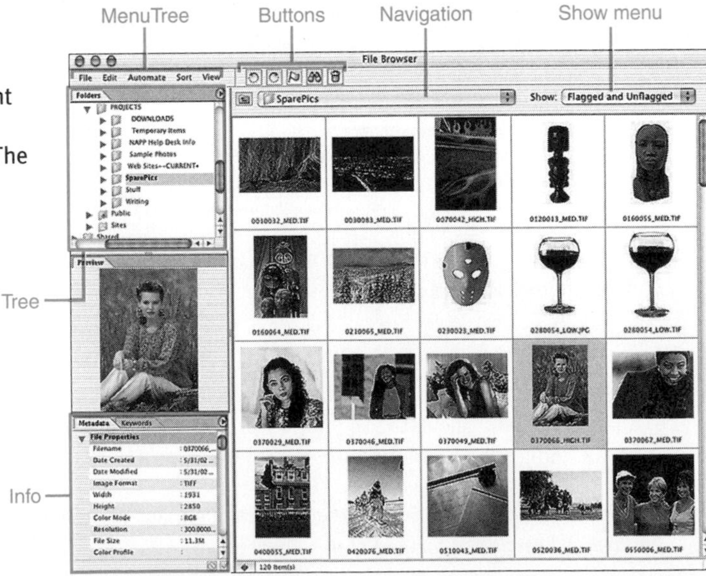


**Figure 8.5**
The large area to the lower right displays thumbnails of the images in the selected folder. The larger version of the selected image to the left is called the *preview*.

# File Browser's Menus

File Browser has its own set of menus, as you can see in Figure 8.6.

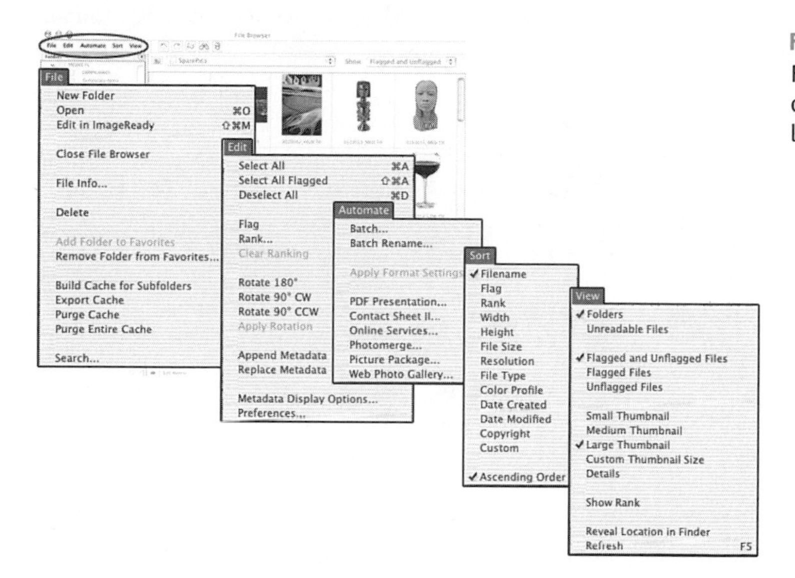


**Figure 8.6**
File Browser has five menus of its own, through which you can regulate most of its operation.

Although most of the commands are self-explanatory, some deserve clarification:

- **File**—In the File menu, note the command Edit in ImageReady. You can now open files from File Browser into ImageReady directly. The *cache* is the file in which File Browser stores information about the images in a particular folder. Included in the information are the previews generated by File Browser. The first time you access a folder, File Browser generates previews of the images, which it stores in the cache. Subsequently, File Browser need only access the cache rather than regenerating the previews.
- **Edit**—Files can be *ranked*, which enables you to assign any one of a number of identifiers to the files, and they can also be *flagged*, which singles out those files from the unflagged ones in the folder. Rotating an image through File Browser's Edit menu changes only the preview. However, if the image is then opened in Photoshop, the rotation is applied (but not saved unless the file is saved). The *metadata* (discussed later in this chapter) is information saved with the file.
- **Automate**—Many of the commands available in Photoshop's File, Automate menu are also accessible from File Browser.
- **Sort**—The Sort menu is used to arrange images within the File Browser. As you can see, there are quite a few choices.
- **View**—The View menu enables you to customize the content and appearance of the thumbnails section of File Browser. The Refresh command is used to update the content of the window.

If you export the cache to a folder of images *before* you burn that folder to a CD or DVD, the previews stashed in the cache will significantly speed File Browser when it accesses that disc.

## Buttons

To the right of File Browser's menus is a series of five buttons (see Figure 8.7). From the left, they can be used to rotate the preview and thumbnail counterclockwise, rotate the preview and thumbnail clockwise, flag the selected file(s), search for a specific file, and delete the selected file(s).

Figure 8.7
Whereas the other four buttons are basically one-trick ponies, the Search button is a bit more complicated. It enables you to find files based on filename, size, creation or modification date, flag status, rank, keywords, captions, and even metadata.

## Navigation

The pop-up menu File Browser uses to locate a specific file includes both Favorite Folders and Recent Folders (see Figure 8.8). You can navigate through your accessible drives quite similarly to the way you would in Windows Explorer or the Mac Finder. Notice, too, the Up One Level button to the left of the pop-up menu. This button is available for both Windows and Mac users to jump to the parent folder in one click.

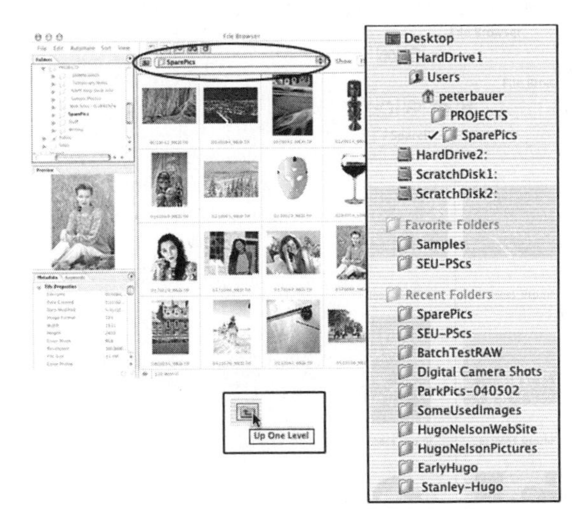


Figure 8.8
The currently active folder is identified with a check mark for the Mac and is highlighted in Windows.

## Show Menu

You can use the Show menu to determine what images will be presented in the thumbnails area. The Show pop-up menu offers the choice of all images (Flagged and Unflagged), only flagged images (Flagged Files), or only unflagged images (Unflagged Files), as shown in Figure 8.9.

**Figure 8.9**
The Unflagged Files option can be handy when used in conjunction with File Browser's File, Delete command to weed out unnecessary images.

## Tree

The hierarchical file structure to the left in File Browser, known as the *Tree* (see Figure 8.10), is a complement to the navigation pop-up menu at the top. Which you use is up to you, and perhaps the location on disk you need to access. You may find it more convenient to use the navigation menu so that you can expand the preview area. Or perhaps you're more comfortable using the Tree to open folders.

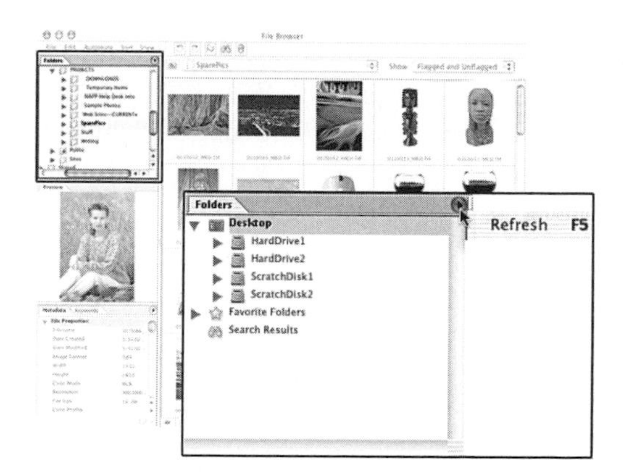


**Figure 8.10**
Note that the Tree includes quick access to favorite folders and saved search results.

## Info

In the lower-left corner of File Browser are the tabs that display a file's information (or *metadata*). You can show (and hide) a variety of information (see Figure 8.11). The Metadata Display Options command from the menu enables you to select which fields to show, and it even offers an option to hide empty fields.

> You can change the widths of the columns in the metadata. Position the cursor over the dots separating the columns and drag.

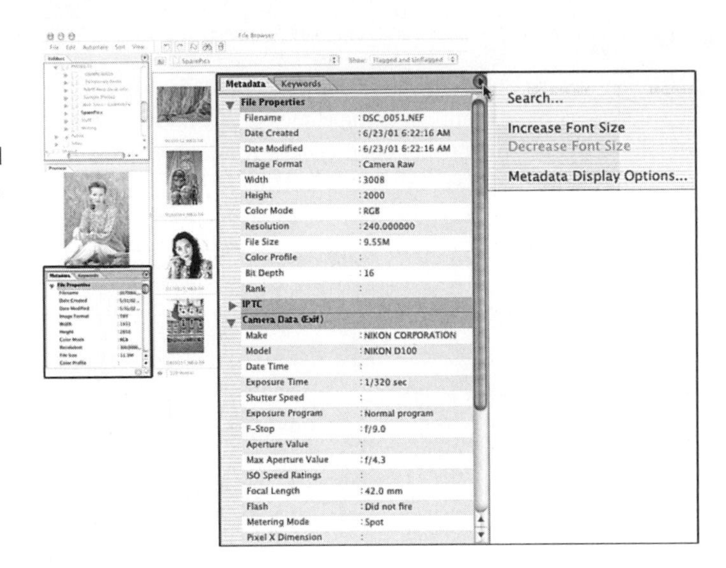


**Figure 8.11**
The IP TC section and the Keywords tab can read keywords tagged to the image by a variety of methods. File Browser can read keywords for stock images from a variety of sources.

# SCANNERS: HARDWARE BASICS

Images can be digitized using scanners as well as digital cameras. Although hardware exists to make accurate three-dimensional scans, the vast majority of scanning for Photoshop involves flat, 2D originals. Most originals fall into one of two categories: reflective materials and transparencies.

*Reflective*, in this situation, indicates that light bounces off the original and is captured when it returns. Paper is the primary example of reflective material. Photographs, pages from books and magazines, and even canvas and brick can be considered reflective materials.

*Transparencies* are film, whether slides or negatives, and come in a variety of sizes (35mm, medium format, and large format). Scanners record film somewhat differently than they record reflective materials. Instead of light bouncing off the surface and being collected, the light passes through the film and the image is captured on the other side.

## Flatbed and Drum Scanners

Flatbed scanners are the most common and least expensive equipment for digitizing reflective artwork. Serviceable scans can be produced by equipment costing under $100. Drum scanners are far more expensive, much more complicated, and produce scans to much more exacting standards. To use a flatbed scanner, you place the object to be scanned on the glass "bed," and the scanning mechanism moves. Drum scanners have the image attached to a spinning drum while the optical mechanism remains stable.

Drum scanners are more likely to be found at service bureaus and print houses, whereas flatbed scanners are common in studios, offices, and homes. Some high-end flatbed scanners can achieve quality comparable to low-end drum scanners.

Flatbed scanners can be connected to your computer via USB, FireWire, or SCSI. FireWire is typically found only on high-end scanners that are designed and intended to capture large amounts of information. If you scan at high resolution on a regular basis, FireWire or USB-2 may be appropriate.



## Flatbed Resolution and Bit Depth

When looking to purchase a flatbed scanner, you should consider several features. The size of the scanner's bed (the largest size it can scan) could be important. The software package that comes with the scanner can perhaps influence your decision. You should also consider the hardware's resolution and bit depth as well as the competence of the scanner's own software.

If you typically scan photos, a Letter- or Legal-size bed is more than enough. If you suspect you'll be scanning larger works, you'll need a larger scanner. When considering bit depth, think about the final destination of the images you'll scan. Both Web and commercial offset press don't require as much color information as fine-art prints.

Resolution is often advertised with two pairs of numbers: the *optical* resolution and the *interpolated* resolution. The first tells you what the hardware can do; the second is all about software. Because you can perhaps more accurately interpolate images in Photoshop, the optical resolution is more important. Optical resolution is typically 600ppi, 1,200ppi, or 2,400ppi. More accurately, scanner resolution should be measured in "samples per inch" (spi). However, there's no practical difference between spi and ppi. Drum scanners can reach resolutions of 9,600spi, and film scanners are typically either 2,000 or 4,000spi.

Color *bit depth* describes how much information the scanner records for each pixel. Although Photoshop can work with 16-bit color, the files are much larger and output options are restricted. Most images in Photoshop, whether RGB, CMYK, or grayscale, use 8-bit color depth.

That having been said, more color information from the scanner is usually better than less. Generally, Photoshop or the output device will eventually discard the excess information, but there's a stronger probability of getting accurate color with a 48-bit scanner than with a 24-bit scanner. Remember, though, that bit depth is dependent on the quality of the scanner's hardware. Although a sub-$100 scanner might offer 42-bit color, that doesn't mean it will produce more accurate scans than a $1,500 36-bit scanner.

The scanner's *dynamic range* should also be considered. The dynamic range, also referred to as the *density*, is the scanner's capability to capture tonal range. The higher the value, the better the scanner reproduces detail in shadow areas. Density rated below 3.2 is marginal. Very high-end flatbed and drum scanners can approach the theoretical maximum of 4.0.

Consider dynamic range to be the thickness of a book and bit depth to be the number of pages. A book that's 3 inches thick and has only 30 very hefty pages is probably just as useless as a book one-tenth of an inch thick with 4,000 pages that are each too flimsy to turn. Both dynamic range and color bit depth are required for a quality scanner.

## Film Scanners Versus Transparency Adapters

Transparencies can be scanned by using film scanners or with transparency adapters for flatbed scanners. (Drum scanners can also digitize transparencies.) Dedicated film scanners generally produce higher-quality scans than do flatbed scanners. The image's tonal range is often captured much more accurately and completely with a film scanner.

If you work only with 35mm film, you'll find film scanners for under $1,000 that do excellent work. If your requirements include medium-format film, expect to pay $3,000 or more. Large-format film scanners cost upward of $10,000.

Transparency adapters are often built in to high-end flatbed scanners costing $1,000 or more. Less expensive flatbeds also offer integrated or add-on transparency capabilities, often at a substantial increase in price and with lower-quality results.

## Scanning Software

The quality of the scanner's software is also important. Some scanners simply acquire images. Others have sophisticated software capable of removing dust and scratches. Online and magazine reviews are often valuable when evaluating scanner software. However, seeing is often believing. If you have the opportunity to put a scanner through its paces before buying, make sure you test its software. If it offers color correction, try it. If the scanner claims to be able to make repairs to damaged originals, give it a test drive. Certainly test its capability to reduce moiré when scanning images printed in books or magazines (you learn more about the problems of moiré in the later section of this chapter, "Moiré Patterns and How to Avoid Them").

Most scanners that would be of interest to a Photoshop user enable you to acquire images by using the Photoshop command File, Import, which opens the images directly in Photoshop. To operate the scanner from within Photoshop, the scanner's acquire module must be located in the correct Photoshop folder. This plug-in is the link between Photoshop and the scanner. In almost all cases, it should be installed or copied to the Import/Export folder within Photoshop's Plug-Ins folder. (Photoshop should not be running when plug-ins are added.)

# SCANNING IMAGES INTO PHOTOSHOP

In most cases, you can use Photoshop's File, Import command to access a scanner's plug-in. The plug-in opens the scanner's software and allows you to control the hardware. Because such a wide range of scanner software is available, this section looks primarily at theory rather than specific examples.

## Resolution

In scanning, the resolution determines the fineness of detail (and file size) of the captured image. In Figure 8.12, the same image has been scanned at four different resolutions.

In the top-left corner, the image was scanned at 72ppi. The top-right image was scanned at 128ppi, a resolution that is

> When preparing to scan, always start from the endpoint. In other words, determine the size and color depth requirements for the final image file before starting to scan.

suitable for many newsprint applications. In the lower-left corner, the image is at 200ppi, appropriate for many magazine printing jobs. The lower-right image was scanned at 400ppi. This resolution isn't typically used for print but can be used to resize an image while scanning.

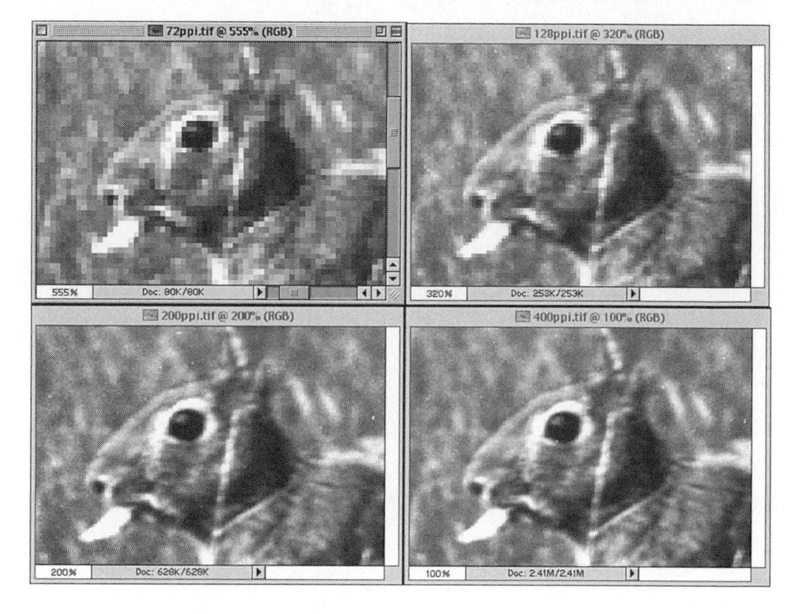


**Figure 8.12**
The four windows have been "zoomed" to show the same area of the image.

Notice the difference in the relative size of the pixels at the various resolutions. When each image occupies the same space, the number of pixels available determines the size of each pixel. The very visible pixels in the 72ppi image (upper left) are more than five-and-a-half times as large as the pixels in the lower-right image. That means the lower-resolution image uses one pixel for an area of detail in the image that the high-resolution image displays with about 30 pixels. For example, the 72ppi image uses approximately 36 pixels to reproduce the rabbit's eye. The 400ppi image uses almost 1,300 pixels for the eye.

Remember that the scanning resolution determines the actual number of pixels in the image, which also plays a large role in the file size. In Figure 8.13, the same four scans are shown, three at 100% zoom and the largest at 66.67% zoom for comparison.

At 100% zoom, each pixel in each image is exactly the same size. The higher-resolution scans require more space onscreen because they have more pixels. Higher-resolution scans also require more space on disk. Because more pixels are being captured, more file information needs to be recorded. Resolution (unless changed in Photoshop) also determines print size. See Table 8.3 for some comparative numbers.

> The terms *ppi*, *dpi*, and *lpi* all refer to *linear* inches. When we say 200 pixels per inch, that's the number of pixels side by side, not in a square inch.

**Figure 8.13**
From back to front, the scans are at 400ppi, 200ppi, 128ppi, and 72ppi.

**Table 8.3** Relative Size at Various Resolutions

| Resolution | File Size | Pixel Dimensions | Print Size at 200dpi |
|---|---|---|---|
| 400ppi | 2,410KB | 1,112×755 | 5.56×3.75 inches |
| 200ppi | 638KB | 562×381 | 2.81×1.905 inches |
| 128ppi | 253KB | 356×242 | 1.78×1.21 inches |
| 72ppi | 80KB | 200×136 | 1.0×0.68 inches |

# Photoshop at Work: Picking a Scan Resolution

The appropriate resolution for an image depends on its final purpose. Images intended to be thumbnails on a Web page don't need to be scanned at the same resolution as photographs that will be printed at 8×10 inches on glossy paper. Nor will either of those images have the same requirements as an image that will occupy three columns at four inches tall in the daily newspaper.

In all cases, the best place to start is at the end. Determine what the final image size must be in *pixels* and then scan to that size. Here is one example:

1. An image will be output on a commercial printing press as part of a page-layout program's document.
2. The document will be printed at a line screen frequency of 133lpi (lines per inch).
3. An appropriate image resolution for 133lpi is 200dpi. (The general rule of thumb is 1.5 or 2 times the line screen is an appropriate image resolution.)
4. The image will occupy a space of 4×6 inches in the document.

> With some scanning software, you can simply input the desired print size and resolution. That eliminates the need to "do the math."

5. The final pixel size must be 800×1,200 pixels. (That's based on 200dpi times 4 inches, by 200dpi times 6 inches.)
6. The original photograph to be scanned measures 5×7.5 inches.
7. The appropriate scan resolution is a mere 160ppi. (800 divided by 5 equals 160; 1,200 divided by 7.5 also equals 160.)

Alternatively, if the original photograph measured only 2×3 inches, the appropriate scan resolution would be 400ppi—800 divided by 2; 1,200 divided by 3.

When you capture the appropriate number of pixels from the start, you eliminate the possibility of image degradation that can be caused by resizing and sharpening.

*Uncertain about scan resolution for transparencies? See "Scanning Resolution for Film" in the "Mastering Photoshop" section at the end of this chapter.*

**Image Resolution for Inkjets**

There is a difference between the "resolution" of an inkjet printer and the appropriate image resolution. An inkjet's 1,440×720 resolution, for example, refers to the ink droplets. It takes several droplets to replicate a colored pixel on a sheet of paper.

The image's resolution refers to the actual pixels in the image. To get the maximum quality from an inkjet printer, you need to use an image resolution of one-third the printer's stated resolution. When two numbers are given, divide the smaller. In the example of a 1,440×720 inkjet resolution, an image resolution of 240 is optimal.

Remember, too, that most inkjet printers are rather limited in the file size they can handle. If your printer can produce 1,440×1,440 droplets per inch, the one-third rule would indicate an image resolution of 480dpi. Run a few tests, and you'll find that there might be no visual difference between 240 and 480dpi for your printer. There could be, however, a huge difference in output time or whether the image even prints at all.

## Scanning for Grayscale

Although most scanners can produce a grayscale image, it's often better to generate a color image and convert from RGB to grayscale in Photoshop. By capturing more color information, you increase the available tonal range. The tonal range determines, among other things, how much detail will be visible in the image's shadow and highlight areas.

*To learn more about working with an image's appearance, see Chapter 17, "Manipulating Color and Tonality," p. 543.*

There are a number of ways to convert an RGB image to grayscale in Photoshop. The easiest is to simply use Image, Mode, Grayscale. Better results are often achieved by using two steps: Image, Adjust, Desaturate and then Image, Mode, Grayscale. However, for even greater control (and a better result), use Photoshop's Channel Mixer (see Figure 8.14).

The Channel Mixer enables you to take the best parts of each color channel and combine them into a single grayscale channel. Open the dialog box with the menu command Image, Adjust, Channel Mixer. To create a grayscale image, click the Monochrome check box in the lower-left corner (see Figure 8.15). Adjust the sliders until you achieve the desired tonal range. Afterward, use the menu command Image, Mode, Grayscale.

For normal key images, try to keep the total of the sliders close to 100. (The value of the Constant slider, negative or positive, should be multiplied by 3 when you're adding to 100.) However, this is not a hard-and-fast rule—different images have different requirements.

Figure 8.14
The image on the left was desaturated and then converted from RGB to grayscale. On the right, the Channel Mixer was used before converting the image to grayscale.

Figure 8.15
The original image, Peppers.jpg, is found in the Samples folder installed by default with Photoshop CS.

# Digitizing Line Art

Resist any temptation to scan line art as RGB. There is no advantage over grayscale, and the size of a 1,200ppi RGB image can create problems.

Scanning line art in bitmap color mode produces an image that contains pixels that are either black or white, with no shades of gray. Scanning line art without *jaggies*, those visible pixel corners that make curves look ragged, requires very high resolution. Instead of being scanned at 300ppi, line art should be scanned at 1,200ppi. For a comparison, see Figure 8.16. Many scanners have special settings for line art, which might also be listed as "bitmap." Even with the higher resolution, the corners of the pixels will be there; they just won't be as visible. Remember that higher resolution means that each individual pixel is proportionally smaller.

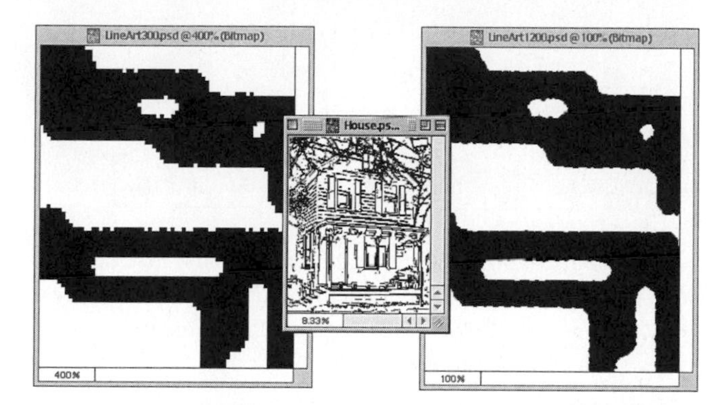

**Figure 8.16**
The two zooms show the same area of the image, at 300ppi on the left and 1,200ppi on the right. The difference in pixel size—and image detail—is apparent.

In addition to scanning at high resolution, you can exercise some control to improve the digitized line art. Scanning in grayscale and then applying the Threshold command can be very effective. The Threshold slider enables you to determine which of the gray pixels will be converted to black and which to white. (When you scan line art as black and white, the scanner's own setting determines the darkness at which any gray pixel is converted to black.) A comparison of Threshold settings is shown in Figure 8.17.

**Figure 8.17**
The Threshold command converts all pixels to either black or white. You use the slider to determine the grayscale value at which the division is made.

8

## Moiré Patterns and How to Avoid Them

One of the most common problems encountered in scanning artwork is moiré patterns. These obvious patterns occur when scanning artwork printed in CMYK. The pattern of dots produced by the printing press, although not visible to the eye, appears quite exaggerated when scanned (see Figure 8.18).

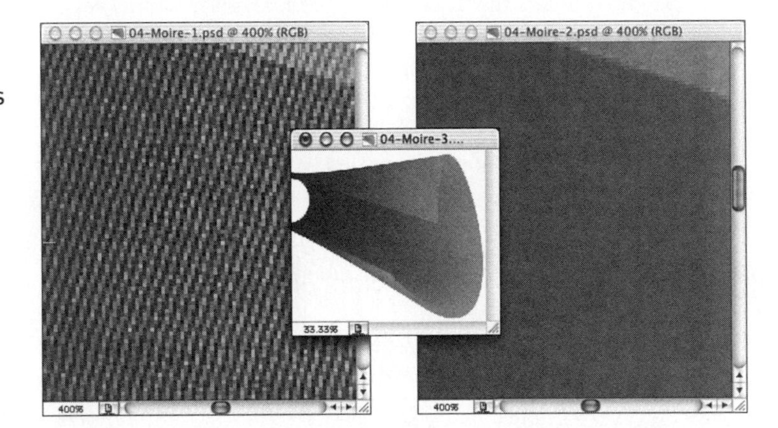


**Figure 8.18**
On the left, the moiré pattern is visible. On the right, the scanner's descreening option was used.

Typically, the easiest way to avoid the appearance of any pattern in scanned artwork is to use the capability built in to most scanners. Whether it's called "Descreening" or "Moire Removal," or perhaps is activated by choosing "Magazine" or "Color Document" as the source, the scanner's software is usually the best tool to use to avoid the problem.

Placing printed artwork on the scanner's glass at a 15° angle can also help reduce moiré. Because the dot pattern no longer aligns with the path of the scan head, the pattern is diminished. In conjunction with this technique (or in place of it, if you have no control over the original scan), you can apply a Gaussian Blur filter to smooth the pattern. The more pronounced the pattern, the greater the blur required. The greater the blur, the more the image is softened.

Although sharpening can reduce the softness introduced by blurring, it can also reintroduce a moiré pattern. Striking a balance between blurring and moiré may be possible, but often it's more feasible to compromise on *where* rather than *how much*. Instead of blurring the entire image and then sharpening the entire image, consider where the focus should be. Work selectively to reduce moiré in key areas of the image, and blur the less important areas to a greater degree. Consider masks or selections to isolate areas of the image and then use the Blur and Sharpen tools to fine-tune those areas.

> A moiré-like pattern can also be found in digital camera images of certain fabrics and textures. The technique of blurring and sharpening can be used to reduce the pattern. Remember, too, that with digital cameras, the pattern may be more pronounced in one channel. You can blur/sharpen each channel individually, according to its needs.

## Photoshop at Work: Why You Should Avoid Resampling

Whether you're working with a scanner, a digital camera, or stock photos downloaded via the Internet, it's always best to start with the correct pixel dimensions. The process of resampling—changing the pixel dimensions of an image without changing its content—can harm the appearance of your artwork. Here's a little exercise to show you what we mean:

1. Open Photoshop and choose the menu command File, Open.
2. Navigate to the Photoshop folder and open Samples.
3. Select the Eagle.psd image and open it.
4. Click twice on the leftmost button at the bottom of the History palette to create two identical copies of the file.
5. With either copy active, use the menu command Image, Image Size. Select the Resample (Bicubic) and Constrain Proportions check boxes, and enter a new width of 212 pixels. Click OK.
6. Switch to the other duplicate Eagle image and use Image Size to change the width to 848 pixels.
7. Zoom in on all three images, as shown in Figure 8.19.

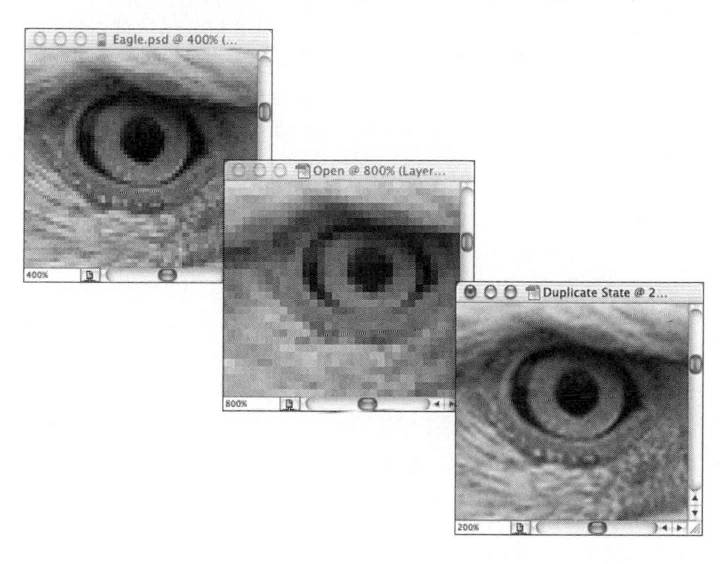


**Figure 8.19**
The original is at the top, the reduced copy is in the middle, and the enlarged copy is at the bottom.

Notice the pixelization of the middle copy. The pupil of the eagle's eye is no longer round. Less noticeable, but nonetheless still there, is a substantial "softening" of the eye that was "upsampled" (the number of pixels in the image was increased). The softness can be reduced by using the Sharp filters; however, if the image had been scanned at a width of 848 pixels originally, there would be no softness.

## Tuning Your Scanner

Just as all scanners are not created equal, so too are areas of the scanner's bed often unequal. Most scanners have a "sweet spot," an area where they seem to work best. Finding the prime position on your flatbed can be as easy as scanning a blank piece of paper at low resolution. Any gray areas in the resulting scan indicate where the image was captured inaccurately. Generally, you'll find that there's a rectangular area in the center of the scanner's bed that gives the best results.

8

Scanning a blank sheet of paper can also indicate whether you need to clean the scanner's glass. (Always follow the manufacturer's instructions for cleaning the glass. Damaging the glass can render the scanner unusable.) Remember, too, that the minutes it takes to clean a scanner's glass can save hours in artifact removal in Photoshop.

To gain practical experience with scanning, let us recommend *The Scanning Workshop* (Que, ISBN 0-7897-2558-4), by our contributing author, Richard Romano.

# STOCK PHOTOGRAPHY AND OTHER EXISTING ARTWORK

Another source of ready-made pixels is stock art. Available on the Web and in collections on CD or DVD, stock artwork consists of photographs, illustrations, clip art, and even audio and motion clips (which cannot be used in Photoshop) prepared by others and licensed for your use. Many programs, including Photoshop, ship with some stock art. (Photoshop CS's default installation includes the Samples folder, inside the Photoshop folder. The stock images are not included with the education version of Photoshop.)

Artwork can also be found on the Internet, in books, and elsewhere. However, you should be aware of copyright laws before using any artwork not created by and for yourself.

## Sources of Stock Images

Stock photography firms abound, and most of the major players have a Web presence. Comstock, SuperStock, PhotoSpin, EyeWire (a division of Getty Images), PhotoDisc, and DigitalVision are just some of the major sources of stock photos. You'll also find vector artwork and, in many cases, fonts. You can search for images that fit your needs from their extensive collections, pay online by credit card or via an account, and download. You can also order collections of images on CD. If you use the same type of image regularly, but don't want to use the same specific image all the time, collections can save you a lot of money.

## Royalty-Free Versus Licensed Images

The images you pay for are not really purchased; rather, they are licensed. The copyright is not transferred, and you are not free to do whatever you want with the images. Even the most lenient licensing arrangements prohibit you from reselling the images as stock art or from using them in defamatory ways. What you can do with the images is governed by the type of license for which you paid.

Royalty-free artwork is licensed to you to use as many times as you like, in whatever manner (except as mentioned previously) you like. The same image can be reused in a variety of works and for whatever purposes you desire.

Traditionally licensed images (also called *rights-protected images*) are much more tightly restricted. You purchase a license to use the images for a specific purpose, for a specific period of time.

Another major difference is availability of the images. Royalty-free images can be and are licensed repeatedly and can appear simultaneously in a variety of different works by different people or studios. You cannot control who else is using the images and for what purpose. (Over the past several years, there has been a preponderance of "perspective" shots—photos taken from a ladder while looking downward at a person. One particular image of a young woman appeared in no fewer than 12 different advertising materials, for 12 different companies, in the space of 4 months. A couple of those companies were direct competitors.)

Rights-protected images can be licensed exclusively for a period of time—no one else will have access to or permission to use those specific images during the license period.

## Copyright Concerns

The licensing agreements for stock images are explicit (and should be read carefully), but rights to other images are not always as clear. Although there is no substitute for advice from a legal professional, you should consider certain guidelines when using artwork that might belong to another:

- If you didn't create it, you probably need to contact the person who did.
- *Derivative works*, those that are made from or include existing artwork, don't transfer copyright. You cannot include another's work in your art without permission.
- There need not be a copyright symbol (©) to indicate protected work. Creative work is automatically copyrighted as soon as it is created.

Other than a practicing legal professional, perhaps the best source of information about copyright law is the law itself. It can be accessed online through the Library of Congress at `www.loc.gov/copyright`.

# MASTERING PHOTOSHOP

## Digital Cameras and sRGB

*According to the EXIF data I see in File Browser, my camera is capturing in the sRGB color space. I thought sRGB was a very limited color space, intended for the Web and not appropriate for general use. What should I do?*

Many cameras indicate in their images' metadata that the embedded profile is sRGB, even when the image was captured in a much broader space. The false sRGB tag is included to ensure that the camera is "Windows compliant." The problem comes when Photoshop actually converts the original colors to that sRGB color space. To prevent this unintentional degradation of the image, go to Photoshop's File Handling Preferences and check the box labeled Ignore EXIF profile Tag.

## Adding, Subtracting, and Preserving Pixels

*What is resampling and why should I avoid it?*

*Resampling* is the process of increasing or decreasing the number of pixels in an image while attempting to maintain the overall look of the image. The content of the image (theoretically) remains the same, but it is created with more or fewer pixels. (This process is in contrast to cropping, which reduces the number of pixels but also changes the image's content.)

When you use Image, Image Size to increase an image's pixel dimensions, Photoshop has to create new pixels to place between (or in place of) the original pixels. It averages the color values of surrounding pixels to determine what color the new pixels should be.

When Image, Image Size is used to reduce the number of pixels in an image, Photoshop averages the color values of a group of pixels and uses that color value to create the replacement pixel(s).

The problem with resampling is that the process of averaging color values introduces a "softness," sort of an out-of-focus look, to the image. When you avoid resampling, you avoid introducing that blurriness.

## Scanning Resolution for Film

*How do I determine the target scan resolution when using a film scanner?*

The formula is the same. Determine the required output size in pixels, measure the original, and divide those dimensions into the pixel dimensions. The only difference is that instead of measuring, say, a 4×6-inch photograph as the original, you may be measuring a portion of a 35mm negative. If you will be using the entire 35mm negative or slide, consider it to be 0.95×1.4 inches. If you'll be scanning only a portion of the film, be sure to place it in a protective sleeve before placing a ruler on it.

## Copyright and "Fair Use"

*I understand that I can use someone else's work in my own under "fair use" standards. What are they, and how is fair use determined?*

As always, this is no substitute for professional legal advice, but here is a summary of the fair use doctrine:

- Under certain circumstances, you can use limited portions of another's work for certain purposes.
- Those purposes are generally held to be commentary, criticism, news reporting, and scholarly work.
- Copyright law states no specific percentage of a work or number of words or musical notes for what constitutes fair use.
- Incorporating someone else's work into your own, with the intent to sell or claim the entire work as your own, does not constitute fair use.

9

# MAKING SELECTIONS AND CREATING MASKS

## IN THIS CHAPTER

Selections are used to identify pixels that are to be the target of your editing. Selections are stored in masks, which can be used to create complex selections. Masks are also used to show and hide parts of a layer or an image. Photoshop has many tools and commands available for creating selections and masks.

This chapter looks at how selections and masks work, as well as the tools and commands you use to make them. You'll also find a discussion of using masks to alter the visibility of layers without deleting original pixels.



# SELECTIONS AND MASKS: TELLING PHOTOSHOP WHERE TO WORK

Whether it's deleting part of an image, adding color, or perhaps applying a filter, you need to let Photoshop know which pixels you want to change. Using a painting tool (or other tool that works with brushes), you need simply select a brush and drag. The size, shape, and hardness of the brush, combined with the course along which the tool is dragged, control what happens.

When working with adjustments, filters, and many other menu commands, you must first identify the target area. You can, of course, apply a filter or other command to an entire layer. By not isolating a section of the layer, you have, in effect, identified where you want the filter to work: the entire layer. However, often you need to apply a filter to only a section of a layer. That's when you need to use selections and masks.

## Selections Defined

Experienced Photoshop users understand that selections are critical to effective use of the program. Understanding the theory behind selections can be a key to mastering their application.

Photoshop has a variety of tools and menu commands available to make selections. Consider a *selection* to be an area of an image that is activated, the part on which you're working. Pixels within the selection can be changed; those outside the selection are protected. Selections can be made with tools and commands and from paths and masks.

Generally speaking, a pixel is either inside a selection or outside a selection. However, under a variety of circumstances, a pixel can be *partially selected*. Any filter or adjustment command applied to the selection is partially applied to any partially selected pixels—the filter or effect is applied with less intensity. Selections that are antialiased or feathered can have partially selected pixels along their edges. Selections made from masks can have up to 256 variations of "selected" among the pixels.

Sometimes it makes sense to think of a selection as *excluding* parts of an image rather than *including* those pixels within the selection. Consider a photo of several blue objects. Some of them look great, but one blue object needs to be adjusted along with the rest of the image. You may be protecting the blue objects that *don't* need adjustment, rather than selecting the bad one as you color-correct.

As an example, consider two selections. One has no feathering or antialiasing: A pixel is either inside the selection or outside. The second selection has two pixels partially selected on either side of the line of selection. When the two selections are filled with black, there are two different results (see Figure 9.1).

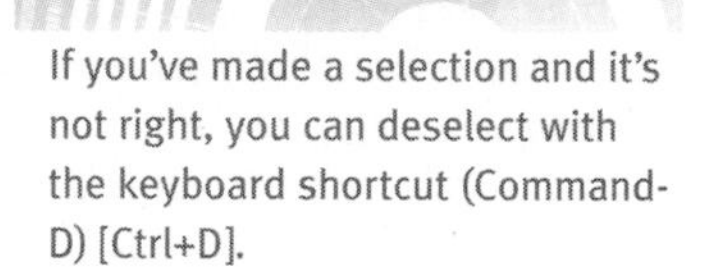

If you've made a selection and it's not right, you can deselect with the keyboard shortcut (Command-D) [Ctrl+D].

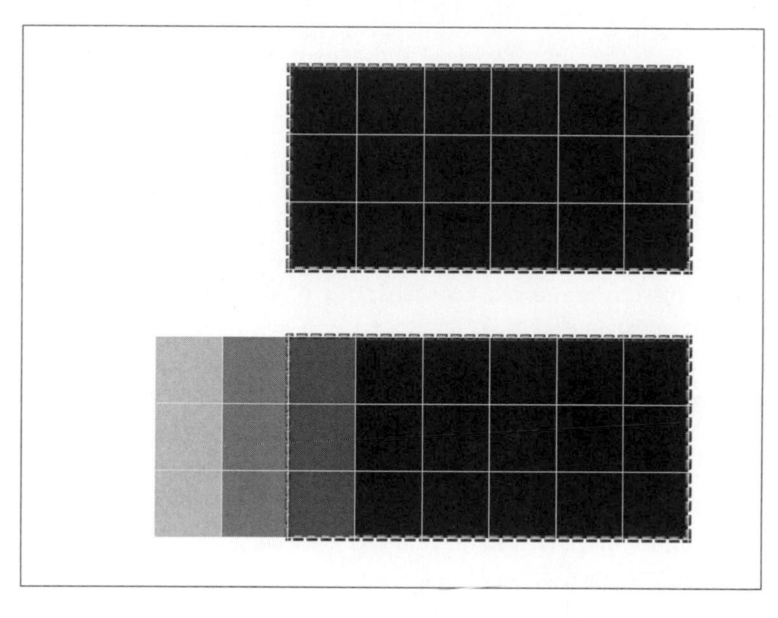

**Figure 9.1**
**At the top, the black fill is consistent and stops at the edge of the selection. Below, the partially selected pixels get filled with black but are partially transparent.**

*Selection border not visible? See "Showing and Hiding Edges" in the "Mastering Photoshop" section at the end of this chapter.*

When a selection is feathered, antialiased, or otherwise contains partially selected pixels, the selection marquee indicates which pixels are at least 50% selected. It is certainly possible to have selections that contain *only* pixels that are less than 50% selected. In such cases, the pixels will be affected by whatever additional steps you take (fill, delete, filter, and so on), but the marching ants will not be visible. Photoshop provides a warning when no selection border will appear or when the feathering was so large that no selection was made at all (see Figure 9.2).

The flashing dashed line that indicates the edge of a selection in Photoshop is technically referred to as a *selection border*, *selection marquee*, or *selection edge*, but you are far more likely to hear the term *marching ants*.

When you're selecting pixels, keep in mind that sometimes it's easier to select the pixels that you *don't* want and then use the command Select, Inverse to swap the selection to the portion that you do want.

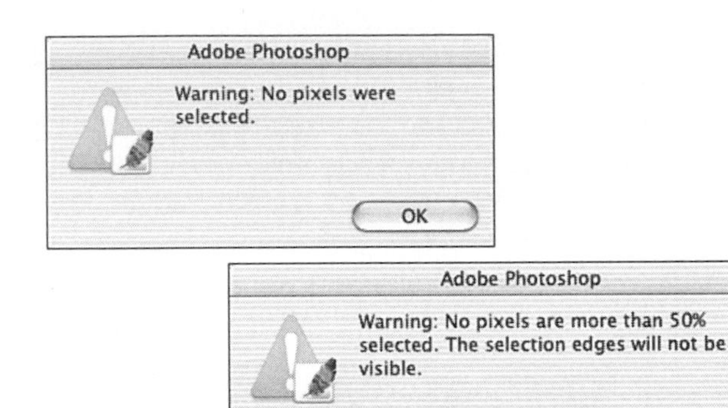


Figure 9.2
When pixels are less than 50% selected, the effect of a filter or an adjustment might be extremely subtle, but the command is executed nonetheless. If no selection is made, no pixels will be changed.

9

## Masks Unmasked

Just as a painter uses masking tape to protect parts of a surface and expose others, so, too, can you use *masks* in Photoshop. Masks are used to create and store selections. (Until a mask is loaded and used as a selection, it has no effect on the appearance of an image.)

Masks can be created from selections or created from scratch. In either case, masks are stored in *alpha channels*, which are grayscale representations of an image. The shades of gray determine levels of selection for individual pixels.

You can use painting tools, selection tools, and even adjustment commands and filters to alter masks. Virtually anything you can do with a grayscale image can be done with an alpha channel.

Photoshop also offers Quick Mask mode, which enables you to make a selection with all the flexibility of masks but without creating an additional channel.

*For more information on creating masks without creating channels, see "Quick Mask Mode," p. 318, later in this chapter.*

# THE SELECTION TOOLS

Photoshop has a collection of tools used to make selections. As shown in Figure 9.3, there are eight primary selection tools: four marquee selection tools, three lasso tools, and the Magic Wand.

When creating a selection, remember that the Shift key can be used with selection tools to add to an existing selection. Likewise, the (Option) [Alt] key can be used with a selection tool to subtract from an existing selection. When both modifier keys are used with a selection tool, anything outside the new selection border is deselected, and anything inside remains selected (see Figure 9.4).

> If one of the warnings in Figure 9.2 appears and you don't know why, take a look in the Options Bar. Make sure your selection tool doesn't have some unwanted feathering.

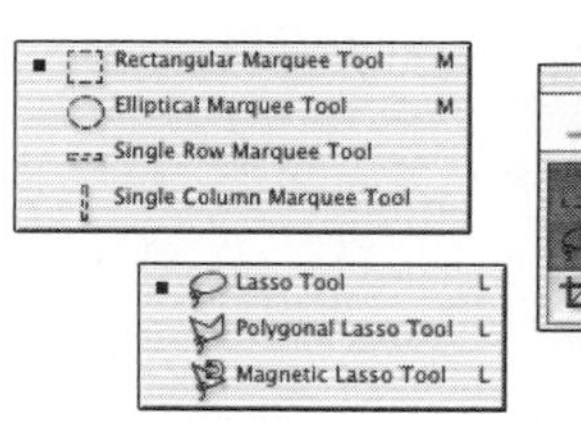


**Figure 9.3**
Click and hold on an icon to show the tools on the fly-out palettes. Hold down the Shift key and use the keyboard shortcut shown in the fly-out to rotate among the related tools.

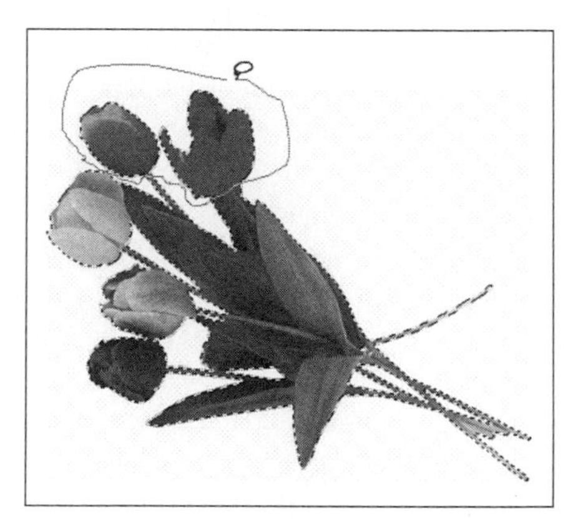

**Figure 9.4**
The Shift and (Option) [Alt] keys are pressed down; therefore, when the mouse button is released, nothing outside the loop being dragged will be selected. Within the loop, only what is already selected will stay selected.

## The Marquee Tools

Photoshop offers two major and two minor marquee selection tools. The Rectangular Marquee and Elliptical Marquee tools have several options and a great deal of flexibility. The Single Row Marquee and Single Column Marquee selection tools are one-trick ponies, with a specific job to do and few options.

> Remember that you can convert any selection to a path by using the Make Work Path button at the bottom of the Paths palette. Likewise, you can convert any selection to a mask by using the Select, Save Selection command.

### The Rectangular and Elliptical Marquee Selection Tools

The Rectangular Marquee tool is used to make rectangular and square selections. Its round counterpart, the Elliptical Marquee tool, creates oval and circular selections. To select squares and circles, respectively, hold down the Shift key while dragging. This constrains the selection to a 1:1 aspect ratio, forcing an identical width and height. You can also hold down the (Option) [Alt] key to drag the selection from the center with either tool. The Options Bar lets you use the tools in several modes (see Figure 9.5).

> You can reposition a selection border while creating it. Continue to hold down the mouse button when using a marquee tool and press the spacebar. You can now move the selection in the image. Release the spacebar and continue dragging. Release the mouse button to finish the selection.

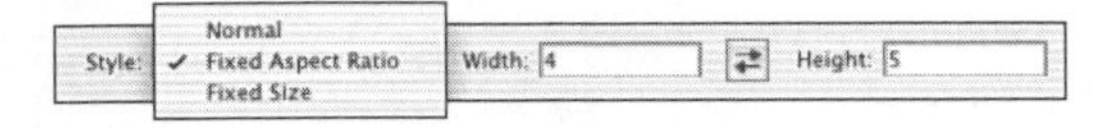


**Figure 9.5**
The pop-up menu is part of the Options Bar when the Rectangular or Elliptical Marquee tool is active.

In Normal mode, the tool can be dragged as you wish, creating a selection of whatever proportions you desire. The Fixed Aspect Ratio option gives you the opportunity to establish a width-to-height ratio in the numeric fields to the right. A ratio of 1:1 creates a square (Rectangular Marquee) or a circle (Elliptical Marquee). You can specify any ratio, constraining the shape of the selection. When you use the Fixed Aspect Ratio option, no matter what size the marquee, the proportions remain the same. The button between the Width and Height fields swaps their values, offering a quick way to switch between landscape and portrait orientations.

The Fixed Size option not only restricts the selection to a set aspect ratio but also determines the selection's actual dimensions. Set the desired size in the Options Bar and then click once with the selection tool. The selection is made to the lower right of the clicked point. The Options Bar assumes the unit of measure specified in the Preferences dialog box. You can use another unit of measure by including the appropriate abbreviation in the fields of the Options Bar. The button between Width and Height is also available in Fixed Size mode to swap the values in the two fields.

*Is your rectangular marquee giving you fits? See "Checking the Options" in the "Mastering Photoshop" section at the end of this chapter.*

The Options Bar also offers several other variables for the marquee selection tools. Normally, the tools are used to create a selection. If a selection already exists in the image, the tool can be set to add to, subtract from, or intersect with that selection (see Figure 9.6).

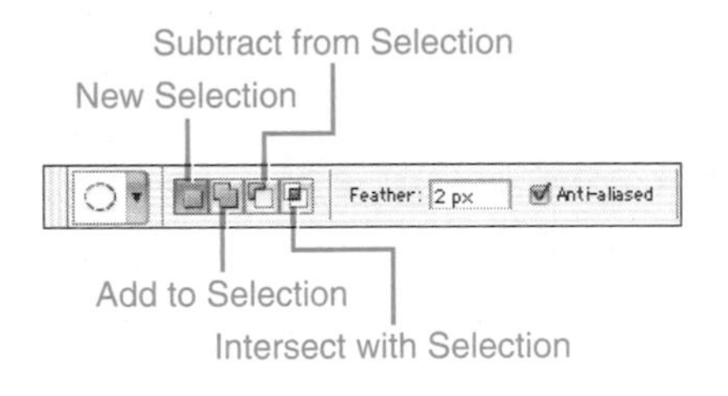


**Figure 9.6**
Feathering and the tool behavior options are the same for both the Rectangular Marquee tool and the Elliptical Marquee tool. With no active selection, the tools create a new selection with any of the four behaviors selected.

The Feather field lets you specify how "soft" to make the edges of the selection. (Remember that feathering lessens the effect of whatever you do on the edges of a selection, whether it's adding a fill, deleting, or applying a filter or an adjustment.) Feathering can be as high as 250 pixels and is always measured in pixels, regardless of the document's unit of measure. Keep in mind that feathering actually affects several times as many pixels as the number specified. To ensure

> The Fixed Aspect Ratio option is invaluable in preparing images for Picture Package and other photograph printing. Dragging with a 5:7 or 4:6 aspect ratio ensures that the image can be properly cropped with the menu command Image, Crop.

that the effect appears seamless, a feather of 2 pixels actually affects a band that is approximately 10 pixels wide along the selection border.

In Figure 9.7, a square selection border is visible, measuring slightly more than 100×100 pixels. With feathering set to 50 pixels, the actual selection border when the mouse button is released is shown by the circular selection within. (Remember that the marching ants are drawn around pixels at least 50% selected.) When the heavily feathered selection is filled with white on a black background, the impact extends far beyond the selection border, as you can see.



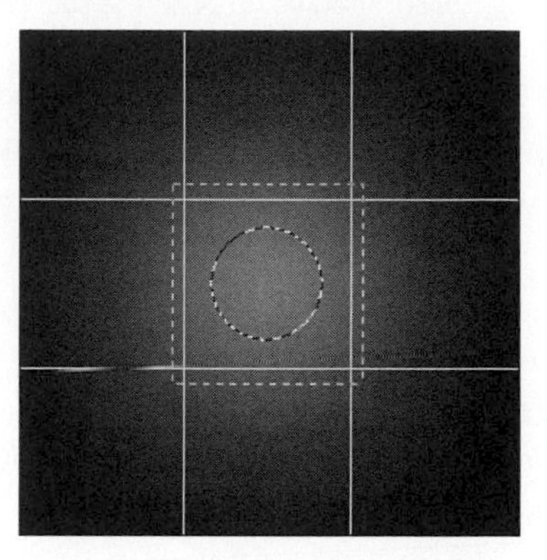

Figure 9.7
The square selection border indicates where the Rectangular Marquee tool (set to Feather: 50 pixels) was dragged. The circular selection edges indicate pixels at least 50% selected. Filling with white affects pixels almost to the corners of the 300×300 pixel black square.

*Antialiasing* softens the edges of curves. It is not available for the Rectangular Marquee, the Single Row Marquee, and the Single Column Marquee selection tools because these tools make selections with straight edges. When an antialiased selection is filled with color or deleted, the appearance of the edges is softened by using pixels that are intermediate in color between the selected area and the background. For example, filling an antialiased selection with black on a white background results in gray pixels to soften the curves (see Figure 9.8).

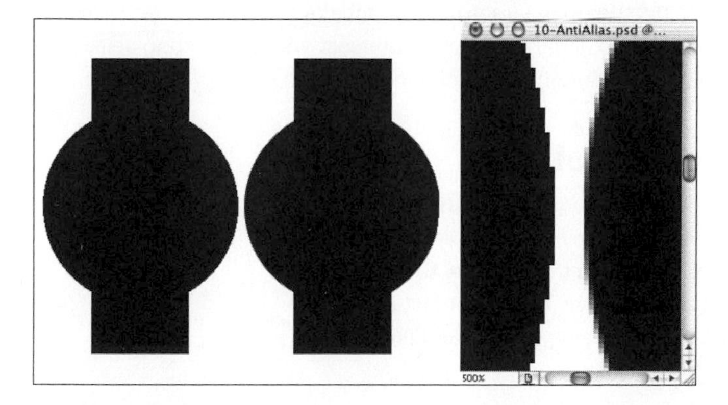


Figure 9.8
On the left, the selection was not antialiased. The selection on the right was. Both were filled with black. The inset shows a close-up comparison of the edges.

Notice, too, that the straight edges of the filled selections form perfect horizontal and vertical lines with and without antialiasing.

The stair-step appearance of curves without antialiasing is often referred to as the *jaggies*.

### Selecting Single Rows and Columns

Photoshop offers two additional marquee selection tools: the Single Row Marquee and the Single Column Marquee. As their names indicate, they select a row or column of pixels exactly 1 pixel high or wide. The row or column extends from edge to edge of the image and is made at the point where you click the mouse.

These tools, set to Feather: 0, are excellent for creating grid lines 1-pixel thick. Click to place the first line and then fill with the foreground color. With the tool still selected and the selection still active, you can use the arrow keys (with or without the Shift key) to reposition the selection for the second line. Each line will be perfectly horizontal or vertical and exactly 1 pixel in width or height.

Although designed to work with 1-pixel selections, the Single Row and Single Column tools do offer the option of feathering. Any feathering with these tools generates a warning that no pixels are more than 50% selected.



## Making Irregularly Shaped Selections

The marquee selection tools are fine for making regularly shaped selections. However, they lack the kind of flexibility needed for many selection jobs. Photoshop's lasso tools are designed to help you make irregular selections, with and without assistance.

### The Lasso Tool

The Lasso tool itself is a freeform tool. Drag it in any shape or direction. When you release the mouse button, the selection will be established. You need not mouse back to the point from which you started—the Lasso finishes a selection with a straight line from the point where you release the mouse button to the point where you started to drag.

Like the marquee selection tools, the three lassos offer buttons in the Options Bar to make new selections or to have the tools add to, subtract from, or intersect with an existing selection. Antialiasing and feathering are also options for the lasso tools.

### The Polygonal Lasso Tool

The Polygonal Lasso tool is not a freeform tool. Rather than drag the tool, you click, move, click, move, click to establish a selection with straight sides. Although the edges of the selection are straight, they can be at any angle, not just horizontal and vertical. Using the antialiasing option can help prevent jaggies along angled edges.

To complete a selection with the Polygonal Lasso tool, position the tool over the start point and click. When the cursor is directly over the start point, a small circle appears to the lower right of the tool's icon. Alternatively, double-click or press the (Return) [Enter] key to complete the selection with a straight segment from the cursor's location to the selection

> Use the (Option) [Alt] key to switch between the Lasso tool and the Polygonal Lasso tool on the fly. While dragging the Lasso, hold down the modifier key and click-move-click to place straight selection edges. When working with the Polygonal Lasso tool, hold down the key and drag to make freeform selections.

start point. (Command)-clicking [Ctrl]-clicking does the same. The Escape key can be used to leave the selection process before a selection is complete.

## The Magnetic Lasso Tool

The third lasso tool is a bit more complex. The Magnetic Lasso tool attempts to follow existing edges in an image to make a selection. Using contrast to identify edges, the Magnetic Lasso is best suited for use on images that have uncomplicated backgrounds (see Figure 9.9).

**Figure 9.9**
This image is a perfect candidate for the Magnetic Lasso tool because of the strong contrast between the foreground and background.



While working, the Magnetic Lasso tool places a series of temporary anchor points as it follows the path you trace. (Note that the tool does not create a path; the anchor points disappear when the selection is completed.) Double-clicking, clicking the start point, and pressing the (Return) [Enter] key all close the selection.

As you move the mouse (or drag it), you can click the mouse button to manually place anchor points at spots where the edge you're tracing takes a sharp turn. If the tool places an anchor point in an incorrect location, press (Delete) [Backspace] to remove it. You can also back up along the edge to retrace a segment.

In addition to the options common to all three lasso tools, the Magnetic Lasso tool has four options of its own (see Figure 9.10).

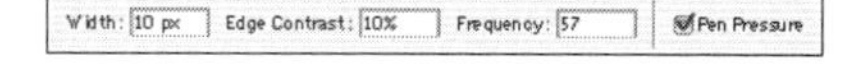


**Figure 9.10**
The first three of these four options are unique to the Magnetic Lasso tool.

Width determines the Magnetic Lasso's search area. It is always measured in pixels and can range from 1 to 256. It follows the line of pixels with the highest contrast within this radius. If the image has few edges, a high Width setting allows you to move quickly and requires less precision. If there are multiple areas of contrast closely placed in the image, a lower width is required, forcing you to keep the cursor precisely along the desired edge. When Photoshop's

> Using the (Option) [Alt] key with the Magnetic Lasso tool gives you access to both the Lasso and the Polygonal Lasso tools. With the key pressed, drag for a freeform selection or click-move-click to create straight selection edges.

Preferences are set to Precise for Other Cursors, the width is displayed as a circle around the tool's crosshair. If you see the tool's icon as the cursor, you need not change the Preferences. Before you start working with the tool, press the Caps Lock key to show the width cursor.

> You can change the Width setting for the Magnetic Lasso on the fly. Think of it as a brush size. The left and right bracket keys increase and decrease the width by 1 pixel. Add the Shift key to jump to the maximum (256 pixels) and minimum (1 pixel) widths.

Edge Contrast can be considered the sensitivity setting for the Magnetic Lasso tool. It ranges from 1% to 100%. Lower values reduce the amount of contrast required to define an edge. However, that can also lead to the selection border being placed along false edges—areas where a texture or shadow/highlight create contrast. Likewise, too high a setting might lead to the tool not finding any edge at all and a very confused selection border.

Frequency determines the automatic placement of anchor points as you drag. Ranging from 0% to 100%, the higher numbers produce more anchor points. Remember that you can manually add anchor points by clicking.

The Pen Pressure check box is used with pressure-sensitive tablets, such as those from Wacom. Increased pressure on the tablet constricts the tool's width, and lighter pressure results in a higher Width setting. The width varies from twice the value in the Options Bar (very light pressure) to 1 (very hard pressure).

## Magic Wand

The Magic Wand tool has its fans and its detractors. Some love it; some find it useless. Designed to select similar colors throughout an image, the Magic Wand enables you to specify a *tolerance* (the range of sensitivity) and click on a sample. Pixels similar in color to that on which you clicked will be selected. Depending on choices in the Options Bar, you can restrict the Magic Wand to the active layer or use all visible layers. (Although the check box is labeled Use All Layers, hidden layers are excluded.) The Magic Wand can also create a selection of all similar pixels throughout the image or only those similar pixels contiguous to the pixel you click.

When Contiguous is selected in the Options Bar, clicking selects all pixels that adjoin pixels of the selected color. If pixels of another color are between the clicked pixel and similarly colored pixels, those pixels are not selected (see Figure 9.11).

Photoshop compares the pixel clicked with the tool to all other pixels in the image. Each color channel value is compared to the clicked pixel. To be included in the selection, each component color for a specific pixel must fall within the tolerance range when compared to the clicked pixel. The Tolerance setting for the Magic Wand can range from 0 to 255.

For example, if you set the Magic Wand to a Tolerance setting of 32 and then click a pixel with the RGB values 200/150/100, the range of color values included in the selection are as follows:

- Red: 168 to 232
- Green: 118 to 182
- Blue: 68 to 132

**Figure 9.11**
To the left, the Magic Wand was set to Contiguous—only similarly colored pixels adjacent to the clicked pixel are selected. On the right, Contiguous was not selected—all similarly colored pixels throughout the image were selected.



To be selected, a pixel must meet *all three* of the criteria. Therefore, included in the selection would be pixels with such different RGB values as 168/18/68 and 232/182/132. However, not included would be pixels with color values of 200/150/133 and 200/150/67, because the Blue component is beyond the tolerance.

You can Shift-click with the Magic Wand to add to a selection and (Option)-click [Alt]-click to subtract from a selection. The Options Bar also enables you to set the tool to add to or subtract from a selection. The tolerance can be changed between clicks as well.

## Photoshop at Work: Removing a White Background

There are a number of ways to extract a subject from a plain white background. One of the simplest uses the Magic Wand:

1. Go to the Photoshop folder, to Samples, and open the image Ducky.tif.
2. In the Layers palette, double-click the layer Background and rename it Layer 0. (Background layers don't support transparency.)
3. Click the New Layer button at the bottom of the Layers palette.
4. Drag the new layer below Layer 0 in the Layers palette.
5. Press D on the keyboard to restore your colors to black and white; then press (Option-Delete) [Alt+Backspace] to fill the layer with the foreground color (black).

Because the Magic Wand selects in a range that extends to both the high and low, you should click a pixel that's in the midtones of the color you want to select.

When you are selecting a uniformly colored background for deletion or want to extract an image, it's usually a good idea to use the menu command Select, Modify, Expand with a setting of 1 or 2 pixels. This helps eliminate any fringe or halo from anti-aliasing.

6. In the Layers palette, click Layer 0 (the Ducky layer) to make it active.
7. Select the Magic Wand in the Toolbox. The default settings in the Options Bar are fine. If necessary, restore the defaults by (Control)-clicking right-clicking the Magic Wand icon at the left end of the Options Bar and selecting Reset Tool.
8. Click once anywhere in the white background of Layer 0. Note that because Contiguous is selected in the Options Bar, the whites of the eyes are not selected.
9. Press the (Delete) [Backspace] key to remove the white background. Your results should be similar to those shown in Figure 9.12.

Figure 9.12
The default settings for the Magic Wand produce a fringe-free extraction from the uniform white background of this image.

## Selections from Paths

Paths can be used to create extremely precise selections. Any path, including work paths and those created with Photoshop's shape tools, can be used to create selections. With the path selected in the Paths palette, either click the Load Path as a Selection button at the bottom of the palette or use the Paths palette menu command Make Selection (see Figure 9.13).

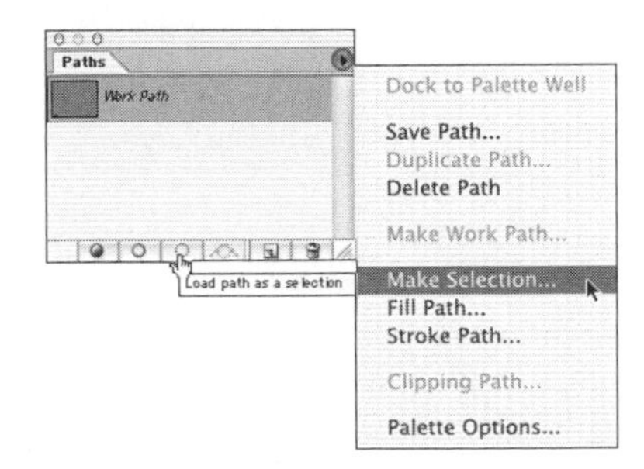


Figure 9.13
Simply clicking the button makes an active selection from the path; the menu command opens a dialog box.

You can also (Command)-click [Ctrl]-click a path in the Paths palette to load it as a selection. Adding the Shift and (Option) [Alt] key adds the path to or subtracts the path from an active selection.

When you choose the Make Selection command, you'll be presented with the Make Selection dialog box. If a selection is already active in the image, you'll be able to add to, subtract from, intersect with, or replace the selection (see Figure 9.14). You'll also be able to specify feathering and choose or forgo antialiasing.

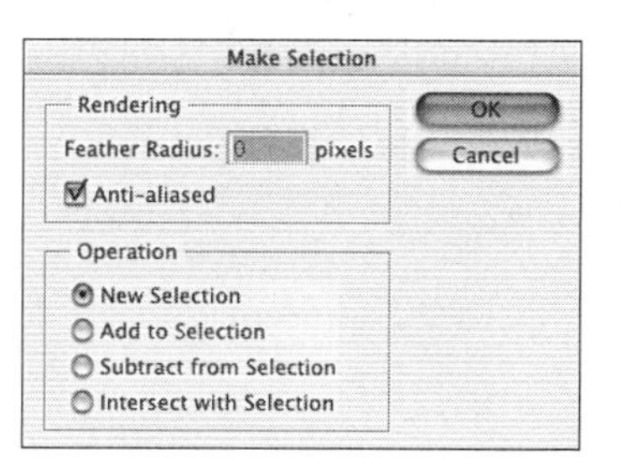


Figure 9.14
The Make Selection dialog box can also be opened by (Option)-clicking [Alt]-clicking the Load Path as a Selection button at the bottom of the Paths palette.



*For an in-depth look at creating and editing paths, see Chapter 11, "The Pen Tool and Shape Layers: Vectors in Photoshop," p. 363.*

# The Type Mask Tools

The Type Mask tool creates selections in the shape of text rather than the vector-based text created by the Type tools. Although the tools have the word *Mask* in their names, no alpha channel is added to the Channels palette when you use these tools. Unlike Quick Mask mode (discussed later in this chapter), there is no mask to save when using these tools. Therefore, you should consider them to be selection tools of a special nature.

The Type Mask tools do not create vector type, nor do they generate type layers. In addition, their result is not "live"—you cannot return to the letter-shaped selections and edit them as you would type by changing fonts or correcting typographical errors.

You can select the Horizontal Type Mask tool or the Vertical Type Mask tool from the Toolbox (see Figure 9.15). All the options for the regular type tools are available when creating type masks.

Photoshop offers both point type and area type masks. To set point type, click once anywhere in the document. A translucent red overlay will appear, much like working in Quick Mask mode (see Figure 9.16). The type mask tools cut holes in this overlay. When you drag the tool, a bounding box is displayed, indicating a type container—a rectangle into which you can place type. Remember that the bounding box can be resized while you work by dragging a handle.

*For a discussion of the difference between point type and area type (and when to use each), see "Point and Paragraph Type," in Chapter 12, "Adding Text: Photoshop's Type Capabilities," p. 392.*

When you have finished typing and click the check mark icon at the right end of the Options Bar or press (Command-Return) [Ctrl-Enter], the type is accepted, the red overlay disappears, and a selection border ("marching ants") appears in the shape of the type. You can then fill, delete, apply adjustments or filters, or do anything else that you can do to a selection in Photoshop.

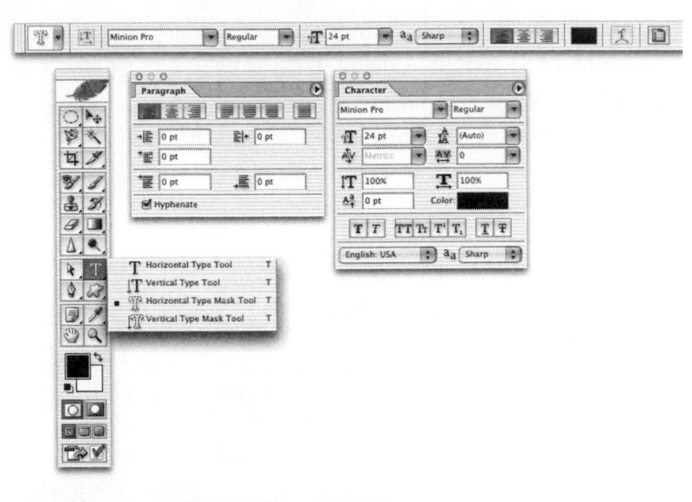


**Figure 9.15**
The Options Bar, Character palette, and Paragraph palette give you the same control over type set as a selection as they do over type set as vectors.

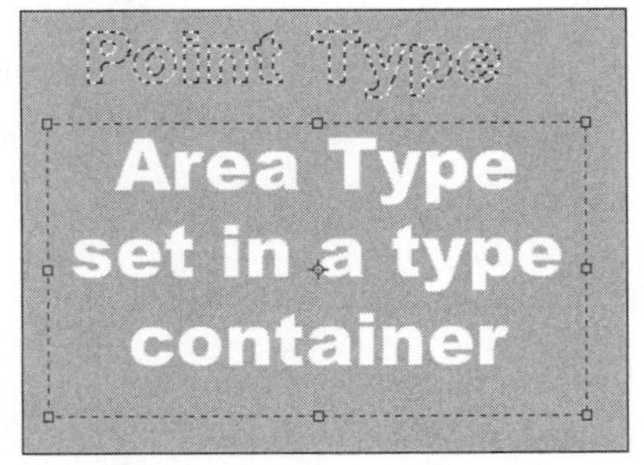


**Figure 9.16**
Area type is currently being set. The "Point Type" selection was an existing selection when a type mask tool was dragged.

*To learn the full capabilities of the type tools, see Chapter 12, "Adding Text: Photoshop's Type Capabilities," p. 389.*

The type mask tools do *not* create layers when you use them. Also, unlike the regular type tools, they are not vector tools—there are no paths for crisp output to a PostScript printer.

## SELECTION COMMANDS

Photoshop's Select menu includes commands in five basic categories (see Figure 9.17). The commands All, Deselect, Reselect, and Inverse can be thought of as the "macro" commands—they work on a large scale. In contrast, the modification commands (Feather, Modify, Grow, and Similar) can be considered the "micro" commands—they fine-tune or adjust an existing selection.

Transform Selection also modifies an existing selection, but it does so on the basis of selection shape rather than content. Selections can be saved as alpha channels (masks) and loaded later. This method is especially useful for protecting the work that went into a complex selection and for modifying a selection as a mask.

Keep in mind when working with the type mask tools that you can create a mask from any selection by using the Select, Save Selection command. Likewise, you can generate a work path from the active selection by clicking the Make Work Path button at the bottom of the Paths palette.

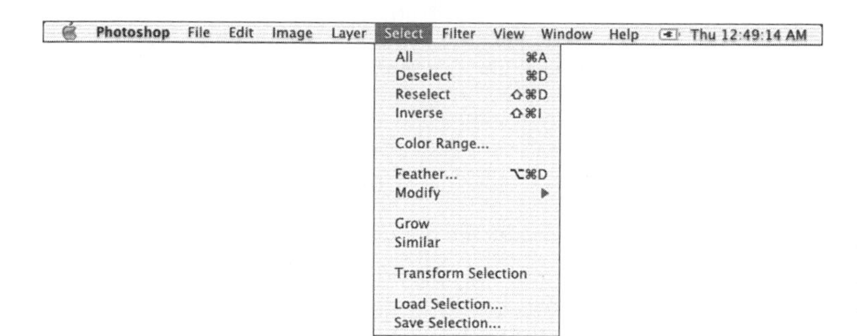


**Figure 9.17**
Although this image shows no commands grayed out for illustrative purposes, not all commands are available at the same time. For example, the command Reselect is grayed out when there is an active selection, so it can't be available at the same time as Deselect.



The Color Range command is also a "macro" selection command, but it's far more complex than simply selecting all or deselecting. It offers the capability of selecting based on one or more colors within an image.

## Basic Selection Commands

The four basic selection commands are rather simple in nature. Select, All makes a selection of the entire active layer. If the layer contains transparency, the transparent pixels are selected with the others. If you were to press (Option-Delete) [Alt-Backspace] next, the entire layer would be filled with the foreground color.

Deselect does exactly what you would expect from the name. It is available only when there is an active selection in the image. After you use this command, no pixels in the image are selected.

Reselect is extremely useful for those occasions, among others, when an unintended click inadvertently deselects. Although you can use the Undo command immediately after deselecting to restore the selection, Reselect is available until another selection is made or the image is closed (or the history purged).

Select, Inverse reverses an active selection—pixels that had been selected are now deselected, and pixels that had not been selected are now selected. Inverse also recognizes antialiasing, feathering, and other partially selected pixels. If, for example, you load a mask containing pixels selected at 25%, Inverse switches them to 75% selected.

## Modifying Existing Selections with Commands

The Select menu offers a number of commands that enable you to modify an existing selection. Feathering softens the edges of a selection, which results in a reduced effect on those pixels. Whether deleting, filling, filtering, or adjusting, you can use feathering to produce a subtle transition between those pixels 100% affected by the command or tool and those pixels that are unaffected. Selecting this command opens a dialog box in which you enter the amount of feathering, which is always measured in pixels.

*Feathering is discussed in more detail earlier in this chapter; see "The Marquee Tools," p. 299.*

> Remember that changing the Feathering amount in the Options Bar after a selection has been made has no effect. Use the Select, Feather command instead.

The Modify commands, accessed through the Modify submenu of the Select menu, are rather clumsy tools and are best applied using very small pixel values. Like Feather, they open dialog boxes into which you enter a value in pixels.

## Border



The Border command creates a new selection and discards the original selection. The new selection is centered on the original selection border, with or without antialiasing and feathering, at the width specified in the Border dialog box. That width, however, extends both inward and outward from the original selection border, so the term *width* is somewhat misleading. The affected area is actually twice the Width value.

The selection created by Border is feathered. Only the two pixels immediately on either side of the original selection border are 100% selected, with the balance of the width tapering to 0% selected. If, for example, you drag a square selection with the Rectangular Marquee tool, use Border with a Width value of 10, and then press (Option-Delete) [Alt+Backspace] to fill with the foreground color, you will not get a beautiful frame around the original selection. Instead, you'll see a line of color that fades inward and outward, with angled corners rather than square.

## Smooth

The Smooth command is designed to eliminate jagged edges in selections. It uses the pixel value you enter into the Sample Radius field to see which pixels should be included in the active selection. It rounds the corners of a rectangular or angular selection.

The Smooth command can be used effectively with the Magic Wand tool and the Color Range command. If your initial selection has numerous unselected pixels scattered around within it, try Smooth set to 1 or 2 pixels.

## Expand

You can move a selection border outward by as much as 100 pixels by using the Expand command. However, any rectangular corners in the original selection become angles (and angles will be rounded) when a selection is greatly expanded. The number of pixels you enter into the Expand By field can be considered a radius from the center rather than a linear measure from the selection border.

The Expand command can be very effective in eliminating a halo. When a background is selected for deletion, expanding by 1 or 2 pixels can eliminate any fringe pixels.

Instead of using Border to create a frame, consider using the menu command Edit, Stroke. If the pixels to be framed are on a separate layer, Layer Style, Stroke is an even better alternative.

## Contract

The Contract command brings in a selection border toward its center. If the active selection consists of a variety of discrete areas, each is contracted individually. Just as Expand can help eliminate a fringe when a background is selected, so, too, can Contract help eliminate a fringe when a foreground is selected.

eate is worth saving. Re-
me consuming. Photoshop
at can be reloaded at will.

ate an alpha channel from
cussed in the "Alpha

sses all pixels of one or
ors, such as the blues in a
bles you to fine-tune your
will be selected.

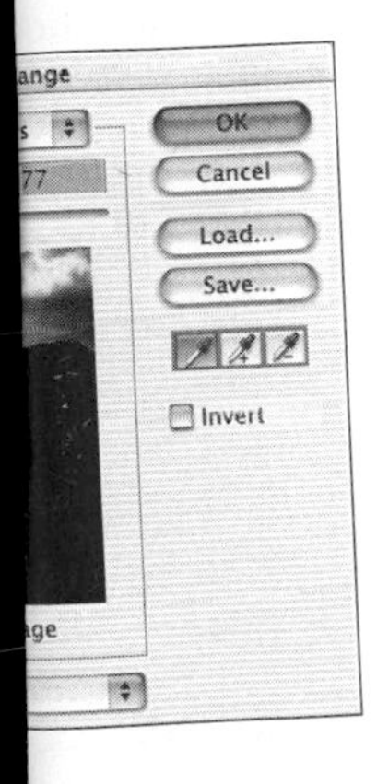


election. To add similar col-
yedropper or use the Add
colors from the selection,
act Eyedropper (the eye-
either the Add Eyedropper

n make a selection before
ng the Color Range dialog
Doing so restricts the final
ion to areas within the ini-
election. Color Range then
s like-colored pixels only
the original selection.

u,
om-
tion
The
and
the
times

## Caution

When a selection extends to the edge of the canvas, neither Expand nor Contract is effective along that edge. A selection cannot be expanded beyond the edge of the canvas, and any selection border on the edge is not affected by the Contract command.

ep-
lored pixels in an image are included in the
t to select a color throughout an image.

distorted by using the Select, Transform
ne active selection (see Figure 9.18).

**Figure 9.18**
The bounding box originates as a rectangle surrounding the selection. You can manipulate it in a variety of ways with the cursor and modifier keys.

on,
cale
ing
d
ail-

the

After you choose the Select, Transform Selection menu command, look again at the menu bar. The Edit menu offers all the standard Transform commands to make transforming a selection much more predictable.

## Saving and Loading Selections

Any selection that takes more than a couple of keystrokes and a drag to c creating a selection might not produce the exact results. It could also be t has the capability to store any selection as an alpha channel—a mask—th

The menu commands Save Selection and Load Selection enable you to cre a selection and to load that channel as a selection. Alpha channels are dis Channels and Masks" section, later in this chapter.

## The Color Range Command

With the Color Range command, you can create a selection that encompa more colors within an image. It is ideal for selecting a range of similar co sky or flesh tones. The Color Range dialog box, shown in Figure 9.19, ena selection much like the Magic Wand's Tolerance setting determines what

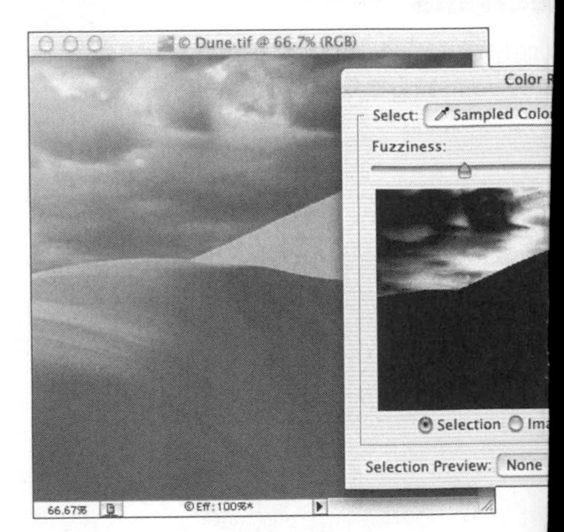


**Figure 9.19**
In this example, the grayscale preview shows that the sky (white and grays) will be selected, but the dunes (black) will not.

The leftmost Eyedropper tool is used to select the primary color of the s ors or other colors to the selection, you can use the Shift key with the E Eyedropper (the eyedropper tool with a plus sign). Likewise, to remove you can use the (Option) [Alt] key with the Eyedropper or use the Subtr dropper tool with the minus sign). You can drag through the image wit or Subtract Eyedropper—or the regular Eyedropper with the Shift or (Option) [Alt] key—to identify a series of colors in one motion.

Use the Fuzziness slider to determine a range of selected pixels, based on the clicked pixel. Dragging the slider to the right increases the number of pixels selected by increasing the amount of color variation allowed. Dragging the slider to the left restricts the selection to pixels that more closely match the selected color.

You c
open
box.
selec
tial s
selec
withi

Below the preview window are radio buttons labeled Selection and Image. Checking Selection presents a grayscale representation of the selection, much like a mask, in the preview window. The preview is updated when you click with an eyedropper tool or drag the Fuzziness slider. Clicking the Image radio button shows you the original image. That preview shows no indication of what areas will be selected, but you can click in the Image preview with any of the eyedropper tools to change your selection.

The Selection Preview pop-up menu offers five choices. They determine how the image window (not the Color Range preview window) will appear while you make your selection. Especially with very large files, the None option can make Color Range updates a bit snappier. The other four options, shown in Figure 9.20, are Grayscale (upper left), Black Matte (upper right), White Matte (lower left), and Quick Mask (lower right).



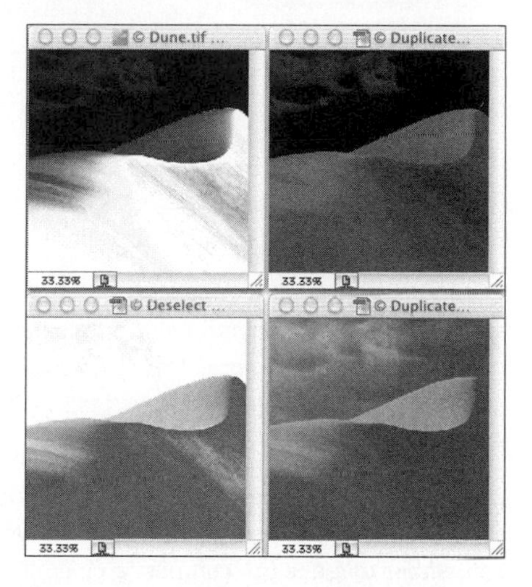


**Figure 9.20**
In all four examples, the dunes are selected. The selection, in this case, is seen most accurately in the grayscale preview to the upper left.

The Color Range dialog box also offers buttons labeled Load and Save. These options do not save the selection but rather the selection *criteria*—the color range information. If you have a series of images that require the same correction (because of a color tint or a light leak, for example), saving a range of color selection criteria can also save a lot of work.

One other capability of Color Range deserves discussion. At the top of the dialog box is the Select pop-up menu. In the discussion to this point, Color Range has been shown (and described) using Sampled Colors mode. However, Color Range can also be used to select predetermined color ranges (see Figure 9.21).

Pixels are selected based on their content of the target color. For example, a pixel with an RGB value of 64/128/75 will be 50% selected when Green is chosen, but only 25% selected if Red is chosen. Neither the Fuzziness slider nor the eyedropper tools are available when you use the presets from the pop-up menu.

Color Range can be especially useful for making selections of hair, branches, and other complex images. It works best when there's a strong contrast between the subject and the background.

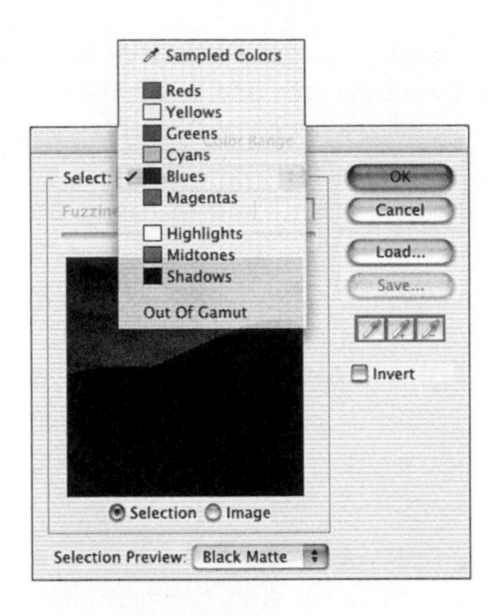


**Figure 9.21**
The Out of Gamut option is available only for RGB and Lab color mode images.



## Selection Tips

Accurate selections, with appropriate feathering or antialiasing, can make or break a project. Quick and efficient selection can make or break deadlines. Here are some tips that can improve your selection procedures:

- (Command)-click [Ctrl]-click a layer in the Layers palette to make a selection of all nontransparent pixels on the layer. (This cannot be done on a layer named *Background* because it relies on transparency, which is not supported on background layers.)
- Open the Channels palette and look at each color channel individually. Your intended selection area may stand out in better contrast on one layer or another. Working with just that layer active improves the performance of the Magic Wand, Color Range, or Magnetic Lasso. After creating the selection, remember to make the composite channel active again in the Channels palette.
- The Filter, Extract command provides an automated way of creating a selection and deleting the inverse—all in one step. You can use the command to make a selection, too. Duplicate the target layer and hide all other layers. Use Extract on the duplicate layer. Click once in the now-transparent background with the Magic Wand. Delete that layer and restore the visibility of others. To finish selecting the subject, use the menu command Select, Inverse.
- If you do a lot of complex selecting that involves hair, fur, glass, clouds, fabric, and the like, you may be best served by a special-purpose plug-in or program. Mask Pro from Extensis and KnockOut from Procreate are two such choices. They are far more capable of making selections of wispy hair, semitransparent objects, and other difficult subjects.
- When a subject has been removed from a background and your selection wasn't perfect, you might see a "halo" around the edges. The command Layer, Matting, Defringe can be used to clean up the selection. Photoshop will search along edges within the specified width to remove remnants of the background color.

- Showing the grid and/or guides and using Snap can give you an added level of precision when working with selection tools.
- A selection can be dragged from one open document to another. You can copy your document, use Levels or Curves to create extreme contrast, make a selection, and then drag that selection back to the original document. With a selection active, use any selection tool to drag from one window to the other.



# ALPHA CHANNELS AND MASKS

When you use the command Select, Save Selection, you're creating an *alpha channel*, a representation of the selection saved in a channel. Alpha channels are stored with the image, whereas selections are lost when deselected. Like other channels, an alpha channel is a grayscale representation. As an 8-bit image, there is a maximum of 256 shades of gray in the channel. In a 16-bit image, there are thousands of levels of gray. Each level of gray represents the level of selection for each pixel. For example, a pixel colored 50% gray in an alpha channel is 50% selected when the channel is loaded again as a selection.

Alpha channels can be created from scratch as well as from an existing selection. As a channel, they can also be edited as though they were grayscale images, with tools, filters, adjustments, and more.

*For a full discussion of channels, see Chapter 16, "Channels: The Ultimate Creative Control," p. 513.*

## Basic Alpha Channel Creation

The easiest way to create an alpha channel to store a selection is to make the selection first. With any selection active in the image, use the menu command Select, Save Selection to open the Save Selection dialog box (see Figure 9.22).

The Document pop-up menu lists all files open in Photoshop that have *exactly* the same pixel dimensions; it also includes the option to create a new document. (Open files that are a different size than the document in which you made the selection do not appear in the list.) Selecting New creates a new document with the same dimensions and resolution as the original. The document consists of only the single alpha channel and is in Multichannel mode. Although the new image contains no color channels and holds only the saved selection, you can convert the document to any color mode (after first converting it to Grayscale). The name selected in the Save Selection dialog box is applied to the channel, not to the new document.

The Channel pop-up menu lists all available alpha channels in the image selected in the Document field. You can create a new channel or add to, subtract from, or intersect with an existing alpha channel. When you're working with an existing channel, the Name field is grayed out.

> Remember that when a pixel is 50% selected, any adjustment or filter is applied at half the intensity compared to a pixel selected at 100%. This behavior also holds true for deleting, painting, and other steps performed on a selection.

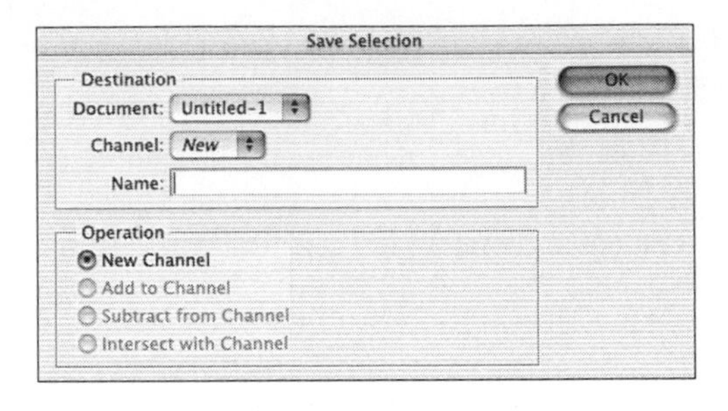


**Figure 9.22**
The Destination area of the dialog box is where you choose both the document and the channel in which to save the selection. You can also select a name when creating a new channel.



With a selection active in the image, you can also create a new alpha channel through the Channels palette (see Figure 9.23). Clicking the Save Selection as Channel button at the bottom of the palette creates a new alpha channel and bypasses the Save Selection dialog box. (The new channel is named Alpha 1 or the next available number.)

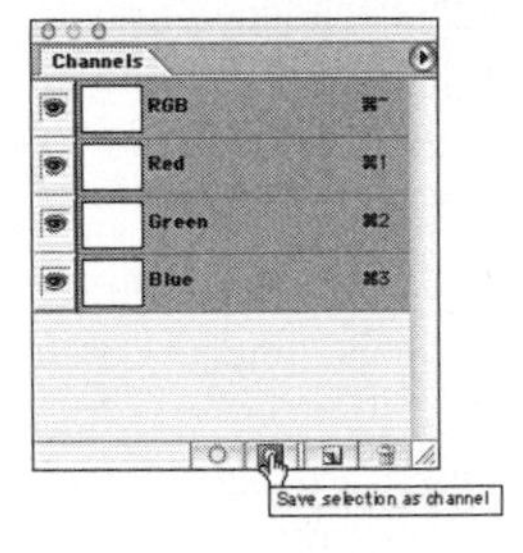


**Figure 9.23**
A new channel added with the Save Selection as Channel button can be renamed by double-clicking the name in the Channels palette.

The third technique for adding an alpha channel from an existing selection is through the Channels palette menu. Select the command New Channel (not New Spot Channel). You'll have an opportunity to name the channel and decide the channel's options (see Figure 9.24).

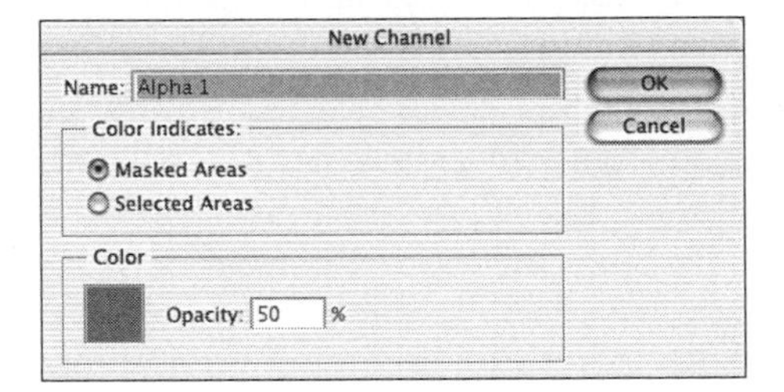


**Figure 9.24**
The Color Indicates and Color options determine the appearance of the mask when it is activated over one or more channels.

## Editing Masks

Whether an alpha channel is saved from a selection or created empty, you can alter its content as though it were a grayscale image. In the Channels palette, click the alpha channel to make it the only active channel. Use all of Photoshop's power to manipulate the shades of gray. Remember that the changes you make in the alpha channel will be reflected in the selection after the channel is reloaded.

> In terms of the actual content of a newly created alpha channel, there is no difference among the Select, Save Selection menu command, the Channels palette Save Selection as Channel button, and the palette menu command New Channel. Each generates the same channel from the same selection.

For example, applying a Gaussian Blur filter to an alpha channel softens edges, much like controlled feathering. If a selection is made within the alpha channel first, the blur can be even further controlled.

The basic tools for adjusting an alpha channel remain the Brush and the Eraser. Using the Brush tool, you can add black to hide areas in the alpha channel, removing them from the selection when the channel is loaded. Likewise, you can erase or paint with white to add areas or an image to a selection. Various shades of gray can be used to create areas of partial selection or feathering (see Figure 9.25).

If your image contains lots of red, or red appears in critical areas, you can certainly change the color of the mask overlay. Click the color swatch in the channel's Options dialog box to open the Color Picker.



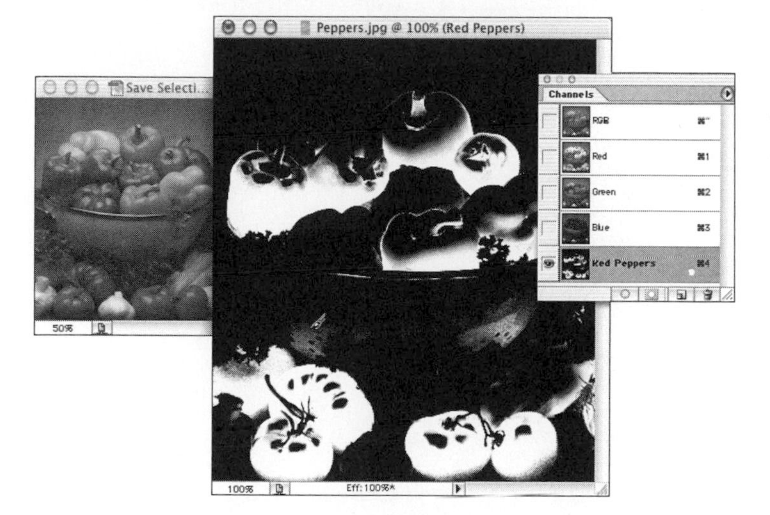


Figure 9.25
Painting with gray results in pixels that will be partially selected when the alpha channel is loaded as a selection.

You can also work on an alpha channel with the image visible behind it. Click the alpha channel in the Channels palette to make it active. Next, click in the visibility column (the "eyeball" icons) next to the image's composite channel to make the color channels visible. (The channel will be named either RGB or CMYK for those color modes.) By default, the areas that are outside the selection when the channel is loaded are covered with a 50% opaque red overlay (see Figure 9.26).

Figure 9.26
Although not apparent in the grayscale version of this image, the background and beak, as well as parts of the eye, are covered by the red overlay. The mask is visible in the thumbnail image of the channel Bird in the Channels palette.

9

## Quick Mask Mode

Photoshop offers a convenient way to edit selections through the use of masks—without ever having to look at the Channels palette. Quick Mask mode takes you directly to a red overlay that is active and ready to be edited as an alpha channel. Simply press Q on the keyboard or click the button in the Toolbox to enter Quick Mask mode (see Figure 9.27). After editing the mask, press Q again or click the opposite button to exit Quick Mask mode.

The Channel Options command from the Channels palette menu can be used to reverse the overlay and to change its color and opacity.

Figure 9.27
The button to the left of the cursor returns you to Standard mode.

When you're in Quick Mask mode, a temporary channel is created in the Channels palette. Just as a work path disappears when it's no longer needed, so, too, is a quick mask deleted when you exit Quick Mask mode. After you exit Quick Mask mode, a selection is active in the image, and you can, of course, save that selection as a regular alpha channel.

In Quick Mask mode, the Channels palette menu also offers the Quick Mask Options command. You can change the overlay's opacity or color and even decide whether it shows or hides the masked areas. You can also open the dialog box by double-clicking the Quick Mask button in the Toolbox.

## Masking Tips

Masks can provide incredible control over selections. With 256 levels of selection available (and thousands of levels in 16-bit color), all through a simple change in gray value, you can create extraordinarily complex selections. Remember that virtually all of Photoshop's capabilities are available to you when editing alpha channels. Here are some suggestions:

Remember to paint in shades of gray when editing a mask. Using colors is deceiving—only the color's luminosity is used.

- Alpha channels are grayscale—edit them with shades of gray. Set the Color palette to Grayscale and use the preset grays in the Swatches palette. Remember that Photoshop can save workspaces for you. Position the palettes you need for mask editing, and use the menu command Window, Workspace, Save Workspace. Name it Mask Editing, and select it when you need to work on an alpha channel.
- The D key sets the foreground color to black and the background color to white. The X key swaps them. When editing a mask, you can quickly switch between "add to" and "subtract from" by switching from white to black, and vice versa.
- Set up the Brush tool with one brush, the Pencil with another, and the Eraser with a third. Switch between them with keyboard shortcuts to speed up editing masks. Remember that erasing to black is the same as painting with black—the only difference being a simple press of the X key.
- Whereas a selection border cannot accurately show feathering, a mask can. To take a quick look at the feathering of a selection, press Q to enter Quick Mask mode. Then press Q again to exit.
- The filter Sharpen, Unsharp Mask can work wonders on detailed and complex masks. However, you might want to isolate certain areas of the channel before applying the filter to avoid harsh edge transitions.
- You can soften the edges of an extremely detailed mask to simulate antialiasing without blurring. Rotate the mask one or two degrees by using Edit, Transform, Rotate and entering the value in the Options Bar. Then rotate it back to the original position, again using the command and Options Bar (not Undo). The effect will be subtle, and that's generally what you want.
- You can create a selection using a type mask tool and save that selection as an alpha channel. You can edit the mask, load it as a selection, and have customized text. Keep in mind, however, that you can't edit the text, and it won't output as vector to a PostScript printer.



## Alpha Channels and File Formats

Alpha channels can be stored in several file formats. Photoshop's native format (PSD) supports multiple alpha channels, as does Photoshop's large image format (PSB). TIFF images in RGB or CMYK mode can support multiple alpha channels, as can PDF files created in Photoshop. The RAW file format can support numerous channels, but it can present problems of its own. For example, when reopening a RAW file, you must know the exact dimensions of the image, the correct number of channels, and whether the color data was interleaved when saved.

A single alpha channel can be saved with BMP, PICT, and Pixar files. The PNG-24 file format can generate an alpha channel to store transparency in an image, but that information cannot be accessed directly or edited. Rather, it is updated if you change the transparency of the image.

*To learn more about the capabilities—and restrictions—of the various file formats, see Chapter 3, "Understanding and Choosing File Formats," p. 79.*

# LAYER MASKS, VECTOR MASKS, AND CLIPPING MASKS

Alpha channels are used to store masks (and, in some cases, to store transparency information), but masks can also be used to show and hide certain areas of a layer. *Layer masks* are pixel-based masks, much like alpha channels. They support variable transparency and can be edited with painting tools. *Vector masks*, on the other hand, use paths to define the visible areas of a layer. They use paths and support only hard-edged transparency. (The term *hard-edged* is used in contrast to variable transparency—a pixel is either completely opaque or completely transparent with vector path transparency.)

## Creating a Layer Mask

You can hide areas of a layer easily with a layer mask. To create a very simple layer mask, you need only make a selection and click the Add Layer Mask button at the bottom of the Layers palette (see Figure 9.28).

**Figure 9.28**
Clicking the Add Layer Mask button leaves the selection visible. (Option)-clicking [Alt]-clicking hides the selection and reveals the rest of the layer.

Layer masks can also be added to the active layer by using the commands in the Layer, Add Layer Mask menu. You can choose to add a mask that hides the entire layer, reveals the entire layer, hides the active selection (if any), or reveals the selection.

Each layer can have only one layer mask (in addition to a clipping mask). Layer masks cannot be applied to *Background* layers. Layer masks create transparency, which background layers do not support.

*Want to get rid of a mask? See "Deleting or Applying?" in the "Mastering Photoshop" section at the end of this chapter.*

After a mask has been added to the layer, it appears in the Layers palette, linked to the layer thumbnail (see Figure 9.29). In the mask's thumbnail, white indicates visible areas of the layer, black is used for hidden areas, and shades of gray show areas of partial transparency.

**Figure 9.29**
The icon to the right of the visibility eyeball indicates that the layer mask is selected for editing. If the layer itself were active, a paintbrush icon would appear in the second column.



## Creating a Vector Mask

In Photoshop prior to version 7, the terms *clipping mask* and *layer clipping path* were used. However, *vector mask* more accurately reflects the nature of the capability. (It also avoids confusion with clipping paths created to selectively show and hide areas of an image in a page layout program, which are still called *clipping paths.*) A vector path is used to determine visibility on a layer. The term *visibility* is used in lieu of *opacity* because there is no variable transparency with a vector mask—a pixel is either inside the path and visible or outside the path and invisible. This does not mean, however, that the *content* of the layer can't have reduced opacity but simply that variable transparency cannot be controlled through a vector mask.

The two biggest differences between vector masks and layer masks are variable transparency (layer masks provide it; vector masks do not) and PostScript output (vector masks provide it; layer masks do not). Vector paths, when output to PostScript-enabled printers, produce crisp, clean edges. This advantage is lost when printing to an inkjet printer, which cannot process the mathematical path description and rasterizes the image.

The process of creating a vector mask is reversed from the layer mask procedure. Instead of identifying the area to be masked and then clicking a button, you click the button *first* and then create the path. To add a vector mask, hold down the (Command) [Ctrl] key and then click the Add Layer Mask button at the bottom of the Layers palette. You can then use the Pen tool or a shape tool (set to Make Work Path) or paste a path to form the mask. It will appear in the Layers palette to the right of the layer thumbnail or to the right of a layer mask thumbnail, if one is present (see Figure 9.30).

> To temporarily disable a mask and show the entire content of a layer, Shift-click the thumbnail in the Layers palette. A large red X will appear across the thumbnail, and the layer will be completely visible. To reenable the mask, Shift-click the thumbnail again.

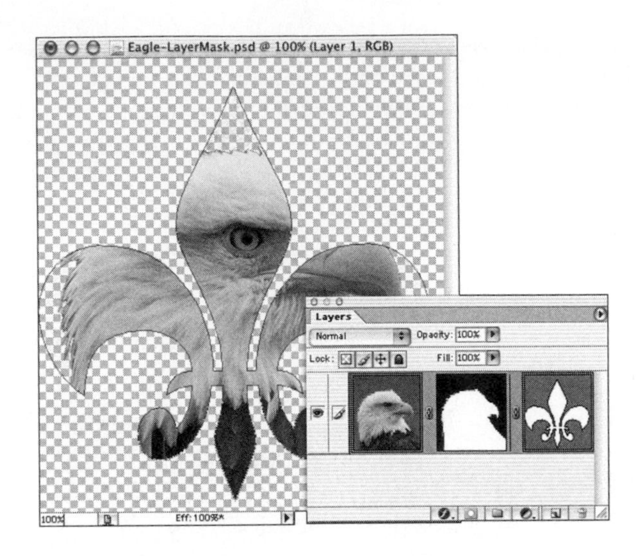


Figure 9.30
The vector and layer masks work together. At the top of the center point, you can see that the background is hidden by the layer mask.

9

## Photoshop at Work: The Two Types of Layer Masks

To get a feel for the difference between vector and raster layer masks, try this:

1. Open an image, any image. If the image is flattened, convert the background layer to a regular layer by renaming it.
2. Select the Custom Shape tool and pick a shape from the Custom Shape palette.
3. In the Options Bar, click the Paths button so that the tool creates a work path rather than a shape layer. (It's the second of three buttons at the left end of the Options Bar.)
4. Drag the shape, creating a path that covers most of the image.
5. Choose the Layer, Add Vector Mask, Current Path menu command.
6. At the bottom of the Layers palette, click the Add Layer Mask button (again, second from left). The layer mask icon will appear in the Layers palette between the layer thumbnail and the vector mask thumbnail. Do not deselect the layer mask thumbnail.
7. Select a gradient tool and set the gradient to black-to-white in the Options Bar.
8. Drag a gradient within your vector mask.
9. In the Layers palette, Shift-click the mask thumbnails to hide one, then the other, and then both.
10. Use the Direct Selection tool to drag the anchor points of the vector mask.

Note the sharply defined edges of a vector mask and how they differ from the gradient layer mask. Vector masks can produce precise masks, whereas a layer mask can be used to create variable transparency on a layer.

## Editing Layer and Vector Masks

Click a mask thumbnail in the Layers palette to make it active and prepare it for editing. Alternatively, both vector masks and layer masks can be edited from the masks' own appropriate palette. Vector masks appear in the Paths palette, and layer masks are found in the Channels palette (see Figure 9.31).

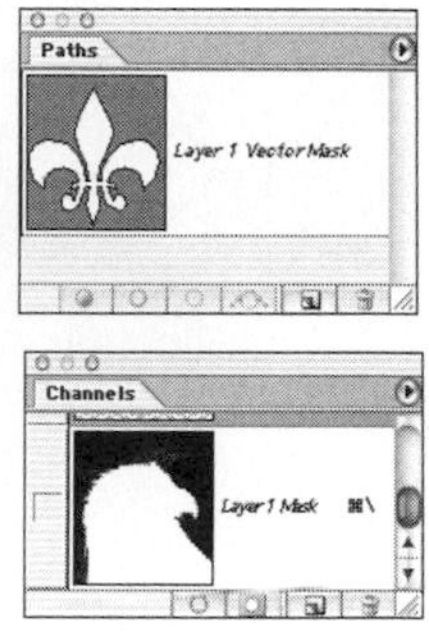


Figure 9.31
Select the mask in its "home" palette to edit it. Note that a vector mask's path will be visible in the Paths palette only when its layer is active in the Layers palette.



A layer mask can be edited much like an alpha channel. You can use shades of gray (as well as black and white) in the image window to edit the mask. Paint and erase in the image to show and hide parts of the layer.

Vector masks are edited with the pen tools, the Direct Selection tool, and the Path Component Selection tool. When the path is selected in the Paths palette, a vector mask can also be manipulated with the Edit, Transform commands.

You can also click the link icon between two thumbnails in the Layers palette to unlink a mask from the layer's content. The mask can then be repositioned in the window. Click the thumbnail and use the Move tool. Click between the thumbnails again to restore the link between the layer and the mask.

## Clipping Masks

A *clipping mask* (known in the previous version of Photoshop as a *clipping group*) is formed when two (or more) layers are joined to selectively show/hide artwork. The opacity on the lowest layer is used to determine what areas of the upper layer(s) are visible. Completely transparent pixels are ignored on the clipping layer, and the rest are used to determine visibility for the upper layers of the clipping mask.

To create a clipping mask, hold down the (Option) [Alt] key and click the line between the two layers in the Layers palette (see Figure 9.32). With the modifier key pressed and the cursor properly positioned, the cursor changes to "wedding rings."

> A layer can have both a layer mask *and* a vector mask. The masks can be created in either order, using the procedures described earlier in this chapter.

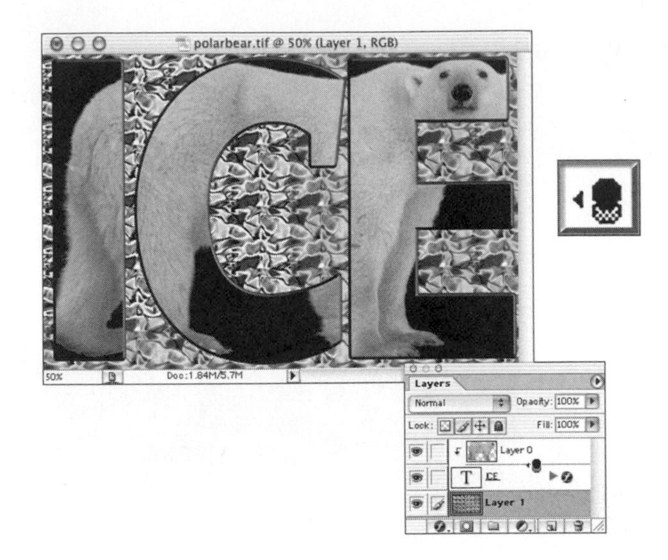


**Figure 9.32**
The "wedding rings" cursor is shown in the inset.



In addition to clicking in the Layers palette, you can create a clipping mask in several other ways. Make sure the upper layer is active in the Layers palette and use the menu command Layer, Create Clipping Mask. When creating a new layer, you can have it automatically grouped with the previous layer. Hold down the (Option) [Alt] key when clicking the New Layer button, or choose the Layers palette menu command New Layer. In the New Layer dialog box, select the Use Previous Layer to Create Clipping Mask check box. You can also drag a layer into an existing clipping mask in the Layers palette.

To clip a number of layers at the same time, you can link the layers in the Layers palette and use the menu command Layer, Create Clipping Mask From Linked (see Figure 9.33).

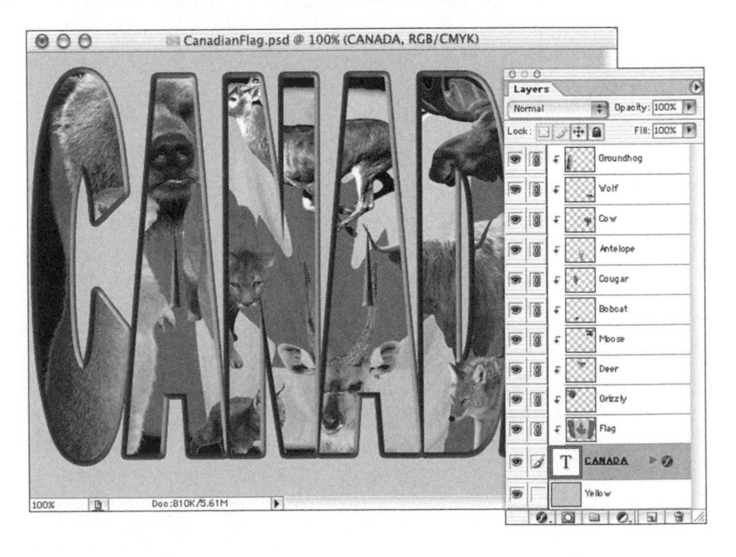


**Figure 9.33**
The linked layers are clipped to the lowermost layer. Any non-linked layer would not be clipped.

# MASTERING PHOTOSHOP

## Showing and Hiding Edges

*I dragged the Rectangular Marquee tool in my image but didn't see any marching ants. I pressed the Delete key to find out if anything was selected and, sure enough, all the pixels in the area I'd selected disappeared. Where did the ants go?*



The keyboard shortcut (Command-H) [Ctrl+H] is used to show and hide "extras." Among the extras is Selection Edges. You can also use the menu command View, Extras to toggle between visible and invisible. To determine what gets included in the extras, open the Show Extras Options dialog box with the menu command View, Show, Show Extras Options. Choose from among Selection Edges, Target Path, Annotations, Grid, Guides, and Slices. Whatever is checked can be hidden and shown with the keyboard shortcut.

## Checking the Options

*I can't get the Rectangular Marquee to behave. Sometimes I try to drag, but it makes a box, and I just drag the box around. Other times it lets me drag, but only certain shapes. Now and then, it doesn't have square corners. What's going on?*

Check the Options Bar. This is good advice for any tool that isn't doing what it used to do. When you're just dragging a box around, it's set to Fixed Size. If the proportions are constant but the size changes, it's in Fixed Aspect Ratio mode. A rectangular selection border with rounded corners is a function of feathering. Switch back to Normal in the Options Bar.

## Deleting or Applying?

*I tried to drag a layer mask to the Trash in the Layers palette to get rid of it, but I got a scary warning message, so I canceled instead. What's the difference between "Discard" and "Apply" for masks?*

If you drag a layer mask or a vector mask to the Trash icon in the Layers palette, Photoshop asks whether you want to keep the layer appearance and throw away the mask, or throw away the mask and the masking, too. The warning dialog box asks, "Apply mask to layer before removing?" It offers three buttons: Discard, Cancel, and Apply. If you discard the mask, it's gone as though it never existed, and the layer is restored to full visibility. If you click Cancel, the mask is retained as it was before you dragged it to the Trash. Clicking Apply uses the mask to edit the layer and then discards the mask. Hidden pixels on the layer are deleted, and areas of partial transparency get reduced opacity. The layer retains the appearance it had with the mask active, but the mask itself is no longer needed.

10

# WORKING WITH LAYERS AND LAYER STYLES

## IN THIS CHAPTER

Layers—along with understanding how layers work with each other—are what make Photoshop such a powerful tool for the digital imagist. Everything else you do in Photoshop is affected by what you do on specific layers.

This chapter looks at how to create and manage layers within a Photoshop document, as well as how to control the visibility of a layer's contents. This is done through opacity changes, layer masks, and clipping masks, which allow you to isolate specific areas to be hidden or revealed. This chapter also looks at how to use layer styles and layer comps to add special effects to layers and experiment with layer combinations.

# WORKING WITH LAYERS



The clear, logical layout of the Layers palette, with the "stacking" of layers one on top of the other, helps you keep track of the images and elements you have on each layer. The topmost layers are the most visible. If the top layer is full-screen and set to Normal blending mode and 100% Opacity, nothing beneath it is visible.

Look at Figure 10.1 and imagine you're starting with a white piece of paper as the background. Add to that your base image and then the shadow of your subject—each added on a piece of clear plastic film. Continue adding your subjects on stacked layers of plastic film.

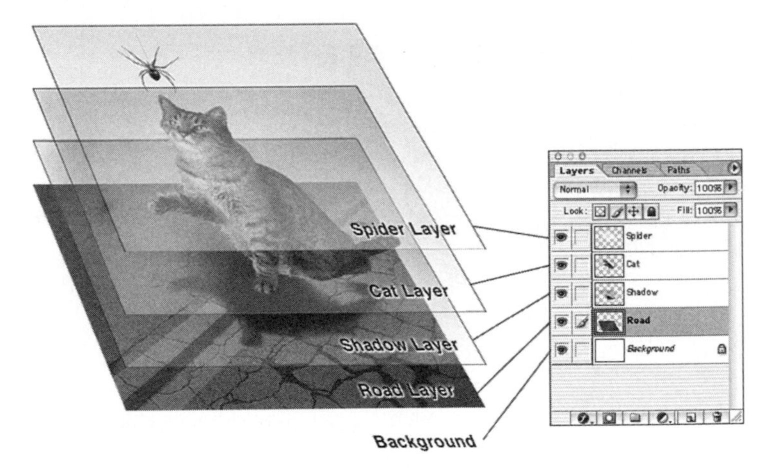


**Figure 10.1**
Consider the arrangement of layers in the Layers palette as images on stacks of film.

The topmost layer is in the foreground, and the subsequent layers are viewed as being beneath it, creating a complete, composited image. In this example, the spider is the topmost layer and is visible in the foreground (see Figure 10.2).

If the topmost image layer is moved beneath the next layer down, it appears to be behind the object in the next layer—just as though you were shuffling stacks of clear film. To reorder layers, click a layer's name in the Layers palette and drag it beneath the next layer in the stack. In this case, the Spider layer is moved under (or behind) the Cat layer (see Figure 10.3).

**Figure 10.2**
A composite can have several layers that make up the final image, with the topmost layers visible in the foreground.

**Figure 10.3**
The Spider layer is moved down one step in the "stack" of layers so that it looks like it is behind the cat's head.

*Unsure about **above, below, in front, in back, over, under,** and the related concepts? See "Relatively Speaking" in the "Mastering Photoshop" section at the end of this chapter.*

# LAYERS PALETTE OVERVIEW

The Photoshop Layers palette provides complete control over how layers are organized and displayed. In addition to reordering layers and turning on and off their visibility, the Layers palette lets you lock various layer characteristics, apply blending modes, and set opacity (see Figure 10.4).

When a layer is named *Background* (in italics) in the Layers palette, it represents a solid layer. Background layers differ from regular layers in a number of ways: They don't support transparency, no layer can be moved below a background layer, and by default they cannot be moved. You can convert a background layer to a regular layer by renaming it in the Layers palette.

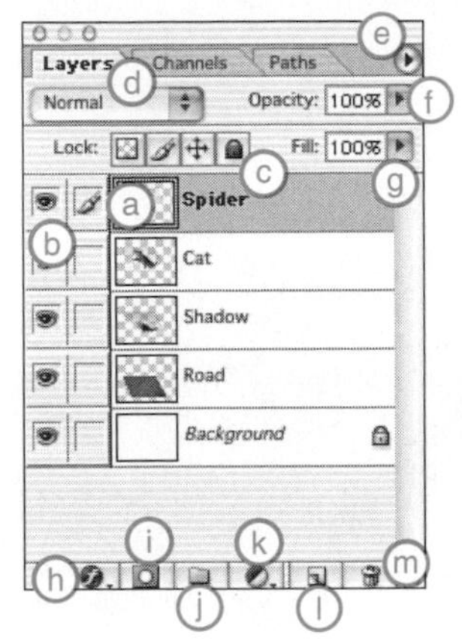


**Figure 10.4**
The Layers palette is one of Photoshop's most powerful features.

a Paintbrush icon indicates that the layer is "active" and anything you choose to do will happen directly to this layer.
b Eye icon indicates whether layer is visible or hidden. Click on this icon to hide the layer, or click on empty space to make it visible again.
c Lock icons allow you to lock individual layers of transparency, paint or editing, movement or lock all.
d Blending modes that can be applied to each layer.
e Layer palette pop-up menu selector.
f Sets Opacity of layer and Layer Styles, effects and masks.
g Sets the Fill opacity of the layer, excluding Layer Styles, effects or masks.
h Adds a Layer Style to the active layer.
i Adds a Layer Mask to the active layer.
j Creates a new Layer Set.
k Creates a new Adjustment or Fill layer.
l Creates a new Layer. You can also drag a layer to this icon to duplicate it directly.
m Deletes the active layer. You can also drag a layer to this icon to delete it directly.

## Showing and Hiding Layers

To hide layers, simply click the eye icon of each layer you want to hide. Click the empty box in the leftmost column to make it visible again. Making a layer visible does not select it or make it active. You must click the layer name itself to make a layer active.

## Linking Other Layers to the Active Layer

One common problem you might experience while working with layers occurs when you don't realize that you're trying to add an effect or paint to a layer that's not selected (active). The selected layer is highlighted in the Layers palette and displays the paintbrush icon to indicate it's active. When a link icon appears in this column, the layer is *linked* to the active layer. You can see the link icon (it looks like a small padlock) in the Background layer in Figure 10.4. If you move the active layer, the linked layer or layers move, too. As long as they are linked, the layers maintain their relative positions. You might also link layers to align or distribute them, to merge them, or to create a layer set.

To link a layer to the active layer, click in the second column next to the layer's name. You can link only to the active layer; however, links are maintained when you make another layer active.

> You can show or hide many layers quickly by dragging through the left column.

## Locking Layers

You can lock the active layer's transparency by clicking the square checkered box in the Lock area of the Layers palette. To lock the editing of a layer, click the paintbrush in the Lock area. Click the four-headed arrow icon to lock the location of the layer's content or the transforming of the layer, and click the padlock icon to lock everything on a layer.

## Choosing a Blending Mode

You use the Blending Mode pop-up menu to select the layer's methods of interacting with the layers beneath it. The default mode is Normal (see Figure 10.5). Try going down the list and selecting the different blending modes to see what effect they have on your image. The blending modes are listed in logical categories: The Multiply, Darken, Color Burn, and Linear Burn modes are grouped together, as are the Lighten, Screen, Color Dodge, and Linear Dodge modes. The Linear Light, Vivid Light, and Pin Light blending modes create very different effects from each other, but all still work in a lightening capacity. These modes are grouped with Overlay, Soft Light, and Hard Light modes.



*The individual blending modes—and how they work—are discussed in "Blending Modes, One by One," p. 597, in Chapter 18, "Mastering the Blending Modes."*

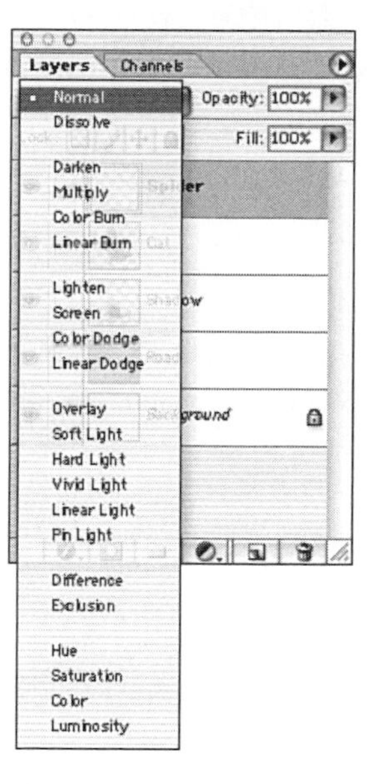


**Figure 10.5**
Select the blending mode in the pop-up menu.

## The Layers Palette Menu

The Layers palette menu contains some commands and options similar to those available with the icons at the bottom of the Layers palette, but it also offers some additional options (see Figure 10.6). You can create new layers, duplicate layers, create layer sets from linked layers, merge layers together, and delete selected individual or grouped layers. You can also dock the palette to the Palette Well at the top of the screen or set palette options from this menu.

*Layer sets, merging layers, flattening images—all are different concepts. Check "Fewer Layers" in the "Mastering Photoshop" section at the end of this chapter.*

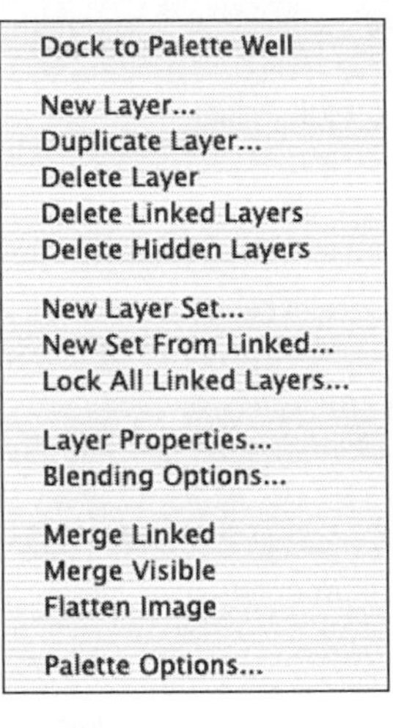


**Figure 10.6**
The Layers palette menu offers several options.



## The Opacity and Fill Settings

There is a fundamental difference between a layer's Opacity and Fill settings. The Opacity setting affects the entire layer, including any masks or layer styles applied to it. The Fill settings, on the other hand, apply only to the layer's content, without affecting anything that has been applied, masked, or stylized. The same is true for adjustment, type, and shape layers as well.

## The Layer Palette Buttons

Across the bottom of the Layers palette are several buttons. Although they duplicate commands in the Layer menu and the Layers palette menu, they are easily accessible doorways to incredible creative power.

### Adding Layer Styles

Layer styles are applied to the pixels of a layer—the layer's content—and incorporate a combination of light, shadow, color, texture, and gradients. You can use layer styles to create 3D and other effects for the image layer. When a layer style is applied, the Layer Style icon is added next to the layer's name in the Layers palette.

When you click the Add Layer Style icon at the bottom of the Layers palette and select an item from the menu (see Figure 10.7), the Layer Style dialog box opens with the selected effect's settings (see Figure 10.8). You can also double-click the layer in the Layers palette (away from the layer name) to open the dialog box.

*For more information on working with layer styles, see "Layer Style Effects Overview," p. 352.*

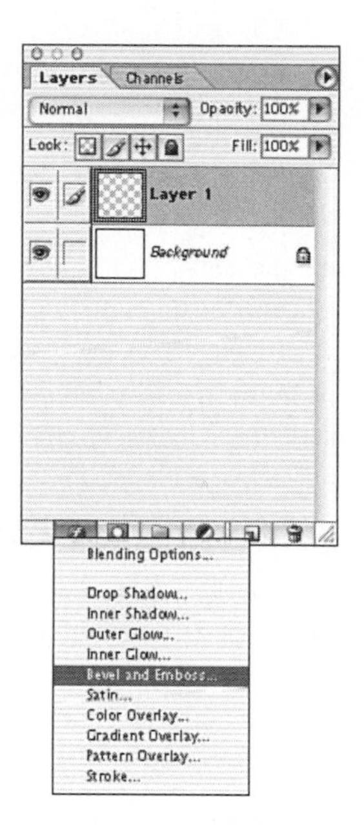


**Figure 10.7**
In the Layer Style menu, select an effect to apply to a layer.



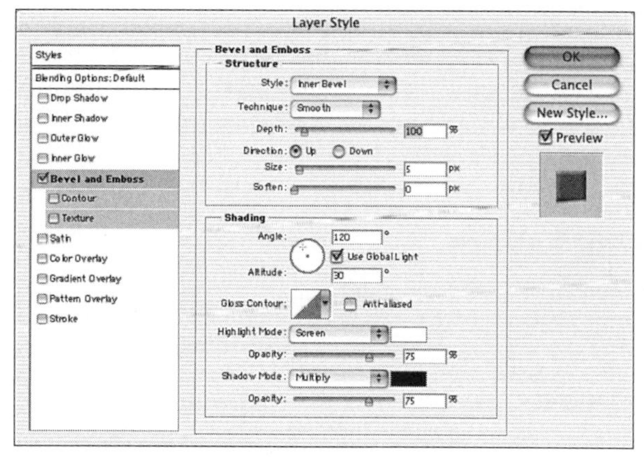


**Figure 10.8**
The selected layer style appears in this dialog box, where you can adjust the settings.

## Adding Layer Masks

Clicking the Add Layer Mask icon once gives you a rasterized (pixel-based) layer mask that you can paint, edit, and fill with selections. Click the icon a second time to create a linked vector mask that can be filled with custom shapes or vectors drawn with the Pen tool. When you click the Layer Mask button, any active selection is used as the basis for the mask.

*For a full discussion of layer masks, see "Layer Masks, Vector Masks, and Clipping Masks," p. 320, in Chapter 9, "Making Selections and Creating Masks."*

## Layer Sets

Click the Create Layer Set icon to organize multiple layers into groups that can be easily hidden or made visible and arranged into folders. You can then move groups of layers within your document's layer hierarchy. (See "Organizing Layers with Layer Sets," later in this chapter.)

In addition to using layer sets to streamline the Layers palette, you can use them to isolate the effects of adjustment layers. Normally, an adjustment layer affects all layers below it in the Layers palette. Likewise, by default, an adjustment layer within a layer set affects *all* layers below it, regardless of whether they're in the set. Changing the layer set's blending mode from Pass Through to Normal prevents any adjustment layer in the set from having an effect on layers outside the set.

## Selecting a Fill or Adjustment Layer



Fill layers can be filled with a solid color, gradient, or pattern. They are often used with a layer mask and a layer style. Click the Layers palette button and select the type of fill layer from the top of the pop-up menu. When you select Color, the Color Picker opens. Select Gradient, and the Gradient Fill dialog box opens. When you select Pattern, the Pattern Fill dialog box appears. A pattern is tiled throughout the layer or an active selection.

Using an adjustment layer is the best way to color-correct the layers beneath it without permanently damaging the image layers. You can reverse or eliminate any modifications, corrections, or effects applied to the adjustment layer without any impact on the original image. Adjustment layers can be reopened at any time to change the settings, unlike changes made with the Adjustments commands. Click and hold the adjustment layer icon and select the type of adjustment layer required from the pop-up menu.

## Adding and Deleting Layers

Among the most basic layer-related steps are creating and deleting layers. The familiar buttons to the right of the Layers palette handle these tasks. You can add a new layer by clicking the New Layer button or using the keyboard shortcut (Shift-Command-N) [Shift+Ctrl+N]. You can quickly duplicate an existing layer—and its content—by dragging the layer from its position in the Layers palette to the New Layer button.

You can delete the active layer by clicking the Trash icon. Alternatively, you can drag a layer (or a layer mask) to the Trash icon to eliminate it.

> You can perform several menu functions by simply (Control)-clicking right-clicking a different area of a layer in the Layers palette. The contextual menus that appear change depending on whether you click the visibility icon, layer thumbnail, or layer name. Available functions include Layer Label Colors, Show/Hide, Layer Properties, Blending Options, Duplicate or Delete Layer, Enable Layer Mask, Rasterize Layer, Copy Layer Style, Paste Layer Style, Paste Layer Style to Linked, and Clear Layer Style.

# PHOTOSHOP AT WORK: CREATING CLIPPING MASKS

The process of creating clipping masks in Photoshop involves linking multiple adjacent layers and using the transparency of the bottom layer of the group as a mask for the other layers. This means that the upper layers are visible only through the "window" created by the transparency of the bottom layer. When layers are in a group, the thumbnails in the upper layers in the Layers palette are indented and shown with arrows, and the line separating the layers is dashed instead of solid. To create a clipping mask, follow these steps:

1. Choose File, Open and select the image file you want to modify.
2. Choose Window, Layers to display the Layers palette. Arrange all the layers to be grouped so that they are adjacent; make sure that the layer to serve as the mask is positioned at the bottom of the group. In the example shown in Figure 10.9, the *Background* layer is at the bottom of the stack, followed by two text layers, a layer with lines drawn with the Paintbrush tool, and a pattern layer.

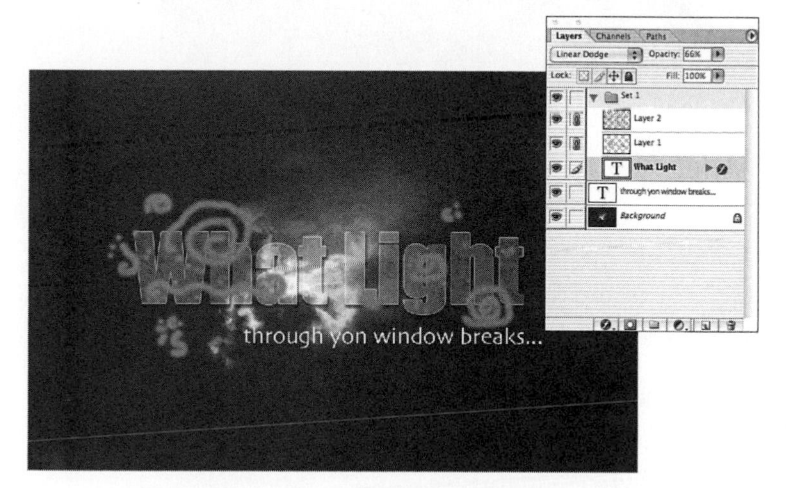


**Figure 10.9**
Arrange clipping mask layers next to each other with the masking layer at the bottom.



3. Link the layers of the group together by clicking the link icon in each layer within the palette. For this example, select the top text layer and then click in the column closest to the layer name to make the chain icon appear. Link the pattern and paint layers to the text layer.
4. Make sure that no layers are linked except for those in the target group. Choose Layer, Create Clipping Mask from Linked (see Figure 10.10). The bottom layer of the group now acts like a mask, revealing the other grouped layers through its visible areas. You can identify clipping masks by the arrow icons to the right of the link icons and by the way the layer names are indented above the bottom mask layer.
5. If you want to ungroup layers in a group, select the layer to be removed from the group in the Layers palette. Choose Layer, Release Clipping Mask. This action ungroups this layer as well as any grouped layers residing above it.

Figure 10.10
Choose Create Clipping Mask from Linked to create the effect.

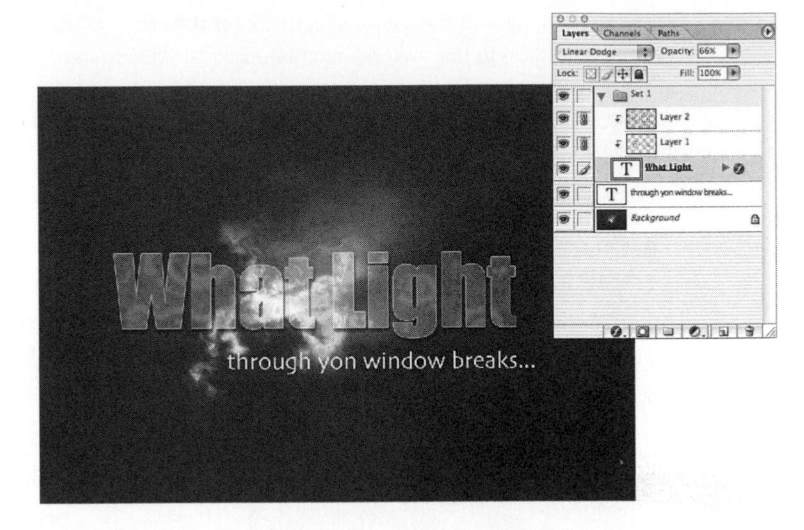


# LAYER BLENDING MODES, OPACITY, AND TRANSPARENCY

A layer's blending mode determines how it interacts with visible layers beneath it, including the layer's opacity and fill.

(Control)-click right-click a layer and select Blending Options from the contextual menu to open the Layer Style dialog box (see Figure 10.11). Although this dialog box has the same name as the one that opens when you select a layer style, choosing Blending Options displays the Blending Options section at the top with the default settings.

Figure 10.11
The Layer Style dialog box doubles as the Blending Options dialog box, with the default settings visible at the top.

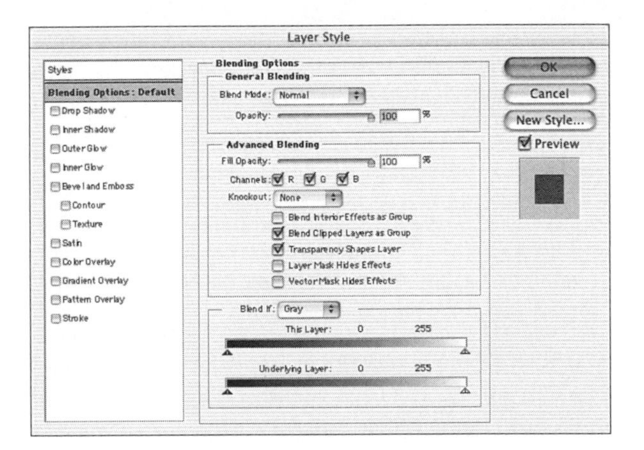


The Advanced Blending section includes options for Fill Opacity (same as Fill in the Layers palette) as well as selectable RGB channels and more. To control the Fill Opacity setting, either type in a percentage for the selected layer or use the Opacity slider, as shown in Figure 10.12.

Figure 10.12
The Opacity slider set to 100% makes the selected layer fully opaque.



Setting the Opacity slider lower decreases the entire layer's opacity, even for the layer styles applied to the layer (see Figure 10.13).

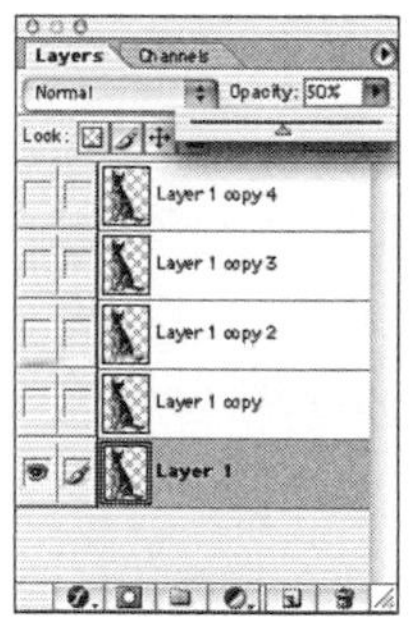


Figure 10.13
The Opacity slider set to 50% adjusts the opacity of the selected layer and its elements.

Adjusting the Fill Opacity slider (or entering a percentage number in the numeric field) affects only the contents of the layer, not the layer styles applied to it. Notice how the stroke outline and drop shadow are still visible, but the layer content is totally transparent (see Figure 10.14).

You can set a layer's blending mode in the Blending Mode dialog box or by simply clicking the Blending Mode pop-up menu in the Layers palette and selecting a mode.

The blending modes are organized into the following groups:

- Normal, Dissolve
- Darken, Multiply, Color Burn, Linear Burn

- Lighten, Screen, Color Dodge, Linear Dodge
- Overlay, Soft Light, Hard Light, Vivid Light, Linear Light, Pin Light, Hard Mix
- Difference, Exclusion
- Hue, Saturation, Color, Luminosity

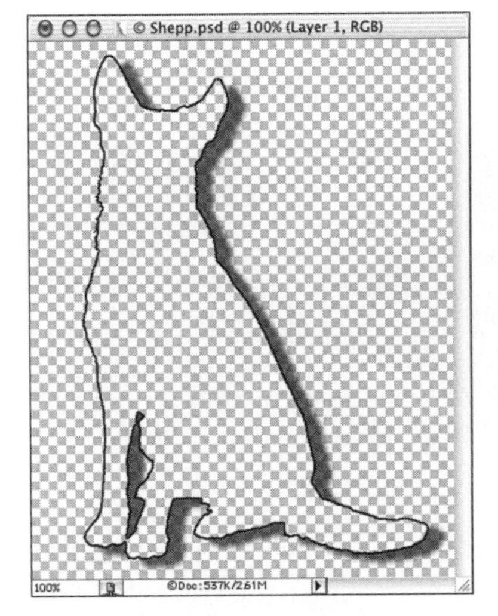


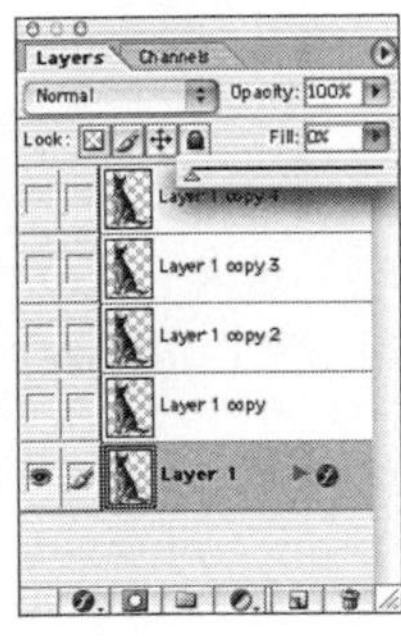


**Figure 10.14**
Only the filled contents of a layer are affected by adjusting the Fill Opacity slider on the selected layer.

The following figures show a few examples of the various blending mode effects. In Figure 10.15, the Plastic Wrap filter was added to the image layer to create contrast and the blending mode was set to Normal (the default setting). The layer is positioned directly above a nonfiltered layer of the same image.

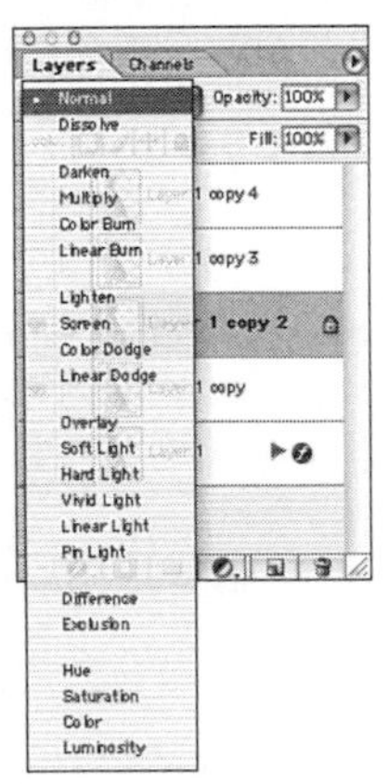


**Figure 10.15**
No animals were actually shrink-wrapped in this example.

With the Multiply mode, the filtered layer increases the saturation of the image layer below it and darkens the highlights and midtones so that very little of the filtered effect appears (see Figure 10.16).

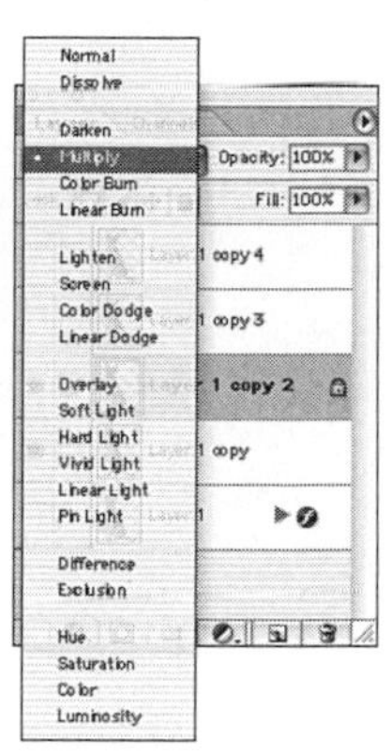


**Figure 10.16**
The Multiply blending mode applied to the filtered layer darkens and saturates the image layer beneath it.

Applying the Lighten blending mode adds the highlights of the applied Plastic Wrap filter. It also lightens the highlights and saturates the midtones of the underlying image (see Figure 10.17).

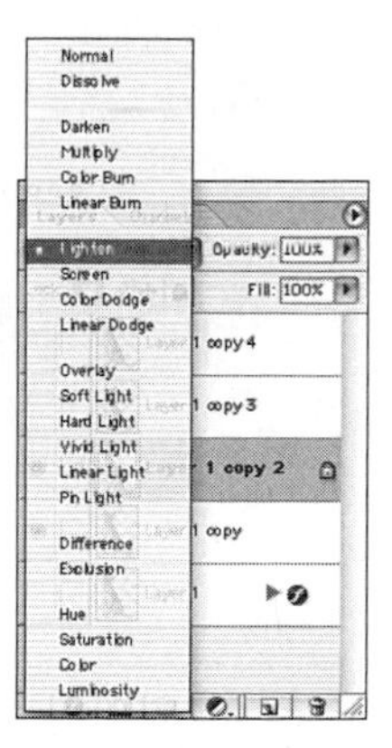


**Figure 10.17**
Only the highlights of the applied filter are visible when the Lighten blending mode is selected.

The Screen blending mode lightens the highlights and midtones and desaturates the image underneath (see Figure 10.18).

Selecting the Difference blending mode shows the differences between the filtered image and the underlying original image layer (see Figure 10.19).

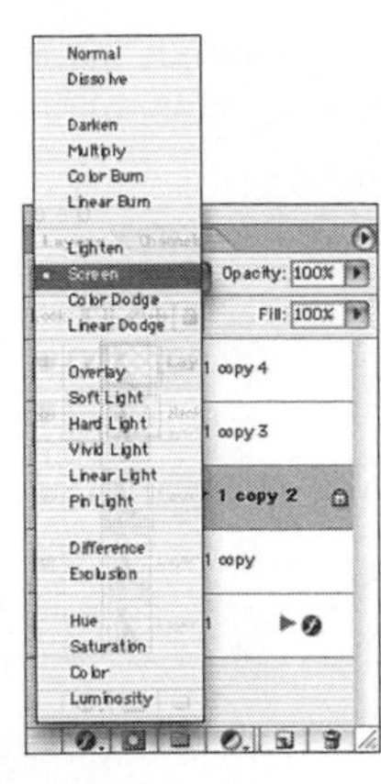


**Figure 10.18**
The Screen blending mode lightens and desaturates the underlying image layer.

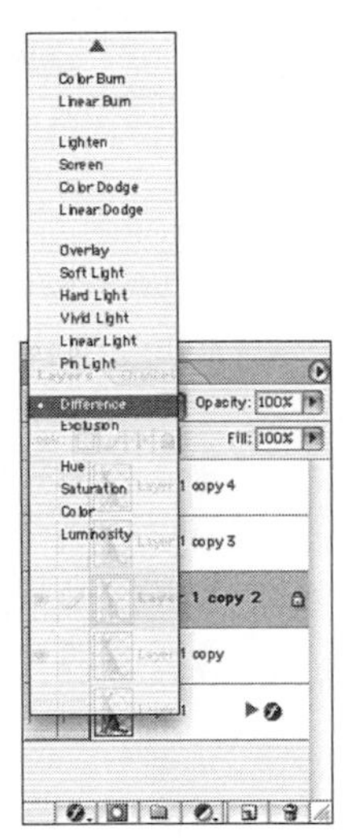


**Figure 10.19**
The difference between the filtered layer and the original image layer is visible when the Difference blending mode is selected.

Luminosity looks similar to the Normal blending mode, working with the blending mode's highlights and midtones (see Figure 10.20).

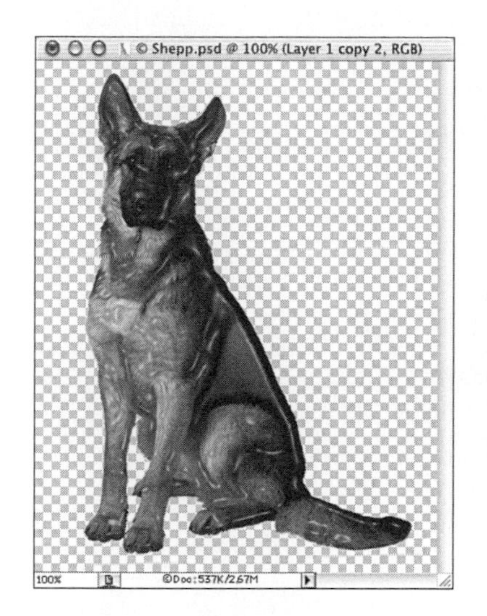


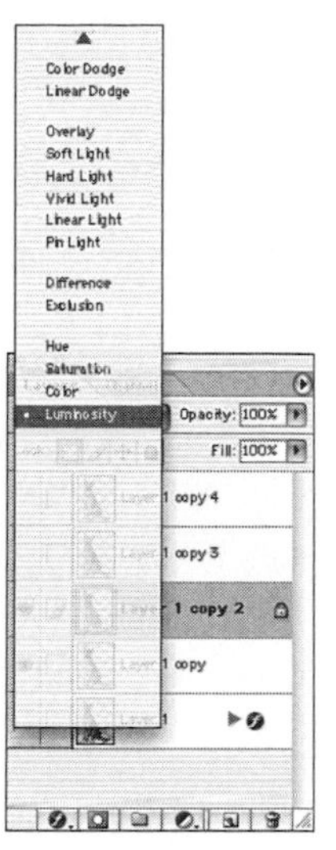


Figure 10.20
The Luminosity blending mode looks similar to Normal but is based on the underlying layer's hue and saturation.



# ORGANIZING LAYERS WITH LAYER SETS

In addition to placing layers in relation to each other, you can organize groups of layers into layer sets, which are "folders" you can create in the Layers palette. You can create a new layer set or create one from existing linked layers. Layer sets can be used to sort large files with multiple layers and can be color-coded for easier organization. To hide or show layer sets, simply click the eye icon associated with the layer set. This method is especially helpful when you're designing multiple-stage button rollovers and animation sequences involving multiple layers.

To create a layer set, select New Layer Set or New Set from Linked from the Layers palette menu, shown in Figure 10.21.

Figure 10.21
Create a new layer set from linked layers.

Give each layer set a unique name and color when you create it to make organization and navigation through your document layers much easier (see Figure 10.22).

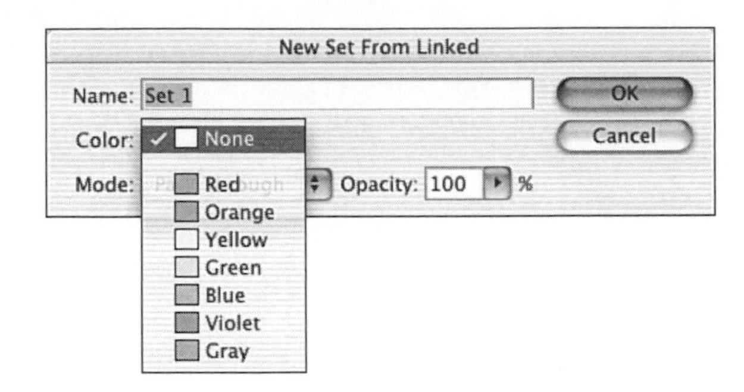


**Figure 10.22**
Name the new layer set and assign it a color for easier organization.

The default blending mode for a new layer set is Pass Through. This is a simple folder that is selectable (on or off) and has no other effect on the layers inside it.

You can select other blending modes that affect all the layers in the layer set and set the opacity for the entire set (see Figure 10.23).



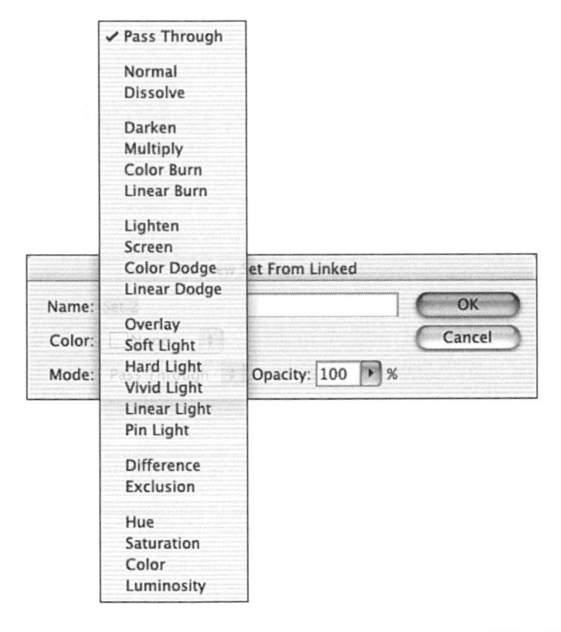


**Figure 10.23**
Configure the layer set's blending mode and opacity to affect all layers inside the set.

Clicking the arrow to the left of the folder icon opens the layer set in the Layers palette. This enables you to continue working with the content of the layers it contains, including layer styles and individual blending modes (see Figure 10.24).

To duplicate or delete layer sets, use the corresponding commands in the Layers palette menu. The layers inside a layer set can be locked as a group or merged into one layer, eliminating the layer set and creating a single merged layer (see Figure 10.25).

> Remember when you're working with a layer set that adjustment layers can be contained within the set or affect all layers below. To keep the effect of an adjustment layer within the layer set, change the set's blending mode from Pass Through to Normal.

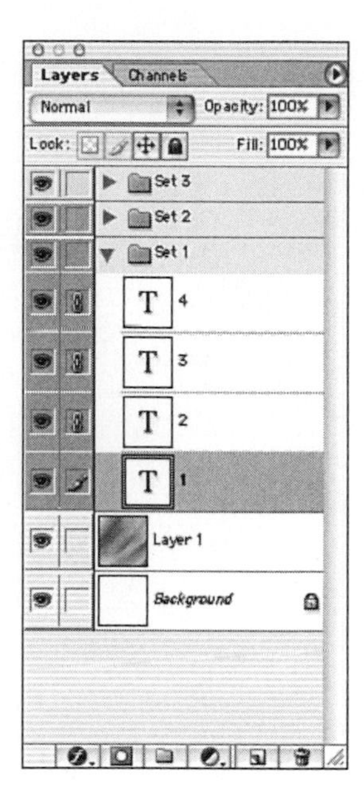


Figure 10.24
You can still work on the individual layers inside a layer set.

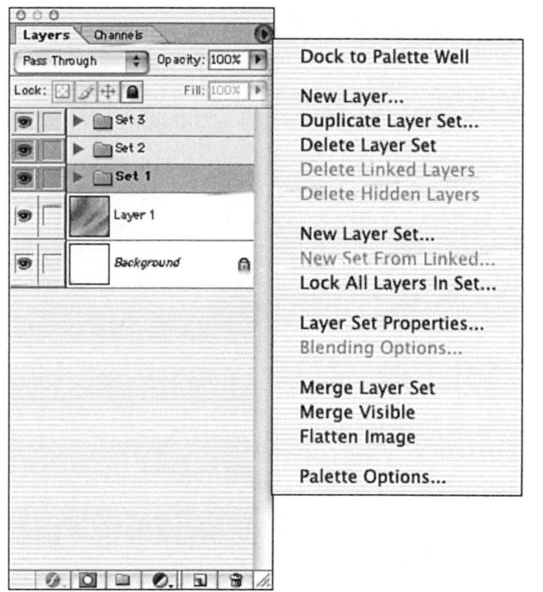


Figure 10.25
Layer sets can be easily duplicated, locked, merged, or deleted from the Layers palette menu.

(Ctrl)-clicking right-clicking a layer set produces a contextual menu, where you can quickly duplicate, delete, or set the layer set properties (see Figure 10.26). You can also duplicate a layer set by click-dragging it to the Create New Layer Set icon at the bottom of the Layers palette, or you can delete it by click-dragging to the Trash icon.

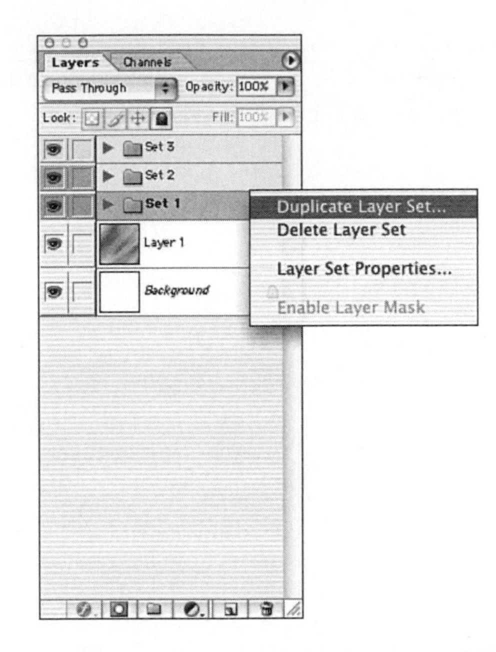


**Figure 10.26**
(Ctrl)-click right-click a layer set to make quick edits or changes to its properties.



Layer sets can also be nested within each other, allowing for an even higher degree of asset organization. With the release of Photoshop CS, you can nest layer sets within other sets in the same way that folders can be stored within other folders in an operating system. In the Layers palette, nested layer sets are indented to show that they are contained within another set (see Figure 10.27).

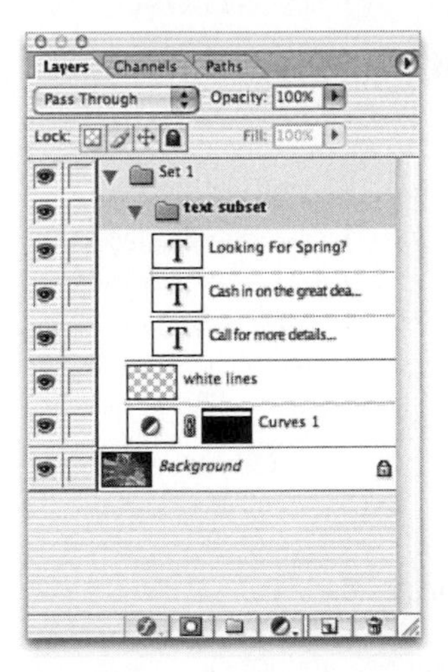


**Figure 10.27**
Nested layer sets appear below the parent layer set and are indented.

The easiest way to nest a layer set is to select it in the Layers palette and drag it to another existing set. The target set will highlight as you do this, showing that the set is being added to its contents. In addition, you can activate a layer within a set and choose the New Set or New Set from Linked command from the Layers palette's Options menu. This will automatically nest the new set, placing it above the active layer.

When you drag a set (or layer) to an existing set in this way, it is added to the bottom of the set's layer stack. It's a simple matter to drag the nested layer set to its desired position within the stack, just as you would a standard layer.

# PHOTOSHOP'S SPECIALTY LAYERS

In addition to layers that contain your artwork's pixels, Photoshop uses a number of other types of layers. Adjustment and fill layers change the appearance of regular layers below them without actually changing their pixels. Type layers contain any text you add to an image. As long as the type layer is not converted to a regular layer (using the Layer, Rasterize, Type command), the text remains editable and vector based for sharp output to PostScript devices. Shape layers, which simulate vector objects, are filled with a color, pattern, or gradient and selectively exposed by using one or more vector paths.



## Adjustment and Fill Layers

Using fill and adjustment layers over a regular layer enables you to create effects and color corrections nondestructively—no pixels are permanently changed. Fill layers can be added to create overall tonal shifting and colorization, patterns, and effects. Adjustment layers are used in place of the Image, Adjustment commands (which make permanent changes to the image). They affect all the layers beneath, not just the adjoining layer, so more layers can be affected globally by the placement of your adjustment layer. You can restrict the effect of an adjustment layer to the one layer immediately below it by (Option)-clicking [Alt]-clicking the line between the layer and the adjustment layer in the Layers palette.

The nondestructive nature of adjustment and fill layers means you can experiment with an image until you're satisfied with the results, without actually changing the original image data or risking a burning contrast or oversaturation that can destroy an image. You can always remove or replace an adjustment layer later with no permanent effect to your image or a drastic increase in the image size. In addition, each adjustment can always be changed, so you can go back and tweak your layers again—you won't have to start over.

Selecting a fill layer gives you the choice of Solid Color, Gradient, or Pattern for the fill. These layers can be used to quickly create a background color or texture. You can use the gradient fill layer as an editable gradient that floats above the image layer so that you can modify it at any time (see Figures 10.28 and 10.29).

> Two different contextual menus are used for the Type tool and type layers. When text is selected or the Type tool is being used to edit, the contextual menu contains font-related and editing options. To access commands that enable you to convert the layer to paths or a shape layer, as well as to access the commands for check spelling and find/replace, make sure the type layer is active in the Layers palette but no text is selected. Then (Control)-click right-click directly on a character with the Type tool.

## Type Layers

Type layers are created with the Type tool. Clicking in the image automatically creates a new layer that contains the vector-based type. The type's appearance is regulated through the Options Bar and the Character and Paragraph palettes. You can rasterize type layers or convert them to shape layers that can be modified as paths. To rasterize the type layer, use the Layer, Rasterize, Type command or (Control)-click right-click the layer and select Rasterize Layer from the contextual menu (see Figure 10.30).

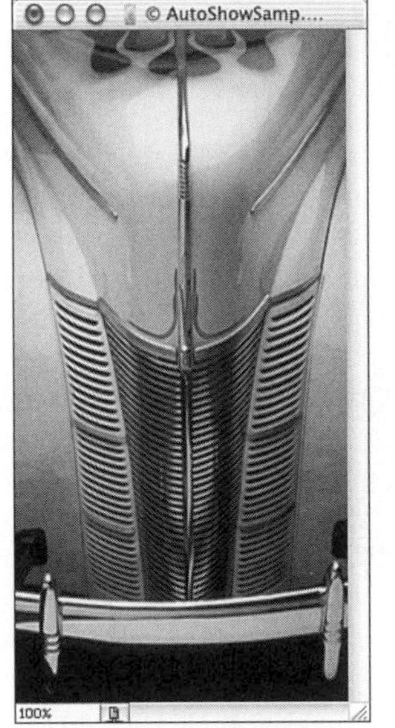


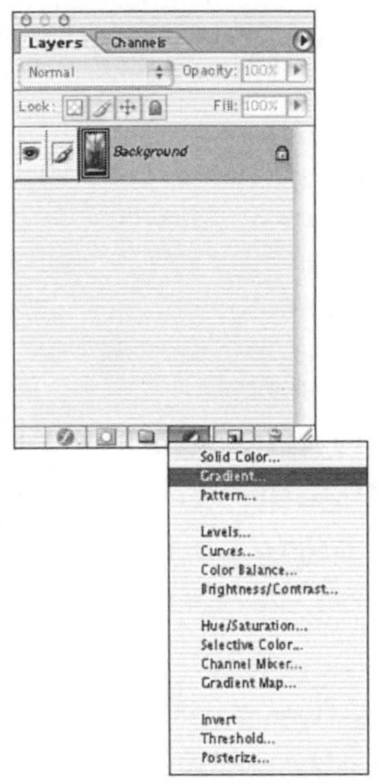


**Figure 10.28**
A fill layer with a solid color, gradient, or pattern can be added to any image.

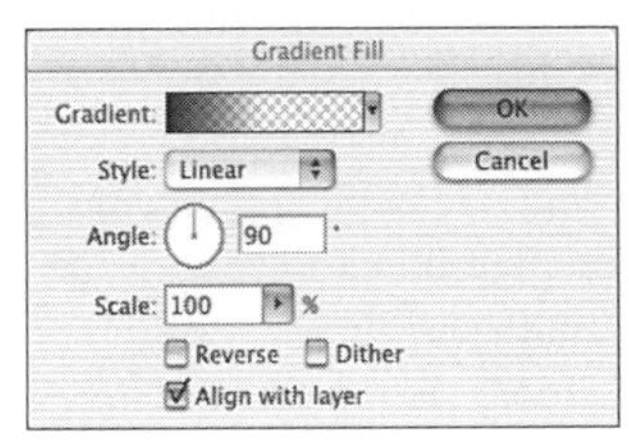


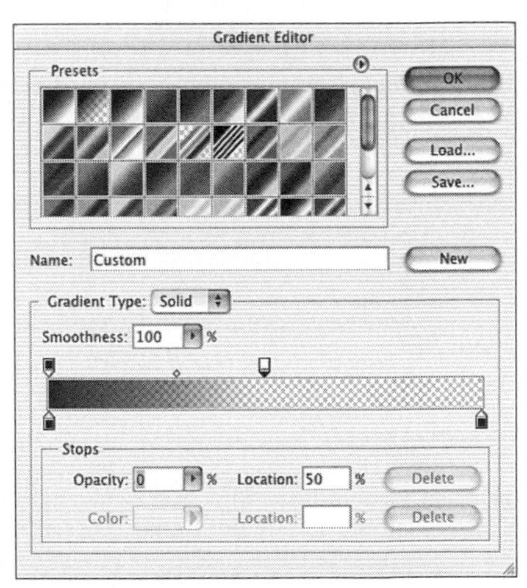


**Figure 10.29**
Use the Gradient Editor to select the appropriate gradient fill for your adjustment layer.

To convert text to an editable custom vector shape, choose the Layer, Type, Convert to Shape command or use the contextual menu's Convert to Shape command. After the text is converted to an outline vector shape, notice that the thumbnails in the Layers palette have changed to a solid fill with a vector mask attached (see Figure 10.31).

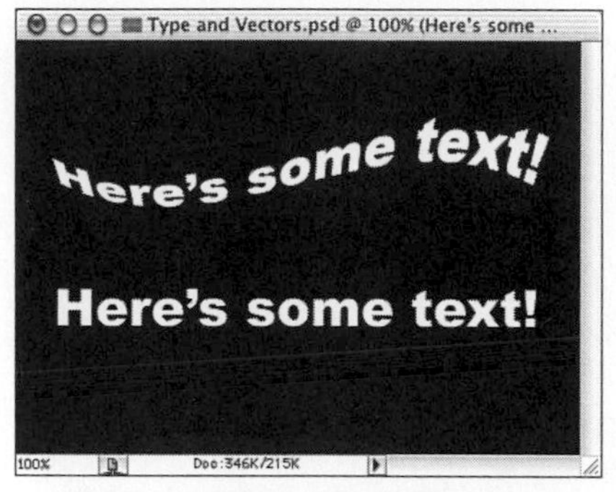


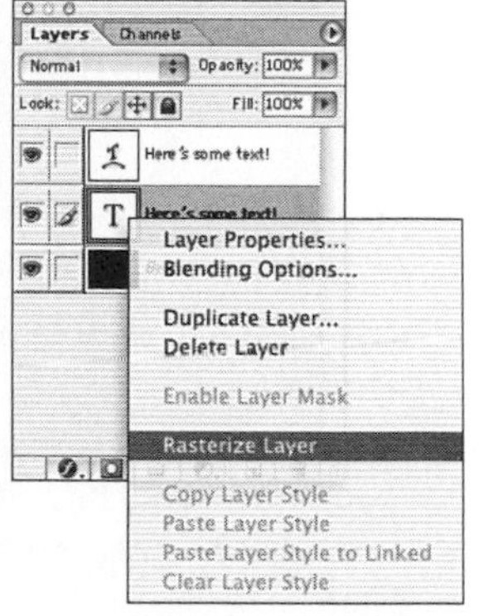


**Figure 10.30**
Type layers can be rasterized so that you can apply filters and liquify effects to them.

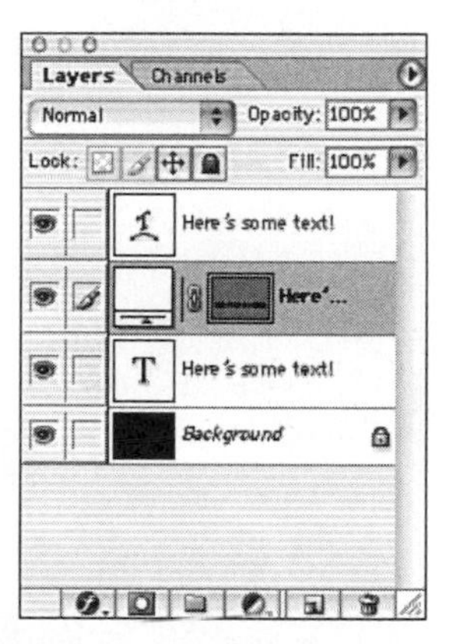


**Figure 10.31**
The text layer converted to an outline shape displays a solid fill with a vector mask.

When type is converted to outline vector shapes, it can no longer be edited in the Character or Paragraph palette; this means, for example, you cannot change the font style and size or run the spell checker. However, you can edit the individual character shapes with the Direct Selection, Path Selection, and pen tools (see Figure 10.32).

**Figure 10.32**
After the font layers are converted to vector shapes, every aspect of the font can be modified with the pen tools.

*For more information on working with text, see Chapter 12, "Adding Text: Photoshop's Type Capabilities."*

> The advantage to maintaining type and shape layers as vector (unrasterized) layers is twofold. Vector artwork can be scaled to any size without losing quality, and when output to a PostScript device, such as an imagesetter or a laser printer, the edges remain crisp and free of jaggies. For more information on the differences between raster and vector artwork, see Chapter 4, "Pixels, Vectors, and Resolutions."

## Shape Layers

Vector shape layers are layers filled with colors, patterns, or gradients that use vector masks on selective exposed parts of the layer. The exposed parts simulate vector objects and appear as artwork in your image. The individual path segments and anchor points of the vector mask can be edited with the Direct Selection and Path Selection tools and the various pen tools (see Figure 10.33).

The Pen tool can also produce a vector mask on a fill layer (see Figure 10.34). You change the behavior of the Pen tool in the Options Bar.

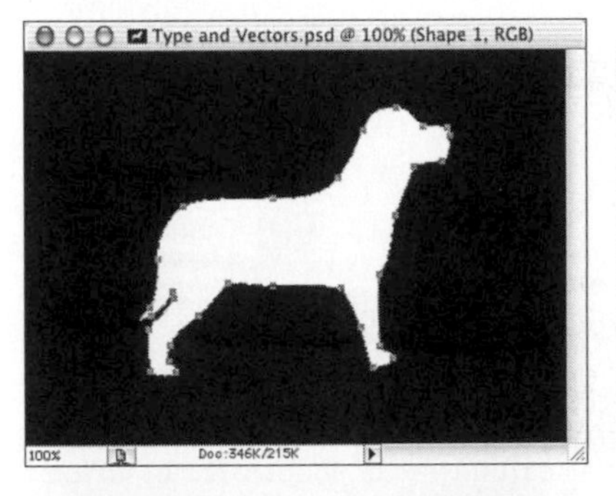


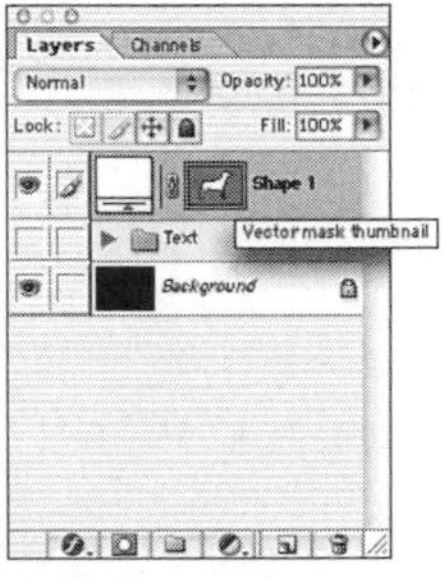


**Figure 10.33**
Create a shape with the Custom Shape tool to produce editable vector points on a vector mask.

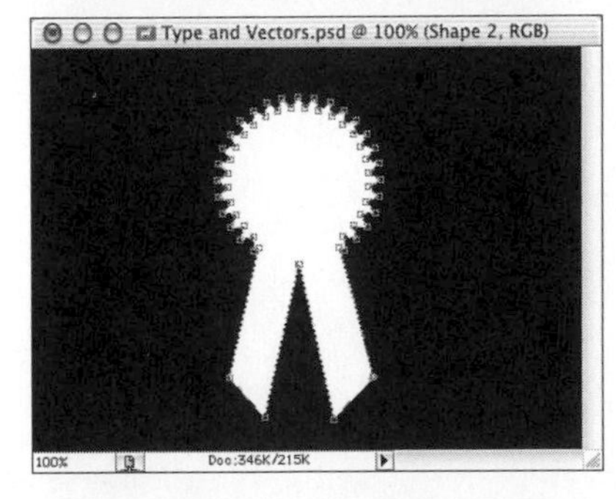


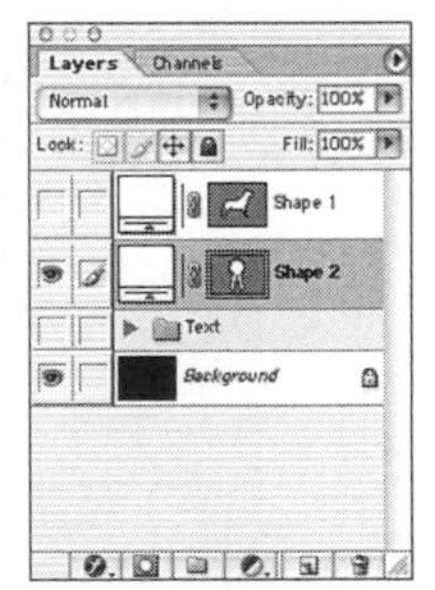


**Figure 10.34**
Use the Pen tool to create solid fill layers with a vector mask custom shape.

You can save custom shapes, whether created by converting a type layer or with the Pen tool, in the Custom Shapes Library. Use the Edit, Define Custom Shape command. You can later reuse these shapes with the Custom Shape tool by selecting them from the Custom Shape Picker.

*To learn more about the Pen tool and other vector objects in Photoshop, see Chapter 11, "The Pen Tool and Shape Layers: Vectors in Photoshop."*

# PHOTOSHOP AT WORK: TRANSFORMING LAYERS

When you *transform* a layer, you modify the position, scale, or proportions of the layer. Transforming a layer is useful for changing the size or placement of a layer, as well as for adding perspective or distortion. You cannot apply the transformation process to the Background layer; you must convert that layer to a standard layer before you can transform it. Double-click the Background layer in the Layers palette and rename it in the dialog box that appears. Alternatively, you can duplicate the layer and transform the copy, leaving the original Background layer untouched. To transform layers, follow these steps:

1. Choose File, Open and select the file you want to modify.
2. Choose Window, Layers to open the Layers palette.
3. In the Layers palette, click the name of the layer you want to transform. In this example, we select the layer that contains a wilting flower (see Figure 10.35).

**Figure 10.35**
Select a layer to transform.



4. Choose Edit, Free Transform to begin the transformation process. A bounding box with handles at the sides and the corners surrounds the layer or the objects on the layer. To transform just a portion of a layer, select the area before choosing Free Transform so that the bounding box covers only the selected area (see Figure 10.36). Background areas left by the transformation will be transparent, allowing lower layers to show through.
5. Apply any of the following transformations to the area in the bounding box:
   - To move the bounding box, place the cursor inside it and drag.
   - To scale the bounding box, click and drag a handle (use the Shift key to keep the original proportions).

- To rotate the bounding box, position the cursor outside it (until the cursor turns into a curved, two-headed arrow) and then drag.
- To distort freely, press and hold (Command) [Ctrl] and drag a handle. To skew, press and hold (Command-Shift) [Ctrl+Shift] and drag a side handle. Press (Return) [Enter] to apply the effect (see Figure 10.37).

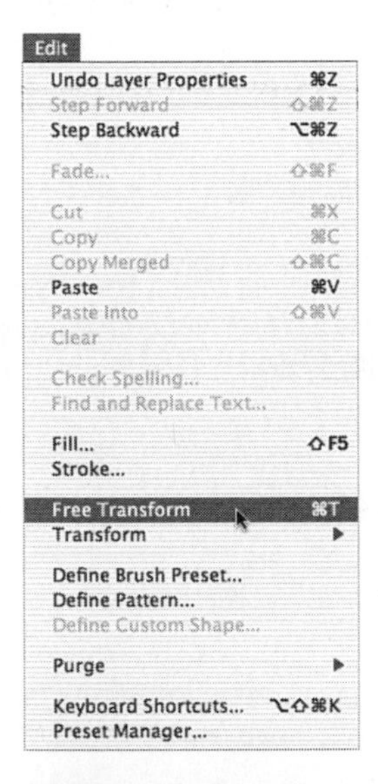


**Figure 10.36**
Select the Free Transform command.

**Figure 10.37**
Transform the layer.

You also can apply individual transformation options by choosing Edit, Transform and then choosing the transformation option you want from the submenu that appears. This approach limits the transformation to only the selected task, such as rotating or scaling. In addition, you can transform a layer with numeric precision by choosing Edit, Transform, Free Transform. In the Options Bar, you can adjust the Position, Scale, Rotation, and Skew options. This approach is especially valuable when you have to repeat the same transformation across multiple unlinked layers.

# USING LAYER STYLES

You can quickly add three-dimensional effects and realism to raster and vector image layers by applying a layer style. Choose from a large variety of layer styles in the Preset Library or create one of your own. You can even modify existing or saved layer styles to create a look that's just right for your project, and you can save the customized style as a preset in your library. You can trade and email custom layer style preset libraries to colleagues and clients. Saved Photoshop files retain the applied style effect on any layer.

Layer style effects range from simple drop shadows and embossed edges to transparent glass and textured 3D patterns. The effects remain with the layer even while you're editing—whether it's a type layer, a vector shape, or a paint layer. Not all effects can be applied to background layers, locked layers, or layer sets.



A layer style can have several effects, and each is fully editable after it has been applied. The layer styles remain fully editable because the layer effects don't degrade or destroy the image layer data (see Figures 10.38 and 10.39). The layer with the layer style effects applied has the Layer Style icon next to the layer name in the Layers palette.

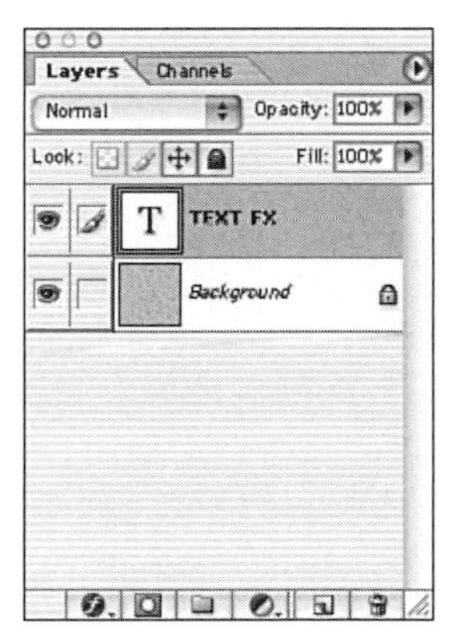


Figure 10.38
No effects are applied to this type layer.

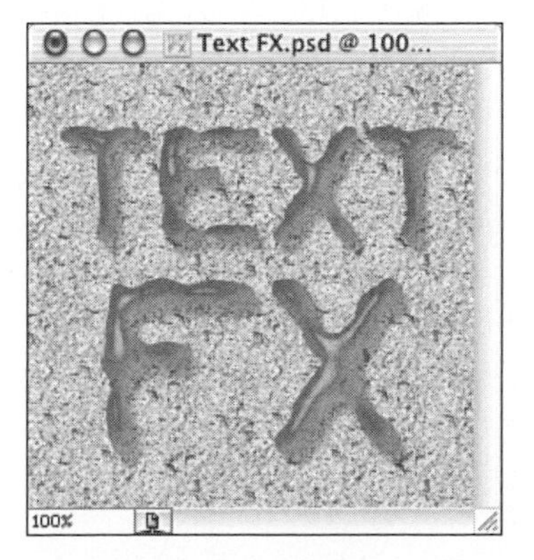


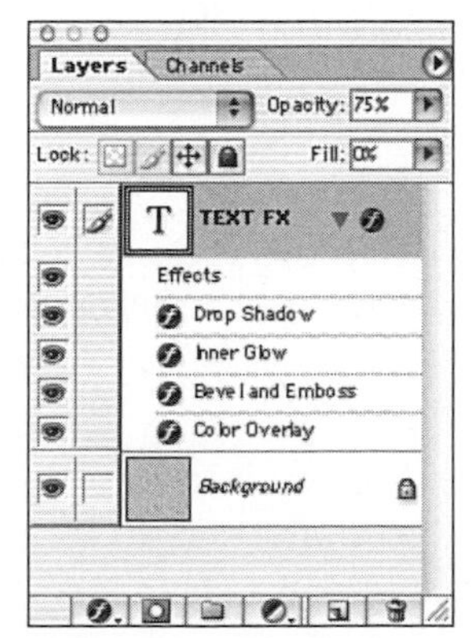


Figure 10.39
A layer style with four effects has been applied to this type layer.

## Layer Style Effects Overview

When you apply a layer style effect to a layer, the Layer Style dialog box opens with the Blending Options section displayed at the top. Click one of the Styles options in the list to the left to apply an effect and modify its settings. You can then create and customize your own layer style effects.

### Drop Shadow

The default Drop Shadow settings, as shown in Figure 10.40, have Multiply as the blending mode, with black as the shadow color and Opacity set to 75%. Generally, these settings are good for most applications. For the angle of the lighting, the Use Global Light option has been selected, which means that all instances of effects lighting are linked together. The distance and size are scalable to the image layer and effect you want to achieve.



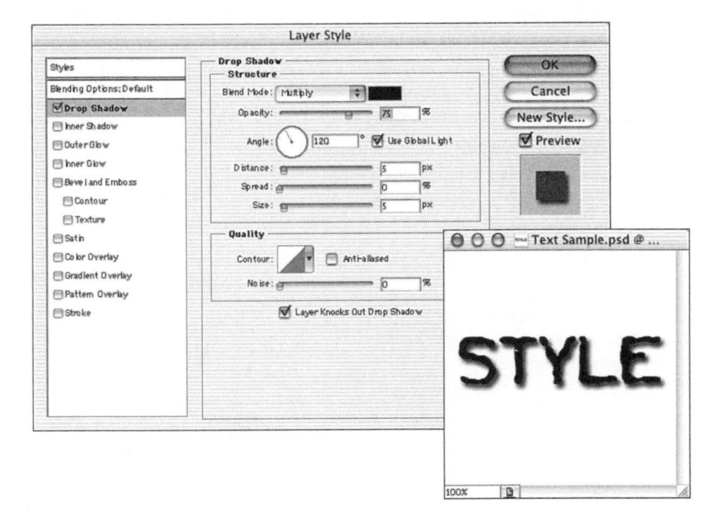


Figure 10.40
The default Drop Shadow settings in the Layer Style dialog box are adequate for most applications.

### Inner Shadow

The Inner Shadow effect places a drop shadow along the inside edges of the image's fill area—such as cutout text—maintaining the layer's fill color and texture (see Figure 10.41). The default blending mode is Multiply, with black as the shadow color and Opacity set to 75%, which is the same as the default Drop Shadow settings.

### Outer Glow

Outer Glow can be used to add a splash of color around an object or a type layer to give it some definition against the background layer. Its primary use is to produce a glow against a dark background, with a default blending mode of Screen; for this example, however, the blending mode has been changed to Normal (see Figure 10.42).

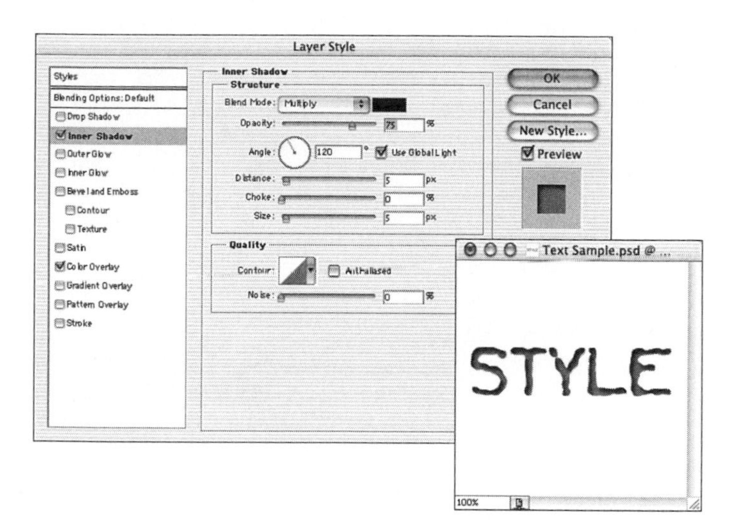


**Figure 10.41**
Inner Shadow simulates a cutout effect from the background layer.

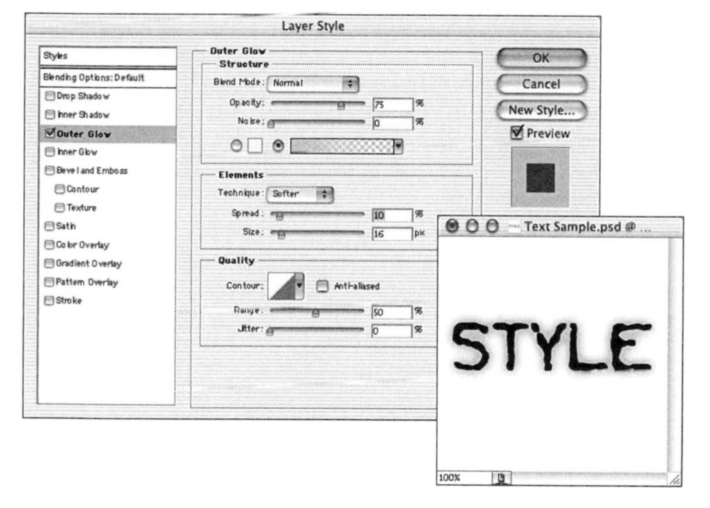


**Figure 10.42**
Outer Glow produces a splash of color around an image layer's fill edges.

## Inner Glow

The Inner Glow effect adds a glow around the inside edges of the image layer's fill area. The blending mode is set to Screen with Opacity at 75% for its default, the same default settings as Outer Glow (see Figure 10.43).

## Bevel and Emboss

The Bevel and Emboss effect gives an object layer the most 3D effect of all the layer style effects. Simply applying the default settings to an image layer gives it a beveled plastic appearance (see Figure 10.44). This effect is usually best accompanied by the Drop Shadow layer style to complete the 3D effect.

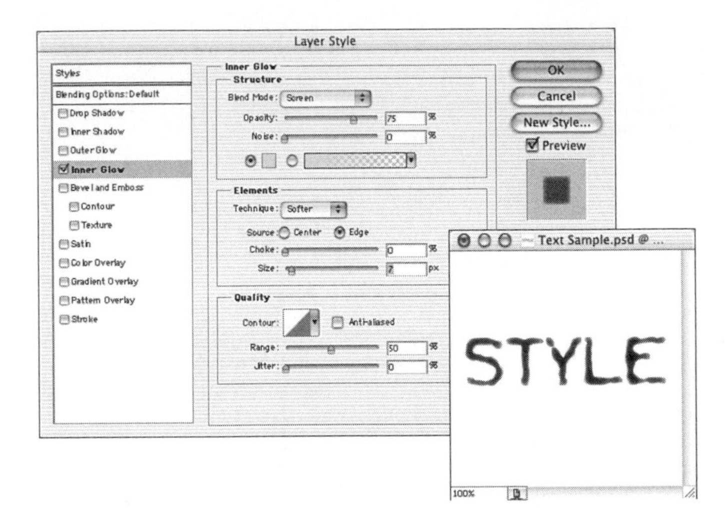


Figure 10.43
Inner Glow adds a glowing rim around the inside of an object image's fill edges.

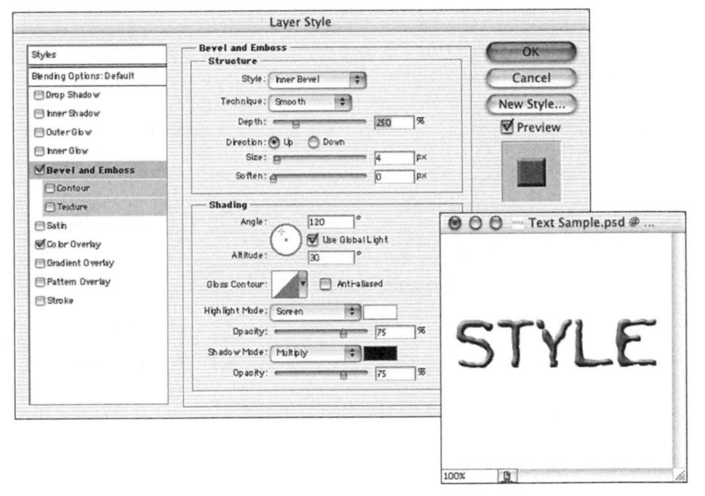


Figure 10.44
The Bevel and Emboss default settings create a basic 3D effect.

To further enhance the 3D effect of the Bevel and Emboss layer style, you can make adjustments to the Contour settings and apply a texture. Similar to the method that sophisticated 3D rendering programs use, adding a texture to the Bevel and Emboss layer style affects the way light hits the surface of the object layer's content. The texture does not affect the image layer's current fill color (see Figure 10.45).

## Satin

Creating more of a two-dimensional surface effect, the Satin layer style uses the edges of the object layer's fill area to produce "waves" across the surface (see Figure 10.46).

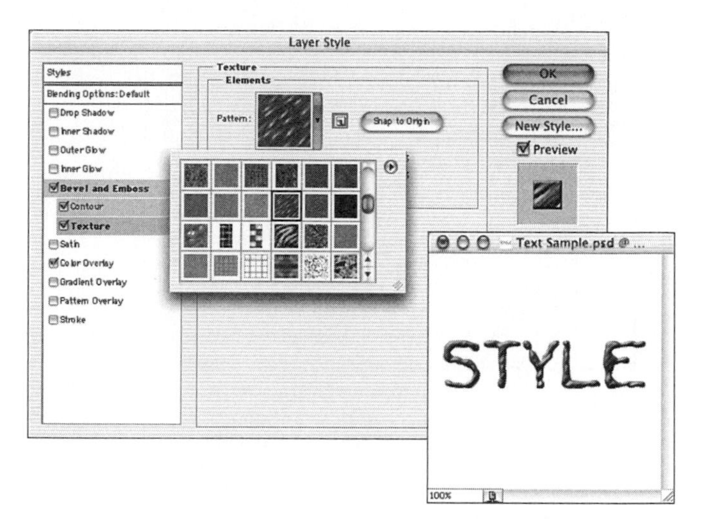


**Figure 10.45**
Adding a texture to the Bevel and Emboss layer style produces a realistic 3D surface-rendering effect.

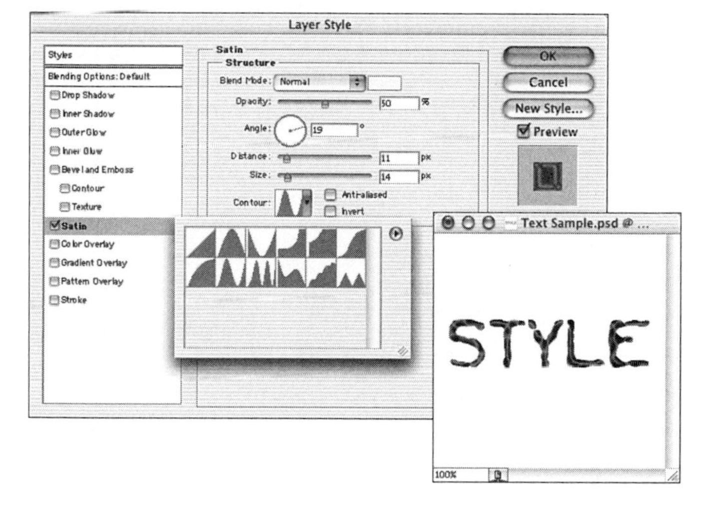


**Figure 10.46**
The Satin layer style produces a wavelike satin finish on the surface.



To edit the contour shape, click the Contour thumbnail in the Structure section to open the Contour Editor (see Figure 10.47).

## Color Overlay

The Color Overlay layer style is a simple but useful feature that enables you to apply a different color to your object layer without changing the layer's fill color (see Figure 10.48). Using the blending mode options gives you the same versatility to work with other layer style effects so that they show through or work together.

## Gradient Overlay

The Gradient Overlay layer style simply applies gradients from the Preset Manager Gradients Library to the image layer's fill area (see Figure 10.49).

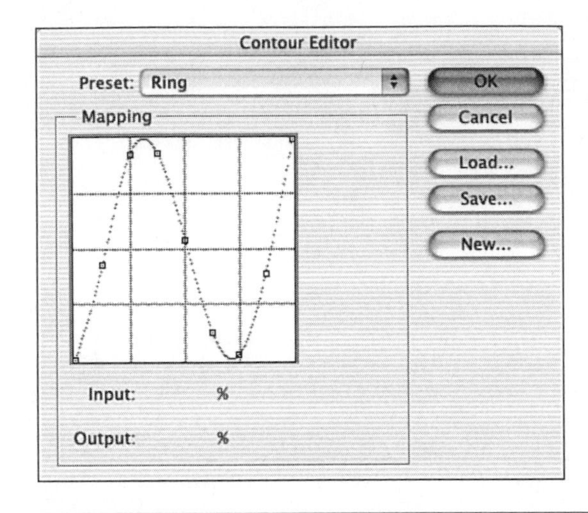


**Figure 10.47**
The Contour Editor enables you to customize the Satin effect for your image.



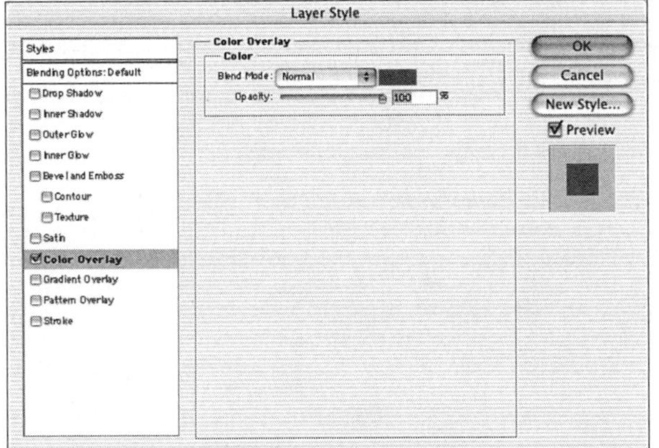


**Figure 10.48**
The most versatile and simplest of all layer style effects is Color Overlay.

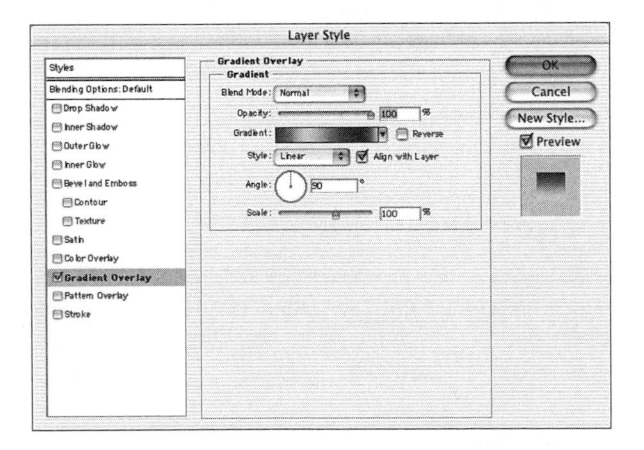


**Figure 10.49**
Scale and angle adjustments enhance the features of the Gradient Overlay layer style.

Clicking the gradient thumbnail in the dialog box opens the Gradient Editor, where you can fine-tune your gradients (see Figure 10.50).

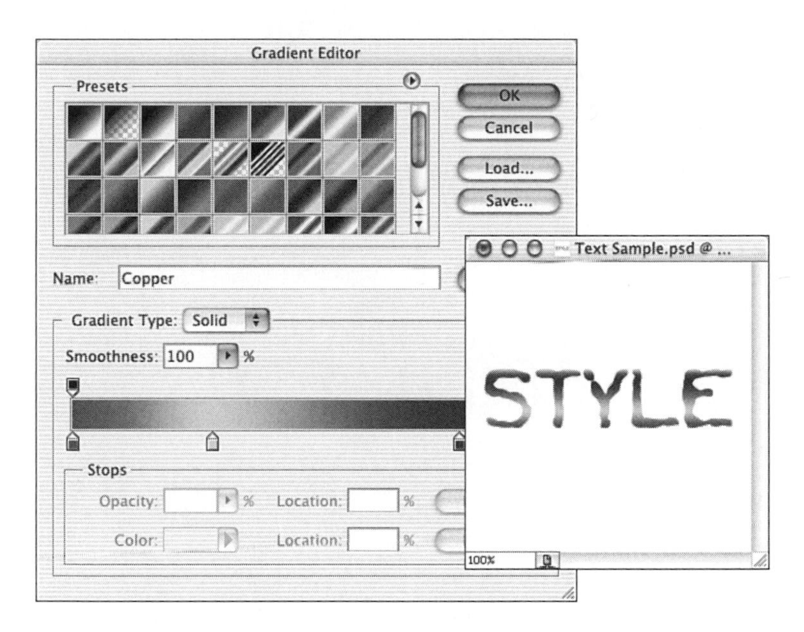


**Figure 10.50**
Modify existing gradients or create new ones in the Gradient Editor dialog box.

## Pattern Overlay

The Pattern Overlay layer style works with other layer style effects, especially if the object layer's fill is solid and needs some texture to bring it to life. To apply the Pattern Overlay, select a pattern from the Preset Manager (see Figure 10.51).

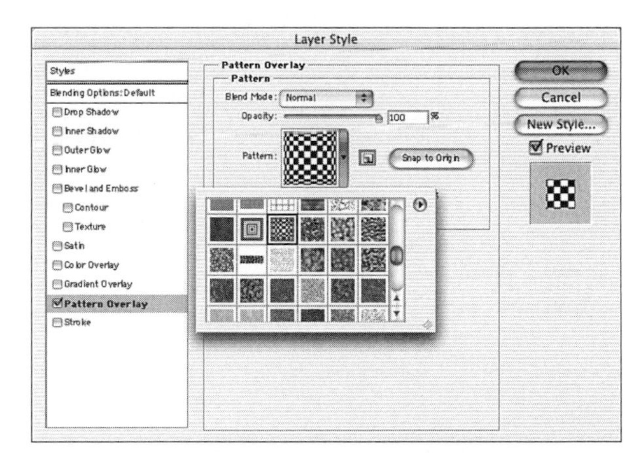


**Figure 10.51**
Select a pattern from the Preset Manager.

The patterns can be scaled to your image layer's content and often produce interesting results (see Figure 10.52). In addition, clicking and dragging inside the image window moves the pattern around inside the object's fill area, so you can align the pattern to its best viewing position.

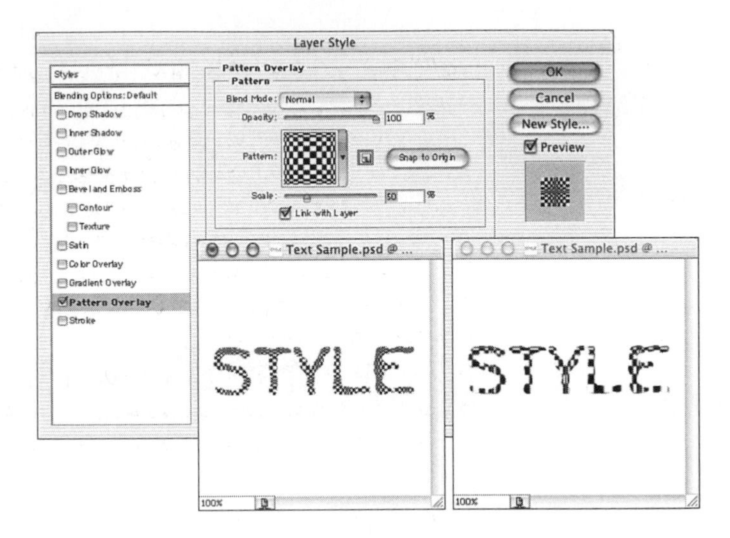


Figure 10.52
Adjusting the scale of the Pattern Overlay layer style.



## Stroke

The Stroke layer style simply creates a smooth outline of the object's fill edges. You can use the Size slider to adjust the pixel width of the stroke and modify the edge orientation in the Position pop-up menu—the choices are Inside, Outside, or Middle. Other options are typical of any color fill, such as Opacity, Blend Mode, and Color (see Figure 10.53).

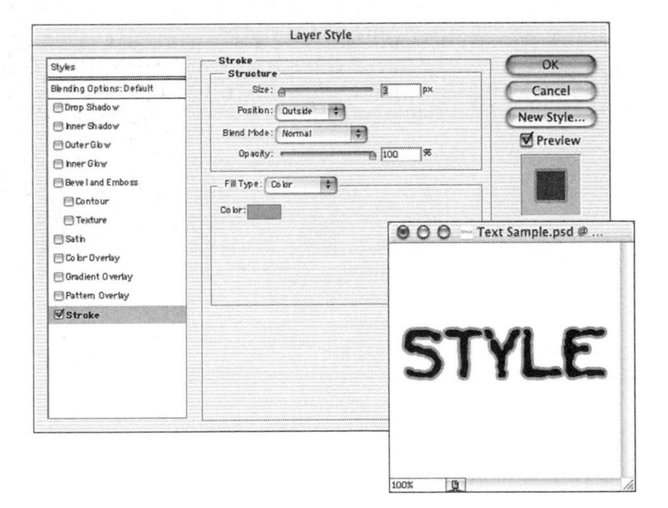


Figure 10.53
The Stroke layer style applies a smooth outline on the object layer's edges.

## Combined Layer Style Effects

The best effects are usually combinations of layer style effects that work together to create a realistic 3D rendered image effect. In Figure 10.54, Drop Shadow, Bevel and Emboss with Texture, and Color Overlay are combined.

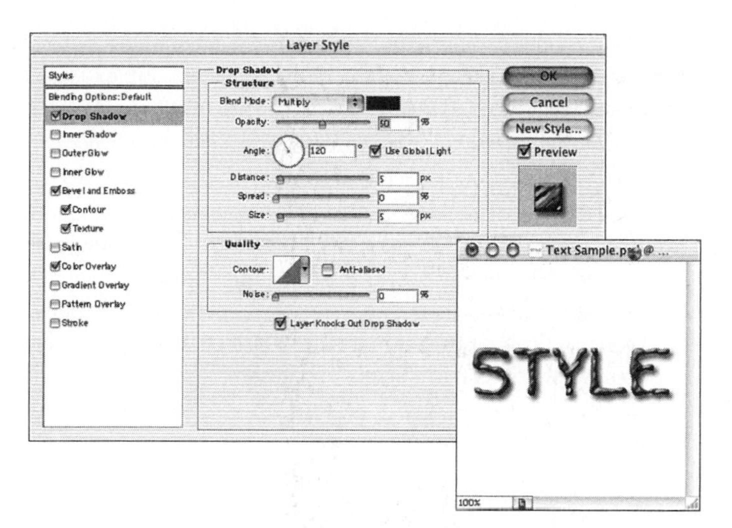


**Figure 10.54**
Combined layer style effects work together to create a 3D effect.



## Selecting Custom Layer Styles from the Preset Library

Many custom layer styles ship with Photoshop CS, and most of them are a good starting point for creating your own special-effects modifications. Remember, you can save any modifications as a new layer style that you can recall for use later or share with colleagues (see Figure 10.55).

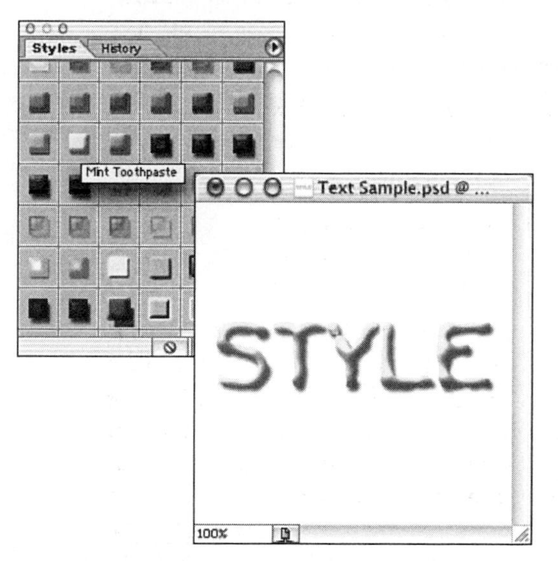


**Figure 10.55**
Select saved layer style presets from the library in the Styles palette.

# USING LAYER COMPS

Layer comps are not actual layers at all. Rather, they are saved layer configurations that preserve the current layer order between all the layers in the Layers palette, as well as any existing settings for opacity, layer styles, and blending modes. Think of them as being similar to snapshots created from the History palette in that they preserve a specific image state that can be loaded and accessed at any time.

This feature is especially valuable for designers who create multilayered montage files with several layers of images, text, adjustments, and shapes. Design success often comes through experimentation, as the designer shifts settings and layer order to modify the composite result. Layer comps give the designer the ability to preserve different design variations and access them with a single mouse click.

Layer comps are created and stored in a separate palette (the Layer Comps palette) that can be opened through the Window menu. To create a layer comp, start by creating a layer configuration as desired, combining layer order, styles, masks, and any other attributes. Click the New Layer Comp icon to launch the Layer Comp Save dialog box and then name the comp, specify which characteristics should be preserved, and add comments about the current state. Click OK to create the comp, which now appears in the Layer Comps palette. You can create and access multiple layer comps by clicking them in the Layer Comps palette. You can also click the forward and back arrows at the bottom of the palette to cycle through the list of layer comps.



# MASTERING PHOTOSHOP

## Relatively Speaking

*I'm a little confused by all the layers lingo and how layers are arranged.*

When we discuss the relative order of layers, we're talking about the *stacking order*. Think of the layers as pieces of paper—or, perhaps better, sheets of transparent plastic. When these sheets are placed on top of each other, it's easy to determine which is on top. If you draw on each sheet of plastic and stack the sheets, artwork on an upper sheet might block artwork on a lower sheet. Moving a sheet below another one changes which artwork hides other artwork.

The Layers palette is arranged the same way: The lowest sheet is on the bottom. When you change the order of layers in the Layers palette, you change the stacking order. Dragging a layer downward in the palette moves the layer's content lower in the image.

## Fewer Layers

*My Layers palette is too full. What's the difference between merging and flattening layers? Do layer sets do the same thing?*

Merging layers combines the content of two or more layers into a single layer. The image might still have multiple layers, but the merged layers become one. Merging all the layers of an image differs from flattening the image in an important way: Flattened images don't support transparency. On the flip side, many file formats don't support transparency, either, so an image must be flattened or saved as a copy.

Layer sets are unrelated to merging or flattening. Think of them as a way to organize the Layers palette. Because you can expand and collapse layer sets to show and hide the layers within, they are an excellent way to streamline the Layers palette without losing information. If you need to reduce the number of layers rather than simply hide them, merging is a possibility. Remember, though, that if the layers have overlapping artwork, the lower pixels might be lost. Both merging and flattening limit future editing possibilities.

11

# THE PEN TOOL AND SHAPE LAYERS: VECTORS IN PHOTOSHOP

## IN THIS CHAPTER

Although Photoshop is primarily a raster image–editing program, it does have some rather powerful vector tools. If you've had experience working with Adobe Illustrator, paths and vector shapes are familiar ground. (Remember, though, that there are *substantial* differences between Illustrator's objects and Photoshop's shape layers.) If you don't work with the Pen tool and vectors in Photoshop, you may be surprised at the level of precision they can make available to you. And with Photoshop CS's new type-on-a-path capability, the Pen tool grows in importance.

This chapter gives an overview of how Photoshop works with vector artwork, describes how to create and edit paths in Photoshop, and then looks at special uses of paths in the program.

# PHOTOSHOP'S PATHS

Photoshop uses vector paths in a variety of ways, for a variety of purposes. As you learned in Chapter 4, "Pixels, Vectors, and Resolutions," vector paths are nonprinting, mathematical descriptions of shapes and lines, also called *Bézier curves*. They can be used to precisely define selections, create "objects" in the artwork, and even show a page layout program what should be visible in an image.

## Vectors in a Strange Land



Photoshop is primarily a raster image–editing program, designed to work with the pixels that make up a digital image. However, it does offer some rather powerful vector capabilities. Vector type, clipping masks, vector masks for layers, and Photoshop's shape layers are examples of vectors in raster images.

Chapter 4 offers a detailed description of vector art, paths, lines, and points, but briefly, vector artwork is based on paths that are recorded in a file as mathematical descriptions. The advantage of vectors is that artwork and images can be scaled to any size without loss of quality. Raster images, in contrast, can be drastically degraded when scaled either up or down (see Figure 11.1).

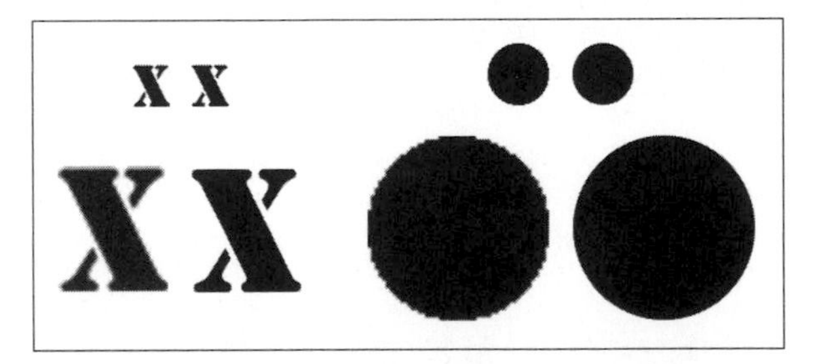


**Figure 11.1**
The X and circle on the left in each pair of images are raster; the ones on the right are vector. The lower pairs have been scaled to 300%. Vector artwork retains its appearance better than raster when scaled.

*For more information on the differences between raster and vector, see "Shapes Versus Objects," p. 381, later in this chapter, and Chapter 4, "Pixels, Vectors, and Resolutions," p. 129.*

Programs such as Adobe Illustrator are designed to work with vector art and have some capability to edit raster images. Illustrator's artwork consists primarily of vector-based objects, with the capability to incorporate placed raster artwork. Photoshop, on the other hand, incorporates its vectors into its raster images. Illustrator doesn't have Photoshop's incredible image-editing power, nor does

Photoshop have Illustrator's vector-manipulation capability—two programs, two purposes, some overlap.

## The Many Faces of Paths

Vector paths in Photoshop can exist independent of a layer, or they can be tied to a layer to create artwork. Vector type layers, for example, must contain nothing but the vector type (keeping in mind that any path on which you place type is independent of the layer). Likewise, shape layers can have no other artwork unless the layer is rasterized. Paths not used directly to create vector shapes or type can be used to create selections or masks for layers and can be stroked or filled.

Keep in mind that the Paths palette commands Stroke Path and Fill Path do not create vector objects. Rather, they color pixels on a layer according to the shape of the path. These commands are comparable to using a painting tool to draw a shape and to filling a selection with the Paint Bucket tool, respectively. They are also comparable to using the menu commands Edit, Stroke and Edit, Fill with selections.

*Unsure about the difference between vector objects and stroked and filled paths? See "The Chicken or the Egg?" in the "Mastering Photoshop" section at the end of this chapter.*

Photoshop can use vector paths in a variety of ways:

- **Type layers**—Although you can't edit the paths directly, type on a type layer consists of filled vector paths. (However, don't overlook the command Layer, Type, Create Work Path. It creates editable paths from the letters.) Photoshop CS can also use paths to bend and warp type baselines.
- **Shape layers**—Photoshop's shape layers are actually layers filled with color, a gradient, or a pattern and selectively exposed using vector masks. When a shape layer is selected in the Layers palette, the path is visible (and selectable) in the Paths palette. When the layer is not active, its path is not visible in the Paths palette.
- **Clipping paths**—The term *clipping path* describes those vector paths that determine areas of visibility for raster images placed into page layout documents. (*Clipping path* and *clipping mask* were also used in earlier versions of Photoshop as the names for paths used to show/hide areas of a layer. The term *vector mask* is now used.) When placing a raster image into a page layout program, you can use a clipping path to selectively hide the background (see Figure 11.2).
- **Vector mask**—Paths can be used to selectively show and hide areas on a layer, much as a clipping path is used for an image as a whole.
- **Selection definition**—A path can be used to precisely define a selection in Photoshop. The Paths palette offers a button that will convert any selected path to a selection.
- **Stroke and fill**—Using the Paths palette menu, you can place color along an active path. Consider the Stroke and Fill commands to be ways to precisely control a painting tool. Remember that unlike true vector objects, if you stroke and/or fill a path and then move the path, the colored pixels remain behind. A path retains no connection to a stroke or fill in Photoshop.

Figure 11.2
The left image was placed into a page layout document with a clipping path. To the right, the same image was placed without a clipping path.

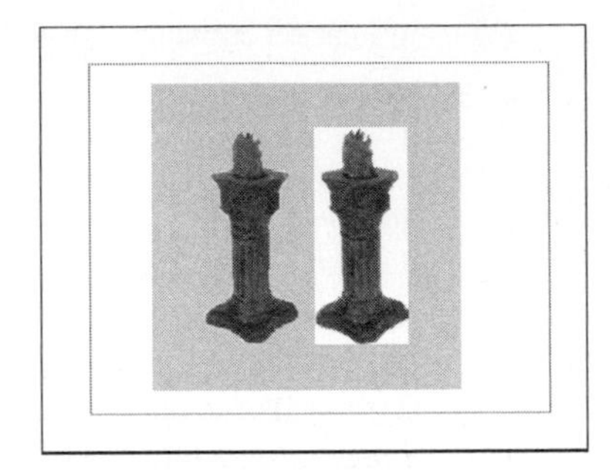

To learn more about vector masks and using paths to create selections, see "Layer Masks, Vector Masks, and Clipping Masks, p. 320, in Chapter 9, "Making Selections and Creating Masks."

## The Anatomy of a Path

The term *path* in Photoshop actually applies to an entry in the Paths palette. The path might or might not contain several subpaths, which work together to form the path (see Figure 11.3). In contrast, Illustrator considers any independent series of path segments to be a distinct path, even if there is but a single path segment.



Figure 11.3
The Paths palette shows a single path, although there are four distinct subpaths.

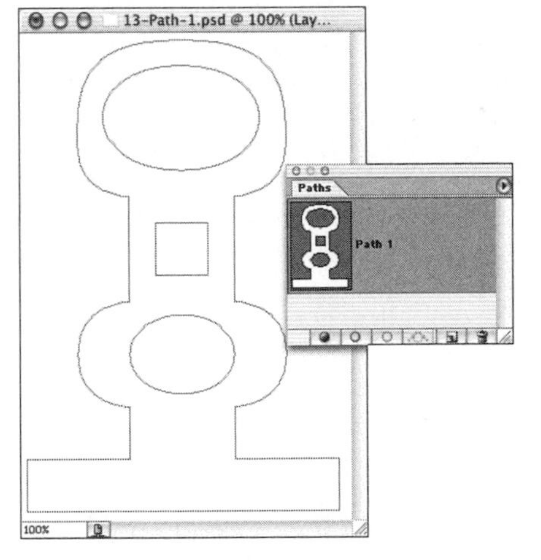


A path consists of one or more *path segments*, the lines you see on the screen. Each segment can be curved or straight. The path itself can be closed, with no discernable endpoints, or open, with two recognizable ends. When filling an open path or creating a vector mask, Photoshop assumes a connecting segment that runs straight between the endpoints. When stroked, only the existing path segments will be colored. Open paths cannot be used as clipping paths.

A path's shape is determined by *anchor points*. There is one anchor point on either end of each path segment. When path segments are connected, they are joined at a single anchor point. Each anchor point in a closed path has a path segment extending on either side. The endpoints of open paths have only one path segment connected. No anchor point can have more than two segments adjoining.

*For a visual representation of the path-related concepts in this section, see "What Is Vector Art?" in Chapter 4, "Pixels, Vectors, and Resolutions," p. 131.*

The position of the anchor points is not key to a path's shape; rather, the relationship among the points determines the path shape. Remember that paths are vector artwork and can be scaled to any size. The relative positions of the anchor points, rather than their exact positions, are the key. In Figure 11.4, the two paths are identical except for size. Although the distance between anchor points is different, the relationship among them is the same—you could scale the smaller path up or the larger path down to create identical objects.

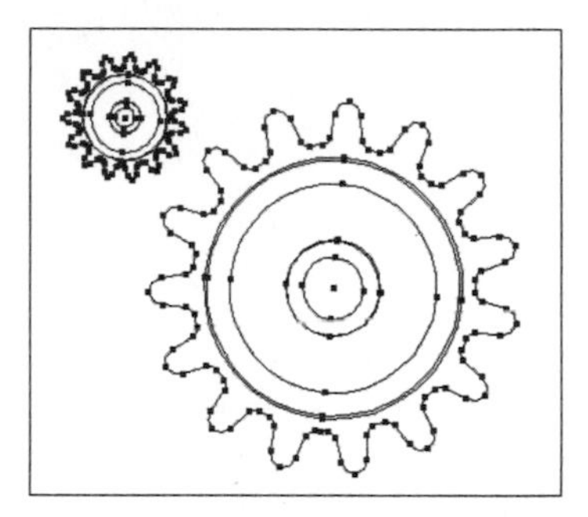

**Figure 11.4**
The smaller path is an exact copy of the larger one, simply scaled to one-third size.

The same path can often be drawn with different numbers of anchor points. In Figure 11.5, three paths have different numbers of anchor points yet present the same shape.



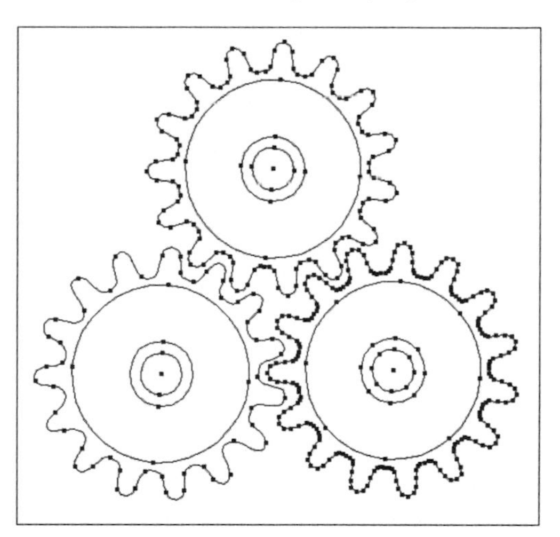

**Figure 11.5**
The top gear has 122 points, the gear on the left has half as many, and the one on the right has twice as many. The shapes on the top and right are identical; the one on the left is nearly identical.

## How Anchor Points Work

There are two types of anchor points in Photoshop: smooth and corner. A smooth point is one through which the adjoining path segments flow in an uninterrupted curve. At a corner point, the path typically (but not always) changes direction. Smooth anchor points are always abutted by a curved path segment on either side. Corner points can have two straight path segments, two curved path segments, one of each, or—as an endpoint—only one of either type. Anchor points are visible when a path is being created or edited.

All smooth anchor points and some corner anchor points have *direction lines*. Direction lines extend from anchor points (smooth or corner) when the point is bordered by a curved path segment (see Figure 11.6). Direction lines determine the shape of the adjoining curved path segment. They are visible only when an anchor point for a curved path segment (or the segment itself) is selected in the image. Selected anchor points are seen as filled squares, and unselected points are hollow squares.

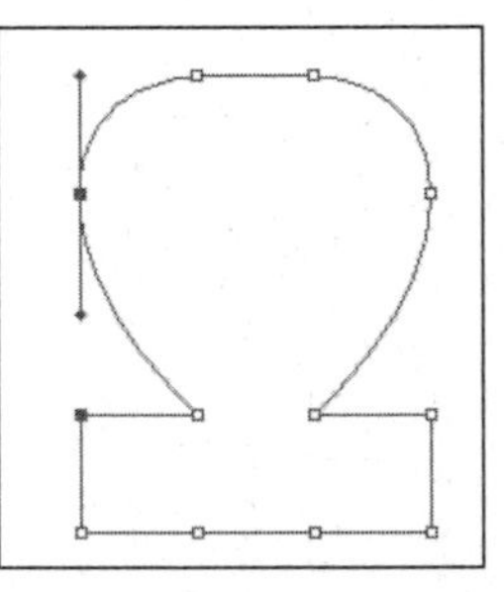

**Figure 11.6**
There are 12 anchor points for this path. Two are selected. The corner point has no direction lines, but the selected smooth point has a direction line for each of the bordering curved path segments.



At the end of each direction line is a *direction point*, which is used to manipulate the direction line and, therefore, the shape of the curved path segment. The Direct Selection tool is used to drag direction points. Both the length and angle of direction lines affect the curve of a path segment.

*Corner points through which a path runs smoothly? How can this be? See "Smooth Corner Points" in the "Mastering Photoshop" section at the end of this chapter.*

When a direction point for a smooth anchor point is dragged, the direction lines—and curves—on both sides of the anchor point are affected (see Figure 11.7).

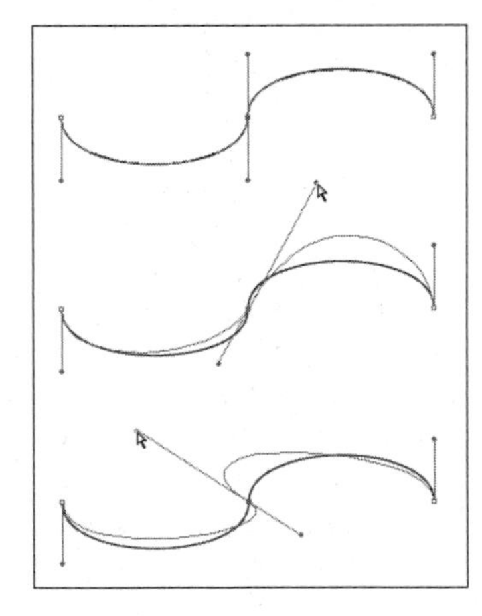

**Figure 11.7**
The original curve is shown at the top. As the Direct Selection tool drags a direction point, the curves are altered.

Note that in the lower examples in Figure 11.7, the direction line on the opposite side of the anchor point changes angle to stay 180° opposed but does not change length.

Direction lines for curves on either side of a corner anchor point function independently. In Figure 11.8, a smooth anchor point (top) and a corner anchor point are compared.

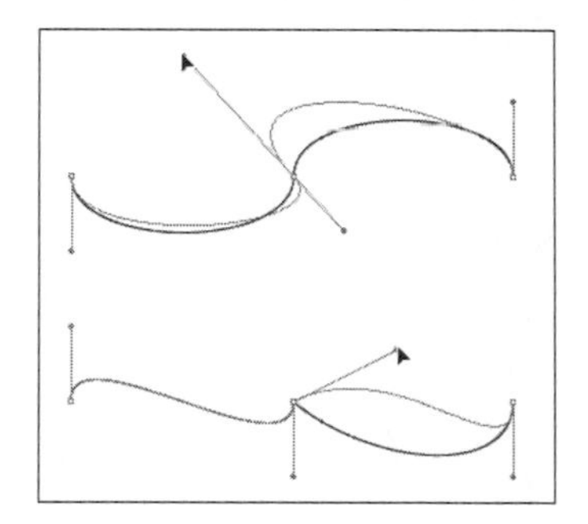

**Figure 11.8**
**Dragging a direction point for a corner anchor point alters only one path segment.**

# CREATING PATHS IN PHOTOSHOP

Paths can be created in a variety of ways. The pen tools can be used to create paths from scratch, selections can form the basis of paths, shape layers are created with paths, and type can be converted to paths. Photoshop uses the Paths palette to manage paths.

A path is called "Work Path" until saved. There can be only one work path at a time. With a work path selected in the Paths palette, you continue to add subpaths. If the existing work path is *not* active in the Paths palette when you begin to create a new path, it will be replaced by the new path (which then assumes the name "Work Path"). The prior work path is lost. Renaming a work path saves it. You can change the name by double-clicking "Work Path" in the Paths palette and overtyping or by using the Paths palette menu command Save Path.



Remember that when a path is active in the Paths palette, creating another path with the Pen tool adds a subpath. Converting a selection into a path replaces an existing work path or, if the active path has been saved, starts a new work path.

## The Paths Palette

The appearance of a path's name in the Paths palette gives you a good indication of what type of path it is. The palette also offers several buttons for use with paths (see Figure 11.9).

The Paths palette menu offers commands to create a new path or new work path; to duplicate, delete, fill, and stroke a selected path; and to convert a path to a selection or a clipping path. When a work path is selected in the palette, you can also use a menu command to save it, which opens a dialog box in which you can assign a name. However, you can achieve the same result by double-clicking the name "Work Path" in the Paths palette and typing a new name.

> To rearrange the order of paths, you can drag them up and down in the palette. This has no effect on their appearance.

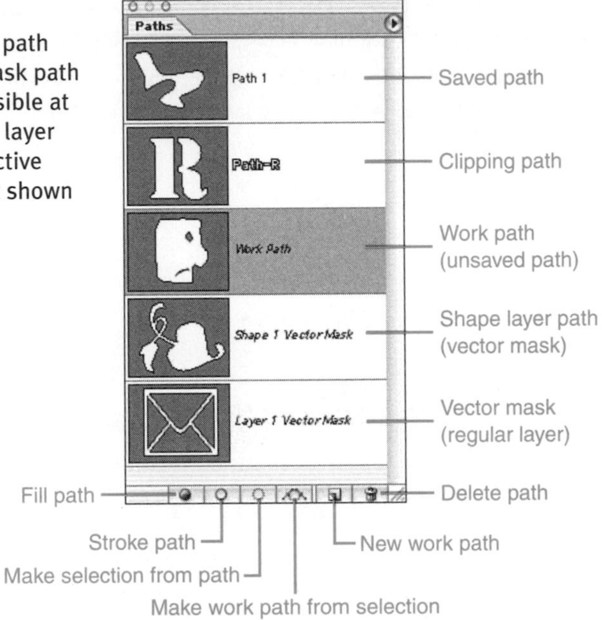


Figure 11.9
The Shape 1 Vector Mask path and the Layer 1 Vector Mask path would not normally be visible at the same time—only one layer can be active, and an inactive layer's vector mask is not shown in the palette.



## Using the Pen Tool

The Pen tool enables you to place each anchor point individually as you work, deciding between corner and smooth points on the fly.

You should remember a few basic concepts when working with the Pen tool:

- To place a corner anchor point with the Pen tool, simply click.
- To create a smooth point, click and drag. The direction and distance dragged set the anchor point's direction line and determine the appearance of the curved path segment.
- To close a path, click (or click and drag) the first endpoint. The Pen tool cursor shows a small circle to the lower right when it's directly over the path's start point. Clicking elsewhere with the Pen tool then starts a new subpath.
- To end an open path, either switch tools or (Command)-click [Ctrl]-click away from the open path.
- To add to an existing open path, select the path in the Paths palette, click once with the Pen tool on an endpoint, and then continue creating anchor points.

Creating a path with the Pen tool can be as simple as clicking in two different locations—a straight path segment will be created between the points. More complex paths can be created by clicking and dragging. The key to creating paths with the Pen tool is understanding how dragging affects curved path segments. In Figure 11.10, four paths were created by clicking and dragging with the Pen tool. In each case, the Pen was clicked and dragged straight down to form the left anchor point.

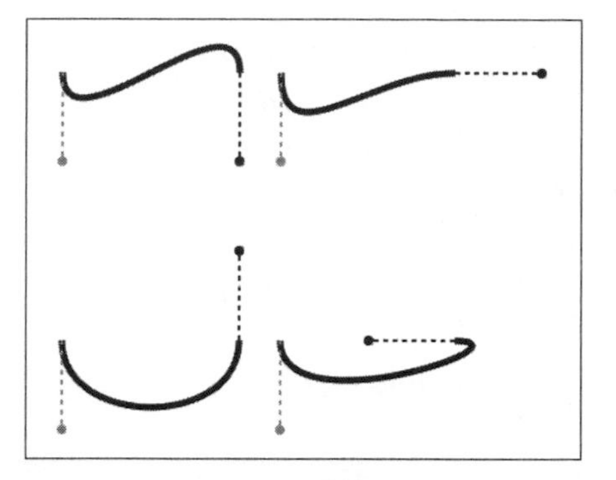

**Figure 11.10**
The dashed lines show the direction and distance of drag for each anchor point. Note that the left points for each of the path segments were created with identical drags.

The only difference among the four path segments shown in Figure 11.10 is the direction in which the Pen tool was dragged when creating the right-side anchor point. (The distance is identical in each case.)

The multiple-segment paths shown in Figure 11.11 illustrate the difference between dragging in opposite directions at each end of a path segment and dragging in the same direction. In the line shown at the left of the figure, each anchor point was created by dragging the Pen tool in the same direction. The second path was created by dragging in alternating directions. However, as you can see in the pair of lines on the right side of the figure, the actual direction lines for the anchor points between path segments look identical.



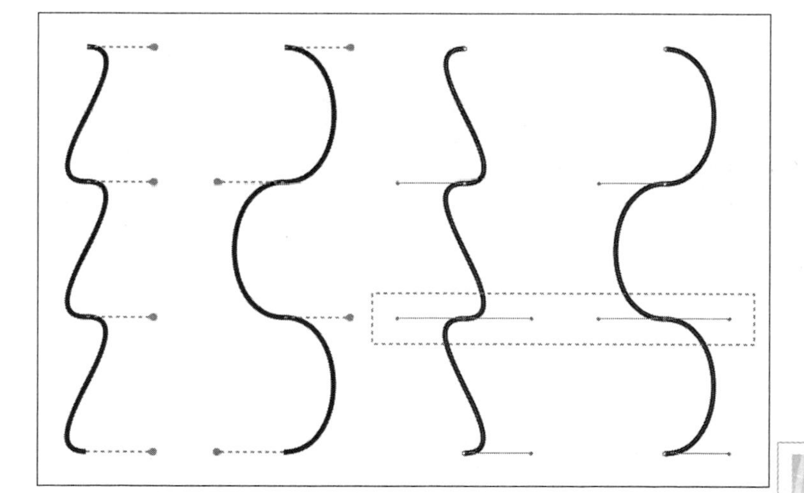

**Figure 11.11**
In the pair of images on the left, the dashed lines show the direction and distance of drag for each anchor point. The pair on the right show the direction lines for the anchor points.

Note on the right of Figure 11.11 that, although only the two anchor points within the dashed box are selected (their squares are filled), one direction line for each of the neighboring points is visible. Even though those neighboring points aren't selected, the direction line for the path segment bordering the selected anchor point is available. This enables you to use the Direct Selection tool to modify the path segments from either end.

Both sets of curves in Figure 11.11 are excellent examples of smooth anchor points. Observe that the direction lines for both selected anchor points are 180° apart—parallel to each other—and the path flows smoothly through the anchor points.

## Pen Tool Options

When the Pen tool is active, the left part of Photoshop's Options Bar offers you the choice of creating a work path or a shape layer (see Figure 11.12). (The option to create an area filled with the foreground color isn't available with the Pen tool.) You can also easily switch to the Freeform Pen tool or any of the shape tools.

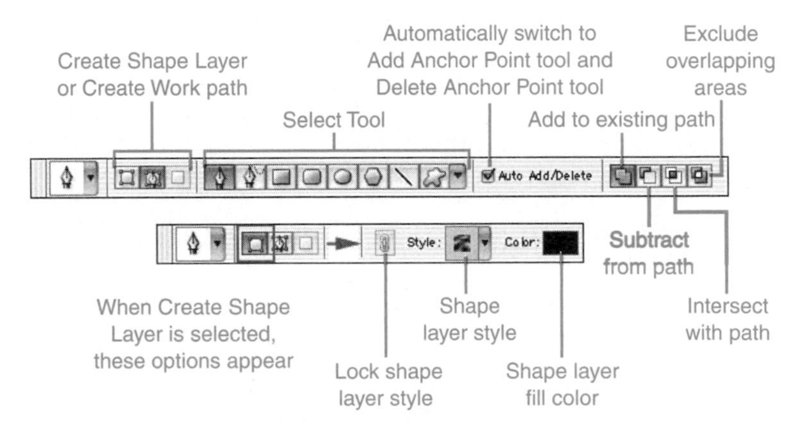


**Figure 11.12**
**The Options Bar differs, depending on whether Create Shape Layer or Create Work Path is selected.**



When set to create a work path and a path is active in the Paths palette, the right side of the Options Bar offers several different behaviors for a new subpath. You can add to, subtract from, intersect with, or exclude overlapping areas. The icons in the Options Bar show the differences.

Selecting the Auto Add/Delete check box in the Options Bar enables the Pen tool to automatically change to the Add Anchor Point and Delete Anchor Point tools. If this option is selected and the Pen tool is positioned over a path segment, it automatically prepares to add an anchor point when you click with the tool. When this option is activated and the tool is positioned over an existing anchor point, it can be used to delete the point.

> When paths are placed close together, disabling Auto Add/Delete can make it easier to start a new subpath. Enabling the option in other situations can save you time switching tools.

When the Pen tool is set to create or edit shape layers, additional options enable you to apply a style and color directly in the Options Bar. You'll notice a "link" icon to the left of the Style example in the Options Bar. When a style is selected, using the Style Link button links the Style pop-up palette to the active layer. Changes made to the style through the pop-up palette in the Options Bar are applied to the active layer. When the link is not selected, changes to the style made in the Options Bar do not affect the active layer.

> The style link button in the Options Bar (available with a pen tool or a shape tool active) applies only to the Style pop-up palette in the Options Bar. Changes made using the regular Styles palette are unaffected by the link status.

Clicking the down arrow to the right of the shape tools in the Options Bar exposes some additional tool-related options. For the Pen tool, you have the Rubber Band check box. With Rubber Band activated, the Pen tool previews the path that will be created by tracking the cursor's movement with the mouse button up. Without Rubber Band, you won't see the path until you click and drag. Additional options for the Freeform Pen tool are discussed in the following section.

## The Other Pen Tools

In addition to the Pen tool, Photoshop offers the Freeform Pen, Add Anchor Point, Delete Anchor Point, and Convert Point tools. The Freeform Pen tool can be used to drag a path, much like using the Pencil or Brush tool. Instead of you clicking to add anchor points, the points are added automatically as you drag. (You can also add an anchor point to the path manually by clicking.) How closely the path follows the cursor's movement is a function of the additional tool options (accessed through the arrow to the right of the shape tool icons in the Options Bar). The default Curve Fit setting of 2 pixels is usually a good balance between path accuracy and complexity. Higher numbers (to a maximum of 10 pixels) reduce the number of anchor points, but accuracy can suffer (see Figure 11.13).

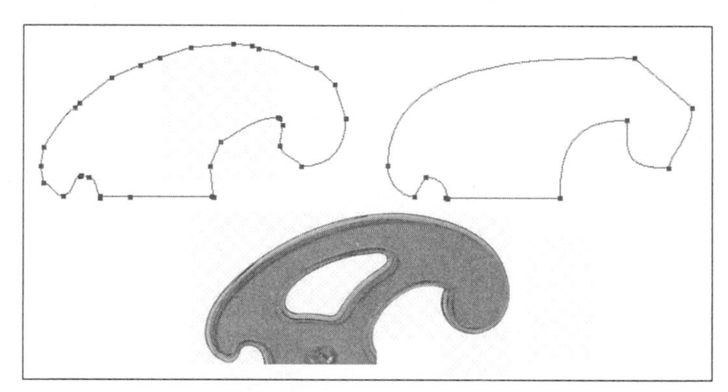

**Figure 11.13**
The image at the bottom was traced with the Freeform Pen tool twice. On the left, Curve Fit was set to 2 pixels. On the right, the setting was 10 pixels.



The Magnetic option for the Freeform Pen tool enables it to follow edges. It uses contrast to determine where an edge exists. The Magnetic option is best suited for use on images with plain backgrounds.

When working with the Magnetic option, the Freeform Pen places a series of anchor points as it follows the path you trace. As you drag, you can click the mouse button to manually place anchor points at spots where the edge you're tracing takes a sharp turn. If the tool places an anchor point in an incorrect location, press (Delete) [Backspace] to remove it. You can also back up along the edge to retrace a segment. Clicking the start point closes the path. Double-click the tool, and it will attempt to follow the nearest edge back to the start point. Pressing the (Return) [Enter] key finishes the path and leaves it as an open path.

> When using the Freeform Pen tool with the Magnetic option, you can temporarily disable the capability by holding down the (Option) [Alt] key. With the key pressed, drag a freeform path without regard for following edges. Release the modifier key to resume using the Magnetic option.

With the Freeform Pen tool selected, click the arrow to the right of the shapes in the Options Bar to set the Magnetic option's behavior. Width determines the radius within which the tool will search for an edge to follow. Contrast, measured in percent, governs how different the pixel color must be to constitute an edge. Frequency controls how often an anchor point will be placed as you drag.

With an existing path selected in the image, the Add Anchor Point tool enables you to add both corner (click) and smooth (drag) anchor points to the path. Similarly, the Delete Anchor Point tool removes existing anchor points from a selected path when you click them. You can use the Convert Point tool to change a smooth anchor point to a corner point (by clicking it) or to convert a corner point to a smooth point (by clicking the point and dragging).

*Wondering about the Auto Add/Delete option? See "Shutting Down the Auto" in the "Mastering Photoshop" section at the end of this chapter.*

The (Option) [Alt] key converts the Pen tool to the Convert Point tool when the cursor is over an anchor point. You can use it to convert corner anchor points to smooth, and vice versa. Click and drag a corner point to create direction lines for a smooth point. Click once on a smooth point to change it to a corner point.

## Editing Paths

Paths as a whole can be edited, or you can work with subpaths or even individual anchor points and path segments. To select an entire path, click it in the Paths palette. You can stroke, fill, delete, and use the Edit, Transform commands.

To isolate a subpath from the entire path, use the Path Selection tool, whose icon is a plain black arrow (see Figure 11.14). Click the subpath in the image window to select it.



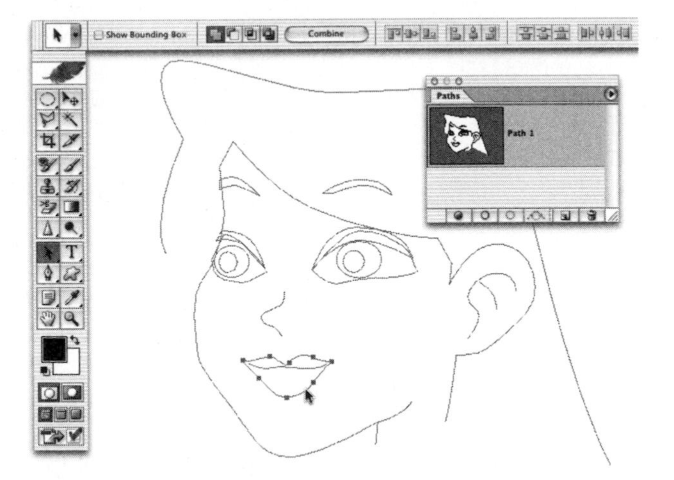


**Figure 11.14**
**The path must be selected in the Paths palette to make it visible. You can then use the Path Selection tool to select a subpath, making its anchor points visible.**

When you use the Path Selection tool to select a subpath, all the anchor points are selected. If you drag with the tool, you can reposition the subpath. You can also use the Paths palette menu commands to stroke or fill a selected subpath.

You can control the operation of the Path Selection tool in the Options Bar using these techniques:

- When Show Bounding Box is selected, you can manipulate a path with the Path Selection tool much like using the bounding box with the Free Transform command. Drag a side or corner anchor to scale the path. Holding down the Shift key while dragging constrains the proportions, maintaining the original height-to-width ratio. You can use the (Option) [Alt] key (with or without the Shift key) to scale from the center. Add the (Command) [Ctrl] key for skew and perspective transformations. The Edit, Transform commands are available with paths; for numeric transformations, you can use the Options Bar.

- Shift-clicking multiple subpaths with the Path Selection tool activates several buttons in the Options Bar. You can combine the paths by adding, subtracting, intersecting, or excluding areas of overlap. Select the preferred operation and then click the Combine button.
- Multiple subpaths can also be aligned or distributed, according to their centers or any side. Shift-click the subpaths or drag across them with the Path Selection tool and then use the appropriate buttons in the Options Bar.

To select an individual anchor point or path segment to edit the shape of a path, use the Direct Selection tool, identified by the white arrow icon (see Figure 11.15). The Direct Selection tool has no options in the Options Bar. Selected anchor points are identified as filled squares; anchor points in the same subpath that are *not* selected appear as hollow squares. (Other subpaths are visible, but their anchor points are not.) If a selected anchor point has direction lines, they will be visible.

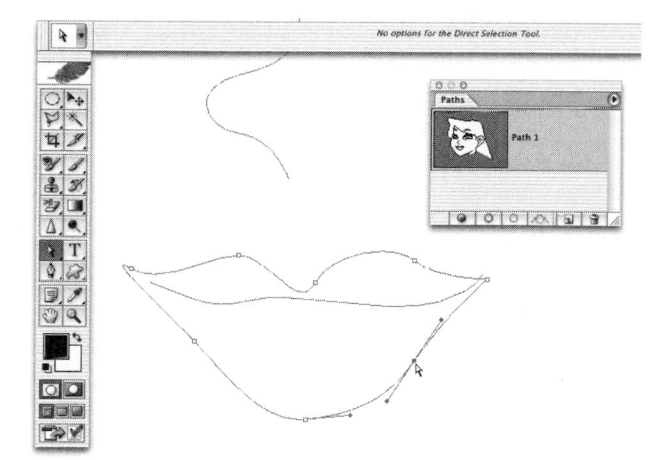


**Figure 11.15**
The direction lines for the selected anchor point are visible, as is one direction line from each of the neighboring points. The additional direction lines are visible so that you can edit the path segments connected to the selected anchor point.



The Direct Selection tool can be used to drag an anchor point or a path segment or to drag direction points, which alters the shape of a curve. Remember that dragging a direction point for a smooth anchor point affects the direction lines—and curves—on *both* sides of the anchor, but changing a direction line for a corner point alters only the curve on that side (see Figure 11.16).

> To alter a curve connected to a smooth anchor point without disturbing the adjoining curve, hold down the (Option) [Alt] key and drag a direction point. The smooth anchor point is converted to a corner anchor point with direction lines.

The Direct Selection tool can also be used to drag path segments. When a straight path segment is dragged, the neighboring anchor points move as well, altering not only the segment dragged but also those on either side. When you drag a curved path segment, the adjoining anchor points remain in place and the neighboring path segments are undisturbed. Note that dragging a curved path segment automatically converts any adjoining smooth anchor point to a corner point. In Figure 11.17, dashed lines represent the original paths, and you can see how dragging path segments affects shapes.

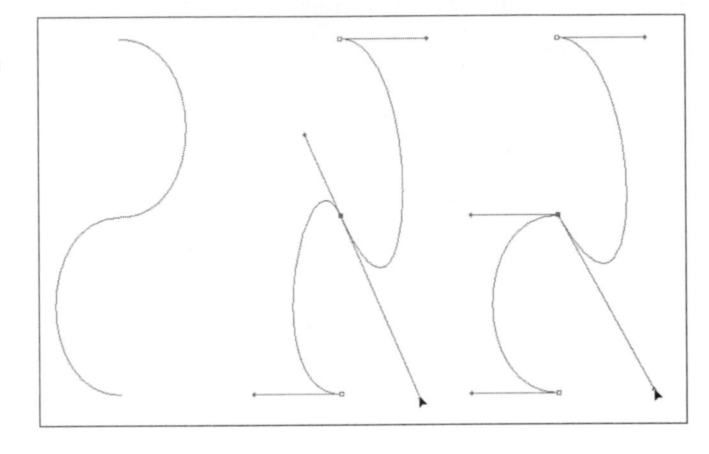

**Figure 11.16**
On the left is the original curve. In the center, you can see how dragging either of a smooth anchor point's direction lines changes the path segments on each side. On the right, the same curve with a corner anchor point has independent path segments.

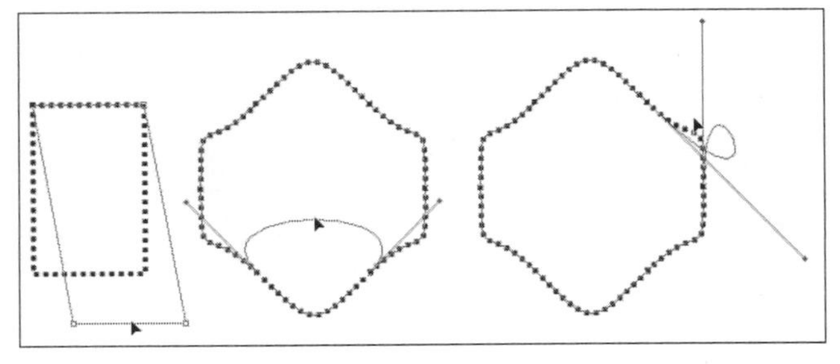

**Figure 11.17**
To the left, a straight path segment is being dragged. In the center, a curved path segment is being dragged straight up. On the right, you can see one example of what can go horribly wrong when dragging a curved path segment. To avoid the unexpected, click and drag in the middle of a path segment.



## Stroking and Filling Paths and Subpaths

To add color to an image, you can stroke and fill paths and subpaths. Use the Path Selection or Direct Selection tool to make the target path active. Make sure you're on the correct layer in the Layers palette. Use the Paths palette buttons or the commands from the Paths palette menu (see Figure 11.18), which open dialog boxes.

The Stroke Path dialog box (or Stroke Subpath, depending on the active selection) offers all the tools that use brushes. You can even apply the Healing Brush, Clone Stamp, and Pattern Stamp tools along paths for incredible precision.

> In Figure 11.18, a second window is open to show the effect of stroking and filling without the distraction of the visible paths. Choose Window, Arrange, New Window for [filename] to create the second window. It will automatically be updated with changes made to the working window.

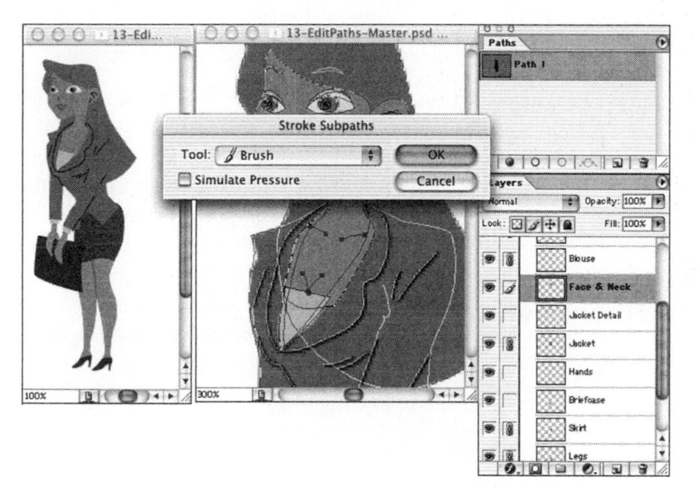


**Figure 11.18**
The buttons at the bottom of the Paths palette use the settings selected in the Stroke and Fill dialog boxes. Open the dialog boxes using the Paths palette menu, select the appropriate options, and afterward you can simply click the buttons to use the same settings.

**Changeable Names**

When your path consists of a single subpath, the commands are Fill Path and Stroke Path. When you have multiple subpaths and all are selected, the commands and dialog boxes also show Fill Path and Stroke Path. When there are multiple subpaths and only one is selected, the commands and dialog boxes are Fill Subpath and Stroke Subpath. When you have multiple subpaths and some but not all are selected, the commands and dialog boxes adapt themselves grammatically and read Fill Subpaths and Stroke Subpaths.



The Fill Path (or Fill Subpath) options include filling with the foreground or background color or with a pattern, history state, black, white, or 50% gray. You can select a blending mode, opacity, feather radius, and antialiasing for the fill. Remember that filling an *open path*—a path with two identifiable ends—fills an area that includes a straight line between the start and end anchor points.

## Paths from Selections

The Paths palette offers two ways to create a path from a selection. At the bottom of the Paths palette, the Make Work Path from Selection button loads an active selection as a work path. Alternatively, the Paths palette menu offers the Make Work Path command, which opens a dialog box where you can specify a tolerance setting. Ranging from 0 to 10 pixels, the Make Work Path command tolerance setting determines the accuracy with which the path will be created as well as the complexity of the final path.

After you stroke or fill a path, the menu command Edit, Fade is available. You can use this command to change the opacity or blending mode of the stroke or fill. Remember that Fade is available only immediately after you apply the stroke or fill.

If a selection is heavily feathered or created from a mask, the path will follow the marching ants (selection border), which indicates pixels at least 50% selected. If no pixels are at least 50% selected and you attempt to create a work path, a work path appears in the Paths palette, but there will be no anchor points or path segments.

Compound paths can be created from selections, as shown in Figure 11.19. You can create the selection with selection tools, from a mask, or by using selection commands.

Compound paths can be used as vector masks for layers and as clipping paths for images to be placed in page layout programs (see Figure 11.20).

**Caution**

Remember that when you create a path from a selection, you're creating a work path. It will replace any existing work path in the Paths palette. And, unless saved, it will be lost as soon as you start another work path (although you can add more subpaths). Save a work path by renaming it in the Paths palette.

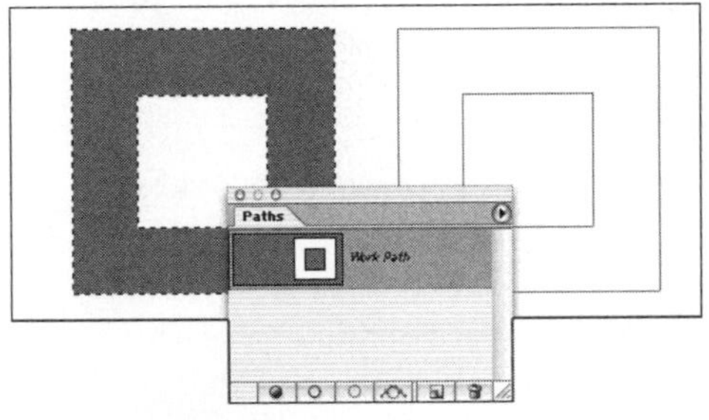


**Figure 11.19**
When the (Option) [Alt] key is used along with a selection tool, areas within a selection can be deselected. The Options Bar also offers this capability for selection tools.



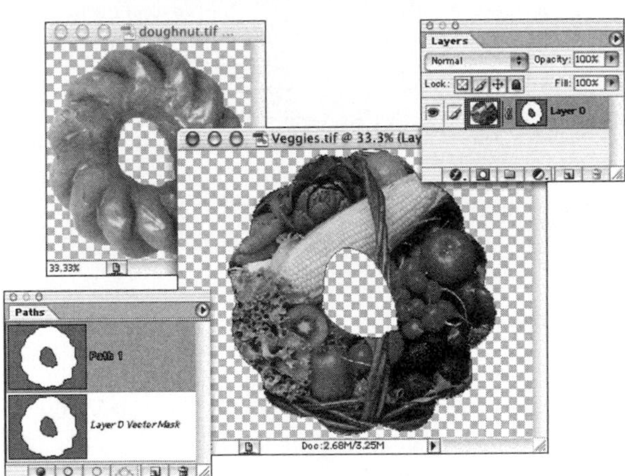


**Figure 11.20**
A compound path was created from a selection of the doughnut and used to mask an image of vegetables. Then the path was duplicated in the Paths palette and the copy converted to a clipping path. When placed into a page layout program, only the pixels between the paths are visible.

## Converting Type to Paths

Editable paths can also be created from vector type. With a type layer selected in the Layers palette, use the menu command Layer, Type, Create Work Path. The original type layer is untouched, and a work path is created in the shape of the letters (see Figure 11.21). Although the original type layer remains editable as text, the work path is no longer type. Before filling or stroking a work path, make sure you are on the appropriate layer.

**Caution**

Creating paths from large amounts of small type can cause problems. The paths can be too complex to output properly.

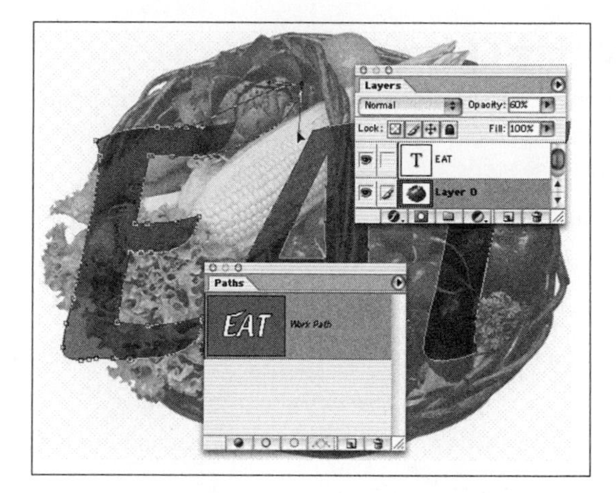


**Figure 11.21**
The two existing layers have reduced opacity to better show the work path. The Direct Selection tool can be used to move anchor points and direction points, customizing the letter shapes. The paths can then be filled or stroked.

### A Note About Illustrator Paths

You can copy and paste paths between Photoshop and Illustrator. However, when you're copying from Illustrator, it's important that the Illustrator Preferences be set correctly. In Illustrator's File Handling & Clipboard preferences pane, select AICB (Adobe Illustrator Clipboard) in the Copy As area. If you'll be copying paths, click Preserve Paths.

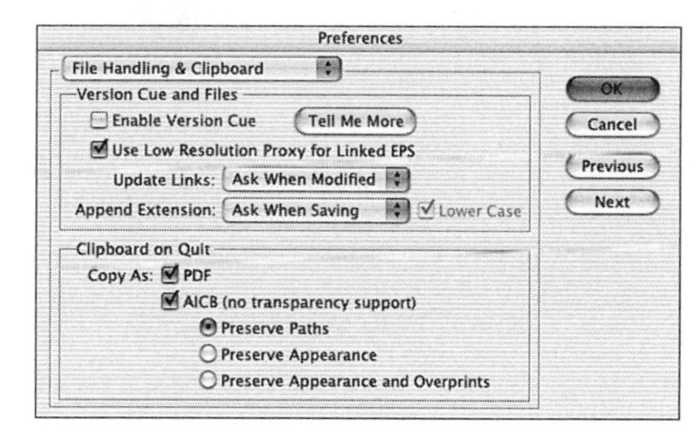


The PDF option can be used along with AICB, but when you're working with Photoshop, AICB must be selected.

When you've copied one or more objects from Illustrator and switched to Photoshop, the Paste command opens a small dialog box. You have the option of pasting from the Clipboard as pixels, as just paths, or as a shape layer.

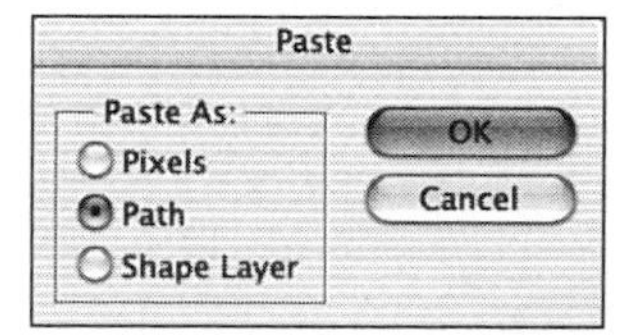


You can, in fact, use the Paste command twice—once to paste the path, and again to paste the pixels. The two will remain separate, and they don't become a vector object. However, you'll have both the substance (paths) and appearance (pixels) of the original object.

## Photoshop at Work: Editing Character Shapes

Although you probably won't want to customize each character in a paragraph of type, altering the shape of a few letters here and there can add a special *something* to your artwork. To practice editing character shapes, follow these steps:

1. Open a new document in Photoshop. Since we're working with vectors, make it 800×600 pixels, RGB, filled with white.
2. Select the Type tool in the Toolbox.
3. In the Options Bar, select a sans serif font. (Boring old Arial is an excellent choice.) Set the size to 150 points.
4. Click in the image window and type **`Pool Hall`**. Press (Command-Return) [Ctrl+Enter] when you're done.
5. Use the menu command Layer, Type, Convert to Shape.
6. From the Toolbox, select the Direct Selection tool. (The tool's icon is a white arrow. You'll find it in the Toolbox below the black arrow of the Path Selection tool.)
7. Click the upper-left anchor point at the top of one of the *L*'s and drag the anchor point upward until the letter is about twice its original height. Drag the anchor point just a little to the right. Drag the upper-right anchor point of that same letter up and to the left just a bit. The top anchor points should be almost right next to each other. (The letter should now resemble a pool cue in shape.)
8. Repeat this for the other two *L*'s.
9. Click the outside edge of one of the *O*'s to activate the path. Shift-click each of the anchor points of the inner path (the inside of the letter).
10. With all the inner anchor points selected, use the menu command Edit, Transform Points, Scale.
11. Hold down the (Option) [Alt] key and drag one of the bounding box's corners inward to shrink the size of the inner path.
12. Repeat this for the other *O*'s.
13. Using 24-point type, add a couple number 8's and move them into the centers of the *O*'s. Your result should look something like what's shown in Figure 11.22.

**Figure 11.22**
Any vector type can be converted to work paths or a shape layer and edited with the Direct Selection and Pen tools.

11

14. Click one of the number 8 type layers and use the menu command Layer, Type, Create Work Path.
15. Choose Edit, Copy.
16. In the Layers palette, make the shape layer active. In the Paths palette, click Pool Hall Vector Mask to make it active.
17. Choose Edit, Paste. The work path is now added to the shape layer's path.
18. Repeat this for the second type layer.
19. The two type layers can now be deleted, as can the work path. You can save this "artwork" as a custom shape, ready for use again at any time.

# PHOTOSHOP'S SHAPE LAYERS

Photoshop simulates vector objects with shape layers. A *shape layer* is actually a layer in the image, completely filled with the selected color or pattern. The layer is selectively shown and hidden by a path called a *vector mask*. The pixels on the layer inside the path are visible; those outside the path are hidden (see Figure 11.23).



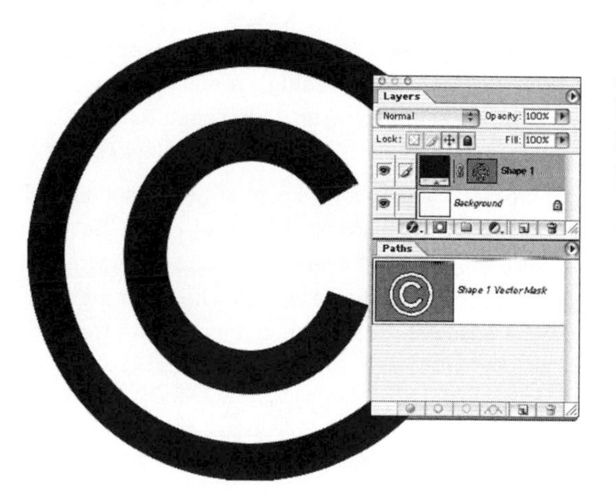


**Figure 11.23**
A shape layer's vector mask is visible in the Paths palette when the layer is selected in the Layers palette.

In the Options Bar, you can assign a color for a shape layer. With the shape layer selected in the Layers palette, you can use the menu command Layer, Change Layer Content to assign a gradient or pattern to the layer, or to convert the layer to an adjustment layer. You can also use the Layer, Layer Content Options command to adjust the fill of a shape layer.

## Shapes Versus Objects

Unlike the vector objects created in Illustrator (and other vector-based programs), Photoshop's shape layers are actually pixel based. The layers are clipped with a vector mask, but they contain pixels.

The path itself can be scaled without risking output quality, but the pixels used to stroke or fill remain raster.

Unlike filled paths, altering the vector mask of a shape layer actually *does* change the appearance of the artwork (see Figure 11.24). Because altering the path changes where the layer's fill is shown and hidden, in appearance it is somewhat akin to editing a true vector object.

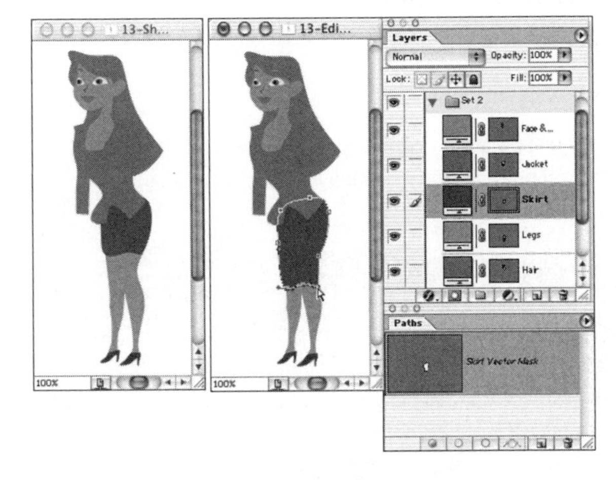


**Figure 11.24**
The original is on the left. Using Photoshop's Direct Selection tool to select and drag anchor points, you can change the artwork when working with shape layers.

11

Shape layer paths in Photoshop can be stroked only by using the Layer Styles command. They can have only one of each layer effect, limiting them to a single stroke and one each of the Satin, Color Overlay, Gradient Overlay, and Pattern Overlay effects. (Other than the stroke, these effects are applied only to the fill of the shape layer and are in addition to the layer's own fill.)

Because of these limitations, Photoshop's shape layers cannot be stroked and filled in the same way that you can change a path's appearance in Illustrator. In Figure 11.25, the same object has been created in both programs. In Photoshop, the shape layer path was duplicated and, on a new layer, the Fill Subpaths and Stroke Subpaths commands were used (the latter, three times). The Illustrator object was created with the Appearance palette's menu command Add New Stroke.

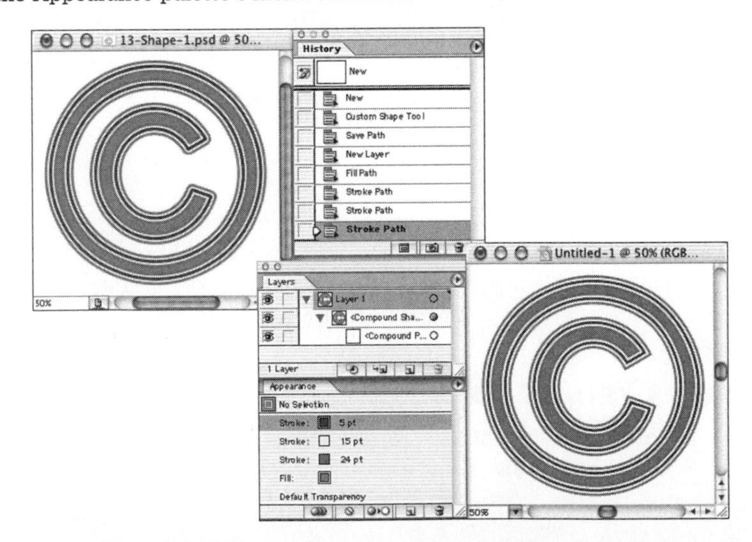


**Figure 11.25**
Although the appearance is identical, the nature of the artwork differs. In Photoshop, there are pixels on a layer and a path. In Illustrator, there is an object.

One of the biggest differences between these two "objects" is what happens when the path is edited. In Photoshop, because the commands Fill Subpaths and Stroke Subpaths were used, the image's appearance is unaffected by the path being edited—the pixels remain in place and only the path is changed. In Illustrator, editing the path results in changes to the object itself (see Figure 11.26).

When you drag the anchor points of a shape layer's vector clipping path, the appearance of the artwork changes. When you've used the Stroke Path and Fill Path commands (and their subpath counterparts), you've added pixels to a layer. Editing the paths does not move the pixels added to the layer.

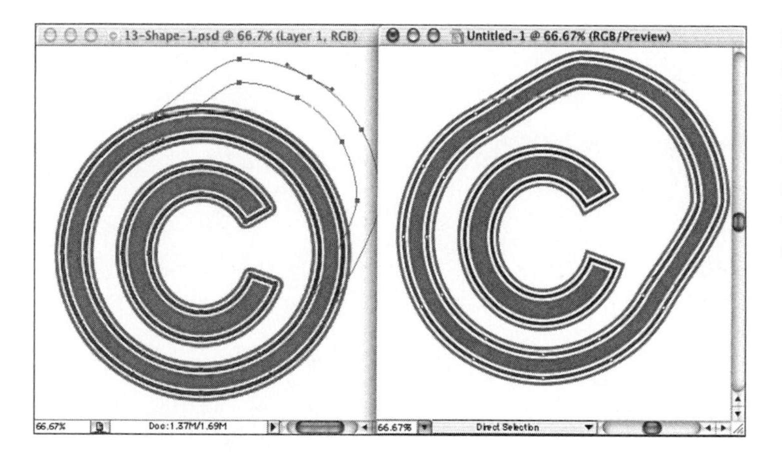


Figure 11.26
On the left, selecting anchor points and dragging them in Photoshop doesn't change the artwork's appearance. On the right, a true vector object is changed when the path is manipulated.



## Using the Shape Tools

The shape tools are, at their heart, scalable preset paths tools. When you use a shape tool, you create one of three things: a shape layer, a work path, or colored pixels in a specific shape on an existing layer. The choice is made by selecting one of the three buttons to the left in the Options Bar.

The shape that is created can be selected in the Toolbox or the Options Bar (see Figure 11.27). The standard preset tools include Rectangle, Rounded Rectangle, Ellipse, Polygon, and Line. Custom shapes can also be selected from a palette, which can be loaded with Photoshop-supplied shapes, third-party shapes, or custom shapes you define.

Regardless of which shape is selected, or whether you're creating a shape layer, a work path, or a filled region, the basic operation of the shape tools is the same: Click and drag. (When size options are selected, you need only click.) Use the Shift key to constrain the shape to its original height-width ratio; use the (Option) [Alt] key to create the shape from the center. The two modifier keys can be used together.

Each of the individual shape tools has characteristics that you can control through the Geometry palette of the Options Bar (see Figure 11.28).

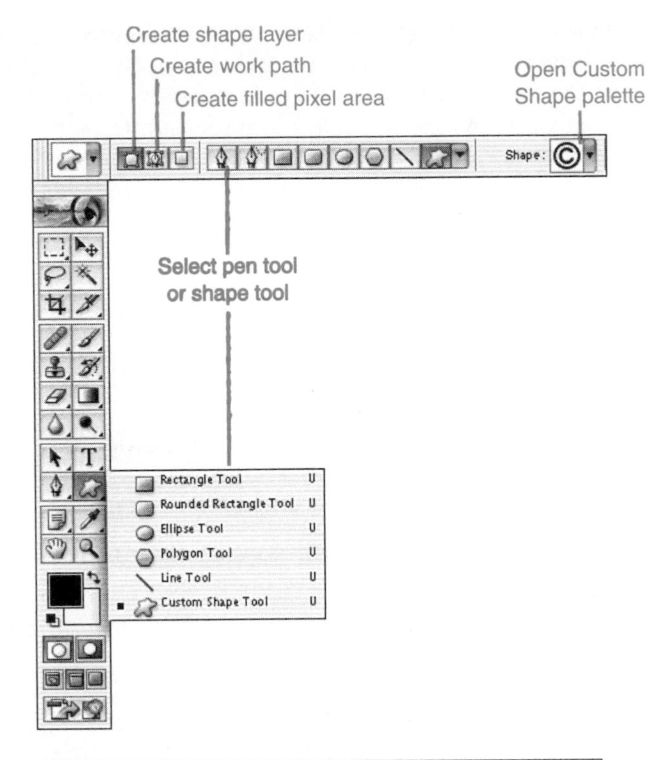


**Figure 11.27**
There is no difference between selecting the tool in the Toolbox or the Options Bar. The shape tools are available in the Options Bar with any shape tool or a pen tool active.



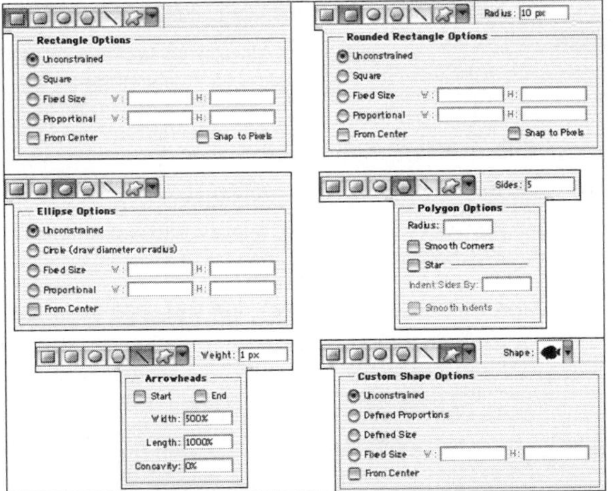


**Figure 11.28**
To open the Geometry palette, click the down arrow to the right of the Custom Shape tool icon.

Most of the geometry options are self-explanatory, but several deserve explanation:

- When the Rounded Rectangle tool is selected, you'll see the Radius field in the Options Bar. The value entered here determines the curve of the corners.
- Snap to Pixels is primarily used when creating Web graphics. By snapping the horizontal and vertical edges of the shape to pixels, this option ensures that Web graphics will be crisp. The

option is used only with the Rectangle and Rounded Rectangle tools and is not available for the shapes that don't have horizontal and vertical edges.

- The Polygon tool offers the option to create stars. When it's checked, you have the opportunity to specify the indentation of the star's arms. Percent is the unit of measure.
- The Line tool can have arrowheads at either or both ends. However, when you have arrowheads at both ends, they must be identical. (You can, of course, transform the line later.)
- The Defined Proportions and Defined Size options for the Custom Shape tool refer to the size and proportions at which the custom shape was originally created.

## Editing Shape Vector Masks

The vector masks that selectively show and hide the fill of a shape layer can be edited like any other path in Photoshop. The path, of course, must be selected in the Paths palette. For the path to be visible in the palette, the shape layer must be selected in the Layers palette. The Path Selection tool selects all the anchor points in a path or subpath, enabling you to move the entire path or subpath as a unit.

The Direct Selection tool enables you to select one or more individual path segments or anchor points to manipulate. It is also used to drag the direction points of anchor points adjoining curved path segments.

*For full information on editing paths in Photoshop, see "Editing Paths" earlier in this chapter, p. 374.*



## Using, Creating, and Saving Custom Shapes

Custom shapes are selected from the Custom Shape palette (see Figure 11.29). This palette, opened through the Options Bar, is available only when the Custom Shape tool has been selected in the Toolbox or the Options Bar.

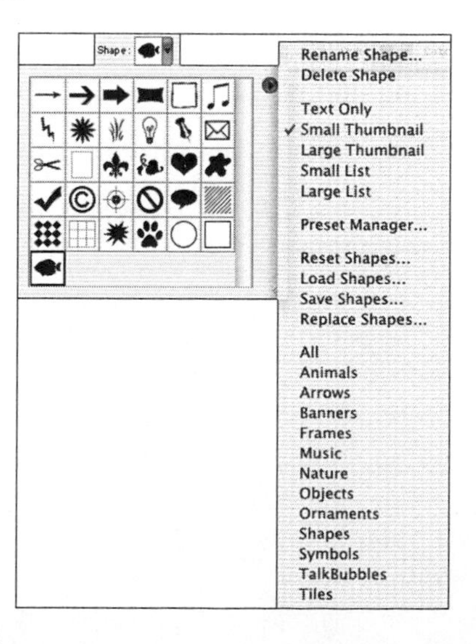


**Figure 11.29**
The Custom Shape palette's menu offers available sets of custom shapes at the bottom. The newly added shapes can be added to or replace those already in the palette.

After you have selected a custom shape from the palette and set options in the Geometry palette, it can be added to the image like any other shape. Shape layers, work paths, and filled pixel regions can all be added with custom shape tools.

You can create custom shapes and add them to the Custom Shape palette. Create a path or select an existing path and then use the menu command Edit, Define Custom Shape. You'll have the opportunity to name the new custom shape (see Figure 11.30).

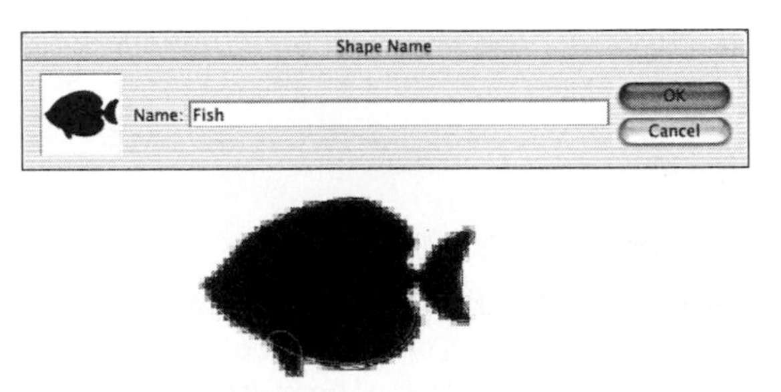


Figure 11.30
Naming the shape is the only option. It is saved at the size created, although as a vector, the original size is insignificant.

Remember that custom shapes are not saved when you add them to the palette. Rather, you must use the palette's menu command Save Shapes. Should you need to replace your Preferences file or reinstall Photoshop, any unsaved shapes you have defined will be lost. The shapes are, by default, added to Photoshop's Custom Shapes folder within the Presets folder, but you have the option of choosing another location. Shapes (and brushes, tool presets, styles, and other such elements) can also be saved in sets using the Preset Manager, found under the Edit menu.



## Photoshop at Work: Styles for Shape Layers

A shape layer in and of itself is rather boring—a layer filled with color and a vector mask. However, styles can be applied, the mask can be edited, and once the shape layer is rasterized, you can even apply filters. Here's how:

1. Open a new document in Photoshop (500×500 pixels, Resolution set to 72, filled with white, RGB color mode).
2. Select the Custom Shape tool from the Toolbox.
3. Pick a custom shape from the Custom Shape palette in the Options Bar.
4. In the Options Bar, click the first of the buttons to the left. The tool is now set to create a shape layer.
5. Drag the Custom Shape tool in the image, starting in the upper-left corner and ending in the lower right. This fills the image with the new custom shape. (The foreground color is insignificant because a layer style will be applied.)
6. In the Options Bar, select the style named "Color Target (Button)" from the Style pop-up palette. It will be applied to the shape layer.

> Consider creating a folder outside the Photoshop folder for custom shapes, Actions, styles, tool presets, and the like. If you save them within the Photoshop folder, you might accidentally delete them during a reinstall of the program.

7. Use the Layer, Rasterize, Layer menu command to convert the shape layer to a regular layer of pixels. The layer style is unaffected.
8. Select the Smudge tool from the Toolbox and choose a hard-edged brush of about 40 pixels in diameter. In the Options Bar, set Mode to Normal and set Strength to 100%.
9. Click in the visible pixels on the layer and drag. Repeat this, smudging a couple of different areas.
10. Change the Strength to 50% and drag again.
11. In the Layers palette, use the Merge Down menu command to create a single layer of pixels in this image.
12. Apply the filter Pixelate, Crystallize with a cell size of 15.

Creating a shape layer and applying a style can be just the beginning of the creative process. When rasterized or merged, the content of the shape layer can become pixels on which you can apply filters, adjustments, and more.

# CLIPPING PATHS AND VECTOR MASKS



Clipping paths and vector paths serve the same purpose—identifying what will be visible or invisible—but they do so at two different levels. Clipping paths are used with images destined for page layout programs, delineating areas of visibility for the image as a whole. Vector masks are used in a similar manner to show and hide areas of individual layers within an image.

Open, closed, and compound paths can all be used to create both clipping paths and vector masks. You must name a work path to save it before you can convert it to a clipping path. Double-clicking a work path in the Paths palette and renaming it will save it, and you can then use the Paths palette menu command Clipping Path.

**Caution**

The Clipping Path dialog box includes a Flatness field. Never enter a value for flatness unless your imagesetter is having trouble outputting curves. The field overrides the device's native setting for vector reproduction.

You can create a vector mask for a layer in either of two ways. You can first create the path and then assign it as a vector mask, or you can create the vector mask and then define it with a path. With or without an active path, use the menu command Layer, Add Vector Mask. Alternatively, you can (Command-Option)-click [Ctrl+Alt]-click the Add Layer Mask button at the bottom of the Layers palette.

*To learn more about creating vector masks and clipping paths, see "Layer Masks, Vector Masks, and Clipping Masks," p. 320, in Chapter 9, "Making Selections and Creating Masks."*

# MASTERING PHOTOSHOP

## The Chicken or the Egg?

*I'm not sure that I understand the fundamental difference between the way Illustrator and Photoshop handle paths to which color is applied. Which comes first, the color or the path?*

Unlike the never-ending question about the order of appearance between the chicken and the egg, the path comes first with both Photoshop's stroked/filled paths and with Illustrator's objects. In Photoshop, the path tells the program where to apply pixels—along the path for a stroke and within the paths for a fill. In Illustrator, it's basically the same—the path is defined and then color is applied.

The difference lies in what happens afterward. When you're working with true vector objects, the colors are bound to the path and are not applied until the path is defined in the image. If the path needs to be scaled because the print size changes, there's no change in the overall appearance of the image—the stroke and fill are applied *after* the path is recalculated and added to the image. In Photoshop, on the contrary, once the stroke or fill is applied, it's there for good. Yes, you can scale the pixels, but they are not tied to the path and can therefore lose quality.



## Smooth Corner Points

*My friend bet me that I can't create a corner anchor point through which a path runs smoothly—she doesn't think my stylus hand is steady enough. Can I win this bet?*

The bet is a lead-pipe cinch! You don't even need your Wacom tablet. Straight is smooth, isn't it? Use Show Grid and Snap to Grid. Click once with the Pen tool. Move the cursor to the right and up a bit. Click again. Move the cursor back down and add a third anchor point to the right. It should be on the same grid line as the first anchor point (aligning the points horizontally). End the path by pressing (Return) [Enter]. Now press A (or Shift+A) to activate the Direct Selection tool. Drag that middle point down until it's in line with the other two points. The path now flows smoothly (straight) through the three points, although none are smooth points.

## Shutting Down the Auto

*Why would I want to turn off the Auto Add/Delete function of the Pen tool in the Options Bar? It seems to me that this is a very useful function.*

If paths are placed very closely together in an image, at times you might find that you're trying to start a path, but the Pen tool is converting to the Add Anchor Point or Delete Anchor Point tool. Unchecking the option in the Options Bar enables you to start that new path.

12

# ADDING TEXT: PHOTOSHOP'S TYPE CAPABILITIES

## IN THIS CHAPTER

Although Photoshop cannot be mistaken for a page layout program, it does have some rather sophisticated type-handling features. You can add a single character, word, or line of type. You can add paragraphs of type that automatically adjust to changes in the enclosing rectangle. New in Photoshop CS is type on a path, the capability to have a line of type follow a path created by the Pen tool or a shape tool. Both spell checking and find/replace for text are built in to Photoshop. You also have incredible control over the appearance of text, especially when using OpenType fonts.

This chapter looks at the type and text capabilities built in to Photoshop CS, the tools and palettes you use to take advantage of those capabilities, and issues involving fonts and font embedding.

# PHOTOSHOP'S TYPE CAPABILITY

As the subject of type and text in Photoshop is discussed, it's important to keep one basic concept in mind: Photoshop is an image-editing program. It is not designed to be a page layout program, nor a word processor. As such, don't consider Photoshop's type-handling capabilities to be substandard; rather, think of them as a bonus. If you have large amounts of text to add to a document, or need to work with very small type, consider Adobe InDesign or Adobe Illustrator.

Just a few versions in the past, Photoshop's type capability was restricted to creating masks in the shape of letters. (The biggest problem with type masks is that the type isn't "live." You can't edit the words or change the typographic attributes without re-creating the entire type element (see Figure 12.1).

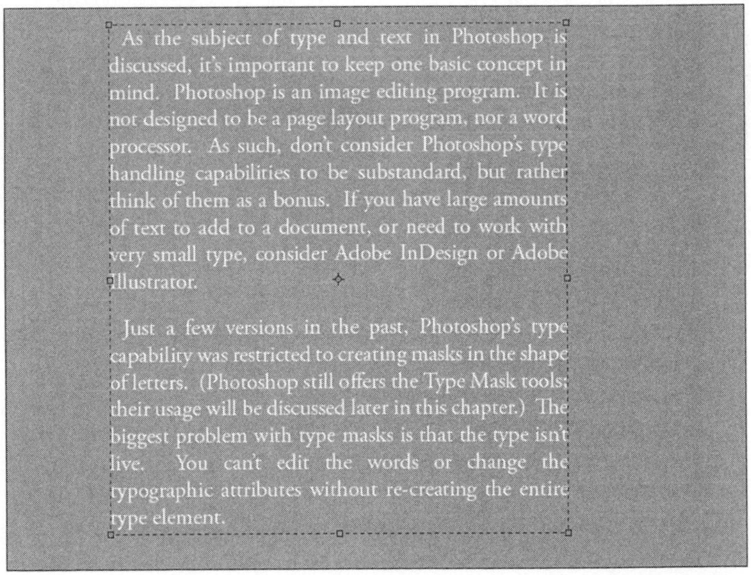

**Figure 12.1**
After a type mask is set, it becomes nothing more than filled pixels. Changing the font or even one misspelling might mean re-creating the entire image when type is added as a mask.



*Photoshop still offers type masks; their use is discussed in "The Type Tools," later in this chapter.*

Photoshop 5 introduced type layers, and Photoshop 6 added vector type. Photoshop 7 refined the type engine and added both a spell checker and the find/replace capability. Photoshop CS goes a bit further with type on a path and support for type layers in 16-bit color and layered PDF files.

## Vector Type

As discussed in Chapter 4, "Pixels, Vectors, and Resolutions," there are numerous advantages to vector artwork. For example, when printed with a PostScript output device, the artwork's edges remain crisp and clean, without the so-called *jaggies*—the visible stair-step edges of pixels along a curve. Vector artwork can be scaled in an illustration program or by a PostScript printer and still retain those high-quality edges. Because it consists of mathematically defined paths, it can also be manipulated in ways impossible with raster art. Figure 12.2 shows the difference between scaling vector type and raster type.

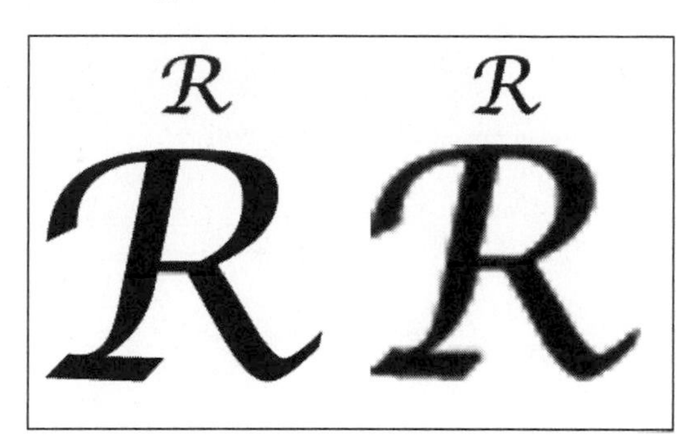


**Figure 12.2**
The original letters are shown for comparison. Notice the dramatic difference in quality when vector and rasterized type are scaled to 400%.

The primary advantage of raster art is its capability of reproducing fine transitions and gradations in color. Because type is usually a single color, that is not of particular value. However, Photoshop's vector type can be rasterized whenever necessary.

## Saving Images with Type

The difference between vector and rasterized type is primarily of importance during the creation process and when preparing artwork for placement in a page layout program. In most other circumstances, the type is automatically rasterized. Remember that with the exception of Scalable Vector Graphics (SVG) and Flash (SWF), formats not supported by Photoshop, Web artwork is raster. Similarly, most inkjet printers don't take advantage of vector type. (Only PostScript printers can actually work with vectors as such.) When you're outputting to an inkjet printer, saving images for the Web, or using a non-PostScript file format, type is automatically rasterized.

In Photoshop, the PostScript file formats, those that support vectors, are limited to these:

- Photoshop (.psd)
- The large image version of Photoshop's format (.psb)
- Encapsulated PostScript (.eps)
- Portable Document Format (.pdf)
- Desktop Color Separations (.dcs)

> **Caution**
> EPS and DCS support vector type when you're saving from Photoshop. However, reopening either of these image formats in Photoshop results in rasterization. PDFs saved without layers are also rasterized when reopened in Photoshop. After you save a file with vector text in one of these formats, don't reopen it in Photoshop. It's a good idea to keep the original in Photoshop's own PSD format.

The enhanced TIFF file format can also support vector type layers, but full implementation of the format's advanced features outside Photoshop is very limited.

When saving in a format that can maintain vector artwork or type, you'll need to ensure that the Include Vector Data option is selected. In Figure 12.3, you can see the check boxes for the various PostScript file format options. Note that both the EPS Options dialog box and the DCS 2.0 Format dialog box warn about reopening files in Photoshop, but the PDF Options dialog box does not.

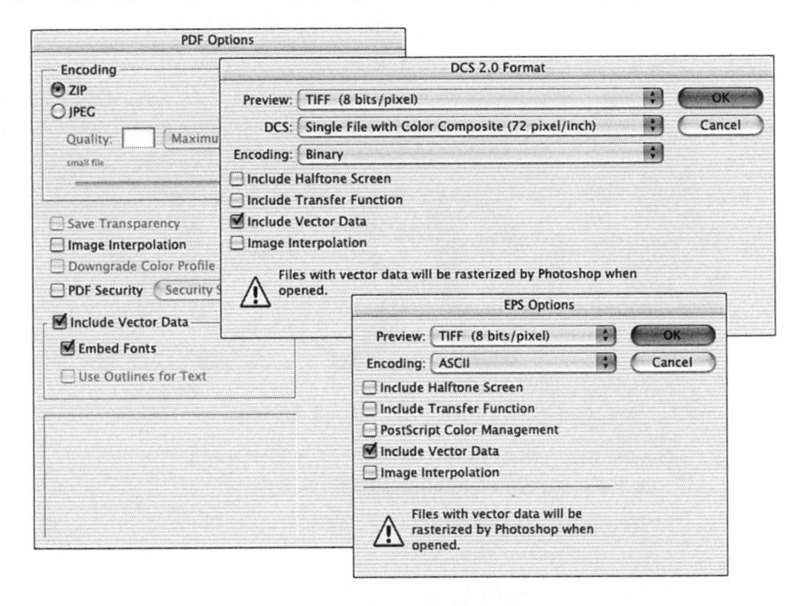


**Figure 12.3**
EPS, PDF, and DCS file formats all offer (but don't require) saving vector data in a file. If there are no vector paths or type in the image, the option is grayed out.

## Point and Paragraph Type

In addition to the differentiation between vector and raster, type in Photoshop can be categorized as *point type* or *paragraph type*. Point type is added to a document at a specific location (or point) in the image. In contrast, paragraph type (also called *area type*) fills a portion (or area) of the image. Figure 12.4 illustrates the difference.

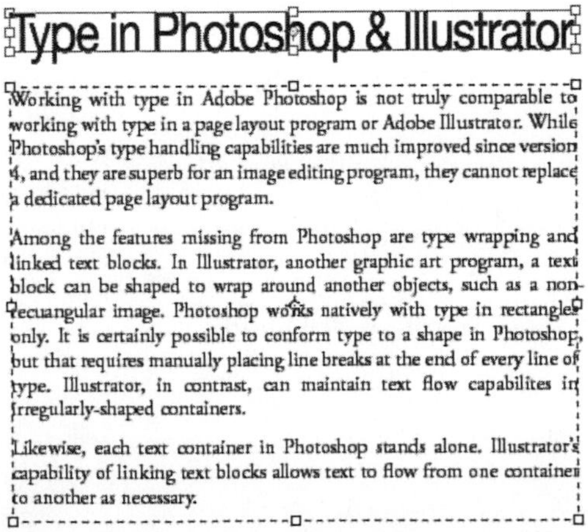

Type in Photoshop & Illustrator

Working with type in Adobe Photoshop is not truly comparable to working with type in a page layout program or Adobe Illustrator. While Photoshop's type handling capabilities are much improved since version 4, and they are superb for an image editing program, they cannot replace a dedicated page layout program.

Among the features missing from Photoshop are type wrapping and linked text blocks. In Illustrator, another graphic art program, a text block can be shaped to wrap around another objects, such as a non-recuangular image. Photoshop works natively with type in rectangles only. It is certainly possible to conform type to a shape in Photoshop, but that requires manually placing line breaks at the end of every line of type. Illustrator, in contrast, can maintain text flow capabilites in irregularly-shaped containers.

Likewise, each text container in Photoshop stands alone. Illustrator's capability of linking text blocks allows text to flow from one container to another as necessary.

**Figure 12.4**
Point type is often used for one or a couple lines of text, such as headlines, whereas paragraph type is used for large blocks of text. Note the difference between the transform bounding box (top) and the paragraph type container (bottom).

These two types of text have a number of important differences:

- Point type continues in a straight line unless you press the (Return) [Enter] key to insert a line break. Paragraph type automatically wraps to the next line when the text reaches the boundary of its box.
- The space occupied by point type continues to expand as more characters are added. Paragraph type is restricted to the designated rectangle; characters that don't fit in the rectangle are hidden.
- Point type is added from the specific spot in the image where the Type tool was clicked. Paragraph type is added from the top of the bounding box.
- To add point type, click with a Type tool. For paragraph type, drag with a Type tool to create a rectangle to fill with the type.
- Resizing the bounding box around point type scales the type. Resizing the container rectangle for paragraph type forces the text to reflow within the container; the type maintains its original size and proportion.

Consider point type to be similar to headlines in a newspaper or magazine. It typically occupies one line, but might require two or three lines. To add lines, type to the desired width, press (Return) [Enter] to move to the next line, and continue typing. Paragraph type, on the other hand, can be compared to the body text of a newspaper or magazine. It flows from one line to the next, and if you go back to the beginning and add a word, the text repositions itself, automatically adjusting the line breaks. This is called *reflowing*.

Consider, if you will, the difference (or one of the differences) between a typewriter and a word processor. With a typewriter, you must be aware of the warning bell that indicates you've reached the end of a line, the edge of the paper. You then advance the paper, return to the left margin, and begin typing on the next line. With a word processor, you can continue typing and the text will automatically wrap from line to line.

With a typewriter, if you need to go back to the first line to add a word, the length of that line is thrown off. If it's a long word, you can't just erase the top line and retype it; you have to retype the entire paragraph. Adding a word to the opening line with a word processor simply moves all the text to the right and, if necessary, down to the next line—the text reflows. A comparison is shown in Figure 12.5.

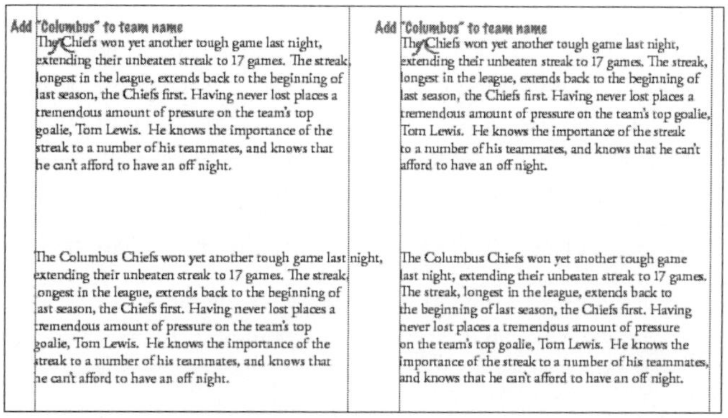

**Figure 12.5**
Compare the pairs. Observe how adding a single word extends the point type past the acceptable boundary but simply causes the paragraph type to reflow without affecting the width of the type container.

12

## Type on a Path

Photoshop CS now has the long-awaited capability of adding type along any path. If you change the size or shape of the path, the type will adapt. What's more, the type remains editable, as long as the type layer isn't rasterized. Type can be placed along a path or even inside a path (see Figure 12.6).

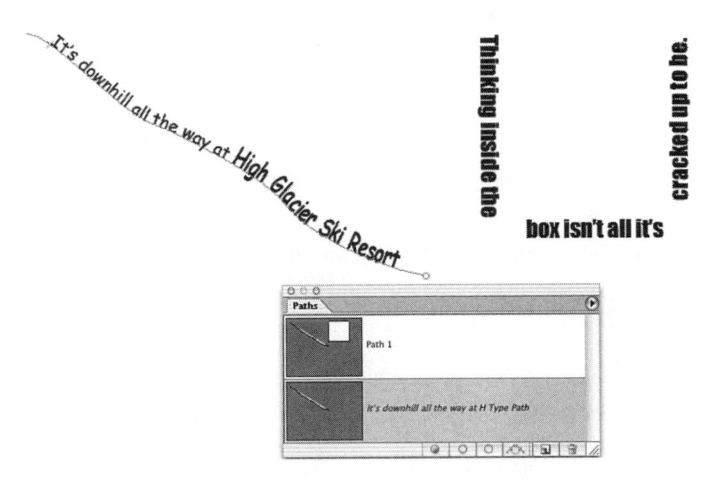


Figure 12.6
To the left, type has been placed along a path created with the Pen tool. To the right, the type is inside a path created with a shape tool. As you can tell from the Paths palette and the visible path, the type layer of the left-side object is active.

Working with type on a path requires knowledge of both path creation/editing and placing type in Photoshop. (Paths and the Pen tool are discussed in Chapter 11, "The Pen Tool and Shape Layers: Vectors in Photoshop.") Here are the basic steps for creating type on a path in Photoshop:

- Create or paste the path and then click it with the Type tool. To add type inside the path, simply click inside the path. The Type tool's cursor changes appearance to indicate that you're adding type on a path.
- Type on a path can be adjusted with the Character palette. For example, Baseline Shift can be used to raise the type from a path that will be stroked or filled (see Figure 12.7). (The Character palette is discussed later in this chapter.)
- When you've finished editing the type, press (Command-Return) [Ctrl+Enter] to accept the type editing. Press it again to hide the path.
- With the Type tool active, click in the type, hold down the (Command) [Ctrl] key, and position the Type tool near the type to alter its position in relation to the path. Drag the beginning and ending points to move the type along the path. Drag the cursor across the path to flip the type upside down. When the cursor is not near the type or the type isn't being edited and the modifier key is depressed, you (as usual) have the Move tool available.
- The Path Selection tool (the "black arrow" tool) can also be used to manipulate type on a path.
- The original path is retained separately in the Paths palette. A duplicate of the path is visible in the Paths palette when the type layer is active in the Layers palette. (This behavior is comparable to that of shape layers and their paths.)

- Type paths cannot be stroked or filled (because you cannot add pixels to a type layer). However, because the original path is retained, you can add a new layer and then stroke or fill *that* path (see Figure 12.7).
- Shape layers can be used as type containers. Select a shape tool, make sure it's set to create a shape layer in the Options Bar, and drag. Switch to the Type tool, position the cursor inside the shape, and click. The shape layer's vector clipping path is copied and serves as a type container. Remember, too, that shape layers can be created with the Pen tool.

When type is placed inside a rectangle or other shape with tight corners, Photoshop does *not* compensate for the corners. Use the spacebar to add some distance around the corner so that characters don't overlap.

- Using the Warp Type feature disassociates the type from the path but does warp the type from its path-based shape.
- If you need to add regular point or paragraph type near an existing path, either deselect the path in the Paths palette first or hold down the Shift key when clicking or dragging the Type tool.

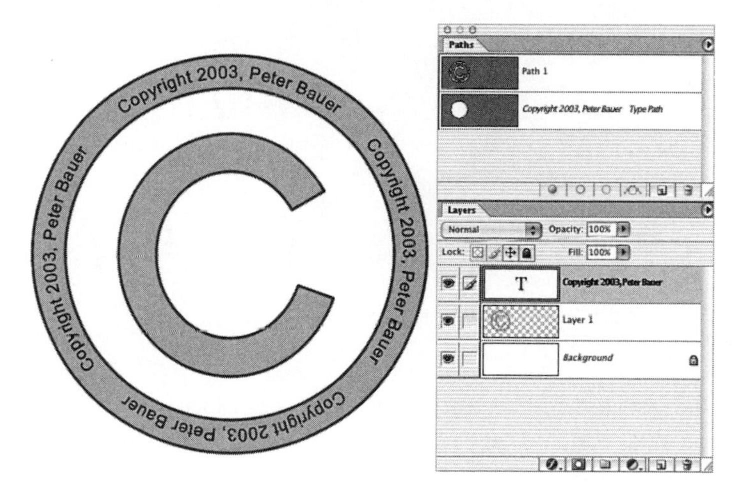


**Figure 12.7**
A custom shape was used to create the copyright-shaped work path. Type on a path was added (and the baseline increased 10 points) and then the original path was stroked and filled.

## Photoshop at Work: Working with Type on a Path

Type on a path is more than just a gee-whiz new feature. It can be very handy for various sorts of artwork, illustration, and layout. One of the most common uses might become adding text around a circle. Let's work with one example:

1. Start a new document (800×600 pixels, RGB, white fill, 72dpi).
2. Select the Ellipse shape tool in the Toolbox. In the Options Bar, set it to create a work path.
3. Press (Command-R) [Ctrl+R] to show the rulers. If they're not set to pixels, (Control)-click right-click either ruler and select Pixels.

4. Position the cursor at about 100 pixels below the top and 200 pixels from the left. Shift-drag a circle 400 pixels in diameter.
5. In the Paths palette, double-click Work Path and rename the path to save it.
6. With the path still active, switch to the Type tool. In the Options Bar, select a font and set the size to 60 points.
7. Position the cursor on the path and observe the change in cursor. Instead of being enclosed in a dotted box, the "I-beam" will have a small slash across it. Click once on the circle, near the top.
8. Type **`Around the world in 180 days`**. If the type runs past the start point, reduce your size or choose another font. (In Figure 12.8, the font is Lithos Pro.)

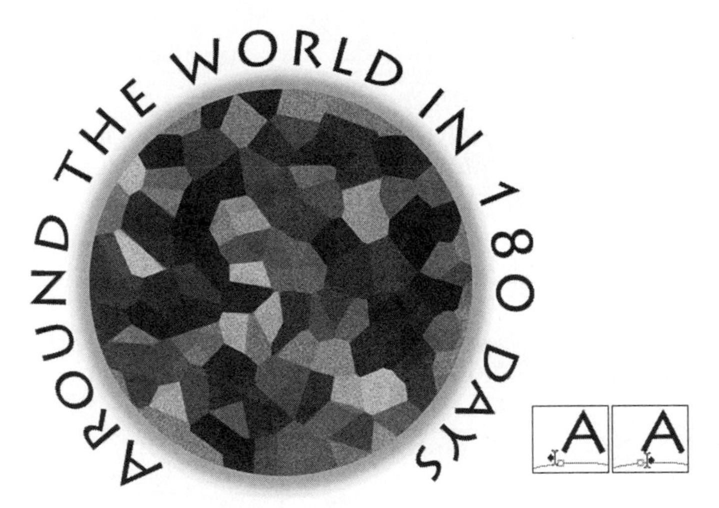


Figure 12.8
In prior versions of Photoshop, the characters would have had to be placed individually around the circle to achieve this effect.



9. In the Toolbox, click the Path Selection tool.
10. Position the cursor near the small hollow square at the top of the path. Move the cursor to the right and left of the square and watch the change in its appearance. To the right of the square, an arrow will point to the right, indicating that you can drag the type's start point. To the left, the arrow points the other way, indicating that if you drag, you'll change the type's endpoint. (The two cursors are shown in the inset of Figure 12.8.)
11. Keeping the cursor outside the circle, position the cursor toward the *right* of the small square and drag to the *left*, rotating the type's start point counterclockwise around the circle. Observe how each letter appears as there is space for it between the new start point and the endpoint. Don't release the mouse button.
12. Now continue to drag outside the circle, but this time, drag clockwise, past the original start point, to about the 6 o'clock position. Notice how characters disappear as they reach the endpoint. Don't release the mouse button.

13. Rotate the cursor back around the outside of the circle to the 12 o'clock position and, with the mouse button *still* depressed, move the cursor inside the circle to flip the type across the path. Release the mouse button. If the type disappears, drag to move the start or endpoint.
14. Position the cursor near the path again and drag the endpoint to the 5 o'clock position, moving the type back to the outside of the path.
15. Move the type's start point to the 7 o'clock position.
16. In the Layers palette, add a new layer.
17. In the Paths palette, click the original path. Stroke the path with blue. (In Figure 12.8, the Brush tool was used, with the Airbrush option and a 35-pixel soft brush at 70% opacity.)
18. Make the foreground color green and fill the path. (In Figure 12.8, a selection was made of the area inside the path, the Noise and Pixelate filters were applied, and then Pixelate was faded.)
19. In the Layers palette, select the Type layer and, with the Type tool, click within the type. Select All.
20. In the Character palette, adjust the baseline and other attributes as you see fit. (In Figure 12.8, the baseline is plus 25.)

## Working with Type Layers

As long as type remains part of a type layer, it remains editable. You can return to the type layer at any time and make changes to the character and paragraph characteristics, or you can edit the text itself. After the layer is rasterized or merged or the image is flattened, the type can no longer be edited as type. (You can, of course, edit the pixels, but you cannot, for example, highlight a word with the Type tool and overtype to correct a spelling error.)

In many ways, type layers are comparable to other nonbackground layers. Layer styles can be applied, type layers can be moved in the Layers palette, they can become part of a layer set, and adjustment layers can be applied (see Figure 12.9).



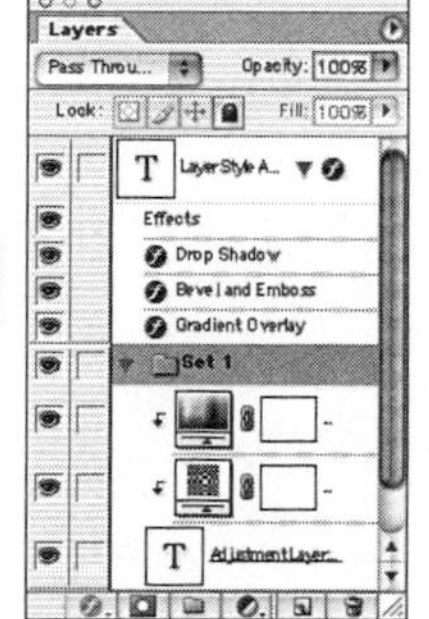


**Figure 12.9**
The Layers palette indicates what effects and adjustments have been applied to the type layers.

A type layer is always indicated by the letter *T* in place of a layer thumbnail in the Layers palette. As with other layers, you can click the layer's name and rename it. (By default, Photoshop names a type layer using the first characters of the layer's content.) You can change the blending mode and opacity of a type layer and create layer-based slices from type layers.

Unlike with other nonbackground layers, you cannot add pixels to a type layer. You cannot paint on a type layer, nor can you stroke or fill a selection. The adjustment tools (Blur, Sharpen, Dodge, Burn, Sponge, Smudge) cannot be used on type layers.

## Warping Type

Among the most fun tools in Photoshop is Warp Text. You can apply preset distortions to type and customize their effects, and the type remains completely editable. You can apply layer styles to the warped text as well (see Figure 12.10).

**Figure 12.10**
Each of the five examples is on a separate type layer.



The Warp Text dialog box can be opened with the button to the right of the color swatch in the Options Bar (when a Type tool is active) or with the menu command Layer, Type, Warp Text. The dialog box allows you to select any of 15 shapes and then use three sliders to adjust the result (see Figure 12.11).

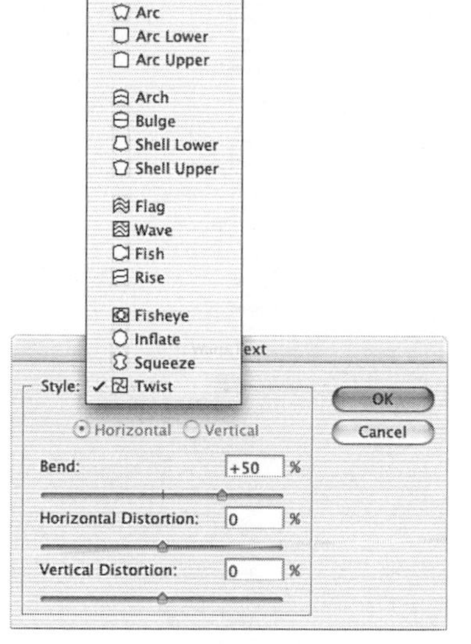


**Figure 12.11**
To remove an existing warp effect, select None from the top of the Style pop-up menu.

# THE TYPE TOOLS

Photoshop offers four related tools for adding type to an image. The Horizontal Type tool (usually referred to as simply the *Type tool*), the Vertical Type tool, the Horizontal Type Mask tool, and the Vertical Type Mask tool are shown in their flyout palette in Figure 12.12.

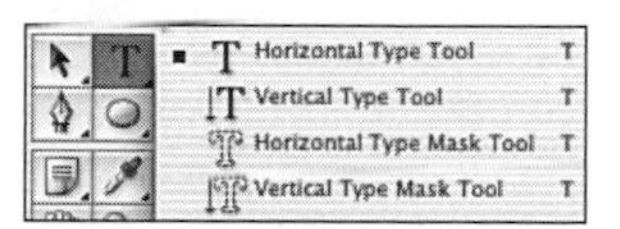


**Figure 12.12**
To open the flyout palette, click and hold on whichever Type tool icon is visible in the Toolbox.

## The Horizontal and Vertical Type Tools

The only difference between the Horizontal Type and Vertical Type tools is the orientation of the characters added to the image. Note in Figure 12.13 the difference between vertical type and horizontal type that has been rotated.

Both the Horizontal and Vertical Type tools create type layers when used. Unless you've rasterized the type, as long as the file remains in a format that supports layers (Photoshop's native format, the Photoshop Large Document Format, or TIFF or PDF with layers), the type remains editable. You can change the font, size, or other attributes as well as change the content of the text. You can click with either tool anywhere in an image window to create a new type layer and add point type. You can also drag with either tool to create a type layer and add paragraph type.

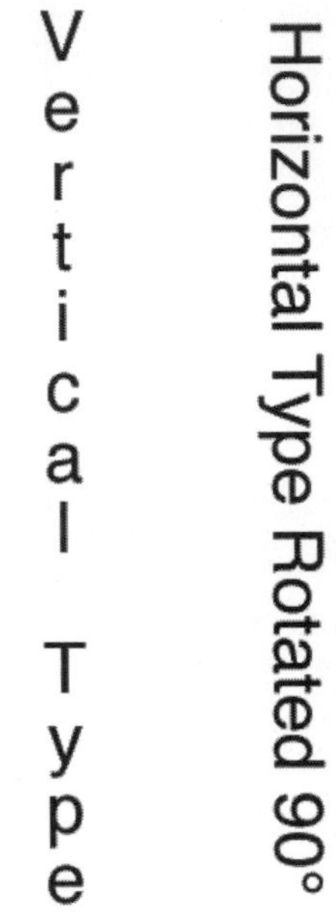

Figure 12.13
Consider vertical and horizontal to be references to the relationship among letters.

Vertical Type

Horizontal Type Rotated 90°

To edit existing type, click and drag with either tool to make a type selection. Changes are restricted to the selected type. A number of shortcuts are available when selecting type:

- Click twice in a word with the Type tool to select the whole word.
- Click three times to select the entire line of type.
- Clicking four times selects the entire paragraph.
- After clicking in existing type with the Type tool, hold down Shift and use the left and right arrow keys to add letters to the selection. The up and down arrow keys select all characters to the same location in the next line above or below the blinking cursor.
- Pressing (Shift-Command) [Shift+Ctrl] and the right or left arrow key adds or subtracts adjacent words from a selection.
- Clicking at one point and Shift-clicking at another selects all characters in between.

> To make changes to an entire type layer, don't select any type; merely select the type layer in the Layers palette. You can change any attributes in the Character or Paragraph palettes, and the change is applied throughout the type layer.

## The Type Mask Tools

Also available for horizontal and vertical type, the Type Mask tools do not create type layers. Rather, they create masks in the shape of the letters. (A nontype layer must be active in

> To better evaluate changes being made to selected type, especially color changes, use (Command-H) [Ctrl+H] to hide the selection highlighting.

the Layers palette.) These masks become selections when you change tools, click the check mark in the Options Bar, or press (Command-Return) [Ctrl+Enter].

Using the Type Mask tools is comparable to using Photoshop's Quick Mask mode. Like in Quick Mask mode, the temporary mask that is created is not retained after the selection is made. You'll see the translucent red overlay while adding the type, but the mask itself is lost when the type is converted to a selection (see Figure 12.14).

> If you want to save the type mask, choose Select, Save Selection immediately after changing tools or otherwise accepting the type mask input.

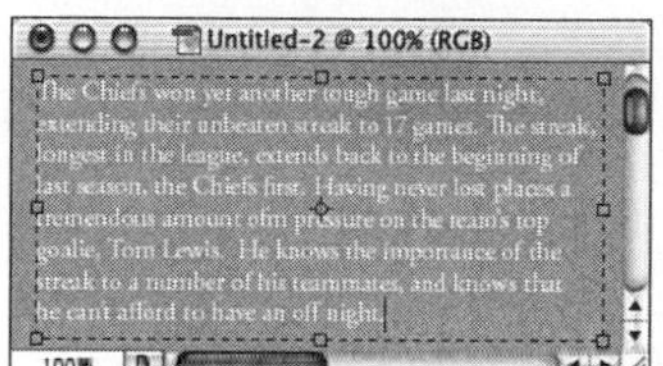


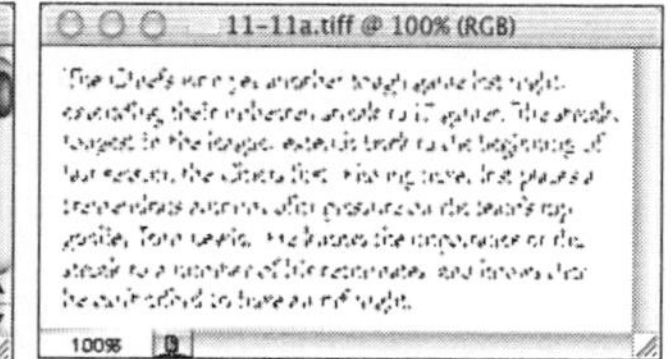


Figure 12.14
On the left, the mask is visible while the type is being set. On the right, the type is a selection and the mask is discarded. This happens automatically when you change tools or otherwise accept the type.

*For a full discussion of Quick Mask mode, see "Quick Mask Mode," p. 318, in Chapter 9, "Making Selections and Creating Masks."*

Type masks are often used to create layer masks in the shape of letters. A Type Mask tool is usually not the tool of choice for creating large amounts of text, and it's especially inappropriate for small type sizes.

# THE TYPE PALETTES AND COMMANDS



In addition to the Type tools in the Toolbox and the Options Bar, some 16 menu commands and two palettes are designed for use specifically with type. Some of the commands duplicate options found in the Options Bar (such as antialiasing), which allows you to access the capabilities without having the Type tool active. (Check Spelling and Find and Replace Text will be discussed separately, later in this chapter.)

In addition, virtually all other commands and palettes can be used with type in one way or another. Styles can be applied, colors can be changed, transformations are available—these are just some of the ways that Photoshop enables you to work with type.

## Type Commands Under the Layer Menu

The Type submenu found under the Layer menu offers 13 commands, each of which is available only when a type layer is active in the Layers palette. Two of the commands can be used to convert the editable type into vector paths, either as work paths or as shape layers.

## Create Work Path

The Create Work Path command converts the type layer from editable type to a work path. The work path consists of all the subpaths used to create the vector type. Photoshop does nothing with the work path, nor does it change your type layer in any way. You can, however, open the Paths palette and save the work path, you can use it to create a layer mask or clipping mask, you can stroke the paths (on a separate layer, not on the original type layer), or you can use the work path as a basis for a selection. Paths created from type can also be exported to Illustrator. In addition, you can edit the individual anchor points of the subpaths to customize the type (see Figure 12.15).

**Caution**

Be aware that paths created from type are very complex. When created from large amounts of text, they can be complex enough to cause output problems for imagesetters and printers. Unlike Illustrator, Photoshop has no Simplify command to reduce the complexity of paths.

**Figure 12.15**
The type has been converted to a work path, and the Direct Selection tool is being used to edit the letterforms. The path can be converted to a selection and filled or stroked.



In Figure 12.16, you can see the number of anchor points for the converted type. Note the density of points in the type.

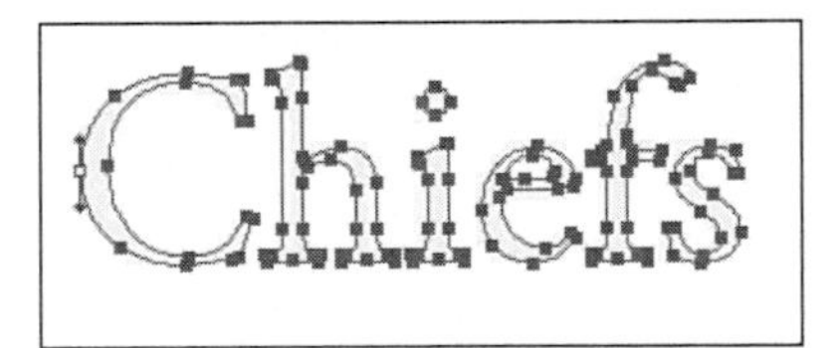


**Figure 12.16**
The type is set at a relatively large 18 points. The density of the anchor points would be increased at lower font sizes because the number of points per character remains the same.

The font used can play a major role in the number of anchor points created when type is converted to work paths. Serif fonts and some script fonts often require a substantially higher number of anchor points to be reproduced as editable paths. Multiply the increased number of anchor points, as shown in Figure 12.17, by the number of letters in a several-word type layer, and you can calculate the increased complexity of the work path.

**Figure 12.17**
The fonts are Arial (27 anchor points), Times New Roman (38 anchor points), Brush Script (74 anchor points), and Lucida Calligraphy (34 anchor points).

## Convert to Shape

Like the command Create Work Path, the Convert to Shape command uses a vector type layer to create paths. However, rather than creating a work path, this command produces a shape layer. The original type layer becomes a layer comparable to those produced by Photoshop shape tools. A shape layer consists of a filled layer with a layer clipping mask. The clipping mask selectively reveals areas of the filled layer (see Figure 12.18).

*Shape layers and the shape tools are discussed in Chapter 11, "The Pen Tool and Shape Layers: Vectors in Photoshop," p. 363.*

**Figure 12.18**
The Layers palette shows the layer thumbnail as well as the layer clipping path created from the type layer. The Paths palette shows the clipping path as a vector mask.



The new shape layer is filled with the same color that was originally applied to the type. If more than one color is applied to the type, the shape layer is filled with the color of the first character. When a style has been applied to the type layer, it is retained in the shape layer.

The paths created by the Convert to Shape command are identical to those created by the Create Work Path command. The caution presented earlier also applies to the shape layer path—paths with too many anchor points can create output problems.

Take a look at the Layers palette in Figure 12.18. Note that the original type layer is still there, but hidden. (You hide the original type layer by clicking its eyeball icon in the Layers palette.) It's always a good idea to create a shape layer from a *copy* of the type layer.

## Antialiasing Type

Antialiasing is the process of adding transitional pixels along the edges of objects in Photoshop images to soften the appearance of curves. These pixels are added in intermediary colors between the subject and the background colors or as semitransparent pixels when working on a separate layer. Antialiasing is used with selection tools as well as type.

Both Convert to Shape and Create Work Path are available for type that has been warped. The paths that are created, whether work paths or layer clipping paths, follow the contours of the warped type. You can also use these commands with type on a path.

Selection tools offer the option of antialiasing or not, but Photoshop's type engine is more sophisticated, offering several levels of antialiasing. Because the appearance of type is usually critical, and because different fonts and type sizes have different requirements, Photoshop's type engine offers these antialiasing options:

- **Anti-Alias None**—Antialiasing smoothes the edges of type onscreen. This command removes all antialiasing, which can result in jagged-edged type (see Figure 12.19). However, None is often the appropriate choice for very small type and small type at low resolution.

Figure 12.19
Although the differences in the other four types of antialiasing are virtually impossible to spot in the examples in this figure, None (at the upper left) is certainly apparent.

- **Anti-Alias Sharp**—This option results in the lowest amount of antialiasing. If the type appears rough or jagged along curves, select another option.
- **Anti-Alias Crisp**—High-contrast edges take precedence over smoothing with the Crisp option.
- **Anti-Alias Strong**—The Strong option adds antialiasing outside the character in an attempt to maintain the individual character's width.

- **Anti-Alias Smooth**—The greatest amount of antialiasing is applied. with this option. If characters become blurry, consider Crisp or Sharp. If the characters seem to lose optical weight (the strokes appear too thin), opt for Strong.

Antialiasing makes curves and angled lines appear smoother by adding colored pixels along edges. Think of the transitional pixels as a mini gradient, blending from the foreground color to the background color. When you look at black type on a white background, the added pixels are shades of gray (see Figure 12.20).

Figure 12.20
The number 2 has no antialiasing applied, but the letter *S* is set to Crisp. The inset is at 100%, and the image behind is at 800% zoom.

At 100% zoom, the jagged edges of the character without antialiasing are visible. With Crisp antialiasing, the curves appear smoother.

The colors used for the transitional pixels depend on the colors of the type and the background. For example, if the type is yellow (RGB 255/255/0) and it's placed on a background that's blue (0/0/255), the transitional pixels could be RGB 238/238/17, 187/187/68, 136/136/119, 119/119/136, 68/68/187, and 17/17/238.

The differences among the four type antialiasing options are subtle. Even when zoomed to 1,200%, it takes a close look to see variations (see Figure 12.21).

In this particular example, the area of greatest variation is the left edge of the letter *O*. The Strong antialiasing (bottom left) is substantially darker than the others. Sharp (top left) and Smooth (bottom right) are nearly identical in both placement and coloring of the transitional pixels.

Keep in mind that antialiasing is not always a good idea. Very small type can become quite blurry onscreen when antialiased. Especially when you're preparing images for the Web, think carefully about antialiasing. Using larger type, particularly the more linear sans serif fonts, such as Arial, can do far more to improve legibility and appearance than antialiasing. In addition, if the image is to be saved as a GIF or PNG-8 file, remember that antialiasing introduces several new colors to the color table, potentially increasing file size.

Remember, too, that antialiasing is not used when you print vector type to a PostScript printer.

Figure 12.21
The top row shows Sharp and Crisp, and the bottom shows Strong and Smooth.

## Other Type Commands

A number of additional commands in the Layer, Type submenu can be used to change the orientation, antialiasing, and a couple other attributes of the selected type or type layer. The submenu also holds commands that enable you to compensate for missing fonts:

- **Horizontal**—A check mark appears next to this command when the type layer contains horizontal type. If the check mark does not appear, you can select this command to convert the type from vertical to horizontal.
- **Vertical**—A check mark appears next to this command when the type layer contains vertical type. If the check mark does not appear, you can select this command to convert the type from horizontal to vertical.
- **Convert To Paragraph Text/Convert To Point Text**—As discussed earlier in this chapter, there are several key differences between point type and paragraph or area type. Perhaps most important, paragraph type can automatically reflow, adjusting the placement of words on each line, if the type container is changed or if text is added or subtracted. Multiple lines of point type, in contrast, must have line breaks (returns) manually entered at the end of each line. These commands allow you to convert between the two. Which command is visible in the menu depends on the content of the active type layer. Type on a path is point type, but cannot be converted to paragraph type.
- **Warp Text**—Using this command is equivalent to clicking the Warp Text button in the Options Bar. Unlike the button, this command is available even when no Type tool is selected. The Warp Text dialog box and the effects of warping are discussed in the section "Warping Type," earlier in this chapter.

- **Update All Text Layers**—When you open a Photoshop file containing type from a prior version or from Photoshop Elements, you might get a message saying that the type layers need to be updated before they can be output as vector type. If you don't update the type layers upon opening, this command gives you another opportunity. Be aware that all type layers in the image will be converted to vector, not just the active layer.
- **Replace All Missing Fonts**—If an image is opened that contains one or more fonts that are not available to Photoshop (for example, not present on the computer), a warning will appear. Layers containing one or more missing fonts are not updated. When a font is missing, you have the option of selecting the type layer in the Layers palette and assigning a font. If you choose to have Photoshop replace the missing font(s) using this command, the results could be less than satisfactory.

One other command deserves special attention. The menu command Layer, Rasterize, Type converts a vector type layer to pixels, and the type is rasterized at the image's resolution. This command is not available if the active layer in the Layers palette is not a type layer (identifiable by the *T* symbol in place of the layer thumbnail).

## The Options Bar and the Type Tools

Photoshop's Options Bar includes the capability to save tool presets. This is a great way to speed your work with the Type tool. If you regularly use certain fonts at certain sizes, they can be saved as presets in the Tool Presets Picker at the left end of the Options Bar (see Figure 12.22).

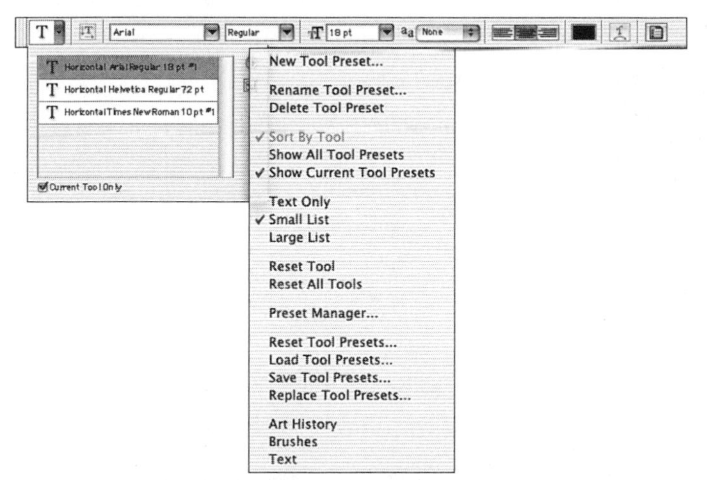


**Figure 12.22**
Select the font, size, antialiasing, alignment, and color, and then use the palette's menu command New Tool Preset. You'll have the opportunity to name the new configuration.



Each of the settings in the Options Bar can be changed for a preset. The values in the Character and Paragraph palettes are recorded as well. Note that the Horizontal Type tool and the Vertical Type tool have separate presets. The Tool Presets palette is available only when the Type tool is selected, but not in the act of adding type to the image. (When you're actually adding type, the preset palette's button is grayed out.)

*Presets gone haywire? Not sure why the type you add doesn't look like the type you want? See "Character Check" in the "Mastering Photoshop" section at the end of this chapter.*

Because the Options Bar is contextual, these fields and buttons are available only when the Type tool is active. However, when a type layer is active in the Layers palette, no matter what tool is selected, all these capabilities are available in the Character and Paragraph palettes or via the Layer, Type menu.

Immediately to the right of the Tool Presets Picker button is a button that allows you to switch existing type between horizontal and vertical. The button is available when a type layer is active in the Layers palette, regardless of whether the type itself is selected in the window. Swapping the type orientation applies to the entire type layer; you cannot change part of a sentence from horizontal to vertical.

With a Type tool active, you can use the Options Bar to change the font, font style (when the font has multiple styles available), type size, antialiasing, alignment, and color. To the right, the Options Bar offers four additional buttons. Just to the right of the color swatch is a button to open the Warp Text dialog box. The only difference between using this button and the menu command Layer, Type, Warp Text is convenience.

To the right of Warp Text is a button that toggles the visibility of the Character and Paragraph palettes. Again, this is comparable to using the appropriate commands in the Window menu to show and hide the palettes. Next are the Cancel Current Edits and Commit Current Edits buttons, which are visible only while a Type tool is in action. Clicking the Cancel button returns the type layer to its previous state (or cancels a new type layer), and the Commit button accepts the type entry or edit. The keyboard shortcuts for these two buttons are Escape and (Command-Return) [Ctrl+Enter].

## Photoshop at Work: Type Tool Presets

Often you need to precisely set many options to make your type look "just right." After you find a combination of settings that produces what you want, you'll likely want to use it in other projects. Photoshop's Tool Presets palette can make reproducing a specific look a snap. To set tool presets for large or headline type, follow these steps:

1. Select the Type tool from the Toolbox.
2. In the Options Bar, select a font you typically use for large type.
3. Select options that are appropriate for large type. Font size, tracking, scaling, color, and leading are some of the choices you need to make.
4. Click the Tool Presets palette tab or use the Window, Tool Presets command to bring the palette forward.
5. From the Tool Presets palette menu, choose New Tool Preset or click the New Preset button at the bottom of the palette.
6. Name the new preset appropriately. The name might contain such words as *Headline* or *Large* and the font name.

*Tracking*, as a preset option, adjusts the spacing among all the letters on a line of type. *Leading* determines the distance between lines of type. You learn more about these and other options for adjusting type appearance in "Character and Line Spacing," later in this chapter.

7. Change all parameters necessary, including font and size, to set the Type tool for body text.
8. Save the new settings, using the Tool Presets palette menu.
9. Open the Presets Manager by using the Edit menu or the Tool Presets palette menu.
10. Shift-click your Type tool presets. Click the Save button to create a set of type tools for future projects.

Remember that creating tool presets doesn't save them. Should you need to reset your Tool Presets palette, your custom tool presets are lost unless they're saved as a set.

## The Character Palette

You can show and hide the Character palette (see Figure 12.23) through the Window menu or a button in the Options Bar when a Type tool is active. The palette replicates many of the fields and options available in the Options Bar for Type tools. Unlike the type-related fields in the Options Bar, the Character palette is also available when a non-Type tool is active.

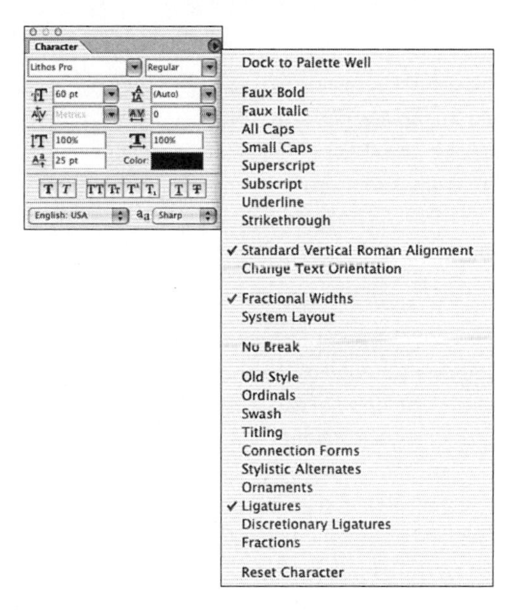


**Figure 12.23**
Not all menu options are available at the same time or with all fonts.

The Character palette can be used in several ways:

- It can be used without any active type layer to establish presets for the Type tools. This affects all type that is entered later, until additional changes are made in the Character palette or the Options Bar.
- With a type layer active in the Layers palette but no type selected in the image, changes can be made to the entire layer. These changes affect all type on the layer, but only type on that layer. The changes remain in effect in the Character palette and Options Bar.

> When adding type, you can show and hide the Character and Paragraph palettes by pressing (Command-T) [Ctrl+T].

- When some type on a type layer is selected with a Type tool, changes can be made to that portion of the type without affecting the rest of the type layer. Such changes affect only the selected type and remain in effect.
- If a Type tool is active and in use, the Character palette can be used to set the characteristics of type that has not yet been entered. All type entered from that point on has the new characteristics, but previously entered type is unaffected.

In the Style field, you can jump only to styles available for that font. If you press I for italic and the current font doesn't offer italic, you'll hear an error tone.

The Character palette has 12 fields and eight style buttons (the eight buttons are duplicated by commands in the palette's menu). You can navigate among the fields in the Character palette with the Tab key. Tab advances you to the next field, and Shift+Tab returns you to the previous one. Note that this method works even with the Font Family (name) and Font Style fields. In these fields, you can type the first letter of an entry in the pop-up list to jump to it.

## Font Family

The Font Family pop-up menu includes a list of all fonts available to Photoshop on your system. Font families include Helvetica, Times New Roman, Arial, and so on. All properly installed TrueType, Type 1, and OpenType fonts should appear. This menu selects only the font family.

You can preview how your type will look in a particular font. Select the type layer in the Layers palette (or select some type with the Type tool). Click once in the Font field of the Character palette or the Options Bar. Use the up and down arrow keys on the keyboard to navigate through the fonts, which changes the appearance of the type in the image. Take a snapshot in the History palette first, because each change is registered there.

## Font Style

The Font Style pop-up menu shows the font styles and weights built in to the font itself. The options can include Regular or Roman, Bold, Italic, Semibold, Condensed, Expanded, and combinations of these options, such as Semibold Italic. Some fonts, such as Stencil and Techno, are designed at a single weight and style, in which case the menu's arrow is grayed out.



For really large projects, you can work around Photoshop's font size limitation. Enter the text at 1296 points and then choose Edit, Transform, Scale. Make the type larger than you need. You can now return to the Font Size field and enter any point size up to the scaled size.

## Font Size

The Font Size field determines how large the font will appear in the image. In addition to the preset values in the pop-up menu, you can type any size between 1/10 of a point and 1296 points. By default, Photoshop uses points as the unit of measure for font size. One point is equal to 1/72 inch. You can change the unit in Photoshop's Preferences. In addition, you can type any unit of measure directly into the field. For example, typing **28 px** makes the font size 28 pixels. The other available abbreviations are in (inches), cm (centimeters), pica (picas), and pt (points). Fractional values can be entered as decimals.

**Styles and Weights**

When we talk about *style* for variations in a font's appearance, we're often misusing the term. Styles include condensed, extended, italic, roman, small caps, strikethrough, and underline. The terms *bold*, *light*, *regular*, and *semibold* are actually referring to a font's *weight*. Think of weight as the thickness of the stroke used to create the character. Consider style to be what you do to the characters: pushing and pulling, tilting and leaning, adding lines through and under.

There's no real reason to differentiate between style and weight in Photoshop, but typographers know the difference.

## Character and Line Spacing

In addition to controlling the appearance of type through fonts, you can determine positioning among characters and between lines of type using these options:

- **Leading**—Pronounced like the metal rather than the verb *to lead*, this measurement determines the distance between lines of type. Like size, leading is normally set in points, but you can enter values in any unit of measure. The pop-up menu defaults to Auto, which sets the leading at 120% of the font size (although this can be changed in the Justification dialog box, opened through the Paragraph palette's menu). You'll find that the values in the pop-up menu mirror those of the Font Size field. Remember that leading is based on the tallest character in a font.

*Changing the leading doesn't change anything? See "Adjusting Line Spacing" in the "Mastering Photoshop" section at the end of this chapter.*

- **Kerning**—Kerning is the space between a pair of characters. It affects only those two adjoining characters. Each font is designed with specific kerning for various pairs of characters, applied with the default setting of Metrics, but you can fine-tune the appearance of type with judicious use of kerning. Kerning is especially valuable when letters of different font size adjoin (see Figure 12.24).

  To adjust kerning, select a Type tool and click between the letters that need adjustment (do not select the letters). Use the pop-up menu or enter a numeric value in the Kerning field. Pressing (Return) [Enter] will commit the change. If you change your mind while still in the numeric field, you can use (Command-Z) [Ctrl+Z] to undo the change, or you can simply press Escape to cancel.

  Kerning is measured in 1/1000 em, a unit of measure based on the particular font's size. One em in a 24-point font is equal to 24 points.

Reducing the tracking can be an excellent way of squeezing type into a space that's just a little too small. Whether you're working with paragraph or point type, tightening the tracking can be far preferable to scaling or resizing the type.

12

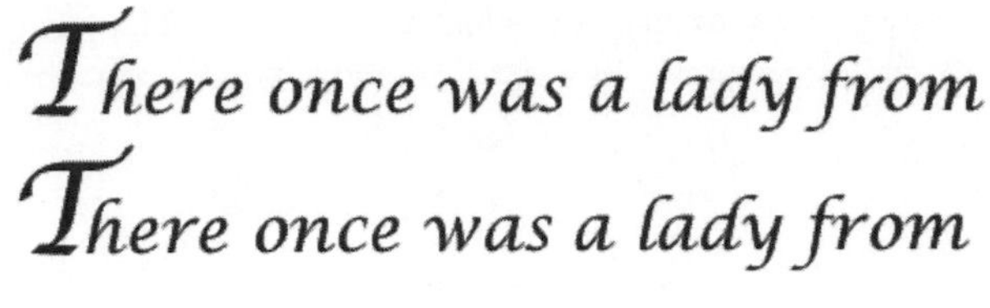

*There once was a lady from*

*There once was a lady from*

Figure 12.24
The top example shows the default kerning. By manually changing the Kerning value, you can improve the overall appearance, as was done in the bottom example.

- **Tracking**—Whereas kerning sets the distance between two letters, tracking adjusts the spacing among a group of selected letters. Tracking is measured like kerning. It can also be applied to an entire type layer by selecting the layer in the Layers palette and then making the change. When tracking is adjusted for a group of letters in a selection, the first letter doesn't move. All selected letters beyond it (by default, to the right) shift to meet the adjustment. Consider tracking to be the addition or reduction of space to the right of selected characters.

## Changing Scale, Shifting, Coloring, and Styling

Photoshop's Character palette enables you to change the vertical and horizontal scaling of one or more characters as well as to move a character up or down in relation to the baseline. You can also assign a specific color to a character or block of type and add style characteristics not built in to the font, such as bold, italic, strikethrough, and even antialiasing. Here are the Character palette fields that govern these options:

- **Vertical Scale**—Because Photoshop's type is vector based, you can scale it without loss of quality. The Character palette allows you to adjust the height of selected characters from 0% (invisible) to 1000%. The font's default appearance is always 100%. You can apply vertical scaling to selected type or to an entire type layer. Keep in mind that this scaling is independent of the menu command Edit, Transform, Scale. The Character palette still shows 100% after a scale transformation.



- **Horizontal Scale**—Useful for simulating expanded or compressed font styles, horizontal scaling can be adjusted from 0% to 1000%. When used proportionally with vertical scaling, the effect is comparable to changing the font size.

- **Baseline Shift**—The *baseline* is the imaginary line on which most letters in a font rest. (Some letters, of course, extend well below the baseline, such as *g*, *j*, *p*, *q*, and *y*; others extend slightly below the baseline, such as *e* and *o*.) Shifting a letter above the baseline creates a *superscript*; shifting a letter below the baseline produces a *subscript* (see Figure 12.25).

  Baseline shift can be adjusted by using (Option-Shift) [Alt+Shift] with the up and down arrow keys. Adding the (Command) [Ctrl] key changes the increment from 2 points to 10 points.

True superscripts and subscripts are typically smaller than the other characters in the text. Shifting the baseline changes the position of the character(s) without changing the size.

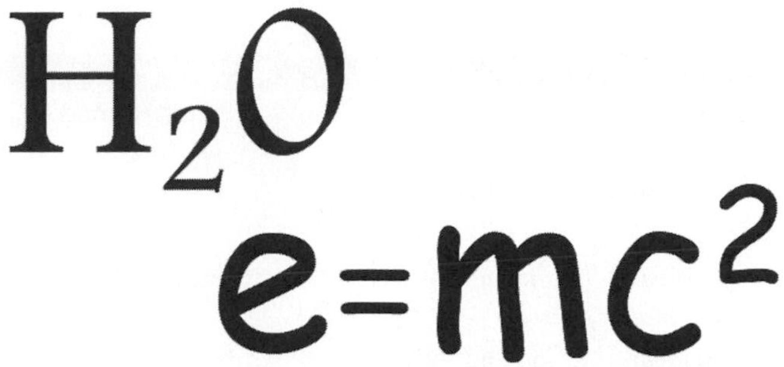

$H_2O$

$e=mc^2$

Figure 12.25
These "2" examples show a common use of subscript and perhaps an equally familiar superscript.

- **Text Color**—The swatch in the Character palette indicates the current type color. Click it to open the Color Picker. Remember that Photoshop allows multiple colors in a single type layer, so each letter can be a different color, if desired. Use a type tool to select text to change, or select a type layer in the Layers palette to apply the change to the entire layer.
- **Style Buttons**—From the left, the buttons are Faux Bold, Faux Italic, All Caps, Small Caps, Superscript, Subscript, Underline, and Strikethrough.

  When the selected font offers a bold weight or an italic style, it's definitely preferable to choose it in the Font Style pop-up menu than to apply the faux style. On the flip side, using Photoshop's Superscript and Subscript buttons is usually easier than working with Baseline Shift and then scaling the character. Remember, too, that Photoshop does not allow you to warp type to which faux bold has been applied (see Figure 12.26).

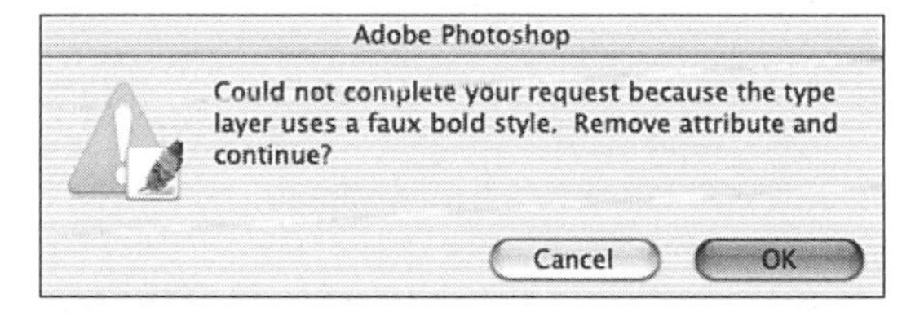


Figure 12.26
The other faux styles do not interfere with warping.

- **Language**—You use this pop-up menu to select the dictionary to use for spell checking and hyphenation (paragraph type only). All available dictionaries will be listed. Photoshop allows you to mix languages on a type layer. Select a word or words with a Type tool and then select a language in the pop-up menu.
- **Anti-Aliasing**—You have the option of applying one of four types of antialiasing to selected type or a type layer or having no antialiasing applied. (Antialiasing is discussed earlier in this chapter and in the section "Antialiasing Type.")

## Character Palette Shortcuts

A number of keyboard shortcuts, listed in Table 12.1, can be used to adjust type, even when the Character palette isn't visible.

**Table 12.1** Type Shortcuts

| To | Macintosh | Windows |
|---|---|---|
| Increase the font size by 2 pts (selected text) | Command-Shift-period | Ctrl+Shift+period |
| Increase the font size by 10 pts (selected text) | Command-Option-Shift-period | Ctrl+Alt+Shift+period |
| Decrease the font size by 2 pts (selected text) | Command-Shift-comma | Ctrl+Shift+comma |
| Decrease the font size by 10 pts (selected text) | Command-Option-Shift-comma | Ctrl+Alt+Shift+comma |
| Increase leading by 2 pts (one or more lines of type selected) | Option-down arrow | Alt+down arrow |
| Increase leading by 10 pts (one or more lines of type selected) | Command-Option-down arrow | Ctrl+Alt+down arrow |
| Decrease leading by 2 pts (one or more lines of type selected) | Option-up arrow | Alt+up arrow |
| Decrease leading by 10 pts (one or more lines of type selected) | Command-Option-up arrow | Ctrl+Alt+up arrow |
| Increase kerning by 20 pts (insertion point between two characters) | Option-right arrow | Alt+right arrow |
| Increase kerning by 100 pts (insertion point between two characters) | Command-Option-right arrow | Ctrl+Alt+right arrow |
| Decrease kerning by 20 pts (insertion point between two characters) | Option-left arrow | Alt+left arrow |
| Decrease kerning by 100 pts (insertion point between two characters) | Command-Option-left arrow | Ctrl+Alt+left arrow |
| Increase tracking by 20 pts (one or more characters selected) | Option-right arrow | Alt+right arrow |
| Increase tracking by 100 pts (one or more characters selected) | Command-Option-right arrow | Ctrl+Alt+right arrow |
| Decrease tracking by 20 pts (one or more characters selected) | Option-left arrow | Alt+left arrow |

| To | Macintosh | Windows |
|---|---|---|
| Decrease tracking by 100 pts (one or more characters selected) | Command-Option-left arrow | Ctrl+Alt+left arrow |
| Increase baseline shift by 2 pts (one or more characters selected) | Shift-Option-up arrow | Shift+Alt+up arrow |
| Increase baseline shift by 10 pts (one or more characters selected) | Command-Shift-Option-up arrow | Ctrl+Shift+Alt+up arrow |
| Decrease baseline shift by 2 pts (one or more characters selected) | Shift-Option-down arrow | Shift+Alt+down arrow |
| Decrease baseline shift by 10 pts (one or more characters selected) | Command-Shift-Option-down arrow | Ctrl+Shift+Alt+down arrow |

Remember that the difference between changing kerning and changing tracking is the selection. If the cursor is between two characters and there is no selection, the shortcuts adjust kerning. If one or more letters are selected, the tracking is changed. Otherwise, the keystrokes are identical.

Also keep in mind that adjusting leading might show no effect unless the entire line is selected. If part of a line has leading set to 24 and another part of the same line has a leading of 48, the entire line appears as 48-point leading. Leading is applied to an entire line, but baseline shift can be applied to individual characters.

## The Character Palette Menu

The Character palette's menu contains a number of commands that simply duplicate the style buttons found in the palette itself. Faux Bold, Faux Italic, All Caps, Small Caps, Superscript, Subscript, Underline, and Strikethrough show a check mark to the left when the style is applied to the selected type or type layer. To select or deselect a style, simply choose the style from the menu or use the palette's button.

The palette's other menu commands deserve additional attention:

- **Dock to Palette Well**—Docking the Character palette to the Palette Well makes it easily accessible.
- **Standard Vertical Roman Alignment and Change Text Orientation**—The option Change Type Orientation rotates type. Horizontal type is rotated to vertical, and vertical is rotated to horizontal. However, when the option Standard Vertical Roman Alignment is applied to one or more characters, those characters are reoriented to the top of the image. In Figure 12.27, the word *Vertical* can be set with the Vertical Type tool or by changing the text orientation of horizontal type. The word *Rotated* uses the Standard Vertical Roman Alignment option. In the words *Mixed Rotation*, the *M* and *R* have standard alignment; the rest of the characters do not.

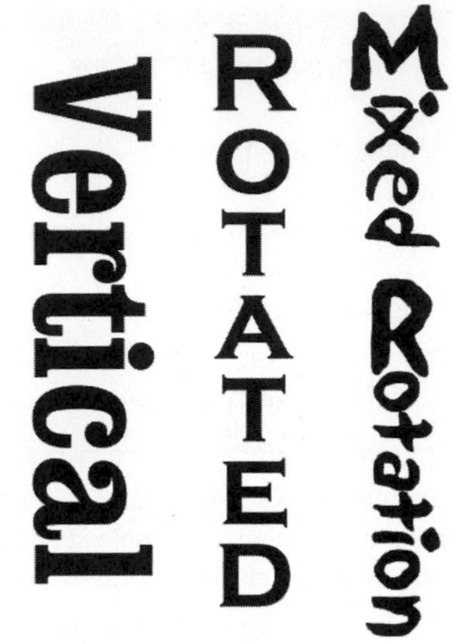

Figure 12.27
Standard Vertical Roman Alignment orients characters to the top of the page.



- **Fractional Widths**—When this option is selected, Photoshop can adjust spacing between letters on an individual basis, using fractions of a pixel. Although this method often improves legibility for large type (20 points and over), it can cause problems for smaller type sizes. It is especially inappropriate for small type destined for the Web. Fractional widths can be applied only to entire type layers.

- **System Layout**—Selecting this option simplifies the characteristics of the selected type layer to match as closely as possible the type of Windows Notepad or Apple's SimpleText and TextEdit. This option's settings include Kerning:0, Tracking:0, Vertical Scaling:100%, Horizontal Scaling:100%, Baseline Shift:0, and Anti-Aliasing:None, and it disables the Fractional Widths option. It does not change font, font size, leading, character style settings, color, or dictionary. System Layout is used primarily for screen mockups and user interface elements.



- **No Break**—This option disables hyphenation in paragraph type. It can be applied on a word-by-word basis by selecting the type with a Type tool and then selecting the command from the menu. No Break can be applied to specific letter combinations to force the break to occur elsewhere in the word. It can also be applied to a group of words to force Photoshop to keep those words on the same line. It is not used with point type because all breaks are inserted manually with the (Return) [Enter] key.

- **Old Style, Ordinals, Swash, and so on**—These options are available only for those fonts that have the specific capabilities built in, primarily OpenType fonts. (Fonts with the word *Pro* in the name are OpenType fonts.) *Ligatures* are two or three letters combined into one character to improve the look of certain letter combinations (see Figure 12.28). Old Style refers to number

> Many non-OpenType fonts have the *fi* and *fl* ligatures built in, and you can add them with (Shift-Option-5) [Shift+Alt+5] and (Shift-Option-6) [Shift+Alt+6]. You'll find ligatures in such common fonts as Times and Geneva, but not in many others, including Arial, Helvetica, and any all-caps fonts.

characters. These are lowercase numbers, used primarily with lowercase type. Many old-style numerals have ascenders and descenders, as shown in Figure 12.28.

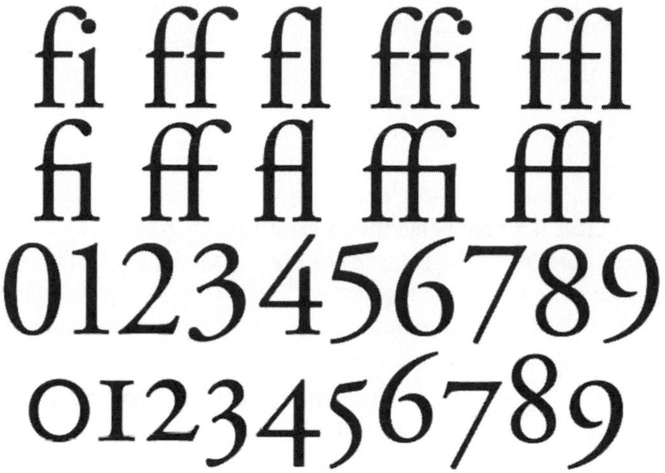

fi ff fl ffi ffl
fi ff fl ffi ffl
0123456789
0123456789

**Figure 12.28**
The top two lines compare the same letter combinations without and with ligatures. The lowest line shows old-style numerals with their natural baseline. (The font is Adobe Garamond Pro.)

- **Reset Character**—This command returns the Character palette (and any selected type or type layer) to the default settings. You can reset selected type or an entire type layer. Either use a Type tool to highlight type on a type layer or select the type layer in the Layers palette. The default settings are not user definable.

## The Paragraph Palette

When nested with the Character palette (as it is by default), the Paragraph palette can be shown and hidden by using the button in the Options Bar or the (Command-T) [Ctrl+T] shortcut while editing or inputting type. You can also show and hide the Paragraph palette through the Windows menu. This palette and its menu, shown in Figure 12.29, govern the appearance of a body of type. Photoshop considers a "paragraph" to be any amount of text followed by a return.

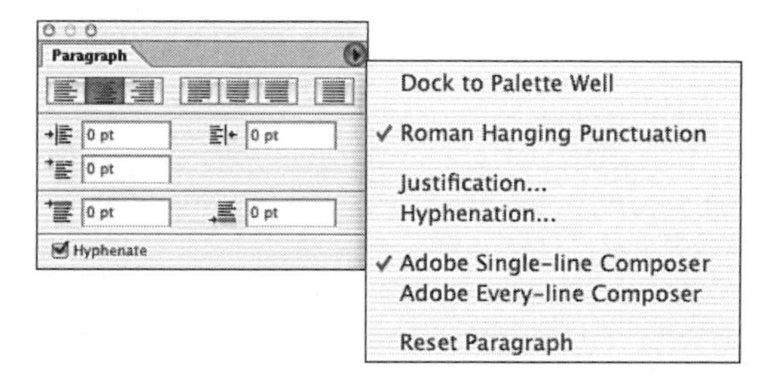


**Figure 12.29**
Some of the Paragraph palette menu commands are not available when point type is selected.

All options in the Paragraph palette can be set individually for each paragraph. The entire paragraph need not be selected; simply click with the Type tool in a paragraph to indicate that it's the target of the changes. You can highlight one or more characters from several paragraphs to select them all. If you don't click in the text, Photoshop assumes that changes made in the Paragraph palette should be applied to the entire type layer. If no type layer is active in the Layers palette, any changes made are used the next time type is added to the image.

> Point type that appears on a single line without a return at the end is considered a paragraph for Photoshop's alignment options.

Across the top of the palette are seven buttons that govern the alignment and justification of paragraphs. What they do to a paragraph of text is apparent from the button icons. The first three buttons are for alignment—arranging the text to have an even margin on the left, have each line centered, or have an even margin on the right. In each case, the text remains within the boundaries of its rectangle. Photoshop's criteria for justifying text are set in the Justification dialog box opened through the Paragraph palette's menu. (Justification rules are discussed in the next section.) When applied to point type, the left align, center, and right align text buttons determine where the type will appear in relation to the spot you clicked with the Type tool.

The four remaining buttons at the top of the Paragraph palette determine justification. *Justified* text has even margins on both the left and right. These four options govern the last line of a paragraph. When the final line is not full—that is, it does not naturally stretch from the left to the right margin—Photoshop offers several options. The final line can be aligned left, centered, aligned right, or justified. To justify the final line, space is added between words and, if necessary, letters. Should the final line be substantially shorter than the others, the amount of whitespace added can be unsightly and interfere with legibility (see Figure 12.30).

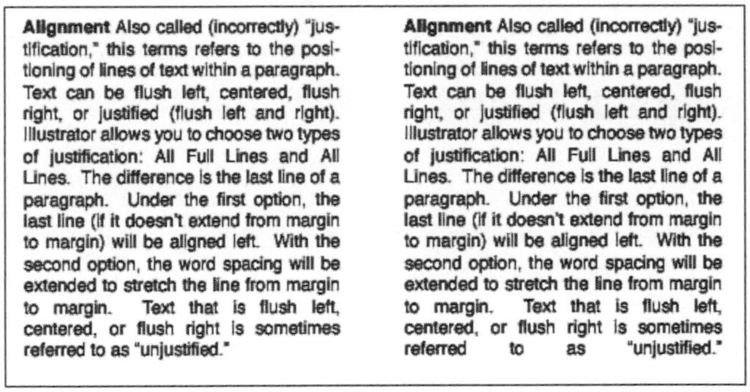

**Alignment** Also called (incorrectly) "justification," this terms refers to the positioning of lines of text within a paragraph. Text can be flush left, centered, flush right, or justified (flush left and right). Illustrator allows you to choose two types of justification: All Full Lines and All Lines. The difference is the last line of a paragraph. Under the first option, the last line (if it doesn't extend from margin to margin) will be aligned left. With the second option, the word spacing will be extended to stretch the line from margin to margin. Text that is flush left, centered, or flush right is sometimes referred to as "unjustified."

**Alignment** Also called (incorrectly) "justification," this terms refers to the positioning of lines of text within a paragraph. Text can be flush left, centered, flush right, or justified (flush left and right). Illustrator allows you to choose two types of justification: All Full Lines and All Lines. The difference is the last line of a paragraph. Under the first option, the last line (if it doesn't extend from margin to margin) will be aligned left. With the second option, the word spacing will be extended to stretch the line from margin to margin. Text that is flush left, centered, or flush right is sometimes referred to as "unjustified."

Figure 12.30
The same text is shown with Justify Last Left and with Justify Last All. Note the difference in the final line of each paragraph.



The second section of the Paragraph palette governs indenting. Entire paragraphs can be indented to the left, to the right, or both (the upper pair of buttons), and you can specify indenting separately for the first line of a paragraph (the lower button in the middle section of the palette). By default, the unit of measure for indenting is points. That can be changed in Photoshop's Preferences under Units & Rulers. The Paragraph palette uses the unit of measure specified under Type. Figure 12.31 shows how indenting can be used effectively. (The first lines of the subparagraphs are indented with a negative number to shift them to the left.)

Also visible in Figure 12.31 is paragraph spacing. Using the lower set of buttons in the Paragraph palette, you can specify spacing before a paragraph (left), or space can be added after a paragraph (right). Like indenting, the unit of measure specified for type in the Preferences is used.

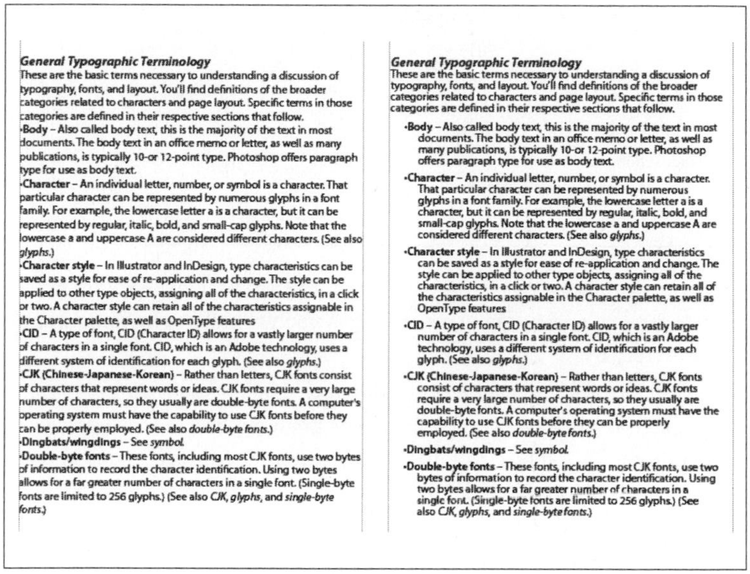

***General Typographic Terminology***

These are the basic terms necessary to understanding a discussion of typography, fonts, and layout. You'll find definitions of the broader categories related to characters and page layout. Specific terms in those categories are defined in their respective sections that follow.

- **Body** – Also called body text, this is the majority of the text in most documents. The body text in an office memo or letter, as well as many publications, is typically 10-or 12-point type. Photoshop offers paragraph type for use as body text.
- **Character** – An individual letter, number, or symbol is a character. That particular character can be represented by numerous glyphs in a font family. For example, the lowercase letter a is a character, but it can be represented by regular, italic, bold, and small-cap glyphs. Note that the lowercase a and uppercase A are considered different characters. (See also *glyphs*.)
- **Character style** – In Illustrator and InDesign, type characteristics can be saved as a style for ease of re-application and change. The style can be applied to other type objects, assigning all of the characteristics, in a click or two. A character style can retain all of the characteristics assignable in the Character palette, as well as OpenType features
- **CID** – A type of font, CID (Character ID) allows for a vastly larger number of characters in a single font. CID, which is an Adobe technology, uses a different system of identification for each glyph. (See also *glyphs*.)
- **CJK (Chinese-Japanese-Korean)** – Rather than letters, CJK fonts consist of characters that represent words or ideas. CJK fonts require a very large number of characters, so they usually are double-byte fonts. A computer's operating system must have the capability to use CJK fonts before they can be properly employed. (See also *double-byte fonts*.)
- **Dingbats/wingdings** – See *symbol*.
- **Double-byte fonts** – These fonts, including most CJK fonts, use two bytes of information to record the character identification. Using two bytes allows for a far greater number of characters in a single font. (Single-byte fonts are limited to 256 glyphs.) (See also *CJK*, *glyphs*, and *single-byte fonts*.)

***General Typographic Terminology***

These are the basic terms necessary to understanding a discussion of typography, fonts, and layout. You'll find definitions of the broader categories related to characters and page layout. Specific terms in those categories are defined in their respective sections that follow.

- **Body** – Also called body text, this is the majority of the text in most documents. The body text in an office memo or letter, as well as many publications, is typically 10-or 12-point type. Photoshop offers paragraph type for use as body text.
- **Character** – An individual letter, number, or symbol is a character. That particular character can be represented by numerous glyphs in a font family. For example, the lowercase letter a is a character, but it can be represented by regular, italic, bold, and small-cap glyphs. Note that the lowercase a and uppercase A are considered different characters. (See also *glyphs*.)
- **Character style** – In Illustrator and InDesign, type characteristics can be saved as a style for ease of re-application and change. The style can be applied to other type objects, assigning all of the characteristics, in a click or two. A character style can retain all of the characteristics assignable in the Character palette, as well as OpenType features
- **CID** – A type of font, CID (Character ID) allows for a vastly larger number of characters in a single font. CID, which is an Adobe technology, uses a different system of identification for each glyph. (See also *glyphs*.)
- **CJK (Chinese-Japanese-Korean)** – Rather than letters, CJK fonts consist of characters that represent words or ideas. CJK fonts require a very large number of characters, so they usually are double-byte fonts. A computer's operating system must have the capability to use CJK fonts before they can be properly employed. (See also *double-byte fonts*.)
- **Dingbats/wingdings** – See *symbol*.
- **Double-byte fonts** – These fonts, including most CJK fonts, use two bytes of information to record the character identification. Using two bytes allows for a far greater number of characters in a single font. (Single-byte fonts are limited to 256 glyphs.) (See also *CJK*, *glyphs*, and *single-byte fonts*.)

**Figure 12.31**
As you can see in this comparison, adding space before or after paragraphs and indenting can improve the appearance and legibility of text.

At the bottom of the Paragraph palette is a check box that turns hyphenation on and off in the paragraph. Like the other Paragraph palette options, hyphenation can be set on a paragraph-by-paragraph basis. Specific rules for hyphenation are set by using the Paragraph palette's menu command of the same name (discussed in the following section).

## The Paragraph Palette Menu

Several commands appear in the Paragraph palette's menu. Like most palettes, the top command, Dock to Palette Well, enables you to add the palette to the Palette Well.

Roman Hanging Punctuation is an advanced typesetting option. With paragraph type, certain punctuation marks fall outside the margins to the left and right, creating a "cleaner" look to the margins (see Figure 12.32).

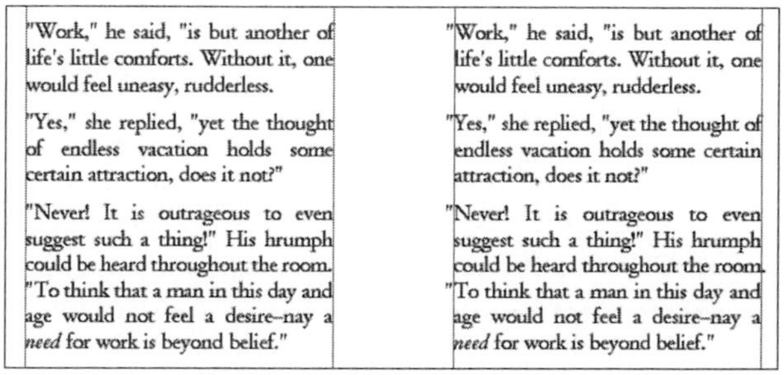

"Work," he said, "is but another of life's little comforts. Without it, one would feel uneasy, rudderless.

"Yes," she replied, "yet the thought of endless vacation holds some certain attraction, does it not?"

"Never! It is outrageous to even suggest such a thing!" His hrumph could be heard throughout the room. "To think that a man in this day and age would not feel a desire–nay a *need* for work is beyond belief."

"Work," he said, "is but another of life's little comforts. Without it, one would feel uneasy, rudderless.

"Yes," she replied, "yet the thought of endless vacation holds some certain attraction, does it not?"

"Never! It is outrageous to even suggest such a thing!" His hrumph could be heard throughout the room. "To think that a man in this day and age would not feel a desire–nay a *need* for work is beyond belief."

**Figure 12.32**
Hanging punctuation allows the larger letterforms to align to the margins. This option gives the text more of a "block" look, producing the illusion of straighter margins.

The Justification dialog box (shown in Figure 12.33) controls how Photoshop justifies paragraphs. Making changes here allows you to make tiny adjustments to how Photoshop spaces words and letters to create full justification.

**Figure 12.33**
Other than Auto Leading, these values are applied only when text is justified.

**Justification**

| | Minimum | Desired | Maximum |
|---|---|---|---|
| Word Spacing: | 80% | 100% | 133% |
| Letter Spacing: | 0% | 0% | 0% |
| Glyph Scaling: | 100% | 100% | 100% |

Auto Leading: 120%

OK
Cancel
Preview

Word Spacing establishes minimum, maximum, and target amounts for space between words. A value of 100% represents the font's built-in spacing plus any changes you've made to tracking in the Character palette. Values can range from 0% to 133%.

Letter Spacing determines how much change Photoshop can make to spaces between letters within words. Justifying relies on letter spacing only after word spacing has been applied and only if necessary. Although percents are shown in the dialog box, the unit of measure is actually fractions of an em. Inputting 0% in all three fields turns off letter spacing.

Glyph Scaling, a method of last resort, actually changes the width of individual characters to create justification. Sacrificing the appearance of the letters for the appearance of the margins is rarely a good idea. A value of 100% represents the original width of each character.

At the bottom of the dialog box, you can specify what percentage of a font's size will be used for the Auto setting in the Character palette's Leading pop-up menu.

The Hyphenation dialog box, shown in Figure 12.34, is opened with the Hyphenation command on the Paragraph palette's menu. It controls what rules Photoshop applies when breaking words at the end of a line. Photoshop uses the assigned dictionary to determine where a word is hyphenated; these settings determine whether a word is hyphenated at all.

The default values for justification in Photoshop CS are appropriate for most purposes. Make changes to the settings when you need to tweak the type a little, perhaps to make a specific amount of text fit in a specific area or to adjust the overall appearance of the text.



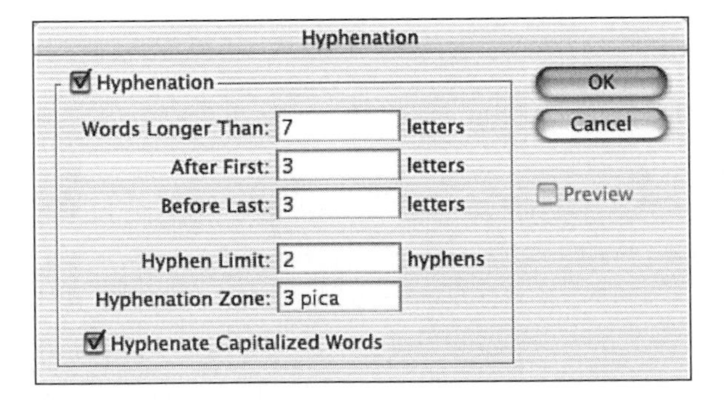


**Figure 12.34**
Remember that only paragraph type can be automatically hyphenated.

You use the Hyphen Limit field to control how many consecutive lines can end with hyphens and the Hyphenation Zone field to establish a distance from the right margin in which words will not be hyphenated. For example, if the preceding word enters the designated zone, the following word is moved in its entirety to the following line. Likewise, if a word to be broken does not have a dictionary-defined break within the zone, the word remains unhyphenated.

If you deselect the Hyphenate Capitalized Words check box at the bottom of the dialog box, words that begin with a capital letter cannot be hyphenated. This includes proper nouns as well as words that start sentences. (The possibility that a word is long enough to both start a sentence and require hyphenation in Photoshop indicates very narrow columns or a very long word.) This setting has no effect on type set in all caps or entered with the Caps Lock key locked down.

The difference between the Adobe Single-line Composer and the Adobe Multi-line Composer commands is the approach to hyphenation. Single-line looks at one line, decides the appropriate hyphenation, and then moves to the next line. Multi-line examines all the selected text before making decisions, which usually produces fewer word breaks and a generally more pleasing look to the text.

The Reset Paragraph command restores the Paragraph palette to its default settings.

# SPELL CHECK AND FIND/REPLACE

Introduced in the previous version of Photoshop, the Spell Check and Find/Replace features are indispensable tools when you're adding large amounts of type to a project.

## The Spell Checker

The menu command Edit, Check Spelling opens Photoshop's Check Spelling dialog box (see Figure 12.35). Similar to spell checking systems found in many word processing programs, this tool offers suggestions and allows you to input your own changes in the dialog box. In addition, you have the choice of ignoring that particular word, ignoring all instances of that word in the image, changing that instance to a suggested spelling or a word you type in the Change To field (thus changing all instances to the selected new spelling), or adding the word to the dictionary.

**Caution**

Think twice about using the Add button in Photoshop's spell checker because the dictionaries are not editable. After you add a word, it's there for good. Instead, rely on the Ignore and Ignore All buttons unless the word will appear often—and you're absolutely certain the spelling is correct.



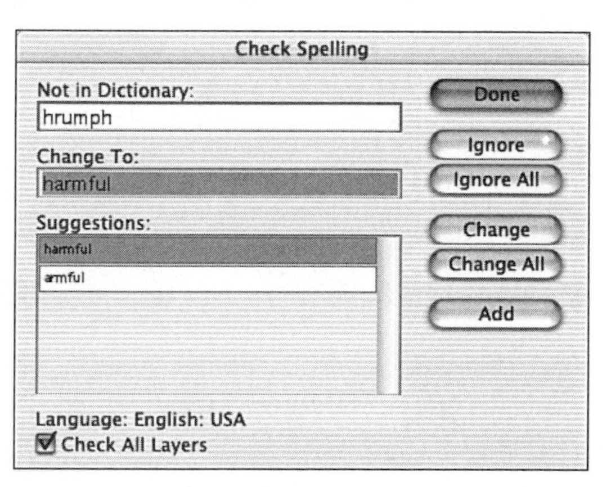


Figure 12.35
The spell checker is rather basic, but it certainly is functional.

The spell checker uses the dictionary assigned to the selected text. If more than one dictionary is assigned, it automatically switches to the appropriate dictionary on the fly. The spell checker does not check grammar.

## Photoshop at Work: Creating a Dictionary Backup

It's always a good idea to protect your dictionaries. Here's a way to ensure that you won't waste a lot of time retyping all your custom words if you need to replace a dictionary:

1. Start a text document in your favorite word processor.
2. Type in all the words that you want to add to Photoshop's dictionary. Check them carefully, and then use the Select All command and copy them.
3. Open a document in Photoshop.
4. Select the Type tool, drag a type container in the document, and then paste. (It doesn't matter if the text exceeds the container size.)
5. Now run the spell checker and click the Add button to put these terms into the dictionary. (If you work in multiple languages, make sure you're adding the terms to the correct dictionary.)
6. Save the Photoshop document for future use, just in case you need to reinstall Photoshop or replace the dictionaries. You can add to or subtract from the list as much as you'd like.

If you have to remove words from the dictionary, reinstall the default dictionary and then reload your custom words from the saved Photoshop document.

## Find/Replace



The Find and Replace Text command, also located under Photoshop's Edit menu, functions much like the Find and Replace command in a basic word processor (see Figure 12.36). Unlike MS Word, however, it doesn't allow you to search by format or style, nor can it search for special characters.

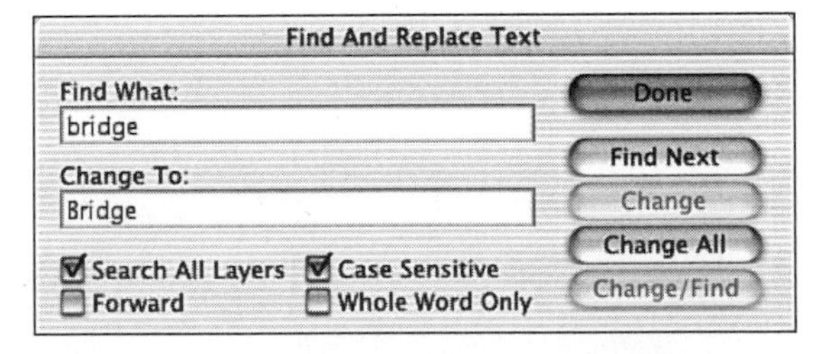


Figure 12.36
To find without replacing, simply enter the word or phrase and click Find Next. You can then click Done without making any changes.

Enter the word or phrase that you want to find and then enter a replacement word or phrase. The Find Next button initiates the search. When an instance of the word or phrase is located, it is highlighted in the text. You have the option of changing that instance, changing all instances in the image, or changing and continuing the search for the next instance (Change/Find). You can also click Change All immediately after entering the target and replacement words.

You have the option of restricting the search to the active type layer or searching all type layers. You can make the search case sensitive, requiring a match in capitalization as well as spelling. When you select the Forward check box, Photoshop searches from the current Type tool insertion point to the end of the text. Selecting the Whole Word Only check box prevents Photoshop from finding matches within longer words. For example, when this option is deselected, a search for *ten* also returns such words as *often*, *intent*, *tension*, and *tents*.

# FONTS AND FONT EMBEDDING

Many types of fonts are currently available in various qualities. Photoshop, like most high-end computer programs, works best with high-quality fonts. Although you can get good results with inexpensive and free fonts, they are often troublesome. TrueType and Type 1 fonts are the most common high-quality fonts available, with more and more OpenType fonts reaching the marketplace. (Adobe has discontinued support for multiple master fonts.)

Fonts (also called *typefaces*) classified as TrueType, Type 1, multiple master, and OpenType typically perform flawlessly with Photoshop. (Any font, however, is subject to corruption over time and might need to be reinstalled.) Bitmap fonts should not be used with Photoshop.

## Fonts and Font Families

Technically, a certain typeface at a certain size in a certain style constitutes a *font*. More generally, we tend to use the term to refer to an entire family of fonts. For example, Times 12 pt is different from Times 24 pt and Times (Italic) or Times (Bold). Each was designed to serve a separate purpose. Colloquially, we refer to all the Times typefaces as a single font. Technically, Times is a font family, with numerous individual fonts.

When does terminology make a difference? Primarily, the subject comes up in marketing. Such-and-such a laser printer may have 52 fonts installed, and a competitor might claim more than 250 fonts. One font package could include more than 1,000 fonts, and another might have 85 font families. As long as you are aware of the difference in terminology, you can make informed decisions.

Although Photoshop can use multiple master fonts, it cannot take advantage of the special characteristics of these fonts. Unlike Illustrator, Photoshop has no provisions for customizing the appearance of multiple master fonts.

12

## Sources of Fonts

Photoshop ships with a number of fonts, which are installed by default. In addition, other installed software has likely added fonts to your computer. Free and low-cost fonts can be purchased as collections on CD or downloaded from a variety of sites on the Internet. Because Web sites come and go so fast, it's impossible to provide a current and accurate list.

Many fonts come in both Macintosh and Windows versions. Make sure you install the appropriate font. OpenType fonts can use the same font file on either platform.

Commercial Web sites that offer high-quality fonts for sale, on the other hand, are reasonably stable, and many of these sources are likely to be around for quite some time. You'll find fonts on a wide variety of Web sites. Here are some notable sites:

- **Adobe (www.adobe.com/type)**—In addition to one of the largest collections of top-quality fonts, you'll find a wealth of information about how fonts work—and how to use them effectively.
- **Agfa | Monotype (www.agfamonotype.com)**—Over 8,000 fonts are available. You'll find fonts from Adobe, ITC, and other major foundries.
- **Berthold (www.bertholdtypes.com)**—Another of the top foundries, where you'll find a large collection of fonts.
- **Letraset (www.letraset.com)**—To an entire generation, this company's name is synonymous with rub-on letters. It also has an extensive collection of digital fonts.
- **Xerox (www.font.net)**—In addition to a wide variety of fonts, you'll find a wealth of background information.

Most of the major stock photography sites also offer fonts. Some collections are quite extensive. Specialty fonts are available at independent sites as well. A huge list of links can be found at www.microsoft.com/typography. Here are several exceptional sites:

- **The Chank Company (www.chank.com)**—Chank Diesel's work includes custom fonts for a variety of packaging. A walk down the aisles of your local supermarket will take you past many examples. Chank.com offers a variety of fun and quirky fonts, perfect for grabbing attention.
- **House Industries (www.houseindustries.com)**—Fun, funky, powerful fonts are available individually or in collections.
- **Linguist's Software (www.linguistsoftware.com)**—Fonts for over 600 languages are available from this organization.
- **ParaType (www.paratype.com)**—This site specializes in foreign language fonts. A large selection of Cyrillic, Hebrew, Greek, Arabic, Armenian, and Georgian fonts are available. You'll also find a wide variety of the more-familiar Latin alphabet fonts and even some experimental fonts.



If you are inclined to create your own fonts, you can explore Macromedia's Fontographer (www.macromedia.com/software/fontographer) and FontLab (www.fontlab.com) as well as software from such companies as DTPSoft (www.dtpsoft.de) and High Logic (www.high-logic.com).

## Adding and Removing Fonts—Macintosh

Generally speaking, if a font is properly installed on your computer (and it is a PostScript font), it will appear in Photoshop's Font menu.

Mac OS X users have fonts in three or more locations (see Figure 12.37).

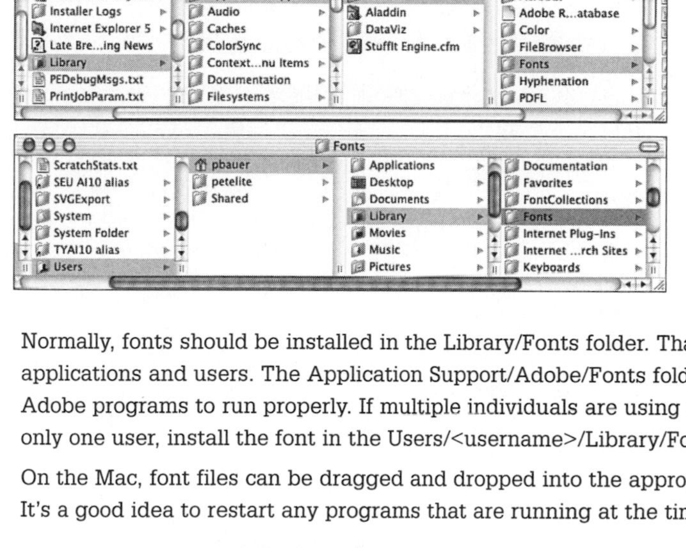


**Figure 12.37**
The top two windows show font locations in a pair of locations in the same Library folder. The Users folder, seen in the bottom window, is also on the startup disk.

Normally, fonts should be installed in the Library/Fonts folder. That makes them available to all applications and users. The Application Support/Adobe/Fonts folder holds those fonts critical for Adobe programs to run properly. If multiple individuals are using a computer but a font is licensed to only one user, install the font in the Users/<username>/Library/Fonts folder.

On the Mac, font files can be dragged and dropped into the appropriate font folder to install them. It's a good idea to restart any programs that are running at the time of font installation.

## Adding Fonts in Windows XP

Windows users should open the Control Panel. The Fonts pane of the Windows Control panel shows all installed fonts. To add a font, use the menu command File, Install New Font (see Figure 12.38).

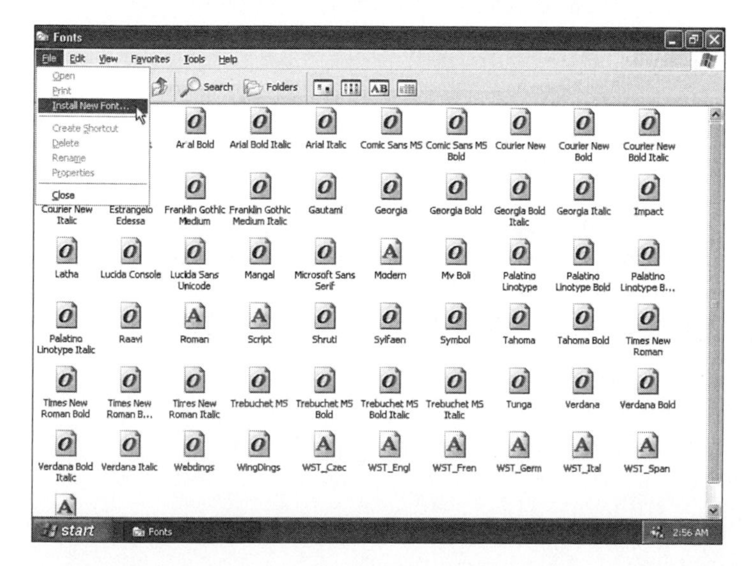


**Figure 12.38**
It's important that new fonts be installed properly, not just for Photoshop, but to ensure that Windows runs correctly.

To install a new font, follow these steps:

1. In the Fonts pane of the Control Panel, navigate to the location of the new fonts.
2. Open the folder that holds the font you want to install.
3. Click the Select All button or Ctrl-click to select individual fonts from the list shown in the upper pane (see Figure 12.39).

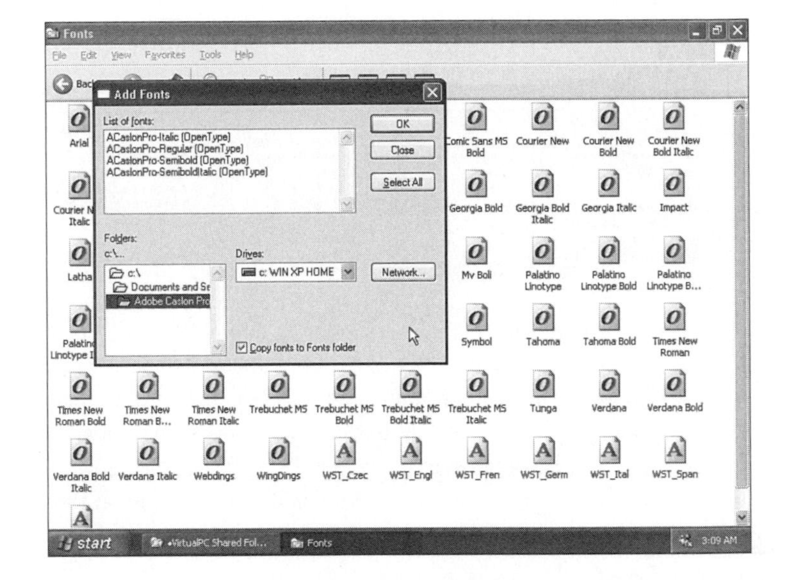


**Figure 12.39**
In this instance, several varieties of an OpenType font are listed as available in the selected folder.

4. Select the Copy Fonts to Fonts Folder check box to leave the originals undisturbed, or deselect the check box to move the original files, deleting them from their original locations.
5. Click OK to move/copy the fonts to the Fonts folder.
6. Restart any program running during font installation to ensure that the new fonts are available to the program. It is not necessary to restart Windows.



## Font Management

Too many installed fonts can slow Photoshop (and other programs) to a crawl. There are a number of font-management utilities available for all platforms. Typically, a font-management utility creates collections of fonts that can be activated when needed. This allows the system (and programs) to run without the overhead of hundreds of fonts that may or may not be needed during a particular work session.

# MASTERING PHOTOSHOP

## Character Check

*I've established presets for my Type tools using the Options Bar, but when I actually try to add type to an image by using the presets, the text is distorted. What's the problem?*

It's a good idea to have the Character and Paragraph palettes open when establishing presets. The settings there are included in the preset, whether the palette is visible or not. It sounds as though the character height and width were not set to 100% when you created your presets. Every field and button in each of the two palettes is also recordable in a preset, including the spell check dictionary.

## Adjusting Line Spacing

*I've changed the leading for a line of type, but don't see any change. What's wrong?*

Make sure you've selected the entire line of type—it's not enough to simply click in a word. If you're reducing the leading, it's also very important that you select the *entire* line of type. Just one letter at the higher leading setting forces the whole line to that value.

13

# PHOTOSHOP'S PAINTING TOOLS AND BRUSHES

## IN THIS CHAPTER

At its heart, *painting* in Photoshop is nothing more than applying color to pixels using tools. Unlike many other Photoshop techniques that require a selection to identify where pixels will be edited, painting tools use *brushes*. Consider a brush to be sort of a moving selection. The brush defines an area within which pixels are altered. Like a selection, a brush can be round, square, or irregularly shaped, and it can be feathered or hard edged.

More broadly, the term *painting* can also encompass some menu commands, including Stroke and Fill and the comparable commands in the Paths palette menu. These commands apply color to the image along selection edges or paths, using painting tools or a specific pixel width, comparable to using a brush. However you define it, Photoshop's painting capabilities give you the incredible power to apply and manipulate color directly at the pixel level.

Photoshop's painting capability took a huge leap with the previous release of the program, Photoshop 7. Photoshop CS continues to refine the Brushes palette and adds one new brush, the Color Replacement tool.

This chapter looks at the basic concepts behind painting in Photoshop CS, explains the highly complex Brushes palette, and discusses defining custom brushes and sets of brushes.

# PAINTING IN PHOTOSHOP

There are three primary painting tools (Brush, Pencil, and Eraser), a couple painting tools that don't use brushes (Gradient and Paint Bucket), and a number of tools that use brushes but modify pixels rather than paint them. All these tools are grouped in the Toolbox (see Figure 13.1).

> Photoshop CS includes one new brush-using tool, the Color Replacement tool. It's discussed later in this section.

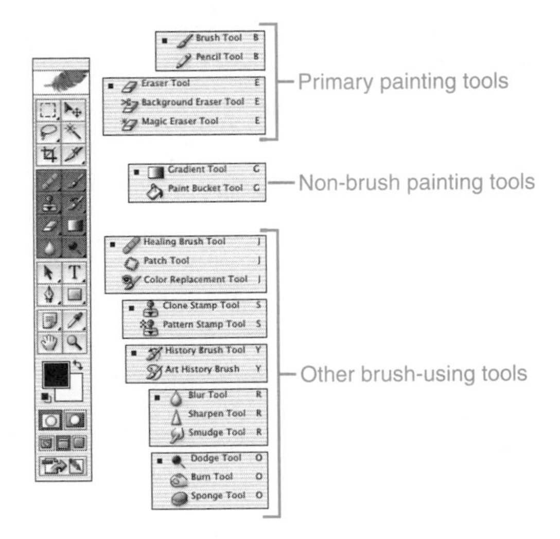


**Figure 13.1**
These tools are grouped in the Toolbox because they use brushes, are painting tools, or are related to a tool that falls into either category.

## Basic Painting Terms and Concepts

Before we start a discussion of painting capabilities in Photoshop, certain terms must be clarified:

- **Airbrush**—Airbrush is an option for the Brush and Eraser tools. It enables the tool to function much like a traditional airbrush, regulating the application of color through movement of the tool.
- **Angle**—Changing the angle of a nonround brush tip produces a calligraphic tool. The line you create changes shape, depending on the direction you drag the tool. (See also *brush tip.*)
- **Blending**—The painting tools can have assigned blending modes. The selected mode determines how color applied by the tool interacts with color already applied to that layer.
- **Brush**—The Brush is Photoshop's primary painting tool.
- **Brush tip**—Selected from and customized in the Brushes palette, the brush tip determines the area affected by the brush-using tools. (Using the Brushes palette is discussed thoroughly in "The Brushes Palette," later in this chapter.) A variety of characteristics can be modified, as you'll learn throughout this chapter.
- **Diameter**—Using the Brushes palette, you can scale any brush tip—round, square, or otherwise. The Diameter slider controls the size of the brush tip.
- **Dynamics**—These are settings that control variations in the brush tip as the tool is used.
- **Hardness**—Available only for round (or elliptical) brush tips, the Hardness setting (0%–100%) determines the sharpness of a brush tip's edges. The higher the setting, the sharper the edge. The lower the setting, the greater the feathering of the edges. The term *soft-edged brush* is often used to describe a tool using a brush tip with a low Hardness setting. Hardness is used only with round brushes.
- **Instance or brush instance**—An *instance* is a single impression of the selected brush tip. If the selected tip is round, a circle results from a single instance. If a custom brush is selected, you get a single impression of the artwork from which you defined the brush. (See also *shape* and *spacing.*)
- **Jitter**—Used with several settings in the Brushes palette, *jitter* can be defined as variation or change. When jitter is greater than 0%, you introduce variation in the placement or appearance of the individual instances of a brush's tip.
- **Media Brushes**—Brush tips that simulate traditional painting techniques and effects include the media brushes, which replicate the behavior of such media as charcoal, crayon, and watercolor, among others.
- **Paintbrush**—See *brush.*
- **Roundness**—Brush tips designed in the Brushes palette can be round or elliptical. Roundness (0%–100%) determines the relationship between width and height of all brush tips, not just round tips.

- **Scattering**—Scattering refers to the distribution of the individual instances of the brush tip along the path of the brush. Instead of aligning each mark left by the brush tip along the path of the cursor, Scattering enables you to vary them along the cursor's path.
- **Shape**—Clicking the mouse with a brush-using tool active is comparable to tapping the point of a pencil on paper. The mark created is the *shape* of the tip (see also *instance*). A brush tip can be round or elliptical when created in the Brushes palette, or it can be any other shape or pattern when created from artwork via the menu command Edit, Define Brush.
- **Spacing**—The Spacing setting in the Brushes palette determines how closely each brush tip shape will be placed. When these shapes are placed very close together, the brush appears to create a continuous line. Actually, however, dragging the cursor with a painting tool creates a series of instances of the brush tip. When the Spacing amount is high, the individual instances are visible. (See also *instance*.)
- **Texture**—Brush tips can have a specific texture built in so that they replicate the appearance of ink or paint on a specific surface.
- **Tip**—See *brush tip*.

# The Primary Painting Tools

The Brush and the Pencil tools use brushes to define the area where they will affect the image. As you drag the tool in the image window, the foreground color is added to the image within the area defined by the brush, according to the opacity and blending mode specified in the Options Bar.

*For specific information on selecting and defining brushes, see "The Brushes Palette," p. 446, later in this chapter.*

## Opacity and Blending for Painting Tools

The opacity of the tool is *combined with* the opacity of the layer on which you use it. Compare the contents on the two upper layers in Figure 13.2. On the left side of the image, the Brush's opacity is 50%, and the layer's opacity is 50%. On the right, the Brush's opacity is again 50%, but the layer's opacity is 100%.

Unlike opacity, the blending modes of the tool and the layer are not combined. Rather, the opacity of the Brush or Pencil tool is applied only on that layer—the tool's blending mode affects how it interacts with colors already on the layer, and then the layer's blending mode determines how the layer interacts with those below. The exception is Dissolve, which appears to interact with lower layers, regardless of the layer's blending mode. Dissolve, however, is less a blending mode and more a dispersal pattern.

> The contextual menu gives you instant access to the Brushes palette. You can also change blending modes by holding down the Shift key when you open the contextual menu. Remember, too, that Mac OS X, like Windows, can use a multibutton mouse.

Figure 13.2
To determine the effective transparency of the Brush or Pencil tool, multiply the layer's opacity by the tool's opacity. On the left 50%×50% is 25%. On the right, 100%×50% is 50%.

*For information about Photoshop's blending modes and how they affect color, see Chapter 18, "Mastering the Blending Modes," p. 585.*

## The Brush Tool's Airbrush and Flow Options

The Options Bar for the Brush tool has, in addition to blending mode and opacity, a pair of controls. Flow is designed for use with the Airbrush option but can be used alone. The Airbrush button is to the right of the Flow field in the Options Bar (see Figure 13.3). When the Airbrush option is selected, the button appears darkened.

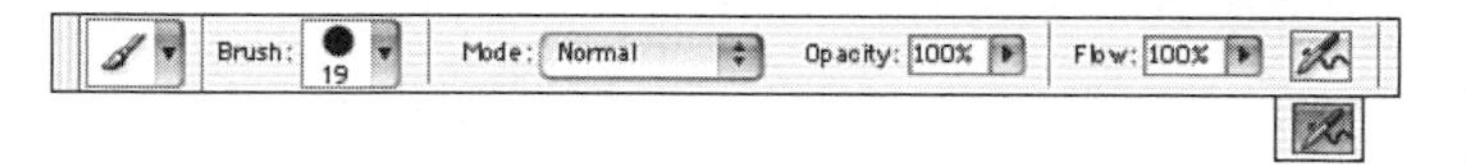

Figure 13.3
The lower Airbrush button shows you how it appears when the option is selected.



*Flow* influences how the Brush tool applies color according to the selected Spacing option. When you reduce flow, the tool treats each brush instance (using Spacing) as a separate application of the brush tip. The Flow setting is available both with and without the Airbrush option. In Figure 13.4, you can see a comparison of reduced opacity and reduced flow. In all three examples, the foreground color is black and the brush tip is set to 50% spacing.

With 50% Spacing, the brush tip is applied at an interval of one half the brush's diameter. With Flow set to 100%, the tool applies a continuous color, with the brush tip's shape (round) visible at the specified interval. With reduced flow, however, each instance of the brush tip (using Spacing) is treated as a separate application of the tool visually (not in the History palette). The areas of overlap darken, as though the Brush tool had been applied repeatedly. The appearance is the same as if you had clicked the Brush tool, moved it slightly, clicked it again, moved it slightly, clicked, and so on, with Flow set to 100%.

Figure 13.4
The brush is applied along three identical paths. At the top, the tool is set to 100% Opacity and 100% Flow. In the middle, the Opacity is reduced to 50%, with Flow at 100%. At the bottom, the Opacity is 100% and Flow is reduced to 50%.

When the Airbrush option is selected, Flow governs the density of color applied by the Brush tool. Think of it as determining how quickly "paint" is applied. The speed with which you move the cursor, in combination with the Opacity and Flow settings, governs both how wide the stroke will be and how much of the foreground color will be applied. Figure 13.5 shows basic airbrush application.

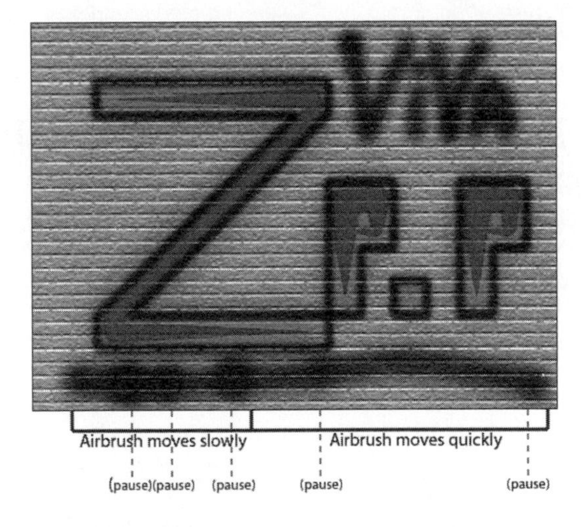


Figure 13.5
The more slowly you drag the Airbrush, the more color you apply. Where you pause the tool while dragging, color builds up.



## The Pencil Tool and Auto Erase

The Pencil tool is designed to be used with hard-edged brush tips but can be used with any brush (although the result is always hard edged). The Pencil doesn't offer the Airbrush and Flow options but does have Auto Erase (see Figure 13.6).

> Although the Hardness slider is available with round brush tips when the Pencil is active, it will have no effect on the tip. The Pencil tool *always* produces a hard-edged line.

With the Auto Erase option selected, if the center of the Pencil's cursor is over the foreground color when you drag, the tool uses the background color. If the cursor is over any color other than the foreground color, it applies the foreground color. If you click with the tool on an area of the foreground color and begin dragging, the background color is applied wherever you drag, not just over the existing foreground color.

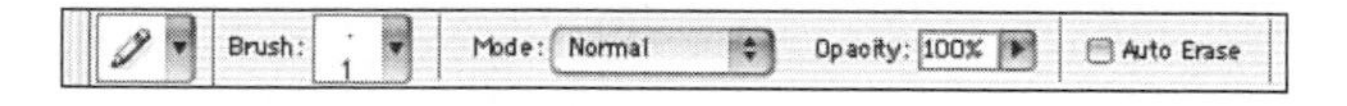


**Figure 13.6**
The term *Auto Erase* is slightly deceptive. Instead of erasing, the option enables you to replace the foreground color with the background color.

# Eraser

In a flattened image, the Eraser paints with the background color. In an image that supports transparency or on a layer above a background layer, the Eraser makes pixels over which it's dragged transparent. In the Options Bar, you can set the Eraser to use the current settings for the Brush tool, the Pencil tool, or a simple hard-edged square (called the *Block eraser*). You control opacity, flow, and the Airbrush option in the Eraser's Options Bar. You also have the option Erase to History, which uses the currently selected state of the History palette, restoring the pixels below the tool to their earlier state.

# Background Eraser

The Background Eraser erases to transparency, converting a background layer to a regular layer, as necessary. It uses the same Limits, Tolerance, and Sampling options discussed later in this chapter for the Color Replacement tool. It has one additional option: Protect Foreground Color, which enables you to designate a "safe" color that will not be erased.

*For a full explanation of Limits, Tolerance, and Sampling, see "Color Replacement Tool," later in this chapter, p. 436.*

# Magic Eraser

The Magic Eraser tool is a close relative of the Magic Wand tool. Rather than making a selection based on similarity of color among pixels, it erases based on pixel color. Click once with the tool, and pixels similar in color to those under the brush tip will be erased—not just under the brush tip, but elsewhere, too. You can limit the tool to contiguous pixels of similar colors, or you can erase similarly colored pixels throughout the layer, or even on all visible layers. Like the Magic Wand, the Background Eraser, and the Color Replacement tools, the Magic Eraser uses a Tolerance field to recognize a range of colors. The Opacity field in the Options Bar determines the transparency to which the tool will erase. When this field is set to 100%, the pixels are erased completely. When it's set to 30%, the pixels remain 70% opaque.

When editing masks, you're painting with black, white, and shades of gray. Set the Brush tool to one brush tip size and use the X key on the keyboard to switch between the foreground and background colors. Set the Eraser to a different-size brush tip and use it, in conjunction with the X key, as a different-sized Brush tool. Switch between the Eraser and the Brush with the B and E keys.

### The Art History Brush: Painting or Not?

Although it uses brushes and applies color, the Art History Brush can't quite be put into the same category as the Brush and Pencil tools. Like the History Brush, it uses data from a history state (designated in the History palette) to modify the image. Whereas the History Brush restores pixels to their previous appearance, the Art History Brush uses that earlier history state to stylize the area over which you paint. (The History Brush is often referred to as "undo in a brush," whereas the Art History Brush could be considered more of a "filter in a brush.") The following figure shows one example of how the Art History Brush can be used to create a "painterly" effect.

The original is shown in the background. The Open state (the original) is used here as the source history state. The Art History Brush applies Impressionistic brush strokes based on the designated history state.

The Art History Brush cannot use Scattering, Dual Brush, Airbrush, or Smoothing, but the Color Dynamics option is available. In addition, after using the Art History Brush, you'll find that the Edit, Fade Art History Brush command offers only the Opacity slider, not the blending modes.

Regardless of whether you classify the Art History Brush as a painting tool or as an effect-in-a-brush, you might find the tool to be more controllable at high resolution. Use the Image, Image Size command to triple the pixel dimensions and then use it again to downsample to the original size after using the Art History Brush. Remember, too, that you can copy a selection of the image to a new document, work with the Art History Brush, and then paste back into the original.



## Color Replacement Tool

The Color Replacement tool is new with Photoshop CS. It uses the foreground color to replace an existing color in the image, retaining the original luminosity. (By changing the tool's blending mode in the Options Bar, you can also work with hue, saturation, and luminosity.) It's similar to setting the Brush tool to the Color blending mode, but it does a bit better job of preserving the original luminosity. In addition, the Color Replacement tool has a variety of controls in the Options Bar that extend its flexibility (see Figure 13.7).

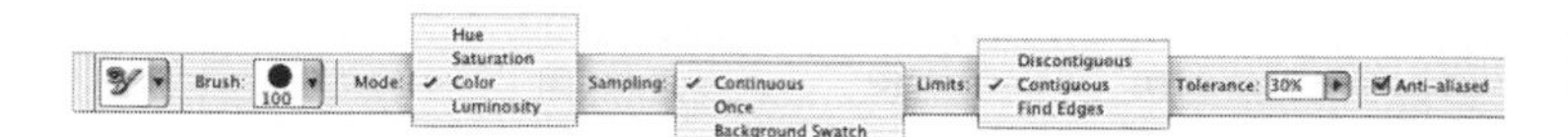


**Figure 13.7**
The additional options make the Color Replacement tool far more powerful than simply using the Color blending mode to paint.

The Color Replacement tool uses brushes, as does the Brush tool, with a full range of options. It offers the four blending modes shown in Figure 13.7. Here are the tool's additional options:

- **Sampling**—This pop-up menu governs how the Color Replacement tool determines what color should be replaced. When Sampling is set to Continuous, the Color Replacement tool replaces whatever color is below the brush with the foreground color. The Once option replaces the color in the image you first click, substituting the foreground color for it wherever you drag. When Sampling is set to Background Swatch, you tell the tool what color to change, by setting the background color in the Color palette or the Toolbox. When Sampling is set to Background Swatch, you designate the color to be replaced by choosing it as the background color in the Color palette or the Toolbox. (Click the background swatch in the Toolbox or Color palette to open the Color Picker.)
- **Limits**—Use this pop-up menu to restrict *where* the Color Replacement tool replaces color. When Limit is set to Discontinuous, the tool replaces the color anywhere it is found under the brush tip. When Contiguous is selected, it replaces the color only in pixels that are connected to each other as you drag the tool. Find Edges attempts to preserve the edges within the image.
- **Tolerance**—Use this field to control the range (based on similarity) of colors to be replaced. When set to a low tolerance, the tool will replace only colors that are quite similar to the sampled or designated color. At higher settings, more variations of the color will be replaced.
- **Antialiased**—As with other tools and features in Photoshop, antialiasing is used with the Color Replacement tool to smooth the transition between colors.

Use the Color Replacement tool's Find Edges option in conjunction with the Sampling option Once or Background Color. If you use Continuous with Find Edges, every time you drag over an edge, the tool will resample and start replacing that new color across the edge.

## Photoshop at Work: Exploring the Color Replacement Tool

Photoshop CS's new Color Replacement tool is a bit of a hybrid. It combines the Background Eraser's capability of identifying color as you drag with the Color blending mode's capability to change color without affecting tonality. Think, if you will, of the Replace Color adjustment in a brush. It's certainly a feature that's worth exploring, which is what you do in the following exercise:

Because the Color Replacement tool does such a good job at preserving luminosity, it is impossible to show examples of the tool's work in grayscale images.

1. In Photoshop, open the file Waterfall(16bit).tif from the Samples folder inside the Photoshop folder.

2. Select the Color Replacement tool from the Toolbox (nested below the Healing Brush and the Patch tool). In the Options Bar, select a 70-pixel brush with a Hardness of 50%. Set Mode to Color, Sampling to Once, Limits to Contiguous, and Tolerance to 20%.
3. Set your foreground color to a dark brown. (The final swatch in the Swatches palette is a fine choice.)
4. Click the image in the center of the foliage in the lower-right corner and drag the Color Replacement tool around the greenery there; then drag straight across the water and paint the foliage across the stream. Do this in a single drag, without releasing the mouse button.
5. Undo. Change the Limits pop-up menu to Discontiguous and then click and drag through the same area.
6. Undo. Change the Sampling field from Once to Continuous and again drag through the foliage on both sides of the stream. Note the difference in the tool's behavior as you cross the water.
7. Undo. Switch to the Eyedropper tool, set it to 5×5 Average in the Options Bar, hold down the (Option) [Alt] key, and click the foliage near the point where you've been starting to drag. That sets the background color to green.
8. Change back to the Color Replacement tool and in the Options Bar, set Mode to Color, Sampling to Background Swatch, and Limits to Contiguous. Leave Tolerance at 20%.
9. Drag through your usual path once again.
10. Undo. Change the Tolerance to 30% and repeat the drag one final time.

Now that you've seen for yourself what the major features of this tool are, you can likely imagine its power to quickly and easily make changes in an image. Replace the color of a dress or a shirt? No problem. Simply set Sampling to Once and set Limits to Find Edges, and you probably only need to click and drag from a couple different places to change the entire garment. A studio backdrop? Setting Sampling to Continuous might be the best choice. As you work with this tool, you'll become more comfortable with the options and, who knows, you might start using the Background Eraser as well!

## The Non-Brush Painting Tools



Photoshop includes two other tools that can be considered "painting" tools: the Paint Bucket tool and the Gradient tool. Both tools add color to the image but do so in ways that don't use brushes.

### The Paint Bucket

The Paint Bucket applies the foreground color or a pattern to the image. By default, it fills all contiguous pixels of the clicked color with the foreground color. The Options Bar enables you to select a pattern for the fill, deselect the Contiguous option, and choose a blending mode and opacity for the tool. In addition, you can set the Tolerance field to specify how closely colors must match to be filled with the

> To constrain the Paint Bucket to a certain part of an image, you can make a selection first, enclosing the areas of color you want to change.

Paint Bucket. The Paint Bucket can be antialiased, and you can elect to fill a target color on all layers or just the active layer.

## The Anatomy of a Gradient

*Gradients* are areas of multiple colors that smoothly blend from one color to the next. No matter how many colors are assigned to the gradient, only adjacent colors will blend (see Figure 13.8).

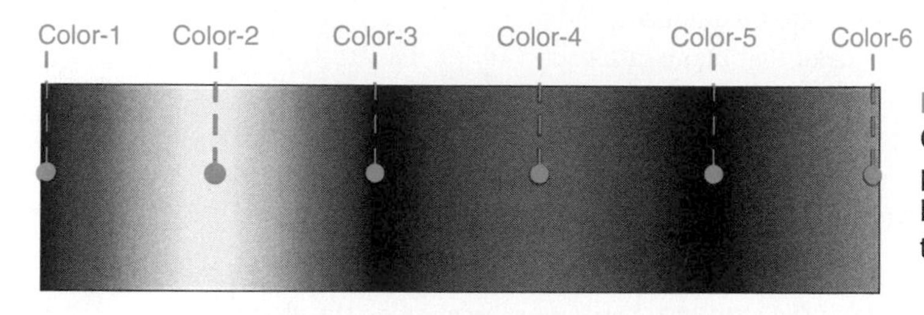


**Figure 13.8**
Color-1 blends to Color-2, but not past it. In no case does a color blend through an adjacent color to the color beyond.

The structure of a gradient is defined in the Gradient Editor. To open the Gradient Editor dialog box, select the Gradient tool in the Toolbox and then click the sample of the gradient in the Options Bar (see Figure 13.9).

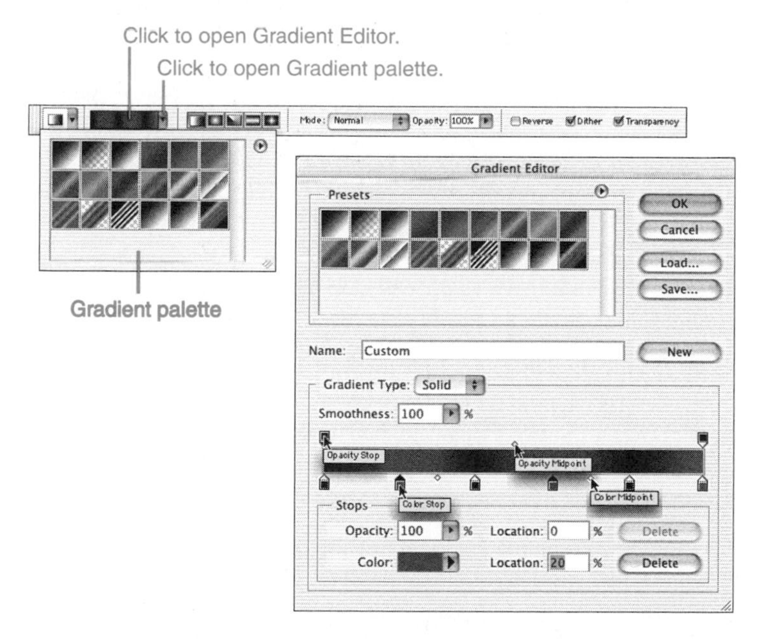


**Figure 13.9**
Click the arrow to the right in the Options Bar to open the Gradient palette; click the gradient itself to open the Gradient Editor.

Although the Gradient Editor might appear to be complicated, it's actually reasonably simple. The upper portion shows all the gradients currently available in the Gradient palette. You can click any one to use it as the basis for your custom gradient. Note that to the left of the OK button is a little triangle that gives you access to the Gradient palette menu, including view options and several sets of predefined gradients that you can load into the palette. (Try viewing the gradients in Small List view. In addition to the sample, you'll see the name.)

Here are the options available to you in the dialog box as you edit gradients:

- **Load and Save**—Sets of gradients can be saved and loaded into the Gradient Editor and Gradient palette. Photoshop CS, by default, installs several sets of gradients in the Presets folder in your Photoshop folder.
- **Gradient Type**—You can create the familiar Solid gradients, which are bands of color that blend into each other, or you can create Noise gradients. A *Noise gradient* uses a randomly generated series of colors within parameters you set. (See "Noise Gradients" later in this chapter for more information.)

As soon as you open the Gradient Editor, Photoshop automatically activates the Eyedropper tool, which enables you to quickly and easily assign colors from anywhere onscreen. Remember that you can click in your image, keep the mouse button down, and drag to any color, anywhere on your screen (not just in Photoshop), to sample that color.

- **Smoothness**—Smoothness, which ranges from 0%–100%, governs the abruptness of the transition between colors in the gradient. The lower the number, the sharper the transition. At the highest settings, the transition is gradual. The Smoothness setting is universal for the gradient—you can't specify different Smoothness values for different parts of the gradient. You can, however, create a sharper transition by using two color stops of the same color next to each other on either end of the transition. Positioning the middle two stops close together creates a sharper transition.
- **Opacity Stop**—Opacity stops regulate the transparency for a particular section of the gradient. To add a stop, click above the sample gradient. To duplicate an existing stop, hold down the (Option) [Alt] key and drag the stop to the new location. When a stop is selected, the little triangle of the slider is filled. Unselected stops have hollow triangles. At the bottom of the Gradient Editor, you can input numeric values for a selected stop's opacity and location. The arrow to the right of the Opacity field opens a slider. The Location field represents the distance from the left end of the gradient, in percent. You can remove an opacity stop by dragging it straight up or down, away from the gradient sample.
- **Opacity Midpoint**—Located above the gradient you're editing, the opacity midpoint represents the point between two opacity stops where their influence is balanced. By default, the midpoint is at the 50% point, halfway between the two stops. You can, however, drag the stop to a new location or click it to make it active (the diamond is filled for the active midpoint) and specify a numeric value for the position in the Location field.
- **Color Stop**—Color stops, located below the gradient you're editing, are the heart of the Gradient Editor. You use them to assign colors to the gradient and to determine where the blends occur (via the Location field or by dragging the color stops). As with an opacity stop, you click a color stop to make it active. Also like an opacity stop, the color stop's triangle becomes black when selected. You click the color swatch to open the Color Picker. Alternatively, you can assign the foreground color or the background color by using the triangle to the right of the Color field. When Foreground or Background is selected from the menu, the gradient automatically assumes the appropriate color from the Color palette when selected. You can also designate the color as User Color from the menu, in which case the color remains static, regardless of the current foreground and background colors.

- **Color Midpoint**—As with an opacity midpoint, the diamonds between color stops determine where the blending is balanced. You can skew a blend toward one or the other color stop, or you can accept the default value of 50%, which balances the blend between the two stops.

*Unsure about how the Foreground and Background designations affect gradients? See "Auto Gradients" in the "Mastering Photoshop" section at the end of this chapter.*

## Working with Gradients

Gradients can be applied to selections or the active layer. The Gradient tool has five variations, which you can select through the Options Bar (see Figure 13.10). They differ in the pattern used to apply the selected gradient.

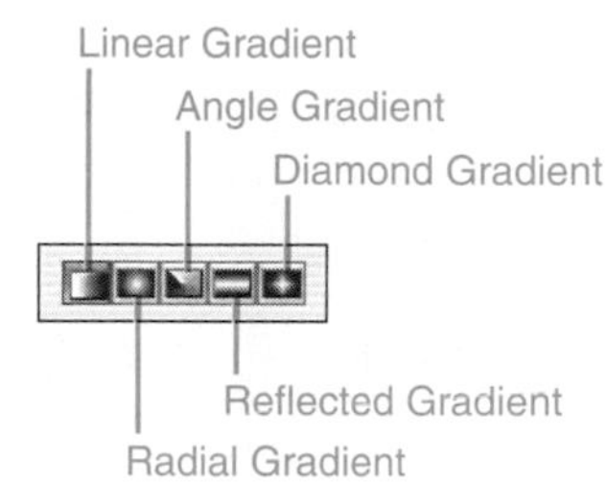


**Figure 13.10**
The five gradient variations all apply the selected gradient; they just apply it in different directions.

The appearance of the gradient depends both on which tool is selected in the Options Bar and on how you drag the tool through the selection or layer. Here are the basic capabilities of the five gradient tools:

- **Linear Gradient tool**—When you drag a linear gradient, the colors are distributed perpendicularly to the line of drag (see Figure 13.11, top left). The distribution of color starts where the drag begins, and it ends where the button is released (or stylus lifted). Any selected areas outside the drag are filled with the first and last colors of the gradient (or transparency, if built in to the gradient). Everything before the drag is the first color; everything after is the last color. The Linear Gradient tool is typically dragged all the way across a selection.
- **Radial Gradient tool**—The colors in the gradient form concentric circles from the start to the end of the drag (see Figure 13.11, top center). Any areas beyond the drag are filled with the last color. Remember that transparency in the gradient and selections can limit the outer fill. The Radial Gradient tool is typically dragged from the center (or somewhat off center) of a selection to the edge.
- **Angle Gradient tool**—The Angle Gradient tool "wraps" the gradient around the line of drag (see Figure 13.11, top right). Consider the line of drag to be the minute hand of a clock. The gradient is applied clockwise, centering on the point where you start the drag. Like the Radial Gradient tool, the Angle Gradient tool is typically dragged from the center to the edge of a selection.

- **Reflected Gradient tool**—The Reflected Gradient tool produces the same gradient extending outward from either side of the line of drag (see Figure 13.11, bottom center). Think of the start of the drag as the point from which the reflection will begin and the length and direction of drag as the extent of the gradient. For that reason, the Reflected Gradient tool is typically dragged from the center of a selection outward.
- **Diamond Gradient tool**—The Diamond Gradient tool is somewhat of a cross between the Reflected Gradient and Angle Gradient tools (see Figure 13.11, bottom right). Multiple copies of the gradient are produced (like the Reflected Gradient tool), but they rotate around the line of drag (like the Angle Gradient tool). Regardless of the shape of the selection, the Diamond Gradient tool always produces gradients along straight lines. Note that in the sample image, if the tool had been dragged to a side of the selection rather than a corner, the pattern would be a diamond rather than a square—picture the gradient rotated 90° with the square selection remaining oriented to the page.

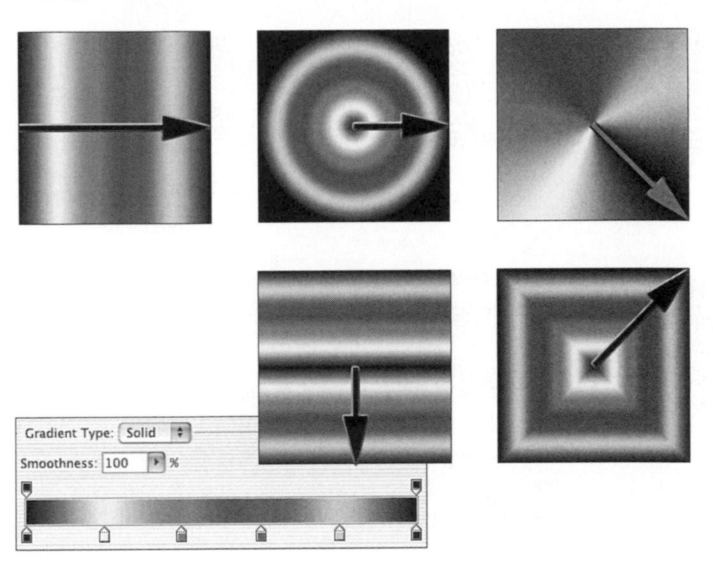


**Figure 13.11**
In the top row, you see gradients made (from left to right) with the Linear Gradient, Radial Gradient, and Angle Gradient tools. The second row gradients demonstrate the Reflected Gradient tool (left) and the Diamond Gradient tool (right). The arrows show the start and direction of drag. The sample gradient is shown in the lower-left corner.



The Options Bar offers three additional gradient tool options. Reverse simply switches the order of the colors in the gradient. (You can simply drag the Linear Gradient tool in the opposite direction, but the same trick doesn't work with the other four tools.) Dither helps reduce banding in very large gradients and for gradients in images that will be changed to Indexed Color mode. The Transparency option works with opacity stops in the gradient. If the gradient is designed with reduced opacity at one or more places, this check box must be selected to accurately apply the gradient. If the option is not selected, transparency in the gradient is ignored, and the adjacent colors are used at 100% opacity.

## Shading with Gradients

Gradients, especially those using black, white, and shades of gray, can be very valuable for simulating depth and 3D. Figure 13.12 shows three examples. The book and the spheres use simple linear and radial gradients, respectively. The boot was created in Adobe Illustrator using a gradient mesh.

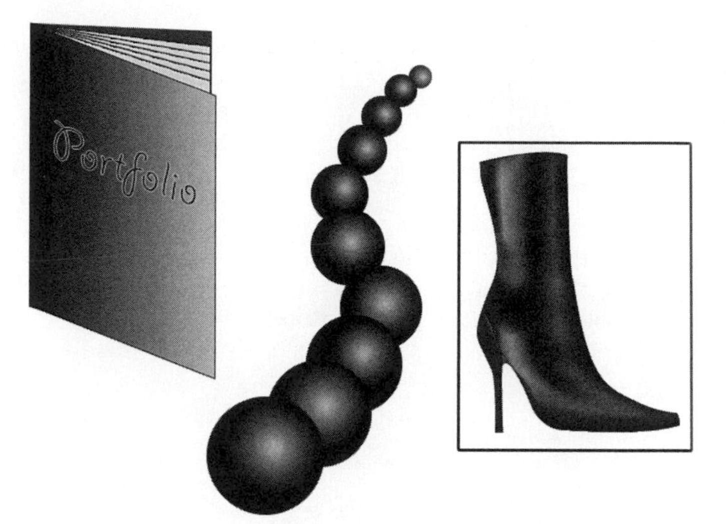


Figure 13.12
Although it's certainly possible to re-create the boot in Photoshop, you'd have to make quite a few selections and apply many gradients individually.

*To learn about Illustrator's more powerful gradient-handling capability, see Chapter 33, "Working with Gradients and Gradient Meshes" in the Adobe Illustrator section of this book, p. 985.*

## Noise Gradients

Instead of blending between pairs of colors, noise gradients are patterns of color that Photoshop selects at random, from within parameters you specify. When you select Noise for the Gradient Editor's Gradient Type setting, the dialog box changes (see Figure 13.13).

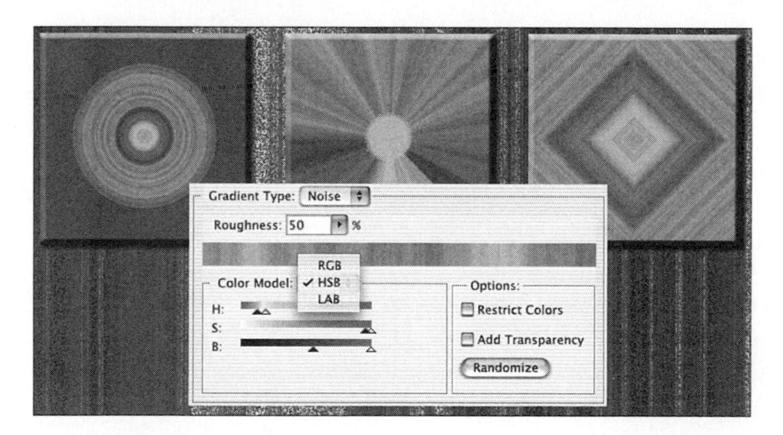


Figure 13.13
Several noise gradient examples are visible, including the background.

Use the Roughness slider to specify the spread of the individual colors within the noise gradient (0%–100%). High settings result in definite, identifiable stripes of color, and very low settings can smooth the gradient to the point where the noise isn't apparent (see Figure 13.14).

**Caution**

High Roughness levels with nonlinear gradients (or linear gradients at an angle) can produce severe pixelation.

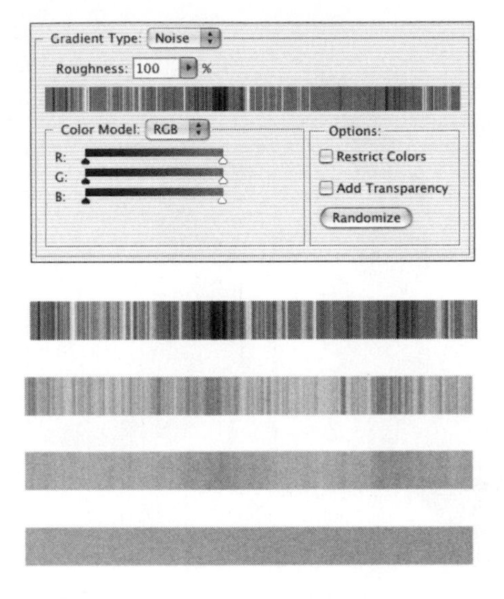


Figure 13.14
The only difference among the upper gradients is the Roughness setting. The lowest gradient shows a Roughness setting of 0% with a broader range of colors.

Use the Color Model pop-up menu to determine how you define the color range for the noise gradient. HSB and Lab are more appropriate for gradients that concentrate the colors within a specific range. RGB is better for noise gradients with a large variety of colors. If you switch color models, the sliders remain in position—they do not shift to select comparable values because the color models do not have comparable sliders.

The Restrict Colors option prevents oversaturation of colors, which keeps most colors within the CMYK gamut. The Add Transparency option introduces variable opacity to the gradient. When you click the Randomize button, the gradient is regenerated with the specified settings—if you don't see a gradient you like, keep clicking Randomize until the sample shows a gradient that is close to your needs. You can fine-tune by dragging the sliders after Randomize has created a gradient.

To create a grayscale noise gradient, use HSB color mode and drag both triangles for the S slider all the way to the left—no saturation produces gray.

## Other Brush-Using Tools

A variety of other tools in Photoshop also use brushes. The basic concepts of brushes remain the same, but some of the brush options do not apply. The specific options are discussed later in this chapter and the various tools elsewhere in the book. Here is a summary of which brush options are available for the various brush-using tools:

- **Healing Brush**—Only the Brush Tip Shape options can be modified for the Healing Brush. Access the options through the mini Brushes palette at the left of the Options Bar rather than the full-size Brushes palette.
- **Clone Stamp and Pattern Stamp**—All brush options except Color Dynamics and Smoothing are available for both of these tools.

Remember that the New button adds your noise gradient to the palette, just as with any other gradient, making it available for future use. But also keep in mind that the gradient isn't saved until you use the Save button.

- **History Brush**—All brush options except Color Dynamics are available for the History Brush.
- **Eraser tools**—The Eraser cannot use Color Dynamics and Wet Edges. The Background Eraser uses only Brush Tip Shape variables, accessed through the Options Bar rather than the Brushes palette. (The Magic Eraser is not a brush-using tool; rather, it relies on a Tolerance setting, as the Magic Wand does.)
- **Focus tools**—The Blur and Sharpen tools can be adjusted for Brush Tip Shape, Shape Dynamics, Scattering, Strength Jitter (Other Dynamics), and Noise. The Smudge tool uses Brush Tip Shape, Shape Dynamics, and Strength Jitter.
- **Toning tools**—The Dodge, Burn, and Sponge tools are adjustable for all brush options except Color Dynamics and Opacity Jitter (Other Dynamics).

In place of Flow Jitter (Other Dynamics), you will see Strength Jitter and Exposure Jitter for tools whose options are so named.

# The Paint Commands

Two menu commands and two palette commands serve as "painting commands." In the Edit menu, you'll find both Fill and Stroke. The Stroke command is available only when there's an active selection in the image. Each command opens a dialog box, shown in Figure 13.15.

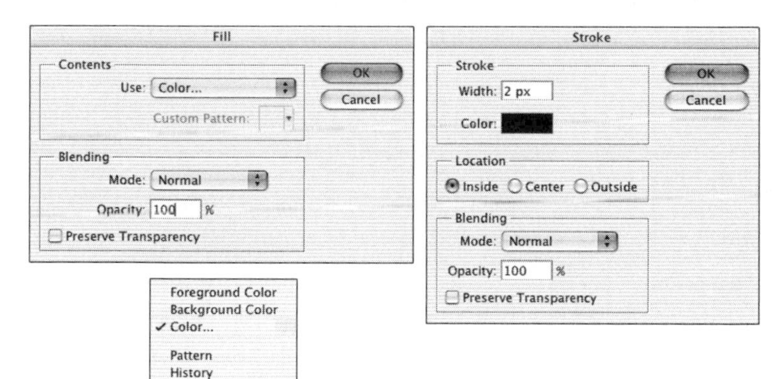


**Figure 13.15**
The menu below the Fill dialog box shows the basic choices for the Use option.



Both the Edit, Fill command and the Edit, Stroke command respect antialiasing and feathering of the selection. With the Stroke command, feathering overrides the specified stroke width. If, for example, you stroke a heavily feathered selection with a 1-pixel width, the resulting stroke fades gradually over a distance of several dozen pixels.

When stroking a selection with sharply angled corners, you may find that the corners are rounded off. To maintain the crispness of the corners, use a slightly larger selection and select Inside as the stroke location.

The Paths palette menu has its own Stroke and Fill commands. These commands are available only with an active path in the Paths palette. They can be used with work paths or saved paths and vector clipping masks, but they are not available for shape layer vector masks. Paths can be stroked with any of the brush-using tools. The tool's current settings and the foreground color are used.

When you're filling a path, the Contents and Blending options are the same as when filling a selection. However, filling a path also enables you to specify antialiasing and/or feathering for the fill. This is comparable to converting the path to a selection, feathering the selection, and then filling.

When stroking a path, instead of specifying a width and location in relation to a selection border, you choose a tool. The command then uses the brush, blending mode, and opacity currently selected for that tool.

Buttons at the bottom of the Paths palette enable you to convert selections to paths and paths to selections.

Set up a brush-using tool before using the Paths palette menu command Stroke Path. Also, remember that the focus, toning, stamp, and history tools, as well as the new Color Replacement tool, can be applied along a stroke.

# THE BRUSHES PALETTE

The Brushes palette is the heart of Photoshop's painting capabilities. This palette is the doorway to an exciting level of creativity in Photoshop. Understanding how the palette works—and what it offers—is the key to that doorway. New in Photoshop CS are "locks" that can be used to maintain a brush attribute, even when you switch brush tips. This section looks at the Brushes palette layout and its menu.

## The Palette Layout

Like the Layer Style dialog box, the Brushes palette's Expanded View mode uses a two-column configuration (see Figure 13.16).

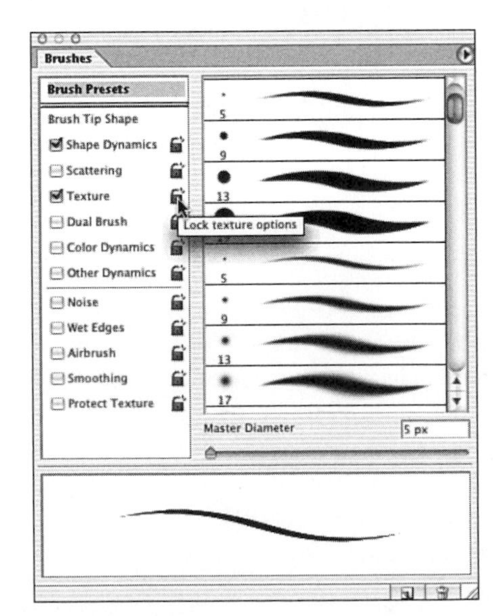


Figure 13.16
Use the palette's menu to select and deselect the Expanded View. When Expanded View is not selected, only the brush thumbnails or names are visible. Note the new "lock" icon, which preserves the current settings for each category.

As in the Layer Style dialog box, you click a heading in the left column to show its options in the right column. (A preview is shown at the bottom.) Also like in the Layer Style dialog box, you can click a check box on the left to activate the option with the current settings (and uncheck the box to disable those options). To see the settings, however, you must click the name.

If the Brushes palette content is grayed out and unavailable, select a brush-using tool from the Toolbox. You can also use keyboard shortcuts to activate a tool, such as B for the Brush tool.

## The Brushes Palette Menu

To access the Brushes palette menu when the palette is docked in the Palette Well, click the arrow in the Brushes tab. When the palette is free-floating in a window, click the triangle in the upper-right corner of the palette. The only difference in the menu between the configurations is the Dock to Palette Well command, which is logically not available when the palette is already docked (see Figure 13.17).

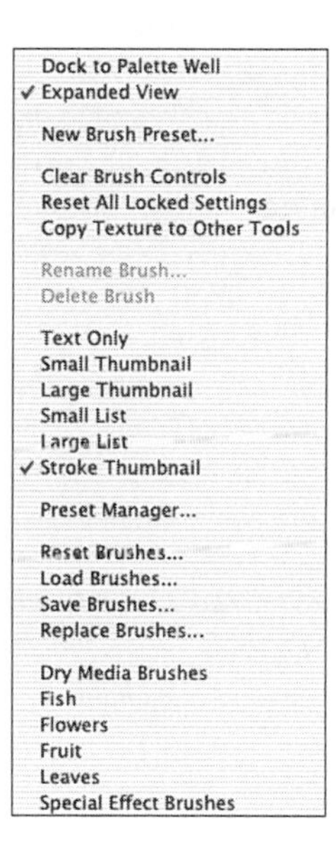


**Figure 13.17**
The list of brush sets at the bottom of the menu contains all the sets available in the Presets, Brushes folder in the Photoshop folder.

Although most of the menu commands are straightforward, a few require additional clarification.

13

## Expanded View

The default Expanded View mode for the Brushes palette, seen earlier in this section, enables you to customize brushes using all the brush options. If you have already created all the brushes you'll need and selected their options, you can simplify the palette by deselecting this option from the menu.

The six configurations shown in Figure 13.18 are the same six available in the Expanded View mode for the right column of the Brushes palette.

When Expanded View is not selected, the Brushes palette reverts to a simplified version, similar to that in ImageReady, in any of the six configurations listed in the menu (see Figure 13.18).

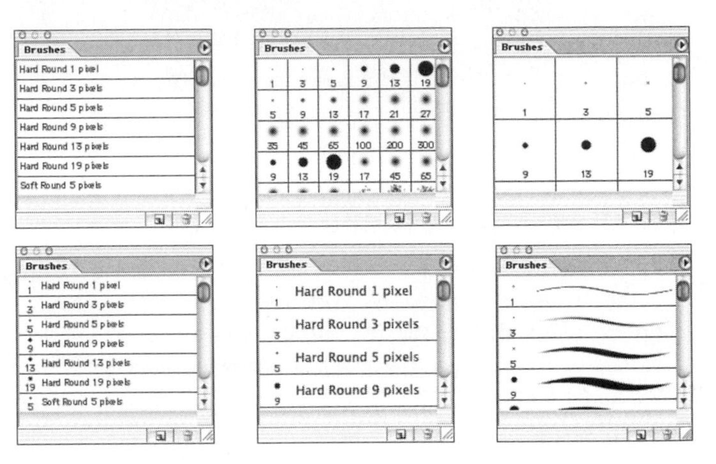


**Figure 13.18**
From left to right, top to bottom, the configurations are Text Only, Small Thumbnail, Large Thumbnail, Small List, Large List, and Stroke Thumbnail.

You select a preset brush by clicking it. Double-clicking enables you to change the brush's name. The content of the palette can be changed by using the palette's menu, but in the simplified view, the brushes themselves cannot be edited.

## Clear Brush Controls

The Clear Brush Controls command deselects all the user-definable settings for the selected brush. The brush reverts to the basic brush tip shape, using the Angle, Roundness, Hardness, and Spacing settings with which it was originally defined. (See "Brush Settings, Pane by Pane," later in this chapter, for specific information about each of the options.)

Clearing the controls does not permanently change the brush, but you can clear the controls and then use the New Brush command to save the changes.

*Cleared a brush's controls and can't reset them? See "Restoring Cleared Brush Controls" in the "Mastering Photoshop" section at the end of this chapter.*

## Copy Texture to Other Tools

When you painstakingly prepare a texture for a specific brush, you can use the New Brush command to save your work. However, if you quickly whip up a texture for a little touch-up to an image, you might want to simply use the Copy Texture to Other Tools command to make that texture available for the editing job at hand. For example, if you match the grain of an image for the Burn tool, instead of going through the process again for the Dodge tool, you can use this command. The tools to which the texture will be matched are Brush, Pencil, Eraser, Clone Stamp, Pattern Stamp, History Brush, Art History Brush, Dodge, Burn, and Sponge.

Copying a custom texture doesn't *apply* it to the other tools; rather, it makes the texture available to the tools. If you change tools, you might still need to open the Brushes palette and select the Texture check box to activate your custom texture.

## Preset Manager

This command opens the Preset Manager, which enables you to customize the content of the Brushes palette. You can also open the Preset Manager through the Edit menu. Customizing the Brushes palette can streamline the search for the appropriate brush. Remember, too, that you can save sets of brushes that can be loaded through the Brushes palette menu or selected as the default in the Preset Manager.

# BRUSH SETTINGS, PANE BY PANE

In the Expanded View, the brushes palette contains eight different panes or windows, and an additional five options that have no variables. Each pane is selected in the left frame or column of the palette, and the variables appear on the right. At the bottom of the palette is a preview that updates automatically as you change settings. Remember that you can click a check box to activate or deactivate a set of options, or you can click directly on the name to open the options pane (see Figure 13.19).

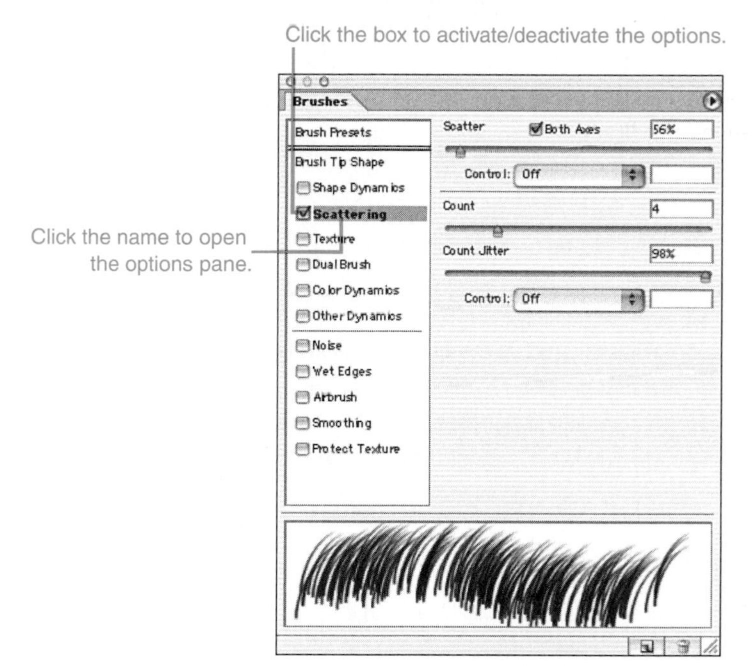


**Figure 13.19**
The five lowest entries in the left column do not have separate panes because they have no variables to change. Clicking the name or the check box activates/deactivates the option.

13

*Can't find the Brushes palette options? See "Expanding the Brushes Palette" in the "Mastering Photoshop" section at the end of this chapter.*

## Brush Presets

At the top of the left column in the Brushes palette is the Brush Presets option. Click the name to open the current palette contents in the right column (see Figure 13.20). (Note that there is no check box for Brush Presets—this is not an option but rather a pane in which you select from the available brushes.)

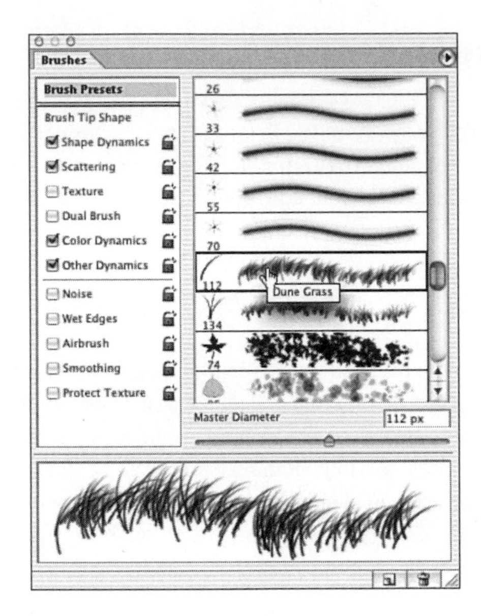


Figure 13.20
The preview window does not show the brush to scale beyond 48 pixels in diameter.

To change the content of Brush Presets, use the following palette menu commands:

- **Reset Brushes**—Restores the default set as specified in Preset Manager
- **Load Brushes**—Adds to or replaces the content of the palette
- **Save Brushes**—Creates a set that can be loaded at another time
- **Replace Brushes**—Deletes the current content and adds a different set of brushes

The Brush Presets pane is the only one in which these menu commands are active. You can delete and rename individual brushes by using the palette menu.

After you have selected a brush, you can adjust its size by using the Master Diameter slider in the Brush Presets pane. You can also move to other panes of the Brushes palette to modify the brush's appearance and behavior.

13

## Brush Tip Shape

The Brush Tip Shape pane includes thumbnails of the brushes currently loaded in the palette (which can make the Brush Presets pane unnecessary when working with brushes that are already loaded). Click a thumbnail to select the brush. You can then modify the Diameter, Angle, Roundness, Hardness (for round brush tips only), and Spacing values by entering numeric values or, for three of the options, by using sliders. As you can see to the right in Figure 13.21, you can also modify the angle (top) and roundness (bottom) by dragging the anchors in the small preview window.

When you're experimenting with the various brush capabilities, it's easiest to see what each does when you disable all the others. For example, when determining optimal spacing for a brush tip, uncheck the dynamics options in the Brushes palette.

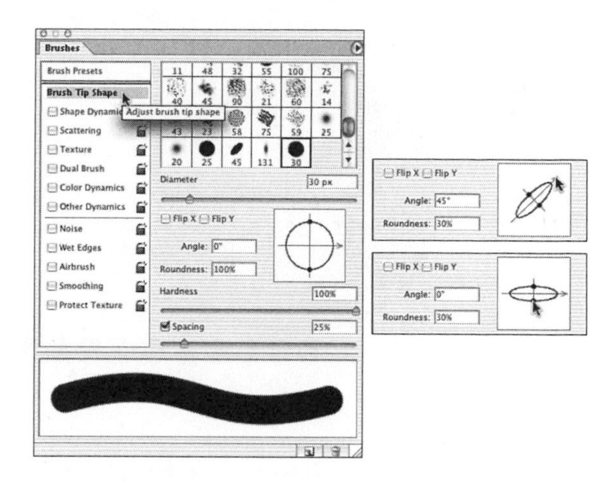


Figure 13.21
The Hardness slider determines feathering for the brush tip. It is available only for round brushes.

When a custom or square brush is selected, the Use Sample Size button is available above the Diameter slider in Brush Tip Shape. You can click it to reset the brush to the size at which it was designed.

New in Photoshop CS are the Flip X and Flip Y check boxes. In Figure 13.22, you can see that they use the vertical and horizontal axes determined by the Angle field.

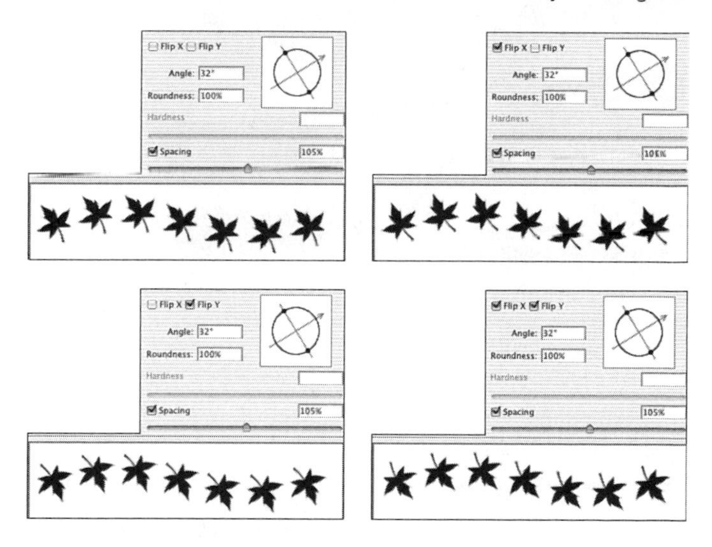


Figure 13.22
Flip X and Flip Y are best visualized with Spacing set beyond 100%.



The Spacing variable determines the distance between instances of the brush tip. Rather than as a continuous flow of ink from a pen, think of Photoshop's brushes as a series of imprints of the brush tip (see Figure 13.23).

When the brush tip instances are very closely spaced, they overlap, and you see what appears to be a continuous line of color. When spacing is increased, you see the individual instances (see Figure 13.24).

Figure 13.23
Instead of as a continuous stream of ink, think of the brush as a stamp or pattern wheel.

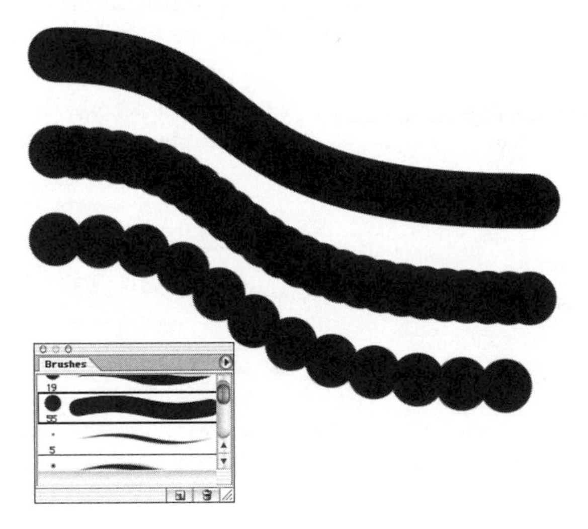


Figure 13.24
From the top, three identical paths are stroked with a 55-pixel hard round brush with a Spacing setting of 1%, 40%, and 83%, respectively.



When the Spacing option is turned off in the Brush Tip Shape pane of the Brushes palette, the spacing is governed by the speed of your drag. The faster you drag, the greater the spacing (see Figure 13.25).

> You can create dashed lines in Photoshop. Select a square brush of the appropriate size, reduce the Roundness setting to 10%–25%, and increase the Spacing variable to 110%–200%. Shift-drag (or click and Shift-click) to create straight dashed lines.

## Controlling the Dynamic Options

Before we discuss the additional Brushes palette panes, an explanation of the Control pop-up menus is appropriate. Many of the options explained in the following sections are "dynamic" options—they produce variations in the placement or appearance of the brush instances as the brush is used.

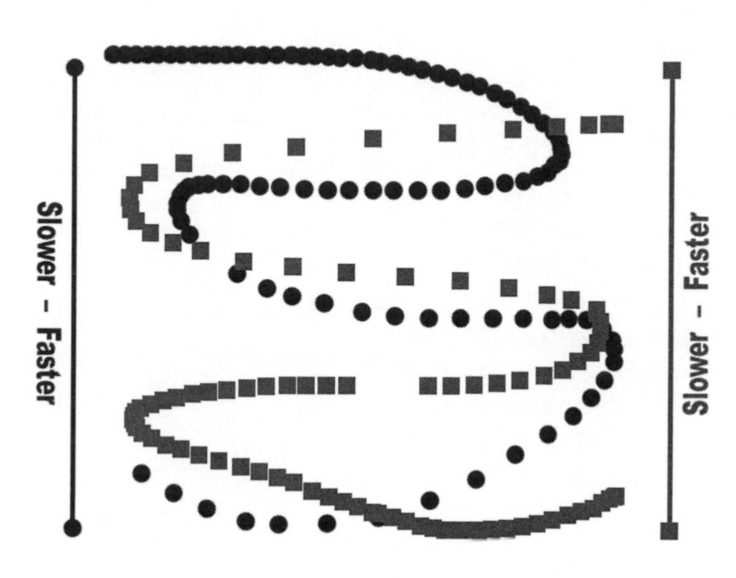


Figure 13.25
As indicated, the mouse is dragged at increasing speed through the curves.

The variety of brush instances adds a randomness to the stroke that would be time consuming to create manually. Photoshop enables you to exercise even more control over the "randomness" of the variations when you use a drawing tablet.

## Off

When Control is set to Off, Photoshop applies the selected jitter randomly and throughout the length of the brush stroke. The stroke is unregulated.

## Fade

You can use the Fade option to taper off the dynamic effect on the brush. Fade is available with or without a pressure-sensitive tablet. When Fade is selected, the field immediately to the right of the Control pop-up menu is active. You specify a value between 1 and 9999. If you set a jitter slider to 0% and specify a value, the Fade command specifies either the value to which the stroke fades or when the specific jitter ends along the stroke. Figure 13.26 shows the difference.

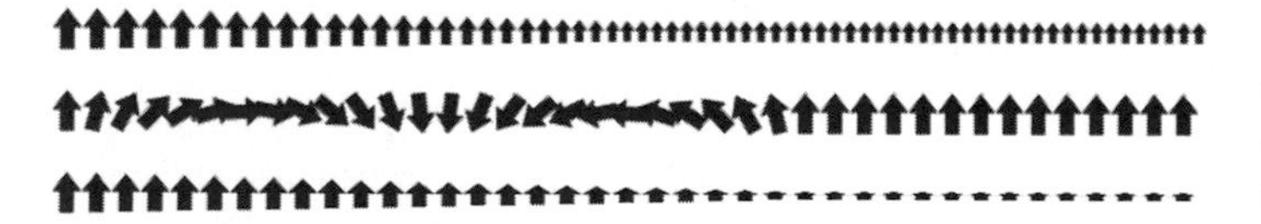

Figure 13.26
All three examples use the same brush, with Fade set to 25. Only one jitter option is active for each. The active option in each row is (from top to bottom) Size, Angle, and Roundness.

The only difference among the three strokes shown in Figure 13.26 is one jitter setting. The brush uses the same tip and a Spacing setting of 100% to best illustrate the differences in the effects of the Fade setting. Here are the specifics:

- The top example shows Size Jitter set to 25%, with a minimum diameter of 50%. Note that the Fade option forces the brush tip size to the 50% diameter after 25 instances of the brush.
- The middle example shows a stroke with the Angle Jitter set to 0% and Control set to Fade, 25. The brush tip "angles" 360° over the first 25 instances. After completing the selected jitter, the stroke returns to its original appearance for the 26th instance and beyond.
- The bottom stroke has Roundness Jitter set to 0%, Control set to Fade with 25 as the number of steps, and a Minimum Roundness setting of 20%. Like the top example, the stroke reaches the desired roundness (20%) after 25 instances.

The best way to learn how each option works is to isolate it. Deselect all but one brush option, and set that option's jitter slider to 0% and the Control pop-up menu to Fade. Now drag the brush around a blank layer and see how it works. Remember, too, that the Spacing setting plays a large role in any brush's appearance.

For the first and third examples, the Fade field's value represents the number of instances the stroke uses to reach the value specified for the jitter. In the middle example, the stroke uses the number entered in the Fade field as the extent or duration of the jitter. You learn how these and other dynamic options work in "Shape Dynamics," later in this chapter.

## Pen Pressure

The Pen Pressure option is used with a pressure-sensitive tablet, such as those from Wacom. Increasing the pressure of the stylus on the tablet *decreases* the amount of jitter—the greater the pen's push, the less variation in the stroke. Figure 13.27 shows examples of Size, Angle, and Roundness Jitter with Pen Pressure activated.

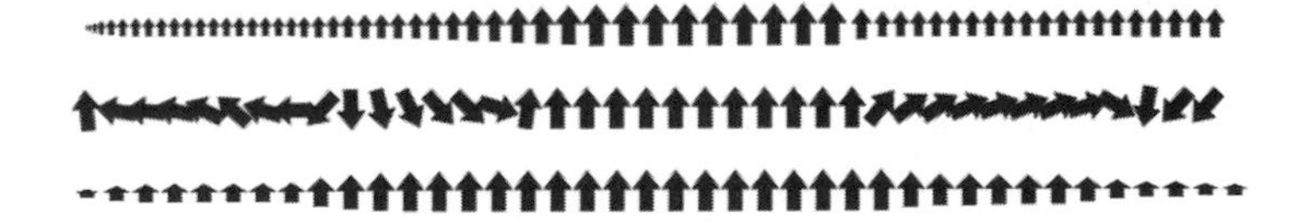

Figure 13.27
In all three examples, the pen pressure is light on the ends and heavy in the middle.

13

## Pen Tilt

Pen Tilt reads the angle rather than the pressure of the stylus on the tablet to adjust the jitter. It is especially useful for airbrush artists using the Brush tool with the Airbrush option. (Not all drawing tablets support Pen Tilt.)

## Stylus Wheel

Some tablet accessories, such as Wacom's Intuos and Intuos2 airbrushes, include a fingerwheel. When available, the wheel can be used to regulate the amount of variation when Stylus Wheel is selected in the Control pop-up menu.

## Initial Direction

Available for the Angle Jitter option only, the Initial Direction option determines the orientation of the brush instances as you drag. In Figure 13.28, the settings are identical for both examples. The Angle Jitter is set to 25%, constraining the brush angles to –90° to +90°. The top example, created from left to right, varies the angle in relation to the top of the page. The lower example, dragged from right to left, reverses the orientation.

Using an Angle Jitter of 0% and Control set to Direction keeps the brush tip oriented to the path. This is a great way to use custom brushes to draw dashed or dotted lines, borders, dividing lines, and even railroad tracks and roads.

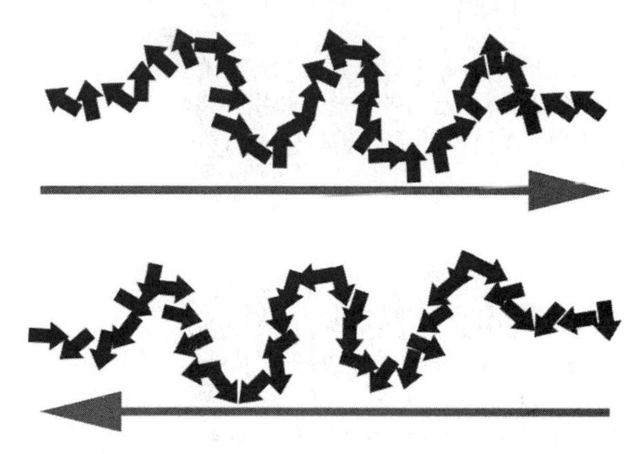

**Figure 13.28**
The 25% setting for Angle Jitter restricts the brush tip angle to one quarter of a circle (90°) in either direction from the original brush orientation.

## Direction

Also available for the Angle Jitter option only, the Direction option orients the brush tip to the path rather than to the page. In Figure 13.29, the Angle Jitter is set to 0% to best show the orientation of the brush to the paths.

**Figure 13.29**
The initial direction of drag when using Direction determines which way the brush tip instances are pointed. The two examples to the right illustrate the difference.

## Shape Dynamics

The Shape Dynamics pane of the Brushes palette, shown in Figure 13.30, controls three aspects of the stroke appearance: size, rotation, and perspective. The variations for each parameter are specified with sliders.

Examples of the shape dynamics are shown in Figure 13.30. Here are descriptions of the Shape Dynamics settings:

- **Size Jitter**—This slider determines the variation in size in the individual incidents of the brush's tip. With a jitter of 100%, the smallest brush tip instance may be less than one-tenth the brush size specified. In no case will Size Jitter create instances of the brush tip larger than the Diameter selected in Brush Tip Shape or the Master Diameter selected in Brush Presets. In Figure 13.30, the cat face brush shows the size jitter. The first cat stroke has Size Jitter set to 50%. The second has Size Jitter at 100%, and the third shows the effect of Size Jitter at 100% combined with a Minimum Diameter of 50%.
- **Minimum Diameter**—You can constrain the size of the smallest instances by using the Minimum Diameter slider.
- **Tilt Scale**—When the Control pop-up menu is set to Pen Tilt, the Tilt Scale slider regulates how much the angle of the stylus affects the brush stroke.
- **Angle Jitter**—With nonround brush tips, the angle of application can be varied. The Angle Jitter setting determines the degree of variation. At a setting of 25%, the brush tip's orientation varies from –90° to +90° In the figure, the hockey mask strokes illustrate Angle Jitter. The first has a variance of 10%, and the second shows an Angle Jitter of 50%.
- **Roundness Jitter**—The Roundness Jitter slider controls variation in the proportion of a brush tip. When it's set to 0%, each instance of the brush has the same width-to-height relationship. As you increase Roundness Jitter, you add variation. At 100% jitter, the height of the brush instances varies between approximately 5% and 100% of the size specified in the Brushes palette. Roundness Jitter never increases the height beyond that selected with the Diameter or Master Diameter sliders. In the two rows of stop sign strokes shown in Figure 13.30, the first row shows a Roundness Jitter of 50%, and the second row shows a Roundness Jitter of 100%, restricted to a minimum of 20%. Note the difference between Roundness Jitter and Size Jitter. With Roundness Jitter, the width of each brush instance remains the same—only the height is varied.

Remember that, by default, the angle is relative to the orientation of the page rather than the path of the stroke—even if you drag a circular stroke, the variation in angle remains relative to the top of the image. Orient the brush tip to the path by changing the Control pop-up menu under Angle Jitter to Direction. (You don't need to change the Angle Jitter from 0%.)

When you're working with the dynamic brush options, think of the slider as representing the amount of variation/variety/change in the individual brush instances along the stroke and think of the pop-up menu as the control for that variation.

- **Minimum Roundness**—You can constrain the Roundness variations by using this slider. It sets the smallest instance that the brush will produce when Roundness Jitter is activated.

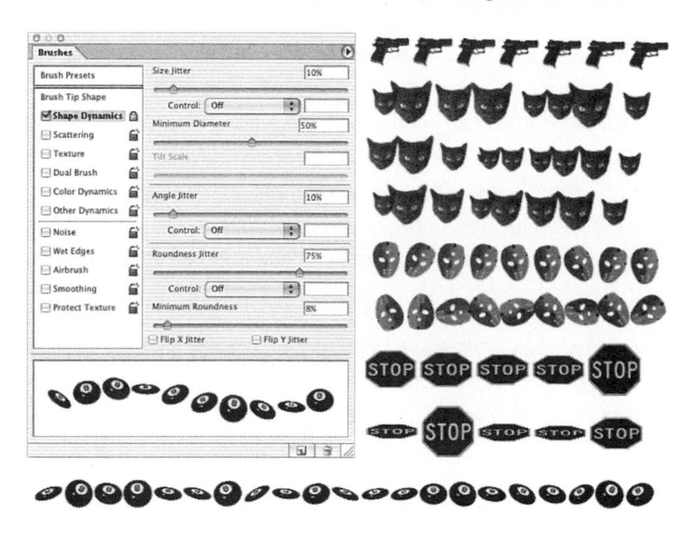


Figure 13.30
The top stroke has no shape dynamics applied; the bottom row has the shape dynamics shown in the palette's settings. In all cases, Spacing is set to 110% for each custom brush.

## Scattering

Scattering spreads copies of the brush tip as instances along the path of the stroke. Figure 13.31 illustrates how spacing affects scattering and shows the influence of the Count and Count Jitter options.

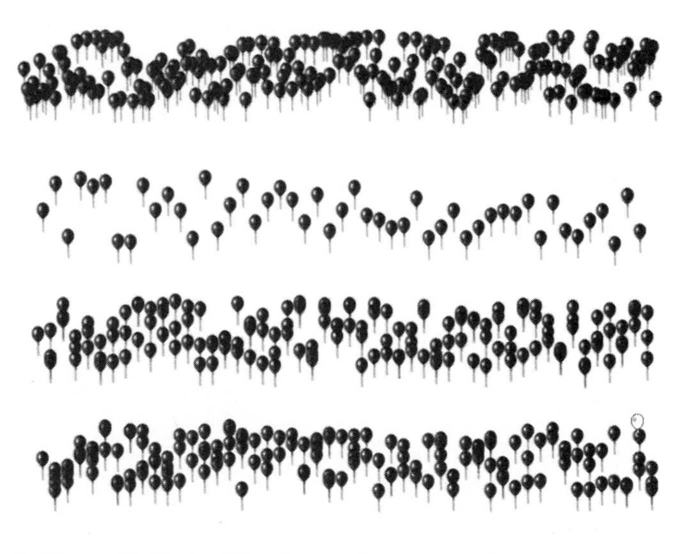

Figure 13.31
The four samples use the same brush with the settings identified in the numbered list in the text, going from top to bottom.

In Figure 13.31, the following settings are used:

1. Spacing 25%, Scatter 220%, Count 0, Count Jitter 0%
2. Spacing 100%, Scatter 220%, Count 0, Count Jitter 0%

3. Spacing 100%, Scatter 220%, Count 3, Count Jitter 0%
4. Spacing 100%, Scatter 220%, Count 3, Count Jitter 60%

Using Spacing to create a specific density of brush instances results in substantial overlap in places as well as some areas of "clumping," where many instances occur in a small space. Using the Scatter and Count options, especially along with Count Jitter, produces the appearance of random distribution, yet does a better job of preserving individual brush instances.

The Scattering pane of the Brushes palette also offers the Both Axes check box. In the first set of examples, only one axis is used for distributing the brush instances. The scattering is perpendicular to the path. Adding the second axis enables you to randomize the scattering along the path as well (see Figure 13.32).

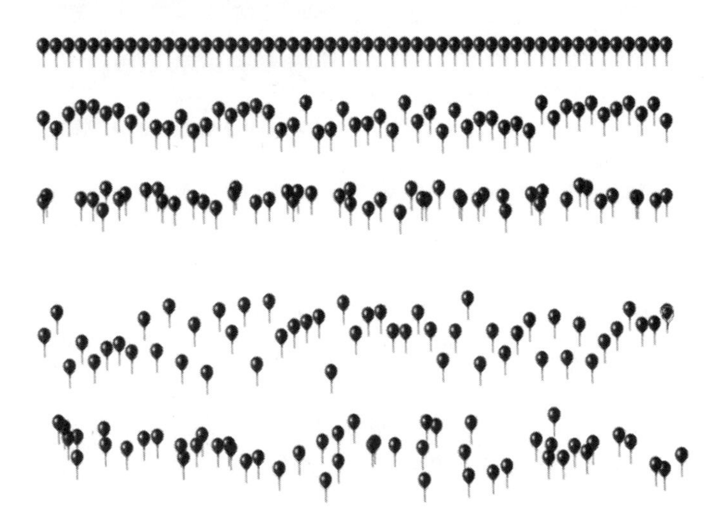

**Figure 13.32**
These five examples, all set to Spacing 100%, do not use the Count option, so they better illustrate the effect of adding a second axis of distribution.

Here are the settings used in Figure 13.32, going from top to bottom:

1. No scattering
2. Scatter 100%, one axis
3. Scatter 100%, both axes
4. Scatter 250%, one axis
5. Scatter 250%, both axes

Enabling the Both Axes option produces a result much like using a reduced Spacing setting—some clumping of the brush instances occurs as the distribution is varied along the path of the stroke.

> When Count and Count Jitter are used and Scatter is set to Both Axes, a very random pattern can be produced, but you're likely to see brush instances bunched together in groups. Add some Roundness Jitter (in Shape Dynamics) to produce an illusion of depth.

## Texture

The Texture option in the Brushes palette applies a pattern to your stroke to give the appearance of a patterned surface underlying the "paint" you've laid down (see Figure 13.33).

Any pattern available in the Pattern Picker for the Edit, Fill command or for the Paint Bucket is also available as a brush texture. You can invert the pattern by selecting the Invert check box to the right of the pattern sample. Inverting reverses the pattern's grayscale values. The blending mode determines how the pattern interacts with the foreground color, the color that will be applied with the brush.

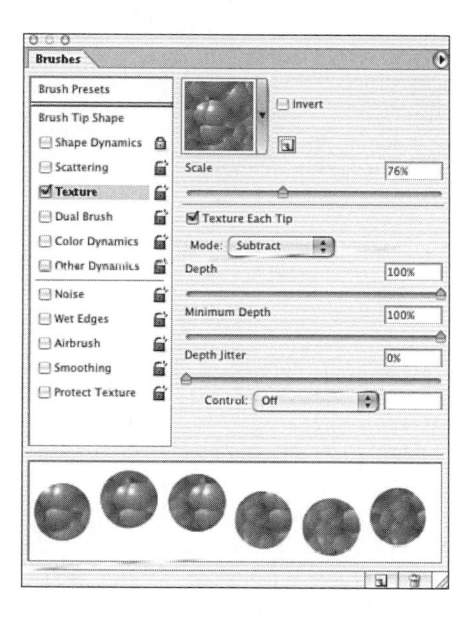


**Figure 13.33**
Click the arrow to the right of the sample pattern to open the Pattern picker.

The Texture Each Tip option applies the pattern individually to each instance of the brush tip. Instead of treating the brush stroke as a whole, this option treats each application of the brush tip separately. Several options are available for Texture Each Tip:

- **Mode**—The blending modes available for Texture are Multiply, Subtract, Darken, Overlay, Color Dodge, Color Burn, Linear Burn, and Hard Mix. The blending mode affects how the overlapping brush instances interact and how the brush itself interacts with other colors already on the layer.
- **Depth**—Depth looks at the texture as a three-dimensional object, with the light and dark areas representing high and low points. Changing the Depth setting alters what grayscale values are affected. At 0% Depth, the pattern is completely eliminated. At 100% Depth, the texture is reproduced normally.
- **Minimum Depth**—Used with Depth Jitter, this slider restricts the lowest jitter value.

The Pattern Picker menu enables you to load sets of patterns. Some of the patterns in the Artist Surfaces set are especially appropriate for use as brush textures.

- **Depth Jitter**—This slider regulates the amount of variation in depth over the course of the stroke. At 0%, there is no variation, and the Depth slider determines the appearance of the brush. The Control options are discussed earlier in this chapter in the section "Controlling the Dynamic Options."

> The Hard Mix blending mode is available only in the Texture and Dual Brush panes of the Brushes palette. Each of the brush's component color values is compared to the existing color on the layer. If the brush's component color is darker, the existing color is darkened. If it's lighter, the existing color is lightened.

## Dual Brush

The Dual Brush option adds another brush tip to the tip selected in Brush Presets or Brush Tip Shape. The second tip is overlaid using the blending mode at the top of the Dual Brush pane of the Brushes palette (see Figure 13.34).

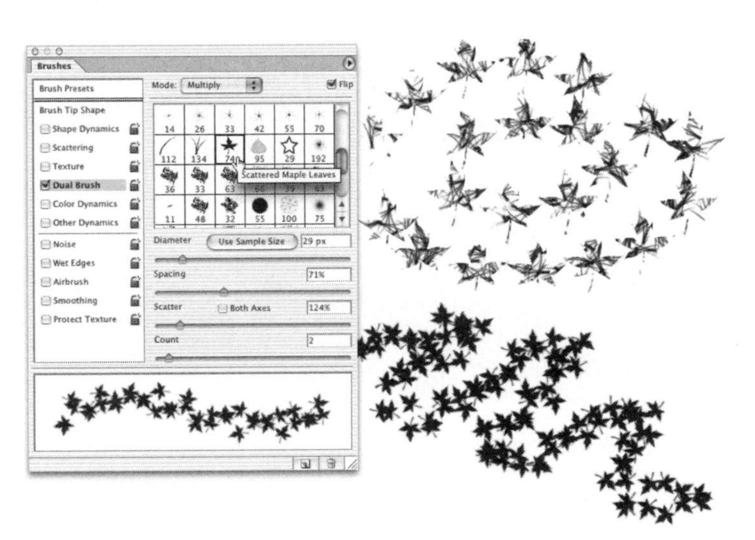


Figure 13.34
You can use Dual Brush to add a texture to a brush (top example) or to add a custom brush within a shape defined by the initial brush tip (bottom example). Select the shape that you'll be filling in Brush Tip Shape and then select the brush tip with which you'll fill in Dual Brush.

The Dual Brush pane is a cross between the Brush Tip Shape and Scattering panes. In addition to selecting the second brush tip and blending mode, you adjust the second tip for diameter, spacing, scatter, and count.



## Color Dynamics

The Color Dynamics pane gives you the opportunity to blend the foreground and background colors for the brush. Each instance of the brush uses only one color, but you can vary the proportions of the foreground and background colors with the sliders.

The Foreground/Background Jitter slider enables you to vary the color of the brush instances between the foreground and background colors, using various colors that are combinations of the two. When Control is set to Fade, the number specified is the number of different colored brush instances that occur before the color reverts to the foreground. (The Control options are discussed earlier in this chapter in the section "Controlling the Dynamic Options.")

When the Hue Jitter slider is set to a low percent, the stroke's hue remains close to the foreground color. As the percent grows, the background color is introduced. By about 25%, some additional color can be detected. At 100%, all the hues of the color wheel are used. Using black, white or gray as the foreground color renders Hue ineffective.

The Saturation Jitter slider affects only the saturation of the stroke. When the slider is toward the left (low percent value), the saturation remains close to that of the foreground color. Likewise, the Brightness Jitter slider varies from that of the foreground color (left) to the full range of brightness (right).

The Purity slider is not a "jitter" option. Rather, it works directly with the saturation value of the stroke. Set to 0%, the slider has no effect. Negative numbers reduce the saturation, with –100% creating a completely desaturated (gray) stroke. At +100%, the stroke is completely saturated. Purity does not override the Saturation Jitter slider; rather, it restricts the setting.

If you leave Control set to Fade and the Foreground/Background Jitter slider at 0%, the color reverts to the background color after the specified number of steps.

After you know how each of the options works, you are better prepared to combine them in a single brush stroke. For example, foliage in nature has leaves of different sizes and colors, at different angles and distances. You combine Shape Dynamics, Scattering, and Color Dynamics to create those variations.

## Other Dynamics

The options in the Other Dynamics pane can be considered the paint dynamics or the tool option dynamics. The Opacity Jitter and Flow Jitter sliders vary the stroke's appearance up to but not beyond the values specified in the Options Bar for the Brush tool. These options are not available for other brush-using tools.

## Additional Brush Palette Options

The five options at the bottom of the left column in the Brushes palette don't have separate panes. You activate them on an on/off basis and can click the check box or the name. Here are the available options:

- **Noise**—When a brush is defined from artwork, noise is added to gray areas of the brush with this option. Areas of the brush tip defined as solid black are not affected.
- **Wet Edges**—Simulating watercolors, the paint collects along the edges of the brush stroke.
- **Airbrush**—The Airbrush option in the Brushes palette activates and deactivates the Airbrush button on the Options Bar for the Brush tool.
- **Smoothing**—Designed for use with drawing tablets, this option reduces the sharpness of some curves. If your stroke *should* have sharp angles, don't enable this option. Also be aware that it can reduce system responsiveness—your screen redraw might be slower.

**Caution**

If you have an underpowered system or your video card is strained by your monitor resolution and color depth, make sure to disable Smoothing. The slower your system, the greater the delay you will experience with this option.

- **Protect Texture**—Just as the Global Light option in Layer Style ensures consistency in lighting effects, so, too, does Protect Texture protect against anomalies in your image. Select this check box, and all the brushes that can use textures will use the same texture.

## Photoshop at Work: Using Photoshop Brushes and Brush Options

It seems that at one point or another, everyone who uses Photoshop needs to create foliage in an image. It's easy to prepare for that day ahead of time and, at the same time, get some practice managing brush sets. Follow these steps:

1. Open the Photoshop Brushes palette.
2. From the palette menu, choose Reset Brushes.
3. Click the OK button rather than the Append button.
4. Put the *Special Edition Using Adobe Photoshop CS* CD into your optical drive and let it mount.
5. From the Brushes palette menu, choose Load Brushes.
6. Navigate to the Brushes folder on the CD (inside the Goodies folder) and load Pete's Custom Brushes.
7. In the Brushes palette, (Option)-click [Alt]-click all non-leaf, non-grass brushes to remove them from the palette. (Tip: Start with the first brush, and the palette will bring the next one to you—you don't have to move the cursor until it's time to skip a brush you want to keep.)
8. For each of the brushes, set appropriate Shape Dynamics, Scattering, and Color Dynamics options.
9. Use the Brushes palette menu command Save Brushes. Name the set Foliage.abr (don't skip the file extension), and save the set to a location where you'll be able to find it when you need it.

# DEFINING CUSTOM BRUSHES AND BRUSH SETS



To take full advantage of Photoshop's paint engine, you need to use custom brushes. You can load existing sets of brushes into the Brushes palette, or you can create your own.

## Defining a Custom Brush

Photoshop's menu command Edit, Define Brush creates a custom brush from artwork you designate. The brush itself is always grayscale, so it's best to either work in Grayscale mode or desaturate your colored artwork (Image, Adjustments, Desaturate). If the artwork for the brush tip is alone on the layer, you need only use the Edit, Define Brush command. If there is other artwork on the layer, isolate the brush tip with a selection. You can define a brush on a layer filled with white or a background layer, and you can use irregularly shaped and feathered selections to define brushes.

When you define a mask, Photoshop considers black to be 100% opaque, white to be transparent, and all other shades of gray (and colors) to be partially opaque. Where you add black to the artwork that will become a brush, you will later be painting with 100% opacity of the foreground color (allowing for tool and Brushes palette options, of course). In that respect, defining a brush is much like creating a mask, filter texture, or spot color channel—black is 100%, white is 0%, and everything else is in between. When you paint with the brush, that's how the foreground color will be added.

**Caution**

Remember that your custom brushes are not permanently recorded until saved in a brush set. If you replace the content of the palette before saving, your custom brushes are lost.

## Loading and Saving Brush Sets

Both the full-sized Brushes palette and the mini palette available in the Options Bar enable you to load and save sets of brushes. The brush sets found in Photoshop's Presets folder (inside the Photoshop folder) appear at the bottom of the Brushes palette's menu. To add one of those sets to the palette, simply select its name from the menu. You'll be asked whether you want to append the brush set (adding the new brushes to the bottom of the palette) or replace the palette's current content.

Although you cannot add individual brushes to the palette (unless they are saved as a set of one), you can delete brushes from the palette. Deleting removes them only from the palette, leaving them intact in their original set. The palette menu and the contextual menu both include the Delete Brush command. In the Preset Manager or the Brushes palette's Brush Presets pane, you can also (Option)-click [Alt]-click a brush to delete it.

The palette menu also offers the Save Brushes command. The current content of the palette, regardless of whether the brushes already belong to a set, will be saved together. Delete the default and other extraneous brushes from the palette before saving your custom brushes as a set. That keeps your new set tidy and makes the custom brushes easier to locate. You can reload the other brushes afterward.

Save your custom brushes someplace outside the Photoshop folder—you don't want to lose them should you ever need to reinstall the program. It's always a good idea to keep a backup copy.



# MASTERING PHOTOSHOP

## Auto Gradients

*How do the Foreground and Background options for color stops work?*

When Foreground or Background is assigned to a color swatch in the Gradient Editor, the gradient automatically updates itself when selected. For example, say that a gradient has been defined with black and white as the foreground and background colors. Later, perhaps even in another project, that gradient is selected from the Gradient palette. If the foreground color happens to be red and the background color is blue, for example, the gradient is updated to reflect those colors for any color stops for which Foreground or Background is assigned.

Using Foreground and Background rather than specific colors can make a gradient far more flexible. These options are also very useful for complex gradients designed to integrate a subject and a background. Instead of having to identify and assign prominent colors from the image, you can simply use the Eyedropper tool and the Color palette to make those colors the foreground and background before selecting your gradient.

## Restoring Cleared Brush Controls

*I used the Brushes palette menu command Clear Brush Controls on one of the preset brushes, and I need to get the scattering back. Any way of doing it?*

If you are in the Brushes palette's Brush Presets pane, simply click the brush again—the controls will be restored. If you are in the Brush Tip Shape pane, change to Brush Presets and click any other brush. Then return to Brush Tip Shape and click the brush you need to restore. If all else fails, remember that you can reload any brush set.

## Expanding the Brushes Palette

*I can't find any of Photoshop's advanced brush options. All I see is the old-fashioned Brushes palette.*

From the Brushes palette menu, choose Expanded View to show the options. When the Brushes palette is docked to the Palette Well, click the tab to open the palette and then click the small arrow in the tab. Remember that ImageReady doesn't use the new painting engine—you'll see only the "old-fashioned" palette.

14

*by Richard Ramano*

# SELECTING AND APPLYING FILTERS

## IN THIS CHAPTER

When the layman thinks of Photoshop—or digital image editing in general—there are two things that immediately come to mind: the Clone tool and filters, two ways that Photoshop lets you completely stylize an image. It is by applying filters that you make an image completely unidentifiable from its original. Filters enable you to transform a photo into a work of art.

This chapter will provide an overview of working with filters—what they are, where they are, what they do, and how generally to get the most out of them. Some new filter management tools (such as the Filter Gallery) will be discussed here as well.

A complete discussion of the nuances of every filter is way beyond the scope of this book. Given how many filters are included in Photoshop, such a discussion would require a book along the scope of James Michener's *Filters*.

# WORKING WITH FILTERS

The effects you can create with Photoshop's filters can be as subtle as slightly sharpening or blurring an image or as radical as transforming a photograph into a watercolor painting. Regardless of the actual effect, all the filters tend to operate in basically the same way. All the filters use a similar interface that lets you adjust the filter's strength as well as see a live preview of the effect that the filter is having on the image.

Filters are located in the Filter menu, where they are grouped into several submenus.

## Production Versus Creative Filters

Filters can be divided into two "unofficial" categories: production and creative. Production filters are designed to enhance, fix, and clean up images. Production filters include such things as Sharpen, Despeckle, and Unsharp Mask, to name three. Creative filters are designed to stylize images—either a little or a lot. Creative filters include Color Pencil, Watercolor, Solarize, Emboss, and myriad others. Perhaps the best way to distinguish the two types of filters is this: Production filters let you make a photographic image look as much like the reality that was photographed as possible. Creative filters, on the other hand, let you make that image look as *un*like the reality that was photographed as possible.

*For specific detail about the production filters, see Chapter 19, "Repairing and Enhancing Images with the Production Filters," p. 613. For specific detail about the creative filters, see Chapter 20, "Adding Special Effects with the Filter Gallery and the Creative Filters," p. 639.*

## Filter Groupings

Without going into massive amounts of detail about each of the filters, here are the basic filter submenus:

- **Artistic**—In this submenu are filters that let you give images the look of a drawing or a painting, or add other related artistic textures. Some filters in this submenu include Colored Pencil (shown in Figure 14.1), Paint Daubs, and Watercolor, to name a few.

Figure 14.1
The Colored Pencil filter lets you transform a photographic image into a drawing.

- **Blur**—In this submenu is a combination of creative and production filters that let you blur images in a variety of ways. The Blur, Blur More, Gaussian Blur, and the new Lens Blur filters let you soften images or create realistic depth-of-field effects, whereas the Gaussian Blur, Motion Blur (shown in Figure 14.2), and Radial Blur filters let you add more extreme blur effects to images, often to convey a sense of motion or excitement.

Figure 14.2
The Motion Blur filter lets you add the illusion of motion to otherwise static images or objects within images.

- **Brush Strokes**—In this submenu is a variety of filters, related to the Artistic filters, that let you apply a variety of painting and drawing effects to images. Some filters in this submenu are Angled Strokes, Crosshatch (shown in Figure 14.3), Spatter, and Sprayed Strokes, to name a few.

Figure 14.3
The Crosshatch filter lets you add a brush stroke–related texture effect that simulates cross-hatching.

- **Distort**—This submenu includes a variety of creative effects that generate volume, 3D, and distortion effects. Some filters in this submenu are Glass (shown in Figure 14.4), Pinch, Ripple, Spherize, Twirl, and Zigzag, to name a few.

Figure 14.4
The Glass filter lets you add a frosted glass effect to images, for that shower door look.



- **Noise**—In this submenu is a variety of filters, both production and creative, that let you either add noise (to simulate film grain) or remove noise-like effects such as dust and scratches. Some filters in this submenu are Add Noise, Despeckle, Dust & Scratches (shown in Figure 14.5), and Median.

Figure 14.5
The Dust & Scratches filter does a pretty good job of removing dust, debris, and detritus from scanned images.

- **Pixelate**—This submenu contains a set of filters used to group pixels together and then stylize them en masse. Filters in this submenu include Color Halftone, Crystallize, Mezzotint, and Pointillize (shown in Figure 14.6), to name a few.

Figure 14.6
Que Seurat Seurat. The Pointillize filter lets you turn an image into something that vaguely resembles a pointillist painting, or basically a low-resolution Georges Seurat.

- **Render**—In this submenu are filters that create 3D, lens, and lighting effects. Filters in this set include 3Clouds, Difference Clouds, Fibers, Lens Flare, and Lighting Effects (shown in Figure 14.7).
- **Sharpen**—This submenu contains a set of production filters that lets you correct any minor blurriness or softness that images may have. Filters in this submenu include Sharpen, Sharpen Edges, Sharpen More, and Unsharp Mask (shown in Figure 14.8).
- **Sketch**—This submenu includes various artistic filters that let you turn images into sketches or drawings. Filters in this group include Chalk & Charcoal (shown in Figure 14.9), Graphic Pen, Plaster, and Water Paper, to name a few.

Figure 14.7
The Lighting Effects filter lets you add dramatic lighting to images.

Figure 14.8
The perhaps contradictorily named Unsharp Mask filter lets you sharpen slightly blurred or soft images.

- **Stylize**—This submenu includes a variety of filters that primarily apply various types of edge effects to images. Filters in this group include Diffuse, Emboss, Glowing Edges (shown in Figure 14.10), and Tiles, to name a few.

Figure 14.9
The Chalk & Charcoal filter lets you transform a photographic image into a chalk and charcoal drawing.

Figure 14.10
The Glowing Edges filter lets you give an image a stylized neon-light effect.

- **Texture**—In this submenu are filters that let you add depth and textures to the surfaces of images. Filters in this group include Craquelure, Grain, Mosaic Tiles, Patchwork (shown in Figure 14.11), Stained Glass, and Texturizer.

**Figure 14.11**
The Patchwork filter lets you give an image the look of small ceramic tiles or a patchwork quilt (a fine line, really).

- **Video**—These filters are used for video editing and for working with still images captured from video.
- **Other**—This submenu is a mélange of filters not easily classified under the other submenus. These include the ability to create custom filters, tiled images, and so on.
- **Digimarc**—This submenu lets you embed watermarks in images, which aids in protecting copyrighted images. Watermarks are invisible to the naked eye, but they can be detected by Photoshop and can be used to track purloined images.

## Applying Filters

When you select a filter from the Filter menu, you will get a small palette that gives you all the various controls for that filter (see Figure 14.12).

Depending on the filter, you may have one slider or you can have several sliders, pop-up menus, radio buttons, and check boxes that control various aspects of the filter. In the case of the Ripple filter, for example, the slider can control whether you want small, medium, or large ripples and how "ripply" you want them. Other filters have controls that let you determine what type of brush stroke to use, how "strong" those strokes should be, and so on.

Most filter palettes have a preview window that lets you see the effect the filter is having on the image. Beneath a preview window are two buttons: - and +. These reduce and enlarge, respectively, the size of the preview, allowing you to see the entire image or a zoomed-in portion of it.

Three other "filters" are also located under the Filter menu—Extract, Liquify, and Pattern Maker. These will be covered in more detail in Chapters 19 (Extract) and 20 (Liquify and Pattern Maker).

Some filters—primarily various types of artistic filters—are controlled using the Filter Gallery rather than through a single filter palette. The Filter Gallery will be covered in the next section.

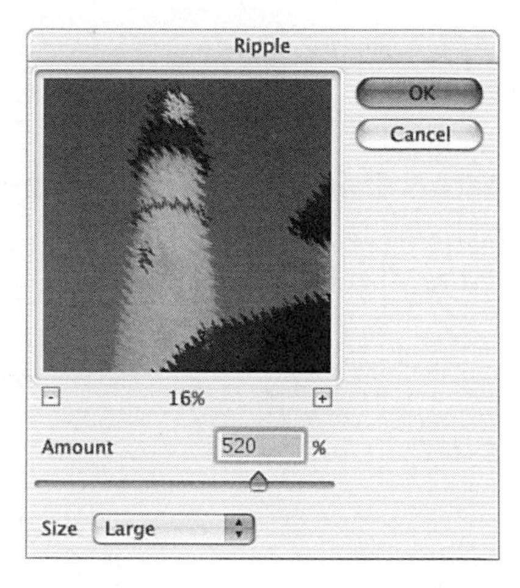


**Figure 14.12**
Each filter has its own palette that lets you vary the effect of that filter.

Clicking in the preview window will do two things. First, the cursor will turn into a hand, and you can click and drag around the preview window to see other portions of the image. Second, when you click, the image will return to its unfiltered state until you release the mouse button. This is a quick and useful way to toggle the effect of a filter on and off to see what effect it is having. Some filters tend to be more subtle than others.

When you click OK in the filter's palette, Photoshop will apply the filter. Again, depending on the speed of your computer and the filter you are applying, this can be a fast or slow process.

Not all filters have live previews—and some don't even have palettes. Radial Blur only has a representation of what the filter will do to the image, which will require some use of your imagination.

If you select Blur, Blur More, Sharpen, or Sharpen More, for example, Photoshop will skip the palette-based adjustment process entirely and just apply the filter using a predetermined amount. You have no control over the extent to which these filters are applied. Pros tend to avoid them, but in truth these filters can provide a good, quick way to sharpen or blur an image in small increments. These filters are best used with your fingers on (Command-Z) [Ctrl+Z] (the Undo command's keystroke combination), however, should the result not turn out to your liking.

> Depending on the speed of your computer and the filter, there can be a slight (or a not-so-slight) delay between changing a filter setting or zoom amount and seeing an updated preview in the preview window. A blinking line underneath the preview percentage below the preview window indicates that Photoshop is still updating the preview. (If you have a fast computer, you'll likely not see the blinking line.)

*For more detail about working with blurring and sharpening filters, see Chapter 19, "Repairing and Enhancing Images with the Production Filters," p. 613.*

The best part about working with filters is that you can have a great deal of fun experimenting with different filters and settings.

> For best results when sharpening or blurring images, use Unsharp Mask or Smart Blur, respectively.

*Are the built-in Photoshop filters the only filters available? See "Third-Party Filters" in the "Mastering Photoshop" section at the end of this chapter.*

## Applying Filters to Selected Portions of an Image

Applying a filter, in general, is not an all-or-nothing affair; you can apply a filter to only a portion of an image, if you desire. In other words, you can create a selection and apply a filter only to that selection.

The first step, as you would expect, is to select the portion of the image to which you'd like to apply the filter. This can be done in any of a variety of ways—by creating paths and/or selections, for example, or by using a Quick Mask.

*For more detail about selecting portions of an image and using the Quick Mask mode, see Chapter 9, "Making Selections and Creating Masks," p. 295.*

In Figure 14.13, a Quick Mask was applied to a portion of an image and a selection created from it.

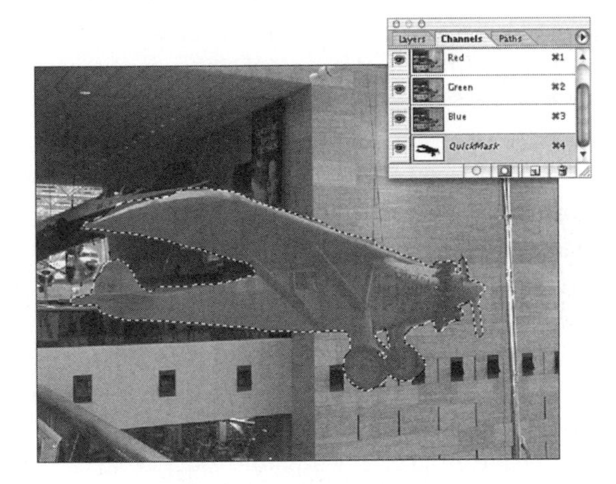


**Figure 14.13**
A Quick Mask is used to create a selection within an image.

Once the appropriate portion of the image is selected, a Motion Blur can be applied to it, as shown in Figure 14.14.

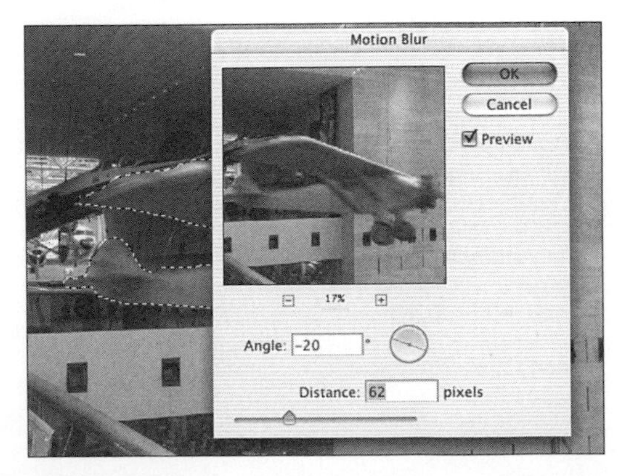


**Figure 14.14**
The Motion Blur filter is only applied to the selected portion of the image.

When the filter is applied and the selection area deselected, the plane in the image has the illusion of motion (see Figure 14.15).

**Figure 14.15**
With the Motion Blur filter applied only to the plane, it has the illusion of movement. (Cloning out the wires suspending it from the ceiling would complete the illusion!)

*Does the Fade command work with filters? See "Fade Away" in the "Mastering Photoshop" section at the end of this chapter.*

# USING THE FILTER GALLERY

New to Photoshop CS is the Filter Gallery, which, as its name implies, is a way of accessing a variety of filters from one central location.

You have two ways in which to enter the Filter Gallery. The first is to select Filter, Filter Gallery. The second is to select a filter from the Filter menu that is included in the gallery. The gallery includes these filters:

- All filters in the Artistic submenu
- All filters in the Brush Strokes submenu
- The Diffuse Glow, Glass, and Ocean Ripple filters in the Distort submenu
- All filters in the Sketch submenu
- The Glowing Edges filter in the Stylize submenu
- All filters in the Texture submenu

The Filter Gallery is divided into three panels, as shown in Figure 14.16.

The left-side panel provides a preview of the image with the selected filter applied. At the bottom of this panel are the "-" and "+" buttons, which let you adjust the size of the preview. Next to these buttons is a pop-up menu with a set of common zoom percentages, including the Fit in View option, which fits the image to the panel. This is useful for seeing the entire image at one time.

**Figure 14.16**
The Filter Gallery is where you select, apply, and customize an assortment of artistic filters.

The center panel is the gallery of filters itself, with iconic representations of all the filters organized by submenu (or folder). When you click a folder, the panel will display all the filters in that submenu. If you then click a filter, Photoshop will generate a preview of that filter applied to the image.

The right panel is where you customize the specific settings for the selected filter.

The right-side panel has a pop-up menu that lists all the available filters (listed alphabetically rather than organized by submenu or type of filter). Below the pop-up menu is a set of sliders and controls that vary by filter. These sliders are where you control the strength of the filter and how it is applied.

## Adding Effect Layers

You can also combine filter effects in a seemingly infinite number of ways. This is done by adding effect layers. At the bottom of the right-side panel is the New Effect Layer button (see Figure 14.17).

If you click the New Effect Layer button, Photoshop will duplicate the filter effect you have already added. You can then click the pop-up menu at the top of the right-side panel of the Filter Gallery (or select a filter from the center panel, if you have it open) and Photoshop will generate a preview of how these two filters interact with each other. Each effect layer has its own independent set of sliders and controls with which you can vary the settings and strength of those filters. By clicking the eyeball icon next to each effect layer, you can toggle that layer's visibility.

> Once you have selected a filter, click the arrow at the top right of the center panel. This hides the gallery itself and gives you more room to see your preview image. Even after you close the center panel of the Filter Gallery, you still have access to many of the filters via the pop-up menu at the top of the right-side panel.

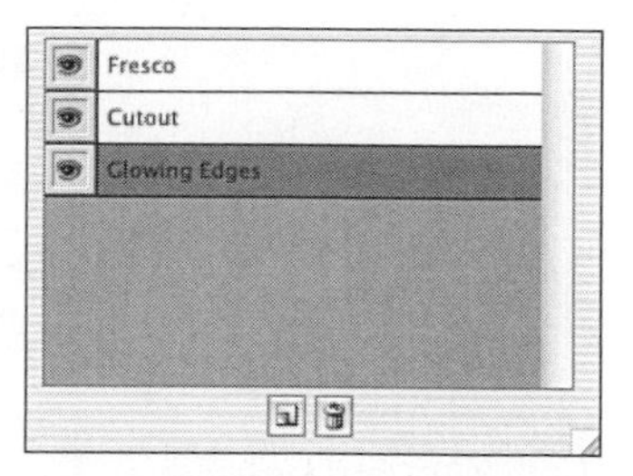


Figure 14.17
You can apply filters on top of filters to create truly unique images.

You can also click and drag each effect layer on top of or beneath other effect layers. The order of the effect layers determines the order in which filter effects are applied to the image. If you apply the Fresco filter to an image, you can then add the Glowing Edges filter. If you drag the Glowing Edges effect layer to the top of the list of effect layers, the Glowing Edges filter will be applied to the original image first, and the Fresco filter will be applied to the resulting image. In other words, the order in which effect layers are applied is from the top down, which is the opposite of how layers interact with each other in the Layers palette in general.

Of course, you can also delete effect layers by clicking the Delete Effect Layer button at the bottom of the right-side panel of the Filter Gallery.

# ADDITIONAL FILTER EFFECTS

Filters can also be combined with other Photoshop features to create even more effects. Not only can filters be applied to selected portions of images, they can be applied to individual layers as well as individual channels.

Just as you can make selections and apply individual filters to those selected areas, so, too, can you make selections and then open the Filter Gallery. You will have the full gamut of gallery filters, which will only be applied to the selected area.

## Applying Filters to Layers

Sometimes you want to use a filter, but not at "full strength." In this case, you can apply the filter to a layer and adjust the opacity accordingly.

For example, say you want to add a slight pencil-drawn feel to an image, but still have it remain fairly photorealistic. Duplicate the background layer and apply the desired filter to the top layer. After you click OK and apply the filter, you will have the filter applied to the top level at full-strength, or 100% opacity (see Figure 14.18).

By selecting the top layer and moving the Opacity slider to the left, you can modulate the effect of the filter (see Figure 14.19).

Filters can be applied to any layer, regardless of whether that layer is a duplicate. You can even apply filters to type layers, to create an infinite assortment of text effects.

**Caution**

If you do apply a filter to a text layer, you will be instructed to rasterize the layer first, thus rendering the text uneditable. So be sure your type is exactly how you want it—and that it is spelled correctly—before you apply a filter to it.

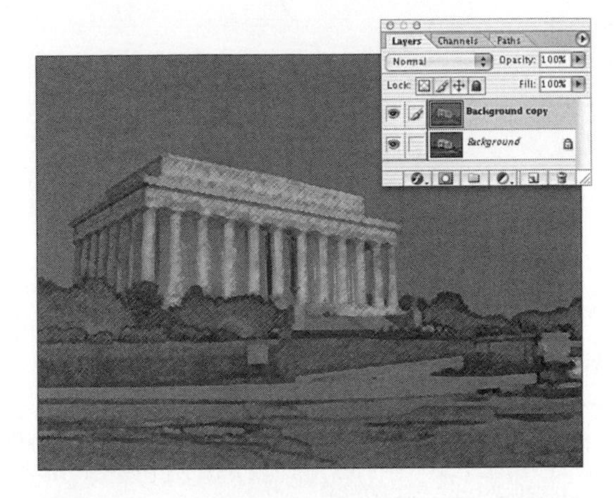


**Figure 14.18**
When an image's background layer is duplicated and a filter (in this case, Colored Pencil) is applied to the top layer, the result is a full-strength application of the filter.

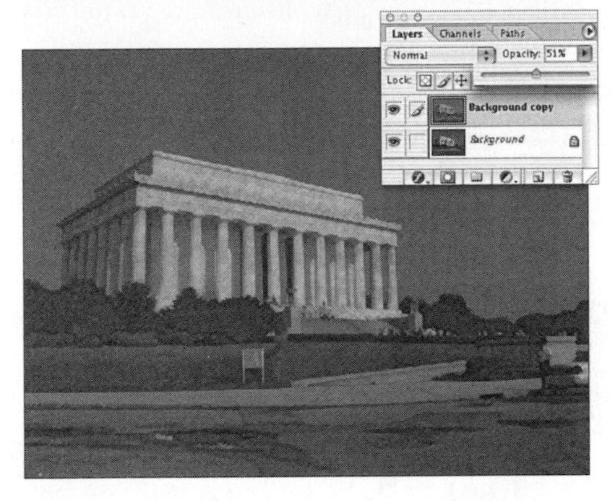


**Figure 14.19**
When the opacity of the top (that is, filtered) layer is reduced, the resulting image has a more "photorealistic" hand-drawn look.

*For more detail about working with layers, see Chapter 10, "Working with Layers and Layer Styles," p. 327.*

*Can I use blending modes with filters? See "Power Blending" in the "Mastering Photoshop" section at the end of this chapter.*

## Applying Filters to Channels

Likewise, you can also apply filters to individual channels—red, green, and/or blue in the case of RGB images, and cyan, magenta, yellow, and/or black in the case of CMYK images. By selecting a single channel in the Channels palette, you can have a filter's effect only apply to that channel. This is useful for adding special effects or, more commonly, for selectively applying sharpens and blurs to individual color channels to correct specific noise problems without overcorrecting the entire image.

*For more detail about applying filters to channels to correct noise problems, see Chapter 19, "Repairing and Enhancing Images with Production Filters," p. 613.*

# MASTERING PHOTOSHOP

## Third-Party Filters

*Are the built-in filters that come with Photoshop the only filters there are?*

Heck no! Way back when, Photoshop created a plug-in architecture for its filters that allowed a cottage industry of independent software companies to emerge and add even more filters and plug-ins than Photoshop has natively. There are literally hundreds of filters and plug-ins that do everything from performing highly controlled unsharp masking to adding edge effects, to employing advanced color correction, to adding bear fur to images, to...well, you name it. Some popular makers of Photoshop filters include A Lowly Apprentice Productions (ALAP), Alien Skin, AutoFX, Corel, Extensis, Flaming Pear, LizardTech, Right Hemisphere, and many, many more. A good resource is Plug-Ins World, found at www.pluginsworld.com, which has overviews of tons of Photoshop filters and plug-ins, with links to software vendor sites. And remember, many plug-in vendors let you download free demo versions of filters, so you can try them to see if you like them before committing money to them.

## Fade Away

*Does the Fade command work with filters?*

Yes. As you know, Edit, Fade lets you adjust the opacity and/or blending mode of an effect added in Photoshop. The trick to the Fade command is to access it immediately after the filter has finished rendering. As you know, the Fade command fades away if any other action (even a save) is performed.

## Power Blending

*Can I use blending modes with filters?*

Absolutely. If you have duplicated a layer and applied a filter to the duplicate layer, you can adjust its blending mode (that is, the way it interacts with the layer beneath it) in the same way that you can alter its opacity. (Blending mode is changed by using the pop-up menu in the Layers palette.) Playing with the blending mode can also yield some unusual effects.

*For more about working with blending modes, see Chapter 18, "Mastering the Blending Modes," p. 585.*

15

# IMAGE CROPPING, RESIZING, AND SHARPENING

## IN THIS CHAPTER

Photoshop offers powerful tools for creating images, but it's also packed with features for photo retouching and repairing. In this chapter, we'll look at basic ways to use Photoshop to improve the look of your digital images. Almost every image can use some post-processing improvement, whether it's tone balancing, sharpening, or just a simple crop to enhance overall composition. Here, you learn how to perform all of these tasks, using Photoshop CS.

# A FEW NOTES ON IMAGE COMPOSITION

When working with stock photography, you try to find the most appropriate picture for your project. When you're taking original photos for a project, there are a few ideas you can keep in mind that will make your work easier.

## Planning the Project

At some point, every project has a layout. In some cases, the layout isn't finalized until the project is actually finished, but it's a better practice to work with a final concept in mind. If you work in an advertising agency, you're probably used to working from a sketch or preliminary design, a plan that has been approved by the client. If you are an artist, you might create as you go along, letting the image form itself as you work. The plan could be as simple as a quick scribble on a piece of paper (see Figure 15.1).

**Figure 15.1**
Although not fancy, even a simple sketch lets you know the general size and location of the subject in the final work.

You can save a lot of image correction and composition work in Photoshop if you take photos that are designed to fill a specific area of the final project. Having a properly composed original can also protect image quality by eliminating the need to resize the picture.

## Arranging the Subject

When you're shooting the image or selecting stock art, consider the overall layout. In Figure 15.1, the subject of the layout is off center. Instead of shooting the image with the dog in the middle of the frame and then cropping, you can shoot the image with the dog in the proper position. Compare the images in Figure 15.2.

Figure 15.2
Either of these images might be appropriate for the idea sketched out earlier. The photo on the right, however, is shot for the concept.

Because the image on the right requires less cropping, it retains more of the original pixel data when resampled to print resolution. (This might not be a factor, depending on your camera's capability, and it's not an issue with properly focused film cameras.) In this situation, the purpose-made photo is appropriate (see Figure 15.3).

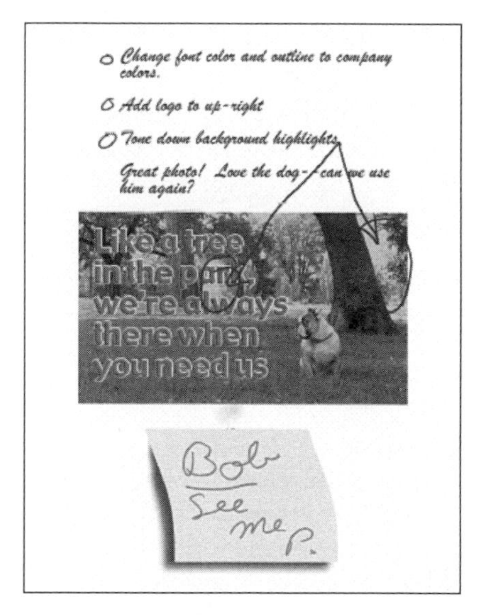


Figure 15.3
Many stock photo and royalty-free suppliers can custom-shoot to your requirements.

# CROPPING TO IMPROVE COMPOSITION

Whether recomposing a picture for artistic reasons or because of space limitations, you must sometimes crop an image. Cropping deletes (or in some cases, *hides*) part of an image. Photoshop offers a number of ways to crop, including commands and tools.

## Cropping Versus Resampling

Cropping an image differs from *resampling* (resizing by changing the number of pixels portraying the same image) in a couple of important ways. Cropping typically maintains the image resolution and alters the picture by discarding some of the image data. Resampling typically maintains the image's visual content but changes the number of pixels presenting it. Figure 15.4 shows the difference.

Figure 15.4
The original image is shown at the top. On the left, the image has been resampled (resized, downsampled) to a specific size. On the right, the image has been cropped to the identical size.

The image on the left in Figure 15.4 has the same content as the original, but it uses a smaller number of pixels to portray the image. (Note that the top image is shown at 66.67% zoom, and both of the lower images are at 100% zoom.) The process of resampling (or in this case, *downsampling* because the new image is smaller) has robbed the painting of its texture.

*For detailed information about resampling, see "Resizing Canvases and Images," later in this chapter.*

The image on the right in Figure 15.4 is exactly the same size as that on the left but contains less of the original image. Cropping has deleted areas of the original. However, the section of the painting that remains uses exactly the same pixels as the corresponding area of the original, so there is no loss of quality.

You can think of *cropping* as changing the canvas size and *resampling* as changing the image size. The nondigital equivalent of the example shown in Figure 15.4 would be this: To crop the image, retaining only a portion of the original without changing that portion, the artist could use scissors or a knife to cut the original canvas down to size. To resize the image, maintaining the entire image portrayed in the original, the artist would paint the picture again, this time on a smaller canvas.

## The Crop Command

The Image, Crop menu command has no dialog box and no options. It changes the canvas size based on an active selection. The selection need not be rectangular, and it can be feathered. The selection shown in Figure 15.5 on the left crops to the image shown on the right.

**Figure 15.5**
The Crop command always produces a rectangular canvas, cut to the nearest edge of the active selection.

When you're preparing a selection for the Crop command, the Rectangular Marquee tool offers you a couple important features. Using the Fixed Size option enables you to crop an image to an exact size, using any unit of measure:

1. Select the Rectangular Marquee tool in the Toolbox.
2. Choose Fixed Size for Style in the Options Bar.
3. Enter the desired width and height in the numeric fields in the Options Bar. You can use any of Photoshop's units of measure—follow the number with "px" for pixel, "in" for inches, "cm" for centimeters, and so on (excluding the quotation marks).
4. Click once in the image window with the Rectangular Marquee tool. A selection of the specified size will appear to the lower right of the cursor.
5. Position the cursor inside the selection border and drag to move it. You must have a selection tool active to reposition a selection marquee.
6. Use the Image, Crop menu command to complete the crop.

The Rectangular Marquee tool also has an option that enables you to make a selection based on a height-width ratio rather than a specified size. To use it, follow these steps:

1. Select the Rectangular Marquee tool in the Options Bar.
2. Choose Fixed Aspect Ratio from the Style pop-up menu in the Options Bar.

3. Instead of an exact size, enter a relationship between width and height, without any unit of measure. For example, you can enter **8** for Width and **10** for Height to prepare for an 8×10 print. Alternatively, you can enter **468** for Width and **60** for Height if you're making a standard-sized Web banner ad.
4. Drag the tool in the image window. The selection border will maintain the exact height-width ratio designated in the Options Bar. Remember that you can reposition the selection border while still dragging by holding down the spacebar. When you release the spacebar, you can continue to drag the selection in its new position. Also keep in mind that the (Option) [Alt] key enables you to drag a marquee from the center.
5. After you release the mouse button, you can reposition the selection border by positioning the cursor inside the selection and dragging.
6. Use the menu command Image, Crop to make the crop.
7. In the Image Size dialog box, select the Resample check box and then enter your target width or height and desired resolution. Click OK.

When working with the Rectangular Marquee tool using Style: Normal, you can refer to the Info palette for the size of the current selection. The W and H fields give you the reading in the document's unit of measure (see Figure 15.6).

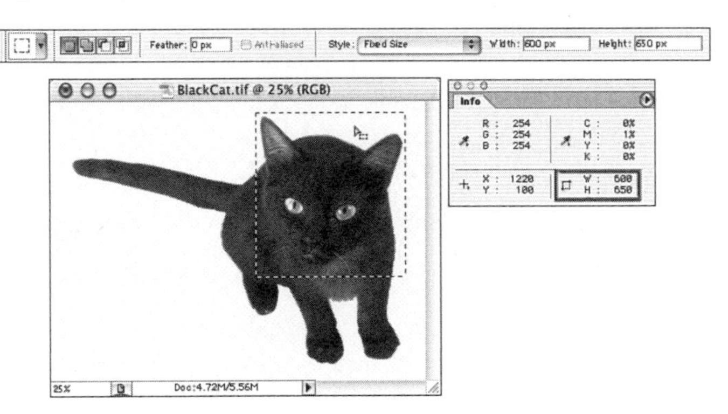


Figure 15.6
The box indicates the area of the Info palette where selection size is visible. In this example, the Rectangular Marquee tool is set to Fixed Size in the Options Bar, and the cursor is ready to reposition the selection border.

# The Crop Tool

The Crop tool works on a basic principle: You position a marquee so that it includes the area you want to keep, accept the change, and anything outside the marquee is eliminated from the image. The image's pixel dimensions are reduced to those of the marquee. The tool has several options that make it more flexible. Like several other Photoshop tools, the Crop tool's Options Bar has different configurations when you select the tool and when you're actually using it.

## Initial Crop Tool Options

When you select the Crop tool in the Toolbox or press the keyboard shortcut C, the Options Bar changes to the configuration shown in Figure 15.7.

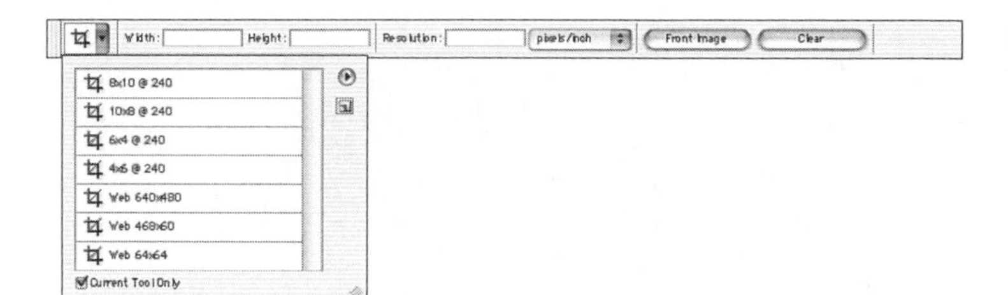


Figure 15.7
The palette shown to the left of the Options Bar contains custom configurations you store by using the Tool Presets palette.



Before you drag a crop marquee (also known as a *crop bounding box*), the Options Bar offers you the opportunity to determine one or more characteristics of the resulting image:

- The three numeric fields in the Options Bar govern not only the size of the crop marquee but also the size of the resulting image. You can specify one, two, or all three variables. If only width or height is specified, the marquee is not constrained and you can drag any rectangular crop marquee. If both width and height are specified, the aspect ratio of the crop is constrained—the rectangular bounding box maintains its shape, regardless of how you drag.
- The resolution of the resulting image can be specified in pixels per inch or pixels per centimeter.

When any of the numeric fields are used with the Crop tool, the image is resampled. When the fields are empty, the image is *not* resampled. Resampling with the Crop tool uses the algorithm specified in the Preferences, General pane for Interpolation.

- Clicking the Front Image button automatically inputs the dimensions of the foremost image open in Photoshop. If you have two images that should match in size and resolution (to composite or collage, for example), this option can automatically set the specs that you need. Bring the image with the desired specs to the front, select the Crop tool, and click the Front Image button. You can then bring the target document to the front and use the Crop tool. The resulting document will match the first document in both pixel dimensions and resolution.
- The Clear button empties the numeric fields in the Options Bar and enables you to use the Crop tool without constraints. The resulting image maintains the original image's resolution and is of the pixel dimensions of the bounding box you drag.

*To learn about Photoshop's three resampling algorithms, see "The Five Interpolation Options," later in this chapter.*

## Refining a Crop Marquee

You can drag the Crop tool in any direction. Holding down the Shift key while dragging constrains the width-height ratio to a square. After you've dragged the Crop tool, a crop marquee or bounding box is visible (see Figure 15.8). By default, the area outside the bounding box is *shielded*, shown with a colored overlay. (This option is discussed in the following section.) The bounding box has eight handles, one in each corner and one in the middle of each side.

15

**Figure 15.8**
**The area within the bounding box or crop marquee is retained; the pixels outside are discarded by default.**

You can resize and reposition the crop marquee in a variety of ways:

- Position the cursor on any handle and drag to resize the bounding box. When on a side handle, the cursor changes to a vertical or horizontal two-headed arrow. On a corner handle, the cursor becomes a diagonal two-headed arrow.
- Hold down the Shift key while dragging a corner handle to maintain the original width-height ratio.
- Hold down the (Option) [Alt] key while dragging to resize from the center.
- The Shift and (Option) [Alt] keys can be used together.
- Position the cursor inside the bounding box and drag to move the crop area without resizing it.
- Position the cursor just outside the bounding box to rotate. (Rotating a crop is discussed in the section "Crop Rotation," later in this chapter.) When positioned to rotate, the cursor shows as a curved two-headed arrow. The Shift key snaps the rotation to increments of 15°. Images in Bitmap mode cannot be rotated with the Crop tool.
- Reposition the crosshair to change the point around which the bounding box is rotated and from which it is scaled. The *target*, as it is sometimes known, is located in the center of the bounding box by default. It can be dragged to any point in the image window, inside or outside the bounding box.
- When being resized or rotated, the bounding box brings an edge or a handle within 8 pixels of the image's edge, and the handle snaps to that edge. You can override this behavior with the Ctrl key. Keep in mind that if the bounding box is rotated, only the handle being dragged will snap—if another handle goes slightly past the edge of the bounding box, you'll have no warning.
- If resizing or rotating extends the bounding box beyond the edge of the image window, when the crop is executed, one of three things happens, depending on the content of the image:
    - If the image is flattened (contains only a single layer named *Background*), the area beyond the image window is filled with the background color.

- If the image is not flattened, the area beyond the image window is filled with transparent pixels.
- If the image contains hidden pixels (pixels that exist in that area beyond the image window's edge), the pixels will be visible.

- The Esc key cancels a crop. The (Return) [Enter] key executes the crop.

When the bounding box has been rotated at least 10°, you can *skew* it to produce special effects by (Option)-dragging [Alt]-dragging a corner handle (see Figure 15.9). After skewing, you can rotate and resize the bounding box again. A skewed bounding box still produces a rectangular crop.

Figure 15.9
The skewed bounding box is shown in the large image window. The smaller image shows the result of the skewed crop.

## Active Crop Marquee Options

When a bounding box is active in the image window, the Crop tool's options change in the Options Bar (see Figure 15.10).

The following are the additional Crop tool options:

- **Cropped Area: Delete/Hide**—The option of hiding rather than deleting the cropped area is not available when the image consists of a background layer only. Adding an empty layer to a flattened image activates this option. When hidden, the cropped area remains part of the image. The Move tool can be used to reposition a layer to change what area is "cropped." Remember that any hidden pixels are lost when the image is flattened, and until the image is flattened, the crop does not reduce the file size.

> Renaming the background layer also activates the hide option. Flattening reverts the name to "Background" and discards the hidden image information.

**Figure 15.10**
The secondary options are not available until the Crop tool has been dragged in the image window.

- **Shield**—This option masks the part of the image to be deleted.
- **Color**—By default, Photoshop uses gray to shield parts of an image to be cropped. Click the swatch to change the shield color. Remember, too, that the color is not dependent on the image's color mode—any RGB color is available, even when you're working with an image in Grayscale or Bitmap mode.
- **Opacity**—By default, Photoshop shields at 75% opacity. Use the slider or type in the numeric field to change the opacity. Click the word *Opacity* in the Options Bar to automatically select the content of the field. You then simply type the new value.
- **Perspective**—The Perspective option allows you to adjust the cropping marquee to correct perspective errors. This option is essentially an extension of the capability to rotate the crop marquee to correct the horizontal/vertical axes. It is designed to work primarily with architectural photography and is discussed later in this chapter in the section "Perspective Crop."

When you use the Hide option, cropping does not reduce the file size—the cropped pixels remain part of the image. The menu command Image, Reveal All expands the image window to show all hidden pixels. Hidden image data is maintained in Photoshop (PSD) and TIFF file formats.

*Want to get rid of hidden pixels, but don't want to flatten the image? See "Trimming the Fat" in the "Mastering Photoshop" section at the end of this chapter.*

# Crop Rotation

You can rotate an active crop marquee to realign the image to the image window. This method is especially useful for images that were scanned at an angle and photographs taken with a handheld camera. Rotating results in resampling (the image must be re-created) and therefore introduces some softness to the appearance. Rotating in 90° increments does not resample.

*Sharpening to remove the out-of-focus look that can be introduced by resampling is discussed later in this chapter. See "The Science of Sharpening."*

Rotating with the Crop tool can be as simple as dragging a bounding box, moving the cursor outside it, and dragging. However, you can use a few basic techniques to make your rotation more precise:

- Keep the Info palette open, especially if you need a precise rotation. The A: field in the upper-right corner of the Info palette shows the angle of rotation while you work.
- Drag the Measure tool along a straight edge in the image to find the precise angle of rotation.
- The farther the cursor is from the bounding box, the greater your control of rotation.

A common method of minimizing moiré patterns when scanning printed images is to place the original on the scanner at a 15° angle. Afterward, rotate the image in Photoshop with the Transform command or when cropping.

Generally speaking, if the image contains even one line that should be horizontal or vertical, you can get a precise rotation by using these simple steps:

1. Drag a crop marquee. Align one corner with the end of a vertical or horizontal line (see Figure 15.11, top left).
2. Drag the point-of-rotation target crosshairs from the center of the bounding box to that corner (Figure 15.11, top right).
3. Rotate the bounding box until one edge aligns with the edge in the image (Figure 15.11, bottom left).
4. Drag the side handles of the bounding box to finish framing the crop (Figure 15.11, bottom right).

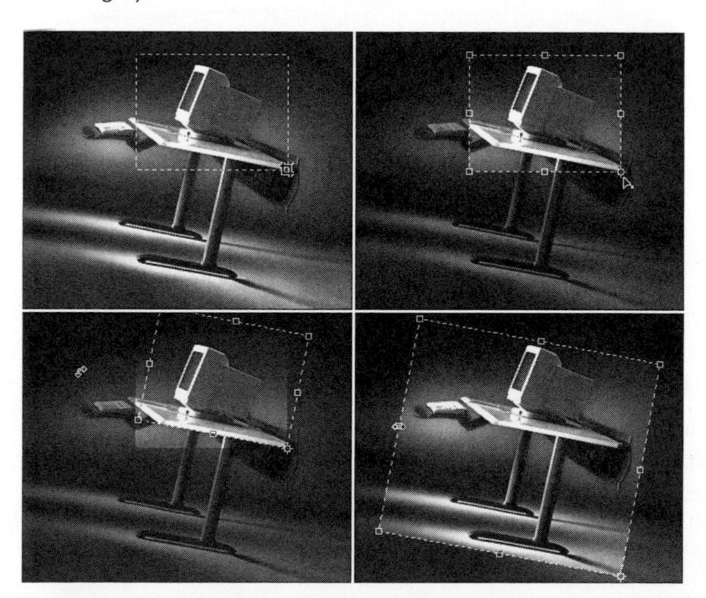

**Figure 15.11**
The four steps shown ensure a precisely rotated crop.

*Unable to get an exact rotation for your crop? See "Rotate, Then Crop" in the "Mastering Photoshop" section at the end of this chapter.*

## Perspective Crop

The Crop tool can be used to correct keystoning and off-angle images. *Keystoning* is the perspective distortion that comes from photographing a tall object or shooting upward or downward. When there's an active crop marquee in the image window, you can select the Perspective check box. This setting allows the corners of the marquee to be repositioned (see Figure 15.12). When the crop is executed, the corners of the bounding box are pulled or pushed to again form a rectangle, and the image is re-created to match.

Figure 15.12
Each of the corner points can be dragged to a new position. The goal is to make the four sides of the bounding box align with the four edges of the subject. The result of this crop is shown in the inset.

If you attempt to crop to a perspective that couldn't exist in nature, Photoshop refuses to execute it, and a warning message appears, giving you the option to choose Cancel or Don't Crop. If you click Don't Crop, the crop marquee is dismissed and you start over. Clicking Cancel, on the other hand, returns you to the image with the existing bounding box so that you can adjust it and try again.

You can avoid this message by ensuring that your bounding box edges align with the actual vertical and horizontal lines of the subject. Here's how to do it:

1. Drag a crop marquee anywhere in the image (see Figure 15.13, Frame A).
2. In the Options Bar, select the Perspective check box (see Figure 15.13, Frame B).
3. Position the corners of the bounding box so that the sides of the marquee align with any part of the image that should be rectangular (see Figure 15.13, Frame C). The four selected edges need not be the outer edges of the subject. The bounding box will not be rectangular.
4. Zoom in to fine-tune your alignment (see Figure 15.13, Frame D). Although you can't switch to the Zoom tool while cropping, you can use the keyboard shortcuts (Command-plus) [Ctrl+plus] and (Command-minus) [Ctrl+minus] to zoom and use the spacebar to reposition the image in the window with the Hand tool. You might find it easier to work with Shield turned off.

5. Drag the side handles (not the corner handles) of the bounding box outward to encompass the entire area to be cropped (see Figure 15.13, Frame E). Using the side handles ensures that the relationship among the corners is maintained.

6. Drag the crosshair symbol to the position that you estimate should be the center of the corrected image (see Figure 15.13, Frame F).

7. Use the (Return) [Enter] key or the check mark button in the Options Bar to execute the crop.

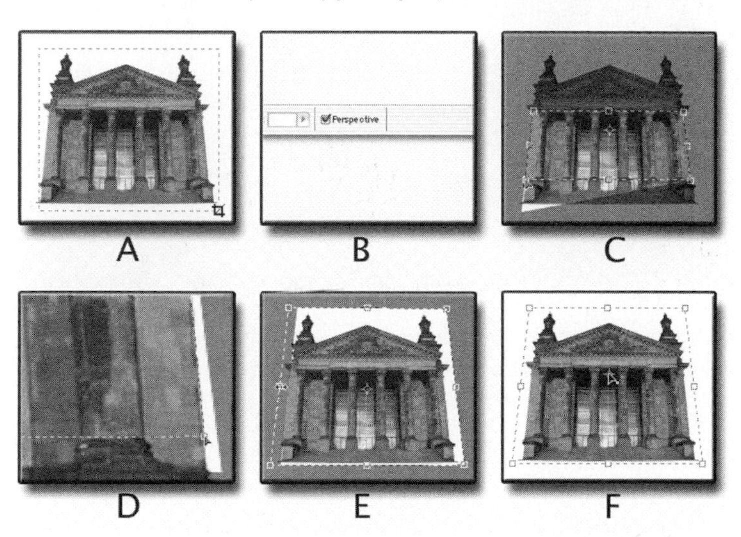


Figure 15.13
Aligning the bounding box edges.

The perspective crop feature can be used for more than just keystone correction in architectural photography. In Figure 15.14, a photograph of a mirror was taken off-center, to avoid showing a reflection of the photographer, and then corrected with a perspective crop.

Figure 15.14
The perspective crop bounding box was aligned by using corresponding points on the frame rather than the mirror itself.

If you compare the left and right inner edges of the frame in Figure 15.14, you'll see a slight discrepancy that perspective cropping cannot remove. To the left, the inner edge of the frame is visible, but it is not visible on the right (see Figure 15.15).

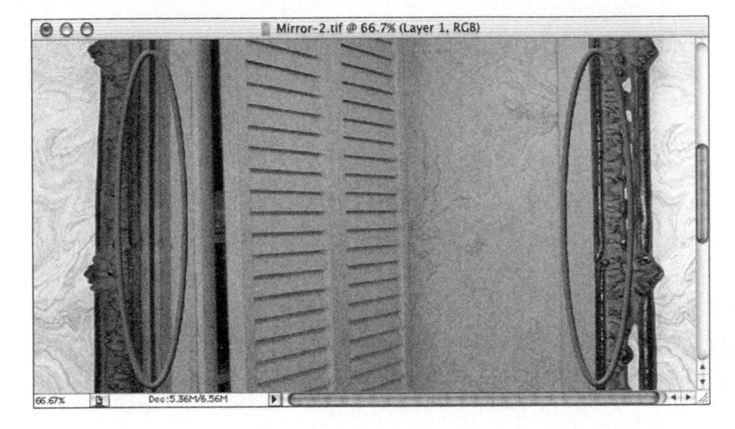


**Figure 15.15**
The ovals identify the areas of concern.

An even more dramatic example of this phenomenon is shown in Figure 15.16. The inner edge of the left side of the arch is visible in the original photo, but the inner part of the right side is not. After cropping, the face of the structure is perfectly aligned to the "camera," but it's apparent that the image is unnatural.

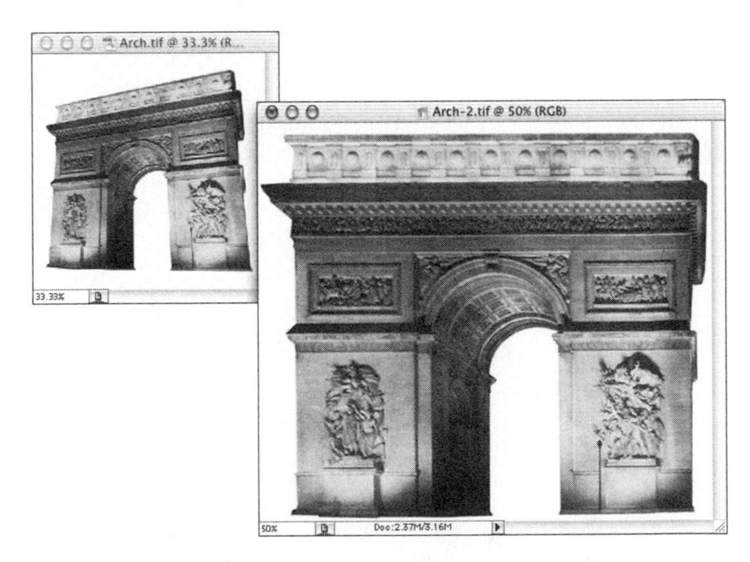


**Figure 15.16**
Because the left side of the inner arch is visible, it appears that the passageway runs at an angle under the arch, rather than straight through.

Perspective cropping is suitable for two-dimensional images; it cannot correct for depth presented in a third dimension. You'll find this problem when correcting photos that were taken at an angle. In some cases, such as the arch shown here, the problem is significant enough to make the image unacceptable. In other cases, the problem might be minor enough to overlook or correctable through cloning.

## Enlarging a Canvas with the Crop Tool

The Crop tool can also be used to enlarge an image, much like the Canvas Size command. Zoom out and enlarge the image window so that empty gray shows around the actual image. Drag the Crop tool, and then drag one or more of the side or corner handles of the bounding box beyond the existing image (see Figure 15.17).

**Figure 15.17**
Use (Return) [Enter] to execute the canvas enlargement. If the image contains a background layer, the background color is added. If not, transparent pixels are added.

## The Trim Command

The Trim command, like the Crop command, is found under the Image menu. It can be considered a "selective crop" command. It removes pixels from an image and reduces the image size based on color. It is especially useful for scans that include a bit of surrounding black or white.

> Enlarging a canvas is often done to allow room for a border. If the image is flattened, make the border color the background color before enlarging—your border will be automatically added.

The Trim dialog box, shown in Figure 15.18, offers the choice of trimming transparent pixels or pixels based on whatever color is found in the image's upper-left or lower-right corner. You can also protect one or more edges by unchecking the boxes in the dialog box before clicking OK. The pixels—and canvas—are deleted only to the extent that the image remains rectangular.

15

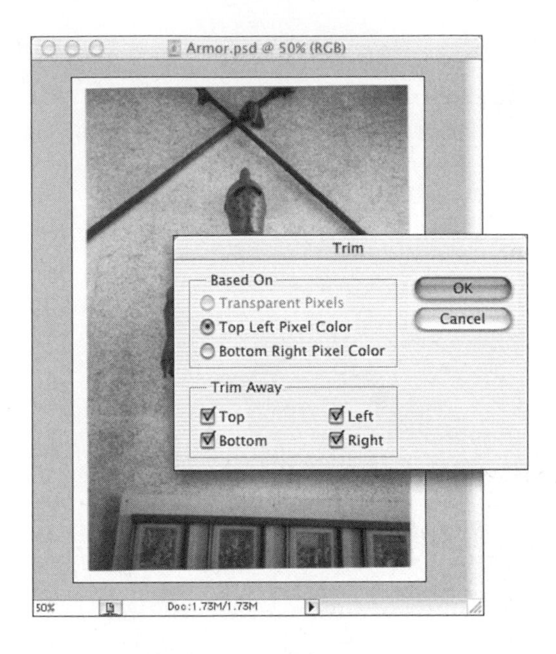


Figure 15.18
The color in the corner need not be black or white, but Trim removes only pixels that exactly match the color found.

# RESIZING CANVASES AND IMAGES

The Image menu contains a pair of commands that change an image's size. The Canvas Size command works like the Crop tool in its normal mode, deleting (or adding) an image area without changing the image that remains. Image Size resamples the image, maintaining the image appearance as much as possible while increasing or decreasing the number of pixels used to portray the image.

If the Trim command isn't getting everything you want it to remove, try using the Magic Wand and deleting first to create a uniform area to trim. Consider using Trim before any technique that relies on a histogram, too. Removing those excess pixels gives you a more accurate read of the image.

*Resampling* is the process of changing the number of pixels used to create the same picture. *Interpolation* is the formula for calculating the new pixel colors to best re-create the original image.

## Image, Canvas Size

The Canvas Size command can enlarge or reduce the actual image area of a file. Blank pixels can be added or parts of the image can be deleted. Whether you're enlarging or reducing the canvas, the part of the original image that remains is untouched—it has exactly the same pixels it had before. The Canvas Size dialog box gives you precise control over the amount of canvas added or subtracted, but limited control over *where* it is added or subtracted (see Figure 15.19).

The upper section of the dialog box, Current Size, tells you the starting point. The lower set of numbers, including the new file size, are updated as you make changes. If you change the unit of measure, Photoshop automatically calculates an equivalent value.

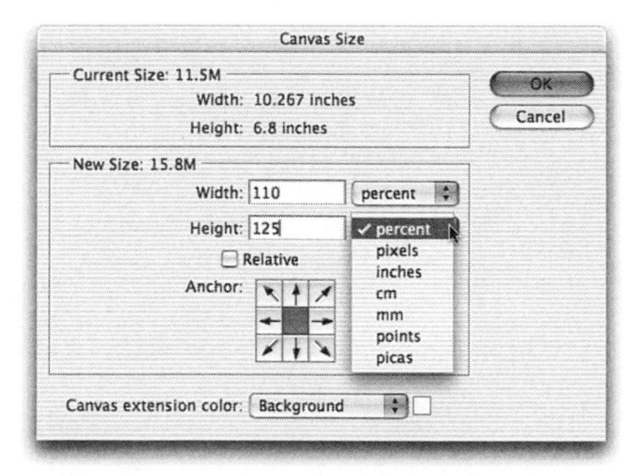


Figure 15.19
The Width and Height pop-up menus offer the same units of measure. Using 100% results in no change to the image's size.

The Relative check box is a relief to the math-weary Photoshop user. Instead of being forced to do addition or multiplication to determine the desired size of the canvas, you can now select the check box and enter the amount you want to add (or subtract). For example, if you want to add a 50-pixel border around the image in Figure 15.19, you simply select Relative, set the unit of measure to Pixels, and enter **50** for both the Width and Height fields.

The 3×3 grid to the right of the word *Anchor* in the dialog box is referred to as the *proxy*. Click a box to show where you want the original artwork in relation to the new canvas size. If you leave the proxy in the middle (the default), the new pixels are split top/bottom and left/right; half of the new width goes to either side, and half of the new height goes to the top and half to the bottom. If you select the upper-left box of the proxy, all the new pixels are added to the right and the bottom. The proxy shows with arrows where the new canvas will be added.

When you enter a value for width or height that is *smaller* than the original, a message appears onscreen, warning that your image will lose some pixels. Where the canvas is chopped is determined by the proxy—the proxy's arrows indicate parts of the image to be deleted.

The final pop-up menu allows you to specify the appearance of the background canvas as it's added around the current image. You can select Background or Foreground from the menu to choose the current values for these options, or you can select white, black, or 50% gray. To select a custom color, choose Other from the menu, or simply click the small color swatch to the right of the menu. Either action will launch the Color Picker, allowing you to select the desired background color.

The currently selected color is shown in a box next to the pop-up menu, which can also be clicked to open the Color Picker.

## Image, Image Size

You can use the Image Size command to do one or both of two things: You can use it to change the image's *resolution*, which tells the printing device how large or small to make each pixel. You can also use it to change the number of pixels used to create the image, known as *resampling*. The Image Size dialog box is shown in Figure 15.20. The lower dialog box is set to change the resolution without resampling the image. The upper part of the dialog box is grayed out, indicating that no change will be made to the actual pixel content of the image.

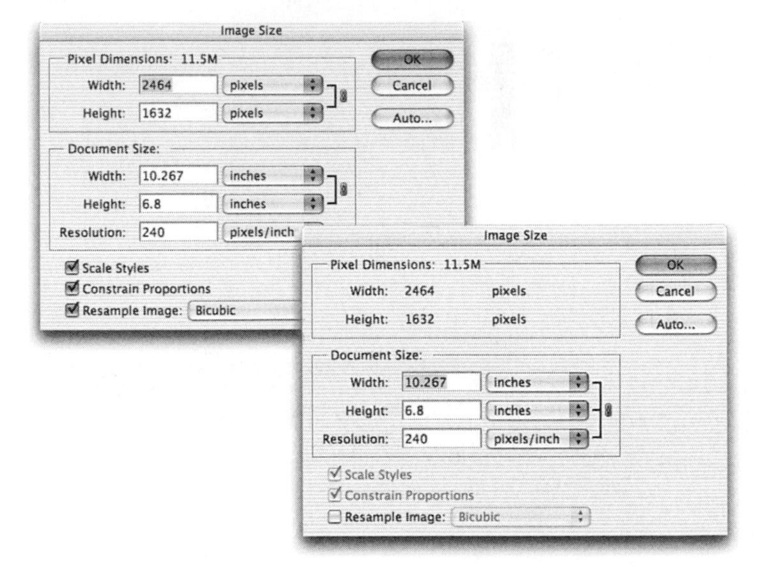


**Figure 15.20**
If the image will be resampled, the pixel dimensions change, and the file size is reflected at the top of the dialog box.

When the Resample check box is not selected, you change only the print information for the image. Whether for commercial offset printing or inkjet output, resolution determines the size of the image on the printed page and the fineness of the printed image's detail. Resolution has no effect on the image's appearance onscreen. Web graphics, for example, occupy a particular amount of space in a Web browser's window based strictly on pixel dimensions—resolution is insignificant for Web graphics.

*For a full discussion of resolution, see "Image Resolution," in Chapter 4, "Pixels, Vectors, and Resolutions."*

When the Resample check box *is* selected, Photoshop changes the number of pixels used to create the image. The artwork is maintained (to the greatest degree possible), but the number of pixels with which it's portrayed changes. (Resolution and print dimensions can be changed at the same time.) Consider resampling as the process of re-creating the image with more or fewer pixels.

## Two Types of Resampling

When resampling with Image Size, you make the image either larger (increase the number of pixels) or smaller (decrease the number of pixels). Certain other operations in Photoshop also resample, such as cropping to a specified size or resolution. Rotating or scaling a selection or image also resamples but maintains the exact number of pixels in the image. The pixels are recalculated to re-create the image with the new size or rotated appearance.

Increasing the number of pixels in an image is called *upsampling*. Reducing the number of pixels in an image is *downsampling*. Figure 15.21 shows a comparison. The top image is the original. The middle image was downsampled to 75% of the original size. The bottom image was upsampled to 125% of the original size.

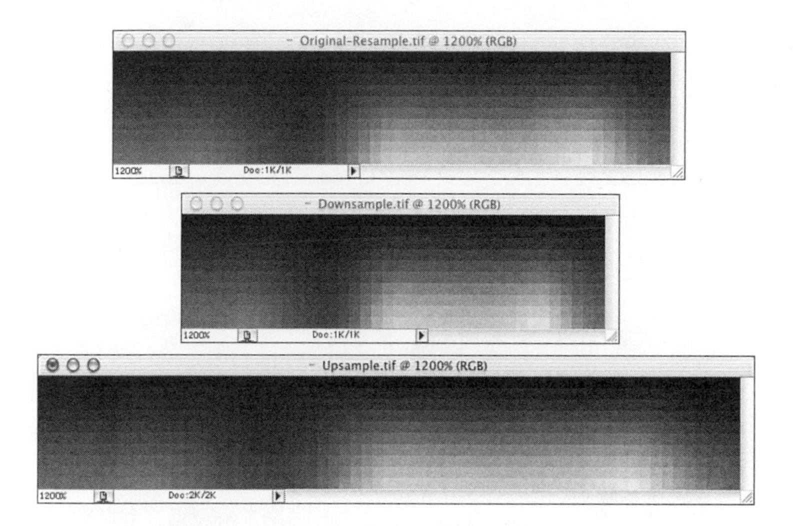


**Figure 15.21**
All three images are zoomed to 1200% so that the individual pixels are visible. The same basic gradient pattern is maintained, but the three images use different numbers of pixels to do so.

To get a feel for how Photoshop resamples, take a look at Figure 15.22. The original image in the center consists of exactly 8 pixels, 4 black and 4 white. For each of the resampled copies, Photoshop has determined what pixels to add or subtract to best maintain the image's appearance.

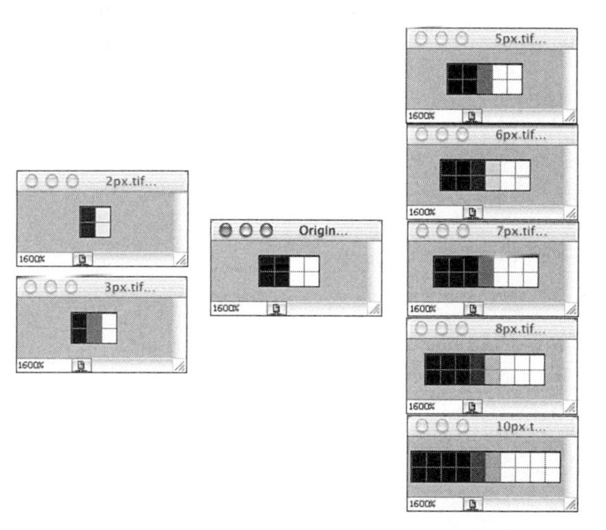


**Figure 15.22**
To simplify the demonstration, only the width of each sample image was changed. The resampling method was Bicubic.

To the left, two copies have been downsampled. On top, Photoshop had no tough calculation—a pair of black and a pair of white pixels were deleted. On the bottom, the resampling process introduced an intermediate color, a compromise between the two abutting colors.

To the right of the original, the copies were upsampled. In each case, one or two columns of intermediary pixels were added. At the top, you can see that a single column of gray pixels has been added between the black and white pixels. Immediately below that sample, the 6-pixel-wide sample has two columns of gray pixels—one dark gray, one light gray. When a copy was upsampled to 7 pixels wide, Photoshop added a column of gray in the middle *in addition to* a column of black to the left and a column of white to the right. Both of the upsampled copies at the lower right had two gray columns to create a transition between black and white.

When Photoshop has a slightly more complex image, it must calculate the relationships among all the surrounding pixels to determine the new color value for each pixel. Figure 15.23 shows how more and more intermediately colored pixels must be introduced as the same image is upsampled several times.

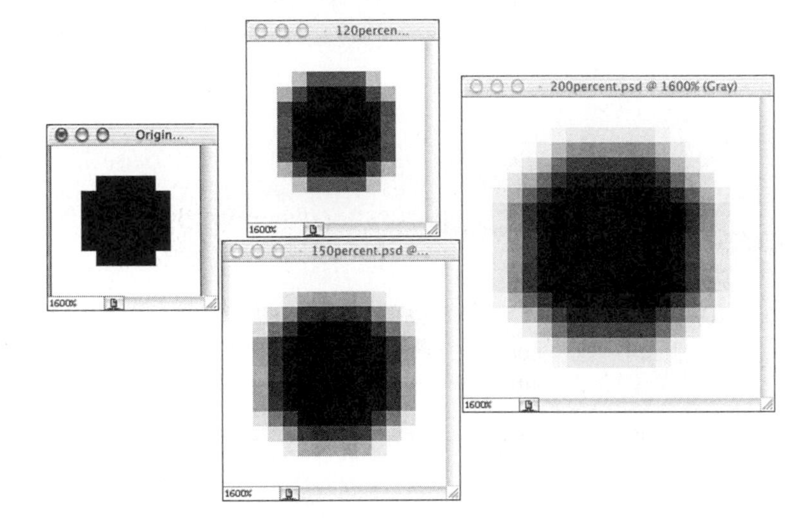


Figure 15.23
The original image is on the left. It was copied and upsampled. Then the copy was duplicated and upsampled, and yet again to create the largest version.

When working with photographic images, Photoshop follows the same basic procedure outlined here. The color values of neighboring pixels are compared and an intermediary color is used. As you can see in Figure 15.24, downsampling, throwing away image data, can have a negative effect on image detail. Upsampling, on the other hand, can introduce *softness*, an out-of-focus look to an image.

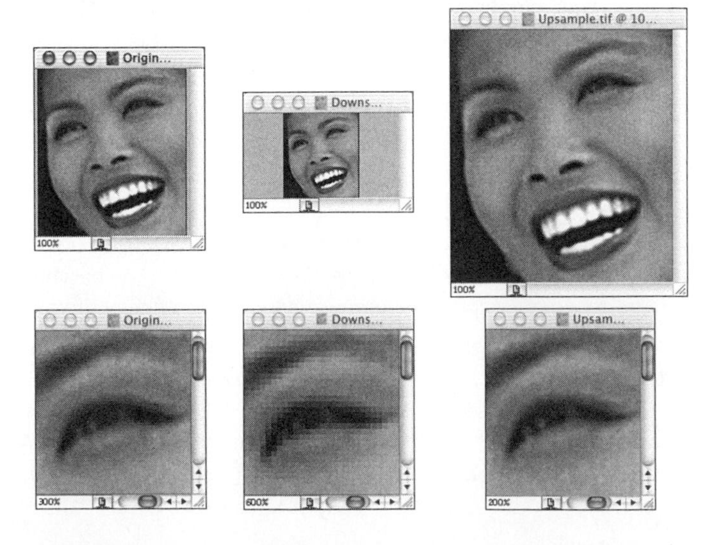


Figure 15.24
The original image (left) was downsampled to 50% width and height (center) and upsampled to 150% width and height (right).

Generally speaking, when you're preparing images for print, it's better to scan at a higher resolution than necessary and downsample rather than scan at a lower resolution and upsample. When you must upsample, consider using a sharpening filter afterward. (Sharpening is discussed later in this chapter.) Your best bet, however, is to calculate the size you'll need and scan to that size whenever possible.

*Wondering what's the easiest way to determine how to scan to size? See "Pixel Size, Please" in the "Mastering Photoshop" section at the end of this chapter.*

## The Five Interpolation Options

The Image Size dialog box and Photoshop's General Preferences offer a choice of five types of resampling. The selection made in the Preferences is used for scaling and rotating selections and images. Each time you open the Image Size dialog box, you can choose the method of interpolation:

- **Bicubic Sharper**—A comparison is made of all surrounding pixels, and a compromise value is assigned with enhanced edge contrast to sharpen the overall result.
- **Bicubic Smoother**—A comparison is made of all surrounding pixels and a compromise value is assigned with reduced edge contrast to smooth the overall result.
- **Bicubic**—A comparison is made of all surrounding pixels, and a compromise value is assigned.
- **Bilinear**—A comparison is made of the immediately adjoining pixels, and a compromise value is assigned.
- **Nearest Neighbor**—The color of one adjoining pixel is duplicated.

The Bicubic interpolation methods are the most appropriate for photographic and other continuous-tone images. Use Bicubic Sharper when applying significant downsampling and Bicubic Smoother when applying a high degree of upsampling. The standard Bicubic setting is often effective when you're upsampling and downsampling in smaller increments. With all Bicubic options, it's important to remember that the actual characteristics of the photograph will dictate the best solution. As a result, you may want to experiment with several Bicubic settings and compare the results.

For non-photographic images, Nearest Neighbor is often the best choice, especially for line art and artwork that contains areas of solid color with distinct edges. Figure 15.25 shows a comparison of Nearest Neighbor and Bicubic for a piece of artwork that consists of solid colors.

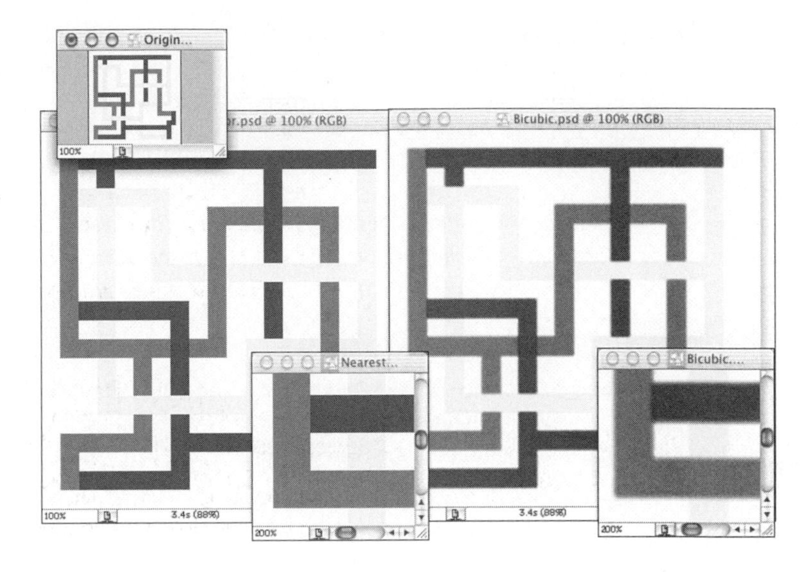


Figure 15.25
At the top left, the original. To the left, a copy was scaled to 400% using Nearest Neighbor. To the right, another copy was scaled to 400% using Bicubic interpolation. The insets are zoomed to show the detail.

# THE SCIENCE OF SHARPENING

Sharpening is the process of emphasizing the detail of an image. By increasing the contrast along edges and areas of contrast within the image, you can make the picture look "crisper" or more focused. Sharpening is especially important after an image has been upsampled. Photoshop's Filters menu offers four sharpening filters, and you'll find the Sharpen tool in the Toolbox.

## How Sharpening Works

The Sharpen tool and the Sharpen and Sharpen More commands increase the contrast between neighboring pixels. They affect every pixel within the image or selection (commands) or under the brush (tool). Figure 15.26 shows the result when Sharpen More is applied to a selection.

The Sharpen Edges command looks for areas of high contrast to identify edges in an image. The sharpening is applied only along those edges (see Figure 15.27).

The Unsharp Mask command is far more complicated than the other sharpen commands. It creates a copy of the image or selection, blurs it, and compares it to the original to identify edges. The contrast along those edges is then increased by lightening and darkening the pixels on either side. In a nutshell, Unsharp Mask finds areas of contrast and emphasizes that contrast. Unlike the other three sharpen commands, Unsharp Mask gives you control over its application with a dialog box (see Figure 15.28).

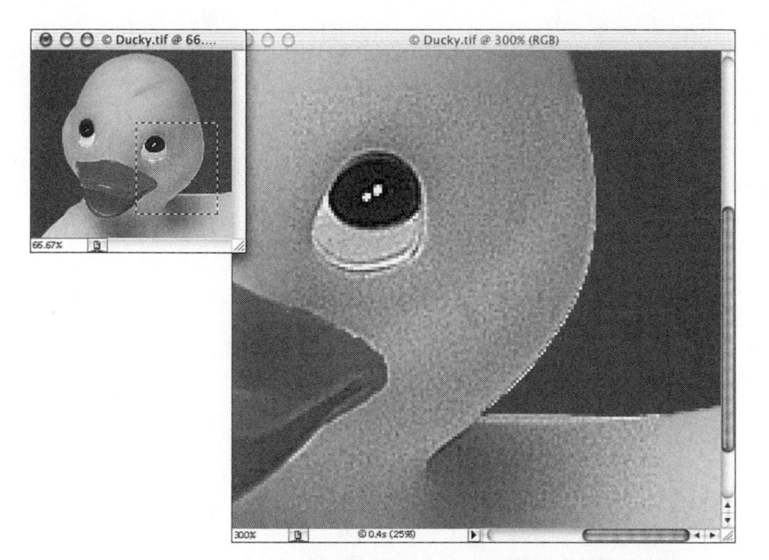


Figure 15.26
The edges of the selection are evident in the zoomed version, even without "marching ants." The Sharpen More filter has increased the contrast among all pixels.



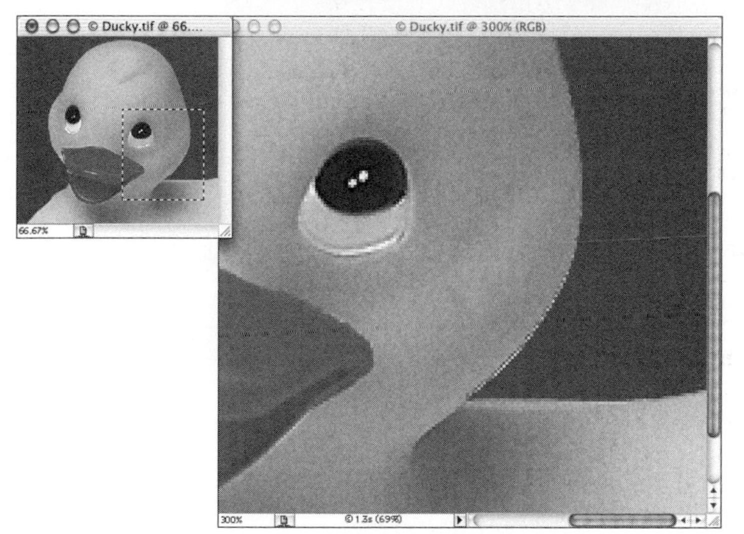


Figure 15.27
In contrast to the Sharpen and Sharpen More filters and the Sharpen tool, Sharpen Edges attempts to apply sharpening only along lines of great contrast.

## Working with the Unsharp Mask Filter

To increase the amount of contrast along an edge, Unsharp Mask creates a pair of "halos," one on either side of the edge (see Figure 15.29). These light and dark halos, emphasized in the sample image, in effect outline the edges to make them more noticeable.

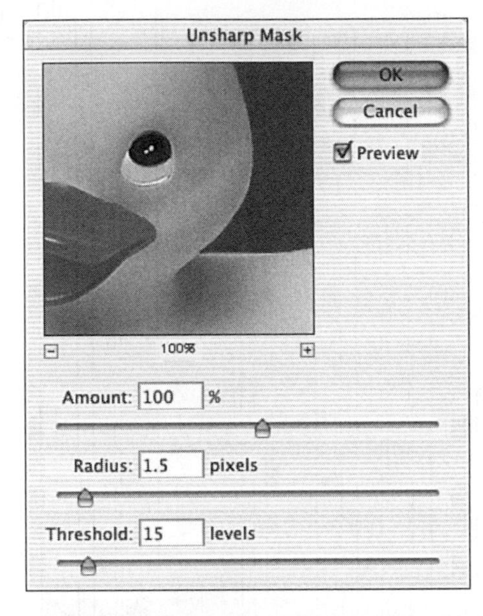


**Figure 15.28**
The Amount setting indicates the level of contrast that will be applied. The Radius setting determines the width of the area along edges to which the contrast will be applied. The Threshold setting determines how much a pixel must vary from the adjoining pixels to be considered an edge.

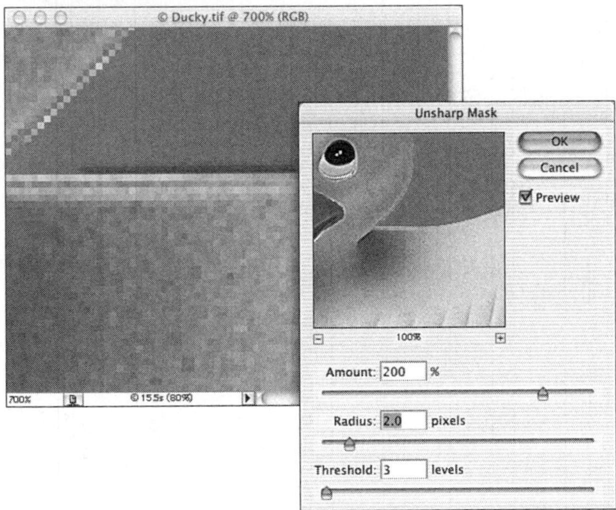


**Figure 15.29**
A large amount of sharpening has been applied to emphasize the halos along the edges.

Areas with lots of small detail require special care. In Figure 15.30, oversharpening makes the selected area look garish and unnatural.

Instead of reducing the amount of sharpening, an increase in the Threshold setting improves the result (see Figure 15.31).

Figure 15.30
The Unsharp Mask filter is being applied to the right half of the photograph only. The settings are shown in the dialog box.

Figure 15.31
Increasing Threshold for this image applies the sharpening between the leaves and the fruit and between the leaves and the shadows, but does not attempt to sharpen the leaves themselves.

Understanding the three Unsharp Mask sliders is key to knowing how to apply the filter:

- **Amount**—This setting determines the amount of contrast to be added wherever Unsharp Mask finds an edge. Consider it to be the brightness of the halos. The value can range from 1% to 500%. Typically, an Amount setting of 100% is a good starting point for a low-resolution image, and 150%–200% is more appropriate for high-resolution images.
- **Radius**—Ranging from 0.1 pixel to 250 pixels, the Radius setting determines how wide an area will be affected where Unsharp Mask finds an edge. Think of this setting as the width of the halo. For most images, 1 or 2 pixels is adequate to restore detail.

- **Threshold**—Threshold can range from 0 to 255, just as any other 8-bit value. It determines how much a pixel must vary from the neighboring pixels to be sharpened. Threshold is used to actually find the edges. When 0 is chosen, Unsharp Mask sharpens all pixels in the image. Threshold also helps prevent the filter from introducing noise into areas of relatively uniform color. Typically, a value between 2 and 20 is entered.

Unsharp Mask can introduce color shifts, especially when applied to images in CMYK mode. Here are three techniques for avoiding color shifts near edges:

- Convert the image to Lab mode, apply the Unsharp Mask to the L channel, and then return to RGB or CMYK mode. This technique restricts the effect of the filter to the brightness of each pixel.
- Apply the Unsharp Mask filter normally and then immediately use the menu command Edit, Fade Unsharp Mask. Switch the blending mode from Normal to Luminosity. (This technique is the same as applying the filter to the L channel in Lab mode, without the need to switch color mode.) You can also reduce the effect of the Unsharp Mask, if necessary, with the Opacity slider.
- When working in CMYK mode, apply the filter to the Black channel only. (It is usually better to sharpen in RGB mode before converting the color mode, but if the image is already in CMYK mode, don't change mode just to sharpen.)

## Selective Sharpening

Different areas of an image might require different amounts of sharpening. This is especially true for images that have a detailed subject against a detailed background. Sharpening the foreground to a greater degree can make it much more distinct (see Figure 15.32).

Figure 15.32
The original image (left) can certainly be improved by sharpening. However, using a mask (center) allows the castle to be sharpened separately from the immediate foreground and the very detailed background (right).

# PHOTOSHOP AT WORK: USING THE BLUR FILTER TO SHARPEN IMAGES

Although it may sound paradoxical, you actually can use the Blur filter to ***sharpen*** an image. Specifically, you can blur one area of your image to make the other area look sharper. In this example, you intentionally soften the background areas of an image, making the subject appear sharper in comparison. This is a good approach for images that are too soft to be remedied using the Unsharp Mask filter alone. Here are the steps to follow:

1. Choose File, Open and select the file you want to modify.
2. Choose Filter, Sharpen, Unsharp Mask and sharpen the image as desired. Begin by sharpening the image as much as you can (see Figure 15.33).

**Figure 15.33**
Begin by applying an Unsharp Mask filter to sharpen the overall image as much as possible.

3. Using Photoshop's selection tools, select the area of the background to which you want to apply the blur. In this example, I've selected the buildings on the right side of the image (see Figure 15.34).
4. Choose Select, Feather. Then, in the Feather Selection dialog box, specify the desired pixel value. The amount of feathering you choose depends on the overall resolution of the image and the subject matter. Click OK to apply the effect.

Figure 15.34
Select the background area to be softened.

5. Choose Filter, Blur, Gaussian Blur to open the Gaussian Blur dialog box. Adjust the Radius slider until the proper blur amount appears in the window; when you are finished adjusting the blur, click OK. Figure 15.35 shows the image after the Gaussian blur was applied.

*Feathering* softens the edges of a selection, helping it to blend with unselected areas. Gauss was a mathematician; the *Gaussian blur* effect is based on his mathematical formulas.

Figure 15.35
Apply the Gaussian Blur filter to soften the background selection.

6. Press (Command-D) [Ctrl+D] to deselect the selection. Then select the Blur tool from the Toolbox and brush in the smaller areas to complete the blur transition.



# MASTERING PHOTOSHOP

## Trimming the Fat

*My file size is bloated from lots of hidden data. Is there a way to get rid of the excess pixels without flattening my image?*

You have a couple options. You can drag a crop marquee that fills the window and then choose Delete rather than Hide, or you can do it much more easily and precisely with two commands: Select, Select All and then Image, Crop. All done!

## Rotate, Then Crop

*Even using the steps shown, I can't rotate my crop exactly right. Is there anything else I can do?*

Try this:

1. From the Toolbox, select the Measure tool. You'll find it under the Eyedropper.
2. Click at one end of a visible line in your image. The edge of a building, a doorjamb, a window ledge, a curb, a distant highway or horizon, even a pencil line you add before scanning will work. Drag the Measure tool along that line. Remember, too, that you can zoom in for precision.
3. Check the Info palette's A: field for the precise angle of the Measure tool's line.
4. Drag a small crop marquee with the Crop tool.
5. Position the cursor far outside the bounding box and drag until the Info palette shows the same rotation recorded for the Measure tool.
6. Drag the side handles of the bounding box to include the area you want in the cropped image. Then press (Return) [Enter].

Alternatively, you can drag the Measure tool as described, and then use the Image, Rotate Canvas, Arbitrary menu command. The Measure tool's angle will already be input for you, so you need only click OK. Now you can crop the image without worrying about rotating the crop bounding box.

# Pixel Size, Please

*All right, your advice is to scan at the size I need for output. But how do I do that?*

The key is calculating the pixel dimensions of the final image and acquiring (scanning) that number of pixels. To scan at your print size, multiply the print dimensions by the print resolution to get the required pixel size. Divide the pixel size by the size of the original in inches. That gives you the required scanning resolution, as shown in this example:

- In your page layout document, the image will occupy a space 3×4 inches, and the line screen frequency for the press that will print the job is 133lpi (lines per inch).
- You know that image resolution should be 1.5 (or 2) times the line screen frequency, so the final image should have a resolution of 200ppi/dpi. (The terms *pixels per inch* and *dots per inch* are often used interchangeably.)
- Therefore, the pixel dimensions of the final image should be 600×800. (That's 3 inches times 200ppi, and 4 inches times 200ppi.)
- The original photo is, let's say, 8×10 inches, but the area of the image that you're going to use in the layout measures only 4.5×6 inches—the rest you either won't scan or will crop out in Photoshop.
- The appropriate scan resolution, therefore, is 133ppi. (That's 600 pixels divided by 4.5 inches, and 800 pixels divided by 6 inches.)

Some scanners make it easy and let you simply type in the print dimensions and resolution. The scan module then calculates the required scan resolution and produces an image of the appropriate pixel dimensions.

III

# POWER PHOTOSHOP

## IN THIS PART

16

# CHANNELS: THE ULTIMATE CREATIVE CONTROL

## IN THIS CHAPTER

Photoshop is about color. It's about assigning the correct color to individual pixels. Whether we're working with commands or tools, filters or adjustments, or even paths and type, it's all about making sure the final pixels are the right colors. And all the color information is stored in channels. Manipulating channels gives you incredible power over the appearance of an image, and Photoshop CS adds a new Histogram palette that allows easy access to information about what's in each channel.

This chapter looks at the nature of channels and discusses ways you can work with channels to improve your images. A number of channels-related commands are discussed and the new Histogram palette is introduced.



# THE THREE TYPES OF CHANNELS

Channels are used by Photoshop to store image color information. Every image has at least one channel, just as it has at least one layer (even if that layer is empty). The layers hold artwork, and the channels hold the color information for that artwork. When an image has only a single layer and a single channel, the Layers and Channels palettes may look the same, but they hold different information.

In Photoshop CS, an image can have up to 56 total channels, up from 24 in previous versions of Photoshop. (The total does not include the composite channel, RGB, CMYK, or Lab, which doesn't actually hold color data.) There are three types of channels.

Component color channels contain the basic color information for the image. They are used with RGB, CMYK, and Lab color modes. The single channel in a Grayscale mode image can also be considered a component color channel. Component color channels store the color information for all artwork on layers in the image.

Spot channels are used in CMYK images to hold special color information. A spot channel represents ink that will be printed independently of and in addition to the component inks (cyan, magenta, yellow, and black). Spot colors and their channels are independent of the layers in the image and are defined only in the spot channel.

Alpha channels do not hold color information. Rather, they are saved selections and are referred to as *masks*. Black, white, and shades of gray are used to store the selection information. A hard-edged selection made with the Rectangular Marquee tool would appear by default as a white rectangle on a black background. A heavily feathered selection made with the same tool would appear as an area of white blending through gray to black. Alpha channels can also be used to store transparency information for a variety of file formats.

*For more information on masks and saving selections in Alpha channels, see Chapter 9, "Making Selections and Creating Masks," p. 295.*

> As discussed in Chapter 5, "Color, in Theory and in Practice," in Photoshop, the *color mode* is used to specify how the colors are recorded in the actual image file. The term *color model*, also called a *color space*, refers to a system of defining color. The color mode (with the color model) determines what *component colors* are used to create the specific colors in the image.

For information on how the new maximum number of channels affects compatibility, see "Too Many Channels" in the "Mastering Photoshop" section at the end of this chapter.

## Component Color Channels



Each color mode has different requirements for the Channels palette, but they all have one thing in common: The data that makes up each pixel's color is stored in one or more channels. The basic content of the Channels palette is always one channel for each of a color mode's *component colors*. Consider the component colors to be the ingredients from which an image is put together. In the case of an RGB image, each pixel's color is a function of the red, green, and blue components. You can manipulate the information in a component color channel to edit image color.

*For information on each of the color modes and how they work, see Chapter 5, "Color, in Theory and in Practice," p. 159.*

The Channels palette always has one channel for each component color and, in some cases, a *composite channel* (see Figure 16.1). The composite channel isn't really a channel, in that it doesn't store color information. Rather, its purpose is to enable you to manipulate or edit all the component channels at the same time.

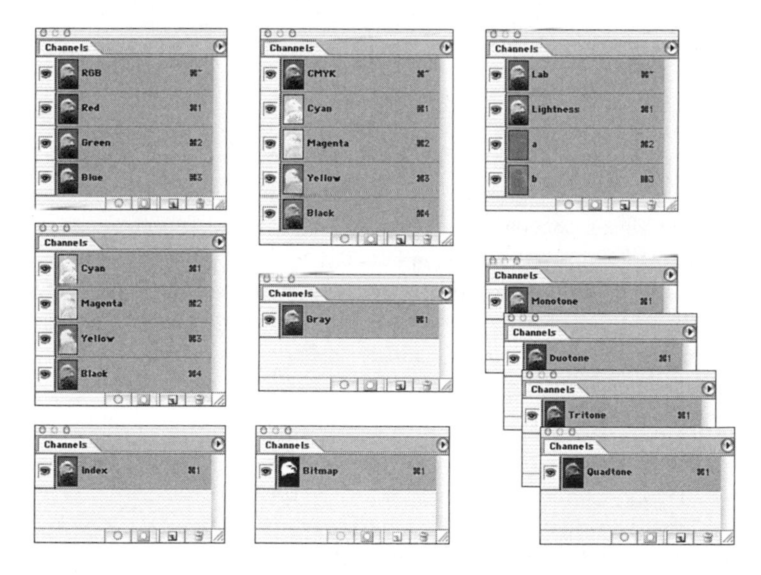


**Figure 16.1**
Photoshop offers eight basic color modes, with Monotone, Duotone, Tritone, and Quadtone lumped together under the label Duotone.

Three of the color modes include composite channels (RGB, CMYK, Lab), four have only one color channel (Grayscale, Duotone, Indexed Color, Bitmap), and one mode has a variable number of channels (Multichannel). The basic channels of each color mode are described in the following sections as they are presented in Figure 16.1, from left to right, top to bottom.

### RGB

In RGB color mode, the component color channels are Red, Green, and Blue, and the composite channel is named RGB. Each pixel's color is determined by the amount of the three component colors, represented by the gray value of the pixel in each of the color channels. The lighter the appearance of a pixel in an individual component color channel, the more of that color in the pixel in the image. When a pixel has high levels of all component colors, it is very bright. Low levels produce darker pixels. Equal amounts of each color, whether high or low, produce shades of gray.

The amount of each component color is measured from 0 to 255, with higher numbers representing more of that color. Typical RGB notation shows the red, green, and blue values for a pixel in order. Examples of RGB notation include 140/133/70 and R:138 G:189 B:212. RGB is used for onscreen work (including Web graphics) and video.



## CMYK

The component channels of the CMYK color mode are named for the four primary inks used in commercial printing—cyan, magenta, yellow, and black. (Black is abbreviated *K* to avoid confusion with blue.) This color mode has a composite color channel, named CMYK. The amount of each ink that will be applied to paper is recorded from 0% to 100%. The higher the amount of each ink, the darker the pixel. CMYK values are always recorded in order, such as 21/18/79/28 or 47C 3M 9Y 0K.

The CMYK color mode is used almost exclusively for preparing images for commercial printing on offset presses. It can, however, also be used with color laser printers, inkjet printers with hardware or software RIPs (raster image processors), or other PostScript devices.

## Lab

Technically known as *CIE Lab* and also seen as *L*a*b*, this color mode is used in Photoshop primarily for image correction and as an interim mode during color conversions. Lab is somewhat different from the other color modes. Instead of having component colors that are combined to create a pixel's color, Lab separates the color into two components and records the lightness of the pixels separately. The lightness is recorded in the *L* channel on a scale from 0 (black) to 100 (white). The *a* channel represents the color value on a scale from green to red, measured from –120 (green) to +120 (red). The *b* channel represents blue to yellow, ranging from –120 (blue) to +120 (yellow). Lab also uses a composite channel (called Lab, of course) in the Channels palette. Lab notation typically records a pixel's color value as 56/–3/39 or 73L –23a –20b, although you might also see the negative numbers in parentheses: 56-(3)-39 or 73L, (23a), (20b).

To understand how the green-red/blue-yellow channel arrangement works, consider the four points of a compass. When North and West pull hardest, the object moves to the northwest. When North and South exert equal pull, and East pulls harder than West, the object moves due east. This is how the *a* and *b* channels influence color. When red and blue are more prominent than green and yellow, they "pull" the color toward purple or pink (depending on the L value). When the *a* channel is at zero, a positive or negative value for the *b* channel determines the color, "pulling" it toward either blue or yellow.

When all channel values are equal, the proportions of the colors are equal, the pixel is in the center of the color wheel, and the pixel is gray. The specific shade of gray (or any other color, for that matter) is determined by the *L* value, the brightness of the pixel, and *b*.

## Multichannel

Pictured in the middle left of Figure 16.1, the Channels palette in Multichannel mode holds one channel for each color but does not have a composite channel. Multichannel mode is used primarily for print, often as a way of gaining direct control of the channels in a Duotone image.

Because the Multichannel color mode is designed primarily for commercial printing, conversion from RGB produces CMY channels, and conversion from CMYK results in only the loss of the composite channel. (However, because Multichannel mode is not color-managed like CMYK, a color shift is likely.)



Conversion to Multichannel from Lab mode produces three alpha channels. When a Duotone image is converted to Multichannel mode, the original color channel is split into a separate spot channel for each assigned color. There is no standard notation for color values of a Multichannel mode because the number and color of the channels vary from image to image. Multichannel documents can consist exclusively of spot color channels.

## Grayscale

Grayscale images have only one component color and, therefore, only one component channel—Gray (with no need for a composite channel). The gray value of each pixel is recorded as a percentage, with 0% representing white and 100% representing black. Keep in mind, however, that grayscale images actually support 256 different levels of gray, despite the 0%—100% scale. Grayscale mode can be used for Web and print.

Although Grayscale uses only 101 variations of color from white (0) to black (100), you can work with more. If you convert an image from Grayscale mode to RGB mode, as long as the three component colors are equal, you still have gray. Your 256 values can range from 0/0/0 (black) through 128/128/128 (mid-gray) to 255/255/255 (white).

## Duotone

A blanket term for Monotone, Tritone, and Quadtone images, as well as Duotone, this color mode has only one channel, regardless of whether one, two, three, or four colors are used in the image. Each of the colors is applied to each pixel. The proportions of the colors are controlled through duotone curves.

*Adjusting duotone curves is discussed later in this chapter. See "Working with Duotone Channels," p. 533.*

## Indexed Color

Instead of having component color channels, Indexed Color mode relies on a *color table*, a listing of up to 256 individual colors that can be included in an image. The Index color channel shown in the palette can be considered comparable to a composite color channel—it enables you to manipulate all the pixels in the image at one time. Only RGB and grayscale images can be converted to Indexed Color mode. A pixel's specific color is recorded as its RGB or Grayscale value. Indexed Color mode is used almost exclusively with Web graphics, in the file formats GIF and PNG-8.

## Bitmap

Each pixel in a Bitmap color mode image is either black or white—there are truly no shades of gray. A pixel's color is recorded, therefore, as black or white or as 0% gray or 100% gray. Bitmap mode is used for some print and Web images, including the WBMP file format (designed for wireless Internet devices and cell phones).

**Caution**

If you ever need to use the Eyedropper tool with an image in Bitmap color mode, set it to Point Sample. Using 3 by 3 Average or 5 by 5 Average is likely to show gray values, which do not exist in the image. However, because the pixels are either black or white, sampling isn't typically required.



## Photoshop at Work: Expanding the Range of Grays

A tip earlier in this chapter pointed out that you can increase the number of different shades of gray by working in RGB color. Here's the explanation:

1. To begin, let's show that Grayscale mode actually supports 256 levels of gray, even when you're working with percentages. Open a new document that's 800×600 pixels in Grayscale mode.
2. Press D on the keyboard to set the colors to black and white and then drag a linear black-to-white gradient across the image.
3. Select the Eyedropper tool and open the Info palette. Set the first color readout to Actual Color (Grayscale) and the second to RGB. You can do this using Palette Options from the Info palette menu or by clicking the Eyedropper icon to the left of each readout in the palette.
4. Zoom in and move the cursor very slowly across the gradient, while watching the Info palette. You'll see that the RGB values can change while the Grayscale reading maintains a single "percent" value. There are as many as three separate shades of gray, all lumped into one "percent" value (see Figure 16.2).

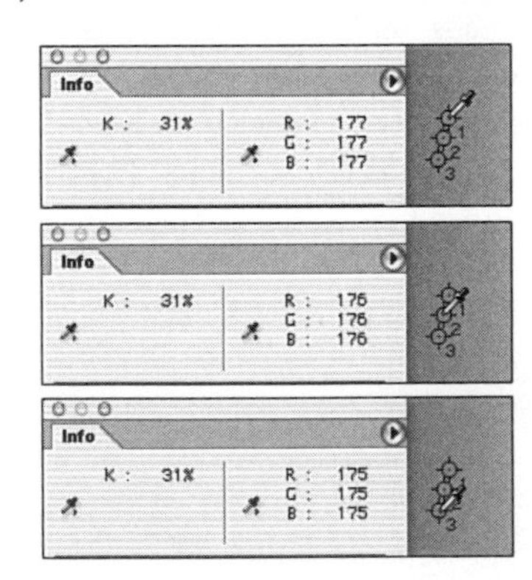


Figure 16.2
Take a look at the three Info palette readings. In this Grayscale image, three different values of gray are all being recorded as 31%.

5. Now, to actually be able to work with 256 levels of gray, use the menu command Image, Mode, RGB.
6. Assign all your color values using equal amounts of red, green, and blue to ensure that they are gray.
7. When you're finished, use the menu command Image, Mode, Grayscale.

*Want to see how the Grayscale percent values compare to RGB? See "Matching the Grays" in the "Mastering Photoshop" section at the end of this chapter.*

**Caution**

Images containing spot channels should be placed into a page-layout program in the DCS 2.0 file format. Although the TIFF format supports spot colors, your page-layout program might not recognize the additional channels or generate color separations from them.



## Spot Color Channels

Spot color channels are primarily used with CMYK and Multichannel documents. They are designed to provide a channel for additional inks to be used in commercial printing. The location in the image where the ink should be applied is stored in the spot channel. A separate printing plate is generated, and an additional run through the press is required. This usually increases the cost of the print job. (Remember that Photoshop can now work with as many as 56 channels.)

If you need to ensure an exact match for a corporate logo, you might want to use a spot color. Another typical use is extending an image's color range beyond what can be produced by using CMYK inks. You can also add neon and metallic colors to an image with spot channels. Spot channels are also used to identify areas of an image over which a varnish will be applied.

*Want to know how to make spot colors lower your printing costs? See "Stopping Some Presses" in the "Mastering Photoshop" section at the end of this chapter.*

A spot channel is added to the image—and to the Channels palette—by using the Channels palette menu command New Spot Channel. In the dialog box, click the color swatch to open the Color Picker (see Figure 16.3).

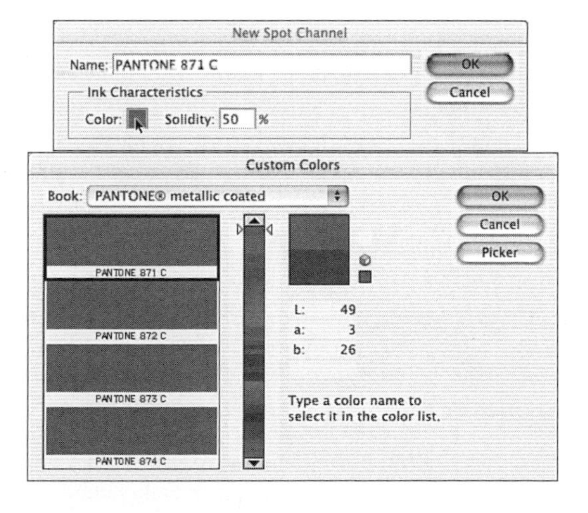


**Figure 16.3**
Spot colors are typically selected from a Custom book in the Color Picker.

The name of the color selected is automatically updated in the New Spot Channel dialog box, as is the swatch. Solidity refers to how the spot channel will be viewed onscreen—it has no effect on printing at all. When set to 100% solidity, the spot color will be completely opaque onscreen in areas where it will be printed at 100% ink density. (Lesser tints of the ink, identified in the channel by gray values under 100%, will be proportionately reduced in opacity.) Setting the solidity to 0%, however, does *not* make the spot color transparent. Rather, it simply reduces the opacity of the spot color areas. Solidity has no effect when the spot channel is the only visible channel.

The Solidity field is previewed live in the image, so you can experiment with various settings before closing the dialog box. You can also reopen the spot color options to change the setting by double-clicking the spot channel in the Channels palette.

Spot channels don't interact with layers, so adding a type layer in a spot color is out of the question. Instead, create a type mask in the spot channel and fill the selection with black.



There are three basic techniques for identifying where a spot color will be applied:

- Make a selection in the image before using the New Spot Channel command.
- Create the new spot channel and then use Photoshop's various tools and commands to create a grayscale representation of the spot color.
- Make a selection with one or more channels active, copy or cut, and then paste into the spot channel.

Spot channel information does not appear in the Layers palette. You edit the spot color information by editing the spot channel. Remember that the spot channel is a grayscale representation (even when the preferences are set to show it in color). Paint with shades of gray, not the spot color itself, in the spot channel. Painting with black produces areas of 100% spot color tint. To show onscreen where the spot color will print, the spot channel must be visible in the Channels palette.

## Alpha Channels

Instead of being used to record color information, alpha channels are masks. Each alpha channel represents a selection. An alpha channel can be created by using the Channel palette's menu command New Channel, the New Channel button at the bottom of the palette, the palette's Save Selection as Channel button, or the menu command Select, Save Selection. The third and fourth techniques require that you have an active selection to create the alpha channel.

As with any channel, you can edit an alpha channel as a grayscale image. By default, areas of the channel that are black will be completely excluded from the selection, and white areas will be completely selected. Use shades of gray to create partially selected areas or gradients and feathering.

*To learn more about creating alpha channels, see "Alpha Channels and Masks," in Chapter 9, "Making Selections and Creating Masks," p. 315.*

The New Channel dialog box, shown in Figure 16.4, enables you to name the channel, determine whether to reverse black and white, and choose how the mask will appear onscreen when active with one or more color channels.

When you choose Color Indicates Selected Areas, the mask is reversed. Painting with black includes areas within the mask, and they will be selected when the channel is loaded as a selection. This option also reverses the appearance of the mask's overlay (see Figure 16.5). The dialog box offers a choice of color for the mask overlay as well as variable opacity.

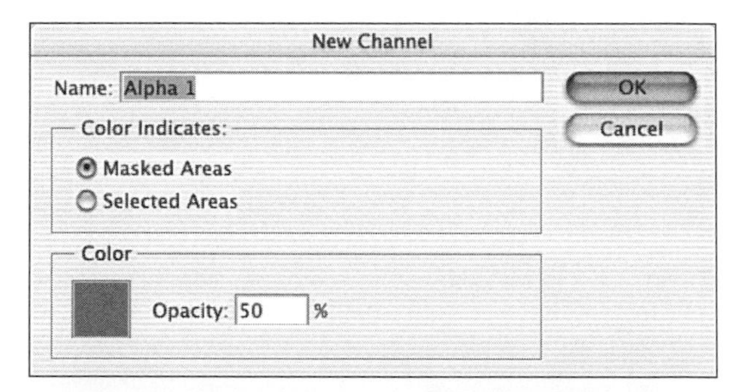


**Figure 16.4**
The color and opacity you select in this dialog box affect only the onscreen appearance of the mask when color channels are also visible.



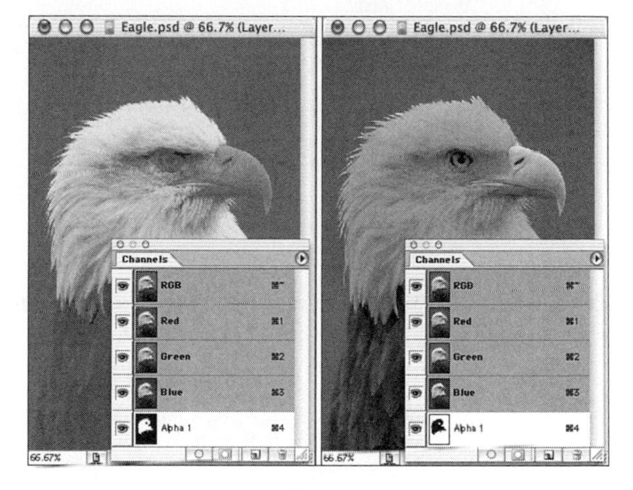


**Figure 16.5**
On the left, the overlay indicates masked areas. On the right, the overlay indicates selected areas. As you can see, the thumbnail in the Channels palette is also reversed.

In Figure 16.5, in both examples, the mask is visible, but the color channels are active. To edit the mask, click the alpha channel in the Channels palette to activate it.

The selection represented by the alpha channel is activated by using the menu command Select, Load Selection and then choosing the alpha channel from the pop-up menu. You can also load a mask as a selection directly from the Channels palette—(Command)-click [Ctrl]-click the alpha channel in the palette.

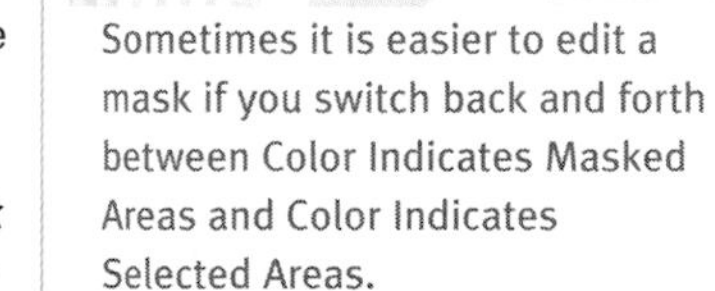

Sometimes it is easier to edit a mask if you switch back and forth between Color Indicates Masked Areas and Color Indicates Selected Areas.

*Need to save a Quick Mask as an alpha channel? See "Quick Channels" in the "Mastering Photoshop" section at the end of this chapter.*

# THE CHANNELS AND HISTOGRAM PALETTES

Both color channels and alpha channels are stored and managed in the Channels palette. You can show and hide channels, select one channel to isolate those color values for manipulation, and even apply adjustments and filters to specific channels, individually or in groups.

The new Histogram palette gives you a good look at the content of each channel. It shows the distribution of pixels in the image according to color or tonal values. Use it to evaluate the color in the image. Understanding the mechanics of the palettes simplifies working with channels.

Remember that keyboard shortcuts can be used to activate individual channels. When the image has a composite channel (RGB, CMYK, and Lab modes), use (Command) or [Ctrl] with the tilde key (~), located to the left of the number 1 on standard keyboards. The other channels are activated with (Command) or [Ctrl] and the number keys, in the order in which the channels appear in the Channels palette. Only the first nine channels get shortcuts.



## The Anatomy of the Channels Palette

The component color channels—those channels that are built in to the document's color mode—always appear at the top of the Channels palette. Any spot color channels or alpha channels also stored in the palette appear below the component colors. To make a channel active, click on it in the palette. You can Shift-click to activate multiple channels. Clicking the composite channel (when the color mode has one) activates all component color channels, but not alpha or spot channels. An alpha channel appears as a grayscale image when it is the only active channel, but it appears as a translucent red overlay (by default) when one or more color channels are also visible.

The Channels palette identifies the individual channels by name and shows a thumbnail of the content (see Figure 16.6). Spot channels and alpha channels can be renamed, but the component color channels and the composite channel cannot. To rename a spot or alpha channel, double-click its name in the Channels palette and type the new name.

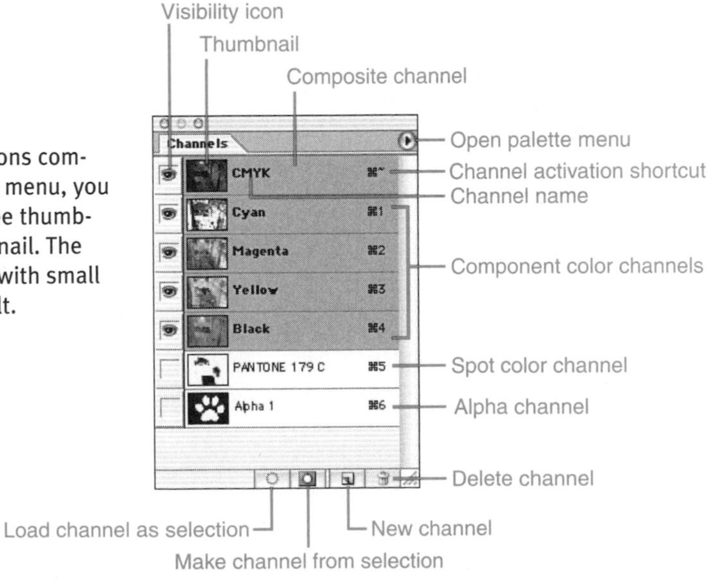


**Figure 16.6**
Using the Palette Options command from the palette menu, you can choose any of three thumbnail sizes or no thumbnail. The palette is shown here with small thumbnails, the default.

In the Channels palette, composite channels (including the Index and Duotone channels) are shown in color. Component color channels for RGB, CMYK, Lab, and Multichannel images are, by default, shown as grayscale. (The Gray channel of a Grayscale document and the Bitmap channel of a Bitmap image are, of course, shown in their respective color modes.) Photoshop's Display & Cursors preferences offer the option of showing the color channels in color. In addition to the thumbnails in the Channels palette, this affects the display when a single channel is active in the palette. Rather than a grayscale image, the channel is portrayed as shades of the component color. When working with RGB images, you may find this option helpful. However, the yellow and cyan channels of most CMYK images are too pale to be of much use when displayed in color.



## The Channel Palette Menu

In addition to duplicating the functions of the buttons at the bottom of the palette, the Channels palette menu provides several powerful tools (see Figure 16.7).

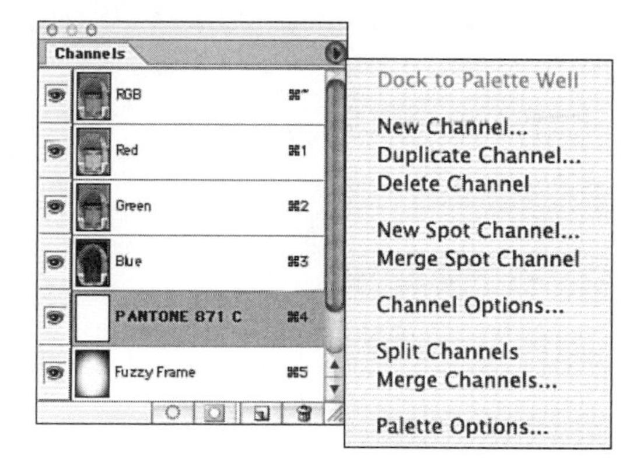


**Figure 16.7**
Not all menu commands will be visible at the same time. For example, Split Channels requires a multichannel document to be open, and Merge Channels is available only with multiple single-channel images open.

*The Split Channels and Merge Channels commands are discussed later in this chapter. See "Splitting and Merging Channels," p. 537.*

The New Channel command opens the New Channel dialog box and creates a new alpha channel. If there is no selection active at the time, the mask fills the image. Duplicating a channel by using the menu command is the same as dragging a channel to the New Channel button at the bottom of the palette—a copy of the channel is created as an alpha channel—but it also opens a dialog box. You can rename the channel, invert it, and copy it to a new document or another open document of the same pixel dimensions. Using the Delete Channel command removes the channel from the palette, just like dragging a channel to the trash icon in the palette.

The New Spot Channel command opens the dialog box shown previously in Figure 16.3, in which you choose the spot color, name, and solidity for onscreen viewing. The Merge Spot Channel command is available only for CMYK and RGB color modes. Merging a spot channel removes the channel from the palette and attempts to duplicate the appearance using the component color channels. Photoshop calculates the nearest equivalent color using the CMYK or RGB component colors and adding appropriately to each of those channels. The Solidity value selected in the channel

> Merging a spot channel into the component color channels will preserve the appearance of the image as much as possible, while eliminating the need for—and expense of—a spot color in print.

options also plays a part in the image's appearance after the merge. Photoshop attempts to maintain the image's *onscreen* appearance—when solidity is reduced, the spot channel is semi-opaque. Also be aware that Merge Spot Channel requires a flattened image.

The Channel Options command is available only when a single spot or alpha channel is active in the palette. It opens the Spot Channel Options dialog box or the Channel Options dialog box, depending on whether a spot or alpha channel is active (see Figure 16.8).

To create a spot channel from an existing color channel, duplicate the channel and then use the Channel Options command to convert it from an alpha channel to a spot color channel.



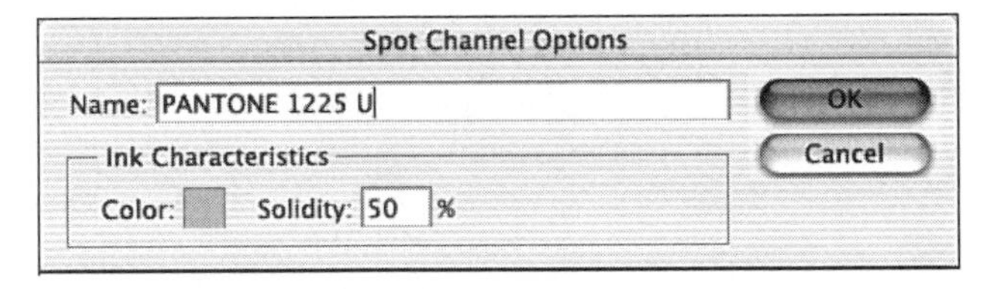


Figure 16.8
The Color setting for a spot channel is the ink color, but an alpha channel's Color option refers only to the onscreen overlay when the mask is being edited with other channels visible.

The Palette Options command offers a choice of thumbnail sizes for the Channels palette. You can show small (the default), medium, or large, thumbnails, or no thumbnails at all. You can also change thumbnail size by (Control)-clicking or right-clicking in an empty area below the channels in the palette and selecting from the contextual menu (see Figure 16.9).

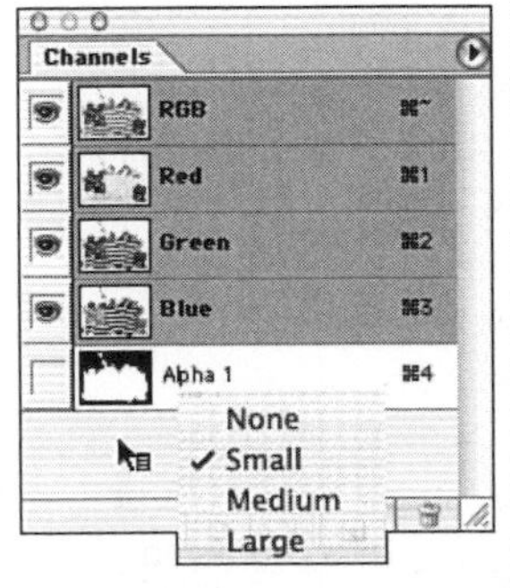


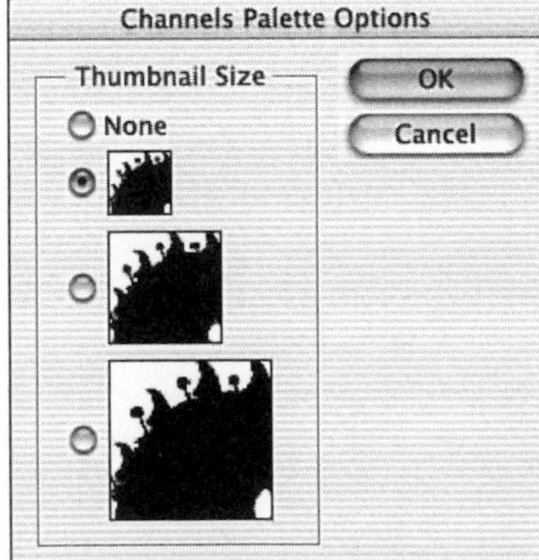


Figure 16.9
The Channels Palette Options dialog box is opened through the palette menu, and the small contextual menu is opened by (Control)-clicking or right-clicking at the bottom of the palette, as shown.

## The Channels Palette Content by Color Mode

The basic content of the Channels palette varies depending on the document's color mode. As mentioned earlier, all color modes have one or more component color channels, and some modes also have a composite channel. The composite channel actually represents the activation of all the document's component channels at the same time. Shift-click to activate multiple channels in an image without a composite channel. In addition to the component color channels, some color modes can have spot color channels and alpha channels. Table 16.1 shows the content of the Channels palette by color mode.



**Table 16.1** Color Mode and the Channels Palette

| Color Mode | Number of Component Colors | Composite Channel | Spot Channels | Alpha Channels |
|---|---|---|---|---|
| Bitmap | 1 | No | No | No |
| Grayscale | 1 | No | Yes | Yes |
| Duotone | 1* | No | Yes | Yes |
| Indexed Color | 1 | No | Yes | Yes |
| RGB | 3 | Yes | Yes | Yes |
| CMYK | 4 | Yes | Yes | Yes |
| Lab | 3** | Yes | Yes | Yes |
| Multichannel | *** | No | Yes | Yes |
| 16-Bit Grayscale | 1 | No | Yes | Yes |
| 16-Bit RGB | 3 | Yes | Yes | Yes |
| 16-Bit CMYK | 4 | Yes | Yes | Yes |
| 16-Bit Lab | 3** | Yes | Yes | Yes |

*Duotone color mode includes Monotone, Duotone, Tritone, and Quadtone images. Each has only one color channel.

**Rather than component color channels, Lab mode has two channels for color and one channel for the luminosity value of each pixel.

***Multichannel mode contains one channel for each color.

*Confused about spot channels in nonprint color modes? See "Spot Colors in RGB and Lab" in the "Mastering Photoshop" section at the end of this chapter.*

## Channels Palette Shortcuts

Using shortcuts can simplify and speed your work with channels. Table 16.2 presents the most common Channels palette shortcuts.

### A Note About 16-Bit Color

Photoshop permits you to work in 16-bit color for RGB, CMYK, Lab, Multichannel, and Grayscale color modes. When each component color is recorded with 16 bits of information rather than 8 bits, the file size doubles. However, the number of possible colors for each pixel increases exponentially. Instead of 256 possible values for each pixel in each color channel, 65,536 possible values are available. With more than 65,000 possible values for each of the three channels in an RGB image, the theoretical number of colors available is overwhelming. (The actual number is over 281 *trillion*. Consider that the distance from the earth to the sun is some 93 million miles. Multiply that by 3 billion, and you're in the neighborhood of the number of possible colors in a 16-bit RGB image.) Needless to say, each image will contain only a minute fraction of the theoretical number of colors.

Although most output devices can't handle the additional color information or don't have the capability of reproducing such fine variations among similar colors, 16-bit mode can be printed. Some film recorders, especially with grayscale images, can show improved tonal range.

Photoshop CS eliminates many of the disadvantages of working in 16-bit color. You can now take advantage of layers, cut/paste, filters, and most of the rest of Photoshop's creative capabilities without losing the additional color information.

**Table 16.2** Channels Palette Shortcuts

| Procedure | Shortcut |
|---|---|
| Show/hide the Channels palette. | Press F7 (when the Channels palette is docked with the Layers palette). |
| Add new channel and open the New Channel dialog box. | (Command)-click or [Ctrl]-click the New Channel button. |
| Convert an alpha channel to a spot color channel. | Use the Channel Options dialog box. |
| Activate a channel. | Use the shortcut shown to the right of the channel name in the hannels palette. |
| Rename a spot or alpha channel. | Double-click the channel's name in the Channels palette (component and composite channels cannot be renamed). |
| Change the thumbnail size. | (Control)-click or right-click in the empty area below the channels in the palette or use the Channels palette menu command Palette options. |
| Load a channel as a selection. | Click the Load Channel button in the Channels palette; (Command -click or [Ctrl]- click the channel in the palette; or hold down (Option) [Alt] and use the channel activation shortcut. |
| Add a channel to a selection. | (Command+Shift)-click or [Ctrl+Shift]-click the channel in the palette. |
| Subtract a channel from a selection. | (Command+Option)-click or [Ctrl+Alt]-click the channel in the palette. |
| Intersect the channel with a selection. | (Command+Option+Shift)-click or [Ctrl+Alt+Shift]-click the channel in the palette. |

## Photoshop's New Histogram Palette

Photoshop CS adds the new Histogram palette, which provides a huge amount of information—or, if you prefer, just enough information. Histograms, which display graphically the distribution of pixels in the image according to their tonality or color, are used to evaluate an image. The palette can show statistical information, and it can even show all channels at once. By making the histogram more accessible and more informative, the Photoshop development team has also made it more valuable. Even if you've never used it before, you may find yourself consulting the now-handy graph to see what impact your editing will have on the distribution of color in the image.

> Remember that you can see a histogram for part of an image simply by making a selection. The histogram calculates only the pixels within the selection.



The Histogram palette can be arranged any of five ways. You make the selection in the palette menu based on what information you need to have available for evaluating your image. The variations, four of which are shown in Figure 16.10, are as follows:

- **Compact View**—In Compact View, only the histogram itself is visible (see Figure 16.10, upper left). This default view saves screen space.
- **Expanded View**—A larger histogram is displayed in Expanded View, and you can switch among the channels and the information source using pop-up menus (see Figure 16.10, middle left). Expanding the palette gives you a better view of the distribution.
- **Expanded View, Show Statistics**—The palette includes numeric data below the histogram (see Figure 16.10, lower left). With numeric data visible, this configuration is most comparable to the Histogram in earlier versions of Photoshop.
- **All Channels View**—Each of the component color channels is displayed in a separate histogram within the palette, in addition to the master histogram. In All Channels View, you can elect to display the individual channels' histograms in black (the default) or in their own colors with the palette menu command Show Channels in Color (see Figure 16.10, right).
- **All Channels View, Show Statistics**—In addition to the individual histograms for each component color, the numeric data is visible. (This is not shown in Figure 16.10.)

> When the Image Cache preference (Preferences, Memory & Image Cache) is set to a value higher than 1, the Histogram palette can refresh faster using a representative sampling of data, but it will be less accurate. The palette will display a warning triangle to indicate that cached data is being used. To view precise information, you can double-click the histogram, choose the Uncached Refresh option in the palette menu, or click the Uncached Refresh button to the right of the Channel pop-up menu. Generally speaking, if you need to use the histogram, you need accurate data—set Image Cache to 1 in the Preferences.

Visible in Figure 16.10 in the middle left are the two pop-up menus within the Histogram palette (these don't appear when you work in Compact View). The Channel menu enables you to select from the composite channel (which includes all the component color information), the individual component color channels, any spot channels in the image, the luminosity values within the image, or the Colors option. The Colors option overlaps each of the individual histograms—including those for spot channels—in the main graph, each in its own color (see Figure 16.11).

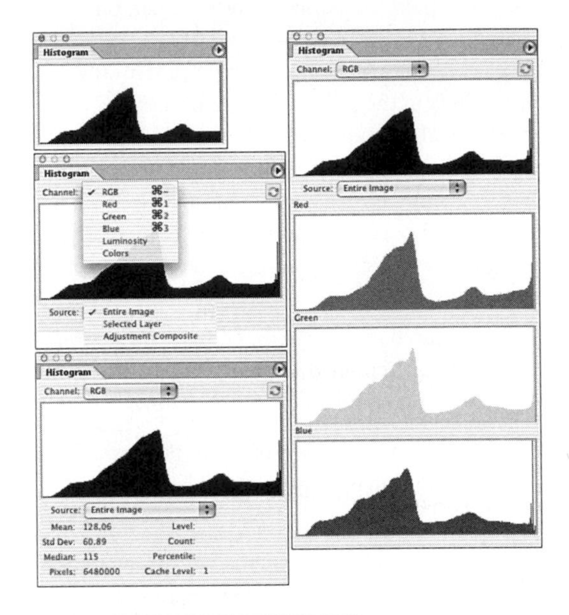


**Figure 16.10**
All Channels View, with Show Statistics active, displays the numeric data (visible in the lower left) below the top histogram, just as it appears in Expanded View, with Show Statistics active.



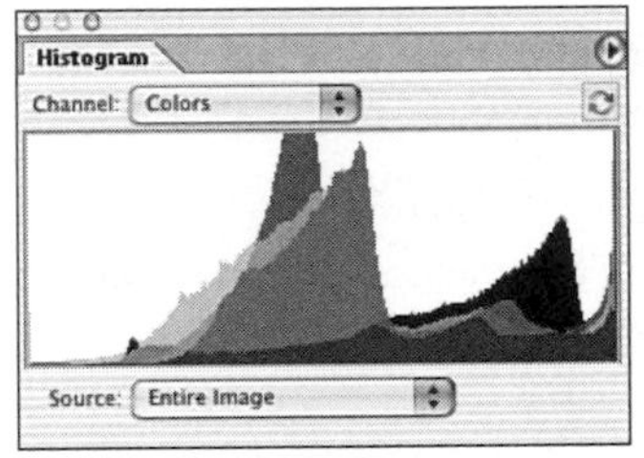


**Figure 16.11**
With the main histogram set to Colors, there's a lot of information in a small space, but the comparison can be valuable.

The Source pop-up menu determines where the palette gets its information. When the option is set to Entire Image, all layers are included, visible or not. You can choose Selected Layer to view a histogram for the active layer in the layers palette. You can also select Adjustment Composite, which displays the histogram for an adjustment layer selected in the Layers palette and all the layers below it. This option enables you to see the effect of the adjustment layer.

*So, now you know what the Histogram palette looks like and a bit about how it's used. For more on how to use this information, see "Evaluating Images" in Chapter 17, "Manipulating Color and Tonality," p. 546.*

Position the cursor within the histogram itself to see numeric data for that particular level. (The Show Statistics option must be selected in the Histogram palette menu.) You can also drag in the histogram to see statistics for a range of values.

# WORKING WITH CHANNELS

Editing channels in Photoshop gives you perhaps the ultimate control over an image's appearance. You can individually manipulate each component color value of each pixel or change a single component color for all pixels. You can even change *all* color values for *every* pixel.

Even if you've never opened the Channels palette, you've worked with channels before. Every time you've used levels or curves, you've directly manipulated the channels. At a more basic level, every time you change any pixel in any way, you're making a change to one or more color channels. Remember that without the channels, the pixel doesn't have color. Without color, the pixel is invisible. This section describes how you work with channels directly and some advanced channel-manipulation techniques.



## Color Channels: Grayscale at Heart

The key to working directly in the Channels palette is remembering that each channel is nothing more than a grayscale image. You can treat the channel as a single-layer grayscale image and use the same tools and commands that you would use on the layer of a grayscale image. Each pixel can be any of 256 different "gray" or brightness values. When considered with the other component color channels of the image, that value is actually the proportion of the channel's color.

To edit an individual channel, click it in the Channels palette. By default, the image will appear in grayscale, with only the values of the selected channel visible. Changes made are applied to only that active channel.

You can also make two or more channels active at the same time by Shift-clicking them. When multiple color channels are active, the image appears in color, using a blend of the selected colors (see Figure 16.12).

You can also work with one or more channels active and all channels visible. By clicking in the left column next to the composite channel, or next to any channel of your choice, you can make it visible without being active. Likewise, you can hide the active channel by clicking the eyeball icon. At least one channel must be visible at all times.

Photoshop's Display & Cursors preferences offer the option of showing individual channels in color. When one channel is active, you'll see a monotone image in that channel's color rather than a grayscale image. Although this may be a handy reminder of what channel is active, it can be very difficult to see detail in the Yellow and Cyan channels when they're shown in color.

## The Relationship Between Channels and Layers

The color channels in the Channels palette show the content of the currently visible layer or layers. Remember that you can edit only one layer at a time, so the appearance of the Channels palette might not match the pixels with which you're actually working. Likewise, when working with the Layers palette visible, you must be aware of which channel or channels are active.

When modifying a channel, click in the left column (the so-called *eyeball column*) next to the composite channel so that you can monitor the effect of your changes on the image's overall appearance.

For example, compare the Layers and Channels palettes in Figure 16.13. On the left, the layer with the five blue balloons is active, as is the composite channel. If you edit the layer, you're editing all color channels. On the right, only the Blue channel is active—changes made to the layer will affect only the blue component of each pixel.

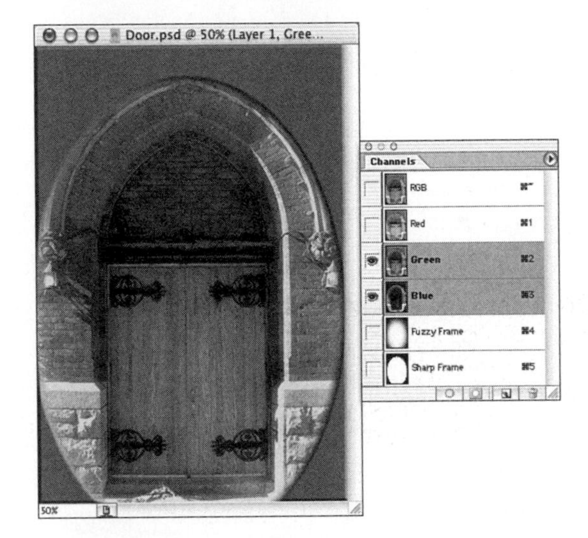


**Figure 16.12**
The Green and Blue channels are active in the Channels palette, so the window displays the image in a combination of greens and blues rather than grayscale.



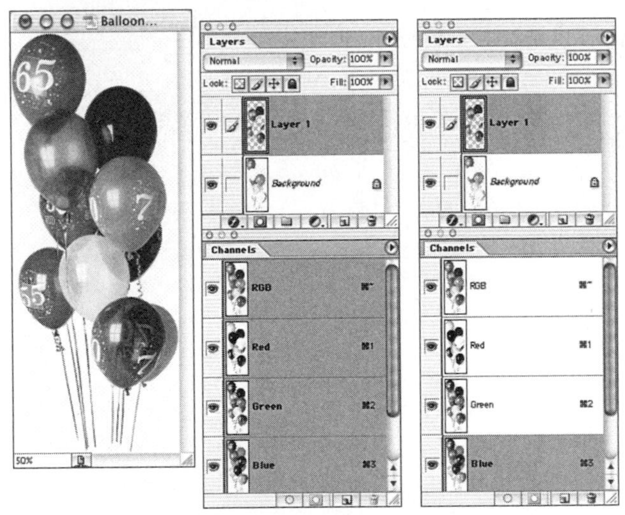


**Figure 16.13**
On the right, only the Blue channel is active, but all channels are visible. Unless the Channels palette is open, it's not immediately evident that changes will be made to only one channel.

Remember, too, that a layer can be active but not visible, or visible but not active. Likewise, you can have a single channel active but not visible—although this makes it impossible to judge the effect of your actions.

Spot color channels, however, are a different story. The pixels for a spot channel don't exist in the Layers palette—they're only a function of the spot channel itself. To edit the spot color in the image, you work with black, white, and shades of gray directly in the spot channel.

## Filtering and Adjusting Individual Channels

Photoshop's filters can be applied to channels individually. You might do this to control the impact of a filter, to produce a special effect, or to fix a problem that occurs in only one or two channels.

Digital camera images often have a lot of noise. When you examine the channels individually, you'll often find that the noise is primarily or exclusively in the Blue channel. Instead of applying a Gaussian Blur or Dust & Scratches filter to the entire image, which results in a general softening of detail, you can filter only the noisy channel, retaining detail in the other channels. Figure 16.14 shows one example.



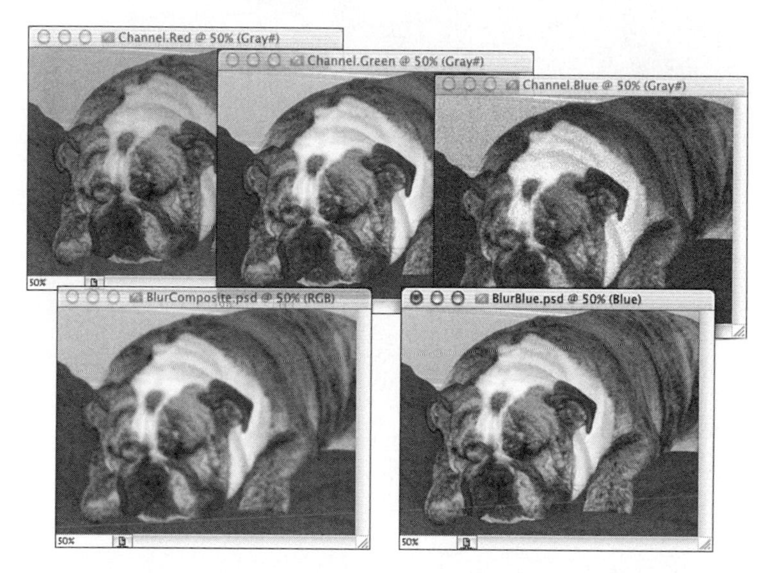


**Figure 16.14**
The original three channels are shown. The Blue channel contains the noise. Blurring the composite channel (left) softens the image far more than blurring only the Blue channel (right).

Likewise, image adjustments can be applied to one channel rather than the entire image. In Figure 16.15, the darkness of the Blue channel thumbnail in comparison to the Green and Red channels is an indication that the skin tones are too yellow.

You can approach single-channel correction in a pair of ways. You can select the channel in the Channels palette to make it the only active channel and make your corrections, or you can use the adjustment dialog boxes to work with a single channel (see Figure 16.16).

When multiple channels (but not the composite channel) are selected in the Channels palette, the dialog boxes show which channels are selected, and the menu includes only those selected channels (see Figure 16.17).

> Multichannel color mode doesn't have a composite channel, so to apply a filter you can Shift-click each channel in the Channels palette, or you can apply the filter to each channel individually. Use (Command+F) [Ctrl+F] to reapply a filter with the same settings to each additional channel.

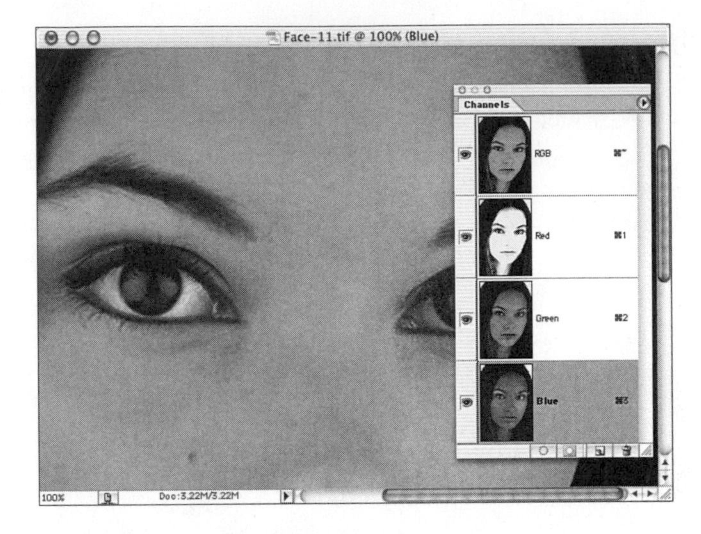


**Figure 16.15**
You don't need to see this image in color to recognize a problem—the thumbnails in the Channels palette tell the tale.

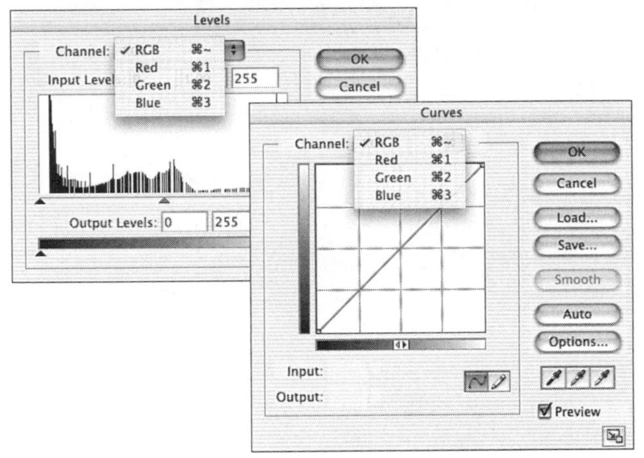


**Figure 16.16**
The image adjustment dialog boxes include menus from which you can select the channel to adjust.

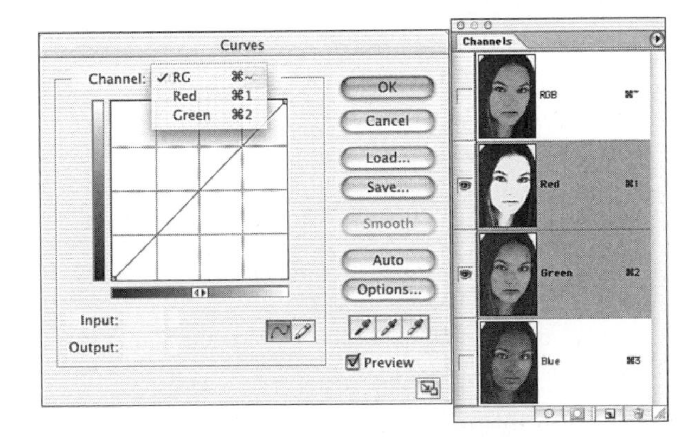


**Figure 16.17**
If the Red and Blue channels were selected, the dialog box would show RB and list only those two channels.

## Working with Duotone Channels

Duotone images use channels differently than other color modes. You can make changes to the image's appearance by using the Channels palette, but the application of color is done through the Duotone Options dialog box (see Figure 16.18).

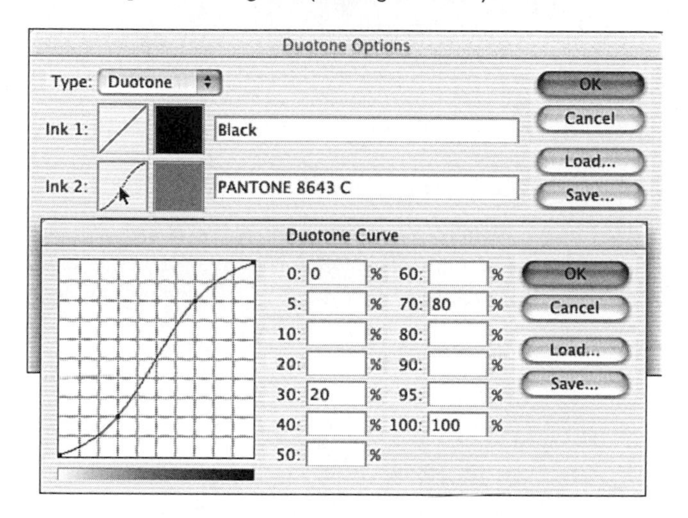


Figure 16.18
Clicking the curve thumbnail in the Duotone Options dialog box opens the duotone curve for that ink.

You can change the curve for each ink independently. Typically, a duotone image uses black and one other ink. The black ink creates a grayscale image, which is tinted with the second color. By adjusting the curve of the second color, you can customize the appearance of the duotone. Figure 16.19 shows three variations of the same image.

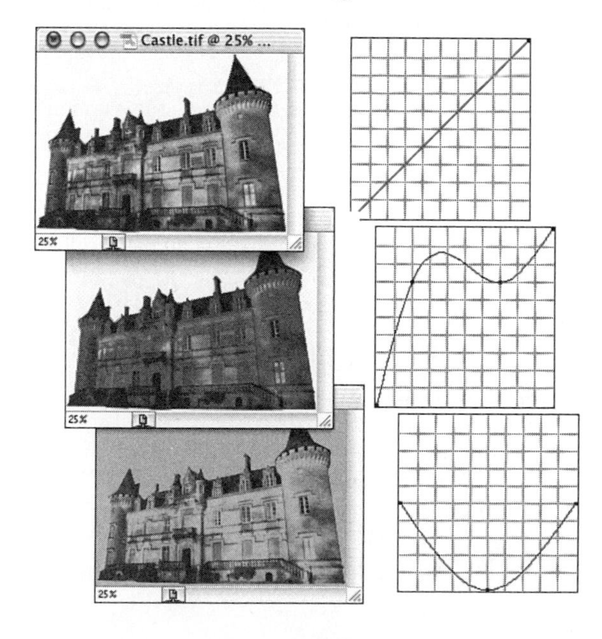


Figure 16.19
The black ink curve is identical for each image. The top image retains the default curve for the second ink. The lower two images use the curves shown.

Remember, too, that you can convert a Duotone image to Multichannel mode, which creates a regular color channel for each ink. Multichannel images can be saved as Photoshop (PSD) files or prepared for print using DCS 2.0.

# ADVANCED CHANNEL MANIPULATION

Photoshop includes some very sophisticated tools for manipulating channels. You can use them to modify existing channels or even to create new documents from channels.



## Channel Mixer

The menu command Image, Adjustments, Channel Mixer opens the dialog box shown in Figure 16.20. You can adjust the content of a color channel by using the content of the other channels as source material. In Figure 16.20, the gorilla is too red. The content of the channel can be modified by copying some of the information from the Green and Blue channels.

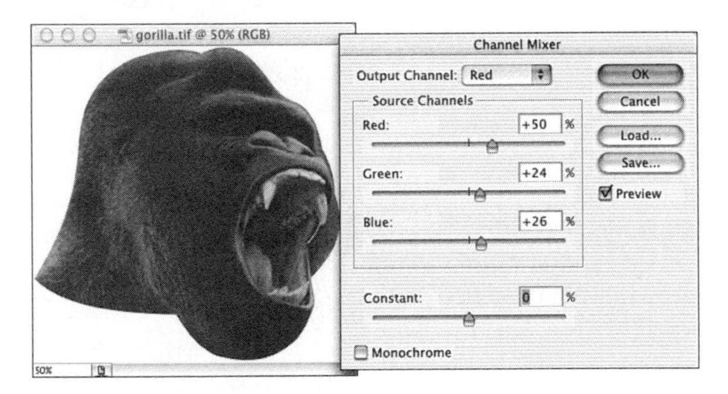


**Figure 16.20**
In this example, the Channel Mixer reduces the intensity of red by making that channel's content closer to that of the other channels, thus "neutralizing" the overly intense reds.

You can use the Channel Mixer to completely replace the content of one channel with that of another channel. Select the target channel from the menu at the top of the dialog box and then move its slider to 0% and the replacement channel's slider to 100%.

The Channel Mixer gives you incredible control when creating a grayscale image from a color image. Select the Monochrome check box, and the output channel automatically switches to Gray. Adjust the sliders to take the best of each channel. After you click OK, use the menu command Image, Mode, Grayscale to complete the transformation.

Here are some tips for using the Channel Mixer:

- Channel Mixer is available only when the composite channel is active in the Channels palette.
- You can make adjustments to one channel and then switch to another to change it without leaving the dialog box. All channels can be adjusted before you click OK.
- Using a negative number inverts the channel's content before adding it to the output channel.
- Reducing the Constant slider adds black uniformly across the output channel; increasing the value adds white.

- You can select the Monochrome check box to desaturate the image, and you can uncheck the box to add a tint to the image.
- To maintain the overall tonality of the image, try to keep the output channel's value close to 100%. If you adjust the Constant slider with the Monochrome option selected, multiply its value by 3 when adding to or subtracting from the total percentage.
- Make a selection before opening the dialog box to restrict the change to part of an image. You can use this technique along with the Monochrome check box to force parts of a CMYK image to appear only in the Black channel. This is an excellent way to ensure that shadows print with black ink only.



## Photoshop at Work: Perfect Grayscale from Color

Using the Channel Mixer is an excellent way to create grayscale images from color pictures. To see for yourself, try this:

1. Open a copy of an RGB image.
2. If it has multiple layers, flatten it.
3. Click twice on the leftmost button at the bottom of the History palette. This makes a pair of copies of the image. Zoom out, if necessary, and position the windows so that you can view all three images onscreen at the same time. (Don't forget the menu command Windows, Arrange, Tile.)
4. Use the Image, Mode, Grayscale menu command to convert one image.
5. Click another copy of the image. Use the Image, Adjustments, Desaturate menu command followed by Image, Mode, Grayscale.
6. Switch to the third copy and use Image, Adjustments, Channel Mixer to open the dialog box.
7. Click the Monochrome check box.
8. Set the Red, Green, and Blue fields to 40, and change the Constant slider to –7.
9. Concentrate on an area of extreme highlight or extreme shadow. Slowly move the sliders back and forth, juggling the amounts of each channel you add or subtract. Watch how you can target certain tonal ranges, depending on the content of each channel.
10. As you work, compare this image with the others. Look for a balance in your mix that makes the image "pop" and provides the best tonal range.
11. When the image looks perfect, click OK and then use Image, Mode, Grayscale.

You can even make selections and work on different areas on an image according to their needs. Generally speaking, for a normal key image, you'll want the total of the sliders to equal about 100. When doing the math, triple the value—positive or negative—of the Constant slider.

## The Calculations and Apply Image Commands

The menu command Image, Calculations creates an alpha channel, a selection, or a new document (consisting of a single alpha channel). You blend the values of two channels, with or without a mask, to create the final product (see Figure 16.21).

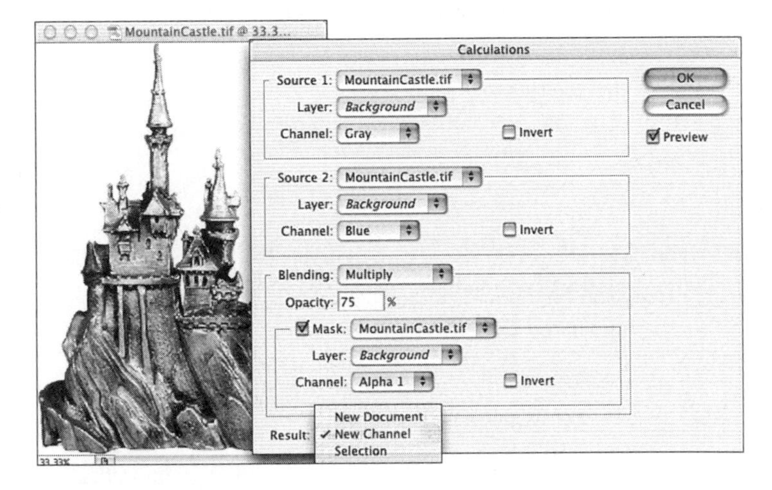


**Figure 16.21**
The Gray channel used as Source 1 is equivalent to a grayscale copy of the RGB image. The Calculations command also has the capability of using channel information from a single layer or from Merged—a composite of all layers.

Calculations can also be used with multiple images—but they must have exactly the same pixel dimensions (see Figure 16.22). Two images can supply source channels, and a mask can be created from an alpha channel in a third image.

**Figure 16.22**
In this example, Calculations uses a channel from each image and a mask from the Bride image to create the new document on the right.

The Apply Image command, also found under the Image menu, is similar to using Calculations with two documents. You specify a target layer and channel before opening the dialog box, and then you choose the source layer and channel from another (or the same) image (see Figure 16.23).

The Calculations and Apply Image commands do very little that you can't do manually in the Layers and Channels palettes. One difference between them and copying and pasting layers and channels is the addition of two blending modes: Add and Subtract. These blending modes are found nowhere else in Photoshop.

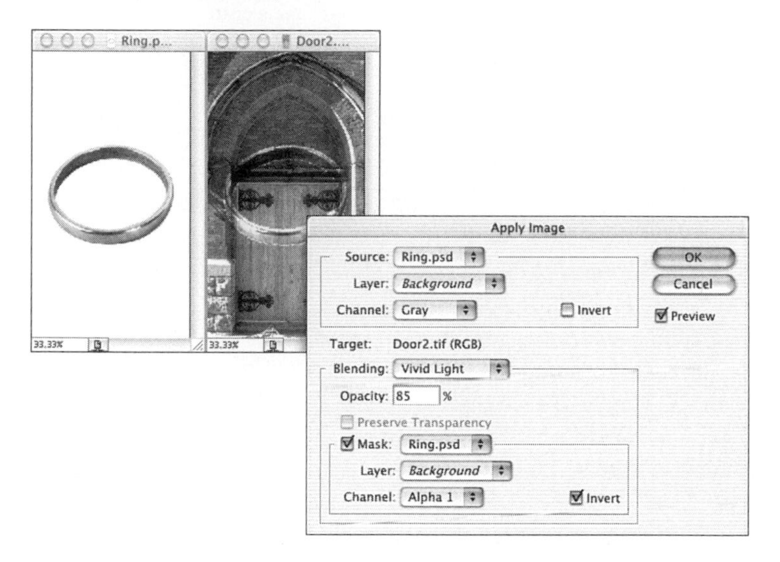


Figure 16.23
If the target image has multiple layers, you need to flatten or select a specific layer before you open the dialog box.



The Add and Subtract blending modes perform simple mathematical calculations on the channel values for each pixel. The value from each channel (0 to 255 for RGB images) is added or subtracted. The Scale factor is then applied. Ranging from 1.0 to 2.0, consider it the divisor. When Scale is set to 2, the combined value is averaged. The Offset field enables you to supply a constant that is either added to (positive) or subtracted from (negative) each pixel value. Offset can range from –255 to +255. When Scale is set to 1, you can use Offset to prevent too many of the pixel values from being either 0 (black) or 255 (white).

## Splitting and Merging Channels

The Channels palette menu contains a pair of very powerful commands: Split Channels and Merge Channels. The Split Channels command creates a grayscale document from each of the channels in the Channels palette (except the composite channel, which is not truly a color channel). The original image is not retained, and your result is a series of one-channel grayscale images. Every color, spot color, and alpha channel is converted to a separate document. Split Channels requires a flattened image and is not available for Indexed Color or Bitmap color mode images. Duotones, regardless of the number of colors, create a single grayscale image from the Duotone channel, plus an image for each spot or alpha channel.

The resulting channels are named for the original image, followed by a dot and the channel name. If you'll be recomposing the image using Merge Channels, retain these filenames. If you'll be using the individual files separately, remember to assign a more reasonable name. For example, if you split an RGB image named Door.psd, the resulting files will have working names of Door.psd.Red, Door.psd.Green, and Door.psd.Blue (Macintosh) or Door_R.psd, Door_B.psd, and Door_G.psd

(Windows). Additional channels in the image will have a numeric suffix starting with 4 rather than a color designation. You'll want to assign filenames that have a dot only at the end of the filename, immediately before the file extension, if the image will stand alone.

The Merge Channels command is designed to re-create a document that has been divided by using the Split Channels command. However, it can be used on any open grayscale documents that have identical pixel dimensions, are flattened, and have only a single channel (see Figure 16.24).

Whether working with documents created by Split Channels or other grayscale images, the Merge Channels command opens two dialog boxes in sequence (see Figure 16.25).

If Multichannel mode is selected for the merged document, a series of dialog boxes, such as the one shown in the center of Figure 16.25, appear. You assign a document to each channel. If you choose RGB, CMYK, or Lab color mode, a single dialog box is used to assign documents to channels. You can click the Mode button to change your selection for the merged document's color mode. Merge Channels uses the Split Channels names, if available, to automatically assign the images to their original color channels (see Figure 16.26).

If you have an image that's too large to fit on the available removable media or to send as an email attachment, Split Channels may be the answer. Each of the resulting documents is substantially smaller than the original. The separate files can be combined later by using the Merge Channels command.

**Caution**

There is no Undo with Split Channels—not even the History palette can reverse this command. Remember that the original image is lost (unless it's saved on disk) and can be re-created only with the Merge Channels command.

**Figure 16.24**
The three images can be combined by using Merge Channels because they all are flattened grayscale images with only one channel and have exactly the same pixel dimensions.

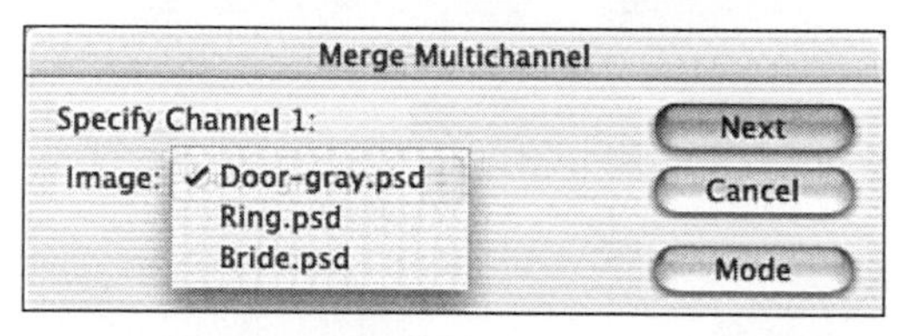


Merge RGB Channels
Specify Channels:
Red: Bride.psd
Green: Door-gray.psd
Blue: Ring.psd
OK
Cancel
Mode

**Figure 16.25**
The top dialog box appears first. The CMYK Color option is available if four or more appropriate images are open.

**Figure 16.26**
Merge Channels uses the dot-channel-name suffixes created by Split Channels to assign the images to their original channels.

## MASTERING PHOTOSHOP

### Too Many Channels

*What happens if I try to open a Photoshop CS image with more than two dozen channels in Photoshop 7?*

You'll get a warning message with the option of canceling the open operation or discarding the extra channels (see Figure 16.27). If you elect to continue, Photoshop 7 simply lops off channels from the bottom of the Channels palette, deleting them from the image.

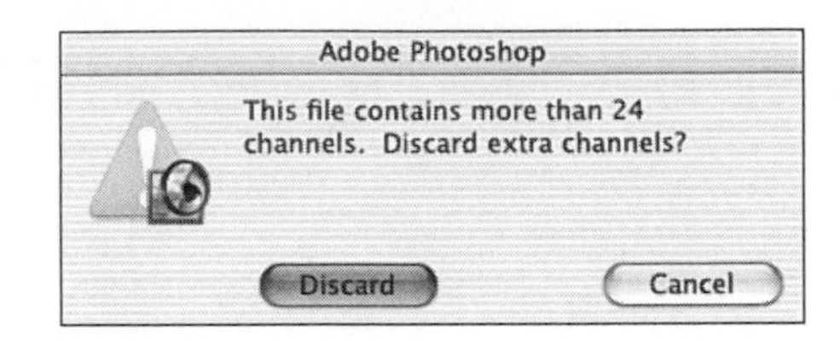


Figure 16.27
The Maximize PSD File Compatibility preference (in the File Handling section of Photoshop's Preferences) has no effect on the number of channels.



InDesign can handle as many spot channels as you care to pay for. However, rather than saving your many-spot-channel image as a Photoshop (PSD) file, you can create a DCS 2.0 file with File, Save As. For convenience, consider using a single file rather than creating a separate file for each of the spot channels.

## Stopping Some Presses

*I want to use spot colors in my design, but the client doesn't want to pay for a fifth or sixth color. How can I keep the cost down?*

Consider skipping CMYK and using just one or two spot colors and black. Work in a monotone or duotone, and add a splash of spot color for a logo or other point of emphasis. The results can be striking and less expensive than a full four-color press run because you're using fewer colors. Be sure to check with the print shop before getting too far into the project.

## Quick Channels

*I like to work in Quick Mask mode, but when I exit, I lose my channel. Can I save it?*

Quick Mask mode deletes the temporary channel when you return to normal editing mode, but you can create an alpha channel from the Quick Mask channel. After exiting Quick Mask mode, use the Select, Save Selection menu command. Even easier, however, is creating the alpha channel *before* exiting Quick Mask mode. Simply duplicate the Quick Mask channel by dragging it to the New Channel button in the Channels palette, or select Duplicate Channel from the Channels palette menu or the contextual menu. Don't duplicate the channel until you've finished editing it; otherwise, it won't be an exact copy of the Quick Mask.

## Spot Colors in RGB and Lab

*Spot colors are for commercial printing, so why can I add them to RGB and Lab images?*

Remember that conversion to CMYK color mode often happens late in a workflow. You can add the spot color channels at any time—they're maintained when you do your final preprint color conversion. In addition, you can use a spot channel as an interim step in an RGB image. Create the spot channel, and apply the color. Because the spot color is in a separate channel, it is protected while you continue editing and adjusting the rest of the image. Later, use the Channels palette menu command Merge Spot Channel to integrate that channel into the RGB channels.

## Matching the Grays

*How do the 0%–100% grayscale values compare to the 256 levels or gray I can work with in RGB mode?*



When you define your grays in RGB mode, you can take advantage of the full 8 bits of grayscale available. Table 16.3 provides a handy Grayscale/RGB Gray conversion chart.

**Table 16.3** Grayscale–RGB Conversion

| Gray Percent | RGB Gray |
|---|---|
| 0% (white) | 255/255/255 |
| 10% | 229/229/229 |
| 20% | 204/204/204 |
| 30% | 179/179/179 |
| 40% | 153/153/153 |
| 50% | 128/128/128 |
| 60% | 102/102/102 |
| 70% | 76/76/76 |
| 80% | 51/51/51 |
| 90% | 26/26/26 |
| 100% (black) | 0/0/0 |

17

# MANIPULATING COLOR AND TONALITY

## IN THIS CHAPTER

This chapter is an exploration of the capabilities you use to change color and tonality in an image. Remember the word *manipulating*, not *correcting*, in the chapter title. Indeed, much of the work done in Photoshop is improving images, making them look more natural. But that's not all there is to it. You may need (or want) a special effect. Perhaps you've decided to emphasize a color cast rather than remove it. Maybe your project requires something futuristic or spacey or retro. Understanding how the features work enables you to do with them what you will, what you need.

This chapter looks at what's meant by *color adjustment*, a process you can use to determine what (if any) adjustment is necessary, and the features you use to make those changes.

# COLOR ADJUSTMENT THEORY



Whether your goal is exact reproduction of an image on paper or screen, or creating a special effect, manipulating the tonality and color of an image can be key. *Tonality*, the brightness of an image's pixels, can be the cumulative product of an image's component color channels, or it can be controlled through a separate channel (Lab color mode). Color (as well as grayscale and black-and-white values) is always stored in color channels. Manipulating these values can improve—or at least *change*—the appearance of your image.

*To learn more about color channels and how they work, see Chapter 16, "Channels: The Ultimate Creative Control," p. 513.*

## Why Adjust?

In the vast majority of situations, you adjust color and tonality to produce an image that most closely reflects reality. You want the skin tones to match those of the person photographed, and you want the sky to be blue. The shadows should be black rather than dark purple. You want white highlights, not pale yellow or cyan or red.

The untrained human eye, in many circumstances, is very forgiving color-wise. Generally speaking, a shopper doesn't care if the type on laundry soap packaging is Pantone 1935 or Pantone 193. Nor can the eye tell the difference between the two shades when they stand alone.

On the other hand, slightly too much yellow in a skin tone or a bit too much blue in foliage can be disturbing, even to an inexperienced viewer. When an image portrays nature, whether flora or fauna, normally you want your image to be reproduced as exactly as possible. The goal is accurate output, whether to paper or screen.

You'll hear and read a variety of terms used to refer to the same thing. Brightness, luminosity, and lightness all refer to how close a pixel is to black or white.

*Looking for information about making people in your images look natural? See "The Skinny on Skin," in the "Mastering Photoshop" section at the end of this chapter.*

## The Need for Calibration and Color Management

You can't adjust what you can't evaluate. If your monitor shows bright red (RGB 255/0/0) as pink or magenta, you can't use your image's onscreen representation to make decisions. Certainly you can do all your corrections "by the numbers," evaluating color only through the Info palette, but that is not particularly efficient. Your monitor should be properly calibrated before you attempt to color-correct any image.

Unless you have disabled color management, virtually every color and tonality correction you make relies on the profiles you've selected in Color Settings.

Color management is also important. Consider it to be correcting for the vagaries of various devices. Just as a golfer compensates for the pitch of a green when putting, or a sailor tacks against the wind, so, too, does color management help you produce the result you want by adjusting color to meet the circumstances of its display or reproduction. If, for example, a printer tends to make images a little too dark, you can lighten the originals before printing to produce perfect output.

*For information on preparing your equipment and settings for accurate color reproduction, see Chapter 6, "Color Management in the Adobe Creative Suite," p. 189.*



## The Eyes Have It

Even if you use color samplers and the Info palette to determine exact color values in an image, the final decision still rests with your eyes. The Info palette might indicate that the subject's skin is within your target range, but it's your *eyes* that have determined what that range should be. In the end, you use your own judgment when deciding whether an image or a print is acceptable.

## Highlights and Shadows

It's important that you understand the concepts of highlights and shadows before adjusting an image's tonality. The key is knowing that shadow and highlight areas of an image are *not* completely black and white. They *should* have some detail. Even pictures of clouds and snow have some detail, and only the deepest shadows hold no detail.

When you're preparing images, especially for offset printing, consider the capabilities of the press. If the smallest dot that can be printed is 8%, your highlight areas should be filled with a very light gray pattern, created with 8% dots. Likewise, if the largest dot that can be reproduced without spreading into a solid area of black ink is 90%, that's where your shadows should be mapped.

There are actually two types of highlights in many images. *Specular highlights* are the pure white flashes of light created by reflections from metal or glass or otherwise occurring in a photograph. Specular highlights have no color information and are typically very small areas of pure white. *Diffuse highlights* are the "real" highlights of an image and should be reproduced with faint detail.

*Controlling the highlight and shadow points, the endpoints of an image, is discussed in the section "The Levels Eyedroppers," p. 557.*

# EVALUATING IMAGES

Photoshop has a number of tools that can help you evaluate images. Some, such as the Proof Colors command, rely on accurate monitor calibration and proper color management. Others, such as the Info palette and the new Histogram palette, objectively measure color but are still dependent on profiles selected in Color Settings.

The Info palette is tied to the Eyedropper tool, whose options determine the sample for the palette's readings. If the Eyedropper is set to Point Sample in the Options Bar, a single pixel's value is displayed. To avoid false readings, set the Eyedropper to 3×3 Average for low-resolution images and 5×5 Average for high-resolution images.

## The Info Palette

The Info palette, shown in Figure 17.1, can give you two different color readings for the cursor location and color readings for up to four separately designated points in an image.

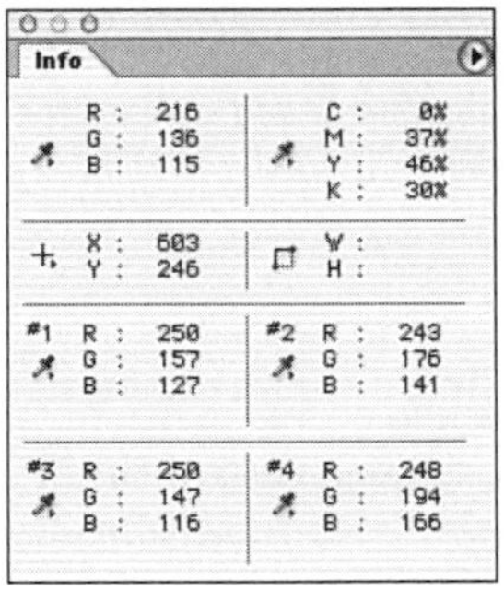

**Figure 17.1**
Regardless of which tool is active, the Info palette displays your choice of color readouts in the top two fields.

The four numbered fields at the bottom of the Info palette display readings for *color samplers*, which can be considered bookmarks placed in the image to track color at specific locations. (Color samplers are discussed in the following section.)

You choose what color information is displayed in the top two fields by clicking the eyedropper button to the left of either field or by using the Info palette menu command Palette Options (see Figure 17.2).

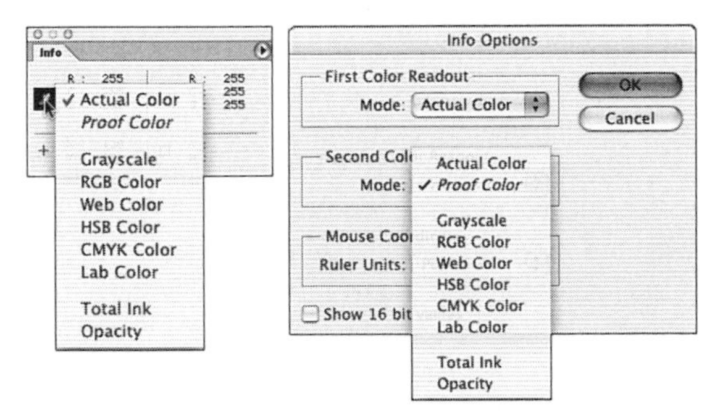


**Figure 17.2**
The First Color Readout and Second Color Readout menus offer the same list of options.

While a color adjustment is being made, the Info palette displays a pair of values for each color reading (see Figure 17.3). The value on the left is the original; the value on the right is updated as you make the adjustments.

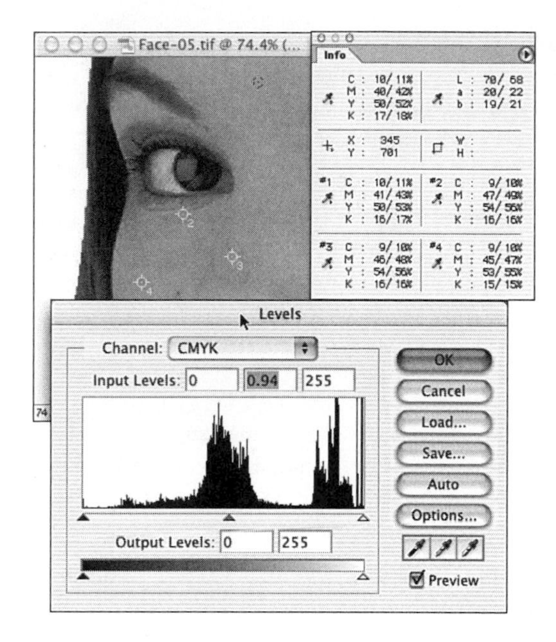


**Figure 17.3**
Observe the position of the cursor. The Info palette shows the values for the image pixels below the cursor, despite the dialog box. For the Mac, the dialog box is transparent to the Info palette.



## Color Samplers

Color samplers represent points in an image that you designate for color evaluation. Color samplers can be placed in highlights, shadows, midtones—any part of the image for which you want information. The samplers appear in the image as numbered crosshairs (see Figure 17.4). You can place them or drag to move them by using the Color Sampler tool or by holding down the Shift key and using the Eyedropper. The Color Sampler tool is found in the Toolbox, grouped with the Eyedropper. Delete a color sampler by dragging it out of the image window.

**Figure 17.4**
The color sampler markers adapt their own color to contrast with the pixels behind them.

Color samplers are visible onscreen when painting, focus, toning, hand, or zoom tools are active. They are hidden when selection, pen, or type tools are active.

By default, the Info palette shows values for each color sampler in the document's color mode. You can change that reading by clicking the eyedropper icon for that sampler in the palette, as shown in Figure 17.2 for the primary readouts.

Remember that, like the top readings in the Info palette, the color sampler readings use the sample size specified for the Eyedropper tool in the Options Bar. These readings update automatically if you change the sample size. Likewise, color samplers display dual readings during an image adjustment.

In photographs, objects are rarely a single color. A face, an apple, and a sky all have a series of similar colors rather than a single color. Therefore, you should place color samplers in several areas to properly evaluate your work.

## Histograms

*Histograms* show the distribution of pixels at various luminosity values for an image or an active selection. The Histogram palette, shown in Figure 17.5 in Expanded View (with Show Statistics) and All Channels View, not only shows you the distribution of pixels at varies values, it provides feedback during an image adjustment.

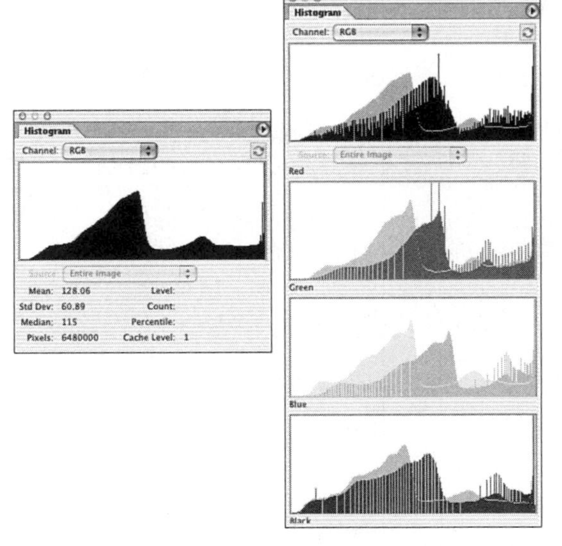


**Figure 17.5**
On the right, you can see how the Histogram palette shows you a faint image of the pre-adjustment values, providing feedback before you click the OK button.

Also note the button in the upper-right corner of the Histogram palette, just below the button to open the palette's menu. The Uncached Refresh button reloads the histogram from the actual pixel data, which is more accurate than using cached data.

*The Histogram palette is introduced in Chapter 16, "Channels: The Ultimate Creative Control," p. 513.*

The histogram is used primarily for evaluating an image. It shows the distribution of pixels at each of the 256 possible values of brightness (composited for Luminosity or as computed for the individual color channel selected). The taller a black column at a given level, the more pixels in the image share that value.

When the bulk of the information in the histogram is to the right end, the image is very bright and said to be *high-key*. When the concentration is to the left, the image is dark and said to be *low-key*. Figure 17.6 shows a comparison.

Figure 17.6
The image on the left is low-key. On the right is an example of a high-key image. The Histogram palette is shown in Compact View.



You can use the histogram to check for *posterization* as you correct images. Posterization occurs when similar color or luminosity values are consolidated in a single value. Gaps in the histogram appear, as shown in Figure 17.7. On the right, the histogram shows signs of posterization (gaps in the data) as well as clipping—the data ends before the lightest and darkest values.

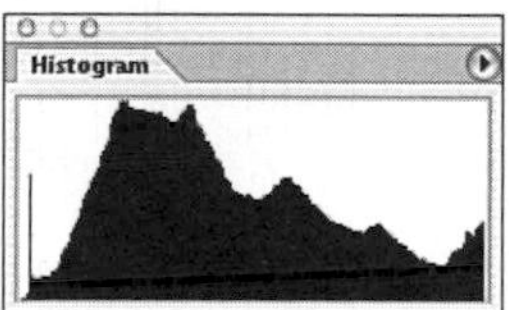


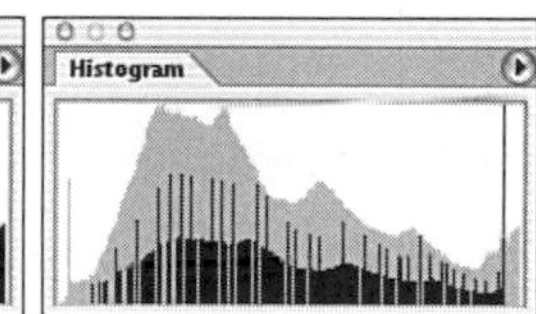


Figure 17.7
Note that the Histogram palette shows a "ghost" of the original histogram while an adjustment is being made.

*If your histogram is showing a wildly impossible distribution, see "Evaluate What You're Evaluating" in the "Mastering Photoshop" section at the end of this chapter.*

You'll also find histograms in the Levels and Threshold dialog boxes. They function as part of those image adjustments and are discussed with their respective commands.

## Proofing Colors

Photoshop's View menu includes a couple commands used for *soft proofing*—the process of evaluating onscreen how an image will appear when printed. Even with the most accurately calibrated monitor and most precise device profiles, soft proofing can never be 100% perfect. Remember that the monitor must use RGB color to simulate CMYK inks and that the way the light reaches your eye is different for RGB and CMYK. However, you can use soft proofing to get a general idea of how an image will print, and it might reveal potential problems so you can resolve them before printing the image.

The View, Proof Setup command determines what color setup you'll be using with the Proof Colors command. Your options include the currently selected CMYK working space, each of the individual color plates for that space, the combined working space CMY plates, and three RGB color spaces: Windows, Macintosh, and your monitor's profile. You can also prepare to proof in another color profile by choosing Custom from the Setup pop-up menu (see Figure 17.8).

ICC profiles record the device-specific information for hardware that displays or reproduces images, including scanners, monitors, and printers. ICC profiles are loaded in Photoshop's Color Settings dialog box as working spaces. Color profiles are discussed in Chapter 6, "Color Management in the Adobe Creative Suite."

17

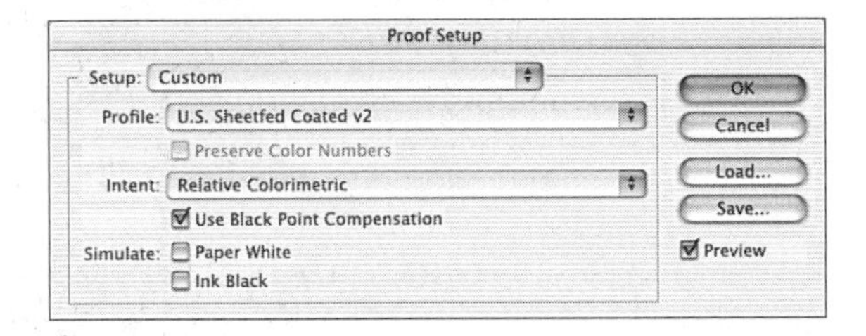


Figure 17.8
All the available ICC profiles appear in the Profile menu.

Depending on the profile that's selected, Photoshop can also attempt to simulate how CMYK inks will interact with paper (Simulate Paper White) and how black will be generated (Simulate Ink Black).

Selecting View, Proof Colors shows onscreen what the image should look like when output. A check mark appears next to the command name that's active. To return to your normal working view, deselect Proof Colors.

You'll also find the Gamut Warning command under the View menu. Instead of simulating how an image will appear in print, it shows you what RGB colors in the image cannot be reproduced using the device whose CMYK profile you've loaded. By default, an opaque gray is shown for problem areas. You can change the appearance of the gamut warning in the Transparency & Gamut pane of Photoshop's Preferences.

# ADJUSTING TONALITY

The range of lightness and darkness in an image is often critical to its appearance. If the whites aren't bright enough, they look gray. If the brighter parts of the image are *too* bright, the highlights are "blown out" and lack detail. Likewise, if too many pixels are too dark, you get muddy, detail-less shadows. Photoshop offers quite a few tools for correcting the brightness of an image. You'll find several powerful tools in the Image, Adjustments menu. Adjusting the tones of an image is often referred to as *remapping*.

Hold down the (Option) [Alt] key when selecting the Adjustments commands that have dialog boxes and they will open with the most recently used settings. You can use the earlier adjustment again or use it as a starting point for a new adjustment.

Remember that you can use the menu command Edit, Fade immediately after applying a tonal adjustment. The Fade command can lessen the impact of the adjustment and apply a blending mode.

# Adjustment Layers: The Live Corrections

Most of the commands in the Image, Adjustments menu can be applied as *adjustment layers*. An adjustment layer changes the image's appearance according to the adjustment you make, but does so without actually changing any pixel color values. In addition to preserving the original image data, adjustment layers are "live." That is, they can be reopened and settings changed. They can also be deleted at any time.

There are several advantages to using adjustment layers rather than the Image, Adjustments commands:

- Adjustment layers do not make any permanent change to the image. As long as the adjustment layer isn't merged or the image flattened, you will not have made any change that cannot be undone.
- Adjustment layers enable you to experiment. At any time you can reopen the adjustment dialog box and change the settings for the adjustment layer.
- You can hide adjustment layers in the Layers palette to temporarily remove the adjustment.
- An adjustment layer applies the adjustment to all layers below it in the Layers palette by default. However, you can also restrict the adjustment to a single layer or a layer set.
- You can change the blending mode and opacity of an adjustment layer to fine-tune the effect. As with all layers, blending mode and opacity changes made in the Layers palette are "live" and can be changed.
- Layer and vector masks can be used to control the effective area of an adjustment layer. Masks can also be edited at a later time.
- You can drag an adjustment layer to the Trash icon in the Layers palette to permanently remove it from the image.



## Adding an Adjustment Layer

You can add an adjustment layer through the Layers palette or the Layer menu (see Figure 17.9). Click and hold the Add Adjustment Layer button at the bottom of the palette and select the type of adjustment from the list. Alternatively, use the menu command Layer, New Adjustment Layer and choose from the submenu.

An adjustment layer is always accompanied by a mask, even if the mask is empty. If there's a selection active when you create the adjustment layer, the selection automatically forms the basis for the mask. If there's no selection, the adjustment layer is applied to the entire image.

After you've made the adjustment and clicked OK in the adjustment dialog box, the adjustment layer appears in the Layers palette. By default, it is added above the active layer. The Layers palette shows two thumbnails for each adjustment layer (see Figure 17.10). To the left, you'll see an icon representing the type of adjustment layer, and to the right, a thumbnail of the layer's mask. The Channels palette shows the mask of an adjustment layer only when that layer is selected in the Layers palette.

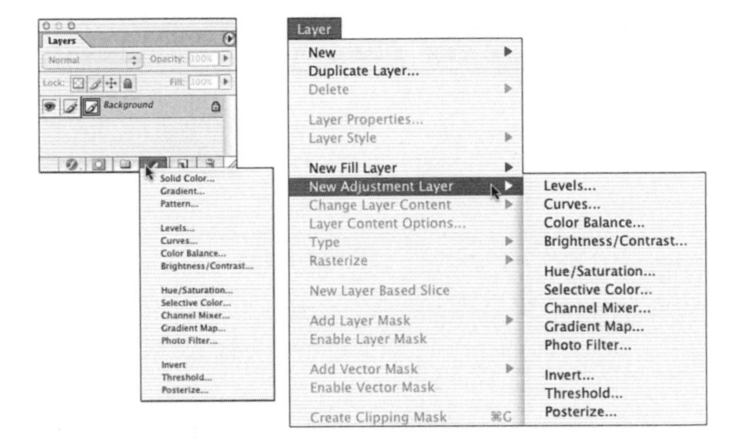


**Figure 17.9**
After you select the type of adjustment layer, the appropriate dialog box opens. Note that you can't add adjustment layers for the Auto commands, Desaturate, Replace Color, Equalize, and Variations.

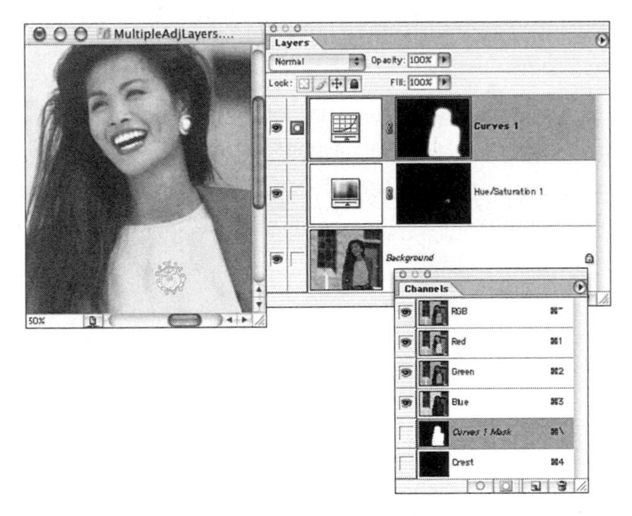


**Figure 17.10**
In this example, if you click the Hue/Saturation adjustment layer in the Layers palette, the Channels palette hides the Curves 1 Mask alpha channel and shows Hue/Saturation 1 Mask in its place.

You can hide adjustment layers and temporarily remove their effects by clicking the visibility column (the eye icon) in the Layers palette. You can lock adjustment layers to prevent movement, but because they don't contain pixels, there's no need to lock them for transparency or editing.

## Changing an Adjustment Layer

You can double-click the left-side thumbnail of an adjustment layer in the Layers palette to reopen the dialog box and change your settings. The dialog box opens with the original settings, and the image is automatically updated when you click OK. The dialog box can also be opened with the Layer, Layer Content Options menu command. You can change the type of adjustment layer with Layer, Change Layer Content.

You can edit an adjustment layer's mask by clicking once on its thumbnail in the Layers palette and then painting in the image window with black, white, or gray. The mask itself won't be visible unless you show it by clicking next to it in the visibility column of the Channels palette.

*To learn more about creating and editing masks, see "The Three Types of Channels," p. 514, in Chapter 16, "Channels: The Ultimate Creative Control."*

If you click the link icon between the adjustment layer icon and the mask thumbnail in the Layers palette, you unlink the mask from the adjustment. You can click the mask thumbnail and use the Move tool to reposition the mask in the image window. Click between the icon and the thumbnail again to relink the mask and adjustment layer.

## Restricting the Effect of an Adjustment Layer

By default, an adjustment layer affects all layers below it, including any other adjustment layers. To restrict the adjustment layer's effect to a single layer, group the adjustment layer with the layer below it in the Layers palette. (Option)-click [Alt]-click the line between the layers to link them (see Figure 17.11).



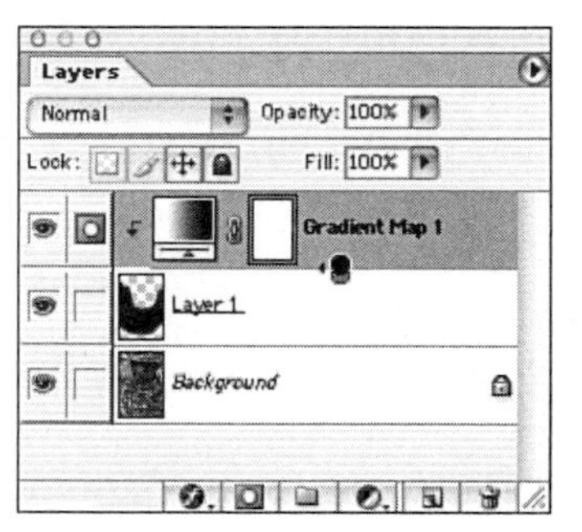


Figure 17.11
The cursor shows the "wedding rings" icon (below the word *Gradient*) when positioned correctly to group two layers. Note that the grouped layer is indented in the Layers palette to indicate its status.

The menu command Layer, Group With Previous also restricts the adjustment layer's effect to the layer or layers with which it's grouped. Additional layers can be added to the group by (Option)-clicking [Alt]-clicking the dividing lines. Adjustment layers can also be used with layer sets. To restrict the effect of an adjustment layer in a layer set, you can group all the layers or change the layer set's blending mode from Pass Through to Normal.

You can also use the Layers palette menu command Merge Down to permanently combine an adjustment layer with the layer below. The effect of the adjustment layer is applied to the layer with which it is merged and then is removed from any other layers below it.

## Fill Layers

Using the New Adjustment Layer button in the Layers palette, you can also add *fill layers* to. an image. A fill layer has no effect on underlying layers, except through blending modes (as do regular layers). A fill layer can be filled with a solid color, a gradient, or a pattern. You can create a fill layer with a selection or closed path active in the image to create a layer mask. The advantage of using a fill layer over a regular layer and the Edit, Fill command is that the fill layer is "live." Like an adjustment layer, you can reopen the dialog box to change the content of the layer.

## Brightness/Contrast and Auto Contrast

Brightness/Contrast is the easiest to understand and use of the tonal adjustments, but it's also the least flexible and the least powerful. The Brightness/Contrast dialog box, shown in Figure 17.12, consists of a pair of sliders and their related numeric fields, along with OK and Cancel buttons and a Preview check box. It can be used on the active layer or an active selection. It always affects all selected color channels equally, but you can apply it to channels individually by selecting the target channel(s) in the Channels palette.

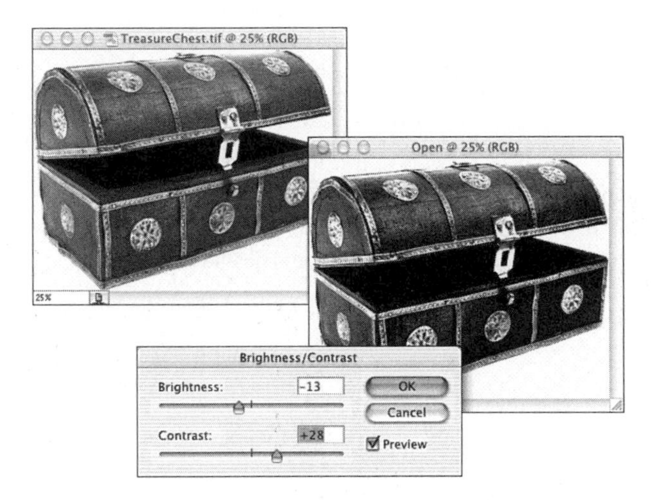


**Figure 17.12**
Each of the sliders ranges from –100 to +100.



Dragging the Brightness slider to the right lightens the image (or selection), and dragging to the left darkens the image. The Contrast slider, in effect, increases or decreases the difference between light and dark pixels. Dragging the slider to the left (reducing the contrast) makes the image more gray and consolidates the pixels' luminosity values in the midranges; dragging the slider to the right distributes the luminosity values (see Figure 17.13).

The Auto Contrast command adjusts image tonality by making light pixels brighter and shadows darker. It attempts to preserve the overall color relationship in the image while making the change.

## Levels and Auto Levels

The Levels adjustment dialog box, shown in Figure 17.14, works with shadows, highlights, and overall gamma (the brightness of an image's midtones) independently. It also gives you separate control over input and output values, includes special eyedropper tools for identifying the highlight and shadow areas of an image, and offers a neutral gray eyedropper for removing color casts.

### Input Levels

One of the most common uses of Levels is to expand an image's tonal range. Typically, the left and right sliders are dragged inward to the beginning of the image data in the Levels histogram. The middle slider is repositioned under what is likely to be the "center mass" of the histogram—the average value, or *mean*, rather than the median (see Figure 17.15).

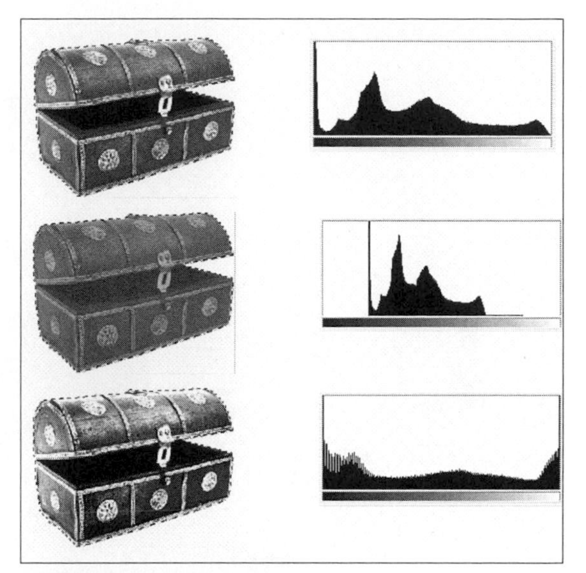

Figure 17.13
The top image represents the original. In the middle, Contrast has been changed to –50. At the bottom, Contrast is changed to +50. Note that Brightness/Contrast was applied only to the subject, not the white background.



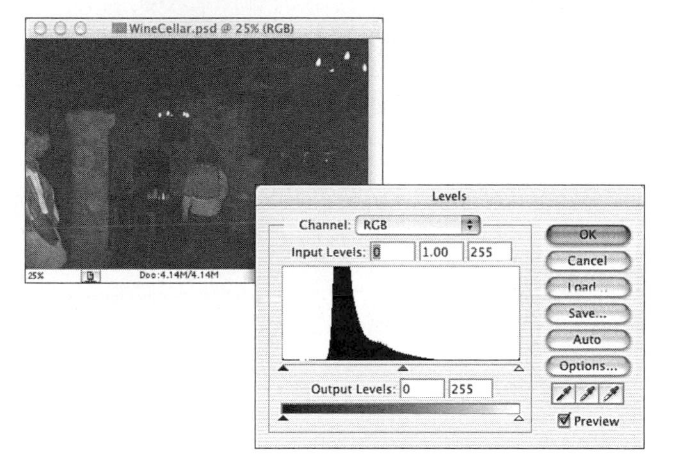


Figure 17.14
The image's tonal range is very compressed. Using Levels spreads the range out by moving values apart to reveal more of the image's details.

Levels works by adjusting the brightness of pixels. The left and right sliders, and their corresponding Input Levels fields, are used to define where black and white begin. For example, in Figure 17.16, the left slider is at 25, meaning that any pixels that have a brightness between 0 and 25 will be changed to 0 and become black. The right slider is at 225, so any pixels with a brightness higher than that become white (255).

As the left and right sliders are brought closer together, the number of possible brightness values in the image decreases. In Figure 17.16, the image will go from 256 possible tones (0–255) to 201 possible tones (25–225). Figure 17.17 shows what the histogram looks like *after* the adjustment in the previous figure is applied. The 201 values that were retained in the previous adjustment (25–225) are now spread over 256 total tonal values (0–255).

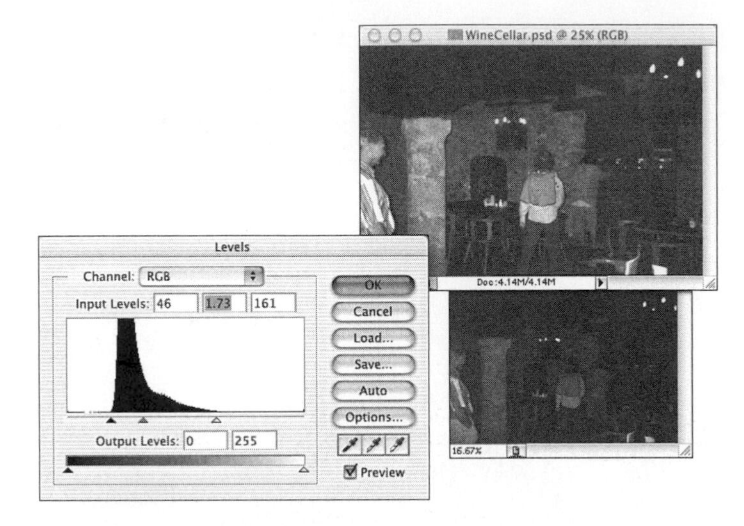


**Figure 17.15**
Note that the few stray pixels to the far left and right of the histogram are ignored and the adjustment concentrates on the bulk of the pixel values in the image.



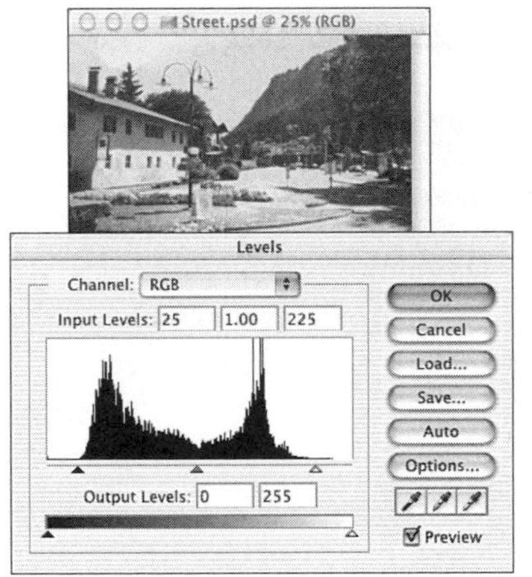


**Figure 17.16**
The middle slider, gamma, repositions itself automatically and remains set to 1.00 as the left and right sliders are changed.

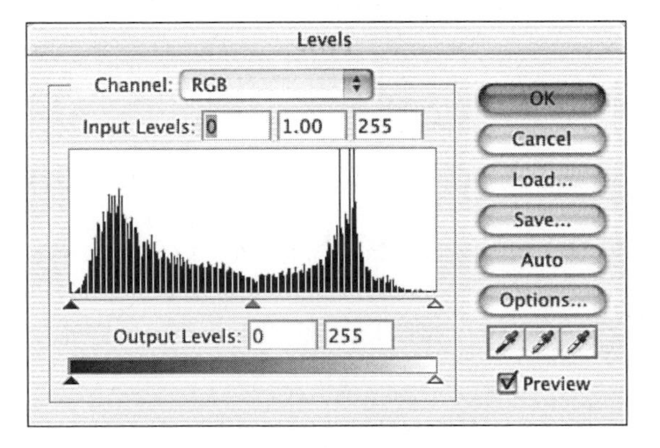


**Figure 17.17**
Notice the new empty columns in the histogram. Levels didn't create any new brightness values; rather, it redistributed the values that were retained in the previous adjustment.

## Output Levels

The lower slider in the Levels dialog box controls the tonal range of an image from a different direction. It is used to compress the range (which reduces contrast) and to *clip* highlights and shadows. (Clipping occurs when multiple tonal values at either end of the tonal range are compressed into a single value.) These sliders can be used very effectively with the gamma (middle) slider below the histogram. In Figure 17.18, the correction is being made to the foreground only. This method not only provides a more accurate histogram, it also maintains the brightness of the white background.

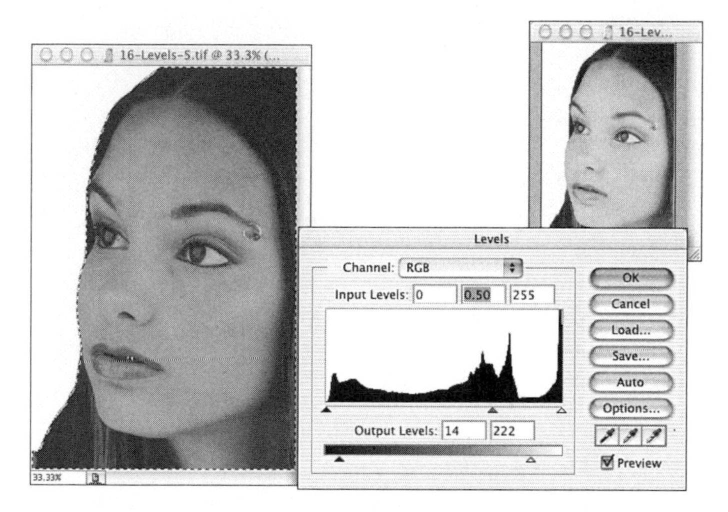


**Figure 17.18**
The original image, shown in the upper right, is skewed to brightness. Changing the Output slider on the right trims the highlights, and using the middle slider below the histogram adjusts the overall gamma.



Adjusting the Output sliders prevents pixels from becoming completely black or white. By bringing the left slider to level 14, the darkest a pixel can be is approximately 95% gray. Similarly, dragging the right slider from 255 to 222 results in the brightest pixel *in the selection* being 16% gray. (The white background is not affected because it is not selected.)

## The Levels Eyedroppers

Using the Output sliders to determine an image's shadow and highlight points can compress the tonal range. Using the eyedropper tools in Levels to set the black and white points enables you to specify which *pixels* should be black and white, rather than which *tones*.

The first step is to identify the actual shadow and highlight pixels. In the Levels dialog box, you can find them by using the (Option) [Alt] key and the Input sliders. Hold down the modifier key and begin dragging the right slider. The image (or selection) will turn black. As you drag to the left, the first white areas you see will be your highlights—ignore colors and drag until you see white. Ignore any specular highlights, too. You want to identify the diffuse highlights.

Similarly, hold down (Option) [Alt] and drag the left slider to the right. Again, ignore color and drag until you see black appear. Those areas are your image's darkest points.

> When you identify the shadow and highlight pixels with the Input sliders, release the (Option) [Alt] key—keeping an eye on your target point—and move the cursor to those pixels. Shift-click to place a color sampler for later reference.

*The Threshold command offers another way to find the darkest and lightest areas of an image. See "Photoshop at Work: Finding Highlights and Shadows," p. 580, later in this chapter.*

There is one advantage to using the Output sliders rather than the eyedroppers to establish black and white points: Output Levels can be recorded in an Action. Although this is not as precise as selecting pixels with the eyedroppers, it can be far more practical in a production environment.

After you've identified the shadow and highlight points, you can click with the black and white eyedropper tools. The histogram changes to reflect the new distribution of tonal values. You still have the option of adjusting the gamma slider separately.

The middle eyedropper tool is used for color balance. If the image contains an area that you know should be a neutral gray, you can click it with the middle eyedropper. Remember that you can leave the Info palette open and maneuver the cursor around the image to check existing color values.

The values that you assign with the eyedroppers are set by double-clicking each of the tools' icons in the Levels dialog box. That opens the Color Picker. For average-key images intended for print, black points can be set to RGB 10/10/10 or CMYK 65/53/51/95 for a rich black. White points can be set to RGB 244/244/244 or CMYK 5/3/3/0. High-key images can have a higher black point, which reserves additional tonal steps for detail in the highlights. Likewise, low-key images can get better shadow detail when the white point is set somewhat lower.



### The Auto Button and Auto Levels

Clicking the Auto button in the Levels dialog box is comparable to using the menu command Image, Adjustments, Auto Levels. The tonal range of each component color channel is maximized. By correcting each channel individually, rather than working with just brightness (as does Auto Contrast), this command can correct (or introduce) color casts. The lightest and darkest values for each channel in the image are mapped to the Shadows and Highlights values assigned in the Auto Color Correction Options dialog box.

## Auto Color Correction Options

You'll find Options buttons in both the Levels and Curves dialog boxes. The Auto Color Correction Options dialog box, shown in Figure 17.19, controls how the Auto buttons in Levels and Curves work as well as the performance of the Auto Contrast, Auto Levels, and Auto Color commands.

Here are the options available for the Auto commands and buttons:

- **Enhance Monochromatic Contrast**—Used by the Auto Contrast command, this option adjusts the image by preserving the existing color relationships in the image and increasing the contrast. Highlights get brighter, and shadows get darker. All component color channels receive the same correction to avoid introducing a color cast. This adjustment is rather simplistic, best suited for images that already show good color and perhaps simply need a bit of a contrast boost. The Auto Contrast command can be recorded in an Action for a production environment.

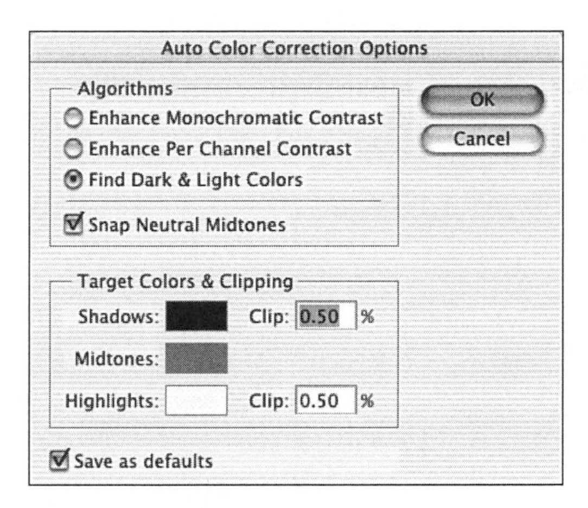


**Figure 17.19**
Remember to save your changes as the defaults, unless you intend to return to the prior values.



- **Enhance Per Channel Contrast**—Instead of the image as a whole being adjusted, each channel is adjusted individually, thus maximizing the tonal range within the channel. This is the technique applied by Auto Levels. Because each channel is adjusted individually, color casts can be eliminated with this option. However, color casts can also be *introduced* if one component channel is substantially restricted. This option, which can be recorded in an Action through Auto Levels, is appropriate for images that need to look good but don't require exact color correction.
- **Find Dark & Light Colors**—This option minimizes the unintentional clipping of highlights and shadows while still increasing an image's tonal range. The brightest pixels are averaged, as are the darkest, to determine the adjustment. This is the algorithm used by Photoshop's Auto Colors command. It is generally effective on most photographic images but can produce unacceptable results in some radically colored images.
- **Snap Neutral Midtones**—Comparable in some respects to using the gray eyedropper in the Levels or Curves dialog box, this option finds a near-neutral color in an image and maps the gamma to it. The color is made truly neutral, and other colors in the image are adjusted accordingly. This option, used by the Auto Color command, can substantially reduce or eliminate color casts.
- **Shadows**—Click the swatch to open the Color Picker. Typically, a shadow value of RGB 10/10/10 (CMYK 65/53/51/95) is appropriate for print; Web designers are better served by a shadow value of 0/0/0. This is the color to which your image's black will be mapped.
- **Clip Shadows**—Clipping shadows eliminates stray pixels from the determination of what constitutes a shadow. By clipping extremes, theoretically, the true shadows are identified. Clipping prevents a single pixel or two from being recognized as black in an image. Generally, 0.5% to 1% clipping is acceptable.
- **Midtones**—The neutral gray value for an image is almost always RGB 128/128/128. If you need to make an adjustment, click the swatch to open the Color Picker. To ensure that the gray is "neutral" and won't introduce a color cast to your image, enter equal values for red, green, and blue. It's best to define neutral gray in RGB or as 50% gray, even when you're working with a CMYK image.

- **Highlights**—Click the swatch to open the Color Picker and assign a highlight value. Images to be printed are likely to benefit from a highlight of RGB 244/244/244 (CMYK 5/3/3/0); Web-oriented images should use RGB 255/255/255.
- **Clip Highlights**—The clipping percent, which should be between 0.5% and 1.0%, identifies "white" in the image. The clipping value tells Photoshop which pixels it can ignore. This setting prevents a situation in which the highlight for an entire image is established by a single out-of-whack pixel.
- **Save as Defaults**—When this option is selected, clicking OK establishes the values in the dialog box for the appropriate menu commands and the Auto buttons of the Levels and Curves dialog boxes. When this check box is not selected, you're prompted to save the options nonetheless when closing the adjustment dialog box.

The Auto Color Correction settings, once saved, are used for all the commands—you cannot set different options for the various Auto commands.



## Curves

The most powerful of Photoshop's image-correction tools is, without a doubt, Curves, although with that power comes complexity. The dialog box itself (see Figure 17.20), however, is not particularly complicated after a few basic techniques and concepts are clear.

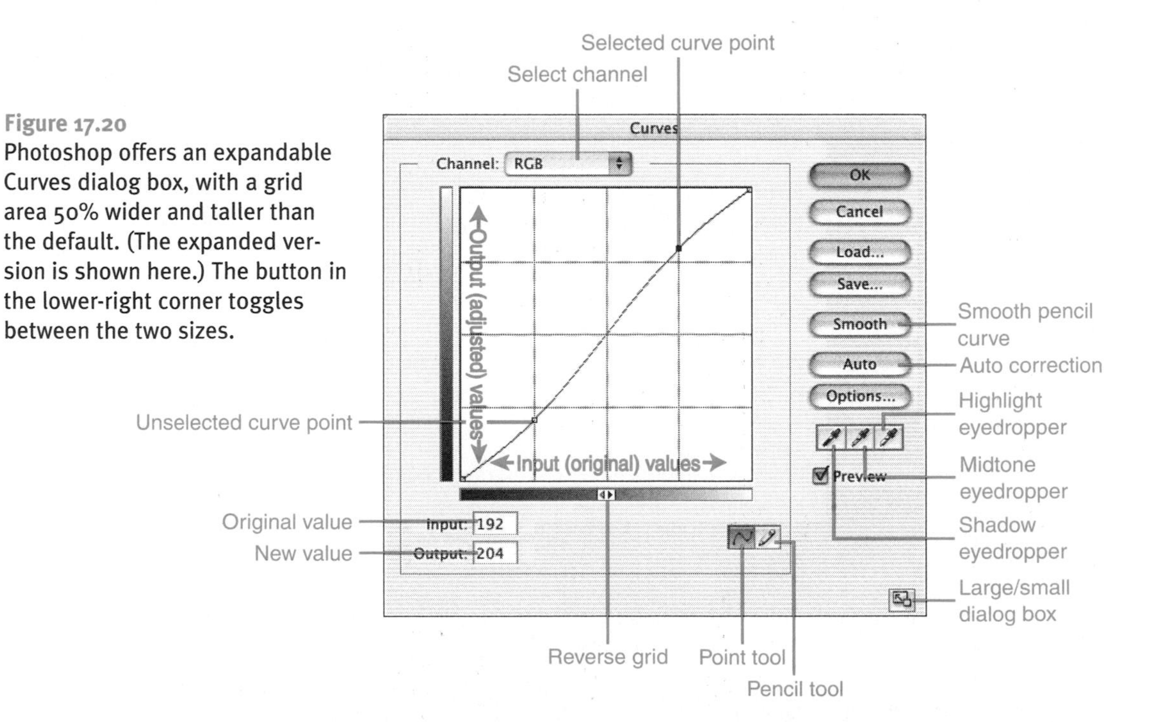


**Figure 17.20**
Photoshop offers an expandable Curves dialog box, with a grid area 50% wider and taller than the default. (The expanded version is shown here.) The button in the lower-right corner toggles between the two sizes.

Curves can be applied to a flattened image, an active layer, a channel, or a selection. Curves adjusts images much as Levels does but uses 256 separate values (RGB) or 100 values (other color modes) rather than just the three available in Levels. (When adjusting 16-bit images, you still see the 256 or 100 value scale.) The eyedropper tools in Curves work the same way they do in Levels.

When you're working with an RGB or a Lab image, shadows are to the left of the grid and highlights are to the right. With CMYK, Grayscale, and Multichannel images, brightness is to the left and shadows are to the right. You can reverse the grid by clicking the two-headed arrow in the gradient below the grid. This also switches the number of levels from 256 to 100, or from 100 to 256.

The horizontal axis represents the original value, and the vertical axis represents the new value. When you first open the dialog box, the "curve" is a diagonal line because each input value is equal to its corresponding output value. The grid's default three vertical lines represent the quarter tones, midtones, and three-quarter tones of the image. (Option)-click [Alt]-click the grid to switch to a 10×10 grid for a more precise view of the curve values.

To simplify the Curves dialog box in your mind, picture it *without* the horizontal grid lines. The vertical grid lines help you identify input values—drag points straight up and down and watch the Output field.

Dragging an anchor point up or down on the curve can have an effect on the entire curve. To keep a section of the curve stable, place pairs of anchor points at either end of that section of the curve. You can use two closely spaced anchor points to prevent changes from flowing past a specific value.

A curve can have up to 16 distinct anchor points (including the endpoints). Drag a point to reposition it, and drag it out of the box to delete it. You select an input level by clicking the curve itself and then you drag the point up or down to change the image's appearance. Curve adjustments can be saved and later loaded to apply the same adjustments to another image. This option is especially useful when a scanner or digital camera regularly produces a color cast.

When Curves is set to the image's composite channel (RGB or CMYK), you are adjusting the brightness of the image. When it's set to a single color channel, you're working only with that color component throughout the image and are, therefore, correcting color.

The Pencil tool can be used to replace a section of the curve with a custom adjustment. Simply select the tool and draw the segment you want. The Smooth button progressively straightens a curve drawn with the Pencil tool to ease the transitions. You can click multiple times, and only the segments of the curve created with the Pencil tool are affected.

## Curves Dialog Box Shortcuts

There are also a number of shortcuts that make working with Curves easier:

- Shift-click to select multiple points. (Command-D) [Ctrl+D] deselects all points. You can also deselect by clicking away from the curve in the grid.
- Ctrl+Tab and Shift+Ctrl+Tab move through the existing points on a curve.
- Use the arrow keys to adjust selected points. Add the Shift key to increase the increment of movement.

- Move the cursor over the image and click to identify where that area falls in the curve. (Remember that you're using the Eyedropper tool's setting—Point Sample, 3×3 Average, or 5×5 Average.) Shift-click to add a color sampler to the image.
- (Command)-click [Ctrl]-click in the image to add a point to the curve. Add the Shift key to place the points in the color channels but not in the composite channel.
- Hold down the (Option) [Alt] key and the dialog box's Cancel button becomes Reset.
- You can manipulate two (or three) color channels at the same time by Shift-clicking them in the Channels palette before opening Curves.

## Making Tonal Adjustments with Curves

Images that already look good can often benefit from some additional help to make them look even better. Typically, adjusting the *quarters* (the quarter tones and the three-quarter tones) is all that is necessary to provide that additional help. The quarter and three-quarter marks are easily identifiable when the Curves dialog box is set to its default four-column/four-row configuration (see Figure 17.21).



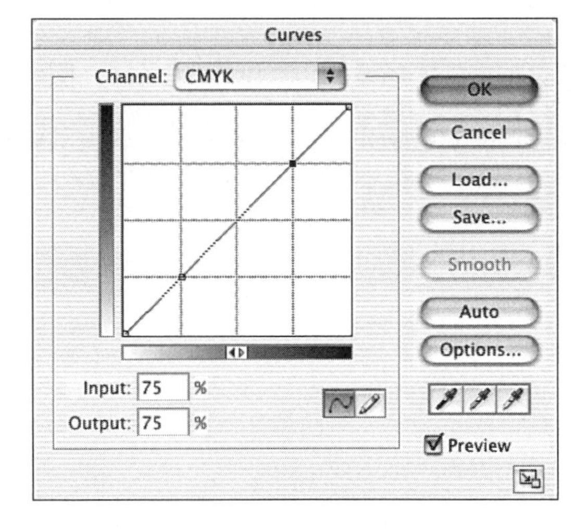


Figure 17.21
By default, vertical grid lines appear at the 25%, 50%, and 75% levels.

Figure 17.22 shows a pair of common Curves adjustments. The adjustment shown in the upper figure tones down hot highlights and lightens dark shadows. In the lower example, the contrast of the image is increased by moving the quarters away from each other.

> When you're working with RGB images, the Input and Output fields are calculated from 0–255 rather than 0–100. The 25% equivalent is 64, 50% is equal to 128, and 75% is comparable to 191.

You can also make more complex adjustments, even targeting specific groups of pixels in an image. Shift-clicking in the image with the Curves dialog box open places color samplers, which can be used with the Info palette to track adjustments as you make them. In Figure 17.23, as you can see from the smaller original in the upper-right corner, the highlights on the forehead are too light and the shadows lack detail. The Curves adjustment targets those specific areas.

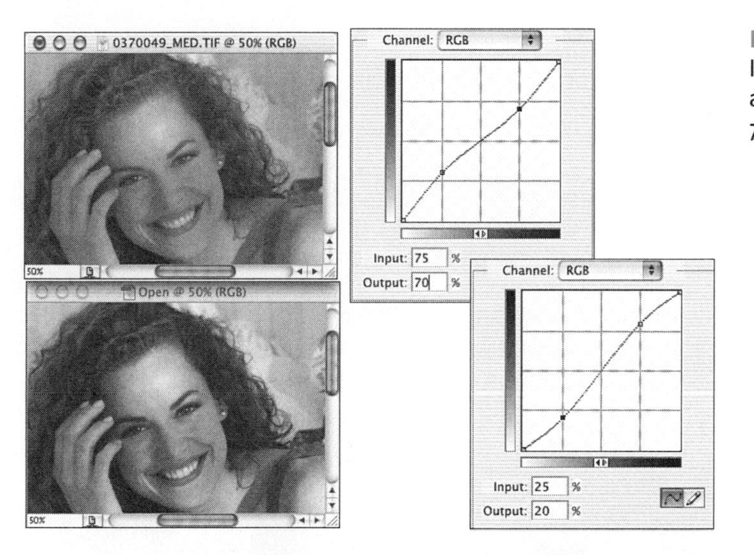


**Figure 17.22**
In each example, the adjustments are small—25% to 20% or 30%, 75% to 80% or 70%.



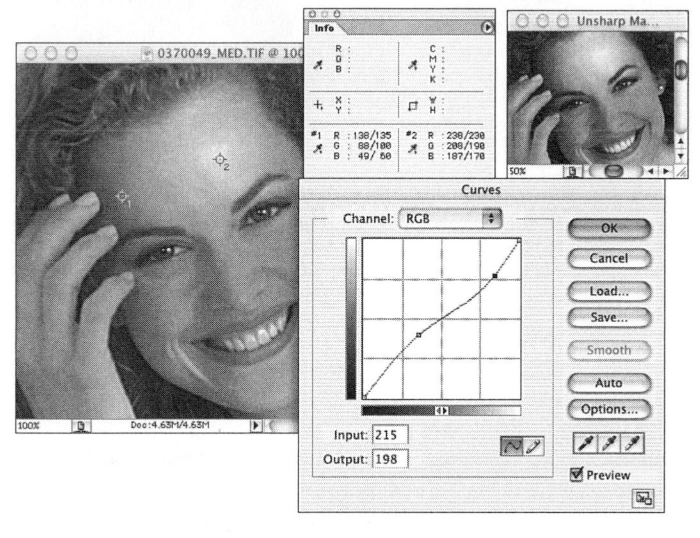


**Figure 17.23**
In the Info palette, the numbers to the left are the original color values, and those to the right are the values after the correction is applied.

Hold down the (Command) [Ctrl] key and click in an image to place a point on the curve at that value. In this example, you can (Command)-click [Ctrl]-click the color samplers to add points.

## Color Correction with Curves

The Channel menu at the top of the Curves dialog box enables you to target a correction to a single component color in an image. Color casts can be removed by adjusting the individual channels. Keep in mind the relationship among the RGB and CMYK component colors:

- When working in RGB, you can increase or decrease yellow in an image by adjusting both the Red and Green channels (R+G=Y).
- In an RGB image, cyan can be adjusted by increasing or decreasing green and blue (G+B=C).
- Magenta in an RGB image is a function of red and blue (R+B=M).
- In a CMYK image, a blue cast can be corrected by reducing both cyan and magenta (C+M=B).
- The amount of red in a CMYK image is adjusted through the Magenta and Yellow channels (M+Y=R).
- Green in a CMYK image is a function of cyan and yellow (C+Y=G).

Curves can also be used with channels in combination. In Figure 17.24, the RGB image has yellow accent lighting that is too prominent. To adjust the yellow lighting without destroying the color in the remainder of the image, you can isolate it by using Select, Color Range.



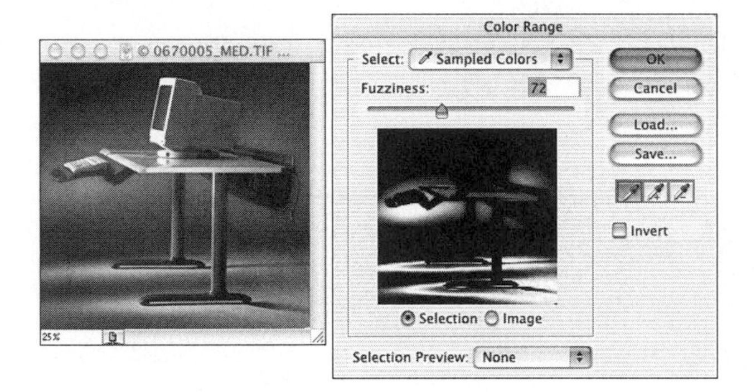


**Figure 17.24**
Curves can be applied to a selection. Color Range is an excellent tool for creating that selection.

In Figure 17.25, you can see that the Red and Green channels are active in the Channels palette, but that all channels are visible. That allows you to work on a pair of channels and continue to monitor the overall effect on the image. In this example, the Red and Green channels are active because, combined, they are responsible for the yellow content of an RGB image.

## The Curves Eyedroppers

The shadow, midtone, and highlight eyedroppers in the Curves dialog box function much like those in the Levels dialog box. First, you identify the darkest shadow and the brightest diffuse highlight (not specular highlight). Next, click with the appropriate eyedropper. The midtone eyedropper can be used to correct a color cast *if* there is a neutral gray in the image.

# Auto Color

Photoshop's Auto Color command is much more powerful than Auto Contrast or Auto Levels. The key to its accuracy in color correction is based on its method of evaluating the image. Instead of looking at the histogram to determine shadows, highlights, and midtones, it examines the image itself. Using the values you specify in the Auto Color Correction Options dialog box, it clips the highlights and shadows, identifies the image's midtone, and neutralizes the color by balancing the component color values. You can open the Auto Color Correction Options dialog box by clicking the Options button in the Curves or Levels dialog box.

In many cases it makes good sense to try Auto Color first, before making any corrections with Curves or Levels. If Auto Color does a good job, great! If not, simply use Undo.

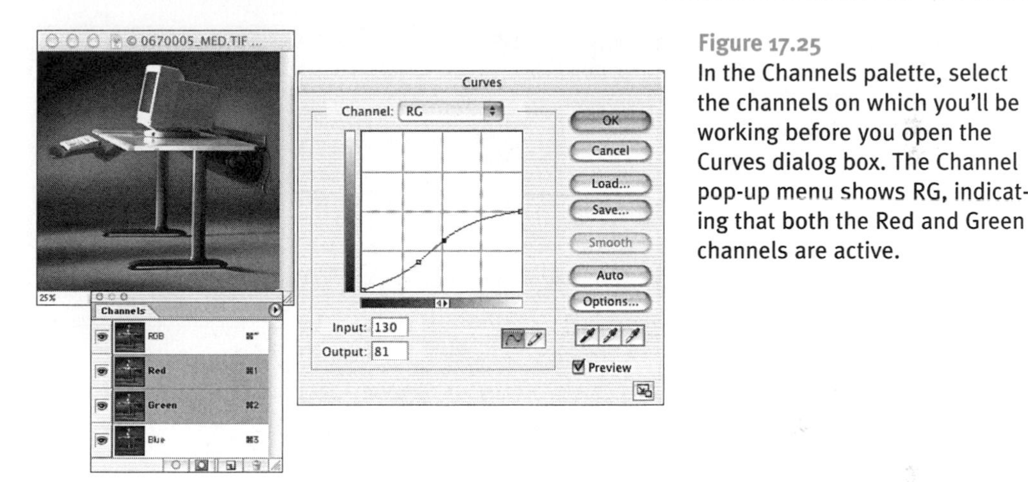


**Figure 17.25**
In the Channels palette, select the channels on which you'll be working before you open the Curves dialog box. The Channel pop-up menu shows RG, indicating that both the Red and Green channels are active.

*For information on establishing the parameters for the Auto Color command, see "Auto Color Correction Options," p. 558, earlier in this chapter.*

# The Toning Tools

Photoshop offers a pair of tools, known as the *toning tools*, for touching up the tonality of an image. The Dodge and Burn tools selectively lighten and darken areas of an image as you drag. The settings in the Options Bar enable you to concentrate on the shadows, midtones, or highlights as well as set an exposure value, which determines the strength of the tools. The toning tools are brush based—you select a brush appropriate for the size and shape of the area you are adjusting.

The Dodge tool is used to selectively lighten an image or selection. It takes its name and icon from the darkroom technique used to lighten an area of an image during exposure. By using an opaque piece of cardboard on a stick and a circular motion, a photographer is able to block some of the light passing through a film negative and onto the photographic paper, lightening the final printed image in those areas. This operation is known as *dodging*. Similarly, photographers burn or darken an area of an image by selectively exposing an area to more light in the darkroom while protecting the surrounding area around from exposure.

Be aware that choosing shadows, midtones, or highlights for the Dodge or Burn tool does not *restrict* the tool to the selected tonal range; rather, it concentrates the effect in that range. In Figure 17.26, the Dodge tool was used on a black-to-white gradient. At the top, the tool was set to Shadows; in the middle, to Midtones; and at the bottom, to Highlights. In all three cases the Exposure setting was 100%. Note that even when set to Highlights, the Dodge tool lightened the darkest areas of the image slightly.

Figure 17.26
The Dodge tool's options have an impact on how strongly it affects a particular tonal range, but the tool can affect the entire range, no matter the setting.

A third tool is grouped with the toning tools in the Toolbox and is sometimes considered with them. The Sponge tool can saturate or desaturate areas of an image. It, too, is a brush-based tool, with an option that determines the strength of its impact (Flow). When used on a Grayscale image, the Sponge tool increases or decreases contrast.

## Photoshop at Work: Removing Redeye

Redeye—that all too common flash photography phenomenon—is easily fixed with the toning tools. Follow these steps to use the Sponge tool to remove redeye from an image opened in Photoshop:

1. Open a photograph of a person whose eyes seem to be glowing red. (Or perhaps you've got a photo of a beloved pet with glowing green eyes.)
2. Zoom in on one of the eyeballs.
3. From Photoshop's toolbox, choose the Sponge tool. In the Options bar, select a hard round brush the size of the red spot and make sure the tool is set to Desaturate and Pressure 50%.
4. Click with the Sponge tool a time or two to desaturate the red area, leaving the natural-looking reflections.

That's usually all it takes, but sometimes you may need to click a time or two with the Burn tool as well. Make sure it's set to a low Exposure value so you don't darken the area too much.

**Pre-Photoshop Image Preparation**

The best way to make sure you've got great tonal range and color in your output is to start with good input. You can do a number of things to make your color and tonal corrections easier *before* the image arrives in Photoshop:

- **Including black, white, and gray swatches**—When you control the environment, add a target card in the bottom or side of the subject area before you snap the shot. It should have three squares of equal size: one black, one neutral gray, one white. (Keep them the same size to avoid skewing your histogram.) The card need not be large; actually, it should be as small as possible. Place it in the image near the subject and then take the picture. When you bring the image into Photoshop, use the eyedropper tools in the Curves dialog box on the squares to correct the image and then crop to remove the swatches.

  The target card should be printed on the brightest white stock available and mounted on a stiff board. To prevent reflections, don't use glossy paper. The targets can be printed from a black-and-white laser printer to avoid any color cast. You can also purchase commercially prepared target cards, including cards with color swatches.

- **Scanning adjustments**—Scan your target card into Photoshop and check the black and neutral gray squares with the Eyedropper tool. If they show a color cast (the RGB values aren't equal), you can create a correction curve that can be loaded and applied to every scan. For more accuracy, create an 11-step black-to-white gradient.

  In addition, try scanning a blank white sheet of paper. See how evenly the scanner scans. Most flatbed scanners have a "sweet spot" in the middle where they produce the brightest, most accurate scans.

- **Knowing your digital camera**—If you shoot with a digital camera, learn about and experiment with its settings. Read the manual and any electronic documents available from the camera manufacturer's Web site. Find out what capabilities it has and use them.

  Although it is easy and convenient to shoot with the camera in Auto mode, that might not be appropriate for your needs. Remember, too, that taking an hour to read the manual and experiment with the controls could save you hundreds of hours in color correction and noise reduction later.

- **Setting the set**—When possible, set up your photo shoot with an eye toward your computer. Take the lenses out of eyeglasses. A little hairspray on highly reflective surfaces can tone them down. Use fill lighting and reflectors to avoid too-dark shadows.



# COLOR ADJUSTMENT AND EFFECTS COMMANDS

Photoshop has a number of commands for directly altering the color of an image. Consolidated under the Image, Adjustments menu, they offer a variety of techniques and procedures to give you ultimate control over the appearance of your image.

The color adjustment and effects commands can be used with Curves and Levels. Remember that proper monitor calibration and appropriate color-management settings are critical to getting good results with these commands. If you are not accurately seeing color onscreen, your decisions are not based on the actual image content. Likewise, if your color-management profiles are inappropriate for the image's destination, the colors you see are unlikely to be the colors actually produced.

*For a discussion of ensuring accurate color, see Chapter 6, "Color Management in the Adobe Creative Suite," p. 189.*

Remember that you can use the menu command Edit, Fade immediately after applying a color adjustment command. The Fade command can lessen the impact of the adjustment and apply a blending mode.

## Color Balance

The Color Balance command is available only when the composite channel is active in the Channels palette. The selection you make in the Tone Balance section of the dialog box enables you to concentrate (but not restrict) the effect in shadows, midtones, or highlights. The Preserve Luminosity option protects the image's tonality. Typically, this command is used to compensate for color casts.

If you ever forget the relationship among the RGB and CMY component colors, open Color Balance. The inverse color pairs are evident in the slider labels.

In Figure 17.27, note that each of the sliders represents a pair of color opposites. Moving the top slider to the right increases red in the image, which is the same as reducing the amount of cyan. The other sliders work similarly. Color Balance can be used with a flattened image, an active layer, or a selection.

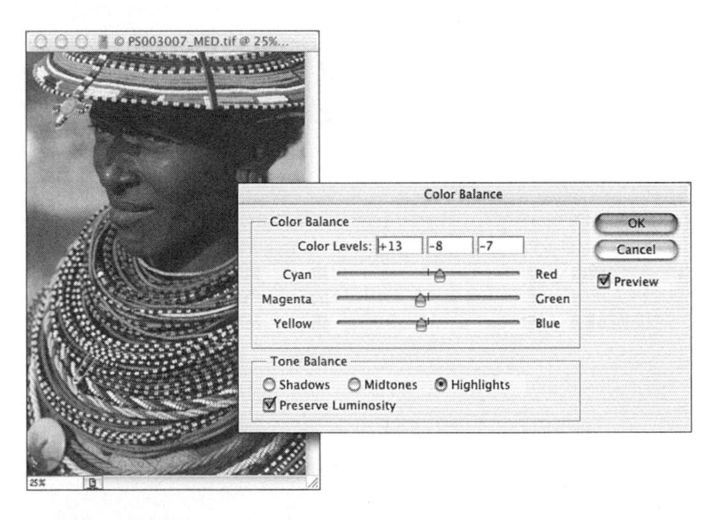


**Figure 17.27**
The numeric fields across the top correspond to the three sliders, from top to bottom.

With Preserve Luminosity selected, moving all three sliders to the right equally has no effect on the image. Without the option, such a change would lighten the image by uniformly increasing the amounts of red, green, and blue throughout the image. Likewise, moving the three sliders equal distances to the left darkens the image when luminosity is not preserved.

## Hue/Saturation

> If the skin tones in your image look good, make sure to exclude them from any selection before using Hue/Saturation.

The Hue/Saturation command actually works with hue, saturation, and lightness. It can be used to correct or add a color cast, increase (or decrease) the saturation of an image, or generally lighten or darken. When used in combination, the three components of Hue/Saturation can produce dramatic effects and subtle adjustments. It can be used with flattened images, active layers, and selections, and you can manipulate the composite channel (all colors at once) or individually selected colors (see Figure 17.28).

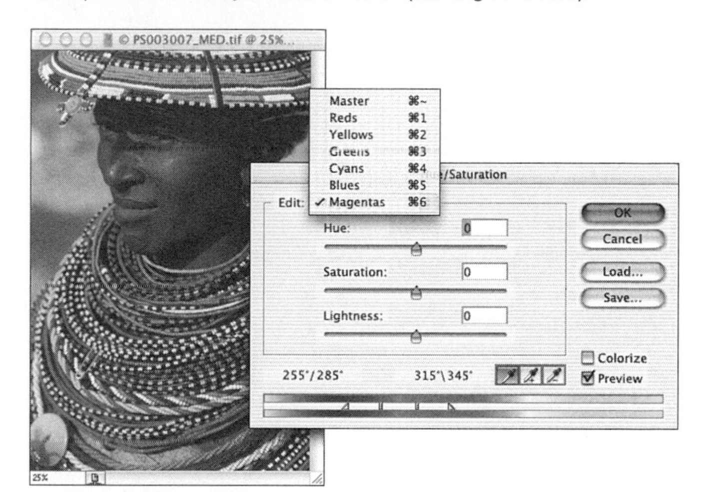


**Figure 17.28**
All six component colors can be adjusted individually, regardless of whether the image is RGB, CMYK, Lab, or Indexed Color mode. Photoshop CS enables you to use Hue/Saturation (and the other adjustments) with 16-bit images in appropriate color modes.



## The Hue Slider

Think of the Hue slider as a color-substitution slider. When Hue/Saturation is set to Edit:Master, you change the entire image or selection. At the bottom of the dialog box, the two gradient bars represent the original color (top) and the color that you'll be substituting (bottom). As the Hue slider is dragged, the lower gradient bar shifts. Moving it realigns the two bars so that you can see the color substitution. (When a specific color range is selected rather than Master, the substitution is limited to that color. The other hues in the image remain unchanged.)

For example, at +120, red (in the center of the top bar) is replaced by green throughout the image. Likewise, blue is replaced with red, cyan is replaced by magenta, and so on. At –120, the color shift is in the opposite direction, with red being replaced by blue, blue by green, and cyan by yellow.

The Hue slider is based on the standard color wheel, so it ranges in value from –180 to +180. Think of degrees around the circle. The key values for the Hue slider—and their results—are shown in Table 17.1.

**Table 17.1** Color Changes with the Hue Slider

| Hue Value | Original Color | Substituted Color |
|---|---|---|
| –180 | Red | Cyan |
| | Green | Magenta |
| | Blue | Yellow |
| | Cyan | Red |
| | Magenta | Green |
| | Yellow | Blue |
| –120 | Red | Blue |
| | Green | Red |
| | Blue | Green |
| | Cyan | Yellow |
| | Magenta | Cyan |
| | Yellow | Magenta |
| –60 | Red | Magenta |
| | Green | Yellow |
| | Blue | Cyan |
| | Cyan | Green |
| | Magenta | Blue |
| | Yellow | Red |
| 0 | (no changes) | |
| +60 | Red | Yellow |
| | Green | Cyan |
| | Blue | Magenta |
| | Cyan | Blue |
| | Magenta | Red |
| | Yellow | Green |
| +120 | Red | Green |
| | Green | Blue |
| | Blue | Red |
| | Cyan | Magenta |
| | Magenta | Yellow |
| | Yellow | Cyan |
| +180 | Red | Cyan |
| | Green | Magenta |
| | Blue | Yellow |
| | Cyan | Red |
| | Magenta | Green |
| | Yellow | Blue |

Note that the –180 and +180 settings have identical results and, in effect, simply invert the image's colors.

## The Saturation Slider

If you need to simulate dusk or dawn, or even night, try reducing Lightness *and* increasing Saturation. Instead of just making the image dark, it makes the image dark and vivid—often a more realistic effect.

The Saturation slider works in absolutes. Ranging from –100 (completely desaturated, grayscale) to +100 (completely saturated), it adjusts the vividness of the colors in the image or selection.

When the Saturation slider is dragged to the right, the primary component color (or colors) in a hue is increased, and the other colors (or color) are decreased to compensate. For example, if a pixel is RGB 220/60/60 (red) and the Saturation slider is dragged to +50, the resulting color is RGB 250/30/30 (without compensation for color profiles). A yellow pixel with a CMYK value of 2/17/73/0, on the other hand, would not likely be affected much by a Saturation of +50 because it is already about as saturated as most CMYK profiles can produce.

Dragging the Saturation slider to the left reduces the primary component color(s) and increases the other component color(s). The closer that all the component colors get to equal values, the closer the pixel is to gray. When all three component colors meet, gray is the result.



## The Lightness Slider

Like the Saturation slider, Lightness works in absolutes. A setting of +100 turns every pixel pure white, and –100 turns every pixel pure black. Smaller adjustments, in effect, increase the brightness of pixels by raising all three RGB component values or lowering the CMYK values (depending on the color mode).

## Adjusting a Specific Color Range

When you select a color from the Edit pop-up menu, the Hue/Saturation dialog box adds some controls to the lower part of the dialog box (see Figure 17.29).

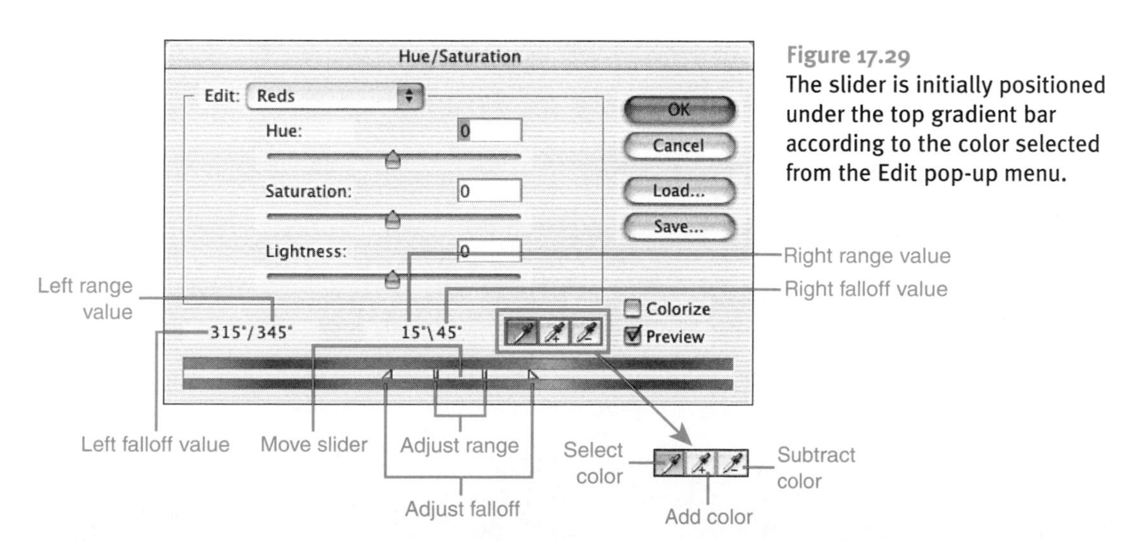


**Figure 17.29**
The slider is initially positioned under the top gradient bar according to the color selected from the Edit pop-up menu.

The slider consists of a pair of vertical bars bracketing the selected color range and a pair of wedge-shaped icons that adjust *falloff*. Think of falloff as a sort of feathering for color—it gradually fades the adjustment from the selected core color to the colors adjacent in the color wheel. The degree readings above the top gradient bar enable you to track the number of degrees of falloff to the left (the left pair), the actual range of color (the middle two numbers), and the right falloff (the right pair).

Falloff prevents posterization or visible banding when you make substantial adjustments to a color range in Hue/Saturation. The default value of 30° on either side is typically very good. However, to restrict the effect of your adjustment, you might need to reduce falloff on one side or both.

Dragging the middle portion of the slider repositions the entire slider without changing the range or falloff amounts. If you drag it to another color, the menu at the top of the dialog box is updated to reflect the new position. Dragging the outer wedge-shaped icons inward reduces the amount of falloff, and dragging them outward increases it. Repositioning the vertical bars changes the targeted range of color.



If you need to adjust similar colors but must leave an intermediate hue untouched, you can create related color ranges. In Figure 17.30, the oranges and purples are selected, but the reds are not. Notice, however, that the Edit pop-up menu has named the two selections Reds and Reds 2. You could even have all six selection ranges within one color name.

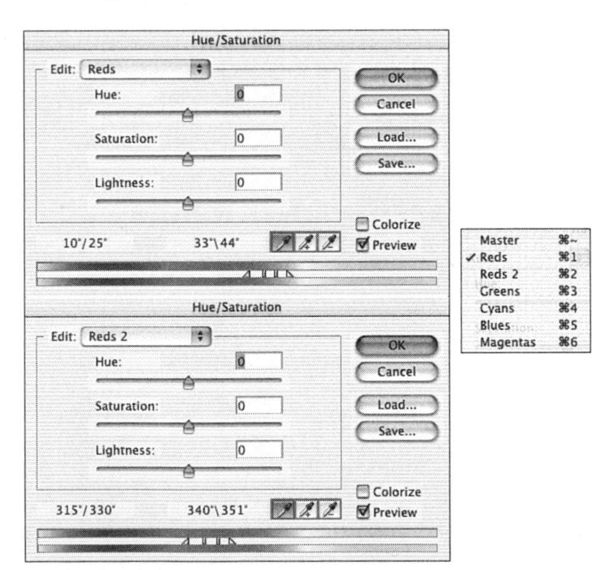


**Figure 17.30**
Despite the related names, each color selection is manipulated individually in the Hue/Saturation dialog box. Change the selection, change the slider, switch to the next selection, change the sliders again, and then click OK.

## Photoshop at Work: Colorizing with Hue/Saturation

You can simulate the look of a Duotone image without ever leaving RGB mode. (A great way to simulate two-ink printing with inkjet printers.) To use the Hue and Saturation sliders to colorize an image opened in Photoshop, follow these steps:

1. Open an image in Photoshop.
2. Add a Hue/Saturation adjustment layer. (Using an adjustment layer rather than an image adjustment enables you to come back later and fine-tune the color. You may need to compensate for a color shift from your printer.)
3. In the Hue/Saturation dialog box, check the Colorize box in the lower-right corner. When you select the check box, the preview shows a desaturated image with a second color applied.
4. Adjust the sliders to your needs or taste and then click OK.

As you may have noticed, Photoshop doesn't provide a Desaturate adjustment layer. At least not directly. Simply add a Hue/Saturation adjustment layer with the Saturation slider at –100.

To colorize a grayscale image, first convert it to RGB mode and then use Hue/Saturation.



## Desaturate

The Image, Adjustments, Desaturate menu command removes the color from an image but does not convert the image to Grayscale mode. The original channels are retained. The brightness values of the pixels are retained, but the component colors RGB or CMY are equalized to create gray. Desaturate can be applied to a flattened image, an active layer, or a selection.

Selective use of Desaturate can be an excellent way to simulate a spot color in an RGB or a CMYK image. Simply make a selection of an area you want to keep in color, invert the selection, and desaturate. You can invert again and use the Hue/Saturation Colorize feature as well.

## Match Color

Match Color, new in Photoshop CS, compares the colors of two images, layers, or selections and adjusts one to match the other. Using a selection, you can match, for example, the grass in one image to the grass in another. A series of similar images, shot under similar conditions, can also be matched. Do not, however, expect Match Color to use a beautifully exposed image from a studio to correct a photograph taken while on your vacation. The images or selections must already be similar for Match Color to perform correctly.

To further clarify, if you take a series of head-and-shoulder shots of the same person in one sitting, you can color-correct or stylize one shot and then use Match Color to adjust the rest. You could not, on the other hand, use a head-and-shoulder shot of a brunette in a red sweater to adjust a full-length shot of a blonde in a blue dress. When the content of the photos is not similar in pixel distribution among colors, the Match Color command is an inappropriate choice.

To use Match Color, open the image to be corrected and the image you want to use for the correction. If you'll be correcting a portion of the image, make the necessary selections in both images. (Remember, too, that you can match colors between layers in the same document.) With the image to be corrected active onscreen, use the command Image, Adjustments, Match Color to open the dialog box shown in Figure 17.31.

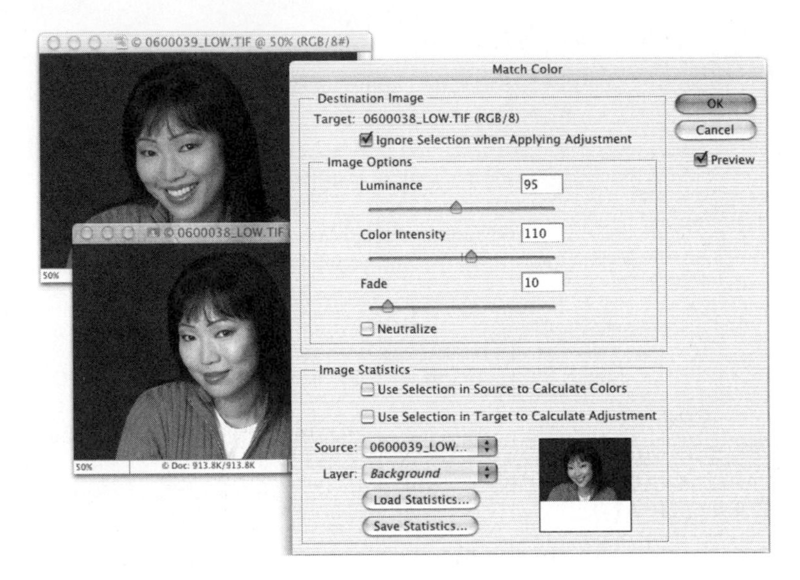


**Figure 17.31**
*Target* refers to the image being corrected, whereas *Source* is the image, selection, or layer that is used as the model for the adjustment.

Note the Load Statistics and Save Statistics buttons near the bottom of the dialog box. If an image will be used as the basis for correction for a series of images, you can open that image, open Match Color, and save the color information in a file (using the .sta file extension). Later that information can be loaded to adjust additional images.

> You can also use Color Match without a source image or selection to neutralize a color cast or adjust an image's color or luminosity. Use the sliders and/or the Neutralize option with the Source pop-up menu set to None.

Also be aware of the difference between the options Ignore Selection When Applying Adjustment and Use Selection in Target to Calculate Adjustment. If a selection is active in the image being adjusted, the upper check box is used to ignore the selection. (When unchecked, only the selected area of the image is adjusted.) The check box in the lower portion of the dialog box has a different function. When a selection is active in the target image and the box is checked, Match Color compares the source image's color information to the selected pixels in the target image and then adjusts the *entire* target image, not just the selected pixels (unless, of course, the Ignore Selection When Applying Adjustment box is not checked).

## Replace Color

Photoshop's Replace Color capability is an incredibly powerful feature that combines Color Range with Hue/Saturation. You select a range of color in an image and change it, all in one step (see Figure 17.32).

You can choose the color to replace by clicking with the Eyedropper tool in the preview window or the image window. Additional colors can be added or subtracted with the plus and minus eyedropper tools, and you can fine-tune the selection by using the Fuzziness slider.

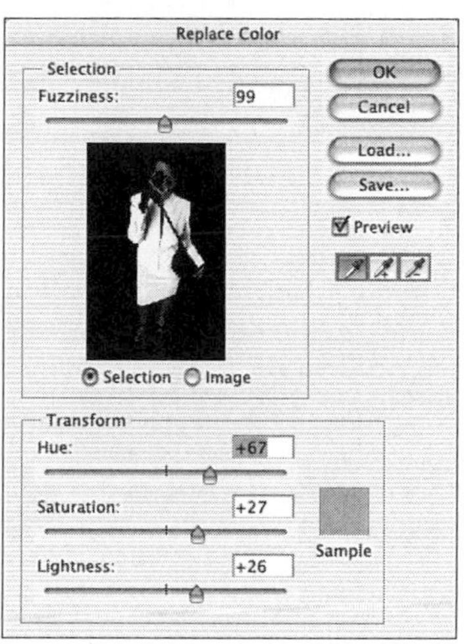


**Figure 17.32**
The original suit was red, but Replace Color has produced several different color variations, while leaving the rest of the image virtually untouched.



## Selective Color

*Selective color replacement* is a technique that controls the amount of each component ink used to create a primary color. For example, blue in a CMYK image is primarily a blend of cyan and magenta inks. However, magenta is also one of the primary components of red in a CMYK image. Selective Color enables you to adjust the magenta in the blues without affecting the reds at all (see Figure 17.33).

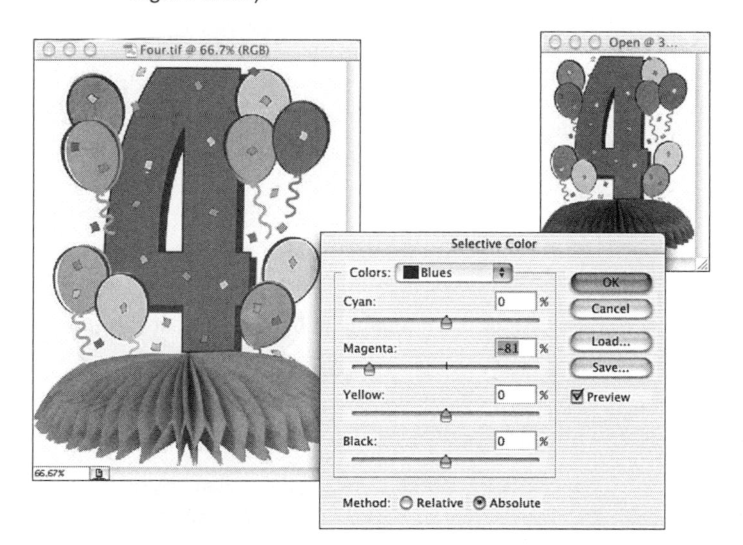


**Figure 17.33**
The original image is in the upper right. Substantially reducing the magenta component of the blues turns them to cyan. Note that the reds are untouched.

In addition to the six primary component colors (red, green, blue, cyan, magenta, and yellow), you can use Selective Color to adjust an image's highlights (Whites), midtones (Neutrals), or shadows (Blacks) by selecting the appropriate "color" from the pop-up menu in the dialog box.

Using the Relative adjustment option changes the color content based on the original content, and the Absolute adjustment option uses the actual ink values. For example, if a color will be reproduced with 80% magenta, a –25% Relative adjustment reduces the ink to 60% (80×0.75=60). On the other hand, a –25% Absolute adjustment would reduce the magenta to 55% (80–25=55).

## Channel Mixer

You can adjust the content of a color channel by using the content of the other channels as sources. You make the adjustments with sliders. You can also completely replace the content of one channel with that of another channel. Select the target channel from the pop-up menu at the top of the dialog box and then move its slider to 0% and the replacement channel's slider to 100%.

*For a full discussion of the Channel Mixer, see "Advanced Channel Manipulation," p. 534, in Chapter 16, "Channels: The Ultimate Creative Control."*

*As you learned in Chapter 16, the Channel Mixer is an excellent way to create grayscale images from color pictures.*



## Gradient Map

Gradient Map creates a new image from a color image, using two or more colors identified in a gradient. The gradient can use as many colors as you want, but the feature is designed for use with two-color gradients.

The leftmost color in the gradient is mapped to the image's shadows, and the rightmost is mapped to the highlights. If there are additional color stops in the gradient, they're apportioned according to their position in the gradient and the image's tonal range. The Gradient Map dialog box offers the options of dithering and reversing the gradient.

Generally speaking, you'll want a dark color on the left end of the gradient and a lighter color on the right. Reversing the setup can produce a "night vision" effect, however.

## Photoshop at Work: Gradient Map "Duotones"

Another excellent technique for creating eye-catching pseudo-duotone images from color pictures uses the Gradient Map command. To give the process a try, follow these steps:

1. Open a copy of an RGB or CMYK image in Photoshop and position it to one side of the screen. Hide your palettes with the Tab key if your monitor isn't huge.
2. Use the menu command Image, Adjustments, Gradient Map. Position the dialog box off in a corner, even partially hanging off the edge of the screen if necessary, so that you can see your image.
3. In the dialog box, click once directly on the gradient to open the Gradient Editor.

4. Create a gradient with the following color stops (see Figure 17.34):
   - Location: 0%, Color: RGB 0/0/0
   - Location: 25%, Color: 64/64/64
   - Location: 50%, Color: 128/128/128
   - Location: 75%, Color: 191/191/191
   - Location: 100%, Color: 255/255/255

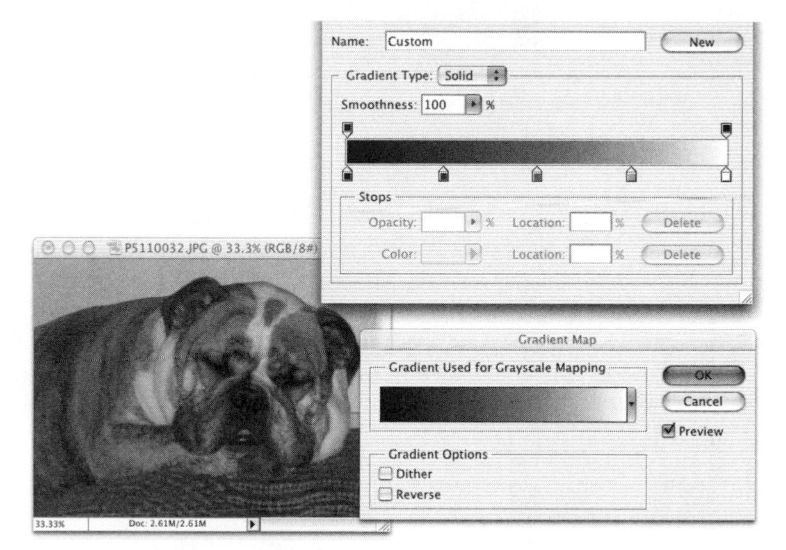


**Figure 17.34**
The gradient, as shown, doesn't differ from a simple black-to-white gradient. However, as you adjust the color stops, you control the tonality of the image.



5. Move the Gradient Editor dialog box to the side so that you can see your image. Drag the color stops back and forth to see the effect on the image.
6. Click the center color stop to make it active.
7. Click the Color swatch to open the Color Picker. Move the Color Picker to the side so that your image is visible.
8. Try RGB 125/120/60. Experiment with other colors for a variety of highly controllable pseudo-duotones.

## Photo Filter

Don't let the name fool you—Photo Filter is an adjustment, not a filter. It replicates the standard photographic filters that screw onto the end of lenses. As you can see in Figure 17.35, Photoshop CS includes a variety of filters and enables you to adjust the density of the "filter."

Photo Filter can compensate for slight color casts. A yellow cast can be reduced with a cooling filter, whereas a warming filter compensates for a bluish image.

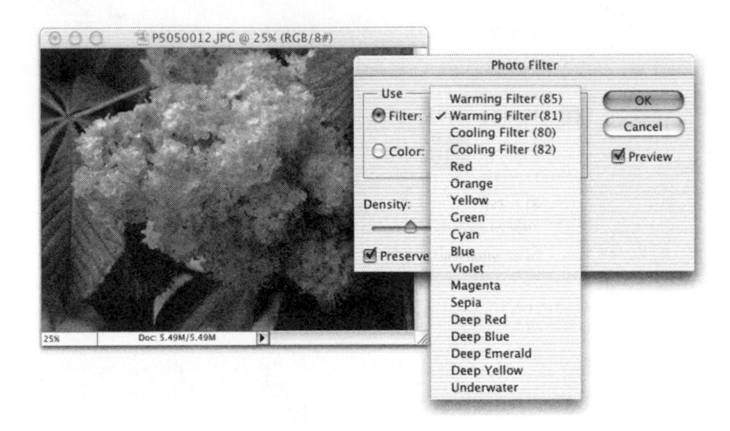


Figure 17.35
The Photo Filter adjustment's Density slider ranges from 0% to 100%. A setting of 25% is usually a good place to start.

## Shadow/Highlight

The new Shadow/Highlight command is designed to give you control of the far ends of an image's tonal range (see Figure 17.36). If a flash overexposes the subject of a photo, you can adjust the highlights. If the subject is in shadow because the image was exposed for a bright background, you can adjust the shadows.

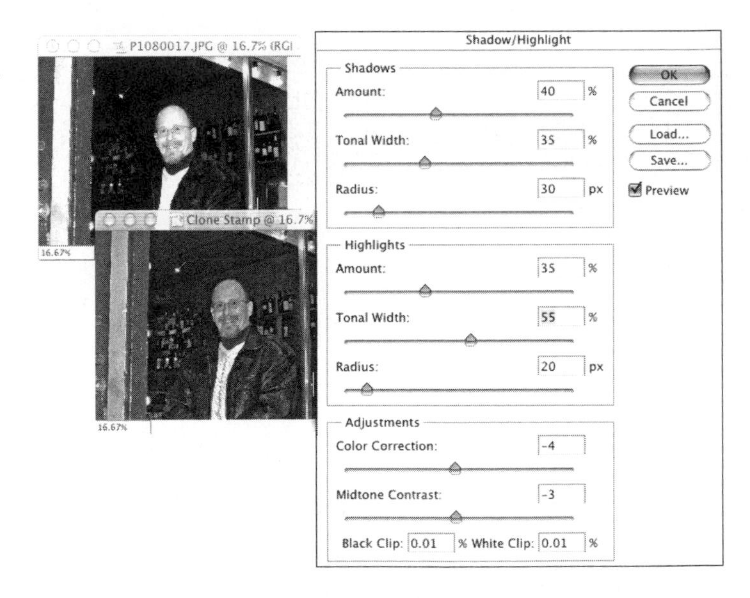


Figure 17.36
The Shadow/Highlight dialog box also offers a Save As Defaults button and can be minimized to show only the Shadows and Highlight sliders.

Tonal Range determines how much of the image will be considered highlight or shadow. Reducing the value prevents alteration of the image's midtones. You use the Radius slider to identify the specific pixels that will be adjusted. A low value tends to select all very dark/light pixels individually. A higher Radius value includes the surrounding pixels. When Radius is too high, the entire image is adjusted.

The Color Correction slider helps remove color casts from newly lightened shadows. It affects only those pixels identified for adjustment by the Radius and Tonal Width sliders.

Midtone Contrast will reduce an image's contract (negative numbers) or increase the contrast (positive numbers). Clipping the shadows or highlights forces more colors to black or white. Higher clipping values can produce posterization in the shadows and highlights, causing a loss of detail.

## Invert

Invert is used primarily to create grayscale images from scanned black-and-white negatives. It is not appropriate for use with scanned color negatives because of their orange mask. When Invert is used with a color image, each channel is calculated independently.

Using the 256 possible values for each pixel in each color channel, Invert simply flips the color across the midpoint. Pixels with high values in one channel get low values, and vice versa. For example, a pixel with an RGB value of 240/130/65 changes to 15/126/190. To calculate this, subtract the beginning value from 255 and you'll get the resulting value.



## Equalize

The Equalize command identifies the darkest and lightest pixels in an image and maps them to black and white. The pixels in between are evenly distributed throughout the tonal range. Equalize generally distributes the pixels much more evenly than Auto Levels or Auto Contrast.

Equalize is not appropriate for high-key and low-key images. It works best with average-key images that lack true white and black. It can be very effective for images with compressed tonal ranges.

## Threshold

The Threshold command converts every pixel in an image to black or white. Use it prior to the Image, Mode, Bitmap command to control the black-and-white image, or before saving in the WBMP file format. Threshold can also be used to simulate line art. You set the level at which the conversion is made in the Threshold dialog box with the slider or by entering a value in the numeric field (see Figure 17.37).

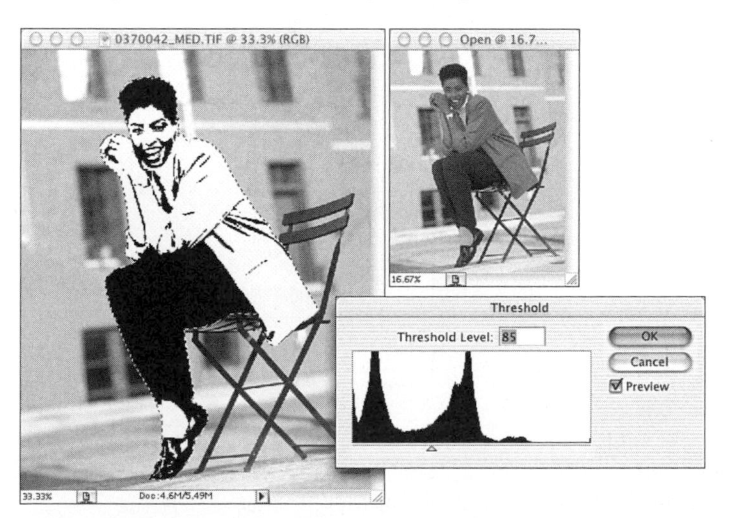


Figure 17.37
Threshold can be applied to a selection (as shown), a flattened image, or an active layer.

If an image is to be printed as line art, you should convert it to Bitmap mode (Image, Mode, Bitmap) after applying Threshold. The Threshold command does not change the number of color channels; rather, it forces the content of the channels to black and white. Remember, too, that resampling or blurring an image after applying Threshold converts some pixel values to grayscale, unless the image has been changed to Bitmap mode.

## Photoshop at Work: Finding Highlights and Shadows

Threshold is the method of choice for finding an image's true shadow and highlight points. Instead of using the Levels sliders, you can use Threshold to easily identify the diffuse highlights and the shadows in an image (see Figure 17.38).



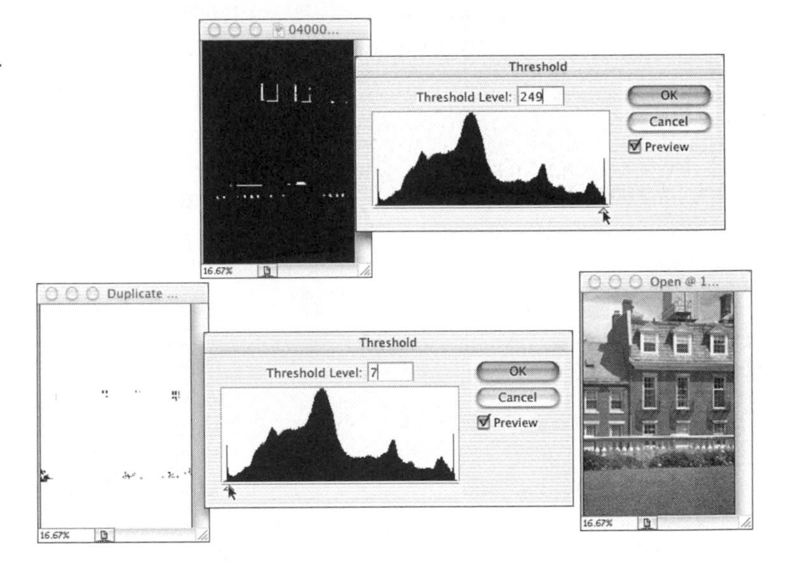


**Figure 17.38**
The top image illustrates identifying highlights, and the bottom example shows finding shadows.

Here's how to do it:

1. Open the image in Photoshop.
2. Choose Image, Adjustments, Threshold.
3. Drag the slider to the far right.
4. Slowly drag the slider to the left until white areas begin to appear. These are the highlights of the image.
5. You can Shift-click a highlight area to mark it with a color sampler. Make sure you choose a diffuse highlight rather than a specular highlight (an area of pure white, such as a reflection off glass or metal). Don't click the OK button.
6. Drag the slider to the far left and slowly bring it to the right until shadows appear.

> You can also use Threshold to edit layer masks. If the mask has fuzzy edges where it should be sharp, use Threshold to force pixels to black and white. Remember to click the mask thumbnail in the Layers palette in order to edit the mask rather than its layer.

7. Use a color sampler to mark a shadow point.
8. Click Cancel rather than OK.

Accurately identifying the highlight and shadow points in an image can be important for using the eyedropper tools in the Curves or Levels dialog box.

You can produce a watercolor effect with Posterize. For best results, blur the image a bit before applying the adjustment. You can also use Posterize to simplify an image's colors for better results when creating vector art with Adobe Streamline.

## Posterize

The Posterize command works similarly to Threshold, but instead of reducing the image to two brightness values (0 and 255), you can specify a number of tones for each channel. The available range is 2 through 255. A smaller number produces a much more pronounced effect (see Figure 17.39).

Figure 17.39
The original image is on the left. In the center, Posterize is applied with four levels. On the right, Posterize is applied with 64 levels. Note that there is little difference between the original and the image on the right.



## Variations

The Variations command helps you make tonal and color-correction decisions by presenting different head-to-head choices in a gigantic dialog box (see Figure 17.40).

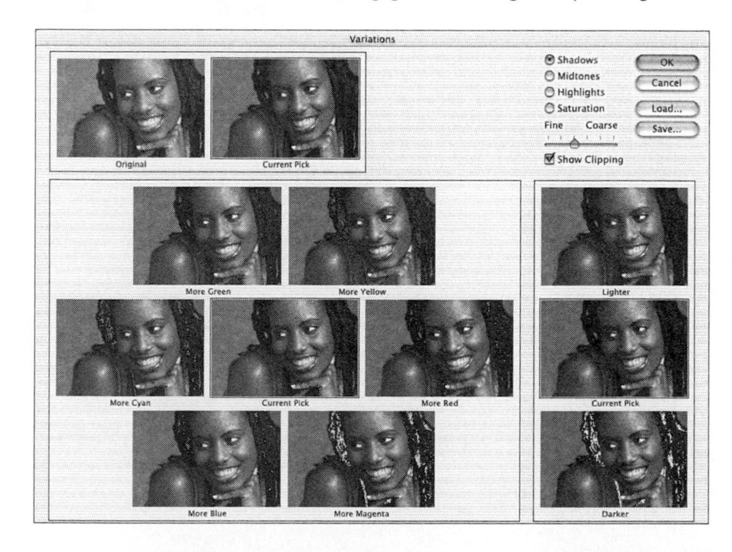


Figure 17.40
This dialog box is not resizable, nor is there an option for smaller previews.

Although the dialog box looks busy and complicated, using Variations is actually quite simple.

Your original image (the picture before you opened Variations) is always available for reference in the upper-left corner. Next to Original is Current Pick. This version shows what you'll get if you click OK. Current Pick is also displayed in the center of the color-correction area to the lower left and the tonal-correction area on the right. To make a change to the image, click the preview image that looks best. It then becomes Current Pick and all the other previews are updated.

Note that the previews around Current Pick in the main Variations area are arranged in the order of the color wheel. Opposites are directly across from each other—Red/Cyan, Green/Magenta, Blue/Yellow.

In the upper right, you choose whether to work with the image's shadows, midtones, or highlights. You can adjust only one range at a time. Remember, though, that selecting Shadows doesn't mean that your choices won't affect the highlights, too, but that the changes will be concentrated in the shadows. Selecting Saturation strips out all previews except the pair at the top and three in the middle. You'll see Less Saturation, Current Pick, and More Saturation. Click the left or right preview to change the image's saturation. The Fine/Coarse adjustment determines how radical the proposed changes will be. Each step on the scale doubles the amount of difference each preview shows. When Show Clipping is selected, Variations indicates with neon color any pixels that will be clipped. This includes pixels that will be forced to black or white as well as pixels that will become oversaturated.



Holding down the (Option) [Alt] key changes the Cancel button to Reset. Clicking Reset enables you to start over without exiting the dialog box. You can save corrections and apply them later to similar images by using the Load button.

# MASTERING PHOTOSHOP

## The Skinny on Skin

*Is there a magic formula for correcting skin tones? The people in my images never seem to look right.*

Producing accurate flesh tones is among the greatest challenges in Photoshop. One of the reasons for the difficulty is that we see and evaluate skin colors constantly: "You look a little pale." "Too much sun this weekend?" "You must be freezing!" In part because of how aware we are of the appearance of people around us, we are sensitive to the appearance of skin in images, too.

There is no single color mix for skin. There is no single relationship among component colors for skin. There is a tremendous range of skin tones in nature and, therefore, in images. Remember, too, that an individual's skin has a range of colors. The top and bottom of the forearm are typically different colors, as are the area beneath the chin and the chin itself. Parts of the body exposed to sun are typically darker, and how much darker often depends on the time of year.

In addition, the way an image is captured presents differences in skin tones. Because of reflections and lighting, foreheads, cheekbones, and noses might be lighter than the areas below the eyes, along the jaw, and the neck.

That having been said, here is some *general* guidance on skin color:

- Even when working with RGB images, evaluate skin in terms of CMYK. Set the Info palette's second color reading to CMYK. Also, use color samplers set to CMYK in key areas, such as the forehead, the side of the nose, cheeks, and chin.
- The key component is magenta. Determine appropriate cyan and yellow proportions based on the magenta content.
- Too much yellow makes the skin look jaundiced. Too little yellow creates sunburn. In Caucasians, too much cyan produces grayish skin.
- Don't think in terms of specific percent values for each of the component colors; rather, consider the relationship among the three values. The actual percentage of each CMY ink depends on the image's tonality.
- The skin of babies and northern Europeans can have a yellow content only slightly higher than the magenta. Southern Europeans may range to 25% more yellow than magenta. American blacks might have only slightly more yellow than magenta. African blacks may show equal values. Asians may have 30%–50% again as much yellow as magenta. Native American skin might even show more magenta than yellow, but only slightly.
- Cyan values should be very low for pale skin and babies. The cyan component might be only 10% of the magenta. Darker Caucasian and Asian skin may have cyan equal to 30% of the magenta. Cyan for Africans and African–Americans can range from 50%–75% of the magenta value. Tanned skin typically needs a higher cyan value than "winter-white" skin.
- With the exception of shadow areas, there should be little if any black ink in northern European and Asian skin tones. There may be trace amounts in darker Caucasian tones. African-Americans and Africans can range from 25% of the magenta value to as much as 75%.

Although it can serve as only a general guide, Table 17.2 provides *sample* skin tone values that *may or may not* be comparable to the values you find in your image. These CMYK values are for illustrative purposes only and are based on studio lighting, proper calibration, and appropriate color management.

**Table 17.2** Hypothetical Flesh Tone CMYK Values

| Skin | Location | CMYK |
|---|---|---|
| Pale Caucasian | Highlights | 4/17/15/0 |
| | Midtones | 14/35/35/0 |
| | Shadows | 31/63/71/31 |
| Dark Caucasian | Highlights | 11/35/42/0 |
| | Midtones | 14/38/49/0 |

17

**Table 17.2** Continued

| Skin | Location | CMYK |
|---|---|---|
| | Shadows | 35/64/73/27 |
| African-American | Highlights | 5/14/22/0 |
| | Midtones | 23/50/63/5 |
| | Shadows | 35/67/72/52 |
| Asian | Highlights | 3/11/13/0 |
| | Midtones | 12/35/42/0 |
| | Shadows | 29/60/56/25 |

There are two schools of thought when it comes to skin tone correction:

- Get a good monitor, calibrate it properly, work with controlled lighting, and trust your eyeballs.
- Ignore the onscreen appearance and work with the CMYK values.



I will confess to being from the first school, although I do keep my Eyedropper tool handy and my Info palette open. The skin tones usually are only *part* of an image—they must look appropriate within the context of the entire image. With the exception of portrait work, the skin is not usually the focus of the image. Although unnatural skin tones are certainly noticeable, make sure that you're not sacrificing the image's overall appearance to apply a formula.

## Evaluate What You're Evaluating

*My Histogram palette can't possibly be right! It's showing that my image is high-key, with all the pixels stacked to the right, yet the image itself is rather dark. What's going on?*

Check to see if there's an active selection. If so, the histogram reflects only those pixels. If you're looking at the histogram in the Levels dialog box, remember that it shows only the active layer.

18

# MASTERING THE BLENDING MODES

## IN THIS CHAPTER

# UNDERSTANDING BLENDING MODES

Any time two colors overlap, whether on separate layers or when the second color is added with a painting tool, one of two things can happen: The upper color can block (or replace) the lower completely, or the two colors can interact. Opacity and blending modes determine how one color interacts with colors below it.

This chapter explains what blending modes are and what they do. It then looks at how you use blending modes in Photoshop and explores the individual blending modes, one by one.

## Color and Pixels

When a file is saved or outputted (either to screen or in print), each pixel can be only one color. (File formats that support transparency can also have pixels with *no* color—invisible pixels.) The color of a pixel can be changed in a variety of ways in Photoshop. Painting tools can apply a color or alter an existing color. Adjustment commands and layers can be applied. Layers can be added, with colors overlapping colors.

Photoshop's native file formats (PSD and the new large document PSB), PDF, and the advanced capabilities of TIFF permit layers to be saved in a file. Each layer can have a different color value for any specific pixel. Each layer can be considered a separate set of pixels, so any given location in an image can have one pixel on each layer. Although that results in a four-layer image having four different pixels in a single location, in the end only one color is printed or viewed in a Web browser. The specific color is the result of the interaction among the colors on the various layers. However, if the pixel on the top layer is opaque, the color on that layer is the color of the pixel, regardless of pixel colors on the lower layers (see Figure 18.1).



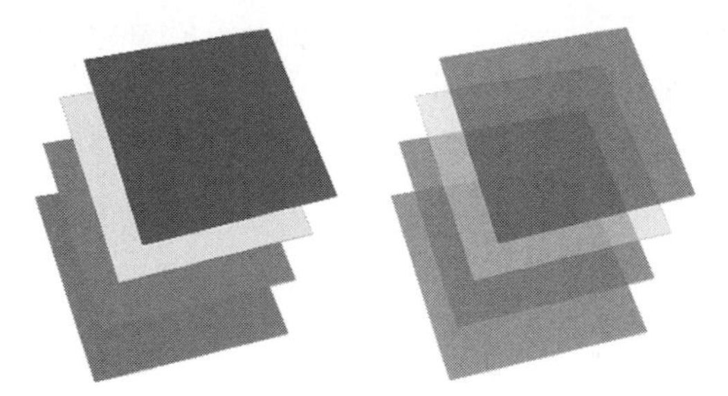

**Figure 18.1**
Consider a single pixel in an image with four layers. If the layers are all at 100% opacity, the top color is visible (left). If the layers have partial transparency, a combination of the layers' colors is visible (right).

*Unsure about the concept of layers? See "Plotting the Pixel's X,Y Coordinates" in the "Mastering Photoshop" section at the end of this chapter.*

## Transparency Versus Blending

Two ways that colors can interact are *transparency* and *blending*. When the opacity of a layer or painting tool is reduced (making the pixel partially transparent), the color's impact is reduced uniformly, much like using a tint in a page layout or an illustration program. Also like a tint, transparency is measured in the percent of opacity. Opacity can be controlled for both layers and painting tools.

Whether applied with a painting tool or on a layer, blending modes allow you to control *how* a color interacts with an existing color on that layer (painting tool blending mode) or on layers below (layer blending mode). The various blending modes use different attributes of the colors being blended to produce an effect. With blending layers, the hue, saturation, and lightness are the attributes of the base and blend colors that can be used, depending on the blending mode selected. When you're using a blending mode with a painting tool, the existing and new colors are compared to create the result color. Transparency and blending are contrasted in Figure 18.2.

In a discussion of blending modes, the terms *base color*, *blend color*, and *result color* are used. The base color is the color on the lower layer or the original color. The blend color is the color on the upper layer or a color that is being added by the painting tool. The result color is the color that results from the interaction.

**Figure 18.2**
On the left, the umbrella is on a layer with reduced transparency. On the right, the layer's opacity is set to 100%, but the blending mode has been changed. (The blending mode shown in the example is Hard Light.)



In Photoshop, you can use the term *transparency* much as it is used in photography, where it refers to the amount of light passing through the film's emulsion. However, rather than measure an object's transparency, you work backward and describe its *opacity*. An object can be from 100% opaque (solid) to 0% opaque (invisible). In simpler terms, an object's opacity refers to whether (or how much) you can see an object below it in the image. In Figure 18.3, a black-to-transparent gradient is shown against a transparency grid.

Remember that layer blending modes work downward only. The lowest layer of an image appears the same, regardless of blending mode. The exception is the Dissolve blending mode, which does have an effect on a layer, even when there's nothing below. Transparency, on the other hand, is apparent even on the lowest layer.

**Figure 18.3**
The grid's visibility is dependent on the opacity of the gradient at a given point.

Opacity is not the same as color value. Figure 18.4 compares transparency with color. Although the results might seem comparable in the image, an object's interaction with other objects can depend on the difference between color and opacity changes.

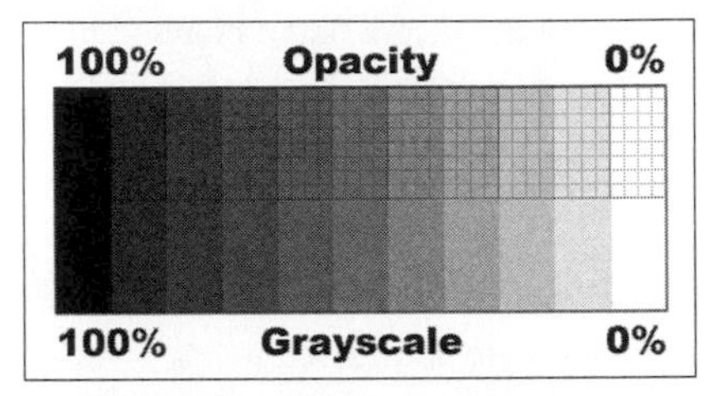


Figure 18.4
A black-to-transparent 11-step gradient (top) is contrasted with a comparable black-to-white gradient. Note that the transparency grid is not visible behind the lower gradient.

# WORKING WITH BLENDING MODES

You can use Photoshop's blending modes while working with painting tools or when applying them to a layer. When a blending mode is applied to a layer, every pixel on the layer is affected. (Each blending mode is explained individually later in this chapter.) Keep in mind, too, that layer blending modes are *live*, meaning they can be changed at any time, as long as the image's layers are intact.

Blending modes enable you to make artwork interact in ways that would be very difficult to replicate manually. For a look at some of the incredible things that can be done with Photoshop's blending modes, explore Juice Drops from Digital Juice (`www.digitaljuice.com`).



## Layer Blending Modes

When a layer's blending mode is changed from Normal to another mode, the relationship between the layer's pixels and those below changes. In Normal mode, each pixel interacts with those below it according to the pixel's color and the layer's transparency. If, for example, a group of pixels is filled with a solid color, the layer's blending mode is Normal, and the opacity is set to 100%, the pixels block those below. On the other hand, if the layer is set to most of the other blending modes or the opacity is reduced, the lower pixels are likely to be at least partially visible.

A layer's blending mode can be assigned in the Layers palette or the Layer Style dialog box (see Figure 18.5). The Layer Style dialog box, which can be opened with the leftmost button at the bottom of the Layers palette or through the Layer menu, also offers some advanced blending controls. The advanced options, discussed in the section "Layer Style Blending," also calculate the values of pixels on different layers but are not blending modes.

Blending modes can also be applied to layer sets. By default, the layer set's blending mode is Pass Through. In effect, Pass Through results in the layer set itself having no blending mode; the modes of the layers within the set interact with lower layers as though they were not part of a set. When the layer set's blending mode is changed from Pass Through, two

> The blending mode of a layer named *Background* (in italics) cannot be changed. Not only are background layers locked, but also nothing can be below them, so there's no reason to change the blending mode from Normal. To move a background layer above another in the Layers palette, first change its name. You'll then be able to change its blending mode, too.

things happen. First, the layers within the set are isolated from the rest of the image, and their blending modes affect only the lower layers within the layer set. Second, the layer set is treated as a single entity for blending, and the layer set's blending mode is used to determine how it interacts with layers below. The difference is shown in Figure 18.6.

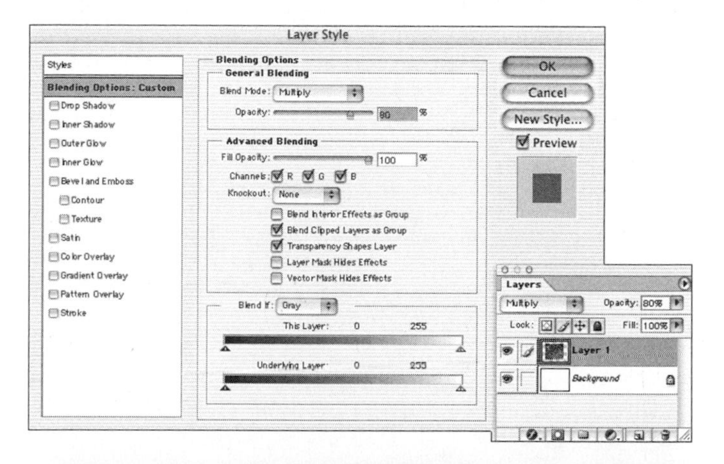


**Figure 18.5**
The General Blending area of the Layer Style dialog box offers the same options as the top of the Layers palette. Changes made in one are reflected in the other for a layer.

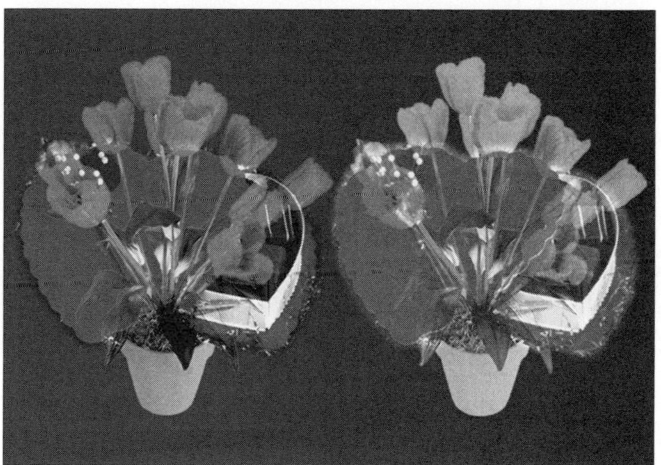

**Figure 18.6**
On the left, the layer set's blending mode is Pass Through. Each layer interacts with all layers below. On the right, the layer set is assigned the Lighten blending mode, so the layers within the set are composited first and then Lighten is applied.



When any nonpainting tool is active in the Toolbox, you can change the active layer's blending mode with one of the keyboard shortcuts listed in Table 18.1. (If a painting tool is active, the shortcuts change the tool's blending mode.)

**Table 18.1** Blending Mode Shortcuts

| Mode | Option-Shift (Mac) Alt+Shift (Windows) |
|---|---|
| Normal | N |
| Threshold (Bitmap and Index Color) | N |
| Dissolve | I |

**Table 18.1** Continued

| Mode | Option-Shift (Mac) Alt+Shift (Windows) |
|---|---|
| Behind (painting tools only) | Q |
| Clear (painting tools only) | R |
| Replace (Healing Brush only) | Z |
| Darken | K |
| Multiply | M |
| Color Burn | B |
| Linear Burn | A |
| Lighten | G |
| Screen | S |
| Color Dodge | D |
| Linear Dodge | W |
| Overlay | O |
| Soft Light | F |
| Hard Light | H |
| Vivid Light | V |
| Linear Light | J |
| Pin Light | Z |
| Hard Mix | L |
| Difference | E |
| Exclusion | X |
| Hue | U |
| Saturation | T |
| Color | C |
| Luminosity | Y |
| Pass Through (layer sets only) | P |
| Next Blending Mode | Shift+plus key |
| Previous Blending Mode | Shift+minus key |



## Photoshop at Work: Using Blending Modes with Painting Tools

Several of Photoshop's blending modes are best used with painting tools to enhance images. You can create a layer, set the blending mode, and paint with shades of gray to improve shadows, highlights, or both. Other blending modes can create dramatic effects when used with a pair of color images. To see for yourself how blending modes work, try this:

1. Open a photographic image in Photoshop. A suitable picture for this experiment has a number of different colors, many of them bright and well saturated. It should also have definite shadows and highlights.

2. In the Layers palette, click the New Layer button.
3. On that new layer, make a rectangular selection of the lower third (or so) of the image.
4. In the selection, drag a black-to-white linear gradient.
5. Make another rectangular selection, this one across the top third of the image.
6. In the new selection, drag a linear Rainbow gradient.
7. Change through the layer blending modes, seeing how the grayscale and color gradients differ from blending mode to blending mode. Keep track of which are most appropriate for correcting the image's shadows and highlights by painting with gray on a separate layer. (And make note of which blending modes make you say "Cool!" out loud.)

## Layer Style Blending

The Layer Style dialog box offers some sophisticated blending capabilities. Used with or instead of the blending modes, the Advanced Blending and Blend If capabilities give you more control over the interaction between layers.

The Fill Opacity slider enables you to change the opacity of a layer's content without changing the opacity of drop shadows, outer glows, or outer bevels. Anything (including effects) within the bounds of the original layer content is reduced in opacity, but effects outside the original pixels remain at the layer's opacity level (see Figure 18.7).



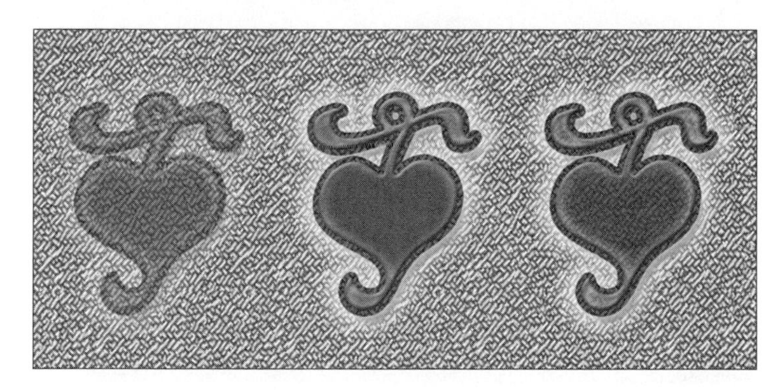

Figure 18.7
The original object, at 100% opacity, is in the middle. On the left, the layer's opacity is reduced to 50%. On the right, the fill opacity is at 50%. Note that the rightmost object's stroke, shadow, and glow are unaffected by the reduction in opacity.

Below the Fill Opacity slider are check boxes for the image's color channels. (The boxes match the image's color mode.) Unchecking a box is equivalent to erasing that layer's content from the corresponding color channel.

The Knockout options are a simple way of using one layer to assign transparency to one or more lower layers. The pixels on the top layer, when set to Shallow or Deep Knockout, serve as a digital cookie cutter, chopping through the intervening layers. When set to Shallow, the layer knocks out to the bottom of its layer set or clipping group. Set to Deep, the layer cuts through to the background layer, or to transparency if there is no background layer.

Below the Knockout pop-up menu are five check boxes for changing the way that selected layer effects appear in the document:

- **Blend Interior Effects as Group**—When checked, this option applies the blending mode and opacity to certain layer effects before the layer is blended with underlying layers. The interior layer effects include Inner Glow, Satin, and Overlay.
- **Blend Clipped Layers as Group**—The blend mode of a clipping group's base layer can be applied to all the layers in a group, or each layer's blend mode can appear individually.
- **Transparency Shapes Layer**—If this option is not selected, effects are applied to the entire layer, regardless of transparency. For example, if a layer contains text and the layer effect Pattern Overlay is selected, this option determines where the pattern is applied. When this option is checked, the pattern is restricted to the pixels that make up the type. When it's unchecked, the entire layer is filled with the pattern.
- **Layer Mask Hides Effects**—Layers to which both effects and layer masks are applied can be treated one of two ways: The mask can clip the content of the layer and then the effects are applied, or the effects can be hidden as part of the layer (see Figure 18.8).
- **Vector Mask Hides Effects**—This is comparable to the preceding option.

*For more information on when to use which type of layer mask, see "Layer Masks, Vector Masks, and Clipping Masks" in Chapter 9, "Making Selections and Creating Masks," p. 320.*



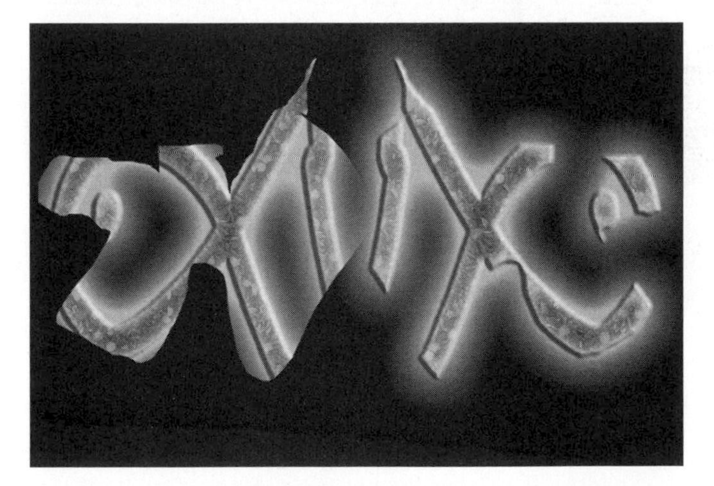

Figure 18.8
On the left, the mask (layer or vector) is set to Hide Effects. On the right, the effects are applied after the layer is masked.

The Blend If sliders enable you to control the interaction of the pixels on the upper and lower layers based on color. To use the Blend If option, select a channel from the pop-up menu (Gray represents the composite channel in RGB and CMYK modes, affecting all channels). Adjust the sliders to determine what pixels should become transparent. The upper slider, This Layer, controls transparency based on the values of the selected layer. Dragging the sliders inward makes the darkest and lightest pixels transparent. Using the (Option) [Alt] key enables you to spilt the slider controls and create a fade.

For example, when the dark slider is split and dragged to the values 245 and 230, the layer is affected like this:

- Pixels darker than 245 become transparent.
- Pixels between 245 and 230 gradually fade from transparent to opaque.
- Pixels lighter than 230 are unaffected and remain opaque.

The lower slider, Underlying Layer, forces visibility of pixels on the lower layer in much the same way. By dragging the sliders, you can determine which pixels will be visible, regardless of the opacity of the upper layer (see Figure 18.9).

**Figure 18.9**
The original images are shown in the lower center. On the left, the white background was made transparent with the right controller of the This Layer slider. To the right, the wine was also made transparent by switching to the Red channel and using the left controller, too.



## Photoshop at Work: Removing a White Background

If you use stock imagery that includes subjects on a plain white background, using the Layer Styles blending options can be a real timesaver for you. To use them to remove a white background, follow these steps:

1. From the Samples folder inside the Photoshop folder, open Ducky.tif.
2. In the Layers palette, double-click the layer *Background* and rename it Layer 0. That converts it from a background layer (which doesn't support transparency) to a regular layer.
3. Click the New Layer button.
4. Fill the new layer with a pattern, gradient, or a color other than white. (You can use the Edit, Fill command.)
5. In the Layers palette, move Layer 0 (the Ducky layer) above this new, colorful layer.
6. With Layer 0 (the upper layer) still active in the Layers palette, open the Layer Style dialog box. You can use the pop-up menu at the bottom of the Layers palette, the menu command Layer, Layer Style, Blending Options, or you can simply double-click Layer 0's thumbnail in the Layers palette.

7. In the Layer Style dialog box, grab the control on the right for the This Layer slider and drag just a hair to the left. You want the value to change from 255 to 254 (see Figure 18.10). The white background should drop away.

The completeness with which the background disappears depends on its purity. You may need to drag the slider control a bit farther to the left. Be aware of any white in the image! If you drag too far, you could lose pixels you don't intend to blend (such as Ducky's eyes).

> **Caution**
> When working with the Blend If sliders, you cannot isolate a section of the layer with a selection or mask. Nor can you use the History Brush to restore portions of a layer. Blend If is a live effect, not a change to actual pixels.

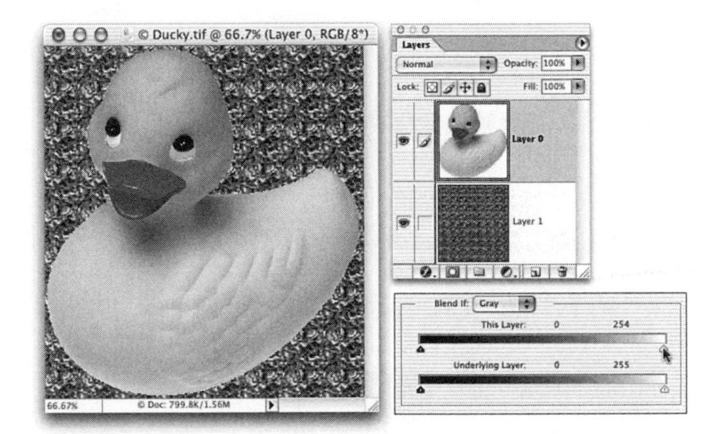


**Figure 18.10**
As you can see in the Layers palette, the white pixels are still there, you just can't see them anymore.



If you work with a *lot* of stock imagery on white backgrounds, continue on, doing this:

1. Right after you knock out the white background, open the Styles palette.
2. At the bottom of the Styles palette, click the New Style button.
3. In the New Style dialog box, name the style, uncheck the Include Layer Effects box (see Figure 18.11), check the Include Layer Blending Options box, and click OK.

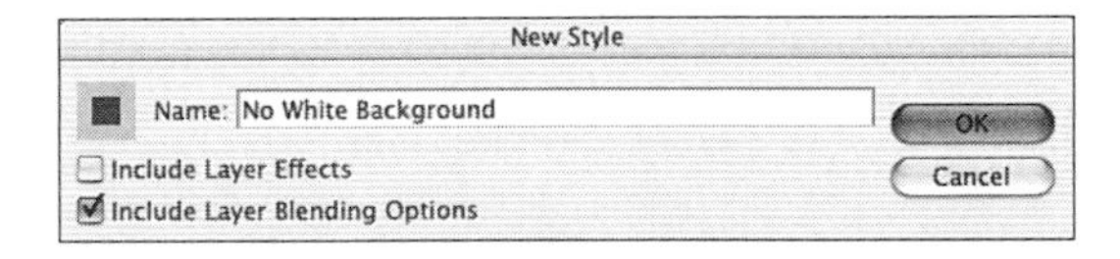


**Figure 18.11**
To eliminate white background in other images, simply change the Background layer to a regular layer by renaming it and then click your new style.

Remember that styles (like Actions, swatches, and tool presets) are not *really* saved until you use the Save Styles command from the Styles palette menu or save the style in the Preset Manager.

## Blend Modes for Painting Tools

Unlike the layer blending modes, which affect how pixels on the selected layer interact with those on layers below, the painting tools work on a single layer. By changing a tool's blending mode, you change the way it adds color over an existing color or fill on a layer. With the exception of Dissolve, the blending modes have no effect on color applied to an empty layer.

The painting tools have several blending modes that are not available for layers. The keyboard shortcuts for the painting tools' blending modes are included in Table 18.1, earlier in this chapter. Not all blending modes are available for all painting tools. Table 18.2 shows which modes are available for which tools.

The standard blending modes are those not identified in Table 18.1 as being of limited availability. The nonstandard blending modes in this table are Behind, Clear, Replace, and Pass Through. (The blending modes Add and Subtract are used only with the Apply Image and Calculations commands and are not included in the table.)

**Table 18.2** Painting Tools' Blending Modes

| Tool | Blending Mode |
|---|---|
| Brush | (All standard blending modes, plus Behind and Clear) |
| Pencil | (All standard blending modes, plus Behind and Clear) |
| Healing Brush | Normal, Replace, Multiply, Screen, Darken, Lighten, Color, Luminosity |
| Color Replacement | Hue, Saturation, Color, Luminosity |
| Clone Stamp | (All standard blending modes, plus Behind) |
| Pattern Stamp | (All standard blending modes, plus Behind) |
| Gradient Tool | (All standard blending modes, plus Behind) |
| Paint Bucket | (All standard blending modes, plus Behind and Clear) |
| Blur | Normal, Darken, Lighten, Hue, Saturation, Color, Luminosity |
| Sharpen | Normal, Darken, Lighten, Hue, Saturation, Color, Luminosity |
| Smudge | Normal, Darken, Lighten, Hue, Saturation, Color, Luminosity |

# The Shape Tools and Edit Commands

When a shape tool is set to Fill Pixels (see Figure 18.12), blending modes are available. In effect, when creating a filled region on an existing layer, the shape tools work like painting tools—they add colored pixels. The shape tools, when adding pixels, can use all the standard blending modes, plus Behind and Clear.

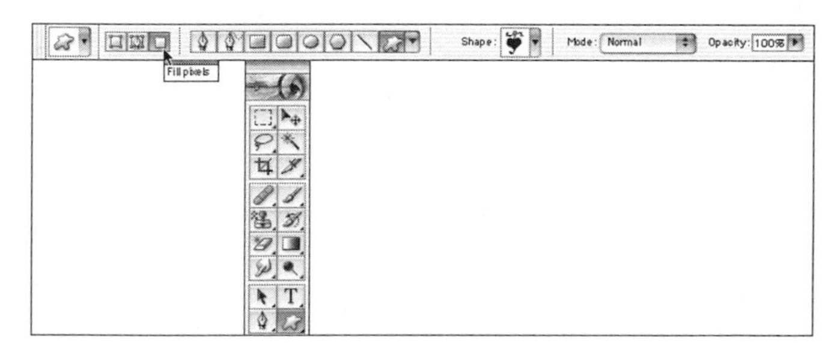


**Figure 18.12**
When set to create shape layers or work paths, the shape tools do not use blending modes.

18

Likewise, the Edit commands Fill and Stroke work like painting tools and therefore have blending modes. You can fill and stroke using all the standard blending modes, plus Behind and Clear.

## Color Mode Restrictions

Some blending modes, for both layer and painting tools, are not available in all color modes. Obviously, those color modes that don't support layers (Bitmap, Indexed Color, Multichannel) don't support layer blending modes. They also can't support some of the painting tools' modes, including Behind and Clear, which rely on layers. Here is a summary of the blending modes available for various color modes:

New in Photoshop CS is extended support for images in 16-bit color. High-bit color images can now include layers and have a full range of blending modes available.

- **RGB, CMYK**—All blending modes for both layers and painting tools are available.
- **Grayscale, Duotone**—The blending modes that are dependent on color are not available, including Hue, Saturation, Color, and Luminosity.
- **Bitmap**—No layer modes are available, and painting tools are restricted to Threshold, Dissolve, Darken, and Lighten.
- **Indexed Color**—No layer color modes are available, and painting tools can be used only in Threshold and Dissolve blending modes.
- **Lab**—All layer and painting tool blending modes are available, except Darken, Color Burn, Lighten, Color Dodge, Difference, and Exclusion.
- **Multichannel**—There are no layer blending modes, and the painting tools do not use Behind, Clear, Hue, Saturation, Color, or Luminosity.

18

*What happens when you convert an image to a color mode that doesn't support your blending modes? See "Color Mode Conversion" in the "Mastering Photoshop" section at the end of this chapter.*

## Blending Clipping Groups

By default, the blending mode of the lowermost layer in a clipping group is used to calculate interaction with lower layers in an image. Alternatively, you can restrict that layer's blending mode to the layer itself, allowing all the layers of the clipping group to maintain their own blending modes and, therefore, their original appearance.

To control the blending of a clipping group, open the Layer Style dialog box for the lowest layer of the clipping group. Select or deselect the Blend Clipped Layers as Group check box.

## The Fade Command

Located under the Edit menu, the Fade command can be used to alter the effect of a filter, an adjustment command, a painting tool, or an eraser tool. It is available only immediately after the application of the command or tool. Fade enables you to change the opacity and blending mode of the filter, adjustment, or tool.

> Rather than convert to Lab color mode to sharpen, use the Unsharp Mask filter in RGB or CMYK mode and then choose Edit, Fade Unsharp Mask and change the blending mode to Luminosity. You accomplish the same thing, without changing color modes.

# BLENDING MODES, ONE BY ONE

Photoshop now offers a total of 31 blending modes. Some, such as Dissolve, are almost always available. Other blending modes are used for one specific purpose, such as Replace for the Healing Brush and Pass Through for layer sets. The blending modes are presented here generally in the order in which they appear in menus. (Remember that not all blending modes appear in all menus.) Photoshop groups the blending modes according to general effect.

Most of the layer blending modes are shown with a sample image consisting of a background and seven additional layers (see Figure 18.13). For each example, all of the seven additional layers are set to the blending mode under discussion, and in each case the opacity is set to 100%.

Figure 18.13
In this figure, each layer is set to Normal.



You will see references to base, blend, and result colors in the Photoshop User Guide and Help, this book, and elsewhere. As mentioned earlier, for layer blending modes, they are, respectively, the lower color (base), the upper color (blend), and the color produced by combining base and blend colors using a given blending mode (the result color). For painting tools, these colors are the original color, the added color, and the color that is produced.

> The figures reproduced here in grayscale to show the blending modes are also available in this book's color insert.

## Normal

Normal is the default, and the most common, blending mode. With this setting, the top color supersedes the bottom color. Figure 18.14 shows the sample image, with all layers set to the Normal blending mode.

Figure 18.14
With all layers set to Normal, it is apparent which layer is on top in areas of overlap.

Assuming an opacity of 100%, pixels on layers set to Normal block pixels on layers below. The result color remains the blend color.



## Threshold

Threshold, available for Indexed Color and Bitmap modes only, is the "Normal" blending mode for Indexed Color and Bitmap images. These color modes support limited color tables (256 colors for Indexed Color, two colors for Bitmap). That limitation prevents such images from using most of Photoshop's blending modes. The result color remains the blend color.

## Dissolve

The Dissolve blending mode affects semitransparent pixels, which include pixels applied with a tool or technique with reduced opacity, and edge pixels in antialiased artwork. Pixels are replaced randomly in this blending mode. The effect scatters the pixels of the base or blend color (see Figure 18.15).

## Behind

When working on a layer with transparency, the Behind blending mode allows a painting tool to add the blend color to transparent pixels only, protecting the base color. This blending mode is available only for painting tools. You cannot use Behind on layers with locked transparency.

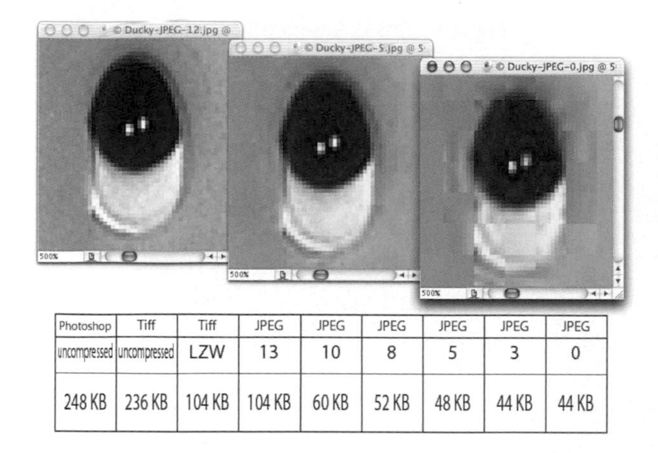


| Photoshop | Tiff | Tiff | JPEG | JPEG | JPEG | JPEG | JPEG | JPEG |
|---|---|---|---|---|---|---|---|---|
| uncompressed | uncompressed | LZW | 13 | 10 | 8 | 5 | 3 | 0 |
| 248 KB | 236 KB | 104 KB | 104 KB | 60 KB | 52 KB | 48 KB | 44 KB | 44 KB |

**Figure 3.18** illustrates the difference in quality among JPEG compression settings. From the left, the JPEG quality is set to 12, 5, and 0.
(See "Optimization Options," **p.99.**)

**Figure 4.1** helps define the nature of raster artwork, which is constructed of little squares called "pixels" (from "picture elements"). (**See** "What is Raster Art?" **p. 130.**)

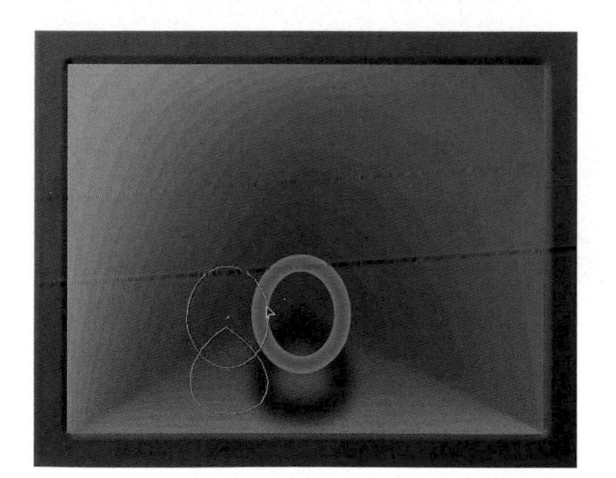

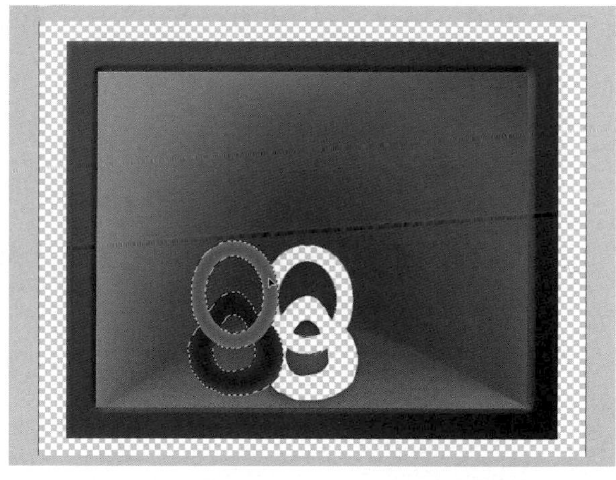

**Figure 4.10** and **Figure 4.11** show one of the major differences between vector artwork (left) and raster artwork (right). Vector artwork consists of "objects" that can be rearranged in the image. Unless the raster file is capable of supporting layers, the artwork cannot be manipulated as "objects." When moving an object in vector art, the underlying objects are undisturbed. In a raster format that doesn't support layers, there is no artwork below the selected pixels. (Most raster file formats do not support layers.)
(**See** "Comparing Vector and Raster," **p. 135.**)

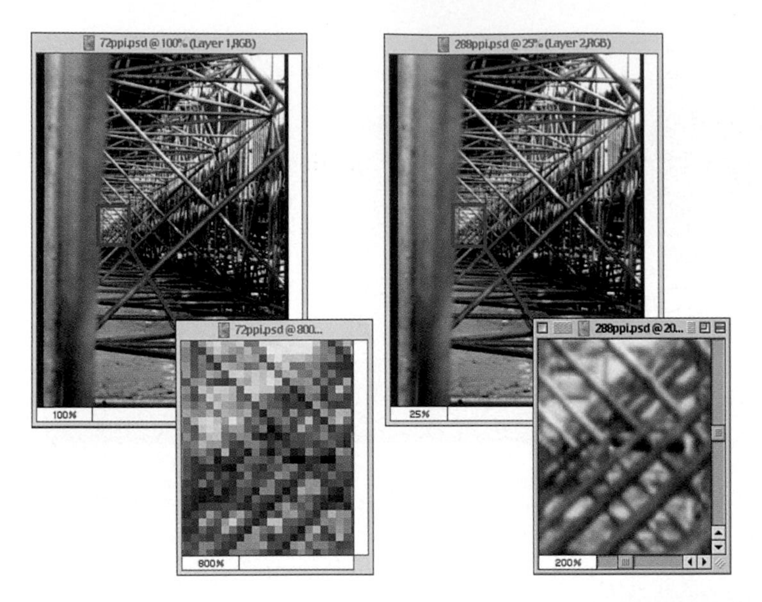


**Figure 4.28** is an excellent example of how low-resolution images have less fine detail than do high-resolution images. At 100%, as an image would be seen in a Web browser, the image to the left looks fine. However, when zoomed in, you can see that the image on the right has far better detail. (**See** "Displayed and Captured Resolutions," **p. 149**.)

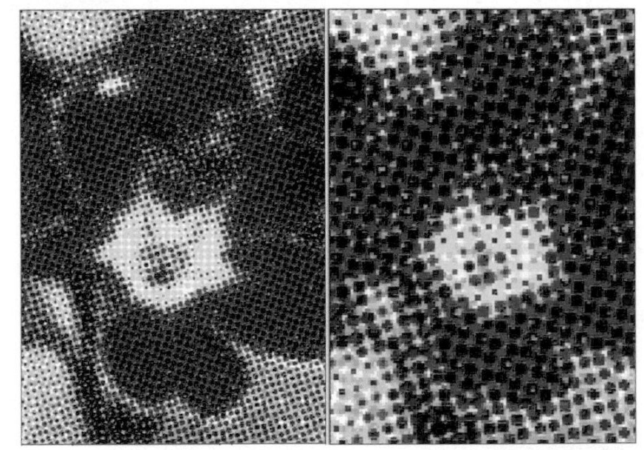

**Figure 4.30** illustrates a comparison of two different line screen frequencies used by commercial printing presses. On the left, you see a close-up of the image as it would be printed on a press using a line screen frequency of 150 lpi (lines per inch). On the right, a close-up of the same image as it would appear printed at 85 lpi. (**See** "Resolution with Raster and Vector," **p. 150.**)

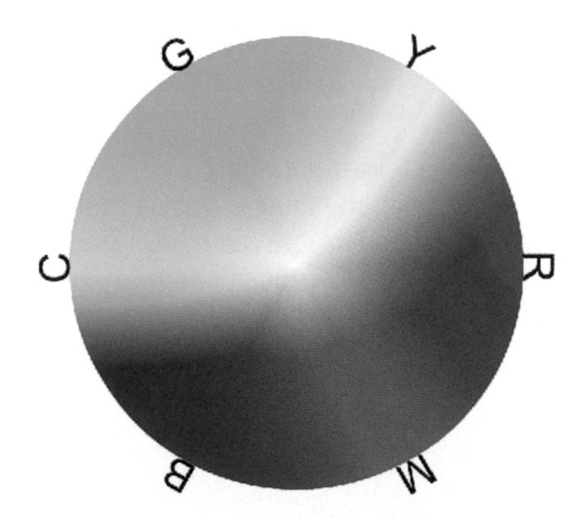


**Figure 5.3** is a sample color wheel, showing the relationship among the RGB and CMY colors. (**See** "The Relationship between RGB and CMY," **p. 164.**)

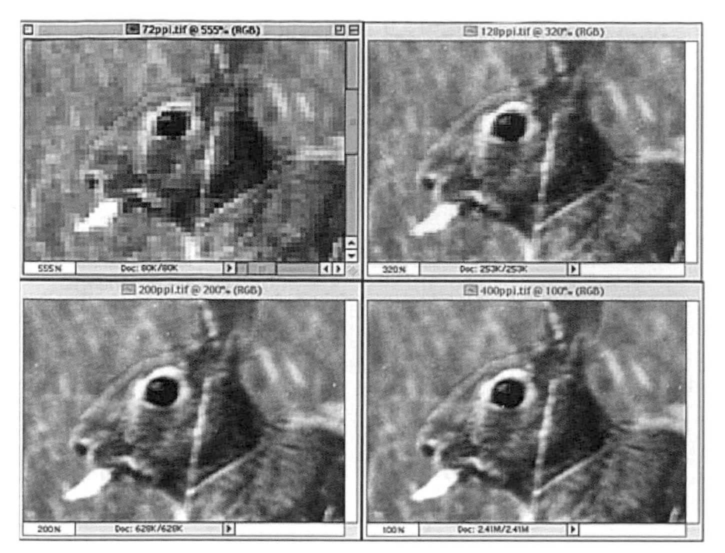


**Figure 8.12** compares the size of individual pixels when the same image is scanned at different resolutions. The higher the resolution, the smaller the pixels. The smaller the pixels, the finer the detail. But remember that higher resolution also produces larger file sizes. (**See** "Resolution," **p. 284.**)

**Figure 8.13** shows one image scanned at four different resolutions. All four images are shown at 100% zoom. When you scan at higher resolution, the file has larger pixel dimensions—and a larger file size. (**See** "Resolution," **p. 284.**)

**Figure 8.18** compares a pair of scans. When scanning an image that was printed on an offset press, the pattern of ink droplets can produce a moiré pattern, as seen in the scan on the left. Most scanners have built-in "descreening" algorithms that can eliminate the pattern from the scan. The image on the right was scanned using a descreening option. (**See** "Moire Patterns and How to Avoid Them," **p. 290.**)

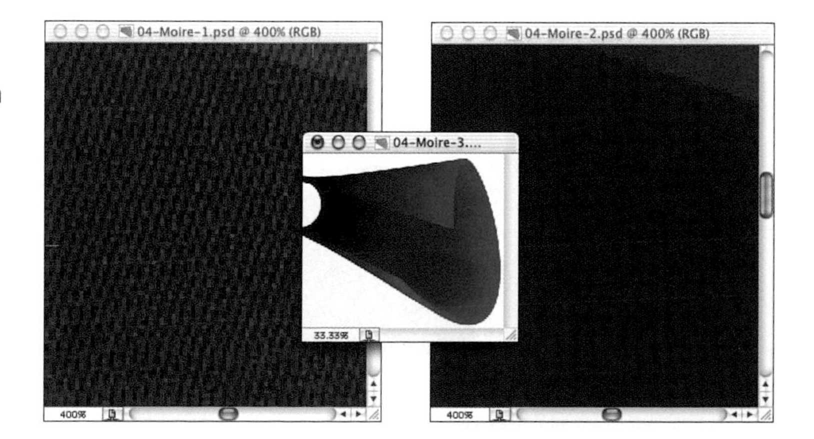

**Figure 28.33** shows a gradient mesh object with a mesh point selected. Mesh points occur at the intersection of mesh lines and have one direction line for each intersecting mesh line segment. (**See** "Editing a Mesh Object," **p. 896**.)

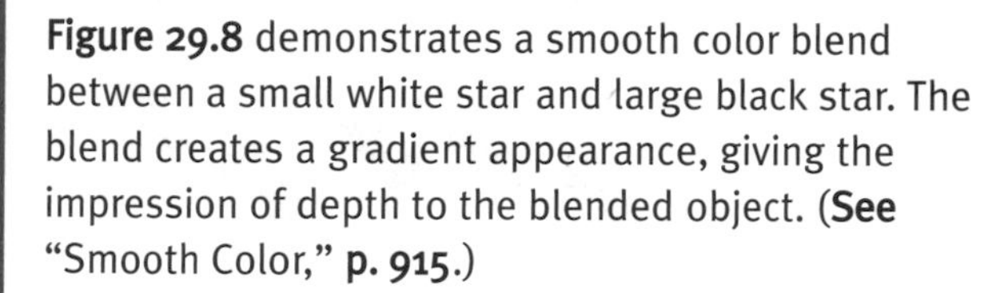

**Figure 29.8** demonstrates a smooth color blend between a small white star and large black star. The blend creates a gradient appearance, giving the impression of depth to the blended object. (**See** "Smooth Color," **p. 915**.)

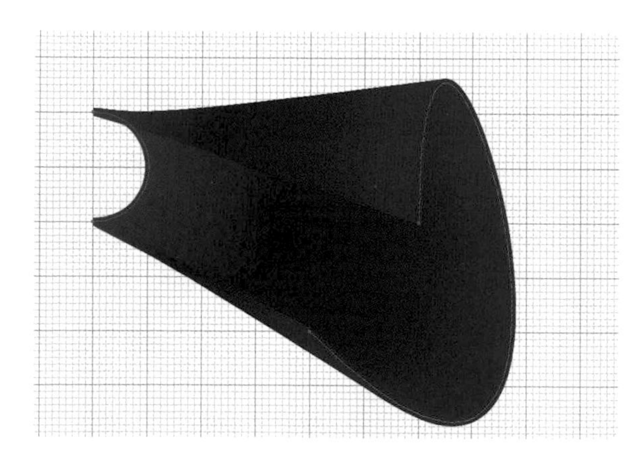

**Figure 29. 9** contains an object created by blending two simple curved paths. Using the Smooth Color blending option produces the appearance of a single surface along the object. (**See** "Smooth Color," **p. 915**.)

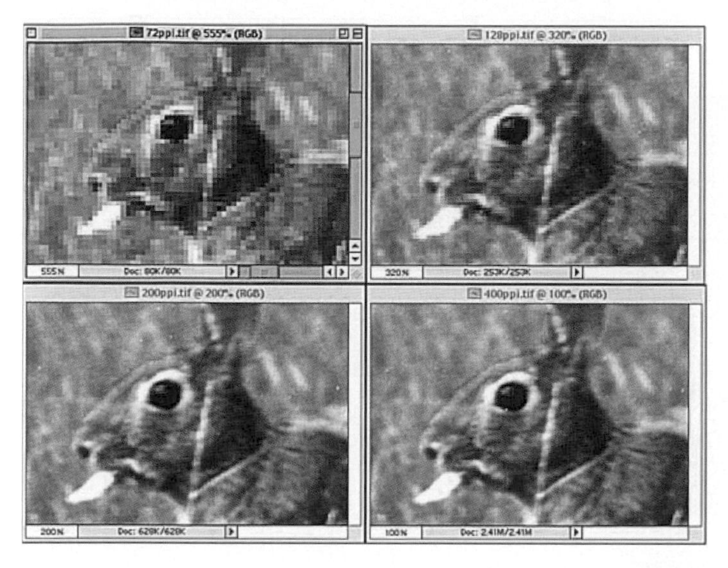


**Figure 8.12** compares the size of individual pixels when the same image is scanned at different resolutions. The higher the resolution, the smaller the pixels. The smaller the pixels, the finer the detail. But remember that higher resolution also produces larger file sizes. (**See** "Resolution," **p. 284**.)

**Figure 8.13** shows one image scanned at four different resolutions. All four images are shown at 100% zoom. When you scan at higher resolution, the file has larger pixel dimensions—and a larger file size. (**See** "Resolution," **p. 284**.)

**Figure 8.18** compares a pair of scans. When scanning an image that was printed on an offset press, the pattern of ink droplets can produce a moiré pattern, as seen in the scan on the left. Most scanners have built-in "descreening" algorithms that can eliminate the pattern from the scan. The image on the right was scanned using a descreening option. (**See** "Moire Patterns and How to Avoid Them," **p. 290**.)

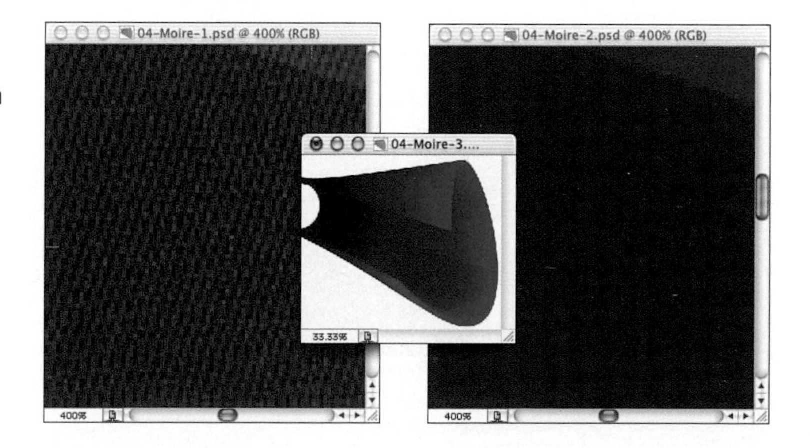

**Figure 9.11** provides an example of the effect of using the Magic Wand's Contiguous option. To the left, the option is selected and only pixels of the appropriate color range that are adjacent to the point clicked are selected. To the right, Contiguous is deselected and all pixels within the color range are selected. **See** "Magic Wand," **p. 304.**)

**Figure 9.12** shows the result of selecting a plain white background with the Magic Wand tool and deleting. In this case, the black layer below shows in the now-transparent areas of the upper layer. (**See** "Photoshop At Work: Removing a White Background," **p. 305.**)

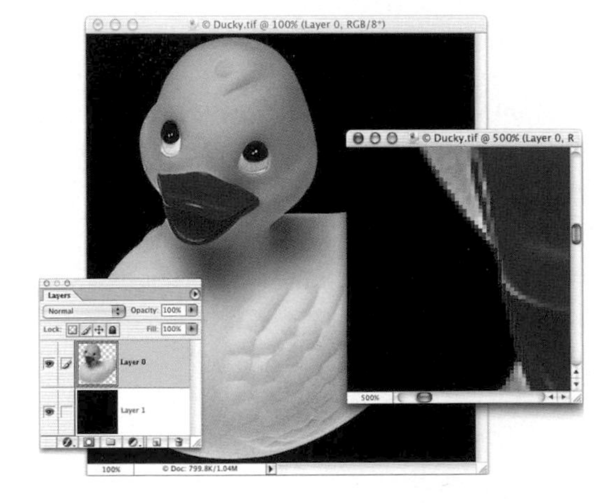


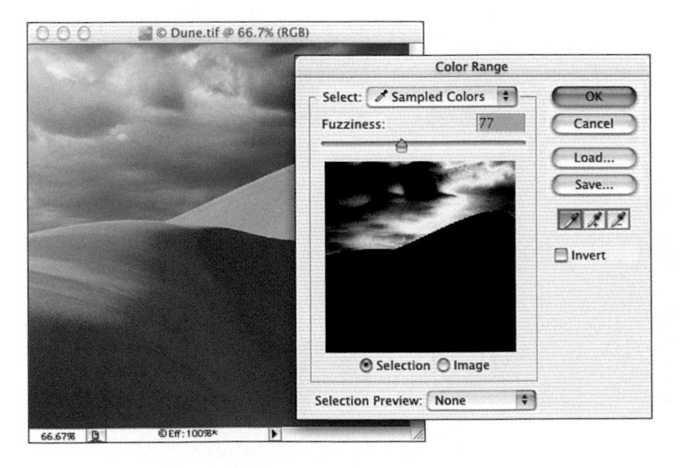


**Figure 9.19** illustrates how the Color Range preview can use a grayscale image to show what is being selected with the command. In this case, the white and grays areas in the sky will be selected but the black areas (the dunes) will not. (**See** "The Color Range Command," **p. 312.**)

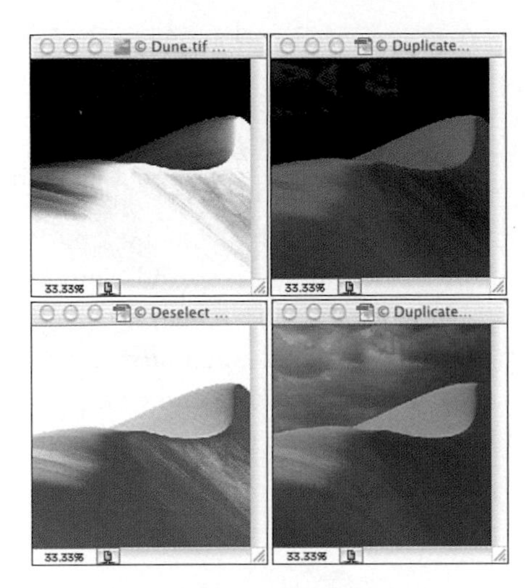


**Figure 9.20** shows four options for the preview feature in the Color Range dialog box. In all four examples, the dunes are being selected. Clockwise from the upper-left: grayscale preview, black matte, Quick Mask, and white matte. (**See** "The Color range Command," **p. 312.**)

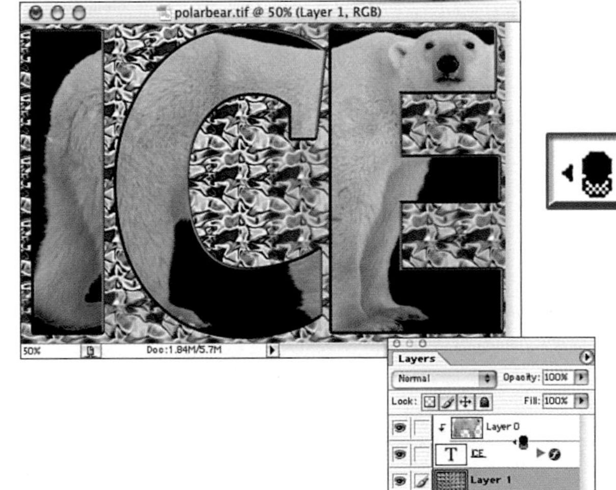


**Figure 9.32** demonstrates a layer clipping mask. The visibility of the top layer is controlled by the pixels on the layer immediately below. Where the lower layer has pixels, the upper layer is visible; where the lower layer is transparent, the upper layer is hidden. (**See** "Clipping Masks," **p. 323.**)

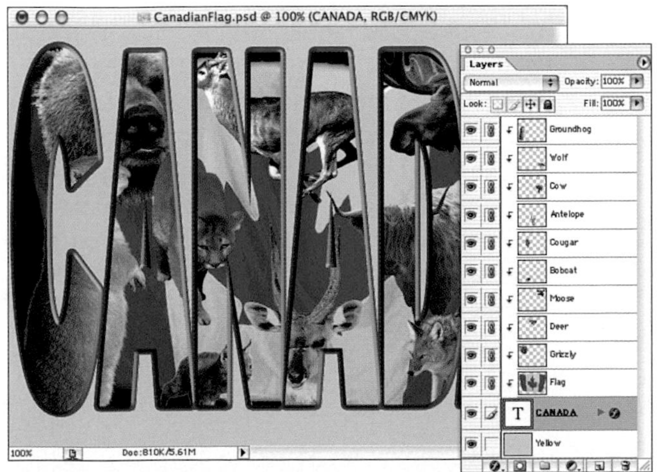


**Figure 9.33** has a single type layer used as a clipping mask for 10 image layers. Each of the images is masked by the type layer, not by the layer immediately below it.
(**See** "Clipping Masks," **p. 323.**)

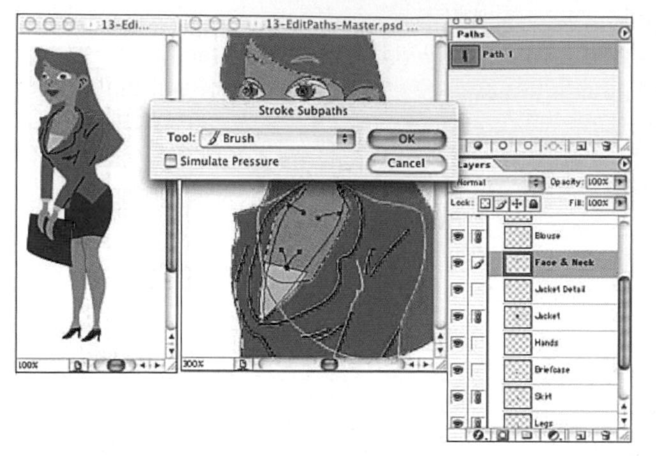


**Figure 11.18** shows the Stroke Subpath dialog box, which is used to determine how the Stroke Path button at the bottom of the Paths palette will behave. The image is reproduced here, however, to better illustrate how opening a second window for an image can given you a better view of your work. The menu command Window, Arrange, New Window for [filename] opens the additional view, which is updated automatically as you work. (**See** "Stroking and Filling Paths and Subpaths," **p. 376.**)

**Figure 12.21** includes type that has been converted to paths. The path for the *E* is being modified with the Direct Selection tool. (**See** "Converting Type to Paths," **p. 378.**)

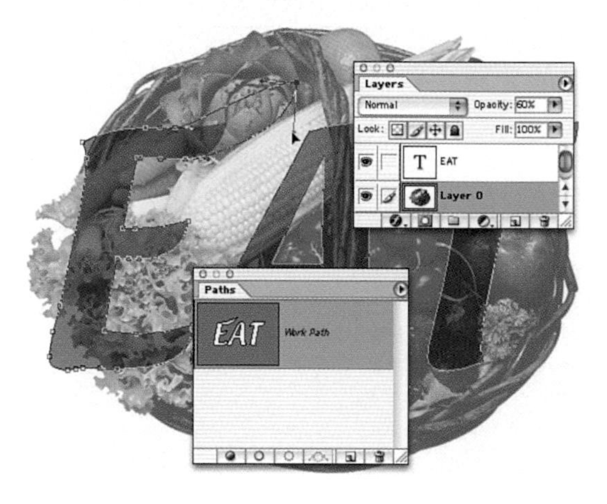


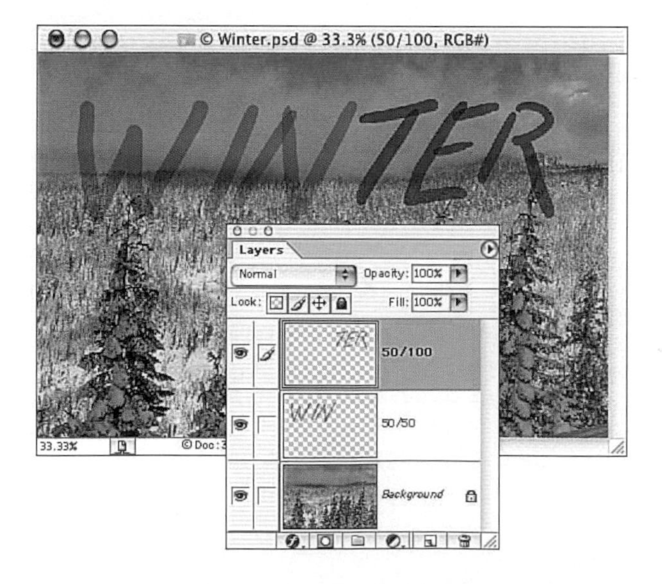


**Figure 13.2** presents the concept of cumulative opacity. If a painting tool with reduced opacity is used on a layer with reduced opacity, the opacity of the painted area is doubly-reduced. On the left, "WIN" was painted at 50% opacity on a layer with 50% opacity (resulting in pixels appearing at 25% opacity). On the right, "TER" was painted at 50% opacity on a layer at 100% opacity (with the pixels appearing at 50% opacity). (**See** "Opacity and Blending for Painting Tools," **p. 432.**)

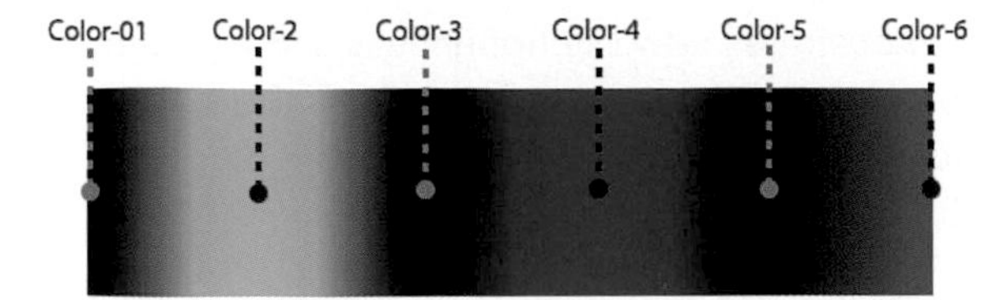


**Figure 13.8** is an example of a linear gradient. Note that each of the adjacent colors blends smoothly into the next. Also observe that none of the colors blends past an adjacent color. If you needed to blend from green to black to green, for example, the first and third "color stops" would be green, with a black color stop in between.
(**See** "The Anatomy of a Gradient," **p. 439.**)

**Figure 13.11** contains examples of the five types of gradients available in Photoshop, along with the gradient from which the samples were created. The gradient types are linear, radial, angle, reflected, and diamond. The arrows show the directions and distance of drag for the Gradient tool. (**See** "Working with Gradients," **p. 443.**)

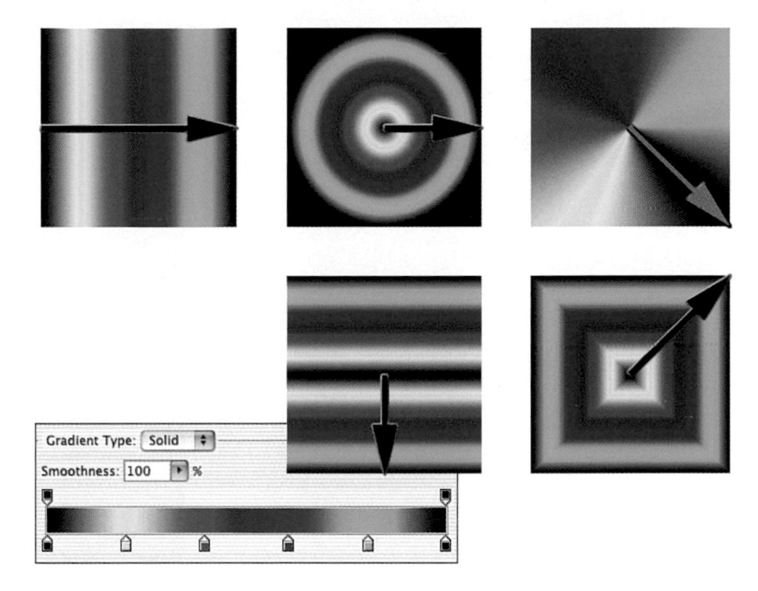


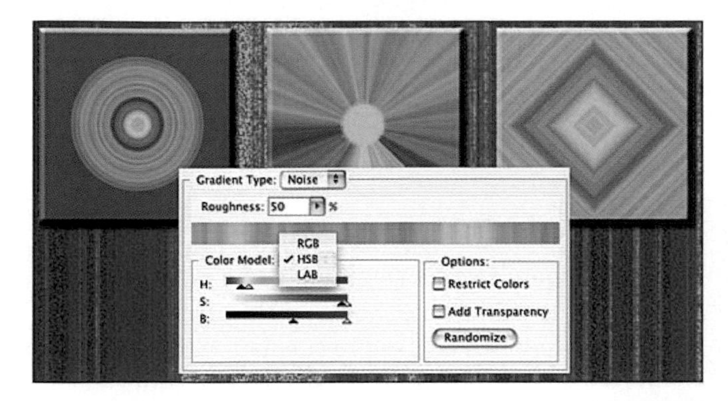


**Figure 13.13** includes three sample noise gradients, displayed on a background that is also a noise gradient. The colors of a noise gradient are selected within parameters specified in the dialog box. In addition to presenting unusual and colorful arrangements, noise gradients can be used effectively with blending modes to texture an image.
(See "Noise Gradients," **p. 443.**)

**Figure 13.14** demonstrates how the Roughness setting determines the smoothness of a noise gradient. From the top, the Roughness slider is at 100%, 75%, 50%, 25%, and 0%. (**See** "Noise Gradients," **p. 443.**)

**Figure 14.6** shows an example of the Pointillize filter's effect. It changes an image into something that resembles a pointillist painting. (**See** "Working with Filters," **p. 466.**)

**Figure 14.11** is an example of the effect produced by Photoshop's Patchwork filter. The result can be used to simulate ceramic tiles or a patchwork quilt. (See "Working with Filters," **p. 472.**)

**Figure 16.5** shows how an alpha channel can indicate the selected areas or unselected areas with a red overlay. On the left, the overlay covers the masked areas; on the left it covers the selected areas. (**See** "Alpha Channels," **p. 520**.)

**Figure 16.12** demonstrates how an image appears when a pair of channels are active in the Channels palette. The image will appear in shades of those color channels active.. *(***See** "Color Channels: Grayscale at Heart," **p. 529***.)*

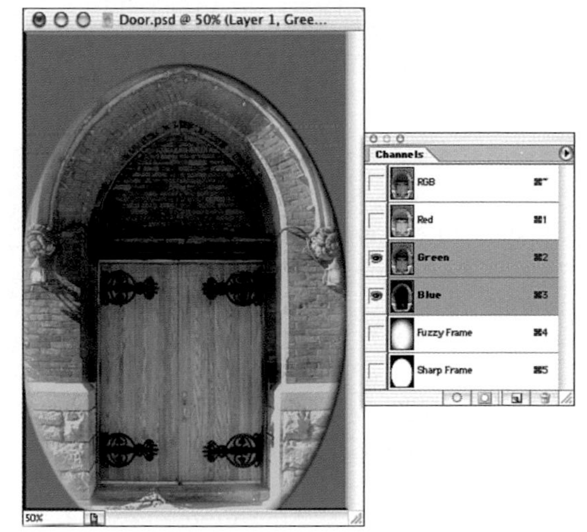


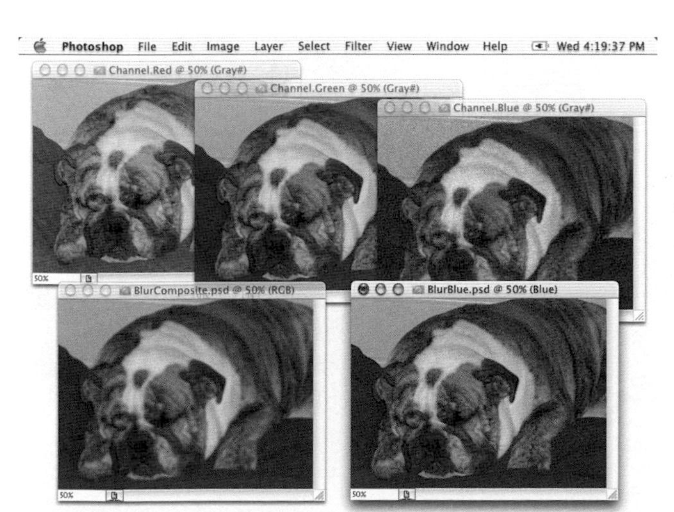


**Figure 16.14** "Noise," the undesirable red, blue, or green pixels scattered through an image, often occurs in one or two channels of a digital photo. Applying a blur filter to the channel(s) that have noise, and not the other channel(s), helps preserve the image quality. In this instance, the two lower images compare blurring all channels (left) versus blurring only the problem Blue channel (right). (**See** "Filtering and Adjusting Individual Channels," **p. 531**.)

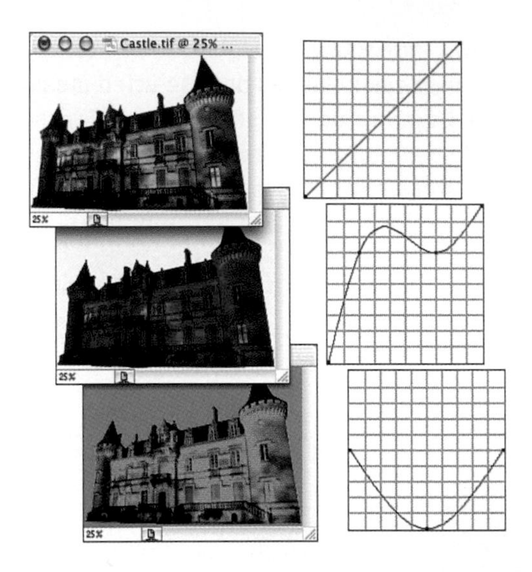


**Figure 16.19** compares three versions of the same duotone image. The black ink curve is identical for each, but changes to the duotone curve for the red ink produce substantially different images. *(***See** "Working with Duotone Channels," **p. 533.***)*

**Figure 17.6** compares a "low-key" image and its histogram (left) with a "high-key" image and histogram (right). The terminology refers to whether an image portrays a dark scene or a light scene. Most images taken in daylight would be considered "normal key." (**See** "Histograms," **p. 548**.)

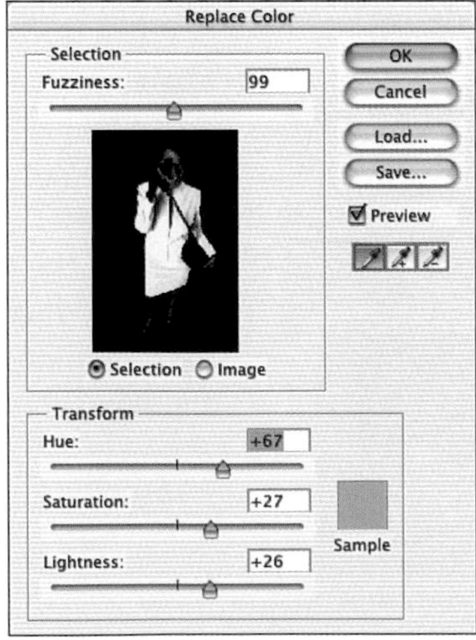


**Figure 17.32** gives one example of using the Replace Color command. The dialog box enables you to make a selection based on color (like the Select, Color Range command), then alter that color in the image (like a Hue/Saturation adjustment). (**See** "Replace Color," **p. 574**.)

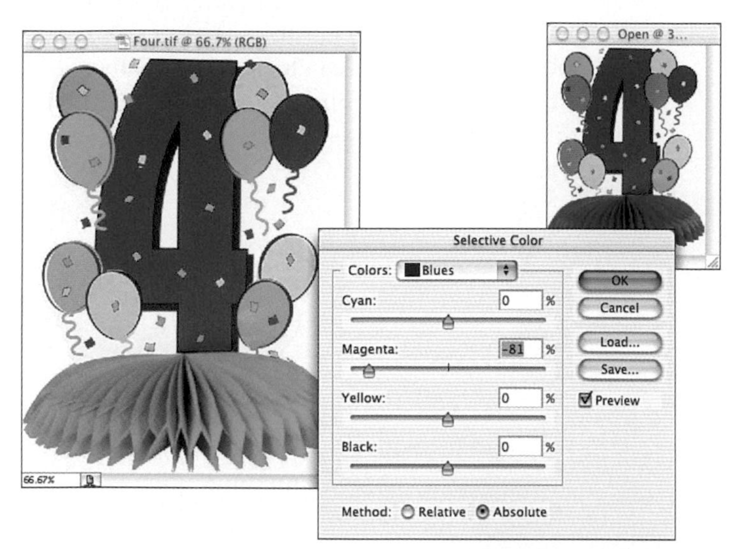


**Figure 17.33** shows how a single component color can be adjusted throughout an image. Selective Color is often used to compensate for a color shift in printing, but can also be used as a creative tool. The dialog box's pop-up menu enables you to select each of the RGB and CMY colors, as well as highlights (Whites), neutrals, and shadows (Blacks). (**See** "Selective Color," **p. 575**.)

**Figure 17.39** demonstrates how the Posterize adjustment can be applied in a couple of different ways. The original, full color, image is on the left. In the center, Posterize was applied with four levels. To the right, 64 levels were used in Posterize. Visually, there is little difference between the image on the left and right. (**See** "Posterize," **p. 581**.)

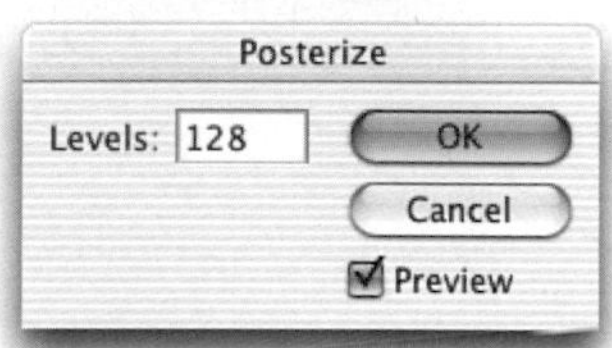

**Figure 20.2** shows how the Colored Pencil filter can be made more subtle. Duplicate the layer, apply the filter to the upper layer, then reduce that layer's opacity. (**See** "The Artistic Filters," **p. 641**.)

**Figure 20.4** illustrates how the Dry Brush filter can be used to create a watercolor effect in an image. (**See** "The Artistic Filters," **p. 641.**)

**Figure 20.18** presents the effect of using the Glowing Edges filter on a photo, turning a pastoral Maine landscape into an image ready for the Las Vegas strip. (**See** "The Texture Filters," **p. 653.**)

**Figure 21.5** shows proper registration (left), slight misregistration (center), and extreme misregistration (right). When printing presses are not properly registered, image degradation occurs. (**See** "Terms and Concepts," **p. 674.**)

**Figure 21.6** includes the four CMYK color separations (the outer images) and the color composite they will produce when the press run is complete. Each color separation determines where one ink will be placed on a page. The composite is the combination of all inks used. (**See** "Terms and Concepts," **p. 674**.)

**Figure 26.13** shows the difference among the colorization options when creating custom scatter, art, and pattern brushes in Illustrator CS. From the top, the options shown are None, Tints, Tints and Shades, and Hue Shift. (**See** "A Note About Colorization," **p. 833**.)

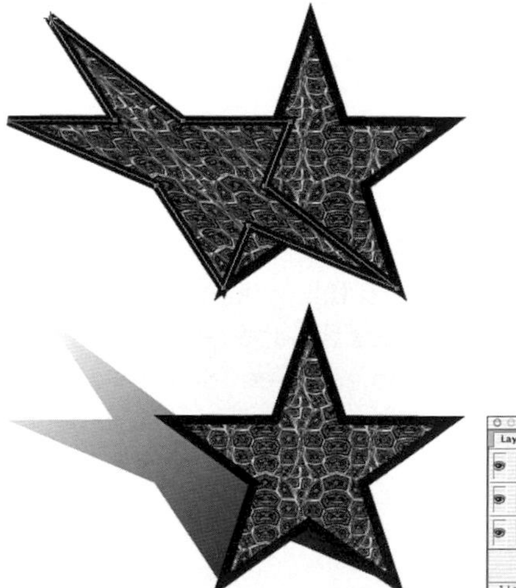

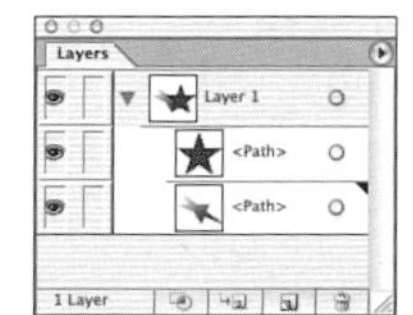


**Figure 28.21** Illustrator's Shear tool comes in very handy when creating cast shadows. Unlike drop shadows, cast shadows cannot be created with an effect or filter. (**See** "Illustrator At Work: Cast Shadows with the Shear Tool," **p. 887**.)

**Figure 28.33** shows a gradient mesh object with a mesh point selected. Mesh points occur at the intersection of mesh lines and have one direction line for each intersecting mesh line segment. (**See** "Editing a Mesh Object," **p. 896**.)

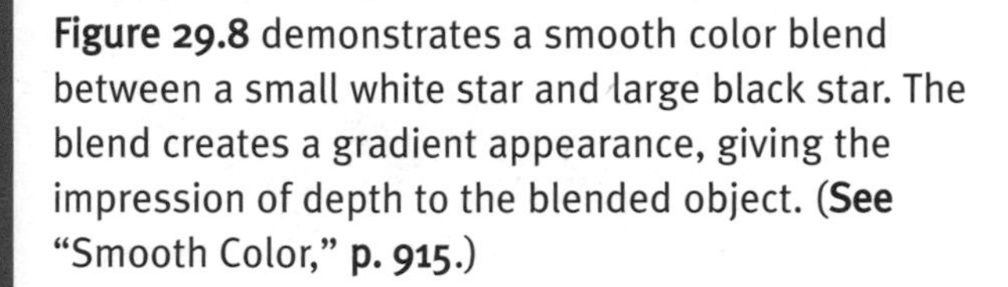

**Figure 29.8** demonstrates a smooth color blend between a small white star and large black star. The blend creates a gradient appearance, giving the impression of depth to the blended object. (**See** "Smooth Color," **p. 915**.)

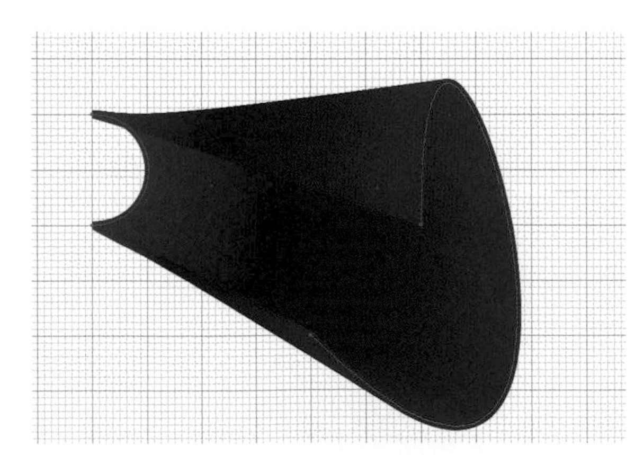

**Figure 29. 9** contains an object created by blending two simple curved paths. Using the Smooth Color blending option produces the appearance of a single surface along the object. (**See** "Smooth Color," **p. 915**.)

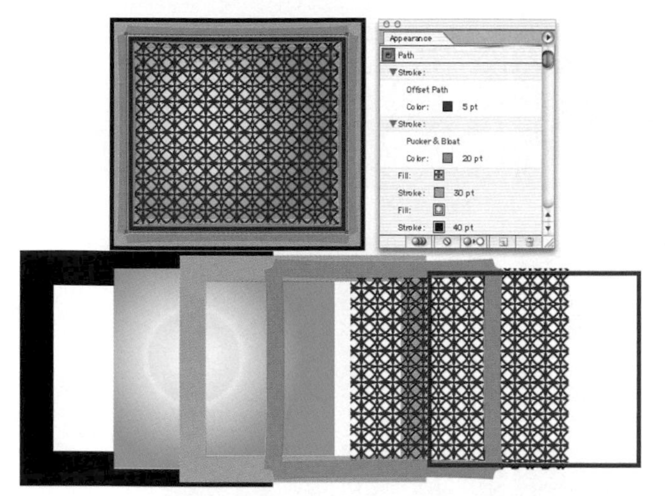


**Figure 32.12** shows an object with A number of appearance characteristics applied (top, with the Appearance palette). Below, the appearance has been expanded using the command Object, Expand Appearance. Expanding the appearance of an object can cure some printing problems. (**See** “Expanding Appearances,” **p. 983**.)

**Figure 33.11** contains a pair of simple gradients (left objects), a pair of gradient mesh objects (middle), and the meshes used to create those objects(right). Gradient meshes give you incredible control over the appearance of objects. (See "Gradient Meshes," **p. 993**.)

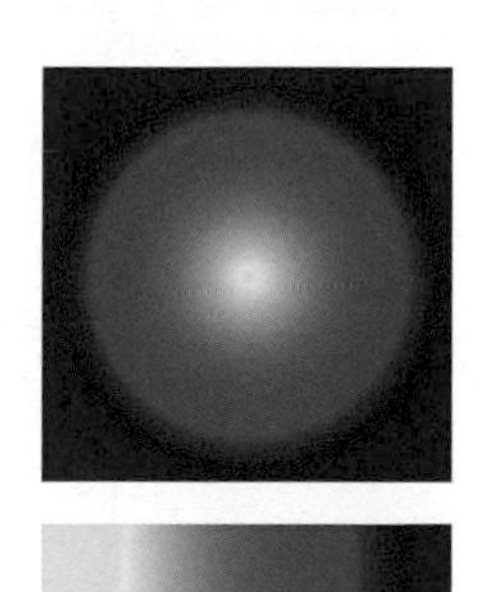

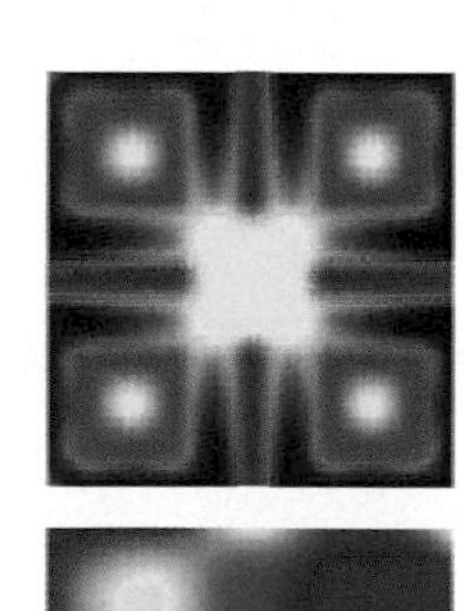

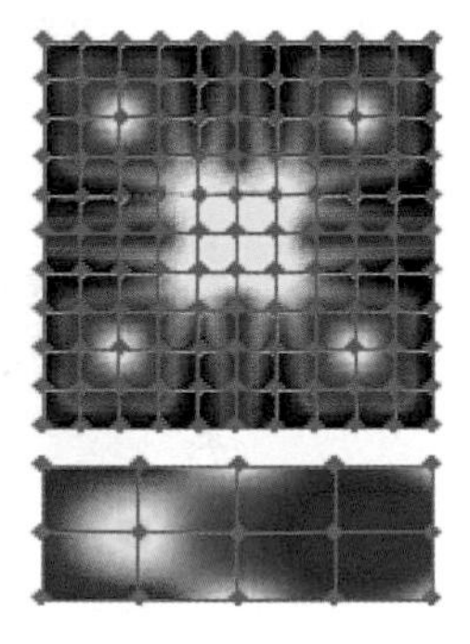

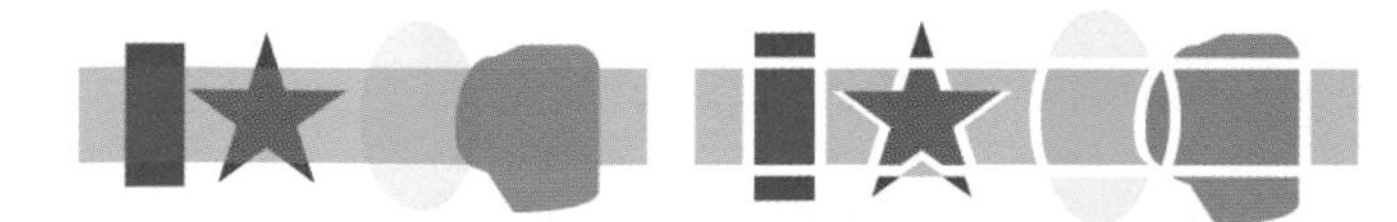

**Figure 34.20** contrasts the use of transparency (left) with creating artwork using a series of single-color objects (bottom). To Re-create the appearance of a semi-transparent rectangle overlapping several other objects requires 19 separate objects (right). (**See** “The Transparency Theory,” **p.1015**.)

**Figure 35.38** includes examples of each of Illustrator's Artistic filters/effects. (See "Artistic (Filter/Effect)," **p. 1058**.)

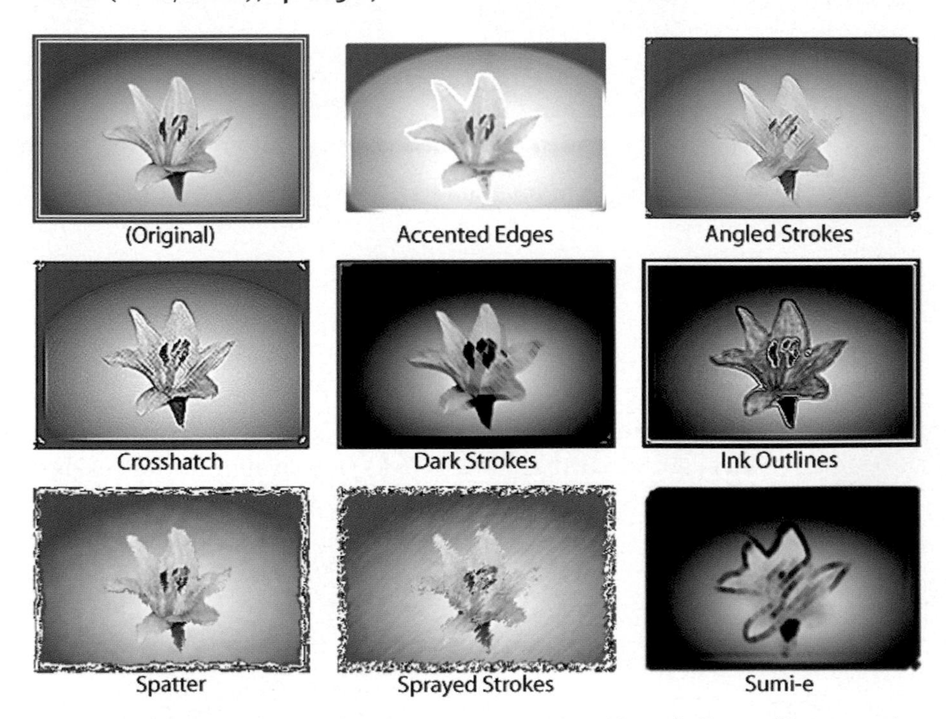


**Figure 35.41** shows each of Illustrator's Brush Strokes filters/effects. (**See** "Brush Strokes (Filter/Effect)," **p. 1061**.)

**Figure 18.15**
Note that the effect is most evident in the partially transparent areas of the flames and along the antialiased edges of the other artwork.

## Clear

Using the Clear blending mode is similar to using the eraser tools: Pixels are changed to transparent. (Clear is used only with the painting tools and is not available for use on background layers or layers with locked transparency.) Unlike the Eraser, which controls the resulting opacity based on the tool's setting, the Clear blending mode makes pixels transparent according to their original opacity. Pixels that were completely opaque become transparent. Pixels that were 75% opaque become 25% opaque. Pixels that were 50% opaque remain 50% opaque.



## Darken

The Darken blending mode compares the individual color components of the base and blend colors. It retains the lower value (RGB) or higher percent (CMYK) for each component color. In all cases, the darker value for each component color is retained. If the base pixel has a color value of RGB 25/100/215 and the blend color is 100/200/50, the result color will be 25/100/50. White is ignored on the blend image (see Figure 18.16).

**Figure 18.16**
Generally, you can expect dark colors on the upper layer to be retained, but dark base colors will have more influence on the result color than lighter base colors.

## Multiply

The Multiply blending mode calculates the color values (RGB or CMYK) of both the blend and base colors and multiplies them. Because this is a multiplication calculation, the result color is darker than the original blend color. Figure 18.17 shows the sample image when the upper layers' blending modes are set to Multiply.

**Figure 18.17**
The Multiply blending mode always results in a darker color, except when the lower color is white (which results in no change). Multiplying with black produces black.



In the figure, observe how the flames show prominently through the lighter areas of the dartboard and the flag.

> The Multiply blending mode is a great help for overexposed or too-high-key images. Duplicate the layer (or a selection of the layer) and change the upper layer's blending mode to Multiply. Duplicate *that* layer if you need to darken things up more. Repeat as necessary.

## Color Burn

Color Burn simulates the darkroom technique used to darken areas of an image by increasing exposure time. Blending dark colors over a base color results in darkening. Blending with white produces no change in the lower color (see Figure 18.18).

**Figure 18.18**
Note that the pure white areas of the clouds show through the flames and trophy.

## Linear Burn

The Linear Burn blending mode is similar to Color Burn in that it results in a generally darker image, except where the base color is white (see Figure 18.19). Color Burn increases contrast, but Linear Burn decreases brightness to produce the result color.

Figure 18.19
In contrast to the Color Burn sample, this image has much less white showing through from the base layer. Rather, the brightness of the overlying images is increased.

## Lighten



The Lighten blending mode is the complement to the Darken blending mode. It determines whether the blend or base color is lighter and makes changes accordingly. If the base color is lighter, it is left unchanged. If it is darker, the upper color is blended (see Figure 18.20).

Figure 18.20
To the left, the white clouds show through the dark dartboard. Only the highlights of the trophy are visible.

In this blending mode, the base and blend colors are compared, with the result color being whichever is lighter.

## Screen

Screen is, mathematically, the opposite of Multiply. The inverse of each color value is multiplied. The result color is always lighter. Figure 18.21 shows the result of changing the blending mode of the upper layers to Screen.

Figure 18.21
If the upper color is black when you use Screen as the blend mode, the result color is the base color. White, however, always produces white when screening.



Screening red on blue (or blue on red) produces magenta; screening red on green (or green on red) yields yellow; and screening blue on green (or green on blue) gives you cyan.

## Color Dodge

*Dodging* is a darkroom technique designed to lighten certain areas of a photograph. When you partially block the light before it reaches the paper, the image in that area is neither as dark nor as saturated. The Color Dodge blending mode is typically used with lighter blending colors. Blending with black produces no change (see Figure 18.22).

Like Multiply, Screen is an invaluable blending mode. Areas of an image that are too dark can be copied to a new layer and that layer's blending mode set to Screen. Repeat as required.

Figure 18.22
Black in the upper layers becomes transparent and white becomes opaque.

## Linear Dodge

Comparable to the way Color Dodge works with contrast, Linear Dodge works with brightness. It compares the base and blend colors and then increases the brightness of the base color to produce the result color (see Figure 18.23).

Figure 18.23
Blending with white produces white; blending with black produces no change.

## Overlay

Overlay serves as a cross between Multiply and Screen (see Figure 18.24). The base color's values for brightness are retained (highlights and shadows). If the base color is dark, it is multiplied and becomes darker. If it is light, it is screened and becomes lighter. Often a hue shift also occurs.

Figure 18.24
Overlay can be comparable to reducing the opacity of the upper layer with extreme highlights and shadows.

Desaturated images (in RGB or CMYK mode) can be colorized by adding a layer of solid color set to Overlay. Adding an Overlay layer of gray can intensify highlights or shadows. Grays near 50% produce subtle changes.

## Soft Light

Soft Light is a mixture of Color Dodge and Color Burn. If the top color is light, the bottom color is lightened; if the top color is dark, the lower color is darkened (see Figure 18.25). The effects of Soft Light are more subtle than many of the other blending modes. Some shifting of hues can be expected.

**Figure 18.25**
Soft Light can be similar to a less-intense version of the Overlay blending mode.



Adding areas of light or dark gray to a layer with the Soft Light blending mode selected produces an effect comparable to Dodge and Burn. Unlike in several other blending modes, pure black and pure white as blend colors do not produce black and white result colors.

## Hard Light

The Soft Light blending mode can be similar to shining a diffused spotlight on the base colors, but Hard Light is much more vivid (see Figure 18.26). When a layer is set to Hard Light, you can paint with dark grays to darken and light grays to lighten.

**Figure 18.26**
Like in many blending modes, using black or white for the blend color leaves it unchanged as the result color with the Hard Light blending mode.

Blending with shades of gray and Hard Light is effective for adding highlights and shadows to an image. Like some other blending modes, Hard Light acts like Multiply when colors are dark and like Screen when colors are light.

## Vivid Light

Vivid Light produces a result similar to a very saturated version of Overlay (see Figure 18.27). The increased saturation produces a more vivid result color than does Overlay.

**Figure 18.27**
Vivid Light increases or decreases contrast based on the blend color.

## Linear Light

A complement to Vivid Light, Linear Light works with brightness rather than contrast (see Figure 18.28). Consider it a combination of Linear Dodge and Linear Burn. If the blend color is light, the brightness of the base color is increased to produce the result color. If the blend color is dark, the base is darkened to generate the result color.

**Figure 18.28**
In the color version of this figure, you'll see that Linear Light retains the hue of the blend color much more than Vivid Light does.

## Pin Light

Pin Light is similar to both Darken and Lighten. If the blend color is dark, base colors darker than the blend color are retained, and those that are lighter are replaced. If the blend color is light, the lighter base colors are retained and the darker pixels are replaced (see Figure 18.29).

Figure 18.29
Not apparent in the grayscale version of this image are the slight hue shifts that Pin Light can produce.



## Hard Mix

New to Photoshop CS is the Hard Mix blending mode. It posterizes the image, forcing colors that are similar to a single value. To see how this blending mode posterizes, drag the background layer of a digital photo (or other single-layer image) to the New Layer button in the Layers palette. Change the upper layer's blending mode to Hard Mix and slowly drag the Opacity slider to the left.

Hard Mix can also be used to increase contrast, using a layer filled with gray, set to Hard Mix, and with the Opacity setting substantially reduced. (An Opacity setting of 10% is typical when Hard Mix is used to work with contrast.) Fill with darker grays or black to work with the shadows, and use light gray or white to adjust highlights.

## Add and Subtract

Available only for the Apply Image and Calculations commands (in the Image menu), these blending modes simply add or subtract the component color values for each pixel. They are used only when combining channels.

*For more information about the Add and Subtract blending modes, see Chapter 16, "Channels: The Ultimate Creative Control," p. 513.*

## Difference

Difference can create among the most dramatic of blending changes. The brightness values of the upper and lower colors are compared and then the color values of the lesser are subtracted from the greater. Because black has a brightness of zero, no change is made. When you're blending with white, expect colors to be inverted. In Figure 18.30, light gray and white areas in the upper layers produce extreme color changes.

Want to know *exactly* what's different about two copies of the same image? Flatten copies of each (if they have layers). From the Layers palette, Shift-drag the layer "Background" to the window of the other copy. Change the upper layer's blending mode to Difference. Every pixel that is identical will appear black. Any pixel that's different will appear as white or a color.

**Figure 18.30**
**Even in grayscale, the results of the Difference blending mode are noticeable.**



## Exclusion

The results of blending with Exclusion are very similar to, but less dramatic than, those of the Difference blending mode. Result colors tend toward grays, with a less contrasting look (see Figure 18.31). Blending with white inverts colors, and black produces no change.

## Hue

The Hue blending mode uses the saturation and brightness of the base color and the hue of the blend color. As you can see in Figure 18.32, blending with imperfect blacks and whites can produce speckling.

## Saturation

In contrast to the Hue blending mode, Saturation uses the hue and brightness from the lower color and the saturation of the upper color. When the upper color is a shade of gray, that neutral saturation overrides the hue. In Figure 18.33, note that using only the saturation of the upper layers produces shadowy silhouettes of the artwork.

**Figure 18.31**
Exclusion has a tendency to flatten contrast when working with brightness values approaching 50% in the blend color.

**Figure 18.32**
Hue uses a simple substitution to produce the result color, substituting the blend color's hue for that of the base color.

**Figure 18.33**
The flames seem to have disappeared, but they're still there—although the sky behind is already well saturated. The black and white squares of the flag obviously have comparable (and very low) saturation.

For the Saturation blend mode, the result color is a product of the base color's hue and brightness, with the saturation of the blend color. Painting with gray produces no change.

## Color

The brightness of the base color is retained in the Color blending mode, and the other two components (hue and saturation) are contributed by the blend color (see Figure 18.34).

**Figure 18.34**
The flag and trophy areas of this sample image are similar to the preceding figure because of the blend colors' saturation values, but several other areas are dramatically different.



## Luminosity

Using the brightness (luminosity) of the blend color and the hue and saturation of the base color, Luminosity is the reverse of the Color blending mode (see Figure 18.35).

**Figure 18.35**
Using the highlights and shadows of the blend color produces well-defined representations of the artwork on the upper layers.

**Simplifying: Hue, Saturation, Color, Luminosity**

The four blending modes, Hue, Saturation, Color, and Luminosity, take HSB values from the lower or upper color to create the resulting color. Understanding which values are used can help you choose the most appropriate blending mode for your artwork. Table 18.3 simplifies the equation for you.

**Table 18.3** HSB for Blending Modes

| Blending Mode | H | S | B |
|---|---|---|---|
| Hue | Upper | Lower | Lower |
| Saturation | Lower | Upper | Lower |
| Color | Upper | Upper | Lower |
| Luminosity | Lower | Lower | Upper |

## Pass Through

The Pass Through blending mode is available only for layer sets, and it's the default layer set blending mode. This mode results in the layer set itself having no effect on the image's compositing or appearance. Consider Pass Through a neutral mode, allowing the layers to interact both within the layer set and with layers below.



## Replace

When working with the Healing Brush (and only the Healing Brush), the Replace blending mode helps ensure that grain and texture near the edges of the brush stroke are preserved.

# MASTERING PHOTOSHOP

## Plotting the Pixel's X,Y Coordinates

*How can there be more than one pixel in the same place?*

When the file is saved in a format that doesn't support layers or is sent to a printer, there is, in fact, just a single pixel in each location in the image. However, when working with layers in Photoshop (or TIFF) file format, you can have one pixel for each location on each layer. The location, measured from the upper-left corner as an X,Y coordinate, exists on each layer independently.

## Color Mode Conversion

*L*a*b color mode doesn't support Darken, Lighten, and a couple other blending modes. What if I've used them and have to convert my image to Lab?*

When you use the menu command Image, Mode, Lab Color, you'll be offered an opportunity to flatten your layers. If you do, the appearance will be preserved. If you don't, any layer that uses an unsupported blending mode will be converted to Normal mode. This can have a substantial impact on the overall look of your artwork. Consider, for example, a layer set to Lighten that contains black. In Lighten, the black is transparent; in Normal, it is opaque black.

19

*by Richard Romano*

# REPAIRING AND ENHANCING IMAGES WITH THE PRODUCTION FILTERS

## IN THIS CHAPTER

Back in the days before digital images, people who worked with photographic images were often stuck with what came out of their camera. These days, we're not subject to the slings and arrows of outrageous photography. We can fix the images that come out of the camera (or the scanner, or wherever it is they come from). For example, if an image is blurry, we can sharpen it to crystal clarity (well, within reason). If it's too sharp, we can blur it to a soft focus. If the color is off, we can fix the color. If the subject of an image looks like she has malaria, we can take the green out of her skin (or put it in).

Photoshop offers three basic ways to fix images: color correction, restoration tools, and filters. Color correction is covered in Chapter 17, "Manipulating Color and Tonality," and the various editing and retouching tools are covered in Chapter 15, "Image Cropping, Resizing, and Sharpening," which leaves filters for this chapter.

As mentioned in Chapter 14, "Selecting and Applying Filters," Photoshop has two types of filters: production and artistic. In this chapter, we focus on the use of production filters—a category that includes the following:

- The Blur and Sharpen filters
- Noise filters such as Despeckle and Dust & Scratches
- Video and "Other" filters

To this list, we can also add some newer filters in the Photoshop arsenal, such as the Extract filter and the Pattern Maker.

This chapter details the ways that images can be fixed and enhanced—from such minor things as sharpening blurry images and removing dust and blemishes from scanned images, to extracting foreground objects from backgrounds and creating custom patterns from portions of images.



# SHARPEN FILTERS

You know how it is. You take a bunch of digital pictures, and when you start downloading them you find that the one you really want to use is blurry. Now, when it comes to images, there is blurry and then there is *blurry*. In the former case, we're talking about images that are a little soft or slightly out of focus. In the latter case, we're talking about images that are little more than indistinguishable blurs. Photoshop's tools can fix the slight softness, but they're not going to resurrect a hideously out-of-focus image.

Probably the most basic way of repairing an image in Photoshop is to sharpen it. Photoshop sharpens an image by increasing the contrast between adjacent pixels. You access the sharpen filters by choosing Filter, Sharpen. There are four sharpening options:

- Sharpen
- Sharpen Edges
- Sharpen More
- Unsharp Mask

The following subsections discuss each of these sharpening options in detail.

## Sharpen and Sharpen More

Two tempting but ultimately unsatisfactory sharpen filters are Sharpen and Sharpen More. These filters are ultimately unsatisfactory because you have no way to control the amount of sharpening they apply—they operate in predetermined amounts. They're a one-size-fits-all solution, and one-size-fits-all solutions rarely work effectively.

Applying these filters is pretty simple. With an image open (or a portion of an image selected), just select Filter, Sharpen or Filter, Sharpen More and the filter is applied. The difference between Sharpen and Sharpen More, as you would expect, is that Sharpen More applies an extra-strength sharpening effect. Sharpen More applies about three to four times as much sharpening as is applied by the Sharpen filter. If your image has a slight amount of softness, either of these filters is worth a quick try. If the result is ineffective, just select Undo and try something else.

## Sharpen Edges

Blurriness or softness is caused, in part, by decreased contrast between the "edges" in an image. An *edge* in an image is where adjacent pixels demonstrate major color changes. Major color changes provide detail in an image, and when these edges are softened, a loss of detail results. An example would be the detail in Figure 19.1: the windows versus the side of the house, the slats in the siding itself, the house versus the sky, the individual pickets in the fence, and so on.

**Figure 19.1**
For the purposes of sharpening, an edge can be considered any place where adjacent pixels demonstrate major color changes, such as windows versus the side of the house, the slats on the picket fence, and so on.



Sharpen Edges looks for those edges and boosts the contrast between them. Figure 19.2 is a before-and-after look at the Sharpen Edges filter on a zoomed-in portion of the image.

Like the Sharpen and Sharpen More filters, Sharpen Edges applies a factory-preset amount of sharpening, which makes it of limited use. But, again, it's sometimes worth a try to see if this filter works on a given image.

Figure 19.2
(Left) A close-up portion of the image in Figure 19.1 before the Sharpen Edges filter was applied. (Right) The Sharpen Edges filter enhanced the contrast in areas where significant color changes existed between pixels.

## Unsharp Mask

Now we're talking. Unsharp Mask is the most useful of the sharpening filters, primarily because it lets you adjust the amount of the sharpening in three ways, using the Amount, Radius, and Threshold sliders. When you select Filter, Sharpen, Unsharp Mask, you will get the Unsharp Mask palette (see Figure 19.3).

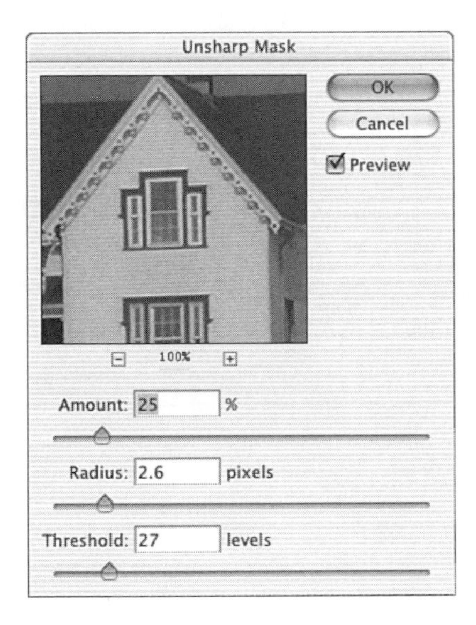


Figure 19.3
The Unsharp Mask palette lets you finesse the sharpening of an image.



The three sliders have these effects:

- **Amount**—This slider controls how much Photoshop will increase the contrast of adjacent pixels. The higher the percentage, the more pronounced the effect. Photoshop's documentation recommends an amount between 150% and 200% for high-resolution images, but, depending on the image, that may be far too much.
- **Radius**—This slider refers to the number of pixels surrounding the edge pixels that will be affected. Therefore, the greater this number, the more pixels affected. A Radius setting of 1 will affect only those pixels right on the edge. You'll rarely want to go beyond 2 pixels.

- **Threshold**—This slider determines how different pixels must be from each other to be considered "edge" pixels. A setting of 0 will consider every pixel an edge pixel and thus sharpen all of them. Such sharpening can be too drastic, so you won't want to use the 0 setting in most cases.

There is no single formula for working with these sliders. Make sure the Preview check box is selected and watch the effect as you drag the sliders back and forth. Too much sharpening can introduce noise and graininess, and make edges look harsh and overblown.

Unsharp masking effects are more noticeable onscreen than in print, so if your image looks a little oversharpened onscreen, that's not necessarily a bad thing. Try printing the image to an inkjet printer and see if the printed result is acceptable.

*Is there an advantage to sharpening individual color channels? See "Looking Sharp" in the "Mastering Photoshop" section at the end of this chapter.*

**The Original Unsharp Mask**

For those who like a sense of history, the term *unsharp mask*—which, let's face it, sounds a tad contradictory in light of the fact that it is used to sharpen images—dates from pre-digital graphic arts photography. The original "unsharp mask" was a somewhat blurry, low-contrast photographic negative produced from a transparency and placed on top of that transparency (like a mask) when making color separations. The light passing through the mask was refracted, which resulted in a color correction to compensate for hue errors inherent in process color inks. One accidental side benefit of unsharp masking was that it enhanced (actually, exaggerated) the edges in the image, yielding greater detail on the color separation negatives.

Although the unsharp mask is perhaps an anachronistic term these days, it is this latter effect that has made the leap to the digital sphere, and we tend to think of the color-changing attributes of the filter as a problem and seek ways of avoiding it.



# BLUR FILTERS

Whereas the sharpen filters enhance the contrast between adjacent pixels, the blur filters do the opposite: They smooth transitions between adjacent pixels. Sometimes, images (especially images taken with a digital camera) have noise or graininess; applying a slight blur can eliminate some of that noise.

The Filter, Blur submenu includes the following filters:

- Average
- Blur
- Blur More
- Gaussian Blur
- Lens Blur

- Motion Blur
- Radial Blur
- Smart Blur

The following subsections discuss these filters in detail.

## Blur and Blur More

Like the Sharpen and Sharpen More filters, the Blur and Blur More filters apply a blurring effect in predetermined and uncontrollable amounts. The Blur More filter applies a blurring amount that is about three to four times as potent as the regular Blur filter.

As always, the recommendation for using these filters is to try them, see if they have any useful effect, and, if not, undo them and try something else.

## Gaussian Blur

The Gaussian Blur filter is an all-purpose blur filter that gives you some degree of control over the blur effect, going from a slight softening to a glaucoma-vision effect (see Figure 19.4).

Figure 19.4
The Gaussian Blur filter lets you adjust the potency of the blurring effect.



The Gaussian Blur filter can be applied to the background of an image to enhance the depth of field or to dramatically highlight the subject of an image. The first step is to separate the object you want to highlight from the background—and the easiest way to do that is to add a Quick Mask to the foreground. When you exit Quick Masks mode, you'll make a selection out of the unmasked area; then you can apply the Gaussian Blur filter to the selected area.

*For specific detail about making selections and using the Quick Mask mode, see Chapter 9, "Making Selections and Creating Masks," p. 295.*

Once the background area is selected, select Filter, Gaussian Blur. With the Preview check box selected, adjust the Radius setting until you have the effect you want (see Figure 19.5).

Figure 19.5
The subject in the foreground was isolated using a Quick Mask. Notice that some of the ground in the foreground was left unselected. This will help ensure a more realistic effect.

After the Gaussian Blur was applied to the image in Figure 19.5, the foreground ground still looked a bit unnatural. Through the use of the Blur tool, the foreground-to-background boundary can be softened (see Figure 19.6).

*For specific detail about the Blur tool, see Chapter 13, "Photoshop's Painting Tools and Brushes," p. 429.*

Figure 19.6
The Gaussian Blur filter lets you adjust the potency of the blurring effect.



For another way of accomplishing this effect, see the "Lens Blur" section, a bit later in this chapter.

## Smart Blur

The counterpart to Unsharp Mask (no, not called Sharp Mask, which would be a correspondingly ironic term for a blurring tool) is the Smart Blur filter. Smart Blur provides a way to precisely control the blurring effect. Selecting Filter, Blur, Smart Blur brings up a palette not unlike the one for the Unsharp Mask filter (see Figure 19.7).

The controls available in the Smart Blur palette are detailed in the following list:

By the way, *Gaussian* is a reference to German mathematician Carl Friedrich Gauss and refers to the method (based on a process devised by Gauss for solving certain types of algebraic equations—which is *way* beyond the scope of this book!) by which Photoshop applies a weighted average to pixels. It's really not an all-pixels-blurred-evenly filter. Rather, the Gaussian Blur filter adds low-frequency detail.

- **Radius**—Like the Unsharp Mask filter's Radius slider, this slider refers to the number of pixels surrounding the edge pixels that will be affected. The greater this number, the more pixels affected.
- **Threshold**—Like the Unsharp Mask filter's Threshold slider, this slider determines how different pixels must be from each other to be considered "edge" pixels. A setting of 0 will consider every pixel an edge pixel and thus blur all of them.
- **Quality**—This pop-up menu lets you determine whether you want a high-, medium-, or low-quality blur. Somewhat counterintuitive, the Low quality setting tends to preserve image detail, whereas the High quality setting can produce a posterization effect. These differences are really only detectable at high-blur radii and thresholds.
- **Mode**—This pop-up menu has three options: Normal, Edge Only, and Overlay Edge. Normal applies a smart blur to an entire selection or image, whereas Edge Only and Overlay Edge are only applied to high-contrast adjacent pixels. In the case of Edge Only, Photoshop applies black-and-white pixels to the entire image, and Overlay Edge applies only white pixels to the edges (see Figure 19.8).



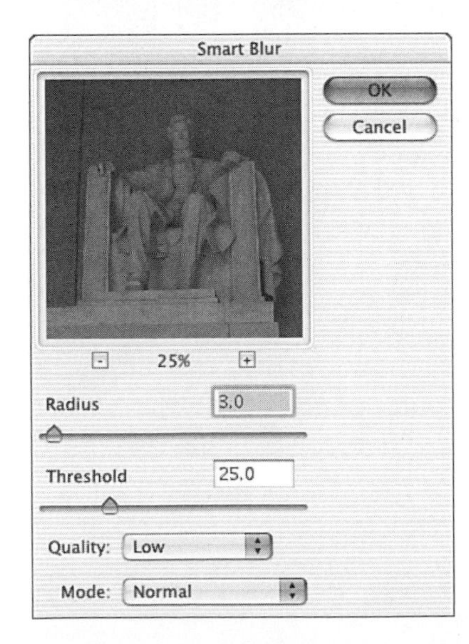


Figure 19.7
The palette for the Smart Blur filter lets you precisely control the blurring effect.

Figure 19.8
(Left) Edge Only applies white pixels to image edges and black pixels to non-edge pixels. (Right) Overlay Edge applies white pixels to edges but leaves the rest of the image alone.

Although it can be considered an artistic effect rather than a strict enhancement, when either the Edge Only or Overlay Edge mode is applied to a copy of an image layer, and the Opacity slider and/or blending modes are adjusted, the resulting effect can provide some degree of edge enhancement.

## Average

The Average filter is new in Photoshop CS. This is another uncontrollable, all-or-nothing filter, but in this case that's not a bad thing. This filter averages the colors of all the pixels in a selected area. Naturally, you don't want to use this filter on an entire image (it will just turn the entire image a single color). When used in conjunction with Select, Color Range to select a range of colors, however, the Average filter can be used to remove noise from and/or equalize the color in selected areas. It can also be used to create a manual posterization effect, giving images a "cartoony" look.

## Lens Blur

The Lens Blur filter is a photography-centric filter that can be used to simulate camera lenses of different focal lengths, allowing you to change the depth of field. This effect is akin to what you saw earlier with the Gaussian Blur filter, but the Lens Blur filter makes it easier and more effective to add these types of effects.

Selecting Filter, Blur, Lens Blur opens up the Lens Blur dialog box (see Figure 19.9).

The first step in applying the Lens Blur filter is to create an "optimization mask." This is basically an alpha channel that isolates the subject of an image—in other words, what you want to be sharp. Follow these steps to create the optimization mask and apply the Lens Blur filter:

1. Create an optimization mask by going into Quick Mask mode and painting a Quick Mask over the foreground object.
2. Exit from Quick Mask mode to load the unmasked area as a selection.
3. Create an alpha channel by going to Select, Save Selection and then make sure New is selected from the Channel pop-up menu. Name the channel Alpha Channel or Optimization Mask—or whatever you'd like to call it. Click OK.

> Here is where Photoshop's monitor recommendations come into play. You will need at least a 1,024×768-pixel monitor to display this entire dialog box.

Figure 19.9
The Lens Blur dialog box lets you precisely control depth of field and focus effects.

4. Open the Channels palette and click your alpha channel to select it. You can see that the entire background is masked out (see Figure 19.10).

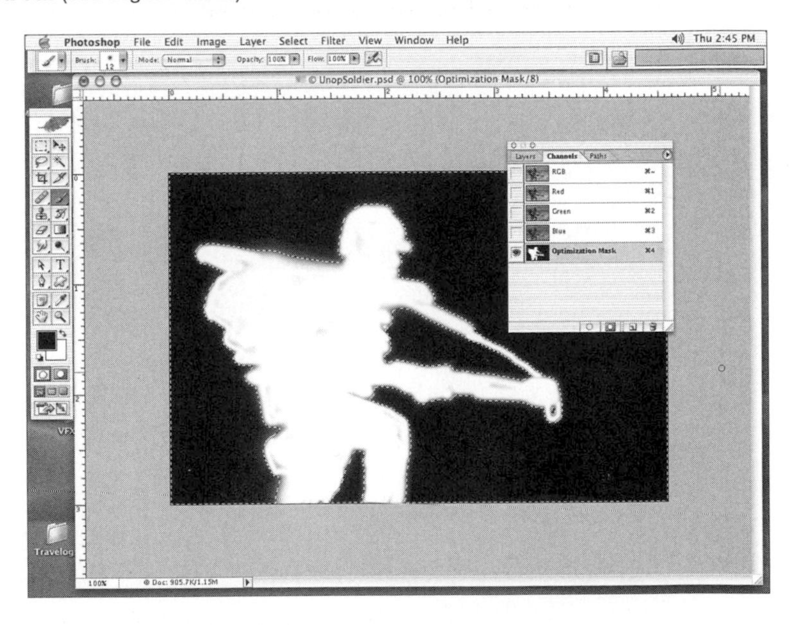


Figure 19.10
The alpha channel isolates the foreground object by masking out the background.

5. For better results, use a gradient transition instead of a strict alpha channel mask. To do this, select the alpha channel in the Channels palette, go to Select, Load Selection, and select your alpha channel from the Channel pop-up menu. On the Tools palette, make sure black is the foreground color and white is the background color; then select the Gradient tool and draw a gradient from the top of the image to the bottom (see Figure 19.11). This will make the mask

vary in strength from the top of the image (the far background) to the bottom (the near background). This will enhance the depth of field effect.

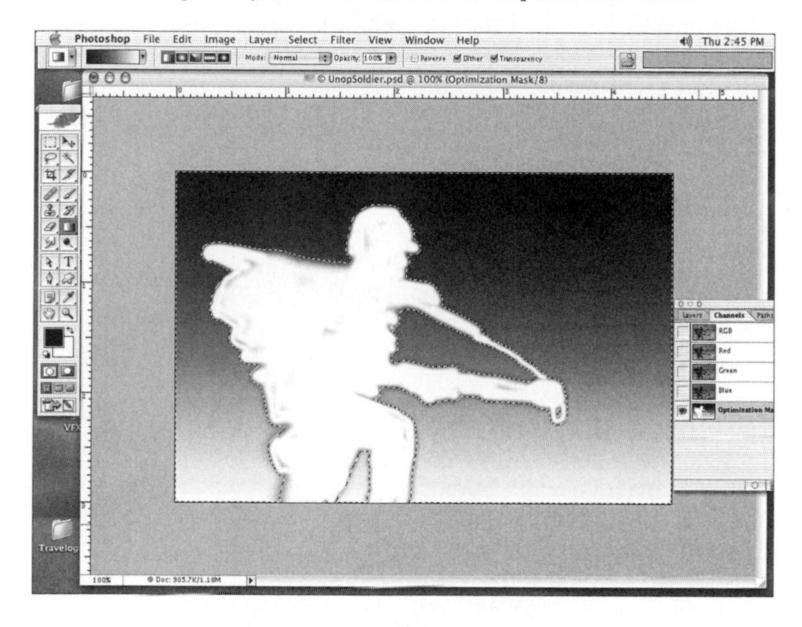


**Figure 19.11**
Using a gradient as a mask will enhance the depth of field effect when the Lens Blur filter is applied.

6. Make sure that the visibility of the alpha channel is turned off in the Channels palette. Then select Filter, Blur, Lens Blur.
7. In the Source pop-up menu in the Depth Map section of the Lens Blur dialog box, select the alpha channel you just created to isolate the foreground object.
8. The Blur Focal Distance slider lets you vary the depth of field from the masked portion of the image. Dragging it up to 30 produces a satisfactory blurring effect, at least on this particular image. All images can vary, so experiment to see what value yields the best result.

*For specific detail about creating masks, see Chapter 9, "Making Selections and Creating Masks," p. 295. For more information on creating alpha channels, see Chapter 16, "Channels: The Ultimate Creative Control," p. 513.*

Part of the advantage of this filter is that you can have highlights simulate the shape of a camera lens aperture, providing for a more realistic photographic effect.

A camera's *aperture* is the hole through which light passes from the lens to the film (or CCD, depending on whether it is a traditional or digital camera). Usually, the aperture is not a perfectly round hole; it is formed by the blades of the iris in the lens, and different cameras have a different number of blades, often six or eight blades, although some expensive lenses can have more blades. Only when the lens is at full aperture is the hole a perfect circle; all other times, it is

> When you create an alpha channel mask, it doesn't matter if you create the mask from the background or the foreground—do whichever is easier—because you can use the Invert check box in the Depth Map section of the Lens Blur dialog box to toggle between the background and the foreground.

octagonal, heptagonal, hexagonal—maybe even triangular, depending on the number of blades comprising the iris and the aperture size. (The size of the aperture itself is controlled by adjusting the camera's *f-stop*, which controls how much light is allowed to pass into the camera.) This discussion gets a tad beyond the scope of this chapter, let alone this filter. Suffice it to say, you will probably only notice any difference in aperture shape when photographing subjects with out-of-focus highlights or lens flares, which produce globs of light, the shapes of which are determined by the aperture shape.

Thus, under Iris, you can choose to change the shape of the lens aperture. Dragging the Radius slider to the right increases the overall blur effect. The Blade Curvature slider increases the "roundness" of the simulated iris, whereas Rotation changes the amount of the iris rotation. You can also change the brightness of the specular highlights (or very bright "speckles" of light), as well as, via Threshold, which pixels should be considered specular highlights.

Figure 19.12 shows the final, previewed image.

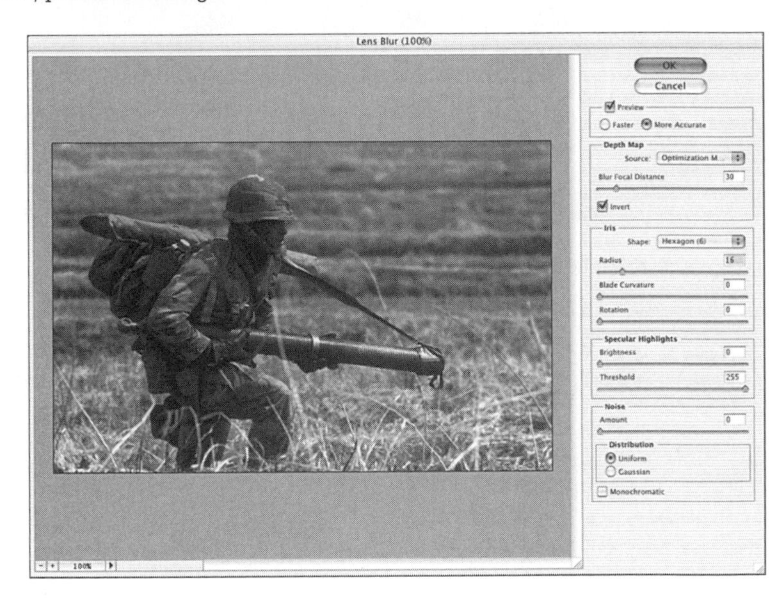


**Figure 19.12**
**With the Lens Blur filter, the foreground object has been brought into sharp focus while the background has been blurred, simulating a high depth of field.**



The key to getting this filter to work as intended is in the preparation: defining masks to isolate the portions of the image that are to be blurred and/or sharpened independently of the rest of the image.

# NOISE FILTERS

Noise filters can be used not only to add noise, but to remove it, as well. If you do a lot of scanning, two filters in particular should be your friends: Despeckle and Dust & Scratches. One of the drawbacks to scanning images is you are likely to capture some degree of dirt, dust, and other detritus from the scanbed as part of the digital image. And just when you

> The other blur filters—Radial and Motion Blur—are creative filters discussed in Chapter 14.

thought that digital photography might alleviate some of that problem, there is also the problem of noise that some digital cameras can add to an image.

For example, Figure 19.13 shows a scanned image. If we were to zoom in to the dark portions of the image, it would seem as if it was scanned during a dust storm.

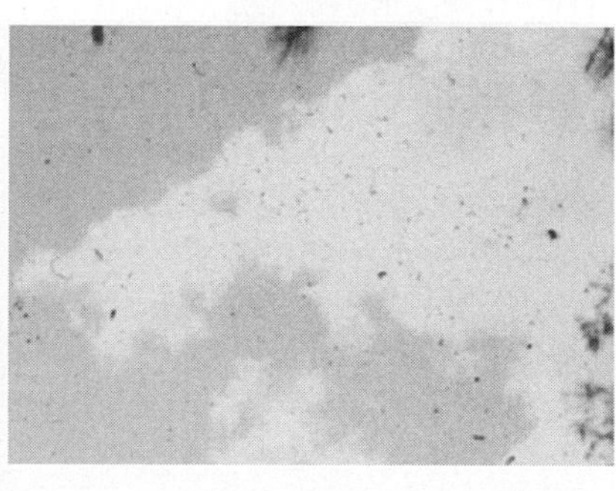

**Figure 19.13**
In dark portions of scanned images, large amounts of dust and debris can be seen (inset). (This has been exaggerated for emphasis.)

Dust and debris are often found in both very light and very dark areas—much like black shoes scuff white and white shoes scuff black.

The following subsections discuss two methods for removing these types of problems.

## Despeckle

The Despeckle filter can be used to remove noise from all or selected portions of an image, or to remove dust and dirt. You access this filter by selecting Filter, Noise, Despeckle. The problem with Despeckle is that, like the Blur and Sharpen filters, you can't control the degree of the despeckling effect (which some people find despeckable). This filter removes tiny highlights that are most likely bits of dirt. Very often, however, tiny highlights are actual image detail. For example, using Despeckle on the entire image back in Figure 19.13 would remove some of the highlights from the treetops in the image. It also tends to eliminate small specular highlights.



Therefore, when you're using the Despeckle filter, it's best to apply it to only certain portions of the image—in the case of Figure 19.11, drawing a selection marquee around the sky and then selecting Despeckle would get rid of most of the dust while retaining the image detail elsewhere in the image.

> In terms of removing digital camera noise, in most cases the noise can be confined to a single color channel—usually the blue channel. If images seem especially noisy, go to the Channels palette and select each channel separately. Whichever one seems the noisiest, run the Despeckle filter on it and see if that helps.

## Dust & Scratches

To clean up images with a bit more finesse, you can use the Dust & Scratches filter (accessed by choosing Filter, Noise, Dust & Scratches). This gives you a palette with two sliders to help eliminate image blemishes (see Figure 19.14).

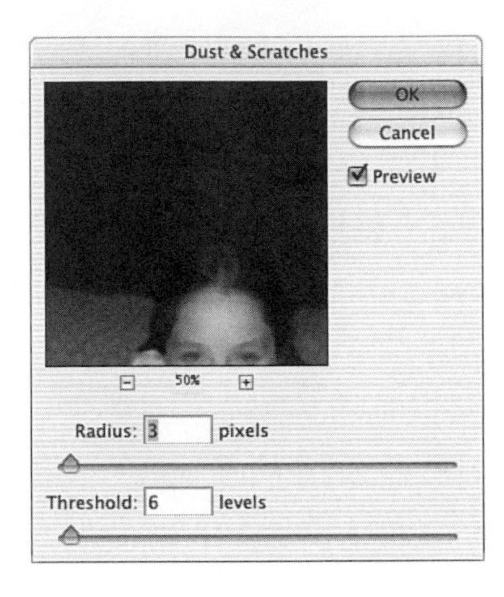


Figure 19.14
The Dust & Scratches filter lets you control how much of a "de-filthing" effect the filter applies.

The two sliders have these effects:

- **Radius**—As with the other filters you've seen in this chapter, Radius determines how far Photoshop searches for anomalous pixels (in other words, how large something can be and still be considered filth). Increasing the Radius value will have the practical effect of blurring the image (or the selected portion of an image) because what Photoshop is doing is smoothing out the differences between adjacent and dissimilar pixels. If that sounds familiar, it's because this is the same modus operandi that the blur filters use. This technique does help get rid of defects, but sometimes—in fact, remarkably often—the difference between dissimilar pixels is actual image detail. So *le secret* with this slider is to find the lowest Radius value that will eliminate dust but not oversoften the image.
- **Threshold**—Again, the Threshold slider lets you determine how different the pixels' values should be before they are eliminated.

Here's the best way to use the Dust & Scratches palette: Start with a Threshold setting of 0. Move the Radius slider up gradually until you reach the lowest possible value before the dust disappears, but don't go beyond that. (It's like when recipes tell you to bring water "just to a boil.") Then, move the Threshold slider way out to the right, and you'll see all the gunk return. Gradually move the slider to the left until the gunk goes away again. In a nutshell, you want the lowest Radius setting and the highest Threshold setting that together produce a clean image with good detail.

After using Despeckle and/or Dust & Scratches, you may also want to run an Unsharp Mask filter to fix any despeckle-induced softness.

Don't worry if you don't get rid of all the defects. Large blemishes and scratches are often best handled by using the Clone tool, the Healing Brush tool, and/or the Patch tool.

*For specific detail about the Clone, Healing Brush, and Patch tools, see Chapter 15, "Image Cropping, Resizing, and Sharpening," p. 481.*

Be sure to not only use the preview window to keep an eye on the disappearing gunk but also to periodically scroll around the image and make sure that you're not losing important image detail elsewhere.

# VIDEO FILTERS

If you work with screen captures taken from video—from broadcast/cable video or from videotape—two filters in the Filters, Video submenu can help solve common problems with these types of images. These filters are the De-Interlace and NTSC Colors filters, discussed in the following subsections.

## De-Interlace

Most video images are created by *interlacing* (or *interlace scanning*), which is a means of drawing an image on a television screen and was invented more than 60 years ago. Interlacing scans an image on a screen by first drawing the odd-numbered lines and then drawing the even-numbered lines. When interlaced video images are captured and brought into Photoshop, the effects of interlacing are visible and look as if there are two frames visible in the same image. The De-Interlace filter removes these interlacing artifacts by deleting either the odd or even fields (see Figure 19.15).

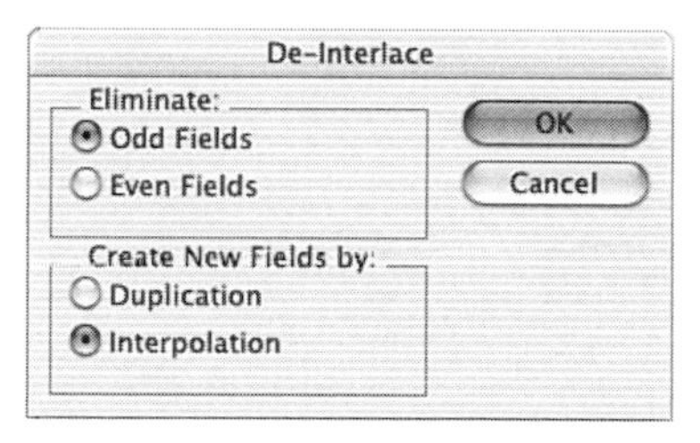


**Figure 19.15**
The De-Interlace filter lets you remove image artifacts caused by interlacing.

You can choose whether to remove the even or the odd lines, and they can be replaced either by duplicating the remaining pixels or interpolating new pixels based on those that remain.

## NTSC Colors

Photoshop is not just used for images designed for print or the Web; it also produces images and graphics suitable for broadcast. However, if you watch TV regularly, you know that certain colors bleed or can be oversaturated. As a result, there is a safe gamut of NTSC (National Television Standards Committee) colors that will not bleed onscreen. Converting images to NTSC colors solves these color-bleeding problems. If you are creating onscreen graphics for broadcast television, this filter remaps the colors to a palette that has been optimized for TV or video.

Digital video and computer screen captures do not exhibit this problem because computer monitors use the alternative to interlacing, *progressive scanning*. Progressive scanning (also used in flat-screen TVs), scans an image on screen by drawing each line of the picture sequentially. The goal in the television industry is to eventually eliminate televisions that use interlacing and have progressive-scan TVs be the wave of the future. That will take a while, so for now, folks who work with digitized broadcast video will have to deal with the interlacing problem.

# OTHER FILTERS

The Other filters submenu is a mélange of filters that are not easily classified into other submenus. The Custom filter enables you to design and save your own filter effects. The

Minimum and Maximum filters modify masks. Each of these filters is described in detail in the following subsections.

## Custom

The Custom filter lets you create your own filters that create unique effects by changing pixel brightness (see Figure 19.16.

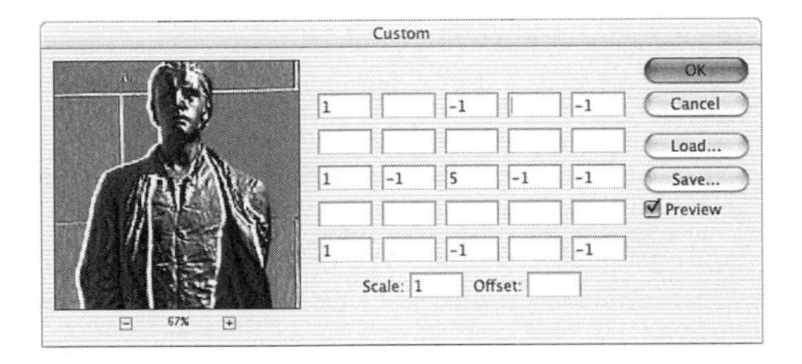


Figure 19.16
It isn't immediately apparent just what the heck this filter does. You'll need to experiment by adding numbers to the boxes and watching the results in the preview window.

The number in the center box represents any given pixel. Changing this number will multiply the brightness of that pixel by whatever number is entered. The surrounding boxes represent adjacent pixels. Entering numbers in them, from –999 to +999, decreases or increases (respectively) the brightness of those pixels. Each pixel is assigned a value based on the value of the surrounding pixels. It's not easy to understand what that means, but adding numbers to boxes and checking out the results in the preview window is a good way to get a sense of what this filter does. It does seem that this filter is good at creating custom emboss effects (see Figure 19.17).

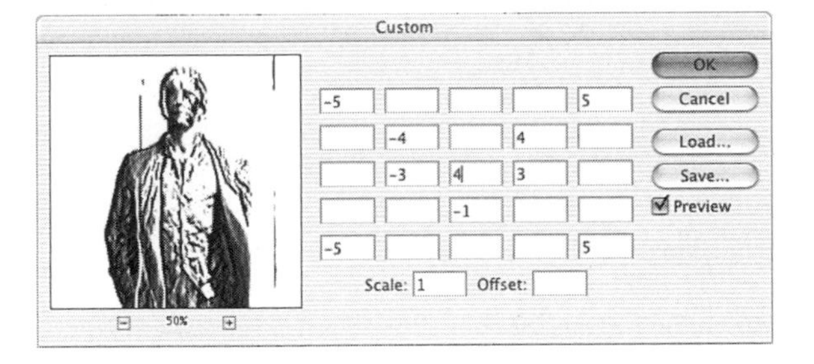


Figure 19.17
Adding numbers to boxes lets you change the brightness of adjacent pixels.

19

If you've managed to create a filter you like, you can click the Save button and save the filter. You can then give copies of your filter to others, who can load them into their own versions of Photoshop by clicking the Load button.

## Minimum and Maximum

The Minimum and Maximum filters are used for modifying masks. The Minimum filter spreads out black areas and shrinks white areas. Within the specified Radius value, the Minimum filter replaces a pixel's brightness with the lowest brightness value of the surrounding pixels.

The Maximum filter, in contrast (so to speak), spreads out white areas and shrinks black areas. Within the specified Radius value, the Maximum filter replaces a pixel's brightness value with the greatest brightness value of the surrounding pixels (see Figure 19.18).

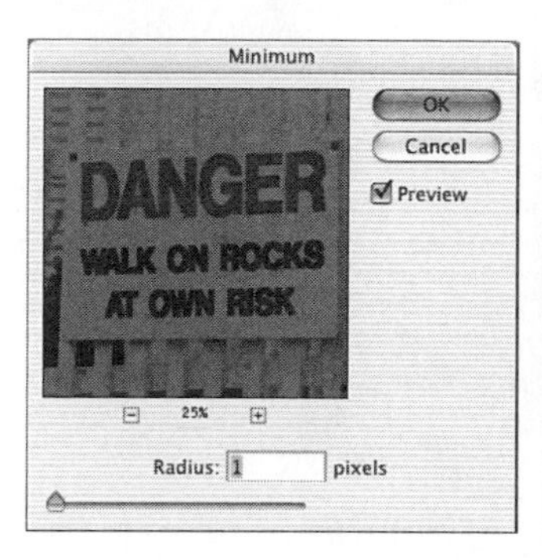

**Figure 19.18**
The Minimum filter (left) spreads the black areas and chokes the white areas, whereas the Maximum filter (right) spreads the white areas and chokes the black areas.

# USING THE EXTRACT FILTER

One of the biggest tricks of working effectively in Photoshop is to isolate objects from backgrounds. This is useful not just for compositing purposes (that is, taking an object out of one image and putting it in front of a completely different background—and we're not just talking about blackmail purposes, either), but also for compositional purposes, such as adjusting the depth of field and so on.

You have a number of ways of isolating objects from backgrounds. You can draw a path around the object in question, for example, and convert that path to a selection, or you can use the Quick Mask mode. The Extract filter offers a new-and-improved way of removing objects from backgrounds (or vice versa) in Photoshop.

## Simple Extraction

When you select Filter, Extract—or press (Option-Command-X) [Alt+Ctrl+X]—you get the Extract dialog box. Like many of the newer filters in Photoshop, this has a larger, more involved interface than the usual small filter palette (see Figure 19.19).

The basic operation of the Extract feature is fairly simple: Use the Highlight tool to trace the edge of the object you want to isolate and then click the Fill tool within the outline you just drew to fill the object with a mask. This will indicate the area(s) you want to retain. Figure 19.20 shows a simple highlighted/masked image.

Next, either click Preview to preview the extraction or go ahead and click OK to begin the extraction process. You will end up with the extracted object against a transparent background (see Figure 19.21).

The Extract filter discards all the background pixels. If you want to keep a copy of the original, duplicate the layer and apply the extraction to the copied layer.

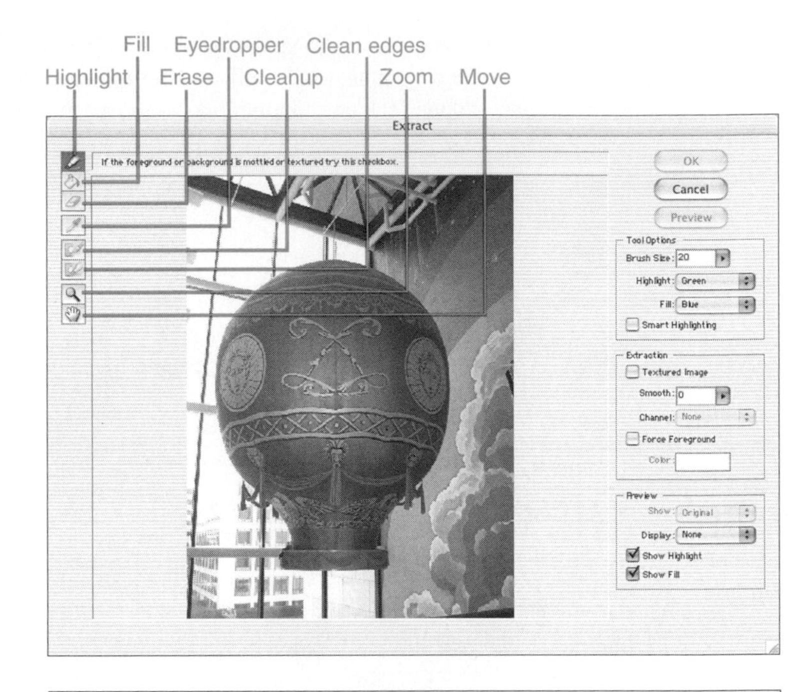


**Figure 19.19**
The Extract dialog box has a set of tools, the controls and setting for those tools, and a large preview window.

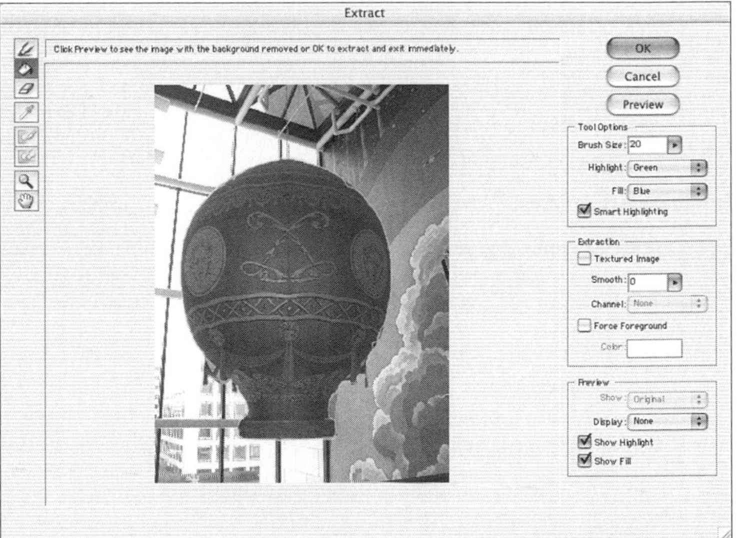


**Figure 19.20**
An outline is drawn around the object with the Highlight tool and then is filled with a mask using the Fill tool.

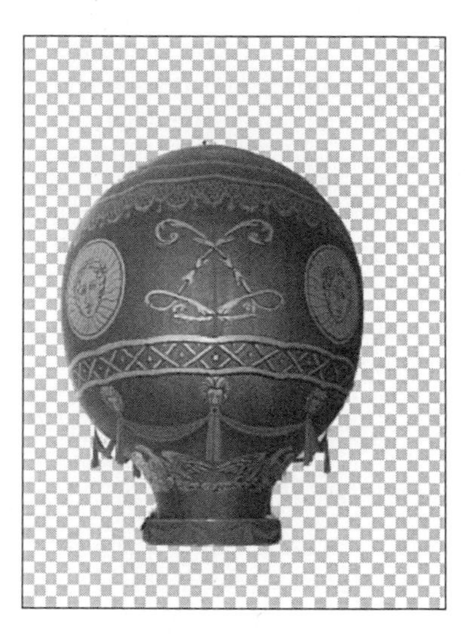

Figure 19.21
The Extract filter strips away the background outside the masked area and leaves you with the extracted object against a transparent background.

## Back in the Highlight Again

There is more to it than that. You can alter the size of the Highlight tool by adjusting the Brush Size slider in the Tool Options portion of the Extract dialog box. You can also choose a different highlight color if the default of lime green disturbs you (or, more importantly, if a similar color is used in the image and you can't see the highlighting).

A good option for many extractions is the Smart Highlighting check box. With this checked, you don't need to precisely draw a highlight around the edge of the object; the tool will automatically seek out the edge and "snap" to the edge of the object. However, the effectiveness of the Smart Highlighting feature (like the Magnetic Lasso tool, if you're familiar with that selection tool) is a function of how distinct the edge of the foreground image is from the background. You may need to do some repair to the highlight after the fact (more about which in a moment).



Enlarge the brush size to cover intricate areas of the object, such as fine hairs, or other parts of the image that are not easily separated from the background. If you are unable to draw a definable border that can be filled (for example, it's hard to draw a highlight around a wispy strand of hair or a blade of grass), highlight all of what you want to include and then check the Force Foreground button. Select the Eyedropper tool and select the color in the highlighted area that you want the Extract filter to base the extraction on. Naturally, this process works best on objects that have large areas of a single color, such as a blade of grass.

If you make a mistake while drawing with the Highlight tool, unlike the Magnetic Lasso tool (or any lasso tool), you can stop, switch to the Erase tool, erase the errant line, reselect the Highlight tool, and soldier on.

**Caution**

If you do stop and start with the Highlight tool and Erase tool, make sure that there are no tiny gaps in the finished, highlighted border; otherwise, the Fill tool will not place a mask within that border, but rather over the entire image. Use the Zoom tool to enlarge the highlighting and inspect it for small gaps. Use the Erase and Highlight tools to fix the border as necessary.

If your highlight is completely out of whack, hold down the (Option) [Alt] key. The Cancel button will change to a Reset button. Click it, and whatever highlight or fill you've drawn will be erased and you can start over without having to exit the dialog box.

Unless you are using a stylus on a drawing tablet (such as Wacom's), you may need to go back over your border and fix any erratic portions of it. After all, a mouse is not a precision drawing tool. Also, this process is less effective if you've consumed a lot of coffee!

If your mouse is not moving smoothly, or only moves about with great effort, it may need a "de-gunking." Unplug the mouse, twist off the bottom ring around the roller ball, and remove the ball. Check to see that there is no gunky buildup (dust and debris picked up by the ball rolling over the mousepad or other surface) on the wheels that press against the ball. If there is, scrape it off with a ballpoint pen tip, an X-Acto knife blade, or your fingernail. Replace the ball, and you'll be surprised how much more smoothly the mouse moves.

## Previewing and Editing Extractions

Once you have drawn a highlight around an object and filled it with a mask, click the Preview button to see a preview of what the extracted object will look like. If the edges are not clean, you can select either the Cleanup tool or the Clean Edges tool.

Clicking and dragging with the Cleanup tool lets you erase portions of the mask, if there is still some background peeking through, either along the edge of the object or in the middle of the object. This is also good for adding "punch-through" parts of an image, such as transparent windows if you are removing a car from a background, for example. Holding down the (Option) [Alt] key while clicking and dragging the Cleanup tool restores the mask, in case you erased too much (see Figure 19.22).

Figure 19.22
In Preview mode, the Cleanup tool lets you erase any portions of the background that got picked up by the mask.

The Clean Edges tool lets you sharpen the edges of the object. Holding down the (Command) [Ctrl] key while clicking and dragging lets you move an edge in or out, if the extraction process "missed."

If you like what you have created, click OK. Photoshop will go ahead and apply the Extract filter.

After you extract an object from an image, you can use any of Photoshop's other retouching tools and filters to make any further corrections or tweaks.

*What if you don't want to completely get rid of the pixels in the background when you extract? See "Weapons of Mass Extraction" in the "Mastering Photoshop" section at the end of this chapter.*

You can, of course, drag the extracted object to a new document to composite it on a new background (see Figure 19.23).

Figure 19.23
An extracted object can be composited over a new background without exhibiting any fringing around its edges.

# WORKING WITH THE PATTERN MAKER

The Pattern Maker lets you create tiled backgrounds and/or textures easily and with a high level of customization.

The Pattern Maker is found at Filters, Pattern Maker. Alternatively, you can access it by selecting (Option-Command-Shift-X) [Alt+Ctrl+Shift+X]. The Pattern Maker dialog box is shown in Figure 19.24.

If you extract an object from the background layer, it is converted to a regular layer, which means you can add a new background by adding a new layer to the document, putting the new background on it, and dragging it under the extracted object's layer in the Layers palette.

## Basic Pattern Generation

It looks complicated, but at heart, it's just complex. On the left side of the dialog box are a scant three tools: a marquee tool, a zoom tool, and a move tool. To create a pattern, first use the marquee to outline a region to use as the source of the pattern (see Figure 19.25).

**Caution**

When you use the Pattern Maker, all the data in the original image is lost. To keep the original image, either save a copy of it or duplicate the layer on which you are making the pattern, and the Pattern Maker will only replace the pixels on that layer.

Figure 19.24
The Pattern Maker dialog box is command central for creating repeating patterns and textures.

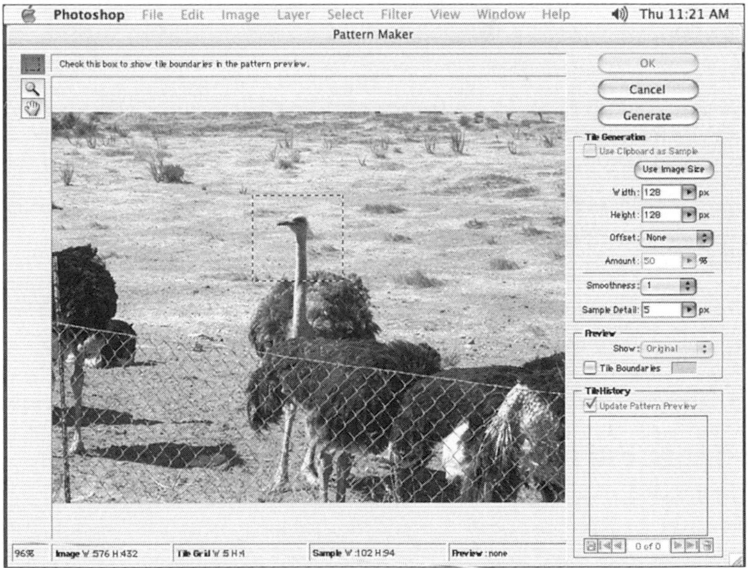


Figure 19.25
Begin the pattern-making process by drawing a marquee around the area of the image to use for the pattern.

Next, click the Generate button. This will create a preview of what your tiled pattern will look like (see Figure 19.26).

The Pattern Maker doesn't always make patterns in the way you'd think it would; it doesn't just take the marqueed area and tile it as is. In other words, it's not designed to be strictly a tile-making tool; instead it goes for a seamless, seemingly random pattern.

*What if you want to simply tile a portion of an image without all that fancy-schmancy pattern stuff? See "Patterns of Force" in the "Mastering Photoshop" section at the end of this chapter.*

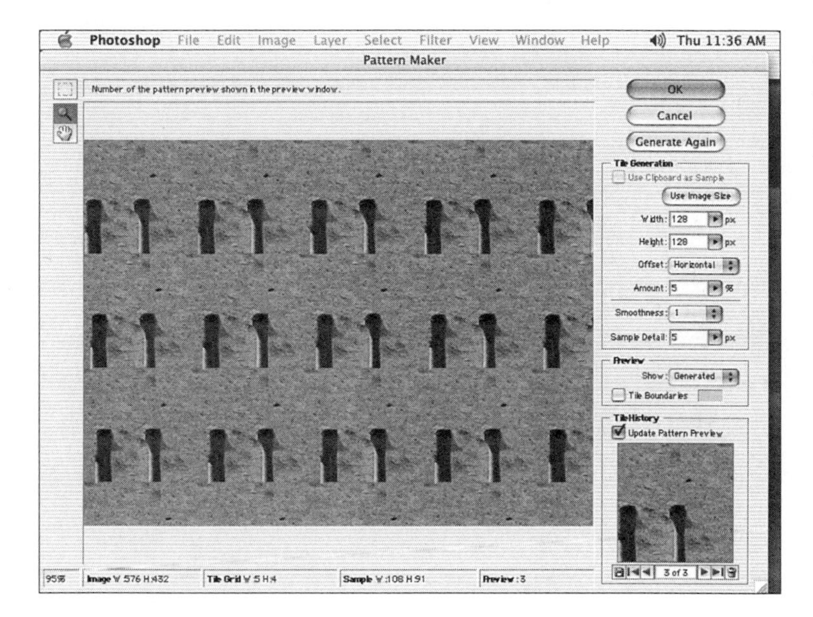


**Figure 19.26**
The Pattern Maker bases the pattern on what you selected; it isn't designed to be a simple tiling tool.

## Editing Patterns

You can continue to make edits to the pattern you created. For example, you can change the height and width of the tile by moving the Height and Width sliders, and you can offset the tiles, either horizontally or vertically, making it so that the tiles will not be in strict rows and columns but will instead be staggered, like seats in a movie theater.

To reduce the sharpness of the tiled image, you can increase the Smoothness value. To increase the detail included in each tile, you can increase the Sample Detail value. To see where the tile boundaries are (which isn't always obvious), click the Tile Boundaries check box.

After each set of changes is made, you can click the Generate Again button and the new changes will be implemented. All the patterns you create are saved in the Tile History box at the bottom right of the Pattern Maker dialog box. This lets you go back to any previous iteration, in case successive edits have sent you farther afield than what you had been going for.



## Saving Patterns

If you click OK, the currently selected pattern will be applied to the entire image.

To save a pattern without applying it to the image, click the (increasingly anachronistic) floppy disk icon at the bottom left of the Tile History box (see Figure 19.27).

If you save your pattern, you can select it from the Patterns palette in the Fill dialog box (see Figure 19.28), or you can paint the pattern using the Pattern Stamp tool.

> The Tile History box only saves a single tile, not the entire pattern. When you select a different tile from Tile History, the Pattern Maker regenerates the pattern from that tile.

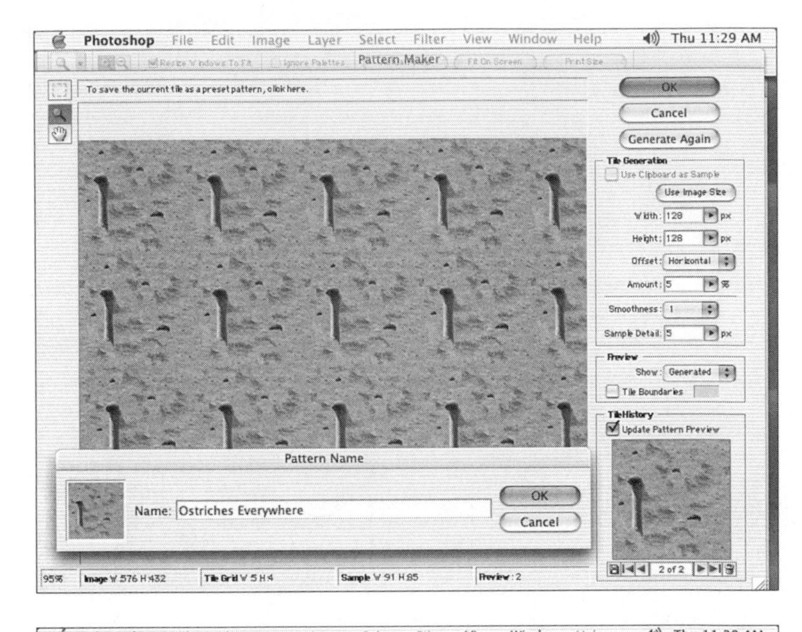


**Figure 19.27**
Click the floppy disk icon at the bottom left of the Title History area to save the current pattern to your Custom Patterns library.

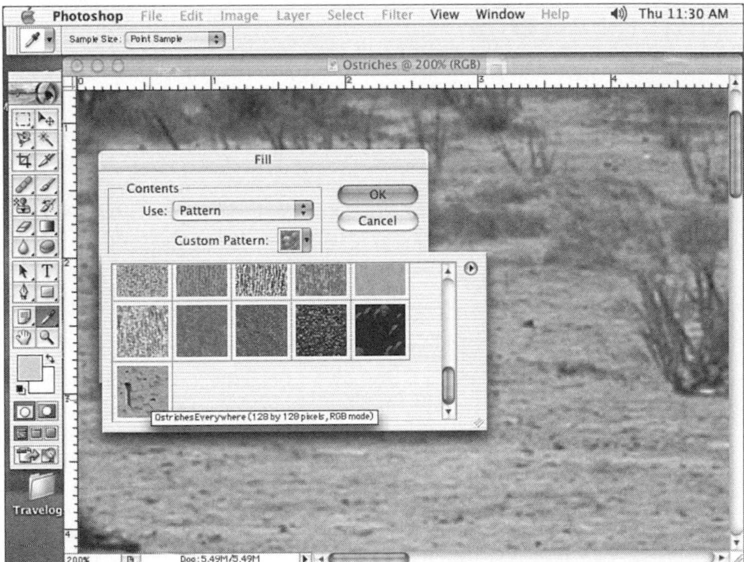


**Figure 19.28**
A saved pattern can be accessed in the Fill dialog box, via the Pattern Stamp tool, or anywhere else you can apply a custom pattern.



# MASTERING PHOTOSHOP

## Looking Sharp

*Is there an advantage to using the Unsharp Mask filter (or any sharpening filter) on individual channels?*

There can be. Unsharp masking can cause color shifts in an image, especially images in CMYK mode. To sharpen just the brightness component of an image rather than the color components of an image, convert the image to Lab mode (Image, Mode, Lab Color), select the Lightness channel in the Channels palette, and apply the Unsharp Mask to just the Lightness channel.

Another option is to apply the Unsharp Mask to just the Black channel (if you are in CMYK mode). This restricts any color shifts to just black—where they are scarcely detectable.

You can also combine the Unsharp Mask with blending modes via the Fade command. Another way to reduce color artifacts from cropping up in images following an Unsharp Mask operation is to immediately go to Edit, Fade Unsharp Mask and then change the blending mode to Luminosity. This lets you apply the Unsharp Mask filter to just the brightness of the image—without having to change color modes.

## Weapons of Mass Extraction

*I really don't want to lose the pixels in the background portion of the image I extract an object from. Do I have to?*

Nope. You can extract an image and simply mask out the background pixels. Here's the trick: First, copy the background layer. In the Layers palette, hide the copied layer by clicking the eyeball icon. Go back to the original background layer and do your extracting. After extraction, use the Magic Wand tool to select the transparent area (that is, the ex-background). If there are any "punch-through" areas, be sure to select them, too. Choose Select, Save Selection and save a mask of the selected area(s). Now delete the extracted layer (don't worry—you really won't need it anymore). In the copied layer you made earlier, choose Select, Load Selection and select the mask you just created. Go to Layer, Add Layer Mask, Hide Selection. Now you have just hidden the background from the extracted image rather than destroying the background.



## Patterns of Force

*I like the Pattern Maker and all, but I really just want to do a simple set of repeating tiles. How do I do that?*

By selecting Filter, Other, Offset. This will divide your image into a set of tiles (see Figure 19.29).

The secret to this filter is to pick a horizontal and vertical offset that is half of the corresponding pixel dimension. The image will be divided into fourths; the point of doing this is to clean up any sharp lines between the tiles so that when the image is itself tiled, the edges aren't as obvious. Once you've cleaned up the tile, reselect the Offset filter. Without adjusting your settings, click OK. Now, this may seem like you're just re-creating your original image, but you have actually softened the edges. Therefore, when the image is tiled, it will blend more seamlessly with copies of itself.

Go to Edit, Define Pattern and add the pattern to the library. If you then fill a blank document with the pattern, the tiles will blend less distractingly (see Figure 19.30).

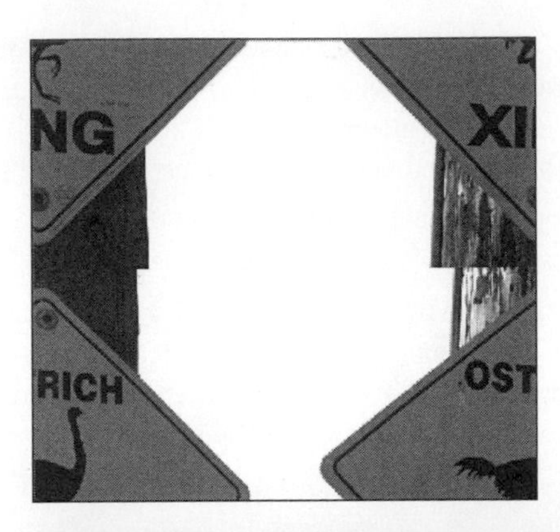


**Figure 19.29**
The Offset filter creates a set of tiles from an image.

**Figure 19.30**
The offset image has been tiled using a pattern fill.

*by Richard Romano*

# ADDING SPECIAL EFFECTS WITH THE FILTER GALLERY AND THE CREATIVE FILTERS

## IN THIS CHAPTER

Chapter 14, "Selecting and Applying Filters," was an introduction to Photoshop's filters and the Filter Gallery in particular. Chapter 19, "Repairing and Enhancing Images with the Production Filters," was a detailed look at how images can be repaired and enhanced using the "production" filters. In this chapter, we will take a closer look at the creative filters, or those filters that let you apply an infinite variety of creative effects to images. We'll also look a bit more closely at using filters in conjunction with other Photoshop tools, such as blending modes. In a nutshell, this chapter is less about fixing images to make them suitable for use and more about using filters to unleash one's creativity. In other words, this is the chapter in which we get to have a bit of fun.

# THE FILTER GALLERY REVISITED

Chapter 14 provided an overview of how the Filter Gallery is set up and how it works. Here, we will plumb the depths of the filters a bit more deeply, although I hasten to add that a detailed look at the ins and outs of every filter is beyond the scope of this chapter. Besides, more than half the fun of working with Photoshop and the filters in particular is trying things on your own. But, then again, you didn't plunk down money for a book that tells you to just go play, so think of this chapter as providing some distinctive highlights to whet your appetite for further experimentation.

If you select Filter, Filter Gallery, you get the Filter Gallery.

*For a detailed "anatomy" of the Filter Gallery, see Chapter 14.*

The Filter Gallery contains six folders of filters:

- Artistic
- Brush Strokes
- Distort
- Sketch
- Stylize
- Texture



The sections that follow talk about the filters contained in the Filter Gallery folders and their effects. Here are a few points to keep in mind when working with the Filter Gallery:

- When you select Filter, Filter Gallery, the Filter Gallery opens onto the last filter you applied, with the last settings you applied.
- Holding down the (Option) [Alt] key changes the Cancel button to a Reset button. Clicking Reset resets the Filter Gallery to whatever filter and settings were active when you entered the Filter Gallery, in case your filtering has gone horribly astray.

All the filters in the Filter Gallery can also be accessed individually via the Filter menu. Selecting one of the filters from the submenus that correspond to Filter Gallery folders will bring you into the Filter Gallery.

- Holding down the (Command) [Ctrl] key changes the Cancel button to a Default button. Clicking Default clears whatever filters and settings you have applied, giving you a blank slate on which to start anew.

# The Artistic Filters

As the folder name indicates, these filters apply painting- and drawing-like effects to images. Many of these filters can be a bit too strong for some people's tastes; in many cases, you'll want to duplicate the layer to which you want to apply them, apply the filters to the copied layer, and decrease the Opacity of that layer so that the net effect of the filters is "half-strength" or so. The best use of a filter will, of course, depend on the image in question, but if you like the *idea* of a filter's effect but think the full-strength version is too potent, try this approach to tone the effect down a bit.

## Colored Pencil

Case in point: the Colored Pencil filter. This is a really cool filter that is used to turn a photograph into a colored pencil drawing. But at full strength, it is far too overwhelming. Decreasing the Pencil Width setting adds more detail, increasing the Stroke Pressure setting darkens the details, and increasing the Paper Brightness setting lightens the background. The "raw" filter applied to an image is shown in Figure 20.1.

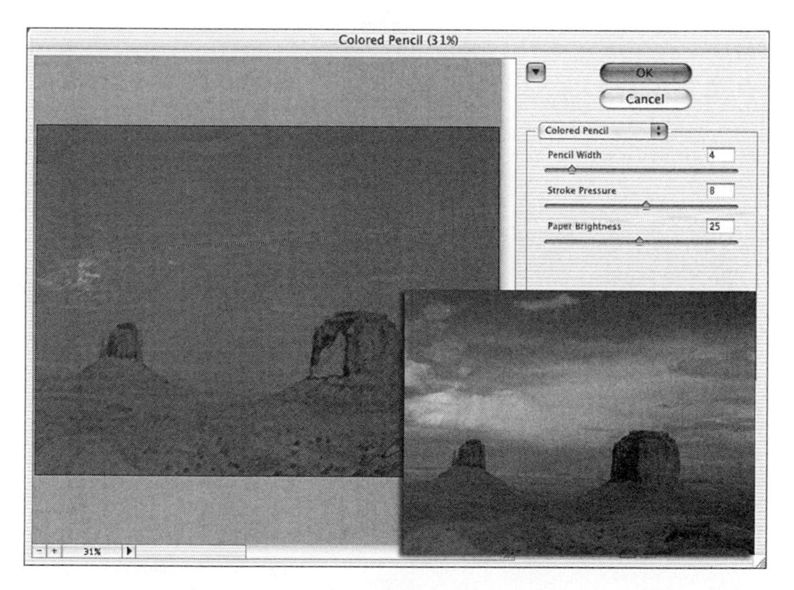


**Figure 20.1**
The Colored Pencil filter, applied to the original image (inset), is a bit too strong.

Changing the blending mode of the filtered layer to Screen and decreasing Opacity to about 60% gives the image a nice, bright, hand-sketched look (see Figure 20.2).

**Figure 20.2**
Changing the blending mode and decreasing the Opacity setting makes the effect of the Colored Pencil filter more pleasing.

## Cutout

If you aren't very proficient at using Illustrator, but want an image to have the look of artwork you created with that program, you can either read Part V of this book or use the Cutout filter. The Cutout filter has the effect of posterizing photographic images. *Posterizing* refers to reducing all the gradations of shade and color into a few sections of flat color. The Number of Levels, Edge Simplicity, and Edge Fidelity sliders all increase or decrease the level of detail and the number of colors the filter applies to the image.

## Dry Brush

Despite the name of this filter, it's actually good for creating pseudo-watercolor artwork, especially watercolors with an Impressionistic sort of feel (see Figure 20.3).

**Figure 20.3**
The Dry Brush filter is good for creating ersatz watercolors.

Again, applying the filter to a duplicate layer and then taking down the Opacity (just a skosh) brings out a little more detail from the original background image (see Figure 20.4).

After you've read Part V, "Illustrator CS," you can import an image filtered with the Cutout filter into Illustrator and autotrace the artwork to create actual vector-based artwork.

## Film Grain

Photographers who have made the transition to digital cameras sometimes miss the effect of having film grain visible in images. For those who want to live in the past, the Film Grain filter can add a touch of grain-based noise (you don't want to overdo it, of course). The secret to this filter is to apply it to a copy of the background and use the Lighten blending mode to make the effect even more subtle.

**Figure 20.4**
By adjusting the filtered layer's Opacity setting, you bring out a bit more detail in the image.

## Fresco

If you're an aspiring Giotto, why bother learning how to make plaster and apply paint to it, when you can use the Fresco filter? For a little of that straight-from-the-Uffizi feel, take down the Brush Size slider and boost the Brush Detail and the Texture sliders (see Figure 20.5).

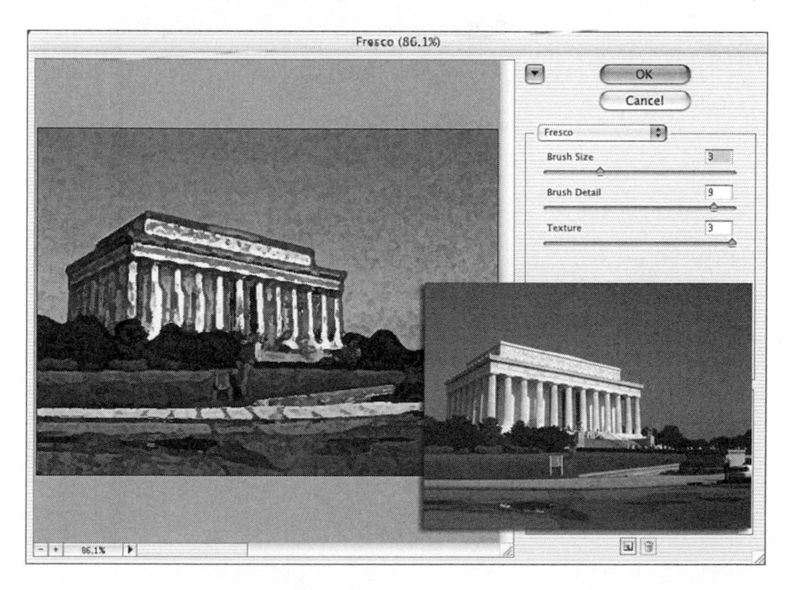


**Figure 20.5**
Painting al fresco. The Fresco filter gives any image that little taste of Florence.

## Neon Glow

Neon Glow suffuses an image with a glow whose color you can customize using the Color Picker, accessed though the Filter Gallery.

> When using the Neon Glow filter, try applying the filter to a duplicate of the background layer and then using the Difference blending mode. This essentially applies a "negative" version of the filter, which produces a more interesting effect than the filter by itself.

## Paint Daubs

Aspiring Rembrandts can avail themselves of the Paint Daubs filter, which makes images look as if they have been painted with thick globs of paint. You can control the brush size and sharpness (to bring out more or less detail) as well as choose from a variety of brush styles (see Figure 20.6).

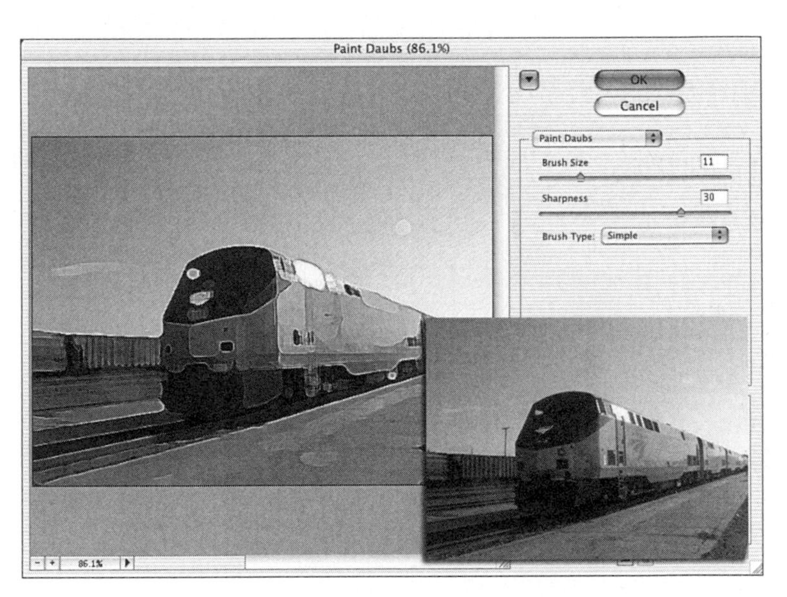


Figure 20.6
Van Rijn's Express. The Paint Daubs filter gives the illusion that a photo has been painted with thick globs of paint.

## Palette Knife

The Palette Knife filter gives the illusion that an image has been painted not with a brush but with a palette knife, and thus has a distinct lack of detail.

20

## Plastic Wrap

The Plastic Wrap filter, perhaps used in packaging applications, gives objects in images the illusion of having been shrink-wrapped.

## Poster Edges

As its name implies, this filter gives images a posterized sort of appearance—much like the Cutout filter. The difference is that this filter adds thick black lines to edges, giving images a cartoon-like effect.

## Rough Pastels

Rough Pastels gives images the look and feel of having been drawn with pastels on a textured surface. You can adjust the Stroke Length and the Stroke Detail sliders, as well as the specific texture (brick, burlap, canvas, or sandstone), the degree of relief, and the light source. You can also choose to load your own texture if you so desire (see Figure 20.7).

**Figure 20.7**
The Rough Pastels filter gives images a pastel-sketched feel.

This is another filter that is nice to use on a duplicate layer with an adjusted blending mode to tone it down.

## Smudge Stick

The principle of the Smudge Stick is a smudged pastel drawing, which gives photos an old-fashioned hand-drawn portrait effect.

## Sponge

The Sponge filter gives the illusion that an image was painted by dabbing a sponge on canvas. You can adjust the brush size (er, sponge size, actually), the definition, and the smoothness. This is another filter best used on a duplicate layer with an opacity and/or blending mode adjustment.



## Underpainting

This filter applies a texture to the image, not unlike the Rough Pastels filter. The primary difference is that Underpainting tends to affect primarily midtones. This is yet another filter that tends to come on a little strong and is most pleasingly handled via an opacity/blending mode adjustment.

## Watercolor

The Watercolor filter gives images the look of a watercolor painting. Brush detail, shadow intensity, and texture can all be controlled (see Figure 20.8).

Figure 20.8
The Watercolor filter, perhaps true to its name, tends to saturate colors—a little more than is desirable.

Taking down the Opacity setting a bit helps make this filter pleasing (see Figure 20.9).

Figure 20.9
The Watercolor filter works nicely with the Opacity setting decreased a skosh.



# The Brush Strokes Filters

The Brush Strokes filters, true to their name, replicate a variety of drawing and painting brush strokes. All the brush strokes vary somewhat in their controls, but they all let you control things such as stroke length and sharpness. You also can control the brush strokes' intensity, which determines how much or how little detail from the original is retained.

The Filter Gallery includes these Brush Strokes filters:

- **Accented Edges**—Applies thick paint strokes to edges within images, with varying degrees of intensity.
- **Angled Strokes**—Paints an image with colored pencil–like strokes of varying direction.
- **Crosshatch**—Replicates a colored pencil or crosshatched sketch.
- **Dark Strokes**—No mystery here: The Dark Strokes filter applies thick dark strokes to edges within images. The trick to this filter is to use it sparingly so that the whole image doesn't get too murky.

The Artistic filters provide nice effects onscreen but will look even better when printed on an inkjet printer using special art paper, such as watercolor paper or canvas. Don't let nice artistic images languish on your hard drive. Print them for everyone to enjoy!

- **Ink Outlines**—Traces an outline around and offset from the edges within the image (see Figure 20.10).

**Figure 20.10**
The trick with the Ink Outlines filter is to ensure that the effect of Dark Intensity isn't too overpowering.

- **Spatter**—Spatter gives images the look of having been created by a spatter airbrush. At low resolutions, the actual effect can look more like a distort filter than the kind of pseudo-pointillist effect it's trying for (see Figure 20.11).
- **Sprayed Strokes**—Similar to Spatter, Sprayed Strokes has an airbrush-generated look, spraying the dominant colors in the image in angled strokes.
- **Sumi-e**—This gives images a black-ink-on-rice-paper kind of look, intended to be reminiscent of a Japanese style of painting. It is most effective on simple images without tremendous amounts of fine detail.

Figure 20.11
The Spatter filter sprays the pixels around the image with varying levels of smoothness and spray radius.

Like the Artistic filters, the Brush Strokes filters also yield the best results when you apply them to a copied layer and adjust the Opacity and/or blending mode.

# The Distort Filters

Although the Distort submenu actually contains 12 filters, only three of them are available through the Filter Gallery: Diffuse Glow, Glass, and Ocean Ripple.

## Diffuse Glow

Not technically a Distort filter per se, Diffuse Glow seems to have more in common with the Neon Glow filter in the Artistic filters submenu. Be that as it may, this filter gives objects the look of being viewed through a soft filter. It adds white noise and graininess to an image, fading the glow from the center of the object outward (see Figure 20.12).

This filter can be good to use on a single object within an image, especially one that has been extracted and pasted on a new layer (see Figure 21.13).



## Glass

The Glass filter gives an image the illusion of being viewed through different types of glass. You can tweak the scaling, distortion, and smoothness, and you can choose from a variety of types of glass types. You also can create and load your own glass surface.

## Ocean Ripple

Ocean Ripple, true to its name, lets you add ripples to an image. This filter is designed to make objects look as if they are underwater. The Ripple Size and the Magnitude sliders can be adjusted, depending on how "choppy" you want the ocean to be.

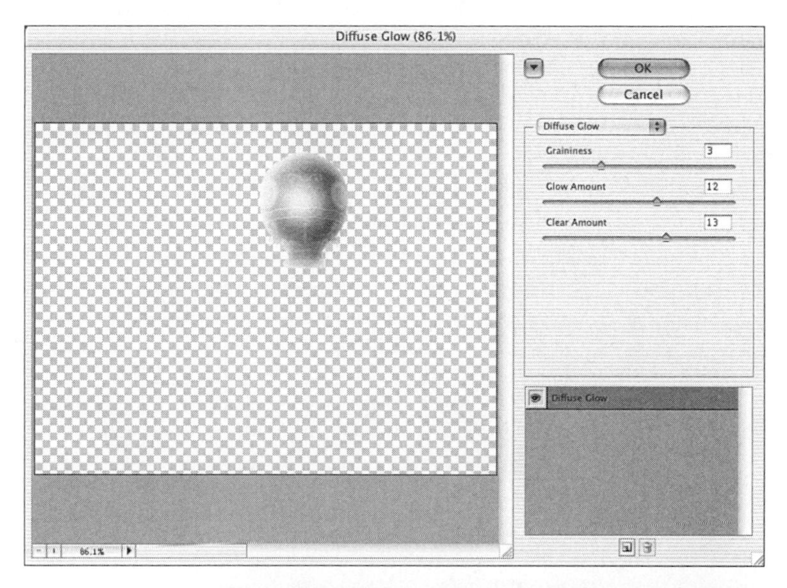


**Figure 20.12**
The Diffuse Glow filter adds noise and graininess to provide the illusion of a soft glow emanating from the center of an object.

**Figure 20.13**
Adding the Diffuse Glow filter to just the extracted layer (the balloon) and adjusting the Opacity setting and blending mode (and perhaps adding feathering to the edge or even tracing over the edge with a very soft Blur tool brush) can give the illusion of a ghost balloon in the sky.

## The Sketch Filters

Just as other filters can let you make your images look like paintings or drawings, the 14 filters in the Sketch submenu can let you make images look like rough sketches of varying types. You can use the Bas Relief, Chrome, and Photocopy filters in this submenu to give images 3D effects, textures, or other primarily two-color effects (which aren't really "sketch" effects per se).

Most of the Sketch filters are based on two colors, using whatever foreground color you have defined for dark areas of the image and whatever background color you have selected for light areas. If possible, pick your two colors before entering the Filter Gallery, because in order to change colors you'll need to cancel out of the Gallery and reenter it when your color change has been made.



### Bas Relief

The Bas Relief filter uses the light and dark portions of an image to create the illusion of a relief sculpture. The height of the relief portions of the image can be adjusted, as can the light direction. The secret to using this filter effectively is to make sure your image has distinct light and dark areas.

## Chalk & Charcoal

This filter converts an image into a chalk and charcoal sketch. The background is rendered in coarse gray chalk, and foreground objects are rendered in charcoal. You can vary the amount of charcoal used versus the amount of chalk used (see Figure 20.14). Charcoal strokes are applied in the foreground color you have selected, whereas chalk strokes are applied in the background color you have defined. Black (or dark gray) and white are the traditional choices for this filter, but you can choose whatever combination of colors you'd like.

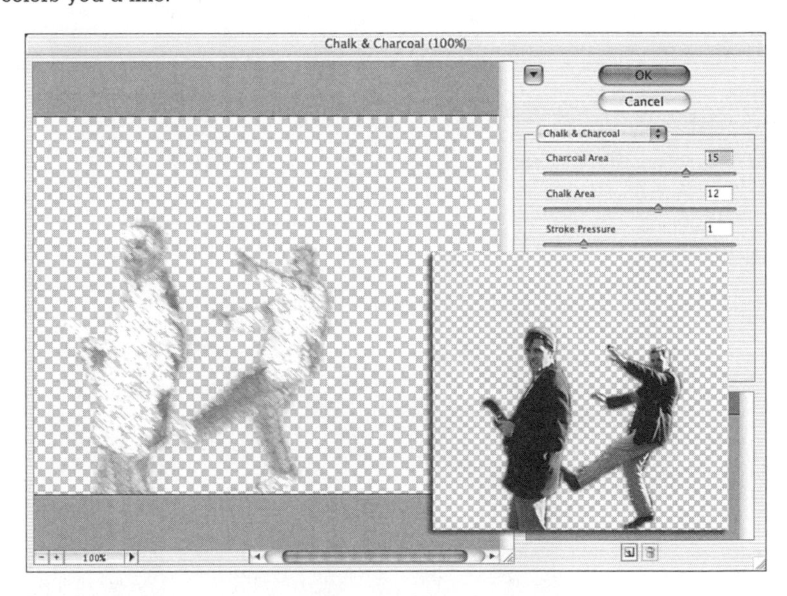


**Figure 20.14**
Chalk & Charcoal can give a hand-sketched feel to images. In this case, making the foreground color white and the background color gray yielded the best results with this image.

By extracting or otherwise isolating part of an image, placing it on a new layer, and applying the filter to the new layer only, you can achieve some interesting special effects (see Figure 20.15).

**Figure 20.15**
A-ha! Applying the Chalk & Charcoal filter to two figures in an image gives a cartoonishly ghostly feel to the image.

## Charcoal

Charcoal is not unlike the Chalk & Charcoal filter, sans chalk. The effect is a more posterized, smudged look than the Chalk & Charcoal filter. Edges are thickly drawn. Charcoal is applied using the foreground color, and the paper is rendered using the background color.

## Chrome

This filter converts an image to polished metal. You can control the detail and the smoothness of the effect. This filter is best used on an extracted or otherwise isolated object in an image. However, applying the Chrome filter to an entire image is a good, quick way to create a textured metal background.

## Conté Crayon

A Conté crayon is a brand of crayon made of graphite and clay, and usually available in black, brown, and red. The Conté Crayon filter draws images in this style, giving images a rough-textured illustration effect. The filter uses the selected foreground color for dark areas of the image and the background color for light areas.

## Graphic Pen

The Graphic Pen filter applies fine, straight pen strokes to give images a pen-drawn look. This filter uses the selected foreground color for the color of the strokes and the selected background color for the color of the paper. You can control the length of the stroke, the light and dark balance, and the direction of the stroke.

## Halftone Pattern

The Halftone Pattern filter simulates an exaggerated halftone dot pattern. You can adjust the size of the dots, the contrast, and the shape of the dot pattern. This filter is useful for simulating the look of old newspaper photos or Roy Lichtenstein paintings.

## Note Paper

This filter is sort of a combination of the Emboss filter and the Grain filter, and it gives images a handmade paper feel. Light areas of the image are rendered in relief (see Figure 20.16).

## Photocopy

To give images the look of a 30th-generation photocopy, you can spend hours at the Xerox machine or you can simply apply the Photocopy filter. You can control the level of detail or, essentially, how many times it appears to have been copied.

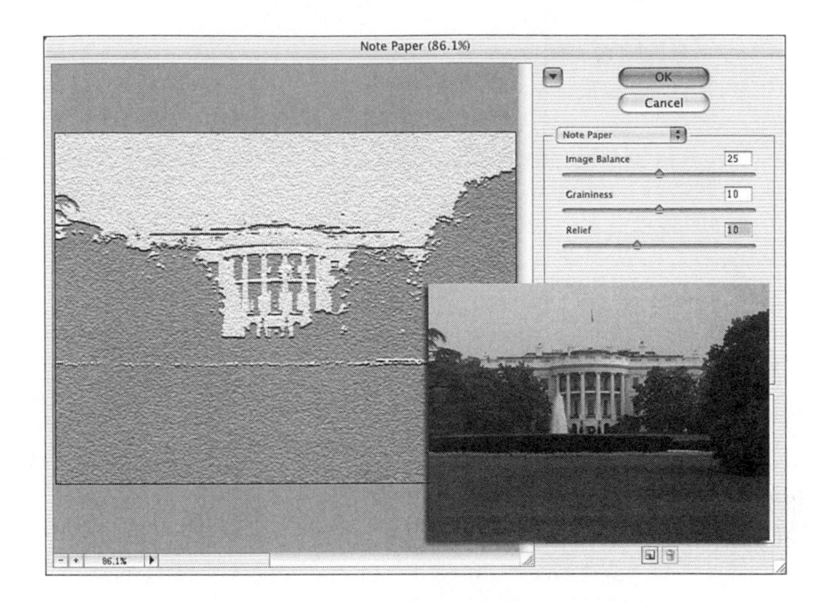


Figure 20.16
The Note Paper filter gives images a handmade paper feel.

## Plaster

This filter creates textured effects that, truth be told, aren't abundantly reminiscent of plaster, but they are interesting nonetheless. You can control the light/dark balance, the smoothness, and the direction of the light source (see Figure 20.17).

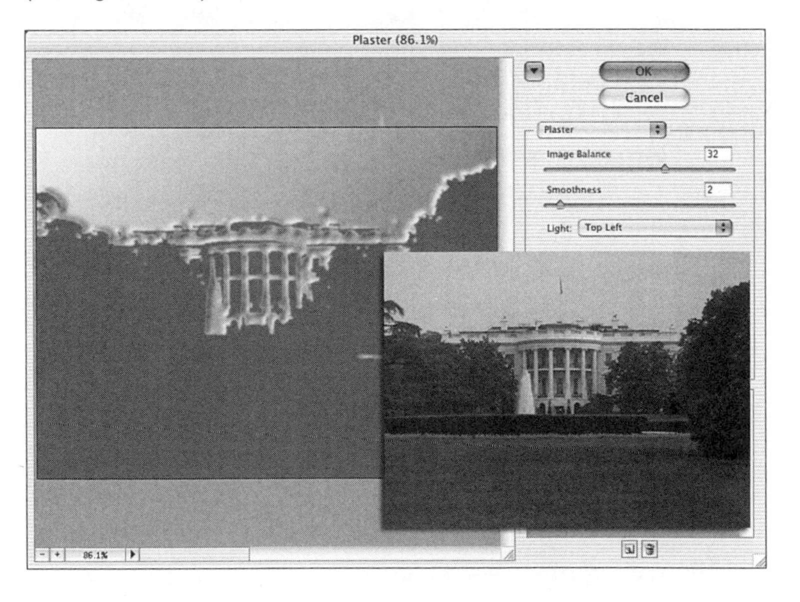


Figure 20.17
The Plaster filter is not apprecia-bly plaster-like, but the 3D effect is nice.

## Reticulation

This filter is said to simulate the shrinking and distorting of film emulsion. In practical application, it can be used to simulate a kind of pointillist illustration.

> Adding an effect layer, choosing a Texture filter such as Craquelure (which you learn about later in this chapter), and placing it on top of the Plaster effect layer can provide a more realistic plaster-like effect.

## Stamp

This filter simulates the look of a rubber or wood stamp, creating a silhouette based on image contrast. This filter is best used on simple illustrations that have large, obvious changes in contrast. Otherwise, this filter will just generate a big blob.

*Can you create custom shapes using the Stamp filter? See "Stamps of Approval" in the "Mastering Photoshop" section at the end of this chapter.*

## Torn Edges

Despite the name of this filter, it doesn't really create an edge effect, or at least not around the edges of the image itself. Rather, like the Stamp filter, it creates a torn-edge effect on edges within the image, seeking out high-contrast areas to which to apply the effect.

## Water Paper

The only full-color filter in the Sketch submenu, the Water Paper filter gives images the effect of watercolor paint on porous paper, complete with bleeding colors and visible paper fibers. Like the Artistic filters, this filter is best used on a duplicate layer with the opacity and blending mode adjusted.

# The Stylize Filter

Although there are nine filters in the Filter, Stylize submenu, the Filter Gallery only includes one of them—which happens to be my favorite: Glowing Edges. The Glowing Edges filter turns any image into what resembles a neon light sculpture, finding areas of high contrast and painting the edges between them with neon tubes (see Figure 20.18).

*For a detailed look at some of the other Stylize filters, see "Additional Creative Filters: Pixelate, Render, and Stylize," later in this chapter, p. 657.*



# The Texture Filters

The six Texture filters available in the Filter Gallery let you add surface effects to images. Like many other filters, the Texture filters are often most effectively used by applying them to a duplicate layer and adjusting the opacity and/or blending mode.

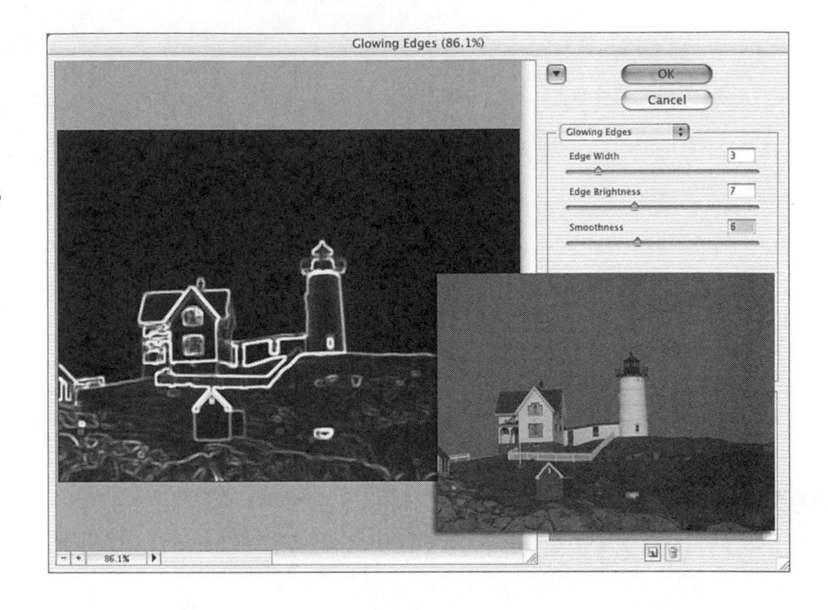


**Figure 20.18**
This is much cooler in color (see the color signature in this book). The Glowing Edges filter can make even a seaside location in Maine look like part of the Vegas Strip.

## Craquelure

The word *craquelure* is defined as "a network of fine cracks or crackles on the surface of a painting caused chiefly by shrinkage of paint film or varnish." That's the official definition, but the filter itself is designed to simulate an image painted onto a rough plaster surface that exhibits the network of fine cracks. Increasing the Crack Spacing slider decreases the overall number of cracks—the image becomes progressively more "uncracked" the higher the Crack Spacing number. Increasing the Crack Depth, though, does indeed increase the crack depth. Decreasing the Crack Brightness slider makes the cracks more pronounced (see Figure 20.19).

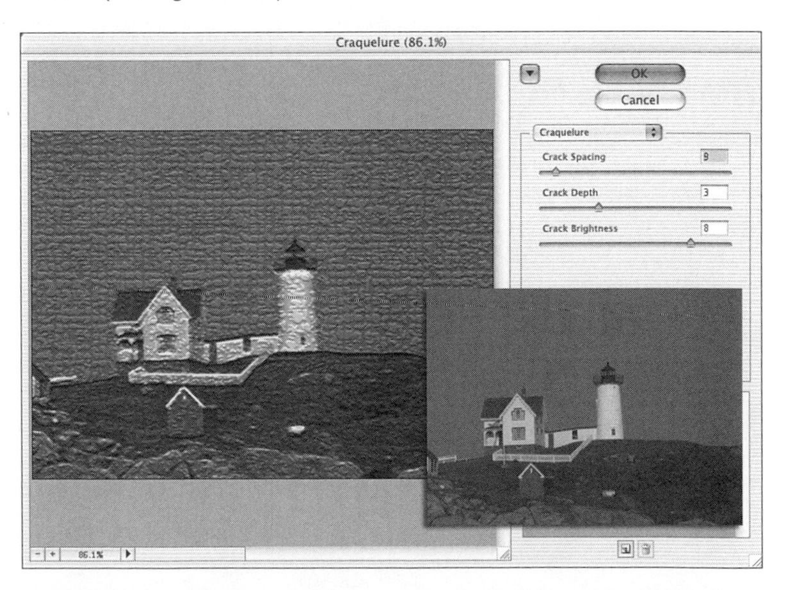


**Figure 20.19**
The Craquelure filter paints the image onto a rough, cracked plaster surface.

## Grain

The Grain filter lets you add a variety of different types of grain to an image—soft, sprinkles, clumped, contrasty, enlarged, stippled, speckle, horizontal or vertical, and of course regular. You can also adjust the intensity and the contrast of the grain that is added. The upshot of this filter is that it adds texture, or a sense of age or motion to an image (see Figure 20.20).

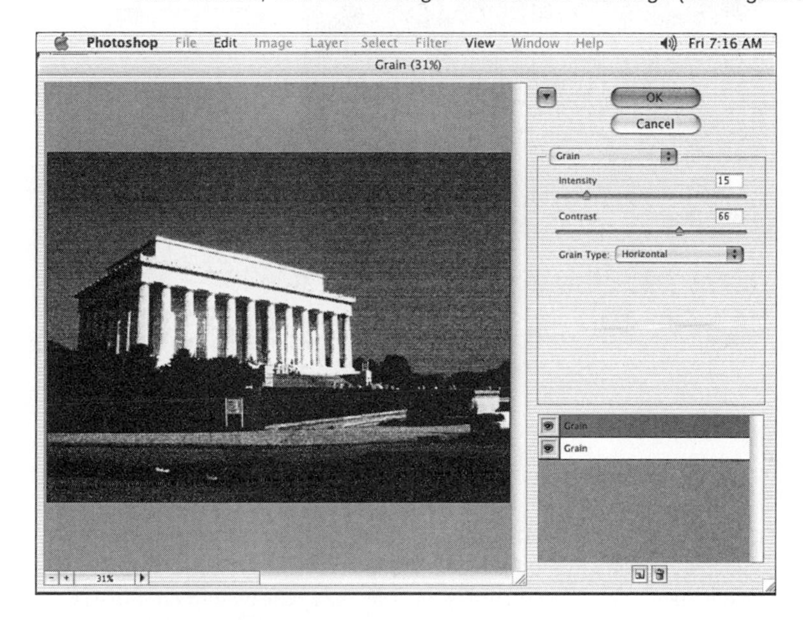


**Figure 20.20**
The Grain filter can be used to add texture, age, or motion to an image. In this case, two effect layers combined Grain effects—Horizontal and Sprinkles—to artificially age this image.

## Mosaic Tiles

At first glance, the Mosaic Tiles filter isn't appreciably different from the Craquelure filter, but Mosaic Tiles creates a more controlled grid pattern. You can adjust the tile size and the "grout" width, and you can lighten or darken the grout (see Figure 20.21).

## Patchwork

Depending on the source images, the Patchwork filter can replicate either a kind of small mosaic/bathroom tile effect or needlework. (And isn't it a fine line, really?) The former tends to be the case with images that have a lot of detail, whereas the latter tends to be the case with images that are fairly simple (see the color signature in this book).

> To make images simple enough to get the most out of the Patchwork filter, try removing color variations. You can use this filter in conjunction with a Poster Edges or Cutout effect layer, or you can select a color range and use Filter, Blur, Average to manually posterize portions of the image.

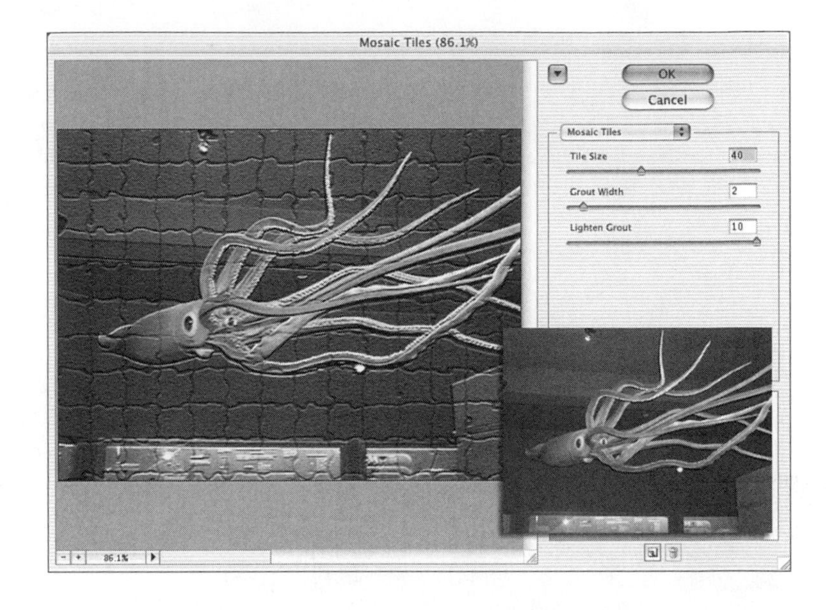


**Figure 20.21**
The Mosaic Tiles filter lets you control the grid and grout spacing more carefully than the Craquelure filter.

## Stained Glass

The Stained Glass filter divides an image up into randomly shaped hexagonal cells, whose size can be increased or decreased. The border between each cell is given the color of whatever foreground color you have selected, and the border thickness can be adjusted, as well. The ultimate effect isn't tremendously reminiscent of stained glass (and probably wouldn't pass muster at Notre Dame cathedral). Instead, it's rather like small, colorful mosaic tiles and can be a cool effect nonetheless. Come to think of it, though, it does tend to give images a sort of Tiffany lamp look.

## Texturizer

Texturizer is an all-purpose texture-generation filter. You can select brick, burlap, canvas, or sandstone (or load your own texture). You can also adjust the scaling, the relief, and the direction of the light source.

# Photoshop at Work: Customized Effect Layers

When you add effect layers in the Filter Gallery, you have no way of changing the opacity or blending mode of those filters; each filter is combined at full strength. As you've seen with many of these filters, full-strength effects can often be far too potent. Here's a way to create your own highly controllable effect layers:

> Any number of the texture filters can be combined by adding effect layers in the Filter Gallery. For a detailed look at how to combine filters using effect layers, see Chapter 14.

1. With an image open, go to the Layers palette and select Duplicate from the Layers palette menu.
2. Making sure the background layer is highlighted, select Duplicate again. You now have two copies of the background layer.

3. Hide the topmost layer by clicking the eyeball icon.
4. Click the middle layer to select it as the working layer and go to Filter, Filter Gallery.
5. Select a filter—say, Colored Pencil from the Artistic folder. Select a combination of Pencil Width, Stroke Pressure, and Paper Brightness that is to your liking. Then click OK. The Filter effect will only be applied to the selected layer.
6. For easy reference, double-click the name of the layer to which you just applied the effect and give it the name of the filter you just applied.
7. Reduce the Opacity slider in the Layers palette to 50%. This applies the filter at half strength, retaining much of the original image detail and color qualities.
8. Select the other copy of the background layer in the Layers palette and go back to Filter, Filter Gallery.
9. Choose another filter—say, Bas Relief from the Sketch folder. Adjust the Detail and Smoothness sliders and select a light direction from the Light pop-up menu. Click OK when the settings are to your liking.
10. Repeat steps 6 and 7 with the layer to which you just added the second effect. Adjust the blending modes, opacities, and even the layer stacking order and see how the different effect layers you just created interact with each other. You can also add as many other effect layers as you'd like.

With this manual effect layer approach, you can combine filters that aren't available via the Filter Gallery, too, adding an Ocean Ripple filter to a Watercolor filter, for example. The possibilities are endless.

# ADDITIONAL CREATIVE FILTERS: PIXELATE, RENDER, AND STYLIZE

The Filter Gallery represents only about half the filters available in Photoshop. Many other creative filters are available via the Filter menu. Some other creative filters worth looking at include the following:

- Pixelate filters
- Render filters
- Stylize filters



## Pixelate Filters

The Pixelate filters function by grouping pixels having a similar color together and inflicting cool and unusual punishment on them. The Pixelate filters apply a number of creative effects, including (among others) halftone, mezzotint, and pointillize. The following subsections discuss these filters in detail.

## Color Halftone

The Color Halftone filter is not used to produce color separations or generate the actual printing halftones. It's merely a special effect.

When a continuous-tone image (such as a photograph) is printed on a printing press, it needs to be converted to what is known as a *halftone*, or a series of dots whose sizes vary, thus producing the illusion of a continuous-tone image. Each of the four color separations used in process color printing (cyan, magenta, yellow, and black) needs its own set of halftone dots, which are printed at certain angles to each other so as to minimize the visibility of them. When four-color dots are overlaid properly, they form a four-color dot pattern called a *rosette*. In ideal color printing, these rosette patterns are not visible unless looked at through a loupe.

However, some designers and other creative types like to use the rosette or halftone pattern itself as a design motif—and thus enlarge and exaggerate the halftone pattern. The Color Halftone filter accomplishes this by simulating large rosette patterns.

## Crystallize

The Crystallize filter has an effect similar to that of the Stained Glass filter you read about earlier, except that it doesn't put any leading between the cells. As with the Stained Glass filter, you can vary the cell size.

## Facet

Facet clumps groups of similarly colored pixels together to make an image look hand-painted. The Facet filter doesn't have a palette; it applies its own predetermined amount of "faceting." As with other filters, that lack of controllability ends up being less than useful.

## Fragment

Perhaps also called the Nausea filter, Fragment creates four copies of the pixels in any given selection (or the entire image), averages them, and then offsets them from each other. This gives the illusion of movement or vibration—or of being able to see the world the way Dean Martin saw it.



## Mezzotint

Interestingly (or perhaps not), the word *mezzotint* is Italian for *halftone*. The difference between the terms as they're used in Photoshop (and in printing), though, is that mezzotint refers to the creative use of converting an image into a pattern of dots, whereas halftone refers to the strict print production use.

Be that as it may, the Mezzotint filter converts an image to a random pattern of dots or lines. You can select the dot or line pattern from the Type pop-up menu.

## Mosaic

Not to be confused with Mosaic Tiles, the effect of using the Mosaic filter is to clump pixels into big chunky blocks (considered "cells"), and this looks like what happens when an image is printed at too low a resolution. You can adjust the size of the cells, and this filter is useful for blurring people's faces to keep them anonymous (see Figure 20.22).

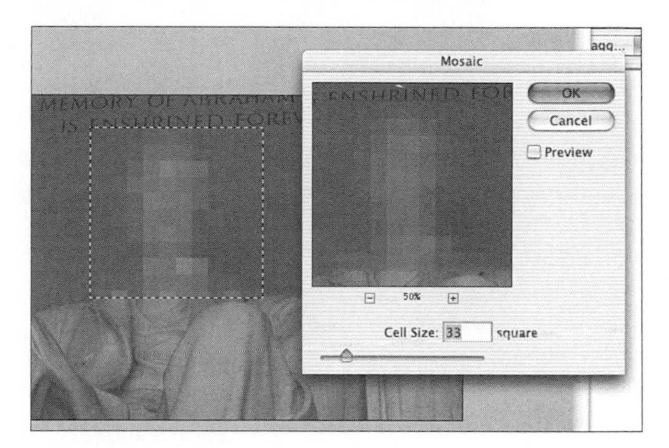


Figure 20.22
Who is it? The Mosaic filter can keep people anonymous.

## Pointillize

Pointillism, an offshoot of Impressionism, made famous by French painter Georges Seurat (especially in his 1886 painting *Sunday Afternoon on the Island of La Grande Jatte*), was based on the idea of portraying the play of light using miniscule brushstrokes of different colors. The Pointillize filter doesn't quite have the same effect (the idea of pointillism wasn't necessarily to see the dots, but perhaps it depended on the output resolution of the artist). However, you can achieve some interesting effects by breaking down an image into tiny dots of color (see Figure 20.23).

Figure 20.23
The Pointillize filter breaks images down into small dots of color.

# The Render Filters

The Render filters are a hodgepodge of different filters that add cloud patterns, textures, backgrounds, and lighting effects.

## Clouds

Yes, if you need to add clouds to an image, here is where you would do it. This filter generates a cloud pattern based on the foreground and background colors currently defined. For a less "overcast" cloud pattern, hold down the (Option) [Alt] key while selecting Filter, Render, Clouds.

The Clouds filter replaces everything in a layer with the clouds, so it is best used on a blank layer, with the opacity and/or blending layer adjusted.

## Difference Clouds

The Difference Clouds filter combines the principle of the Clouds filter with the Difference blending mode. Unlike the Clouds filter, which replaces the pixels on the layer to which it is applied, the Difference Clouds filter adds clouds to an existing image. Applying the filter once yields a negative-image effect, but applying it a second time creates a better effect (see Figure 20.24).

**Figure 20.24**
The Difference Clouds filter, when applied once (bottom left), yields a negative-image effect. When applied a second time (bottom right), it yields an eerie, impending storm effect. The choice of image—and the color qualities therein—will be a big determinant of the specific effect this filter has.



## Fibers

A new Render filter added in Photoshop CS is the Fibers filter. This filter basically creates the illusion of fibers in the image surface, as in paper fibers. The size, distribution, and contrast of the fibers can be adjusted by moving the Variance and Strength sliders. The color of the fibers themselves is based on the foreground color currently selected, whereas the background of the fibers is based on the currently selected background color. There is also a Randomize button, so the fibers can be made to seem less regular (see Figure 20.25).

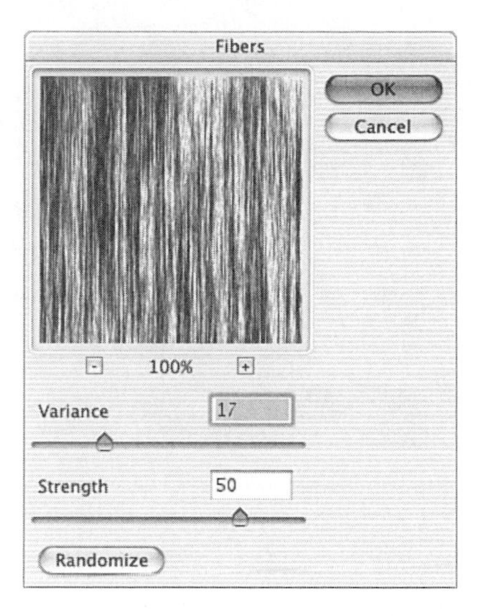


Figure 20.25
The Fibers filter lets you create a paper fiber-based texture that can be intermingled with an image.

This filter is best used on a blank layer with the opacity and/or blending mode adjusted (see Figure 20.26).

Figure 20.26
Using the Overlay blending mode and a 30% Opacity setting adds a fibrous texture to an image.



## Lens Flare

The Lens Flare filter simulates the refraction effect you get when a bright light shines into the camera lens. You can position the light source and the center of the flare by moving the crosshairs inside the preview window. You can also choose a lens type by clicking the radio buttons at the bottom of the Lens Flare filter palette (see Figure 20.27).

Figure 20.27
The Lens Flare filter lets you position a light source and add a refraction effect.

## Lighting Effects

The Lighting Effects filter lets you create myriad lighting effects on an image. You can use this filter to add a spotlight effect to highlight a specific part of an image or to adjust the entire lighting of a scene to change the mood.

# The Stylize Filters

The Stylize filters search out areas of high contrast (such as edges) and apply various types of effects on those areas. These effects can give images the look of being stamped or embossed, apply a hand-drawn look to images, break images into tiles, and add 3D effects to images.

## Diffuse

The Diffuse filter gives images a slightly out-of-focus look that goes beyond a simple blurring effect. The Normal mode shuffles pixels randomly. Darken Only replaces light pixels with dark pixels, and Lighten Only replaces dark pixels with light pixels. Anisotropic moves pixels in the direction of the least amount of color change; the effect is a softening, almost posterizing effect.



## Emboss

One of the most used of the Photoshop filters, Emboss is a utilitarian filter for making buttons or other elements that need a "stamped in metal" effect. The filter has three controls: the Angle wheel lets you set the angle of the emboss effect; the Height slider lets you set how much the object is embossed; and the Amount slider lets you set how pronounced the emboss effect is (that is, if it is lightly stamped or heavily stamped). Figure 20.28 shows an example.

Because the filter works by displacing edges, moving these sliders too far to the right tends to lose the emboss effect in favor of a "double-vision" effect.

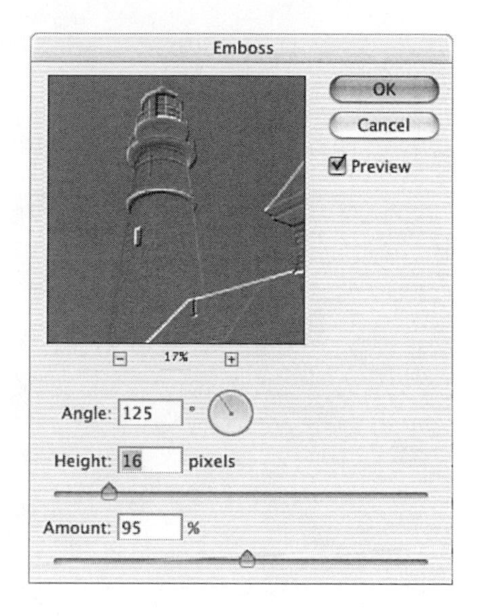


Figure 20.28
The Emboss filter displaces the edges and fills the image with silvery gray to simulate a foil-stamped effect.

## Extrude

The Extrude filter gives a 3D effect to a selection or to an entire image, creating a set of extruded blocks or pyramids that radiate out from the center of the image or selection.

## Find Edges

The Find Edges filter looks for high-contrast areas of an image and replaces them with black lines on a white background. The effect of the filter is to give an image or selection a hand-drawn effect.

## Solarize

The Solarize filter simulates the old photographic solarization technique of briefly exposing a print to light while it's being developed. The effect is a blend of a negative and positive image. The result tends to be very dark. However, boosting the brightness via the Image, Adjustment Levels command can help bring back some detail.

## Tiles

The Tiles filter divides an image into rows of offset tiles. You can specify how many tiles to create and how many are offset. You can also specify what to use as the color between the tiles (either the foreground or background color of the original image, either inverted or unaltered).

For an added 3D effect, apply the Tiles filter on a duplicate of the background layer. Specify a solid background color, such

Colorful images tend to produce colored artifacts along edges and therefore lose the stamped-in-metal look. Grayscale images work best with the Emboss filter. An alternative to converting the image to grayscale is to duplicate the background layer, select Image, Adjustments, Hue/Saturation, and move the Saturation slider all the way to the left. Then apply the Emboss filter to the "grayscale" layer. To restore some of the original image's color, apply the filter to a duplicate layer and adjust the opacity and/or blending mode.

as white, to use between the tiles. After the filter is applied, select the Magic Wand tool and click the color between the tiles. This will select all between-tile borders. Click the Delete or Clear button to convert the white to transparent, allowing the original background layer to show through. Finally, apply a drop shadow or other layer style to the tiles (see Figure 20.29).

Figure 20.29
Using the Tiles filter on a duplicate layer and then applying a layer style to the tiled layer gives images a 3D effect.

### Trace Contour

The Trace Contour filter is rather like the Glowing Edges filter without that touch of Las Vegas. The Level slider lets you determine how "contrasty" adjacent pixels need to be to be considered an edge.

### Wind

The Wind filter adds horizontal lines to edges in an image, simulating wind or movement. This filter is most effectively used by applying it to a selected object within an image.



## THE LIQUIFY COMMAND

The Liquify filter allows you to take an image or part of an image and remold it in a seemingly infinite variety of ways.

The Liquify command is based on the principle of the mesh (and what a mesh you can make of things, too). A mesh is, essentially, a grid to which the original image is mapped. When you use a tool in the Liquify interface, you are basically shifting a portion of the mesh, and the image is remapped accordingly. Figure 20.30 shows what this means.

> To give images the illusion of moving in directions other than left to right (or vice versa), rotate the image (either 90°, 45°, or some arbitrary amount) before adding the Wind filter and then rotate it back.

Figure 20.30
The top of the tower in this image has been warped using the Forward Warp tool. But what really happened is that the mesh was distorted, and the image remapped to the distortion.

That sounds needlessly complicated, but in truth, the Liquify command is, at its heart, tool based: You select a tool and attack the image with it. (We'll get to why the mesh business can be useful shortly.)

## The Liquify Interface and Tools

Selecting Filter, Liquify, or pressing (Shift-Command-X) [Shift+Ctrl+X] brings up the Liquify interface (see Figure 20.31).

The Liquify command gives you access to these tools:

- **Forward Warp**—This tool moves pixels in a brush-like fashion. Adjust the Brush Size, Density, Pressure, and Rate options (more about these in "Tool Options," later in the chapter), align the crosshairs of the cursor with the edge you want to deform, and start clicking and dragging.
- **Reconstruct**—Okay, you've been dragging with the Warp tool (or any other tool) willy-nilly, and you've passed the point at which the result is useful. What to do? Click the Reconstruct tool and drag back over the area(s) you have deformed. Think of it as an "Undo brush."
- **Twirl Clockwise**—This works kind of like a hand blender or automatic spaghetti winder: Place the crosshairs in the portion of the image you want to twirl, and hold down the mouse button. You won't hear a whirring noise, but you can imagine one as you see an eddy forming in the image.
- **Pucker and Bloat**—The Pucker tool gives faces, for example, that "I've just had a lemon ball" look. The Bloat tool lets you make objects inflate. Select either of these tools, hold the crosshairs over the area of the image you want to either pucker or bloat, keep the mouse button pressed, and watch the effect (see Figure 20.32).

You might recall that Photoshop 7 had a Twirl Counterclockwise tool. It is now gone. To twirl counterclockwise, hold down the (Option) [Alt] key while using the Twirl Clockwise tool.

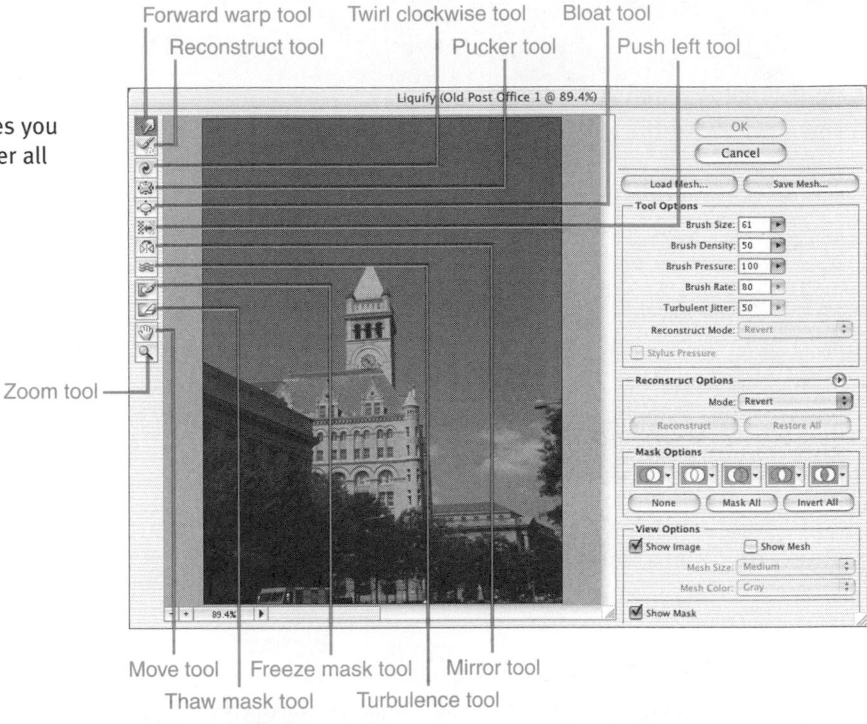


**Figure 20.31**
The Liquify interface gives you nearly infinite control over all aspects of liquefaction.

**Figure 20.32**
(Left) The Pucker tool gives faces a pinched, "I've eaten something sour" look. (Right) The Bloat tool gives people that "I've accumulated the sum total of all knowledge in the universe!" look.

- **Push Left**—When clicked and dragged up, this tool pushes pixels to the left. When dragged down, it pushes pixels to the right. When dragged right, it pushes pixels up, and when dragged left, it pushes pixels down.
- **Mirror**—This tool takes some experimentation to figure out, but basically it spins a portion of an image 180° (see Figure 20.33).

Hold down the (Option) [Alt] key while dragging with the Push Left tool to push pixels in the opposite direction of the normal mode.

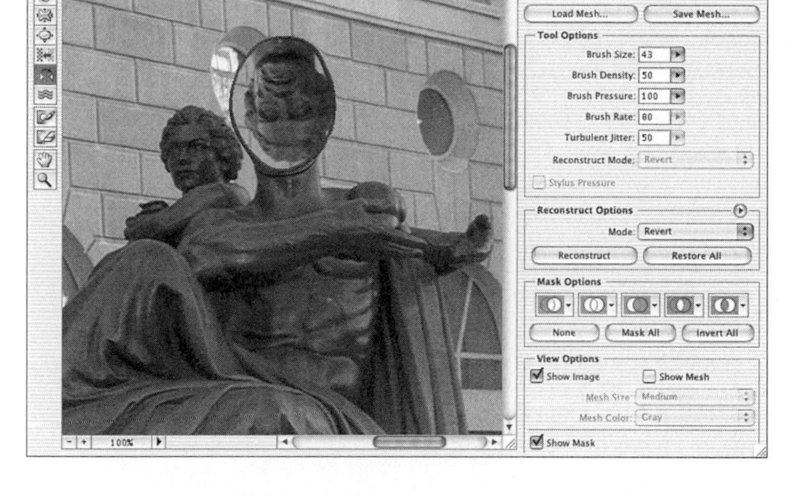


**Figure 20.33**
With the Mirror tool, keep clicking and dragging in a circular motion repeatedly until an upside-down version of the image starts to form and gradually resolves itself.

- **Turbulence**—This tool creates a wavy distortion wherever it is dragged. It's good for giving images those "We're going into a flashback" feel.
- **Freeze Mask and Thaw Mask**—The Freeze Mask tool lets you draw a mask over a portion of the image (it will look like a Quick Mask). With this mask in place, you can use any other Liquify tool on the image, and the masked portion of the image will remain undistorted. The Thaw Mask tool lets you erase all or parts of the mask.
- **Move and Zoom**—These are the usual Photoshop tools for letting you move around an image and zoom into/out of part of the image.

## Photoshop at Work: The Liquify Tools

Here's a hands-on way of seeing how these tools work. Let's apply a simple "big giant head" effect:

1. Find a portrait—either a human or a pet. Basically, anyone or anything that has a head (sorry, if you have a portrait of Charles I of England, it won't work). Open it in Photoshop.
2. Select Filter, Liquify to access the Liquify filter interface.
3. Adjust the Brush Size setting so that the outline of the brush cursor is just about the size of the head.
4. Reduce the Brush Rate setting to about 30 so that you can more easily control the effect.
5. Select the Bloat tool from the Tools palette and place the crosshairs of the cursor in the center of the forehead of your portrait.

> You can freeze areas that have been distorted to keep them immune from further distortions.

6. Click the mouse to start the bloat effect. Click outward from the center of the forehead evenly from left to right so that the bloat effect is applied symmetrically to the head (unless you're trying for an Elephant Man kind of effect).
7. Use the Reconstruct button to remove the last few applications of the Bloat tool, in the event you've applied the effect errantly.
8. Down at the bottom right of the Liquify dialog box, uncheck the Show Image check box and check the Show Mesh check box. See how the filter has distorted the mesh underlying the image? If you want to get compulsively symmetric about this effect, you could use the Bloat tool on just the mesh, ensuring that the gridlines are adjusted precisely. Double-check the efficacy of this change by clicking Show Image and ensuring that the effect is what you intended.
9. After you have created the big giant head, select the Reconstruct tool and brush it over the bottom of the forehead. Notice how you can restore part of the original image, so if the expanding head has affected the face, you can remove that effect and keep the expansion confined to the top of the head.

## Tool Options

The Tool Options portion of the Liquify dialog box lets you customize the tools. Most of the options apply to all tools, and you can control the settings for Brush Size (the diameter of the brush), Brush Density (how many pixels are affected), and Brush Pressure (affects how quickly or slowly changes take place). You can also control the Brush Rate option (only available for the Twirl Clockwise, Pucker, Bloat, Reconstruct, and Turbulence tools), which affects the sensitivity of these tools. The Turbulence tool also lets you set Turbulence Jitter, which controls how tightly pixels are scrambled (not how nervous you are on bumpy flights).

## Reconstruct Options

If you don't like any or all of the distortions you made, you have the option of undoing them—or restoring the original image.

The easiest way to undo a distortion is to repeatedly click the Reconstruct button, which undoes one level of distortion. Unlike Photoshop in general, here the program doesn't consider an entire single brush stroke as one single thing to undo. Getting rid of one quick stroke of the Forward Warp tool may require up to 10 clicks of the Reconstruct button. This is actually helpful, because many times distortions are undone because they have gone too far. Thus, you can back up gradually.

To get back to a "state of grace," just click Restore All.

The Mode pop-up menu has five options for reconstruction, which undo or propagate distortions between frozen and unfrozen areas. For general purposes, the Revert mode gets the job done most effectively.

> To undo everything and restore the Liquify dialog box to the condition it was in when it was opened, hold down the (Option) [Alt] key. The Cancel button will change to a Reset button.

## Mask Options

If you have applied a mask to part of the image or defined a selection prior to entering the Liquify dialog box, you can use the Mask Options to alter those image areas. Use these options to replace the selection with a new one, add to the selection, subtract from the selection, define a new selection that intersects with the previous selection, and invert the selection. To clear all masks and selections, click the None button.

## Saving Meshes

You can save a mesh—basically a set of distortions—by clicking the Save Mesh button. You can apply it to other images by opening a new image, selecting Filter, Liquify, and then clicking the Load Mesh button. Select the saved mesh, and the new image will be mapped to the preset distortions.

*How can you use the Liquify command to create animations? See "Liquid Video" in the "Mastering Photoshop" section at the end of this chapter.*

# MASTERING PHOTOSHOP

## Stamps of Approval

*Can I use the Stamp filter to create custom shapes that can be accessed via the Custom Shape palette?*

Yes. Once you have created a simple, definable silhouette using the Stamp filter, go to Select, Color Range and select the color you used for the silhouette. Once your silhouette is selected, go to the Paths palette menu and select Make Work Path. This draws a path around the edge of your silhouette. Once the path is drawn, go to Edit, Define Custom Shape, give your shape a name, and click OK. Now, when you select the Custom Shape tool, your shape will be available in the Custom Shape palette.



## Liquid Video

*How can I use the Liquify command to make animations?*

Animation can be a complicated topic, but what you're after is a bunch of frames, over the course of which an action gradually takes place. Assume you want a head to melt. Start with a background layer that has the intact head you want to melt. Duplicate the layer and then select Filter, Liquify. Now, the key to effective animation is making very small adjustments that, over several frames, will exhibit movement. In this first duplicated layer, make a small distortion in the head. Apply the effect to the layer and then duplicate the distorted layer. You'll build on the distortion you just made to further the effect. On this second duplicated layer, make the head melt slightly more pronounced.

Apply the effect and then duplicate *this* layer. Repeat this over the course of a dozen or so frames until, by the last frame, the head is melted. If you toggle the visibility of these layers on rapidly, you can see roughly how effective the animation is. You can then open this in ImageReady to create the actual animation.

21

# PREPARING FOR PRINT

## IN THIS CHAPTER

Creating imagery on paper with inks placed by an offset press is part art and part science. It's also part preparation and part faith. As the artist or illustrator, you create the work and perhaps place it into a page layout document. From there, it's transferred into the capable hands of the print shop for processing and the actual printing. The more you understand about what happens *after* the file leaves your hands, the better you can prepare it *before* it's sent out.

This chapter presents the concepts and issues you need to understand to properly prepare images for commercial printing. You should understand the process before researching specific questions.

# PROCESS PRINTING

Photoshop is the most commonly used tool for preparing photographic images for print. Whether reproduced in a newspaper, in a magazine, on a billboard, or on the side of a bus, photos most likely passed through Photoshop. (In contrast, nonphotographic, vector-based illustrations are typically produced using Illustrator or a similar program.) Properly preparing images in Photoshop for process printing—printing on a commercial printing press using the *process* inks CMYK—requires some knowledge of resolution and color and a general understanding of the printing process. (If, on the other hand, you print only to the color printer on your desk, see the sidebar "Photoshop and Inkjet Printers," later in this chapter.)

**Caution**

This chapter deals primarily with techniques and procedures for commercial process and spot color printing. Process printing uses CMYK inks applied by huge mechanical printing presses.

The guidelines and background material in this chapter do not pertain to most inkjet printers. Most inkjets also use CMYK inks, but they use software to convert from RGB colors to the CMYK gamut (with the exception of high-end proofers and fine art printers). Generally, you should not prepare CMYK output for inkjet printers; rather, you should send only RGB data.

## Who Needs to Know What

Commercial printing is a combination of art and science. Generally, just four inks are used to create the entire range of colors needed to reproduce photographic images. Additional colors, called *spot colors*, can be added, but the bulk of the work is done with just four inks. Knowing how and where to put the ink to correctly re-create an image requires a substantial level of expertise. The artist or illustrator's general knowledge of the principles of printing must be supplemented with the press operator's specific knowledge of the individual printing presses and the particular inks and paper being used for the job, and sometimes even weather conditions.

In most cases, you are not expected to know (or even understand) the specific tolerances of a huge piece of machinery in another company's building. The people who work directly with that machinery do, theoretically, know its capabilities and foibles and can compensate for them as necessary.

In contrast, the press operator probably has no need to understand the symbolism in a particular ad campaign or the meaningfulness of a cover shot. The reasons for selecting a specific spot color for a logo might not matter to him or her. As a professional, however, the press operator likely understands that a specific color *was* chosen, that an ad campaign *does* use symbolism, that a cover shot *is* meaningful, and that proper reproduction on paper is important for these images to fulfill their purposes.

**Photoshop and Inkjet Printers**

Both commercial printing presses and home/office inkjet printers use ink on paper to reproduce your artwork. In many cases, they use the same colors of ink, but that's where the similarities end.

On the technical side, huge industrial presses use a series of evenly spaced dots of varying sizes to reproduce color. Stochastic printers, such as most inkjets, use dots of the same size, spaced irregularly, to reproduce an image. That results in differing resolution needs. Some photo-quality inkjet printers can place droplets of somewhat varying size, using larger dots for dense color coverage and smaller droplets for areas with sparse ink coverage. They are, nonetheless, stochastic printing devices.

Most inkjet printers achieve maximum print quality at resolutions of 240 pixels per inch (ppi), although some max out at 480ppi. Images prepared for commercial printing should be at a resolution 1.5 to 2 times the line screen frequency of the press.

Commercial printing usually involves producing large numbers of identical documents, and inkjets are more commonly used to print one or several copies of a single image.

Preparing an image for process printing means converting it to the CMYK color mode. Although you may see those inks under the hood of your own printer, inkjets require RGB images (with some exceptions). Remember that the vast majority of inkjet printers are sold to individuals and businesses who don't have access to software that supports CMYK. Even Photoshop Elements and Photoshop LE have no support for the professional printing color mode. Inkjets are prepared to print from programs such as Excel, Word, PowerPoint, Internet Explorer, and iPhoto, and directly from digital cameras. The software that transfers information from the program to the printer *expects* RGB data. If you send a CMYK image to print, the colors are converted *again*, and are likely to become muddy and dark.

In summary, if you send images to an inkjet printer, keep them in RGB color mode and set your resolution to 240ppi or 480ppi. A couple of tests with slightly higher and lower resolution will tell you what's optimal for your printer. Remember that images with too high a resolution can cause printing problems for inkjets.

# The Role of Page-Layout Programs

Images prepared in Photoshop for commercial printing are almost never sent directly to press. Instead, they are placed in a page-layout or illustration program to be combined with text and/or additional artwork. The document in which an image is placed could be one page long or hundreds of pages. (Each image in this book was prepared in whole or in part in Photoshop and integrated into the book by the fine production staff at Pearson Technology Group.)

The page-layout or illustration program is more than just a carrier for a Photoshop image. Rather, the artwork created or edited in Photoshop is merely an element of the page. Even if the image stands alone, it is an element on a page. When it's printed, there are likely other elements surrounding it, including registration marks, color bars, and crop marks (see Figure 21.1).

For the remainder of this chapter, the terms *printing* and *printer* are used to refer to the commercial printing process, using process and spot inks, unless otherwise noted.

Commercial printing is a combination of art and science. Generally, just four inks are used to create the entire range of colors needed to reproduce photographic images. Additional colors, called spot colors, can be added, but the bulk of the work is done with just four inks. Knowing how and where to put the ink to correctly re-create an image requires a substantial level of expertise. General knowledge of principles of printing must be supplemented with specific knowledge of the individual printing presses and the particular inks and paper being used for the job, and sometimes even weather conditions.

In contrast, the pressman probably has no need to understand the symbolism in a particular ad campaign or the meaningfulness of a cover shot. The reasons for selection of a specific spot color for a logo may be insignificant to him or her. As a professional, however, the press operator likely understands that a specific color was chosen, that an ad campaign does use symbolism, that a cover shot is meaningful, and that proper reproduction on paper is important for these images to fulfill their purposes.

Perhaps the most important guideline when preparing artwork for process printing is the simplest: Talk with your printer or service bureau. In most cases, you are not expected to know (or even understand) the specific tolerances of a huge piece of machinery in another company's building. The people who work directly with that machinery do, theoretically, know its capabilities and foibles and can compensate for them as necessary.

If you are or will be preparing artwork for commercial reproduction, you can benefit from an understanding of the fundamentals of the process. Clarifying some basic terminology and a closer look at some key aspects of printing will set the groundwork for a discussion of preparing projects for print.

Overprinting is controlled for individual objects through the Attributes palette (shown in Figure 24.9). In this palette, you can choose to overprint an object's stroke, its fill, both, or neither. In addition, you can set output resolution, you can show or hide an object's centerpoint, and you can reverse a path that is part of a compound path. The Attributes palette is also used for assigning the target of an imagemap on the World Wide Web. (This behavior has no impact on printing.) You can add notes about a selected object by using the annotation feature of the palette. These notes are included in the PostScript file

**Figure 21.1**
Shown is the black ink color separation for a document that contains columns of text and an image from Photoshop.

It's important to remember the role of the document in which the Photoshop image is placed. The Photoshop image's dimensions, resolution, color mode, and even file format depend on the destination document.

# TERMS AND CONCEPTS

If you are or will be preparing artwork for commercial reproduction, you can benefit from understanding the fundamentals of the process. Clarifying some basic terminology and taking a closer look at some key aspects of printing will set the groundwork for a discussion of preparing projects for print.

The vocabulary presented in this section is not Photoshop specific. Rather, it includes terms related to the commercial printing process, whether directly applicable to Photoshop or applicable to a page-layout or illustration program.

- **Bleed**—The bleed extends the ink past the crop marks to avoid unwanted whitespace around trimmed images. In many cases, the paper is larger than the print area. To ensure that the ink extends all the way to the area that will be cut from the larger paper, a bleed is used. Without the bleed, a tiny error in trimming the paper can result in an unwanted white line in places where the design should go to the edge.
- **Choke**—In trapping, the process of extending the surrounding light color onto an enclosed dark color is called *choking*. (See also *spread* and *trapping*.)
- **CMYK**—Cyan (C), magenta (M), yellow (Y), and black (K) are the four *process colors* used in commercial printing. Artwork being prepared for color printing must be in this color mode. RGB

illustrations and images cannot be separated for printing. (See also *process colors* and *spot colors*.)

*For an in-depth look at color and the color modes, see Chapter 5, "Color, in Theory and in Practice," p. 159.*

It is critical that the proofs be prepared properly and using the correct technique. Digital proofs should not be used for a job that will eventually be printed from film-based plates. Likewise, creating a laminate proof for a digital output job opens the door to inaccuracy.

- **Color stitching**—Color stitching is the undesirable visibility of the transition from vector to raster artwork in an image. It occurs when a printer handles the two types of artwork differently.
- **Contract proof**—The contract proof is the final prototype of a printed piece that must be approved before printing the final separations and printing plates. After the client or other approving authority approves the contract proof, the job should roll. The contract proof is the standard against which the final production project is measured. Final approval of the contract proof is normally in writing, and the contract proof is used to ensure accurate color during the press check. (See also *press check*.)
- **Dot gain**—When ink is placed on paper, it can spread as it is absorbed into the paper. The spreading is called *dot gain* and is measured as a percentage. Coated papers generally have less dot gain that uncoated papers, resulting in more precise dots. However, when the amount of dot gain can be predicted, it can be compensated for by using a proportionately smaller dot of ink.
- **Duotone**—When only two colors are used to create an image, it can be considered a duotone. Photoshop can also produce images using two colors of ink as CMYK images (with two empty channels) or as multichannel color mode documents. (See also *tritone*.)

  In a duotone (or *tritone* or *quadtone*), the inks are generally all spread throughout the image. In an image that uses spot colors, one or more inks can be isolated in a specific area or pattern of the page. The spot colors need not overlap, although they can.
- **Flatness**—Vector curves are not actually printed as curves when you are creating separations and printing on a press. Rather, the PostScript imagesetter creates a series of straight lines that represent the curve. The smaller the flatness number, the shorter the segments used to print curves and, therefore, the greater the number of segments and the more accurate the curve (see Figure 21.2). Flatness is a function of the imagesetter's resolution divided by the document's output resolution.

  In Photoshop, the Clipping Path dialog box contains a field for flatness (see Figure 21.3). Leave this field completely empty unless instructed to enter a value by your service bureau or print shop.
- **Flexography**—This type of printing process uses flexible printing plates and different inks from offset printing. (See the sidebar "Flexographic Printing," later in this chapter.)

Figure 21.2
As you can see with these "circular" clipping paths, the greater the number of segments, the smoother the curve.

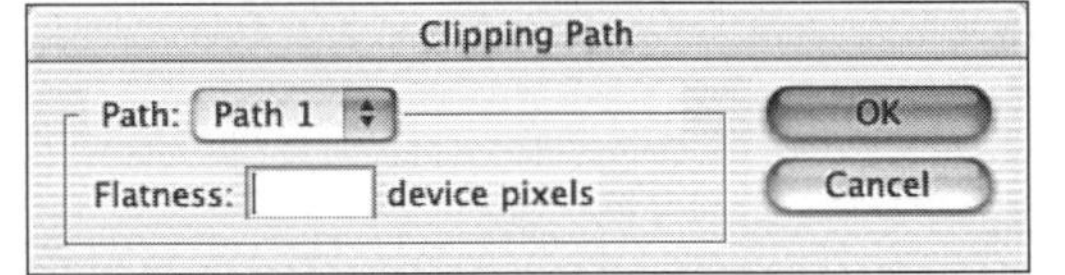


Figure 21.3
Values for flatness can range from 0.2 to 100. The smaller the value, the shorter the path segment—and the more complex and difficult the path is to output.

- **Frequency modulation (FM) printing**—Also called *stochastic printing*, in the FM printing process, dots of ink are all the same size, and an image is created by varying the placement of the dots. This is in contrast to halftone printing, in which the dots are regularly spaced but vary in size. (See *stochastic printing*.)
- **Gradient**—Gradients are smooth and gradual changes in color that are sometimes hard to reproduce in print. Printing presses generally can produce only a few dozen variations in the density of each of the component inks, so transitions from one color to another may not be as smooth as they are when viewed on your monitor. The appearance of a gradient on the printed page is limited by the number of color variations that can physically be printed.
- **Halftone**—One of the keys to producing photographic and other continuous-tone images on a printing press is *halftoning*. The press doesn't produce continuous-tone images; rather, it simulates them with a series of dots. The halftone dots are spaced equidistant in a grid. Each square in the grid, called a *cell*, can be occupied by only one dot. Typically, the distance from the center of one dot to the center of the next is uniform throughout the grid. The illusion of color variation is created with changes in the size of those dots. Figure 21.4 shows halftone dots spaced in an imaginary grid. The dashed lines represent the line screen frequency.

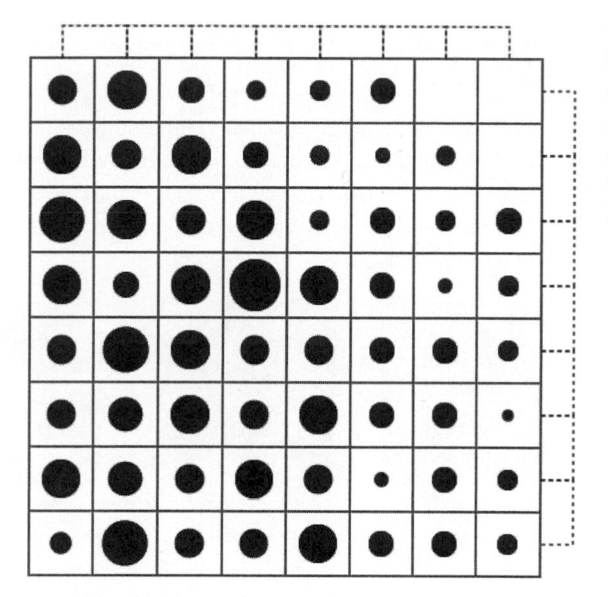

Figure 21.4
Halftone dots are always equidistant in an imaginary grid. The grid spacing is a function of line screen frequency, and the size of the dots determines how much ink is placed.

With a grayscale image, the areas with large dots would appear darker than areas with smaller dots. In the case of color, the ink density of that color would be increased where the dots are larger. The size of the dot in relation to the size of the cell (or the grid square) is described as *tint* or *screen*. The combination of cyan, magenta, yellow, and black dots produce the appearance of various colors in the CMYK gamut. (See also *line screen frequency* and *tint*.)

- **Knockout**—When two or more areas of solid color overlap in an illustration, one of two things can happen. First, the colors can interact, producing another, different color. If, on the other hand, the overlapping color completely blocks the lower, it is said to "knock out" the lower color, thus creating a *knockout*. This is primarily a factor with vector artwork and does not apply to continuous-tone images and raster images. (See also *overprint*.)

- **Limitcheck error**—PostScript printers can return limitcheck errors when overwhelmed by data. Specifically, overly long paths can require more memory than is available in the printer. Photoshop can generate overly long paths with extremely complex clipping paths and shape layers. Using a PostScript Level 3 printer with large amounts of memory can eliminate limitcheck errors.

- **Line screen frequency**—The line screen frequency determines the spacing and size of the dots printed by the imagesetter and used to create the printing plates. It is measured in lines per inch (lpi). The higher the value, the closer the lines and smaller the dots. Small dots and close lines produce a finer image. Line screen frequency must be matched to the imagesetter (or plate maker) that's producing the color separations (or printing plates). Using a line screen frequency that's too high for a lower-resolution imagesetter can seriously degrade the quality of the separations. The PPD for the particular imagesetter usually offers appropriate settings. Refer back to Figure 21.4, which shows halftoning and line screen. The dashed lines in the figure indicate the distance between rows and columns of dots. In an actual halftone, the number of rows or columns per inch is the *line screen*. (See also *halftone* and *PPD*.)

- **Lpi**—This abbreviation stands for *lines per inch*, a measure of line screen frequency. (See also *line screen frequency*.)
- **Misregistration**—As paper is pulled through the multiple units required to place the different colors of inks, slight irregularities in alignment might occur. When the inks are not placed in exact relationship to each other, the press is said to be *misregistered*. The effect on a four-color image can range from virtually unnoticeable to devastating (see Figure 21.5). The term *out of register* is also used. (See also *registration*.)

Figure 21.5
On the left, the original. In the center, one color is slightly out of register. On the right, the same image when the misregistration is more severe.

- **Offset printing**—The majority of printing done worldwide is offset printing. When you think of the production of books, brochures, magazines, and business cards, you're thinking of offset printing. Printing plates press against rollers to pick up ink, and then the plates are applied to paper, transferring the ink.
- **Opacity**—In Photoshop, an object's opacity refers to whether (or how much) you can see pixels below it in the image. A pixel's opacity can range from 100% opaque (solid) to 0% opaque (invisible). (See also *transparency*.)
- **Out of register**—See *misregistration*.
- **Overprint**—When two colors overlap in artwork, it can result in an overprint or a *knockout*. Overprinting puts the upper color over the lower, and with translucent inks, that allows them to interact and create a third color. When an upper color knocks out a lower color, the lower color is not printed underneath the overlapping area. (See also *knockout*.)
- **PPD**—PPD stands for PostScript Printer Description. This file, when loaded, supplies all the variables for your PostScript printer or imagesetter.
- **Press check**—The last chance to ensure that colors, knockouts, trapping, and overprinting are correct, the press check uses pages printed at the beginning of the production press run. The printing presses are actually in motion to produce these samples. The press check should be compared only to the contract proof and should be used only for checking color output. It is too late to correct typographical errors or change the appearance of the artwork. If one ink is printing too lightly or darkly, the press operator can usually adjust its flow to compensate. (See also *contract proof*.)

- **Process colors**—The process colors are cyan, magenta, yellow, and black (CMYK). They are the four standard colors on which four-color printing is based. (See also *CMYK* and *spot colors*.)

For halftone printing, use an image resolution that is 1.5 or 2 times the line screen frequency (measured in lpi) for the press on which the job will be run. If you're printing to an inkjet or other stochastic device, use a resolution that is one-third the printer's resolution.

- **Proof**—A *proof* is a sample used to verify the work, and *proofing* is the process of checking that sample. A proof can be prepared at any step in the creation or production process and in various ways. Proofing is almost always done for client or project lead approval before production. When properly calibrated monitors are used with appropriate printer profiles, proofing can be done onscreen, a procedure referred to as *soft proofing*. Hard proofing is generally considered to be more reliable.
- **Registration**—Registration is the alignment of printing plates to ensure that colors are placed exactly in relationship to each other. (See also *misregistration*.)
- **Resolution**—Resolution refers to the number of pixels per unit of measure for an image. Typically, resolution is recorded in either pixels per inch (ppi) or pixels per centimeter. The image itself simply has pixels. In printing, resolution describes how tightly those pixels should be packed on the paper, which also determines the size of each pixel.
- **Screening**—See *halftone*.
- **Separations**—Color separations are the images from which printing plates are usually made. Each separation represents the distribution of one color of ink on the page. Separations are grayscale images, with a maximum of 256 levels of color for their ink. Some printing operations bypass separations by creating printing plates directly from computer files, a process called *direct to plate*.
- **Soft proofing**—Soft proofing is the procedure of verifying an image's final print colors by simulating them. Because the monitor can only simulate the appearance of ink on paper, soft proofing is generally considered to be not as accurate as actually producing a printed sample. (See also *proof*.)
- **Spot colors**—Spot colors are predefined, premixed inks that produce predictable results in typical circumstances. Sometimes printed work needs to have an exact color match, or a color that's required cannot be reproduced using the four standard inks. Some artwork is overprinted with a protective or glossy varnish. Occasionally, a metallic or neon color must be added to artwork. In all these cases, you use spot colors. They usually require an additional run through a printing press, which can add to the cost of a print job. They are output on a different color separation to produce a separate printing plate. (See also *CMYK*, *process colors*, and *separations*; for more information, see Chapter 5.)
- **Spread**—In trapping, the process of extending a light color into the surrounding dark color is called *spreading*. (See also *choke* and *trapping*.)

- **Stochastic printing**—Dots of ink in stochastic printing are usually all the same size, and an image is created by varying the placement of the dots. (This is in contrast to *halftone* printing, in which the spacing of the dots remains constant but the dots' sizes vary.) Stochastic printing can also be referred to as *frequency modulation (FM)* printing. Inkjet printers can be considered stochastic printers. (See also *frequency modulation [FM] printing* and *halftone*.)
- **Tiling**—Sometimes an image or illustration is larger than the pages on which it is to be printed. When that is the case, the image must be divided into rectangles the size of the selected paper. The various parts of the image are printed as separate pages of the document, which can later be pieced together.
- **Tint**—The size of a halftone dot in relation to the halftone cell determines the darkness or density of an ink in a given area. The diameter of the halftone dot in relation to the halftone cell's height or width is measured as a percentage to give the tint or screen. For example, a 50% tint (or 50% screen) consists of halftone dots that are one-half the size of their cells. (See also *halftone*.)
- **Transparency**—Any object or image in an image that does not obscure everything below it is said to be *transparent*. Although the word *transparent* actually connotes *clear*, it is used in Photoshop to denote various levels of *opacity*, measured as a percentage. However, the opacity level, as controlled in the Layers palette, is not the only factor involved in opacity. An object, a group, or a layer's blending mode can also affect transparency.

*To learn about blending modes and opacity, see Chapter 18, "Mastering the Blending Modes," p. 585.*

- **Trapping**—Trapping is the process of preparing adjacent colors to ensure that no unwanted whitespace appears between them. Because of a variety of factors, miniscule variations can occur during a print run. As a result, the presses can be slightly misregistered. That tiny gap between the point where one ink ends and the next begins is often very visible. Trapping increases the distribution of a lighter colored ink under a darker ink to ensure that no white area shows through. (See also *choke*, *knockout*, *misregistration*, *overprint*, and *spread*.)

*You've heard about trapping, but you don't know if you should be doing it. See "Avoiding the Trap" in the "Mastering Photoshop" section at the end of this chapter.*

- **Tritone**—A tritone is an image that can be reproduced using only three colors of ink. (See also *duotone*.)

# THE BASICS OF PRINTING



Regarding commercial printing, the most important piece of advice I can give you is to simply talk with your printer. Just as a race car driver trusts his mechanic to prepare a multimillion-dollar machine to perform at peak efficiency, so should you trust your printer to run his or her machinery at maximum efficiency. Communication is the key. A mechanic might have to tell a driver, "The car will pull a little to the outside on Curve 3." So, too, might a printer need to tell a client, "With this paper, under these conditions, we'll have to increase the trap by a point."

Commercial printing presses are vastly expensive machines, made up of more individual parts than you can count, some standing two stories tall and costing more than the race car mentioned earlier. The people who run and maintain these monsters should be skilled professionals who know and understand their particular machinery as no other can. On the other end of the project, however, is the client or designer or account executive or artist. This individual has a concept in mind, however fuzzy at the beginning, and wants to achieve that image on paper. Someone must create the digital file that conveys the message; someone must take that series of computerized ideas and turn it from magnetic zeros and ones to ink on paper. One or more individuals can become involved in the process in between.

*What if your printer won't talk with you or can't answer your questions? See "Do I Need More Than an Ink-Slinger?" in the "Mastering Photoshop" section at the end of this chapter.*

When your artwork is printed, it is re-created on paper (or another medium) using inks (or dyes). The artwork itself is actually an electronic recording of what you've created. The image exists in the computer or on the disk as a series of zeros and ones. Those zeros and ones (binary data) represent the pixels and colors and effects that you see on the monitor. Going from binary data to ink on paper can be a complicated process. Fortunately, most of the process is transparent to you a majority of the time—most steps can proceed without your direct control.

You'll discover many variations in offset printing today, including print on demand, direct to plate, PDF workflow, automated form printing, high-fidelity color, and other options, such as flexographic printing (see the sidebar "Flexographic Printing," later in this chapter). This discussion, however, focuses on the most common types of commercial printing. The artwork can be placed in a page-layout program, or the final preparation can take place in an illustration program, such as Illustrator. Typically, in either case, the artwork needs to end up on printing plates, which the presses use to actually place ink on paper. The following subsections cover the basics of the offset printing process.

## Proofs

The only way to really see how a print job will come off the press is to run it through the press. Doing so, however, is prohibitively expensive until every aspect of the job is checked. When the plates are on the presses and the paper starts to feed, it's too late to find a mistake.

*Proofs* are an intermediary stage created before the printing plates are made. Proofs can be actual color separation film (see the next section), bluelines (which are less expensive than film), or laminates to show color. Laminates use the actual film to produce an example of how the project will print. If problems are found, corrections are made. If film or separations have been made, they are replaced by corrected versions. (These corrections, of course, can be expensive.)

Among the most expensive options is *wet proofing*, in which a small press is used to print the proofs, using plates made from the color separations. This procedure is usually reserved for the most color-sensitive, high-volume projects. Wet proofs can be run on the same paper that will be used for the print run.

*Digital proofing* uses high-end color laser or special inkjet printers to create proofs. Typically, such proofers (from Kodak, Iris, and Imation) are calibrated to a specific printing press. They replicate, as closely as possible, the press's halftone dots, dot gain compensation, screen angle, and other press-specific conditions. The paper selected for the actual printing can be used.

*Soft proofing* relies on calibrated color monitors to show onscreen what the final project will look like. The monitor *must* be properly calibrated if color decisions are to be made. If, on the other hand, the job will be run using only colors selected from a swatch book, even an uncalibrated monitor can suffice. The colors onscreen might not be accurate, but using spot colors or color swatches ensures that the printed materials will be accurate. PDF files can be sent to a client or approving authority for soft proofing, if that individual has access to a properly calibrated monitor or understands the limitations of soft proofing.

If problems are found when you are soft proofing or working with digital proofs, making corrections is far less expensive than if color separations have been prepared.

## Halftoning, Line Screen Frequency, and Color Separations

In traditional offset printing, your artwork isn't sent from the computer directly to the printing press. Rather, the press uses printing plates made from *color separations*. The *seps* (one for each of the inks being used) are grayscale representations of parts of your image. Each separation covers the whole illustration but indicates only those areas where its particular ink will be placed. If an image is to be printed in grayscale, one separation is required. Standard four-color (CMYK) printing requires four separations, and more seps can be added for additional colors. (See "Process Versus Spot Colors," later in this chapter.) Sometimes you might also print a *duotone* or *tritone*. Duotones use two colors of ink (most often, black and one spot color); tritones use three inks.

Figure 21.6 shows a comparison of the four CMYK separations with the single image from which they were produced.

The original image, shown in the middle, is the composite. It is made up of all four colors. Keep in mind how the cyan, magenta, yellow, and black interact to produce color. Looking at the separations, you can determine several things about the original, even though it is shown here in grayscale:

- The body of the letters appears dark on the magenta and yellow separations, but it's not present at all on the cyan and black plates. This tells you that the fill for the text will be printed with just magenta and yellow inks; therefore, it is red.
- The text outline appears on all four separations; therefore, it will be black.
- Just a little of the telephone's body appears on the black separation, indicating that the phone is actually dark gray rather than black.

> The resolution of commercial printers is measured in *lines per inch (lpi)*. The number of rows per inch is the *line screen*. Line screen frequencies must be matched to the printer producing the separations. Using a line screen frequency that's too high for a lower-resolution imagesetter can seriously degrade the quality of the separations. For halftone printing, use an image resolution that is 1.5 to 2 times the line screen frequency (measured in lpi) for the press on which the job will be run. If you're printing to an inkjet or other stochastic printer, use a resolution that is one-third the printer's resolution.

- The gravel at the bottom of the bowl is very dark on the cyan separation, but it also appears on the magenta and yellow seps. Expect it to be royal blue.
- The tangle to the left and lower right of the phone is likely wires rather than weeds. Various strands look different on each separation—they are bright yellow, red, blue, and green.

Figure 21.6
Each of the outer images shows one color channel to indicate what information would appear on that color separation.

*For more information on these topics, see the section "Color Issues," later in this chapter, and Chapter 5, "Color, in Theory and in Practice," p. 159.*

The separations are sometimes produced as negatives, reversing the black and white areas. They are printed on *imagesetters* (see the following section). Whether positive or negative, separations are used to create the actual printing plates. The step that creates color separations is skipped when you are working "direct to plate."

Remember that separations are grayscale representations. Because grayscale is 8-bit (eight bits of computer data are available to record the shade of gray), theoretically, each ink can have 256 levels of variation. That would produce almost 4.3 *billion* possible colors (256×256×256×256). In reality, printing presses can produce only thousands of variations of color with the four process color inks.

## Imagesetters

Separations are printed on paper or film from very high-resolution laser printers called *imagesetters*. Whereas the typical office laser printer has a resolution of 600 dots per inch (dpi), imagesetters print at 1,200, 2,400, or 3,600dpi. Most imagesetters are PostScript printers, using PostScript Level 2 or 3.

The paper or film on which the imagesetter prints is then used to produce the actual printing plates. The term *direct to plate* means that the output device actually produces plates rather than film. This device is therefore called a *platesetter*.

## Printing Plates

The plates are *burned* from the color separations. A light-sensitive material is used, and the miniscule dots of the color separation protect areas of the plate when exposed to light. After the plates are burned, the areas that were protected remain capable of transferring ink to paper.

During production, the printing press rolls the plate against inked rollers and then presses it against the paper. The plate picks up ink (where it wasn't burned) from the rollers and deposits that ink on the paper. The machinery and processes are vastly more sophisticated, but the theory is similar to what you may have used in elementary school art classes. As a youngster, you might have applied ink to wooden blocks with patterns cut into them. The area that isn't cut away stands out from the rest, receives the ink, and makes contact with paper, leaving the ink behind. This is also the same as the process of being fingerprinted: The police officer rolls the suspect's fingertips on the ink pad. The fingertips are then rolled onto the card. Only the raised ridges of the fingertips transfer ink, leaving behind their distinctive patterns.

Each ink color requires a separate run through a printing unit. The job may use the standard four colors (CMYK), additional spot colors might be added, or the job can be run as a one-, two-, or three-color product.

### Flexographic Printing

Flexographic printing plates are created from a soft, flexible material. They are wrapped around a roller for printing. Designing for flexography requires that the slight distortion of the design on the plate be taken into account. In addition, the soft plates can result in higher dot gain. Flexographic (or *flexo*) printing, traditionally used for packaging, has been around since the late nineteenth century. At that time, melted rubber was poured into plaster molds to create the plates. The production process took a giant step forward with the introduction, some 50 years later, of metal rollers with tiny etched cells to ink the plates. These little ink holes allowed more precise control over the amount of ink applied to the plate and, therefore, the amount of ink transferred to the paper or other material. Flexography has several advantages:

- It can be used with a wide variety of materials. Unlike traditional offset inks, which require a porous surface, such as paper, flexo inks can be used on polymer films and other nonporous materials.
- Many flexo inks are opaque, which allows them to be used on dark materials.
- Flexo presses come in widths up to twice that of most offset presses, up to 10 feet wide. They can also have cylinders of various diameters, used to alter the size or repeat length of a pattern.

Recent improvements in flexo technology have resulted in plates and presses that have the same level of detail as traditional 133lpi screens.

The details of preparing artwork for flexographic printing are best discussed directly with your printer. The printer might prefer that you allow the printer's in-house team to do any necessary conversion, and you are probably well advised to let experienced people handle that aspect of the work.

# COLOR ISSUES

Four-color process printing requires artwork in the CMYK color mode. Although work can be created in RGB, it must eventually be converted to CMYK for printing. In addition to the process colors, you can incorporate spot colors into your work and even reduce the number of colors below four for artistic or budgetary reasons.

## CMYK Versus RGB Color

As discussed in Chapter 5, the two primary color modes in Photoshop are CMYK and RGB. RGB (red, green, blue) is used by light-generating hardware, such as monitors and projectors. It is the color mode of the World Wide Web because the Web is monitor based. CMYK (cyan, magenta, yellow, black) is the color mode of professional printing, which uses inks of these four colors to reproduce images.

Each color mode has its own *gamut*, or range of colors, that can be reproduced. RGB has an inherently larger gamut, which might need to be constricted when converting to CMYK. The colors that can be reproduced using CMYK inks can vary, too, depending on the inks and paper on which they are applied. Subtle variations in color can also be produced by the printer itself. Printers capable of finer line screens can do a better job of portraying delicate transitions between colors.

CMYK colors are defined by their percentages of the four colors. Photoshop offers CMYK mode in the Color palette and Color Picker (see Figure 21.7).

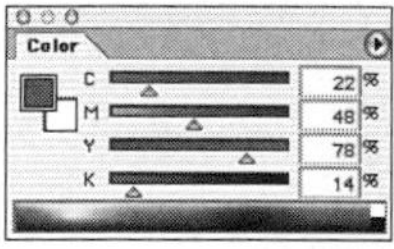


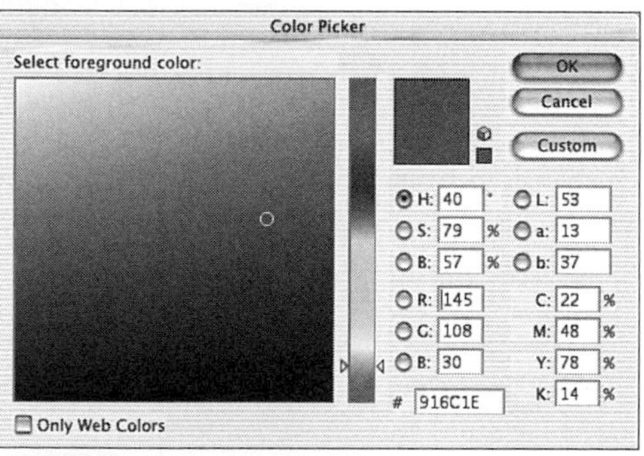


**Figure 21.7**
In both the Color palette and Color Picker, you can define CMYK colors numerically.

In Figure 21.7, note that the Color Picker does not have radio buttons next to the CMYK fields. The buttons next to the HSB, RGB, and Lab fields allow the Color Picker to use each of those components as the basis for color definition. CMYK component colors are not available for this purpose.

When an RGB color cannot be reproduced using standard CMYK inks, it is said to be *out of gamut*. Out-of-gamut colors

> Although RGB has a wider gamut than CMYK, some colors can be printed on paper that cannot be shown onscreen. For example, metallic and neon inks can't be accurately reproduced in RGB.

should be corrected (brought into gamut) to protect the image's color fidelity. (See "Viewing and Correcting Colors," later in this chapter.)

## Process Versus Spot Colors

Although the four process inks (cyan, magenta, yellow, and black) can reproduce only some of the visible spectrum, they can be supplemented with *spot colors*. Unlike RGB or CMYK colors, spot colors are not calculated; rather, they are selected. Choosing from a collection of predesignated values, you can identify the appropriate color for your needs. In Photoshop, you can load collections of spot colors, called *swatch libraries* or *books*, into the Swatches palette by using the palette's menu (see Figure 21.8).

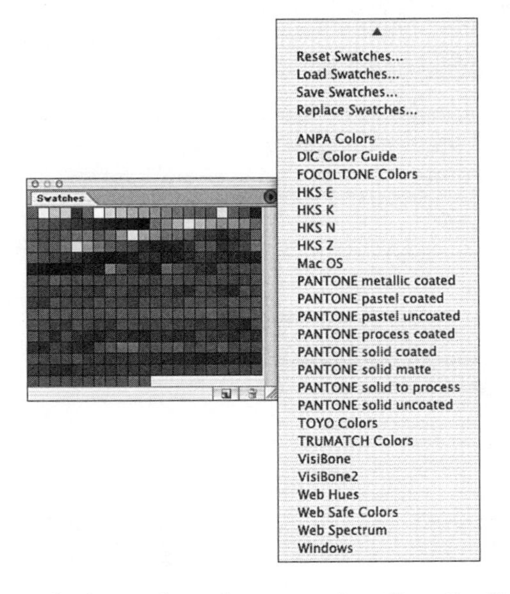


**Figure 21.8**
Photoshop ships with and installs by default a number of spot color libraries.

Photoshop's Color Picker can also be used to select spot colors. Open the Color Picker and click the Custom button (below the Cancel button) to open the Custom color picker (see Figure 21.9).

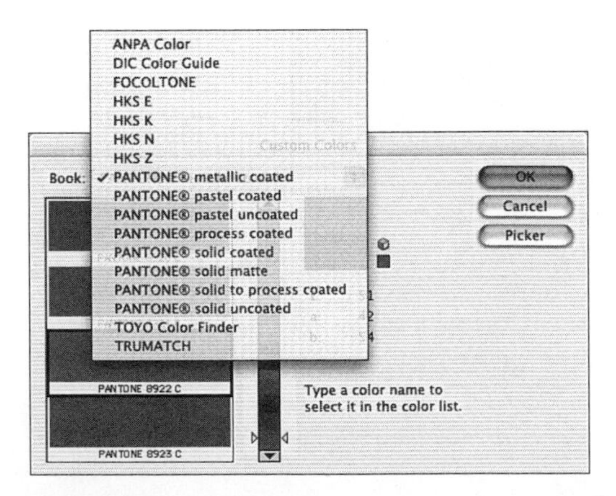


**Figure 21.9**
The same swatch libraries (or books) are available in the Custom color picker and the Swatches palette menu.

Samples of each color printed in books or ink charts showing swatches are typically used to select the appropriate color. Using a printed swatchbook is always better than trusting the appearance of a spot color on a monitor. Also, keep in mind the naming conventions of the swatches. For example, PANTONE 105 CVU and PANTONE 105 CVC are actually the same color—PANTONE 105 CV. The U (uncoated) and C (coated) at the end of the names simply indicate an attempt to simulate onscreen the difference between uncoated and coated paper.

The term *spot color* can refer to two very different types of color. Some spot colors, such as Pantone Process Coated (one of the swatch libraries available in Photoshop), are actually process (CMYK) colors. They are standardized to ensure that the color requested is the color delivered. For example, PANTONE 269-2 CVS is the same as a CMYK blend of 80/0/70/35.

In addition, the term *spot color* can refer to colors that cannot be reproduced by using blends of the cyan, magenta, yellow, and black inks. Pantone solid colors are an example. Metallic and neon colors are also available. These colors are printed separately from the CMYK inks.

Ensure that the spot colors you apply in the Photoshop image can be used on the printing press that will run the job. Check with your printer about how the job will be printed before using spot colors. Of primary importance is the type of paper that will be used. Uncoated paper and coated paper might require different inks. In addition, spot colors used with blends or gradients may need special attention to print properly.

Spot colors that require a separate printing plate (and a separate run through the press) can increase your printing costs substantially. Using a spot color in place of one of the process colors, creating duotones or tritones, and converting the spot color(s) to process colors are ways to keep costs in check.

## Viewing and Correcting Colors

Because the range of color in CMYK is limited and because not all of Photoshop's filters are available in that color mode, design and creation are often done in RGB mode, and the artwork is later converted for print. The difference in gamut, however, allows you to design in RGB with colors that can't be printed in CMYK. Photoshop warns you if you select an RGB color that cannot be reproduced with CMYK inks. In Figure 21.10, you can see the gamut warning for both the Color palette and Color Picker. It is a small triangle with an exclamation point.

Clicking the swatch that appears next to the gamut warning triangle in the Color palette or below the triangle in the Color Picker converts the color to the nearest CMYK equivalent. Photoshop automatically converts all colors to their nearest CMYK equivalents when a document is converted from RGB to CMYK mode.

Photoshop also enables you to soft proof your work. By choosing View, Proof Colors, you can check how your project is expected to print.

Soft proofing is not usually considered an acceptable substitute for hard proofs, discussed earlier in this chapter. Soft proofing is feasible only when the monitor has been properly calibrated and an appropriate profile for the specific printer is available.

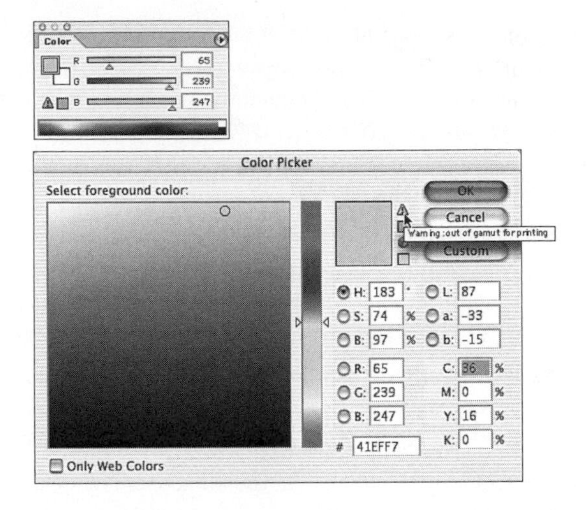


Figure 21.10
The cursor indicates the gamut warning in the Color Picker. The icon is the same in the Color palette.

The View, Proof Setup, Custom command enables you to select a color profile for the printer. You then use the View, Proof Colors command to toggle the preview on and off. The Custom option opens the Proof Setup dialog box, shown in Figure 21.11.

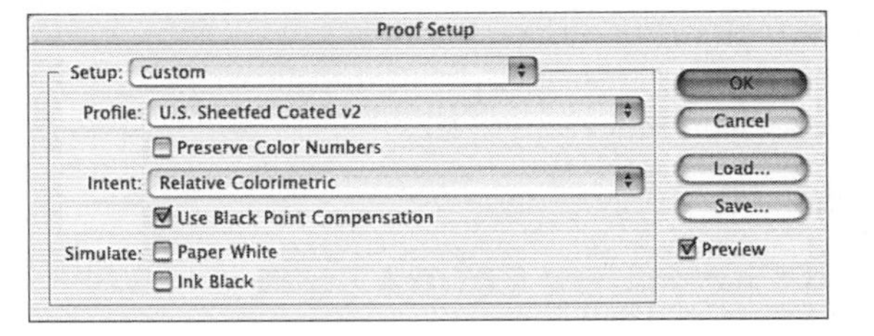


Figure 21.11
Changes made in this dialog box do not change the selections in the Color Settings dialog box.

Selecting the appropriate color profile is critical if Proof Setup is to give you an accurate representation of the image. Your printer may be able to supply you with a profile for the particular press and inks that will be used on your project.

The Preserve Color Numbers option shows you what your artwork would look like if it were just thrown on the press "as is." This setting simulates printing the color values without compensating for the profile space. Normally, you should leave this option unchecked.

The Intent pop-up menu gives you the same four options that you can find in the Advanced section of the Color Settings dialog box:

- **Perceptual**—This option preserves the relationships among colors. The range of colors can be changed, but the visual differences among them are maintained. Color values can also change. Perceptual is not suitable for images, such as logos, that must use specific colors.
- **Saturation**—The Saturation option is not acceptable for print in many circumstances. It attempts to make colors more vivid and is designed for use with presentation graphics.

Using the Custom option enables you to select a CMYK setup other than that selected in Color Settings. You can select Working CMYK to use that setting.

- **Relative Colorimetric**—This option, the default, strives to preserve all colors that fall inside the target gamut, maintaining their color accuracy. Colors that are outside the target gamut are mapped as closely as possible but might overlap with other colors. The extreme highlight of the image (white) is mapped to white in the destination space. If the artwork is within the CMYK gamut, you need to consider only the differences among output devices. These differences are usually minor.
- **Absolute Colorimetric**—Like the Relative Colorimetric option, this one tries to preserve colors that are within the target gamut. However, it does not take the image's white point into account.

Simulate Paper White, when selected, compensates for the medium defined in the profile (if any). Simulate Black Ink simulates onscreen the dynamic range of the selected profile.

# SERVICE BUREAUS, PRINT BROKERS, AND PRINTERS

A graphic artist must do several things to prepare artwork for commercial printing. Some of the other steps, however, may be best left to others. In some cases, one individual serves as designer, artist, and prepress specialist. Understanding who is responsible for what steps, and communicating about those steps, is often the key to successfully completing a project.

## Service Bureaus

It would be lovely if you had a huge budget and an office equipped with the latest and greatest machinery, ready and waiting for any project that comes along. Unfortunately, the reality is that budgets are usually tight, or at least realistic. Spending tens of thousands of dollars for a piece of equipment that you might use only a few times a year is not efficient. Hiring out that particular piece of work a couple of times a year is usually far more practical.

*Service bureaus* have evolved to fill that niche. The typical service bureau offers drum scanners that can produce the highest quality digital images, imagesetters that can produce the films from which printing plates are made, calibrated color-proofing equipment, and various other hardware and services. Finding (and maintaining a good working relationship with) a good service bureau allows a small operation or an independent to offer all the services of a major production house. Within those major production houses, maintaining good relationships between departments is often critical to mission accomplishment. For contractors and independents, most service bureau costs can be built in to a bid, an estimate, or a contract. In-house project estimators should also build in such expenses.

In the offset printing workflow, service bureaus can be used for initial scans, color corrections, color proofs, and separations or film. Most service bureaus can handle Windows as well as Macintosh files and can work with files generated by all major graphics and publishing programs. However, asking which file formats, program versions, and platforms are acceptable before you enter into a working relationship with a service bureau is always a good idea.

## Print Brokers

*Print brokers* are middlemen, outside vendors who coordinate a print job for you. Some print brokers are sales representatives, with a working knowledge of the business and a stable of clients. Other print brokers may be experts in the field, with extensive experience and endless contacts. In either case, they are expected to serve as your representative to and with the printer.

Your communication with print brokers, as with anyone involved with a project, is important. Print brokers need to understand clearly what you (or the client or boss) expect before finding and contracting with a printer. The specific areas of discussion could include color fidelity, image clarity, paper quality, and finishing. If you're using a broker, you'll also want to clearly delineate areas of responsibility. Perhaps you need the broker to price out the job and determine the best printer for the contract. On the other hand, you might need a broker who is able to handle the job from the time it's completed on your computer to the time it's sent to the distribution channel.

## Printers

Some printers have all the capabilities of service bureaus, and some contract out everything except putting ink on paper. The key to a good printer is twofold: fulfilling your requirements at a good price and communicating with you.

After you've received or conceived the project, determine whether any special inks or papers will be involved. If so, one of your first calls should be to the printer. Find out what requirements (and limitations) could have an impact on your creative or production process. You should also know, if you'll be transferring projects digitally, what file formats and program versions the printer can use.

Sometimes you need different printers for different types of jobs, too. One printer may produce superior color fidelity but be too expensive for a two-color insert. Another printer might be able to offer faster turnaround for emergency jobs. Having working relationships with several printers can make it possible to save money or, sometimes more important, time.

# MASTERING PHOTOSHOP

## Do I Need More Than an Ink-Slinger?

*I called my print shop to ask which CMYK profile I should be using in my color settings. All they could say was "I dunno." What should I do?*



Is accurate color reproduction something you don't care about at all? Is it the only print shop in town? Are you or your spouse related by blood to the owner of the print shop? If the answer to these three questions is "No," perhaps a few phone calls are in order.

On the other hand, if you never prepare color-critical work, if the price is right, and if delivery meets the deadline, you might not have a problem. Consider your needs. It could be that having the perfect CMYK profile for that shop's Heidelberg press isn't necessary. If the results are good, whether through precise coordination of digital data or by "Kentucky windage," there's no reason to change.

Remember, too, that you can establish working relationships with different shops for different jobs. You can also use service bureaus or print brokers when necessary.

Although an understanding of trapping can be beneficial, leaving the actual procedure to specialists is usually best. Improper trapping can produce severe output problems. Before attempting to trap an image, speak with your printer or service bureau.

## Avoiding the Trap

*I hear a lot about trapping, but don't see anything about it in Photoshop. Should I be trapping my images? If so, how?*

Photoshop is primarily an image editor, and most Photoshop work involves raster images. Trapping is typically reserved for vector artwork, in which large areas of solid color abut. You don't need to trap most Photoshop images. Service bureaus and printers often have dedicated workstations with specialized software to do trapping. Trapping can be extremely time consuming and, therefore, very expensive. Typically, the workstations and trapping software are run by experienced professionals.

To trap properly, if the occasion does arise, expand the lighter color so that it overlaps with the darker color. Expanding the lighter color minimizes distortion of the image. The darker color's shape remains the same, resulting in less apparent change of the image. There are two basic types of trapping. A *spread* occurs when the lighter color sits on a darker background, and the area of lighter color is expanded. A *choke* occurs when the darker color sits on a lighter background, and the lighter color is extended onto the darker.

IV

# IMAGEREADY

22

# SAVE FOR WEB AND IMAGE OPTIMIZATION

## IN THIS CHAPTER

This chapter discusses the myriad of file optimization options available when prepping files for the Web. Although it's true that Web image optimization hasn't changed much in the past few years, it remains crucial that files are compressed as much as possible, without sacrificing colors or detail. We may be entering the broadband age, but people still have little patience for graphics that load slowly.

Topics in this chapter include file formats, color table optimization, and variable compression with alpha masks.

# GRAPHICS ON THE WEB: OVERVIEW

The World Wide Web has evolved into a visual environment. This graphic-rich environment, however, does have a number of limitations. Because the Web is presented in Hypertext Markup Language (HTML) and related computer languages, graphics must conform to certain rules. Chief among them is the restriction on which file formats can be used. A Web browser will not, for example, display a PSD or TIFF file.

Photoshop and ImageReady are state-of-the-art Web graphic production tools. You can use them to develop a wide range of Web-compatible graphics, from simple logos to rollover buttons to animations.

## File Optimization and Compression

*Optimization* is the process of minimizing file size while protecting image quality. Smaller files download from the Web server to the visitor's computer faster, so they display onscreen quicker. The more quickly the image displays, the less disruption for the site's visitor. The balance between file size and image quality is not an exact science—there is no specific formula for optimization.

Files optimized for Web display are stripped of nonessential data. Image previews and custom icons, for example, are not saved with the file. Such data is not visible over the Web and serves to increase file size, thus slowing download time.

JPEG files use a *lossy* compression scheme. Image data is discarded to reduce file size and is re-created to display the image. The more data that is thrown away, the smaller the file size. However, the more information that must be re-created, the more likely the image quality will be degraded. When a JPEG image is opened onscreen (or printed), the pixels that were deleted during compression must be restored. Because the exact color of the missing pixels is not recorded, the JPEG process estimates their color, based on surrounding pixels. The more pixels that must be re-created, the fewer original pixels that are available from which to estimate.

GIF and PNG (both 8-bit and 24-bit) use *lossless* compression. GIF and PNG-8 file size can be further minimized by reducing the actual number of colors recorded in the file. PNG-24 has no such option. Save for Web has a lossy GIF setting.

Remember that Photoshop and ImageReady are designed to create *graphics*, not to produce Web pages. Although it is certainly possible to produce rudimentary Web pages using only Photoshop and ImageReady, they are *not* Web development tools. Use Adobe GoLive or Macromedia Dreamweaver instead.

## The Role of the Web Browser

A Web page typically consists of both text and images, wrapped up in HTML so that the page can be displayed on the viewer's computer. You use a Web browser to translate that HTML and re-create the page on your screen. The HTML file contains the page's text and tells the browser where to find the images on the Web server. The two major Web browsers are Microsoft Internet Explorer and Netscape Navigator. They, and most of the lesser-used browsers, can interpret HTML and similar languages natively and can use plug-ins for additional capabilities (such as Scalable Vector Graphics). Without the Web browser, the page can't be downloaded and displayed. (However, numerous programs, including some word processors, can efficiently display a Web page if it has been downloaded and saved to your hard drive.)

When designing and producing your Web graphics in Photoshop and ImageReady, you must take into account the capabilities of the Web browsers that your visitors are most likely to use. If your visitors or at least your target audience is likely to be using up-to-date versions of major Web browsers, you can save your graphics in a wider variety of file formats. If it's important that visitors with older browsers not be excluded from the full impact of your graphics, you should restrict yourself to JPEG and GIF.

Remember, too, that cellular telephones and personal digital assistants (PDAs) can access the Internet. PDAs typically use wireless connections and have limited color capability. Although some cell phones are limited to 1-bit color—they can display only black and white (or black and gray or green)—color cell phone displays are becoming very common. If your target audience will be accessing your site with cell phones or PDAs, plan accordingly.

## HTML and Images

Web graphics can be *sliced*—divided into subsections—and with ImageReady you can create special effects associated with the image. The image can change appearance depending on the mouse's location or behavior, and you can even create animations that play in the Web browser window.

These special attributes and behaviors require HTML code associated with the image. The HTML tells the Web browser how to handle the file and when or why to change the image's appearance. HTML can be generated for sliced images in ImageReady or Photoshop, but only ImageReady can create rollovers and animations. (The component images can be generated in Photoshop, but the special attributes must be developed in ImageReady.)

## Saving HTML with Images

If the image has rollovers, is an animation, includes a special background color or background image, or will be used as a tiled background on a Web page, you must save both the image and the associated HTML. With this saving option, HTML code is generated and an .html file is saved along with a folder named, by default, Images.

When working with Adobe GoLive, you can simply add a rollover as a "component" by using Adobe's Smart Objects technology. GoLive generates the HTML automatically.

To incorporate the artwork into an existing Web page, you typically must copy and paste the HTML into the appropriate section of the Web page's HTML document. The Images folder must be saved (and uploaded) with the HTML and other Web page graphics.

## Color: 8-Bit and 24-Bit

Most modern Web browsers (and HTML) support Bitmap (black and white), Grayscale, Indexed Color, and RGB modes. CMYK images cannot be displayed in a Web browser. Indexed color and grayscale images contain a maximum of 256 different colors or shades of gray. RGB images can have millions of subtly different colors in a single image. Because less color information per pixel is required in Indexed Color mode, an image of the same pixel dimensions is typically smaller and displays more quickly in a Web browser because it downloads faster.

*For a discussion of color depth, see Chapter 5, "Color, in Theory and in Practice."*

Indexed Color mode is appropriate for Web graphics that have few colors or large areas of solid color and for any image smaller than 256 pixels. RGB mode is better suited to capture and present the fine gradations of color typically found in photographs.

## Resolution Versus Pixel Size

Web browsers ignore any resolution information recorded in an image. (The exception is Scalable Vector Graphics, which require a plug-in for the Web browser and cannot be created in Photoshop or ImageReady.) Images are displayed onscreen strictly according to their pixel dimensions, not their print dimensions. Consider resolution to be an instruction to the printer about how to reproduce the image on paper, not an instruction to the browser about how to reproduce the image onscreen. As you can see in Figure 22.1, graphics of the same pixel dimensions occupy the same amount of Web page, regardless of resolution.

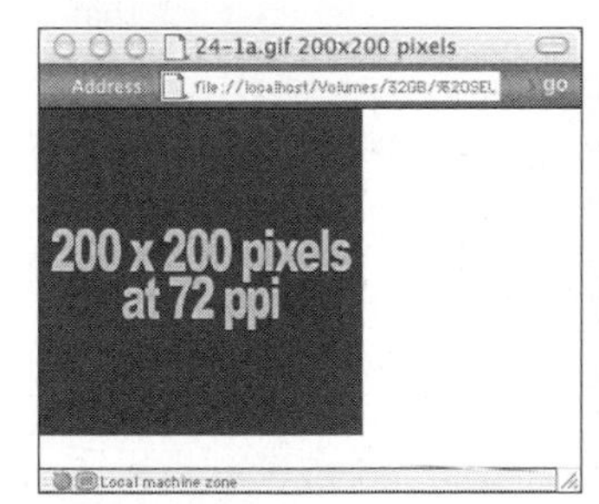

**Figure 22.1**
The two images are shown in separate Internet Explorer windows.

## Transparency on the Web

Every graphic you create in Photoshop and ImageReady is rectangular. If you want the image to appear to be another shape, you must make parts of the rectangle transparent. The pixels will still be there; they'll just be invisible. If you want the image to fade to the background or appear with a translucent shadow, you need partially transparent pixels. When each pixel is either completely opaque or completely transparent, the transparency is said to be *hard edged*. Images that have partially opaque pixels are said to have *variable transparency*.

The key to transparency in Web graphics is understanding the capabilities—and limitations—of the Web-compatible file formats:

> Remember that, with the exception of SVG, all graphics are displayed in a Web browser window at 100% zoom—pixel for pixel—onscreen. Always preview your graphics at 100% zoom.

- **GIF**—You can create images with hard-edged transparency and save them as GIF. The file format does not support variable transparency.
- **JPEG**—JPEG does not support transparency.
- **PNG-8**—Hard-edged transparency is handled automatically in PNG-8—simply create the image on a transparent background and save it as PNG-8. Variable transparency is simulated in PNG-8 with dithering.
- **PNG-24**—Both hard-edged and variable transparency are supported natively by PNG-24.

In Figure 22.2, an image using both hard-edged and variable transparency is shown in the four major Web-related image formats.

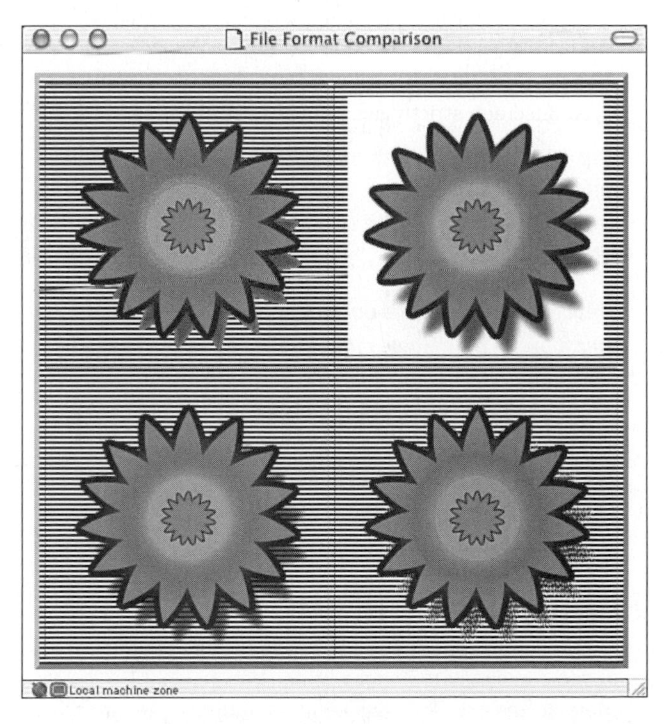


**Figure 22.2**
Clockwise, starting from the upper left, the images are GIF, JPEG, PNG-8, and PNG-24.

*Need to optimize as JPEG, but want transparency too? See "Transparent JPEGs" in the "Mastering ImageReady" section at the end of this chapter.*

## Text for Web

Text appears in a Web page one of two ways: as text, embedded in the page's HTML, or as part of an image. Generally speaking, large amounts of type are typically incorporated into the page as HTML; images that contain type often include buttons and banners.

Type displayed in a Web browser window is displayed as pixels, whether HTML or in an image. Because the type is displayed at 100% onscreen, small type is often blurry or jagged. You can use Photoshop's antialiasing to smooth the curves of type you incorporate into an image. Fonts with strong, even strokes reproduce more cleanly with pixels than do cursive or ornamental fonts.

PNG is not supported by some older Web browsers, but most browsers in use today can properly display PNG images. Remember, however, that a PNG-24 image is typically larger than the same image saved as JPEG.

When possible, use sans serif fonts for Web graphics—their straight, even strokes reproduce more clearly in a Web browser.

*Want more information on type for the Web? See "Letters by Pixel" in the "Mastering ImageReady" section at the end of this chapter.*

# PHOTOSHOP'S SAVE FOR WEB

Web graphics can be created directly from Photoshop, using the Save for Web feature. You can optimize images as GIF, JPEG, PNG-8, PNG-24, and WBMP. Using Save for Web gives you far more control over the optimization process than you have creating JPEG images with the Save As command or exporting to GIF89a in earlier versions of Photoshop.

Save for Web is, in some respects, a separate program within Photoshop. It even creates its own preferences. For the Mac, look for Adobe Save for Web 8.0 Prefs in the same folder as Photoshop's preferences file. In Windows, Save for Web's preferences are written to the Registry.

*What do you need to do to prepare an image before opening Save for Web? See "Pre-optimization" in the "Mastering ImageReady" section at the end of this chapter.*

The Photoshop CS Save for Web dialog box, shown in Figure 22.3, is resizable—you can drag the lower-right corner to increase the size of the preview area. Because this is a dialog box rather than a window, there is no "maximize" box to click.

## The Window Tabs

The four tabs in the upper-left corner of the Save for Web dialog box determine the content of the preview area. You can show the original image alone, a single image that is updated to show you current optimization settings, or you can compare images. When you select 2-Up, a pair of images is visible in the preview area. By default, the original image and an optimized image are shown, although you can change the original to any optimization settings. When you choose 4-Up, you can see the original and three different optimization possibilities for comparison or see four different sets of optimization options.

In both the 2-Up and 4-Up variations, you activate a pane by clicking it. That variation's settings will be shown and can then be changed. Figure 22.3 shows the 4-Up view. When the image is wide and short, the window automatically reconfigures, as shown in Figure 22.4.

## The Tools

To the left of the preview area, you have four tools available. In 2-Up and 4-Up views, the tools can be used only in the active pane. They function similarly to the comparable tools in Photoshop:

- **Hand tool**—When the entire image doesn't fit in the window, click and drag with the Hand tool to reposition it. You can temporarily activate the Hand tool by holding down the spacebar.
- **Slice Select tool**—When the image has multiple slices, you can use the Slice Select tool to choose a slice to optimize. Different slices can have different optimization settings.
- **Zoom tool**—Click or drag to zoom in, and (Option)-click) [Alt]-click to zoom out. You can also change the magnification by using the pop-up menu to the lower left in the dialog box or by using the contextual menu.
- **Eyedropper tool**—The Eyedropper is used to select a color. You can select colors only in the active pane. If the optimization settings selected are GIF or PNG-8, the color you click will be selected in the color table. For 24-bit images (JPEG and PNG-24), the color is shown only in the swatch below the Eyedropper tool on the left.

Below the tools is the color swatch, which shows the color most recently selected with the Eyedropper. (When you open Save for Web, the last selected color is still visible, even if it's not present in the current image.)

The button below the color swatch toggles slice visibility on and off. Clicking the Slice Select tool automatically shows slices, too.

## Settings and the Settings Menu

The heart of the Save for Web dialog box is the area to the right, where optimization options are selected. When in 2-Up or 4-Up mode, click a pane or a slice and then change the options. You can select from a menu of predefined optimization settings, or you can select a file format and choose custom settings (see Figure 22.5).

> Although Save for Web offers preset zoom magnifications from 12.5% to 1600%, you can use the Zoom tool to zoom out as far as 1%. Remember, however, that you should always make your final evaluation of Web graphics at 100% zoom—that's how they'll be seen in a Web browser.

**Figure 22.3**
The right side of the dialog box changes, depending on the file format you select in the Settings area. Note the new Edit in ImageReady button (you learn more about this in "Using Channels and Layer Data to Optimize," later in this chapter.

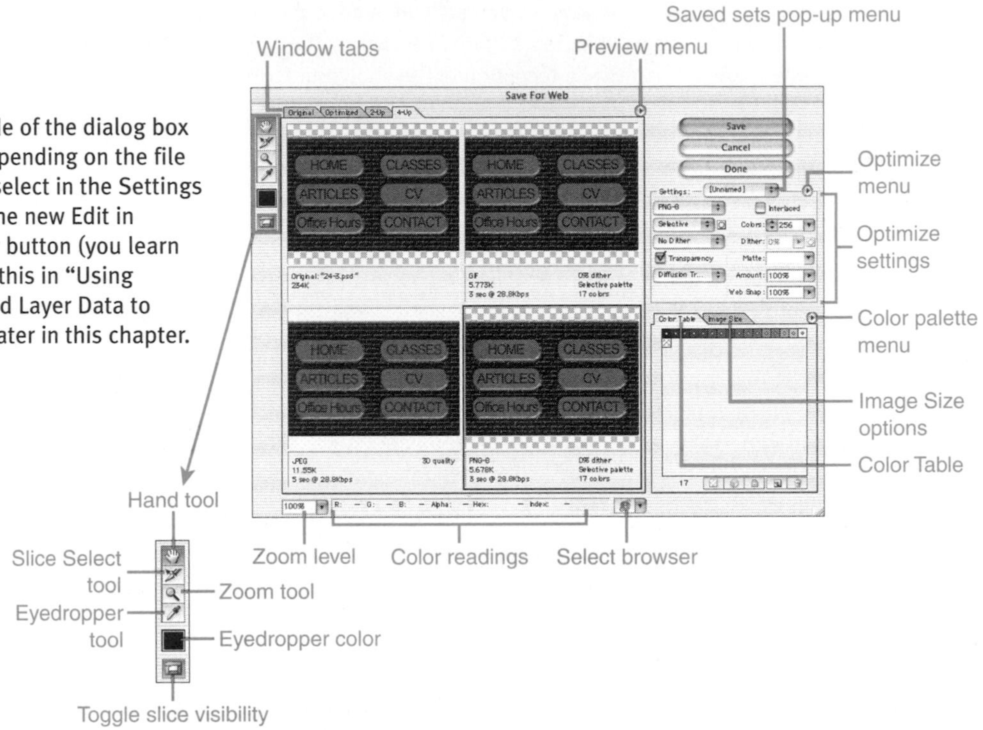

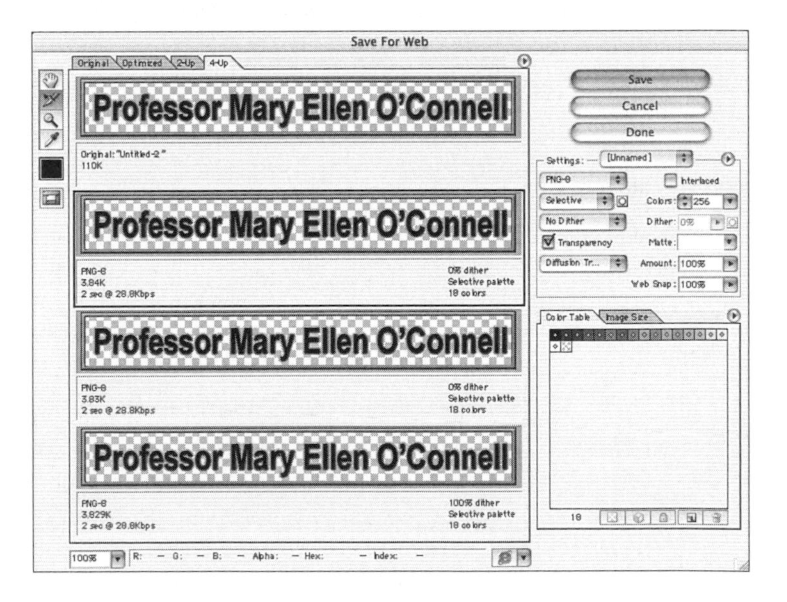


**Figure 22.4**
The active image is highlighted with an outline, and its settings are visible to the right.

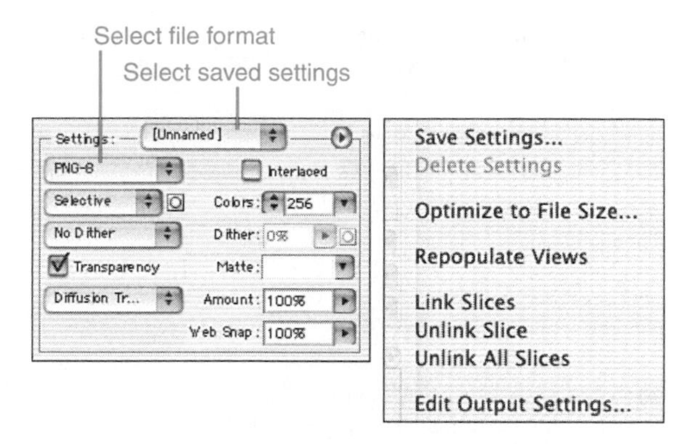


Figure 22.5
The fields and sliders available in the Settings area of the Save for Web dialog box vary from file format to file format. The Settings menu is shown to the right.

*Each of the five file formats has its own options for the Settings area. See "File Format Optimization Settings," later in this chapter.*

You can choose custom optimization settings and save them, using the Save Settings command from the Settings menu. As long as they are saved in the Optimization Settings folder, they will appear in the Settings pop-up menu. Saved settings can also be removed from the pop-up menu by using the Delete Settings command. The file in the Optimized Settings folder is not deleted until you quit Photoshop.

The Optimize to File Size command opens the dialog box shown in Figure 22.6. You select a target file size, and Save for Web generates the most appropriate settings *for that pane*—the other panes in 2-Up and 4-Up are not affected. After you click OK, you can then further adjust the optimization settings, if desired.

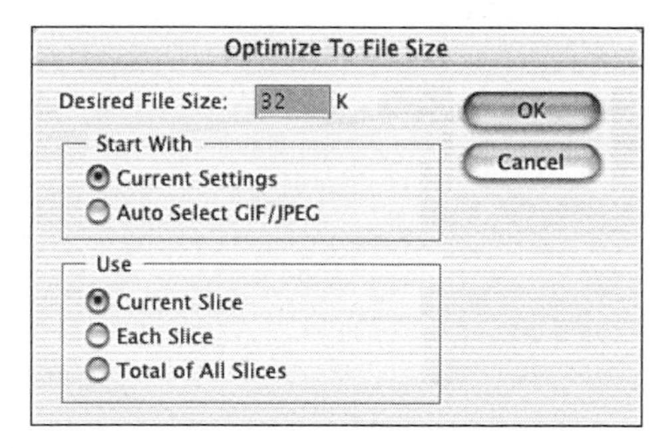


Figure 22.6
You can generate settings to optimize a single slice or an entire image to the specified size.

The Repopulate Views menu command is available only in 4-Up view. It generates a pair of new optimization settings based on the selected pane. The new options use the same file format but different options for comparison. If you've selected the Original pane and changed it to show an optimization configuration, Repopulate Views restores it to Original and replaces the other three panes with their original content.

Even in Save for Web, you can view the Slice Options dialog box. Simply double-click a slice with the Slice Select tool to change the slice's name, URL, target, message, or other options.

You can select multiple slices in an image by Shift-clicking with the Slice Select tool. When more than one slice is active, you can link and unlink them with the commands in the Settings menu. Linking slices enables you to optimize them at the same time.

Perhaps the most important of the Settings menu commands is Edit Output Settings. You use this command to specify how Save for Web creates HTML, names slices, generates an image or a background, and more.

*For specific information about output settings, see "Editing Output Settings," later in this chapter.*

## The Color Table

The Color Table palette shows the individual colors of an 8-bit image. You can edit, delete, and shift each color. The Color Table palette is used only with GIF and PNG-8 images. You cannot directly manipulate the individual colors of images in 24-bit color.

*For specific information about manipulating the colors of an 8-bit image, see "Working with the Color Table," later in this chapter.*

## The Image Size Tab

Docked with the Color Table palette in Save for Web, the Image Size palette enables you to change the size of the image directly in the dialog box (see Figure 22.7).

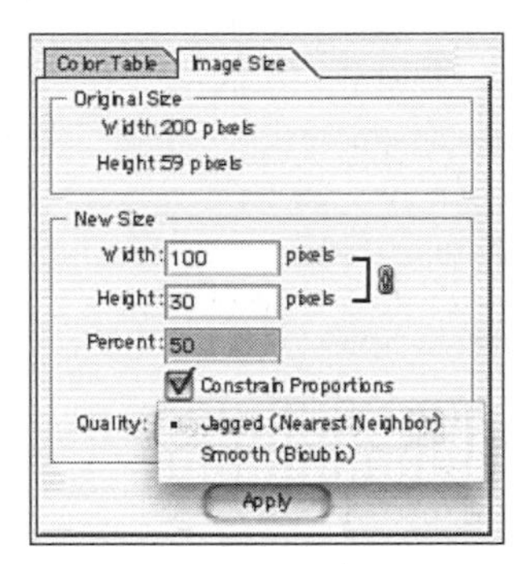


**Figure 22.7**
The Image Size palette has options comparable to those found in the Image Size dialog box (opened with the command Image, Image Size), with the exception of resolution (which isn't required for raster Web graphics).

You can specify an exact pixel dimension or a percentage. Selecting the Constrain Proportions check box automatically maintains an image's width/height ratio (as does sizing by percent). One of the Bicubic options in the Quality pop-up menu should be used with photographic or other continuous-tone images. Use Bicubic Sharper when reducing image size, and use Bicubic Smoother when enlarging an image. Nearest Neighbor is often more appropriate for interface elements and other Web graphics that have large areas of solid color or distinct edges.

## The Preview Menu

Save for Web's Preview menu (see Figure 22.8), accessed through the triangle at the top right of the preview panes, determines how the image will appear in the active preview pane.

> Using the Image Size palette changes all panes of the Save for Web dialog box, including the Original pane. Clicking the Apply button simply resizes the image and does not optimize it.

Browser Dither

Hide Auto Slices

✓ Uncompensated Color
Standard Windows Color
Standard Macintosh Color
Use Document Color Profile

Size/Download Time (9600 bps Modem)
Size/Download Time (14.4 Kbps Modem)
Size/Download Time (28.8 Kbps Modem)
✓ Size/Download Time (56.6 Kbps Modem/ISDN)
Size/Download Time (128 Kbps Dual ISDN)
Size/Download Time (256 Kbps Cable/DSL)
Size/Download Time (384 Kbps Cable/DSL)
Size/Download Time (512 Kbps Cable/DSL)
Size/Download Time (768 Kbps Cable/DSL)
Size/Download Time (1 Mbps Cable)
Size/Download Time (1.5 Mbps Cable/T1)
Size/Download Time (2 Mbps)

**Figure 22.8**
The Browser Dither option is not available for preview panes set to Original.



Browser Dither simulates how the image will appear on a monitor set to 8-bit color. Hide Auto Slices doesn't hide the content of the slices, just the slice lines and numbers for automatically generated slices. Each pane's color simulation can be set individually, using any of the next four options. The colors selected affect the preview in Save for Web, not the saved image. The Size/Download Time options determine what numbers will be displayed in the lower-left corner of each preview pane.

## The Done, Reset, and Remember Buttons

Clicking the Done button makes a record of the current optimization settings (or the settings for the current pane in 4-Up view) and closes the dialog box. The settings are saved in the Save for Web preferences rather than with the image file. The next time you open Save for Web with the same or a different image, the settings you recorded are used.

When you hold down (Option) [Alt], the Done button changes to Remember. Remember stores the current settings for that pane without closing the dialog box.

Although Save for Web doesn't support Undo, you can revert to the settings you had for the active pane or slice when the dialog box was opened (or when you last used Remember). Click in the pane or select the slice and then hold down the (Option) [Alt] key. The Cancel button changes to Reset.

## Using Channels and Layer Data to Optimize

You can use alpha channels or vector layers to govern the application of a number of options when optimizing images. Type and shape layers, or alpha channels you create in Photoshop, can form the basis for where certain settings are applied in an image. The options that can be regulated vary from file format to file format:

- **GIF**—You can use alpha channels and vector layers to regulate the application of dither, lossiness, and color reduction for GIF files.

- **JPEG**—JPEG files can use alpha channels and vector layers to control what level of compression is applied in different areas of an image.
- **PNG-8**—Dither and color reduction can be controlled with alpha channels and vector layers in PNG-8 files.
- **PNG-24**—PNG-24 cannot take advantage of alpha channels or vector layers in optimization.
- **WBMP**—You can control what parts of an image are dithered with an alpha channel or vector layer information when preparing images for WBMP format.

You can use type *and* shape layer data, as well as an alpha channel, for each image or slice. You must create the alpha channels in Photoshop before opening Save for Web.

Using layer data or an alpha channel with Save for Web enables you to maintain quality in key areas of an image while sacrificing quality in other areas to reduce file size. For example, if you have a photograph of a statue in a park to prepare as a JPEG for the Web, you can use an alpha channel to maintain high quality for the statue and compress the background at a lower quality level.

To use layer data or an alpha channel in Save for Web, you click the mask button to the right of the appropriate field in Settings (see Figure 22.9, left). You select a check box for the type of layer data to use, or you can select the alpha channel from the Channel pop-up menu, which lists all available alpha channels.

An alpha channel enables you to set minimum and maximum values for the application of some options. For dithering, lossiness, and JPEG quality, you set a minimum and maximum value by using the slider in the dialog box (see Figure 22.9, bottom right). To use an alpha channel with a color-reduction algorithm, you simply choose the alpha channel (see Figure 22.9, top right).

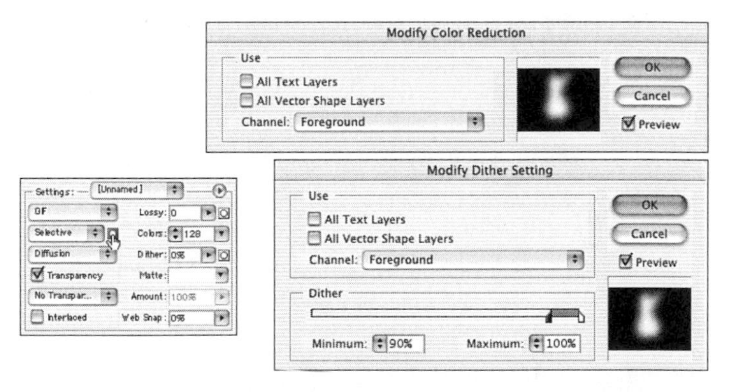


Figure 22.9
The dither, lossiness, and JPEG quality options have identical dialog boxes.

The minimum and maximum values are applied according to the location of black and white in the alpha channel, with intermediate values applied according to grays in the channel.

You can use a separate alpha channel for each setting in GIF and PNG-8, but only one channel can be used for each setting. The exception is, of course, when you're optimizing slices individually; in this case, you can use a different set of channels with each slice. The alpha channels are used during the application of the Save for Web settings but are not retained with the image.

If the image needs more detailed Web optimization, click the Edit in ImageReady button. ImageReady allows for more control over advanced Web optimization features, including GIF animations, image map controls and parameters, as well as detailed slice options and customizable HTML files.

# OPTIMIZING IN IMAGEREADY

The basic tools for preparing images for optimization in ImageReady are the image window, the Optimize palette, the Color Table palette, and the Output Settings dialog box (see Figure 22.10). The optimized image is saved with the File, Save Optimized As command.

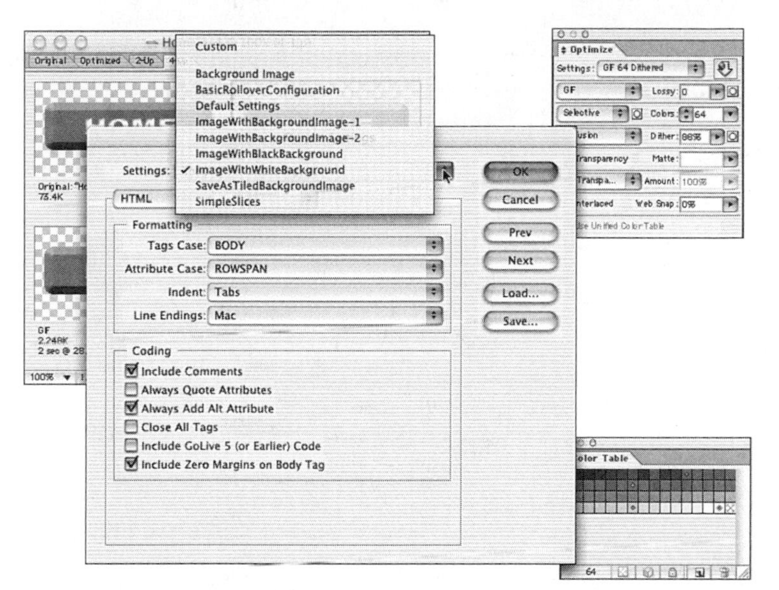


**Figure 22.10**
The image window (left), the Optimize palette (upper right), and the Color Table (lower right) are shown behind the Output Settings dialog box.

## The Image Window

The image window has four configurations that you select by using the tabs at the top of the window. If you want to compare three different optimization configurations head-to-head against the original, use 4-Up (see Figure 22.11). If you need to conserve screen space, one of the other tabs might better suit your needs.

## The Optimize Palette

The Optimize palette fills the role of the Settings area of the Save for Web dialog box. The content of the palette varies, depending on the file format selected. Clicking the two-headed arrow in the palette's tab shows and hides portions of the palette. Click multiple times to rotate through the configurations, shown in Figure 22.12.

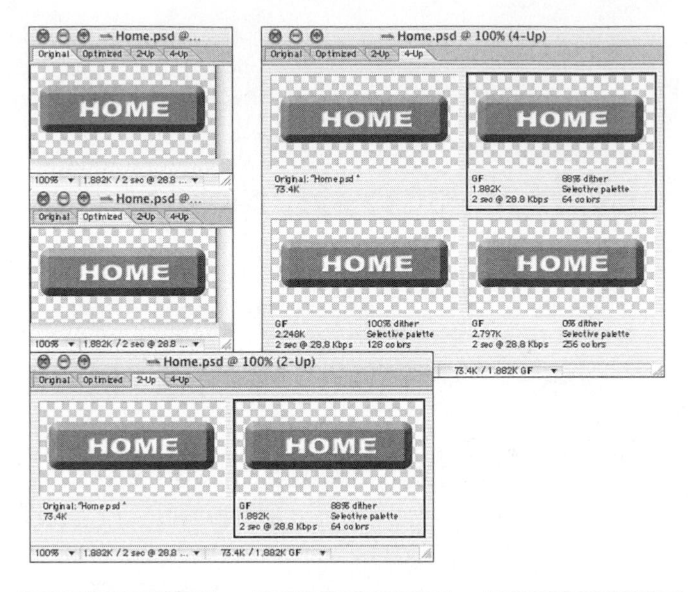


Figure 22.11
The 4-Up tab allows you to compare the original image with three optimized variations.

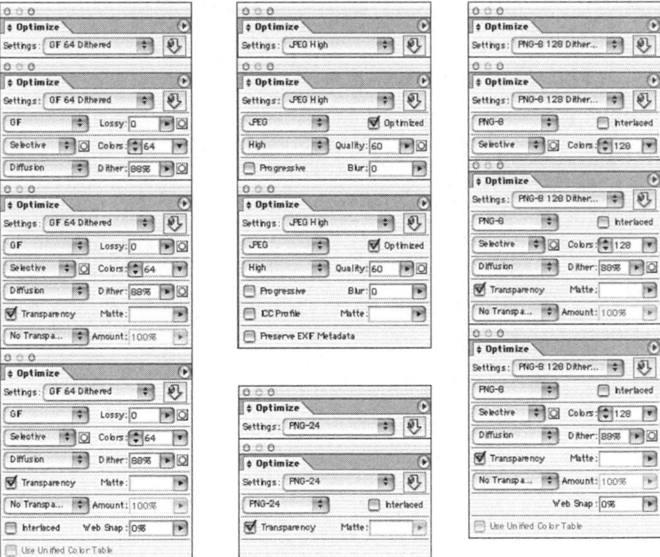


Figure 22.12
The various configurations for each file format are shown. The palette can also show only the tab itself, regardless of the file format.

## The Color Table Palette

The Color Table palette is used only with GIF and PNG-8 files. It is empty when working with JPEG and PNG-24 files and shows only the uneditable black and white swatches for WBMP files.

The Color Table palette can display swatches in two sizes (see Figure 22.13). If you edit colors, the large swatches might be handier—you'll be able to see the difference between the original and edited colors much better.

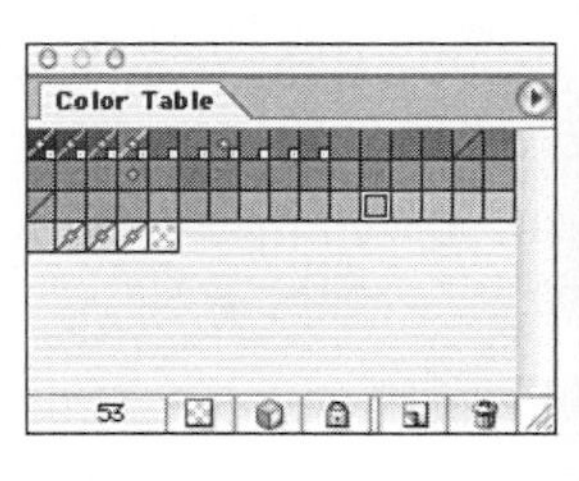


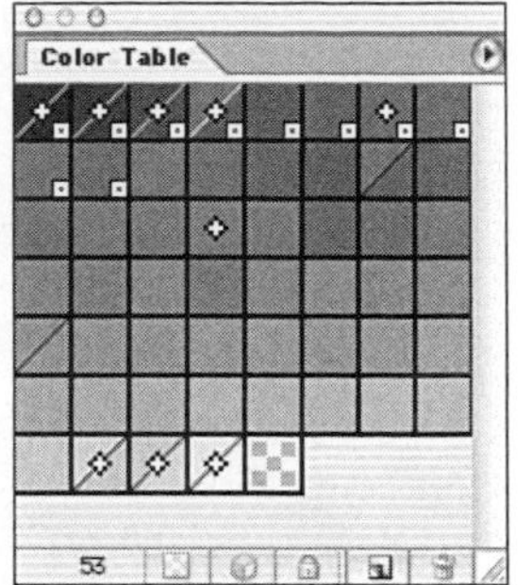


**Figure 22.13**
Change the palette's configuration by using the palette menu.



# FILE FORMAT OPTIMIZATION SETTINGS

Each of the five available file formats has its own options in the Settings area of Save for Web and in ImageReady's Optimize palette. There is considerable overlap between the Save for Web options used for GIF and PNG-8, in that each uses a Color Lookup Table and controls quality and appearance using dither and transparency. As a result, they are discussed together in this section.

## GIF and PNG-8

As you can see in Figure 22.14, the GIF and PNG-8 options in Save for Web are nearly identical. The appropriate options are visible when you select GIF or PNG-8 as the file format from the pop-up menu or when you choose a saved set of GIF or PNG-8 settings in Save for Web or ImageReady.

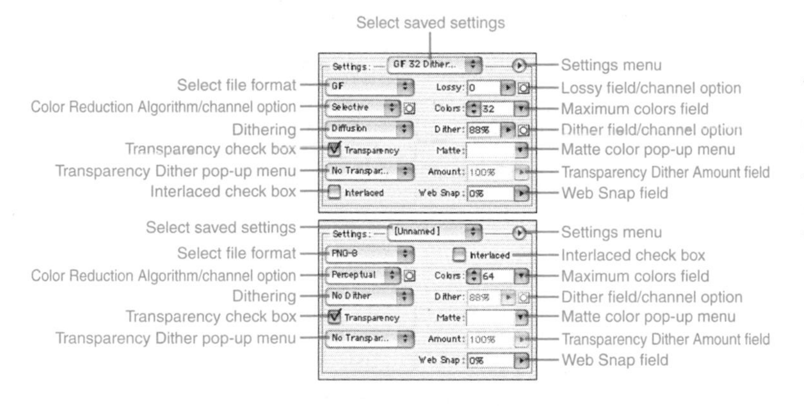


**Figure 22.14**
The only differences between GIF and PNG-8 in the ImageReady Optimize table are the addition of the Lossy field and the Channel option in the GIF settings window.

### Color Reduction Algorithm

Color Reduction Algorithm determines which colors are retained when you reduce the color table. It is discussed at length in the section "Reducing Colors with Algorithms."

*To learn more about using vector layers and channels with the Color Reduction Algorithm, Lossy, and Dither fields, see "Using Channels and Layer Data to Optimize," earlier in this chapter.*

The optimization options are nearly identical in Save for Web and ImageReady. The primary difference is the ImageReady Optimize palette's Create Droplet button. Format-specific differences are discussed in the appropriate sections.

22

## Dithering

Dithering is, in its most basic form, intermixing two colors to simulate a third color. In Figure 22.15, a sample gradient is visible above the Save for Web preview panes. (In color, the gradient runs from blue to red.) In the preview panes, different dithering options are displayed.

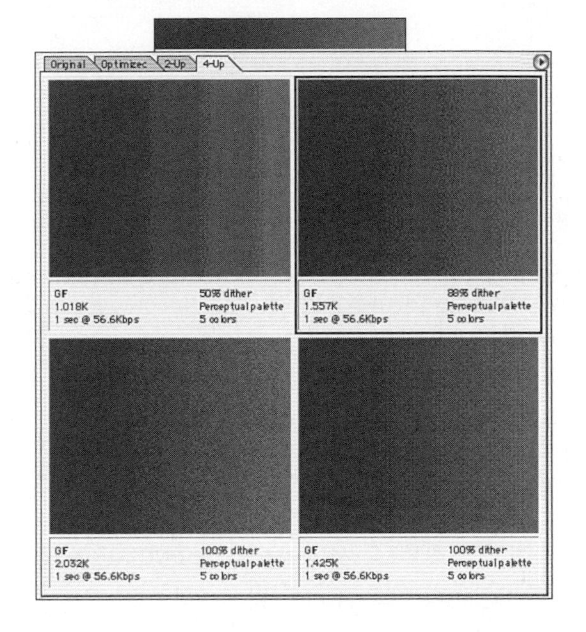


**Figure 22.15**
Top left: Original image. Top right: Diffusion dither, 100%. Bottom left: Diffusion dither, 50%. Bottom right: Diffusion dither, 25%.

When viewed at 100% in a Web browser, the dithering results in a smoother transition between colors than an undithered image.

> You can use dithering to further reduce the number of colors in the color table. When you're optimizing an image, reduce the number of colors to the point where the image is starting to degrade; then select Diffusion from the Dithering pop-up menu and adjust the slider to regain image quality.

## Transparency

When a GIF or PNG-8 image is on a transparent background, you can maintain the transparency by selecting the Transparency check box in Save for Web and ImageReady. When this option is not selected, the transparent areas of the image are filled with the matte color. If the Matte pop-up menu is set to None, white is used. The Transparency check box must be active when you map colors to transparency using the color table.

## Transparency Dither

The Transparency Dither option softens the transition from colors to transparency. It works similarly to the standard Dither option (discussed in the section "Dithering"), but instead of blending colors, it blends from color to transparent.

> If your image should have distinct edges, as for many interface items, set the pop-up menu to No Transparency Dither to prevent softening of the edges.

As with Dithering, you're offered the choice of Diffusion, Pattern, and Noise for Transparency Dither. In addition, when using Diffusion, you can choose the amount by using the slider to the right in the Settings area.

## Interlacing

Interlaced GIF and PNG-8 images appear in the Web browser as they download. Although it *seems* that the image is loading faster, interlacing doesn't actually speed up the process. Rather, the viewer gets feedback while the page loads. Interlacing is recommended for images over a few KB in size.

## Lossy Compression (GIF Only)

The standard implementation of the GIF file format uses only lossless compression. However, when using Save for Web and ImageReady, you can further reduce file size by using the Lossy slider. The more information that is discarded, the smaller the file size. However, image quality can suffer. Complex images, such as photographs, can exhibit speckling or blockiness at higher lossiness settings. Lossy compression is less effective at reducing file sizes of plain images that contain large areas of solid color.

## Maximum Number of Colors

The Colors field governs how many individual colors the image will contain, up to the 8-bit maximum of 256. You can use the pop-up menu, click the arrows, or type a number in the field. Increasing the maximum number of colors does not add new color to an image that starts with fewer than 256 colors. When you select a lower number, Save for Web and ImageReady use the selected algorithm to decide which colors to eliminate.

## Matte

When you deselect Transparency, the matte color is used to fill transparent areas of the image. It can be used to blend the image with a solid-color Web page background. The options are None (no matte), Eyedropper Color (the color most recently selected with Save for Web's Eyedropper tool), White, Black, and Other (which opens the Color Picker). ImageReady doesn't offer the Eyedropper Color option, but it does display a palette of the 216 Web-safe colors from which you can select. ImageReady offers Foreground and Background color as choices, but drops White and Black.

## Web Snap

Increasing the value in the Web Snap field forces colors to the nearest Web-safe color. The higher the value, the more colors are shifted. The percent refers to the tolerance used for changing colors. The higher the Web Snap tolerance, the more change in color that's allowed. Lower tolerances result in only colors closer to their Web-safe counterparts being changed.

> If your image has a transparent background and feathering or antialiasing, selecting your Web page's background color in Matte can prevent or reduce any "halo" around your image.

### Use Unified Color Table (ImageReady Only)

ImageReady's Optimize palette includes the Use Unified Color Table check box, which enables you to standardize the colors used in all rollover states of an image. Selecting this option prevents unwanted color changes in an image's various rollover states. Unifying the color table is available only for GIF and PNG-8 images.

## JPEG

When the file format is set to JPEG in Save for Web or ImageReady, the Settings area changes to the configuration shown in Figure 22.16.

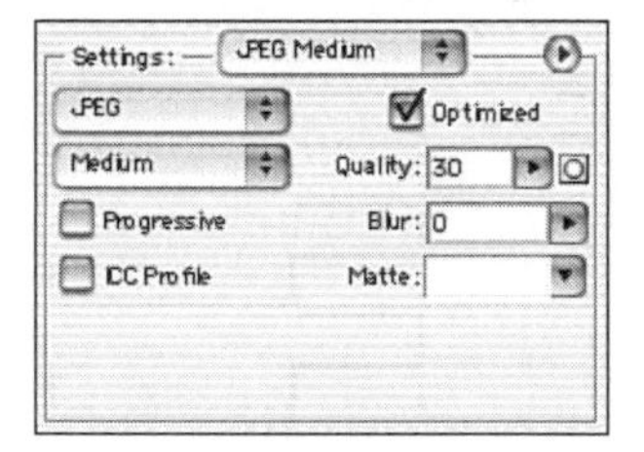


Figure 22.16
The options available remain the same—although their values change, regardless of the level of JPEG compression. ImageReady's Optimize palette also offers a check box that enables you to include a JPEG image's EXIF metadata.

You can select a preconfigured set of JPEG compression options from the pop-up menu at the top of the Settings area, or you can create custom settings. With JPEG selected as the file format, you have the following options:

- **Quality Level**—The pop-up menu directly below the file format pop-up menu offers Low, Medium (shown in Figure 22.16), High, and Maximum. The pop-up menu and the Quality slider are linked—a change to one updates the other. When you select from the pop-up menu, the Quality slider is adjusted to these values: Low: 10, Medium: 30, High: 60, and Maximum: 80.
- **Quality slider**—You can select precise levels of compression by using the Quality slider or by entering a value into the Quality field. The Quality setting is tied to the Quality Level pop-up menu: Quality settings of 0–29 are Low, 30–59 are Medium, 60–79 are High, and 80–100 are Maximum. The Quality Level setting is automatically updated as you change the slider.
- **Blur**—Applying a slight blur to an image can substantially reduce file size when it's compressed as a JPEG. The tradeoff is, of course, a degradation of image sharpness.
- **Transparency matte**—The color you choose in the Matte pop-up menu determines how the JPEG file handles transparency. Because the JPEG format doesn't support transparency, any pixel in the original that has reduced opacity must be filled with color. The matte color is used for any pixel that is 100% transparent, and it's blended with the existing color in any pixel with partial transparency.
- **Progressive**—When the Progressive check box is selected, the JPEG image appears in the Web browser window in stages. Each stage clarifies the image until the final image is displayed. This display option can result in a slight delay in download, but the viewer gets feedback as the image loads, giving the impression of faster loading.

- **ICC Profile**—You can include an ICC color profile with the image. Some Web browsers can adjust the image's appearance according to an embedded profile, but at the expense of increased file size—and therefore a slightly slower download speed. Browsers that do not support ICC profiles display the image as uncorrected.
- **Optimized**—Optimizing a JPEG file can result in a slightly smaller file size. However, some older Web browsers cannot display optimized JPEGs.

In ImageReady, the Optimize palette offers the option of preserving any EXIF data in the image. EXIF data, typically generated by a digital camera, can include information about how and when the image was created and print resolution.

## PNG-24

Unlike the JPEG file format, PNG-24 supports transparency. However, you can also choose to use a matte color in lieu of transparency. As you can see in Figure 22.17, when the Transparency check box is selected, the Matte pop-up menu is grayed out. To select a matte color, uncheck Transparency.

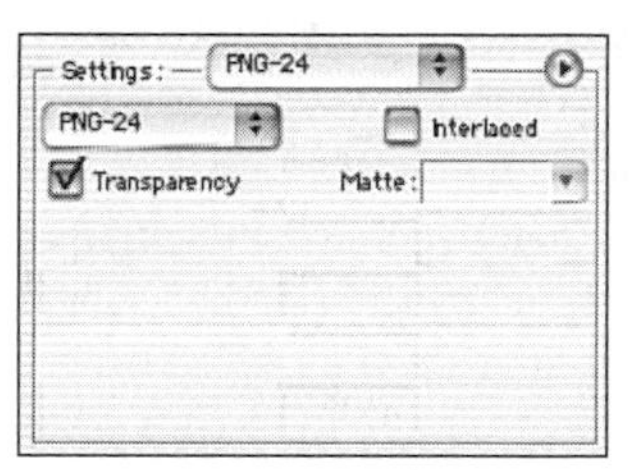


Figure 22.17
Matte choices are None, Eyedropper Color, Foreground, Background, and Other, which opens the Color Picker. ImageReady offers a palette of Web-safe colors rather than the Eyedropper color.

In addition to a choice between transparency and matte, PNG-24 offers interlacing, which is comparable to the JPEG Progressive option and GIF interlacing—the image begins to appear in the Web browser more quickly.

## WBMP

The WBMP file format is intended for the creation of tiny black-and-white image files that transfer speedily to wireless Internet devices, including Web-surfing cellular phones. Because the images are 1-bit color, file size is minimized. As you can see in Figure 22.18, the color table contains only white and black.

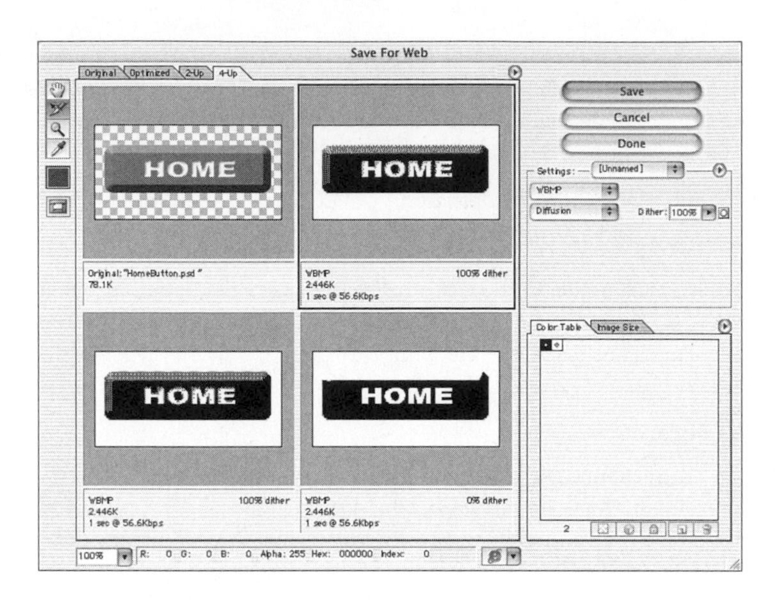


**Figure 22.18**
Save for Web and ImageReady offer the same WBMP options. Displayed clockwise from upper left, this window shows the original, WBMP 100% dither, WBMP 0% dither, and WBMP 50% dither.

# WORKING WITH THE COLOR TABLE

Images in Indexed Color mode use a *color table* to record the colors used in the file. Because such images use 8-bit color, there can be a maximum of 256 distinct colors in a file. The content of the color table is initially determined by the existing colors in the image (or selected slice) and the Colors field in the Settings area of Save for Web or ImageReady's Optimize palette (see Figure 22.19).

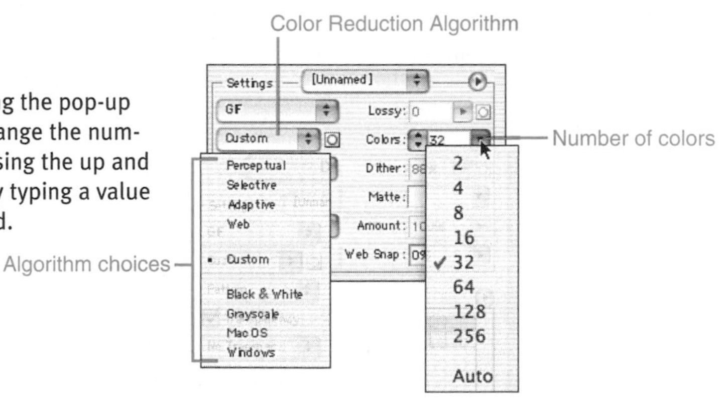

**Figure 22.19**
In addition to using the pop-up menu, you can change the number of colors by using the up and down arrows or by typing a value directly in the field.

## Reducing Colors with Algorithms

When you reduce the number of colors in an 8-bit image, Photoshop makes decisions in accordance with your choice of color-reduction algorithm. You have several options:

- **Perceptual**—Colors are viewed differently by the human eye. Some colors appear more prominent than others. Perceptual color reduction favors the colors that you see with greater sensitivity.

- **Selective**—Like the Perceptual algorithm, Selective favors the colors for which the human eye is more sensitive. However, it also considers the image itself. Areas of broad color are prioritized, and Web colors are retained over similar non-Web colors. The image's overall appearance is best maintained by using Selective, which is the default setting.

> Remember that the color table represents either the colors in the selected pane of Save for Web or those of the selected slice in that pane. Each slice can be optimized separately.

- **Adaptive**—The Adaptive color-reduction procedure evaluates the image and gives preference to the range of color that appears most in the image. For example, color reduction of a picture of a banana preserves most of the yellows at the expense of other colors in the image.
- **Restrictive (Web)**—The colors in the image are converted to Web-safe colors, those 216 colors common to both the Windows and Macintosh system palettes.
- **Custom**—When an image's color table is created by using the Custom option, the colors are "locked in." Further editing of the image won't change the color table. If, for example, you create a custom color table that does not include RGB 255/0/0 (hexadecimal value FF0000) and then attempt to paint with that shade of red, the nearest color already present in the color table is substituted.
- **Black & White**—The color table is reduced to only black and white and consists of only those two colors. The color table is locked after the conversion.
- **Grayscale**—The color table is reduced to grayscale and is then locked.
- **Mac OS**—Only the 256 colors of the Macintosh system palette are used.
- **Windows**—Only the 256 colors of the Windows system palette are used.

## Editing the Color Table

You can also manipulate the colors of the color table individually. In Save for Web, you open the color table (see Figure 22.20) by clicking the palette's tab in the lower-right section of the dialog box. In ImageReady, use the Color Table palette. In 2-Up and 4-Up configurations, either application reflects the currently selected pane. If the image is 24-bit color (JPEG or PNG-24) or 1-bit color (WBMP), the color table is empty.

You can double-click any color in the color table or Color Table palette to open the Color Picker and change the color. Every occurrence of the color in the image is automatically updated. Edited colors appear in the color table with a diagonal line, dividing the swatch into the original color (upper left) and the edited color (lower right).

You can also select a color by clicking once and then using the buttons at the bottom of the color table or the Color Table palette. Making the color transparent or Web-safe changes that color throughout the image. Web-safe colors appear in the table with a diamond in the center of the swatch. Colors you convert to transparency or make Web-safe are divided diagonally, with the original color to the upper left.

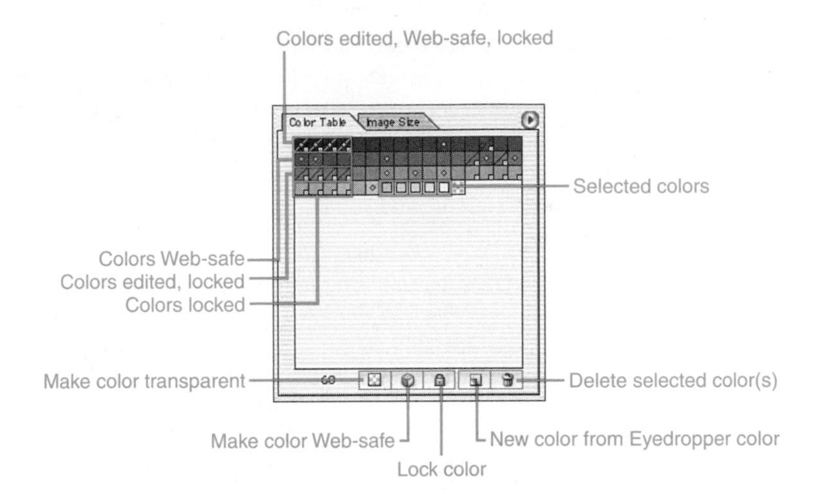


**Figure 22.20**
The color table is used only with 8-bit file formats—GIF, PNG-8, and Grayscale—in Save for Web and ImageReady. It is visible, but uneditable, with WBMP's 1-bit color.

Locking a color prevents it from being deleted if you decrease the number of colors in the image and also prevents a color shift during a color reduction. Locked colors appear in the table with a small box in the lower-right corner of the swatch.

In Save for Web, clicking the New Color button at the bottom of the color table adds a swatch, using whatever color was most recently selected with the Eyedropper tool. You can click anywhere in the active pane to select a color with the Eyedropper. This enables you to select a color that was dropped in a color reduction or to add a color from the original.

When you select and delete a color from the color table, it is replaced in the image with the nearest remaining color. Save for Web and ImageReady attempt to retain the image's appearance as much as possible.

You can select a color in the table by clicking it with the Eyedropper in the active pane of the Save for Web dialog box or ImageReady's image window. You can also hold down the Shift key and click multiple colors. In addition, hold down Shift and *drag* in the active pane to select multiple colors quickly! Deselect all colors by clicking the empty space at the bottom of the color table.

## The Color Table Menu

The menu for Save for Web's color table contains several handy commands. ImageReady's Color Table palette menu mirrors those commands and adds commands to view the palette's colors as large or small swatches (see Figure 22.21).

Many of the commands in the color table menu are self-explanatory, but some deserve further attention:

- **Rebuild Color Table (ImageReady Only)**—When the image has been edited in a way that adds one or more colors, you can regenerate the color table with the Rebuild Color Table command or by selecting an optimization pane in the Optimize dialog box.

**Caution**

After a color is manually deleted from the color table, it is gone, meaning you can no longer increase the number of colors in the image by using the Colors field. In addition, remember that Save for Web has no Undo—however, you can use the Reset button by holding down (Option) [Alt].

**Figure 22.21**
The Save for Web color table menu is not used when optimizing as JPG or PNG-24



- **Map/Unmap Selected Colors to/from Transparency**—Whether you use the menu command or the button at the bottom of the color table, mapping a color to transparency makes that color transparent in the image. This change is "live" and can be reversed by using this menu command again, restoring the color to its original areas in the image. Colors that have been mapped to transparency appear at the end of the table when sorted by Hue or Luminance (see Figure 22.22). The color swatch is divided diagonally, showing the original color to the upper left.
- **Unmap All Transparent Colors**—Instead of just selected colors, all colors that have been mapped to transparency can be unmapped at once.
- **Shift/Unshift Selected Colors to/from Web Palette**—Shifting colors to the Web-safe palette, like mapping to transparency, can be reversed, whether you use the command or the button. The swatches appear in the color table with a diagonal line, showing the original color to the upper left and the Web-safe color to the lower right.
- **Unshift All Colors**—This command returns all colors that have been made Web-safe to their original colors, whether selected or not. It does not affect colors that were originally Web-safe.
- **Unsorted**—Colors are shown in the color table in the original sorting order. Look for reverse order, from highest to lowest, using the hexadecimal value.
- **Sort By Hue**—Using the hue value of the color's HSB value, colors are sorted from 0° to 360°. Neutral colors are placed with the reds at 0°.
- **Sort By Luminance**—Colors in the table are sorted according to the brightness value in the HSB value.
- **Sort By Popularity**—Colors are sorted according to the number of pixels of each color in the image or slice. The most common colors (those with the most pixels per image or slice) appear at the top of the color table.

- **Load Color Table/Save Color Table**—Useful for creating uniformity among a group of images or slices. With this option, you can create color tables that use specific groups of colors. Loading the color table converts the image (or slice) to that set of colors.

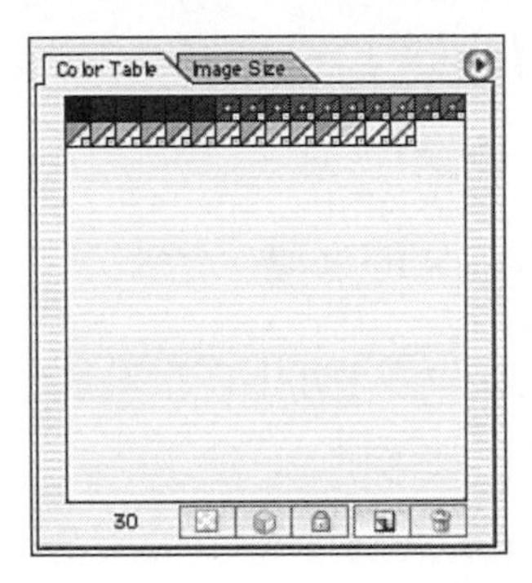


Figure 22.22
All colors mapped to transparency are moved to the end of the table when sorted by Hue or Luminance. Their position is unaffected by mapping when the table is sorted by Popularity.

# PHOTOSHOP AT WORK: OPTIMIZING A COLOR TABLE

The more you work with GIF conversion, the more you realize that the most critical step is in mapping the original colors to a minimal yet representative table set. To most people, it sounds inconceivable that 32 colors can replace the thousands of colors in an image. Although you *can* do it, you must be careful about which colors you keep and which you throw away. Follow these steps to optimize a color table:

1. In Photoshop, choose File, Open. The Open dialog box appears. Select the file you want to convert to the GIF format and click Open. Choose File, Save for Web.
2. From the Colors list, select the lowest number of colors while keeping the file's integrity intact. Click the Optimized tab to review the results.
3. Click the Color Table tab. Click the Eyedropper tool in the Save For Web dialog box and click a prominent color in the image. The corresponding color in the Color Table is highlighted.
4. Lock the selected color by clicking the Lock button (marked with a padlock icon) at the bottom of the Color Table palette (see Figure 22.23). Locking a color prevents it from being removed or dithered. Repeat this step for any critical colors in the image.
5. With the image showing on the Optimized tab, choose Sort by Luminance from the Color Table palette menu. In the color table, select a color close to a locked color and click the Trash Can icon in the Color Table section (see Figure 22.24). The screen redraws to delete the selected color from the image. Continue deleting colors until you get a core set that represents the image well.

Keep in mind that colors mapped to transparency and shifted to the Web-safe palette are permanently converted when you save the image. You cannot use the Unmap or Unshift commands after you've saved the file and reopened it.

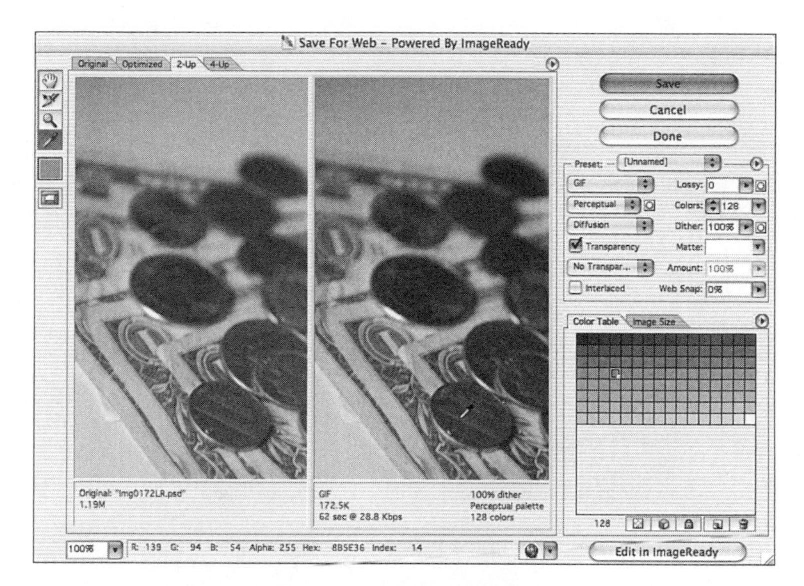


Figure 22.23
Select a color from the image and lock it in the color table.



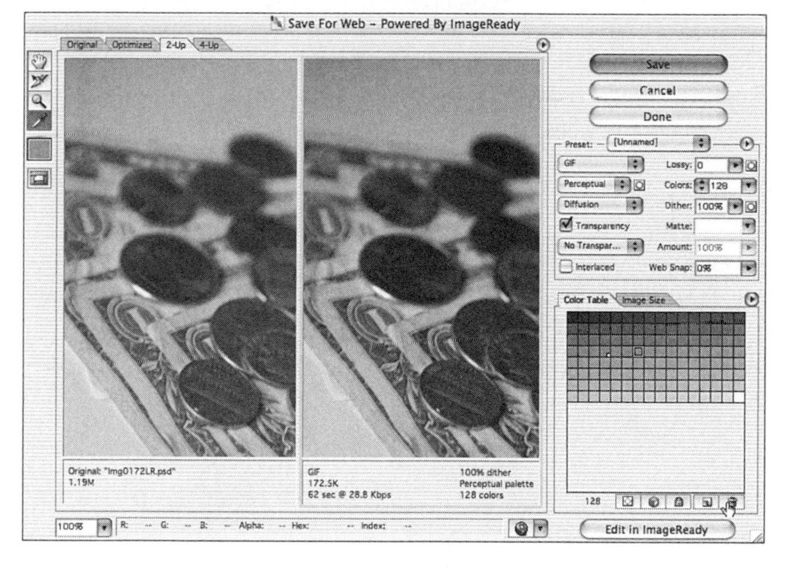


Figure 22.24
Click the Trash Can icon to delete a color.

6. With the important colors locked down, determine whether you need to change other colors. To change color swatches, double-click the color in the color table; the Color Picker dialog box opens (see Figure 22.25). Change the current color, paying close attention to the Web-safe icon in the picker (the three-sided box icon), which shows you the nearest Web-safe color.

7. If you're working with the same kind of image, or you want a series of images to use the same color set, save the color table you just fine-tuned. Choose Save Color Table from the Color Table palette menu. In the Save As dialog box that appears, type a name for the color table and click OK.

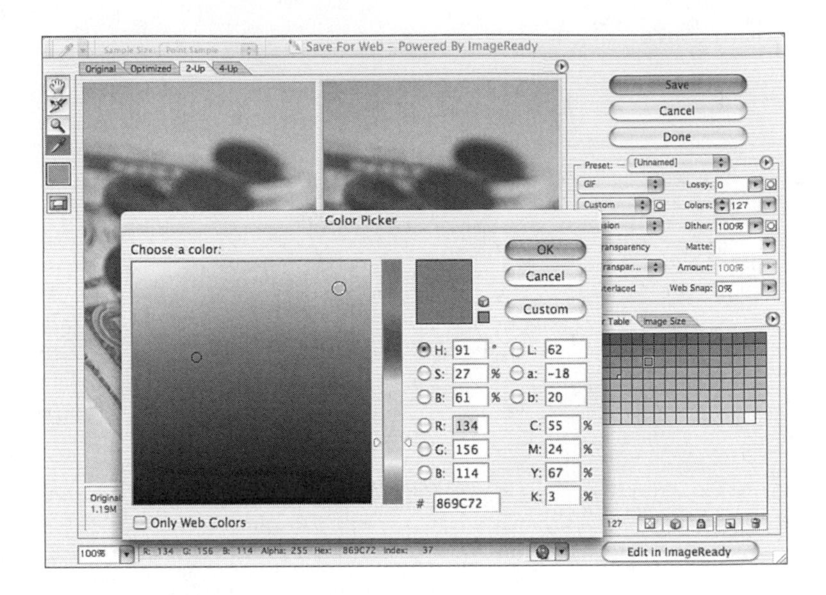


**Figure 22.25**
Double-click a color in the color table to change its value in the Color Picker.

# EDITING OUTPUT SETTINGS

The bottommost command in Save for Web's Settings menu enables you to change how Save for Web handles slices, HTML, the filename, and any background image associated with the file. In ImageReady, use the File, Output Settings command.

Unless an image has been sliced, normally you save only the image itself from Photoshop's Save for Web. Generating an HTML Web page for a single image is possible, but unless the image will be posted as a standalone Web page, there's no need to create the HTML in Save for Web. In ImageReady, you need to save HTML with any artwork that has been sliced, has rollovers, or is an animation.

The Output Settings dialog box has five panes (see Figure 22.26). In addition, you can select from any available saved setting configurations from the pop-up menu at the top of the dialog box.

## HTML Options

The HTML pane of the Output Settings dialog box governs how HTML will be written (see Figure 22.27).

Save for Web offers these HTML options:

- **Output XHTML**—Generates XHTML 1.0 Transitional–compliant code when selected.
- **Tags Case**—The HTML tags can be created in all uppercase, upper- and lowercase, or all lowercase. Web browsers can read tags in any style—this option is primarily for your convenience. If you'll be editing or reviewing the HTML, you might prefer to have the tags stand out by putting them in uppercase.
- **Attribute Case**—Attributes can also be recorded in all uppercase, upper- and lowercase, or all lowercase. Again, it makes no difference to the Web browser.

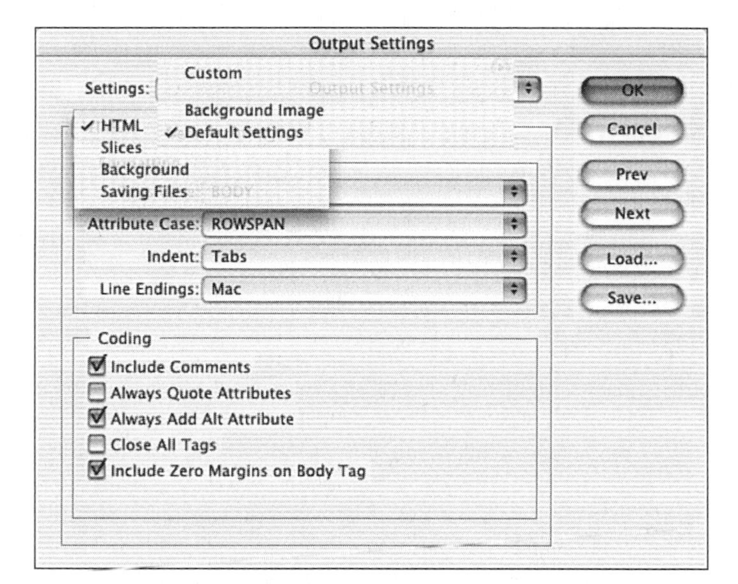


Figure 22.26
The Photoshop Save for Web Output Settings dialog box.

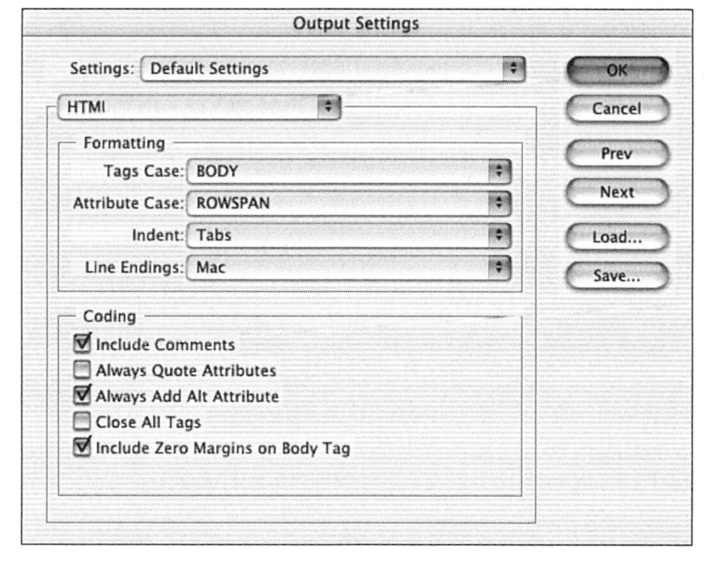


Figure 22.27
These options determine the formatting of the HTML file generated by Save for Web.

- **Indent**—You can format the HTML to indent using tabs or a specified number of spaces. If you'll be editing the HTML in a word processing program, either is appropriate. However, some text editors don't recognize tabs, so specifying a number of spaces better preserves the indenting.

- **Line Endings**—Macintosh uses carriage returns at the end of lines, Unix uses line feeds, and Windows uses both. If you know what platform will be hosting your Web site, choose that platform from the pop-up menu. Generally speaking, however, there is no need for concern.

- **Encoding**—Allows the user to select a customized text-encoding option. Options include ISO-8859-1, Mac OS Roman, and Unicode.
- **Include Comments**—Explanatory comments can be added to the HTML. Comments do not appear in the Web page but rather are used by Web design programs and can be used by ImageReady when updating HTML.
- **Always Quote Attributes**—Strict compliance with HTML standards requires that tag attributes be enclosed in quotation marks. The earliest Web browsers also require the quotes. However, you should leave this option unchecked to allow Save for Web to include quotes only when necessary.
- **Always Add Alt Attribute**—Images are identified in HTML by the <IMG> tag. When a browser can't display the image, it looks for the ALT attribute and displays any text entered there, along with a symbol indicating that the image wasn't found. Without the ALT attribute, nothing is displayed. Save for Web includes the ALT attribute and quotation marks; you open the HTML file in a Web design program, word processor, or text editor to add a message within the quotes. If you don't add any message, just the symbol is displayed. ALT attributes maintain links, even if the image is missing. Be aware that ALT attributes are required for compliance with U.S. government accessibility standards.
- **Close All Tags**—If the HTML will be incorporated into an XHTML page, you should select this check box. It ensures that all tags in the HTML have closing tags to match.
- **Include Zero Margins on Body Tag**—Margins are used by the Web browser much as they are used in a word processing document to offset the document. When you include the margins, you can later simply change the zeros to your desired margin by editing the HTML document (see Figure 22.28).

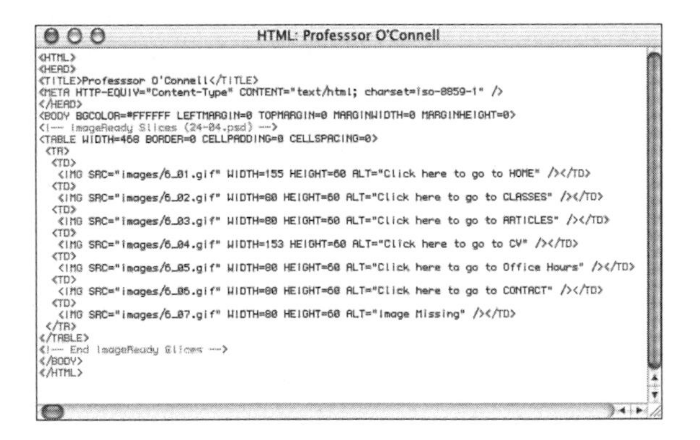


**Figure 22.28**
The source HTML is shown in an Internet Explorer window. You can open the HTML document in a word processor or text editor to change the margin information and add ALT messages.

## Slice Options

Slice options (see Figure 22.29) are necessary only when you're working with a sliced image. They determine how the slice-related information is recorded in the HTML file. To open this pane, you can select Slices from the dialog box's pop-up menu or click the Next button in the HTML pane. In ImageReady, you can select Slices directly from the File, Output Settings submenu.

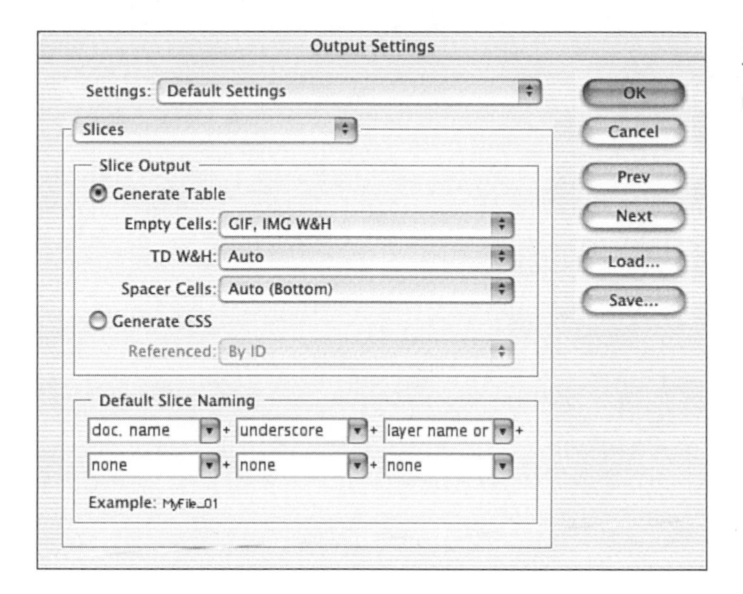


**Figure 22.29**
These options do not pertain to unsliced images.

Save for Web and ImageReady offer these options for slice-related HTML:

- **Generate Table**—When you save a sliced image in Photoshop or ImageReady, you are actually creating a separate image from each slice—the slices are saved as individual files. The Web browser requires HTML to tell it how to arrange those slices back into a cohesive whole, the original image. The browser uses the HTML to reassemble the jigsaw puzzle. You can generate an HTML table within which the slices are placed by using these options:
  - **Empty Cells**—Empty cells, used to ensure correct table spacing, can be recorded as single-pixel GIF images, with their width and height (W&H) recorded with the <IMG> (image) tag or the <TD> (table data) tag. The NoWrap option creates a nonstandard attribute and records W&H in the table data tag.
  - **TD W&H**—You can choose to include the width and height for all table data, never include the width and height, or let Save for Web determine when it is necessary. The Auto option is recommended.
  - **Spacer Cells**—A row or column of empty cells can be generated to ensure that a table displays properly in the Web browser window. Spacer cells are particularly important when slice boundaries don't align. Save for Web can generate the extra cells automatically, always, or never, and you can also choose to have the spacer cells only at the bottom of the table. Auto generation is recommended.
- **Generate CSS**—Instead of producing tables to hold slices, Save for Web can create Cascading Style Sheets (CSS). The slices can be identified by a unique ID, in the <DIV> tag as an inline style, or by class.

For in-depth information on creating and editing code for Web pages, see *Special Edition Using HTML and XHTML* by Molly Holzschlag (Que, ISBN 0-7897-2731-5).

- **Default Slice Naming**—Save for Web offers six fields for choosing names for slices. You choose the name options from pop-up menus for each field. A generic sample name is generated based on your choices and is displayed below the six fields. The available options are shown in Figure 22.30.

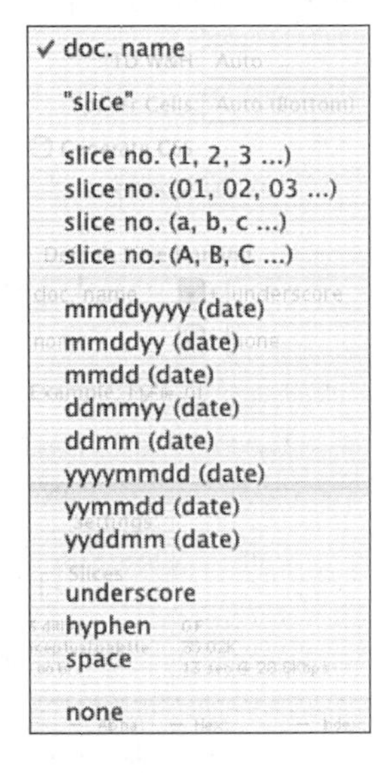


Figure 22.30
The slice names must be unique, so you must include at least one variable that changes from slice to slice.

## Image Maps (ImageReady Only)

When you're working with images that contain image maps, ImageReady offers several ways to encode link information. Client-side image maps use the visitor's Web browser to interpret the links. When you opt to use server-side links, the link information is generated as a separate MAP file, instead of being embedded in the HTML. The browser must query the server before navigating a server-side image map link. Client-side links are generally much faster for the browser to open. However, server-side links can be updated separately from the Web page's HTML file.

When creating server-side links, you can generate code that complies with the NCSA or CERN standard and can elect to include client-side links within the image's HTML as well.

When you generate client-side links, the Placement buttons at the bottom of the Image Maps pane are available (see Figure 22.31). They determine where in the HTML the image map declaration is placed. The information can appear at the beginning or end of the BODY section of the HTML (Top and Bottom options, respectively), or it can be placed directly above the appropriate <IMG SCR> tag (the Body option). The difference is insignificant for the Web browser, but you might have a preference if you edit HTML.

> **Caution**
> You must use client-side links if the image contains slices in addition to image maps. ImageReady cannot generate server-side links for sliced images.

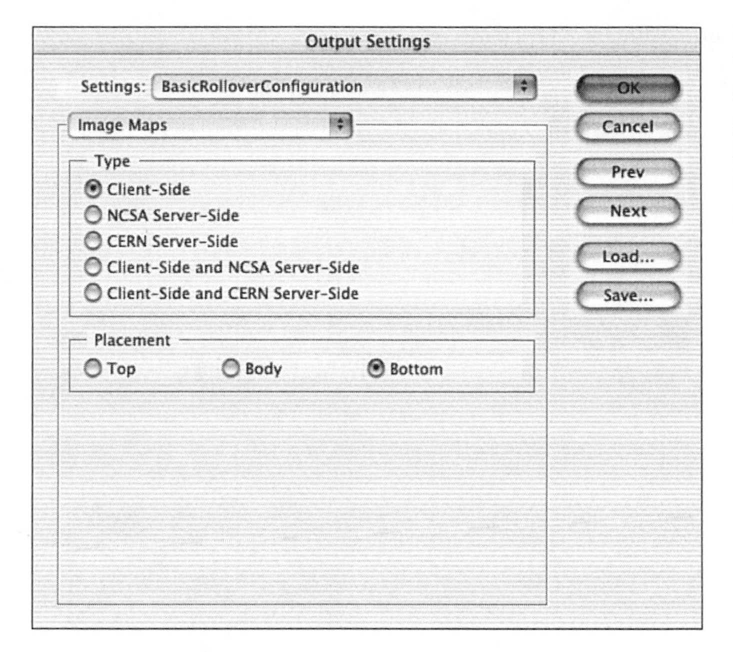


**Figure 22.31**
The Placement buttons refer only to image map information generated for an image's HTML. The buttons are grayed out if you generate only server-side image maps.

## Background Options

Using the Background pane of the Output Settings dialog box (see Figure 22.32), you can opt to save the file as an image or to create a background image to be tiled behind a Web page. When saving as a background, you can also select a color to appear behind the image, filling areas that would otherwise be transparent in GIF and PNG images.

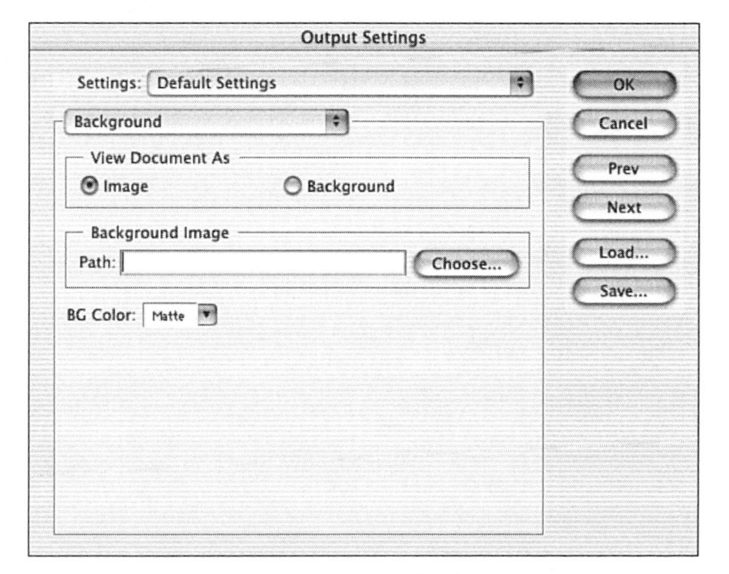


**Figure 22.32**
The Background Image option is not available in Save for Web when you choose Background in the View Document As section of the dialog box.

Choosing Image in the View Document As section saves the image regularly. If you choose Image with a background image or color, you must also choose HTML and Images in the Save Optimized As dialog box. (It opens after you click Save in Save for Web.) To see the image displayed with the tiled background image or the selected background color, you then open the HTML file, not the optimized GIF, JPEG, or PNG file.

When you save an image as a background, you must also generate an HTML document that tells the Web browser to tile the saved image throughout the Web page. See Figure 22.33 for a comparison of saving as an image (left) and as a background (right).

**Figure 22.33**
To tile the image in the Web page, open the HTML document. If you save only the image or choose to open the image rather than the HTML document, only a single instance appears in the browser window.

# File-Saving Options

The Saving Files pane of the Output Settings dialog box, shown in Figure 22.34, enables you to specify how slices will be named (when generated) and several additional options.

When an image is sliced, each slice is saved as a separate image. Save for Web automatically generates a separate file for each slice, using filenames that follow the guidelines you choose in the File Naming section of the dialog box.

Each slice name can contain up to nine elements, the last of which must always be the file format extensions. You select the components from a list in each field (see Figure 22.35). You can also enter text into any of the fields, but remember that file extensions *must* be included at the end.

If you know what type of Web server is hosting the site in which the image will be used, you can uncheck the unnecessary Filename Compatibility options. However, keep in mind that equipment gets upgraded, servers get replaced, and hosting services get changed. Keeping maximum compatibility helps prevent unexpected problems related to server changes.

To generate an HTML document from Save for Web, click the Save button and then choose HTML and Images from the Format pop-up menu in the Save Optimized As dialog box.

If your image will be part of a Web page, consider starting the slice names with the "doc. name" option. That makes it easier to find them among a Web site's images.

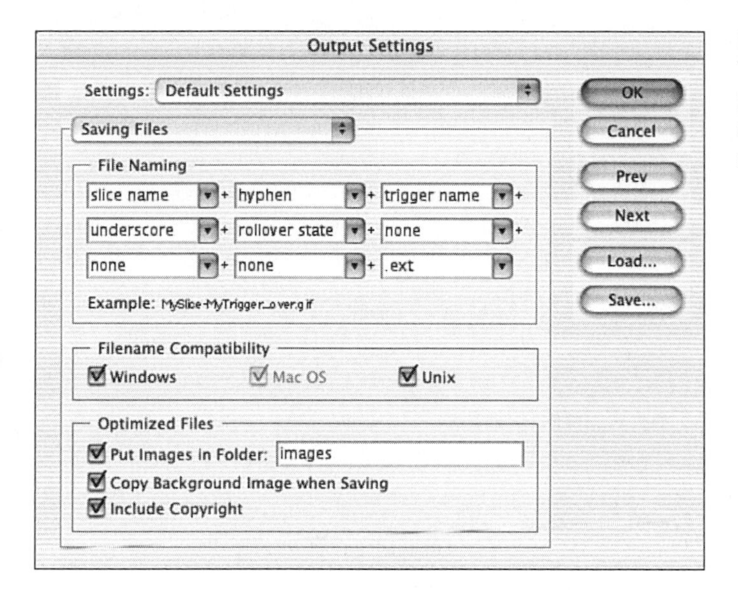


**Figure 22.34**
The upper parts of the dialog box pertain only to slice naming—the options have no effect on unsliced images.

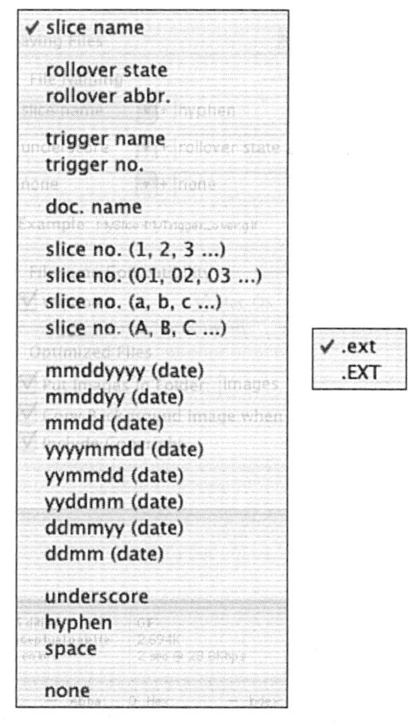


**Figure 22.35**
The first eight fields use the list on the left. The final field selects a lowercase or an uppercase file extension (as shown on the right).

The Optimized Files section of the dialog box offers three options:

- **Put Images in Folder**—You can select a name for the folder that will hold the images created as slices or backgrounds. The default name, Images, is standard for most Web purposes. The folder is created at the location where you choose to save the file. If a folder with that name already exists, the images are added to it.

- **Copy Background Image When Saving**—When you specify a background image to be tiled behind the image you're saving, the file can be copied to the folder you create. If this option is not selected, you must remember to include the background image separately when adding the image to a Web page or site.
- **Include Copyright**—The copyright information and file title in File Info can be automatically added to each image if you select this option. If no information is available in File Info, nothing is added. To add the information, use the File, File Info menu command. Enter the data in the Copyright Notice and Title fields. The copyright information is added to the file but is not visible in the image.

## Saving Custom Setting Configurations

You can save optimization configurations that can be easily accessed in both the Output Settings dialog box and—more important—directly in the Save Optimized As dialog box (see Figure 22.36).

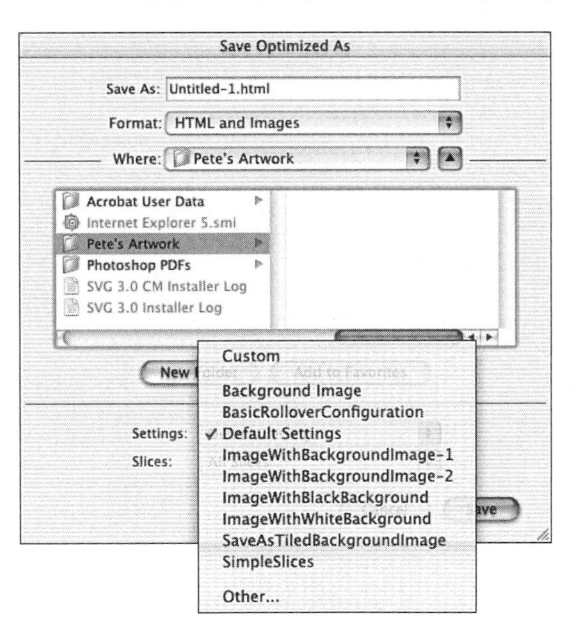


Figure 22.36
Output settings saved in the Presets, Optimized Output Settings folder appear in the pop-up menu for Save for Web.

Output setting configurations can be saved from the Output Settings dialog box, but not from the Save Optimized As dialog box. In addition, the Output Settings dialog box offers the Load button. It enables you to load setting configurations that are saved in folders other than the Optimized Output Settings folder. The setting configurations should be saved with the .iros file extension.

# PHOTOSHOP AT WORK: HOW TO OPTIMIZE FILES WITH ALPHA MASKS

*Variable compression* allows you to alter image compression and quality in different areas of the same image. You can focus more detail around a central character or image while allowing details to erode in unimportant areas, such as the background or flat areas of color. The result is an optimized image that delivers higher quality and lower bandwidth. To optimize files with alpha masks, follow these steps:

1. To create an alpha mask in Photoshop, open Photoshop and select File, Open. From the Open dialog box, select the file you want to optimize (see Figure 22.37).

**Figure 22.37**
Open the original image.

2. Select Window, Channels to launch the Channels palette. Select New Channel from the Channels palette menu. Modify any parameters as desired in the New Channel dialog box (including mask color and area definition options) and click OK to create the new channel.
3. Initially, the new channel will turn the image black. To view the channel and the image as a composite, go to the Channels palette and turn on visibility for all channels, including the new channel you just created.
4. In the final compressed image, white areas of the alpha channel will carry the most detail; black areas will have the least detail. With this in mind, paint the channel to emphasize image detail (see Figure 22.38). When you're finished, turn off visibility for the alpha channel in the Channels palette.
5. Choose File, Save for Web to launch the Save for Web dialog box. In the Save for Web dialog box, select JPEG from the Optimize File Format menu. Click the icon next to the Quality control to launch the Modify Quality Setting dialog box.
6. From the pop-up menu, select the channel created in step 2. With the Preview box checked, adjust the slider to specify the minimum or maximum quality setting to be applied, based on the selected channel (see Figure 22.39). Remember that the pure white channel areas correspond to the maximum settings, and the black areas correspond to the minimum settings. Click OK.

> As you paint, you must have only the alpha channel active; it will display in your open document as your selected mask color (red is the default). Also, remember to name your alpha channel and save the PSD file.

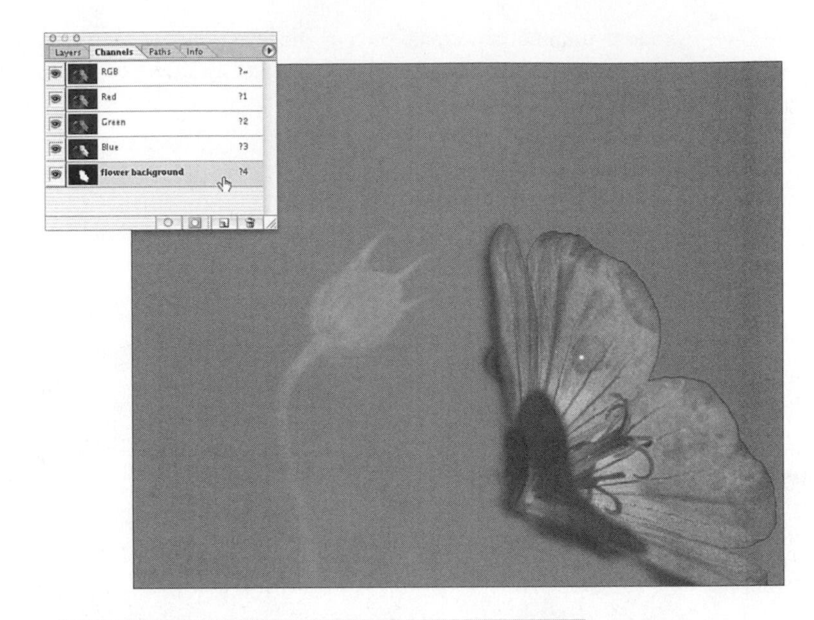


Figure 22.38
Paint the Alpha Mask.

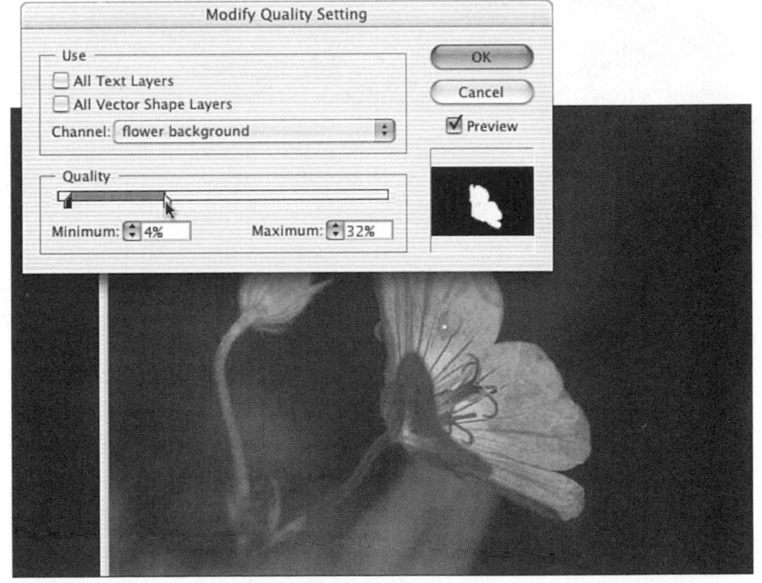


Figure 22.39
Apply JPEG quality adjustment through mask.

7. In the Save for Web dialog box, select GIF from the Optimize File Format menu and set the GIF settings as desired. You can use channels to modify the Dither, Lossy, and Colors settings by clicking the icon next to the associated control to open a dialog box and then by following the process in the preceding step.

If the image contains type or shape layers, you can select the check boxes to use them for optimization as well. The content of type and shape layers is treated like the white areas in a mask, and surrounding areas are optimized with the Minimum quality setting. Type and shape layers, as well as alpha channels, can be used to modify a variety of optimization settings for GIF and PNG-8 images.

When building the mask in Photoshop, use the Blur filter or the Airbrush tool to create soft, graduated areas between light and dark sections of the mask. Doing so reduces the crisp transitions between areas of different quality.



# MASTERING IMAGEREADY

## Transparent JPEGs

*I want to cut out the foreground of my image and see the Web page's background, but I want to keep it as 24-bit color. Any suggestions?*

The first possibility is the PNG-24 file format. Although it produces larger file sizes than JPEG, it natively supports transparency. Remember that some older Web browsers can't display PNG files. That is rarely a problem, however.

Alternatively, you can get the benefits of the JPEG format's smaller file size and wider compatibility by simulating transparency. Here's how:

1. Make a copy of the image.
2. Merge all layers. If the image is flattened, convert the background layer to a regular layer by renaming it.
3. Make a selection of the area that you want to be "transparent" and delete it. (The area should actually become transparent in the image.)
4. Open Save for Web.
5. Select JPEG as the file format and choose your Quality setting.
6. In the Matte pop-up menu, choose Other.
7. Select the Web page's background color. For best results, the Web page (and the matte color) should use a Web-safe color.
8. Save the image.

This technique is *not* recommended for use with Web pages whose background is a pattern or tiled image. It's difficult to ensure that the pattern will be properly aligned. To get the best possible color match, do not save an ICC profile with the JPEG.

## Letters by Pixel

*Why does type look so bad on the Web?*

Type doesn't *have* to look bad on your Web pages. Keep in mind one simple concept as you design and create, and you'll get excellent quality. In a nutshell, you need only remember that everything on the Web is reproduced with square pixels.

Because Web pages are viewed on a monitor, everything is created from pixels, and every pixel is square. Trying to use square, evenly spaced pixels to show the subtle variations and curves of a script font or an italicized type, for example, can be difficult. And the smaller the type, the fewer the number of pixels that can be used for each character. Here are some suggestions:

- Use the largest type size possible. The more pixels you have for each character, the better they will reproduce.
- Sans serif fonts are typically easier to show onscreen. They have uniform stroke sizes throughout the letter and lack the fine details at the end of strokes that often get too fuzzy to see properly.
- Sharp antialiasing is designed for use with type. It's especially effective for smaller font sizes.

*For more information about how pixels are used to reproduce artwork onscreen, see Chapter 4, "Pixels, Vectors, and Resolutions."*

## Pre-optimization

*What do I need to do to get an image ready for Save for Web? What color mode? What resolution? What else?*

Actually, you don't have to do anything—Save for Web automatically converts CMYK to RGB and 16-bit to 8-bit. Layers are flattened, type is rasterized, and blending modes are applied. Save for Web handles all the conversions necessary for the selected file format.

Remember, too, that there's no resolution on the Web. All raster images are displayed according to their pixel dimensions. You don't even need to use Image Size to adjust those dimensions, either. Instead, leave your original as is, and use the Image Size tab in Save for Web to resize the image. You can use the same resampling algorithms as in Image Size, so there's no worry about additional image degradation.

ImageReady, on the other hand, requires 8-bit RGB images. Use the Image, Mode command if necessary before jumping to ImageReady.

# CREATING ROLLOVERS AND ADDING ANIMATION

## IN THIS CHAPTER

Among the ways to dress up a Web page are rollovers and animations. Rollovers are interactive graphics on the page. The graphic or another area of the page changes in response to the visitor's mouse actions. Animations are moving pictures, graphics that change and play, like small movies.

In this chapter, you'll see how rollovers and animated GIFs are created using ImageReady and how to export to the SWF file format for working with Macromedia Flash.



# IMAGEREADY'S ROLLOVERS AND ANIMATIONS: OVERVIEW

Rollovers and animations in ImageReady are based on layers—you show and hide layers to create the different rollover *states* (the different appearances of the graphic) and to create the individual frames of an animation.

## Why Rollovers?

Rollovers are most commonly used as buttons on a Web page, clickable graphics that make something happen. A button may be a link to another page, it may open another window or change a frame, it may alter the current page in some way. The appearance of the image changes when the mouse is moved on top of the graphic (that is, *rolled over* the graphic) or when the graphic is clicked.

Using rollovers enables you to help the visitor keep track of which buttons have been clicked (among other things). For example, a button can have a basic appearance when the page is opened in a Web browser, another appearance when the visitor's mouse is over the button (to indicate that the button is, in fact, a clickable link), and a third appearance to show that the button has been clicked.

In addition to showing the status of a particular button or link on a page, rollovers can be used to display messages, and even as a safeguard against casual theft of your images (as you'll see in "ImageReady at Work: Rollovers as Antitheft Devices," later in this chapter).

## Adding Movement with Animated GIFs

Whereas rollovers can serve a distinct practical purpose, animations are more decorative in nature. They can certainly communicate a message, but the primary use is to attract attention and improve the appearance of a Web page.

Generally speaking, animations involve moving pictures, moving or changing text, or both. You can use them as scrolling banners, flashing icons, or short cartoons.

## Incorporating Rollovers and Animations into Web Pages

ImageReady and Photoshop are designed primarily to create graphics, not Web sites or Web pages. You most certainly can create entire pages with Photoshop and ImageReady, incorporating rollovers, animations, and more. However, the graphics created in ImageReady are actually intended to be placed into a Web page using a Web development tool, specifically Adobe GoLive CS.

Generally speaking, to add an ImageReady rollover or animation to an existing (or new) page, you need to do three things:

1. From ImageReady, save both the HTML and images. (Select this option in the Save Optimized As dialog box from the Format pop-up menu.)
2. Move the images into the Web page or Web site's Images folder so that they are accessible to the page.
3. Copy the appropriate sections of HTML code from the HTML page generated by ImageReady (see Figure 23.1) and paste it into the Web page's HTML at an appropriate place.

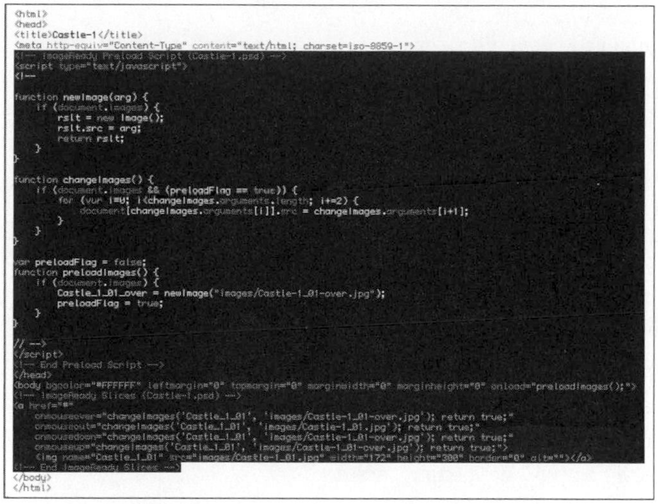

```
<html>
<head>
<title>Castle-1</title>
<meta http-equiv="Content-Type" content="text/html; charset=iso-8859-1">
<!-- ImageReady Preload Script (Castle-1.psd) -->
<script type="text/javascript">
<!--

function newImage(arg) {
    if (document.images) {
        rslt = new Image();
        rslt.src = arg;
        return rslt;
    }
}

function changeImages() {
    if (document.images && (preloadFlag == true)) {
        for (var i=0; i<changeImages.arguments.length; i+=2) {
            document[changeImages.arguments[i]].src = changeImages.arguments[i+1];
        }
    }
}

var preloadFlag = false;
function preloadImages() {
    if (document.images) {
        Castle_1_01_over = newImage("images/Castle-1_01-over.jpg");
        preloadFlag = true;
    }
}

// -->
</script>
<!-- End Preload Script -->
</head>
<body bgcolor="#FFFFFF" leftmargin="0" topmargin="0" marginwidth="0" marginheight="0" onload="preloadImages();">
<!-- ImageReady Slices (Castle-1.psd) -->
<a href="#"
    onmouseover="changeImages('Castle_1_01', 'images/Castle-1_01-over.jpg'); return true;"
    onmouseout="changeImages('Castle_1_01', 'images/Castle-1_01.jpg'); return true;"
    onmousedown="changeImages('Castle_1_01', 'images/Castle-1_01-over.jpg'); return true;"
    onmouseup="changeImages('Castle_1_01', 'images/Castle-1_01-over.jpg'); return true;">
    <img name="Castle_1_01" src="images/Castle-1_01.jpg" width="172" height="300" border="0" alt=""></a>
<!-- End ImageReady Slices -->
</body>
</html>
```

**Figure 23.1**
The selected HTML is copied and pasted into a Web page's HTML to add a rollover to that page.

For rollovers, copy the ImageReady HTML starting with `ImageReady Preload Script` and ending with `End ImageReady Slices`. The HTML looks like this:

```
<!-- ImageReady Preload script (filename.psd) -->
```

```
<!-- End ImageReady Slices -->
```

Although it's not technically necessary to include informative headers, copying them to the page's HTML makes it easier to identify the entire rollover.

For animation GIFs, you need only copy/paste the line of code that starts with `img src`. Here's an example:

```
<img src= "images/filename.gif" width="172" height="300" alt="">
```

There will be some variation. "Images" is the default folder name. The filename is not likely to be "filename." The width and height fields will show the pixel dimensions of the image. The last part of the line, `alt=" "`, may have text that displays in browsers that can't show the animation.

In the Web page's HTML code, you'll need to paste this line into the proper location. Often that will be a specific cell in a table. Sometimes you'll be able to identify the location by finding the name of an adjacent image file or snippet of text on the page.

*Having trouble finding the proper place in a Web page's HTML into which you'll paste your ImageReady HTML? See "HTML Placeholders" in the "Mastering ImageReady" section at the end of this chapter.*

# CREATING ROLLOVERS

23

Creating rollovers in ImageReady is quite simple: Specify the type of rollover in the Web Content palette and then show/hide layers in the Layers palette. That's it! No muss, no fuss. When the image is shown in a Web browser, the visitor's mouse actions determine which state (appearance) of the rollover is visible.

You can create rollovers for an image as a whole or for one or more slices in the image. Each slice can have its own set of rollovers. Keep in mind that each rollover state for each slice is actually a separate image when you save the file. The original PSD file can maintain all the slice and rollover information, but when placed into the Web page, each rollover is a separate image that is visible or invisible, depending on the mouse action.

## The Rollover States

The change in appearance of an image for which you've created rollovers depends on the behavior of the mouse. The viewer moves or clicks the mouse, and the appearance changes. ImageReady can create nine rollover states for each slice or image, although you need not assign all states to any rollover. The rollover states are as follows:

- **Normal**—Normal is the default state for every image in a Web page. When rollovers are created, this can be considered the "nothing happening" state.
- **Over**—The Over state is triggered when the cursor is moved on top of the graphic.
- **Down**—When the cursor is over the graphic and the mouse button is pushed down, the Down rollover state is triggered.
- **Click**—When the cursor is over the graphic and the mouse button is pressed and released (clicked), the Click state is triggered. Some Web browsers leave a button in the Click state after a single click but use the Up or Normal state after a double-click.
- **Out**—After the cursor has been moved over the graphic and then away, the Out state may be used. The Normal state is often used instead. You may want to create an Out state if the Over state triggers a change in the browser window, such as displaying a message. The Out state restores the image to its appearance prior to that created by the Over state.
- **Up**—After the mouse button is clicked on a button, the Up state can be displayed. It's common to have the button return to the Normal state after a click, but you can change the image's appearance with the Up state to indicate, for example, links that have already been followed.
- **None**—The None rollover state saves the current state of the Layers palette but does not create a separate image when you use Save Optimized As.

- **Custom**—The Custom state is triggered by a JavaScript event. To use this state, you must first write the JavaScript and afterward incorporate that code into the Web page. You might use the Custom rollover state in conjunction with, for example, a fieldvalidator.js script in GoLive to show a message about an entry in a form field.
- **Selected**—The Selected rollover state is used to maintain a slice or image appearance, regardless of mouse action. It overrides other rollover states.

If one button's Selected state uses a different view of the same layer as another button's rollover state, and the two buttons might be used in conjunction with each other, you can duplicate the layer. Use the second copy for the second button's rollover states because the selected state supercedes the other button's change to the Layers palette.



## Assigning a Rollover State

To set up rollovers, you need only click the Create Rollover State button in the Web Content palette and make appropriate changes in the Layers palette. Double-clicking the new rollover state in the Web Content palette opens the Rollover State Options dialog box, shown in Figure 23.2.

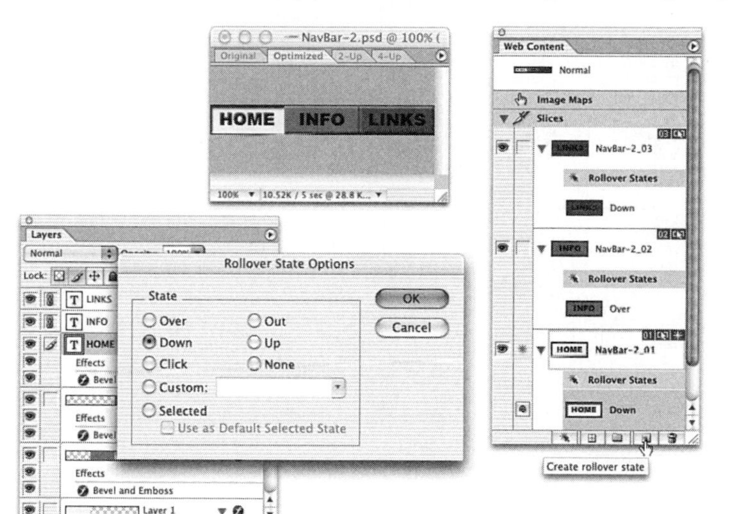


**Figure 23.2**
The Create Rollover State button is shown at the bottom of the Web Content palette. The Rollover State Options dialog box is opened by double-clicking a rollover state in the palette.

With a rollover state active in the Web Content palette, you can change the appearance of the graphic while in that state. Changes you can make include showing and hiding layers; adding, deleting, or changing layer styles; and changing the opacity and blending mode. Remember, though, that changing the *content* of the layer by adding, deleting, or changing the color of the pixels on the layer alters the layer itself and therefore affects all rollover states.

## ImageReady at Work: Rollovers as Antitheft Devices

Although they're no deterrent to a dedicated thief, rollovers can be used to prevent accidental or casual theft of your images. Many Web surfers don't realize that it's a copyright violation to download and use the images on someone else's Web site. They see an image they like and use the contextual menu to download or copy. (Control)-clicking right-clicking an image in a Web browser offers a variety of options, depending on the browser. Generally, those options include copying the image to the Clipboard and downloading the image to the hard drive.

You can use rollovers to help prevent these unauthorized downloads. Here's how:

1. In ImageReady, open an image that you'll be posting on the Web.
2. Add a new layer or layers that indicate that you don't want anyone stealing your picture. In this case, we've added a layer filled with black to hide the image, the international "Don't do it!" symbol in red, and a specific message in English (see Figure 23.3).

When you're using layer styles to differentiate among rollover states and you need several slices or images to have comparable appearances, create a style in the Styles palette. For example, if each button in a navigation bar has a down state that uses the same inverted bevel and outer glow, create a style. Not only will it be easier to apply, but the style ensures consistency among the buttons.

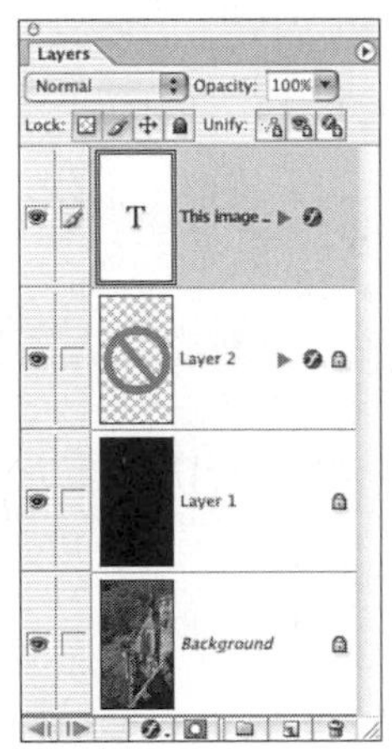


**Figure 23.3**
The message is clear, but not likely to be found offensive by those who accidentally trigger it.

3. In the Layers palette, hide the layer or layers on which you've added your message, leaving only the original image layer visible.
4. In ImageReady's Web Content palette, click the Create Rollover State button to add the Over state (see Figure 23.4).
5. In the Layers palette, make your antitheft layers visible.
6. Save the image using ImageReady's Save Optimized or Save Optimized As command. You can save the file in any of the formats supported by ImageReady except WBMP. Save both the HTML (which defines the table used and actually controls the rollover) and the images. The images are later placed into the Images folder of the Web site, and the HTML is incorporated into the page's HTML document.

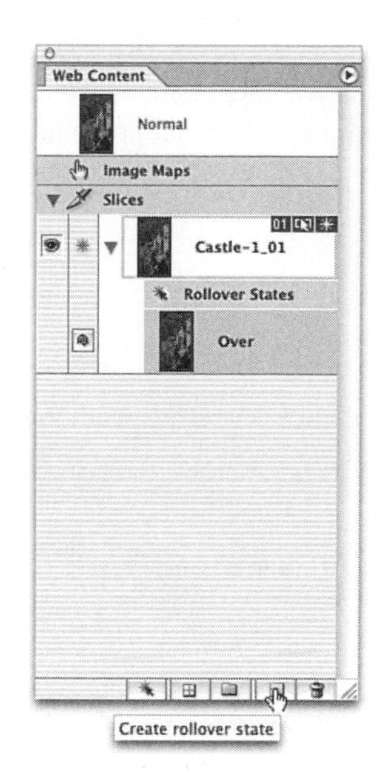


Figure 23.4
The second rollover state is, by default, the Over state.



When the image is displayed in a Web browser, the rollover eliminates the possibility of downloading or copying the image through the contextual menu. When the mouse is moved over the image, with or without a right-click, the page switches from your picture to the "This image is not available for download" message. If the visitor selects Download Image to Disk or Copy Image to Clipboard from the contextual menu, he or she will download or copy your message rather than your image (see Figure 23.5).

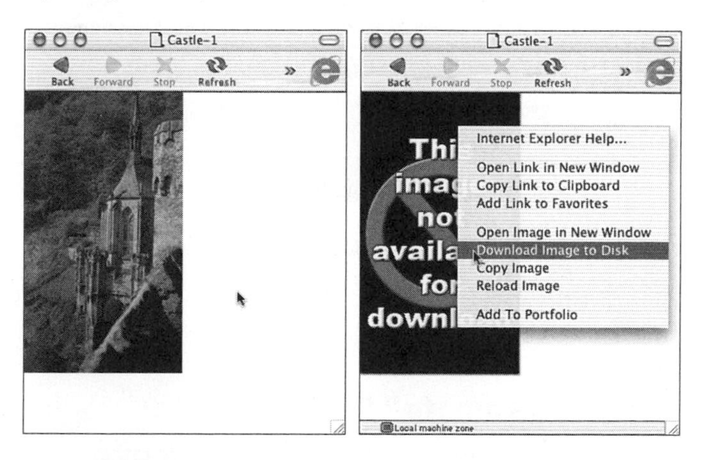


Figure 23.5
If the visitor attempts to copy or download through the contextual menu (left), he or she will get the "This image is not available for download" message rather than the photo.

## Rollover Styles

You can create rollover styles to speed and simplify the process of creating similar rollover elements in ImageReady. Create a layer-based slice, develop your rollovers, and then click the New Style button at the bottom of the Styles palette. Name the style, determine what characteristics you want to copy, and click OK to add it to the palette. To apply your rollover style, create another layer-based slice and click the style in the Styles palette to apply it. Not only will the layer styles be copied, but the actual rollover states will be created automatically, too. As shown in Figure 23.6, rollover styles have a black triangle in the upper-left corner of the thumbnail to differentiate them from layer styles.



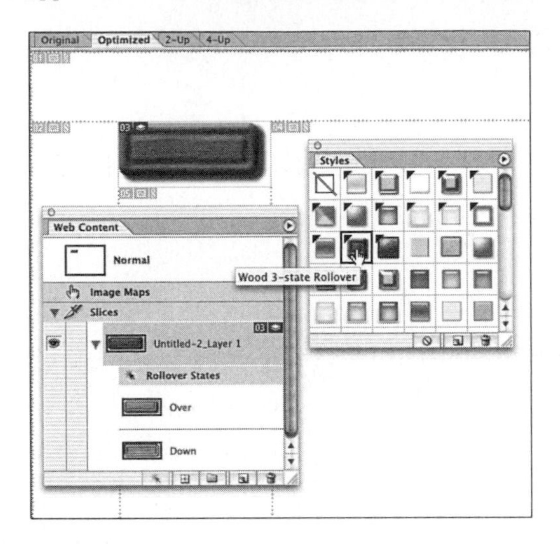


Figure 23.6
A rollover style automatically creates the individual rollover states and applies the various appearance characteristics with which each state was recorded.

## Changing the Default State

When using the same image on multiple pages, you might want to change the default appearance for the image. For example, consider a row of buttons that are links to specific pages. You might want to have the button for a specific page appear in the down state on that page. Not only is this a visual reminder to the visitor about what page is being viewed, it also indicates that there's no sense clicking that button—the page is already visible. Figure 23.7 shows how the default state for rollovers might change, depending on which page is being visited.

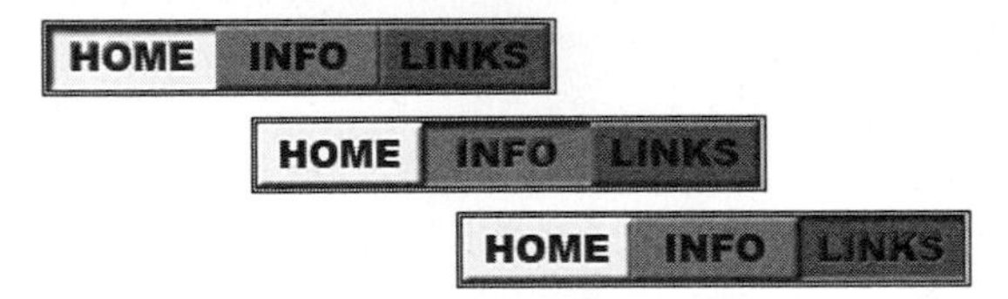


Figure 23.7
The change in the default state indicates which page of the Web site is displayed in the Web browser.

To assign a default state, double-click the state in the Web Content palette and click Selected. Then check the box Use as Default Selected State.

## ImageReady at Work: Creating "Remote" Rollovers

Sometimes you want a rollover to trigger a change to another part of the image rather than to the slice's own appearance. These *remote rollovers* can be very effective in uncluttering a Web page by showing content only when needed. One example is a world population map. As the cursor is moved over a country, it triggers an Over state for a slice, with that country's population appearing in another slice, in another part of the image (see Figure 23.8)

**Figure 23.8**
The population statistics appear in a slice far removed from the slice whose Over state triggered their appearance.

In the Web Content and Layers palettes (see Figure 23.9), you can see that the Over state for a specific slice triggers the visibility of the type layer "Guatemala Total Population," in addition to the already-visible layers that make up the map and the title to the lower left of the image.

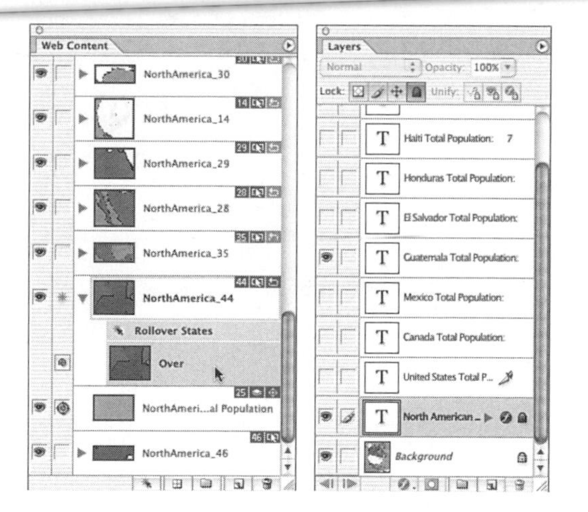


**Figure 23.9**
If the cursor was over a neighboring slice, the layer "Guatemala Total Population" would be hidden and another population statistics type layer would be visible. All the population type layers are stacked in the same slice.

To create a remote rollover you must first create the slices. Next, create the new rollover state in the Web Content palette. To identify the slice that you want to use as the remote rollover, drag the Pickwhip (targeting icon), found to the left of the rollover state in the Web Content palette, onto the slice in the image window (see Figure 23.10).

If you release the mouse button while the cursor is over a spot that cannot be used in the operation, the Pickwhip recoils away and retreats to its icon (see Figure 23.11). The Pickwhip gets its name from this behavior, indicating failure in the targeting process. The heavy black targeting line snaps back to the icon in a whip-like motion.

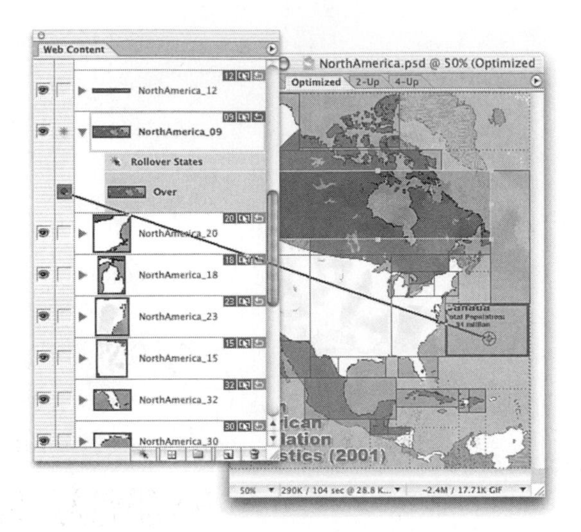


Figure 23.10
Users of GoLive are familiar with the Pickwhip.

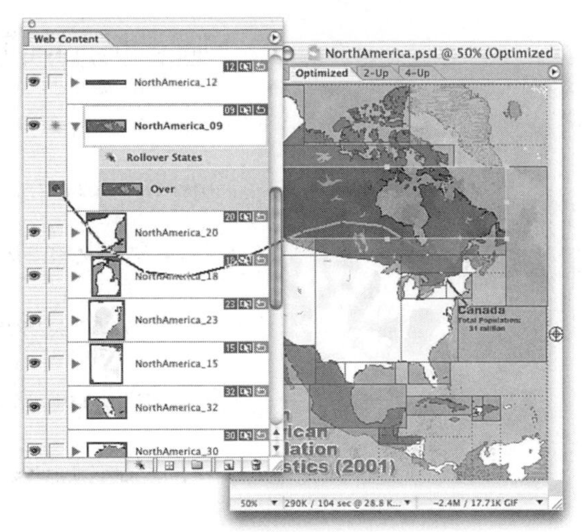


Figure 23.11
Note that the cursor is past the population statistics slice, outside the image window, not over a valid selection for a remote rollover.

# IMAGEREADY'S ANIMATION-CREATION CAPABILITY

Animation is becoming more and more common on the Web as the technology matures. High-speed Internet connections are better able to handle animation, the file formats are becoming compact enough for speedy downloading, and the creation tools are becoming more and more accessible. ImageReady enables you to create animated GIF files and to export animations to the now-common Flash file format.

## Setting the Stage: Terminology

Before discussing the process of creating animations in ImageReady, several terms should be clarified:

- *Animation* itself can be described as a series of images that portray movement or, perhaps more accurately, a series of images that give the illusion of a single image with movement.
- *Animated GIF* is a file in GIF format that simulates motion through the use of frames. Adobe ImageReady uses the individual layers of a file to create the frames of an animation. GIF is a raster image file format.
- *Flash (SWF)* is a version of the Macromedia Flash program's file format. The Flash format supports animation and can include vector and raster artwork, including JPEG images. Most Web browsers either support the Flash format or include a plug-in for Flash support.
- *Frame* refers to a single image within an animation. A series of frames produces the illusion of motion.
- *Frame-based animation* is more akin to a cartoon than to a movie or television program. The frames, rather than being a series of photographic representations of an event, are a series of drawings, if you will. Rather than capture images on film, you create each image individually.
- *Streaming video* refers to video delivered over an Internet connection that is viewed as it downloads. Alternatively, nonstreaming video must be downloaded to the viewer's hard drive as a complete file before it can be seen. (Streaming video is a delivery technology rather than an actual form of animation or file format.) The term *streaming video* can also encompass streaming animation, as long as the concept of viewing-while-downloading is maintained.
- *Tweening* is automated frame creation. You create the initial and final frames in a sequence, and ImageReady creates the intermediary frames. Each of the succeeding intermediary frames will be progressively more like the final frame and less like the first frame.



Animations can be grouped into two categories. *Cumulative animations* build from frame to frame, with objects from the first frame appearing in the second. They are also called *typewriter* animations because each character or object appears one-after-another, much like a typewriter puts letters on a page (or, perhaps, the way a keyboard enters letters on a monitor). *Noncumulative* animations do not build. When the second frame appears, the objects in the first frame disappear. A graphic representation of the difference between frames of a cumulative animation and a noncumulative animation is shown in Figure 23.12.

# ImageReady Animation Basics

ImageReady creates frames of an animation from layers in an image. To change the content of a frame, you show and hide layers. (This is comparable to the way you change the appearance of an image with rollover states.) Consider the three frames shown in Figure 23.13. Each frame has one layer visible in the Layers palette. In an animation, the smiley face would appear to wink as the eye is closed and reopened.

ImageReady uses the Animation palette in conjunction with the Layers palette to create the frames of an animation. Much like creating rollovers, you click the New Frame button in the Animation palette and then configure the Layers palette to show the image as you want it for that frame. The Animation palette is shown in Figure 23.14.

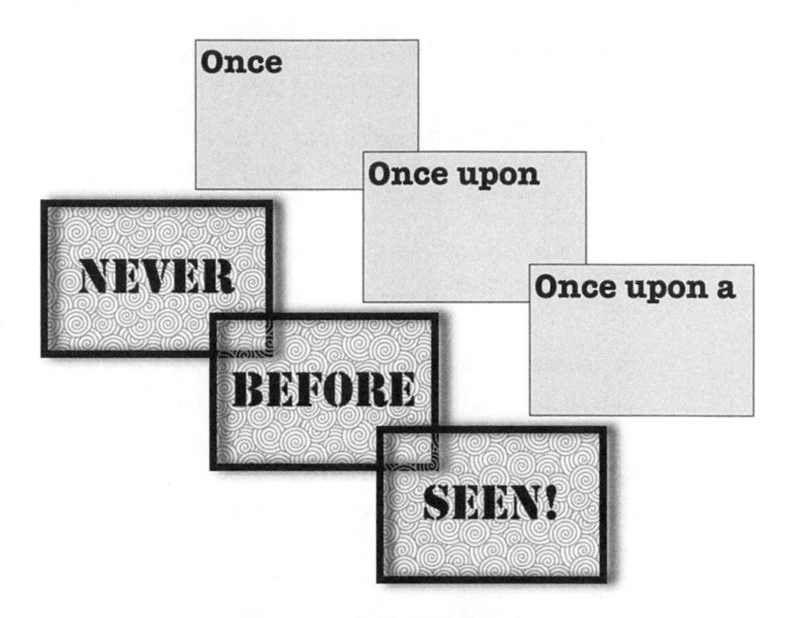


Figure 23.12
The top three frames are cumulative—the content of previous frames remains. The lower example shows a noncumulative animation. Note that even with noncumulative animations, some content can be retained from frame to frame (the background in this example).

23

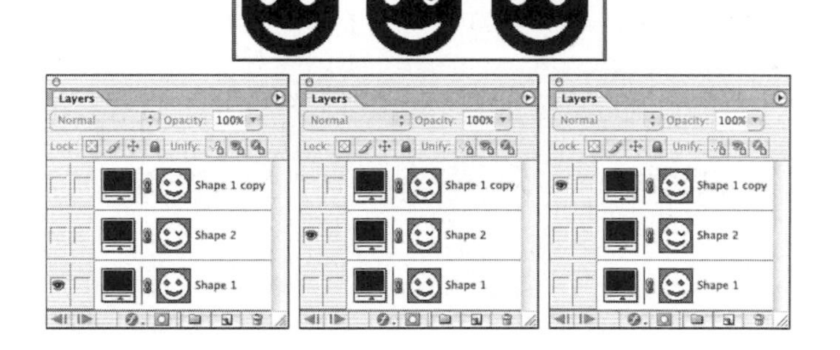


Figure 23.13
It would, of course, be just as easy to use Layer 1 for the third frame because there is no difference between the first and third frames or between Shape 1 and Shape 1 copy.

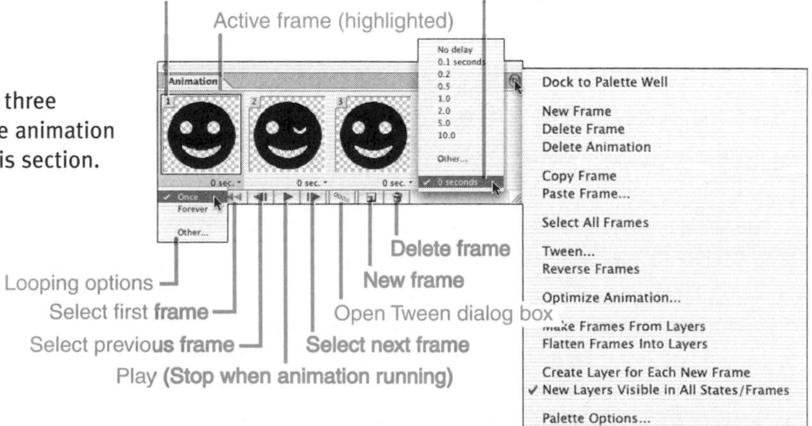


Figure 23.14
The palette shows the three frames from the simple animation discussed earlier in this section.

Most of the features of the Animation palette need no explanation. However, a few items deserve attention:

- **Looping options**—Looping determines how many times the animation will play after it starts. If Once is selected, the animation stops when it reaches the last frame (which remains visible). The Forever option restarts the animation each time it reaches the last frame, until you stop it or the image is no longer open in the Web browser. Other enables you to input a number from 1 to 30,000.

If you select Once for looping and you want the first frame of the animation showing after the animation stops, simply duplicate the first frame and move it to the end of the animation. You can increase the timing for the prior frame to have it visible for a few seconds before the copy of the first frame appears.

- **Open Tween dialog box**—The Tween dialog box is used to create intermediary frames between two selected frames. It's discussed in the following section.
- **Frame Timing**—The Frame Timing pop-up menu enables you to determine how long each frame will show before the following frame appears. With No Delay selected, the animation plays as fast as the Web browser and Internet connection can display it. The Other option enables you to specify a frame delay of up to 4 minutes (240 seconds). You can Shift-click or (Command)-click [Ctrl]-click multiple frames to set them to the same delay.
- **Reverse Frames**—The Reverse Frames command in the Animation palette menu reverses the order of the selected frames in the animation. You can use Select All Frames, then Reverse Frames to reverse the entire animation. You can select a number of frames and then copy, paste, and reverse the newly pasted frames. If you've created frames showing, for example, an elevator rising, copying and reversing is an easy way to show the elevator coming back down.
- **Optimize Animation**—The Optimize Animation command helps you reduce the file size (and therefore speed the download and play time over the Internet). Optimizing animations is discussed later in this section.
- **Make Frames from Layers**—One click can turn each layer into a separate frame in the Animation palette with the Make Frames from Layers command. This command will be grayed out and unavailable if the Animation palette contains more than the default first frame.
- **Flatten Frames into Layers**—When frames are created with several layers visible, the Layers palette can get rather confusing. The Animation palette menu command Flatten Frames into Layers can quickly clarify the situation. When you use this command, a new layer is created in the Layers palette for each frame. Each frame's layer is a merged version of all the layers used in the frame. The original layers are preserved and hidden.
- **Create Layer for Each New Frame**—When the Create Layer for Each New Frame option is selected, a check mark will appear next to it in the Animation palette menu. The new layer will be empty and visible only in the frame for which it's created. Use this option when you'll be adding some new graphic elements to each frame—think of it as a simple laborsaving feature that eliminates the need to manually add a new layer each time you click the New Frame button. However, unless there is a reason for you to add a new layer each time you create a frame, leave this option unselected.

- **New Layers Visible in All States/Frames**—If you'll be adding a new layer to your image and want the content of that layer to be visible in all frames of the animation, select the New Layers Visible in All States/Frames option in the Animation palette menu. When this option is active, a check mark appears next to it. This option is handy for adding a new element to an existing animation. Remember, too, that if you need the content of a new layer visible in *most* frames of an animation, you can select this option, add the layer, and then hide the layer for the frames in which it should not appear.



You can drag frames in the Animation palette to reorder them. You can click any frame and change its appearance by altering the content of the Layers palette.

## Tweening to Create Frames

The term *tween* comes from "in between." You select a pair of frames in an animation and use ImageReady's tweening to create a series of frames that fall between them. The content of the tweened frames is a progression from one frame to the other (see Figure 23.15).

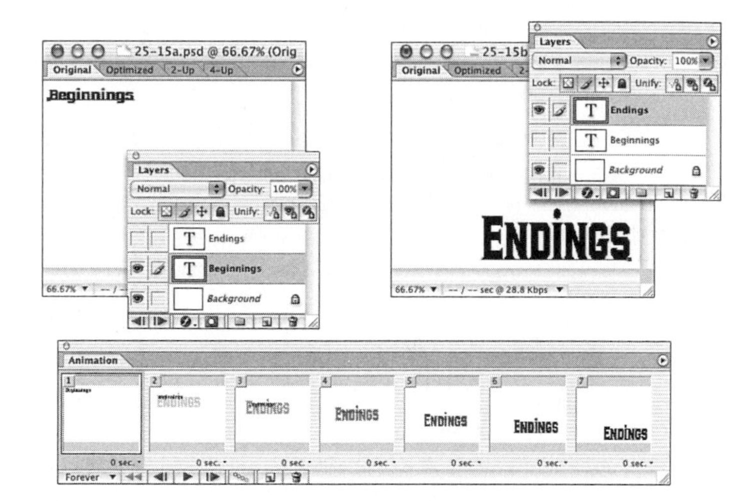


Figure 23.15
The first frame is based on the image in the upper left, whereas the last frame is shown to the upper right. The intermediary frames were tweened.

Before clicking the Tween button at the bottom of the Animation palette or selecting the Tween command from the palette's menu, select a frame or a series of two or more frames. After opening the Tween dialog box, you choose whether to base the tweening on the selected frames or, if only one frame is selected, whether to tween that frame with the preceding or following frame. The number of frames you can add to the animation with tweening ranges from 1 to 100. You also choose whether to tween based on changes in all the layers in the image or just those layers currently selected in the Layers palette.

Tweening can create new frames based on differences in the existing frames for three characteristics:

- **Layer position**—Position the layers as you want them for the first frame. Create a new frame or click the next frame in the Animation palette. Drag the layers to the positions for the last frame. When you tween, the content of the layers will appear to move from frame to frame.

- **Layer opacity**—With the first animation frame active in the Animation palette, set the opacity for each layer. With the last frame active, make the required changes to opacity.
- **Layer style**—Any layer styles applied in the first frame will gradually change to those applied with the last frame active.

Figure 23.16 shows changes between the first and last frame in both layer position and layer opacity. In the first frame, the text on both layers is in the upper-left corner of the image, but the type layer "Endings" has an opacity of 0%. For the last frame, both layers were moved to the lower right and the opacity of "Endings" was changed to 100% and the opacity of "Beginnings" was reduced to 0%.



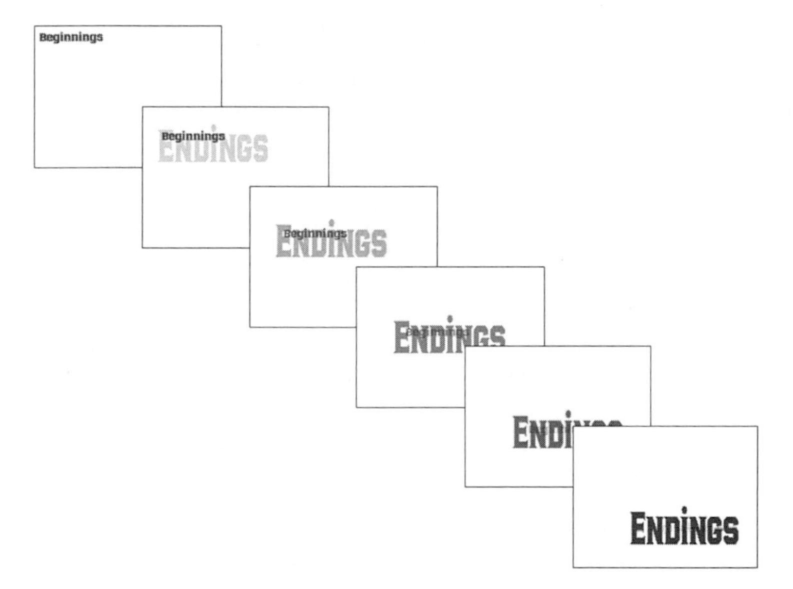


Figure 23.16
Tweening produces an animation that has "Endings" fading in and "Beginnings" fading out, while the words slowly move across the image.

In Figure 23.17, you see a change in layer style. In the first frame, a layer style is applied with a drop shadow angle of 150°, which gives the perception that the light source is to the left of the hourglass. In the last frame, the drop shadow angle is 30° in the Layer Style dialog box, thus "moving" the light source. Tweening shifts the drop shadow effect, frame by frame.

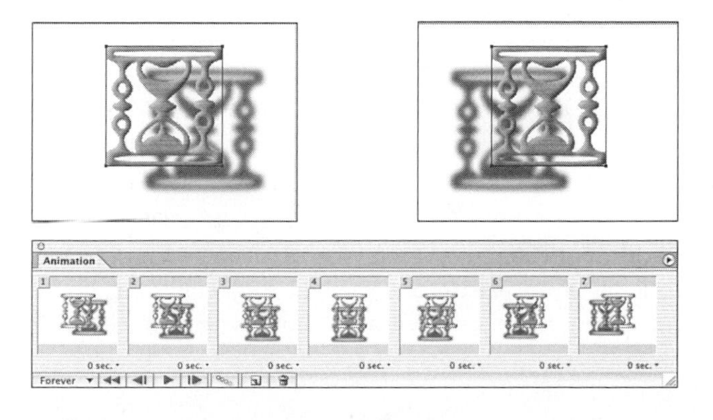


Figure 23.17
When changing the angle of a drop shadow, inner shadow, or bevel/emboss shading, you must uncheck the Global Angle box in the Layer Style dialog box.

*Tweening grayed out? See "Checking the Frame Selection" in the "Mastering ImageReady" section at the end of this chapter.*

Tweening is not only a great laborsaving feature, it can ensure that your animation plays smoothly and precisely. Because ImageReady calculates the content of the intermediary frames, human error is minimized.

Don't confuse ImageReady's tweening with Illustrator's blending capability—tweening does not create new objects in the intermediary frames.



## ImageReady at Work: Tweening to Create Frames

ImageReady's tweening capability can easily and efficiently create animation frames that would otherwise consume lots of your creative time. Consider, if you will, a bouncing ball. If your animation is extremely basic, you create a frame, move the ball's layer a little in the image window, create a frame, move the ball, create a frame, move the ball, and so on. For the most basic bouncing ball, tweening enables you to create the first frame, move the ball to the other end of the bounce, create a new frame, and then tween to create all the intermediary frames.

Here's how to use tweening with a slightly more sophisticated bouncing ball effect:

1. Open a new document in Photoshop. For this example, use RGB, 300 pixels wide and 400 pixels tall, filled with white.

2. Add a new layer. With that layer active, make a circular selection in the bottom center of the image using the Elliptical Marquee tool (about 100 pixels in diameter), and add a slightly off-center radial gradient from the color of your "ball" to black (see Figure 23.18). (We're creating the original artwork in Photoshop rather than ImageReady in order to use the Gradient tool.) After adding the gradient, use the keyboard shortcut (Command-D) [Ctrl+D] to deselect.

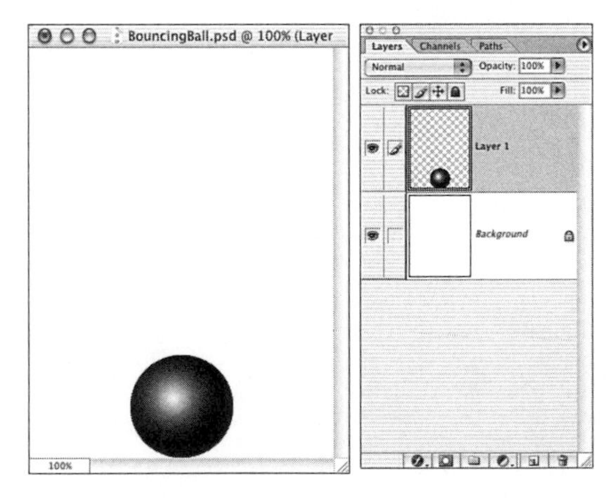


**Figure 23.18**
Make sure your gradient-filled selection is on a separate layer.

3. Because you want to make the ball "squash" a little when it hits the floor, copy its layer (drag to the New Layer button in the Layers palette) and use Edit, Free Transform. Bringing down the top of the transform marquee and sending the sides outward gives you the look you need.

4. To extend the squash, copy the new layer and flatten/widen a little more with Free Transform. You should now have three ball layers in the Layers palette (see Figure 23.19).

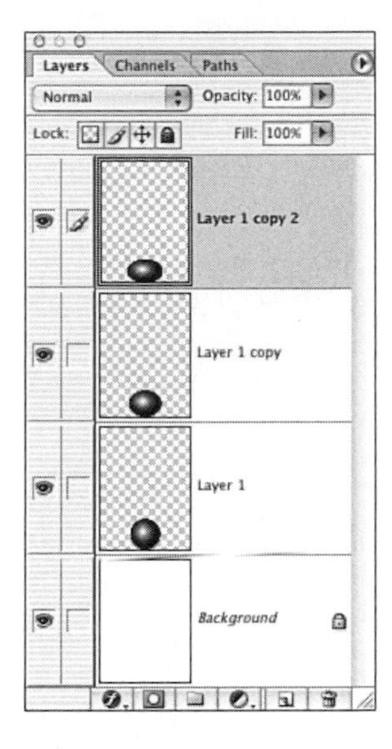


**Figure 23.19**
The ball will bounce downward, but the "squashed" ball layers are above the original ball layer.



5. Although the final animation will have almost 30 frames, you only need to create these three layers. Remember that you produce the frames of an animation by showing/hiding layers and changing the position, opacity, and layer styles of those layers. Click the button at the bottom of the Photoshop Toolbox to jump to ImageReady. You'll start by hiding the two "squashed ball" layers, thus producing the initial animation frame (see Figure 23.20).

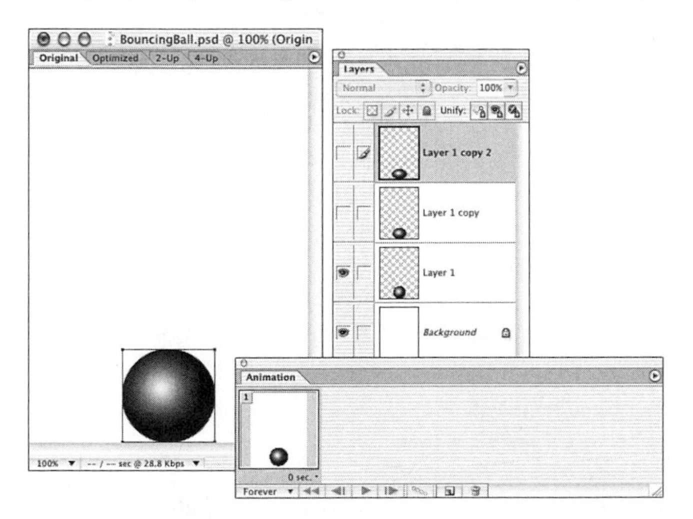


**Figure 23.20**
The Background layer and the original ball layer are visible in the Layers palette, thus creating the first frame in the Animation palette.

6. Add a second frame by clicking the second button from the right at the bottom of the Animation palette. To show the ball at the top of the bounce, you must make sure the appropriate layer is active in the Layers palette and then click and Shift-drag with the Move tool to reposition the ball. (Shift constrains the drag, making sure the ball goes straight up.)

7. Before you start tweening, you should think ahead: What goes up must come down. (Option)-drag [Alt]-drag the first frame to the end of the animation, duplicating it. The Animation palette shows three frames: down, up, down.

8. Here's the easy part: making ImageReady earn its keep by creating frames with the Tweening feature. Select the first two frames by clicking and Shift-clicking. Then click the Tween button at the bottom of the Animation palette or choose the Tween command from the palette menu. As you can see in the Tween dialog box, shown in Figure 23.21, you can choose to create new frames based on changes in position, opacity, or layer effects. You can also elect to make changes to the animation based on one layer or all visible layers.



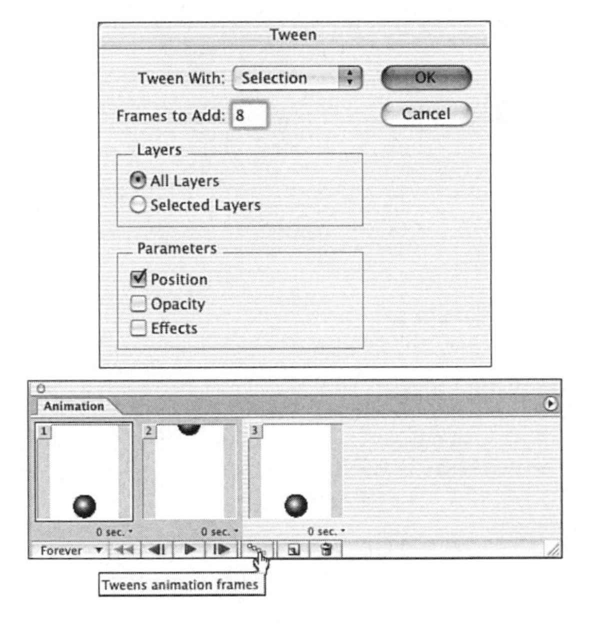


**Figure 23.21**
Your Animation palette should show three frames, with one ball layer visible in each.

9. In this case, you want ImageReady to produce frames using all visible layers (you want the background visible in each frame) and base the new frames on changes in position. You'll generate eight new frames.

10. ImageReady calculates a uniform transition from frame to frame to generate the new frames. Now you'll want to tween between the "up" frame and the second "down" frame, using the same parameters. Again, simply select the frames between which you want the new frames and use the Tween command from the Animation palette menu.

11. Because ImageReady can't tween the scaling of an object, you have to insert your "squashed ball" frames with opacity. Because you want them to appear between the two "down ball" frames (the very last frame and the first frame), you'll add them to the end of the animation. Select the last frame, click the New Frame button, and make the changes in the Layers palette. Keep the background visible, hide the original ball frame, and show the first copy.

12. Select the new frame and the frame immediately prior to it in the Animation palette and then open the Tween dialog box. Add three frames, based on opacity rather than position (see Figure 23.22).

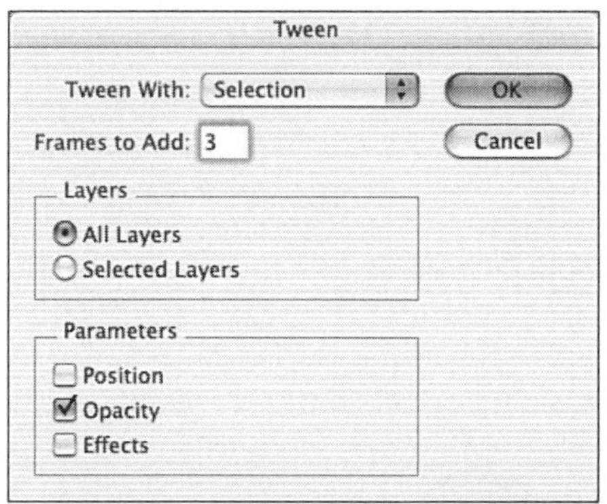


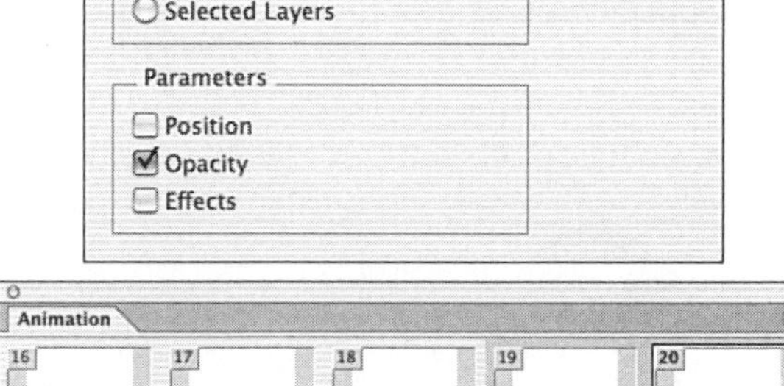


**Figure 23.22**
The three new frames will transition from the "down" to the "squashed" frame by fading out the previous frame and fading in the new frame.

13. You must create another new frame to show the ball in the "fully squashed" position (the second layer copy) and then tween it to transition from the "half squashed" frame. Tween only one new frame, again based on opacity. Click the New Frame button, hide the "half squashed" layer, show the "fully squashed" layer, and then use Tween to add a single frame.

14. Because the ball shouldn't change from "fully squashed" to the "down" position, you'll "unsquash" the ball. Click the last frame of the animation (Frame 25). Now scroll to the left and Shift-click the very first frame of the transition from "down" to "half squashed" (Frame 20).

15. Duplicate this series of frames by dragging to the New Frame button. Now, without deselecting the frame series, use the Animation palette menu command Reverse Frames. Click the Play button at the bottom of the animation palette to preview the bouncing ball. The Play button becomes the Stop button when an animation is playing.

16. Stop the animation. You can now adjust the timing of the frames if desired, but the default value of 0 sec is suitable for this animation. (Remember that you can click the first frame, Shift-click the last frame to select all frames, and then adjust the timing for all by changing the Frame Timing pop-up menu for any selected frame.) However, you can make some frame edits to improve the flow: The ball stays in the "fully squashed" position just a bit too long, so delete Frame 26. You can also delete Frame 20 and then the (newly numbered) Frame 29 to improve the transition from "down" to "half squashed." After deleting those frames, locate the one frame that shows the ball at the top of the bounce (Frame 10) and drag it to the New Frame button to duplicate it. This makes the ball "hang" at the top of the bounce before succumbing to gravity. (Alternatively, simply increase the timing of Frame 10.)

17. The final step is to save the file as an animated GIF. Because of the gradient, dithering is a good idea, and using a reduced color palette can help keep file size small (see Figure 23.23). After setting the options in the Optimize palette, use the menu command File, Save Optimized.

23

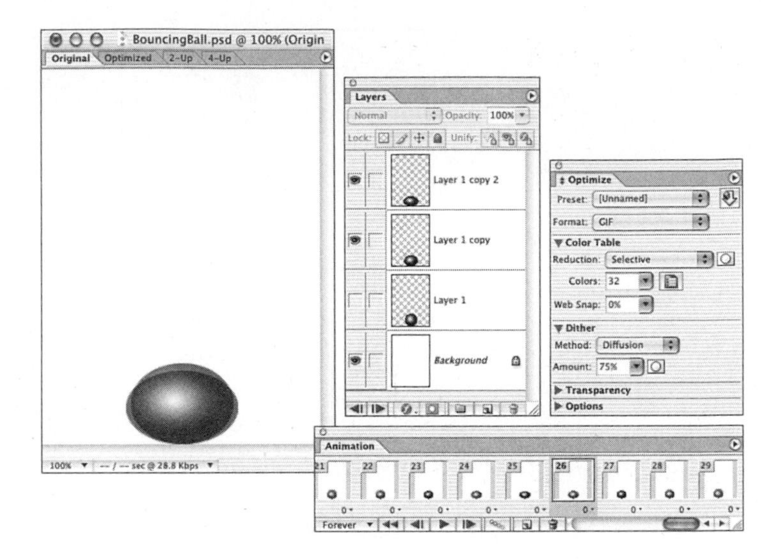


Figure 23.23
The Layers palette and the image window show the frame currently active in the Animation palette. The Optimize palette shows the settings used for this animated GIF.

# Optimizing Animations

File size for an animated GIF file can be substantially reduced by selecting the appropriate optimization method. In addition to choosing GIF settings in ImageReady's Optimization palette, you can select a method of optimizing the frames of the animation. From the Animation palette menu, select Optimize Animation. By default, both Bounding Box and Redundant Pixel Removal are selected.

Optimizing to the bounding box crops each frame to that area that has changed from the preceding frame. This option produces the greatest file size savings. Deselect the option Bounding Box only if the animated GIF will be edited outside of ImageReady in a program that does not recognize the option.

Redundant Pixel Removal compares the pixels of a frame to those of the preceding frame. Identical pixels become transparent.

# Choosing a Frame Disposal Method

How the animation appears onscreen when playing back often depends on the selected frame disposal method. You can change the frame disposal method to create cumulative animations. Generally you'll want to leave the decision up to ImageReady by sticking with the default Automatic settings. However, in some cases you'll want to manually control the settings for a frame or series of frames.

To change the frame disposal method, select one or more frames in the Animation palette and then (Control)-click right-click to open the contextual menu. Here are the options:

> For Redundant Pixel Removal to function properly, you must check the Transparency box in ImageReady's Optimization palette. In addition, do not change the Frame Disposal Method setting.

- **Automatic**—ImageReady evaluates a frame, and if the frame contains transparency, the preceding frame is hidden when the new frame is displayed.

- **Do Not Dispose**—Cumulative animations can be created with the Do Not Dispose option. The content of each layer remains displayed, showing through the transparent areas of succeeding frames. If the content of the frames do not overlap, the image builds onscreen. Places where frames do not have transparency hide the content of earlier frames.
- **Restore to Background**—With this option, only one frame is displayed at a time.



## Adding Animation to Rollovers

To add an animation to a rollover state, select the state in the Web Content palette and select New Animation Frame from the palette menu or click the Create Animation Frame button at the bottom of the palette. (Note that the button is not visible by default, and you much select the option Include Animation Frames in the Web Content Palette Options.) Create the animation in the Animation palette.

As you can see in Figure 23.24, the animation appears in the Web Content palette as a series of frames under the designated rollover state. You can hide the animation frames in the Web Content palette by clicking the triangle to the left of the rollover state or by deselecting Include Animation Frames in the Web Content Palette Options.

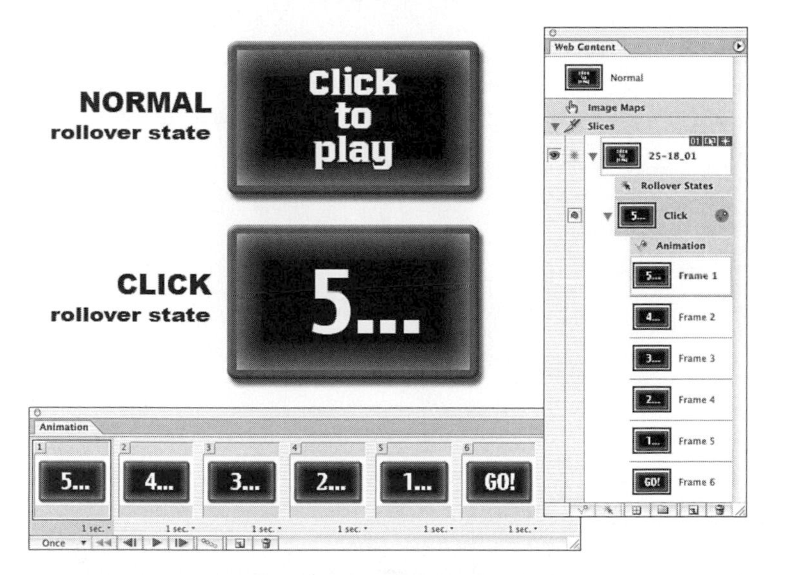


Figure 23.24
The animation is associated only with the Click rollover state. If you assign an animation to the Normal state, the animation plays when the animated GIF file loads.

# ANIMATIONS AND IMAGEREADY'S EXPORT COMMAND

In addition to creating animated GIFs, you can create Flash animations in the SWF format. Exported SWF files can be posted to the Web or opened in Flash (from Macromedia) for further editing. In addition, you can also export the frames of an animation to individual files for use in Flash or another program, and you can export layers to individual files, which can also be used in Flash.

23

## Exporting as Macromedia Flash from ImageReady

The SWF file format supports both vector and raster data in an animation. You can use type layers and shape layers in the animation, and the layer content can be scaled as necessary in Flash without loss of quality. However, although SWF supports raster images, background gradients and textures are exported as solid colors—a Flash image can have only a solid color background and does not support background transparency.

Exporting both frames and layers to individual files can give you greater flexibility when working with Macromedia Flash or Adobe's now-discontinued LiveMotion. Each frame-based file shows every layer visible in that frame. Having the individual layer content also available may make editing and fine-tuning easier.

Another limitation of the SWF file format is lack of support for rollovers. If your image contains rollovers in addition to animation, animated GIF may be a better choice. Not only will the rollovers be dropped, any animation assigned to a rollover state is lost. Slices, image maps, and any URLs associated with them are also discarded on export to SWF.

The File, Export, Macromedia® Flash™ SWF command opens the dialog box shown in Figure 23.25. In the dialog box, you select the options that govern what features and data are recorded with the file.

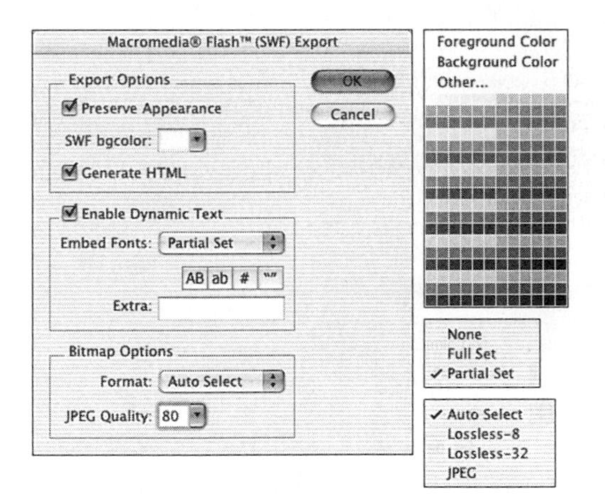


Figure 23.25
The SWF bgcolor, Embed Fonts, and Format pop-up menus are shown to the right of the dialog box.

Here are the options available to you when exporting to SWF format:

- **Preserve Appearance**—When selected, Preserve Appearance helps maintain the visual integrity of the image. This option is especially important when layer styles are used in an animation, and it's absolutely critical when layer styles are applied to unrasterized type and shape layers. When Preserve Appearance is deselected and layer styles are present, they may be discarded on export. Layer effects that would require rasterizing a vector layer are always discarded when the option is inactivated. Flash is, at heart, a vector-based image format, and preserving the integrity of vector art takes precedence over layer effects unless Preserve Appearance is selected.

- **SWF bgcolor**—All SWF files must have an assigned background color. The pop-up menu offers the Web-safe palette, as well as your choice of the current ImageReady foreground or background color and Other, which opens the Color Picker.
- **Generate HTML**—In addition to the SWF image file, an HTML document will be created. Copy/paste from that document into an existing Web page to add the SWF file (and remember to move or copy the SWF file to the appropriate Images folder for that Web page and site).
- **Enable Dynamic Text**—If, and only if, type variables (assigned as data-driven graphics) are used in the image is this option necessary. Text variables will be mapped to Flash dynamic text for use by the Flash plug-in of a Web browser. Don't use this option when an image will undergo further editing in Flash—the dynamic text (and the text variables) will be disregarded.
- **Embed Fonts**—When working with files that will include dynamic text, you can reduce the file size (often substantially) by either not embedding fonts or embedding partial fonts. If you select the Partial Set option, you use the buttons immediately below the Embed Fonts pop-up menu to identify what glyphs to embed. The four buttons are, starting from the left, Capitals, Lowercase, Numbers, and Punctuation. Select the options that cover the characters used in the text variables. The Extra field enables you to type any additional characters necessary for the text variables. For example, all text variables used with the file may consist of numbers and the letters *A*, *B*, and *C*. You could then minimize file size by clicking the number button and typing **ABC** in the Extra field.
- **Format**—The Bitmap Options, Format pop-up menu enables you to determine how raster artwork in your SWF file will be saved. The pop-up menu offers Auto Select (ImageReady will export according to the artwork's current color depth), Lossless-8 (Indexed color mode), Lossless-32 (RGB), and JPEG (compressed RGB). Auto Select is usually a good choice. Specify Lossless-8 or Lossless-32 in situations where you need to force a specific color mode for further editing in Flash.
- **JPEG Quality**—If either Auto Select or JPEG is selected in the Format pop-up menu, the JPEG Quality field determines the compression level used for raster images. When either of the Lossless options is selected in Format, the JPEG Quality field is disregarded.



# Exporting Layers and Animation Frames

ImageReady's Export menu also includes the commands Layers as Files and Animation Frames as Files. These commands are often used to generate files that will later be used in Flash to build animations. You can, however, export to individual files any time you need an image of a specific frame or layer.

## Export Layers as Files Options

The Export Layers as Files dialog box determines how the files generated will be named, which layers will be saved, and what file format and options will be used for each new file (see Figure 23.26).

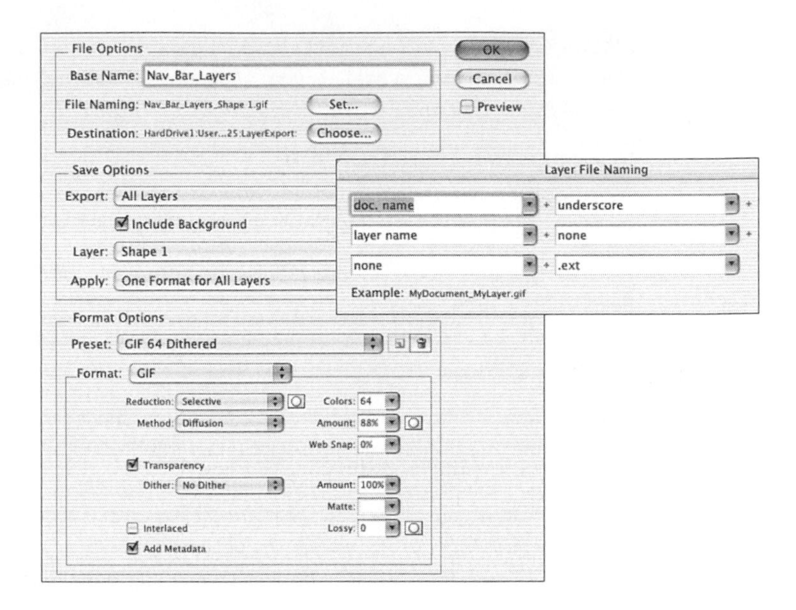


**Figure 23.26**
The Layer File Naming dialog box is opened by clicking the Set button in the Export Layer as Files dialog box.



You determine how the new files will be named and where they will be saved in the upper part of the dialog box. In the Save Options area, you select which frame or frames will be used to generate new frames. The lower section of the dialog box determines the format and options for saved files. If the Apply pop-up menu in the Save Options section is set to Separate Format for Each Layer, you can assign any appropriate file format and options for each of the layers being exported. This is especially valuable if the layers being exported include some layers with large areas of solid color (best exported as GIF or PNG-8) as well as layers containing photographic images or gradients (best saved as JPEG or PNG-24). Other format options include WBMP, SWF, and PSD. Note the two buttons to the right of the Preset pop-up menu. You can save and delete custom preset options combinations. The Preview button shows you the content of the layer as it will be exported.

## Export Animation Frames as Files Options

When you're exporting animation frames to individual files, several of your options are similar to those described for exporting layers to files. You use the same filenaming conventions and the same file format options. The middle part of the dialog box, however, differs between the two Export commands (see Figure 23.27).

When exporting animation frames to individual files, you have the choice of generating files from all frames or just those selected in the Animation palette at the time you selected the Export command. Note that if the Preview box is checked in the upper-right corner of the dialog box, you have the option of seeing how each frame will look after the export. You can select a specific frame from the pop-up menu or cycle through the frames using the buttons to the right of the Preview pop-up menu.

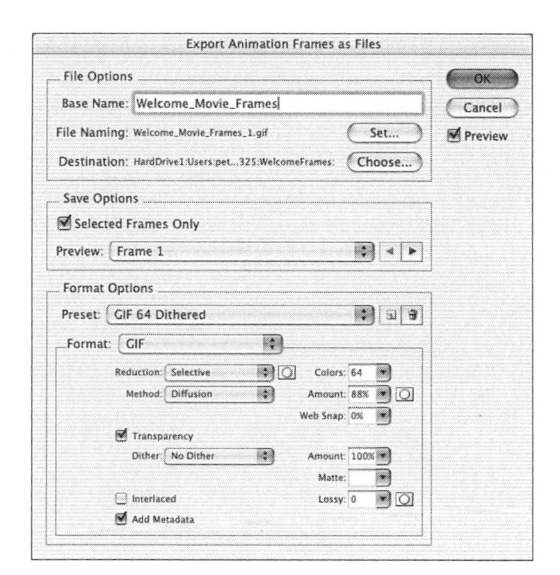


Figure 23.27
Note that there is no provision to customize the file format options for each new file.



# MASTERING IMAGEREADY

## HTML Placeholders

*I often create Web pages first, then later go to ImageReady and create the fancy graphics. Is there an easy way to find the proper place to paste my ImageReady HTML?*

Sure! When creating your original Web page, put in a "placeholder" graphic. Use a GIF file that's the same dimensions as the rollover or animation you'll add later from ImageReady. Save the dummy image using a naming convention such as <placeholder_rollover_1.gif>. When you're ready to paste, do a quick search of the source code to identify the proper place for your ImageReady code.

## Checking the Frame Selection

*I've selected two frames in my animation and want ImageReady to create a series of frames between them, but the Tweening button and command are grayed out. What's the problem?*

The problem may lie with the frame selection. Are the two selected frames next to each other in the Animation palette? Here are your frame-selection options when preparing to tween:

- Select one frame. When tweening, you'll be asked whether to tween with the previous frame or the following frame.
- Select two contiguous frames. If the two selected frames are next to each other in the Animation palette, the Tween command knows exactly where to place the new frames.

- Select the first and last frames of the animation. Tweening then creates frames that follow the last frame. Use this option when you're preparing an animation that will loop—the tweened frames will smoothly transition from the last existing frame to the first, preventing a sudden jump when the animation starts over.
- Select a series of three or more frames by clicking the first and Shift-clicking the last of the series. When tweened, the existing intermediary frames will be altered to ensure a smooth transition from the first to last selected frame.

# ILLUSTRATOR CS

# CREATING AND EDITING PATHS

## IN THIS CHAPTER

The building blocks of Illustrator artwork are paths. With the exception of raster and rasterized objects, paths are the basic component of each item on the artboard. In Illustrator, even type is path based. Understanding paths and how they work is a key to getting the most out of Illustrator's various capabilities.

# PATHS AND VECTOR ART

Illustrator is a vector art program. Although it allows you to do some rather advanced work with raster images and rasterized artwork, it is at heart a vector art program. Vector art is based on the concept of paths. Each item is a path, and the path is stroked and/or filled to produce artwork. Without the path, there's nothing to stroke or fill, so the artwork cannot appear on the page. Likewise, without a stroke or fill, the path may be there, but it is invisible. (Invisible paths are used in Illustrator. They are discussed later in this chapter.) The path defines the basic shape of an object, whereas the stroke and fill (and other characteristics) determine the appearance of the object.

*The differences between the two categories of computer graphics are discussed more fully in Chapter 4, "Pixels, Vectors, and Resolutions," p. 129.*

The concepts *vector* and *raster* are very important in a discussion of computer graphics. To clarify, vector artwork is path based. It consists of paths that determine the shape of objects and the colors that are applied to the path (stroke) and within the path (fill). Raster artwork consists of a series of small colored squares, called *pixels*. Raster artwork can be an object in an Illustrator document, but the raster art itself does not have objects within it. It may appear as a circle or a square, but the raster art is actually just those small, color pixels.

## Basic Path Creation

Every time you add a line or a shape to the artboard, you're creating a path. Rectangles, ellipses, stars, grids, graphs, and flares are just some of the examples of path-based objects that you can add to the artboard with a click and drag. The path is identifiable when an object is selected on the artboard (or in the Layers palette), as shown in Figure 24.1. The left and center objects are selected, and their paths are visible, but the object on the right is not selected and its path is not visible.

If the artboard is looking too complicated or confusing, consider eliminating some of the visual cues. The menu command View, Hide Edges makes the path invisible, even when an object is selected. View, Hide Bounding box is also available.

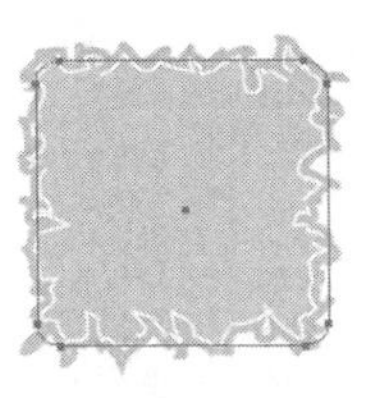
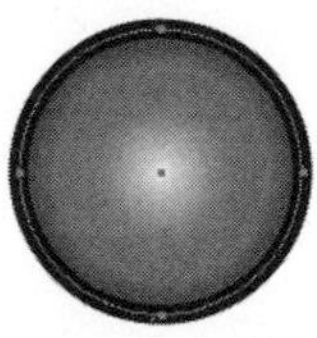

Figure 24.1
The color of the path depends on the layer options, which are assigned through the Layers palette.

Dragging or clicking one of the basic creation tools (Rectangle tool, Ellipse tool, Line tool, and so on) adds a path to the artboard. The path automatically assumes the current stroke and fill characteristics, as well as any characteristics assigned to the layer. (Chapter 30, "Illustrator's Layers, Sublayers, and Groups," discusses targeting appearances to a layer.)

There are many ways to add paths to the artboard in addition to the basic creation tools. The Pen, Pencil, and Paintbrush tools enable you to create paths in any shape. The Graph, Grid, and Flare tools create multiple paths at the same time. The Transform commands enable you to copy an existing path. Paste is another command that can add one or more paths. Figure 24.2 shows a variety of paths.

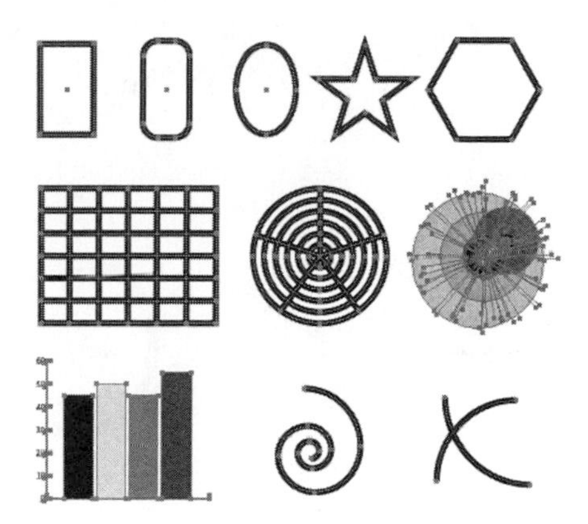

Figure 24.2
From simple objects and lines to grids and graphs, paths are the building blocks of artwork in Illustrator.



## Types of Paths

Paths can be categorized in two ways. They can be either open or closed. A path consists of two or more *anchor points*, which bound a straight or curved *path segment*. Each segment must have an anchor point at either end. Paths can be open (with two distinct endpoints) or closed (with no endpoints). Consider the difference between a piece of string and a rubber band. The string, even if you tie the ends in a knot, has a pair of identifiable ends. The rubber band does not (unless broken). Figure 24.3 shows examples of open paths.

Figure 24.3
All these paths have two identifiable endpoints, so all are open paths.

Notice that the round path in the upper-right corner has two endpoints, even though the path crosses itself. Regardless of the enclosed area within the path, the endpoints make this an open path.

Closed paths, such as those shown in Figure 24.4, have no identifiable endpoints. Each and every anchor point has a path segment on either side of it. There are no endpoints.

**Figure 24.4**
None of these paths have endpoints.

Open paths can consist of a single path segment and therefore can have as few as two anchor points. Closed paths can also have only two anchor points (see Figure 24.5).

**Figure 24.5**
Each of these paths has exactly two anchor points.

**Non-Object Paths in Illustrator**

While the most common paths in Illustrator are, without question, objects, there are a variety of other uses for paths in your documents. Here are some examples:

- Clipping masks are created from paths. They selectively expose parts of an image, hiding the rest of the parts without deleting them. The path defines what part of the image will be visible (inside the clipping mask) and what will be hidden (outside the mask). (Clipping masks are discussed in Chapter 34, "Using Masks, Transparency, and Blending Modes.")
- Crop marks and trim marks, which indicate where a printed page should be cut, are formed from rectangular paths.
- Type on a path uses a path to create the baseline for type.

# HOW ANCHOR POINTS SHAPE PATHS

To understand how paths are shaped, it's important to understand how anchor points work. The path's segments are what we stroke and fill and otherwise use in Illustrator to produce art. However, it's the path's *anchor points* that actually determine the shape of those segments. You edit the shape of a path by manipulating the anchor points.

The location of an anchor point on the artboard is relatively insignificant in shaping a path. Rather, it is the relationships among anchor points that are important. The distance and direction among the anchor points determines the shape of an object. In addition, anchor points determine whether a path segment will be straight or curved.

The paths used in vector art are referred to as *Bézier curves*, named after the French engineer who pioneered their application, Pierre Etienne Bézier.

## Locating, Selecting, and Moving Anchor Points

Each path segment is bordered by exactly two anchor points. The distance and angle between the anchor points is a major factor in determining the shape of the path. With straight path segments, this relationship between the anchor points is *the* determining factor.

*Think you've got an anchor point with more than two path segments coming from it? See "That's No Path!" in the "Mastering Illustrator" section at the end of this chapter.*

When a path is selected, anchor points are shown as small squares along the path and at the ends of open paths. The path segments are indicated by a thin line. Both the path and the anchor points are shown in the color assigned to the layer on which the path is located (see Figure 24.6).

**Figure 24.6**
Anchor points are visible, as are the path segments, when a path is selected on the artboard.

Normally, when an object is selected on the artboard, all the object's anchor points are selected. However, when the Direct Selection tool or the Direct Selection Lasso tool is used, individual anchor points can be selected for manipulation. When selected, an anchor point is shown as a filled square on the artboard (see Figure 24.7). Unselected anchor points are shown as hollow squares.

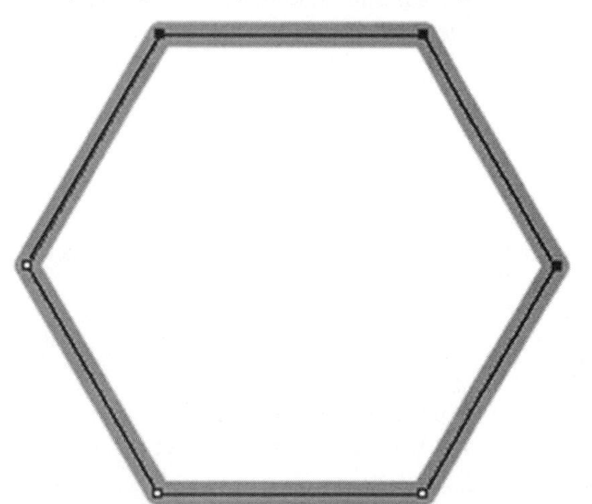

**Figure 24.7**
The selected anchor points are filled squares; unselected anchor points are hollow squares.

When all anchor points are selected and you move an object on the artboard, the object moves as a unit but the appearance itself doesn't change. When some, but not all, anchor points are selected, you change the appearance of the object. In Figure 24.8, you can see that only the anchor points that were selected in Figure 24.7 are being dragged.

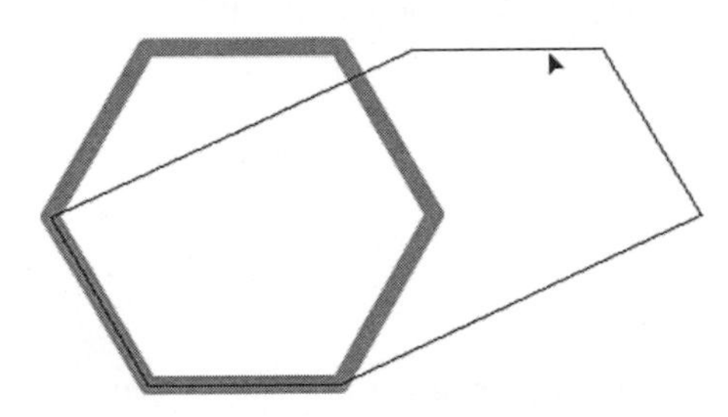

Figure 24.8
The three selected anchor points are being dragged; the other three remain stationary.



If all six anchor points had been selected, the entire polygon would have moved as a unit. Instead, its shape is changed (see Figure 24.9).

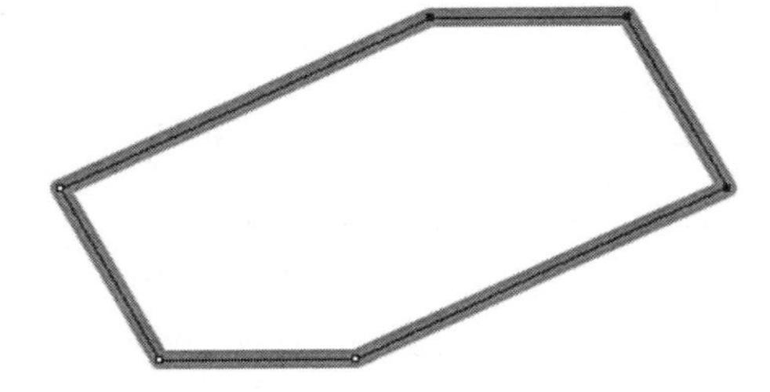

Figure 24.9
The shape that results from the drag operation shown in Figure 24.8.

One or more selected anchor points can also be deleted to change the appearance of a selected object. The tool that you use makes a difference. In Figure 24.10, the two copies of the object on the left had a single point deleted. In the middle, the point was selected with the Direct Selection tool and the (Delete) [Backspace] key was used. On the right, the Delete Anchor Point tool was used. (The Delete Anchor Point tool is discussed in the section "The Other Pen Tools," later in this chapter.)

Figure 24.10
The original object is on the left.

The first technique changed the closed path to an open path. The second simply altered the shape of the path.

## The Types of Anchor Points

In addition to the locational relationship between anchor points, a path segment's shape is determined by the *type* of anchor points. The two basic types of anchor points are *smooth* and *corner*.

In Figure 24.11, the middle anchor points of all six open paths are selected (they are within the dashed rectangles). On the left, all four points are corner points. On the right, both selected points are smooth points.

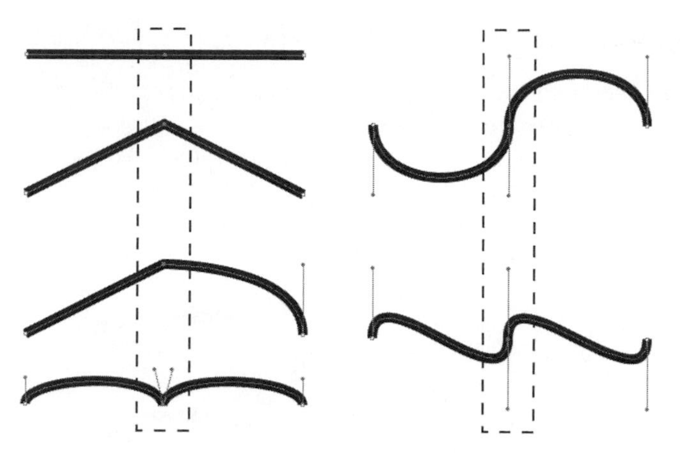

Figure 24.11
The middle of each path on the left has a corner anchor point. The two paths on the right have smooth anchor points in the middle.

(In Figure 24.11 you can also see the *direction lines* and *control points* for a number of the anchor points. These lines, which control the shape of curved path segments, will be discussed in the next section.)



A smooth point has a curved path flowing continuously through it. The curve includes the curved path segments on either side of the smooth point. In contrast, a path abruptly changes direction at a corner point (the exception to this general rule is, of course, three points in a row, such as the top-left path in Figure 24.11—the path doesn't change direction at all). The path segments on either side can both be straight segments, both be curved segments, or can be one of each. As you can see in the lowest example on the left in Figure 24.11, when two curved path segments meet at a point but do not flow smoothly through that point, the point is a corner point.

You may also hear the term *combination point* used. It typically refers to an anchor point where a curved path segment meets a straight path segment. Although these anchor points are technically corner points, the unofficial term is certainly valuable for clarification.

As a general rule, the key to differentiating between a corner point and a smooth point is the shape of the bordering path segments. If the path changes direction at the anchor point, the point is a corner point. If the path flows continuously through the point, it is a smooth anchor point.

*Confused about how to tell a smooth anchor point from a corner anchor point? See "What's in a Name?" in the "Mastering Illustrator" section at the end of this chapter.*

Remember that a straight path segment will always have two corner anchor points. A curved path segment may have two smooth points, one smooth and one corner point, or two corner points bordering it. (If a path segment appears to be perfectly straight but is bordered by one or two smooth anchor points, it is technically a curved path segment.)

The Pen tool creates corner points when you click with it. Smooth points are created by dragging. (Using the Pen tool is discussed in the section "Creating Paths with the Pen Tool," later in this chapter.)

## The Anatomy of an Anchor Point

An anchor point's direction lines determine the shape of bordering curved path segments. Both corner and smooth anchor points can have direction lines. (Remember, though, that an anchor point with no direction lines must be a corner point.) The length and angle of the direction lines determine the shape of a curved path segment. Figure 24.12 shows several examples of how curved path segments can differ, even when their anchor points are exactly the same distance and direction apart.

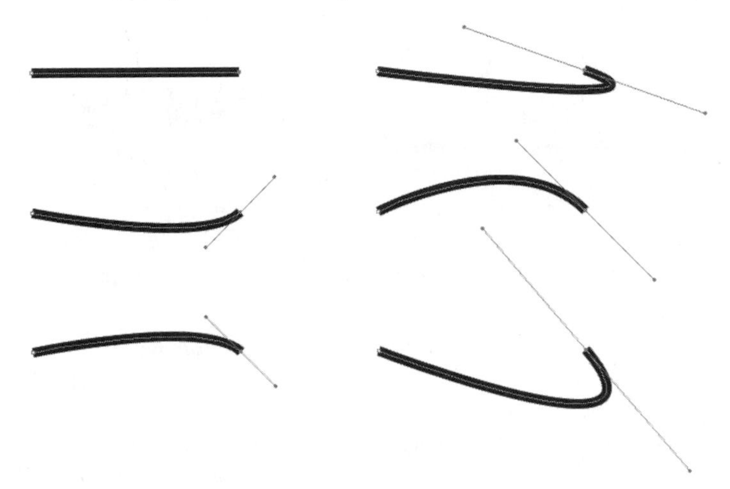

**Figure 24.12**
Each path segment has a corner point to the left. They differ only in the length and angle of the direction lines for the points on the segments' right.



At the end of each direction line is a *control point*, which can be dragged to change the length and angle of a direction line. In Figure 24.13, the path segment's anchor points are shown as a hollow square (left) to indicate an unselected anchor point and a filled square (right) to indicate a selected anchor point. The control points, visible at the ends of the direction lines, are solid diamond shapes.

**Figure 24.13**
The selected anchor point's direction lines (and control points) are visible to the right.

Even if the selected path was unstroked, the path and direction lines would be identifiable, thanks to the difference in appearance of the anchor points and the control points (see Figure 24.14).

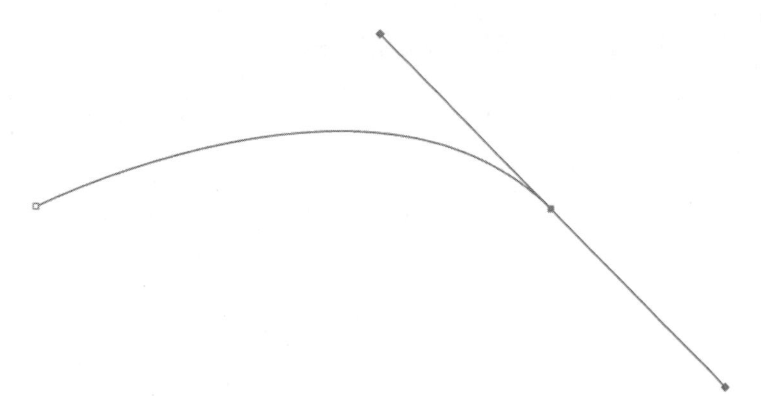

Figure 24.14
A path segment is bordered by squares, hollow or filled. A direction line has an anchor point (square) at one end and a control point (diamond) at the other.



### Straight Curves?

Even if a path segment runs perfectly horizontal or vertical, it may still technically be a curved path segment. If one or both anchor points have direction lines, the segment, despite its appearance, is technically a curve. In the following figure, the path segment's selected point on the right has direction lines, as you can tell from the diamond-shaped control points. Therefore, although the path segment is visibly straight, it is technically a curved path segment.

The anchor point's direction lines run parallel to the path segment.

If we add another path segment directly to the right, with another corner anchor point at the end, the path can continue to run straight, as shown by the upper line.

Each line is a pair of path segments, with three anchor points.

Observe, however, that we can create an exception to the rule stated earlier by placing three corner anchor points in a line (the lower line). The general rule is that a path will make an abrupt change of direction at a corner anchor point. Here, obviously, the path does not change direction at all. The middle anchor point in the lower path is, nonetheless, a corner anchor point because it lacks direction lines.

A corner anchor point can have a single direction line. If the point is bordered by a straight path segment on one side and a curved path segment on the other, there can be but a single direction line, which will be used to control the curved segment (see Figure 24.15).

Figure 24.15
The path segment to the left is straight; the one to the right is curved. The middle anchor point has only one direction line.

*If you've never seen an anchor point with only one direction line (other than endpoints), see "Direction Line Demo" in the "Mastering Illustrator" section at the end of this chapter.*

# THE PEN TOOLS

Although all the vector-creation tools in Illustrator produce paths and anchor points as they add objects to the artboard, one tool gives you extremely precise control over the creation process. The Pen tool enables you to place each anchor point individually as you work, deciding between corner and smooth points on the fly, using either a click (corner) or a drag (smooth). Three additional pen tools assist in the process—the Add Anchor Point, Delete Anchor Point, and Convert Anchor Point tools.



## Creating Paths with the Pen Tool

There are a few simple concepts behind the Pen tool:

- To place a corner anchor point with the Pen tool, simply click.
- To create a smooth point, click and drag. The direction and distance dragged sets the anchor point's direction line and determines the appearance of the curved path segment.
- To close a path, click (or click and drag) on the first endpoint. Clicking elsewhere with the Pen tool then starts a new path.
- To end an open path, either switch tools or (Command)-click [Ctrl]-click away from the open path.
- To add to an existing open path, select the path on the artboard, click once with the Pen tool on an endpoint, and then continue creating anchor points.

The process of creating a path with the Pen tool can be as simple as clicking in two different locations on the artboard. A straight path segment will be created between the points. More complex paths can be created by clicking and dragging. The key to creation with the Pen tool is understanding how dragging affects curved path segments. In Figure 24.16, four paths were created by clicking and dragging with the Pen tool. In each case, the Pen was clicked and dragged straight up to form the left anchor point.

The only difference among the four path segments is the direction in which the Pen tool was dragged when creating the second anchor point. (The distance is identical in each case.)

Multiple-segment paths show the difference between dragging in opposite directions at each end of a path segment and dragging in the same direction (see Figure 24.17).

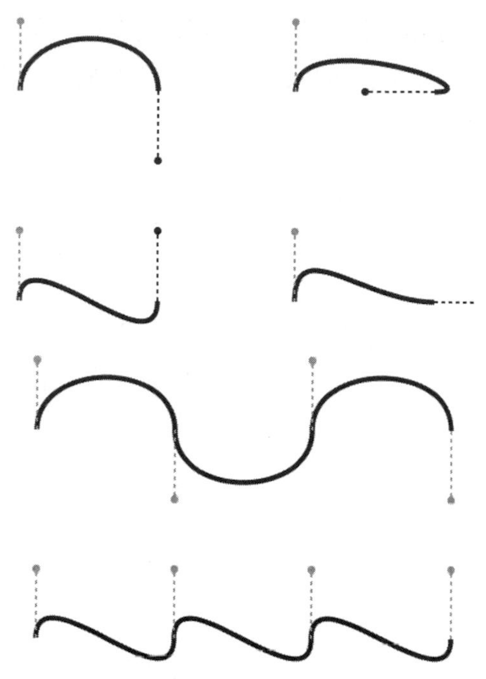

Figure 24.16
The dashed lines show the direction and distance of drag for each anchor point. Note that the points on the left of all the path segments have the same direction line.

Figure 24.17
The dashed lines show the direction and distance of drag for each anchor point.



In Figure 24.17, the actual direction lines for the anchor points between path segments look identical. In Figure 24.18, you can see that, despite the radical difference in the shape of the curves, the direction lines are vertical.

In Figure 24.18, note that although only the two anchor points within the dashed box are selected (their squares are filled), one direction line for each of the neighboring points is visible. Even though those neighboring points aren't selected, the direction line for the path segment bordering the selected anchor point is available. This enables you to use the Direct Selection tool to modify the path segments from either end.

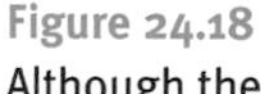

Figure 24.18 shows a pair of excellent examples of smooth anchor points. Observe that the two direction lines for either anchor point are 180° from each other. The direction lines for a smooth point will always be 180° apart.

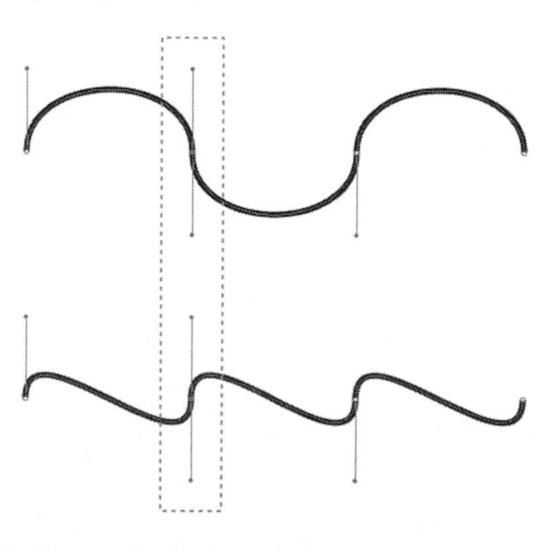

Figure 24.18
Although the direction lines look the same, they were created by dragging in opposite directions.

## The Other Pen Tools

In addition to the Pen tool, Illustrator offers the Add Anchor Point tool, the Delete Anchor Point tool, and the Convert Anchor Point tool. With an existing path selected on the artboard, the Add Anchor Point tool enables you to add both corner (click) and smooth (drag) anchor points to the path. Similarly, the Delete Anchor Point tool removes existing anchor points from a selected path when you click them. You can use the Convert Anchor Point tool to change a smooth anchor point to a corner point by clicking the point, or you can convert a corner point to a smooth point by clicking the point and dragging.

The Toolbox flyout palette that holds these extra tools is shown in Figure 24.19, along with the preference that determines whether or not you'll ever need them—Disable Auto Add/Delete.

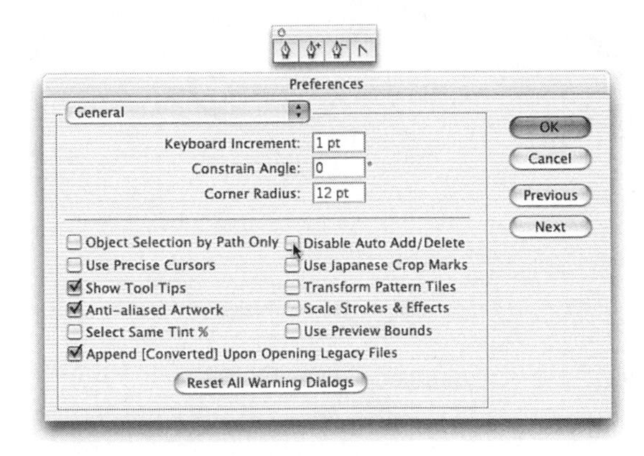


**Figure 24.19**
The three additional pen tools are found in the Toolbox below the Pen tool. The General preferences are accessed through the Illustrator menu in Mac OS X or through the Edit menu in Windows.

*Wondering about that preference setting? See "Shutting Down the Auto" in the "Mastering Illustrator" section at the end of this chapter.*

When you leave the preference Disable Auto Add/Delete unselected, you need never choose these additional pen tools from the Toolbox. Instead, Illustrator will automatically select the correct tool based on the cursor's location on a selected path. If the cursor is over a path segment, Illustrator assumes that you want to add a new anchor point. When the cursor is positioned over an existing anchor point, Illustrator assumes that you want the Delete Anchor Point tool. The cursor will change to indicate which tool is active. A small + or – will appear to the lower right of the Pen tool icon to indicate adding or subtracting an anchor point.

Pressing the (Option) [Alt] key converts the Pen tool to the Convert Anchor point tool.

# EDITING PATHS

Illustrator offers numerous ways to change paths. You can add and subtract anchor points. You can reposition one or more anchor points. You can apply various filters and use various tools to change a path. You can even manipulate a curve by changing the direction lines of one or more anchor points.

## Using the Direct Selection Tool with Points and Segments

When you click an object or drag across it with Illustrator's Selection tool, you select the object as a whole. The object's entire path will move as a unit. Using the Direct Selection tool enables you to select and move individual anchor points, one or several at a time. You can also select and move path segments with the Direct Selection tool.

To select a point, simply click it. The path does not need to be selected first. To help you identify when the cursor is directly over an anchor point, a small hollow square will appear to the cursor's lower right. When the tool is positioned over a path segment, the square will be filled.

You can Shift-click with the Direct Selection tool to add additional anchor points and/or path segments. Both anchor points and path segments can be part of a single selection. You can also drag with the Direct Selection tool. Any anchor points within the drag will be selected.

With the appropriate point(s) and/or segments selected, you can drag to reposition them. The elements of the selection will maintain their relationships to each other but will be shifted in relationship to the other anchor points of the path. In Figure 24.20, the original object is on the left. In each of the other objects, several anchor points were selected with the Direct Selection tool and dragged upward. You can see by the filled squares which points were selected. You can also see how those selected points maintained their relationships as they were dragged.

**Figure 24.20**
Only the selected anchor points were moved.

Selecting and dragging a curved path segment with the Direct Selection tool can help reshape an object without moving anchor points (see Figure 24.21).

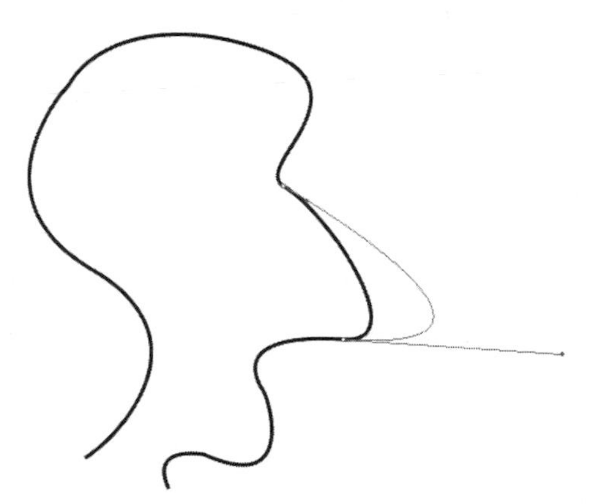

**Figure 24.21**
Click a path segment with the Direct Selection tool and drag to reposition the segment.

Sometimes dragging a path segment can lead to undesirable changes in neighboring paths (see Figure 24.22).

Figure 24.22
Dragging the same path in a slightly different direction causes it to double-back on a neighboring path.



## Manipulating Direction Lines with the Direct Selection Tool

When you select a path segment with the Direct Selection tool, the direction lines that control the segment are active. When you click a single anchor point with the tool, both direction lines for each of the neighboring path segments are activated (see Figure 24.23).

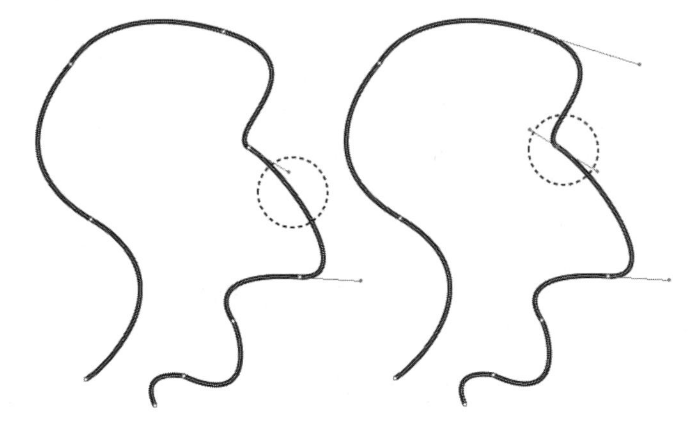

Figure 24.23
The dashed circles indicate the path segment (left) and anchor point (right) that were clicked with the Direct Selection tool.

Note in Figure 24.23 that two direction lines are active for the object to the left, whereas four direction lines are active on the right. When you select a path segment, Illustrator assumes that you will be editing that particular segment. When you select an anchor point, Illustrator is prepared for you to edit the path segments on either side.

You can use the Direct Selection tool to drag the control point of any active direction line. You cannot Shift-click to select multiple control points.

When you drag either control point of a smooth anchor point, the opposite direction line will also move. That preserves the flow of the curve through the anchor point. Although the angle of the opposite direction line changes, the distance does not. The curves on both sides of a smooth anchor point are changed when you drag either direction line's control point.

In Figure 24.24, you can see how dragging one control point moves both direction lines of the smooth anchor point (and alters both adjoining path segments).

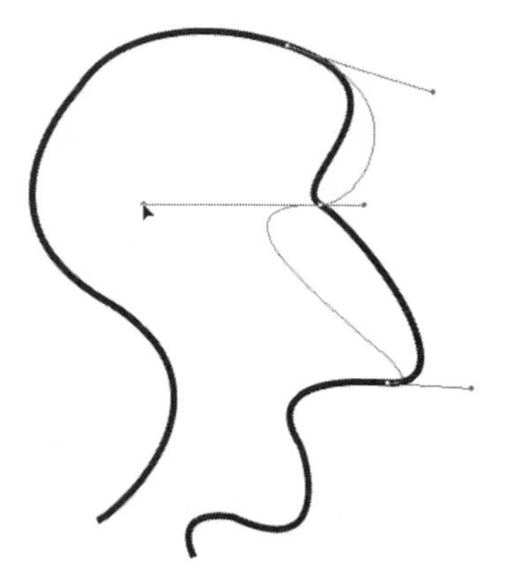

**Figure 24.24**
The anchor point's second direction line changes angle to remain 180° from the direction line being dragged. The second direction line's length remains unchanged.

To edit only one adjoining path segment, the smooth anchor point must be converted to a corner anchor point. Clicking with the Convert Anchor Point tool would convert the anchor point to a corner point but would also delete both direction lines. This would, of course, alter both the path segments.

To alter one direction line while leaving the other untouched, hold down the (Option) [Alt] key and then drag the control point with the Direct Selection tool. The path will no longer flow smoothly through the point, so it can no longer be considered a smooth anchor point. Instead, it becomes a corner anchor point with two direction lines. In Figure 24.25, the original path is on the left, with direction lines visible for the selected anchor point. In the middle, a direction line has been dragged, and the point's second direction line also has been moved. This alters the curved path segment above the anchor point. On the right, the control point has been (Option)-dragged [Alt]-dragged. The curve below the anchor point has been altered without affecting the curved path segment above the anchor point.

Keep in mind that the Direct Selection Lasso tool enables you to select individual anchor points but does not enable you to manipulate them. For that, you'll need the Direct Selection tool, not the Direct Selection Lasso tool. However, you can only use the Direct Selection tool to select anchor points by clicking (and Shift-clicking) them or by dragging a rectangular marquee. In contrast, you can use the Direct Selection Lasso tool to draw a selection marquee of any shape to select anchor points. You can weave in and out among anchor points, selecting with far more discrimination.



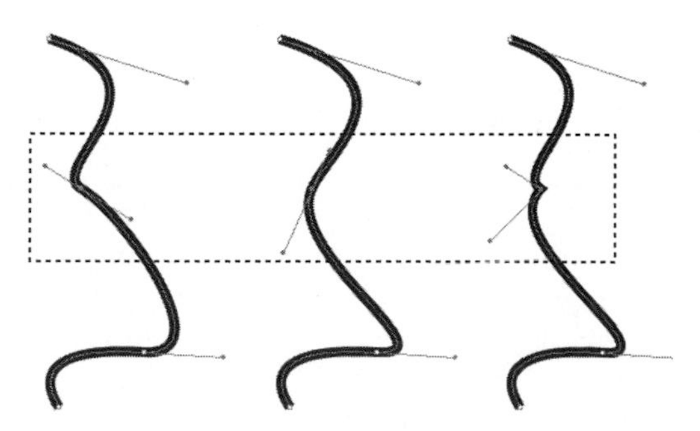

**Figure 24.25**
(Option)-dragging [Alt]-dragging enables you to edit one path segment without disturbing the adjacent curve.

### Effects, Filters, and Paths

Illustrator offers some very sophisticated capabilities for manipulating the appearance of objects. Among them are filters and effects. (They are discussed in Chapter 35, "Illustrator's Effects and Filters.") Filters that are used with vector artwork change the path of an object. Effects, on the other hand, change the appearance without actually changing the path. Take a look at the three objects in the following figure. On the left is the original object. In the middle, the Pucker & Bloat *filter* has been applied. Notice how the path conforms to the shape of the object. On the right, the Pucker & Bloat *effect* has been applied. Notice that the appearance is identical to the middle object, but the path remains identical to the first object. Filters change an object; effects change only the appearance of an object. This enables you to revert to the original appearance if necessary.

All three objects were identical until the filter and effect were applied.

# USING THE PAINTBRUSH AND PENCIL TOOLS

Many of Illustrator's tools create paths while they create objects. A couple tools, however, are designed with path creation, rather than object creation, in mind.

## The Paintbrush Tool

The Paintbrush tool (default keyboard shortcut B) creates freeform paths. The paths can be filled, stroked, and edited like any other path. Although any path can be stroked with a brush, the Paintbrush tool and its cousin the Pencil tool (discussed in the next section) are well equipped to work with the Brushes palette and its content. (Working with brushes is discussed in Chapter 26, "Working with the Four Types of Brushes.")

Here are the specifics of working with the Paintbrush tool:

- Double-clicking the Paintbrush tool in the Toolbox opens the Paintbrush Tool Preferences dialog box. Here, you set the tool's options (see Figure 24.26).
- Fidelity and Smoothness relate to the sensitivity of the tool to the movement of a mouse or stylus on a graphics tablet. In Figure 24.27, the same template was traced four times, using different Paintbrush options. They are, in order, low Fidelity/low Smoothness; low fidelity/high smoothness; high fidelity/low smoothness; and high fidelity/high smoothness. The third example is closest to the actual path as drawn.

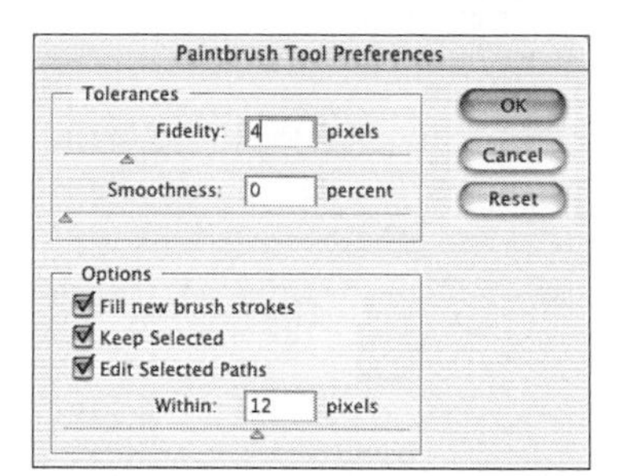


Figure 24.26
The Paintbrush tool is one of several that you can double-click to open a dialog box. It is, however, one of the few that has its own preferences.

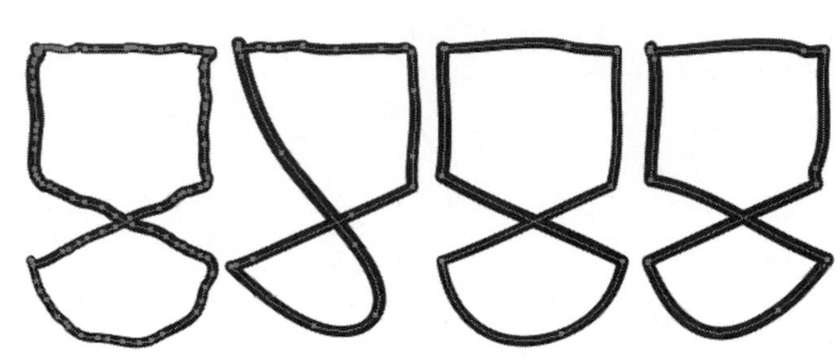

Figure 24.27
Notice the difference in the number of anchor points produced by the Paintbrush at the different settings.



- Fidelity, which can range from 0.5 pixels to 20 pixels, determines how far from a path the stroke can drift to produce a smooth curve. A low Fidelity setting produces more points on a path.
- Smoothness, measured in percent, determines how tightly the stroke can handle corner anchor points. A high Smoothness setting produces rounded paths.
- Fill New Brush Strokes, when unchecked, leaves the path unfilled. This option allows, among other things, pattern brushes to be stroke-only.
- Keep Selected leaves the just-drawn path active and selected after completion. The path is ready for editing or the application of a brush or style.
- Edit Selected Paths, which can range from 2 to 20 pixels, determines how far the cursor must be from a selected path to start a new path. The cursor changes appearance to indicate that the active path will be edited rather than a new path being started. (The small *x* to the lower right of the cursor, the New Path indicator, disappears when the cursor is within the specified distance of an active path.) When two or more paths must be drawn consecutively in a limited area, a small number for this option is preferable.
- Holding down (Option) [Alt] while drawing with the Paintbrush tool results in a closed path. No matter where you release the mouse button, the path is closed with a straight segment to the starting point if (Option) [Alt] is pressed.
- You also can use the Paintbrush tool to edit existing paths. (Command)-click [Ctrl]-click to select a path, release (Command) [Ctrl], and position the Paintbrush tool near the path to begin editing. The cursor must be within the distance specified in the tool's preferences under Edit Selected Paths.

## The Pencil Tool

The Pencil tool (default keyboard shortcut N) is similar to the Paintbrush tool in a number of respects: They both draw open or closed paths, they both use the currently selected brush, and they can both edit paths. You can see one difference in the Pencil Tool Preferences dialog box (see Figure 24.28). Note that this tool lacks the Fill New Brush Strokes option of the Paintbrush tool.

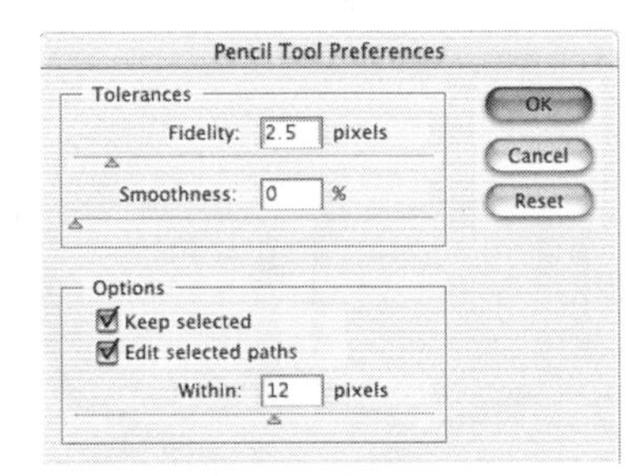


Figure 24.28
Like the Paintbrush tool, the Pencil tool has its own preferences.



Here's what you need to know to effectively work with the Pencil tool:

- Fidelity can be set from 0.5 pixels to 20 pixels. It determines how far from a path the stroke can vary to produce a smooth curve.
- Smoothness, which can range from 0% to 100%, allows the stroke to follow the path precisely or rounds off any corners. Refer to Figure 24.27 for examples of various Fidelity and Smoothness settings with the Paintbrush tool. The Pencil tool behaves similarly.
- Keep Selected leaves a new path active and selected for editing.
- Edit Selected Paths determines how close the tool must be to a selected path in order to edit that path. The lowest setting, 2 pixels, is appropriate when you're drawing several consecutive paths in a limited area. It allows the tool to begin a new path rather than edit the most recently created path. Higher settings, which can go up to 20 pixels, make it easier to begin the editing process when you want.
- While you're drawing with the Pencil tool, pressing (Option) [Alt] automatically forces it to produce a closed path. When the key is down and the mouse button is released, a final path segment is drawn from that point directly to the path's starting point.
- With the Pencil tool selected, but no path being drawn, pressing (Option) [Alt] changes the active tool to the Smooth tool (see the description in the following section of this chapter). As long as the modifier key is pressed, the Smooth tool is active.
- You can use the Pencil tool, like the Paintbrush tool, to edit existing paths. (Command)-click [Ctrl]-click a path to select it; then position the tool near the path and begin redrawing. The distance at which the tool will edit a path is set in the preferences (see the description of Edit Selected Paths, earlier in the list). The cursor changes when it is within the predetermined range of a selected path; the small *x* to the lower right disappears.

### Editing Paths with the Pencil and Paintbrush Tools

When you're first using the Paintbrush or Pencil tool to edit a path, its behavior may seem unpredictable. These tools, however, follow certain rules. Keep these points in mind:

- The cursor must be within a specified number of pixels of a selected path to begin editing. You select that distance in the Pencil Tool Preferences or Paintbrush Tool Preferences dialog box. Double-click the tool's icon in the Toolbox to open the dialog box.
- To alter the shape of one or more segments of an open path without changing the endpoints, start and end the new section with slight overlaps of the existing path. Make sure the starting overlap moves away from the nearest endpoint and that the ending overlap finishes in the direction of the second endpoint. See the following figure for the difference between ending toward and away from the starting point.

Three edits with the Pencil tool (top) and their results (bottom): 1) Editing an endpoint. 2) Pencil tool curving back toward the starting point. 3) Pencil tool curving toward the endpoint.

- When you're editing a closed path, the cursor must start and end on (or near) the existing path to keep it closed.

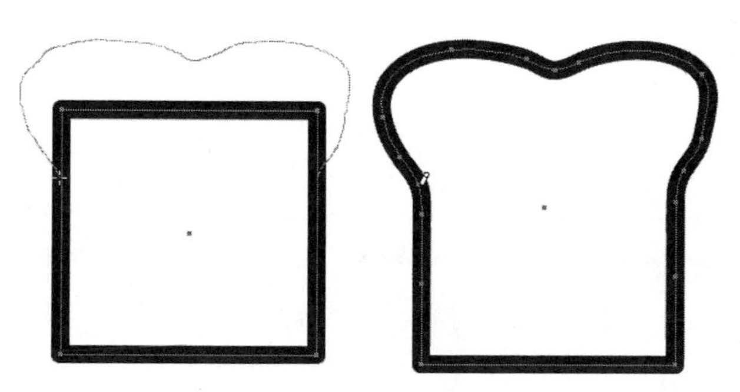

Closed paths stay closed when edited if the drawing tool starts and ends on a segment or an anchor point.

- You can transform closed paths into open paths by starting with the Pencil or Paintbrush tool on the existing path but ending away from the path. An endpoint is added to the first path at the position where the edit started.

The first frame shows the path that was drawn, and the second shows the result. The third frame shows where the new endpoint was inserted into the original closed path.

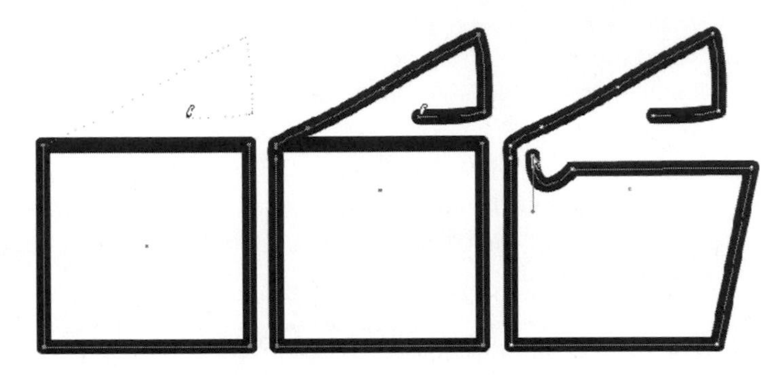



# ADDITIONAL PATH-RELATED TOOLS

Quite a few of Illustrator's other tools can be considered to have path-manipulation capabilities. The transform and liquify tools, for example, change the appearance of objects by altering the objects' paths. (These tools are examined in Chapter 28, "Transforming and Distorting Objects.") Several other tools are designed to work directly with paths, rather than with objects.

## The Smooth Tool

You can find the Smooth tool beneath the Pencil tool. It reduces sharp curves and angles in paths. Often you can simplify a complex path by using this tool. Additional application of the Smooth tool results in additional smoothing, as shown in Figure 24.29.

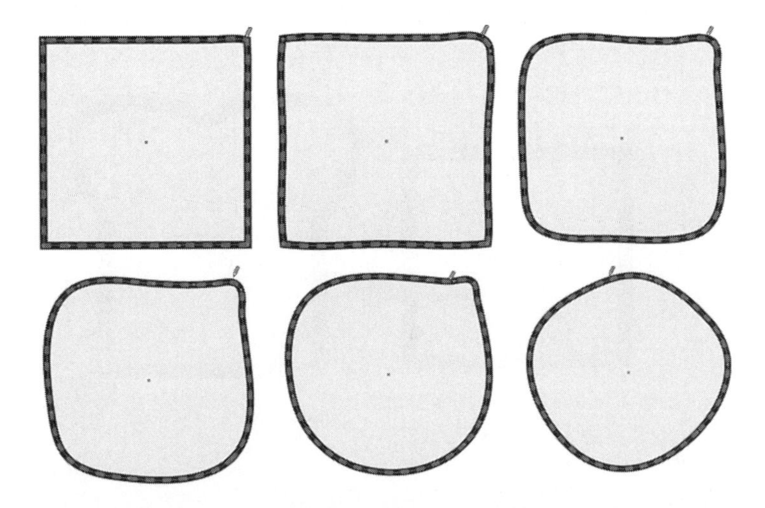

Figure 24.29
Multiple repetitions with the Smooth tool continue to reduce the sharpness of paths. Starting from the left, you see the original square and then the results after 2, 3, 4, 5, and 15 applications of the Smooth tool.

Consider these points when working with the Smooth tool:

- You set preferences for the Smooth tool by double-clicking the tool in the Toolbox. This tool has only two options: Fidelity and Smoothness. As with the Paintbrush and Pencil tools, the sensitivity of the tool toward the mouse or stylus is determined by these two settings.
- Fidelity relates to how closely the path will follow the smoothed movement of the input device. Low values produce more angular corners and typically more complex paths with a greater number of points.
- The Smoothness setting controls what percentage of smoothing is applied to the path as drawn by the input device. Lower values produce paths that are closer to the actual movement of the mouse or stylus. Higher values compensate for minor irregularities of the input device.
- You also can activate the Smooth tool by pressing (Option) [Alt] with the Pencil tool selected.
- Use the Smooth tool along a path. Multiple repetitions continue to reduce sharpness in the path. The Smooth tool also works on corner points.



## The Erase Tool

The Erase tool, located with the Smooth tool below the Pencil tool, removes portions of paths. When you use it on a closed path, the path becomes open and endpoints are created. Figure 24.30 shows one use of the Erase tool.

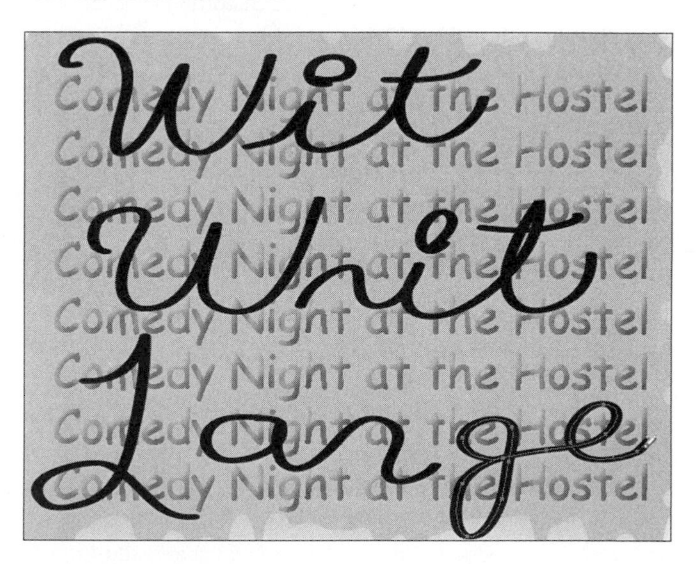


Figure 24.30
Dragging the Erase tool along a path, not across the path, eliminates one or more anchor points or segments. In this case, shortening the tail of the *e* with the Erase tool is easier than adjusting the path.

## The Scissors Tool

The Scissors tool (shortcut C), which has no user-defined settings, divides both open and closed paths. The path need not be selected to apply this tool. Figure 24.31 shows the Scissors tool in action.

Figure 24.31
You can use the Scissors tool to clip off the end of a path. In this case, the upper path can be trimmed on the right to end the pattern with a large star.



## The Knife Tool

The Knife tool is designed for use with closed paths. (It's found below the Scissors tools in the Toolbox.) Dragging the tool across one or more closed paths divides the objects into sections. In Figure 24.32, you'll see the original objects on the left. In the center are the divided objects, with a dashed line showing the path of the Knife tool. On the right, the pieces have been moved apart.

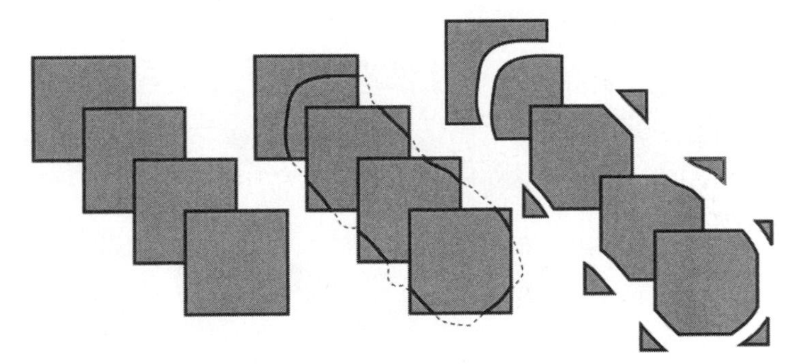

Figure 24.32
The Knife tool divides closed paths.

# ILLUSTRATOR'S AUTO TRACE TOOL

Although no substitute for a dedicated tracing program such as Adobe Streamline, the Auto Trace tool can do an adequate job of creating vector outlines of bitmap (raster) images. The tool has only two options—Tolerance and Tracing Gap—that you set in Illustrator's preferences. The Tolerance setting establishes how close the tool must be to an edge in the image being traced, and the Tracing Gap setting tells the tool which breaks in an edge to ignore. Figure 24.33 shows the Auto Trace tool's preferences, along the bottom of the dialog box, as well as a likely candidate for a successful trace.

**Figure 24.33**
The Auto Trace tool performs best on uniformly colored objects against a contrasting background.



Here's what you need to know to work with the Auto Trace tool:

- The Auto Trace tool works on the basis of color differences. An object that has several areas of different color should be traced manually or in segments.
- The crosshairs should be placed within the object to be traced, no more than 6 pixels from the edge.
- To trace the entire object, click once.
- To trace part of an object, drag the cursor, staying within 2 pixels of the edge.
- To connect Auto Trace paths, drag the second path from an anchor point of the first.
- You can edit Auto Trace paths like any other paths.

Because the Auto Trace tool finds edges based on color differences, you can do several things (in Illustrator or in an image-editing program such as Adobe Photoshop) to improve the tool's performance (remembering, as always, that it's best to work on a copy of the image):

- You can blur images with texture near the edges.
- You can maximize the contrast and slightly decrease the brightness. You can produce a similar effect by using Photoshop's Levels adjustment and moving the middle slider to the far right.
- You can convert the image to Grayscale mode.
- You can use Photoshop's Threshold adjustment to reduce the image to black and white pixels.

# MASTERING ILLUSTRATOR

## That's No Path!

*I have an object on my artboard that seems to have three or four paths coming from each anchor point. How can that be?*

The object is either a gradient mesh or an envelope mesh object. What look like extra paths coming from the anchor points are actually mesh lines. (And the points that seem to have four "paths" coming from them are mesh points, not anchor points.)

## What's in a Name?

*The difference between smooth anchor points and corner anchor points has me quite confused. How do I tell them apart?*

If the anchor point has no direction lines, it's a corner point. If it has direction lines and they are exactly opposite each other (at 180°), it's *probably* a smooth point. If you click the control point at the end of a direction line and drag and the other direction line moves, too, then it's *definitely* a smooth point.



But remember that these are just labels. You usually don't need to know whether an anchor point is a corner point or a smooth point, unless you're going to change a direction line. Click the control point and drag. If it's a smooth point but you needed to change only one path segment, just click Undo. Now you can hold down the (Option) [Alt] button and drag the control point without altering the adjoining path segment.

## Direction Line Demo

*Try as I might, I can't seem to create or find an anchor point with just one direction line. Did they get left off the ark with the unicorns?*

They exist—really, truly. Typically you'll come across them in paths that have been edited. Here's one way to create these elusive creatures in your very own laboratory.

Select the Pen tool and click the artboard. Click in another spot to create a straight path segment. Click and drag to create a curved path segment. (Command)-click [Ctrl]-click away from the path to deselect. Get the Direct Selection tool from the Toolbox. Click that middle anchor point. No direction lines, right? Now click the curved path segment and drag it in any direction. Watch a single direction line grow from that middle anchor point!

## Shutting Down the Auto

*Why would I want to disable the Auto Add/Delete Anchor Point function of the Pen tool?*

If you ever find yourself creating multiple paths in tight quarters, or even starting just one new path within a few screen pixels of an existing path, you'll understand the option. When the Pen tool's cursor is within a few pixels of an existing path, the Auto capability switches tools—even if you're actually trying to start a new path rather than add a new anchor point to an existing path. With Auto Add/Delete disabled, you can even start a new path directly on top of an existing path.

25

# WORKING WITH THE SHAPE, DRAWING, AND GRAPH TOOLS

## IN THIS CHAPTER

If Illustrator offered only the Pen and Gradient tools and the Color palette, we would still be able to use it to create the majority of the artwork we produce today. However, it would take a lot longer and would perhaps not be quite as precise. Thankfully, Illustrator offers a tremendous number of tools, palettes, and commands that make the creation process easier. Many of the capabilities we take for granted are simply shortcuts. The Rectangle tool, for example, does nothing more than create four-sided paths. These are quite easy to produce with the Pen tool, yet we think of the Rectangle tool as a basic component of Illustrator.

Maximizing efficiency means taking advantage of the capabilities Illustrator offers. That includes using the Rectangle tool to drag an object rather than trying to precisely place four corners with the Pen tool. Truly *maximizing* efficiency also includes knowing and taking advantage of the full potential of Illustrator's basic tools.

This chapter looks at the tools and commands available to you for creating and manipulating shapes in Illustrator. You'll also see how Illustrator works with compound shapes and learn how to work with graphs and the graph tools.

# ILLUSTRATOR'S OBJECT CREATION TOOLS



Illustrator's Toolbox holds a variety of tools designed to simplify basic (and somewhat more advanced) object creation through "click-and-drag." Generally speaking, these tools place an object on the artboard, using the current stroke and fill and other appearance characteristics, when you click, drag, and release. The tools also have dialog boxes that allow you to control the creation process numerically. Illustrator's object creation tools are shown in Figure 25.1.

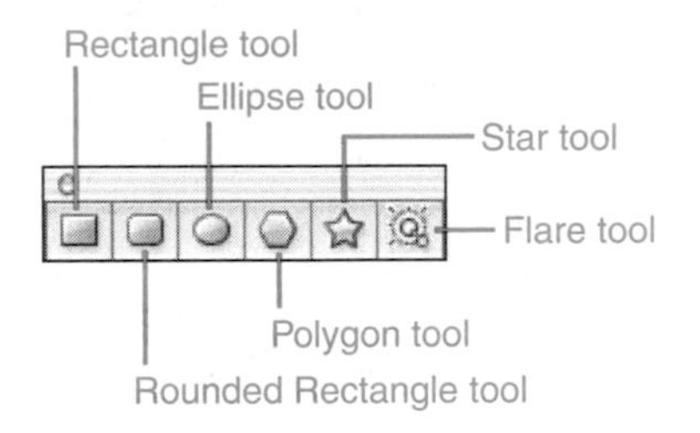


**Figure 25.1**
**These tools can be used to create Illustrator's basic objects (and some more advanced objects, too).**

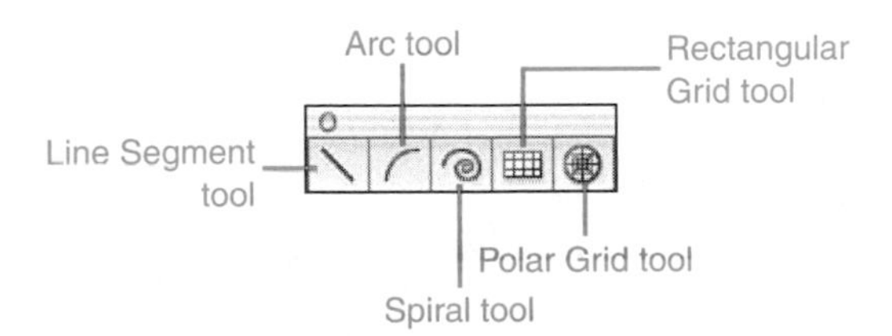


The object creation tools can be classified into a pair of categories: basic and complex. A basic object creation tool produces an object consisting of a single path, open or closed, in one of a variety of shapes. A complex object creation tool produces an object that consists of multiple paths.

# THE BASIC OBJECT CREATION TOOLS

These eight tools include some of the most frequently used Illustrator capabilities. They include the Rectangle, Rounded Rectangle, Ellipse, Polygon, Star, Line Segment, Arc, and Spiral tools.

The basic object creation tools produce objects consisting of a single path, which assumes the current appearance characteristics for stroke, fill, and effects. Each tool is designed to produce a single shape of object, but the dimensions of the object can be varied.

After selecting the appropriate tool in the Toolbox, you can drag to create an object or click the tool on the artboard and enter dimensions numerically in the tool's dialog box. For some of the tools, double-clicking the tool's icon in the Toolbox opens the dialog box so that numeric values can be preset. The dialog box otherwise assumes the dimensions of the object most recently created with that tool.

The following behaviors apply to all the basic creation tools, except as noted:

- You create objects by dragging.
- Clicking once brings up a dialog box, allowing you to enter numeric values for an object at the point clicked. The values you see in the boxes are those of the last object drawn. For the Rectangle, Rounded Rectangle, and Ellipse tools, the object will be created to the lower right of the point clicked. For the Polygon, Star, and Spiral tools, the point clicked will be at the center of the object. The Line Segment and Arc tools' dialog boxes allow you to specify in which direction the path will be created.
- Double-clicking the tool's icon in the Toolbox opens the dialog box for the Line Segment and Arc tools.
- Pressing the spacebar while drawing allows you to reposition the object while continuing to draw.
- Holding down Shift while dragging constrains the proportions of the object for the Rectangle, Rounded Rectangle, and Ellipse tools. (When proportions are constrained, the tools will produce squares and circles.)
- Holding down (Option) [Alt] allows you to draw from the center with several of the tools. You can use this technique in conjunction with the Shift key. This applies to the Rectangle, Rounded Rectangle, Ellipse, Line Segment, and Arc tools. The other three basic tools always create from the center.

When created, objects will assume the current appearance characteristics for stroke, fill, and effects, as well as any appearance characteristics assigned to the layer upon which they are created. More information is available in Chapter 30, "Illustrator's Layers, Sublayers, and Groups," and in Chapter 32, "Using the Appearance and Style Palettes."

## The Rectangle Tool

The Rectangle tool (default keyboard shortcut M) is used to create rectangles and squares (which are simply rectangles with equal height and width dimensions). Select the tool and click once to access the variables. Figure 25.2 shows a series of rectangles and the dialog box for the last one created.

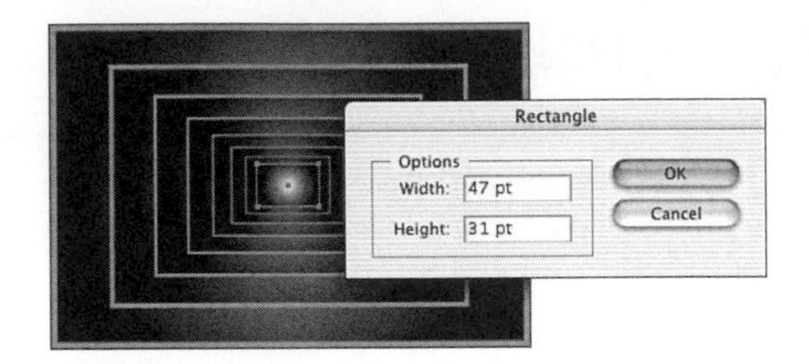


Figure 25.2
The Rectangle dialog box, by default, shows the exact dimension of the last such object created.

## The Rounded Rectangle Tool

The Rounded Rectangle tool functions almost identically to its counterpart, the Rectangle tool, except for the corners of the shapes produced. The corners of the Rounded Rectangle tool can be controlled through its dialog box. Select the tool and click once to access the variables. Figure 25.3 shows the difference between the Rectangle and Rounded Rectangle tools.

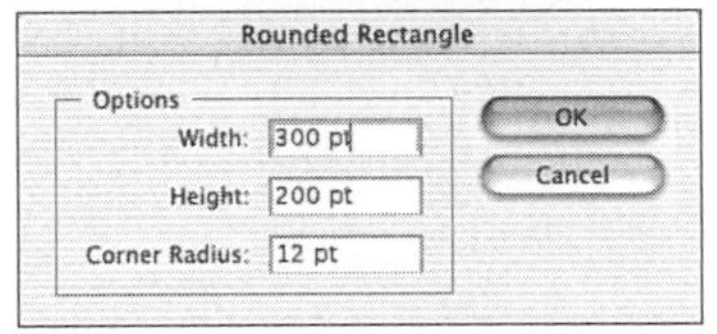


Figure 25.3
The Corner Radius option is not found in the Rectangle dialog box.

The arc of the corners is adjustable from 0.001 points to 8192 points. Notice that the rectangle (left) has four anchor points. The rounded rectangle object has eight anchor points. The rectangle's anchor points are all corner points, whereas the rounded rectangle has smooth anchor points. (The difference between corner and smooth anchor points is discussed in Chapter 24, "Creating and Editing Paths.")

When you click the Rounded Rectangle tool on the artboard, the numeric values shown will be those of either the last rounded rectangle or the object last created with the Rectangle tool, whichever is most recent.

If an image is destined for the Web, you should create it using exact pixel dimensions. If you simply drag a rectangle or rounded rectangle that looks about the right size, it may end up with one or more sides that look "fuzzy" on the Web when the rectangle is resized to pixel dimensions. Instead, drag that "looks right" rectangle and delete it. Click with the Rectangle tool in the upper-left corner and see what the dialog box says. Round the dimensions to the nearest pixel and click OK.

## The Ellipse Tool

The Ellipse tool (default keyboard shortcut L) is also sometimes referred to as the *Oval* or *Circle tool*. It creates elliptical objects, which have four smooth anchor points, as you can see in Figure 25.4.

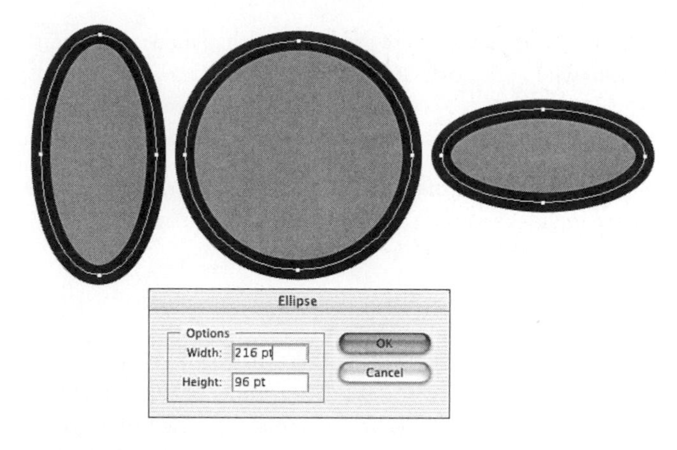


Figure 25.4
From the values in the dialog box, it is apparent that the object on the right was the most recently created.

## The Polygon Tool

The Polygon tool creates multisided closed paths. The sides, which are path segments, are symmetrical in every variation. The minimum number of sides is three (triangle); the maximum is 1,000 sides. At the highest setting, an almost perfect circle is created. Figure 25.5 shows some polygons.

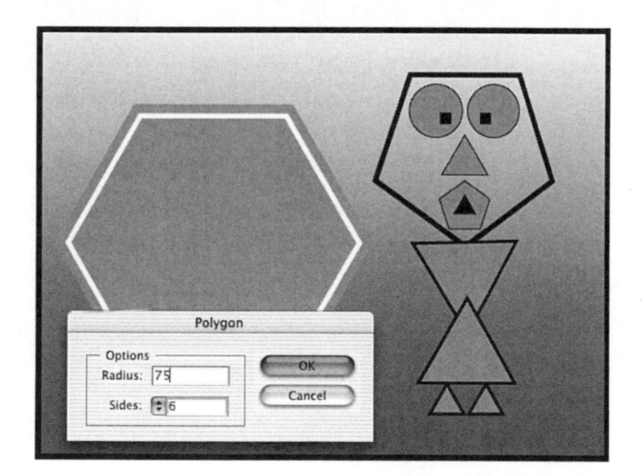


Figure 25.5
The Polygon tool produces closed paths. The circle for the eye on the left has 1,000 segments. The eye on the right has 50. However, there is no visible difference.



Here are the basic techniques you use with the Polygon tool:

- You create a polygon by dragging. The object is drawn from the center, similar to holding down (Option) [Alt] while dragging the Ellipse or Rectangle tools.
- Clicking once with the tool brings up the dialog box, allowing you to enter numeric values for an object at the point clicked. The numbers in the boxes when the dialog box is opened are the dimensions of the most-recently created shape. Radius is the distance from the center of the object to each anchor point.
- Pressing the spacebar while drawing allows you to reposition the object while continuing to draw.

- Holding down Shift orients the object to the top of the page. For polygons, a flat segment always appears at the bottom when you press Shift. With an odd number of segments, a point appears at the top; with an even number of segments, a flat side appears at the top. When you do not press Shift, you can rotate the object while drawing by moving the cursor in an arc.
- The up- and down-arrow keys allow you to make changes to the number of sides of a polygon. Hold down the mouse button while drawing and press the up-arrow key to increase the number of sides or the down-arrow key to decrease the number.

## The Star Tool

The Star tool always creates perfectly symmetrical objects. The number of sides can range from 3 to 1,000. Each star is measured according to two criteria: the distance from the center to the inner points and the distance from the center to the outer points. Figure 25.6 shows some variations among five-pointed stars.

Figure 25.6
Changing the ratio between the inner and outer points affects the general appearance of a star object.

Here's how you use the Star tool:

- You create a star by dragging. The object is drawn from the center.
- Clicking once with the tool brings up a dialog box, allowing you to enter numeric values for an object at the point clicked. The numbers in the boxes when the dialog box is opened are the dimensions of the most-recently created star. By default, the Radius 1 number is the distance from the center of the object to inner points. Radius 2 is the distance from the center to the outer points. However, as you can see in the dialog box in Figure 25.6, the numbers can be reversed. This, in effect, simply flips vertically a star with an odd number of points and has no effect on a star with an even number of points.
- Pressing the spacebar while drawing allows you to reposition the object while continuing to draw.

- When used with the Star tool, the Shift key orients the object toward the top of the page. A point is always straight up, regardless of whether the star has an odd or even number of points.
- Using the up- and down-arrow keys, you can make changes to the number of points on a star. Hold down the mouse button while drawing and press the up-arrow key to increase the number of points or press the down-arrow key to decrease the number.
- Pressing (Option-Command) [Alt+Ctrl] alters the relationship between the inner and outer points of a star. Pressing (Command) [Ctrl] holds the inner points in position while you continue to draw, expanding or contracting the outer points. Pressing (Option) [Alt] holds the segments adjoining the topmost point parallel and at a 90° angle. (This is easiest to see when the Shift key is pressed, orienting the star toward the top of the page. The segments to either side of the top point are level.) This cannot apply to stars with four or fewer points.

## The Line Segment Tool

This tool does one thing and does it very well. The Line Segment tool creates straight path segments, one at a time. It creates a single segment, with corner anchor points for endpoints. Click the tool where the line should start; click again where the segment should end. The path remains selected, yet the tool is ready to create another segment immediately. Without the Line tool, creating a single straight path segment requires clicking with the Pen tool at the beginning point and the endpoint and then (Command)-clicking [Ctrl]-clicking away from the path to deselect and prepare to create the next line segment.



The Line Segment tool's dialog box, shown in Figure 25.7, allows you to specify the length and angle of the segment, as well as offers the option to include a fill. (The fill normally would be unseen but might be necessary when multiple segments are to be joined using a pathfinder command.)

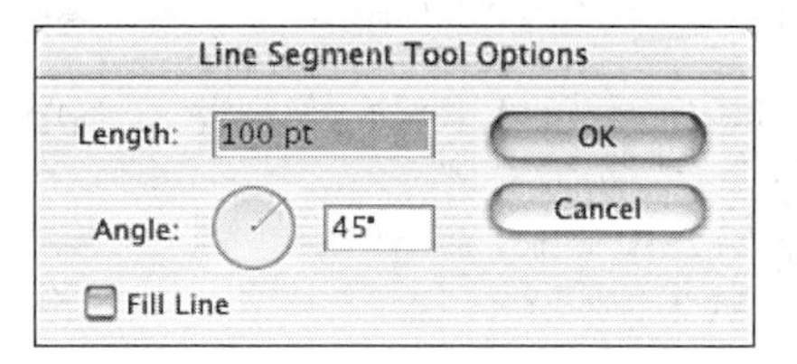


Figure 25.7
The path will extend the distance and direction chosen from the point on the artboard where the tool was clicked.

## The Arc Tool

Like the Line Segment tool, the Arc tool can create a single path segment, bordered by a pair of anchor points. Unlike the Line Segment tool, the anchor points the Arc tool creates have direction lines (although they are corner points, not smooth points). The direction lines allow the anchor points to produce a curved path segment. The Arc tool can also be used to create a closed path with two straight sides and one curved side. The tool's behavior is governed by its dialog box, shown in Figure 25.8, which can be opened by double-clicking the tool's icon in the Toolbox or by clicking the Arc tool on the artboard.

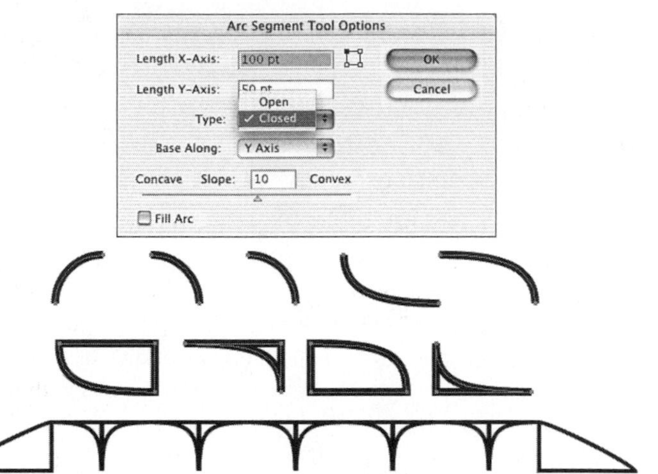


Figure 25.8
The Arc tool can create more than simple curved lines.

Notice in the Arc Segment Tool Options dialog box the four-point grid to the left of the OK button. That grid allows you to specify the point of origin for the arc. For example, when the upper-left box is selected, the arc will be created to the lower right of the spot clicked on the artboard. When the upper-right square is selected, the arc will be created to the lower left.

The other settings in the dialog box determine the width and length of the arc (Length X-Axis and Length Y-Axis), whether the tool will create a single curved line or a three-sided object (Open/Closed), the orientation of the object (Base Along: Y Axis/X Axis), and the shape of the curve (Concave/Convex). There's also a check box that you can use to fill the path.



To see the differences among the settings, refer to Figure 25.8. The objects shown were created with the following settings in the Arc Tool Options dialog box:

- **Top row, left**—50, 50, Open, Base: X-Axis, Convex: 50
- **Top row, second**—50, 50, Open, Base: Y-Axis, Convex: 50
- **Top row, third**—50, 50, Open, Base: X-Axis, Concave: –50
- **Top row, fourth**—100, 50, Open, Base: X-Axis, Convex: 67
- **Top row, right**—100, 50, Open, Base: X-Axis, Concave: –67
- **Middle row, left**—100, 50, Closed, Base: X-Axis, Convex: 75
- **Middle row, second**—100, 50, Open, Base: X-Axis, Concave: –75
- **Middle row, third**—100, 50, Open, Base: Y-Axis, Convex: 75
- **Middle row, right**—100, 50, Open, Base: Y-Axis, Concave: –75
- **Bottom row**—A series of arcs used to create a bridge

## The Spiral Tool

The Spiral tool creates open paths that are, as the name indicates, spirals. You draw the objects by dragging the tool in the document. (See "Controlling a Spiral" for additional information on creating spirals.)

Five basic concepts govern the Spiral tool:

- The Spiral tool draws from the center. Position the cursor where you want the center of the new object.
- Dragging in an arc rotates the spiral.
- Pressing Shift constrains rotation to 45° angles.
- The up- and down-arrow keys add and subtract segments from the spiral.
- Although spirals are open paths, many styles can be successfully applied (see Figure 25.9).

**Figure 25.9**
Some styles are more suitable for spirals than others, often depending on the stroke (or lack thereof) in the style.



## Controlling a Spiral

Like the Line Segment and Arc tools, with which it is nested, the Spiral tool creates open paths. Its open paths can, indeed, be filled and stroked, much like closed paths. There are, however, a number of differences between the operation of the Spiral tool and the Line and Arc tools.

The Spiral tool, like the Polygon and Star tools, draws objects created with segments. These segments differ from those of a star or polygon in a couple ways. First, they are curved. Polygons and stars are always created with straight sides. Second, the anchor points connecting the curved segments are, as you could imagine, smooth points rather than corner points. Once drawn, the anchors' direction lines can be modified with the Direct Selection tool. (The corner points of the stars and polygons must be converted with the Convert Anchor Point tool before they can have direction lines.)

An additional difference between the segments of a spiral and those created in other objects is that the spiral's segments are each one-quarter of a revolution around the object's center (called a *wind*). Because the spiral's segments move away from the center, the segments are not quarters of a circle.

You determine the direction of the spiral in a dialog box. To access the dialog box (shown in Figure 25.10), select the Spiral tool and click once in the document. In addition to controlling the direction of the spiral, you can enter numeric values for a precise object. Note that Decay rates (which can range from 50% to 150%) below 100% allow you to drag the spiral from the outside point. Decay rates above 100% result in drawing from the inner end of the path, and they are a bit tougher to control. A spiral that decays at 100% is an open path shaped like a circle. If the spiral has more than four segments, they overlap.

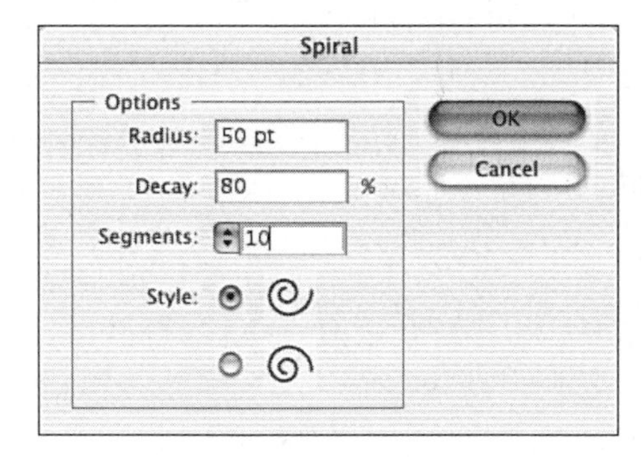


**Figure 25.10**
In the Spiral dialog box, you can select a clockwise or counter-clockwise rotation.



When you're dragging the Spiral tool to create an object, rotating the cursor in an arc rotates the spiral. Holding down Shift constrains the rotation to 45° angles. Pressing the up- or down-arrow key increases or decreases the number of winds, one segment at a time. Hold down (Command) [Ctrl] while dragging to increase or decrease the decay. When you start dragging a spiral and then press (Command) [Ctrl], moving the cursor toward the center of the spiral increases the decay percentage. This opens the center of the spiral and brings the winds closer together until the decay rate reaches 100%. Moving away from the center decreases the decay, thus tightening the center of the spiral and increasing the space between winds.

*Creating objects but their appearance isn't coming out right? See "Checking the Layers Palette" in the "Mastering Illustrator" section at the end of this chapter.*

# THE COMPLEX OBJECT CREATION TOOLS

In addition to the tools that create objects consisting of a single path, Illustrator offers several more-complex creation tools. The objects created by these tools are actually multiple paths, working together to form a single object.

## The Flare Tool

Since the dawn of photography, artists have worked tirelessly to remove unwanted lens flares from their pictures. Adobe Illustrator offers us an easy way to *add* lens flare to an image with two clicks.

A flare consists of the bright center, some halos and rings, and some rays. In Figure 25.11, a flare is shown on the left. On the right, a copy of the flare is selected so that the complexity of its paths is visible. Below, the flare has been separated into component parts. (The Group Select tool can be used to take a flare object apart, and the command Object, Expand will separate it into components.)

**Figure 25.11**
The flare's halo and rays are very subtle accents to the highlights and the rings.



In Figure 25.12, the Flare Tool Options dialog box is shown. Illustrator's default values are visible. Flare Tool Options can be opened by double-clicking the tool's icon in the Toolbox or by clicking the Flare tool on the artboard.

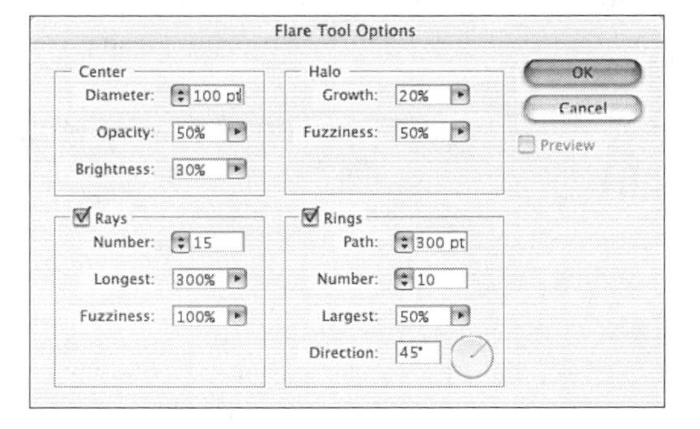


**Figure 25.12**
The center and halo are required parts of the flare. Rings and rays are optional.

You can bypass the dialog box and create flares directly with the Flare tool. Click on the artboard where you want the center to be and then drag to establish the center and rays. Click and drag a second time to create the rings. The process is shown in Figure 25.13.

> You can reset the Flare Tool Options dialog box to its default values. Open the dialog box and press (Option) [Alt]. The Cancel button changes to Reset.

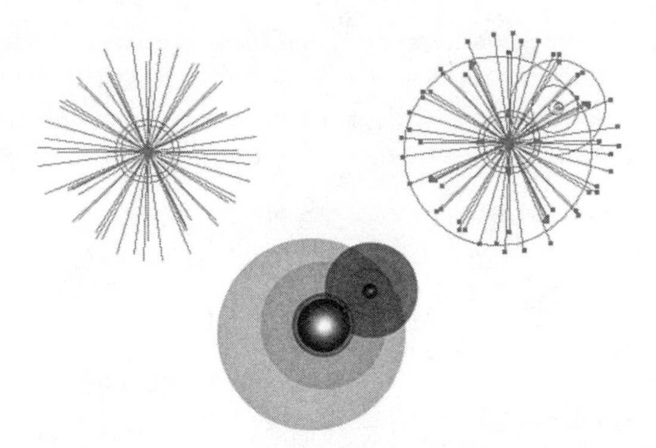

Figure 25.13
In the upper left, the first click and drag produces the center and rays. To the upper right, a second click and drag creates the rings. The finished flare is shown at the bottom.

You can use several modifier keys while creating with the Flare tool:

- Shift constrains the rays to the angles designated in the preferences (by default, 45° angles).
- The up- and down-arrow keys add and subtract rings while you drag.
- In the first part of the flare-creation process, holding down the (Command) [Ctrl] key while dragging will maintain the current size of the flare's center and allow you to continue dragging to change the size of the rays.
- Holding down the (Command) [Ctrl] key while dragging during the second part lets you adjust the halo size.
- Pressing the tilde (~) key while dragging the rings creates new random patterns of rings.



Flare objects can be transformed and otherwise manipulated. Keep in mind, too, that flares are complex objects. Adding too many rays or rings in the dialog box can create objects that are difficult to output.

## The Rectangular Grid Tool

The Rectangular Grid tool creates a grid of vertical and horizontal dividers. You can drag to create a grid or click with the tool to open its dialog box (see Figure 25.14).

The top section of the dialog box allows you to specify the outer dimensions of the grid. To the right, next to the OK button, is a grid that determines where the grid will be drawn in relationship to the point clicked on the artboard.

The dialog box also allows you to specify the number of horizontal and vertical dividers, as well as any skew. Skewing the dividers moves them proportionally closer together. Figure 25.15 shows some examples of skewed dividers.

Want to edit an existing flare? Select it on the artboard, select the Flare tool from the Toolbox, and press (Return) [Enter]. The Flare Tool Options dialog box will open, allowing you to make changes. Check the Preview box to watch your changes in action.

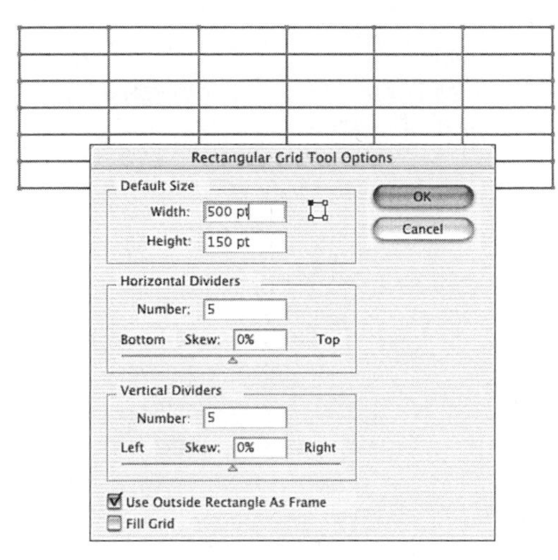


**Figure 25.14**
The Rectangular Grid Tool Options dialog box can be opened by clicking with the tool on the artboard or by double-clicking the tool's icon in the Toolbox.

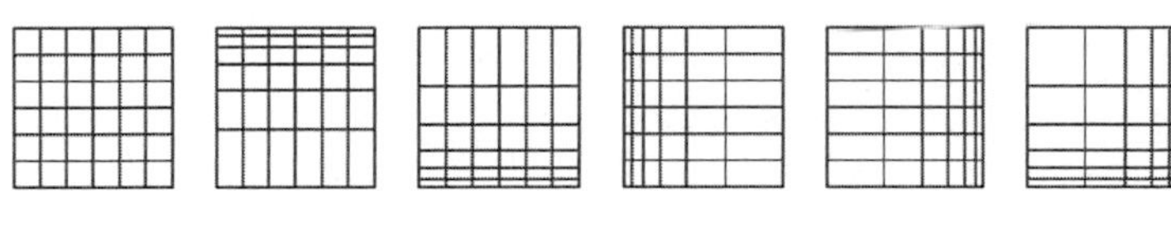

**Figure 25.15**
The examples, starting on the left, are unskewed; horizontally skewed to the bottom and to the top 50%; vertically skewed to the left and right 30%; and skewed both vertically and horizontally 50%.



The check boxes at the bottom of the dialog box allow you to replace the outer dividers with a rectangle and to use the currently selected fill color. (By default, grids are unfilled.)

When dragging to create a rectangular grid, you have a number of modifier keys available:

- Shift constrains the grid to a square.
- (Option) [Alt] creates the grid from the center. Shift can be used in conjunction with (Option) [Alt].
- Holding down the spacebar allows you to reposition the grid as you drag.
- The up- and down-arrow keys increase and decrease the number of horizontal dividers.
- The left- and right-arrow keys decrease and increase the number of vertical dividers.
- F and V decrease and increase the horizontal skew in increments of 10%.
- X and C decrease and increase the vertical skew in increments of 10%.
- The tilde key (~) creates multiple grids as you drag.

## The Polar Grid Tool

You can use the Polar Grid tool to create round grids either by dragging or by entering numerical values in the dialog box (see Figure 25.16).

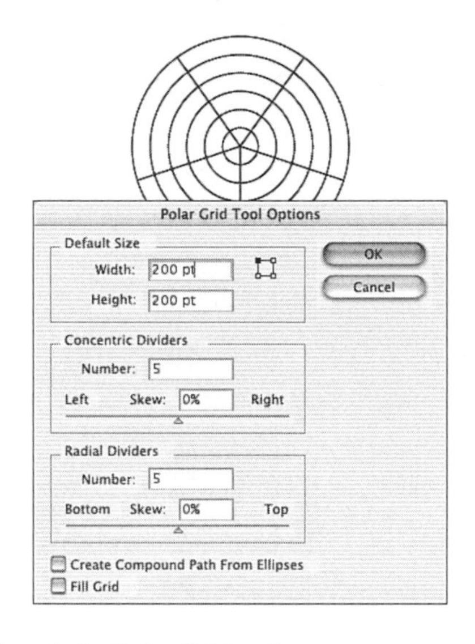


**Figure 25.16**
The Polar Grid Tool Options dialog box can be opened by clicking with the tool on the artboard or by double-clicking the tool's icon in the Toolbox.



Like the Rectangular Grid tool, the Polar Grid tool creates patterns of lines, which divide an object into sections. Rather than rectangles, the Polar Grid tool creates concentric rings with radial dividers.

Skewing to the left and right moves the radial dividers. Skewing toward the bottom and top can perhaps be thought of as moving the concentric dividers inward and outward. Examples of skewing are shown in Figure 25.17.

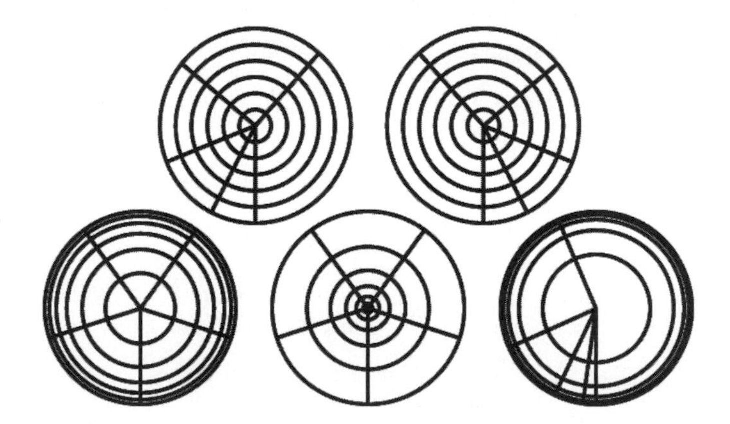

**Figure 25.17**
The examples shown along the top, starting on the left, are skewed right 50% and skewed left –50%. The examples along the bottom, starting on the left, are skewed top 50%, skewed bottom –50%, and skewed right and top 125%.

When dragging to create a polar grid, you have a number of modifier keys available:

- Shift constrains the grid to a circle.
- (Option) [Alt] creates the grid from the center. Shift can be used in conjunction with (Option) [Alt].

- Holding down the spacebar allows you to reposition the grid as you drag.
- The up- and down-arrow keys increase and decrease the number of concentric dividers.
- The left- and right-arrow keys decrease and increase the number of radial dividers.
- F and V decrease and increase the skew of the radial dividers in increments of 10%.
- X and C decrease and increase the skew of the concentric dividers in increments of 10%.
- The tilde key (~) creates multiple grids as you drag.

In addition to creating objects using the tools described in this chapter, Illustrator allows you to create objects and paths of any shape using the drawing tools. The Pen tool creates paths by placing each anchor point individually. The Paintbrush and Pencil tools create freeform paths as you drag, with Illustrator deciding where to put the individual anchor points.

**Easy Targets**

The Polar Grid tool can be used to quickly create simple target objects. Check the box to create a compound object, check the box to fill the object, and then set Radial Dividers to 0.

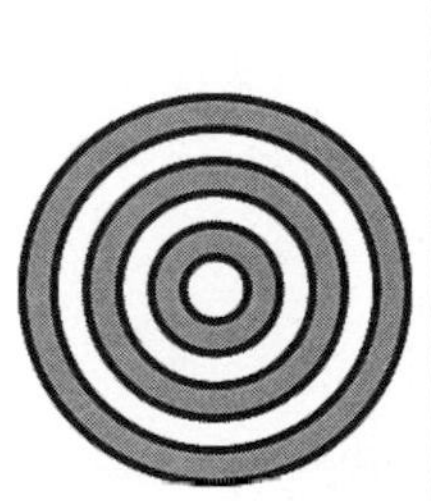

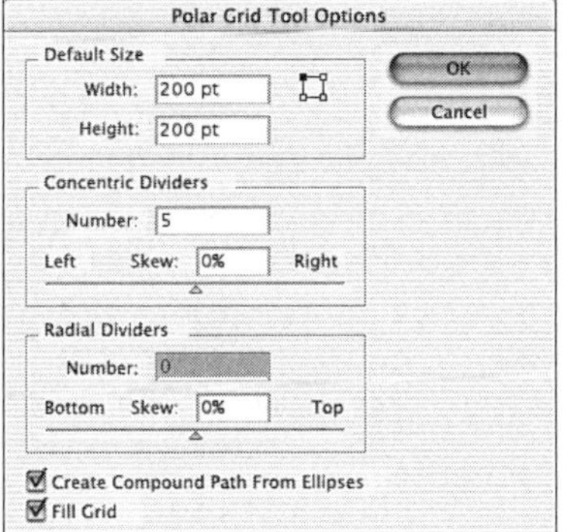


With no radial dividers, the Polar Grid tool creates concentric circles.



# SELECTION TOOLS AND COMMANDS

After objects are created on the artboard, the work is rarely finished. Perhaps appearance characteristics must be applied, or one or more objects need to be rearranged on the artboard. For whatever reason, changes must be made.

Before you can alter an object on the artboard, you have to identify it to Illustrator. This is the process of selection. When an object is selected on the artboard (or through the Layers palette), changes can be made to it. Unselected objects cannot be changed directly.

Illustrator has several tools and commands to help you select objects and paths.

The appearance of unselected objects can be altered if changes are targeted to the object's layer. Targeting layers is discussed in Chapter 30.

## The Selection Tool

The Selection tool (default keyboard shortcut V) selects an entire object. You select an object by clicking it or, if the object is unfilled, its edge. Shift-clicking allows you to select multiple objects. The Selection tool can also be dragged on the artboard. All paths and objects that fall completely or partially within the dragged rectangle will be selected. (Objects partially within the selection marquee will be completely selected.)

By default, a selected object is surrounded by a rectangular bounding box. You can use the bounding box to manipulate the object(s). When the bounding box is visible, you use the Selection tool to change the shape or location of the object. By clicking within the object and dragging, you can move the object. By clicking one of the bounding box's eight handles, you can change the shape of the object. Notice how the cursor changes from the Selection tool to a two-headed arrow when positioned over a handle. The variations in the cursor's appearance are shown in Figure 25.18.

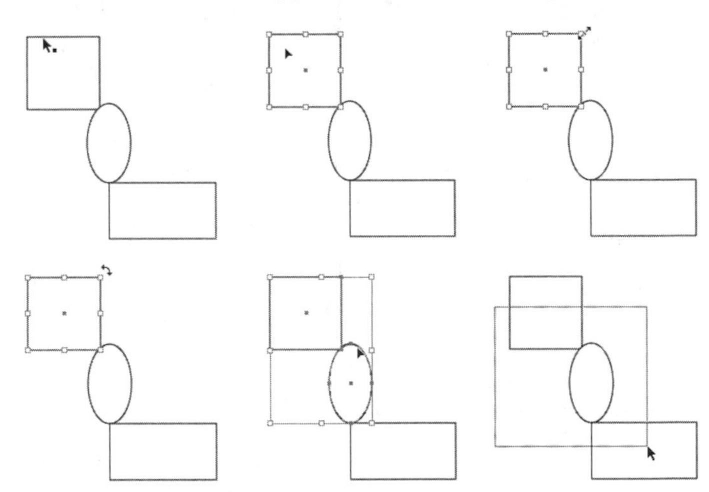

Figure 25.18
The Selection tool examples are as follows: prepared to click an object to make a selection; prepared to move the object; ready to resize the object; ready to rotate the object; Shift-clicking to select multiple objects; and dragging to select multiple objects.



Here are the basic concepts governing the Selection tool:

- You can access the Selection tool at virtually any time by pressing and holding (Command) [Ctrl].
- Click the fill or stroke of an object to select it for movement.
- You can select multiple objects in an image by Shift-clicking with the Selection tool. Dragging with the Selection tool across objects also selects them.
- When multiple objects are selected, Shift-clicking deselects an object.
- Click one of the bounding box's anchor points to edit the general shape of the object. The cursor changes to a two-headed arrow when over an anchor point.

- Holding the Shift key while dragging one of a bounding box's corner points constrains the object's proportions. The object's height-to-width ratio is maintained. If the object starts as a square or circle, it retains that quality; in other words, it does not become a rectangle or an oval.
- (Option)-dragging [Alt]-dragging one or more selected objects with the Selection tool will duplicate them on the artboard.

## The Direct Selection Tool

The Direct Selection tool (default keyboard shortcut A) selects a portion of an object. Specifically, you use it to manipulate an anchor point or a segment of a path between anchor points.

When using the Direct Selection tool, remember these points:

- Click directly on an anchor point or path segment. An anchor point appears filled when selected, hollow when not.
- You can select multiple anchor points or segments by Shift-clicking or dragging.
- When multiple anchor points and/or segments are selected, Shift-clicking deselects each in turn.
- When a segment is selected, the bounding anchor points do not move when the segment is shifted.
- You can select segments and anchor points together by Shift-clicking.

*For more information on working with the Direct Selection tool, see "Manipulating Direction Lines with the Direct Selection Tool" in Chapter 24, "Creating and Editing Paths," p. 774.*

## The Group Selection Tool

The Group Selection tool selects one (or several) items from a group. When a number of objects are "grouped" (linked together as a single object, while retaining their individual attributes), the Selection tool selects them all. The Group Selection tool, on the other hand, can select an individual item from the group without your having to use the command Ungroup. (The Direct Selection tool operates on members of a group as it does with individual items.) With the Group Selection tool, the first click selects an object. An additional click selects the object's group. If that group is part of a larger group, a third click will select it, and so on.

Here are some guidelines for working with the Group Selection tool:

- Using (Option) [Alt] with the Group Selection tool allows you to duplicate (copy) an individual segment.
- To copy more than one segment, (Option)-click [Alt]-click the first segment and, without releasing the (Option) [Alt] key, press the Shift key and click the remaining segments. Moving the cursor and releasing the mouse button completes the copy process.

## The Magic Wand Tool

The Magic Wand tool (default keyboard shortcut Y) allows you to select objects on the artboard based on shared characteristics. Rather than a specific characteristic, such as the command Select, Same (discussed later in this chapter), you can use this tool to select based on a *range* of characteristics. Rather than an Options dialog box, the Magic Wand has a palette, which is shown in Figure 25.19.

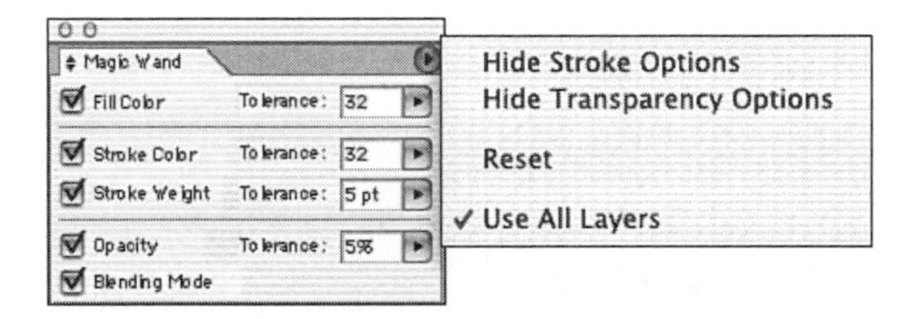


**Figure 25.19**
The Magic Wand tool's palette can be opened through the Windows menu or by double-clicking the tool's icon in the Toolbox.

The Magic Wand palette can be expanded or contracted by double-clicking the palette's tab. You can choose to show just the Fill Color option, the Fill Color, Stroke Color, and Stroke Weight options, or the entire palette. Remember that a selection criterion will be applied, even if that part of the palette is hidden. Also keep in mind that the selection criteria are cumulative. If you check the boxes for Fill Color and Stroke Color, objects will be selected only if they fall within the tolerances for *both* fill *and* stroke color.

Notice in the palette that the Magic Wand has Tolerance sliders for fill, stroke, and opacity characteristics. When you click an object with the Magic Wand, Illustrator will select all objects whose characteristics fall within the specified (and selected) tolerances. For example, suppose you check Stroke Weight in the palette and set the tolerance to 5 points and then click an object with a stroke of 7 points. Illustrator will select all objects with a stroke weight between 2 and 12 points (see Figure 25.20).

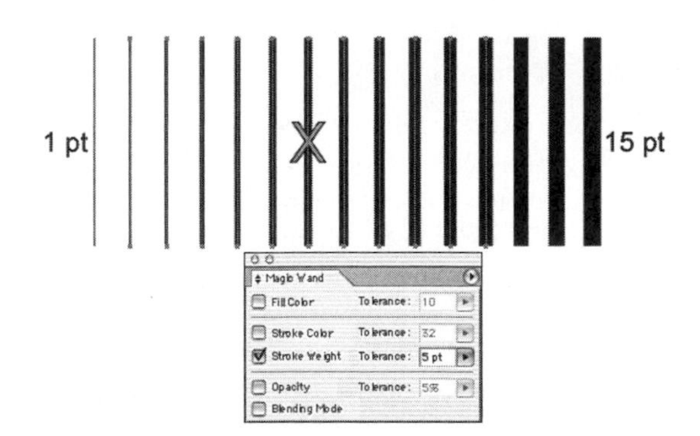


**Figure 25.20**
The stroke weight of the path segments ranges from 1 point to 15 points. The *X* marks the 7-point stroke, which was clicked with the Magic Wand, using the tolerance shown.

The opacity tolerance is also straightforward. It selects any object that falls within the specified tolerance. The Magic Wand is designed to select all objects with a specified blending mode, although that particular capability appears to be flawed.

The Magic Wand tool does not work with type objects, gradient mesh objects, or objects with an envelope distortion.

*Can't get the Magic Wand to behave? See "Choosing What to Select" in the "Mastering Illustrator" section at the end of this chapter.*

The tolerance sliders for the fill and stroke colors require a bit more explanation. When you're working with a CMYK document, the Fill Color and Stroke Color tolerance sliders range from 1 to 100. In RGB mode, the sliders range from 1 to 255.

In Figure 25.21, an RGB document, three objects are shown. Their fill colors are as noted. With the Magic Wand set to a Fill Color Tolerance of 18, the top object (fill: 255/0/0) was clicked. The second object (fill: 253/16/16) was selected, but the bottom object (fill: 252/16/16) was not.

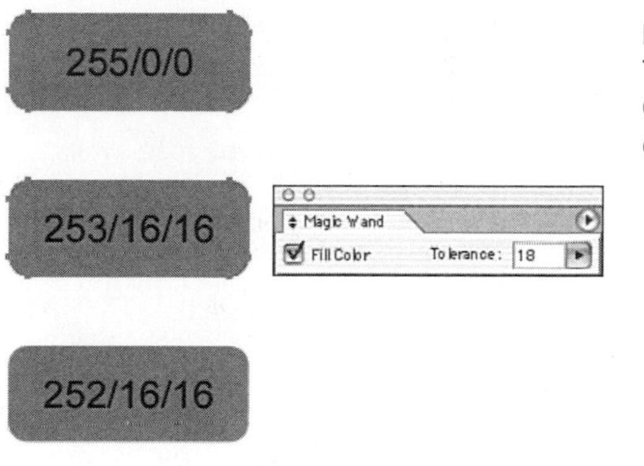


**Figure 25.21**
The Magic Wand was set to Fill Color Tolerance 18 and then clicked on the top object.



Slight variations in color tolerance can produce widely varying results with the Magic Wand tool's selections. The difference between fills 253/16/16 and 252/16/16 was enough to exclude the bottom object from a selection made with Tolerance 18. In fact, the bottom object is not included in the selection until the Tolerance setting is raised to 34.

When the middle object is clicked with Tolerance set to 16 (but not 15), the bottom object (but not the top) is selected. When Tolerance is raised to 18 (but not 17) and the Magic Wand is clicked on the middle object, all three objects are selected.

As with other selection tools, Shift-clicking with the Magic Wand will add to a selection. You can click an object, change the selection options in the Magic Wand palette, and Shift-click the same or a different object.

You can also remove objects from a current selection with the Magic Wand. Set the range of options for the object(s) you want to remove from the current selection and (Option)-click [Alt]-click one of the objects.

## Illustrator at Work: Selecting with the Magic Wand

The Magic Wand can be a very powerful tool, but many long-time Illustrator users prefer the simplicity of the command Select, Same. Working with the Magic Wand is one way to build confidence in its capabilities.

1. Select the command File, Open. In the Open dialog box, navigate to the Adobe Illustrator CS folder, to Sample Files, to Sample Art. Select and open the file named Museum.ai. (Update the text if you get a warning message to that effect.)

2. Double-click the Magic Wand tool's icon in the Toolbox to open its palette.
3. Check only the box for Fill Color and set Tolerance to 25.
4. Click once on the brown box behind the words *Purchase Tickets*. This selects all other objects in the illustration that use that fill color.
5. Switch to the Eyedropper tool and click the gray area in the top center.
6. Undo to reverse the change made in the preceding step.
7. In the Magic Wand palette, deselect Fill and check the box for Stroke Weight, setting Tolerance to 0.
8. Press Y on the keyboard to reactivate the Magic Wand.
9. Click any one of the thin lines in the map that indicate room walls.
10. Click the Stroke swatch in the Toolbox to make it active. Then in the Swatches palette, click the brown swatch. The stroke color of the lines should change.
11. In the Magic Wand palette, click once in the Tolerance field next to Stroke Weight and use the up-arrow key on the keyboard to change the value to 3 pt.
12. Click again on one of the thin lines in the map. Observe how many more lines in the illustration are selected.



Continue to monkey around with the settings, clicking various objects in the artwork. Not only will you see how the Magic Wand tool works, you'll see how the various objects within the illustration are related.

## The Direct Select Lasso Tool

Like the Direct Selection tool, the Direct Select Lasso tool selects individual anchor points. Drag the tool on the artboard to make a selection. All anchor points within the loop dragged will be selected. Although the Direct Selection tool can be dragged to select anchor points as well, it always selects within a rectangular marquee. The Direct Select Lasso tool, in contrast, can be dragged in any shape. You need not close the path of your drag; Illustrator will assume a straight line between the point first clicked and the point where the mouse button was released.

Dragging with the Shift key depressed allows you to add to an existing selection. Holding down (Option) [Alt] and dragging deselects.

The Direct Select Lasso tool cannot manipulate selected anchor points; it is used only for selection.

## The Lasso Tool

Like the Selection tool, the Lasso tool can be dragged on the artboard to select objects. Unlike the Selection tool, the Lasso tool doesn't create a rectangular selection marquee. Rather, you can drag in any irregular pattern, just like with the Direct Select Lasso tool. You need not drag a closed path. When you release the mouse button, Illustrator will assume a direct line from that point to the point where the mouse was clicked. An object whose path falls into the Lasso's loop will be selected. (If the Lasso is dragged entirely within an object, that object will not be selected because the tool did not cross the object's path.)

Holding down the Shift key while dragging adds to a selection. To subtract from an existing selection, hold down the (Option) [Alt] key while dragging.

Like the Direct Select Lasso tool, this tool is used only for selection. You cannot manipulate objects with the Lasso tool.

# ILLUSTRATOR'S SELECT MENU

The Select menu contains a variety of commands that can ease the process of making—or changing—selections (see Figure 25.22).

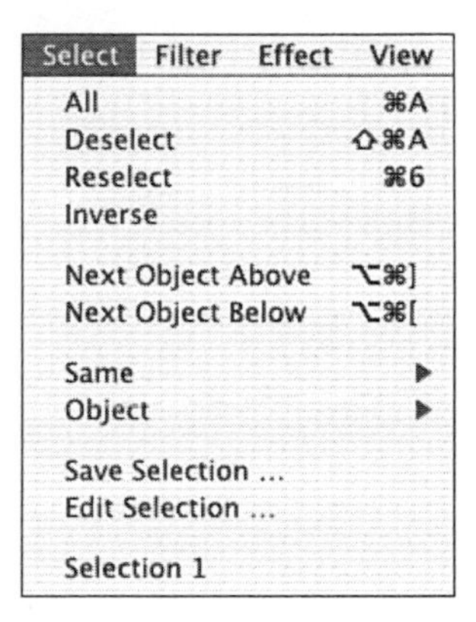


**Figure 25.22**
Saved selections appear at the bottom of the menu, such as Selection 1, shown here.



## Select, All

As in many other programs, this command makes a selection of all available paths and objects on the artboard. Locked objects and groups, as well as objects on locked or hidden layers, will not be selected.

The default keyboard shortcut is (Command-A) [Ctrl+A].

## Select, Deselect

As the name implies, this commands deselects everything.

The default keyboard shortcut is (Shift-Command-A) [Shift+Ctrl+A].

## Select, Reselect

The Reselect command works in conjunction with the Inverse and Select, Same commands. (It is not normally used when an object has been deselected with a selection tool.) Rather than reselecting a specific object or objects, the command applies the last-used selection criteria again. Think of it as "select again," rather than "reselect."

For example, if you have made a selection of all objects with a specific fill color, using one object as an example, you can use a different fill color as a selection criterion again by simply clicking a different object and using the Reselect command.

The default keyboard shortcut is (Command-6) [Ctrl+6].

When many but not all objects on the artboard need to be selected, consider whether or not it would be easier to select the ones you *don't* need and then use Select, Inverse.

## Select, Inverse

The Inverse command reverses the selection on the artboard. Objects that are selected become deselected; objects that were not selected become selected. Only objects that are not locked or hidden are considered.

## Select, Next Object Above

This command considers objects by their position in the Layers palette and the stacking order. When a single object or path is selected on the artboard, using Next Object Above switches the selection to the objects directly above in the stacking order. When multiple objects are selected, the topmost object is considered, and the object above it is selected.

Next Object Above, whose default keyboard shortcut is (Option-Command-]) [Alt+Ctrl+]], ignores layers and sublayers, but it doesn't ignore groups. If the next "object" above is a group, the entire group is selected.



## Select, Next Object Below

Like its counterpart, this command considers objects by their position in the Layers palette and the stacking order. When a single object or path is selected on the artboard, using Next Object Below switches the selection to the objects directly below in the stacking order. When multiple objects are selected, the lowest object is considered, and the object below it is selected.

Next Object Below, whose default keyboard shortcut is (Option-Command-[) [Alt+Ctrl+[], ignores layers and sublayers, but it doesn't ignore groups. If the next "object" below is a group, the entire group is selected.

## Select, Same

This series of commands is housed in a submenu (see Figure 25.23). Illustrator uses one or more already-selected objects as a guide and finds and selects all other objects on the artboard that match, using the selection criterion chosen from the menu.

If multiple objects are selected on the artboard, they must match for Illustrator to use a characteristic as a selection criterion. For example, if you have several items selected on the

The Next Object Above and Next Object Below commands don't take into account at all an object's position on the artboard. These commands look only at the order in the Layers palette, not whether objects are overlapping on the artboard.

artboard and want to use the command Select, Same, Stroke Weight, the already-selected items must have the same stroke weight.

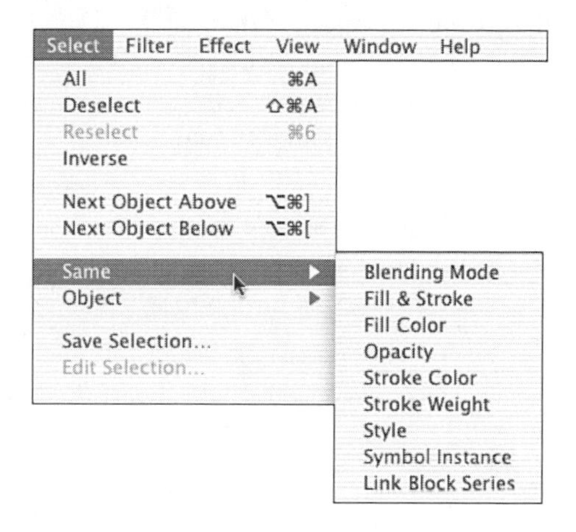


**Figure 25.23**
The submenu command Symbol Instance is only available when a symbol is selected on the artboard. Link Block Series refers to type containers joined using the command Type, Threaded Text, Create.

*Illustrator's Magic Wand tool can select based on a range of stroke weights, fill colors, and more. See "The Magic Wand Tool," earlier in this chapter, p. 802.*

## Select, Object

This series of commands, shown in the submenu in Figure 25.24, is composed of two groups. At the top of the submenu are All on Same Layer and Direction Handles. In the lower part of the submenu are commands to select certain types of objects throughout the document.

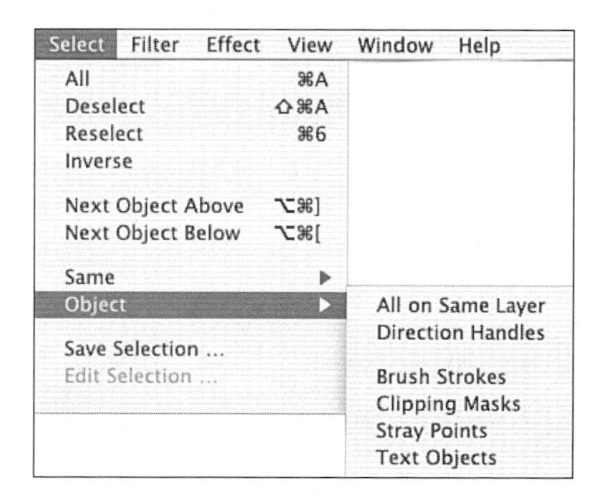


**Figure 25.24**
The two sections of the submenu hold different categories of commands.

The Select, Object commands are described in the following list:

- **All on Same Layer**—This command makes a selection of all unhidden, unlocked objects on the layer of the current selection. If multiple objects from different layers are selected when the command is chosen, all objects on all the represented layers will be selected.

- **Direction Handles**—This command shows the direction lines and control points for all anchor points of objects and paths selected on the artboard. (Remember that not all corner anchor points have direction lines, such as those in the corners of rectangles.) While the direction lines are all selected, you can manipulate only one control point at a time.

> Remember that clipping paths can be stroked and have effects such as drop shadows applied. Selecting all clipping masks allows you to apply appearance characteristics quickly and uniformly.

- **Brush Strokes**—This command selects all objects and paths on the artboard that have a brush stroke (from the Brushes palette) applied. Some of Illustrator's Styles include brush strokes, and objects to which those styles have been applied will be selected.
- **Clipping Masks**—This command selects only the paths being used as clipping masks, not the objects that are being masked.
- **Stray Points**—Stray points are anchor points that are not part of a path segment. They can be produced by accidental clicks of the Pen tool or be left over from various path-editing procedures. It's good practice to select them with this command and delete all stray points as part of the work flow.
- **Text Objects**—The last command in the Select, Object submenu allows you to select all text objects in a document. Type on a path, area type, and point type will all be selected.



## Select, Save Selection

Selections can be saved with a document. The saved selection will be listed at the bottom of the Select menu. (In Figure 25.22, "Selection 1" is a saved selection.) Once a selection has been saved, Illustrator will track the objects. The parts of a saved selection can be moved and edited, and even placed on a different layer or renamed in the Layers palette. When the selection is loaded, Illustrator will be able to find the objects.

To save a selection, first select the objects on the artboard or in the Layers palette. Next, simply choose the menu command Select, Object, Save Selection. You'll have an opportunity to name the selection (see Figure 25.25).

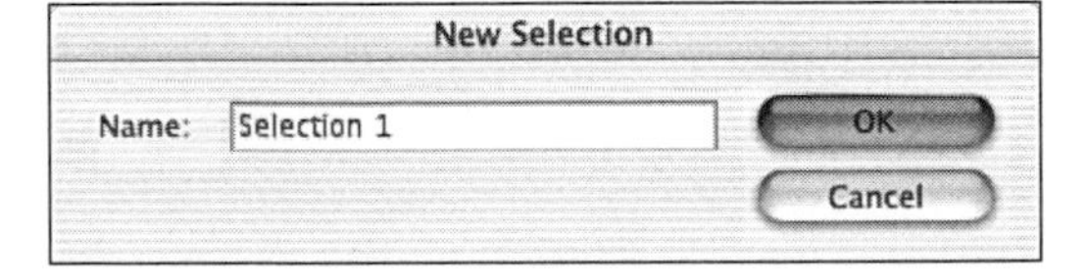


Figure 25.25
Illustrator offers numerically sequential names for saved selections. Descriptive names may be of more value with documents that will be reopened at a later date.

## Select, Edit Selection

The Edit Selection command allows you to change the contents of a saved selection and delete saved selections using a dialog box (see Figure 25.26).

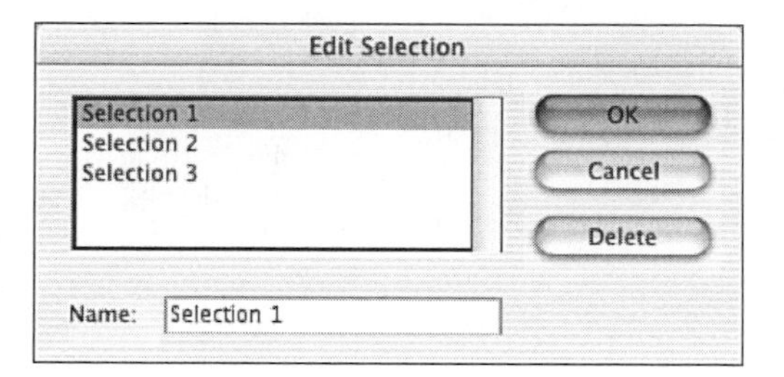


**Figure 25.26**
All selections saved with the document will be listed in the dialog box.

To edit a saved selection, first load the selection by choosing it from the bottom of the Select menu. Add or subtract objects from the selection. Next, choose the Edit Selection command and click the appropriate selection name. Clicking OK overwrites the saved selection.

## The Saved Selections

At the bottom of the Select menu will appear the names of all saved selections. To load a selection, select its name from the list.

# COMPOUND SHAPES AND THE PATHFINDER PALETTE

Rather than creating compound paths from two or more objects, you can now create compound *shapes*. The difference between compound paths and compound shapes is similar to that between filters and effects. Compound paths take two or more objects and combine them into a single object. However, to change the relationship among the parts, the compound shape must be released, the change made, and then the compound path restored. Compound shapes, on the other hand, are "live." You can use the Direct Selection or Group Selection tool to make changes to one of the components of the combined object without having to release or expand it.



## Compound Shapes

Compound shapes are created through the Pathfinder palette (see Figure 25.27). Two or more overlapping objects must be selected on the artboard to create a compound shape. They should not be grouped.

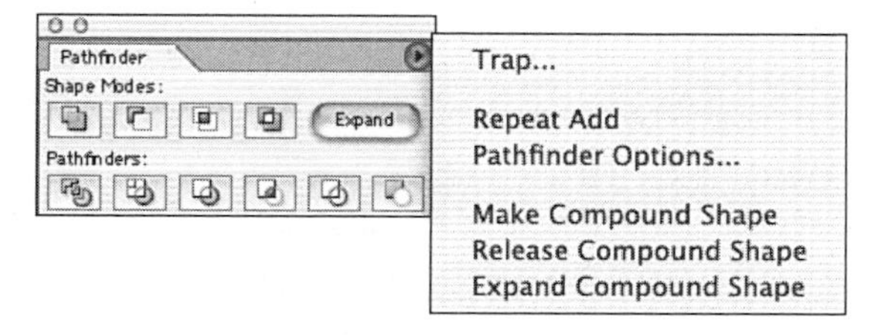


**Figure 25.27**
The buttons in the top row are used to create compound shapes.

Compound shapes combine objects in a variety of ways. In Figure 25.28, the original pair of objects is pictured in the upper left. All the compound shape examples have been created from copies of those objects.

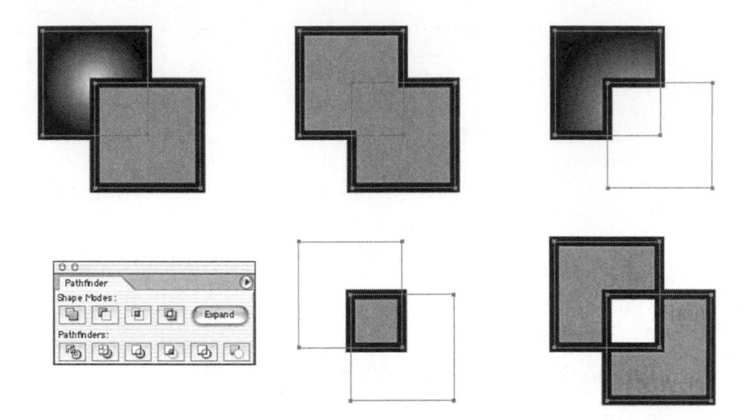


Figure 25.28
The visible paths show that compound shapes are "live" and can be edited.

The first compound shape button adds the selected objects (top row, middle). This replaces the former Unite pathfinder command. The resulting object takes on the fill and stroke of the topmost object.

The second button subtracts the topmost object from the lower object. The remaining object retains its original fill and stroke. Notice, however, that the center of the gradient is shifted to the center of the compound shape rather than remaining at the center of the original object (top row, right).

Intersecting two objects (bottom row, left) retains only the overlapping area of the selected objects. The topmost object's fill and stroke are retained.

Excluding the overlapping area produces the opposite object (bottom row, right). Again, however, the topmost object's fill and stroke are retained.

*Can' t create a compound shape from two selected objects? Check "Compounding Problems" in the "Mastering Illustrator" section at the end of this chapter.*

## Expanding a Compound Shape

Clicking the Expand button in the Pathfinder palette with a compound shape selected on the artboard eliminates any hidden parts of the object. As you can see in Figure 25.29, the paths of the compound shapes are reduced to the visible areas.

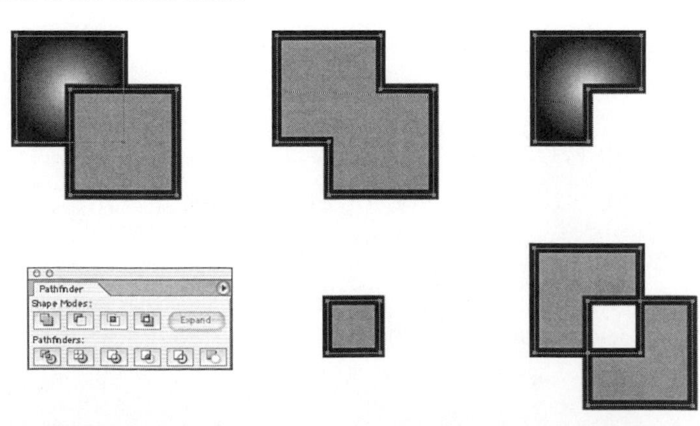


Figure 25.29
The compound shapes from Figure 25.28 have been expanded.

Notice the resulting object in the lower-right corner. In this case, expanding has created a pair of objects. In Figure 25.30, one of the grouped objects has been selected to identify the paths.

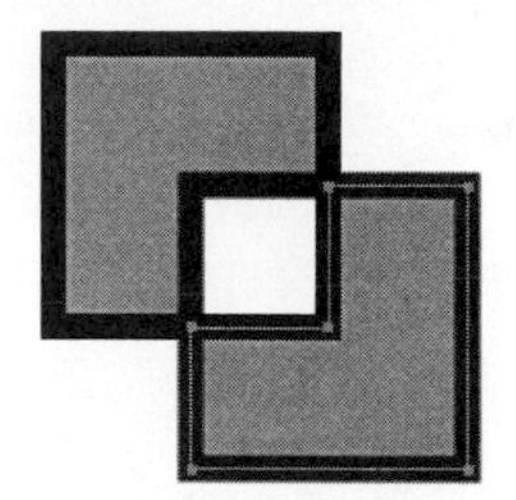

**Figure 25.30**
Expanding such a compound object results in multiple objects, which are grouped.

## The Pathfinder Buttons

The lower half of the Pathfinder palette contains buttons that work with multiple shapes in a different way. The pathfinder capabilities are not live. Once they are applied, they can be removed with the Undo command (until the document is closed), but they cannot be reversed, expanded, or released otherwise.

A number of general rules cover the use of the Pathfinder palette:

- Select objects before you access the Pathfinder palette.
- Resulting multiple objects are grouped.
- Gradient mesh objects cannot be altered from the Pathfinder palette.
- Many of the Pathfinder palette commands create *faces*, which are areas of color undivided by a path. The fill of a simple object is a face.
- Applying Pathfinder palette commands to complex objects, including blends, can be very slow on less-powerful computers.



You can choose from six basic operations in the lower part of the Pathfinder palette:

- **Divide**—Creates objects from overlapping areas, with each face becoming a separate object.
- **Trim**—Deletes hidden parts of objects, removing strokes and leaving objects of the same color as individual objects.
- **Merge**—Deletes hidden parts of objects, removing strokes, and merges objects of the same color as individual objects.
- **Crop**—Uses the foremost object as the "cookie cutter," deleting anything outside it, and creates individual objects of the faces remaining. Strokes are changed to None.
- **Outline**—Creates unfilled open paths from the objects' path segments. Every place that one path crosses another, the paths are both divided.
- **Minus Back**—The foremost object is retained after deletion of any part overlapping any selected object behind it.

## The Pathfinder Palette Menu

The Pathfinder palette's menu allows you to make, release, and expand compound shapes, as well as repeat the last pathfinder operation. (Note that Make Compound Shape assumes the Unite operation.) The two remaining commands—Trap and Pathfinder Options—deserve a closer look.

The Trap command opens the dialog box shown in Figure 25.31. Trapping is a technique used to compensate for possible misregistration during commercial printing operations.

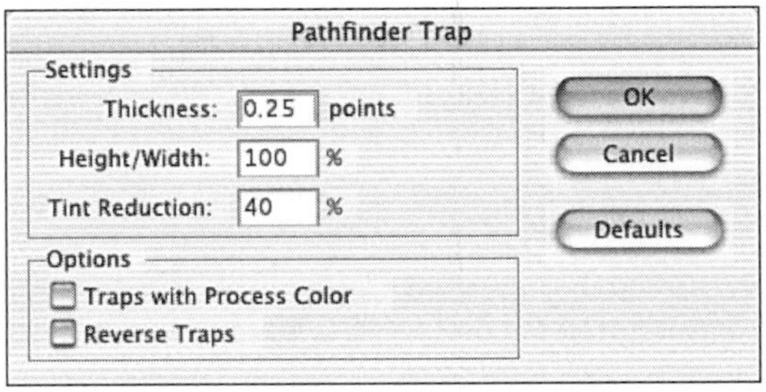

Pathfinder Trap
Settings
Thickness: 0.25 points
Height/Width: 100 %
Tint Reduction: 40 %
Options
Traps with Process Color
Reverse Traps
OK
Cancel
Defaults

**Figure 25.31**
This dialog box offers the same trapping options (in a streamlined package) as those offered by the command Effect, Pathfinder, Trap.

The Pathfinder Options command opens the dialog box shown in Figure 25.32. This dialog box allows you to select the accuracy with which Illustrator executes the pathfinder operations, via the Precision field, and offers a pair of options: Remove Redundant Points, and Divide and Outline Will Remove Unpainted Artwork. Redundant points are those anchor points that duplicate each others' effects on a path after a pathfinder operation. Removing them is usually a good idea. It's also a good idea to remove unpainted artwork after using the Divide and Outline capabilities. Redundant anchor points and unpainted artwork unnecessarily complicate documents and can lead to output problems.



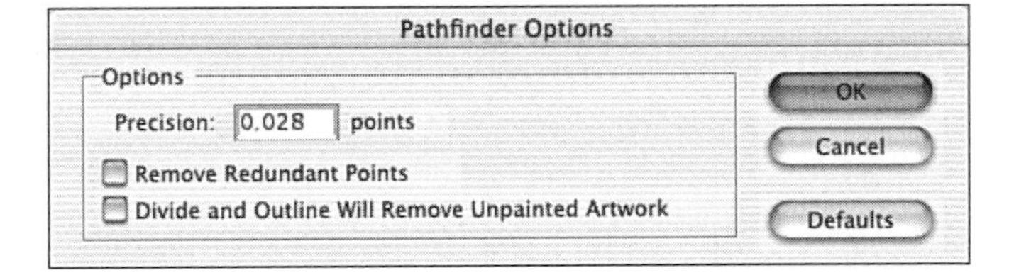


**Figure 25.32**
The Pathfinder Options dialog box allows you to adjust accuracy and to clean up after pathfinder operations.

## Illustrator at Work: Pathfinder Prowess

The Pathfinder palette makes short work of complex path creation. Use it to combine simple shapes into intricate objects. Learn just a few basic concepts and you're on your way! Follow these steps to use the Pathfinder palette to create a path:

1. Start a new document in Illustrator (800×600 pixels, RGB).
2. Under the View menu, show and snap to the grid. In Illustrator's Preferences, set the grid to "Gridline every: 100 px" and "Subdivisions: 4."

> Illustrator also offers the full range of pathfinder operations as effects. The pathfinder effects are explained in Chapter 35, "Illustrator's Effects and Filters."

3. Show the rulers with (Command-R) [Ctrl+R]. From the intersection of the rulers in the upper-left corner, drag to the upper-left corner of the artboard. This resets the 0/0 point.
4. Select the Rectangle tool and drag from the point 100/100 (the first intersection of major grid-lines in the upper left) to the 400 pixel mark horizontally and the 500 pixel mark vertically. You should have a portrait-oriented rectangle.
5. With the rectangle still selected, change the fill to None and change the stroke to a brown swatch with a stroke weight of 10 pixels.
6. Click with the Rectangle tool at the 110/110 grid subdivision intersection and create a rectangle 250 pixels wide and 150 pixels tall.
7. Click again 20 pixels below the lower-left corner of the new rectangle and then click the OK button. You should now have two rectangles of equal size, evenly spaced within the first rectangle (see Figure 25.33).

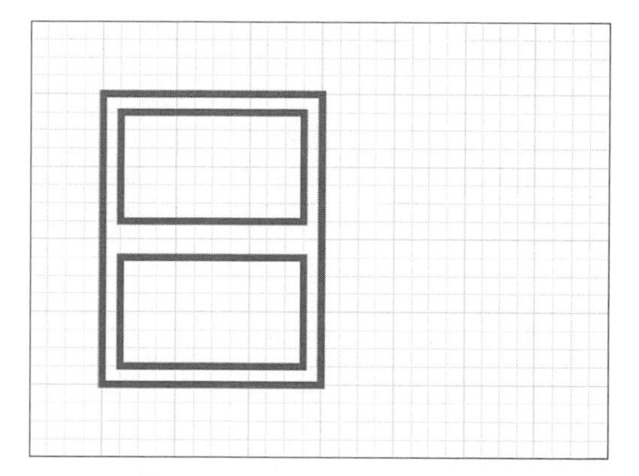

**Figure 25.33**
Your artboard should look like this.



8. Select All. Press Shift-F9 or use the menu command Window, Pathfinder to show the Pathfinder palette.
9. Click the second button from the left in the top row. That intersects the two upper rectangles with the original rectangle.
10. Press X on the keyboard to swap the stroke and fill. Instant window! (See Figure 25.34.)

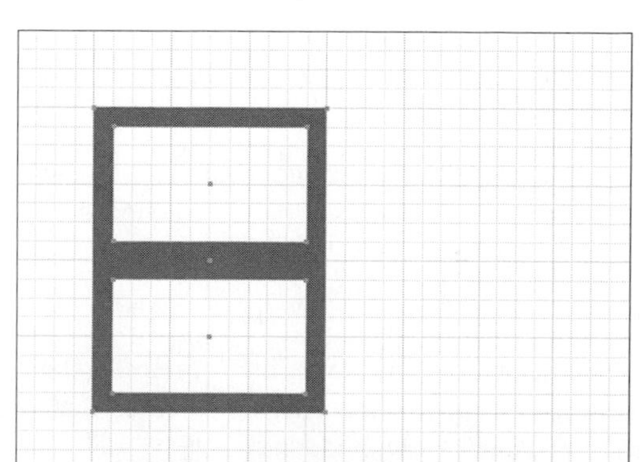

**Figure 25.34**
Notice how the transparency grid shows through the now-empty areas.

11. Activate the Direct Selection tool by clicking it in the Toolbox or by using the keyboard shortcut A.
12. Click any of the anchor points of either of the smaller rectangles and drag inward. When you release the mouse button, observe how the combined object is changed to reflect the new shape.

By default, Illustrator installs several examples of graphs and graph designs on your hard drive. Look in the Sample Files folder.

That's just one simple example of how you can use the buttons in the Pathfinder palette to great advantage. Experiment with different overlapping shapes and watch how the buttons combine them. A pair of vertically overlapping circles can be combined, then their centers subtracted to create a figure 8. A character's hand can be constructed joint by joint, finger by finger, and then the individual objects combined. The beauty of this is that each of the original objects retains its identity, allowing for easy manipulation.

# GRAPHS IN ILLUSTRATOR

Although it doesn't compare to a dedicated graphing tool, Illustrator does offer some rather impressive graphing capabilities. In addition to placing a graph in a document, Illustrator allows you to import data from a variety of sources and update a graph at any time. Nine styles of graphs are offered, any of which can be added to a document in just a few quick clicks.



## The Types of Graphs and Graph Tools

The first step in adding a graph to a document is deciding what type of graph to add. Illustrator offers you nine different types of graphs (see Figure 25.35).

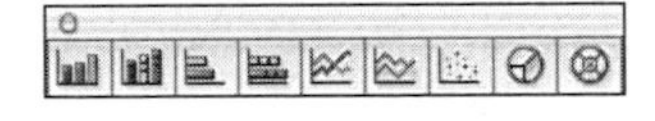

Figure 25.35
The graph tools are shown on a Toolbox flyout palette.

The graph types, which correspond to the graph tools, are detailed in the following list:

- **Column Graph**—The most common type of graph; vertical bars are used to show the comparison between two or more sets of data (see Figure 25.36, top).
- **Stacked Column Graph**—Stacked columns use vertical bars stacked atop each other to produce the column. Each of the stacked pieces represents a subset of the column's value (see Figure 25.36, middle).
- **Bar Graph**—Bar graphs, counterparts to column graphs, use horizontal bars to show values. Like column graphs, each bar represents a single value (see Figure 25.36, bottom).
- **Stacked Bar Graph**—Similar to stacked column graphs, these graphs show partial values as subsections of the horizontal bar (see Figure 25.37, top).
- **Line Graph**—The line graph compares values over time. Typically, the horizontal axis represents time and the vertical placement of points represents value. Such graphs are often used for such data as stock prices (see Figure 25.37, middle).

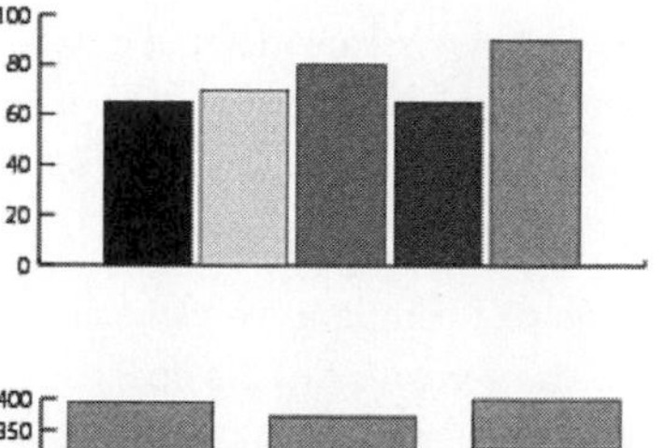


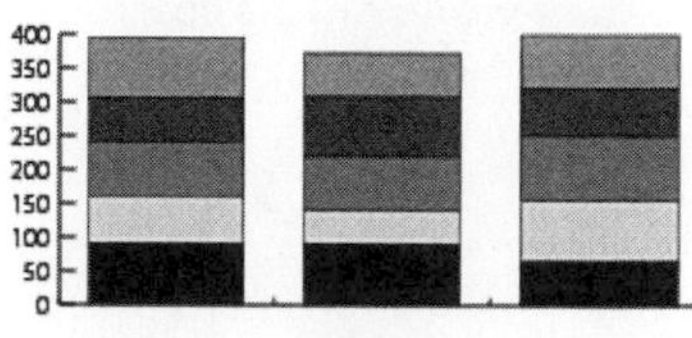


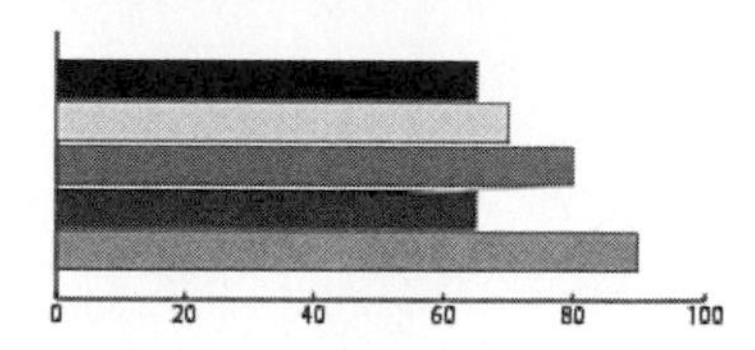


Figure 25.36
Examples of three types of graphs: column, stacked column, and bar.

- **Area Graph**—Area graphs have much in common with stacked column graphs, except they also make it easier to track horizontal comparisons and establish comparative subsections more easily (see Figure 25.37, bottom).

0 50 100 150 200 250 300 350 400

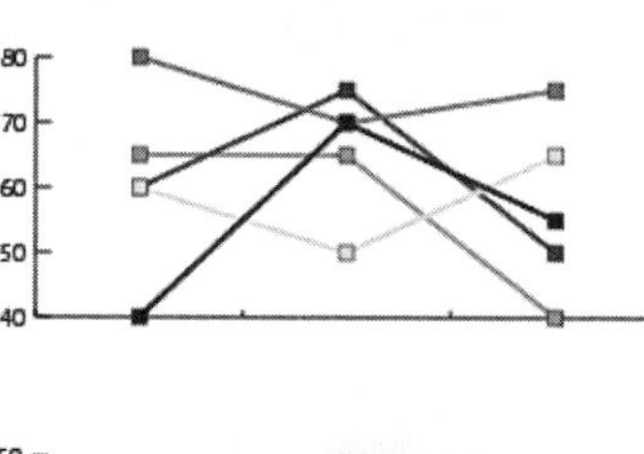


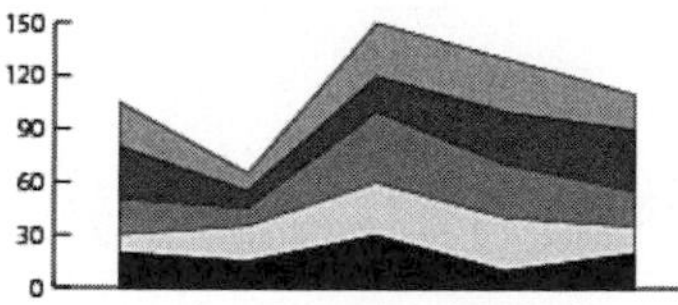


Figure 25.37
Examples of three types of graphs: stacked bar, line, and area.

- **Scatter Graph**—Points are plotted against both the x-axis and the y-axis. These graphs are often used to spot trends or show a relationship between the x-axis and the y-axis variables (see Figure 25.38, top).

- **Pie Graph**—This graph type shows subsections of a value as slices of the pie. Each pie represents a value. When the individual values of multiple pies are different, the diameter of the pies will vary. However, if all the pies total, for example, 100, the pies will be the same size (see Figure 25.38, middle).
- **Radar Graph**—Radar graphs plot comparative values around a circle. The x values are points around the circle, whereas the y values are the spokes (see Figure 25.38, bottom).

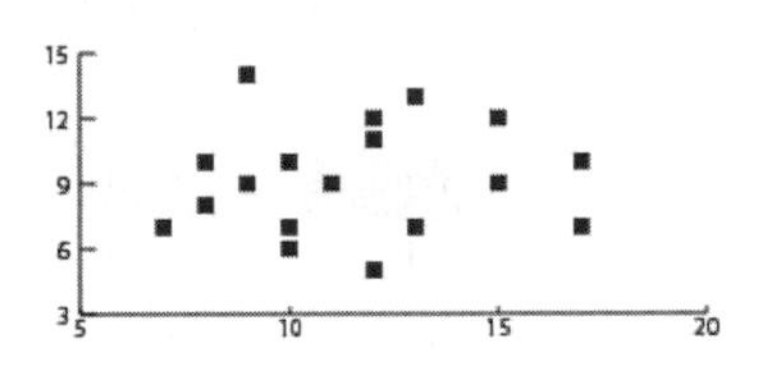


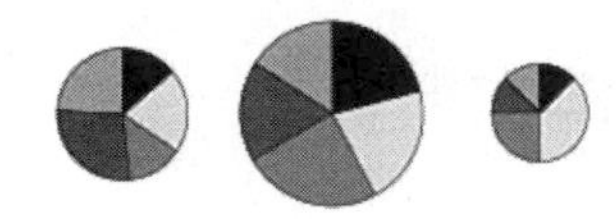

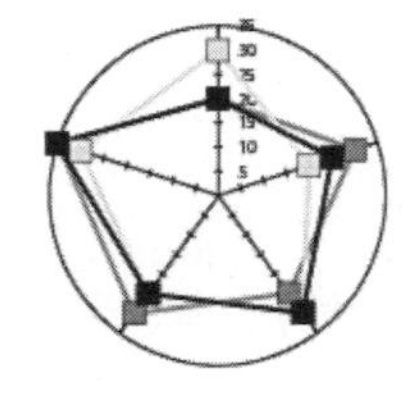

Figure 25.38
Examples of three types of graphs: scatter, pie, and radar.



## Adding a Graph to the Artboard

Once you've decided what type of graph to add, select the corresponding icon from the tearoff palette of the Toolbox and either click once on the artboard or drag to determine the graph's size. Clicking opens the dialog box shown in Figure 25.39, which allows you to specify the dimensions of the graph.

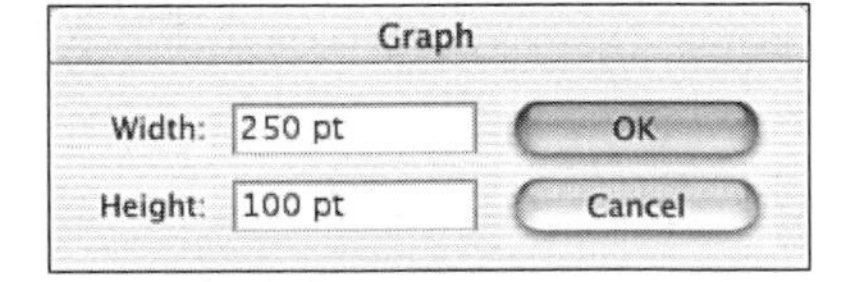


Figure 25.39
Clicking a graph tool on the artboard allows you to specify dimensions.

## Adding Graph Data

Once the dimensions are established, either through the dialog box or by dragging, a data window will appear (see Figure 25.40). You can enter data manually or import it from any tab-delineated text file.

The buttons to the right of the data entry field are, from the left, Import Data, Transpose Row/Column, Switch X/Y, Cell Style (which determines number of decimals and column width), Revert, and Apply. Transpose Row/Column and Switch X/Y are available for the appropriate graph types, and they serve the same basic purpose: If the data across should be the data downward in the table, or vice versa, one click prevents you from having to reenter all the data.

After you've entered the appropriate data, you must either click the Apply button or use the Enter key on the keyboard (the numeric keypad for Macintosh) to use the data in the graph.

When working with rectangular graphs (all except pie and radar), the point you click is where the graph itself begins. The values for the vertical axis may fall to the left of that point. However, the overall width specified in the Graph dialog box includes those labels (if any).

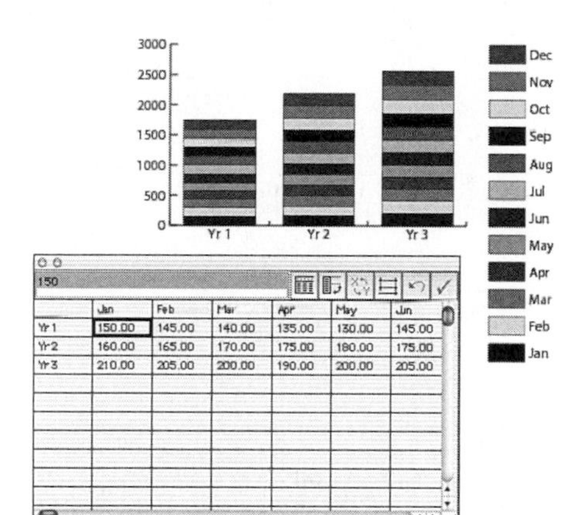


| | Jan | Feb | Mar | Apr | May | Jun |
|---|---|---|---|---|---|---|
| Yr 1 | 150.00 | 145.00 | 140.00 | 135.00 | 130.00 | 145.00 |
| Yr 2 | 160.00 | 165.00 | 170.00 | 175.00 | 180.00 | 175.00 |
| Yr 3 | 210.00 | 205.00 | 200.00 | 190.00 | 200.00 | 205.00 |

Figure 25.40
The data shown is for the graph pictured.

25

## Changing Graph Type and Graph Data

With a graph selected on the artboard, you can use the menu command Object, Graph, Type to open the Graph Type dialog box. You can change the type of graph and specify a variety of settings. Column, stacked column, bar, and stacked bar graphs use the same graph options (see Figure 25.41). The only differences are that for the two types of bar charts, the lower part of the dialog box asks for Bar Width rather than Column Width, and the Value Axis pop-up menu offers Top, Bottom, and Both, rather than Left, Right, and Both.

The line, scatter, and radar graphs use variations of the dialog box shown in Figure 25.42. Scatter graphs, however, do not have the option Edge-to-Edge Lines.

Pie graphs offer the graph options shown in Figure 25.43.

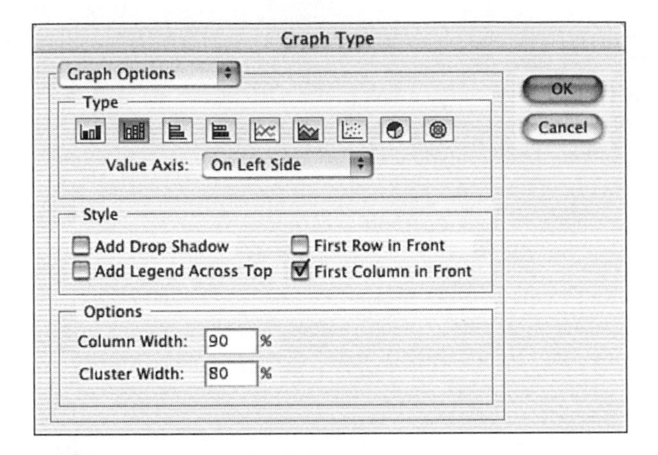


Figure 25.41
The column and bar type graphs have similar options.

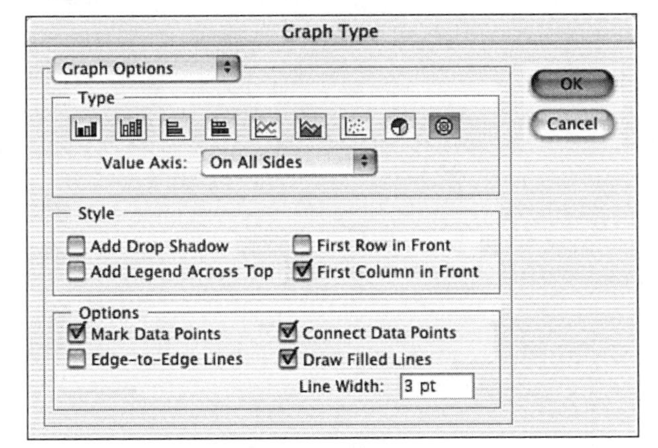


Figure 25.42
Graph options are similar for line, scatter, and radar graphs.

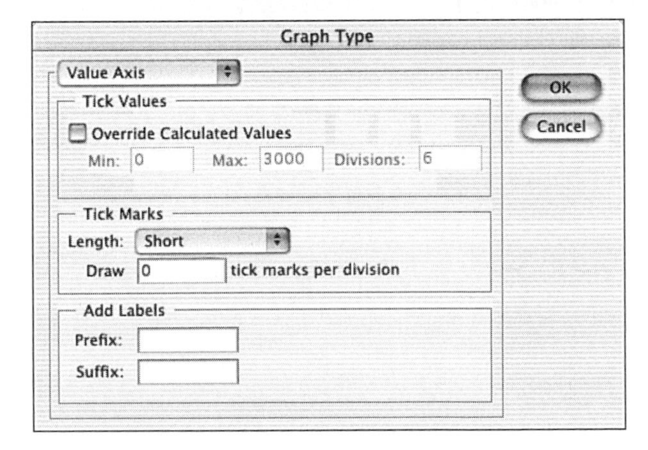


Figure 25.43
The pie graph options are shown here.

Area graphs have no options, offering only the possibility of changing the Style options (as shown in the previous figures).

All the graph types except the pie graphs offer customization of the value axis and the category axis. The options are shown in the dialog box in Figure 25.44.

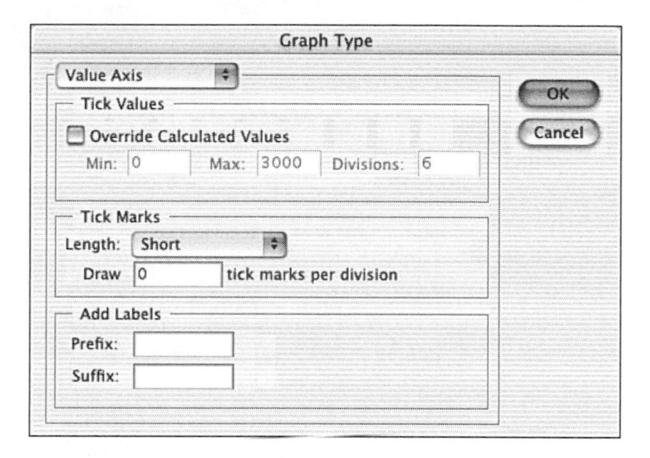


**Figure 25.44**
These settings determine much about how the graph will appear.

Radar graphs have only a value axis. With the exception of the scatter graph, all other graph types can customize the category axis only in terms of the tick marks. Scatter graphs offer the same options for both the value axis and the category axis.

Illustrator also allows you to update a graph's data using the menu command Object, Graph, Data. The current data will appear in the data window. Remember to either click the Apply button or use the Enter key to update the graph.



## Customizing Graphs

One of the easiest ways to customize a graph in Illustrator is to add color. By default, all graphs are created in grayscale. Do not ungroup a graph to make changes to its appearance; the connection to the graph's data will be broken. The Group Selection tool can select elements to add strokes and color, pattern, or gradient fills. Click once to select part of a "stacked" column or bar chart, click a second time to select all like items in the graph, and click a third time to include the identifying item in the legend (if any).

Graphs in Illustrator can be jazzed up with custom symbols to replace the standard bars and columns. Create the artwork, surround it with a rectangle to delineate the boundary (use a stroke and fill of None to make the rectangle invisible), and then use the menu command Object, Graph, Design (see Figure 25.45).

Clicking the New Design button adds the artwork to the list (as shown). You can also paste existing artwork onto the artboard to edit it and delete unneeded designs. (The Select Unused button can make it simple to delete any designs that are not in use in the current document.)

**Caution**

Remember that ungrouping a graph breaks the connection to the data. If the data is finalized, that's not a problem. However, if there's any chance that the data will need to be updated (or otherwise changed), use the Group Selection tools rather than ungrouping.

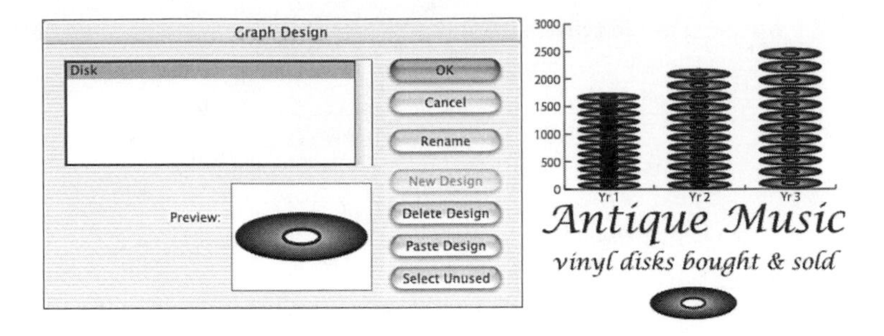


Figure 25.45
The Graph Design dialog box will list all available designs.

To apply custom artwork to a specific graph, select the graph on the artboard and use the menu command Object, Graph, Column or Object, Graph, Marker (depending on whether you want to customize the columns or bars or the value markers). You'll be able to choose from any existing designs, and you'll have the option of how to apply the design (see Figure 25.46).

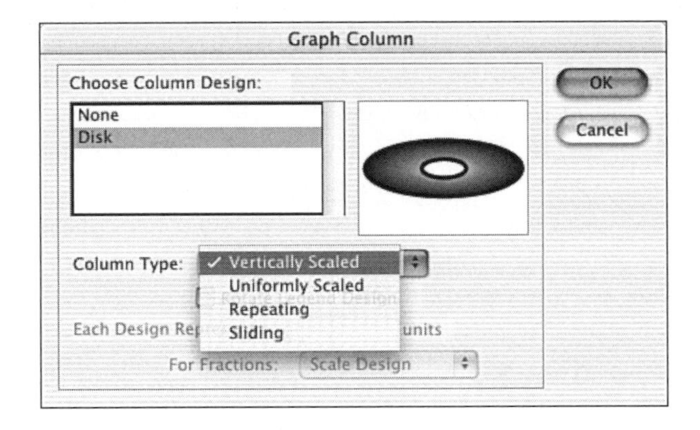


Figure 25.46
You can scale artwork, repeat artwork to show value, or have the artwork slide (distort) to show value.



If you choose to have the artwork repeat, you must enter a value. Each occurrence of the artwork will represent that value.

# MASTERING ILLUSTRATOR

## Checking the Layers Palette

*Simple rectangles and ellipses are showing up on the artboard with all sorts of unexpected looks. What's going on?*

Open Illustrator's Layers palette and take a look. If the layer upon which you're creating the objects has a small filled circle to the right of its name, appearance characteristics have been targeted on the layer. You can click the New Layer button to create an untargeted layer and create on it. (Targeting appearances to layers is discussed in Chapter 30.)

## Choosing What to Select

*I can't seem to get the Magic Wand to select properly. It either gets too many objects or not enough. I've tried fiddling with the settings, but that doesn't seem to help.*

Remember that there are three parts to the Magic Wand palette. Click the palette's tab a couple times until you've got the palette fully opened up. Take a look at the check boxes. In particular, uncheck Blending Mode (unless that's what you're trying to select). Any characteristic checked will be part of the selection criteria, whether visible or hidden by a partially collapsed palette.

## Compounding Problems

*Why can't I create a compound shape from the selected objects?*

Make sure that the objects are not grouped. Grouped objects cannot be used in compound shapes.

26

# WORKING WITH THE FOUR TYPES OF BRUSHES

## IN THIS CHAPTER

Illustrator not only gives you tools with which to draw paths, but it also gives you ways to add art to those paths while you draw them. By selecting a particular brush, you can decorate your path as it is created. Illustrator offers four types of brushes, each with its own capabilities. Brushes are stored in the Brushes palette. They can be applied to existing paths to change the stroke, or they can be used to create new paths with various tools. Figure 26.1 shows the Brushes palette and several examples of each type of brush.

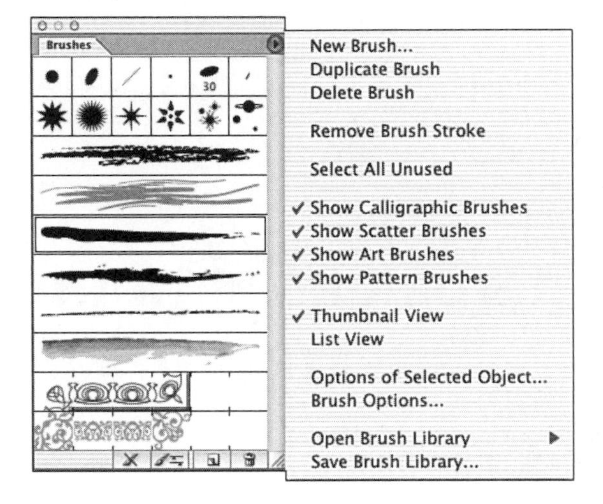


**Figure 26.1**
The Brushes palette menu allows you to streamline the palette's contents by showing only brushes of a certain type or types.

Illustrator's brushes are categorized as calligraphic, scatter, art, and pattern brushes. Several of each are installed by default with the program. In addition to the default brushes, extra sets are available on the hard drive and the program CD, and you can create your own. This chapter looks at how to use and create brushes of all four types.



# WORKING WITH BRUSHES

To add brush artwork to an illustration, you either draw the art with a tool that uses brushes or apply a brush to an existing path. After a brush is applied to a path, the path can still be edited.

## The Four Categories

Illustrator's brushes are grouped into four categories, each with its own unique applications. Descriptions of each of the four categories follow, and examples are shown in Figure 26.2:

- **Calligraphic brushes**—These brushes are designed to replicate calligraphy. The angled points of such pens produce lines that vary in stroke width as they curve.
- **Scatter brushes**—These brushes place copies of a piece of artwork along the path. How the individual objects are scattered is determined when the brush is designed.
- **Art brushes**—These brushes stretch a single piece of artwork along the path.
- **Pattern brushes**—These brushes tile a repeating pattern along the path.

Figure 26.2
From the top, examples of calligraphic, scatter, art, and pattern brushes.

## The Brushes Palette

The Brushes palette, shown earlier in Figure 26.1, stores all four types of brushes. A number of general rules govern brushes:

- You can design and store custom brushes in the Brushes palette.
- When you select List View from the Brushes palette's menu, a small icon appears to the right of each brush to tell you what kind of brush it is.
- You can load brush libraries from other documents by choosing Window, Brush Libraries, Other Library.
- After you use a brush from another library, it is added automatically to your document's Brushes palette.
- With additional brush libraries open, you can drag brushes onto your document's Brushes palette to make them readily available.
- Double-clicking a brush in the palette opens the Brush Options dialog box. Making changes can affect either all the paths in the artwork that use the brush, just those selected, or none. The palette menu also contains the Brush Options command.
- To change a brush without changing preexisting artwork, drag the brush to the New Brush button at the bottom of the palette or use the Duplicate Brush command from the palette menu.
- To change some but not all artwork using a specific brush, select the desired artwork and choose Options of Selected Object. You can also access this command through its button at the bottom of the Brushes palette.
- Illustrator installs dozens of additional brush libraries on your hard drive, ranging from animals to borders. Use the Brushes palette menu's Open Library Brush command. The additional brushes open in a separate palette.

## Brushes and Strokes

The artwork you create with brushes is applied to paths. Both open and closed paths have strokes and can use brushes. You can apply a brush to an existing path in a variety of ways:

- Select the path (or paths) on the artboard with the Selection, Direct Selection, or Group Selection tool and then click the desired brush in the Brushes palette.
- Select the path (or paths) in the Layers palette by clicking the targeting icon and then clicking the desired brush in the Brushes palette.
- Drag the brush from the Brushes palette onto the path.

You can also select a brush for use with a tool. The Pen, Paintbrush, and Pencil tools all can be used with brushes. Any of the object tools also apply a selected brush. (See "Brush-Stroked Type" later in this chapter for information about applying brushes to text.) Figure 26.3 shows three different brushes used with the same tools.

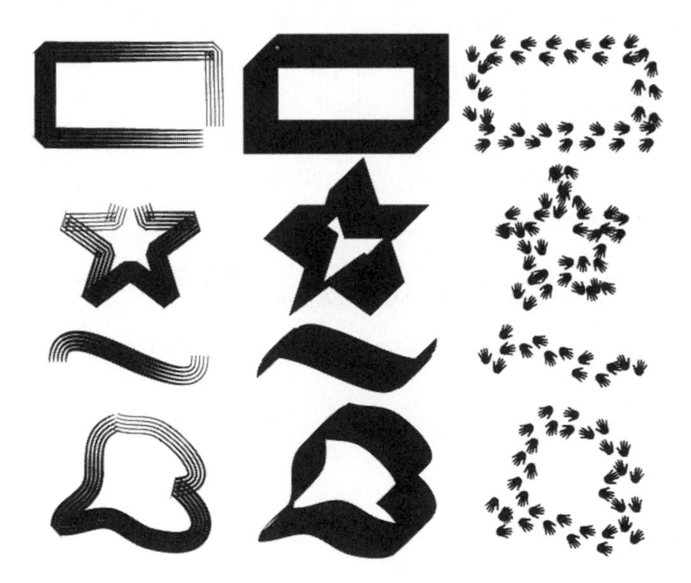

Figure 26.3
Each brush was applied to identical paths created with (from the top) the Rectangle, Star, Pen, and Paintbrush tools.



The stroke weight selected in the Stroke palette affects the appearance of the brush. The brush is scaled to match the weight. Figure 26.4 shows some examples of identical paths at different stroke weights.

Changing the stroke color in the Color palette affects some strokes but not others. Many pattern brushes, for example, are designed with specific color schemes. Some of the scatter brushes are also locked into particular colors. Generally speaking, though, the calligraphic brushes can be changed with the Color palette. You cannot change art, pattern, and scatter brushes unless the brushes were designed to use the stroke color. (Locking in a brush's colors is a function of the Colorization option. See the sidebar "A Note About Colorization" later in this chapter.)

A particular combination of brush and stroke weight can easily be saved for repeated use. Simply make it a style and store it in the Styles palette.

Figure 26.4
The left column shows a stroke weight of 1; the right column shows a stroke weight of 2.

## Editing and Transforming Brushed Paths

When you apply a brush to a path, you can still edit the path. You can move anchor points, reshape segments, and apply transformations. Especially with scatter brushes, identifying the anchor points can be challenging unless the path as a whole is selected. Figure 26.5 shows an example.

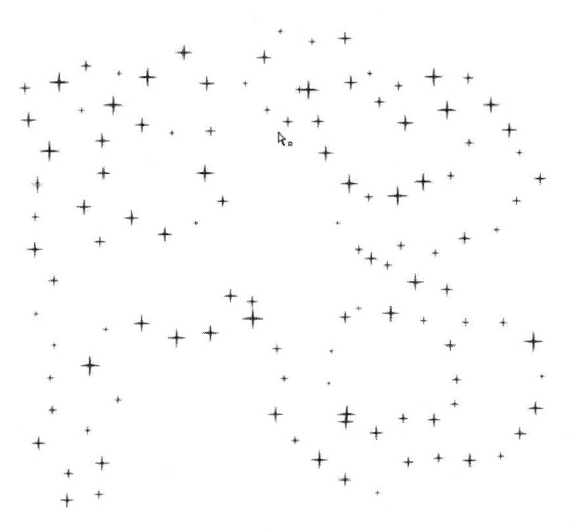

Figure 26.5
This image is an example of the challenge of finding anchor points when a scatter brush is applied. Dragging with a selection tool can help.

You can change a path both by editing its anchor points and by altering its bounding box. In Figure 26.6, a path has been changed using both techniques.

In Figure 26.6, the middle copy of the arrow was edited by dragging up on the top of the bounding box. Notice how the tail and point are relatively unchanged, whereas the body of the arrow has been warped. The direction lines for the center anchor point were correspondingly extended vertically.

Figure 26.6
The original path is shown at the top.

The bottom copy was changed by extending and angling the direction lines of the center anchor point. A different look has been created by curving the arrow throughout its length.

The point where Illustrator starts a brush, particularly the art brushes, may not produce the flow along a closed path that you want. You can alter the brush's appearance by changing the starting point of the path. Use the Scissors tool to cut the path and create a new starting point. Figure 26.7 shows an example.

Figure 26.7
The first star shows the default flow. The center and right stars were divided at the anchor point between the lower points.



The center star in Figure 26.7 was cut with the Scissors tool, and the two resulting anchor points were left, creating an open path. For the star on the right, however, those two points were selected and the command Object, Path, Join was used. In addition to reclosing the path, choosing this command reestablished the original break in the artwork.

The Transform palette and transform commands can also play a large part in editing brushed paths. The dialog box for the Scale command contains a check box labeled Scale Strokes & Effects. The comparable option for the Transform palette appears in the palette's menu. The difference between resizing an object with and without scaling the brush is shown in Figure 26.8.

The original object is shown to the left in Figure 26.8. To the right, the upper object was scaled without the stroke being scaled. The lower object was scaled with the Scale Strokes & Effects option selected.

Figure 26.8
When checked, Scale Strokes & Effects preserves the relationship between the objects and the brushed stroke.

Effects added to a path are also added to the brush's artwork. For example, in Figure 26.9, a drop shadow has been applied to a scatter brush. Note that each element produces its own shadow. Also, note by comparing the upper and lower examples the difference between a fill of None and a white fill. The stroked path is still considered part of the object, and the object as a whole will cast its shadow. The stroke cannot cast its shadow on the fill, even when the stroke is above the fill in the Appearance palette.

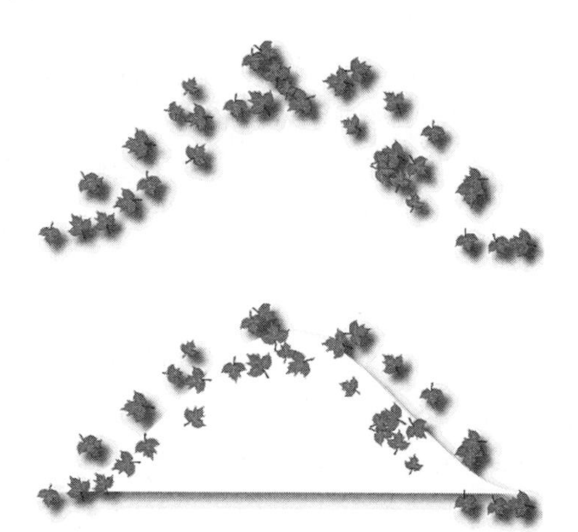

Figure 26.9
Each piece of a scatter brush pattern casts its own shadow, but an object's stroke cannot cast a shadow on the object's fill.



## Brush-Stroked Type

Most appropriate for displaying fonts at very large sizes, Illustrator's brushes can be applied to text. No stroke is required. Examples of each of the four types of brushes are shown applied to text in Figure 26.10.

**Figure 26.10**
The text is Adobe Myriad Roman at 150 points.

## Illustrator at Work: Changing the Color of Brushed Text

After you apply brushes to text, you cannot change the size or color of the brush artwork. You can, however, change the color of the text. To get, for example, blue scatter brush art on black text, follow these steps:

1. Select the Type tool.
2. Set the fill color to the desired shade of blue.
3. Place the text. The text should be the selected shade of blue.
4. Switch to the Move tool by clicking it in the Toolbox. The text should appear within a bounding box.
5. Apply the scatter brush from the Brushes palette. Both the text and scatter brush artwork should be blue.
6. With the text still selected on the artboard, change the fill color to black. The text should change color, but not the scatter brush artwork.

Changing the stroke color in the Color palette or the Toolbox after the brush has been applied does not change the scatter brush artwork. It instead places a stroke around the text. You can also resize this stroke by using the Stroke palette.

*If the artwork applied with the brush seems too large, see "Type Size and Brushes" in the "Mastering Illustrator" section at the end of this chapter.*

# CREATING AND MODIFYING BRUSHES

You can create your own brushes in Illustrator, and you can alter the brushes supplied with the program to fit your needs. Because brushes are stored with a particular file, you can freely alter the default brushes without fear of causing problems for other documents. And, of course, you can reload those default brushes when needed.

*Because brushes are stored with a specific document, the brushes you create or modify are not automatically available for use with other images. Using a simple technique, though, you can make all your hard work available to other documents. See the section "Illustrator at Work: Creating Custom Brush Libraries," later in this chapter.*

The processes of creating and modifying brushes have much in common. In both cases (with the exception of calligraphic brushes), you start with one or more pieces of artwork and define some options. The difference between modifying a brush and creating an original brush is the source of the artwork. When you're modifying an existing brush, the artwork is ready for you rather than being developed specifically for the new brush.

The easiest way to modify an existing brush is to double-click it in the Brushes palette to open the brush's options palette. You can also click a brush once to select it in the Brushes palette and choose the palette menu command Brush Options. You also can modify the artwork used for scatter, art, and pattern brushes. Simply drag the artwork to the artboard, make the changes, and drag it back to the Brushes palette. Illustrator prompts you to pick a type of brush and assign options. This type of change does not affect the original brush. Each of the four types of brushes has its own set of options. Later sections of this chapter discuss each of these brush types in more detail.

If the brush you've modified has been applied in the document, you are asked how you want to handle existing strokes. The dialog box is shown in Figure 26.11.

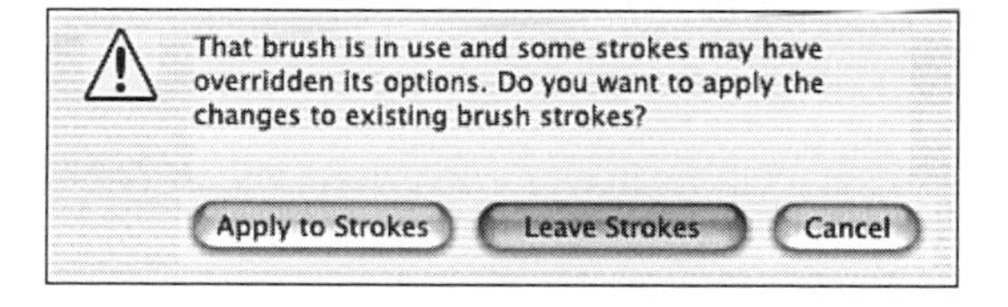
That brush is in use and some strokes may have overridden its options. Do you want to apply the changes to existing brush strokes?
Apply to Strokes
Leave Strokes
Cancel

**Figure 26.11**
You can apply your changes to previously created artwork, leave the older art as it is, or cancel the changes.

Illustrator also allows you to change a brush stroke that has been applied to one or more paths without changing other objects or the brush itself. Select one or more objects that have the same brush stroke and, from the Brushes palette menu, choose the command Options of Selected Object. You can then make modifications that will be applied only to those selected objects.

TROUBLESHOOTING

*If your new brushes—or any brush artwork, for that matter—don't seem to print, see "Expanding Brush Artwork for Print" in the "Mastering Illustrator" section at the end of this chapter.*

Before you spend too much time creating a new brush, check to see whether something similar is already available to you. Your installation of Illustrator includes a large selection of extra brushes. In the Brushes palette menu, go to Open Brush Library.

## Illustrator at Work: Creating Custom Brush Libraries

Creating new brushes or editing existing brushes takes time and effort. However, those brushes are saved only in the file in which you created them. Rather than creating brushes over and over for various files, you can create your own brush library, which you can load just like any other. Just follow these steps:

1. Create or modify the brushes that you want in your custom set.
2. Delete any other brushes from the Brushes palette.
3. Save a copy of the file with the name Custom Brushes or something else that's recognizable.
4. Put the file into the Presets, Brush folder, which you can find inside the Adobe Illustrator CS folder.
5. Restart Illustrator.
6. You can now load this set of custom brushes in any other document by choosing Window, Brush Libraries. Your file shows up right there in the list.

It's generally a good idea to make a copy of such documents and store the copy in a folder outside the Illustrator folder. That way, if you ever need to reinstall Illustrator or upgrade it, you won't accidentally delete your custom brushes.

## Creating or Modifying a Calligraphic Brush

The calligraphic brushes simulate the angled points of their nondigital counterparts. To create a new calligraphic brush or modify an existing calligraphic brush, do either of the following:

- Click the New Brush button at the bottom of the Brushes palette or use the palette's New Brush command. Select New Calligraphic Brush from the New Brush dialog box. The Calligraphic Brush Options dialog box then opens, as shown in Figure 26.12.
- Double-click an existing calligraphic brush in the Brushes palette to open the Calligraphic Brush Options dialog box, as shown in Figure 26.12.



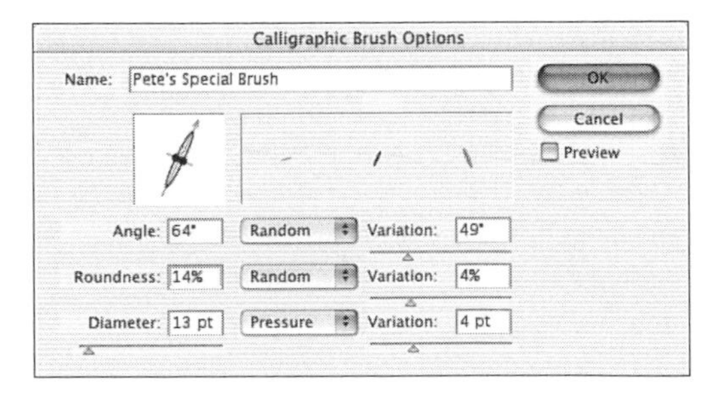


Figure 26.12
Changing the name prevents overwriting an existing brush.

### A Note About Colorization

The scatter, art, and pattern brushes all contain artwork. The colors used to re-create that artwork with the brush depend on the settings selected in the brush's options. In the Colorization section of the Options dialog boxes, you'll find a button labeled Tips. It opens the window shown in the following figure.

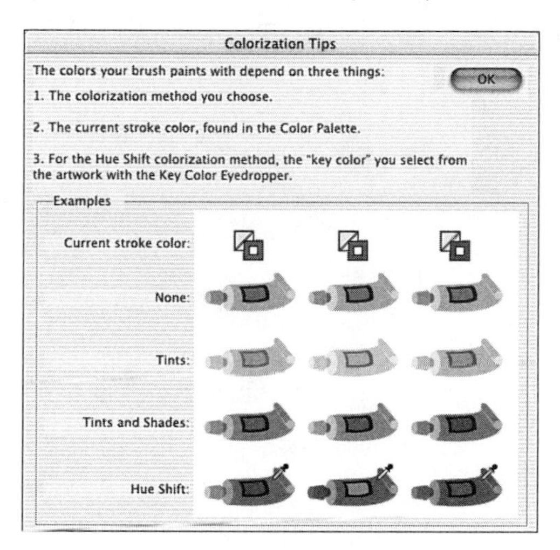


The Colorization Tips are not particularly useful, especially in grayscale.

More complete explanations of the options may be helpful:

- **None**—With None selected, the artwork retains the colors with which it was created. Modification of the path's stroke color does not affect the brush stroke.
- **Tints**—The stroke color is applied to the artwork along the path. The various colors in the original artwork are replaced with tints of the stroke color. Black in the original artwork becomes the stroke color. White stays white. Illustrator uses the saturation and brightness values of the tints to maintain the relationships among the various components of the artwork. If a stroke color is a spot color, Illustrator automatically generates the appropriate tints (but they are not automatically added to the Swatches palette).
- **Tints and Shades**—As it does with tints, Illustrator re-creates the artwork in tints of the stroke color, but black and white are maintained. When you're using a spot color as the stroke color, keep in mind that black is added, which prevents the artwork from separating to a single spot color plate.
- **Hue Shift**—The Eyedropper tool in the brush's Options dialog box designates the key color in the original artwork. The key color usually should be the most important color rather than the most prominent color. The designated color becomes the stroke color, and other colors become tints of the stroke color. Hue Shift maintains any black, white, and gray in the original.

The following figure shows one scatter brush colorized in each of the three ways. Even when the image is in grayscale, very large differences are apparent. (The top row shows the original "uncolorized" artwork, which you can use by selecting None as the Colorize option.)

From the top, these examples are None, Tint, Tint and Shade, and Hue Shift.

In color, the image shows that the last example, Hue Shift, maintained the gray of the pushpin's pin. In the other two examples, the pin is colored with a tint of the stroke color.

In the Hue Shift example, the center of the pushpin's shaft was designated the key color. This area was selected because it represents what could be considered the actual color of the pushpin, without highlight or shadow. Selecting a darker area would substantially lighten the resulting artwork, whereas selecting a lighter area would produce shadows that are too dark.



The Angle and Roundness values can be fixed at a set value, random within a range of values, or set to respond to the pressure of a stylus on a graphics tablet (if one is installed and available). Angle, when set to Random, can range from 0° to 180°. Roundness, as a random value, can range from 0 to the amount specified in the Roundness field. Diameter is similarly limited, ranging from 0 to the number of points in the Diameter box.

You can also make changes by using the cursor to drag points in the sample above the Angle box. Dragging the arrowhead changes the angle (called the *eclipse angle of rotation*), and dragging either of the two side spots can change the roundness of the brush. You can set the diameter either by using the slider or by entering a value in the Diameter box.

## Creating or Modifying a Scatter Brush

A scatter brush consists of a piece of artwork and the instructions for distributing that art along a path. To create a new scatter brush or to modify an existing scatter brush, do either of the following:

- Create or select a piece of artwork on the artboard. Click the New Brush button at the bottom of the Brushes palette or use the palette's New Brush command. Select New Scatter Brush from the New Brush dialog box. The Scatter Brush Options dialog box then opens, as shown in Figure 26.13. The Scatter Brush option is not available in the New Brush dialog box if no artwork is selected.

- Double-click an existing scatter brush in the Brushes palette to open the Scatter Brush Options dialog box, as shown in Figure 26.15.

Scatter brushes cannot be created from artwork that contains gradients, gradient meshes, patterns, or styles.

*If you would like to use a particular style but it knocks out your brush, see "Styles and Brushes" in the "Mastering Illustrator" section at the end of this chapter.*

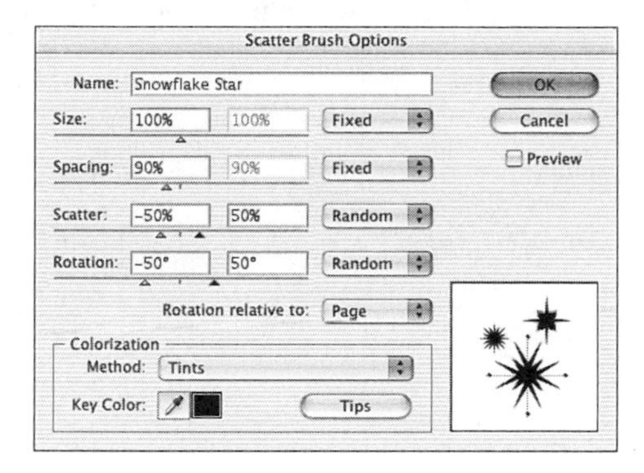


**Figure 26.13**
**You can check Preview to see how the changes will look on the artwork selected on the artboard.**

You can choose from six options for scatter brushes. You can set Size, Spacing, Scatter, and Rotation to a fixed or random value within specified limits. If a graphics tablet is available, you can also set Size, Spacing, Scatter, and Rotation to vary according to the stylus pressure. Each setting is measured as a percentage of the size of the original artwork. You can rotate the artwork in relation to the page or the path. The other two scatter brush options are Colorization Method and Key Color. All four of the Colorization methods are available. (Refer to the sidebar "A Note About Colorization," earlier in this chapter.)

When fixed settings are used for the first four options, each slider has a single adjustment triangle below it. When an option is set to Random, a pair of triangles is available. Use them to set the minimum and maximum values for each setting.

The scatter brush's artwork can also be dragged to the artboard and modified. After you change the artwork, drag it back to the Brushes palette. You then are prompted to select the type of brush, and the appropriate Brush Options dialog box will open. The original scatter brush is not changed.



## Creating or Modifying an Art Brush

Like a scatter brush, an art brush consists of a single piece of artwork that is replicated along a path. To create a new art brush or modify an existing art brush, do either of the following:

Art brushes cannot be created from artwork that contains gradients, gradient meshes, patterns, or styles.

- Create or select a piece of artwork on the artboard. Click the New Brush button at the bottom of the Brushes palette or use the palette's New Brush command. Select

New Art Brush from the New Brush dialog box. The Art Brush Options dialog box then opens, as shown in Figure 26.14. The Art Brush option is not available in the New Brush dialog box if no artwork is selected.

- Double-click an existing art brush in the Brushes palette to open the Art Brush Options dialog box, as shown in Figure 26.14.

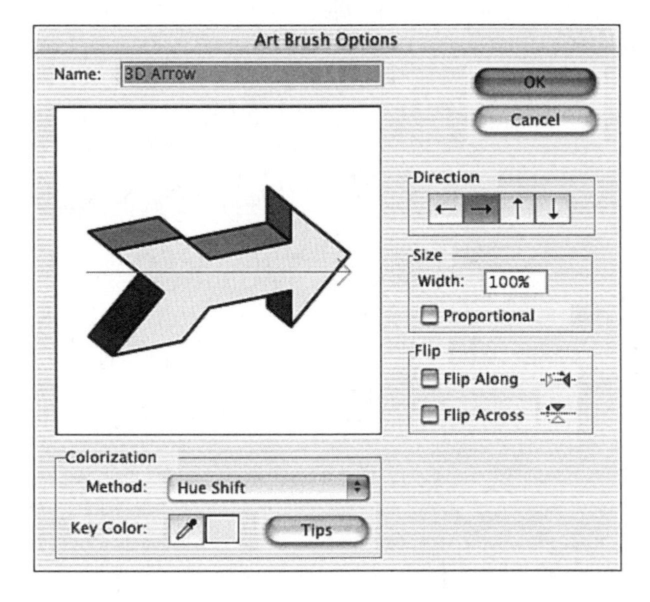


Figure 26.14
The 3D Arrow brush is not part of Illustrator's default collection.



The four Direction buttons indicate how the art will be drawn along the path. The arrow indicates the end of the path. Also important to the appearance of the art are the size and proportions selected. The length of the path determines the length of the artwork, and the width is designated in the Options dialog box. The percentage is relative to the original artwork. Checking Proportional results in a width based not on the original art but rather on the percentage specified for width. Flipping the artwork along a path is similar to using the Reflect tool or command.

Some examples of how the various options affect the appearance of the artwork are shown in Figure 26.15.

The first arrow uses a width of 50%. The second arrow in the figure is identical to the first, except that the width has been changed from 50% to 100%. The middle arrow is set for 100% width, and the Proportional box is checked. The fourth arrow is again at 50% width, but the Flip Along box is checked, changing the alignment of the arrow on the path. The arrow at the bottom of the stack is also at 50% width, but a different Direction button has been selected. Rather than the right-pointing button, the upward-pointing button has been clicked.

> An easy way to create a set of brushes is to make copies of an art brush and use the Options dialog box to flip the artwork. Create the original with neither Flip box checked. Make a copy with Flip Along checked, another with Flip Across checked, and a third with both boxes checked. This way, you'll have a brush pointed in whichever direction you require.

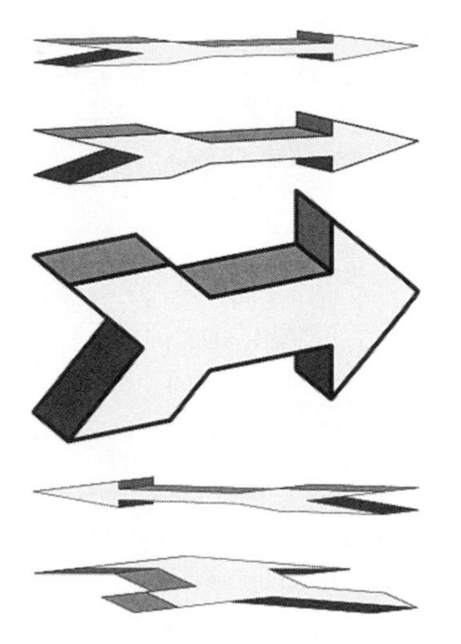

**Figure 26.15**
You can substantially change the appearance of a preset brush.

The Colorization options were discussed earlier in this chapter in the sidebar "A Note About Colorization."

As with a scatter brush, you can drag an art brush from the palette onto the artboard and edit the image. Afterward, you can drag the image back to the Brushes palette, select the type and some options, and a new brush is created, leaving the original untouched.

## Creating or Modifying a Pattern Brush

Using individual tiles, a pattern brush creates a pattern along an open or closed path. When you're modifying a pattern brush, you may see a single tile or as many as five tiles in the Pattern Brush Options dialog box. A side tile, one that places the pattern along segments of a path, is required. Optional are tiles for the beginning and end of open paths, and tiles used for corner anchor points that point inward or outward. To create a new pattern brush or modify an existing pattern brush, do either of the following:

- Click the New Brush button at the bottom of the Brushes palette or use the palette's New Brush command. Select New Pattern Brush from the New Brush dialog box. The Pattern Brush Options dialog box then opens, as shown in Figure 26.16.
- Double-click an existing pattern brush in the Brushes palette to open the Pattern Brush Options dialog box, as shown in Figure 26.16.

*The specifics of creating tiles for pattern brushes are discussed in Chapter 31, "Defining and Applying Patterns."*

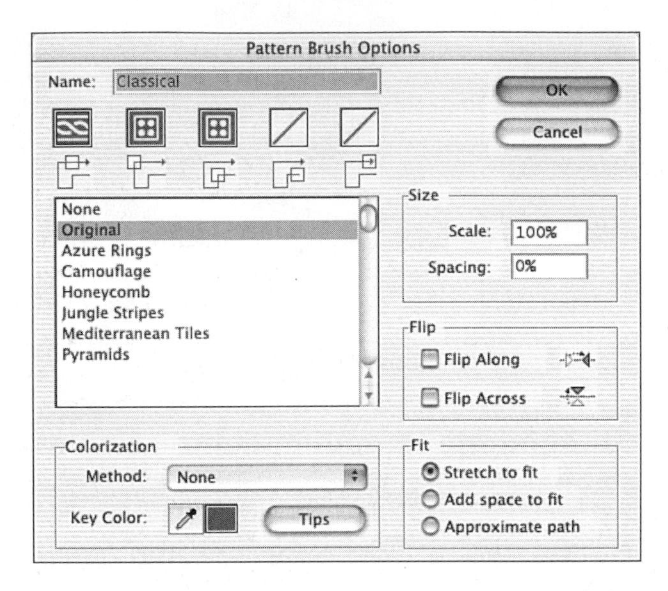


**Figure 26.16**
The Classical pattern is installed by default into the Brushes palette in Illustrator CS.

Creating or modifying the tiles of a pattern brush is a simple matter of designating the appropriate pattern for the type of tile. Here are the basics:

- Near the top of the dialog box, below the pattern's name, are the samples for each of the five types of tiles. The first, Side Tile, is required. The others are Outer Corner Tile, Inner Corner Tile, Start Tile, and End Tile.
- Below the five tile samples is a list of patterns available to create the individual tiles. Shown are the default patterns. (Chapter 31 discusses the specifics of creating tiles for use with patterns.)
- Click one of the five types of tiles and then click the pattern to use.



The Size options, Scale and Spacing, are set for the entire pattern brush, not for individual types of tiles. They are relative to the original artwork's size.

Flipping a pattern along or across the path is comparable to using the Reflect tool or command. The pattern is reversed across the designated axis. You can select Flip Along, Flip Across, both, or neither.

The Colorization options were discussed earlier in this chapter in the sidebar "A Note About Colorization."

Choosing the appropriate Fit setting can drastically affect the appearance of the pattern when it is used with a path that includes corner anchor points (see Figure 26.17).

The first rectangle uses Stretch to Fit, the middle rectangle is set to Add Space to Fit, and the object to the right is set to Approximate Path. Note that the pattern is not centered on the bounding box of the last object (the three objects are of identical size and are aligned through their centers).

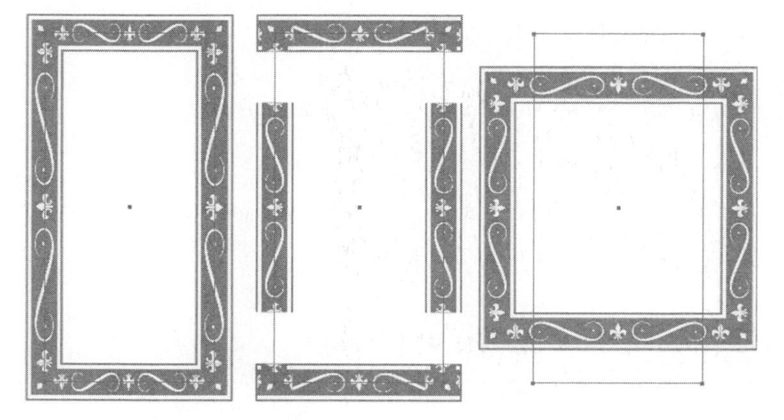

Figure 26.17
The Pattern Brush Options dialog box offers three Fit settings.

## Illustrator at Work: Modifying Brushes for Smaller Text

Although Illustrator's default brushes are too large for most type sizes, that doesn't mean you can't use them. You just need to chop them down to size by following these steps:

1. In the Brushes palette, click the brush you intend to apply.
2. In the Brushes palette menu, select Duplicate Brush.
3. Double-click the copy of the brush to open its Brush Options dialog box.
4. To the right, under the Cancel button, you'll see the Size area. Change the percentage in the Scale box to fit your needs.
5. Click OK and apply the new brush to your text.

# MASTERING ILLUSTRATOR

## Type Size and Brushes

*The art brush seems to overwhelm my font, but I can't find a way to resize it.*

You can't resize the brush work, but you can resize the text. Set your type at a point size that's between one-half and three-quarters the desired size. Apply the art brush. Resize the type to the size you need in the illustration. The brush work should stay the same size.

## Expanding Brush Artwork for Print

*I created these really killer brushes, but my printer seems to lock up every time I try to use them. What can I do?*

The artwork the brushes added to your image is likely very complex. Try expanding it to simplify the printing. Select the object to which the brush is applied and then choose Object, Expand Appearance.

## Styles and Brushes

*I want to add a style to my artwork, but every time I do, it erases my brush.*

Apply the style first; then add the brush. Many styles have a specific stroke assigned to them. That stroke overrides any stroke previously applied (including brushes). After the style is in place, however, you can override the style's stroke with a brush.

# TYPE AND TEXT IN ILLUSTRATOR

## IN THIS CHAPTER

Text is often a critical part of an illustration. Illustrator not only allows you to place and control text in an image, it also gives you advanced typographic capabilities. You can produce individual pages of text with the sort of refinement and precision associated with high-end page layout programs. In addition, letters and words can be used as artwork. Not only can you strategically place characters, but you also can transform them into paths and use them as outlines.

Illustrator CS uses a more powerful type engine than any previous version. Many of the changes are behind the scenes, but if you like to fine-tune the appearance of your type, you'll truly enjoy the new support for OpenType fonts, optical kerning, optical alignment, and the new Every-line Composer. If you work with large amounts of type or in a production environment, the new Character Styles and Paragraph Styles palettes hold great promise. Not only can you apply a complex style easily, you can ensure consistency from project to project with character and paragraph styles.

This chapter looks first at the subject of fonts, then at Illustrator's type-related tools, palettes, and commands. It also includes discussions of ways to work with text containers, create outlines from type, and adjust type attributes.

*For related information, see Chapter 36, "Linking and Embedding Images and Fonts."*

# UNDERSTANDING, ADDING, AND FIXING FONTS

Many types of fonts are available today, in various qualities. Illustrator, like most high-end computer programs, works best with high-quality fonts. Although you can get good results with inexpensive and free fonts, they are often problematic. TrueType and Type 1 fonts are the most common high-quality fonts available today, with more and more OpenType fonts reaching the marketplace.

Fonts (also called *typefaces*) that are classified as TrueType, Type 1, or OpenType typically perform flawlessly with Illustrator. (Any font, however, is subject to corruption over time and may need to be reinstalled.) You can use bitmap fonts, but they don't use all of Illustrator's capabilities and they may not print properly.

## Fonts and Font Families

Technically, a certain typeface at a certain size in a certain style constitutes a font. More generally, we tend to use the term *font* to refer to an entire family of fonts. For example, Times 12 pt is a different font from Times 24 pt and Times (Italic) or Times (Bold). Each was designed to serve a separate purpose. Colloquially, we refer to all the Times typefaces as a single font. Technically, Times is a font family, with numerous individual fonts.

When does terminology make a difference? Primarily today, the subject comes up in marketing. Such-and-such laser printer may have 52 fonts installed, and a competitor might claim more than 250 fonts. One font package could include more than 1,000 fonts, and another might have 85 font families. As long as you are aware of the difference in terminology, you can make informed decisions.

> You may also find some multiple master fonts available, but Adobe has discontinued that technology in favor of OpenType, and Illustrator no longer includes a Multiple Master palette or support for such fonts.

## CID and OpenType Fonts

The CID (Character Identification) and OpenType font families support extended characters rather than being limited to 256 letters, numbers, and symbols. The larger number of characters available makes these types of fonts highly appropriate for CJK (Chinese-Japanese-Korean) character sets. CID fonts are an extension of the Type 1 architecture, so they perform well with Illustrator. CID fonts use ID numbers to index and access characters. This system is more efficient than the name-based access system used by Type 1 fonts.

OpenType fonts are cross-platform, working on both Macintosh and Windows computers. In addition, each OpenType font requires a single file to include the entire font family. Multiple glyphs for each character are incorporated into many OpenType fonts. (*Glyphs* are the individual representations of a character, such as the lowercase and small caps versions of the same letter.)

## Adding and Managing Fonts

In Windows, fonts are stored in a couple different folders. You'll find a folder named Fonts at C:\Program Files\Common Files\Adobe. In it are those fonts installed by Adobe programs. Generally speaking, however, you add new fonts to the main Fonts folder, shown in Figure 27.1. Use the Control Panel (in the Start menu) to add fonts.

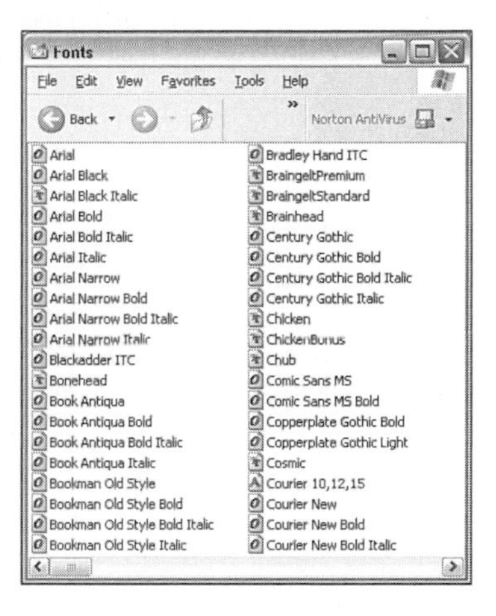


Figure 27.1
In the second column, note the bitmap font Courier 10, 12, 15. This and several other bitmap fonts are required by Windows and should never be deleted. They are identifiable by the red letter *A* icon.

Macintosh users have fonts in quite a variety of places on the hard drive. The primary Fonts folders are found in the main Library folder, the Library folder at the user level (for each user), in the main Application Support folder, and in the Application Support folder at the user level (for each user). Additional Fonts folders might be found inside individual program folders, as well as in a number of other locations (including, if installed, the OS 9 System Folder).

To add fonts in OS X, copy them to one of the two primary Fonts folders. To make the fonts available to all users, add them to the Fonts folder in the main Library folder (see Figure 27.2). If a font needs to be restricted to one or more users, perhaps for licensing reasons, add it to the Fonts folder in the Library folder for that user or users.

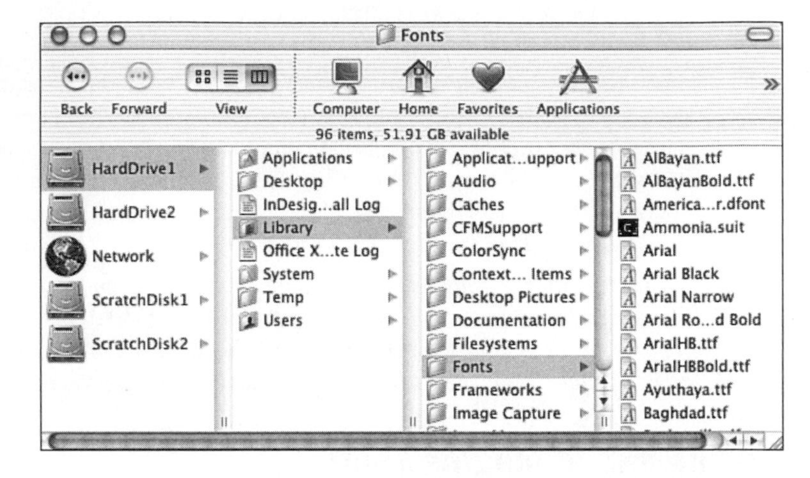


Figure 27.2
You'll find the primary Fonts folder on the hard drive on which the OS is installed, in the Library folder.

Keep in mind that having too many fonts installed and active can slow your programs and may actually overload them. Having more than a few hundred fonts can result in an abridged Font menu in Illustrator, with some fonts missing from the list.

The Macintosh Panther operating system includes Font Book, which can be used to create font collections and activate fonts only when needed. Those using earlier versions of Mac OS X and Windows users can purchase font-management utilities, such as Suitcase from Extensis.

## Fixing Font Problems

Fonts can become corrupted. If you suddenly find that a favorite font is no longer available or you get warnings about missing or bad fonts when opening documents, you may need to replace the font in question.

In Windows, find the font in My Computer/Windows Explorer and double-click it. If the font is in good shape, Windows Font Viewer will launch and display the font. (You can also print a sample sheet of the font from Font Viewer.) If the font has indeed gone bad, Font Viewer likely will have trouble opening it. You can reinstall the font from the original source. If the font is found inside the main Fonts folder, it may have been installed with Windows or with a program, or you might have installed it using the Control Panel. If you can open the font with Font Viewer, the copyright information may give you a hint about the source.



Mac OS X includes KeyCaps in the Applications, Utilities folder. You can use that program to check the integrity of a font. Remember, too, that you can Control-click a font file and select Get Info from the contextual menu. The Get Info box may have information about the source of the font. Panther users can use Font Book's Font Viewer capability to verify fonts.

If the font problem is specific to Illustrator (or another member of the Adobe Creative Suite), the font itself might be in perfect order. The source of trouble might instead be the file AdobeFnt.lst (which may or may not have a two-digit number after AdobeFnt). A search for AdobeFnt with My Computer/Windows Explorer (Windows) or the Finder (Mac) will locate the file (or files). Quit all Adobe programs and delete the AdobeFnt file(s). The font list will be regenerated when you next start each program.

Illustrator CS also provides a warning if fonts are missing (see Figure 27.3). If you click Open, Illustrator substitutes another font. If you click Cancel, the file is not opened. Once the file is open, the menu command Type, Find Font is available. You can have Illustrator highlight text that uses missing fonts. In the Document Setup dialog box's Type section, check the box labeled Highlight: Substituted Fonts.

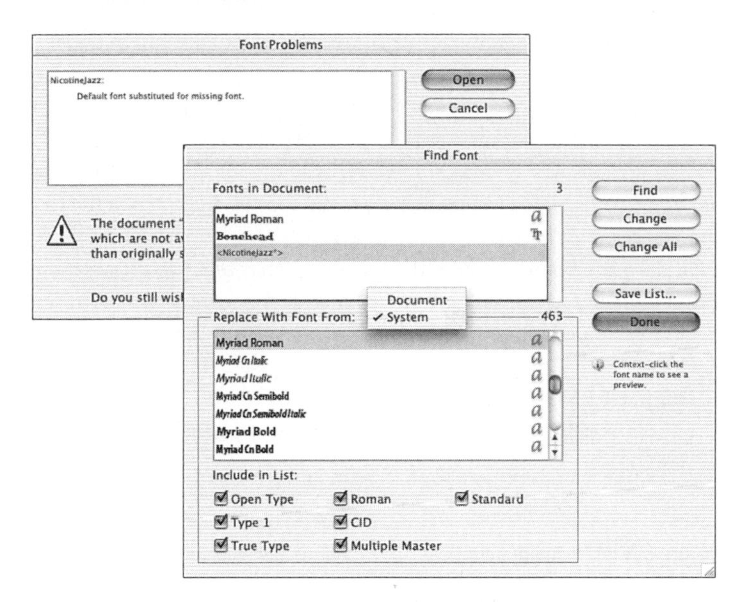


Figure 27.3
Illustrator doesn't offer you a chance to locate the missing font when opening a document (rear dialog box) but does offer a capability to locate a missing font or select a suitable substitute (front dialog box).

*For more information on locating fonts and font substitution, see "The Type Menu," later in this chapter.*

# ILLUSTRATOR'S TYPE TOOLS

The Type tool (default keyboard shortcut T) has six variations. You can choose from horizontal and vertical versions of three different functions. In addition to inserting new text, you can use the type tools to select text that is already present in the document. Click and drag with a type tool to select all or part of a section of text. After you select the text, you can edit the type or change its attributes.

## Type Tool and Vertical Type Tool

The type tools place horizontal and vertical type at any point in a document. Select the tool in the Toolbox and click once anywhere on the artboard to begin entering type. If the point where you need to place text is already occupied by an object, lock or hide that object in the Layers palette to prevent it from being converted to a type container. (Type containers are discussed later in this chapter.)

After you click with the Type tool, you can begin typing your text. While you're in this mode, Illustrator functions as a basic word processor. The single-key keyboard shortcuts (V for the Move tool, M for the Rectangle tool, Tab to show/hide palettes, Return or Enter to accept changes) are not available when you're entering text. Pressing one of those keys, most naturally, adds that letter or special character to the text being entered. After you finish entering text, click another tool in the Toolbox or (Command)-click [Ctrl]-click away from the text to retain the Type tool.

You also can use these tools to create text boxes. Click and drag with either type tool to create a rectangular area in which you can enter text. The text wraps from line to line to stay within the rectangle. Such text boxes are invisible and nonprinting unless you choose to fill or stroke them with color.

If the text you enter doesn't fit in the rectangle, you have several options. In addition to choosing a new font size, shortening the text, or adjusting spacing and leading, you can resize the rectangle or have the text continue in another box. A small indicator appears in the lower-right corner of the rectangle to indicate text overflow. When the small box with the plus sign appears, your text no longer fits in the rectangle. To resize the box, use the Selection tool and drag one of the bounding box handles. If the Type tool is active, you can simply hold down the (Command) [Ctrl] key to activate the Selection tool. Illustrator gives you a live update of how the text will appear by indicating the baselines of the lines of text. As you drag the bounding box, the baselines shift and reposition themselves to show you how the text will flow in the resized box. Figure 27.4 shows how Illustrator indicates both text overflow and text reflow when you're resizing a bounding box.

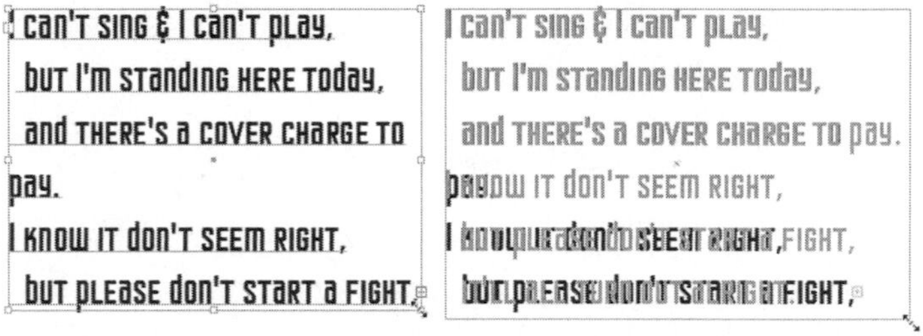

**Figure 27.4**
To the left, the text doesn't fit the bounding box and a plus sign appears in the square near the bounding box's lower-right corner. To the right, the text reflow is previewed as the bounding box is expanded to fit the text.

*Do you absolutely have to make the text fit into a container of a specific size? Can' t stand the thought of reducing your font size any further? See "Copyfitting" in the "Mastering Illustrator" section at the end of this chapter.*

Be sure that you do not have anything else selected when resizing a text rectangle. If more than one object on the artboard is active, Illustrator treats the text within the rectangle as an object, scaling it along with the box. Figure 27.5 shows an example.



**Figure 27.5**
When you have both the text rectangle and object rectangle selected, Illustrator resizes the type.

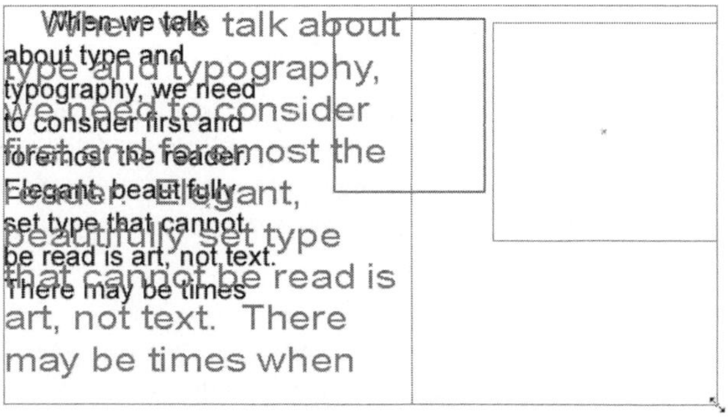

The text within the box is resized along with the rectangle. The overflow text is still not visible, and the text that was visible is distorted in size and shape.

When the Type or Vertical Type tool is positioned over an object or a path, it automatically changes to the Area Type or Path Type tool (or the tool's vertical counterpart).

## Area Type Tool and Vertical Area Type Tool

Using the Area Type tool, you can enter text into any shape, including open paths. Figure 27.6 shows some examples.

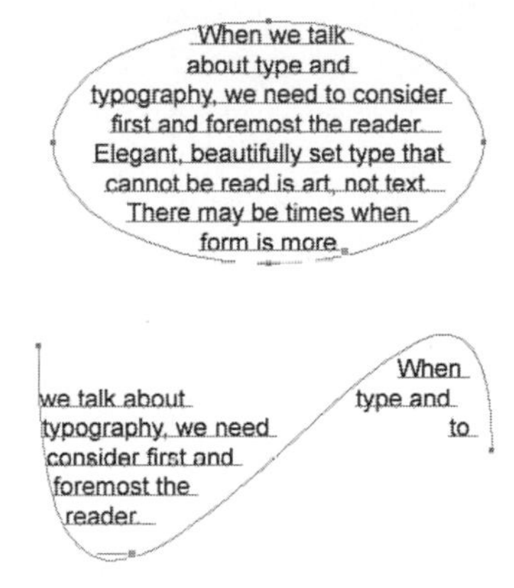
When we talk
about type and
typography, we need to consider
first and foremost the reader.
Elegant, beautifully set type that
cannot be read is art, not text.
There may be times when
form is more
When
type and
to
we talk about
typography, we need
consider first and
foremost the
reader.
When we talk
about type and
typography, we
need to consider
first and foremost
the reader. Elegant,
beautifully set type
that cannot be read
is art, not text.
There may be times
when form is more
important than
function, but
generally speaking,
we should consider
the legibility of our
type as paramount.

**Figure 27.6**
Regardless of whether you create a path with an object tool or the Pen tool and whether it's open or closed, Illustrator can fill the path with text.

Notice that the two text containers to the left in the figure show the text-overflow symbol at the lower right. Also, note that the oval's text is center aligned, whereas the open path and rectangle are left aligned. Alignment is controlled through the Paragraph palette.

When you select an open path, Illustrator fills an area with text, just as it does with the fill color, drawing an invisible straight line between the two endpoints. Area type is also required to wrap text around an object. This will be discussed later in this chapter, in the section "Wrapping Text Around Objects."

By default, any object or path that is filled with text loses its fill and stroke. Any changes made to the fill and stroke swatches with the object and text selected are applied to the text. To add color to the fill or stroke of the text container, select it with the Direct Selection tool and use the Color or Swatches palette to add color. Figure 27.7 shows an example of coloring a text container.

## Type on a Path Tool and Vertical Type on a Path Tool

Just as a text container receives a stroke and fill of None, so, too, does a path along which type has been placed. Using the Type tool, Vertical Type tool, Type on a Path tool, or Vertical Type on a Path tool, you can click a path to have the text flow along it. In Figure 27.8, the text paths are invisible but loosely parallel stroked paths.

**Figure 27.7**
Using the Direct Selection tool, you can select the text container independently of the text.

**Figure 27.8**
The text paths help convey the message.

The text can be repositioned along a path. Using the Selection or Direct Selection tool, click the text. Click directly on the I-beam and drag the text to a new position, as shown in Figure 27.9.

You can also flip text by dragging the I-beam across the path. This technique also works with closed paths. Figure 27.10 shows an example.

The initial direction of text flow is determined by the path's direction of creation. The order in which the path's anchor points were placed determines in which direction the text will flow. Figure 27.11 shows this flow graphically.

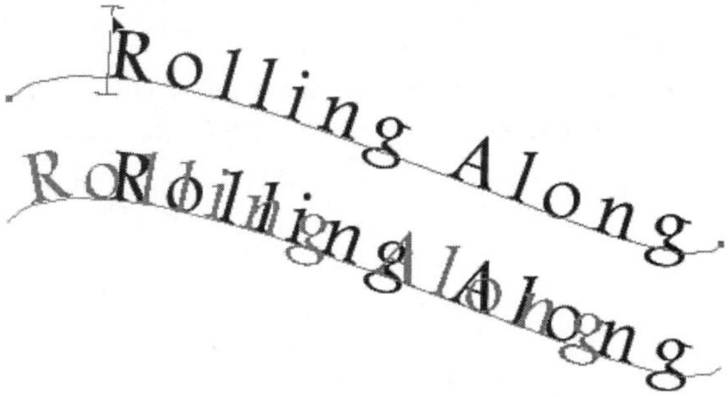

Figure 27.9
The text maintains its flow and attributes when repositioned.

Figure 27.10
The cursor shows the position of the I-beam, which regulates the start position of the text.

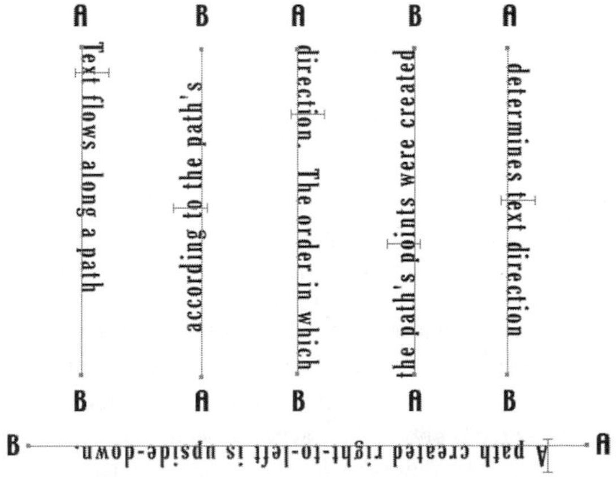

Figure 27.11
Each path was created from *A* to *B*. That is, the Pen tool was clicked near the letter *A* and then near the letter *B* to draw each path.

# Type-Related Preferences

Perhaps the most important Illustrator preference for type is not found with the others. When you open Preferences, Units & Display Performance, you'll find the setting that determines the unit of measure for type. It is shown in Figure 27.12.

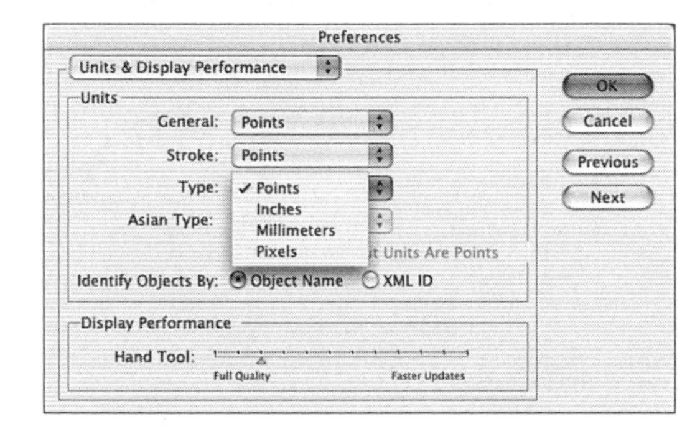


**Figure 27.12**
This dialog box contains several choices for measuring type.

Points are the standard unit of measure for type in the United States. There are 72 points in an inch. Illustrator also offers several alternatives. Inches and millimeters are self-explanatory. Pixels are the same as points when you're working with a standard of 72 pixels per inch (ppi). The unit of measure selected here is used not only for font size but also for all other type-related preferences and palettes.

The remainder of Illustrator's type-related preferences have their own dialog box. You can access the Type & Auto Tracing panel of the Preferences dialog box, as shown in Figure 27.13, by choosing Preferences, Type & Auto Tracing.

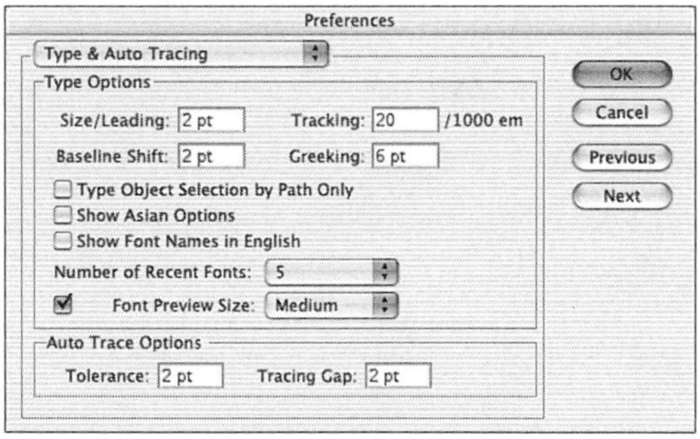

**Figure 27.13**
The Auto Trace Options area has nothing to do with type or text. It merely shares the Preferences dialog box.

The type preferences are global, affecting all documents with editable type opened or created in Illustrator. You can change them at any time, but you cannot save them with individual documents. Three of the preferences listed here involve keyboard shortcuts:

- **Size/Leading**—These preference values determine the increment when you use the keyboard to adjust type size or leading. *Leading* is the amount of space between lines of type, measured from baseline to baseline. The unit of measure is determined by that set for the type size in the Units & Undo panel of the Preferences dialog box. The keyboard shortcuts to increase and decrease a font's size are (Command-Shift->) [Ctrl+Shift+>] and (Command-Shift-<) [Ctrl+Shift+<]. To increase or decrease leading, you use (Option) [Alt] and the up- or down-arrow key.

- **Tracking**—This preference value determines the keyboard increment for both tracking and kerning. (*Tracking* is the spacing between characters in a line of type; *kerning* is the spacing between two adjacent characters.) The unit of measure is determined by that set for the type size in the Units & Undo panel of the Preferences dialog box. The default value is 20/1000 of an em space. An *em space* is a distance equivalent to that needed for an em dash in the particular font being used. An em dash (—) is larger than a hyphen (-) and is historically the width of the uppercase letter *M* in a typeface. You can change tracking and kerning from the keyboard by using (Option) [Alt] and the left- and right-arrow keys. If two letters are selected, kerning is changed. If more than two characters are selected, tracking is adjusted.

> Both the Macintosh and Windows versions of Illustrator use the 72ppi standard. You can verify this unit of measure by opening Preferences, Units & Undo and setting the General unit of measure to Inches. Choose File, New and look at the default dimensions; then click Cancel. Now change the General unit of measure to Pixels and check the default dimension of a new document. That 8.5-by-11-inch document is now listed as 612 pixels by 792 pixels. Dividing 612 pixels by 8.5 inches and dividing 792 pixels by 11 inches gives you 72ppi.

- **Baseline Shift**—This preference value determines the keyboard increment for *baseline shift*, the distance above or below the line along which type is set. The unit of measure is determined by that set for the type size in the Units & Undo panel of the Preferences dialog box. (Option-Shift) [Alt+Shift] and the up- and down-arrow keys adjust the baseline of selected text.

- **Greeking**—Text is *greeked*, displayed as a linear placeholder, when it is too small to be displayed on the monitor. The value entered in the preferences is for use at 100% zoom. If you change the zoom factor to 50%, text at twice the specified size also gets greeked. Figure 27.14 gives a comparable demonstration.

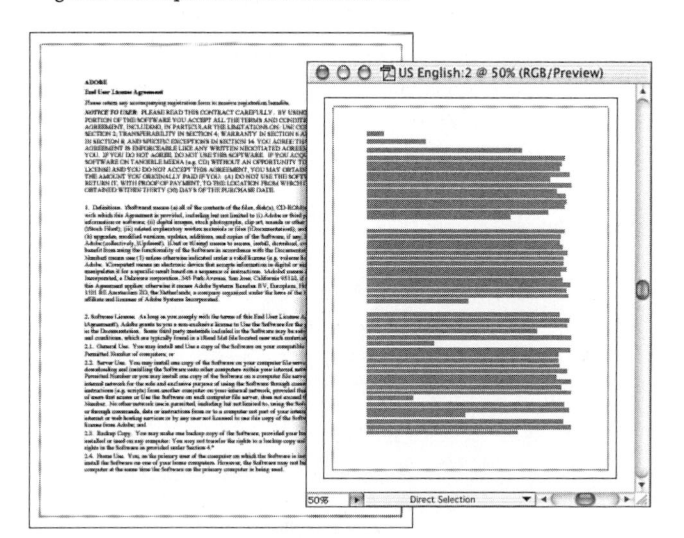


**Figure 27.14**
The inset window is zoomed out to 50%, and the body text must be greeked because it is too small to be displayed properly.

- **Type Object Selection by Path Only**—With this option unchecked, you can click with a selection tool anywhere on text to select it. When this option is checked, you must click the type's baseline to select the text. (In prior versions of Illustrator, this option was named Type Area Select.)
- **Show Asian Options**—Illustrator includes a number of options for fine-tuning the appearance of Asian fonts. When this option is selected in the Preferences dialog box, the Character and Paragraph palettes show options used only with Asian fonts, including those shown in Figure 27.15.

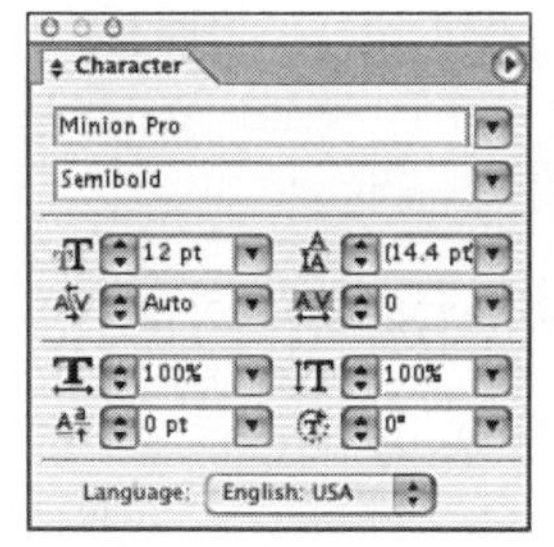


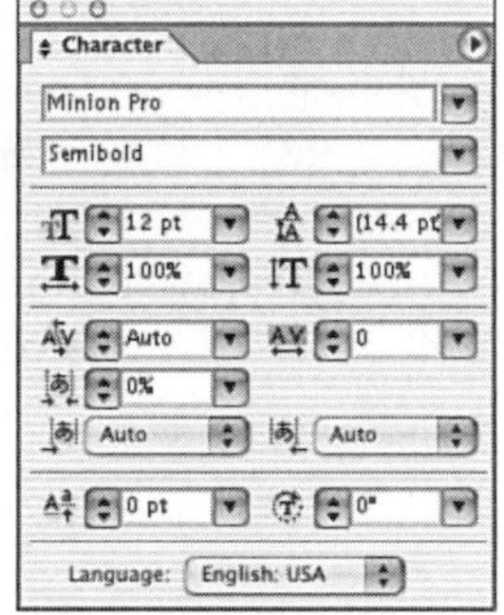


**Figure 27.15**
As you can see, the Character palette is reorganized when the Asian font options are showing. The three additional options visible in the palette configuration to the right control spacing around characters and are used only with CJK fonts.

- **Show Font Names in English**—When you're working with double-byte fonts, specifically CJK (Chinese-Japanese-Korean) fonts, this option determines which language will be used to show the name of the font in the menu and palette listings.
- **Number of Recent Fonts**—New in Illustrator CS is a list of the most recently used fonts in the Type menu. Using the new submenu can save you considerable time when moving back and forth among several fonts. This Preferences option determines how long the list will be.
- **Font Preview Size**—Also new in Illustrator CS is a font menu that shows you the font names in their own font (see Figure 27.16). The options in the Preferences dialog box determine whether or not the handy-but-somewhat-slower new menu will be used (the check box to the left of Font Preview Size) and how large the sample fonts will be in the menu.

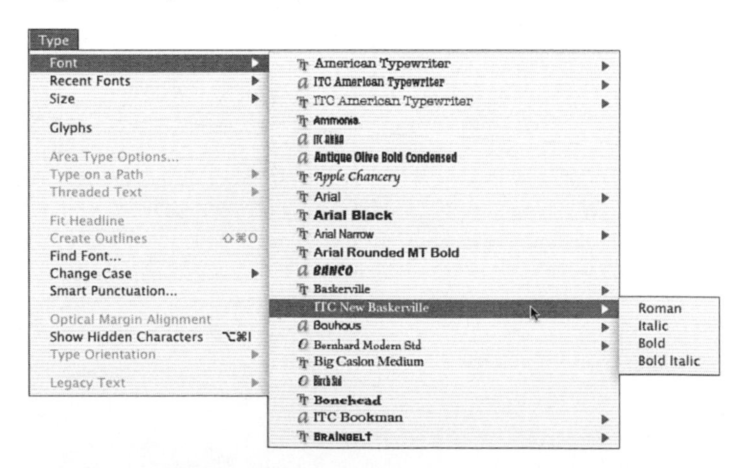


**Figure 27.16**
Note that the new Font menu also shows you what type of font you're selecting. The double-*T* icon indicates TrueType, the *a* symbol is used for PostScript Type 1 fonts, and the stylized *O* tells you the font is OpenType.

## Type Tool Operation

Some general rules cover the Type tools:

- Click anywhere in a document with the Type or Vertical Type tool to start placing text.
- Click any shape with the Area Type or Vertical Area Type tool to place text in that shape.
- Use the Path Type or Vertical Path Type tool to place text along any open or closed path.
- Double-clicking with any text tool within text selects an entire word. Triple-clicking selects an entire paragraph.
- When a block or line of text is not selected, Shift-clicking with any type tool at any point within text automatically highlights text from that point to the beginning of the text.
- Shift-clicking when the text is already active makes a selection from the point Shift-clicked to the previous blinking insertion point.
- When a text tool is active and the cursor is within text, you can hold down Shift and use the right- or left-arrow key to add to or subtract from (or make) a selection one letter at a time. Add (Command) [Ctrl] to add or subtract entire words, one at a time.
- With the cursor inside a block of text, hold down Shift and use the up- or down-arrow key to add an entire line to or subtract it from a selection. (Command-Shift) [Ctrl+Shift] and the up- and down-arrows keys alter the selection a paragraph at a time.
- When you're editing type, you can use any of the Type tools to highlight (select) text.
- Using the Selection tool to alter the bounding box of text set with a type tool (vertical or horizontal) changes the size and shape of the text.
- Using the Selection tool to alter the bounding box of text set with an area type tool (vertical or horizontal) changes the shape of the object and may change the amount of visible text within the object. However, the type retains its size, shape, and other characteristics.
- Using the Selection tool to alter the bounding box of text set with a path type tool (vertical or horizontal) changes the path and the size and shape of the type, and it may change the distribution of type along the path.



# THE PALETTES

Seven of Illustrator's palettes are devoted to text. Like other palettes in Illustrator, they are shown and hidden using the Window menu. However, you'll find them in the Type submenu. The palettes, along with the floating Type tools, are shown in Figure 27.17.

## The Character Palette

The default keyboard shortcut to show and hide the Character palette is (Command-T) [Ctrl+T]. It is normally grouped with the Paragraph palette.

Figure 27.17
Illustrator CS's four new palettes enable you to take advantage of the additional characters in OpenType fonts, as well as to create and apply character and paragraph presets, known as *styles*.

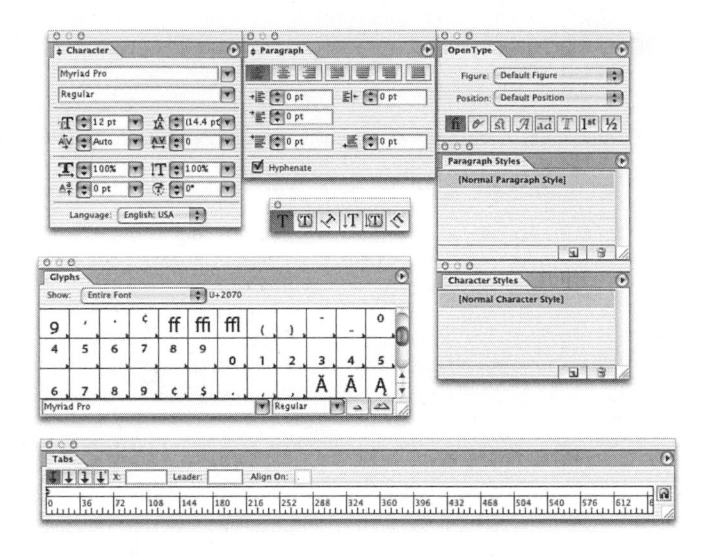


The first of the palette's four sections determines the font. The pop-up menu uses submenus for font styles, such as bold, condensed, italic, and regular. The keyboard shortcut (Command-Z) [Ctrl+Z] works to undo font changes.

The second section determines font size, leading, kerning, and tracking. Briefly, *leading* (pronounced as the metal *lead* rather than the verb *to lead*) is the space between rows of type. *Kerning* is the space between two letters, and *tracking* is uniform space between letters in a word or several words.

The palette's third section, which you show by double-clicking the palette's tab or by choosing the palette menu command Show Options, controls the appearance of individual characters. Using the designated font size, you can increase or decrease the height and width of one or more selected characters. *Baseline shift*, the placement of a character above or below the others as a superscript or subscript character, is also controlled here. New is Illustrator CS is the Character Rotation field (see Figure 27.18).

Figure 27.18
Character rotation can be applied to a single selected character, as shown, or to an entire type object.

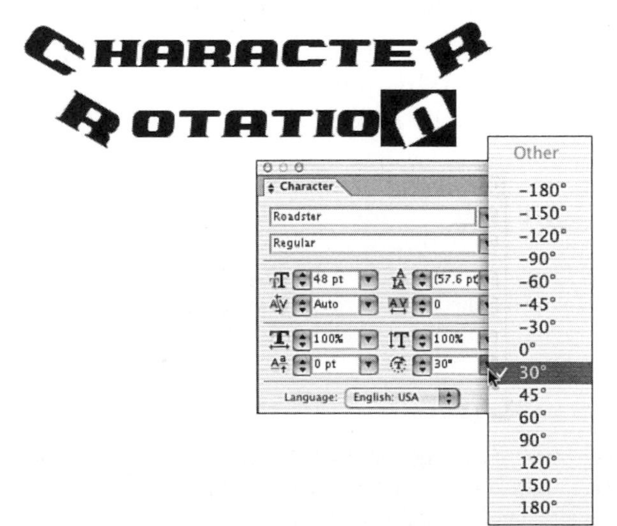

The bottom portion of the palette enables you to select a language for the selected type or type object. The Language option determines what dictionary will be used for checking spelling.

Remember, too, that in Illustrator CS, the Asian font options are shown or hidden in the Character and Paragraph palettes through the Preferences dialog box. (See Figure 27.15 and the section "Type-Related Preferences," earlier in this chapter, for additional information.)

## The Character Styles Palette

Character styles are saved sets of character options. Any option that you can select in the Character palette can be saved in a character style. To create a character style, set some type and use the Character palette to establish the options you want for the character style. Select the text and click the Create New Style button in the Character Styles palette. You can also (Option)-click [Alt]-click the Create New Style button at the bottom of the Character Styles palette and then set the options in the Character Styles Options dialog box (see Figure 27.19). You can change style options in the dialog box by double-clicking the style in the Character Styles palette.

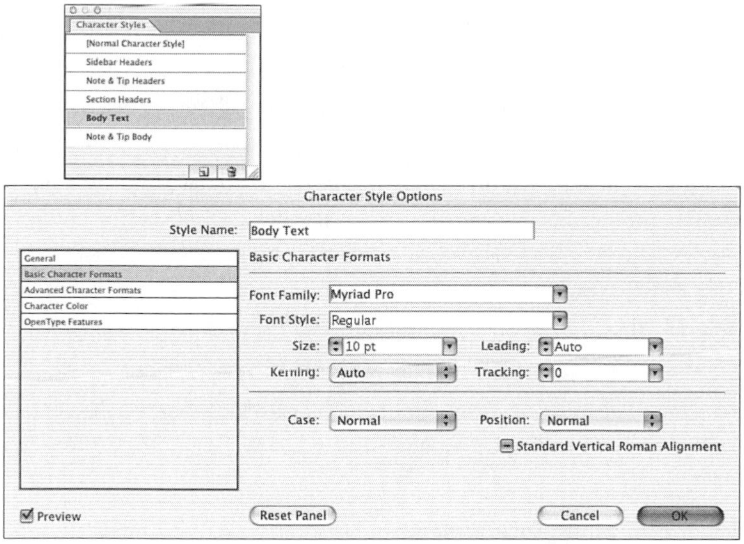

**Figure 27.19**
Double-click the style name in the Character Styles palette to open the Character Style Options dialog box. You can also open the dialog box when creating a new character style by holding down the Option [Alt] key when clicking the Create New Style button in the Character palette.

Use character styles for any type appearance that you may need to replicate in the document. Create a style, select the type to which you want to apply it, and then click the style in the Character Styles palette. You can also use styles to produce consistency from document to document. Save your styles with the first document you create; then, in later documents, use the Character Styles palette menu command Load Styles or Load All Styles to access the original document and load the styles into the current document.

## The Paragraph Palette

You open the Paragraph palette through the Type submenu of the Window menu, or with the default keyboard shortcut (Command-Option-T) [Ctrl+Alt+T]. Figure 27.20 shows this palette with its options visible, as well as the Hyphenation dialog box.

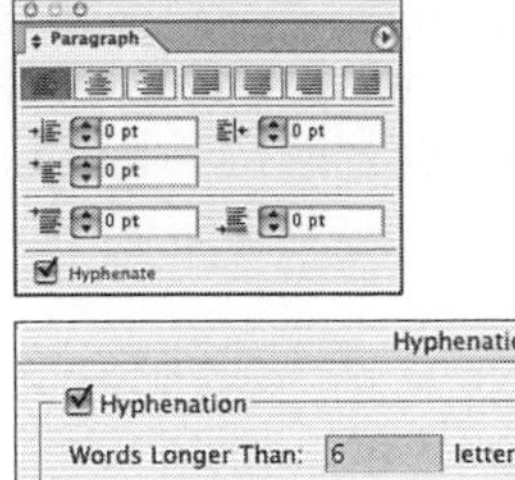


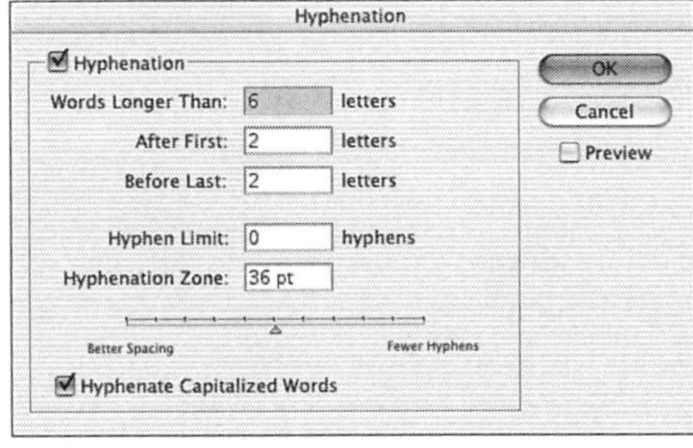


**Figure 27.20**
You access the Hyphenation dialog box through a command in the palette menu.

You can use the Paragraph palette to change the options for a selected paragraph or paragraphs, or, if no text is selected, you can establish options for all later text:

- The seven boxes across the top of the palette control paragraph alignment. Following the left, center, and right alignment buttons are options to justify all full lines and to justify all lines, even if they are not full.
- Below the alignment buttons are two entry fields that control the left and right indent of a paragraph. The unit of measure is that specified for the type size in the Units & Undo panel of the Preferences dialog box. Below the two indent options is an option to indent just the first line of a paragraph. The left indent and first line indent can also be controlled using the tab ruler.
- The third section of the palette offers the option of adding space before each paragraph (left) or after each paragraph (right). The fields are independent and can be used together.
- The Hyphenate check box allows Illustrator to automatically hyphenate long words at the ends of lines. You access the options, shown in the Hyphenation dialog box in Figure 27.20, through the Paragraph palette menu.

The first three hyphenation options are self-explanatory. Hyphen Limit refers to the number of consecutive lines that can end in a hyphen. (Having several hyphens, one below the other, can attract unwanted attention to the right margin of a paragraph.) A value of 0 permits unlimited consecutive hyphenated lines. Hyphenation Zone establishes a protected zone near the right margin in which hyphenation is not permitted. It is used only when Single-line Composer is selected in the Paragraph palette's menu.

Also visible in Figure 27.20 is the Better Spacing/Fewer Hyphens bar. Dragging the slider or clicking a tick mark selects a compromise between an overall improvement in the spacing of the paragraph (at the cost of a possible increase in the number of hyphenated words) and fewer hyphens (which can result in more irregularities in word and character spacing).

Also important to consider when discussing hyphenation is the difference between the Adobe Single-line Composer and the Adobe Every-line Composer. Single-line Composer examines each line of type individually to determine how to adjust spacing. Every-line Composer examines the paragraph as a whole and generally produces a more pleasing appearance. However, you should choose Single-line Composer if you'll be manually tweaking the kerning or tracking of the text.

## The Paragraph Styles Palette

Like character styles, paragraph styles are saved sets of options. Any options that you can set in the Paragraph palette can be saved in a paragraph style. Use paragraph styles to quickly apply a preset collection of options to one or more selected paragraphs. To create a new style, select a paragraph that has the options you want for the style and then click the Create New Style button at the bottom of the Paragraph Styles palette.

In addition to maintaining consistency within a document, you can use the Paragraph Styles palette menu command Load Paragraph Styles (or Load All Styles) to maintain appearance among different documents. If you load the styles from another document into the current file, they'll appear in the appropriate palette, ready to use.

## The OpenType Palette

Adobe has thoroughly embraced the concepts behind OpenType fonts. Not only do they permit a larger number of glyphs (characters), they are completely cross-platform. All Adobe fonts have been converted to OpenType (although you'll have to purchase the new versions). Installing Illustrator added a number of OpenType fonts to your system.

The OpenType palette enables you to specify which of the available glyphs in a font you want to use. (The options available vary from font to font.) You can set the options and then add type, or you can select existing type and apply the options. Some examples of how OpenType alternate glyphs can improve the appearance of your text are shown in Figure 27.21.

Options in the OpenType palette can be saved in a character style.

fi fl ffl 1/8 2/3 3/4
fi fl ffl 1/8 2/3 3/4
1st 2nd 1234 1234
1st 2nd
boot room
boot room

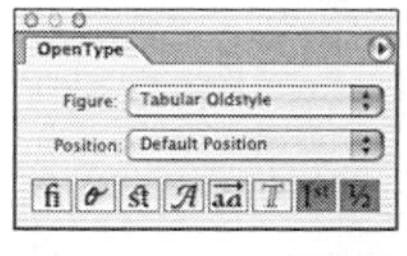


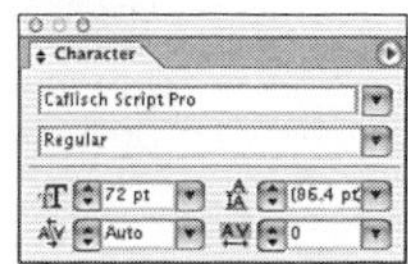


**Figure 27.21**
Using a single glyph for ligatures, fractions, and ordinals can improve the appearance and legibility of type. A ligature, single-character fraction, or a single-character ordinal can also be substantially shorter as well.

## The Glyphs Palette

The Glyphs palette is used primarily in conjunction with OpenType fonts but can be used with any font. You can display all the glyphs in a font or a selected subset (see Figure 27.22). Changing the font at the bottom of the Glyphs palette also changes the active font in the Character palette.

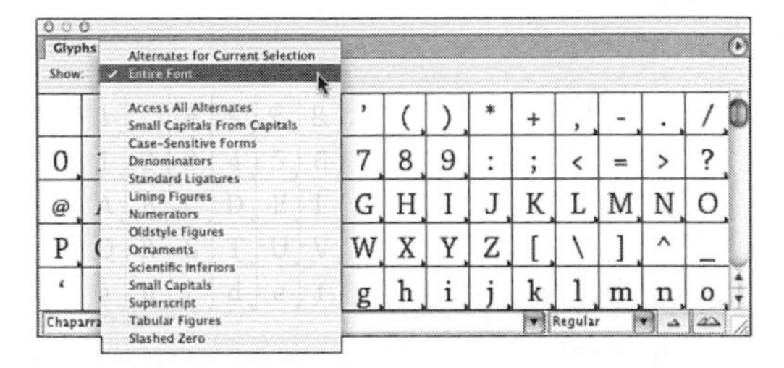


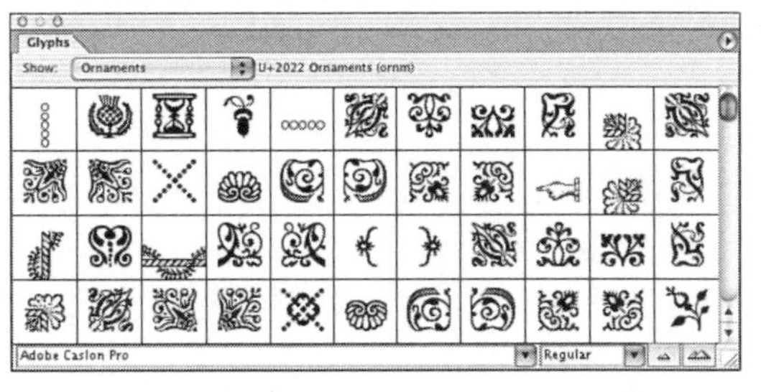


Figure 27.22
The two buttons in the lower-right corner of the palette switch between small and large glyphs. If you're in the process of adding or editing type, double-clicking a glyph adds it to the type.

## The Tabs Palette

Use the Tabs palette to add tabs to a selected block or container of type. Choose one of the four types of tabs in the upper-left corner of the palette. Click in the area above the ruler in the palette to set the tab stop. To snap to the ruler's tick marks, hold down the Shift key while clicking. You can delete a tab stop by dragging it from the palette.

To precisely place a tab stop, enter the location in the X: field. (The Tabs palette uses the unit of measure for type specified in the Preferences dialog box.) The new Leader field allows you to specify a character or a string of characters that will appear between items in your tabbed columns (see Figure 27.23). When using decimal tabs, you can specify the character on which the tab aligns in the Align On field.

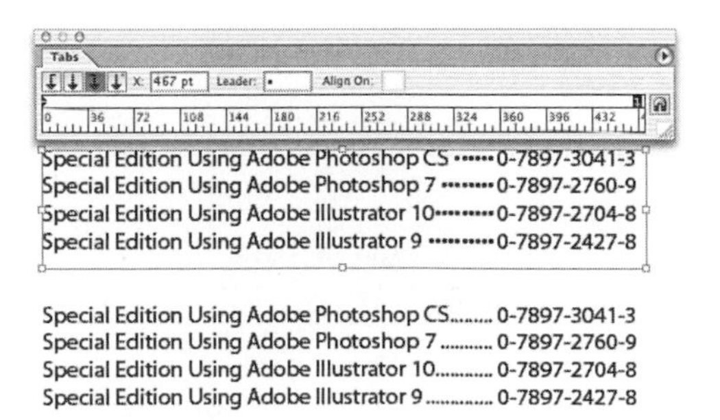


Figure 27.23
The Leader field can reproduce a single character or a string of up to eight characters. You can highlight the character and change its appearance in the Character and OpenType palettes.

The Tabs palette includes a couple other very handy features. Click the magnet icon at the right end of the palette to snap it to the currently selected type object. Create one tab at a specific distance from the indent marker and then choose Repeat Tab from the palette menu to replicate the tab stop at the specified distance across the palette. Use can also select Snap to Unit from the palette menu to ensure that new tab stops align exactly with the units of the ruler.

*Can' t get the tabs where you want them? See "Taming the Tabs" in the "Mastering Illustrator" section at the end of this chapter.*

# TYPE-RELATED MENU COMMANDS

Illustrator uses a number of menu commands related to type. Most are found in the Type menu, with a few under the Edit menu. Many of the commands are available only when a selection has been made. Others can be used to establish settings that will be applied to text placed subsequently.

## The Type Menu

Commands in Illustrator's Type menu (see Figure 27.24) include some that replicate capabilities found in the Character palette (Font and Size), the Window menu (Glyphs), and even Type tool selection (Type Orientation). Most of the commands, however, give you access to features found no where else in Illustrator.

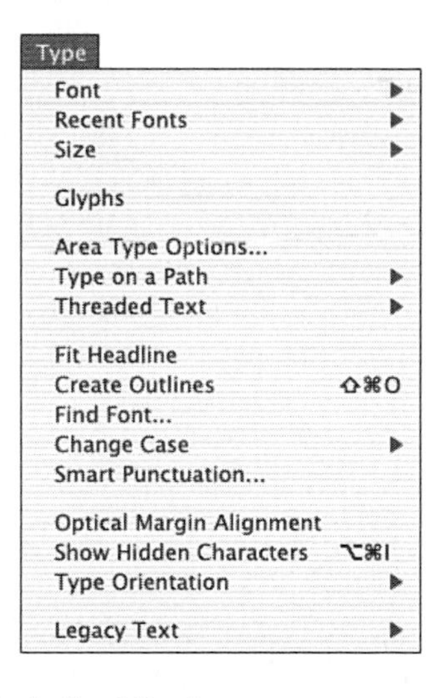


Figure 27.24
Some commands are available only when appropriate text is selected.

The Type menu commands include the following:

- **Font**—A list of all available fonts appears to the right when you drag the cursor to this command. You can have the menu show a sample of the font by checking the box to the left of Font Preview Size in Preferences, Type & Auto Tracing. Pick a font by dragging onto the list and releasing the mouse button while it's over the specific font's name. If multiple variations of the font are available, you'll see a submenu to the right. Use it to choose the specific font of the font family (regular or roman, italic, bold, condensed, and so on).

If text is selected in the document, it is changed to that font, with all other attributes and options unchanged. If None is selected, the font is used for text placed from that point on.

- **Recent Fonts**—New in Illustrator CS, this submenu shows the fonts most recently used in Illustrator. The list is not document specific. Let's say, for example, that you use Minion, Myriad, and New York in one document and then switch to another document and use Arial. All four fonts will appear in the Recent Fonts list, regardless of which document is active. The number of fonts shown can range from 1 to 15 and is set in Preferences, Type & Auto Tracing.
- **Size**—Like Font, this choice can be applied to existing type or specified for type placed in the document subsequently. In addition to the standard font sizes, this list contains the Other option, which opens the Character palette.
- **Glyphs**—The Type, Glyphs command is the same as Window, Type, Glyphs—it shows and hides the Glyphs palette (discussed earlier in this chapter).
- **Area Type Options**—When an area type object is selected, the Area Type Options command is available in the Type menu. The command opens the Area Type Options dialog box, which enables you to precisely configure the type object (see Figure 27.25).

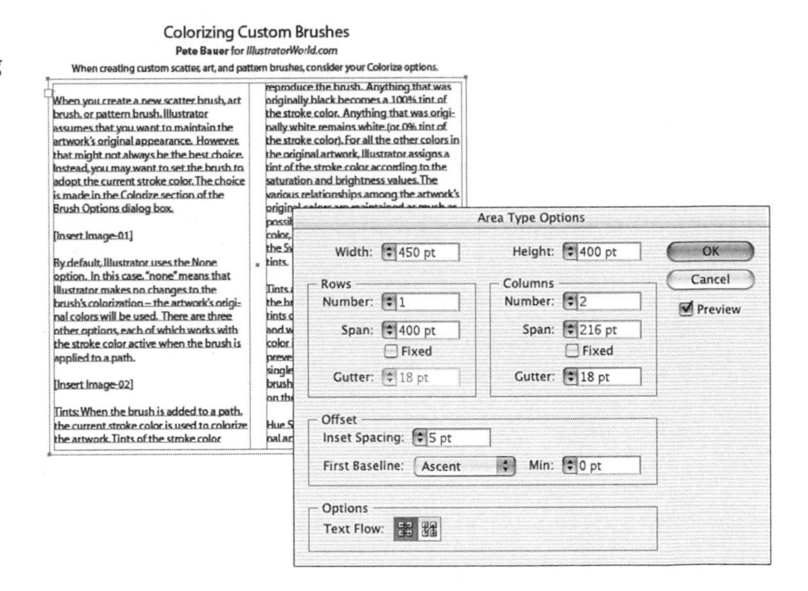


Figure 27.25
The new Area Type Options dialog box supercedes the Rows & Columns feature of earlier versions. The Width and Height fields enable you to change the overall dimensions of the type object.

- **Type on a Path**—With a type on a path object selected on the artboard, you can use this command to apply any of five variations (see Figure 27.26) and adjust the relationship between the type and the path.
- **Threaded Text**—Area type objects and/or type on path objects can be linked (or *threaded*) to permit text to flow from one object to the next. In the Type menu, you'll find commands to create and release threading, and a command to show/hide the threading indicators. The indicators, lines that show the order in which type containers are linked, are shown in Figure 27.27.

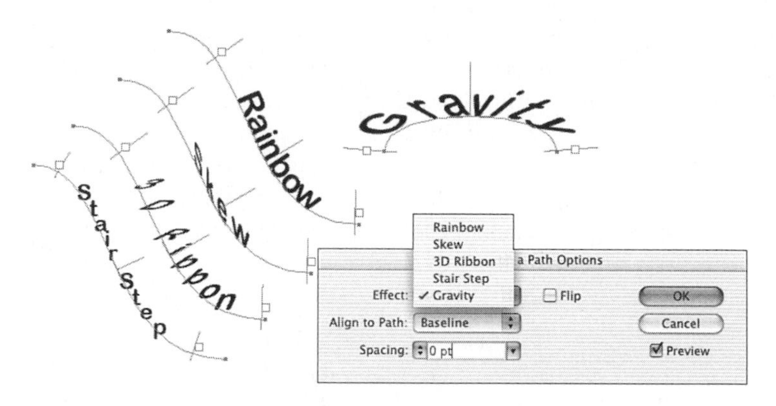


Figure 27.26
The Align to Path pop-up menu enables you to change the positional relationship between the type and the path. Spacing increases or decreases the space among letters, much like tracking.

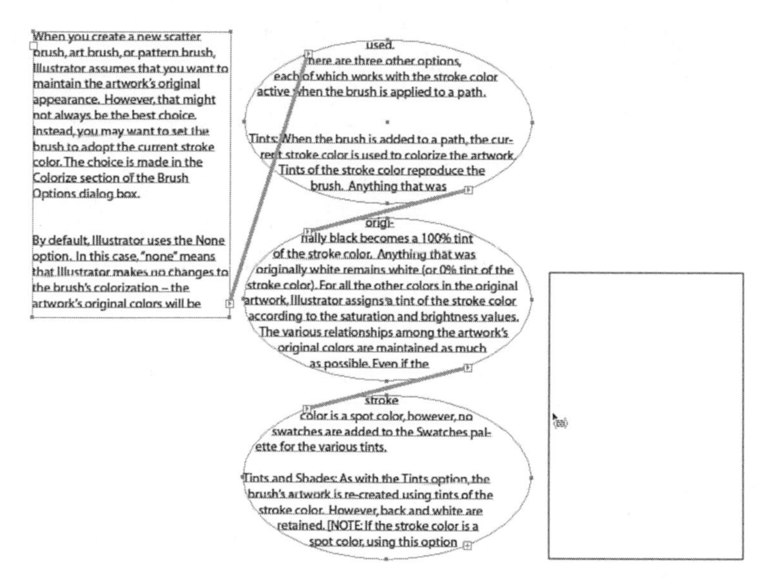


Figure 27.27
Click the text-overflow box (found in the lower right of a type container that can't show all the text) and then click another object or path to add it to the thread. The cursor changes (as shown) to indicate that you're threading text.

- **Fit Headline**—This command is designed to adjust type to fit into its container's width. Tracking is changed to spread or tighten the spacing of the letters. If you try to squeeze too much type into too narrow a container, the tracking may be reduced to the point where letters overlap and become illegible. The options then are to change the font, change the font size, enlarge the type container, and change the wording of the text.

- **Create Outlines**—This command changes type into compound paths. It is similar to the effect Outline Object. Text can no longer be edited after being converted. Create Outlines will also be discussed later in this chapter.

- **Find Font**—A powerful tool, Find Font allows you to find and replace all instances of any font in your document. You can also print lists of included fonts, which can be of great assistance when you're troubleshooting a problem file. Illustrator compiles a list of all fonts used in the document, and you can choose to replace them from a list of fonts already in the document or fonts installed on your system. (Figure 27.28 shows the System option.) To better manage the list of replacement fonts, you can check or uncheck categories of fonts below the window. OpenType, Type 1, TrueType, Multiple Master, and CID (Character Identification) can be considered technical classifications of fonts. (Note that if you want multiple master fonts to appear in the list, you must check the boxes for both Multiple Master and Type 1.) When unchecked, the Standard check box excludes the following fonts from the list: Chicago, Geneva, Helvetica, Hobo, Monaco, New York, Courier, Souvenir, Symbol, and Times. Unchecking Roman removes Western fonts from the list.

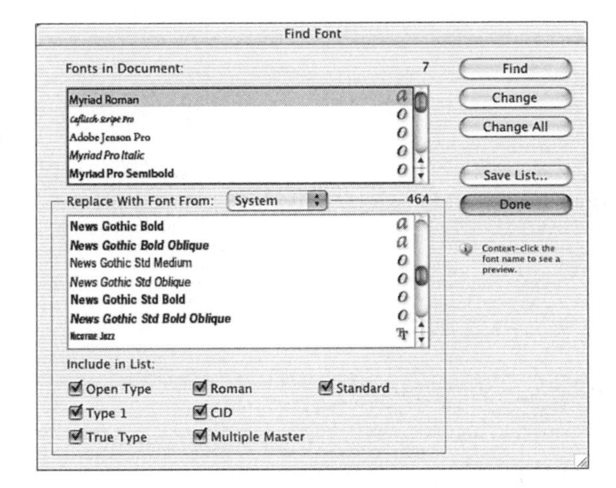


**Figure 27.28**
The Find Font dialog box also displays the type of font. Visible are the symbols for Type 1, OpenType, and TrueType fonts.

- **Change Case**—With 1-byte roman fonts (not CJK fonts), you can change selected text to and from all capital letters, all lowercase letters, and titling (first letter of each word capitalized), and you can return the "sentence case," in which the first word of a sentence is capitalized.
- **Smart Punctuation**—Using a find-and-replace technique, Smart Punctuation searches either the selected text or the entire document and replaces certain characters and symbols with their publishing equivalents. To change selected text, you must highlight it with one of the text tools. The list of possible changes is shown in the dialog box in Figure 27.29.

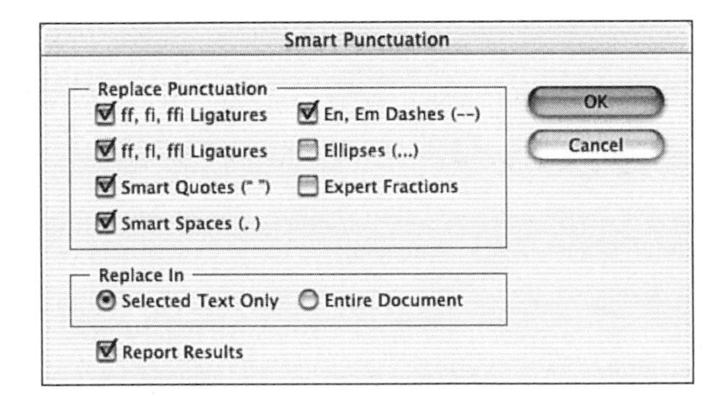


**Figure 27.29**
Smart Punctuation is available whether or not text is selected.

27

Ligatures are the lowercase letter combinations *ff*, *fi*, *fl*, *ffi*, and *ffl*. They are replaced with a single publishing symbol. Ligatures are available only when an appropriate Adobe Expert font is installed. Smart Quotes replaces the straight quotation marks with the "curly" marks used in publishing. Smart Spaces changes a double space after a period to a single space. En, Em Dashes replaces a double hyphen with an en dash and a triple hyphen with an em dash. Ellipses replaces three periods with the correct symbol. Expert Fractions (like Ligatures, available only when an appropriate Adobe Expert font is available) uses a single character for the most common fractions. Smart Punctuation also generates a report, telling you how many characters were changed. Such a report is shown in Figure 27.30.

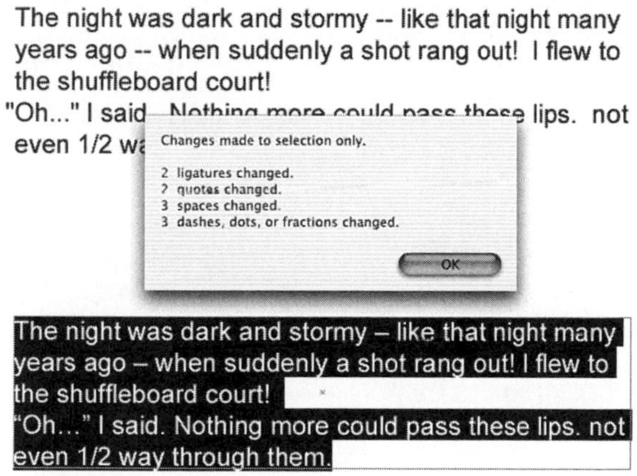

**Figure 27.30**
As you can tell by comparing the two passages, this Adobe Expert font does not contain the single-character fractions.

- **Optical Margin Alignment**—When text is justified (aligned to both margins), you can elect to use optical margin alignment. When this feature is active, punctuation marks and extensions on some letters can extend past the margin to create the appearance of a more regular margin.
- **Show Hidden Characters**—The hidden characters are nonprinting symbols. Among the hidden characters are spaces, tabs, and returns. They can be made visible for editing or troubleshooting. In Figure 27.31, the symbols for line breaks (returns), tabs, and spaces are visible.

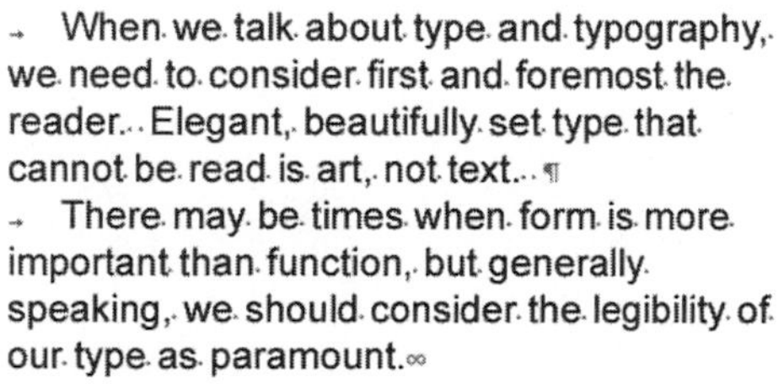

**Figure 27.31**
Whether hidden or visible, the characters that represent spaces, tabs, and paragraph returns can be selected and deleted.



- **Type Orientation**—Selected type can be switched from horizontal to vertical, and vice versa, with this command.
- **Legacy Text**—When you open a document from a previous version of Illustrator that includes type, you'll have the option of updating the text upon opening the document or not updating

the text. Because Illustrator CS uses a new type engine, updating is required for editing type. (Text that is not updated, *legacy text*, is visible in the document and can be moved and printed.) Updating text can change the flow, hyphenation, leading, tracking, and kerning of the text.

You can open a legacy document without updating text and later select specific type objects to update. Double-clicking a legacy type object opens a dialog box that offers the options of updating, creating an updated copy of the type object, and canceling the operation.

When you've elected to copy a legacy type object, all the commands in the Type, Legacy Text submenu are available (see Figure 27.32).

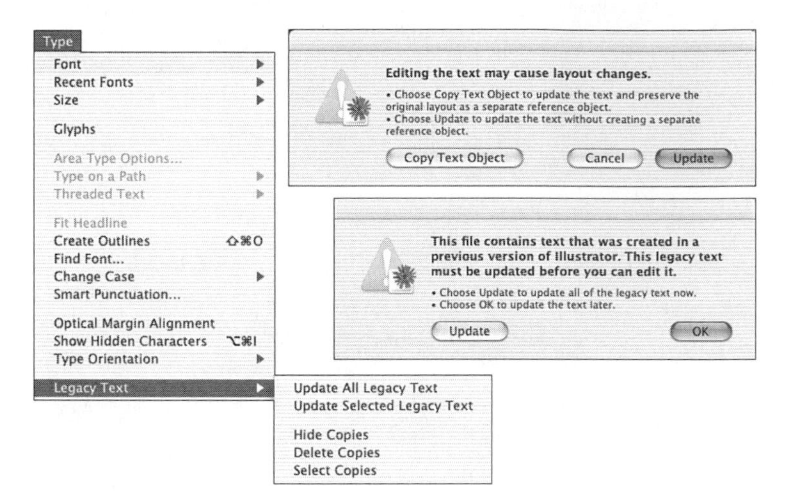


**Figure 27.32**
The dialog box in the upper right appears when you double-click a legacy type object. The dialog box to the middle right appears when you open a file with legacy text.

# Type Commands in the Edit Menu

Illustrator CS moves some of the type-related commands from the Type menu to the Edit menu:

- **Find and Replace**—Illustrator's Find and Replace dialog box, shown in Figure 27.33, enables you to look for a string of characters and replace those characters with others that you specify. Generally, it's used to swap one word or phrase for another. You can search in one or more selected type objects or search the entire document by ensuring that no text is selected before using Find and Replace.
- **Find Next**—Find Next is used in conjunction with Find and Replace. Once a word or character string has been identified in Find and Replace, you can use the Find Next command to select the next instance in the active type object. (The Find and Replace dialog box need not be open to use Find Next.)
- **Check Spelling**—Like Find and Replace, Illustrator's Check Spelling is a reasonably competent, no-frills feature. Any word not recognized is highlighted, and you have the choice of leaving the word as is (Ignore), changing to one of the suggested replacements, typing your own replacement, or adding the word to your custom dictionary.
- **Edit Custom Dictionary**—When words have been added to your custom dictionary, you can delete or change each entry. Illustrator uses a single custom dictionary for all documents.

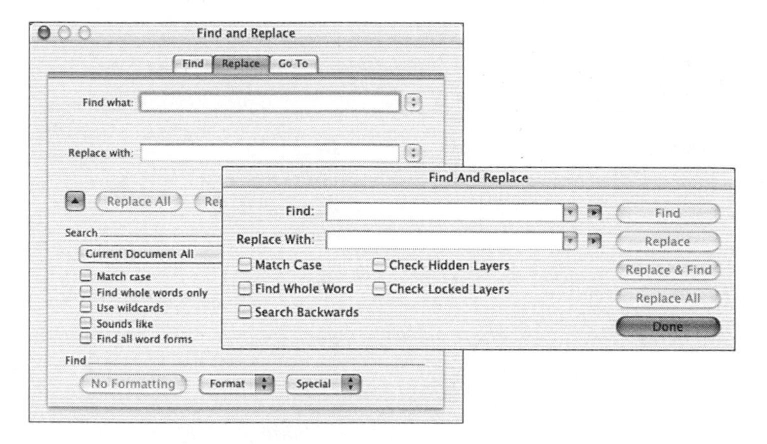


Figure 27.33
Illustrator's Find and Replace capability is not nearly as sophisticated as that found in a dedicated word processor, such as Microsoft Word (shown in the background).

# CUSTOMIZING TEXT CONTAINERS

Any shape can contain text in Illustrator, including open paths. In addition, Illustrator can wrap text outside objects. Type containers can have strokes and fills to customize their appearance.

## Wrapping Text Around Objects

Just as text can be placed inside objects, Illustrator can wrap text around objects and paths. You need to keep in mind a few important concepts:

- You must place a path around placed bitmap images. The text can wrap around identifiable paths only.
- The objects or paths around which the type will be wrapped must be in front of the type.
- Text flows directly against the path. Adding a path some distance beyond an object to create a margin is often worthwhile.
- An unstroked, unfilled path can create an invisible boundary around which you can wrap type. This boundary can be smaller than the object, as long as the object itself is not also selected for wrapping. Figure 27.34 shows an example.

  Note that the capital *T* in Figure 27.34 is technically neither a *drop cap* (top-aligned with the following text) nor a *raised cap* (bottom-aligned with the following text).
- After you wrap paths, you can select and edit them, and the wrap will reconfigure and adapt to the object's new path. This capability can be especially useful with unstroked, unfilled paths, such as described earlier in this list.

To easily create a margin around an object, follow these steps:

1. Select the object.
2. Copy the object using (Command-C) [Ctrl+C].
3. Paste the copy directly in front of the original object using the command Paste in Front. The keyboard shortcut is (Command-F) [Ctrl+F].
4. Choose Effect, Path, Offset Path. Enter an amount equal to the desired margin. Then click OK.
5. Change the stroke and fill of the enlarged copy to None. Then wrap the text around it rather than the original.

Figure 27.34
The unstroked, unfilled path is actually smaller than the capital *T*, allowing the text to wrap a bit more closely.

*The beginning of the Beginning came first, as it is wont to do. It was closely followed by the middle of the Beginning, most logically. To our surprise, however, the next in succession was not the end of the Beginning, but rather the beginning of the End. Most curious, the circumstances surrounding this turn of events. Most curious, indeed. And therein lies the tale...*

Figure 27.35 shows an example of text being wrapped around multiple objects. Notice that each placed bitmap image is surrounded by a path. Also, note that the text is very tightly aligned to those paths.

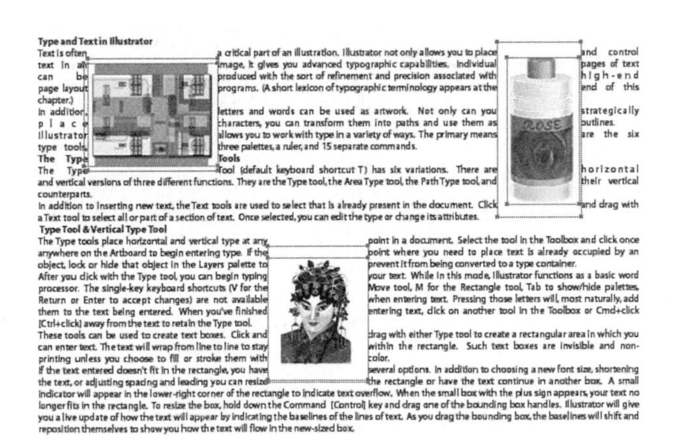

**Type and Text in Illustrator**
Text is often a critical part of an illustration. Illustrator not only allows you to place and control
text in al image, it gives you advanced typographic capabilities. Individual pages of text
can be produced with the sort of refinement and precision associated with high-end
page layout programs. (A short lexicon of typographic terminology appears at the end of this
chapter.)
In addition letters and words can be used as artwork. Not only can you strategically
place characters, you can transform them into paths and use them as outlines.
Illustrator allows you to work with type in a variety of ways. The primary means are the six
type tools, three palettes, a ruler, and 15 separate commands.
**The Type Tools**
The Type Tool (default keyboard shortcut T) has six variations. There are horizontal
and vertical versions of three different functions. They are the Type tool, the Area Type tool, the Path Type tool, and their vertical
counterparts.
In addition to inserting new text, the Text tools are used to select that is already present in the document. Click and drag with
a Text tool to select all or part of a section of text. Once selected, you can edit the type or change its attributes.
**Type Tool & Vertical Type Tool**
The Type tools place horizontal and vertical type at any point in a document. Select the tool in the Toolbox and click once
anywhere on the Artboard to begin entering type. If the point where you need to place text is already occupied by an
object, lock or hide that object in the Layers palette to prevent it from being converted to a type container.
After you click with the Type tool, you can begin typing your text. While in this mode, Illustrator functions as a basic word
processor. The single-key keyboard shortcuts (V for the Move tool, M for the Rectangle tool, Tab to show/hide palettes,
Return or Enter to accept changes) are not available when entering text. Pressing those letters will, most naturally, add
them to the text being entered. When you've finished entering text, click on another tool in the Toolbox or Cmd+click
[Ctrl+click] away from the text to retain the Type tool.
These tools can be used to create text boxes. Click and drag with either Type tool to create a rectangular area in which you
can enter text. The text will wrap from line to line to stay within the rectangle. Such text boxes are invisible and nonprinting unless you choose to fill or stroke them with color.
If the text entered doesn't fit in the rectangle, you have several options. In addition to choosing a new font size, shortening
the text, or adjusting spacing and leading you can resize the rectangle or have the text continue in another box. A small
indicator will appear in the lower-right corner of the rectangle to indicate text overflow. When the small box with the plus sign appears, your text no
longer fits in the rectangle. To resize the box, hold down the Command [Control] key and drag one of the bounding box handles. Illustrator will give
you a live update of how the text will appear by indicating the baselines of the lines of text. As you drag the bounding box, the baselines will shift and
reposition themselves to show you how the text will flow in the new-sized box.

Figure 27.35
If the paths had been at the edge of the bitmap images, the text would have flowed to the very edge of the pictures.

Multiple text containers can wrap around one or more paths or objects. In Figure 27.36, two containers wrap around one path.

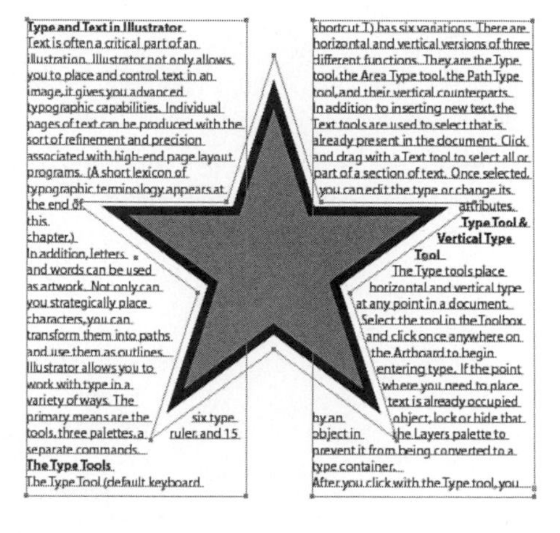


Figure 27.36
Like the previous figure, an additional path has been drawn around the object to prevent the text from wrapping too closely.

## Filling and Stroking Text Containers

By default, when a path or an object becomes a text container, it automatically receives a stroke and fill of None. However, it often makes sense to have a text container with either a stroke or a fill, or both. Illustrator allows you to colorize your text containers, but you must select them independently of the text. Using the Direct Selection tool, click the invisible path that constrains the text. You can then apply a fill and/or stroke as appropriate. Figure 27.37 shows an example.

Figure 27.37
The normally invisible text container was selected using the Direct Selection tool, and a style was applied.

# TYPE OUTLINES AND ATTRIBUTES

Type can be converted to outlines, which can then be edited as any path. This gives you tremendous control over the appearance of individual characters. (Remember, though, that the outlines cannot be selected and overtyped like regular type.)

Illustrator also offers the capability of copying attributes among type objects, using the Eyedropper and Paint Bucket tools. Although this technique is largely superceded by character styles and paragraph styles, it remains functional in Illustrator CS.

## Converting Text to Outlines

In addition to being used for text, type can be used as decorations or objects in an illustration. When type is used in this capacity, the characters may be converted to compound paths. As such, they can no longer be edited as text but rather can be edited as paths. Figure 27.38 shows the difference between a type character and an outline created from that character.

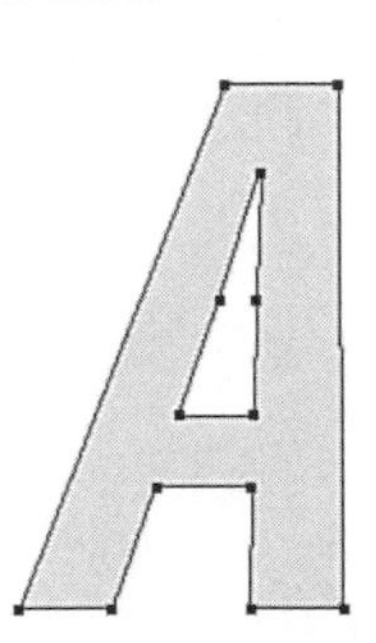

**Figure 27.38**
On the left is a letter; on the right is a compound path that can be edited with the Direct Selection tool.

More useful with type at very large sizes, the command Type, Create Outlines produces compound paths for each letter. Text—whether point, path, or area—must be converted together. You cannot convert, for example, a single word in the middle of a sentence.

### Simplifying Type Outlines

When you're converting text to outlines, Illustrator is very precise. This precision can result in very complex paths. These paths are often too complicated to print properly. Illustrator usually returns a warning when you attempt to use extremely complex paths as masks, too.

The command Object, Path, Simplify can be of great help. You'll find that, in many cases, you can leave Curve Precision set to 100% and still have a dramatic reduction in the path complexity. The following figure shows an example of text converted to outlines and simplified to 90%. The resulting paths, not visually different from the originals, had a reduction in anchor points of more than 80%.

The more angular serif fonts benefit most from simplification, but all type outlines can benefit as well.

Two Blind Sheep:
Following the Leader

Two Blind Sheep:
Following the Leader

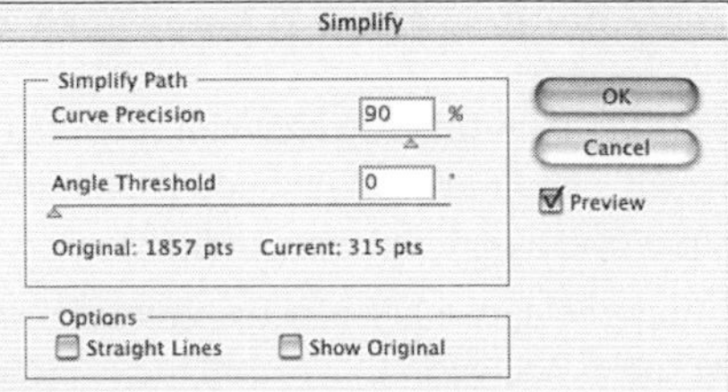

## Copying Type Attributes

Typography can be considered the art of typesetting and printing. Although you can get beautiful results using the type defaults, taking advantage of Illustrator's advanced typographic capabilities can improve virtually any text. One of Illustrator's great timesavers is the capability to copy attributes from one set of characters to another.

The Eyedropper tool, in conjunction with the Paint Bucket tool, allows you to copy type attributes among text in an Illustrator file. The Eyedropper samples the attributes from the source text, and the Paint Bucket applies them to the target text.

You can copy attributes in two ways using the Eyedropper. Here's the first:

1. Use a type or selection tool to designate the text that is to receive the attributes (the *target* text).
2. Use the Eyedropper to click the *source* text, the text whose attributes you want to be copied to the target text.

Alternatively, you can use the Paint Bucket with the Eyedropper as follows:

1. Use the Eyedropper to copy attributes from the source text by clicking it.
2. Switch to the Paint Bucket tool and click the target text, or drag with the Paint Bucket to apply the attributes to only part of the target text.

When either the Eyedropper or Paint Bucket is selected in the Toolbox, you can switch to its partner tool by pressing and holding down (Option) [Alt].

To control which attributes are transferred from source to target, double-click either the Eyedropper or Paint Bucket tool to open the dialog box shown in Figure 27.39.

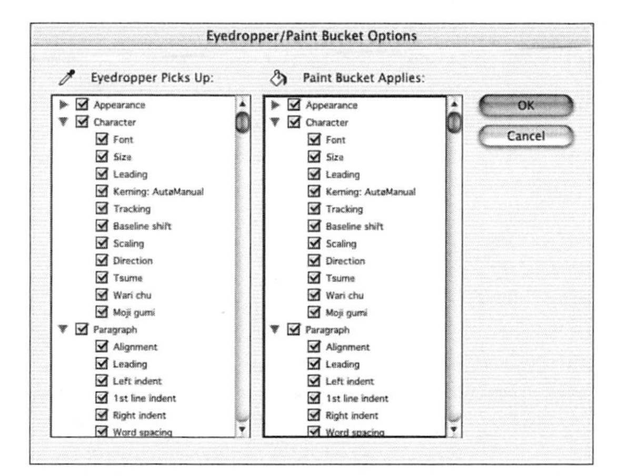


**Figure 27.39**
Checking or unchecking a box determines which attributes are copied.

The following text attributes can be copied:

- **Appearance**—Transparency; Focal Fill color, Transparency, and Overprint; Focal Stroke color, Transparency, Overprint, Weight, Cap, Join, Miter limit, Dash pattern

- **Character**—Font, Size, Leading, Kerning (auto/manual), Tracking, Baseline shift, Scaling, Direction, Tsume, Wari-Chu, Moji Gumi
- **Paragraph**—Alignment, Leading, Left indent, First line indent, Right indent, Word spacing, Letter spacing, Auto-hyphenation, Kurikaeshi Moji Shori, Kinsoku Shori

Note that Leading appears twice, once under Character and again under Paragraph. The first refers to the leading (line spacing) set in the Character palette. The second refers to the amount of space added before a paragraph in the Paragraph palette. (Remember that the latter is available only for area type.)

# MASTERING ILLUSTRATOR

## Copyfitting

*I can't make the font any smaller because it won't be legible, but I need to squeeze another line or two into my text container. What can I do?*

You've got several possibilities, all of which fit under the title *copyfitting*. First, reduce your leading in the Character palette. That will bring the lines of type closer together vertically. Remember that you can use fractions, too, so that the adjustment is the very smallest necessary. Next on the list (if your text is justified rather than aligned) would be word spacing from the Paragraph palette. (If the palette is not visible, expand it by clicking the two-headed arrow in the palette's tab a couple times.) Word spacing, which works only with area type, allows you to change the amount of space between words in the selected text. After that, you've still got letter spacing (also in the Paragraph palette), which reduces the gap between each of the letters in the selected text. Think of it as mass-kerning. Using these three advanced techniques should bring those last two lines of your text into the allotted area.

## Taming the Tabs

*The Tabs palette is something new for me, and I can't seem to get it to work. No matter what I do, I can't get different parts of my text to have different tab stops.*



Tabs established for a block of text apply to the entire block, even if only part of the text is selected. If you need different tab stops for different parts of the text, break the block into two separate text boxes.

In addition, did you know that you can change the indent and first line indent of selected text in the Tabs palette? To the left, above the ruler and below the icon for the left tab stop, are two small triangles. Drag the top one to change the first line indent; drag the lower one to change the paragraph indent.

28

# TRANSFORMING AND DISTORTING OBJECTS

## IN THIS CHAPTER

Illustrator offers a variety of ways to alter the shape of an object or a path. Some are designed for convenience, some for precision, and some are targeted toward creativity. Illustrator's powerful envelope distortions and liquify tools open new doors on productivity and artistry. In this chapter, you learn techniques for transforming and distorting objects in Illustrator, including using the Transformation commands, envelope distortions, and the liquify tools.

Illustrator also offers many of the capabilities discussed in this chapter as effects. Using the commands under the Effect, Distort & Transform or Effect, Warp menu does *not* alter the path of an object. As live effects, only the appearance is changed. The difference between transforming a path and applying an effect is shown in Figure 28.1.

# TRANSFORMATIONS AND DISTORTIONS IN ILLUSTRATOR

When a transformation or distortion is applied to an open or closed path, the anchor points and/or the direction lines for the anchor points are moved. Changing the path will alter not only the appearance of the stroke and fill but also any effects applied to the selection.

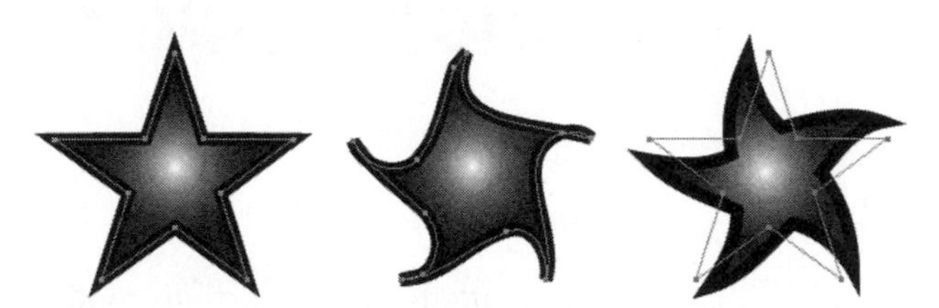

Figure 28.1
The original object is on the left. In the center, the object has been transformed using a liquify tool. On the right, an effect has been applied. Compare the three paths.

Generally speaking, a transformation is applied to paths, objects, or groups selected on the artboard. You can also use most of the transformation commands and tools with selected anchor points to change part of an object or path.

*You can, of course, distort and transform paths manually. For information on manipulating path anchor points directly, see Chapter 24, "Creating and Editing Paths," p. 761.*

## Transform, Envelope Distort, and Liquify

Three basic categories of path manipulation—Transform, Envelope Distort, and Liquify—are discussed in this chapter. Each of these groups of techniques works in a different way to create different results. Each of the three categories has a number of distinct capabilities.

The first and third figures have a star-shaped path. The middle figure, transformed with the Twirl tool, has a path that conforms to its appearance. For more information on the Effect commands, see Chapter 35, "Illustrator's Effects and Filters."

The transformation commands, Selection tool, and Transform palette offer predictable and regular control over the changes to a path (or a portion of a path). They work with the existing anchor points, moving them or changing the length and angle of the direction lines. In some instances, additional anchor points may be added to a path or object. Corner anchor points may have direction lines added, and smooth points might be converted to corner points.

The Envelope Distort commands create mesh objects that are used to alter the shape and appearance of paths or objects. A *mesh object*, which will be explained in depth later in the chapter, uses a series of path-like mesh lines to reshape the fill of an object.

Illustrator's liquify tools alter the shape of a path by adding, subtracting, and moving anchor points. The tools provide a variety of capabilities.

# THE BASICS OF TRANSFORMING

There's nothing in the category of transformations that cannot also be done with the Selection and Direct Selection tools. However, using Illustrator's transformation commands and tools and the Transform palette allows you to quickly and precisely change the shape of paths and objects. Transformations can be performed on objects, open paths, selected anchor points of objects and paths, and on groups. The transformation tools and menu commands and the Transform palette are shown in Figure 28.2.

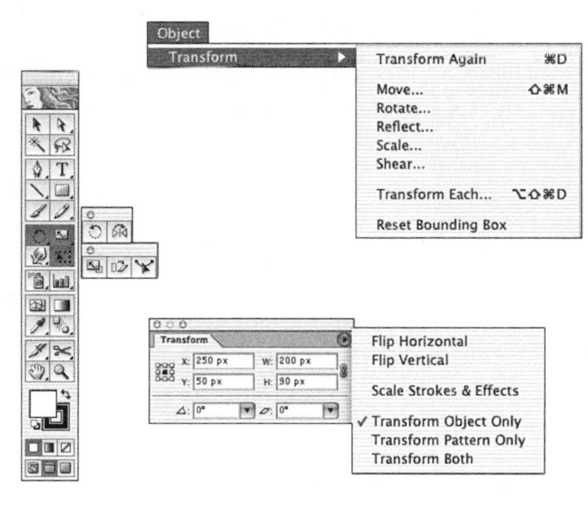


**Figure 28.2**
**Note that the Twist tool is gone from Illustrator CS. The Twirl command and Twist effect/filter remain to provide that capability.**

Illustrator's Toolbox has two hidden palettes that hold transformation tools. The Rotate and Reflect tools share one flyout palette, whereas the Scale, Shear, and Reshape tools share the other. The Free Transform tool (default keyboard shortcut E) sits alone in the Toolbox.

Note that the Rotate, Reflect, Scale, and Shear tools are duplicated by menu commands. The menu also has commands for reapplying the most recent transformation (Transform Again), relocating a selection on the artboard (Move, which is comparable to dragging with the Selection tool), applying a transformation individually to members of a group or selection (Transform Each), and resetting a selection's bounding box (Reset Bounding Box).

The Transform palette, which can be used to move, scale, rotate, and shear a selection, can accept negative numbers and can accept values with precision to one one-thousandth of a point (three decimal places).

This chapter presents each type of transformation and discusses how it can be applied using a tool, a menu command, and the palette (when applicable).

## Transforming with the Selection Tool and the Bounding Box

You'll notice that Illustrator allows you to move an object using a menu command or the Transform palette, but it doesn't have a dedicated transformation tool for the job. The Selection tool is more than adequate for the job. Objects must be selected on the artboard before they can be moved with the Selection tool. By default, selections are surrounded by a bounding box.

The bounding box, which can be shown or hidden using commands under the View menu, by default surrounds all selected objects on the artboard, regardless of whether unselected objects are mixed among them. (Only the selected objects can be manipulated.) The bounding box has eight handles that can be used to change the shape of the selected area and its contents (see Figure 28.3).

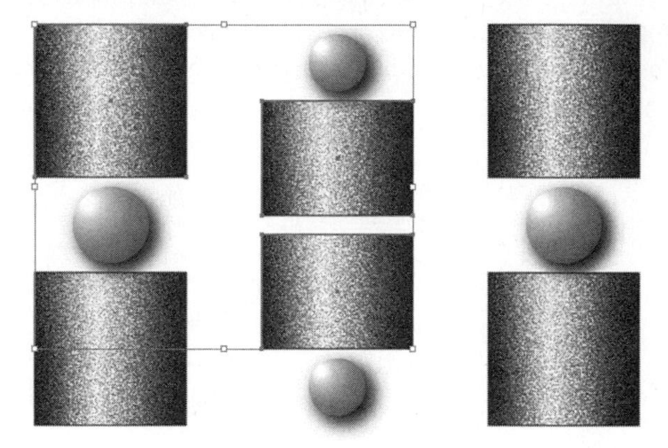

Figure 28.3
The bounding box's handles are found in each corner and in the middle of each side.

*Bounding box not showing up? Check "Showing and Hiding the Bounding Box" in the "Mastering Illustrator" section at the end of this chapter.*

You can reposition (move) selected objects on the artboard by dragging with the Selection tool. You can also use the bounding box and Selection tool to scale (resize) selected objects.

Here are the techniques for scaling an object by selecting it and dragging the handles of the bounding box:

- Dragging a handle on the side of the bounding box will scale the selected object or objects in one dimension only (horizontally or vertically).
- Dragging a corner handle allows scaling in both directions at the same time.
- Holding the Shift key while dragging a corner handle constrains the proportions as the selection is resized.
- The (Option) [Alt] key scales from the center of the bounding box. This maintains the object's general position on the artboard while resizing. Shift and (Option) [Alt] can be used together when scaling.

Scaling can also be accomplished with the Scale tool, the Transform palette, and the Scale menu command. (See the section titled "Scale," later in this chapter.)

## The Point of Origin

One of the most important concepts for properly employing transformations is the *point of origin*. Understanding how the point of origin controls the transformation enables you to position it effectively. The point of origin is the spot on the artboard around, across, or from which a transformation will be calculated. It is represented on the artboard by a crosshair symbol (see Figure 28.4). You can see that it appears in the middle of a selection (the default) even when multiple objects are selected.

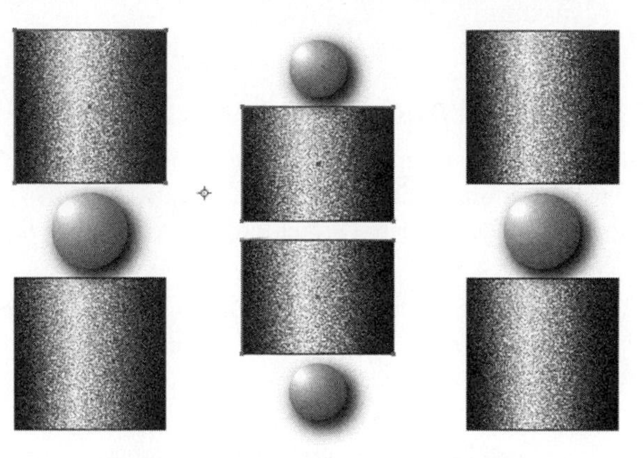

Figure 28.4
The same three rectangles are selected. The point of origin appears in what would be the middle of the bounding box.

The point of origin can be relocated anywhere on the artboard by clicking or dragging. It need not remain within the area of the selection or a selected object. Figure 28.5 shows the difference in rotating an object using different points of origin.

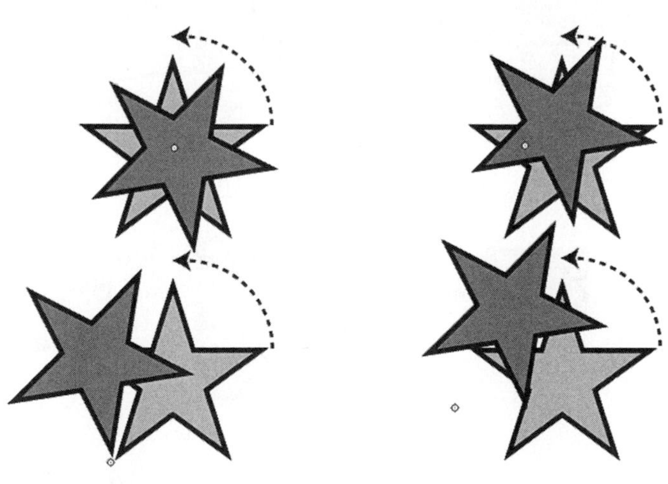

Figure 28.5
In this composite image, the point of origin and rotation are shown for each example.

The original objects are shown behind, with a lighter fill. The top objects were all rotated 45° around the point of origin shown for each.

The point of origin works differently for different transformations. It is not used with the Reshape tool. When you're transforming with a command, the point of origin is assumed to be the center. When using the Transform palette, you can choose one of nine points for the point of origin. The points are the center (default) and the eight handles of the bounding box. When using the Transform palette, you choose the point of origin by selecting one of the squares in the small grid to the left of the palette, called a *proxy* (see Figure 28.6).

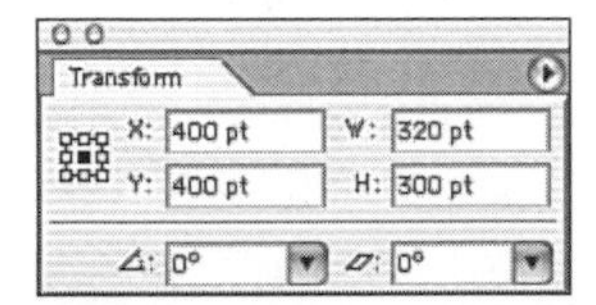


**Figure 28.6**
The proxy is the 3×3 grid of boxes. Click a box to select the point of origin. The center is currently selected.

## Transforming Objects, Patterns, and Both

The Transform commands allow you to transform an object's pattern fill as well as the object itself. You can also elect to transform the pattern without changing the object. (You also have these options available when using the Transform palette. Select the appropriate options in the palette's menu.)

In Figure 28.7, the Rotate dialog box is shown. It offers check boxes to select the object and the pattern for rotation. When both boxes are checked, as shown in the figure, the object and pattern will rotate together.

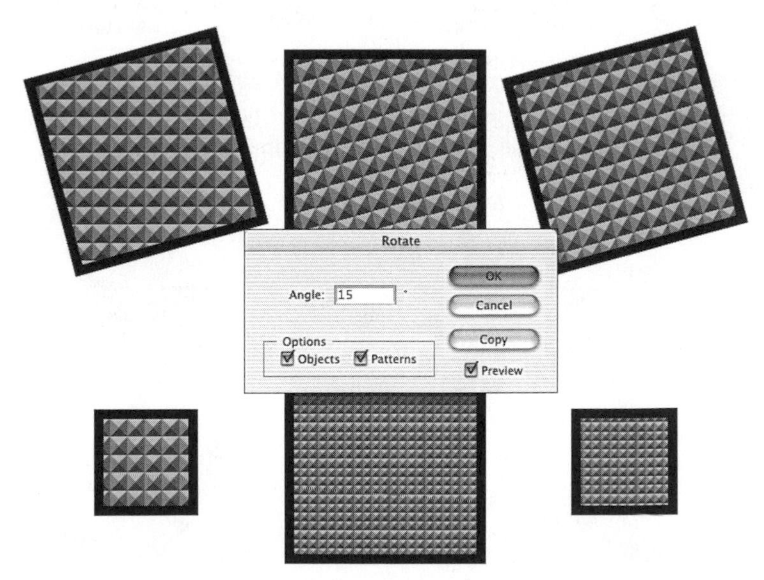


**Figure 28.7**
All the Transform commands offer the option to transform the object, the pattern, or both.

In the figure, Rotate has been applied to the top row. From the left, the objects show Rotate object (not pattern) 15°, Rotate pattern (not object) 15°, and Rotate both object and pattern 15°. In the lower row, Scale has been applied. Again from the left, they show Scale object (not pattern) 50%, Scale pattern (not object) 50%, and Scale both object and pattern 50%.

The Reflect, Rotate, Scale, and Shear tools can also transform patterns without changing the object itself. Hold down the tilde key (~) while using the tool to change just the pattern. (You learn more about these tools and their use in "The Transformations," later in this chapter.)

Using the Transform commands, especially Scale and Rotate, with patterns alone is a great way to customize the look of your artwork. Scaling and rotating patterns can make them proportionally more appealing.

The check boxes in the transform dialog boxes should not be confused with the check box in the General pane of the Preferences dialog box. The Preferences dialog box's Transform Pattern Tiles option primarily affects scaling done by manipulating the bounding box with the Selection tool.

## Scaling Strokes and Effects

In addition to transforming patterns, Illustrator allows you to transform strokes and effects. This allows transformed artwork to retain the proportions and appearance of the original. In Figure 28.8, the original object is in the center. To the left, the object is scaled, but not the strokes. The strokes are proportionally thicker than the original. On the right, the strokes were scaled with the original.

The Transform command dialog boxes and the Transform palette menu offer the option to scale strokes and effects.

Transforming patterns using the Transform commands works with patterns applied from the Swatches palette (and custom patterns) and also with styles that use patterns. It makes no difference whether the pattern was applied to the object using the Swatches palette or the Styles palette.

The General Preferences also offers a check box that gives you the option of scaling strokes and effects. The Scale Strokes & Effects option is used primarily with scaling done with the Selection tool and the bounding box.

Figure 28.8
Transforming strokes and effects allows the artwork to retain the appearance of the original.

# THE TRANSFORMATIONS

The transform capabilities are spread among six tools, one palette, and eight menu commands. Although there is overlap in what they can do, these items differ in how they do it. For example, you can rotate a selection using the Rotate tool, the Transform palette, or the menu command Object, Transform, Rotate. The choice may be one strictly of convenience, or you might need to take advantage of a particular option of one of the techniques. The Rotate tool allows you to set the point of origin anywhere. The Transform palette and the Rotate menu command give you precise control over the amount of rotation. The menu command allows you to preview the rotation. Which you choose depends on your situation. The choices are described in the following sections.

## Free Transform

The Free Transform tool is a multipurpose tool that duplicates the capabilities of several others. It is not itself directly duplicated by a menu command or the Transform palette. This tool can rotate, scale, reflect, shear, and distort:

- To rotate a selected object, simply position the Free Transform tool outside the object's bounding box. The cursor turns into a two-headed arrow, and you can drag it in the desired direction of rotation. The Shift key constrains the rotation to 45° angles.
- To scale an object with the Free Transform tool, position the cursor on an anchor point of the object's bounding box. When the cursor is on a corner point, the Shift key maintains the object's proportions (height-to-width ratio) during the scaling procedure.
- Reflecting with the Free Transform tool is simply a matter of dragging an object's bounding box handle past the other side of the object. The Shift key constrains cursor movement to horizontal or vertical. (This technique provides far less control than the Reflect tool offers.)

- To shear, position the Free Transform tool over a side anchor point (not a corner anchor) of a selected object's bounding box. After you start to drag, press (Command-Option) [Ctrl+Alt]. Figure 28.9 shows the difference between shearing with a side point and dragging a corner point while pressing (Command-Option) [Ctrl+Alt].

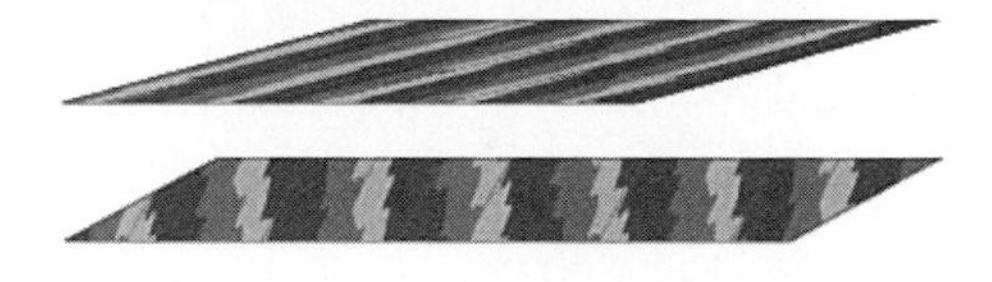

**Figure 28.9**
Although it doesn't appear to be the case, the two objects have identical heights and widths. Additionally, the top and bottom of the upper image are indeed parallel.

- To distort with the Free Transform tool, drag from a selected object's corner point and then press (Command) [Ctrl]. To distort in perspective, hold down (Command-Shift-Option) [Ctrl+Shift+Alt].

## Move

As discussed earlier in this chapter, the most common way to move a selection on the artboard is with the Selection tool. (In addition, the arrow keys can be used to move selected objects when the Selection tool is active.) Illustrator's transform tools don't include a "Move" tool, but the Transform commands and the Transform palette both give precise control over movement. The menu command Object, Transform, Move opens the dialog box shown next to the Transform palette in Figure 28.10.

The Transform, Move command allows you to specify a distance and a direction to move a selection. As you can see in the dialog box pictured in Figure 28.10, Illustrator offers you two pairs of numeric fields. The top pair, Horizontal and Vertical, moves a selection left/right and up/down. (To move a selection to the left or downward, enter negative numbers.) The second pair allows you to specify a precise angle and distance of movement. Illustrator will automatically update all the numeric fields as you enter values into one.

The Move command's dialog box also offers two additional features—Preview and Copy—that can save you tremendous amounts of time. The Preview check box prevents guessing and undoing (as well as those Undos that result from lack of a minus sign before a number), and the Copy button produces a copy of the selection in the new location, leaving the original untouched.

Remember that Illustrator allows you to enter values in any unit of measure into numeric fields. Your entries need not be in the document's unit. You can also enter equations into numeric fields such as this:

```
3 in + 4 px - 2 pt
```

This tells Illustrator that you want it to calculate the value of 3 inches plus 4 pixels minus 2 points. No problem!

Use the Transform palette to move a selection to a specific point on the artboard. Use the Transform, Move command to move a selection a specific distance at a specific angle.

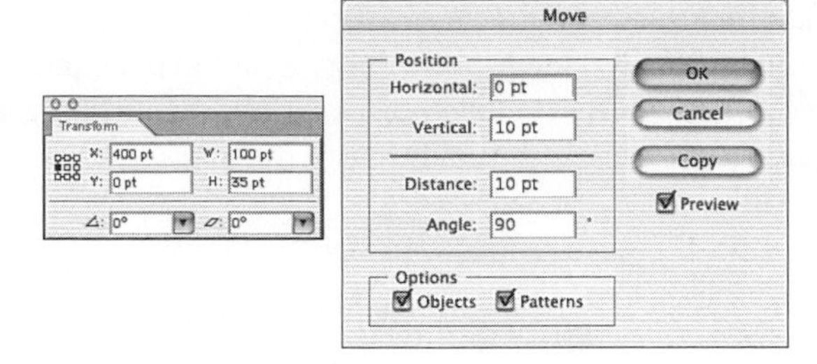


Figure 28.10
The dialog box can only be opened when there is a selection on the artboard.

The two numeric fields on the left of the Transform palette allow you to specify a selection's exact position on the artboard. This is in contrast to the Move dialog box, which calculates a new position relative to the selection's original position. (Remember that, by default, Illustrator measures position from the lower-left corner of the artboard.) The X: and Y: fields give the exact position of a selection. By changing these values, you change the position on the artboard. Numeric values can be entered to three decimal places, ensuring exact placement. When the values are entered, the selection is moved. As soon as you click in another numeric field or use a tool on the artboard, Illustrator makes the change. You can also use the (Return) [Enter] key to register a change.

When using the Transform palette, remember that the position is determined based on the palette's proxy (the proxy is the 3×3 grid to the left of the X: and Y: fields). If the proxy's center box is checked, Illustrator will measure to the center of the selection. To use a corner or a side of an object or selection as the point of reference, change the proxy by clicking any of the outer eight squares.

Also keep in mind that, by default, Illustrator measures to an object's path, not to the edge of a stroke. Therefore, an object with a 10-point stroke, positioned using the lower-left corner of the proxy, will actually extend 5 points (one-half the stroke width) to the left and below the point shown in the X: and Y: fields.

By default, the Use Preview Bounds box is unchecked in Illustrator's General Preferences. While this box is unchecked, any object to which an effect has been applied may not be accurately reflected in the Transform palette. In addition to such effects as drop shadows, stroke weight may be a factor in how accurately the transformation is portrayed.

With the box unchecked, Illustrator calculates an object's position on the artboard based on the location of an object's path. That calculation doesn't take into account anything that extends beyond the path.

For most illustration purposes, it's best to check the Use Preview Bounds box so that calculations in the Transform and Info palettes take into account stroke weight and effects. For some technical and engineering purposes, precision requires that stroke weight be discounted, so unchecking the Use Preview Bounds box is appropriate.

## Rotate

A selection can be rotated using the Rotate tool, the Transform palette, or the menu command Object, Transform, Rotate. In Figure 28.11, the Rotate tool is shown as the selected tool in the flyout palette. Also, the Transform palette is shown, as is the Rotate command's dialog box. The Rotate dialog box can also be opened by double-clicking the Rotate tool's icon in the Toolbox.

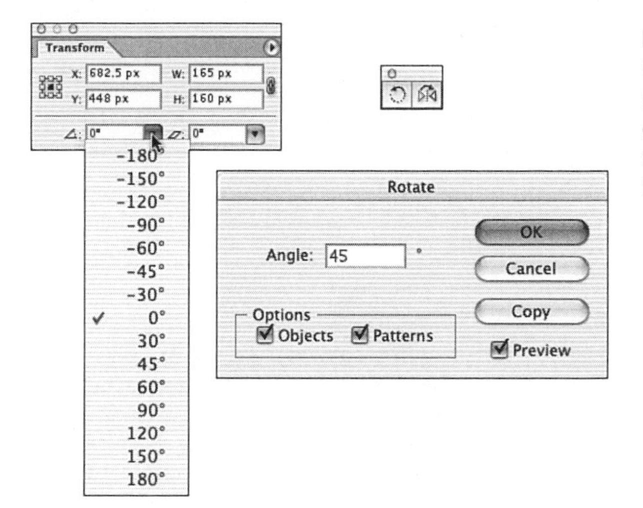


Figure 28.11
Illustrator offers many ways to rotate. Don't forget, too, that you can use the Selection tool and rotate using a selection's bounding box.

The Rotate tool (default keyboard shortcut R) rotates an object or path around a designated point without deforming it. The object or path retains its proportions and appearance, and it's rotated around the point of origin, as shown in Figure 28.12. The Rotate dialog box also allows you to rotate the contents of an object.

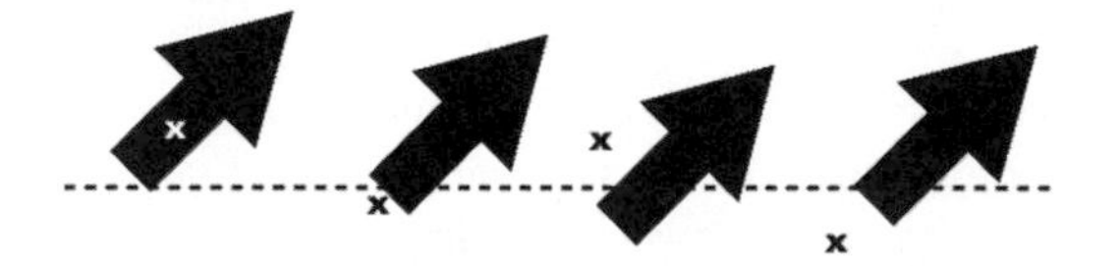

Figure 28.12
The points of origin are shown by the letter *X* for each rotation.

Certain techniques make the Rotate tool more valuable:

- By default, the point around which the object or path is rotated is its center.
- You can change the point of rotation by dragging or clicking. The rotation point does not need to be within the outline of the object itself.
- Holding down Shift while rotating constrains the rotation. By default, the constraint is set to 45° angles. That can be changed in Illustrator's preferences.
- To make copies of an object while rotating, hold down (Option) [Alt]. This technique is especially appropriate for such things as tick marks on the face of a clock and petals on a flower.
- The farther the cursor is from the point of rotation, the finer the control.
- (Option)-click [Alt]-click to set the point of rotation and specify a numeric value. The dialog box also allows you to rotate a copy of the object, leaving the original in place.
- The Rotate tool rotates grouped objects as a group. (To rotate them individually, choose Object, Transform, Transform Each.)

The Transform palette allows you to specify any angle of rotation in the numeric field in the lower-left corner. The field also offers a pop-up menu with common angles of rotation (see Figure 28.13).

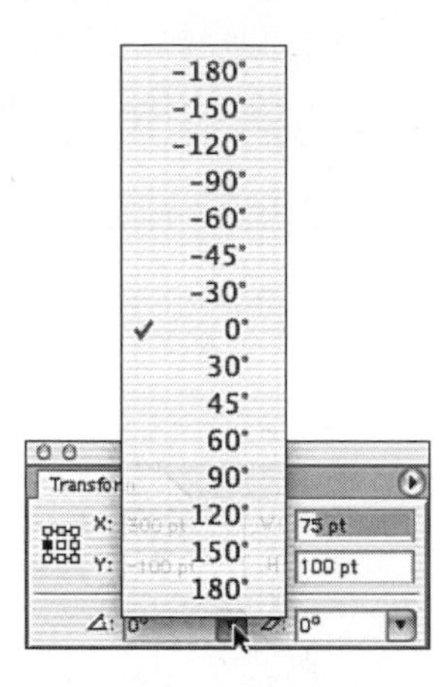


Figure 28.13
Negative numbers rotate counter-clockwise; positive numbers rotate clockwise.

You can open the Rotate dialog box through the Object menu or by double-clicking the Rotate tool icon in the Toolbox. Using the options in the dialog box, you can specify the angle of rotation, choose to rotate objects or patterns (or both), and preview the rotation. In addition, the Rotate dialog box offers the Copy button, which leaves the original selection unchanged, producing a copy with the specified rotation applied.

## Reflect

Reflecting flips a selection across an invisible line, called the *line of reflection*. The result is a mirror image of the original. Illustrator offers the Reflect tool and the Reflect dialog box (see Figure 28.14). However, this capability isn't found in the Transform palette.

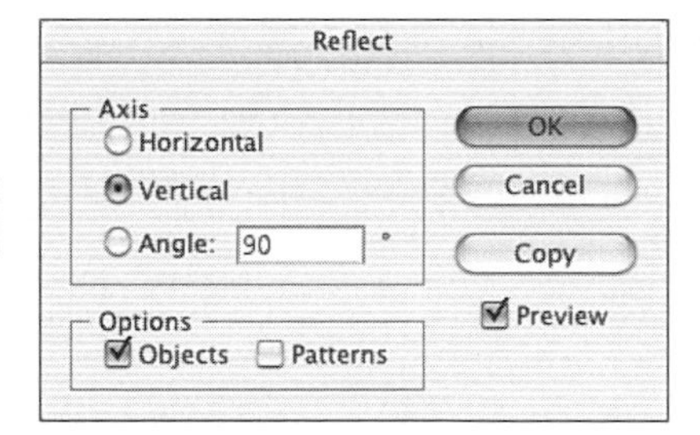


Figure 28.14
The Reflect tool is shown highlighted in the flyout tool palette.

The Reflect tool behaves a bit differently than the other transform tools. Rather than setting a point of origin, you must set a line of reflection.

Here's how to use the Reflect tool effectively:

- With one or more objects selected, click once to set one end of the line across which the selection will be reflected or copied. Clicking at a second point completes the line, and the selection is reflected.
- (Option)-click [Alt]-click at the second point to copy the selection to the new location.
- To see the new location of the reflection, you need to drag rather than click for the second point. Release when the outline is in the desired position. Pressing (Option) [Alt] produces a copy of the object.

28

- Pressing Shift constrains the angle of reflection to 90°.
- Double-click the Reflect tool icon in the Toolbox to open the Reflect dialog box.

Notice in the Reflect dialog box that horizontal and vertical reflections can be selected with radio buttons. Remember that negative numbers can be used and that reflections are measured in degrees. Using the dialog box gives you precise control over the location of the reflected object.

The Reflect dialog box also offers previews, copying, and the capability to transform objects, patterns, or both.

## Reshape

Reshaping is only available through the Reshape tool, which can be used to smoothly distort an object. Selected path segments and points are redrawn as if pulled or pushed by "focal points." You select points and segments to be adjusted normally, by dragging or clicking with a Selection tool. You select the focal point or points by clicking or dragging with the Reshape tool. Figure 28.15 shows the visual difference between focal points and selected points.

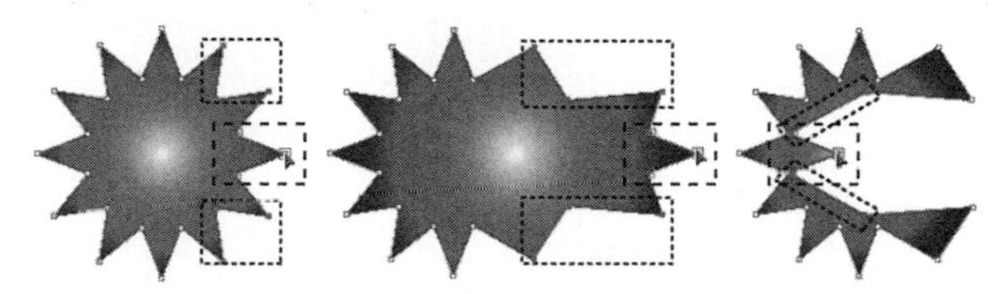

**Figure 28.15**
**The bolder dashed rectangles indicate the focal points. The lighter dashed rectangles show the points that are selected, but not focal points.**

When you use the Reflect tool, the selected points (which are affected by the change) are highlighted normally, whereas the focal points are surrounded by boxes. In the figure, note the effect when the focal points are pushed backward into the object (on the right).

When using the Reflect tool, keep these points in mind:

- Use the Shift key to select more than one focal point.
- The focal points maintain the relationships among themselves, moving as a unit. Unselected points are unaffected. Selected points that are not focal points will move when a focal point is dragged.
- The Reshape tool selects multiple focal points when dragged.
- Altering the shape of an object with the Reshape tool differs from using the Direct Selection tool in that the Reshape tool allows you to change the relationship among segments while reshaping. The Direct Selection tool, in contrast, moves selected points and their segments en masse, altering only those segments connecting the selected and unselected portions of an object.

> Rather than click the Direct Selection tool to prepare an object for reshaping, you can press (Command) [Ctrl] to switch tools. You can even select a point with the Reshape tool with two clicks—clicking once makes it a focal point, and then Shift-clicking makes it a normally selected point.

## Scale

Scaling alters a selection's size on the artboard horizontally, vertically, or in both directions. Objects can be enlarged or reduced through scaling. Selections can be scaled dynamically by dragging with the Scale tool, or numerically, using the Transform palette or the menu command Object, Transform, Scale.

The Scale tool is highlighted in Figure 28.16, shown with the Transform palette and the Scale dialog box.

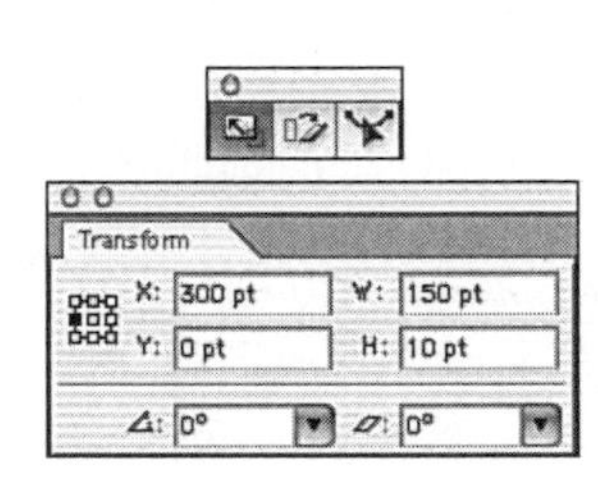


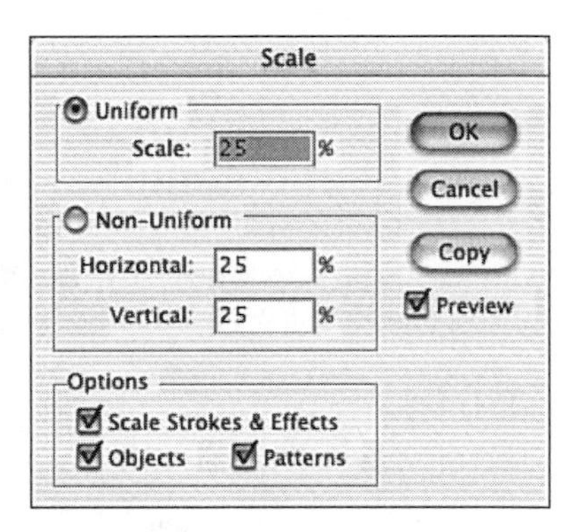


**Figure 28.16**
The Scale tool is, by default, visible in the Toolbox. It can also be found on the flyout palette with the Shear and Reshape tools.

Scaling with the Scale tool is comparable to using the Selection tool with the bounding box of a selection. However, the Scale tool allows you to change the point from which the selection is transformed. The Scale tool allows you to set the point of origin by either clicking or dragging the point of origin marker on the artboard.

You can also scale numerically using either the Transform palette or the Scale dialog box. The dialog box can be opened using the menu command Object, Transform, Scale or by double-clicking the Scale tool's icon in the Toolbox.

The Transform palette allows you to specify exact dimensions for an object or objects using the W: and H: fields. You can enter in any unit of measure or enter a percentage (use the % symbol). The Transform palette accepts numeric input to three-decimal accuracy.

The Scale dialog box allows you to scale only by percent. You can scale uniformly (the same percentage for both vertical and horizontal dimensions) or you can specify different percentages (nonuniform scaling). You also have the option of scaling objects, their patterns, or both.

> You can get the best of both worlds when scaling—you can specify a new point of origin *and* scale numerically. Make a selection on the artboard, choose the Scale tool from the Toolbox, hold down the (Option) [Alt] key, and click to set the new point of origin. Not only will the point of origin move, the Scale dialog box will open. Enter the transformation percentage, check the appropriate boxes, and then click the OK button.

Here are some guidelines for transforming with the Scale tool:

- By default, the Scale tool enlarges or shrinks an object from the object's center.
- Click once with the Scale tool to set a new point of origin. That point need not be within the object. The point of origin marker can also be dragged on the artboard.
- To scale, drag with the Scale tool. You need not position the cursor over the object(s) or on an anchor point.
- Shift-dragging while scaling maintains the object's proportions.
- (Option)-dragging [Alt]-dragging scales a copy of the object. Begin dragging before pressing (Option) [Alt].
- (Option)-click [Alt]-click to set a new point of origin and open the Scale dialog box for numeric input.
- In addition to scaling the object, you can scale its stroke, effects, and patterns by using the dialog box. That also sets the preference for the Scale tool.

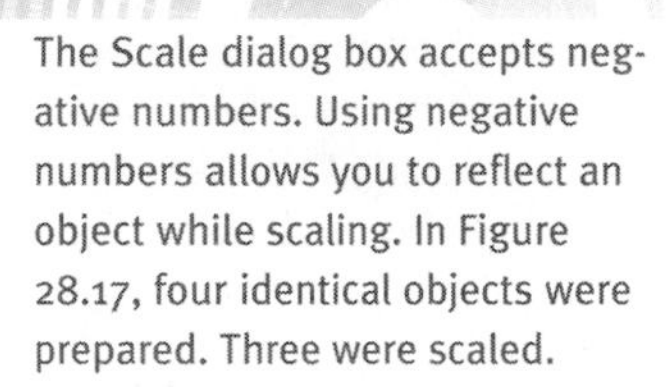

The Scale dialog box accepts negative numbers. Using negative numbers allows you to reflect an object while scaling. In Figure 28.17, four identical objects were prepared. Three were scaled.

To the left is the original object. Next, the object has been scaled nonuniformly, using the values Horizontal:100% and Vertical:50%. The third object was scaled with the values Horizontal:100% and Vertical:–50%. Note that not only was the arrow flipped, the pattern was flipped as well. The fourth object was scaled using the values Horizontal:–100% and Vertical:–100%, which is a uniform scale. The arrow and pattern are flipped in both dimensions. This works even when the point of origin is moved; the selection will be reflected across that point.

*If the Scale tool is producing strange effects, or if it's not producing the effect you want, take a look at "Checking Options" in the "Mastering Illustrator" section at the end of this chapter.*

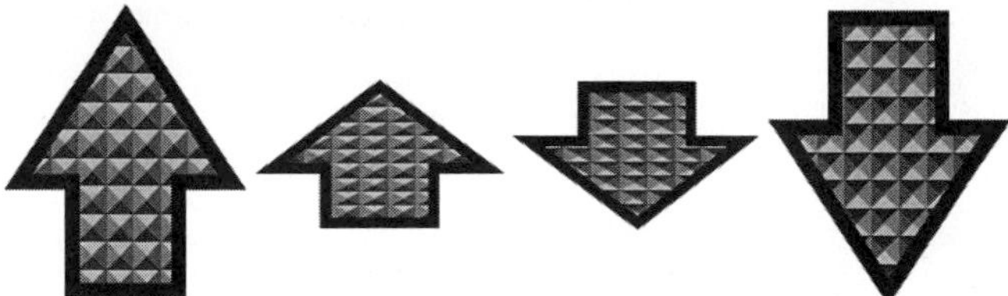

**Figure 28.17**
Scaling with negative numbers results in a reflection as well as a scale.

## Shear

Shearing slants or angles a selection. (Think *Physics 101* and lateral deformation rather than *Animal Husbandry 101* and shaving sheep.) It can be used to show perspective or simply to slant an object. Illustrator offers the Shear tool, a shear field in the Transform palette, and the Shear command (under the Object, Transform menu). The tool is selected in Figure 28.18 and shown with the Transform palette and the Shear dialog box.

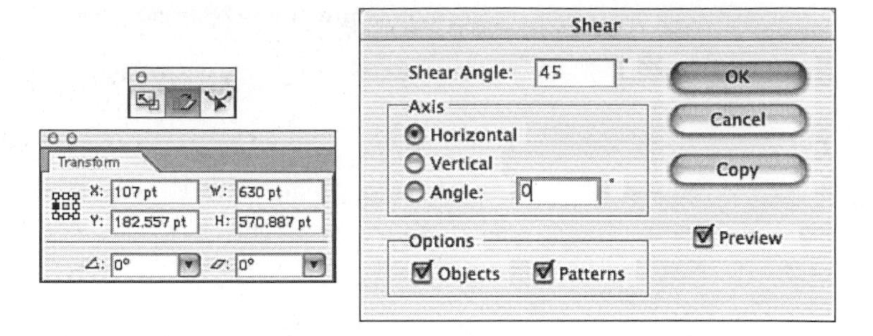


Figure 28.18
The Shear dialog box can be opened by using the menu command Object, Transform, Shear or by double-clicking the Shear tool's icon in the Toolbox.

Working with the Shear transformation is often considered difficult, but it need not be. To have more predictable results when shearing using numeric input in the dialog box, consider these guidelines:

- The Shear dialog box assumes a point of origin in the center of the selection. The exception is when the Shear tool has been (Option)-clicked [Alt]-clicked to open the dialog box. The point of origin is then at the point clicked.
- When Axis is set to Horizontal, the topmost and bottommost anchor points of each selected object move horizontally, but not vertically (see Figure 28.19).
- When Axis is set to Vertical, the leftmost and rightmost anchor points of each selected object will move vertically, but not horizontally (see Figure 28.19).

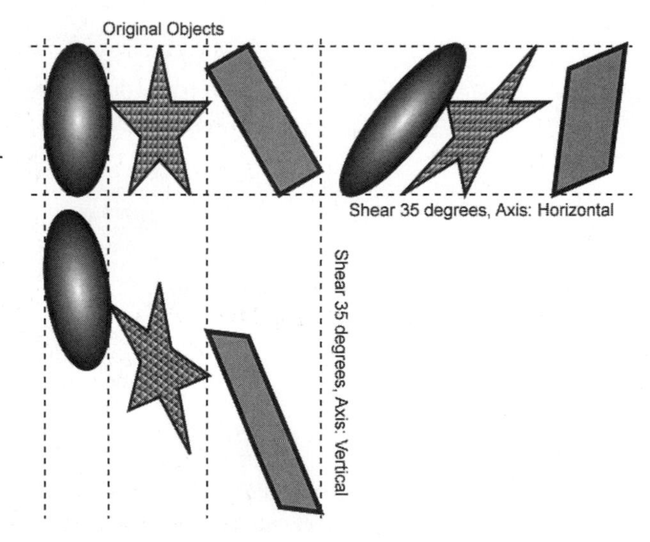


Figure 28.19
When a selection is sheared horizontally, the top and bottom anchor points move right or left. When a selection is sheared vertically, the left and right anchor points move down or up.

- Selecting the Horizontal option results in the top of the selection shearing to the right (positive Shear Angle values) or left (negative Shear Angle values).
- Selecting the Vertical option results in the right side of the selection shearing downward (positive Shear Angle values) or upward (negative Shear Angle values).

- The Shear Angle values can be positive or negative, from 1° to 89°. A value of 90° will generate an error message.
- Inputting values between 91° and 180° is the same as entering the comparable negative value between –89° and 0°. For example, there's no difference between 145° and –35° (see Figure 28.20).
- Entering a value over 180° is the equivalent of entering that value minus 180. For example, there's no difference between 215° and 35°. (See Figure 28.20.) slants or angles a selection

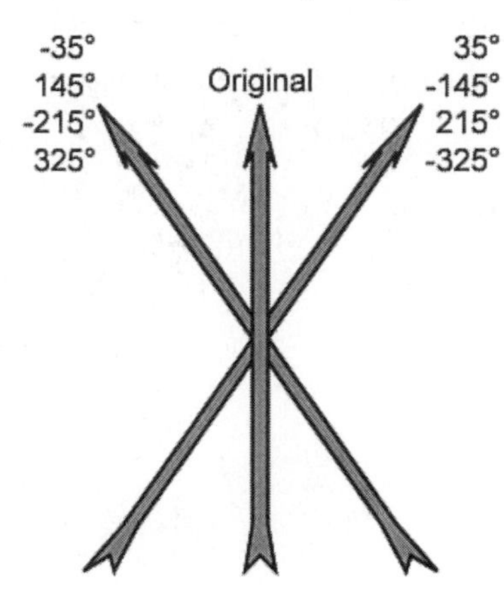


Figure 28.20
Positive and negative Shear Angle values between 1° and 89° are duplicated by higher values.

The Shear tool might seem easier to control than numeric input. It behaves much like the other transform tools. Here are some guidelines for its use:

- Click once to set a new point of origin around which the object will be sheared.
- (Option)-click [Alt]-click to set a new point of origin and open the Shear dialog box. This allows you to specify the point of origin and shear numerically.
- Shift-drag to constrain the tool to horizontal or vertical movement.
- The farther the cursor is from the point of origin, the finer the control you have over shearing. You don't need to click an anchor point or path segment to shear. To get exact placement of an object (or copy) while shearing, click and drag at a distance from the object.
- Pressing (Option) [Alt] after the drag is started copies the object to the new position. This is slants or angles a selectionvery useful for creating cast shadows.

## Illustrator at Work: Casting Shadows with the Shear Tool

Creating a drop shadow (the shadow created when an object is parallel to the surface on which the shadow falls) is easy: Use the Effect, Stylize, Drop Shadow command. Creating a *cast* shadow (when an object is perpendicular to the surface on which the shadow falls) takes a few steps. The Shear tool makes it easy, however:

1. Open or start an Illustrator document.
2. Add a five-point star, orienting it to the top of the page by holding down the Shift key as you drag. Give the star a wide stroke and pick a pattern or gradient fill.
3. Select the Shear tool from the Toolbox.
4. Click the lower-left point of the star to set the point of rotation.
5. Hold down the (Option) [Alt] key to create a duplicate and the Shift key to constrain the tool's movement. Then drag straight left. (This step is shown in Figure 28.21, top.)
6. In the Layers palette, move the new, sheared star below the original star.
7. Give the sheared star a stroke of None. Grab the Gradient tool and drag a black-to-white linear gradient from the top of the sheared star to its base. (Depending on how you've set your gradient, you may have to drag from the base to the top—you want black at the base.) Your cast shadow should look something like that shown in Figure 28.21 on the right.

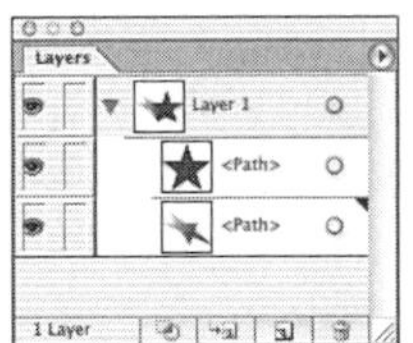


**Figure 28.21**
At the top, the project after step 5. At the bottom, the finished project with the Layers palette.

## The Transform Palette Menu

The Transform palette's menu, shown in Figure 28.22, offers a pair of commands that can be considered shortcuts. Flipping a selection horizontally or vertically is equivalent to using the Reflect tool or command. In addition, the options to transform objects, patterns, and both are available, as is the option to scale strokes and effects. These options are identical to those found in the transform command dialog boxes.

> The Shear dialog box remembers the most recent shear transformation, whether by palette, dialog box, or tool. After transforming with the Shear tool, you can open the dialog box to see the angle of shear.

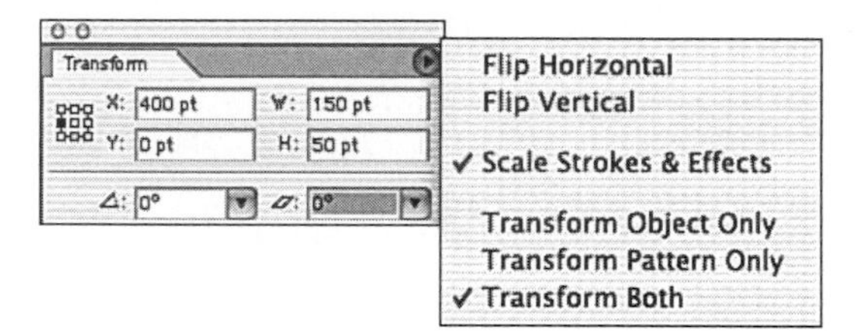


**Figure 28.22**
The Transform palette's menu offers options also found in the transform command dialog boxes.

## The Transform Again Command

In addition to the transform commands discussed earlier in this chapter, the Object, Transform menu offers several other commands. At the top of the Transform submenu, you'll find the command Transform Again, whose default keyboard shortcut is (Command-D) [Ctrl+D]. This command simply reapplies the last transformation, with the last settings used, to the current selection. A typical application of this command follows this pattern: Make a selection. Execute a transformation. Make a new selection. Use the Transform Again command.

## The Transform Each Command

Found under the Object, Transform menu, Transform Each works with selections of more than one ungrouped object. The transform commands work with multiple objects as a single entity, whereas Transform Each transforms the objects individually. Figure 28.23 shows the difference.

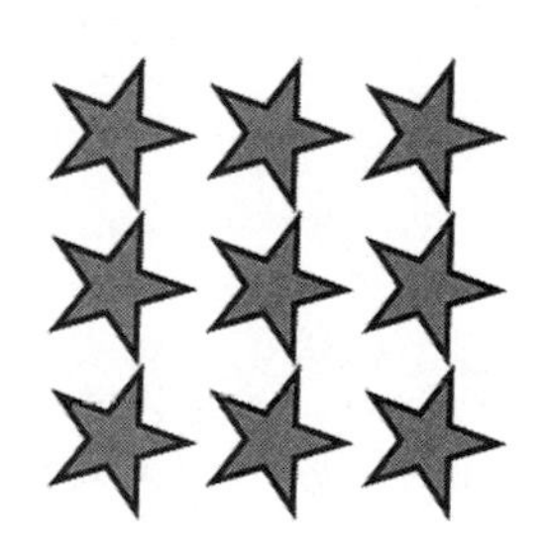

**Figure 28.23**
The stars on the left were rotated –20° with Transform, Rotate. On the right, Transform Each applied the same rotation. Each star remained in its original position and was rotated individually.

The Transform Each dialog box, shown in Figure 28.24, offers scaling, moving, rotating, and simple reflections. It does not offer the shear transformation, nor does it allow you to transform patterns separately from objects or to scale strokes and effects.

Notice below the Reflect check boxes that Transform Each offers the same point of origin proxy seen in the Transform palette. This allows you to choose the center of the selection or any of the eight bounding box handles as the point of origin.

> Keep in mind that Move is a transform command. Simply dragging an object on the artboard constitutes a transformation, at least as far as the Transform Again command is concerned. If you need to reapply a transformation to another object, but Transform Again isn't working, simply open the appropriate dialog box again and click OK.

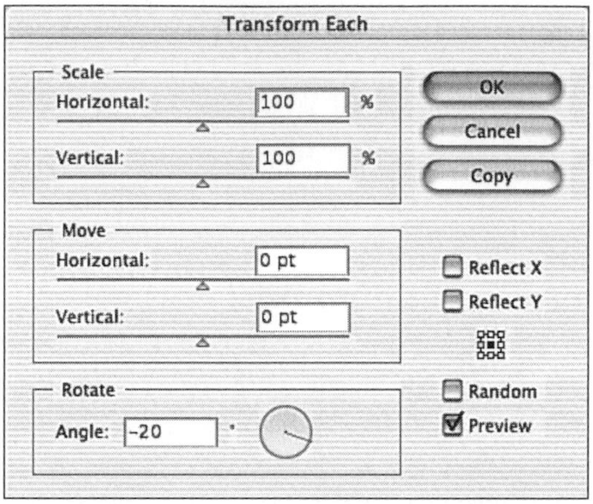

Figure 28.24
The Transform Each dialog box is accessed through the menu command Object, Transform, Transform Each.

Transform Each considers grouped objects to be a single entity and thus rotates them accordingly. In Figure 28.25, the original objects are shown to the left. On the right, Transform Each has been used to rotate –20°. As you can see, the circles, the squares, and the polygons were all grouped with similar objects, whereas the stars were ungrouped. Transform Each treated the selections as one group of circles, one group of squares, one group of polygons, and 25 individual stars.

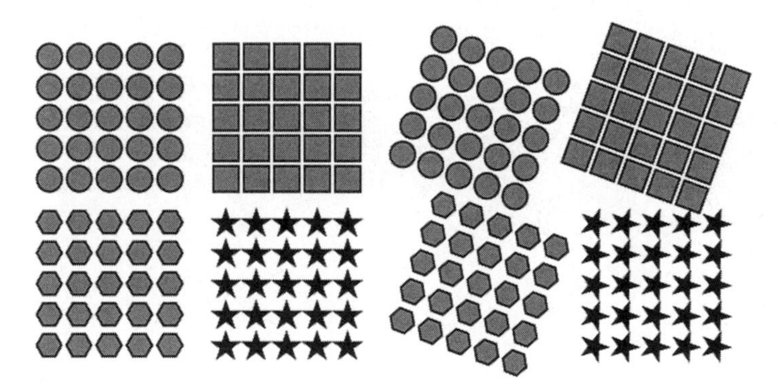

Figure 28.25
All the circles are one group, all the squares are one group, and all the polygons are one group. The stars, however, are ungrouped.

In Figure 28.26, you can see that the black squares were rotated as a group, whereas the remaining gray squares were all rotated individually. Again, Transform Each was used to apply a –20° rotation.

One additional feature of Transform Each deserves special attention. Notice the Random check box near the lower-right corner of the dialog box in Figure 28.24. When you're transforming a number of individual objects, this box varies the amount of transformation to provide a more "natural" look. In Figure 28.27, identical collections of squares have been transformed "randomly" using Transform Each.

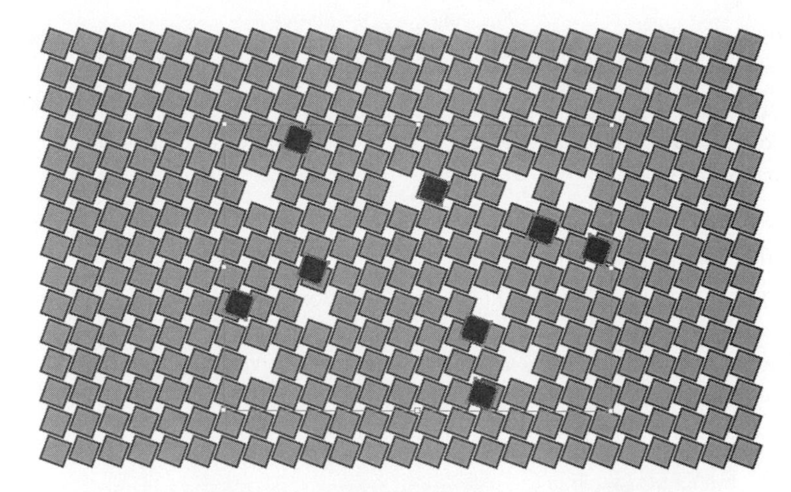

**Figure 28.26**
The black squares were grouped prior to the application of Transform Each.

**Figure 28.27**
The six sets of squares were originally identical.

The "randomized" transformations in Figure 28.27 are as follows:

- **Top row, left**—Rotate 15°
- **Top row, middle**—Rotate 45°
- **Top row, right**—Rotate 135°
- **Bottom row, left**—Rotate 45°, Scale Horizontal 151%, Scale Vertical 151%
- **Bottom row, middle**—Same as previous, but applied twice
- **Bottom row, right**—Same as bottom row, left but applied three times



As you can see, combining transformations and applying Transform Each multiple times can potentially save you a tremendous amount of production time when creating collections of "random" objects or shapes. Remember that you can repeat the transformation using the same settings by pressing (Command-D) [Ctrl+D]. Also keep in mind that you can start with objects of various shapes; they need not all be squares of circles or stars.

When you're working with the Random option, unchecking and rechecking the Preview box will generate a new set of random values, as will changing any value in the dialog box or unchecking and rechecking the Random box.

## The Reset Bounding Box Command

The final command in the Object, Transform menu is Reset Bounding Box. When an object is rotated, the bounding box is also rotated. Using this command realigns the top and bottom of the bounding box to the top and bottom of the artboard. It's not necessary to realign the bounding box, but doing so can make it easier to visualize additional transformations.

# ENVELOPE DISTORTIONS

Among the most powerful features of Illustrator is envelope distortions. This capability is somewhat of a cross between transformations and effects, with a family history that probably includes the Gradient Mesh tool. Like transformations, an object's shape changes. Like effects, the change can be modified or removed. In the manner of gradient meshes, it can be accomplished using mesh lines.

Illustrator offers predefined shapes (called *warps*) that you can use to bend an object, or you can create extremely precise distortions using a mesh or another path. (The 15 preset warps are also available in the Effects menu.) The submenu Object, Envelope Distort contains the seven commands shown in Figure 28.28.

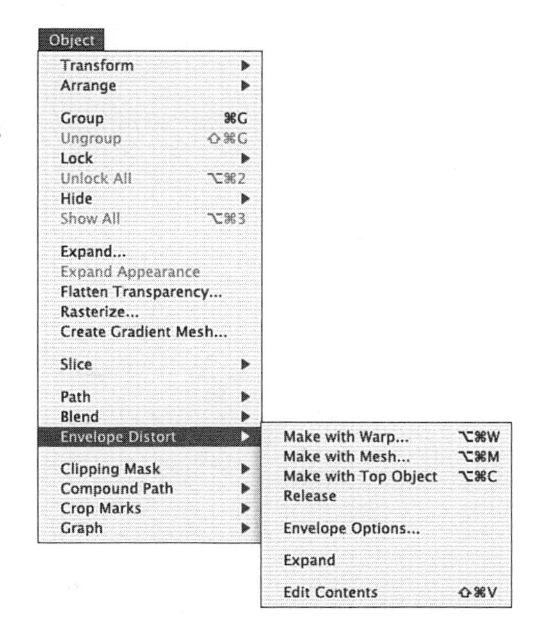


**Figure 28.28**
The top three keyboard shortcuts use the Option and Command keys for Mac, the Alt and Ctrl keys for Windows.

## Using the Make with Warp Distortions

The easiest envelope distortions to make are those that use the ready-made shapes applied with the menu command Object, Envelope Distort, Create with Warp. Illustrator offers a variety of customizable preset distortions (see Figure 28.29).

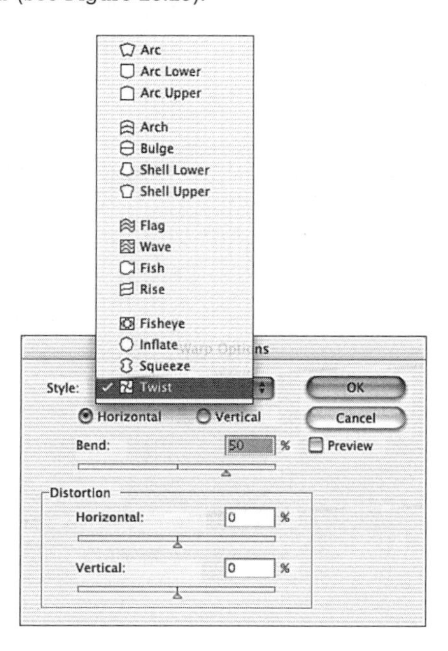


Figure 28.29
Illustrator's 15 preset warps are shown in miniature in the pop-up menu.

Warps can be applied to objects, paths, text, meshes, blends, and placed raster images. They cannot be used with graphs. To apply a warp, make a selection on the artboard and choose the menu command Object, Envelope Distort, Make with Warp to open the dialog box. In the dialog box, choose the desired preset from the pop-up menu, click Horizontal or Vertical, and adjust the sliders to achieve the desired shape.

Although the preset warps do a good job of replicating the shape shown in the pop-up menu, the power of warping comes from the sliders in the dialog box. As you can see in Figure 28.30, adjusting the distortion sliders can add a 3D look to an object.

In the upper-left corner of the figure, the default values are used: Horizontal, Bend 50%, Horizontal Distortion 0%, Vertical Distortion 0%. To the right, the only change was switching from Horizontal to Vertical. In the lower-left example, the settings include distortion: Horizontal, Bend 67%, Horizontal Distortion 50%, Vertical Distortion 50%.

Figure 28.30
These sample warps are all created with the Arc preset.

## Extreme Warping

Extreme warping can make an object appear to be twisted so much that the "back" of the object is visible. In the following figure, for example, the type of the top object appears reversed when the object is warped.

The "back" of the text is visible when warped.

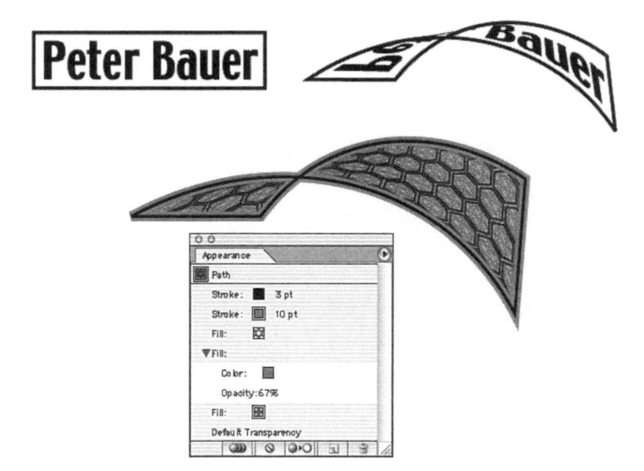


However, keep in mind that Illustrator is not actually manipulating objects in 3D. If it were, then the lower object would show a different fill appearance on the two sides. In the Appearance palette, you can see that there are several layered fills in the object. If the "back" of the object were actually visible, the fills would be stacked in reverse order. Likewise, if a pair of objects are stacked and grouped and then warped, the lower object will not be visible as the "back."



Warps can be applied to a selection that includes multiple objects. Whether the objects are grouped or not, the warp will be applied to the selected objects as a single entity. In Figure 28.31, the difference between applying the same warp to three individual objects (left) is compared to applying a single warp to three selected objects (right).

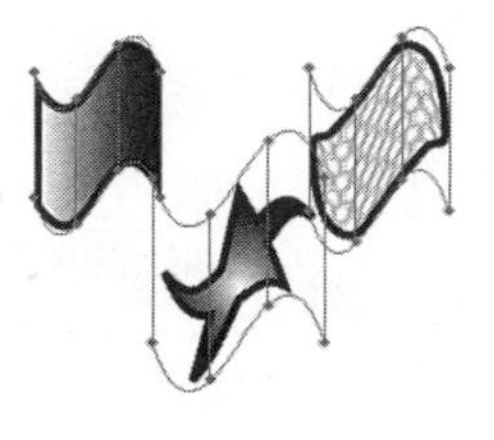

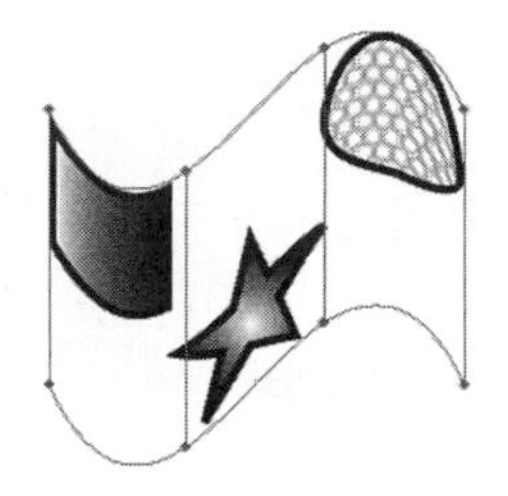

Figure 28.31
On the left, each object was warped individually. On the right, the three objects were selected together and the warp applied once.

## How Meshes Warp

Notice in Figure 28.31 that the warp paths are visible. The warped object becomes a *mesh object*, whose shape is determined by mesh points and mesh lines. A closer examination shows the anatomy of a mesh object (see Figure 28.32).

The parts of a mesh object are as follows:

- **Mesh point**—Mesh points are comparable to a path's anchor points. They are found at every intersection of mesh lines and only at the intersection of mesh lines.
- **Mesh line**—Like path segments, each segment of a mesh line is bordered by two points. Its ends are determined by the mesh point locations, and the shape of the segment is determined by the points' direction lines.
- **Direction line**—Just as path anchor points can have direction lines to determine path segment geometry, so, too, do mesh points. The shape of a mesh line segment is determined by the length and angle of the mesh point's direction line. (A complete explanation of direction lines and how they work is found in Chapter 25.)
- **Control point**—Each direction line has a control point at the end. Dragging the control point determines the length and angle of the direction line.
- **Mesh patch**—An area surrounded by mesh lines can be called a *mesh patch*. Mesh patches can be dragged to reshape a mesh object.

When a mesh line ends at a mesh point, the point may be called an *endpoint*. Mesh points that join only two mesh line segments are *corner points*. Mesh points always have one direction line for each line segment that touches a point. There can be as few as two or as many as four direction lines. Corner points will have two, endpoints will have three, and other mesh points will have four direction lines.

When a mesh point is selected on the artboard, the diamond is filled. Unselected mesh points show hollow diamonds.

When a mesh point is selected on the artboard, its direction lines will be visible. In addition, the direction lines for the mesh points at the far end of each adjoining path segment will be visible. (This is depicted in Figure 28.32.)

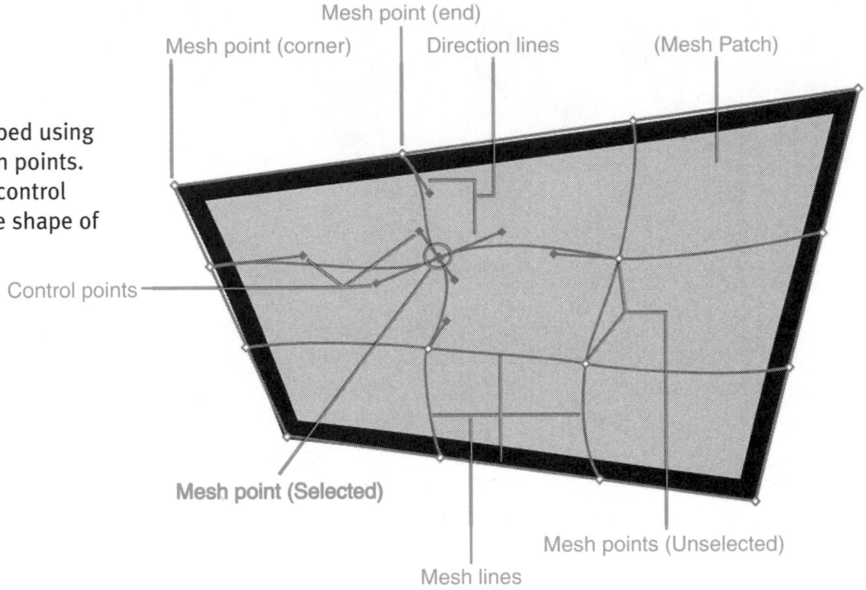

**Figure 28.32**
The selection is warped using mesh lines and mesh points. Direction lines with control points determine the shape of the mesh lines.

## Editing a Mesh Object

Mesh objects are manipulated like gradient mesh objects and, in many respects, paths. (Gradient meshes are discussed in Chapter 33, "Working with Gradients and Gradient Meshes.") Changing the shape and fill appearance of a mesh object is similar to manipulating paths in Illustrator. The Direct Selection tool can be used to modify the mesh points. As you can see in Figure 28.33, mesh points can have as many as four direction lines. Mesh points will be found at the intersection of mesh lines, including corners. Each mesh point will have one direction line for each mesh line segment.

The following guidelines cover manipulating mesh points and mesh lines:

- Each mesh point has at least two direction lines, one for each mesh line segment that meets at the mesh point.
- The shape of the mesh object is governed by the location of the mesh points and the length and angle of the points' direction lines. (This is analogous to the way that anchor points determine the shape of paths.)
- Mesh points can be moved by selecting them and dragging with the Direct Selection tool.
- A direction line is manipulated by dragging the control point at its end. The Direct Selection tool is used to drag control points.
- Shift-clicking with the Direct Selection tool allows you to select and move multiple mesh points.
- Only one control point can be manipulated at a time.
- The Direct Select Lasso tool can be used to select (but not move) mesh points. It cannot be used with control points.

- Holding down the (Option) [Alt] key and clicking a mesh point with the Direct Selection tool will select all mesh points, and dragging will make a copy of the mesh object.
- Mesh lines can be deleted by selecting a mesh endpoint and deleting the point. (Corner mesh points cannot be deleted.)
- Deleting a mesh point at the intersection of two mesh lines deletes both lines.
- The Direct Selection tool can be used to select and drag a mesh patch, an area surrounded by mesh lines. The surrounding mesh lines will be adjusted, but the mesh points' direction lines will remain unchanged in length and angle.
- When a mesh point has a mesh line running smoothly through it, changing the angle of the direction line with the Direct Selection tool will have an equal and opposite affect on the opposite direction line. (The length of the direction line on the other side of the mesh point will not be affected.) This behavior is comparable to that of a smooth anchor point on a path.
- The Convert Anchor Point tool can be used to move a control point without altering the opposite direction line.

**Figure 28.33**
The selected mesh point is at the intersection of two mesh lines. It has four direction lines, one for each line segment.

## The Make with Mesh Command

The Object, Envelope Distort menu also offers a couple ways to create custom envelope mesh objects. The Make with Mesh command opens the dialog box shown in Figure 28.34.

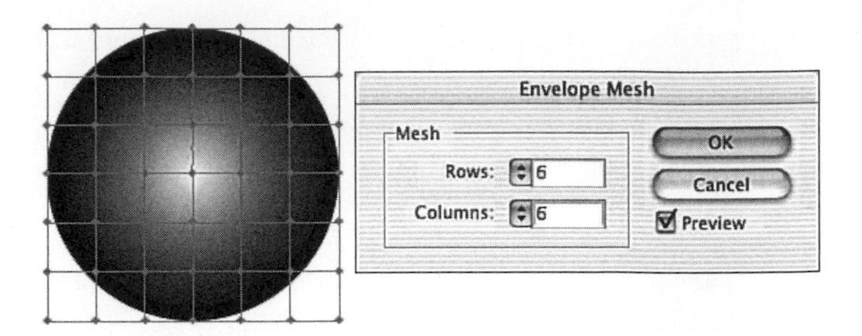


Figure 28.34
This simple dialog box offers tremendous control over the development of an envelope mesh object.

Illustrator will turn the selected object or objects into an envelope mesh object with the specified number of rows and columns. The mesh lines will be organized in an evenly spaced grid.

Creating mesh grids allows you to customize the shape of the envelope from scratch.

## Reopening the Envelope Distort Dialog Box

After a warp distortion has been applied, it can be altered. With an envelope mesh object selected on the artboard, the Object, Envelope Distort menu changes to that seen in Figure 28.35.

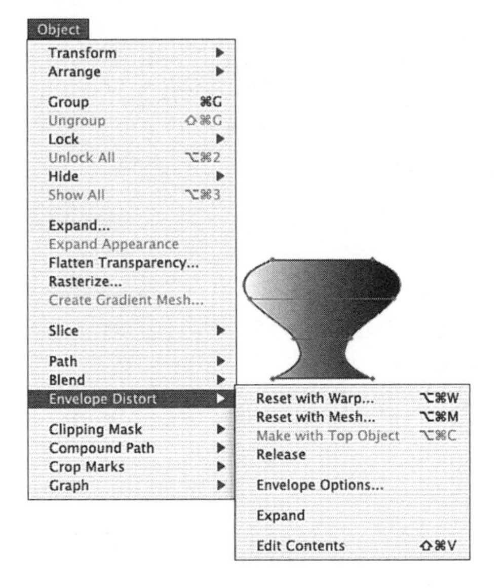


Figure 28.35
Envelope mesh objects can be altered through the original dialog boxes.

Selecting Reset with Warp reopens the Warp Options dialog box, allowing you to change the slider settings or even select a different preset. Using the menu command Reset with Mesh opens the dialog box shown in Figure 28.36.

If the Maintain Envelope Shape box is unchecked, Illustrator will convert the envelope mesh object into a rectangle the size of the original object.

Rather than counting the mesh lines, the Make with Mesh dialog box asks you for the number of rows and columns of *mesh patches*. The actual number of horizontal and vertical mesh lines will be one higher than the number of rows and columns.

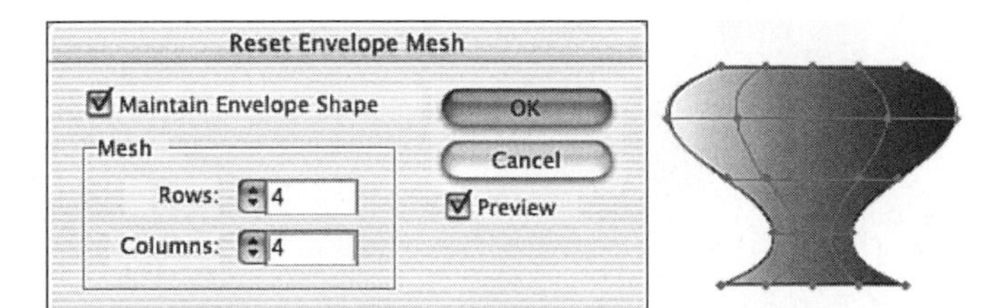


Figure 28.36
You can add or subtract rows and columns.

## Using the Make with Top Object Command

Illustrator allows you to use an object as the basis for an envelope mesh object. Only a single path or mesh object can be used, which excludes compound paths and compound shapes. The command Object, Envelope Distort, Make with Top Object executes without a dialog box. Whatever path is topmost of those selected will be used to create the shape of the mesh object, distorting any selected object(s) below to create the fill. Figure 28.37 shows a pair of examples.

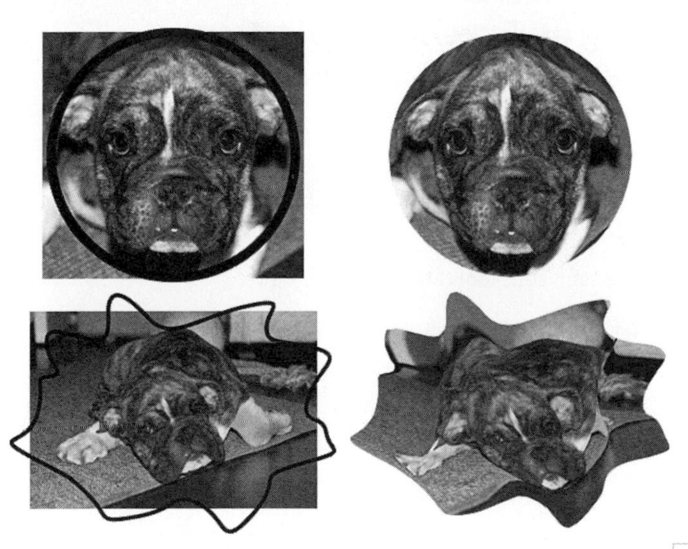

Figure 28.37
The original raster images and the paths used are on the left; the resulting mesh objects are on the right.

Any path—open or closed, stroked and filled, or invisible—can be used at the top object. Illustrator will assume a direct line between endpoints of an open path.

In Figure 28.38, a path has been drawn that maintains the integrity of the upper two-thirds of the photograph, while distorting only the lower one-third.

Where the top path follows the edges of the photo, the distortion is minimal. Where the path flares away from the photo, the distortion is much more pronounced.

When a gradient mesh object is used to create an envelope mesh, only the object's path is used. The gradient mesh lines within are ignored, and colors can no longer be assigned to the mesh points or mesh patches. Similarly, when another object is used to create an envelope mesh from a gradient mesh, the gradient mesh is no longer editable. The gradient mesh object is rasterized to create the envelope mesh object.

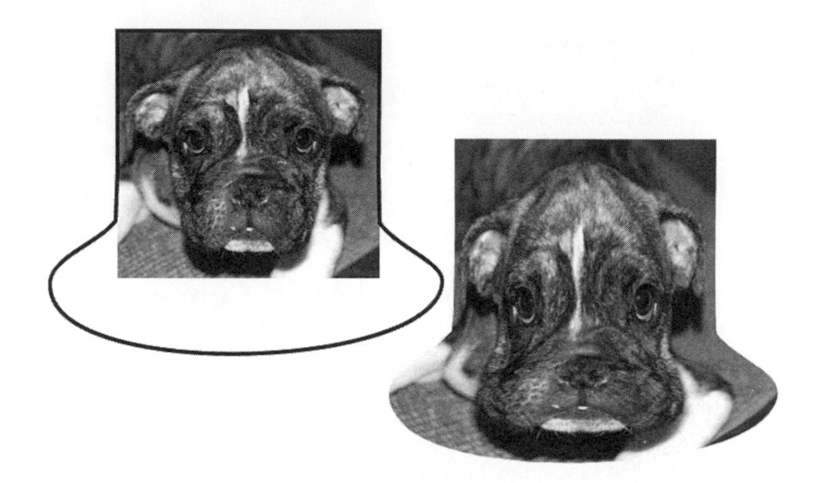

Figure 28.38
The path is shown as a heavy black outline.

## Illustrator at Work: Creating an Envelope Distortion

Make with Top Object can also be very effective with type, although the type will not be editable as long as it's part of a mesh. In order to edit your text, use the Release command, discussed later in this chapter.

To use this Envelope Distort command to distort type, follow these steps:

1. Open or create an Illustrator document.
2. Add some point type, using a sans serif font. Make it rather large.
3. Use the Pen tool to create an irregular path a little larger than the type.
4. Select both objects on the artboard or in the Layers palette.
5. Use the menu command Object, Envelope Distort, Make with Top Object. The type will change shape to conform to that of the path (see Figure 28.39).

Figure 28.39
The top object is the gray path on the left. The mesh path is visible on the right.

Remember that although the type is no longer editable as type, the envelope is still editable. You can use the Direct Selection tool to drag anchor points and direction lines to change the envelope's path, and thus the appearance of the distortion.

## Envelope Options

Illustrator gives you several options that can be preset for envelope distortions. The menu command Object, Envelope Distort, Envelope Options opens the dialog box shown in Figure 28.40.

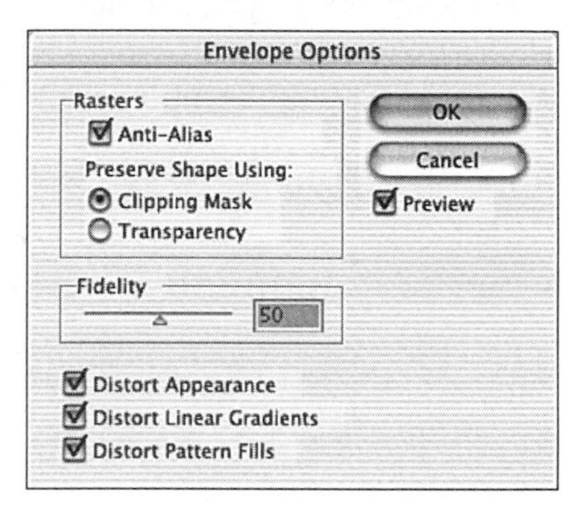


**Figure 28.40**
This dialog box determines what characteristics of an object will be distorted and how precisely.

The top section of the box, which applies only to rasterized artwork, allows you to use antialiasing to smooth the appearance of curves and to choose between a clipping path and a mask (alpha channel) to preserve the appearance of the artwork.

The Fidelity slider controls how closely the distortion will match the path. The slider ranges from 0 to 100, with 50 as the default. Increased fidelity results in more points being added to the resulting object. In addition to requiring more time to produce the envelope distortions, higher fidelity can produce extremely complex paths.

Illustrator also offers the Envelope Options dialog box to determine whether a pattern fill or linear gradient fill will be distorted with an object. You can also elect to scale strokes and effects, much as they can be scaled when you're working with transformations.

The difference between distorting an object and distorting an object and its pattern fill is shown in Figure 28.41.

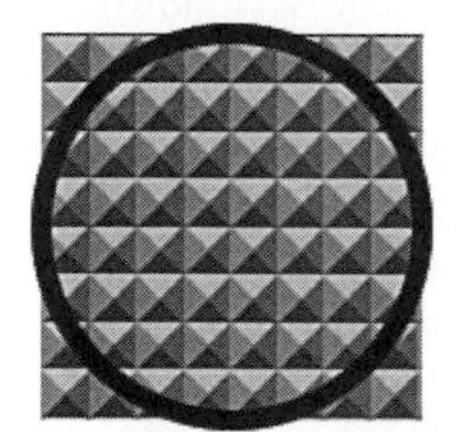

**Figure 28.41**
The original pair of objects is on the left. In the center, the object alone was distorted. On the right, the object and pattern were distorted.

## Releasing and Expanding Envelope Distortions

The menu commands Object, Envelope Distort, Release and Object, Envelope Distort, Expand are discussed together to avoid confusion. In execution, these commands have similarities; in result, they do not. Releasing a distortion restores the object to its pre-distortion appearance; expanding a distortion permanently applies it to the object.

To either release or expand an envelope distortion, the envelope mesh object must be selected on the artboard and the command invoked. Multiple envelope mesh objects can be released or expanded at the same time.

The Release command removes the distortion, returning the object to its original state, and produces an object in the shape of the mesh. It is no longer a mesh object but rather consists of an unstroked path filled with gray. It is always created on top of the original object(s). If it's no longer needed, the mesh shape can be selected and deleted.

The Expand command applies the envelope distortion permanently. The mesh is removed and the object retains the distorted shape.

Figure 28.42 shows the envelope mesh objects from the previous figure released (top) and expanded (bottom).

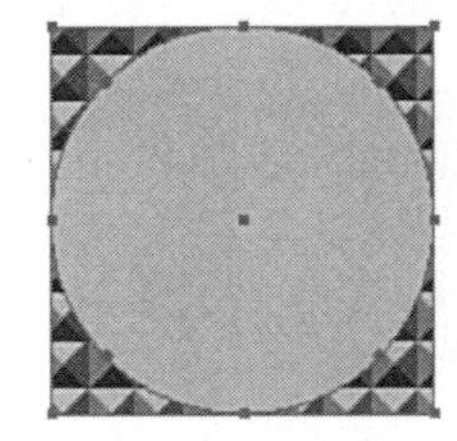
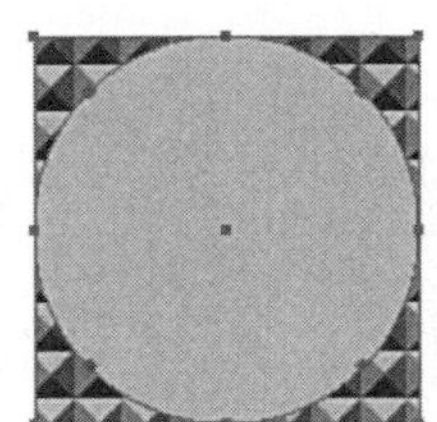
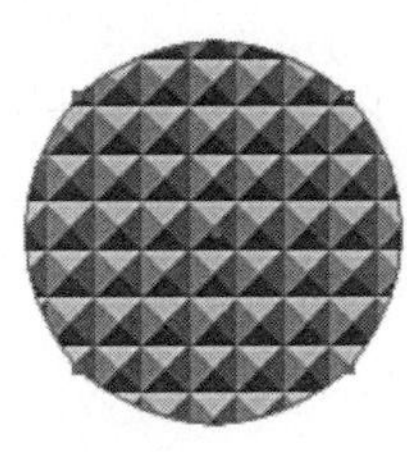
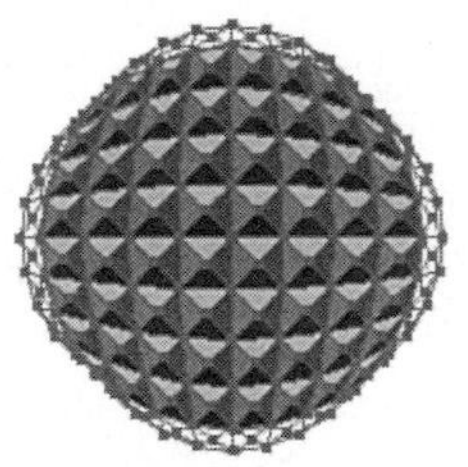

**Figure 28.42**
The two envelope mesh objects from Figure 28.41 have been both released (top) and expanded (bottom).

Note that there is no difference between the two released envelope distortions. Both now consist of the original object and a gray circle.

The expanded objects, however, differ substantially. On the left, only the object was distorted, so expanding the envelope mesh resulted in a simple change of shape from the original square to the circle. On the right, however, both the object and its pattern fill were distorted and expanded. The result is a very complex collection of vector objects. Each section of the pattern has been expanded to a separate object. (There are actually 275 separate vector objects, surrounded by a clipping path.)



## Reusable Distortion Envelopes

If you need to replicate a custom distortion again and again, you need to create it only once and you can apply it as often as you'd like. Make the envelope mesh object and manipulate it until it looks just right. Next, use the menu command Object, Envelope Distort, Release. A plain gray object will be created, representing the envelope mesh shape. Select just that shape and click the New Symbol button in the Symbols palette. The shape will be added to the palette as a symbol.

When you next need to create an envelope distortion with the shape, you can select it in the Symbols palette and either click once with the Symbol Sprayer or drag the shape to the artboard. Position it atop the object(s) to be distorted, and use the menu command Object, Envelope Distort, Make from Top Object.

## The Edit Contents Command

The appearance of an object can be changed even after it is converted to an envelope mesh object. The menu command Object, Envelope Distort, Edit Contents gives you access to the underlying object through the Appearance palette. (After you choose this command, it will change in the menu to Edit Envelope.)

If this command isn't in effect, double-clicking the Contents line in the Appearance palette expands to show the mesh object (see Figure 28.43). No stroke or fill or other appearance characteristic can be applied directly to the mesh.

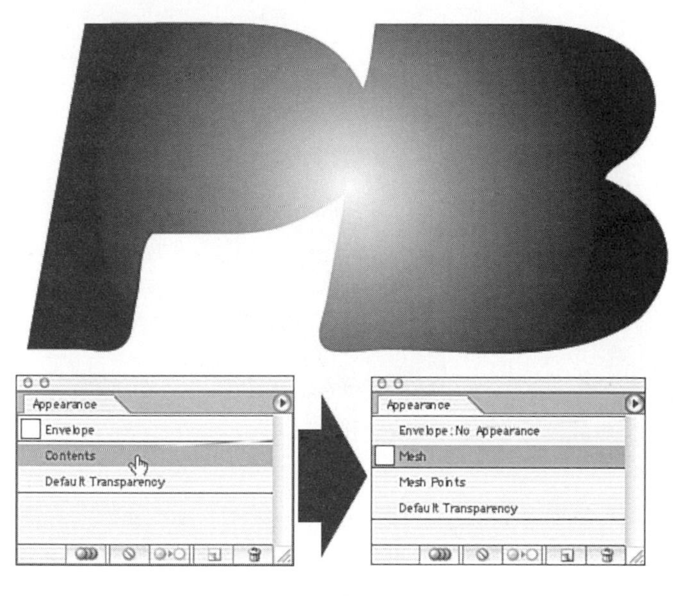


Figure 28.43
With an envelope mesh object selected on the artboard, double-clicking Contents in the Appearance palette (left) opens the palette content to show Mesh (right). Of course, only one Appearance palette will be visible.

After you use the menu command Edit Contents, double-clicking Contents in the Appearance palette gives you access to the underlying object. You can add or change fills, strokes, and opacity characteristics. The envelope mesh remains applied, and the distorted shape remains unchanged. If necessary, Illustrator will re-center the mesh on the original object. Figure 28.44 shows one example of what can be done after an envelope distortion is applied.

The Envelope Distort menu command alternates between Edit Contents and Edit Envelope, depending on which you have chosen most recently. Illustrator does allow you to add strokes and fills directly to an envelope object itself. As you can see in Figure 28.45, adding a simple 1-point stroke to an envelope mesh object can have very interesting results.

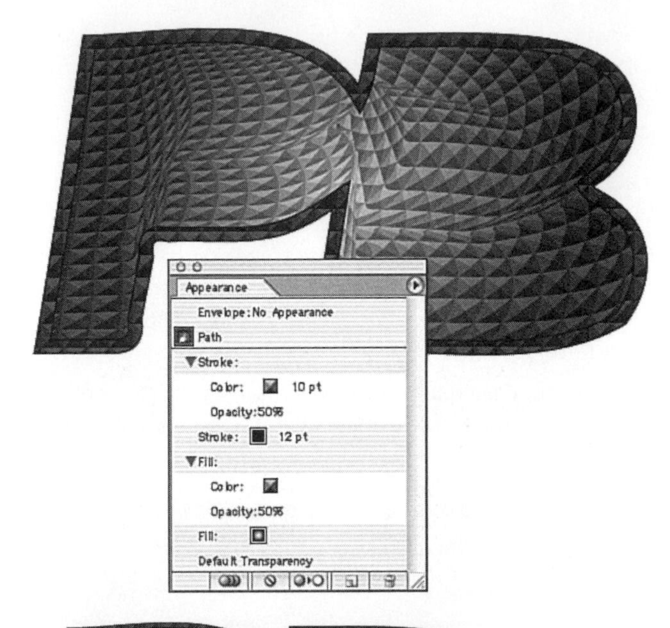


**Figure 28.44**
Once the content is available for editing, additional stroke, fill, and opacity characteristics can be added through the Appearance palette, all without removing the distortion.

**Figure 28.45**
The mesh includes the original object's pattern fill, so the stroke is applied to it as well as the outer path.

# ILLUSTRATOR'S LIQUIFY TOOLS

Illustrator contains a group of tools that enable you to push and pull, swirl and scallop, expand and contract, and generally distort vector shapes (see Figure 28.46).

> The liquify tools have preferences (including brush size) that can be specified by double-clicking the tool's icon in Illustrator's Toolbox.

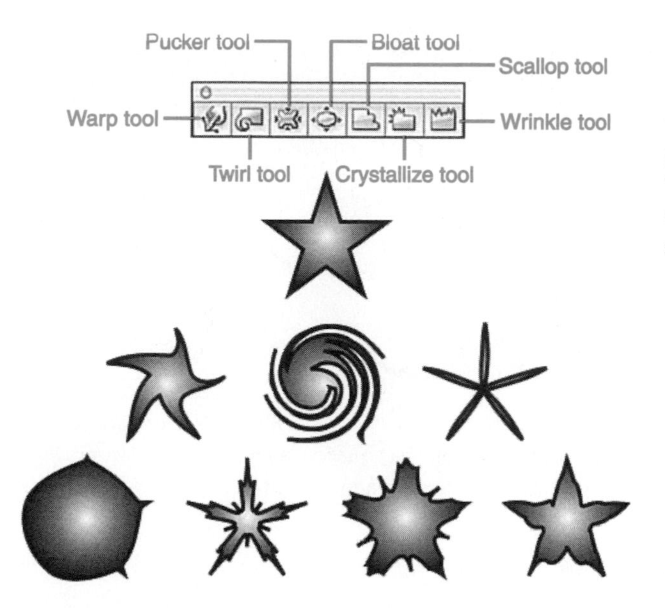


**Figure 28.46**
The flyout tool palette is found under the Warp tool in the Toolbox. The original object is shown at the top. Each tool was applied in turn.

## Working with the Liquify Tools

The liquify tools use round brushes to define the area of application. Selected paths within the diameter of the brush are modified by moving and/or adding anchor points. The following list describes each of the liquify tools:

- The Warp tool pushes and pulls on an object's anchor points as you drag. New anchor points are created as necessary to modify the shape.
- The Twirl tool modifies path segments by adding and moving anchor points and changing direction lines. It does not create smoothly uniform changes to an entire object, such as you can produce with the Twist effect. Rather, it manipulates those path segments and anchor points within the brush's diameter. To use it, select the target object on the artboard and either click and hold to create uniform twirls or click and drag for nonuniform distortions. In Figure 28.47, a single line has been distorted three times with the Twirl tool.

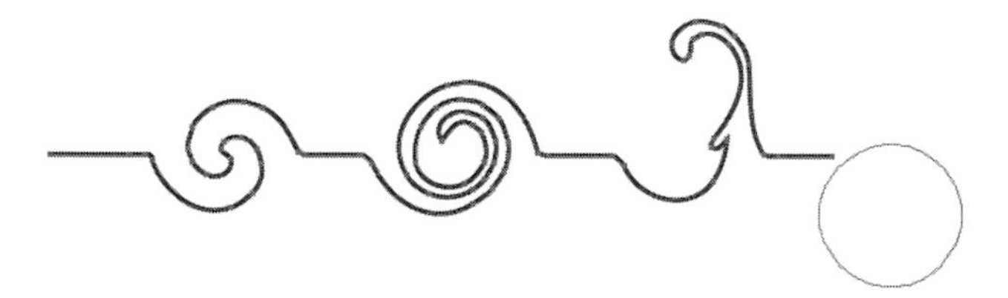

**Figure 28.47**
To the left, the twirl tool was applied with a click-hold-release operation. In the center, the tool was dragged in a small circle. To the right, the tool was dragged upward.

Note the number of anchor points added by the Twirl tool. The original path was a single line segment with two anchor points.

- The Pucker tool collapses the sides of an object inward. It can also be used to drag a path segment. Select an object on the artboard and click and hold to pucker it. In Figure 28.48, three pairs of squares are shown; one of each pair has been puckered. The dashed circles represent the brush size for the Pucker tool.

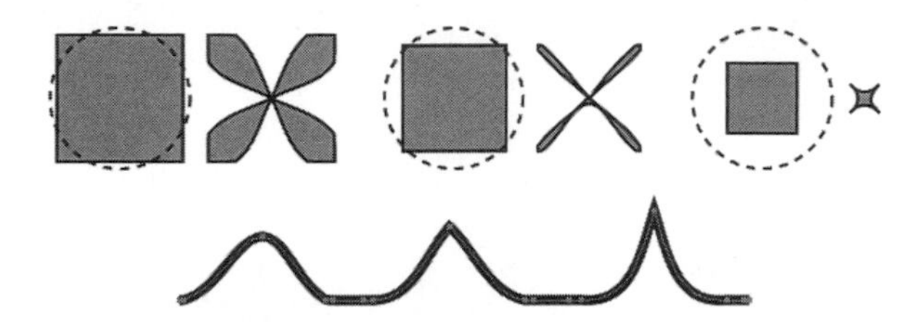

Figure 28.48
Whether or not an object's anchor points are within the brush diameter makes a large difference in the pucker distortion applied.

To the left, you can see that the anchor points and parts of the object's path that were outside the brush remain unaffected. In the center, the square was just slightly larger than the brush diameter. On the right, you can see the result when the entire object is within the brush diameter.

Figure 28.48 also shows the result of applying the Pucker tool to a straight path segment. The speed with which the tool is dragged affects its result. The Pucker tool was dragged upward three times from the path. From the left, the tool was dragged very slowly, slowly, and quickly.

- The Bloat tool is the counterpart of the Pucker tool. It expands the sides of an object. Apply the Bloat tool by clicking or dragging over a selected object. When the entire selected object fits inside the brush diameter, a single click can result in a near-circular object. Smaller brushes are usually more effective. When you're applying the tool to a path segment rather than anchor points, drag in the direction opposite to that in which you want to bloat. Think of it as dragging away to create curves.
- The Scallop tool creates curves along the path of a selected object. Dragging the tool produces curves going in the direction of the drag.
- The Crystallize tool creates pointed segments rather than curves. Drag away from the direction in which the points should go.
- The Wrinkle tool creates a series of angles along a path, like the Crystallize tool, but its angles are restricted by the Liquify options.

## The Liquify Tool Options

Each of the liquify tools has its own options dialog box, which can be opened by double-clicking the tool's icon in Illustrator's Toolbox. The Warp Tool Options dialog box is shown in Figure 28.49.

All the liquify tools use the same Global Brush Dimensions options. In fact, all the tools use the same brush. Changing the Warp tool's brush also changes the brush for each of the other liquify tools.

**Caution**

Consider using the command Object, Path, Simplify after working with a liquify tool. The tools can add many extra points to a path, and Simplify can delete the unnecessary points without changing the path's shape. Simplifying paths can help reduce the chance of output errors.

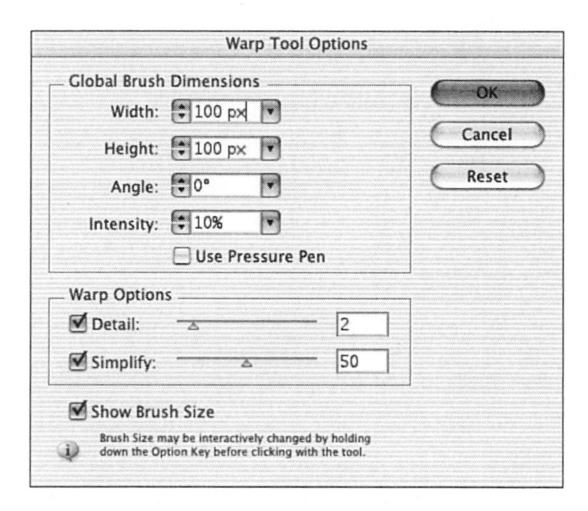


**Figure 28.49**
The Warp Tool Options dialog box is typical of most of the liquify tool options.

Modifying the width and height nonuniformly creates a nonround brush. Adding an angle other than 0° produces a calligraphy-like brush.

Intensity determines how fast or slowly the tool works while the mouse button is held down. The Pressure Pen option is for use with drawing tablets, such as the Wacom Intuos line.

The lower part of the Options dialog box varies from tool to tool. The Warp, Pucker, and Bloat tools use the options shown in Figure 28.49 in the Warp Options area.

The Scallop, Crystallize, and Wrinkle tools use a set of options that differ from the other liquify tools. The Wrinkle Tool Options dialog box is pictured in Figure 28.50. The Scallop and Crystallize tools do not have the Horizontal and Vertical sliders but otherwise offer the same options.

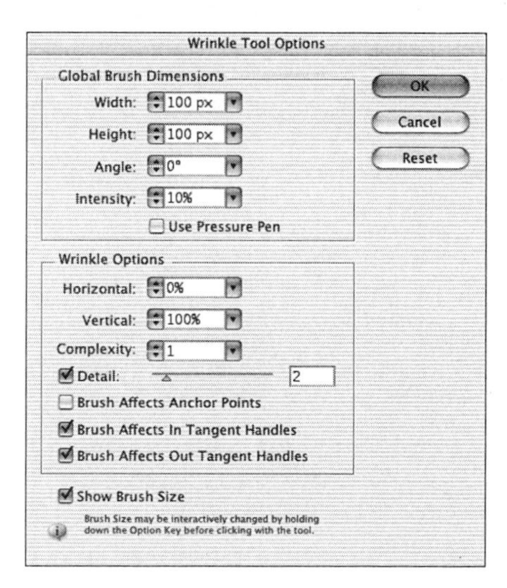


**Figure 28.50**
Changes to the Global Brush Dimensions are applied to all of the liquify tools. The settings in the lower part of the dialog box are unique to each of the tools.

You can modify anchor points and/or either of the tangent handle types, or you can choose just one of the three. You'll typically see little variation between the tangent handle options. However, checking and unchecking the Brush Affects Anchor Points box will typically produce a large difference in tool behavior.

If you find that the liquify tools seem out of control, that they create shapes far too extreme, reduce the Intensity setting in the tool options.

# MASTERING ILLUSTRATOR

Always check the Wrinkle tool options before working with the tool. Specifically, look to see whether you'll be producing changes horizontally, vertically, or both. When horizontal is set to 0%, you'll be adding anchor points to vertical lines without changing the path appearance in any noticeable way.

On the flip side, restricting distortion to either vertical or horizontal allows you to produce uniform perspective, motion, and gravity effects.

## Showing and Hiding the Bounding Box

*Why is the bounding box sometimes visible and sometimes not?*

First, remember that Illustrator uses the bounding box with only the Selection tool and the Free Transform tool. When any other tool is active, the bounding box is not. Second, it's possible to inadvertently hide the bounding box with the Show/Hide Bounding Box command's default keyboard shortcut. (Shift-Command-B) [Shift+Ctrl+B] is very close to the keyboard shortcut for Paste in Back, (Command-B) [Ctrl+B]. You can check to see if the bounding box is hidden by pressing the (Command) [Ctrl] key to temporarily switch to the Selection tool. Assuming that something is selected on the artboard, the bounding box will be visible while the key is depressed.

## Checking Options

*I get some pretty strange results when I use the transform tools. Any suggestions?*

When a transform tool is acting strangely, double-click its icon in the Toolbox and look at the check boxes in the Options dialog box. You may (or may not) be scaling patterns, strokes, and effects as well as the object.

29

# CREATING BLENDS

## IN THIS CHAPTER

A *blend* is a series of objects created to show a linear progression between two objects. Each step (or intermediary object) created by Illustrator in a blend is a unique element, with characteristics of each of the objects being blended. As the blend progresses from one of the original objects toward the other, the balance of characteristics shifts. Blends are created along straight paths (called *spines*), but the paths can be edited as any other. The shapes from which the blend is created can be edited, and the blend is automatically updated.

This chapter looks at creating blends, editing them, and expanding them for editing and to prevent output problems.

# CREATING BLENDS

You can create blends by using the Blend tool or choosing Object, Blend, Make. You can create them among an unlimited number of objects, but Illustrator blends only adjacent objects. See Figure 29.1 for an example.

**Figure 29.1**
The blend among these three objects is actually a pair of blends. The first is a blend between the square and star; the second, between the star and circle.

In Figure 29.1, notice that the path along which the blend was created is visible, as are the paths of the three objects used in the creation of the blend. Making an adjustment to one of the objects produces the result shown in Figure 29.2. The intermediary objects, created by Illustrator for the blend, cannot themselves be edited unless the blend is expanded. (See "Expanding a Blend" later in this chapter.)

Blends can be created between multiple filled or unfilled objects, multiple open paths, or among a combination of open and closed paths. As you can see in Figure 29.3, Illustrator can also blend grouped objects and unfilled/unstroked objects.

Figure 29.2
Using the Direct Selection tool to move an anchor point results in changes to all the intermediary objects in the blend.

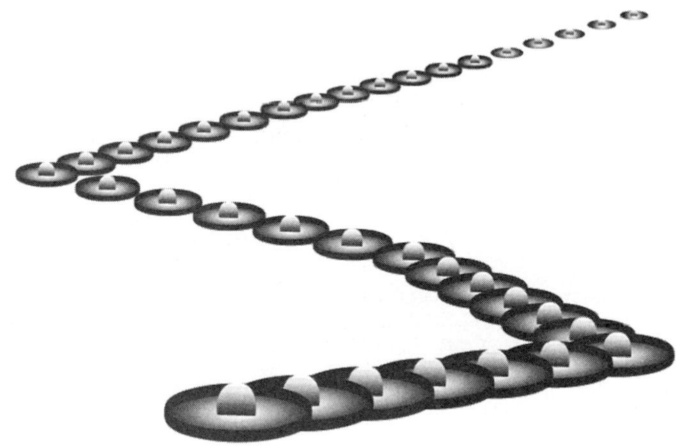

Figure 29.3
The objects appear to fade in because the object in the upper-right corner has a stroke and fill of None. That first object is, of course, not visible.

Depending on the current options, Illustrator produces a specified number of intermediary objects, produces objects at a specified distance from each other, or creates a smooth blend of colors.

The following rules govern the creation of blends:

- The objects must be vector (not rasterized) and cannot be gradient mesh objects.
- The paths can be open or closed.
- You can blend between gradients.
- You can blend between open and closed paths.
- You can create a blend from numerous objects.
- After you create a blend, the parts of the blend are joined into a single object. You can access individual parts of the blend after choosing Object, Blend, Expand.

- You can transform or edit the unexpanded blend like any other single object.
- You can edit the path along which the blend is created like any other open or closed path.
- Intermediary objects are always distributed evenly along the blend spine.
- You can select and manipulate individual points on the blend's original objects with the Group Select tool.
- When you're blending among more than two objects, the order of blend follows the stacking order in the Layers palette.
- You can blend among grouped objects, but when you're blending among members of a group and another object, each group member blends independently.
- Objects with multiple attributes, such as strokes, fills, and effects, can be blended. Illustrator attempts to determine the averages of the attributes to create the intermediary objects.
- When you're blending objects filled with patterns, the pattern of the topmost object overrides the others.
- When you're blending objects with differing opacities, the blend adopts the transparency of the topmost object.
- When you're blending paths with different miter limits, caps, or joins, the intermediary objects assume the appearance of the object uppermost in the stacking order.
- When you're blending objects on different layers, Illustrator moves the entire blend to the layer of the topmost object.
- You can edit the blend itself after creating it by using selection and transformation tools.
- Illustrator attempts to blend multiple effects, fills, and strokes.

Complex blends, especially when you're blending different colors, can substantially slow screen redraw times in Preview Mode. Outline Mode shows only the paths of the original objects and the path along which they were blended. If you create your blend on a separate layer, you can show that individual layer in Outline Mode by (Command)-clicking [Ctrl]-clicking the layer's eye icon in the Layers palette. You can leave the rest of the image in Preview Mode, with just the blend's layer in Outline Mode.

Several issues related to printing involve blends. Illustrator uses process colors to blend between two spot colors or between a spot color and a process color. When you're blending between two tints of the same spot color, the intermediary shapes are also tints of the spot color. To control whether transparent objects in a blend knock out those below, select the blend and expand the Transparency palette to show its options.

# The Blend Menu

The following commands are available in the Blend menu:

- **Make**—Creates the blend according to the options specified.
- **Release**—Deletes all intermediary objects in a selected blend.

- **Blend Options**—Opens the Blend Options dialog box. There, you can specify the number of intermediary objects (Specify Steps) to be created or how far apart to place the new objects (Specify Distance). You also can allow Illustrator to choose the number of steps and their distance by opting to blend for Smooth Color. You can also choose the orientation of the intermediary objects and whether they will be aligned with the page or the path.
- **Expand**—Comparable to the Object option of the menu command Object, Expand.
- **Replace Spine**—Allows you to substitute a new path for the straight path along which the blend was created.
- **Reverse Spine**—Somewhat comparable to using the Reflect tool and reflecting perpendicular to the spine's path. With complicated paths, reversing the spine may give more precise results than Reflect.
- **Reverse Front to Back**—Reverses the stacking order of the original and intermediary objects. If the pattern or transparency of the original topmost object was imposed on the blend, it is not changed.

## Illustrator at Work: Using the Blend Tool

The Blend tool allows you to click objects sequentially to determine the order of blend. In addition, you can click specific anchor points of the objects to force Illustrator to create the blend with the designated points aligning. Follow these steps:

1. Open or create an Illustrator document.
2. Use the Star tool to add a pair of stars to the artboard, one on each side of the artboard. Make one a 5-point star and the other an 11-point star. Assign contrasting fills and strokes.
3. Select the Blend tool from the Toolbox and click in the center of each object. A blend is created.
4. Undo to remove the blend.
5. Click the top anchor point of the 5-point star and the bottom point (or one near the bottom) of the 11-point star. Observe how the blend rotates. (The difference is shown in Figure 29.4.)

**Figure 29.4**
In the lower example, the Blend tool was clicked on the uppermost anchor point of the 5-point star and then on the point indicated on the second star.

6. Undo to remove the blend.
7. Add a third object, any shape, to the artboard.
8. Using a series of clicks and Undo commands, watch how the blend changes according to the order in which you click the objects and which anchor points are clicked.

Designating anchor points with the Blend tool will create a blend that rotates to align the points. This technique can be accomplished only with the Blend tool—the menu command Object, Blend, Make cannot assign anchor points.

Here are the two basic operations you can perform using the Blend tool:

- To simply blend two or more objects, click them sequentially with the Blend tool.
- To rotate a blend between two objects, click corresponding anchor points. For example, if a point at the top of one object and a point at the bottom of the second object are clicked, the intermediary objects appear to rotate through 180°. When the cursor is directly over an anchor point, it changes appearance, darkening and adding a plus sign.

## The Blend, Make Command

The actual process of making a blend can be as simple as selecting two objects on the artboard and choosing Object, Blend, Make. Illustrator uses the currently specified blend options (see the next section).

Unlike the Blend tool, which allows you to specify the order of blend, the Make command uses the stacking order found in the Layers palette. To change the order, you must rearrange the objects, groups, or layers in the Layers palette.

*If an illustration isn't printing properly, see "Printing Blends" in the "Mastering Illustrator" section at the end of this chapter.*

# EXAMINING THE BLEND OPTIONS

In the Blend Options dialog box, shown in Figure 29.5, you can specify that the blend be created with smooth color, a certain number of steps (intermediary objects), or with a specified distance between objects. In addition, you can choose to maintain the orientation of the objects on a curved path or create each object perpendicular to the path.

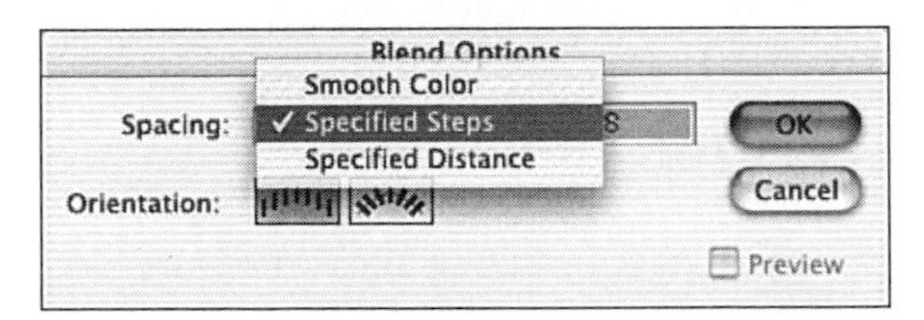


Figure 29.5
For the Specified Distance option, you can input a specific number and unit of measure. Smooth Color has no numeric option.

## Smooth Color

Illustrator determines how many intermediary objects are required to produce a smooth color blend between two objects. If the colors are identical, or if the objects have gradient or pattern fills, Illustrator calculates the number of new objects based on the distance between bounding boxes (see Figure 29.6).

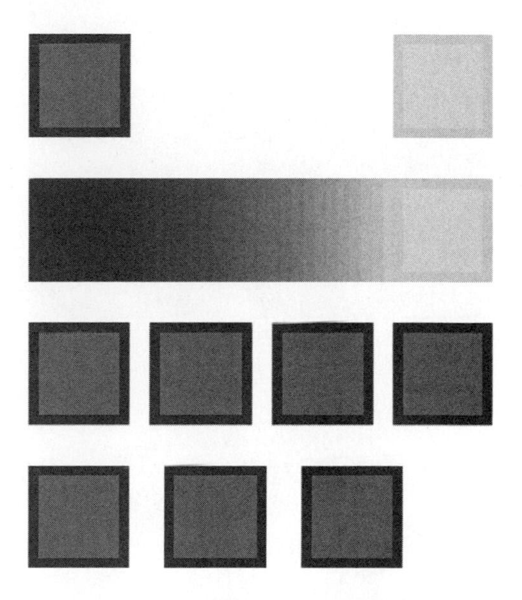

Figure 29.6
The top pair of boxes were blended using Smooth Color to produce the blend in the second row. The third row is a Smooth Color blend of two identical objects.

In Figure 29.6, two squares of differing stroke and fill (shown at the top of the image) were blended. Illustrator created 254 intermediary objects to bridge the gap between the colors. The third and fourth pairs of squares show how Illustrator blends two identically colored squares when Smooth Color is selected. The third pair has two intermediary objects because that is how many would fit between the originals without overlapping bounding boxes.

Figure 29.7 illustrates how the number of intermediary objects created depends on the color difference between the two originals. All the squares have the same color stroke. All the squares on the left have the same fill, an RGB value of 255/0/0. The squares with which they have been blended, on the right, have varying fills. The RGB values are, from the top down, 250/0/0, 240/0/0, 225/0/0, and 200/0/0.

You can use Smooth Color to create shaped gradients. Figure 29.8 shows a star-shaped example. To create this gradient look, the large star was created with a fill, but no stroke. It was duplicated using Copy and Paste in Front. The duplicate was scaled to 25% of its original size using the command Object, Transform, Scale. Its fill was changed to white, and the command Object, Blend, Make was used, with the Blend Options set to Smooth Color.

You also can use Smooth Color to create shaded objects with unusual shapes. Figure 29.9 shows a blend between two open paths.

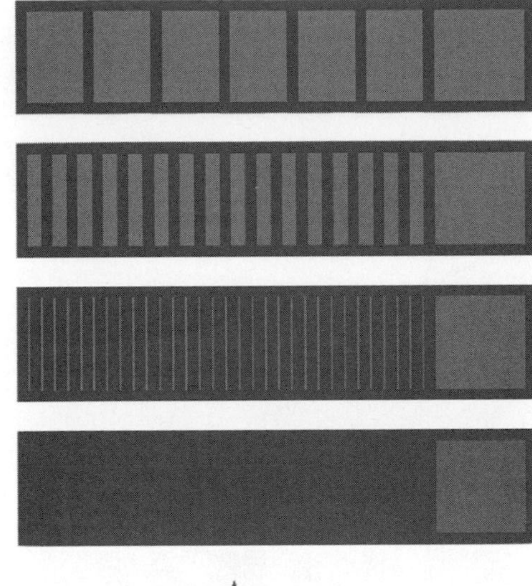

Figure 29.7
To bridge the gap between a red value of 255 and, from the top, red values of 250, 240, 225, and 200, Illustrator has created, respectively, 5, 15, 30, and 57 new objects.

Figure 29.8
The small white star (on top) is blended into the larger star to create the gradient look.

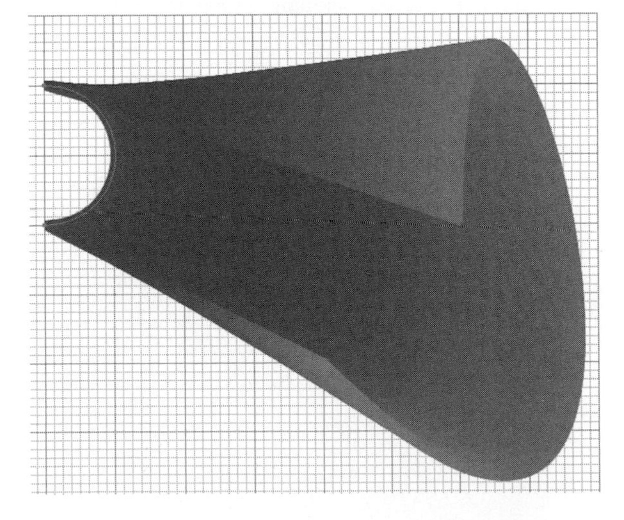

Figure 29.9
Using vector paths and Smooth Color blends can produce precisely proportioned objects.

**Smooth Blends for Graphs**

Smooth Color blends are excellent for customizing certain types of graphs. The following figure provides some suggestions.

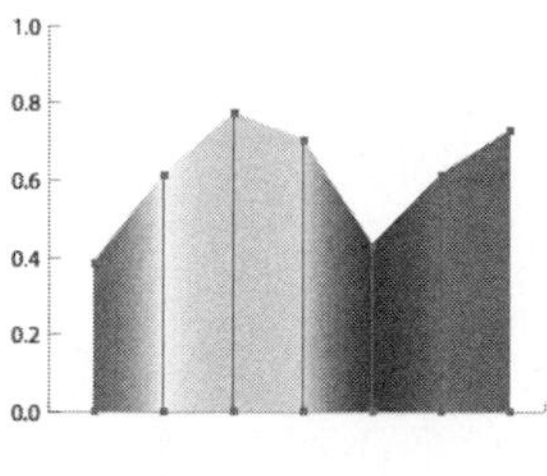


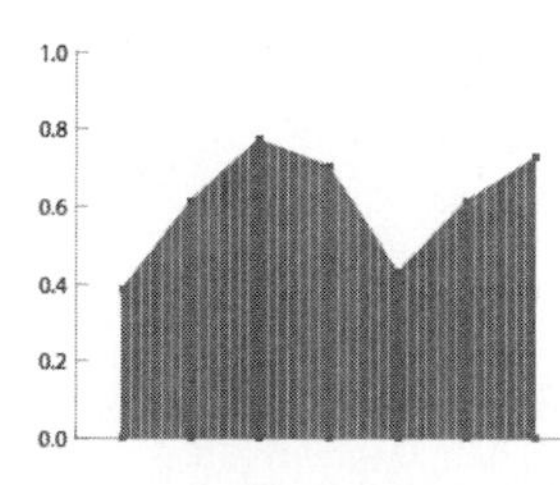


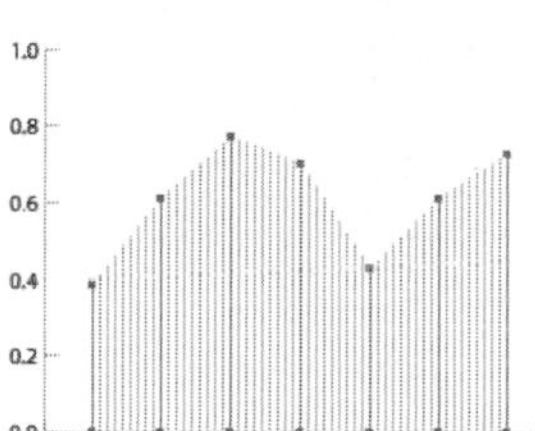


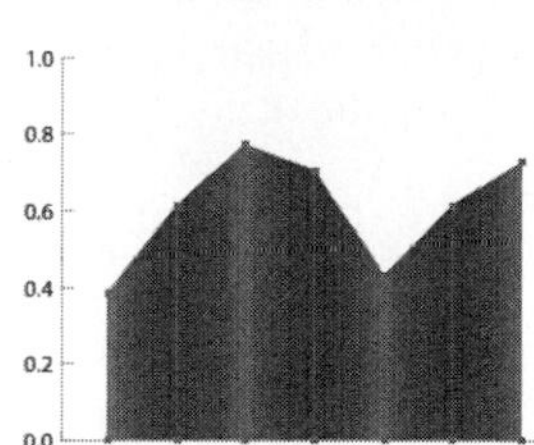


As is evident from the selections, the four graphs use the same seven open paths as values.

The rainbow pattern in the upper left is created by using different color values for each of the seven paths that are blended. In the upper right, grayscale values of 100% and 75% are alternated. To the lower left, the grayscale values are 100% for each path. In the lower right, the alternating grayscale values are 50% and 100%.

You can make blends from graphs created with the Graph tools after ungrouping. Remember, however, that ungrouping a graph prevents further changes to the graph data, styles, and designs (see Chapter 25, "Working with the Shape, Drawing, and Graph Tools").

## Specified Steps

When you select Specified Steps, you are instructing Illustrator on how many intermediary objects to create. The program automatically calculates the proper proportion of each original object's appearance for the intermediary objects. The objects are evenly spaced between the original objects.

The Specified Steps setting is especially appropriate for the creation of Web-based animation. Whether you're working with animated GIF or Flash format illustrations, you can simplify frame-based animation by using Specified Steps blends. After you expand and ungroup the blended objects, choosing Illustrator's Release to Layers command puts each object on a separate layer, ready to become an individual frame of the animation.

*Remember that you can export a layered Illustrator image to Photoshop's PSD format for use with ImageReady.* *See Chapter 23, "Creating Rollovers and Adding Animation," p. 733.*

In Figure 29.10, three objects have been grouped at the beginning of the sequence and copied to the end. Illustrator's Blend command (using Specified Steps) produced the intermediary steps in the sequence. When the blend is expanded, ungrouped, and released to layers, the result is the "frames" of a figure walking across the screen. At a frame rate of 15 frames per second (fps), the walk is just under a second and a half.

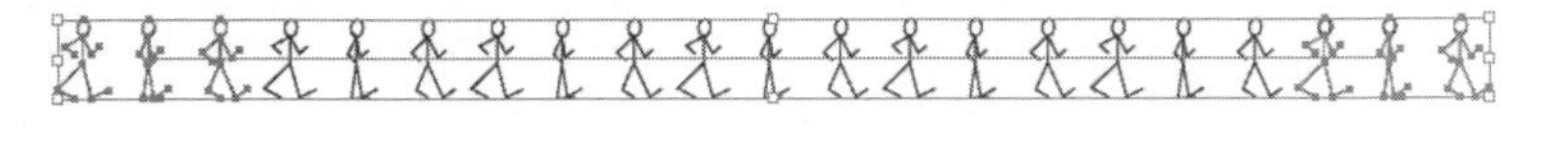

**Figure 29.10**
Separating each object into its own frame results in an animation that shows the figure walking across the page. Enlarged versions of the three original objects are shown below.

Specifying the number of intermediary objects can serve a variety of purposes in addition to creating animation. You can insert virtually anything that you need to uniformly add to an illustration by choosing Object, Blend, Make using Specified Steps. Figure 29.11 shows some varied ideas.

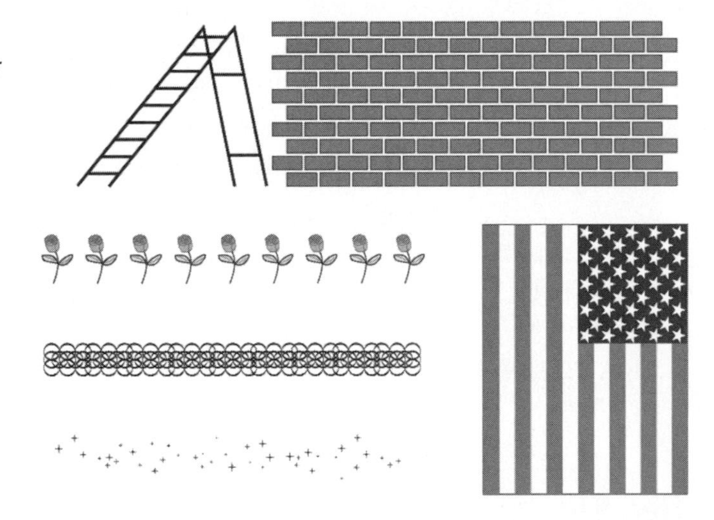

**Figure 29.11**
All these examples employ one or more blends using Specified Steps.

When you're blending multiple objects, keep in mind that blends depend on the stacking order of objects. Even when all objects are on the same layer, the order in which they were drawn determines the order in which they will be blended. Figure 29.12 shows 20 numbered tiles, drawn sequentially, and how they blend.

## Specified Distance

The third choice for spacing in the Blend Options dialog box is Specified Distance. Especially useful for blends that include multiple objects, this option attempts to place intermediary objects at a set distance from the original objects and from each other. However, if the distance isn't a multiple of the specified distance, Illustrator will shift the intermediary objects to maintain uniform distance between all the objects.

When you're using Specified Distance, the relative positions of the original objects being blended are irrelevant to the spacing of the intermediary objects. Specified Distance and Specified Steps are contrasted in Figure 29.13.

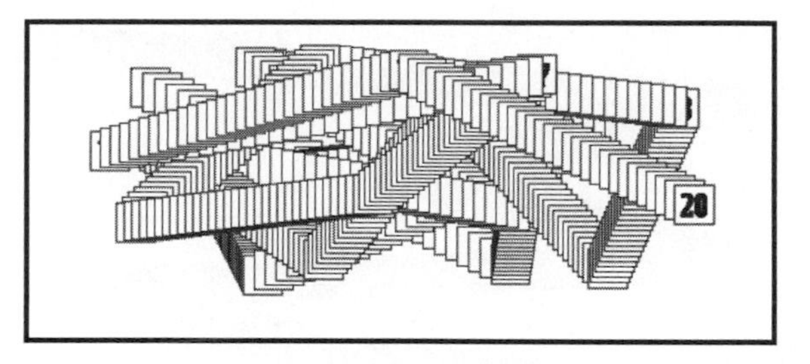


**Figure 29.12**
Note that the spacing of the intermediary objects varies, depending on the distance between the two objects being blended. The number of intermediary objects, however, is the same for each segment of the blend.



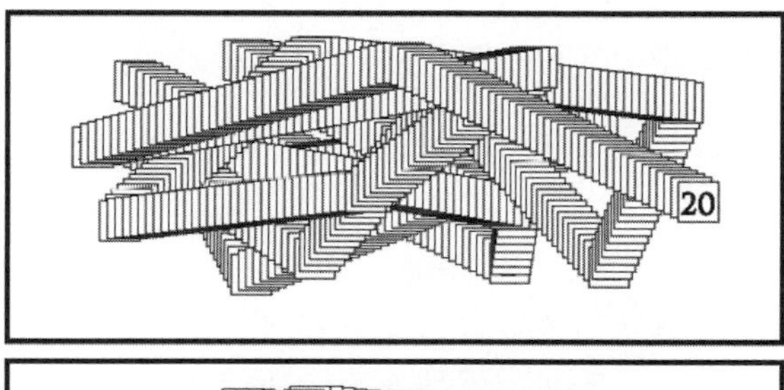


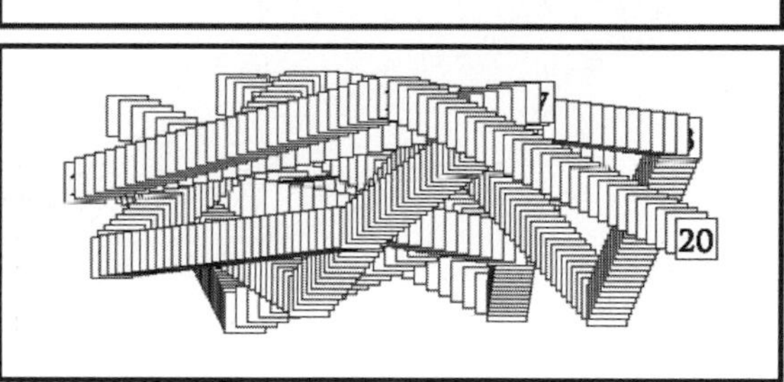


**Figure 29.13**
Compare the upper blend, created with Specified Distance, to the lower blend, from Figure 29.12, created with Specified Steps.

In Figure 29.13, the upper blend has each intermediary object evenly spaced. The lower blend has an equal number of objects in each segment of the blend, but because the distance between blended objects differs, so does the spacing. As you can see in Figure 29.14, with Specified Distance, all intermediary objects are equally spaced, regardless of the spacing of the two original objects bordering the blend.

*If you can' t seem to get that last intermediary object in exactly the right spot using Specified Distance, see "Correcting Blend Spacing" in the "Mastering Illustrator" section at the end of this chapter.*

The spacing of the intermediary objects created with the Specified Distance option is based on paths. Observe in Figure 29.15 how the stroke of a path can change the perception of spacing.

Figure 29.14
The 10 original objects are at the corners, with intermediary objects between.

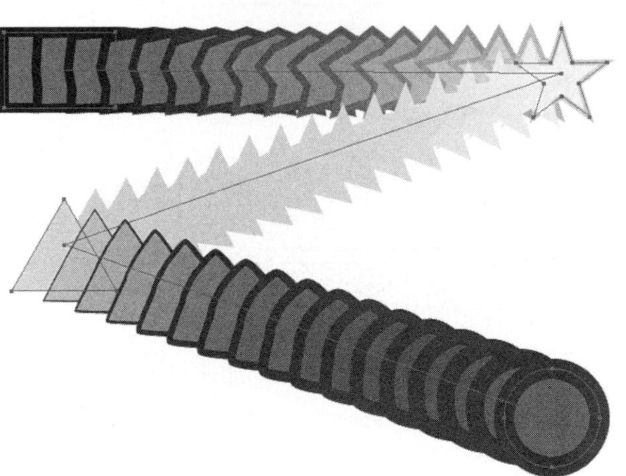

Figure 29.15
Because the stroke of the circle is heavy, the intermediary objects toward the end of the blend appear to be closer together than those near the triangle. They are all equidistant.

An increase in stroke, especially combined with a change in transparency, can alter the perception of distance created with a blend. Figure 29.16 shows two different examples.

## Orientation

The Orientation options in the Blend Options dialog box are Align to Page and Align to Path. The former maintains the vertical orientation of each intermediary object created; the latter rotates each object so that it is perpendicular to the path. Although this pertains to all paths, it is significant only with nonlinear paths. (Editing the straight path of a blend as created by Illustrator is discussed in "Adjusting Blend Paths," later in this chapter.) The difference between the two choices is shown in Figure 29.17.

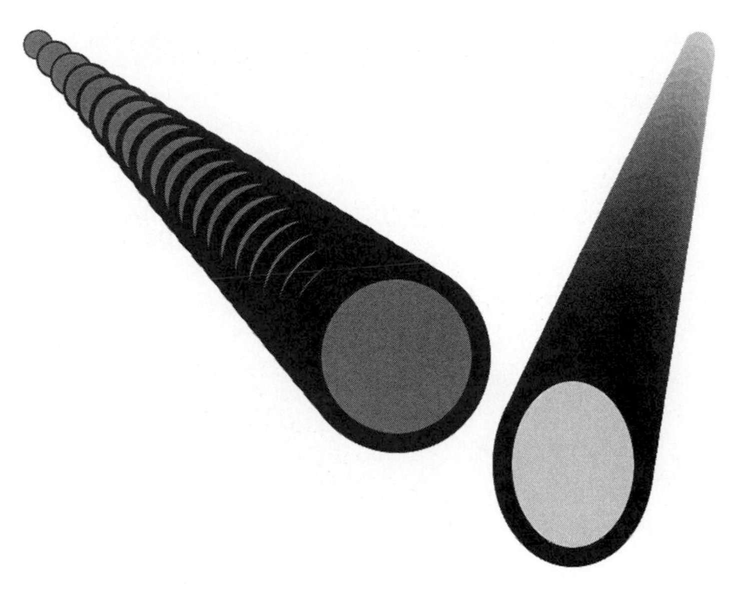

Figure 29.16
The increased stroke on the left adds a perception of distance. On the right, an enlarged stroke is combined with a change in transparency for a different look.



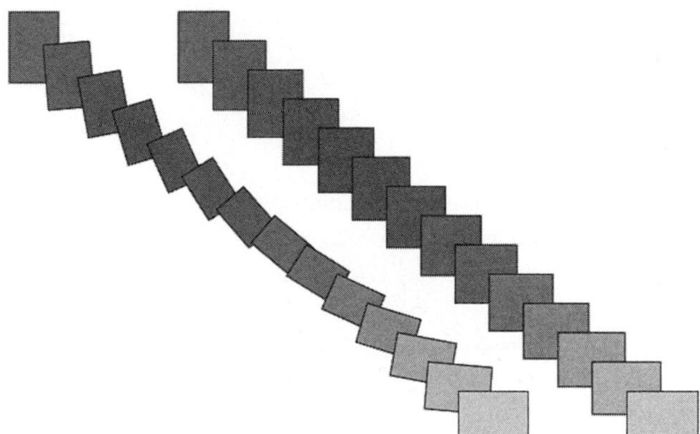

Figure 29.17
On the left, the intermediary objects maintain orientation to the page. On the right, they rotate and remain perpendicular to the angled path.

At first glance, the caption for Figure 29.17 may seem to be reversed. Note, however, that the two original objects (at either end of the blends) are perpendicular to each other. Because of the 90° rotation between the original objects, the intermediary objects in the blend on the right are the ones that are rotated. Note also that the size of the rectangles changes in the blend on the right.

## Illustrator at Work: Comparing Blend Options

The best way to see the difference among the blending options is to play with them. Follow these steps:

1. Open or create an Illustrator document.
2. Add a rectangle and a circle on opposite sides on the artboard. Give them different fill colors, stroke colors, and widths. Select them both.

3. Use the menu command Object, Blend, Blend Options to open the dialog box and set Spacing to Smooth Color. Click OK. (Remember that this doesn't create a blend; it just changes the options.)
4. Use the keyboard shortcut (Option-Command-B) [Alt+Ctrl+B] to execute the blend.
5. Return to the Blend Options dialog box, switch to Specified Steps, and enter **10** for the number of steps. Click the Preview box.
6. Change the number of steps and then uncheck and recheck the Preview box to update the view on the artboard. (Remember that you can move the dialog box out of the way to better view the artboard.)
7. Play with the settings, switching among the three spacing choices and the number of steps and distance.

The Preview box in the Blend Options dialog box is available only when an existing blend is selected on the artboard. It's grayed out even if two objects you *want* to blend are selected but not yet blended. To save a step, consider using the Blend shortcut, regardless of the current settings, *before* you open Blend Options. You'll then be able to preview as you change settings.

Those are basic blends. You can add a couple objects with graphic styles and patterns or gradients and experiment some more using these same basic steps.

# ADJUSTING BLEND PATHS

After you create a blend, you can change the path (spine) along which the intermediary objects were drawn. Illustrator always creates the blend along a straight path. You can edit that spine with the same tools you use to edit any other path. You can also replace it with another existing path.

## Editing Spines

As with any path, the two basic types of editing involve moving anchor points and changing the curve of segments. When you move an anchor point, the appearance of the blend changes. How it changes depends, to a large degree, on the options with which the blend was created. As you can see in Figure 29.18, you can predict the results of editing spines based on the type of blend.

Each of the top three blends was duplicated and its spine edited. In each case, the Direct Selection tool was used to drag the end of the path to the right. The results included the following:

- Smooth Color already added the proper number of intermediary objects to ensure a proper transition between the objects. When the blend was extended, the intermediary objects were simply spread out slightly.
- Specified Steps produced a blend with the exact number of intermediary objects requested. Extending the spine maintained that required number of objects and adjusted their spacing.
- Specified Distance continued to approximate the requested distance between intermediary objects, adding additional objects at the necessary intervals.

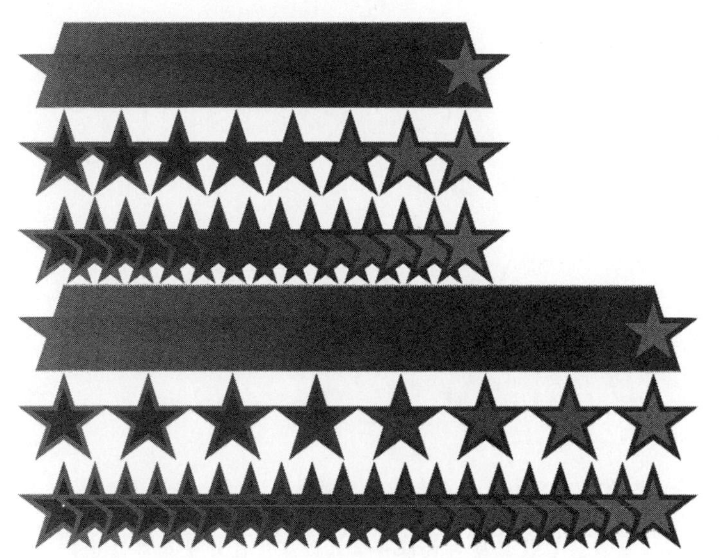

Figure 29.18
The first and fourth blends are Smooth Color; the second and fifth are Specified Steps; the third and last are Specified Distance.

Because a blend is created along a straight path, the spine's anchor points are always corner points. When you use the Convert Anchor Point tool to change a corner point into a smooth point, a straight spine can be curved. Note, however, that even with Specified Distance selected, curving a spine does not change the number of intermediary objects. Figure 29.19 gives an example.

Figure 29.19
Although the number of intermediary objects remains the same and the spacing becomes skewed, the orientation is updated.

As mentioned previously, the orientation blend option is very important to the appearance of a curved spine. Figure 29.20 shows the difference between Align to Page (top) and Align to Path (bottom).

## Replacing Spines

In addition to editing spines, you can replace them with any other path, open or closed. In Figure 29.21, the top blend and the open path just below it have been combined to create the third object at the bottom of the page.

Figure 29.20
Other than the orientation option, the two blends are identical.

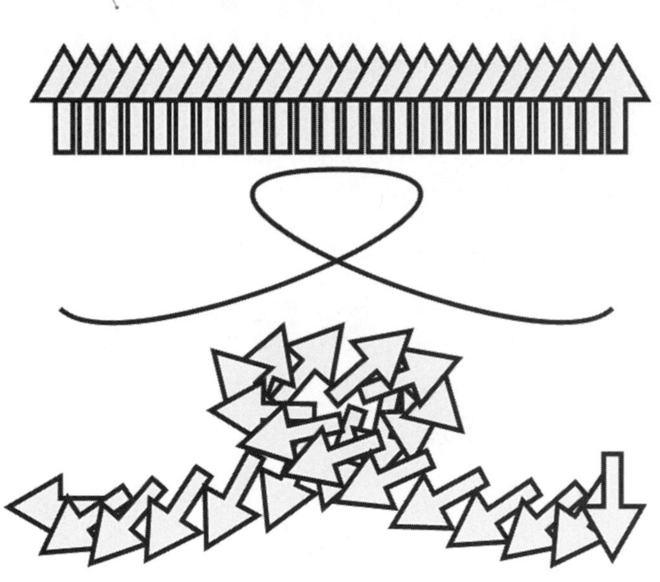

Figure 29.21
The original blend was created with the option Align to Path, resulting in the confusion of arrows after the spine is replaced.

To place a blend along a different path, simply select the blend and new path and then choose Object, Blend, Replace Spine.

*Sometimes Illustrator doesn' t cooperate when you' re trying to wrap a blend around an object. See "Different Spines" in the "Mastering Illustrator" section at the end of this chapter.*

## Reversing

Illustrator also gives you two additional commands for editing blends. As you can see in Figure 29.22, Reverse Spine and Reverse Front to Back are different.

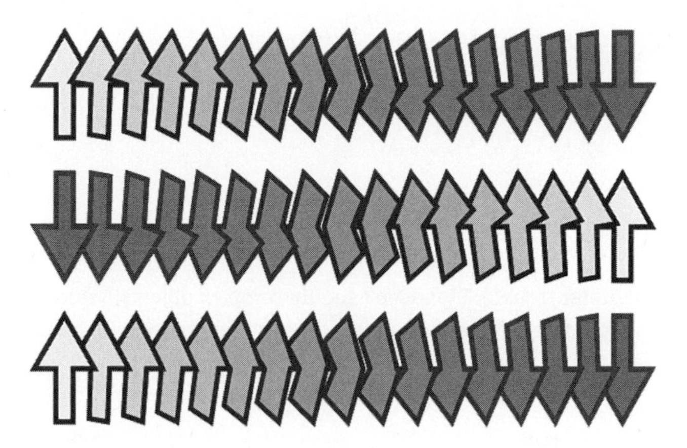

Figure 29.22
The top blend is the original; the middle has the spine reversed; the bottom has the stacking order of the objects reversed by the command Reverse Front to Back.



# EXPANDING A BLEND

Expanding a blend creates editable objects from each of the intermediary objects. There are two major reasons for expanding a blend. First, expanding complex objects is often a cure for printing problems. Second, the objects created with an expanded blend can be used independently. Figure 29.23 shows an example of the latter.

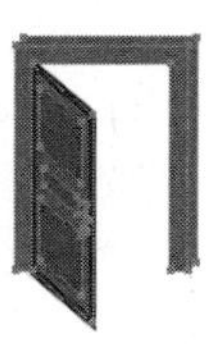
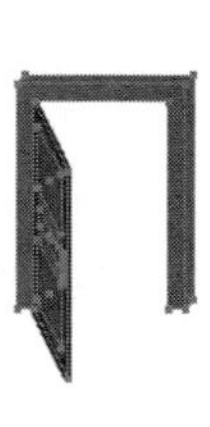

Figure 29.23
Using Specified Steps and a value of 3, a door one-quarter open is produced. The other four doors can be discarded.

For a particular series of illustrations, an image of a partially opened door was required. Because the closed and open doors were available, rather than drawing a new door, a blend was created and expanded. After expansion and ungrouping, the partially open door (the second object) could be moved to the new illustration. The first, third, and fourth doors could then be deleted or saved for future use.

Of course, after a blend is expanded, the individual objects can also be ungrouped and edited as any other path or group. Figure 29.24 shows a smooth color blend used to create color samples.

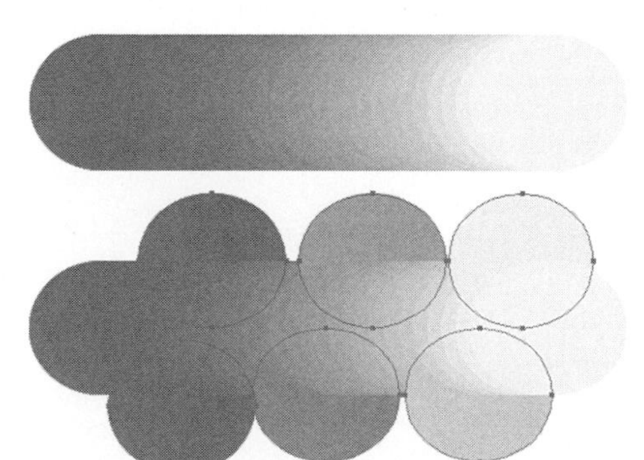

Figure 29.24
Using Smooth Color created the blend at the top. A copy of the blend was expanded and ungrouped, allowing the individual disks to be extracted as color samples.

29

# MASTERING ILLUSTRATOR

## Printing Blends

*Ever since I added a blend, my artwork seems to be crashing my printer. What can I do?*

Expanding blends often cures printer trouble. Blends are highly complex objects, which can put a lot of strain on printers. Expanding the blend creates a series of individual objects, which is much easier for the printer to digest.

## Correcting Blend Spacing

*I've got my distance almost exactly right, but the final blend object is too far away from my last original object. I don't want to move the original object, but it is a noticeable difference in spacing.*

You can do one of several things, including expanding the blend and moving the intermediary objects. But here's an easier way: You're just a little bit off, so count the number of objects created by Specified Distance blending and then open the Blend Option dialog box and switch to Specified Steps. Input that number and click the Preview box. You'll see that the difference in spacing will be spread out among the intermediary objects, resulting in an unnoticeable variation. Click OK.

## Different Spines

*No matter what I do, my blend goes only three-quarters of the way around my object when I choose Object, Blend, Replace Spine.*

The easiest workaround is to create an open path on top of your object. Use the Pen tool to re-create the object, leaving a tiny gap or tiny overlap where the first and last points meet. Give the path a stroke and fill of None and replace the spine of your blend.

30

# ILLUSTRATOR'S LAYERS, SUBLAYERS, AND GROUPS

## IN THIS CHAPTER

Just as objects and paths are arranged back-to-front according to the order in which they are drawn, they can be organized using *layers*. Rather than back and front, the terms *top* and *bottom*, *above* and *below*, and *up* and *down* are used with layers.

Each layer, in and of itself, is transparent. The typical analogy is to a sheet of clear plastic, acetate, or glass. If you put artwork on an upper layer, it obscures the artwork below. You can make the lower artwork visible by moving it to a place not obscured by the upper layer's artwork. You can also make it visible by moving that layer above the other.



This chapter discusses the theory behind and reasons for using layers and explains the Layers palette. You'll also find information on using layers to organize your artwork, using layers as templates, and how to assign appearance characteristics to layers and groups, rather than to individual objects.

# WHY LAYERS?

The primary concepts behind layers are organization and efficiency. By placing related objects on the same layer, it's easy to find and select them. Illustrator enables you to show and hide the content of layers, helping you to streamline and de-clutter the artboard while working. That allows you to see and concentrate on a single aspect of an illustration *and* see how everything fits together with just a few clicks.

Illustrator offers layers and sublayers, as well as the capability to rearrange specific groups of objects and paths within the Layers palette. You can also *target* layers and groups. *Targeting* involves designating a layer, sublayer, group, or object to have an appearance attribute (including style, effect, and transparency) applied to it. Using this capability, you can assign appearance attributes to an entire layer, and any object moved to or created on the layer will assume the attributes. Layers can also work with Illustrator's effects and transparency. Rather than merely a handy way to keep track of your artwork, layers are a very powerful, creative tool.

The power of the Layers palette truly comes into play with very complicated documents. Illustrator gives substantial flexibility with the Show/Hide option. Rather than simply toggle the visibility/invisibility of a layer, you can change a layer to Outline View mode by (Command)-clicking [Ctrl]-clicking the eye icon in the Layers palette. This capability applies only to layers and sublayers; groups and objects cannot be viewed differently than the other content of their layers. Additionally, you can make a layer into a template through its Layer Options dialog box. Templates are discussed in detail later in this chapter.

Another important aspect of Illustrator's layers is their capability to translate into layers in Photoshop and Adobe Acrobat (version 6, using PDF 1.5). With each object or path on a separate Illustrator layer, an image exported to Photoshop's PSD format maintains the independence of each object. Without layers, the Photoshop file would consist of a single layer of pixels—you would not be able to change the stacking order or "move" one object from under another. PDF's new support for layers enables you to add multiple objects in a single location, which can then be shown or hidden in Acrobat 6. This feature can be extremely useful for preparing a single file in multiple versions, for client approval or even different versions for different languages.

## Examining Sublayers

The number of layers in an Illustrator document is theoretically limited only by your system's memory. Each layer can have up to 29 levels of nested sublayers, and each of those levels can have an unlimited number of layers.



A sublayer is, in fact, a layer in and of itself. It works like a layer, has a name like a layer, has content like a layer, has a designated color like a layer, and can be rearranged like a layer. However, it is called a *sublayer* when it is subordinate to a layer. (Sublayers can be moved to the top level and become layers.) The advantage is in having what amounts to groups of layers. Rather than Shift-clicking to select multiple layers, you can just click to select the topmost layer and all its sublayers. An appearance attribute (including style, effects, and transparency) can be applied to the layer and all its sublayers through targeting (explained later in this chapter). Only the top layer (or the highest sublayer you want) needs to be targeted; subordinate sublayers, groups, and objects are automatically selected. Of course, a sublayer can be targeted individually, too. A layer and all its subordinate components can be locked, deleted, or made invisible or a template simply by making the desired change to the top layer (or the highest subordinate layer you want).

## Groups of Objects in Illustrator

The command Object, Group binds selected objects and/or paths together in relationship to each other. The objects remain independent, but they can be manipulated as a single element. Here are some of the behaviors of groups:

- Grouping moves the selected objects or paths to the layer of the topmost of the selected elements.
- Grouping can change the stacking order. If an unselected object is between the topmost and bottommost selected objects when grouped, the unselected object will be moved behind the group.
- Individual objects in a group can be selected with the Direct Selection or Direct Select Lasso tool. The Selection tool and the Lasso tool will select the group rather than an element of the group.
- Groups can contain other groups. That is, groups can be *nested* within each other. (This is similar to the concept of a sublayer.)
- The default keyboard shortcut for the Object, Group command is (Command-G) [Ctrl+G].

The command Object, Ungroup, or (Shift-Command-G) [Shift+Ctrl+G] reverses the Group command for the selected group. If the group was nested within another group, the ungrouped elements remain part of the larger group.

The Group Selection tool selects one (or several) elements of a group. Click once on an object or path to select it; click a second time to select its group. If the object's group is nested, subsequent clicks select each higher group in the hierarchy. As with the other selection tools, use the Shift key to add to a selection, including objects or paths outside the group. Use the (Option) [Alt] key to duplicate by dragging.

Groups can also be managed through the Layers palette with drag-and-drop ease. Rather than select a group on the artboard, ungroup it, deselect one item, and regroup the remainder, you can simply move an object (path) out of a group or add it to a group by dragging within the palette. An object added to a group automatically is moved to the same layer as the group, and it assumes all attributes and styles applicable to that layer, while losing any that were applied to the former layer. Styles and attributes applied specifically to the individual object or path transfer with the object to the new group's layer without affecting other objects in the group.



# THE LAYERS PALETTE

Layers and sublayers are created and organized with the Layers palette. You also use the Layers palette to identify layers, sublayers, or groups for effects or attributes. (This is discussed later in this chapter, in the section "Targeting Layers, Groups, and Objects.")

The features of the Layers palette include the following:

- Thumbnails (icon-sized views of the content of layers and groups, and pictures of individual paths)
- Sublayers and the capability to nest layers
- The capability to target a layer, group, or object for styles, effects, or transparency (discussed separately in this chapter)
- Groups and paths (objects) within the palette
- The capability to move objects and groups among layers directly in the palette
- Increased flexibility in palette display
- Several powerful commands available from the palette's menu, including Locate Object, Collect in New Layer, Release to Layers, and Reverse Order

Figure 30.1 shows the Layers palette.

By default, layer names are capitalized, and the names of groups and paths are enclosed in angle brackets. You can double-click a layer, sublayer, group, or path to open the Layer Options dialog box and rename it. Here are descriptions of the various elements shown in Figure 30.1:

- Show/Hide is the visibility column. An eyeball in this column indicates that the layer, group, or object is visible. When the column is empty, that layer, group, or object is hidden. A hollow eyeball indicates that the layer, group, or object is visible in Outline mode. An icon constructed of a triangle, a circle, and a square indicates that the layer is a template.
- Lock/Unlock determines whether a layer can be changed, edited, altered, added to or subtracted from, deleted, or given a sublayer. A locked layer, indicated by a lock icon in the second column, can be duplicated. When the icon is grayed out, the parent layer or group is locked. Groups and objects can also be locked independently in the Layers palette.

> Be aware that locked objects (paths) and groups can still be deleted if the layer upon which they are found is deleted in the Layers palette.

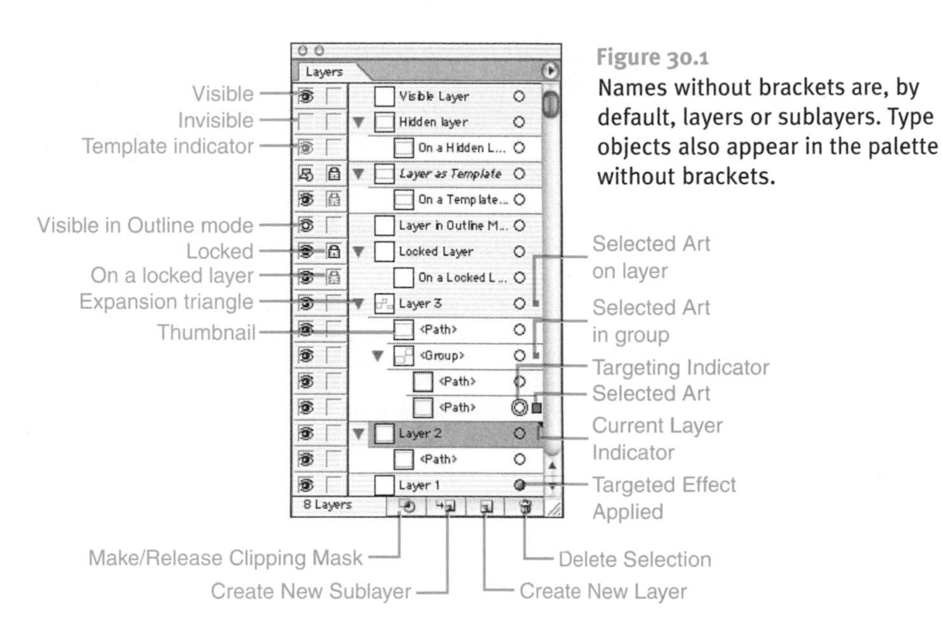


**Figure 30.1**
Names without brackets are, by default, layers or sublayers. Type objects also appear in the palette without brackets.



- Expand/Collapse allows you to view the sublayers, groups, and paths (objects) that are part of a particular layer. You can also expand or collapse sublayers and groups to see their contents.
- Thumbnails give you a visual reference for the content of a layer, sublayer, group, or path. Their visibility and size are controlled through the Layers palette menu.
- An active layer, sublayer, group, or path is highlighted. If you don't want any layer highlighted, you can click in the blank space at the bottom of the Layers palette, below the lowest layer, group, or path. Illustrator, however, still recognizes the active layer through the small black triangle at the far right of the layer's row—the Current Layer indicator. When you click this indicator, all art at that particular level is selected. You should not confuse it with the Selected Art indicator (described next).
- The Selected Art indicator tells you which particular element of your artwork is selected. You can also use it to move artwork by dragging the icon to a different layer. Especially useful when layers or groups are collapsed are the mini-indicators that show on which layer or in which group the selected art can be found.
- A targeted layer, sublayer, group, or object can have one or more appearance attributes assigned to it. Anything created on or added to such a targeted layer has that attribute applied. Any object moved to another layer does not take the particular characteristic with it. The various possible icons are described later in this chapter in the section "Targeting Layers, Groups, and Objects."
- The four buttons across the bottom of the palette perform their functions according to their names. The special capabilities of the Create New Sublayer and Create New Layer buttons are described later in this chapter in the section "Creating New Layers and Sublayers: Advanced Techniques."

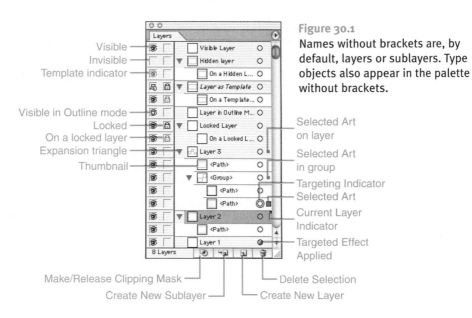

The name of a nonprinting layer will be italicized. The layer options can be used to make a layer nonprinting, and templates are automatically nonprinting.

*If your Layers palette doesn' t show all the thumbnails you would like to see, check "Layers Palette Viewing Options" in the "Mastering Illustrator" section at the end of this chapter.*

The Selected Art indicator can be a great help in locating or moving a specific element in a complicated document. When a large square, in the layer's designated color, appears to the right of the layer's name, the entire layer is selected. When a smaller square appears, a group or object on that layer or sublayer is selected. With all layers collapsed or only top layers showing, you still get an indication of where the particular element is located. You can even move the selected artwork without expanding the layer. Simply drag the icon to another unlocked layer or group.



## Making Selections with the Layers Palette

Clicking the name of a layer automatically selects all objects and groups on that layer. The modifier keys work to add to or subtract from a selection according to the Windows paradigm:

- **Individual selection**—You (Command)-click [Ctrl]-click to add (or subtract) a layer's content or a specific group or object to (or from) the selection.
- **Contiguous selection**—Shift-clicking adds all the items between the originally selected (or items) and the item that is Shift-clicked.

You can also hold down the (Command and Option) [Ctrl and Alt] keys and drag through the Layers palette to make selections.

You also can select an individual object, even when it's part of a group, by clicking the far right of its row (name) in the Layers palette. The Selected Art indicator appears in the row, and the object's bounding box becomes visible in the document, but the row in the Layers palette is not highlighted. An additional indicator, targeting, will be discussed later in this chapter. When an individual object is selected in the Layers palette, it can be manipulated individually, including movement and appearance, without altering any other part of the group. This capability is comparable to clicking the object itself in the document with the Direct Selection tool (white arrow icon) rather than the Selection tool (black arrow icon).

## The Layers Palette Options

A look at the Layers Palette Options dialog box, shown in Figure 30.2, reveals several choices for how the contents of the Layers palette will be presented. The Show Layers Only check box hides all information other than layers and sublayers. The groups and paths themselves are not affected; they simply are no longer visible in the palette.

The Row Size setting adjusts the height of each row in the palette to the thumbnail size. If you set it to Small, no thumbnail appears (rows are minimized to the height of the font). At Medium, the default size, the thumbnail is 20 pixels square. Large thumbnails are 32 pixels square. Custom thumbnails can range in size from 12 to 100 pixels. Text size is not affected by Row Size, and visibility, lock, and target icons appear one pixel smaller in Small Row Size than in the other possibilities.

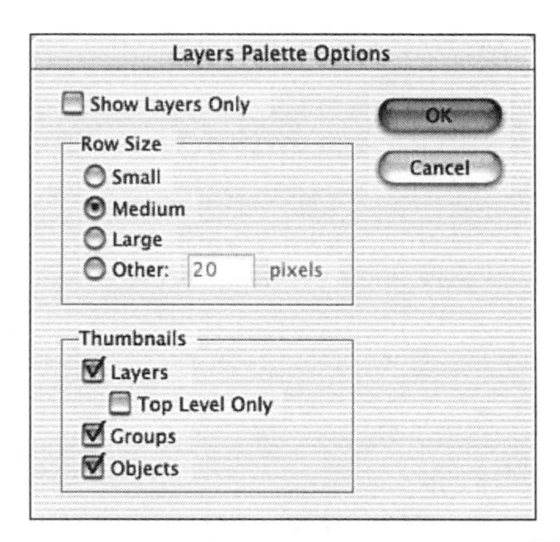


Figure 30.2
In the Layers Palette Options dialog box, you can control how the palette is viewed, as well as how much of it is viewed.



The Thumbnails area of the Layers Palette Options dialog box controls which thumbnails are visible. These check boxes hide only the thumbnail at the left of the row; the rows themselves remain visible. Checking Top Level Only hides the thumbnails of all sublevels nested in other layers.

The procedure for expanding and collapsing the various layers, sublayers, and groups in a complicated document can be streamlined with a modifier key. (Option)-clicking [Alt]-clicking the expand/collapse triangle next to a layer's name expands or collapses all sublayers and groups, as well as the layer itself.

Every element in the Layers palette—layers, sublayers, groups, and paths—has its own options. Double-clicking the item's name opens its Options dialog box. The name and color of a layer or sublayer can be changed; it also can be made a template (discussed later in this chapter), hidden, shown in Preview or Outline mode, locked, made nonprinting, and dimmed to a specified percentage. Groups and objects (paths) can be renamed, hidden, or made nonprinting through their options. (Nonprinting layers, sublayers, groups, and objects are indicated by italicized names in the Layers palette.)

Redrawing the object thumbnails and group thumbnails in the Layers palette can significantly slow down your work. Using the triangle to the left of the layer name to hide nested sublayers, groups, and paths can speed things up. Another way to minimize the amount of time required to show the palette is to name the various layers, groups, and paths so that the thumbnails are unnecessary. Double-click the name of a layer in the Layers palette to bring up the Layer Options dialog box, rename it according to content, and use the Layers Palette Options dialog box to hide thumbnails.

The convention of naming layers with capital letters and using angle brackets for group names makes sense to continue when naming elements in the Layers palette. However, sublayers can be differentiated from layers when renamed by using all lowercase letters. When a specific object warrants its own name, consider using parentheses rather than angle brackets to visually differentiate pathnames from group names.

## Illustrator at Work: Arranging Layers

A thorough understanding of Illustrator's capabilities, including the sublayers, forms the basis upon which you can build your mastery of layers. Even with all the other capabilities, the most important aspects of layers remain your ability to create without destroying artwork below a layer and to organize and rearrange the elements of your artwork. Figure 30.3

shows how layers interact in the most basic fashion. At the top of the figure, the three layers are separated so that the content is visible. To the lower left, they overlap. To the lower right, they are aligned. Also note in Figure 30.3 that lower artwork shows through when nothing is above. (Keep in mind that Illustrator's powerful transparency capabilities make this explanation a bit simplistic. For more details on transparency, see Chapter 34, "Using Masks, Transparency, and Blending Modes.")

> Another visual cue in the Layers palette is color. The Selected Art indicator squares are the same color as the objects' paths for that level in the Layers palette.

**Figure 30.3**
Although each of the three layers is independent and has its own artwork, when viewed together, artwork on an upper layer blocks the artwork below.

To experiment with the capability of rearranging the content of the artboard through the Layers palette, do this:

1. Create a new Illustrator document. The size and color mode are not important.
2. Add a large number 1 to the artboard. Select a serif font and make it black.
3. At the bottom of the Layers palette, click the New Layer button.
4. Add a large number 2 to the artboard, in a different font and color.
5. Add a third layer and the number 3, in a contrasting font and color. Your artboard may look something like Figure 30.4.
6. Select All by Shift-clicking the circles to the right of Layer 1, Layer 2, and Layer 3 in the Layers palette. (Indeed, there are many ways to select everything on the artboard in Illustrator, some more efficient than others, but this exercise is about the Layers palette.)

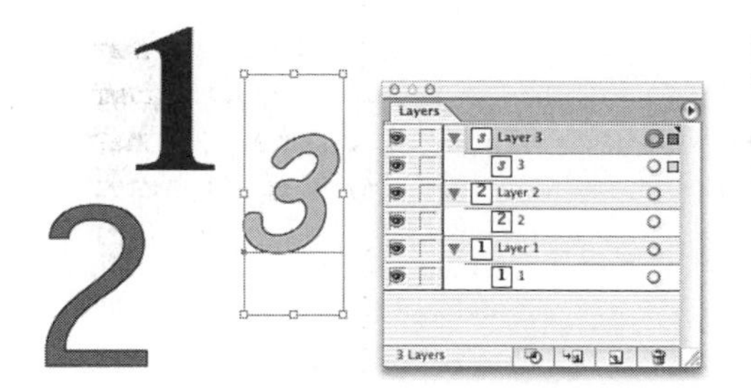


**Figure 30.4**
The placement of the three type objects on the artboard is insignificant at this point.



7. Show the Align palette through the Windows menu or with a keyboard shortcut (default: Shift+F7).
8. In the Align palette, click the second and fifth buttons of the top row, aligning the content of all three layers vertically and horizontally (see Figure 30.5).

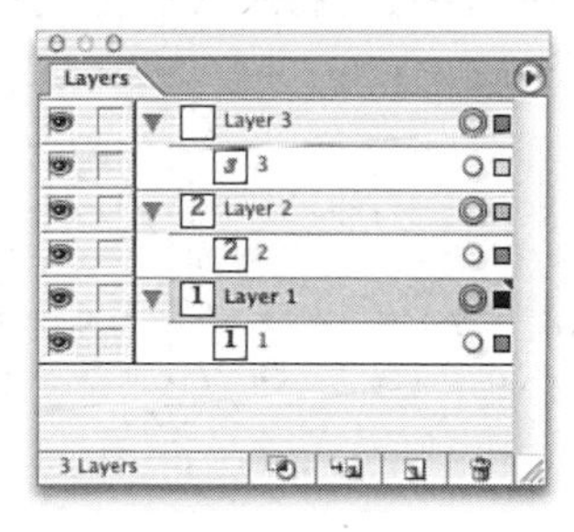


**Figure 30.5**
Because Layer 1 was clicked first, it remains the active layer in the Layers palette.

9. Deselect by clicking in the empty area at the bottom of the Layers palette (or anywhere on the artboard away from the numerals).
10. In the Layers palette, drag Layer 1 up to just above Layer 2 (see Figure 30.6, left). The thick black line under the cursor should extend across the width of the layer name field. (Note the change in the stacking order, and therefore the artwork, on the artboard.)
11. Drag Layer 3 down to between Layer 2 and the object named 2 (see Figure 30.6, center). The thick black line under the cursor should extend from the right edge of the layer name field only as far left as the Layer 2 thumbnail.
12. Drag the object named 2 to between the object named 1 and Layer 2 (see Figure 30.6, right). The thick black line under the cursor should extend only as far left as the top of the Layer 2 thumbnail.

After all the dragging around, your Layers palette should look like this (see Figure 30.7):

- Layer 1 should be at the top. It should have on it the objects named 1 and 2. (They appear under and offset slightly to the right of Layer 1.)
- Layer 2 should be below the content of Layer 1. It should be left-justified with Layer 1.

- Under and slightly to the right of Layer 2 should be Layer 3. On it, and offset to the right, should be the object named 3. (Note that Layer 3 is now a sublayer of Layer 2.)
- The object named 2 should be active in the Layers palette, but the active selection, as indicated by the double circles to the right in the Layers palette, remains Layer 1 and Layer 2.

The menu commands Object, Arrange, Bring to Front or Bring Forward, Send Backward, and Send to Back can also be used to move individual objects or paths, but they cannot be used with layers or sublayers.



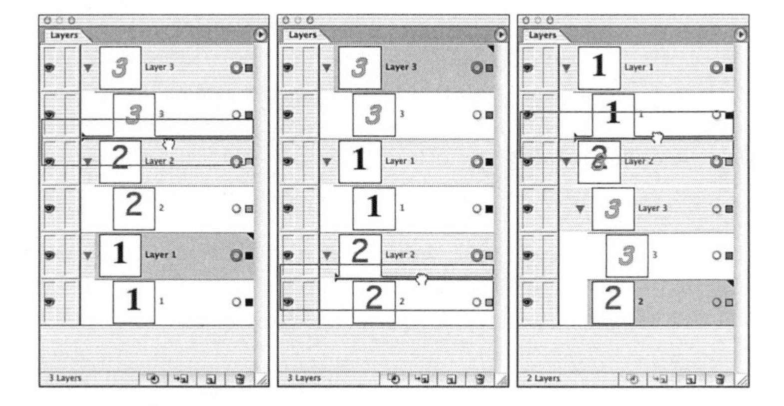

Figure 30.6
For improved clarity, the Layers palette options are set to a thumbnail size of 50 pixels.

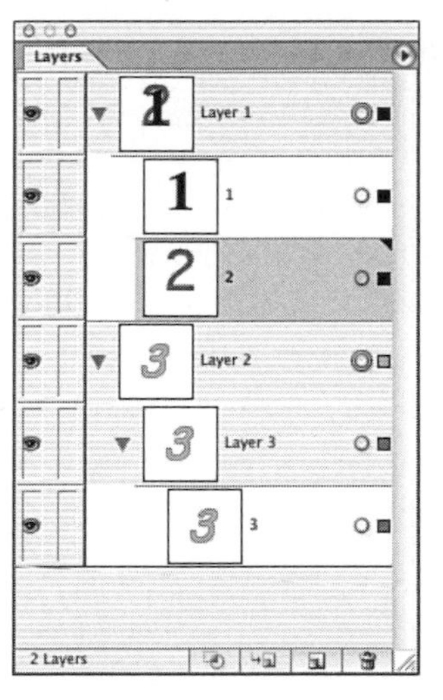


Figure 30.7
Note the thumbnail of Layer 1. It shows the entire content of the layer.

## The Layers Palette Menu

One other aspect of the Layers palette deserves attention. The palette menu, which you access by clicking the triangle in the upper-right corner of the palette, contains numerous commands. Many of these commands, shown in Figure 30.8, need little explanation.

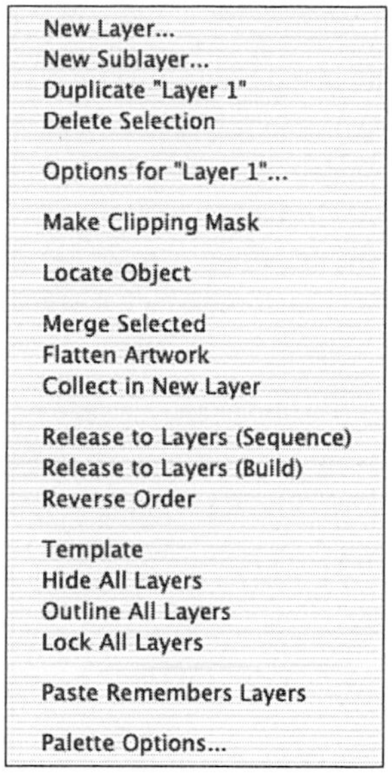

New Layer...
New Sublayer...
Duplicate "Layer 1"
Delete Selection

Options for "Layer 1"...

Make Clipping Mask

Locate Object

Merge Selected
Flatten Artwork
Collect in New Layer

Release to Layers (Sequence)
Release to Layers (Build)
Reverse Order

Template
Hide All Layers
Outline All Layers
Lock All Layers

Paste Remembers Layers

Palette Options...

Figure 30.8
Generally, not all commands will be available at any one time. The commands Duplicate, Delete, and Options For will show the name of the selected item if the command is available for that item; otherwise, they show "Selection."



New Layer and New Sublayer do just that, adding a new layer at the same level as the active layer or a new sublayer under the active layer. Duplicate Layer and Delete Layer are just as you would expect. The command Options for "Selection" (showing the name of the selection, as appropriate) is used to show/hide, lock/unlock, and change the name of that item in the Layers palette. There is, of course, no reason not to perform these operations directly in the palette. Make/Release Clipping Mask functions the same as the commands Object, Clipping Mask, Make and Object, Clipping Mask, Release. The remainder of the palette menu commands deserve specific attention:

- **Locate Object**—Useful for those incredibly complicated illustrations that are possible with so powerful a program, this command finds an object in the Layers palette. Click an object or group on the artboard, select Locate Object from the palette menu, and the Layers palette automatically scrolls to or opens to the object's row in the palette.

- **Merge Selected**—Select layers, choose the command, and the layers are merged. To select layers that are adjacent in the Layers palette, Shift-click the highest and the lowest in the palette. To select layers that are not contiguous in the palette, (Command)-click [Ctrl]-click each of them. Keep in mind that you can merge locked and hidden layers without changing their status. Artwork is merged onto the highest visible, unlocked layer. The content of each layer or sublayer is collected as a group. The stacking order of all objects as they appeared on the artboard is retained on the remaining layer.

- **Flatten Artwork**—This command works much like Merge Selected but affects all layers and sublayers. There is one major difference, however. Rather than automatically creating a group from a hidden layer, Flatten Artwork deletes the layer and its content. You are given a warning that artwork appears on the hidden layer or layers, and you are asked whether you would like to save the artwork or delete it. The artwork is flattened to the active layer. Effects are carried from layers and sublayers into the groups that are created. Effects for the top-level layer are discarded rather than applied to all other art. Illustrator attempts to preserve exactly the look of your art at the time you chose Flatten Artwork. Choosing this command is usually a final step, taken after all creative work is finished, and should be used with a copy of the original file.

- **Collect in New Layer**—You can gather together the contents of various layers, sublayers, groups, or objects and place them on a new layer by using this command. You can select objects and groups on any level of the Layers palette by using the Selection tool or the Direct Selection tool on the artboard. You are, however, limited as to what you can select for collection. Only those items that have their next-higher level in common can be Shift-clicked to select, for example, only objects on the same sublayer or layer. Here is some guidance:



  - You can select only those sublayers that are part of the same higher layer and are themselves at the same hierarchical level. (See Figure 30.9 for a visual guide to the relationships among layers, sublayers, groups, and paths.)
  - All objects in a group are at the same level.
  - All groups on a single sublayer are at the same level.
  - A group on that sublayer and an object in a different group on that sublayer are not at the same level.
  - A group on that sublayer and a group on a different sublayer are not on the same level.

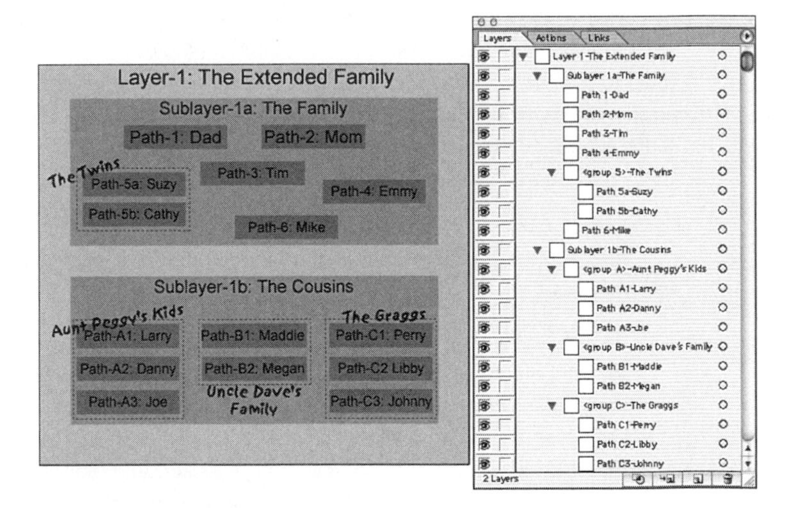


**Figure 30.9**
The relationships among items in the illustration are comparable to those shown in the Layers palette.

The largest box, Layer-1, contains all the other elements. Both Sublayer-1a and Sublayer-1b have elements, but no element can belong to both sublayers. Within the individual sublayers are paths (objects) and groups. Paths can be at the same level as groups. Not depicted here are sublayers within sublayers and groups within groups. Both are available to you in Illustrator.

*The Collect in New Layer command is a great timesaver in Illustrator. If it's grayed out when you're trying to use it in conjunction with the Layers palette, see "Collect in New Layer Unavailable" in the "Mastering Illustrator" section at the end of this chapter.*

- **Release to Layers (Sequence) and Release to Layers (Build)**—These commands will be discussed independently later in this chapter.
- **Reverse Order**—Like the Collect in New Layer command, Reverse Order works only with items that can be selected together: Layers, sublayers, groups, and objects that are all part of the same group, sublayer, or layer and must be immediately subordinate to that "parent" level.

Depending on what is selected in the Layers palette, you may see Hide All Layers instead of Hide Other in the palette menu. The same holds for the Outline and Lock commands.



- **Template**—This command will be discussed independently, later in this chapter.
- **Hide Others/Show All Layers**—With one or more layers selected, the Hide Others command makes all other layers and sublayers and their contents invisible. In the Layers palette, invisible artwork, both groups and objects (paths), are indicated by grayed eye icons in the visibility column. For layers and sublayers that are hidden, nothing appears in that column. Any new layers or sublayers created while this command is active are visible. The Show All Layers command restores visibility.
- **Outline Others/Preview All Layers**—These commands work like Hide Others/Show All Others, except that instead of becoming invisible, the nonselected layers, sublayers, groups, and objects are viewed in Outline or Preview mode. The fact that these other elements retain their visibility means that they can be selected, moved, deleted, edited, and so on. Hidden elements cannot be selected.
- **Lock Others/Unlock All Layers**—Designed primarily to prevent unintended alteration of artwork, this is another command that is available only when you have selected one or more layers or sublayers. This command can be very effective when used in combination with Outline Others, allowing you to unclutter the artboard and speed screen redraw.
- **Paste Remembers Layers**—When this command is active, a check mark appears next to it in the Layers palette menu. When it is active, you can choose Edit, Paste, or one of its related commands (Paste in Front or Paste in Back), to place an object from the Clipboard onto its original layer (assuming you copied it from a layer in the existing document). If that layer has been renamed or deleted, a new layer is created. When this command is unchecked (inactive), the Paste commands add from the Clipboard to the active layer. If more than one layer is active, the lowest layer receives the artwork.
- **Palette Options**—This command was discussed earlier in this chapter.

### Working with the Paste Commands

You can find the Paste commands, used in conjunction with the Paste Remembers Layers command, under the Edit menu. Here's how they work with Paste Remembers Layers active:

- **Paste**—The command places the content of the Clipboard onto the layer from which it came. If multiple objects are on the Clipboard and they came from different layers, they are returned to the layers from which they came. Objects are pasted in the center of the layer.
- **Paste in Front**—Objects are pasted to their original layers, in front, but rather than being pasted into the center of the layer, they are pasted in their original positions. If an object or path is selected, the Clipboard's contents are pasted in front of it.
- **Paste in Back**—Objects are pasted to their original layers, in back, but rather than being pasted into the center of the layer, they are pasted in their original positions. If an object or path is selected, the Clipboard's contents are pasted in back of it.

If no layer has the same name as the layer from which the objects came, a new layer is created and given the original layer's name, and the Clipboard content is pasted there. The original layer need not exist, merely a layer with the same name.

Here's how these commands work with Paste Remembers Layers inactive:

- **Paste**—This command places the content of the Clipboard into the center of the active layer. If more than one layer is selected, the lower layer receives the objects. The artwork is pasted to the front of that layer.
- **Paste in Front**—Pasting into the artwork's original positions on the active layer, it becomes the frontmost artwork. If a group is selected, it becomes part of the group.
- **Paste in Back**—Pasting into the artwork's original positions on the active layer, it becomes the rearmost artwork. If a group is selected, it becomes part of the group.

Remember, too, that Paste Remembers Layers works when pasting (or dragging and dropping) between Illustrator documents.

# ORGANIZING WITH LAYERS

In early versions of Illustrator, the Layers palette was a convenience for organizing artwork. Now, not only can you arrange your artwork on layers, but you also can use the Layers palette to rearrange those elements. No longer do you need to select an object or a path on the artboard to move it from one layer to another. The procedure is as simple as dragging and dropping right in the Layers palette.

## Creating New Layers and Sublayers: Advanced Techniques

When you click the Create New Layer button at the bottom of the Layers palette, a new layer is created directly above your currently active layer. This new layer is always at the same hierarchical level as your current work. In other words, if you are working on a sublayer that is a sublevel of a sublayer, the Create New Layer button gives you a new sub-sublayer. The Create New Sublayer button creates a sublayer, below the currently active layer.

To speed up your workflow, use the modifier keys with both the Create New Layer and Create New Sublayer buttons of the Layers palette:

- **Create New Layer (menu command/button alone)**—Creates a new layer directly above the active layer, at the same hierarchical level.
- **(Command) [Ctrl] with Create New Layer**—Creates a new layer at the top of the Layers palette (the highest hierarchical level).
- **(Option) [Alt] with Create New Layer**—Creates a new layer directly above and at the same level as the active layer (as normal) and opens the Layer Options dialog box.
- **Create New Sublayer (menu command/button alone)**—Creates a new sublayer directly below and subordinate to the active layer.
- **(Option) [Alt] with Create New Sublayer**—Creates a new sublayer as normal, but also opens the Layer Options dialog box.



The Shift key has no effect on either button, and the (Command) [Ctrl] key has no effect with Create New Sublayer.

New layers can also be created with the Layers palette menu (the triangle at the upper-right corner of the palette). Both the Create New Layer and Create New Sublayer menu commands automatically open the Layer Options dialog box. The default keyboard shortcut for New Layer is (Command-L) [Ctrl+L]. (In the Keyboard Shortcuts dialog box, you can find the New Layer command under Menu Commands in the Other Palette category.) This keyboard shortcut creates a new layer or sublayer at the same level as the currently active layer.

## Moving Elements in the Layers Palette

The Selected Art indicator in the Layers palette (shown at the beginning of this chapter in Figure 30.1) tells you what layer, sublayer, group, or object is currently selected on the artboard. You can move that element to another (unlocked) layer by dragging its name to the new layer and releasing the mouse button.

To make this process even easier for you, the Layers palette shows a smaller version of the Selected Art indicator throughout the element's location hierarchy. Smaller boxes indicate the selected object's group and its layer. If the group is on a sublayer or part of another group, those intermediate levels are also designated with a smaller box.

*If you're having trouble with the appearance of an object or objects changing when moved from layer to layer, see "Moving a Group or Object Changes Appearance" in the "Mastering Illustrator" section at the end of this chapter.*

The little boxes that indicate the location hierarchy of the selected artwork are more than just indicators. Even with the Layers palette collapsed to Top Layers Only, you can rearrange your artwork. Simply drag the little box to a different layer and release. You don't need to open all the layers, sublayers, and groups to find the particular element you want to move.

# Illustrator at Work: Releasing to Layers

The Release to Layers commands are located in the Layers palette menu, which you access through the triangle in the upper-right corner of the palette. Release to Layers (Sequence) places each object of a selected group or layer onto its own sublayer. Release to Layers (Build) puts the first object on one layer, the first and second on the next layer, the first, second, and third on the third layer, and so on. (These commands are invaluable in the creation of Web-based animation.)



Let's see how these commands work:

1. Create a new Illustrator document (RGB, 800×600 pixels).
2. Add a series of objects on Layer 1, perhaps similar to those shown in Figure 30.10.

The objects on a layer or sublayer or in a group are each placed on a new layer according to their stacking order. The objects behind the others are placed on a layer lower than the others. When you're preparing illustrations for separation to layers, it is a good idea to rearrange the elements in the Layers palette before using the Release to Layers command. The success or failure of an animation depends, in part, on the layers (frames) being displayed in the correct order.

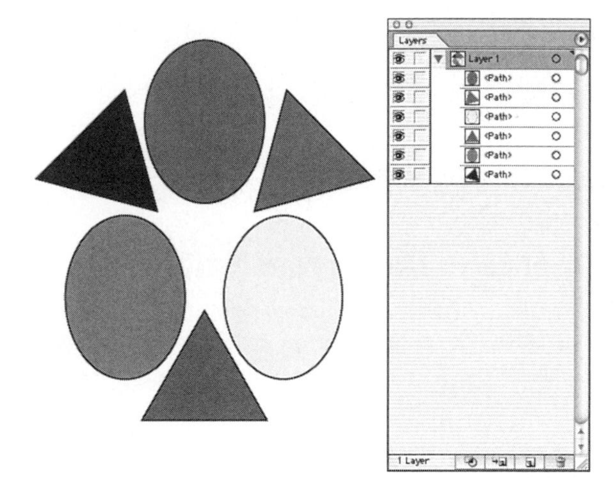


**Figure 30.10**
In this example, it is important to click Layer 1 to make it active prior to choosing Release to Layers.

3. Note the order in which the objects appear in the Layers palette. This is the order in which the individual sublayers will be created.
4. The layer that contains the objects or groups (or the group that contains the objects) must be active; otherwise, the Release to Layers commands will not correctly produce a series of layers. With Layer 1 active, select the command Release to Layers (Sequence) from the Layers palette menu. The result should be similar to that shown in Figure 30.11.
5. Undo to reverse the Release to Layers command.
6. Now select the Layers palette menu command Release to Layers (Build). Your results should be similar to those shown in Figure 30.12.

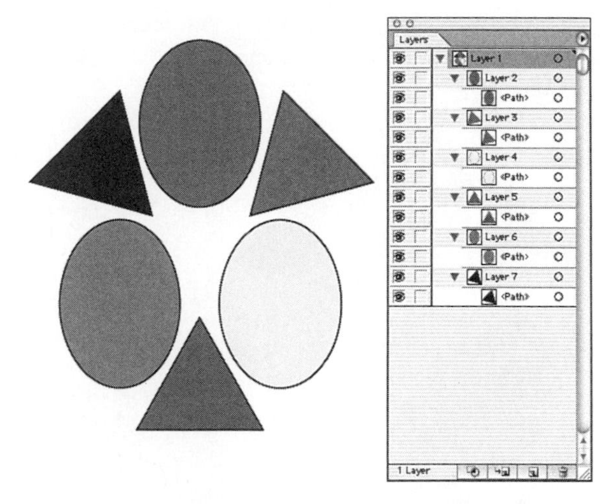


Figure 30.11
The newly created sublayers appear in the order in which their objects appeared. Note that each layer contains only a single object. Layer 1, of course, contains all the sublayers.

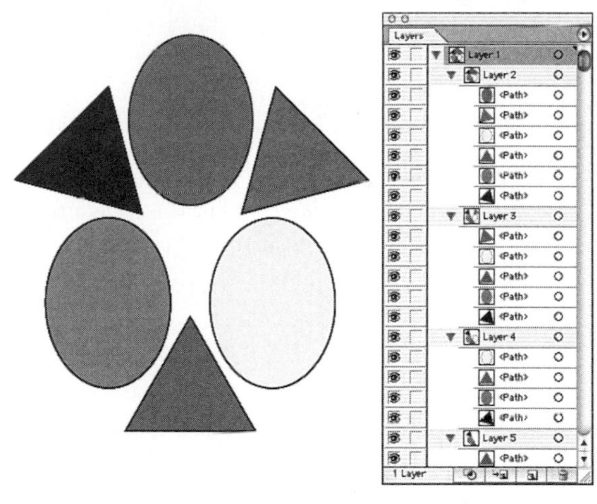


Figure 30.12
Notice how, from the bottom up, each layer incorporates the content of the previous layer.

The command Release to Layers (Sequence) is perfect for preparing artwork for export to Photoshop's PSD format. You're more likely to use Release to Layers (Build) for animation. It produces what can be called a "typewriter" effect. In such an animation, objects appear cumulatively. That is, in the first frame (or layer, in this case), Object #1 appears. In the second frame, Object #1 remains and Object #2 appears. In the third frame, Objects #1 and #2 remain, and Object #3 appears. And so the string continues throughout the animation. Just as new letters appear after the old on a typewritten sheet, so do the objects appear onscreen in a parade of images.

In Figure 30.12, note the order in which Illustrator has created the sublayers. The first-created layer (with just one object) is at the bottom. If your animation program produces a backward graphic from this sequence (objects leaving the picture rather than entering), you have an easy solution:

1. Click the bottom sublayer that contains a frame (or image) for your animation.
2. Hold down the Shift key and click the top sublayer of your future animation (not the top layer in the Layers palette, just the top sublayer of the animation).

3. Now choose Reverse Order from the Layers palette menu. The sublayers are then swapped from top to bottom, leaving you with your required frame order. Figure 30.13 shows the result.



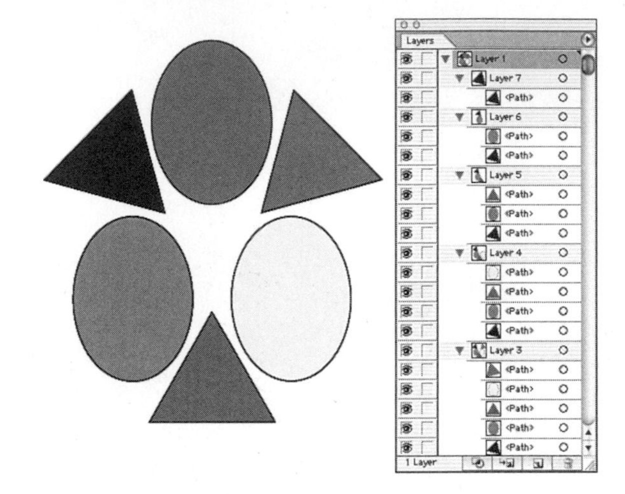


**Figure 30.13**
Although the order of the sublayers is reversed, their names and content remain unchanged.

# DESIGNATING LAYERS AS TEMPLATES

Double-clicking the name of a layer or sublayer opens the Layer Options dialog box. A check in the Template box makes several decisions for you. Templates are automatically made nonprinting and locked. They are dimmed to a default of 50% opacity, but that level can be adjusted on an individual basis, layer by layer. Three changes take place in the Layers palette:

- The eye icon is replaced by the template icon, a triangle-circle-square.
- The locked icon appears in the second column.
- The name of the layer or sublayer appears in italics to indicate that it is a nonprinting layer.

You'll also notice that all subordinate sublayers, groups, and objects have a dimmed locked icon in the second column of the Layers palette. The icon is dimmed to indicate that the locked status has been applied to a higher level in the hierarchy and must be removed at that level.

Templates are designed to allow you to trace over an item or to use it for reference. By default, checking Template in a Layer or Sublayer Options dialog box automatically switches the view mode to Preview. If you would rather have an object or group in that template in Outline view, select the layer to be made a template and give it a sublayer. Move the elements that are to be in Outline view to the sublayer. (Command)-click [Ctrl]-click the eye icon to change the view mode of the sublayer to Outline. Now change the original layer to a template, and the elements on the sublayer remain in Outline view. Figure 30.14 shows an example of how this works.

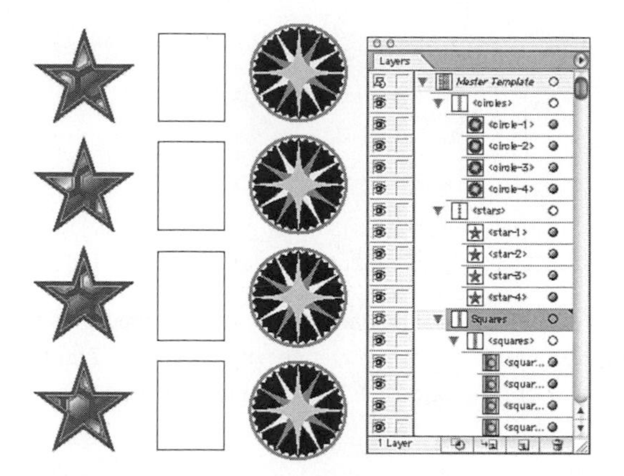


**Figure 30.14**
Although the circles and stars must be in Preview mode because the top layer is a template, the Squares sublayer remains in Outline mode. This change in view mode must be made prior to the top layer becoming a template because all subordinate elements of templates are locked.



# TARGETING LAYERS, GROUPS, AND OBJECTS

As you read earlier, targeting involves designating a layer, sublayer, group, or object to have an appearance attribute (including style, effect, and transparency) applied to it. A targeted layer and all its subordinate elements take on the specific appearance when applied. From that point forward, any element added to that particular layer, sublayer, or group will also assume the attribute. If an object, group, or sublayer is moved from a layer to which an attribute has been targeted, the attribute is left behind, and the element moves to its new layer or sublayer, as originally created. Any change to appearance that is applied directly to an individual element remains intact when the element is relocated.

*If you're having trouble with the appearance of an object (or objects) changing when it's moved from layer to layer, see "Moving a Group or Object Changes Appearance" in the "Mastering Illustrator" section at the end of this chapter.*

The Layers palette tells you at a glance the targeting status of any layer, sublayer, group, or object:

- In the Layers palette, to the right of the row's name, a single hollow circle indicates that the layer, object, or group is not targeted.
- A double concentric circle icon indicates that the layer, sublayer, group, or object is currently targeted, but no attribute has been applied.
- A single filled circle means that an attribute has been applied to the layer, sublayer, group, or object but that the layer, group, or object is not currently targeted.
- A filled circle in a hollow circle tells you that the level is currently targeted and has already had an attribute applied.

Figure 30.15 shows the four variations of the targeting indicator.

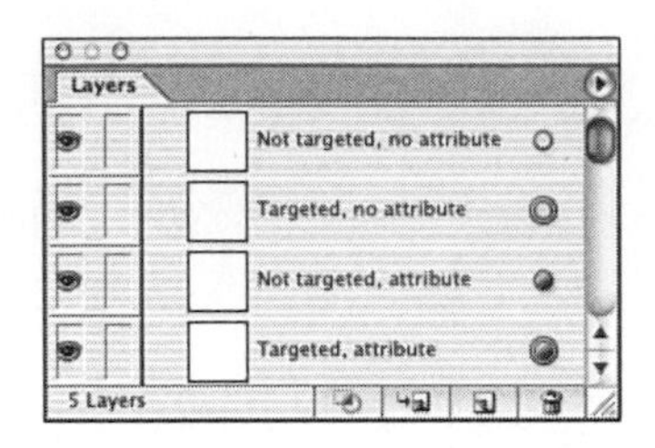


Figure 30.15
The layers' names indicate their status.



The first layer in the Layers palette has no appearance attribute applied, nor is one targeted. The second layer has been targeted, but no attribute has yet been applied. The third layer has an attribute applied, but it is not currently targeted. The last layer in the Layers palette has an attribute applied and is targeted.

If, at this point, an effect or other attribute is selected, it will be applied to both the second and fourth layers (both are targeted), but not the first and third. You can think of the outer circle of the Layer Targeting icon as a visual bounding box. Just as a selected object on the artboard has its bounding box visible, so too does a targeted layer have a "bounding circle" around the Layer Targeting icon.

Expressed in simplified form, the rules governing targeting are reasonably easy to understand, as you will note in the following lists. When a layer is targeted and an appearance attribute (style, effect, or transparency) is applied

- Every item (sublayer, group, and object) already on the layer is modified according to the new attribute.
- Every item added to the layer receives the new attribute.
- Any item moved from the layer loses the attribute.

When an item is moved to a layer, sublayer, or group to which an appearance attribute has been applied

- The element adopts the attribute of the layer.
- The element retains any attribute applied to it individually *and* attempts to apply the attribute of the layer, even if a conflict occurs. For example, an object that has individually been given the style Starburst, when moved to a layer that has been given the style Caution Tape, attempts to display both styles (see Figure 30.16).

When an item is moved from a layer, sublayer, or group that has had an appearance attribute applied to it

- The item loses the attributes of the layer, sublayer, or group.
- The item retains any attribute applied individually to it, as well as its original stroke and fill.
- The item adopts any attribute applied to the new layer, sublayer, or group.

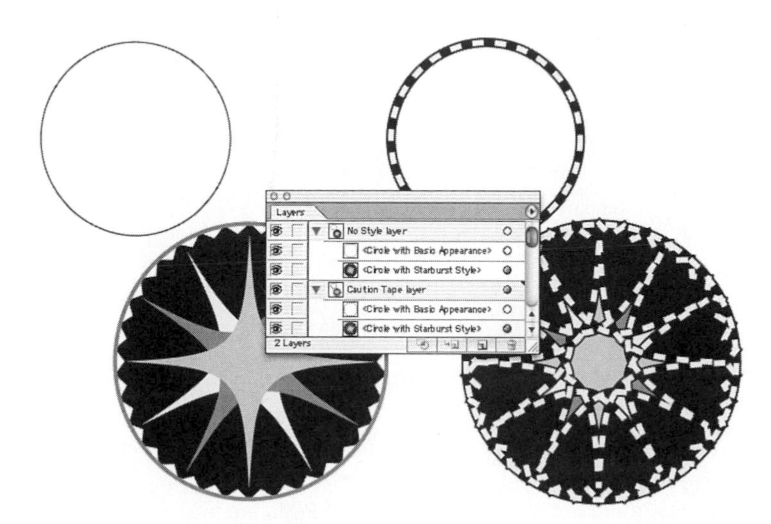


**Figure 30.16**
Two circles on each layer, one black and white, and one with the Starburst style applied. To the left, the objects on one layer have no additional applied characteristics. On the right, the layer has the style Caution Tape applied.



Appearance attributes can be dragged from element to element. (Option)-dragging [Alt]-dragging copies rather than transfers the attributes. Dragging from the Layer Targeting icon of a layer or sublayer to another layer or sublayer transfers some, but not all, attributes to existing elements on that layer. New objects created on the layer have all the attributes. When you're transferring or copying from layer to layer, attributes such as effects, transparency, and drop shadows are applied to existing objects. Strokes and fills do not override the element's existing attributes, unless they have been applied through targeting.

*One potential problem with dragging attributes from layer to layer is discussed in "Disappearing Objects During Attribute Transfer" in the "Mastering Illustrator" section at the end of this chapter.*

Copying or transferring by dragging the Layer Targeting icon from a layer or sublayer to a group likewise does not apply all attributes to the elements of the group—the original fill and stroke are not replaced, unless applied through targeting.

Copying or transferring from a layer or sublayer to an individual object (path) overrides all previous attributes.

Dragging the Layer Targeting icon from a group or an object to a layer, sublayer, another group, or another object works the same way.

The following can be applied to layers, sublayers, groups, and objects (paths) using targeting:

- Fill color
- Stroke color
- Stroke weight
- Calligraphic, Scatter, Art, and Pattern brushes
- Style
- Transparency
- Gradient

- Fill pattern (swatch)
- Printing attributes (Attributes palette)
- Object menu commands
- Effects
- Filters

Filters can also be applied using targeting in the Layers palette. However, unlike effects, filters permanently change all objects targeted or on the targeted layer, and they are applied to only those objects that exist at that time.



When you apply effects and filters through the Layers palette, Illustrator follows the same rules and guidelines as when you apply them directly. As an example, most filters are available only for RGB images. (For more information, see Chapter 35, "Illustrator's Effects and Filters.")

In the preceding list, you can see that Object menu commands are available to targeted layers. Because targeting, in effect, selects the groups and objects on a layer, the Transform commands, as well as such commands as Rasterize, Clipping Mask, and Compound Path, are available. Note that these commands work differently from attributes. They are available only when objects appear on a layer. They affect only those objects already on the layer, not any objects later added to the layer. They do not affect locked objects (paths).

# SPECIAL UTILIZATION OF LAYERS

The use of layers can make many tasks in Illustrator much simpler. You can accomplish some tasks, however, *only* by using layers. Animation is discussed earlier in this chapter. Using the standard Web file formats, you can create animation from Illustrator artwork only through layers.

The Layers palette can be a major tool in the actual design of Web pages and sites. Using the layers for individual pages and sublayers for the components of those pages, you can design an entire Web site in a single Illustrator document.

Effects can be applied much more easily when targeted to a layer rather than applied individually to a series of objects. Not only is this approach easier, it is often more accurate. Getting the same effect setting used 20 minutes earlier on some forgotten object is much more difficult than simply (Option)-dragging [Alt]-dragging an effect within the Layers palette.

One example of using effects with layers is simulating depth of field. By applying increasing amounts of blur to deeper and deeper layers, you can achieve an illusion of distance in your illustration. The foremost layer, the subject of the illustration, should be in sharp focus, as in a photograph. Objects immediately behind the subject can be slightly out of focus. Objects in the near distance should be a bit more out of focus, and objects in the far distance can be blurry (see Figure 30.17).

In Figure 30.17, each path has the same style applied, and each of the sublayers has a 2-pixel Gaussian blur targeted. Because the sublayers are sublayers of each other, the effect is cumulative. The lowest sublayer effectively has a total of four 2-pixel blurs applied.

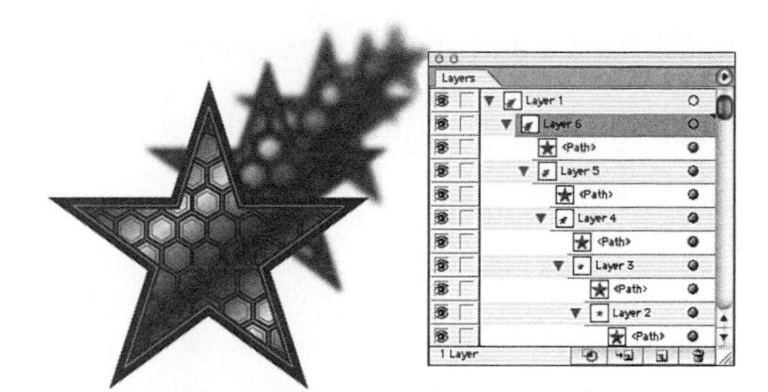


**Figure 30.17**
The blur effect is cumulative.



# MASTERING ILLUSTRATOR

## Layers Palette Viewing Options

*I can't see thumbnails for any of my objects, groups of objects, or sublayers in the Layers palette. How do I get to view them?*

The Layers palette menu, which you access by clicking the triangle in the upper-right corner of the palette, has the Palette Options command. Open the Layers Palette Options dialog box with this command and look in the lower part of the dialog box. Put check marks in the boxes next to Layers, Groups, and Objects, and make sure that no check mark appears next to Top Level Only. After you click OK, you'll see the thumbnails for all the elements of your illustration.

## Collect in New Layer Unavailable

*I have a number of objects that I want to put together on a separate layer, but I can't Shift-click to select them all in the Layers palette. How do I use the Collect in New Layer command?*

The Collect in New Layer command, located in the Layers palette menu, is available only when you have selected elements at the same level hierarchy (when selecting in the Layers palette). You can use this command with objects of any level that are selected on the artboard. Shift-click the objects themselves, rather than their names in the Layers palette. When you're working in the palette, each object or group needs to be part of the same group, sublayer, or layer—whichever is the next level up in the Layers palette.

## Moving a Group or Object Changes Appearance

*I dragged a group and a few objects from one layer to another, and they look completely different. Why did they change appearance?*

Either the layer they came from or the layer they went to, or both, were targeted for attributes. Look in the Layers palette. To the right of each layer's name is a circle. If the circle is filled, the layer has one or more attributes applied to it. Those attributes, because they are at the layer level rather than applied to an individual object, affect every object added to the layer. Likewise, when an object is moved from the layer, it loses the layer's attributes.

## Disappearing Objects During Attribute Transfer

*I transferred the attributes of one layer to another, and everything on my first layer disappeared. Is something broken?*

The fill and stroke of the objects was transferred to the second layer. The objects are still there, but they're invisible because they now have a fill and stroke of None. To maintain attributes on the first layer and apply them to the second, hold down (Option) [Alt] when dragging the filled circle of the Layer Targeting icon from one layer to another.

31

# DEFINING AND APPLYING PATTERNS

## IN THIS CHAPTER

Patterns, like colors, can be customized, saved, and applied to individual objects. The two basic types of patterns are fill patterns and brush patterns. Brush patterns are intended to be applied to paths, including the stroke of an object. They are used exclusively with pattern brushes. Fill patterns, on the other hand, are designed for use as an object's fill. Fill patterns are stored in the Swatches palette; you can load them through the Swatch palette's menu. Brush patterns are stored in the Brushes palette; you can load them with the palette's menu command Open Brush Library. (Brushes and the Brushes palette are discussed in Chapter 26, "Working with the Four Types of Brushes.")

Loosely, a *pattern* is a piece of artwork that repeats throughout the object into which it is placed (or along a path). This repeating is called *tiling*, much as a kitchen floor or a bathroom wall is made of individual tiles that repeat a pattern. A pattern is artwork that is available for fills or paths and is stored in the Swatches palette.

This chapters looks at the concepts governing the creation and employment of patterns as well as looks individually at the two types of patterns—those used as fills and those used with brushes.



# GENERAL RULES GOVERNING PATTERNS

A pattern can contain objects and text, paths and compound paths, and fills or no fill. Several tools and techniques *cannot* be used to create patterns:

- Other patterns
- Gradients and gradient meshes
- Blends
- Brush strokes
- Bitmap images
- Placed files
- Graphs
- Masks

To see how you can use varying levels of transparency in a pattern, look at Figures 31.1 and 31.2, in which a simple target pattern was developed. The progressive circles are all set for 25% opacity in the Transparency palette, and the cross is set at 100% opacity. These figures show how the different opacities interact with each other and the background.

To see some of the differences in behavior between fill patterns and pattern brushes, see Figures 31.3 and 31.4.

In Illustrator, you can use transparency with objects, paths, and text that are destined to become parts of a pattern. The transparency affects not only the interaction among the parts of the pattern, but also the pattern itself. Chapter 34, "Using Masks, Transparency, and Blending Modes," describes how such interactions are controlled.

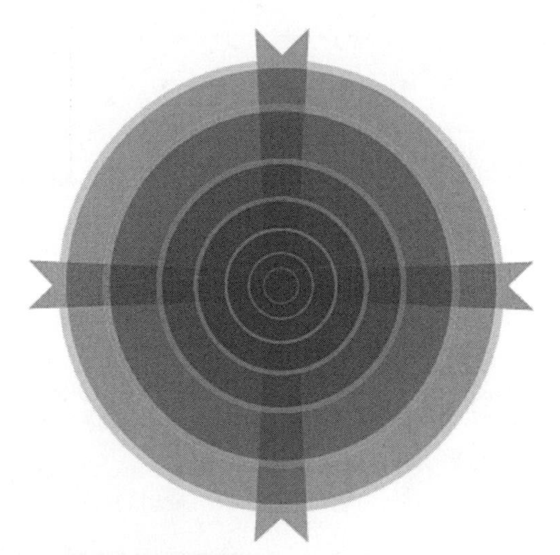

**Figure 31.1**
As the number of semi-transparent circles increases, the visibility of the background cross decreases, particularly within the inner pair of circles.

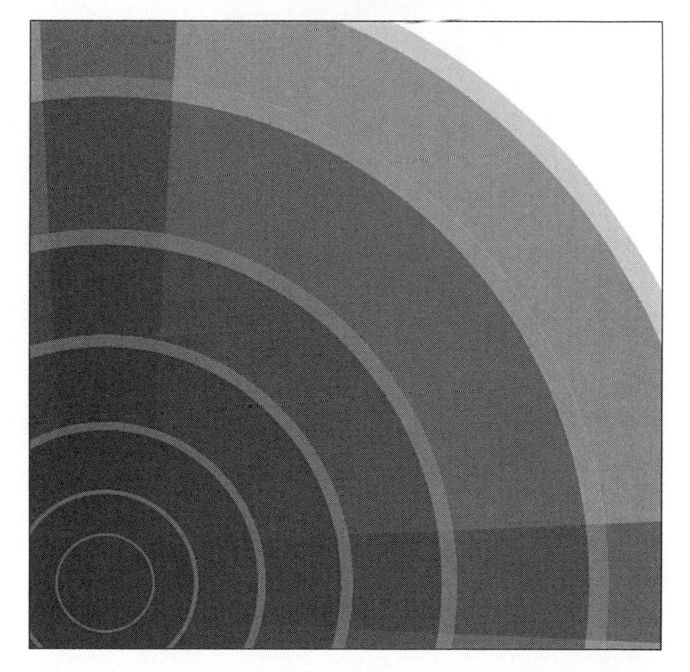

**Figure 31.2**
This close-up view shows how the cumulative opacity of the pattern in the foreground eventually obscures the background cross.



In Figure 31.3, the rectangles in the left column have the pattern fill and no stroke; the center column shows no fill and a stroke of 15 points; the right column has both the pattern fill and a stroke of 15 points. Note how the patterns flow seamlessly outward from the fill into the stroke.

In Figure 31.4, observe the difference between fill patterns and brush patterns when they're applied to a stroke. A brush pattern (bottom row) normally rotates around the object, whereas a fill pattern (top row) remains oriented to the vertical and horizontal axes.

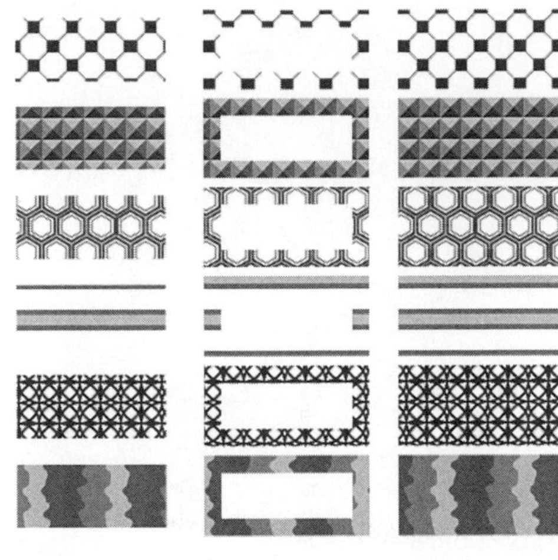

Figure 31.3
Use the Illustrator Swatches palette menu command Other Library to load any of the more than two dozen sets of patterns supplied with the program. Look inside the Illustrator folder, inside Presets, for the patterns folder.

Figure 31.4
The top three objects have fill patterns applied to their strokes; the lower three have brush patterns.

Fill patterns tile (replicate to cover an area or stroke) from the ruler's point of origin. By default, the zero-zero point of the ruler is in the lower left of the document. When the rulers are visible, you can change this point by dragging from the intersection of the rulers in the upper left of the screen to the new point of origin. From the point of origin, patterns tile from left to right, from bottom to top. You can shift a pattern within an object or along a stroke (not a path) by holding down the tilde key (~) and dragging.

The tilde key can also be used in conjunction with the Rotate, Scale, and Reflect tools to change a fill pattern without altering the object itself. As with any use of these keys, the object must first be selected before it can be altered with the specific tool. You also can use these tools to transform fill patterns applied to strokes, but you cannot use them with brush patterns. Also, be aware of the Transform Pattern Only command from the Transform palette pop-up menu. When this option is used, the pattern is altered without affecting the object itself.

# FILL PATTERNS

Fill patterns can be complex or simple, plain or ornate. All, however, have several things in common. As discussed earlier, a number of tools and techniques cannot be used to create patterns. In addition, all fill patterns tile from the ruler origin. All fill patterns are stored in the Swatches palette and are kept with a particular document. More complex patterns should be smaller for efficiency. Simple patterns can be larger. Most fill pattern swatches should be between 1/2- and 1-inch square.

Bounding boxes are great for planning and for regulating space around your artwork within the pattern. They are not, however, always necessary. If, for example, you want a simple star as your fill pattern, you just draw the star, select it, and choose Edit, Define Pattern. That's all there is to it. Your star will repeat in nice, orderly rows throughout any object you choose.

The process of creating a fill pattern is rather simple. You draw the artwork, place a *bounding box* behind the artwork to designate what will be included in the pattern, and save the pattern to the Swatches palette by choosing Edit, Define Pattern. Creating a good fill pattern, however, requires some planning.

The bounding box controls the size of an individual tile of the pattern. A bounding box substantially larger than the artwork it surrounds produces lots of whitespace between elements in an object filled with the pattern. Although it isn't required, a bounding box is useful for regulating how each tile aligns.

You can think of fill patterns as falling into two distinct categories: repeating patterns and seamless patterns. A *repeating pattern* has individual elements that are obvious in the object that is filled. *Seamless patterns*, on the other hand, have hidden edges. They are meant to appear as one continuous pattern within the object rather than as a series of tiles. Examples of the two types are shown in Figure 31.5.

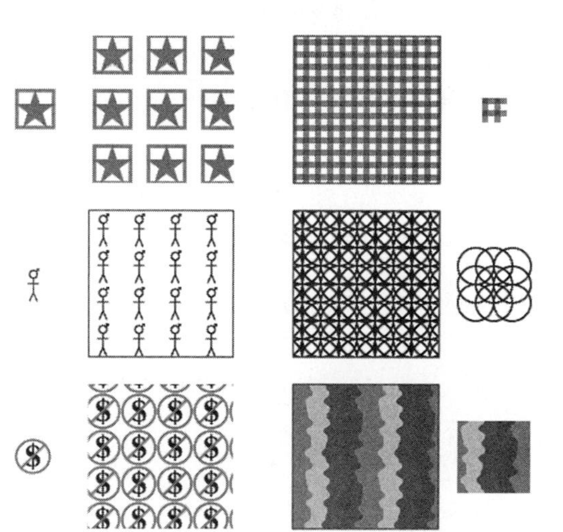

Figure 31.5
The objects on the left are filled with repeating patterns. The right column shows objects filled with seamless patterns. Individual tiles of each pattern are shown at the size at which they were designed.

The basic technique for creating a seamless pattern is to have elements that cross the boundary of one tile into the neighboring tile. Although this isn't possible because only a single tile is used, you can create such an illusion. When an element starts on the left side of the tile, appears to go off the edge, and then reappears on the right side, the eye cannot tell where one tile ends and the next begins. Two approaches are shown in Figure 31.6.

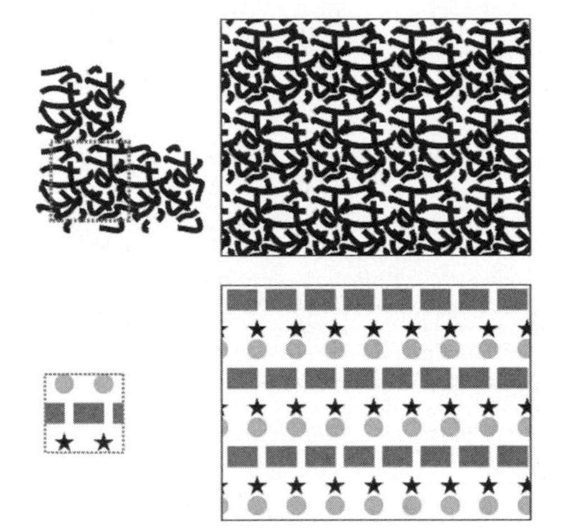

Figure 31.6
With bounding boxes indicated by dashed lines, the difference in the two techniques is apparent.



In the upper example in Figure 31.6, duplicates of the pattern were dragged above and to the right to add the ends of the lines that extended past the bounding box. Those parts of the lines that extend beyond the dashed lines to the left and the bottom are reproduced in the right and top of the box by the copies. The bounding box, in the process of producing the pattern, chops off any part of the pattern sticking out of it. The lower example is much more straightforward. Elements of the pattern are "halved" in the creation process, with one half on each side of the pattern.

## Illustrator at Work: Creating Repeating Fill Patterns

To create a fill pattern, follow these basic steps:

1. Draw a square of the required dimensions (but typically no larger than 1 inch × 1 inch). It will become your bounding box and must be the furthest back of any object in the pattern.
2. Within the bounds of the square, draw and color your art. Remember which techniques cannot be used in a pattern. (See "General Rules Governing Patterns" at the beginning of this chapter.)
3. Group your art (but not the bounding box).
4. Select the bounding box; then give it a fill of None and a stroke of None.

> **Caution**
>
> Patterns, especially very complex patterns, can cause trouble for printers. Rather than waiting for a printer error, consider the complexity when you're designing your custom patterns. Remove any unnecessary artwork (including details that will be obscured by other artwork placed on top). Objects of the same color should be grouped so that they are adjacent in the stacking order. Arranging similarly colored items in the stacking order can affect layers, so planning is required.

5. With the bounding box still selected, Shift-click your grouped artwork to select it as well.
6. Choose Edit, Define Pattern to open the New Swatch dialog box.
7. Give your pattern a name and click OK.

## Illustrator at Work: Creating Seamless Fill Patterns

If you want to create a seamless pattern, as shown in the upper half of Figure 31.6, the technique is a bit different:

1. Establish your future bounding box and begin drawing your art as described in the preceding steps. Artwork can extend past all four sides of the bounding box for this procedure.
2. When the art is ready, select it all and the bounding box.
3. Ensure that Snap to Point is selected under the View menu.
4. Press (Shift-Option) [Shift+Alt] and drag the selection toward the bottom of the bounding box. When the edges of the boxes are aligned and snap together, release the mouse button.
5. Release the modifier keys, click again on the still-selected artwork, press (Shift-Option) [Shift+Alt] again, and drag at a 45° angle until the copied artwork aligns with the right side of the original bounding box.
6. Release the modifier keys, click again on the still-selected artwork, press (Shift-Option) [Shift+Alt] again, and drag at a 45° angle until the copied artwork aligns with the top of the original bounding box.
7. Release the modifier keys, click again on the still-selected artwork, press (Shift-Option) [Shift+Alt] again, and drag at a 45° angle until the copied artwork aligns with the left side of the original bounding box.
8. Delete the four surrounding boxes, leaving only the original bounding box.
9. Select all the artwork (but not the bounding box) and group it.
10. Select the original bounding box. (It should be the only one left.) Give it a fill of None and a stroke of None.
11. Shift-click the grouped artwork. Everything, including the bounding box, should now be selected.
12. Choose Edit, Define Pattern to open the New Swatch dialog box.
13. Give your pattern a name and click OK.

*If you're having trouble getting your new patterns to appear properly in the Swatches palette, see "Trouble Defining Patterns" in the "Mastering Illustrator" section at the end of this chapter.*

## Editing Patterns

You can edit a pattern after adding it to the Swatches palette. To do so, simply drag the swatch to the artboard, ungroup it if necessary, do the editing, and (Option)-drag [Alt]-drag the modified swatch back on top of the original in the Swatches palette. All objects in the document that had been filled with the original pattern are updated to the new pattern. And, of course, anything new to which the pattern is applied uses the edited version.

Often you can solve printing problems with documents that contain complex patterns by using the Expand command. The Object, Expand command can turn an object filled with a pattern into an object filled with objects.

If you want to edit the pieces of an object whose fill has been expanded, you can do so. You'll often see masked objects and paths that extend well beyond the limits of the original object. Select the pattern and start with a couple of Ungroup commands (until the command is grayed out in the Edit menu). Next, zoom in very closely on a corner of the visible fill. Using the Direct Selection tool, and watching its cursor change to indicate that you're over a point, click to select the invisible bounding box. Press Delete twice. The once-masked objects and paths are now available for you to edit or copy as you will.

*Images with complex (or many) patterns can drown a printer in data. If your image isn't printing, check "Expanding Patterns for Print" in the "Mastering Illustrator" section at the end of this chapter.*

# BRUSH PATTERNS

A brush pattern is actually a series of patterns combined into one brush. Unlike a fill pattern, a brush pattern must be able to rotate around corners and adapt to curves. To create such a pattern, you must actually create the individual parts that serve as the outer and inner corners. See Figure 31.7 for the difference between these two types of corners. If the brush pattern is to be used with open paths, start and end tiles must also be created.

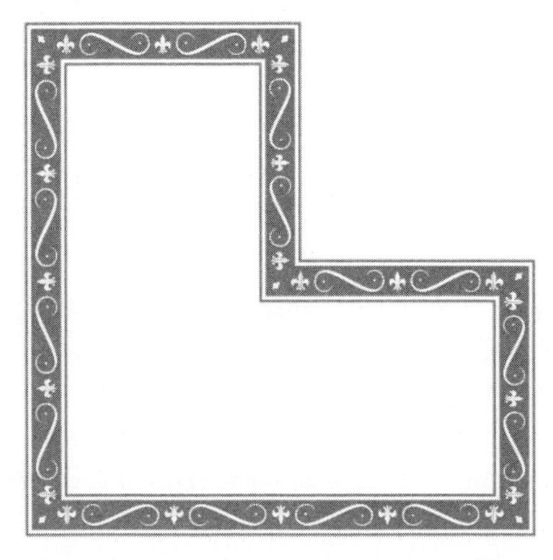

Figure 31.7
This pattern contains five outer corners and one inner corner.

Notice how, in making all the corners except one, the brush pattern has pointed the fleurs-de-lis outward, away from the corner. They are outer corners. The one exception (in the center of Figure 31.7) is the inner corner, in which the fleurs-de-lis are pointed toward each other. When you're designing a nonsymmetrical pattern brush, you must construct both outer and inner corners.

When you're drawing with the Pen tool or the Pencil tool, Illustrator assumes, for the purposes of applying a pattern, that you are working clockwise. See Figure 31.8 for a visual explanation.

Figure 31.8
When you're using the Pen tool from a central point, Illustrator orients a pattern with the assumption that you are working clockwise.



In Figure 31.8, from point A to point B, the pattern points to the left. From A to C, it points upward. From A to D, the top of the pattern points to the right. From A to E, it's toward the bottom. This rule applies to any tool utilizing a pattern brush.

## Illustrator at Work: Creating a Brush Pattern

You can create a new brush in two ways. In the first method, you simply use the built-in Illustrator artwork found through the Brushes palette, as described in Chapter 26. Using the Brushes palette's pop-up menu, select New Brush. In the dialog box, choose New Pattern Brush. Illustrator gives you a large selection of parts with which to work.

You also can use the Brushes palette pop-up menu in the creation of original pattern brushes. All parts of the new brush pattern must be saved as patterns in the Swatches palette before you can access them from the New Pattern Brush dialog box. The process of creating a brush pattern is not as complicated as it seems. (The specifics of creating side, corner, and end tiles will follow.) To create a brush pattern, follow these steps:

1. Create the side tile of your new brush and choose Edit, Define Pattern to add it to your Swatches palette.
2. Create the corner pattern or patterns (you need both outer and inner corner patterns if you're creating a nonsymmetrical pattern) and use the Define Pattern command.
3. Create end patterns and add them, too, to the Swatches palette.
4. After you've created all your required parts, click the Brushes palette tab to make it visible.
5. From the palette's pop-up menu, select New Brush.

6. Choose New Pattern Brush, which opens the New Brush dialog box, shown in Figure 31.9. Your new swatches should appear in the list of available art in the Pattern Brush Options dialog box, also shown in Figure 31.9.

7. At the top of the dialog box are five squares, each with a depiction of its purpose. From left to right, they are Side Tile (straight segment), Outer Corner Tile, Inner Corner Tile, Start Tile, and End Tile. Click the leftmost one and then select your side tile pattern from the list below.

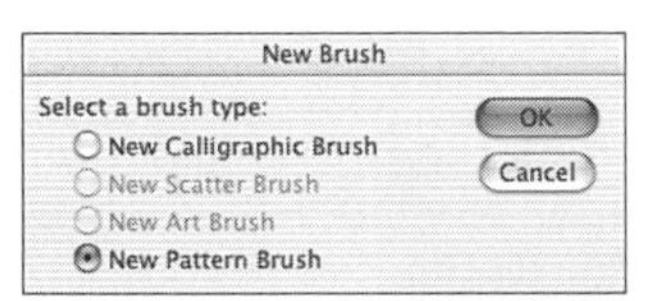


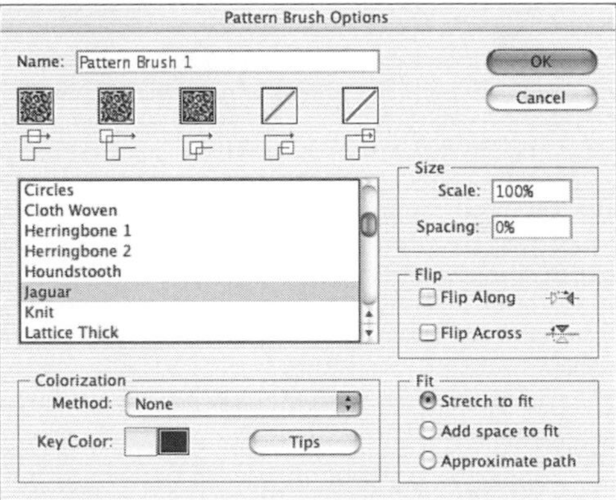


**Figure 31.9**
The Pattern Brush Options dialog box shows all available patterns from the Swatches palette.

8. Do the same for all other required parts. If you accidentally choose the wrong artwork, simply reclick the correct swatch's name. If you add a swatch where you would rather have no swatch (an end tile, for example), you can choose None from the top of the list.

9. In the Size area of the Pattern Brush Options dialog box, select the appropriate size ratio. Choosing 100% tiles the brush pattern at the original creation size. The value must be between 1% and 10000%, although very large values are usually impractical. Consider a pattern designed and created at 1/4 inch × 1/4 inch. A size value of 10000% would produce tiles 25 inches × 25 inches.

10. Choose one, both, or neither Flip option. Flip Along reverses each tile, whereas Flip Across changes all tiles by swapping the top and bottom.

11. Choose the appropriate Fit setting (see Figure 31.10).

When you click a tile button at the top of the Pattern Brush Options dialog box, the selection automatically jumps to the top of the list of patterns. You can jump right back to where you need to be by pressing the first letter of the name of your pattern. For example, after clicking the Outer Corner Tile button, you can press J on the keyboard to jump to the first pattern whose name starts with that letter.

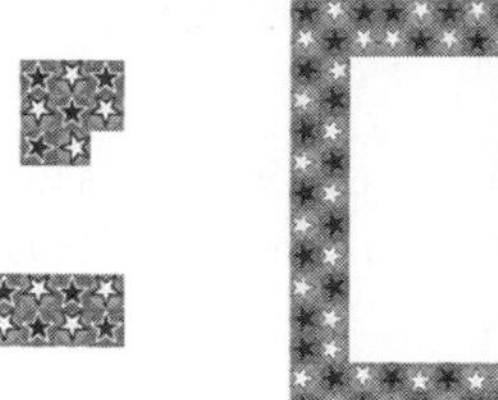

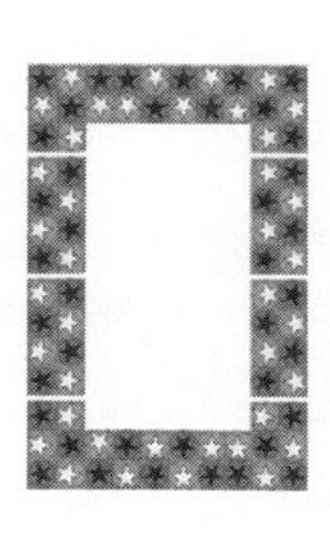

Figure 31.10
The Pattern Brush Options dialog box offers three Fit settings.

To the left in Figure 31.10 are an outer corner and a side tile from this particular pattern brush. The first rectangle uses Stretch to Fit, the middle rectangle is set to Add Space to Fit, and the object to the right is set to Approximate Path. Note that the pattern is not centered on the bounding box of the last object (the three objects are of identical size and are aligned through their centers). Also, be aware of the lack of corner tiles and the fact that only a single tile is used vertically, which distorts the pattern. Some other types of pattern brushes, however, behave excellently with this setting.

12. Choose your method of colorization. None keeps the pattern's colors as they were when created. Tints uses the currently active stroke color. The darkest parts of the brush pattern will be that color, whites will remain white, and everything in between will become a tint of the stroke color. Tints and Shades keeps black and white, and it creates shades (and tints) of the stroke color for the rest of the pattern. This option is designed to be used with brushes created from grayscale art. (See the warning following these steps.) Hue Shift is designed for use with color patterns. It takes the dominant color (key color) and transforms it into the currently active stroke color. Other colors in the pattern are transformed accordingly. Black, white, and gray retain their respective values. You can designate a new key color by using the Eyedropper and clicking a color in one of the tiles at the top of the dialog box. Note that you should select your desired stroke color prior to opening the New Brush dialog box.
13. If you haven't yet, assign a name to your new pattern brush.
14. Click OK. The pattern is automatically applied to any currently selected object. It is added to the bottom of the Brushes palette as a new pattern brush.
15. (Optional) You can now delete your artwork from the Swatches palette unless you have further use for it.

**Caution**
The Tints and Shades colorization option adds black to the pattern brush's color palette. When you're working with a spot color for your pattern brush, be aware that this option could prevent the artwork from separating completely to a single plate. The addition of black could result in part of the pattern brush's stroke appearing on a spot color plate and the rest on the black plate.

## Designing Brush Patterns for Pattern Brushes

Several key concepts deserve attention during the planning of a brush pattern:

- As side tiles are placed along the path, the top always faces "outward" from the center of an object.
- No artwork can protrude beyond the bounding box without being chopped off in the pattern.

- Like fill patterns, brush patterns should be kept as simple as possible to avoid long redraws and potential printing problems.
- The more complex a pattern, the smaller the individual tiles should be. Although more tiles are required to complete the path, the file itself will be less likely to present printing problems.
- A side tile should usually be from 1 to 2 inches long and half that high.
- Corner tiles must be square; each end of the pattern meets up with the same size tile. The pattern must be centered along the two sides where it will meet the side tiles (assuming that the side tiles are also centered).
- There are both continuous patterns and repeating patterns for both fill and brush. A continuous pattern would be one without a discernible repetition of elements. A repeating pattern, while perhaps having neither beginning nor end, does have individual elements that can be seen to reoccur. See Figure 31.11 for a visual comparison.
- If the pattern is symmetrical from top to bottom, the same tile can be used for outer and inner corners.



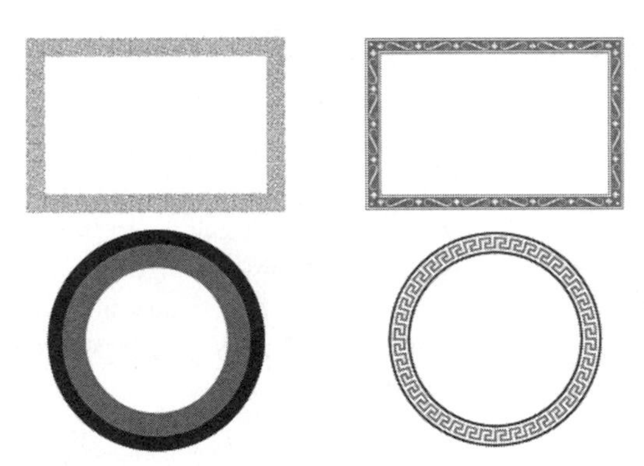

**Figure 31.11**
The examples on the left are continuous patterns; they have no obviously repeating elements. The double-line border, for example, has just one of each of the two lines. The examples on the right have repeating patterns.

*If the brush pattern you've designed just doesn't seem to be proportional to your artwork, see "Resizing Brush Patterns" in the "Mastering Illustrator" section at the end of this chapter.*

# Creating Brush Pattern Side Tiles

Among the handiest features of Illustrator for use during the brush pattern–creation process are grids and guides. The use of the commands View, Show Grid and View, Guides, Show Guides should be part of setting up the workplace for this type of operation.

As noted previously, the best dimensions for a side tile are between 1/2 and 1 inch tall and 1 to 2 inches wide. Simpler patterns are more efficient at larger sizes because fewer copies are required to cover a path.

If your brush pattern is to be a repeating pattern, you must decide whether you want the end of each tile to be in the middle or at the edge of an object. You can see the difference in Figure 31.12.

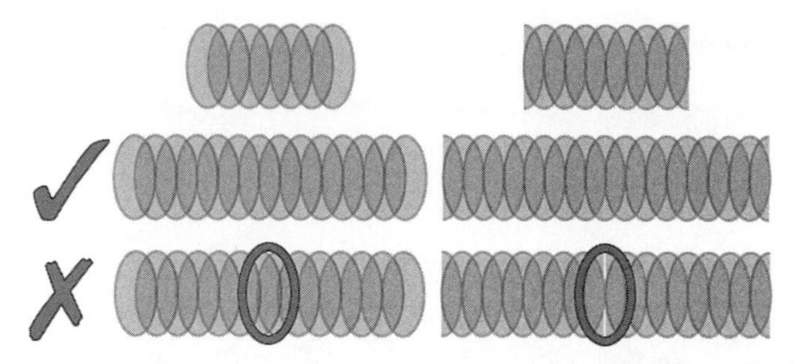

Figure 31.12
The patterns are shown at 200% zoom.

In Figure 31.12, the top row shows single tiles that end at the edge and in the middle of an object. The second row shows how two of the tiles should match. The third row shows what is to be avoided. Notice the misalignment of the center ovals on the left, which leads to a slight doubling of the stroke for the objects in the middle (where the pattern tiles join). On the right, the pattern is just a bit too short, resulting in a gap between tiles. A gap in the middle of an object is far more distracting than it would be between objects.



To create "seamless" patterns, many designers split each tile in the middle of an object rather than at its edge. When the object matches with the other half of the object in the abutting tile, the illusion of flow is maintained. The eye is prevented from seeing any place that the pattern could be split vertically. In the top example in Figure 31.13, the black and white blocks align, allowing the eye to see a potential seam between tiles. In the bottom example, a "seamless" pattern, no such break is visible between tiles. This illusion is maintained because the top block and bottom block do not align. The original patterns for the two lines are shown below with their bounding boxes visible.

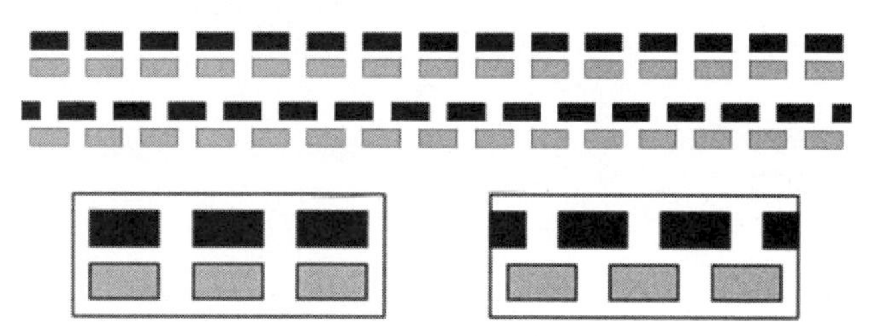

Figure 31.13
The two lines of blocks are actually the same length, although the upper line looks shorter because of the whitespace at the end of the tiles.

In addition to the decorative borders with which you are familiar, brush patterns can serve in more mundane (yet important) ways. Maps, for example, can contain patterned lines that represent such things as warm and cold fronts (weather maps), unit sector borders and minefields (military maps), and, of course, the borders that appear on political maps. Figure 31.14 shows some examples of various delineation and border patterns, along with examples of their side tiles.

The first example in Figure 31.14 is a very basic combination of rectangles and circles. The second through fourth examples were created with two filled paths (the third pattern also has a third path for the yellow line). The bottom pattern is created with basic shapes. Note that items of similar color are grouped individually to ensure that they are on the same stacking order to simplify the pattern. Observe how the lack of corner tiles in the first, fourth, and fifth examples results in irregular spacing when the path changes direction sharply. (Creation of corner tiles is discussed in the next section.) Also note how irregular spacing is not a problem with the bottom example, which consists of discrete objects rather than a continuous segment.

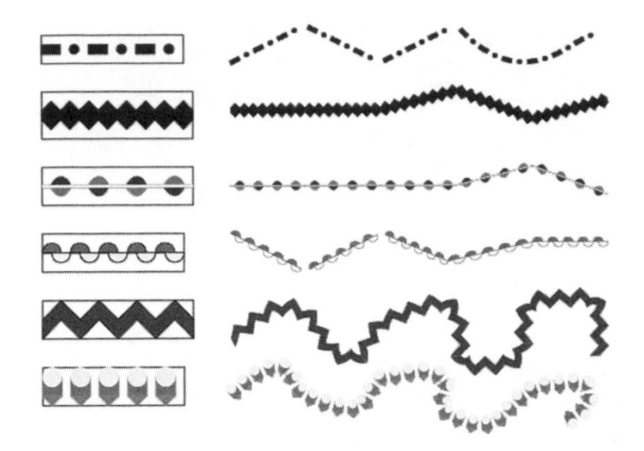

Figure 31.14
Using pattern brushes is the easiest way to make and store such delineation markers.

Maps can also contain features such as roads, railroads, rivers, and other items that may be a bit more complex. See Figure 31.15 for some examples of more complex brush patterns.



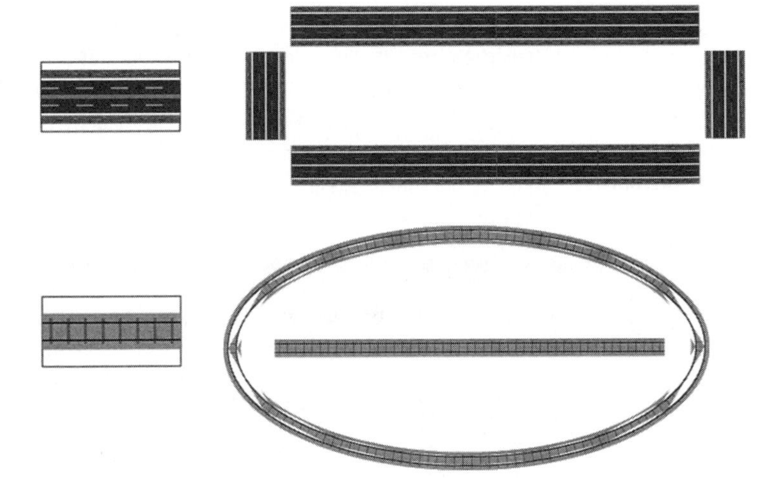

Figure 31.15
Brush patterns differ in complexity, resulting in a variety of potential concerns.

The two brush patterns shown in Figure 31.15 require some additional effort to design. To minimize the complexity of the top pattern, layered lines of varying sizes were used, rather than duplicating the edge lines and center lines. Although both of these brush patterns appear fine in the horizontal and vertical examples, the lack of corner tiles ruins the effect for rectangles and ovals.

## Creating Brush Pattern Corner Tiles

As you saw previously in this chapter, corner tiles are an important part of most (but not all) brush patterns that are applied to curves and shapes. Corners come in two types: outer and inner. (Refer to Figure 31.7 for a visual depiction of the difference.) The construction of a corner tile can be a very simple or an arduous task, depending in part on the complexity of the pattern. Using a simple pattern, you can examine many of the techniques of corner construction.

Remember that a corner tile's bounding box must be square to properly match both the vertical and horizontal side tiles. The center of the corner pattern will be centered on the adjoining sides.

In Figure 31.16, you can see how Illustrator handles curves differently from actual corners. The star pattern was added as a corner tile to the pattern brush. When the Pen tool is used with this pattern, corner tiles are placed only where corner anchor points exist. When smooth anchor points are created, the pattern continues without a corner tile.

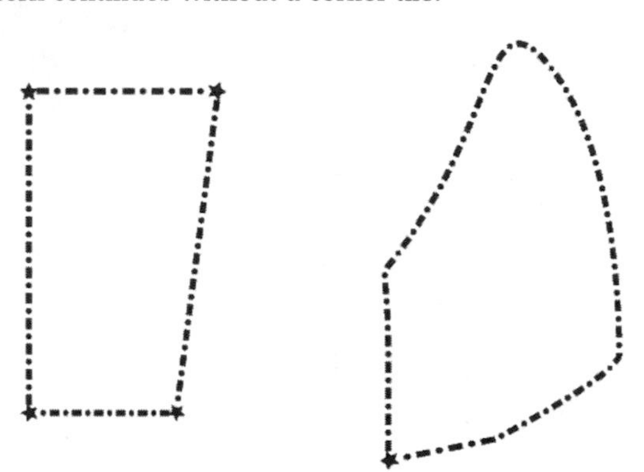

Figure 31.16
Chapter 24, "Creating and Editing Paths," described the difference between a corner anchor point and a smooth anchor point. These two examples show yet another reason why the difference is important.



If you want to explore the differences among square, curved, and angled corners, a continuous pattern is suitable. The pattern in Figure 31.17 is constructed of two stacked lines. The bottom line is 21 points wide, and the top is 7 points. The corner tiles are shown below, with bounding boxes simulated by dashed lines. The square and curved corner tiles are also two stacked lines with the same stroke specifications as the side tile. The angled corner, however, requires (at a minimum) that a path be drawn from corner to corner for each of the two lines, as shown in Figure 31.18.

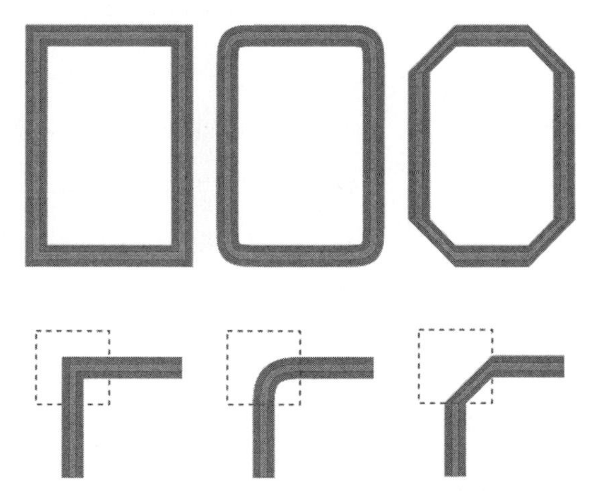

Figure 31.17
These three objects use the same side tiles, but the corner tiles differ, as shown.

Each of the two lines of the square corner tile's path was constructed with the Pen tool and consists of a simple three-point open path with corner anchor points. The curved corner tile is a two-point open path with smooth anchor points on each end. The angled corner tile was constructed by making paths that outline the two lines (see Figure 31.18).

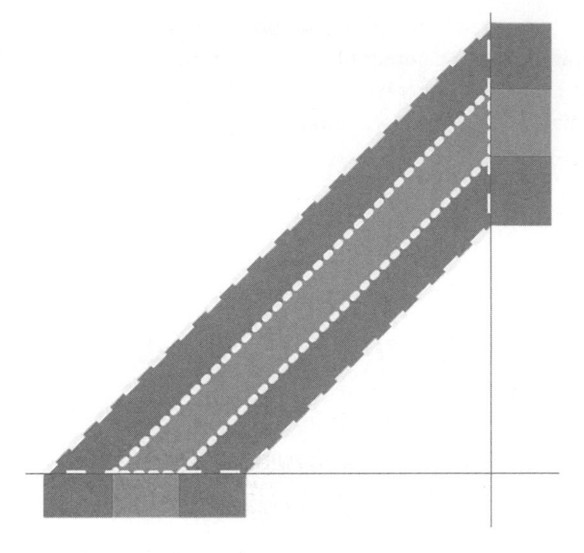

Figure 31.18
This image represents the paths required to produce the angled corner tile in Figure 31.17.



The dashed lines indicate the two paths that were drawn with the Pen tool to create the two lines. Both of the paths are set to a stroke of None and the appropriate fill color. With a stroke of None, the corners of the paths can easily match those of the horizontal and vertical side tiles. With a positive value for the stroke, the line caps force the edges beyond the desired point of junction.

Note that the angled corner tile shown in Figures 31.17 and 31.18 has thinner lines than the side tiles. To compensate for the angle, the outer edges of each line must be offset slightly. Figure 31.19 shows the difference.

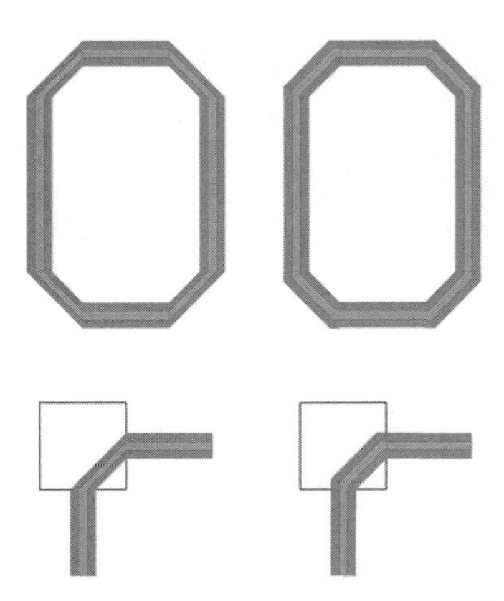

Figure 31.19
Notice the difference when angled corners are offset to maintain line width (right).

The corner tile on the left was drawn corner to corner (or point to point). Notice how much thinner the lines are across the angle than they are in the vertical and horizontal strokes. To maintain the integrity of the pattern's lines (or other elements in various patterns), the outer edges of the lines must be extended slightly beyond the point where the inner edge angles away. Look at the corner tile on the right as three distinct lines, from the inner (right) side to the outer (left). The right edge of the right (innermost) line begins to angle from the bottom toward the top directly at the edge of the bounding box. The outer edge of the rightmost line proceeds vertically for a short distance before angling off. The edges of the other two lines follow similar patterns.

As you saw in Figure 31.19, drawing a path on an angle that maintains the width of the vertical and horizontal strokes is a bit more complicated than simply going corner to corner. The outer corners of the elements must be offset slightly, but determining how much requires some work. Figure 31.20 shows how a grid and guides can be used to determine offset.

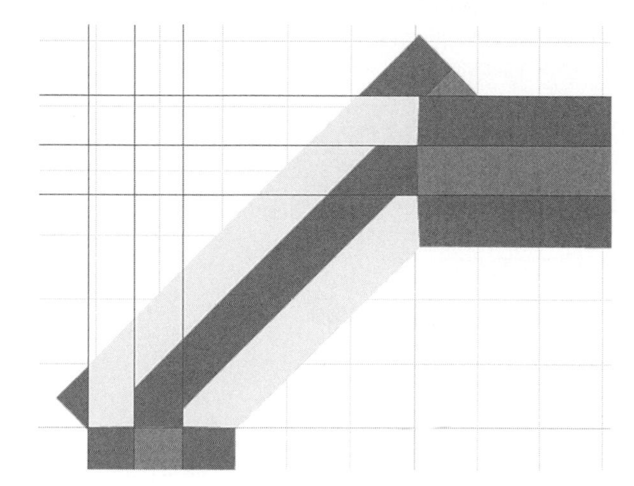

**Figure 31.20**
The grid and guides can help you determine angles when creating offset corner tiles.

A curved corner tile, in addition to being easier to create than an angled corner, is appropriate for many uses. Paths like the one shown in Figure 31.21 can use the same tile for both outer and inner curves.

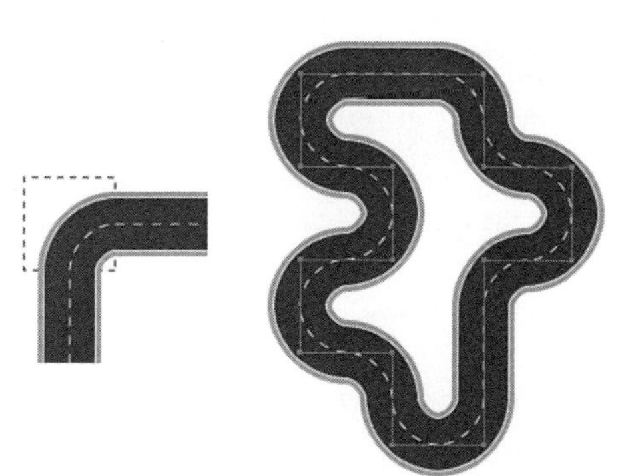

**Figure 31.21**
A simple curve can often be used for both inner and outer corner tiles.

The curved corner tile in Figure 31.21 was made by simply copying the side tile and curving it using a combination of the Direct Selection tool and the Convert Anchor Point tool. The test-track path to the right is shown with the path itself selected.

## Creating Brush Pattern Start and End Tiles

End tiles are required only when a brush pattern will be used with an open path, and not all patterns require end tiles for open paths. Unlike corner tiles, the bounding boxes of end tiles do not have to be square because they abut on only one side. Some patterns require closure at the start and end, such as those patterns that utilize a fine line or border near the top and bottom and patterns designed specifically for open paths. Figure 31.22 shows a couple examples.

Although the bounding box of a corner tile must be square, there is no requirement that it be the same size as the side tile's bounding box. Remember, though, that the center of the corner tile's bounding box must align with the center of the side tile's bounding box.

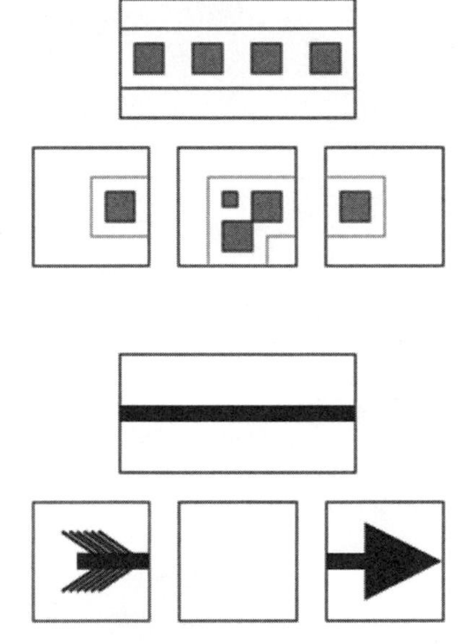

**Figure 31.22**
Both patterns show their side tile above and the start, corner, and end tiles below.



Because of the line at the top and bottom, the upper example requires end tiles when used with open paths. In this case, the start tile was simply reflected vertically to create the end tile. The lower example requires start and end tiles for obvious reasons. It does not require a corner tile because the side tile consists of a simple line.

# MASTERING ILLUSTRATOR

## Trouble Defining Patterns

*When I define a new pattern, sometimes all I get is a blank white box. Other times I get a border around my pattern that I don't want. What am I forgetting?*

To ensure that your artwork actually becomes part of the pattern, make sure the objects are selected (and grouping them is a good idea) before choosing Edit, Define Pattern. To avoid an unintended box around your pattern, check that your bounding box has a stroke (and fill) of None.

## Expanding Patterns for Print

*When I send my image to the printer (or image setter), things start off fine and spooling is proceeding, but then everything locks up. What's the cure?*

If the image contains complex patterns, blends, or gradients, select them and choose Object, Expand to create objects and paths from the more complex data. Printing should go much more smoothly.

## Resizing Brush Patterns



*I spent hours and hours designing the perfect pattern brush, but it looks terrible because it's too big to fit around my objects. Have I wasted all that time?*

No, you haven't. In the Brushes palette, double-click your design. When the Pattern Brush Options dialog box opens, reduce the percentage in the box labeled Scale.

32

# USING THE APPEARANCE AND STYLE PALETTES

## IN THIS CHAPTER

Appearances and graphic styles are among the most powerful tools in Illustrator. They allow you to change the look of an object without actually changing the object itself. You can later edit the original object and have all the appearances update themselves automatically. Whether you need to change the size, shape, color, or effects applied to an object, the other characteristics will conform to the new look. They can be applied to objects, groups, or layers.

This chapter looks at appearances and styles as well as the palettes you use to work with them.

# APPEARANCES AND GRAPHIC STYLES

Appearance characteristics are applied to objects and groups and can be assigned to layers. All the following items are appearance characteristics:

- Fill color, gradient, and pattern
- Stroke color, weight, and brush
- Effects
- Transparency

A selected object's characteristics are shown in the Appearance palette (see Figure 32.1).



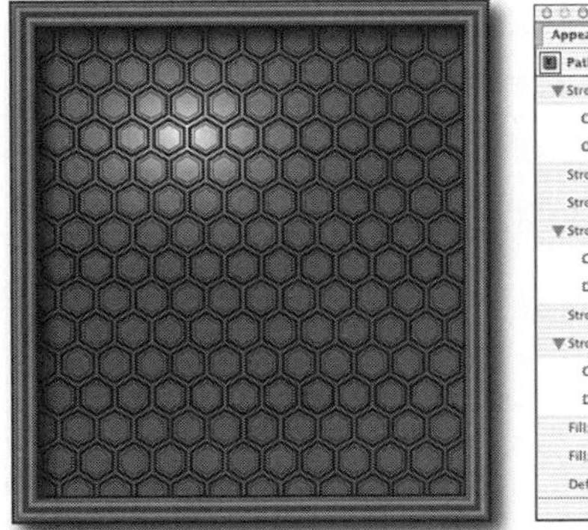

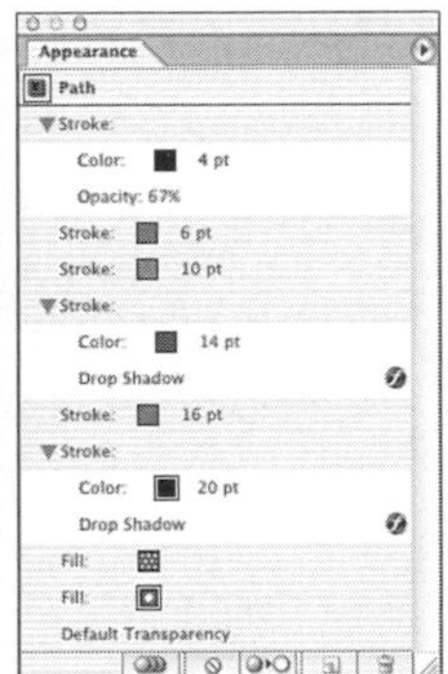


**Figure 32.1**
This is a single object, a rectangle, with multiple appearance characteristics.

Appearance characteristics are sometimes referred to as appearance *attributes*. However, because that term is also used in Illustrator to refer to the Attributes palette (which contains printing and image map information), the term *characteristic* will be used throughout this discussion.

Styles are the various appearance characteristics, collected, named, and saved in the Graphic Styles palette. You can apply a style by selecting an object and clicking the style in the palette. Developing consistency and ease of application are the two main reasons to use styles. Style libraries can be loaded when needed, and custom libraries can be saved and opened in other documents.

In Figure 32.2, you can see that another object has been created with the same characteristics as the rectangle in Figure 32.1. Instead of being applied individually, these characteristics are from a custom style named Grated Moon.

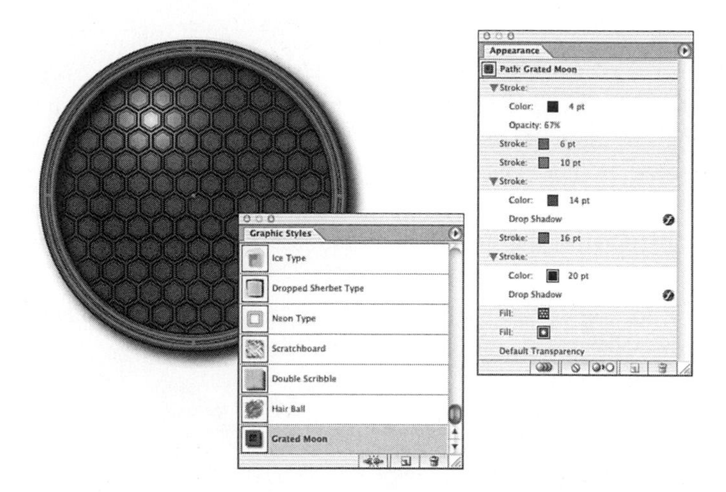


Figure 32.2
Notice that the name of the style is visible to the right of the word *Path* in the Appearance palette.

*If you've created elaborate appearances or styles and now your document won't print, see "Expanding Appearances" in the "Mastering Illustrator" section at the end of this chapter.*

# THE APPEARANCE PALETTE

The Appearance palette shows a list of every characteristic of the selected object or group. Before you even create an object, the Appearance palette is recording the characteristics: The current fill, stroke, and transparency settings are automatically tracked in the palette (see Figure 32.3).

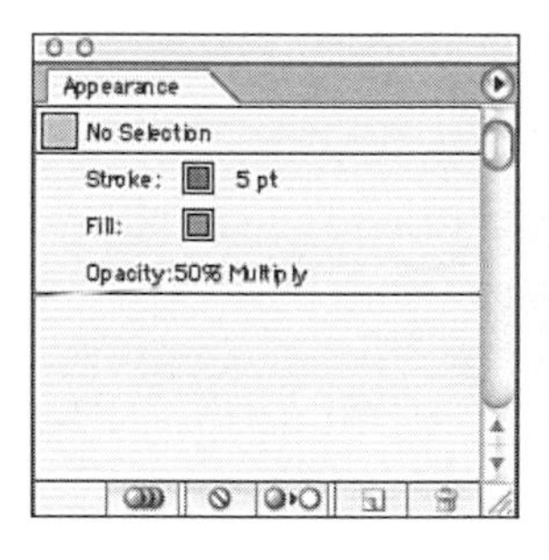


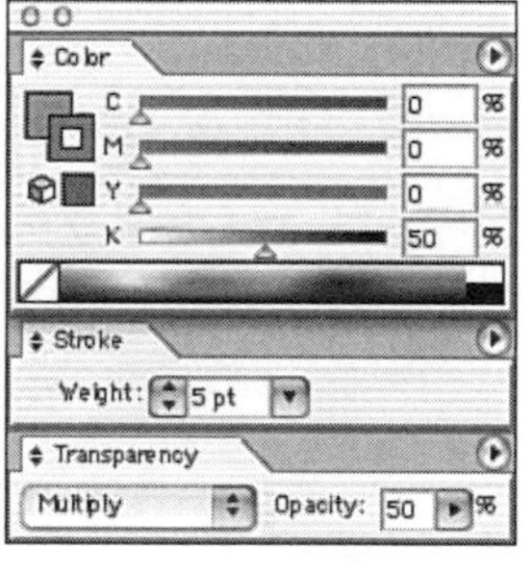


Figure 32.3
The Appearance palette allows you to track various settings, even when the individual palettes are not visible. For example, a glance at the Appearance palette can tell you the current settings in the Color, Stroke, and Transparency palettes.

The Appearance palette also allows you to view a layer's characteristics. In addition to fill, stroke, and transparency, any effects are shown (see Figure 32.4). (Effects and filters are discussed in Chapter 35, "Illustrator's Effects and Filters." Also, see the following sidebar, "Effects Versus Filters.")

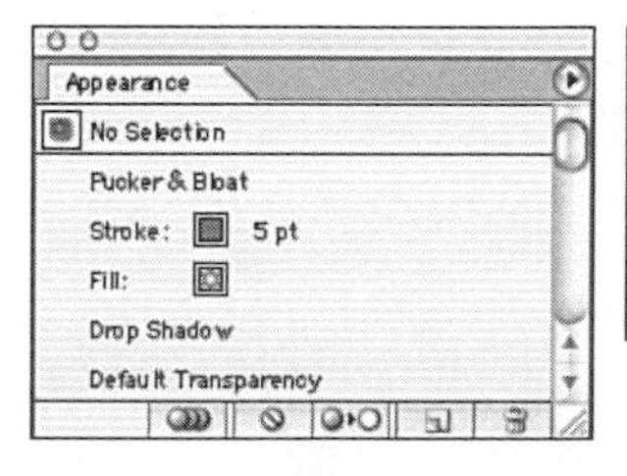


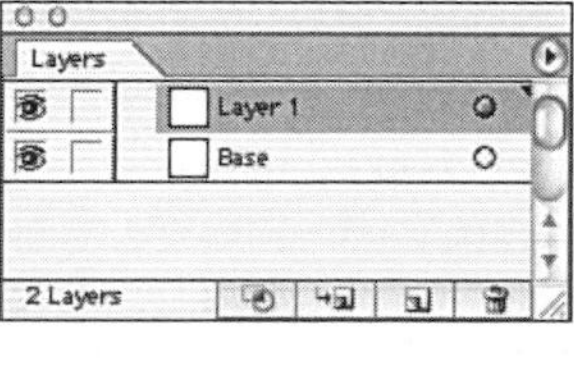


Figure 32.4
Any object created on or moved to this layer assumes the layer's characteristics, which are shown in the Appearance palette.

### Effects Versus Filters

Illustrator supports a wide range of effects and filters. Discussed in Chapter 35, they can change the appearance of an object or group in many ways. Of key importance to a discussion of appearances and styles is the primary difference between effects and filters.

When something is applied as an effect rather than as a filter, you can edit or remove changes by using the Appearance palette. The effects of a filter, on the other hand, cannot be altered or removed except with the Undo command.

A filter, when applied, changes an object. If you apply the command Filter, Distort, Pucker & Bloat to an object, the object's path is permanently changed.

**When you're distorting with a filter, you can return the path's anchor points and control lines to their original positions only by using the Undo command.**

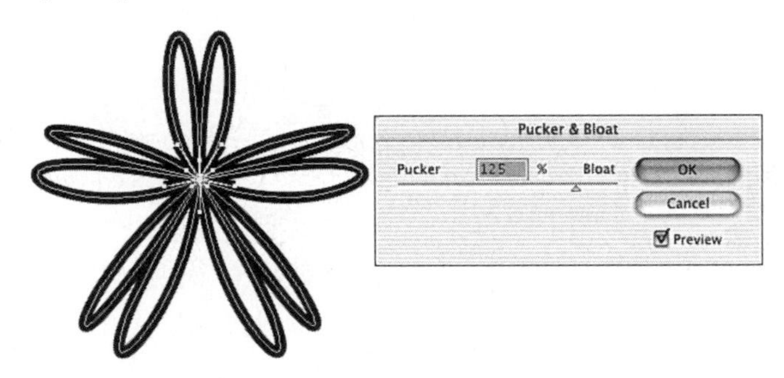




In comparison, when you're applying the same distortion as an effect, the path's anchor points and control lines are not changed; merely the appearance is altered. In the following figure, notice that the effect's preview does not show new anchor points, as does the filter's preview. The original object's shape, now visible as a star, is unchanged by the effect.

**An effect produces an appearance change rather than an actual change in the object itself.**

In Figure 32.5, the characteristic Pucker & Bloat was double-clicked in the Appearance palette to reopen the effect's dialog box. The setting can now be changed, and the object's appearance will be automatically updated. To remove an effect from an object, drag it from the Appearance panel to the Trash Can or use the palette menu command Remove Item.

Filters applied to an object or a group cannot be reversed, as can effects. They, therefore, are not visible in the Appearance palette. You may, however, see one or more of the filter's options listed. They include settings that override the layer's setting, such as transparency. Figure 32.6 shows the application of a drop shadow as a filter. The drop shadow actually becomes rasterized pixels with an assigned opacity, which can be changed through the Appearance palette.

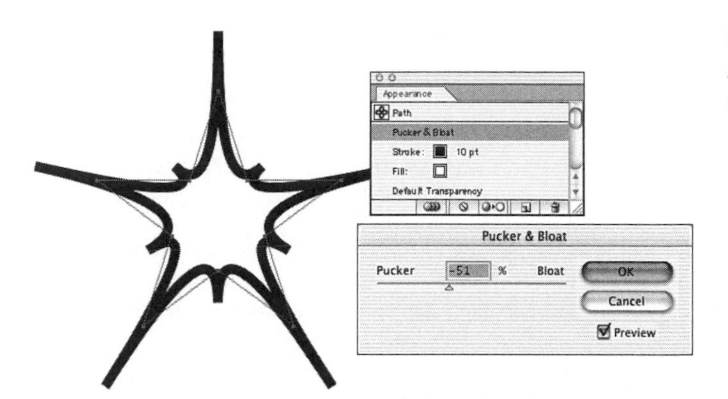


**Figure 32.5**
Any changes are automatically reflected in the object.

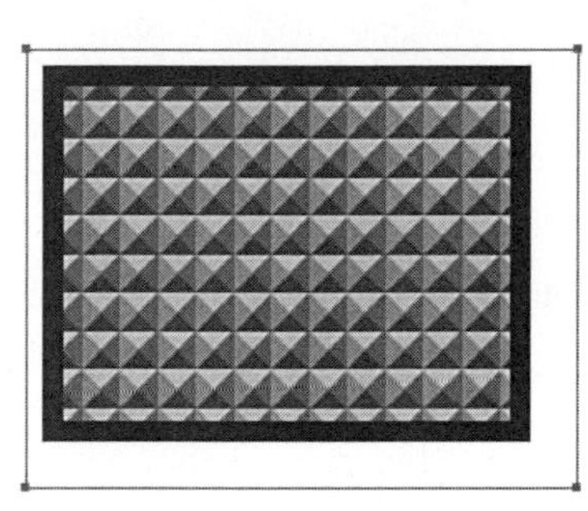

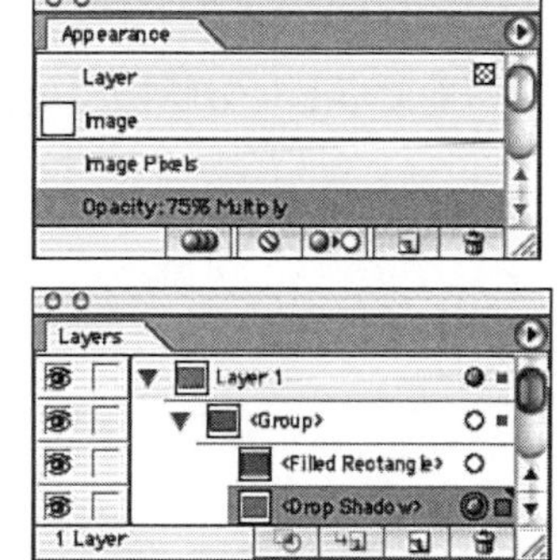


**Figure 32.6**
The drop shadow's opacity and blending mode differ from that of the layer, so they are listed. Even though a filter was applied, double-clicking allows you to change the settings.

When several appearance characteristics have been applied to a single object, they often interact. Here are some guidelines:

- By default, a new characteristic is added on top of existing characteristics. Therefore, a wider stroke must be below a narrower stroke in the Appearances palette if the narrow stroke is to be visible.
- The order in which effects appear in the palette determines the order in which they are applied. This can have a dramatic effect on appearance.
- Effects can be applied to an object or a path as a whole, or they can be applied to a single fill or stroke. Click the specific stroke or fill and then apply the effect.

You can drag an object's appearance from the Appearance palette to another object. Grab the icon to the left of the word *Object* or *Path* and drag it to an object on the artboard. The source object should be selected; the destination object should not be selected.

When more than one effect is applied to an object, take time to see how they interact by changing their order in the Appearances palette.

## Illustrator at Work: Building Roads with Style

The Appearance palette can be used to create graphic styles of a particularly handy nature. This simple example of layering strokes can save you hours of work creating roads. Simply build the style, save it, and apply it to virtually any path. Here are the steps to follow:

1. Open or create an Illustrator document.
2. Press D on the keyboard to return to the basic appearance of a black 1-point stroke and a white fill.
3. Use the Line tool to add a single path segment to the artboard. You don't need to have an object selected on the artboard to add or change the appearance characteristics, but it helps to see what you're doing. (Keep the path segment selected throughout this exercise so that changes are applied to it.)
4. Open the Appearance, Stroke, and Swatches palettes.
5. Change the stroke weight to 60 points.
6. Drag the 60-point stroke to the Duplicate Selected Item button at the bottom of the Appearance palette, to the left of the Trash icon.
7. Change the stroke weight to 50 points and the stroke color to white.
8. Duplicate the new stroke and change the color to black and the weight to 48. The road should start taking shape.
9. Duplicate *that* stroke and change the new copy's color to white and the weight to 25 points. Still in the Stroke palette, check the Dashed Line box and enter **12 pt** and **6 pt** in the first two boxes. (If the Dashed Line option isn't visible, double-click the tab of the Stroke palette and then double-click again.)
10. Add another black stroke, 24 pixels wide. Remember to uncheck the Dashed Line box for this stroke.
11. If the style will be applied to straight or gently curving line segments, you'll want a dashed yellow centerline. If, on the other hand, you'll be applying the style to curving or mountain "roads," you'll need the double yellow line of a "no passing" zone. Here's how to create each type:
    - The dashed centerline is a single yellow stroke, 1 point wide, dashed at the 12 pt/6 pt interval used in Step 9.
    - For the double yellow line, add an undashed yellow stroke 2 points wide and a solid black stroke 1 point wide.
12. Add one more stroke, green and 100 points wide. In the Appearance palette, drag this stroke down below the 60-point black stroke.
13. To preserve your work, click the New Graphic Style button at the bottom of the Graphic Styles palette. (But keep in mind that the style isn't really saved and protected until you use the Save Graphic Style Library command or save the document itself. You'll find this discussed later in this chapter.)

You can, of course, adapt the stroke widths for your needs. And remember that although a single path can't show both the dashed yellow and double yellow centerlines, two paths can be abutted, one with each style (see Figure 32.7).

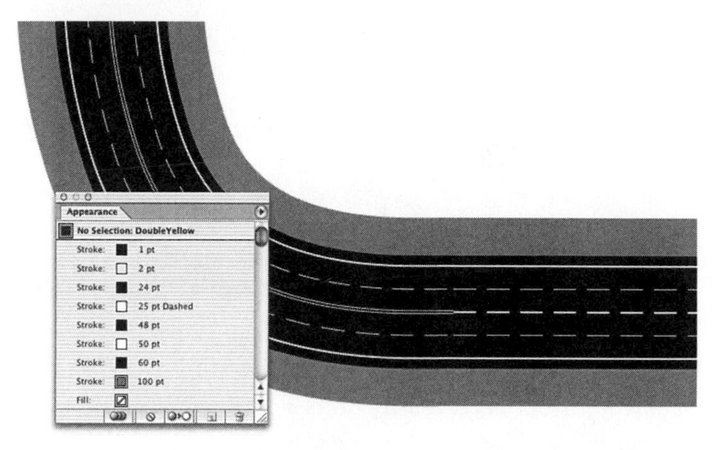


Figure 32.7
To ensure a proper match between the styles, the endpoints of each segment were selected and the command Object, Path, Average was used to stack the two anchor points.

# THE APPEARANCE PALETTE MENU



You can access the Appearance palette menu, shown in Figure 32.8, through the small triangle in the upper-right corner of the palette.

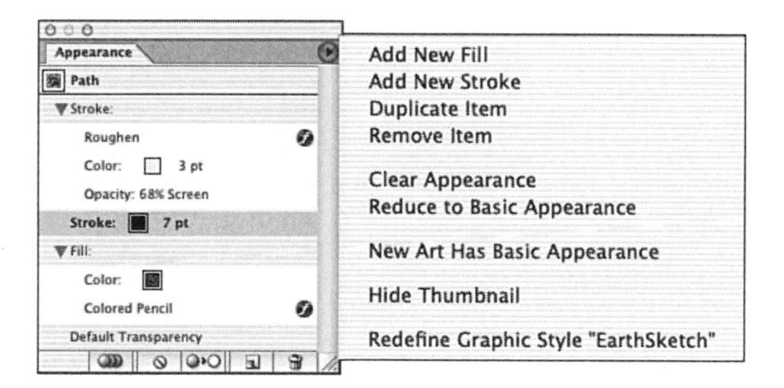


Figure 32.8
Not all the commands are available at all times. Some are usually grayed out because they aren't applicable to the current situation.

The command Add New Stroke actually adds another stroke on top of the one or more strokes already in place for an object. (The Add New Fill command behaves similarly with fills.) This is comparable to duplicating strokes as you did in the section "Illustrator at Work: Building Roads with Style," earlier in this chapter. Although you could create the same appearance by creating several objects and aligning them next to each other, there is no reason why you cannot do it by layering strokes in a single object.

Using the Appearance palette, you can create superior text effects. You can add additional strokes and fills to type objects, as shown in Figure 32.9.

Remember that you can also add brushes to an appearance or style. However, keep in mind that you cannot apply multiple strokes and fills to the text within type objects. The appearance characteristics can be applied to the container, but the text inside the container will accept only one stroke and one fill. When you're creating complex text, it's usually best to choose Object, Expand Appearance before you print.

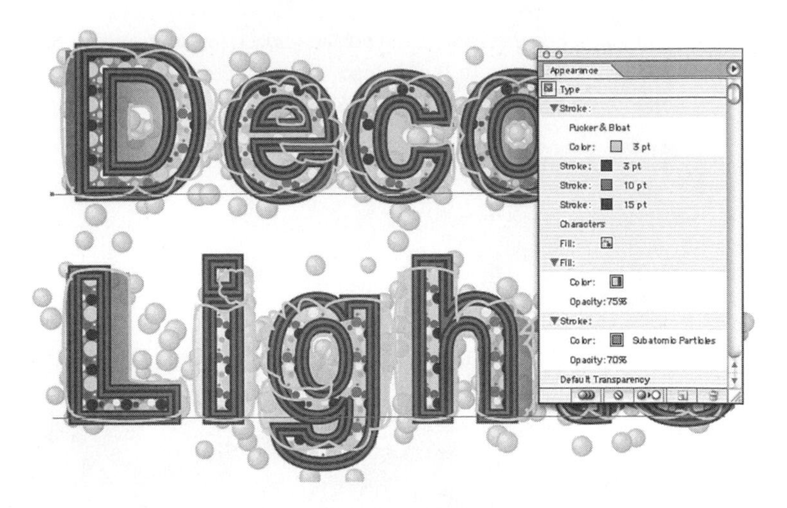


**Figure 32.9**
The type object remains editable.

*There is a difference between multiple appearance characteristics and a style. See "Appearances Versus Styles" in the "Mastering Illustrator" section at the end of this chapter.*

You can duplicate individual appearance characteristics by using the Duplicate Item command from the Appearance palette menu or by dragging the specific characteristic to the Duplicate button at the bottom of the palette. You can also remove an appearance characteristic by using a menu command or the appropriate button at the bottom of the palette.

32

The commands Clear Appearance and Reduce to Basic Appearance are similar and can have the same effect. However, if an object or group is on a layer to which appearance characteristics have been applied, the two commands perform different jobs. Clear Appearance reduces an object to a fill and stroke of None, and it will show only characteristics targeted to the layer that the object is on. Reduce to Basic Appearance removes targeted effects and appearance characteristics, and the object retains its originally assigned fill and stroke. When selected, the Appearance palette's command New Art Has Basic Appearance has a check mark next to it in the menu. When this option is checked, any new objects will have the fill and stroke active in the Toolbox (plus any characteristics applied to the layer). When this option is unchecked, new objects will assume the characteristics of that object most recently created or edited.

The Appearance palette also allows you to show or hide thumbnails and replace a style in the Graphic Styles palette. When a selected object has an assigned style and a modification has been made, the menu offers you the option of updating the style in the Graphic Styles palette. Doing so generally updates all objects with the assigned style to the new appearance. (Styles will be discussed later in this chapter.)

> The Appearance palette commands Duplicate Item and Remove Item and their button counterparts use the term *item* to refer to a specific appearance characteristic, such as a stroke, fill, or effect. The object on the artboard is not duplicated or removed, simply the one characteristic.
>
> To duplicate or delete an object or group, use the Layers palette.

## Illustrator at Work: Applying Appearances to Layers

Just as appearance characteristics can be applied to objects, they also can be applied to groups and layers. By default, any object added to a group or layer is automatically updated to show the appearance characteristics assigned. Conversely, any object removed from a group or layer that has assigned characteristics loses them. As discussed earlier, this is controlled in part by the Appearance palette's menu command Layer/Group Overrides Color.

See how targeting appearances to layers works by trying these steps:

1. Open or create an Illustrator document.
2. Press D on the keyboard to set the appearance to the default.
3. Create a square.
4. Add a new layer by clicking the third button from the left at the bottom of the Layers palette.
5. Click the circle to the right of the name Layer 2 in the Layers palette to "target" the layer.
6. Click the Neon Type style in the Graphic Styles palette.
7. In the Layers palette, drag the <Path> for the square from Layer 1 to Layer 2. Because the graphic style is applied to the layer, the square picks up the style.
8. Open the Appearance palette and click the square with the Selection tool. Note that the object itself still has the default appearance. If you drag it back to Layer 1 in the Layers palette, the graphic styles remains behind.
9. Click Layer 1 in the Layers palette and add another square to the artboard.
10. With the square still selected, click the Parchment style in the Styles palette. This style is applied to the object, not the path.
11. In the Layers palette, drag this new object from Layer 1 to Layer 2. Illustrator will apply both the object's Parchment style and the layer's Neon Type style.

The same behavior that you see with layers also applies to groups:

- Characteristics assigned to a layer or group are applied to any object created on the layer or added to the layer or group.
- Characteristics already assigned to an object are retained when added to a layer or group.
- A layer or group's characteristics are left behind when an object is removed from the layer or group.

*Confused by how appearances work with groups and layers? See "Stationary Characteristics" in the "Mastering Illustrator" section at the end of this chapter.*

32

# THE GRAPHIC STYLES PALETTE

Styles are collections of appearance characteristics (attributes) that are named and saved. They can be applied together to an object or a group or assigned to a layer. Styles can be saved in the Graphic Styles palette (see Figure 32.10), and collections of styles (called *libraries*) can be loaded into a document.

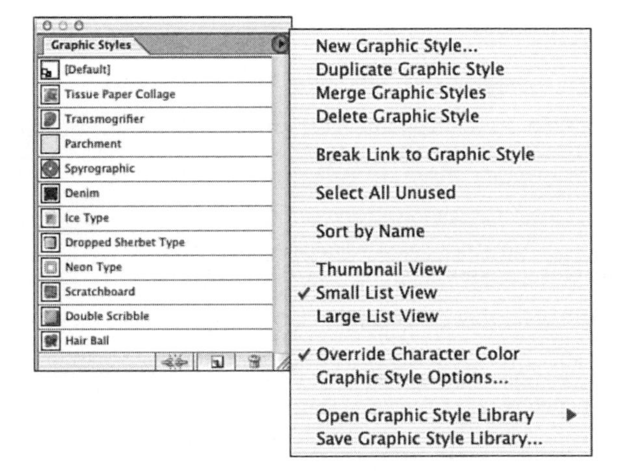


**Figure 32.10**
The Graphic Styles palette is shown with its menu open and set to Small List View.



Because styles are based on appearance characteristics, they can be edited and reversed later, even after the file has been closed and reopened. Styles themselves can be deleted, duplicated, or edited and reapplied.

To create a style, you need not have an object selected on the artboard. In fact, you can develop a style before you even create an object. Stroke color, weight, and brush; fill color, pattern, and gradient; and effects can all be selected without an object in the document. After you make these choices, you can click the New Style button at the bottom of the Graphic Styles palette or select the New Style command from the palette's menu. Likewise, clicking the button or selecting the command creates a new style from a selected object's appearance characteristics.

Several guidelines affect styles:

- Styles can include strokes, fills, effects, patterns, gradients, blending modes, and transformations.
- Styles are nondestructive. The original object is not changed; merely its appearance is changed. When a style is removed, an object reverts to the basic appearance (black stroke, white fill, 100% opacity).
- To apply a style to a selected object, group, or layer, you simply click it in the Graphic Styles palette. You can also apply a style by dragging it from the palette onto an object.
- You can apply a style to layers, groups, objects, or type (although some restrictions apply with type).

- When you're applying a style to type, you must select the entire type object. Styles cannot be applied to individual words or characters within a text object.
- You cannot apply a style to fixed-outline (outline-protected) fonts or bitmap fonts.
- You can apply multiple fills (with transparency) and strokes to a style.
- You can change a style globally. In other words, when you modify a style, all objects, groups, and layers to which it has been applied are automatically updated.
- When you apply a style to a layer, any object added to the layer adopts the style.
- Selecting an object and changing an attribute break the link between that object and the style. The attributes of the style remain (unless changed), but if the style is modified, that object is not updated.
- The Graphic Styles palette can display swatches of each style or list them by name with a large or small thumbnail.
- You can apply a style by selecting an object (or targeting a group or layer in the Layers palette) and clicking the style in the Graphic Styles palette. A style can be dragged from the palette onto an object, whether or not the object has been selected.
- To create a new style, assign the desired attributes to an object and drag the object to the Graphic Styles palette or the New Style button at the bottom of the palette.
- Double-clicking a style in the palette opens the Style Options dialog box, allowing you to rename the style.
- Choosing New Style from the Graphic Styles palette menu allows you to name a style while you're creating it.
- (Option)-dragging [Alt]-dragging an object from the artboard on top of a style in the Graphic Styles palette globally replaces that style with the new style applied to the object.
- Using the Appearance palette command Redefine Graphic Style also creates a global change.
- You can delete styles from the palette by selecting them and then clicking the Delete Style button at the bottom of the palette, or you can drag them to the button's Trash icon.
- You can select multiple styles in the Graphic Styles palette by (Command)-clicking [Ctrl]-clicking.
- You can select multiple styles and use the command Merge Styles from the palette menu to create a new style with all the other styles' attributes.
- You can duplicate a style by using the Duplicate Style command from the palette menu or by dragging the style to the New Style button at the bottom of the palette. The duplicate style, which you can use as a template for a new style, will have the original style's name, followed by a numeral.

- You can disassociate a style from all objects, groups, and layers by highlighting it in the palette and clicking the Break Link to Style button at the bottom of the palette. There will no longer be a connection with objects, groups, or layers that have the style applied. The palette menu contains the comparable command.

# GRAPHIC STYLES LIBRARIES

Illustrator installs, by default, numerous libraries of styles. One appears in the Graphic Styles palette; the others are available to load from the Adobe Illustrator folder on the hard drive. The default library for the document's color mode is automatically loaded when the file is opened (unless the document has been saved with changes made to the Graphic Styles palette).

The palette menu command Open Graphic Style Libraries enables you to add additional sets of styles to the document. The libraries appear in a separate floating palette. Figure 32.11 shows the list of basic libraries.

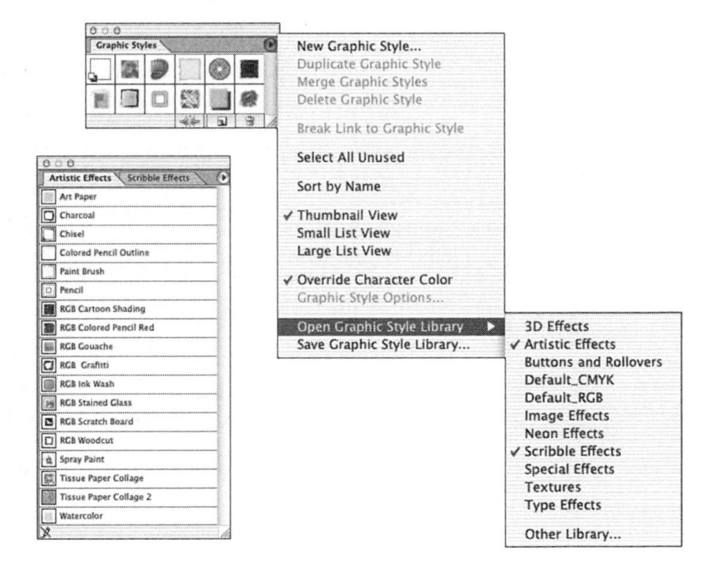


**Figure 32.11**
A check mark next to a library's name indicates that it is available in the floating palette opened for the additional libraries (lower left).

When a style from an additional library is used in the document, it is automatically copied to the document's Graphic Styles palette. It is then saved with the document. If the style is discontinued in the document, it is not automatically deleted from the palette.

When a style has been created and saved in another Illustrator document, you can load it by choosing Open Graphic Styles Library, Other Libraries. You must then navigate to the document in the dialog box and select it. The styles available in that document (including default styles, if loaded into the document's Graphic Styles palette) are

> You can add your own custom sets of graphic styles to the list of libraries in the Graphic Styles palette menu. Create the styles and save the Illustrator document in the Graphic Styles folder, inside the Presets folder that you'll find within the Illustrator folder. When you next start Illustrator, that AI file's name will appear in the list shown in Figure 32.11.

loaded. They, like other loaded libraries, appear in a separate floating palette. Also like other libraries, when a style is used in a document, it is added to the document's Graphic Styles palette.

The Graphic Styles palette menu offers the command Select All Unused. Selecting and then deleting styles that aren't used in a document slims the document a little, and it streamlines the Graphic Styles palette. This is especially useful when a document contains numerous custom styles.

# MASTERING ILLUSTRATOR

## Expanding Appearances

*I've spent a lot of time getting my appearances just right, but now the illustration doesn't output. What can I do?*

Appearances and styles can be expanded to simplify printing. Expanding (by choosing Object, Expand Appearance) creates a separate object from each stroke and fill of the object. The various components maintain the assigned effects and brushes. Figure 32.12 shows an example.

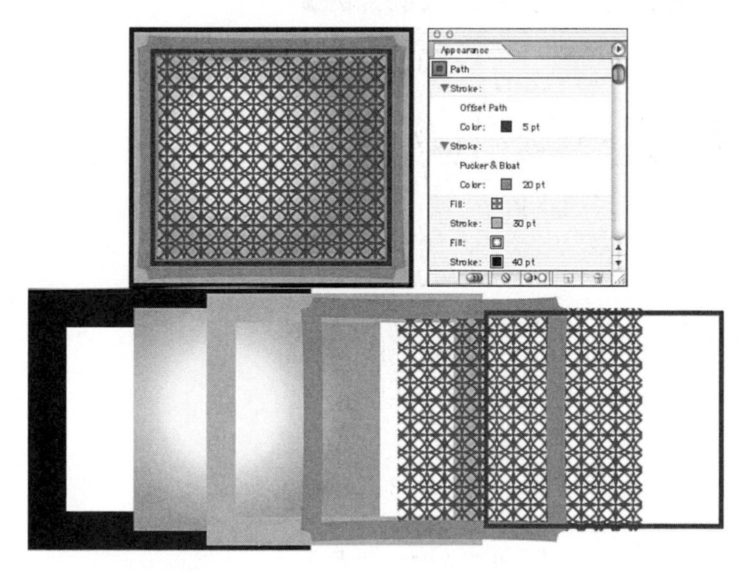


**Figure 32.12**
The top object, whose various characteristics are shown in the Appearance palette, is expanded and separated below to show the individual objects.



## Appearances Versus Styles

*I've assigned multiple strokes and fills to my object. Is that a style or not?*

It's not a style until you give it a name and save it in the Graphic Styles palette. Until then, you've got an object, group, or layer with a bunch of appearance characteristics.

## Stationary Characteristics

*How do appearances and styles work with layers and groups? When does an object change and when doesn't it?*

The layer or group can be assigned appearance characteristics. When an object is added to the layer or group, it puts on that appearance, just like slipping on the blazer from your new country club. If you are asked to leave the country club, you'll take off the jacket. So, too, will an object moved from a layer or group leave behind appearance characteristics assigned to that layer or group. However, you were wearing your own slacks and shirt when you put on that blazer; likewise, the object will retain any characteristics it had before being added to the layer or group.

33

# WORKING WITH GRADIENTS AND GRADIENT MESHES

## IN THIS CHAPTER

The Gradient and Gradient Mesh tools produce blends between colors. These subtle blends from one color to another help Illustrator produce the illusion of three dimensions and light. These tools enable you to produce top-notch illustrations. The simple addition of a gradient or two can change a piece of flat, two-dimensional artwork into an image with depth and perspective. Figure 33.1 shows the difference between shapes filled with color and those same shapes filled with simple gradients.

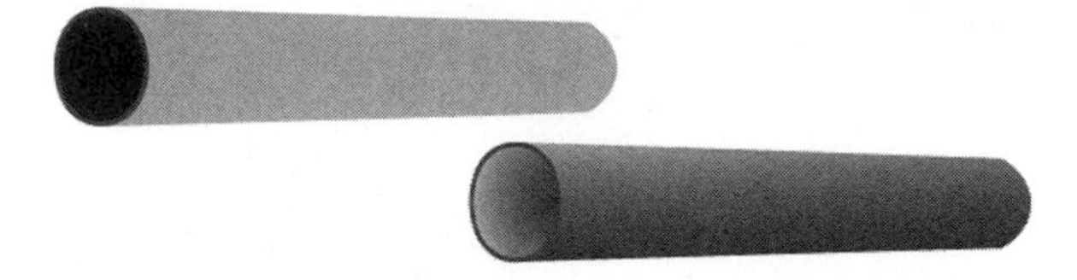

**Figure 33.1**
The addition of gradients gives the illusion that the "pipe" is round and hollow.

Gradients are blends of two or more colors, either in a straight line or as concentric rings of color. Gradient meshes, on the other hand, allow you to blend numerous colors, and at whatever angle is necessary (see Figure 33.2).

**Figure 33.2**
A gradient mesh object (left), with its mesh visible on the right (the dashed line indicates the object's path). Note that in the ankle area, the mesh extends beyond the path.



Gradients and meshes, however useful, can present some production problems. You might need to rasterize them before printing. The Document Settings dialog box contains fields for automatically selecting rasterization resolutions for gradients and gradient mesh objects. You can find them in the Printing & Export panel.

This chapter looks at how you work with gradients and gradient mesh objects in Illustrator.

# WORKING WITH GRADIENTS

Gradients are designed and applied primarily through the Gradient palette, Color palette, Swatches palette, and Gradient tool. The Gradient palette determines which type of gradient you will be using and, in conjunction with the Color and Swatches palettes, allows you to customize the colors and blending. Also valuable in the development of a gradient are the Transparency and Appearance palettes and the Object and Effect menus.

After you design gradients, you can save them in the Swatches palette for future use. You can load them, like any swatches, into the current document from another by choosing Window, Swatch Libraries, Load Library.

## The Anatomy of a Gradient

Whether linear or radial, a gradient can contain numerous colors, but only two colors can be blended at a time. A single color in the middle of a gradient blends with each color on either side, but each side blends independently. For example, in Figure 33.3, the gradient goes between left and right, through the color in the center. However, this is (for practical purposes) not one gradient, but two color blends. The color on the left blends with the color in the center, and then it stops. That color does not continue past the midpoint. The center color then blends with the color on the right. At no time does the color on the left pass through the center; at no time does the color on the right pass through the center.

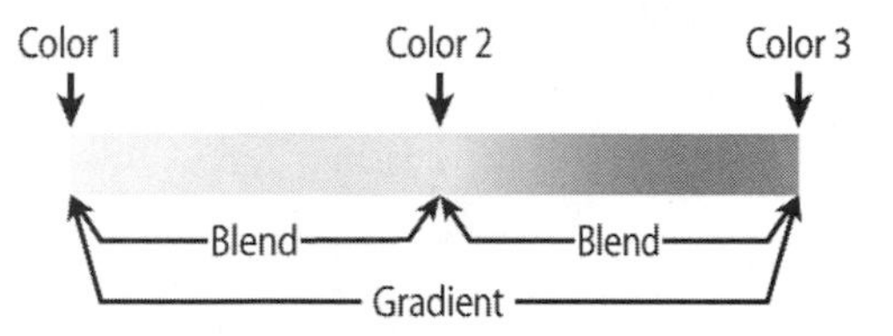


Figure 33.3
Each gradient is a series of colors, blended two at a time.

The point in a gradient that represents an unblended color is called a *stop*. From the stop, the color then begins to blend with the neighboring color. A gradient can have as many color stops as you would like, although there is a practical limit of about 25, unless you expand the palette. More than that and the gradient bar in the Gradient palette gets too crowded to select individual stops. You can add (and delete) stops in the Gradient palette and control them by using the sliders (see Figure 33.4).

> The gradient bar in the Gradient palette is rather small, which makes it difficult to see subtle changes in the gradient as you edit. Drag the palette out away from the edge of the screen and drag the lower-right corner. You can increase the height of the palette to over 200 pixels and the width to 2,000 pixels—plenty of palette in which to see your gradient!

A stop consists of a small square color swatch and the triangle above it. A darkened triangle, as shown for the middle stop in Figure 33.4, represents the active stop. The stop's location, given in percent, is shown in the palette. You can drag stops to reposition them. (Option)-dragging [Alt]-dragging a stop duplicates it.

The diamond above the gradient bar represents the 50% point between two colors. At this point, the two colors being blended are at equal strength. You can reposition it by dragging, which changes the distribution of the blend. As you drag it, the Location field is updated to show the position of the midpoint between the two color stops (in percent).

The Angle field represents the direction of the gradient when applied (see Figure 33.5). Rather than a particular gradient slider, this field affects the entire gradient. Dragging from left to right on the artboard creates an angle of 0, and the colors blend in that direction. Angle is available only for linear gradients.

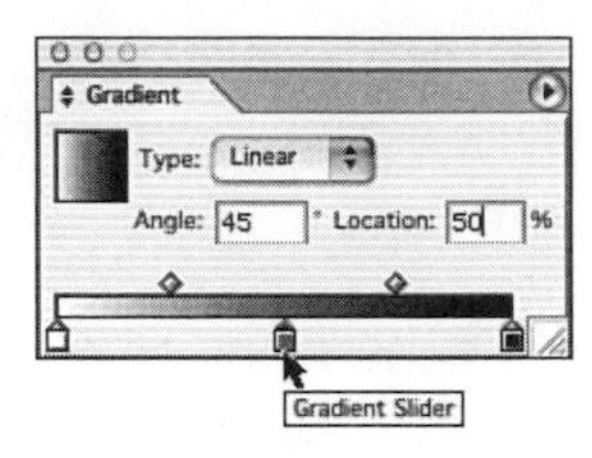


Figure 33.4
Each gradient slider represents a color stop.

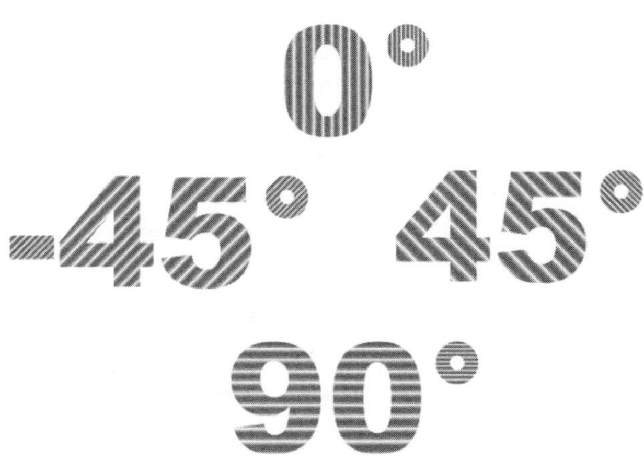


Figure 33.5
The Angle field in the Gradient palette determines the direction of the blends.

The Gradient palette shows you a thumbnail of your work. As you add, move, and change stops and midpoints, Illustrator updates the preview in the upper-left corner of the palette.

## Using the Gradient Sliders

The area between two stops on a gradient slider is blended from one color to the other seamlessly. The default gradient has two color stops, one at each end. They are black and white, and their color mode is grayscale. When you're creating a custom gradient, it is often easier to use one from the Swatches palette as a starting point.

To edit an existing gradient or create a new one, choose Linear or Radial from the Gradient palette's Type pop-up menu. Choosing one of these options automatically makes the default or last-used gradient the fill and makes it available in the palette for editing. Most of the changes to a gradient are made through the sliders. Several rules govern changes to them:

- You can copy an existing color stop (with its assigned color value) by (Option)-dragging [Alt]-dragging it along the gradient bar. You can drag past an existing stop to place the new stop.
- You can click any place along the gradient bar to add a new color stop. It automatically assumes the color value directly above it.
- To change the color of a stop, click it and use the Color palette. If the Color palette isn't visible, double-click the slider.
- To delete a stop, drag it off the bar.

- You can drag a swatch from the Swatches palette onto a stop to change its color.
- (Option)-clicking [Alt]-clicking a swatch in the Swatches palette assigns that color to a selected stop in the Gradient palette.
- You can drag a swatch from the Swatches palette directly onto the gradient bar to create a new stop of that color.
- You cannot have a color stop with a color value of None, nor can you use patterns or other gradients in a gradient.
- You can assign the locations of stops precisely by clicking a stop and typing the location (in percent) in the Location field.

By default, the blend is smooth and consistent, with the midpoint representing 50% of each color value. You can adjust the flow from one color to another by dragging the slider positioned above the gradient bars. You cannot drag the slider closer than 13% to either color stop. (Less than 13% gives a severe and distinct change in color, with little or no blending.)

If you plan to create a complex gradient, create swatches for the stops first. Using the Color palette, define each color and then add it to the Swatches palette by clicking the New Swatch button. After you have all the colors you need, creating the new gradient is simply a matter of dragging the swatches to the gradient bar in the Gradient palette.

*Do you have gradients that print okay but look lousy onscreen? Check "Monitor Settings" in the "Mastering Illustrator" section at the end of this chapter.*

## Saving and Applying Gradients

After you create a gradient, you can save it in the Swatches palette for future use:

- Drag the gradient thumbnail from the Gradient palette to the Swatches palette.
- Drag the gradient swatch from the Fill swatch of the Toolbox or Color palette to the Swatches palette.
- Click the New Swatch button at the bottom of the Swatches palette.
- Use the New Swatch command from the Swatches palette menu (which you access by clicking the black triangle in the upper-right corner of the palette).

Gradients added to the Swatches palette in one document can be used in other documents. Choose the Swatches palette menu command Open Swatch Library, Other Libraries and navigate to the file that contains the gradients. That file's gradients, along with all other swatches, are loaded into a separate floating palette. Swatches can be dragged from that palette into the Swatches palette, or they can be applied directly to an object. After a swatch (a gradient or any other swatch) is applied to an object from the new palette, it is added to the open document's Swatches palette.

After you create gradients, you can apply them to one or more objects in various ways:

- Select one or more objects on the artboard and click the gradient swatch at the bottom of the Toolbox, the gradient swatch in the Gradient palette, or the gradient swatch in the Swatches palette (if the gradient has been saved).
- Dragging the Gradient tool applies the current gradient to an object.
- If you select more than one object, the Gradient tool creates a gradient that encompasses the entire area of the selected objects. Parts of the gradients appear, as appropriate, in the selected objects. Figure 33.6 shows the difference. To the left, the gradient is applied to each object individually. To the right, the gradient works on the objects as a single entity.

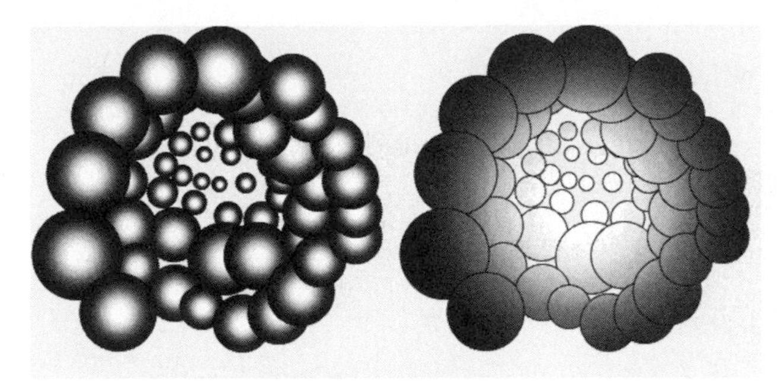

**Figure 33.6**
The same gradient as it appears on individual objects and on a collection of objects.

- You can reapply a gradient by re-dragging the Gradient tool.
- The direction in which you drag the tool determines the direction in which the gradient's colors are applied.
- The angle at which you drag the tool determines the angle of a linear gradient and is shown in the Gradient palette.
- Shift-dragging constrains the Gradient tool to 45° angles.
- You can start dragging the Gradient tool from outside the object or from well inside the object. A gradient need not be applied from stroke to stroke. Areas before the start or after the end of the drag are the color of the last stop.



**Linear Versus Radial**

A linear gradient blends colors in straight lines, whether vertically, horizontally, or at an angle. Radial gradients use concentric circles. They are designed and constructed in the Gradient palette the same way. When you use the Gradient tool to create a linear gradient, the color on the left of the gradient bar (in the Gradient palette) is the start point and appears at the place clicked. With radial gradients, that point is the center of the gradient. That point does not have to be located in the center of the object. You can drag from any point, including outside the image, to create the effect you want. Figure 33.7 shows how both radial and linear gradients are dragged.

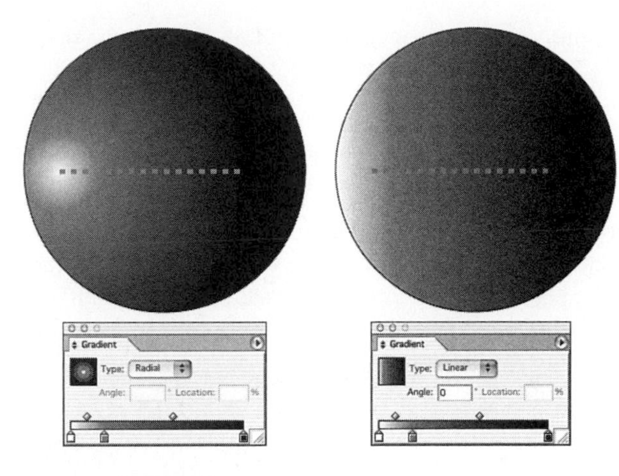


Figure 33.7
The Gradient tool was dragged along the dashed line. Note that in both cases, it was dragged from left to right.

## Combining Gradients

You can create complex patterns of gradients by layering fills within an object. In the Appearance palette, you can add additional fills to a selected object. (The Appearance palette menu command Add New Fill adds a fill to the palette.) Gradients are assigned to fills by selecting a fill in the Appearance palette and dragging the Gradient tool or clicking the appropriate gradient in the Swatches palette.

If you use lessening opacity from bottom to top, a number of gradients can interact in a single object. Before you print, however, such an object is a likely candidate for high-resolution rasterization. Figure 33.8 shows several radial gradients applied to the same object. In the Appearance palette, note that the opacity of each layer is low, allowing those below it to show through.

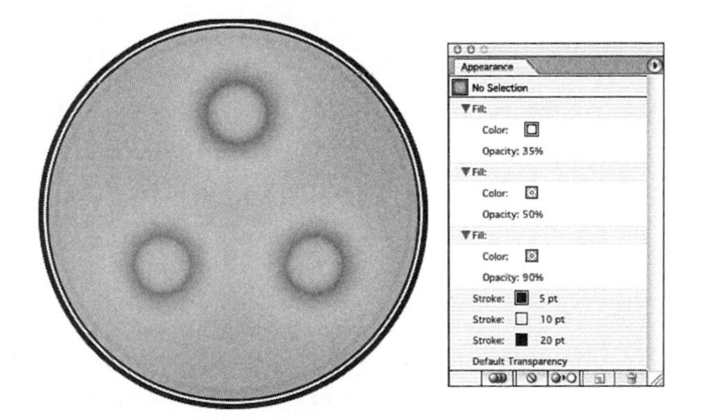


Figure 33.8
The higher the gradient is in the stacking order, the lower the opacity. The center points of the three radial gradients are identifiable as concentric circles.



## Illustrator at Work: Creating Custom Gradients

Although Illustrator supplies you with hundreds of excellent gradients in 19 libraries, there are times when you need a custom gradient. Sometimes it may even be easier to create a gradient than to search through the libraries for an appropriate premade gradient.

Remember that if, at any time during the following exercise, you click a swatch rather than drag it, you'll deactivate the Gradient palette. Simply press (Command-Z) [Ctrl+Z] to undo the change of fill and continue editing the gradient. Also keep in mind that the Locations field in the Gradient palette can show very precise values. You need only come within a percent or two of the values listed in the exercise. Follow these steps:

1. Drag the Gradient palette to the middle of your screen. Drag the lower-right corner down as far as it will go and to the right, until the palette is double its normal width.
2. Use the menu command Window, Open Swatch Libraries, Neutrals. Dock the two palettes. (Drag the Neutrals palette's tab from its window to the bottom edge of the Gradient palette. When the thick black line appears at the bottom of—not all the way around—the Gradient palette, release the mouse button.)
3. From the Neutrals palette menu, choose Large Thumbnails and drag the lower-right corner of the palette to form two rows of swatches. With the work area looking much like Figure 33.9, you're now ready to get started.

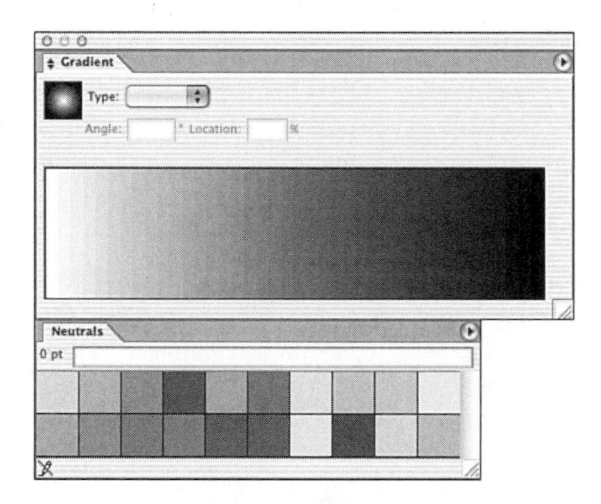


Figure 33.9
Having the swatches near the Gradient palette makes defining colors much easier.



It's far easier to create a custom gradient using near-by swatches than it is to define each stop in the Color palette. Before starting to create a complex gradient, define your color stops and save them as swatches.

4. Delete the leftmost color stop on the gradient by dragging it down and out of the Gradient palette. Now drag the first swatch (top row, left) from the Neutrals palette to *near* the left end of the Gradient palette's sample. The Location field should show about 5%. (The first color stop need not be at the end of the gradient.)
5. Drag the fourth swatch from the Neutrals palette to Location 20%.
6. Hold down the (Option) [Alt] key, click that second color stop (the one just added), and drag it to about Location 35%.
7. Drag the third color swatch from the Neutrals palette to Location 45% on the gradient. Above the gradient sample and to the left of the new swatch is a small diamond. Drag it to the left until the Location field reads about 32%. (Remember that the 32% setting represents the distance between the two adjacent color sliders, not from the start of the gradient.)
8. From the regular Swatches palette, drag a white swatch to Location 60%.

9. Drag the first color swatch to the gradient, to Location 65%. Move the diamond above and to the left to 65%.

10. Add another copy of the white swatch (immediately to the left of the most recent color stop) by (Option)-dragging [Alt]-dragging *past* the swatch to its right, to Location 75%.

11. Add a copy of the third color swatch at 85%. Drag the diamond between it and the swatch to the left to about 70%.

12. From the regular Swatches palette, add a black color stop at the 100% mark. (If your Gradient palette started with the White, Black Radial gradient, that color stop may already be set.) Move the diamond above the gradient to 62%. Your gradient should look something like that shown in Figure 33.10.

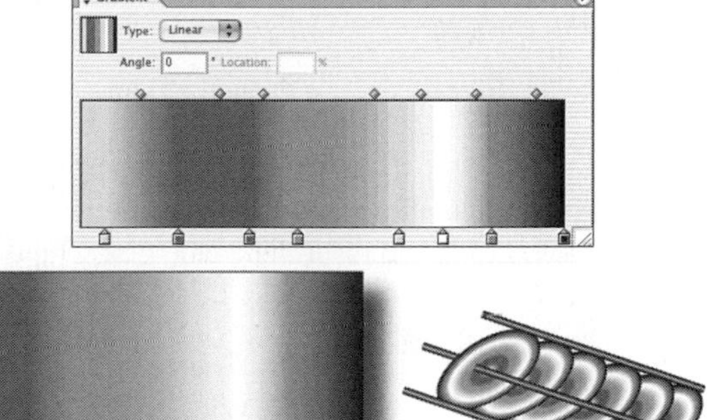


**Figure 33.10**
With a rectangular object and no stroke, this gradient can produce the appearance of a subtle curvature to the surface.

Don't forget to click the New Swatch button at the bottom of the Swatches palette if you want to save your gradient.



# GRADIENT MESHES

Gradient mesh objects can be created from vector objects or raster images embedded in an Illustrator document. A *mesh* is a single object with colors blending in various directions. The difference between objects with gradient fills and gradient mesh objects is shown in Figure 33.11.

A gradient mesh is created from an existing object or image and can then be edited. *Mesh points*, which control the placement of color, can be added, deleted, and moved, and the color can be changed, as can the spread of the color. The mesh points, which appear on *mesh lines*, appear as diamonds rather than squares on the lines. Regular anchor points (seen as squares) can also appear, but they lack the capability of affecting color.

**Caution**

When an object is turned into a gradient mesh object, only the Undo command can convert it back to its original state. There is no way to convert a mesh object to a vector object. For that reason, it is usually a good idea to work with a copy of an object, with the original hidden away on an invisible layer.

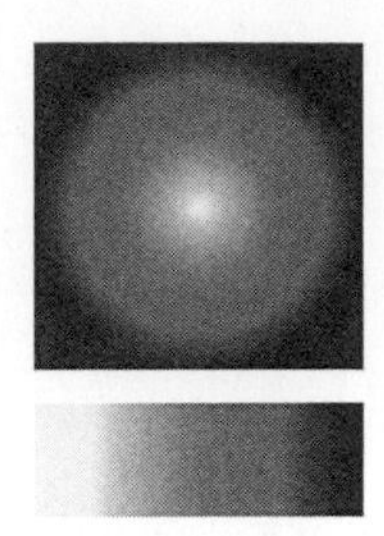
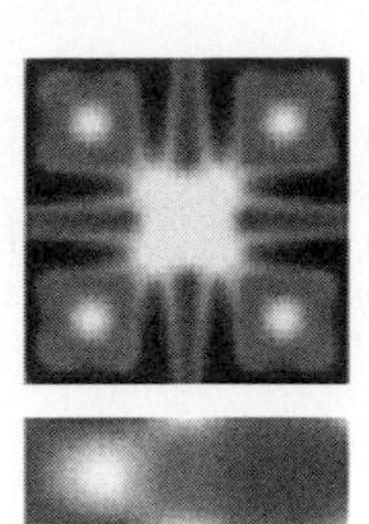
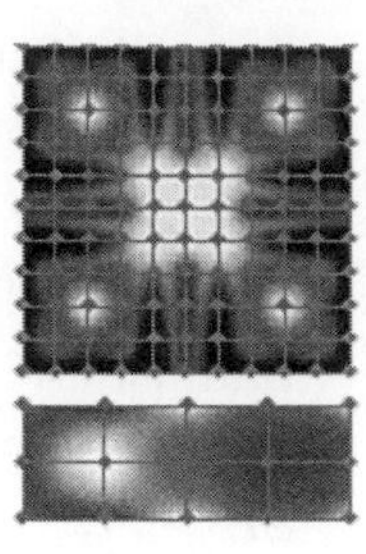

Figure 33.11
To the left are simple gradients. In the center are gradient mesh objects created from those gradients. To the right, the meshes used to create the objects are visible.

## Creating Gradient Mesh Objects

With an object or embedded raster image selected, you can create a gradient mesh in three ways:

- Choose Object, Create Gradient Mesh.
- Click the object's stroke or fill with the Gradient Mesh tool.
- If the object is filled with a gradient, you can choose Object, Expand and then choose the Gradient Mesh option.

When you use the Create Gradient Mesh command, you can specify the number of rows and columns and what type of mesh to start with in the resulting dialog box. The options are shown in Figure 33.12.

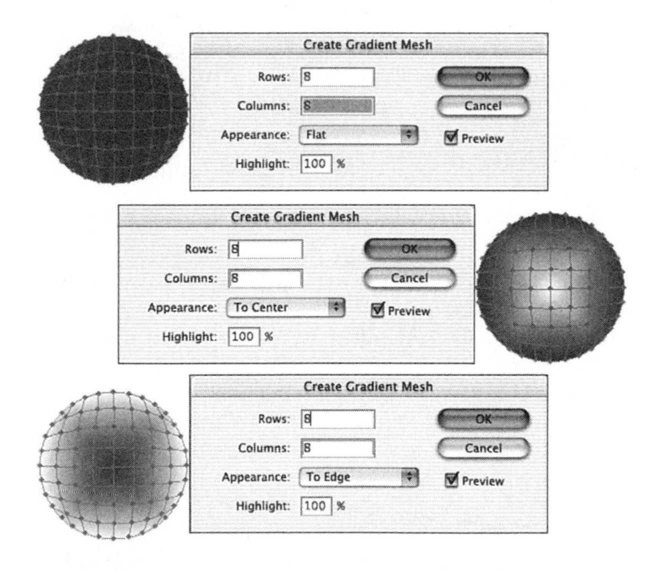


Figure 33.12
When applied to a vector object, the Create Gradient Mesh command produces either a solid color (Flat) or a two-color gradient (To Center, To Edge), no matter what the object's original fill. Colors in rasterized objects retain their general locations when a gradient mesh object is created with either of the latter Appearance options.

Although *Rows* and *Columns* are handy terms to work with, they actually refer to the spaces between the lines. A gradient mesh object is controlled with the points at the intersections of the lines.

When you select Flat for Appearance, the gradient mesh object has a solid color fill, the same color as the original object's fill. When you select To Edge or To Center, that color is blended in a gradient with a shade of itself determined by the Highlight percentage. A value of 100% produces white; lesser values give you a color closer to the original. When you're working with spot colors, tints are produced.

Using the Gradient Mesh tool to produce a mesh object is simply a matter of clicking the object's fill or path. When you click the fill, a pair of mesh lines with a single mesh anchor is produced. When you click a path (stroked or unstroked), a single mesh line, perpendicular to the path, is created (even with curved lines). You can click as many times as necessary to create the number of mesh lines you'll need. After you click the Gradient Mesh tool on an object, it is converted into a mesh object. You can use the Gradient Mesh tool only on vector objects; it is not available for raster images.

When you expand a gradient object using the command Object, Expand, the option to create a gradient mesh object is available (see Figure 33.13).

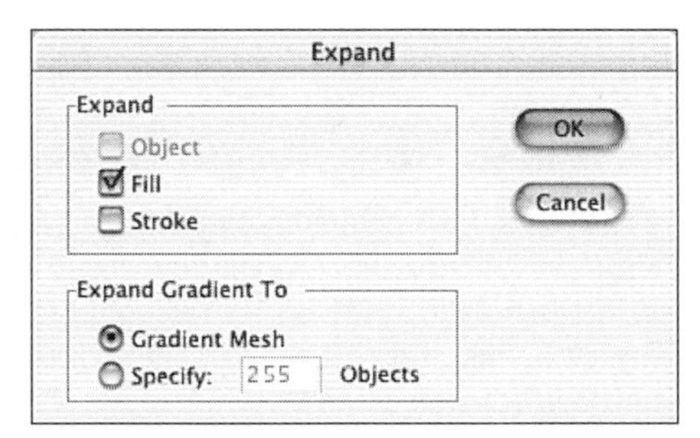


Figure 33.13
If Stroke is selected in the dialog box, the mesh will include the object's stroke as mesh patches.

When you use the Expand command to create a gradient mesh object, the object is given mesh lines that correspond to the color stops in the gradient. That pertains to both radial and linear gradients, as shown in Figure 33.14.

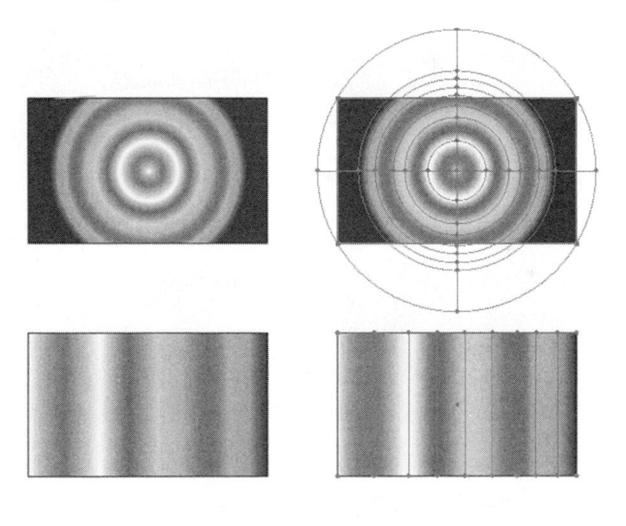

Figure 33.14
The mesh lines are visible, along with their mesh points. Note that the original rectangle shape serves as a clipping mask for the mesh object.

There are several guidelines and restrictions for the creation of gradient mesh objects in Illustrator:

- The Gradient Mesh tool creates the minimum number of mesh lines and points necessary when converting an object. Typically, that will be two lines with their endpoints and a fifth point where the lines intersect.
- If a specific point on an object requires a specific color (a highlight or button, for example), click that point with the Gradient Mesh tool when converting an object.
- You can use the Create Gradient Mesh command to specify a number of rows and columns, producing a given number of mesh points.
- You cannot create a gradient mesh object from a linked raster image, a compound path, or text.
- When an object becomes a gradient mesh object, it can no longer be considered a vector object, although the shape can still be manipulated.

## Creating Gradient Mesh Objects from Raster Images

Linked and embedded raster images can be turned into gradient mesh objects. However, a linked image, after it is converted, becomes a mesh object and loses its link. In addition, gradient mesh objects from images can create very large files and may lead to print problems. One way to limit the size of the files is to compromise on the amount of detail and control. Figure 33.15 shows a comparison of two different settings for Create Gradient Mesh.

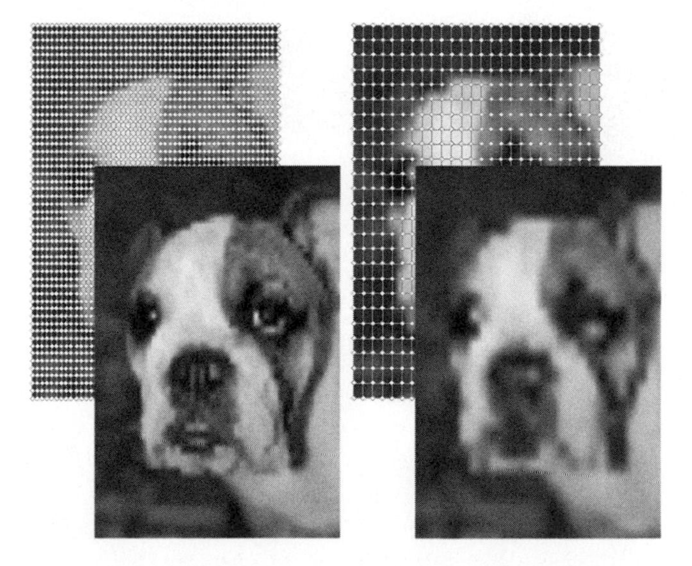

**Figure 33.15**
The meshes for the two objects are shown behind. On the left is a 50×50 mesh; on the right is a 25×25 mesh.



The number of mesh points makes a great difference in file size. The 50×50 mesh in Figure 33.15 produced an Adobe Illustrator file almost two and a half times bigger than the 25×25 mesh setting. However, notice the difference in detail between the two mesh settings. Obviously, images with more detail demand finer meshes.

You can minimize printing problems if you create and combine several smaller mesh objects rather than make one large object. The image in Figure 33.15, for example, can be quartered in an image-editing program, and separate mesh objects can be created from each.

*Having trouble outputting a gradient mesh object to an inkjet printer? See "Outputting Gradient Mesh Objects" in the "Mastering Illustrator" section at the end of this chapter.*

One way to reduce file size when you're creating a gradient mesh object from a raster image is to reduce the area of the image that is being used. Make a copy of the raster image and crop it down to just the part that needs to be turned into a mesh; then add both the full-size and smaller images to your Illustrator document. After creating the mesh object, position it above the full-size raster image.

Don't forget that you can simulate gradient meshes by using objects and the Blend command. If a gradient mesh is proving difficult to print, you might be able to easily simulate the mesh using blends. Figure 33.16 shows an example of blended objects that produce an effect similar to the gradient mesh shown in Figure 33.2.

## Editing Gradient Meshes

After you create a gradient mesh object, whether from a vector object or raster image, you can edit it. To understand the process of editing a gradient mesh, you need to understand the components. Examining Figure 33.17, you'll see parts that look familiar from path editing and some parts that look strange.

Figure 33.16
The stacked objects are shown on the left; the blend, on the right.

As you can see in Figure 33.17, gradient mesh objects, like other objects, are constructed of points and lines between those points:

- **Mesh point**—A mesh point, which is always shown as a diamond, can exist at the end of a mesh line or somewhere along the line. These points always exist at the intersection of two lines. (See also *corner mesh point.*) Mesh points control the coloring of a mesh object. The color is applied to a point, and it spreads from there, based on the relationship to the point's direction lines and neighboring points. When a mesh point is located at the end of a mesh line, it has two direction lines. When it is found at a location where two mesh lines cross, it has four direction lines. Like path anchor points, mesh points are hollow when unselected and are filled when selected, as shown in Figure 33.17.
- **Corner mesh point**—Like any other mesh points, these points have direction lines and can be colored. They, too, exist at the intersection of two mesh lines. They are created when an object

that contains corner anchor points is converted into a mesh object. An object's smooth anchor points are converted into regular mesh points when they coincide with mesh lines. Otherwise, they may be left as smooth anchor points.

- **Direction line**—Just as control points and direction lines regulate the shape of paths, so do they regulate the shape of mesh lines. In addition, however, they also determine the interaction of colors (see Figure 33.18).

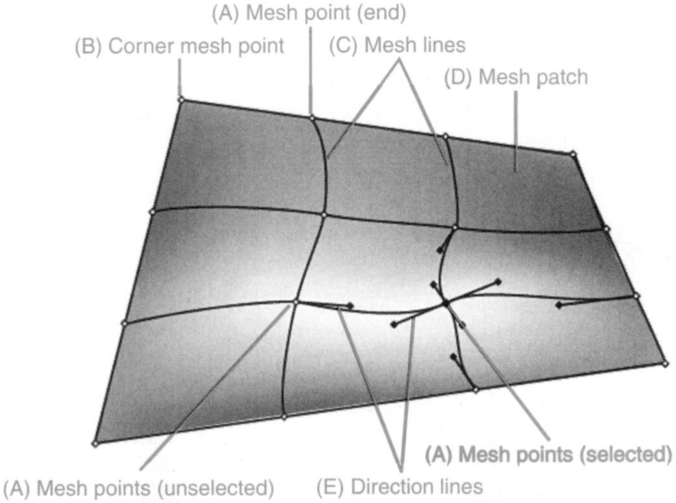

**Figure 33.17**
Mesh points have much in common with anchor points, but they have several important differences.

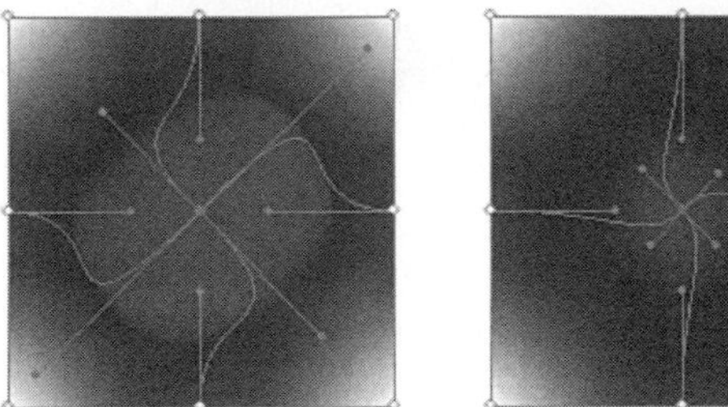

**Figure 33.18**
The difference between these two examples is only the length of the direction lines from the center mesh point. Note that, in addition to the color change, the direction lines control the shape of the mesh lines, just as with paths.

- **Mesh line**—You can add mesh lines by using the Create Gradient Mesh command or the Gradient Mesh tool. Mesh lines always extend completely across an object, whether horizontally or vertically. Every place where two mesh lines intersect, a mesh point is created. When you're converting an object, path segments may be subdivided by mesh points.

- **Mesh patch**—The area bounded by mesh lines is referred to as a *mesh patch*. It always has four mesh points on its perimeter, even if there are not four places where mesh lines intersect (see Figure 33.19).

- **Path anchor point (not identified in Figure 33.17)**—Regular anchor points can be retained when a mesh object is created. Path anchor points differ from mesh points in two respects. First, they cannot have an assigned color. Second, they appear at the ends of path segments rather than at intersections of paths. As usual, they are shown as squares on the artboard. (Mesh points are shown as diamonds.) You can add and delete these points by using the appropriate Pen tools.

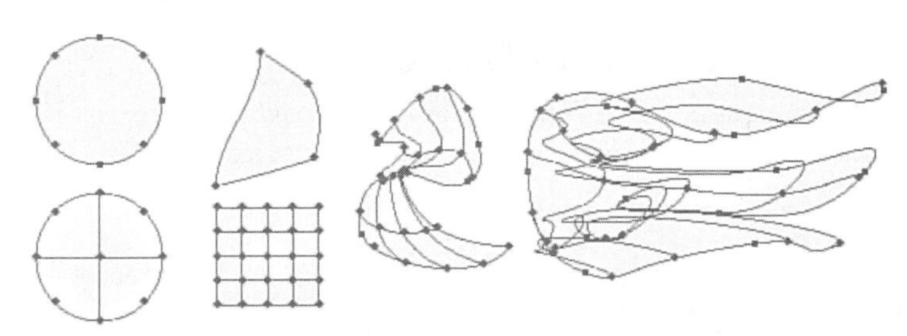

**Figure 33.19**
The top-left object has only one mesh patch and its four mesh points. It also has the original four smooth anchor points. Knowing that each patch has exactly four mesh points can help in deciphering the object on the right.

You can edit mesh objects by changing the color of mesh points, moving mesh points, adding mesh points (and the corresponding mesh lines), and deleting mesh points (and their lines). Here are some items to keep in mind:

- Before you can change the color of a mesh point, you must select it with the Direct Selection or Gradient Mesh tool.
- To add or change the color of a selected mesh point or points, you can use the Color palette, Swatches palette, or Paint Bucket. Gradients and patterns cannot be used.
- Clicking with the Direct Selection tool in a mesh patch selects the four surrounding mesh points.
- Clicking in a mesh patch with the Gradient Mesh tool adds a pair of mesh lines, perpendicular to each other, extending across the object.
- Clicking with the Gradient Mesh tool on a mesh line adds a single line, perpendicular to the existing line.
- If the mesh object is already colored, you can add a mesh point and corresponding mesh lines of the same color by Shift-clicking with the Gradient Mesh tool.
- (Option)-clicking [Alt]-clicking a mesh point with the Gradient Mesh tool deletes the point.
- You can modify direction lines for an active mesh point by dragging the control points at the ends of the direction lines.
- To relocate a mesh point along the mesh line without disturbing the line itself, use the Gradient Mesh tool and hold down the Shift key.
- You can manipulate mesh points and mesh lines by using the Transform commands and tools.

> Many of the effects available in Illustrator produce outstanding results with gradients and gradient meshes. Of particular note are the Artistic effects.

*Having difficulty manipulating mesh points? See "Working with Mesh Points" in the "Mastering Illustrator" section at the end of this chapter.*

## Illustrator at Work: Creating a Gradient Mesh Object

Creating gradient mesh objects may appear to be a very complex and difficult task. It doesn't need to be that way. The best way to learn how to control a gradient mesh is to do just that.

1. Open a new Illustrator document (RGB, 800×600 pixels).
2. With the Rectangle tool, click once in the upper-left part of the artboard. Add a rectangle 400 pixels wide and 300 pixels tall. (Remember that you can type **`400 px`** and **`300 px`** regardless of the document's unit of measure.)
3. With the object selected on the artboard, use the menu command Object, Create Gradient Mesh. In the dialog box, opt for five columns and four rows with Appearance set to Flat.
4. With the Direct Selection tool, click away from the object to deselect it; then click in the lower-right corner. (This is a quick-and-easy way to deselect all the mesh points and then reselect the object.) If the fill color of the original rectangle is white, it will disappear, but you should have no trouble clicking the invisible object.
5. Click the mesh point at the lower-right corner of the mesh patch in the upper left. (If the mesh lines were numbered 1 to 5 from left to right, and 1 through 6 from top to bottom, this point would be the intersection of 2-2.)
6. Click a yellow swatch in the Swatches palette or mix a bright yellow in the Color palette, such as RGB 255/255/0. At this point, your object should look like the one shown in Figure 33.20.

33

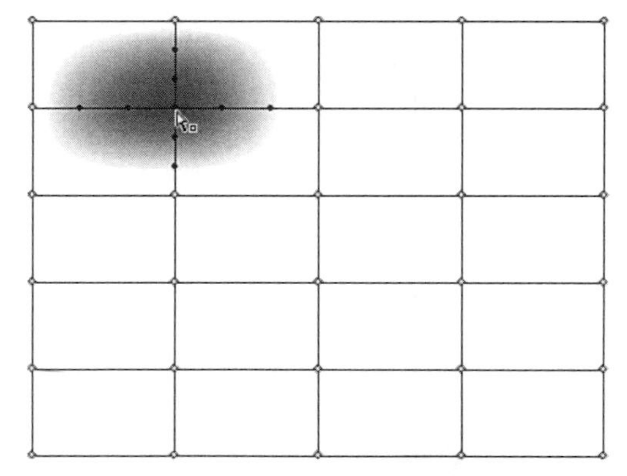

**Figure 33.20**
One mesh point is selected and color has been added. The remaining mesh points and patches have the object's original fill color (white in this case).

7. Shift-click to select each of the mesh points immediately surrounding your yellow patch. (Make sure to select all eight of the surrounding mesh points, but not the yellow point.) Add a very pale blue to these points, perhaps RGB 130/230/255.
8. Select the top three mesh points in the fourth mesh line from the left as well as the first three mesh points on the fourth mesh line from the top. Add a medium blue (RGB 50/105/255) to the six selected mesh points.

9. Select all the mesh points on the mesh line on the right and all the mesh points on the fifth mesh line from the top, plus the one as-yet-unselected mesh point at the intersection of the fourth mesh line from the left and the fourth mesh line from the top. Make them dark blue (perhaps RGB 0/30/255).

10. The last four not-yet-colored mesh points are along the bottom mesh line, starting in the lower-left corner. Give them a nice rich green color, such as RGB 0/170/55. All mesh points should now have an assigned color. From the top down and from left to right, the mesh point colors are shown in Table 33.1.

**Table 33.1** Mesh Point Colors (RGB Notation)

| Mesh Row | Left | 2nd | 3rd | 4th | Right |
|---|---|---|---|---|---|
| Top | 130/230/255 | 130/230/255 | 130/230/255 | 50/105/255 | 0/30/255 |
| 2nd | 130/230/255 | 255/255/0 | 130/230/255 | 50/105/255 | 0/30/255 |
| 3rd | 130/230/255 | 130/230/255 | 130/230/255 | 50/105/255 | 0/30/255 |
| 4th | 50/105/255 | 50/105/255 | 50/105/255 | 0/30/255 | 0/30/255 |
| 5th | 0/30/255 | 0/30/255 | 0/30/255 | 0/30/255 | 0/30/255 |
| Bottom | 0/170/55 | 0/170/55 | 0/170/55 | 0/170/55 | 0/30/255 |

11. Click away from the gradient mesh object to deselect it, hiding the object's mesh. You should see an Impressionistic sun over a grassy hill. More or less. We'll now fine-tune the image using the Direct Selection tool.

12. Click somewhere on the lower-right part of the mesh object to show the grid; then click the mesh point in the center of the yellow area. Drag the mesh point slightly up and to the left; then shorten its direction lines and extend the direction lines of the surrounding mesh points. Make the "sun" a bit smaller and rounder.

> Use (Command-H) [Ctrl+H] to show and hide the mesh while you're working. That gives you a better look at transitions between colors.

13. Click the mesh point to the lower-right of the yellow area's point. Adjust its direction lines and those of the mesh points to the right, lower right, and below to better round the transition from light blue to dark blue. Keep in mind that you can drag the mesh points into new positions, too.

14. Drag the upward-pointing direction lines for the green mesh points farther up to extend the hill. Drag the direction lines for the points directly above downward to sharpen the transition from blue to green. Depending on how much creative license you've taken with the preceding steps, your final mesh should look similar to that in Figure 33.21.

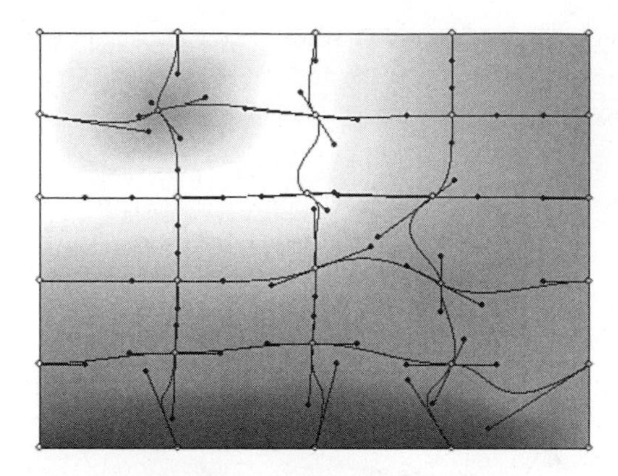

Figure 33.21
The mesh points' direction lines will not all be visible at once. They're shown here for illustrative purposes.

# Printing Gradients and Gradient Meshes

Printing gradients and especially gradient meshes can be a problem. The complexity of the objects can choke an imagesetter or result in banding. The following guidelines pertain primarily to preparing CMYK images for four-color process printing:

- Short, distinct blends print better than longer, more subtle blends.
- Lighter colors blend better than darker colors. Blending between a very dark color and white is worst.
- Use PostScript Level 3 devices when possible. When you must print a gradient mesh or gradient to a PostScript 2 device, be sure that you have appropriate settings in the Printing & Export panel of the Document Setup dialog box.
- Some lower-resolution printers are not well equipped to handle gradients. Try deselecting the Use Printer's Default Screen option.
- Ensure that the imagesetter's resolution and line screen frequency allow the full range of 256 levels of gray. Using too high a line screen actually reduces the number of grays available.



When printing to low-resolution or inkjet printers, you may be able to solve problems by simply rasterizing the gradient or gradient mesh object.

You should also keep in mind several rules that Illustrator uses for separating and printing colors in gradients and mesh objects:

- If a process color and a spot color are blended in a gradient, all colors are converted to process colors.
- When you're blending a spot color with a tint of itself, the gradient separates as a spot color.
- When you're creating a gradient between a spot color and white, make "white" a 0% tint of the spot color. This technique ensures that the gradient will separate to a single plate.
- When you're creating separate plates for spot colors, make sure you have the correct options in the Separations Setup dialog box (which you access by choosing File, Separation Setup). See Figure 33.22 for an example of the dialog box.

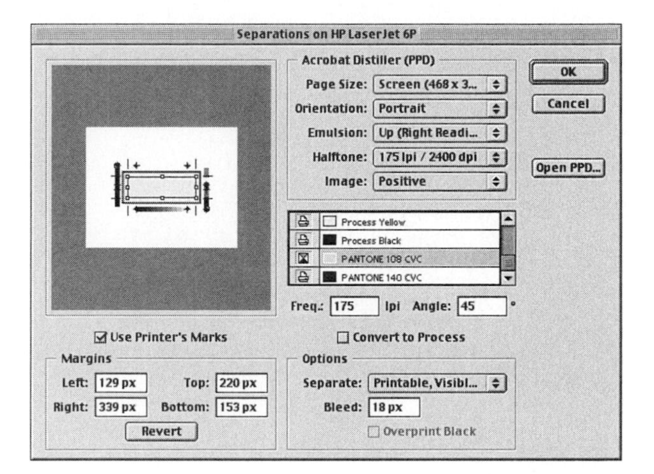


Figure 33.22
The printer icon next to a color's name in the list indicates that a separation will be printed. The four-part square indicates that a spot color will be converted to process colors.

# MASTERING ILLUSTRATOR

## Monitor Settings

*My gradients look very dithered or banded onscreen, but when I send them to my inkjet printer, they come out fine. What's the solution?*

Your monitor is probably set to too few colors. See Figure 33.23 for an example.

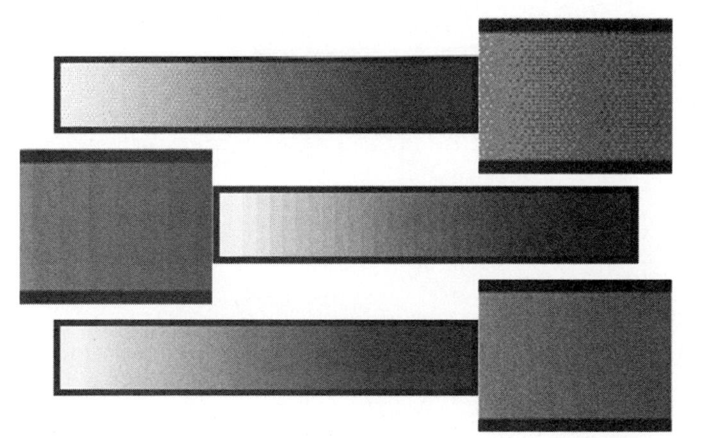

Figure 33.23
The same gradient—with zoomed views—as displayed on monitors set to (from top) 256 colors (8-bit), thousands of colors (16-bit), and millions of colors (24-bit).

For Macintosh OS X, changes to monitor settings are made in the Displays panel of the System Preferences. For Windows, you make changes to the monitor color depth using the Control Panel (found in the Start menu). In the Control Panel window, click Display and open the Settings tab. Look for the Color Palette option.

## Outputting Gradient Mesh Objects

*I'm having problems printing gradient meshes on my inkjet printer. What can I do?*

Rasterize. The gradient mesh object is a combination of vector and raster information. Converting it to all-raster makes it easier for your printer to handle.

## Working with Mesh Points

*Trying to get that perfect look for a gradient mesh is driving me nuts! I can't seem to get the points to cooperate with each other.*

First, keep in mind that having more points is not always better. Every time you add a mesh point, you're actually adding one or two mesh lines, with new mesh points every place they cross existing lines. Next, keep in mind that each mesh patch has four mesh points controlling it. When mesh lines curve and overlap, you may have trouble recognizing that fourth point. Click somewhere in the patch, and the four points will automatically be selected. One more tip: When a color fades as it moves away from a mesh point, but a second mesh point stands in the way, remember that you can use the HSB sliders in the Color palette to make the second point a tint of the fading color.

34

# USING MASKS, TRANSPARENCY, AND BLENDING MODES

## IN THIS CHAPTER

Masks, blending modes, and the Transparency palette are just some of the ways to manipulate visibility in Illustrator. Changing the stacking order of overlapping objects affects visibility, as does increasing or decreasing the width of a stroke, or changing a stroke or fill to None.

However, masks, transparency adjustments, and blending modes are far more powerful than those simple techniques. They offer an incredible amount of control over how overlapping objects appear—or how an object alone appears. Generally speaking, a mask controls visibility for an object or group of objects broadly. Artwork inside the mask is visible; artwork outside the mask is invisible. Blending modes determine how overlapping colors will appear, in conjunction with any other changes in the Transparency palette.

You can, of course, hide items using the Layers palette, but that's a different sort of procedure—the hidden objects and paths, or the content of a hidden layer, are no longer part of the artwork, temporarily or permanently.

These features rank among the most powerful capabilities in Illustrator. Understanding how to use them—and how to output them properly—will vastly increase your creative flexibility.

## TRANSPARENCY AND OPACITY

Any discussion of Illustrator's transparency and masking capabilities must start with a few words about terminology. When the term *transparency* is used, it generally refers to an object or path's *opacity*. When an object is transparent, you can see through it. When it is opaque, you cannot. When an object has an opacity of 25%, you could think of it as 75% transparent. (This is, however, not quite accurate. The object would be better referred to as *translucent*.) Reserve the term *transparent* for that state of 0% opacity—completely invisible.

There are also two different types of transparency or opacity. The hard-edged border between opaque and transparent areas, like that formed by path-based masks and clipping paths, uses pixels that are either transparent *or* opaque, with no variations. Transparency that fades, such as that used for drop shadows, can be considered *variable transparency*. This can be created with a gradient mask, Illustrator's effects, and the impact of a blending mode on a gradient or gradient mesh object.

It's important to keep in mind that some file formats support only one kind of transparency or the other. When working with the TIFF file format, you can use a clipping path to define what part of an image will be visible. However, when placed into a page layout document such as InDesign, each pixel will be either 100% opaque or 100% transparent. TIFF images can't have a shadow that gently falls across other elements of the page. InDesign CS's support for Adobe's Smart Object technology enables it to use shadows, blending modes, and reduced opacity with Illustrator's AI file format, as well as Photoshop's PSD files (see Figure 34.1).



For the Web, GoLive supports Adobe's Smart Objects technology, which enables it to work with Illustrator and Photoshop files. However, there are restriction in the file formats that can be used for optimized images.

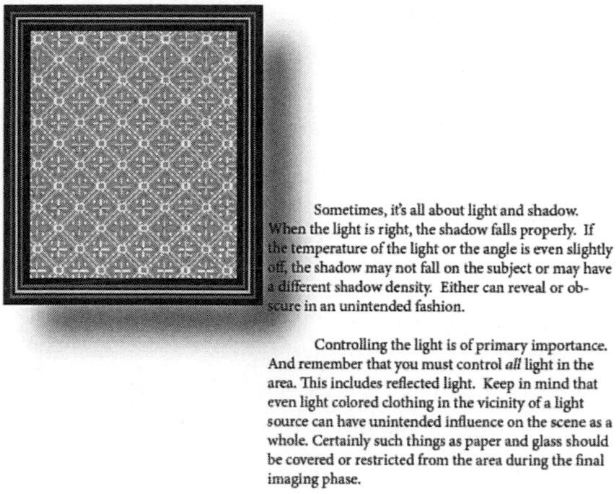

Sometimes, it's all about light and shadow. When the light is right, the shadow falls properly. If the temperature of the light or the angle is even slightly off, the shadow may not fall on the subject or may have a different shadow density. Either can reveal or obscure in an unintended fashion.

Controlling the light is of primary importance. And remember that you must control *all* light in the area. This includes reflected light. Keep in mind that even light colored clothing in the vicinity of a light source can have unintended influence on the scene as a whole. Certainly such things as paper and glass should be covered or restricted from the area during the final imaging phase.

**Figure 34.1**
This InDesign layout includes Illustrator artwork that employs a drop shadow. Note that the shadow, which is above the type elements on the page, does not obscure the type.

Most graphic images on the World Wide Web are in JPEG or GIF file format. Both of these are raster formats. As such, the issue of whether areas of color should be vector or raster disappears when you save images in either of these formats. The entire illustration or image becomes a single raster image. The file is automatically flattened and becomes a series of individually colored pixels. (See Chapter 4, "Pixels, Vectors, and Resolutions," for a full explanation of the difference between vector and raster.) PNG is another raster image format for the Web, although it's not fully supported by all Web browsers.

The term *transparency* applies to Web graphics in another sense as well. GIF images can have irregular outlines with uncolored areas becoming transparent on the Web. JPEG, on the other hand, can have no such transparency. Every JPEG image must be rectangular. If an area of an illustration is not filled with color, it appears as white in a Web browser.

*For information on which Web-related file formats support transparency—and which kind—see Chapter 22, "Save for Web and Image Optimization," p. 695.*

# CLIPPING MASKS

Masks in Illustrator come in two varieties: clipping and opacity. *Clipping masks* hide part of an object or image. *Opacity masks* use a pattern or gradient to selectively expose parts of an object or image. A practical difference is that opacity masks can be semitransparent, whereas clipping masks cannot. Figure 34.2 shows an image and how it can be affected by the two types of masks.

**Figure 34.2**
The selection in the center shows how the clipping mask hides part of the image. To the right is an opacity mask using a pattern.

A clipping mask is like a frame that covers part of an image. In this case, the frame is usually invisible, and it makes the hidden part of the image invisible, too. An opacity mask, on the other hand, has a fill, and that fill reacts with the image underneath. Clipping masks can contain multiple paths and mask multiple objects or images. Clipping masks are grouped with the objects they mask, and the group is referred to as a *clipping set.*

Clipping masks, which can be any shape or size, are created with a menu command. They typically have no stroke or fill. They can be locked or unlocked so that you can reposition the artwork within the mask or the mask in relation to the artwork.

In some respects, clipping masks are similar to the compound shape mode Intersect (found on the Pathfinder palette). As with Intersect, the artwork is restricted to the area of overlap.

It's easier to comprehend the topic of masks when the terminology is clear:

- **Clipping paths**—Define areas of visibility and invisibility. They are paths and can be edited like those used to create objects.
- **Clipping masks**—The clipping paths in action. A clipping mask is used to reveal and hide portions of an underlying object or objects. Normally, the clipping mask is not visible, consisting of a clipping path or paths with a stroke and fill of None. Multiple clipping paths can be used in one clipping mask.
- **Clipping groups**—Compound paths used as clipping paths.
- **Clipping sets**—Clipping masks grouped with objects that they mask.

## Creating Clipping Masks

A clipping mask, at its most basic, consists of a piece of artwork that is partially hidden and the path that defines the visible area. To create a mask, simply select the artwork to be masked and the path that will be doing the masking; then choose Object, Clipping Mask, Make. The following are some basic guidelines for creating clipping masks:

- Any vector object can be used as a clipping mask, regardless of its fill or stroke.
- The path or object to be used for the clipping mask must be on top of the artwork to be masked.
- Both the fill and stroke of the upper path become None when the command is invoked (see Figure 34.3). The masking path's fill and stroke can be changed after it becomes a mask, however.

**Caution**

Clipping masks, especially those that use complex paths, can create printing problems. Overly complex paths can choke an imagesetter.

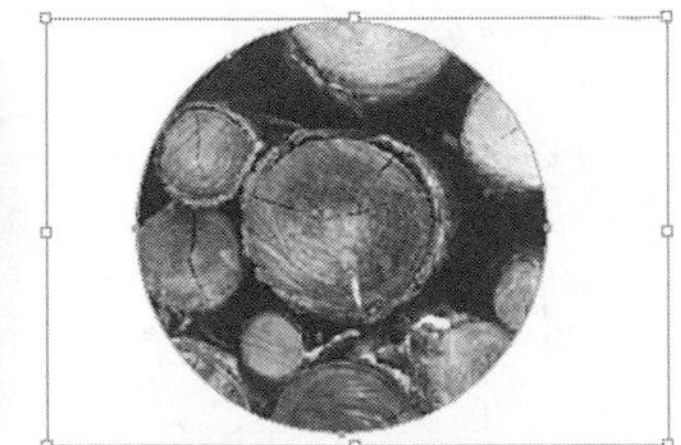

**Figure 34.3**
The gradient in the circle is lost when you choose Object, Clipping Mask, Make.

- Raster images and gradient mesh objects cannot be used as masks, but can themselves be masked by vector objects.
- If the object to be masked and the masking path are on separate layers, unselected objects on intervening layers are ignored.
- Text can be used for masking. (See "Type as Clipping Masks," later in this chapter.)
- Compound paths and compound shapes can be used as masks. Figure 34.4 shows a comparison of a simple path as a clipping mask and a compound path as a clipping mask or a compound shape as a clipping mask.

When clipping masks are causing printing problems, the standard advice is to simplify the paths used to make the clipping masks or avoid using clipping masks completely. Before you do that, though, make a copy of the document and try rasterizing the masked objects and images. When rasterized, the vector path that may be causing the problem is eliminated.

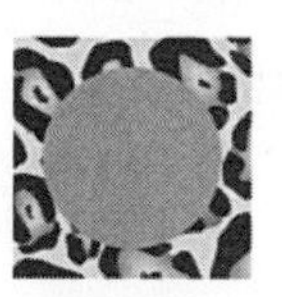
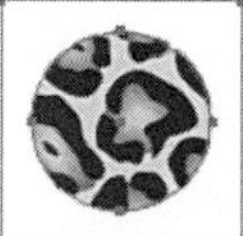
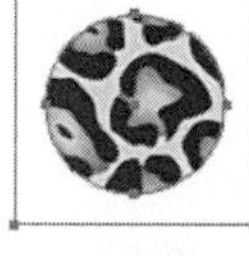

**Figure 34.4**
You can use compound paths (Object, Compound Path, Make) or a compound shape created with the Pathfinder palette as a mask.

- Choosing Object, Clipping Mask, Release undoes a selected clipping mask but does not restore the original fill and stroke of the object used as a mask. The path that had been used as a mask will have a stroke and fill of None, unless you have specifically applied a stroke or fill.

*Having trouble creating a clipping mask? See "Clipping Creation Conflicts" in the "Mastering Illustrator" section at the end of this chapter.*

## Editing a Clipping Mask

You can edit clipping masks in a variety of ways after you create them. The path being used as a clipping mask can be assigned a fill and stroke, and it remains a path, subject to manipulation.

Both fills and strokes can be assigned to a path being used as a clipping mask. The stroke is visible, but the fill remains hidden unless the object being masked has reduced opacity, is hidden, or does not occupy the entire area of the mask. If you select the clipping mask's path with the Direct Selection tool, you can assign a stroke and fill as you would to any other object.

Interestingly, reducing the opacity of the fill of a path being used as a clipping mask has no effect unless the mask is released. While acting as a clipping mask, the fill's opacity will not be changed. If the mask is released, the reduced opacity will be apparent. You can, however, control the opacity for both the object that is being masked and, by using the Appearance palette, its fill.

You can use the Direct Selection tool to manipulate individual anchor points on the clipping mask, just as you would any other path. You can also, when the mask is selected, change the path's appearance attributes. Figure 34.5 shows an example.

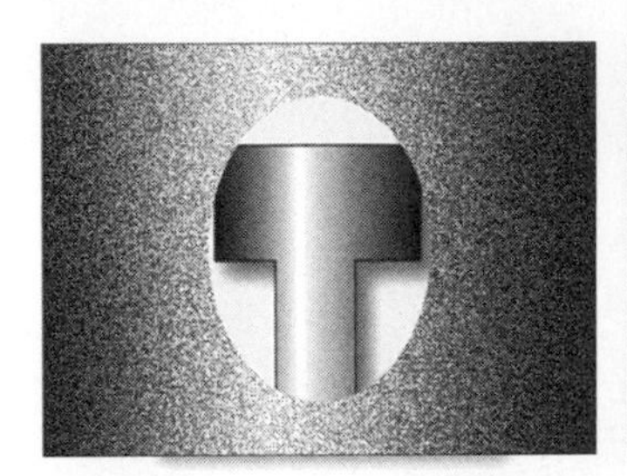

Figure 34.5
In this example, a stroke has been applied to a compound path being used in a clipping mask.

The Group Selection tool enables you to reposition a clipping mask. This includes repositioning a path that is part of a compound path being used as a mask (see Figure 34.6).

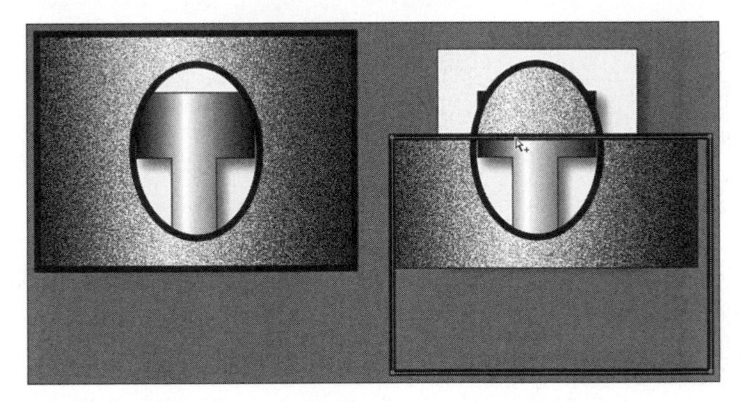

Figure 34.6
On the right, you can see the mask being dragged. The rectangle and ellipse are a compound path being used as a mask on the frontmost rectangle.

Illustrator enables you to cut an object from the artboard and then use the Paste in Front and Paste in Back commands to add it to a clipping mask. To determine where the new object will be added, use the Direct Selection tool to select a member of the clipping set. Keep in mind that Paste in Front and Paste in Back remember the object's location on the artboard. Position the object before cutting. Likewise, you can use the Direct Selection tool to select an object to be removed from a clipping set. Choosing Edit, Cut or pressing Delete [Backspace] removes a selected object from the artboard without disturbing the rest of the clipping set.



## Type as Clipping Masks

You do not need to convert type to outlines to use it as a clipping mask. As you can see by the Type tool selection in Figure 34.7, the text remains fully editable.

Note that the type loses its drop shadow when it's made into a clipping mask. The shadow can be reapplied to the type while the type is being used as a mask, but the shadow isn't visible unless the mask is released.

Large amounts of type or area type can provoke a warning from Illustrator that previewing and printing might cause problems. See Figure 34.8 for such an example.

Figure 34.7
The word *Mask* is selected and can be overtyped to edit.

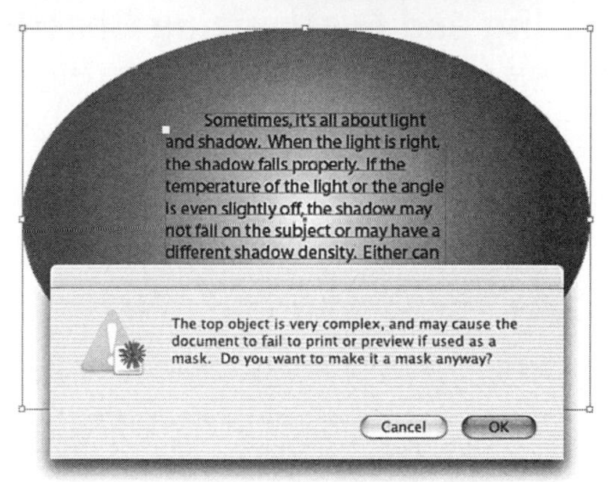


Figure 34.8
Text is created from complex compound paths, which can lead to problems.

*Having trouble printing but are afraid to rasterize? See "Protecting Editable Type" in the "Mastering Illustrator" section at the end of this chapter.*

## OPACITY MASKS

Opacity masks use the luminosity of the uppermost object to produce a transparent pattern on lower objects. When the masking object is filled with a solid color, the mask is uniform. If the luminosity is high (bright colors), the mask appears to have little or no effect. If the masking object is filled with a dark color, the artwork below appears more transparent. When the masking object is filled with a pattern or a gradient, the results can vary substantially. Figure 34.9 compares opacity masks created with various solid color, gradient, and pattern fills.

**Caution**

Illustrator's warning is not to be ignored. Overly complex clipping masks can prevent a job from printing or even prevent the screen from redrawing correctly. The clipping group can, however, be rasterized.

Figure 34.9
On the left are the original objects. To the right, the background image has been divided into five pieces and different opacity masks have been applied to each (from the top: white, neutral gray, black, pattern, and gradient).

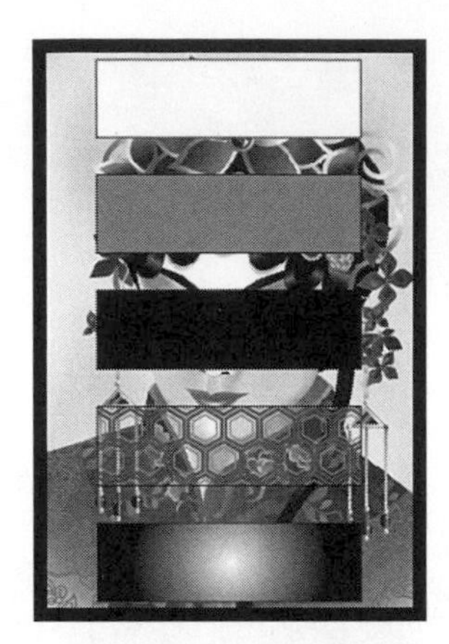

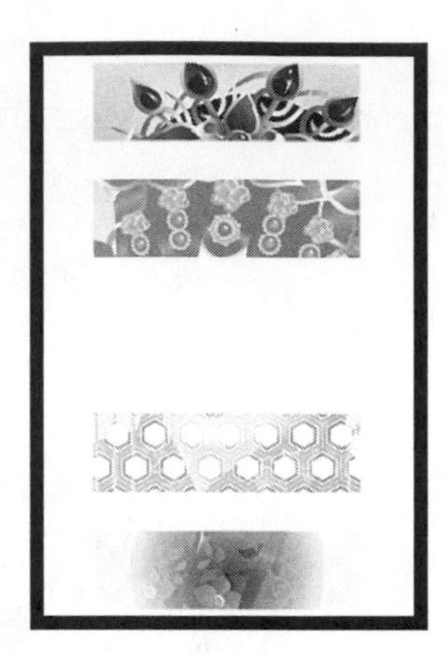

## Illustrator at Work: Creating and Customizing Opacity Masks

Gradients and objects with pattern fills make the most interesting opacity masks. Here's an example:

1. Create a new Illustrator document (Letter size, RGB).
2. Use the command File, Place to add a photograph to the artboard. (If you don't have a digitized photo handy, check the Goodies folder on this book's CD.)
3. Drag a rectangle over the photo and give it a radial white-to-black gradient fill.
4. Select All. Both the rectangle and the photo must be selected to create an opacity mask.
5. From the Transparency palette's menu, choose Make Opacity Mask. Note that in the Transparency palette, the topmost object, your gradient-filled rectangle is visible as a thumbnail (see Figure 34.10).

Figure 34.10
Where the gradient is black, the photo will be completely hidden. Where it's white, the photo will be completely visible. The blend area will have opacity comparable to its gray value.

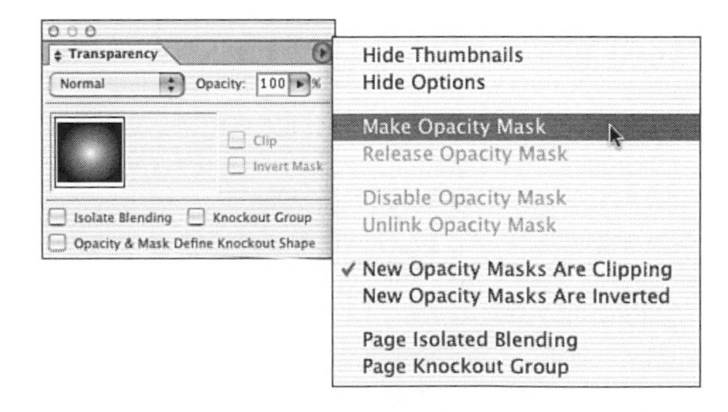


6. In the Transparency palette, click the thumbnail of the gradient opacity mask to make it active.
7. In the Gradient palette, drag the white color stop toward the middle and drag the diamond above the gradient sample closer to the black color stop. The change in the gradient will be reflected in the opacity mask (see Figure 34.11). Try clicking the Invert Mask box a couple of times to watch the opacity mask reverse itself.

**Figure 34.11**
You can adjust the opacity mask to create a perfect vignette for your photo.

8. Keeping the photo-and-mask object selected on the artboard and the opacity mask thumbnail selected in the Transparency palette, experiment with different gradients. Remember that the luminosity value of the gradient is used, so gray color stops will give you a better indication of how the gradient will behave as an opacity mask. In Figure 34.12, a second fill has been added to the object being used as an opacity mask, and that fill's opacity has been reduced. This enables *both* the object's fills to work as part of the mask.

**Figure 34.12**
Note in the image and the Appearance palette the effect of increasing the stroke.

*For information on creating and editing gradients, see Chapter 33, "Working with Gradients and Gradient Meshes," p. 985.*

9. From the Transparency palette menu, choose Disable Opacity Mask. Take a look at how a red X is placed across the opacity mask's thumbnail in the palette; then use the palette menu command Enable Opacity Mask.

10. Click the left thumbnail in the Transparency palette, the thumbnail for the photograph. From the palette's menu, choose Unlink Opacity Mask. (This can also be accomplished by clicking the link symbol between the two thumbnails.) Click the mask's thumbnail. Use the Selection tool to drag the gradient-filled rectangle on the

> After repositioning an opacity mask, you can relink it and the object below, either by clicking once between the thumbnails in the Transparency palette or by using the palette's menu command Link Opacity Mask. Before either method can be used, however, the left thumbnail in the Transparency palette *must* be active.

artboard. Watch how repositioning it moves the opacity mask and its effect on the photo. Use the Direct Selection tool to edit the mask's path itself. Click an anchor point and drag. The mask updates to conform to the new shape.

11. From the palette's menu, select the command Release Opacity Mask. (If the command is grayed out, click the left thumbnail and try again.) Delete the gradient-filled rectangle, add a star-shaped object, fill it with a pattern, and experiment. Click a couple of times on the Clip box in the Transparency palette to see how the star's path is used as a clipping mask. With a star, you'll want to take a look at the Effect, Distort & Transform, Twist command (see Figure 34.13).

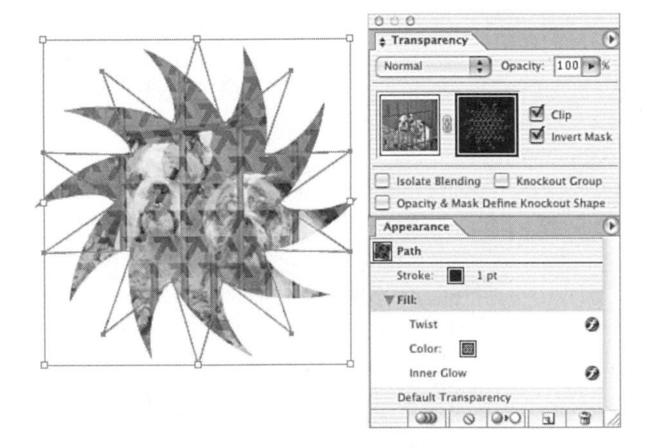


**Figure 34.13**
In the Appearance palette, you can see that the Inner Glow effect is applied to the fill. Using a large radius, with black as the color and Multiply or Overlay as the blending mode, a pattern can be softened with Inner Glow.

## Type as Opacity Masks

You also can use type as opacity masks. Figure 34.14 shows a type opacity mask.

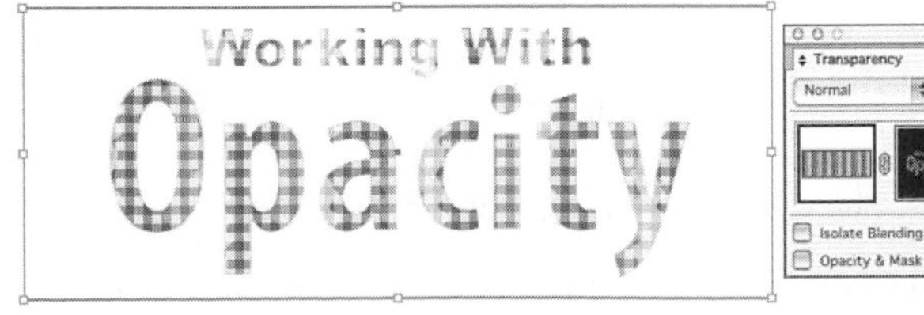


**Figure 34.14**
The Transparency palette shows the background object and opacity mask.



You can still edit type after you create the opacity mask. However, the mask itself must be active in the Transparency palette. Click the mask's thumbnail in the Transparency palette and use the Type tool to select the text for editing (see Figure 34.15).

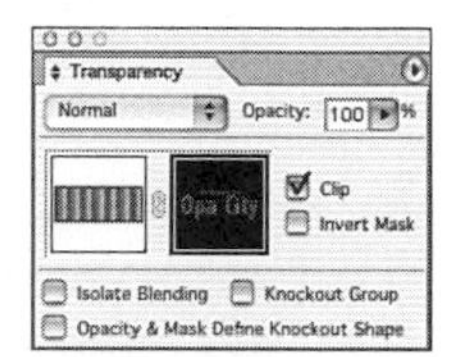


**Figure 34.15**
With the mask active in the Transparency palette, you can edit the type.

# WORKING WITH TRANSPARENCY IN ILLUSTRATOR

The *appearance* of transparency has always been available in Illustrator, but in the past, it has been difficult to achieve. For example, a drop shadow can be simulated with a gradient, as shown in Figure 34.16.

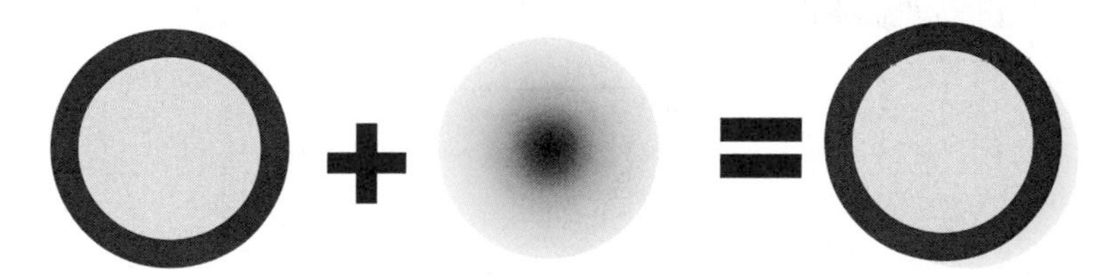

**Figure 34.16**
Placing a copy of an object that is filled with a black-to-white gradient behind the object can simulate the transparency of a drop shadow.

The gradient runs from black to white and in the shape of the object. In this case, with a simple circle, a radial gradient suffices. Drop shadows that can be directly applied rather than simulated with another object are just one example of transparency effects and filters in Illustrator. You can apply transparency to an object, its fill or stroke, or a group, or you can even assign it to a layer.

## The Transparency Theory

Although *transparency* is the term we use, it's not exactly correct. Transparent objects, technically, are clear, such as window glass. In the case of Illustrator, that would make them invisible with a stroke and fill of None. *Translucent*, on the other hand, is also not quite appropriate for our purposes. It implies distortion of the light coming through, such as frosted glass.

In Illustrator, we can use the term *transparency* much as it is used in photography, where it refers to the amount of light passing through the film's emulsion. However, rather than measure an object's transparency, we work backward and describe its opacity. An object can be from 100% opaque (solid) to 0% opaque (invisible). In simpler terms, an object's opacity refers to whether or not (or how much) you can see an object behind it on the artboard. In Figure 34.17, a series of rectangles show the range of opacity against Illustrator's grid. The rightmost rectangle, with an opacity of 0%, is selected.

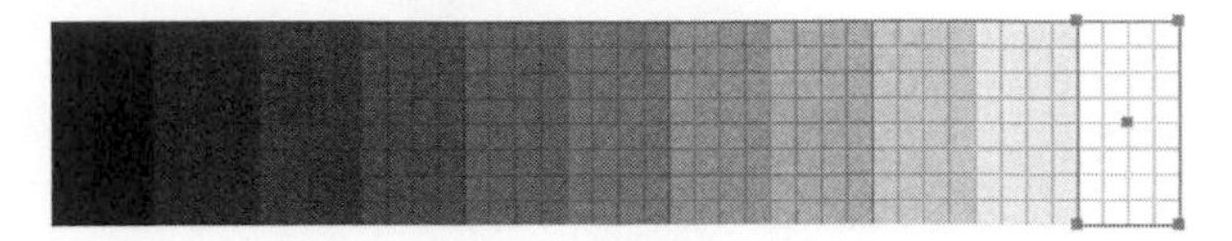

Figure 34.17
If the rectangle on the far right was not selected, it would not be visible.

*Confused about the difference between transparency and opacity? See "Two Terms, One Concept" in the "Mastering Illustrator" section at the end of this chapter.*

Opacity is not the same as color value. Figure 34.18 compares transparency with grayscale fill values, each in increments of 10%. Although the results may appear comparable on the artboard, an object's interaction with other objects may depend on the difference between tinted fill and opacity changes.

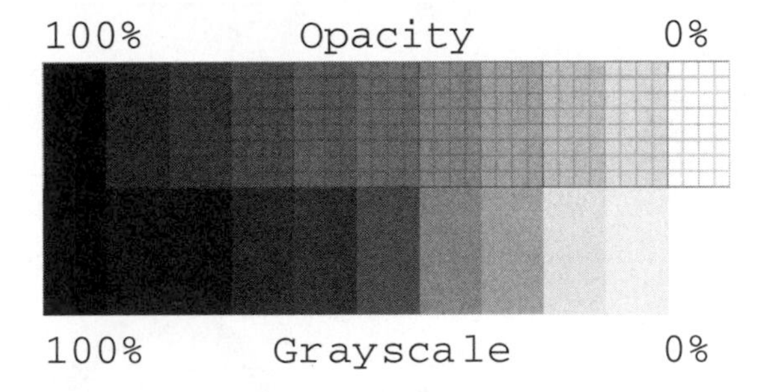


Figure 34.18
Note that the grid is not visible behind the color value swatches.

In addition, observe in Figure 34.19 that only in a couple of these cases do grayscale tint and opacity produce comparable appearances at comparable values.

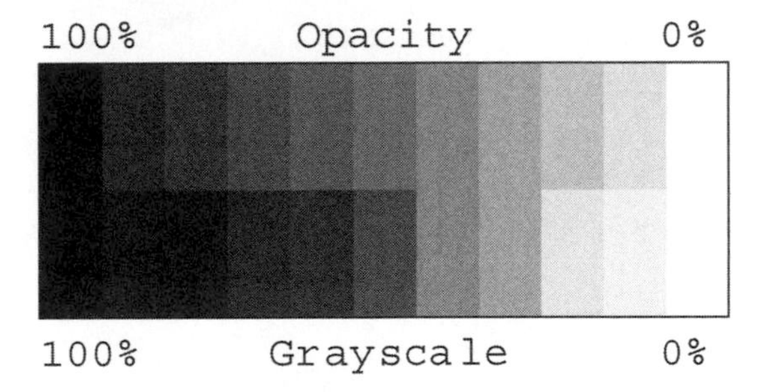


Figure 34.19
You can see that 100%, 40%, and 0% (invisible at the right end of the bars) produce comparable appearance for both grayscale and opacity using the current color settings.

Opacity allows objects to interact in ways that are difficult (but not impossible) to reproduce. For example, in Figure 34.20, a single rectangle with an opacity of 50% overlaps several objects of different colors and different opacities. At the top, several objects are selected. Below, you can see how many objects it would take to re-create this look without opacity. Each individual object would be filled with a specific blend of the two colors to simulate the overlap.

The grayscale "matches" illustrated here are examples. Your choices in the Color Settings dialog box will determine how Illustrator displays color. In this example, the monitor profile is selected for RGB and the CMYK working space is ColorSync.

34

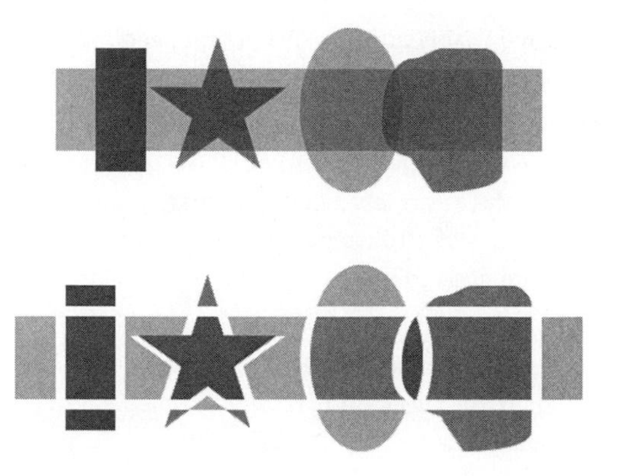

Figure 34.20
One object using opacity to overlap four other objects requires 19 separate objects to re-create without opacity.

Bear in mind that the example shown in Figure 34.20 is actually very simplistic. All the objects have simple, one-color fills and are unstroked. Adding strokes or complex fills greatly increases the difficulty of simulating transparency.

The division of overlapping objects into discrete components (as shown in Figure 34.20) is related to the way Illustrator prepares transparency for printing to both PostScript and non-PostScript printers. (This subject is discussed in more detail later in this chapter.)

Transparency works by calculating the effect of the two or more superimposed images upon each other. You can alter this interaction by changing an object's *blending mode*. Changing the blending mode, discussed in depth later in this chapter, alters the way two or more colors are calculated as they overlap.

## The Transparency Palette

The primary way to control transparency in Illustrator is to use the Transparency palette. The palette allows you to specify a percentage of opacity, blending mode, and several other variables. You can expand or reduce the palette, shown in Figure 34.21, by clicking its tab to cycle through the views. This figure shows it fully expanded, with the palette menu showing.

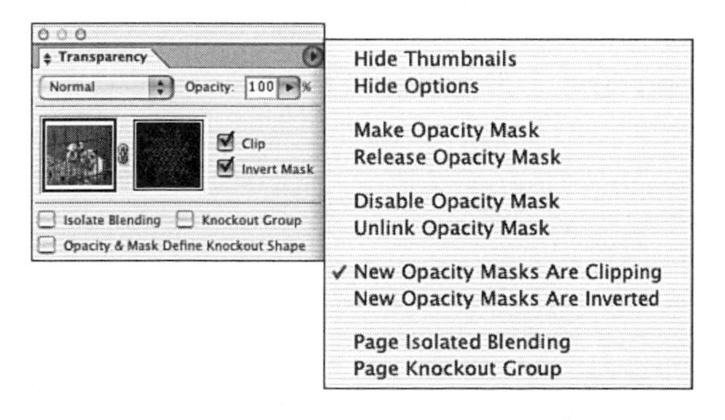


Figure 34.21
Not all of the palette's menu items will be available at the same time.

34

You can change the transparency of an object selected on the artboard either by typing a new value (default: 100%) or by using the Opacity field's slider. You change the blending mode (default: Normal) by choosing from the pop-up menu. The middle section of the palette controls opacity masks, which are discussed earlier in this chapter. The lower section is used primarily for printing preparation and is discussed later in this chapter.

You also can use the Transparency palette in conjunction with the Layers and Appearance palettes. Using the Layers palette allows you to target a group or layer. Every object created in or pasted into that group or layer then assumes the designated level of transparency. When used with the Appearance palette, multiple fills and/or strokes can be applied to an individual object. Lowered opacity and/or blending modes are used to prevent one fill or stroke from hiding those below.

Transparency can affect groups differently from individual objects. When transparency is applied to individual objects in a group, their opacity is cumulative. When the change is applied to the group as a whole, the opacity affects how the group interacts with objects it overlies, but not how the members of the group affect each other.

Figure 34.22 shows three identical groups. The first group and the individual squares within it all have an opacity of 100%. In the middle, the three squares were selected individually, and their transparency was changed to 70%. Note how they interact with each other. The cumulative opacity in the center almost completely blocks the background. On the right, however, the group was targeted in the Layers palette. The changes affect the group as a whole. The relationship among the squares is consistent, and the group has a uniform level of difference with the background.

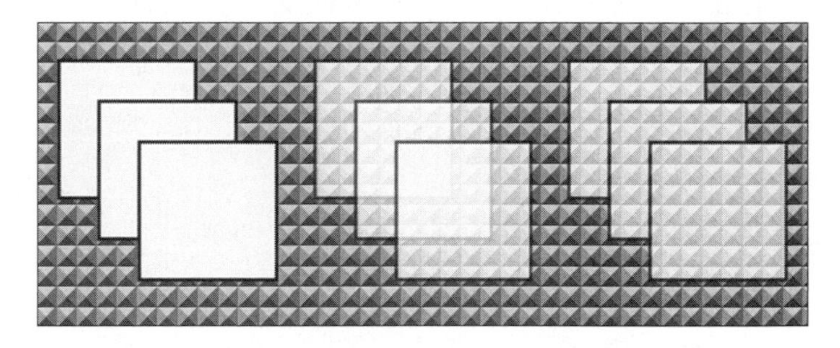

Figure 34.22
Targeting groups for opacity changes can protect the color relationships among the elements of the group.

*Unsure about how group and layer opacity affects objects with opacity values other than 100%? See "Multiple Transparencies" in the "Mastering Illustrator" section at the end of this chapter.*

## Transparency Preferences and Other Settings

Several settings affect transparency in Illustrator. In the Files & Clipboard preferences, for example, you can control how Illustrator handles transparency when copying. The Document Setup dialog box, shown in Figure 34.23, regulates on a document-by-document basis the printing and export of transparency, as well as some interface issues.

The transparency grid, designed to aid visibility of objects with lowered opacity, is controlled with Document Setup, but shown and hidden through the View menu. The command is View, Show Transparency Grid, and the default keyboard shortcut is (Command-Shift-D) [Ctrl+Shift+D]. The transparency grid was visible earlier in this chapter in Figure 34.17 and Figure 34.18.

The transparency grid is not limited to the artboard; it extends across the entire work area. The size of the grid (determined in the Document Setup dialog box) is relative to the screen, not the artboard.

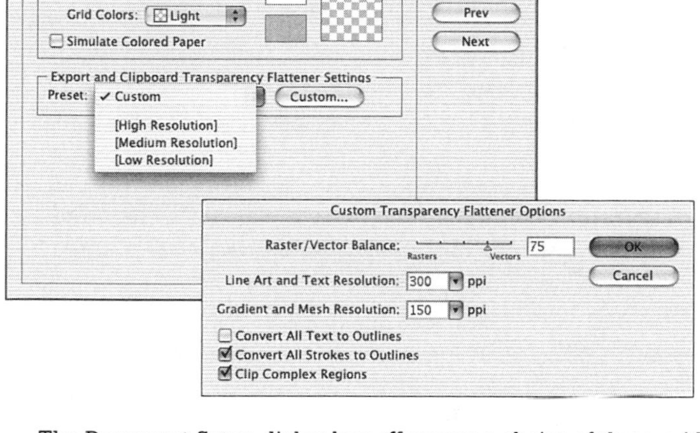


**Figure 34.23**
You access the Document Setup dialog box through the File menu.

The Document Setup dialog box offers you a choice of three grid sizes, as well as three shades of gray and five preset colors. In addition, you can designate your own color for the grid by choosing the Custom option. You can also click either of the two color swatches to open the Color Picker and designate custom color combinations for the grid. The upper swatch controls the background (paper) color, and the lower swatch controls the grid squares themselves.

The Document Setup dialog box also offers the option Simulate Colored Paper. The color for the paper is controlled through the upper swatch in the Document Setup dialog box. Like the transparency grid, the color of the simulated color paper extends throughout the work area and is not limited to the artboard or the page tiling. Also like the transparency grid, it is nonprinting.

*Wondering what use you might have for simulated color paper? See "Picturing It on Paper" in the "Mastering Illustrator" section at the end of this chapter.*

When you're working with grayscale objects of variable opacity, it's often better to designate a bright color for the grid. When you're working with illustrations that are primarily of a specific hue, using a contrasting color rather than gray for the transparency grid often makes it more effective.

The Export and Clipboard Transparency Flattener Settings area establishes the settings that Illustrator uses when preparing the document for output to a printing device. The pop-up menu offers three preconfigured sets of options and a Custom button. Clicking the button or selecting Custom from the pop-up menu opens the Custom Transparency Flattener Options dialog box, shown in Figure 34.23.

You can click the Raster/Vector Balance slider to choose from five levels of compromise between quality and printing speed, or you can drag the slider to any value in between. What follows are Adobe's descriptions of the five levels of Quality/Speed (from Rasters on the left to Vectors on the right):

**Caution**

Remember that working with the medium or dark gray grid settings can alter the apparent tint of objects with opacity below 100%.

- The entire illustration will be rasterized. Use this setting for printing or exporting very complex illustrations with many transparent objects. Ideal for fast output at low resolution; higher resolution will yield higher quality but increase processing time. Size of saved files or print spool files may be large.
- Maintains simpler vector objects, but rasterizes more complex areas involving transparency. Ideal for artwork with only a few transparent objects. Some printers may yield rough transitions between bordering vector and raster objects and make hairlines appear thicker. Appropriate for low-memory systems.
- Maintains most objects as vector data, but rasterizes very complex transparent regions. Generally the best setting for printing and exporting most illustrations. With some printers, improves transition issues between bordering vector and raster objects.
- Maintains most of the illustration as vectors, rasterizing only extremely complex areas. Produces high-quality output that is generally resolution independent. Higher occurrences of transparent regions will increase processing time. With some printers, improves transition issues between bordering vector and raster objects.
- The entire illustration is printed or exported as vector data, to the greatest extent possible. This produces the highest quality resolution-independent output. Processing of complex illustrations may be very time and memory intensive.

## The Flattener Preview Palette

New in Illustrator CS, the Flattener Preview palette gives you an opportunity to see how your artwork will be prepared for printing by Illustrator. It uses the settings selected in the Document Setup dialog box (discussed in the preceding section). The Flattener Preview palette is shown with its options visible in Figure 34.25.

After making adjustments, you can save the changes as a defined preset and/or send the changes to Document Setup. Both commands are available through the palette's menu. Any presets you save appear in the Document Setup pop-up menu.

The options that have any actual effect on the image as output are the same as those found in the Custom box of Document Setup. (For specific information, see the previous section of this chapter. The options are shown in Figure 34.23.)

> If you create graphics only for the Web and/or non-PostScript devices (such as most inkjet printers), you can ignore Flattener Preview.

### Outputting Transparency

Transparency can be a problem for printing. When two objects with 100% opacity overlap, Illustrator need print only the top object because the lower object is totally obscured. When the upper object has an opacity of less than 100%, or a blending mode other than Normal is applied, additional objects may have to be created from the area of overlap.

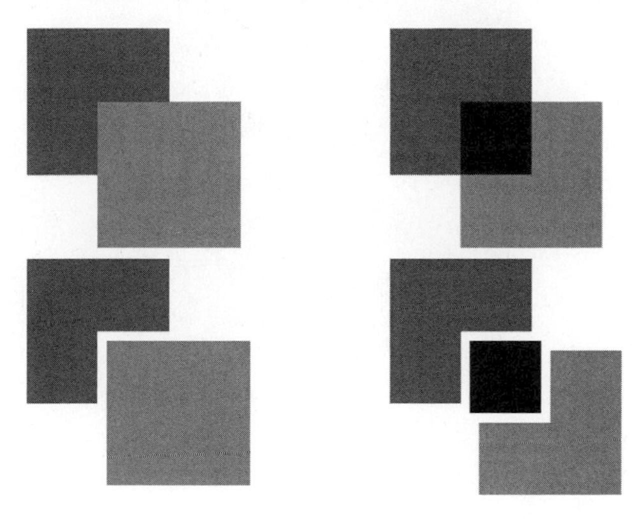

The figures on the top left (Normal blending mode) would be printed as two objects, as shown in the bottom left. The figures on the top right (Multiply blending mode) would be printed as three objects, as shown on the bottom right.

Although the example in the preceding figure seems simple enough, complex illustrations can lead to extremely complex printing problems. Merely adding strokes to the objects in the preceding figure complicates matters. Rather than three separate objects, the number balloons to nine, as you can see in the following figure.

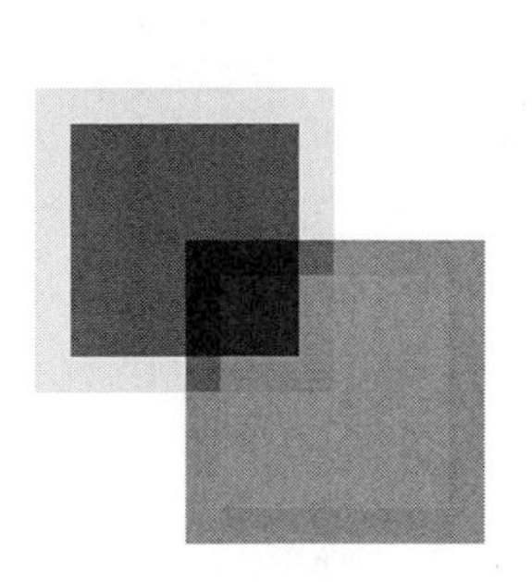

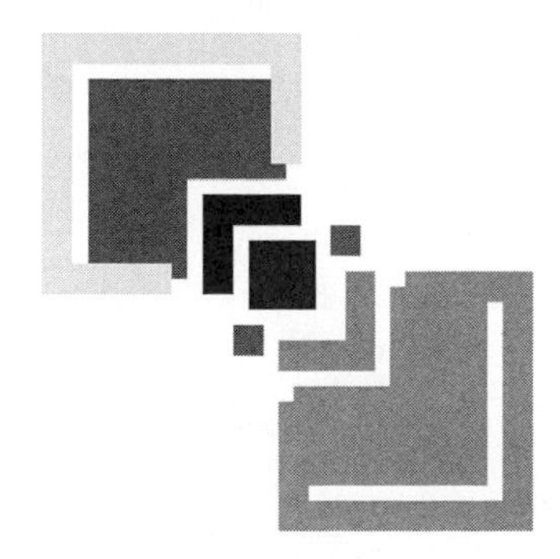

When a lowered opacity or blending mode is used, each area where two colors overlap becomes a separate color.

Adding additional objects and multiple layers of overlap, as well as gradients, can make matters extremely complicated. Figure 34.24 shows an image that requires a great deal of calculation before printing.

Figure 34.24
Every place where a blending mode changes or opacity is reduced results in additional work for printers.

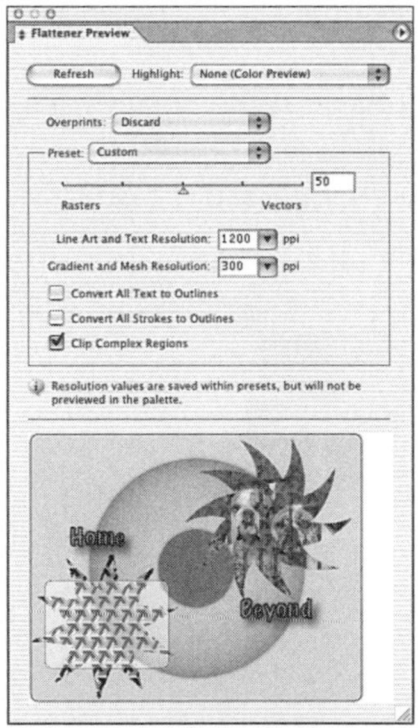


Figure 34.25
The Flattener Preview palette is expanded using the palette menu command Show Options. You can drag the lower-right corner of the palette for a larger preview area.



The Flattener Preview palette also offers a few options that change only the appearance of the preview in the palette. You can elect to discard, simulate, or preserve any overprints in the image. Flattener Preview will also highlight with a red overlay any of a variety of potential problem areas. The Highlight pop-up menu includes Rasterized Complex Regions, Transparent Objects, All Affected [*sic*] Objects, Affected [*sic*] Linked EPS Files, Expanded Patterns, Outlined Strokes, Outlined Text, and, as you saw in Figure 34.25, None.

After making changes in the palette's settings, click the Refresh button to generate a new preview. On extremely complex illustrations, the preview can take a little while.

## Illustrator at Work: Flattener Preview Demo

To get a feel for what the Flattener Preview palette does, how it does it, and whether it's for you, try this:

1. In Illustrator's Open dialog box, navigate to the Illustrator CS folder, to Sample Art, and open the file named Tech Wars.ai.
2. Open Document Setup through the File menu and switch from Artboard to Transparency. In the section Export and Clipboard Transparency Flattener Settings, set the Preset pop-up menu to [High Resolution].
3. Open the Flattener Preview Palette and drag it to the upper-left area of the screen.
4. If they're not showing, display the palette's full range of features with the palette menu command Show Options.
5. Drag the lower-right corner of the palette until it nearly fills the height of your monitor and about half the width. The artboard can be hidden.
6. Click the Refresh button. The preview area should show the artwork in full color. If you see a grayscale image, select None (Color Preview) from the Highlight pop-up menu.
7. Change the Highlight pop-up menu to Outlined Strokes and click Refresh.
8. Move the cursor to the preview area—it will turn into the Zoom tool—and click four times on the highlighted (red) stroke that arcs between the *H* and the *A*. (Wait for the preview to refresh before each click.) Now switch from Outlined Strokes to None (Color Preview).
9. Drag the Raster/Vector slider to the leftmost tick mark, click Refresh, and zoom in again on the same spot.
10. Open some of the other complex images from the Sample Art folder and see if Flattener Preview can help you find areas that would be degraded by using a low setting in Document Setup's Custom Transparency Flattener Options.



# USING BLENDING MODES

Any time two colors overlap, one of two things can happen: The upper color can block the lower completely, or the two colors can interact. Blending modes determine how a color interacts with colors below it. As you can see in Figure 34.26, blending modes are controlled through the Transparency palette.

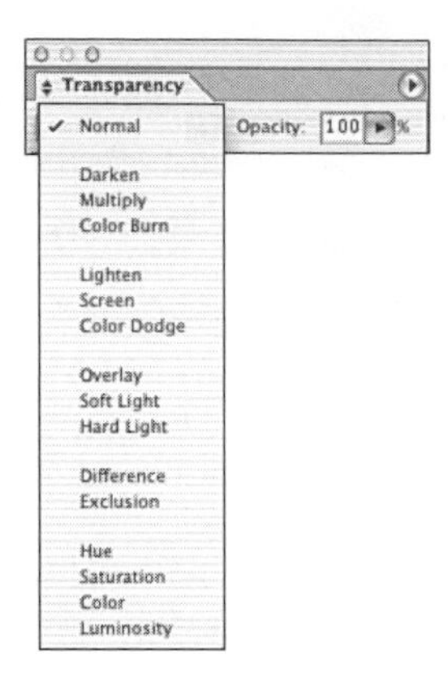


Figure 34.26
Several of the 16 blending modes have near-identical effects on a specific pair of two colors but may have radically different effects on two other colors. Select an object on the artboard or in the Layers palette to change its blending mode.

*Illustrator uses a subset of the blending modes found in Photoshop. For more information on blending modes, see Chapter 18, "Mastering the Blending Modes," p. 585.*

In a discussion of blending modes, Illustrator uses the terms *base color*, *blend color*, and *resulting color*. They are, respectively, the color in back or below, the color in front or above, and the color that results from their interaction.

Here are descriptions of Illustrator's blending modes and how they work with color:

- **Normal**—Normal is the default, and the most common, blending mode. The top color supercedes the bottom color.
- **Multiply**—The Multiply blending mode calculates the color values (RGB or CMYK) of both the top and bottom colors and multiplies them. Because it is a multiplication calculation, the resulting color is always darker than the original top color.
- **Screen**—Screen is, mathematically, the opposite of Multiply. The inverse of each color value is multiplied. The resulting color is always lighter.
- **Overlay**—Overlay serves as a cross between Multiply and Screen. The lower color's values for brightness are retained (highlights and shadows). If the background color is dark, it is multiplied and becomes darker. If it is light, it is screened and becomes lighter. Often a hue shift also occurs.
- **Soft Light**—Soft Light is a mixture of Color Dodge and Color Burn (explained later). If the top color is light, the bottom color is lightened; if dark, the lower color is darkened. The effects of Soft Light are more subtle than many of the other blending modes. Some shifting of hues can be expected.
- **Hard Light**—Although pure black or white is ineffective with the Hard Light blending mode, shades of gray are very effective for adding highlights and shadows to an image. Like some other blending modes, Hard Light acts like Multiply when colors are dark and like Screen with light colors.

34

- **Color Dodge**—*Dodging* is a darkroom technique designed to lighten certain areas of a photograph. When you partially block the light before it reaches the paper, the image in that area is neither as dark nor as saturated. The Color Dodge blending mode is typically used with lighter blending colors. Blending with black produces no change.
- **Color Burn**—Color Burn is the complement to Color Dodge. Whereas dodging is a darkroom technique to lighten parts of an image, burning results in darkening of an image. Blending dark colors over a base color results in darkening. Blending with white produces no change in the lower color.
- **Darken**—The Darken blending mode does a comparison of the upper and lower colors. If the underlying color is lighter than the blending color, it is darkened. If the lower color is already darker than the upper, it is unchanged.
- **Lighten**—The Lighten blending mode is the complement to the Darken blending mode. It determines whether the upper or lower color is lighter and makes changes accordingly. If the lower color is lighter, it is left unchanged. If it is darker, the top color is blended.
- **Difference**—Difference can create among the most dramatic of blending changes. The brightness values of the upper and lower colors are compared and then the color values of the lesser are subtracted from the greater. Because black has a brightness of zero, no change is made. When you're blending with white, expect colors to be inverted.
- **Exclusion**—The results of blending with Exclusion are very similar to, but less dramatic than, those of the Difference blending mode.
- **Hue**—The Hue blending mode uses the saturation and brightness of the lower color and the hue of the upper color.
- **Saturation**—In contrast to the Hue blending mode, Saturation uses the hue and brightness from the lower color and the saturation of the upper color.
- **Color**—The brightness of the lower color is retained in the Color blending mode, and the other two components (hue and saturation) are contributed by the upper color.
- **Luminosity**—Using the brightness of the upper color and the hue and saturation of the lower color, Luminosity is the reverse of the Color blending mode.

The last four blending modes—Hue, Saturation, Color, and Luminosity—take HSB values from either the lower or upper color to create the resulting color. (Remember that Illustrator refers to the upper color as the blending color and the lower color as the base color.) Table 34.1 simplifies the equation for you.

The Hue, Saturation, Color, and Luminosity blending modes do not work with spot colors. Convert both upper and lower spot colors to process colors before applying these blending modes.

34

**Table 34.1** Blending Modes

| Blending Mode | H | S | B |
|---|---|---|---|
| Hue | Upper | Lower | Lower |
| Saturation | Lower | Upper | Lower |
| Color | Upper | Upper | Lower |
| Luminosity | Lower | Lower | Upper |

## Restricting the Effects of Blending Modes

Unless you specify otherwise, an object's blending mode affects its interaction with all colors below it. In the Transparency palette, you can choose the option Isolate Blending. When this option is checked, the interaction of colors created by a blending mode is constrained to a group. As you can see in Figure 34.27, you can have members of a group interact with all colors below (left) or restrict the blending to the group itself (right).

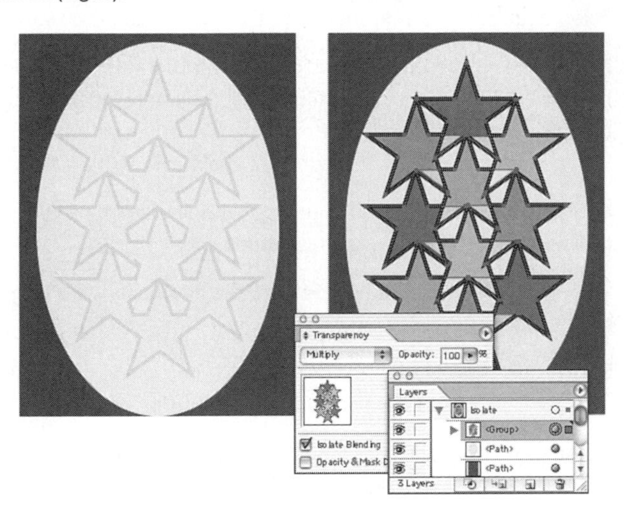


Figure 34.27
The stars on both the left and right have the blending mode Multiply. On the left, the stars are blended with each other and with the oval and rectangle below. On the right, with Isolate Blending checked, the stars blend only with each other.



# MASTERING ILLUSTRATOR

## Clipping Creation Conflicts

*I can't seem to create a clipping mask. What could I be doing wrong?*

First, make sure you have both (or all) objects selected. Second, make sure the path to be used for clipping is on top. Third, remember that the clipping mask cannot be made from a raster or gradient mesh object.

## Protecting Editable Type

*I can't print, yet I can't rasterize my clipping set. I'll need to change the text later. Suggestions?*

Elementary. Make a copy of the file, rasterize the clipping set in the copy so that it will print, and keep the original for future editing. Assuming you have the storage space, it's a good idea to save a copy of any image with its vector art before rasterizing any artwork.

## Clarifying Opacity

*I don't understand how opacity masks work. I see the examples and think they are something I want to use, but I just don't get the concept.*

Opacity masks are based on the masking object's *luminosity*. Luminosity is the lightness value of a given color. Using the Hue-Saturation-Brightness (HSB) color model (also known as Hue-Saturation-Lightness), you can break down any given color into three values. Hue is the color, saturation is the purity or the amount of gray in the color, and brightness (lightness) is the relative darkness or brightness of the color. (Color theory is explained in depth in Chapter 5, "Color, in Theory and in Practice.")

Opacity masks look only at the lightness/brightness value of the color. By default, the darker the color's lightness/brightness, the more transparent the resulting image will be in that area. (You can, of course, reverse this by selecting the Invert Mask option in the Transparency palette.)

In other words, the actual color of the mask is ignored. The transparency applied to the object or image below is based strictly on the lightness or brightness of the mask.

## Two Terms, One Concept

*What exactly is the difference between opacity and transparency?*

Opacity is the way you measure transparency in Illustrator. An object through which you can see other objects below it on the artboard is said to be transparent. *How* transparent is a question of opacity. Using the Transparency palette's slider, you can assign an opacity of 0% to 100% to an object. In this respect, transparency and opacity are opposites; an object that has a 75% opacity setting is 25% transparent.

Don't forget, too, that there's more to transparency than just opacity. An object with an opacity of 100% can still be partially or fully transparent, depending on its blending mode and the interaction of its fill and stroke with colors below. In addition, an object with an opacity of 100% is still fully transparent if the fill and stroke are both None.

## Multiple Transparencies

*What happens if an object with, say, 75% opacity is moved to a layer that has, say, 50% opacity? Which takes precedence?*

You could say that neither takes precedence. The effects are cumulative. Therefore, the object no longer is 75% opaque, nor is it 50% opaque. Its opacity is $50 \times .75 = 37.5\%$.

## Picturing It On Paper

*Why would I want to use the Simulate Paper setting?*

Not all projects are printed on white paper. Remember that inks are not truly opaque and that the color of the paper shows through. When you're printing on bright white stock, coated or uncoated, this is not a particular problem. This option allows you to see what your illustration will look like as it goes to print on colored stock. It can also be very valuable when you're preparing jobs that will run on white paper of a lower brightness.

35

# ILLUSTRATOR'S EFFECTS AND FILTERS

## IN THIS CHAPTER

# ABOUT FILTERS AND EFFECTS

Filters and effects, in most cases, are simply shortcuts. They do automatically—or with the drag of a slider and the click of a button—what could take hours to do manually. In fact, some filters and effects would be almost impossible to replicate step by step in Illustrator. Illustrator installs, by default, nearly 140 filters and effects.

This chapter looks at the difference between effects and filters and examines each of the commands and their capabilities.

## What They Do and How They Do It

Most of the filters and effects in Illustrator work in one of two ways. They either manipulate the appearance of an object by changing the way its path looks, or they alter the appearance by rasterizing and manipulating pixels. (Some do both, and therefore fall outside these general statements.) The difference can be categorized as similar to the difference between vector and raster artwork. One works with paths; one works with pixels. (And one set of effects is for use strictly with scalable vector graphics files.)

An example of a path-manipulation effect/filter is shown in Figure 35.1.

Figure 35.1
The original object is on the left; the Pucker & Bloat filter/effect has been applied on the right.

In Figure 35.2, two raster-based effects have been applied to the same object.

*Filter grayed out and unavailable? See "Circumventing the Unavailable Filter" in the "Mastering Illustrator" section at the end of this chapter.*

Most filters and effects parallel one another; the same appearance can be generated by a filter and its effect counterpart. However, some filters are not duplicated by effects, and some effects do not have comparable filters.

> Some of Illustrator's "raster" filters and effects are not available for use with CMYK images. All can be used with both RGB and Grayscale images. Because these raster filters and effects work by manipulating the color information, the difference between RGB's three color channels and CMYK's four color channels presents a barrier.

## Filters Versus Effects

The primary difference between filters and effects is permanence. When applied as a filter, a change to an object's appearance can only be reversed with the Undo command. When altered with an effect, the object's appearance can be restored; changes to the effect can be made at any time. The effect does not actually alter the object; it just changes the appearance. Filters, on the other hand, do make changes to the object itself.

**Figure 35.2**
On the left, the effect Brush Strokes, Spatter has been applied. On the right, the effect is a Gaussian Blur.

In Figure 35.3, the original object is seen on the left. In the center, the Pucker & Bloat filter has been applied. On the right, the Pucker & Bloat effect has been used. Observe the difference among the paths.

**Figure 35.3**
When an effect is applied, the object's path is unchanged. A filter, however, changes the path to match the new shape.

The object in the middle has a different path from those two either side. The original object has the path with which all three objects were created. The object that has an effect applied (on the right) retains that original path, although the appearance is changed. In the center, the filter has changed the path to match the appearance.

The same Pucker & Bloat effect was applied to three more identical objects to show how effects maintain the original object. In Figure 35.4, all three objects had the same effect applied. On the left, the effect is unaltered (for reference). In the center, the effect was removed using the Appearance palette. On the right, the Direct Selection tool was used to alter the object's path. Notice how the effect was updated to match the change in the object's path. (Dragging an anchor point with the Direct Selection tool is, of course, a permanent change to the path and not an effect.)

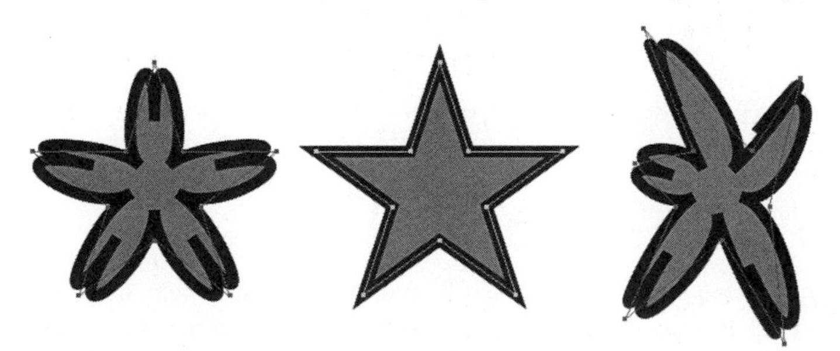

**Figure 35.4**
If the Pucker & Bloat filter had been used instead of the effect, you would have to manipulate the puckered path.

## "Live" Effects

We often use the term *live* when referring to effects in Illustrator. This simply means that an effect can be removed or its settings altered at any time. Many of Illustrator's other capabilities can also be considered live. Strokes, fills, and even styles can be applied and removed at will. Compound paths and crop marks can be made and released. Type can be edited. (Consider, if you will, how much more difficult working with type would be if it were not live. To make a simple change of a word or to apply kerning would require resetting an entire text block.)

On the other hand, many of the things we do in Illustrator are not live. If you use the Direct Selection tool to drag an object's anchor point, that point can be restored to its original position with the Undo command or by dragging it back. If you close and reopen the file, Undo is not available. Trying to put an anchor point back to exactly the same spot later could prove to be an exercise in frustration. Likewise, the Liquify tools are not live, nor is the simple process of deleting an object. (The "live" equivalent of deleting an object would be to hide it using the Layers palette's visibility column.)

One of the keys to working with the concept of live in Illustrator is the Appearance palette. When an effect (not a filter) has been applied to an object, you can reopen the effect dialog box and change the settings. Simply double-click the effect in the Appearance palette (see Figure 35.5). Likewise, you can use the Appearance palette to remove an effect from the object by dragging it to the trash icon at the bottom of the palette.

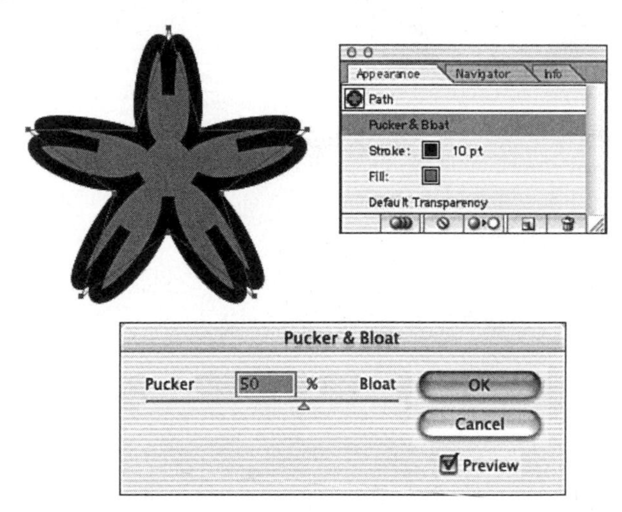


Figure 35.5
The Appearance palette allows you to change or remove an effect.

Remember, too, that effects can be applied to only a stroke or a fill. In the Appearance palette, you click a stroke or a fill and *then* apply the effect (see Figure 35.6).



## Why Use Filters?

The advantages of using an editable effect rather than a permanent filter are obvious. It's usually a good idea to protect the original artwork as much as possible, just in case you need to make changes from an earlier state. However, there are several situations in which a filter is preferable to its effect counterpart:

- Images with filters applied rather than effects can be substantially smaller.
- Using a filter rather than an effect minimizes the chance that artwork will be inadvertently altered.
- If the file will be saved in an earlier version of Illustrator or exported as a raster image, the advantages of live effects will be lost.
- Additional editing of a path may require that a filter be applied to make permanent changes first. In some cases, the fact that an effect retains the original path can limit additional editing.

> Keep in mind that you can duplicate an object before applying a filter and then hide the copy by turning off its visibility in the Layers palette. Should you later need to return to the prefiltered object, it's right there—delete the filtered original and simply show the unfiltered copy.

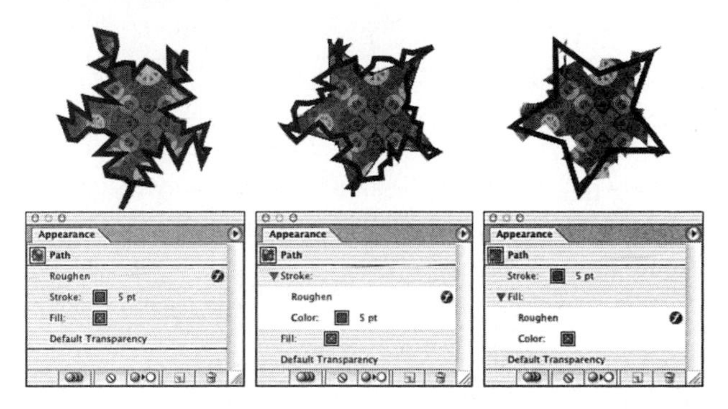


**Figure 35.6**
**As these Appearance palettes show, the Roughen filter has been applied to (starting on the left) the object, the object's stroke only, and the object's fill only.**

# ILLUSTRATOR'S FILTER AND EFFECT MENUS

Filters and effects fall into two categories: those applied to vector (Illustrator) objects and those applied to rasterized artwork. At the top of each menu are a couple commands that allow you to quickly reapply a filter or effect. The Effect menu also has a command that governs rasterization. The remainder of the two menus are divided into two sections. Generally, the commands located in the middle section of the menus are for vector, whereas those in the lower parts are raster filters (see Figure 35.7). Such filters as Drop Shadow can be applied to both vector and rasterized artwork.

> In the descriptions that follow you'll see notations about whether particular capabilities are available as filters, effects, or both. In addition, any differences in the behavior or interface between filter and effect versions will be noted.

*Want to remove an effect but forgot how? See "Back to Normal" in the "Mastering Illustrator" section at the end of this chapter.*

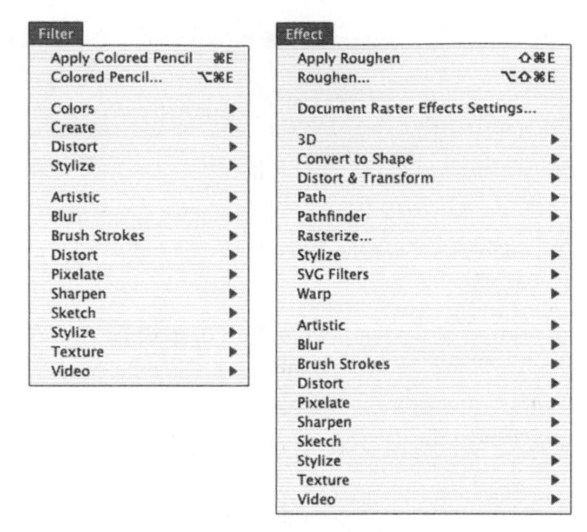


**Figure 35.7**
The top two commands in each menu are available only after a filter or effect has already been applied.

# THE TOP OF THE MENUS

At the top of the Filter menu, you'll find a pair of commands that make reapplying the last filter quick and easy. The upper portion of the Effect menu has comparable commands, as well as one that controls how effects are rasterized.

## Apply Last Filter/Apply Last Effect

When a filter has been applied, the first command in the Filter menu shows its name. Likewise, when an effect has been applied, it will show in the top command of the Effect menu. Using the Apply Last Filter/Apply Last Effect command reapplies the filter or effect, with whatever settings were last used, to the current selection.

## Last Filter/Last Effect

When a filter or effect has been applied, its name is shown in this spot. Using the Last Filter/Last Effect command opens that command's dialog box. It will not be applied until you have had a chance to make any changes and have clicked the OK button.

## Document Raster Effects Settings (Effect Only)

These settings, shown in Figure 35.8, determine how Illustrator will work with objects when applying certain effects. With some commands, objects must take on a rasterized appearance. Such effects as glows and drop shadows are raster themselves. Screen resolution (72ppi) is appropriate for Web graphics and other low-resolution work. Higher resolutions should be reserved for print. Note the field at the bottom, used to add empty space (called *whitespace*) around the object being rasterized. If you want the object alone, enter **0** in this field.

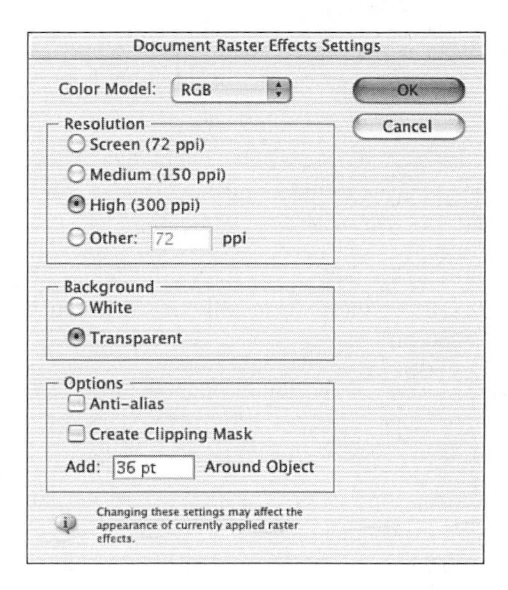


**Figure 35.8**
These settings affect existing effects as well as those applied later.

# THE MIDDLE OF THE MENUS—VECTOR

The filters and effects listed in the middle of the menus are, as mentioned previously, designed for use primarily with vector objects.

## Colors (Filter Only)

The following set of filters works with one or more selected objects. The object's stroke color or fill color (or both) can be adjusted, depending on the specific filter selected:

- **Adjust Colors (filter)**—This command's dialog box uses sliders to change the percentage of each component color in an object (see Figure 35.9). The object can be converted between the document's color mode and grayscale, but not between RGB and CMYK. (Illustrator supports objects of only one color mode per document.) The changes can be applied to the object's fill or stroke. Tints can also be adjusted. Adjust Colors can be used with both vector and raster objects.

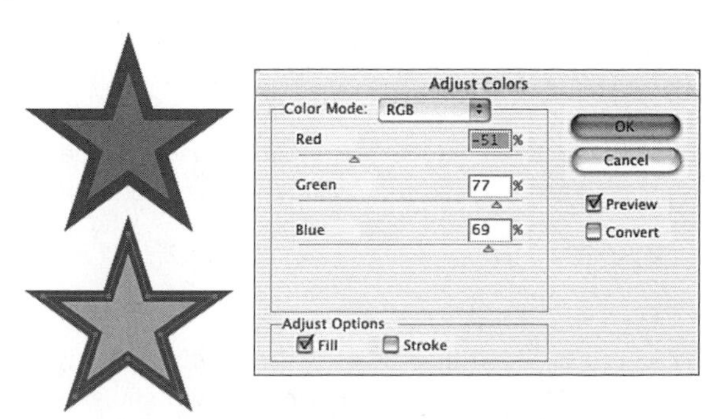


**Figure 35.9**
You have the option of adjusting the fill, the stroke, or both. In this example, the lower object's fill is being modified.

- **Blend Front to Back (filter)**—Working with three or more objects, this filter creates intermediate colors in the objects between the front and rear objects. It works only on fills, ignoring all strokes and fills of None.
- **Blend Horizontally (filter)**—Like the other Blend filters, this one works with three or more objects, changing those in the middle to intermediate shades and tints. As the name implies, stacking order is ignored over placement from left to right.
- **Blend Vertically (filter)**—Like the other Blend filters, this one works with three or more objects, changing those in the middle to compromise shades and tints. As the name implies, stacking order is ignored over placement from top to bottom.
- **Convert to CMYK (filter)**—Available only for documents in CMYK mode, this command can bring grayscale objects into the CMYK gamut. However, the color value is still gray. Convert to CMYK can be used with both vector and raster objects.
- **Convert to Grayscale (filter)**—Any selected objects, regardless of the document's color mode, are converted to grayscale. After you execute this command, you can reverse it only by choosing Undo. Using a command to convert back to RGB or CMYK produces an image in the correct color mode but does not restore the former colors. Gradients and patterns cannot be converted to grayscale with this command. Convert to Grayscale can be used with both vector and raster objects.
- **Convert to RGB (filter)**—This command is grayed out when a CMYK document is active. In RGB documents, it can change the color space of a grayscale object to RGB, although it does not change the actual colors of the fill and stroke. Convert to RGB can be used with both vector and raster objects.
- **Invert Colors (filter)**—When you use this command, you should have the Color palette visible. You'll see the sliders for each value jump to positions opposite their original spots. Invert Colors can be applied to RGB, CMYK, or grayscale images. Each color changes to its opposite on the color wheel. Invert Colors can be used with both vector and raster objects.
- **Overprint Black (filter)**—Overprinting determines how overlapping colors are printed. This command works with selected objects to determine how black ink will be applied. Note that the selected objects must create black through the K color value to be able to overprint it; any black created by mixing CMY or through transparency is not affected with this command.
- **Saturate (filter)**—The vibrancy of a color can be adjusted with this command. Most colors can be lightened by reducing the saturation. You cannot adjust patterns and gradients with this command, however. Although grayscale objects are already completely desaturated, Illustrator adjusts their brightness levels when you use this command on them.



## 3D (Effect Only)

Perhaps the most hyped new feature in Illustrator CS is the 3D effect. Certainly showy, and definitely something new, its usefulness depends on your creative bent. If you already work with 3D, you likely have a fully featured, more robust program on hand. If you're just starting to experiment with 3D, you may find this effect hard to use. If you keep working with it and learn to control it, you may find yourself wishing for some fully featured, more robust 3D program.

For those who want to occasionally add a three-dimensional object to an illustration, or perhaps need to show packaging in context to a client now and then, or for those who might find it useful to rotate a two-dimensional object rather than using the Transform commands, the 3D effect is a welcome addition.

Illustrator's 3D offers three effects: Extrude & Bevel, Revolve, and Rotate. Each does a different job, but their dialog boxes share several features. Their various options are shown in Figure 35.10.

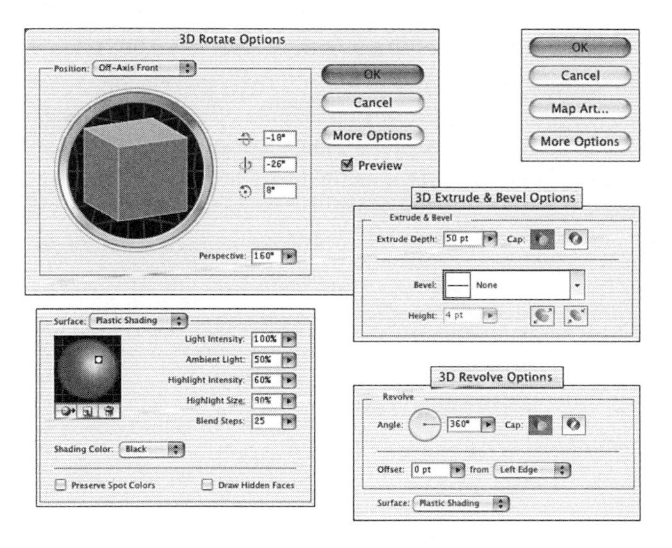


**Figure 35.10**
All three dialog boxes share the options shown for 3D Rotate Options. 3D Extrude & Bevel Options and 3D Revolve Options share the lighting options shown; 3D Rotate Options offers only Diffuse Shading with Light Intensity and Ambient Light options. Map Art is also not available with 3D Rotate Options.

*For a look at the 3D effect lighting controls, as well as mapping artwork, see "Illustrator at Work: Creating 3D Objects," later in this chapter, p. 1041.*

You use the top of the dialog box, shown in Figure 35.10 as the 3D Rotate Options dialog box, to position the object, rotating it in three dimensions. 3D Extrude & Bevel Options simply extends the 2D object along the z-axis, adding depth, much like creating a blend between two identical objects. (Imagine extruding a rectangle into a book, with the original rectangle as the cover.) 3D Revolve Options spins the object (or path) around an imaginary line to create a 3D object. (Consider spinning a circle into a ring, with the original circle a cross section of the ring.) You can adjust the lighting that falls on the object with a variety of controls. 3D Rotate Options rotates a two-dimensional object in three dimensions.

> You can use the 3D effects with compound objects, objects using patterns, and objects without fills. You *cannot* use the 3D effects with gradient mesh objects or raster images. You *should not* use the 3D effects with large groups, objects without strokes, and some overly complex objects. Not only will you have incredibly long screen redraw times in most cases, you'll also run the risk of bizarre errors and mistakes in 3D object generation.

The key to working with 3D in Illustrator is rotating an object to present the appearance your illustration requires. There are three primary techniques for changing the rotation of a 3D object:

- You can select 1 of 16 preset angles from the Position pop-up menu.
- You can click the cube-shaped proxy in the Position window and drag.
- You can enter precise values, positive or negative, in the three fields.

The Perspective slider permits up to 160° of offset, simulating lens distortion.

### The Z-Axis

Before looking too closely at the 3D effect, it's a good idea to understand what is meant by the term *three dimensional*. Any object on the artboard with a stroke and/or fill has two dimensions: height and width. (An unstroked path has only length.) Naturally, we refer to height in terms of the top and bottom of the window or screen, and width refers to the distance from right to left. Consider the third dimension to be from the screen of the monitor to the back of the monitor—heading directly away from you as you look at the screen.

Width uses the *x-axis*, height uses the *y-axis*, and depth uses the *z-axis*. Illustrator measures the x-axis and y-axis from the lower-left corner of the window, the default point of origin for the rulers. The z-axis isn't measured in Illustrator but can be considered to be centered on the individual object's place in the Layers palette.

To see how Illustrator measures the z-axis, do this:

1. Create a small filled and stroked circle in the middle of your artboard.
2. Select Effect, 3D, Extrude & Bevel.
3. In the dialog box, select Top from the Position pop-up menu and check the Preview box. You'll be looking "straight down" at the top of the 3D object.
4. Increase the Extrude Depth by dragging the slider to the right. The object becomes longer in the z-axis (now running up and down onscreen because you're viewing it from above).

Because the additional length is centered on the object's path, we can consider Illustrator to be measuring the z-axis equally in both directions from the path. However, rather than the artboard being the 0-point of the z-axis, it's actually the *object's position in the stacking order*. No matter how much longer an object is than another object above it in the Layers palette, the lower object will never overlap the object above it. Likewise, a longer object will never overlap another object below it in the stacking order.

Illustrator's other 3D effects are explained in the following list:

- **3D Extrude & Bevel (effect)**—*Extruding* a two-dimensional object adds the third dimension, depth. You can consider it to be stretching an object from front to back. *Bevel* options determine how the effect handles the edges of the object. The 3D Extrude & Bevel Options dialog box is shown in Figure 35.11, along with some examples of its work.

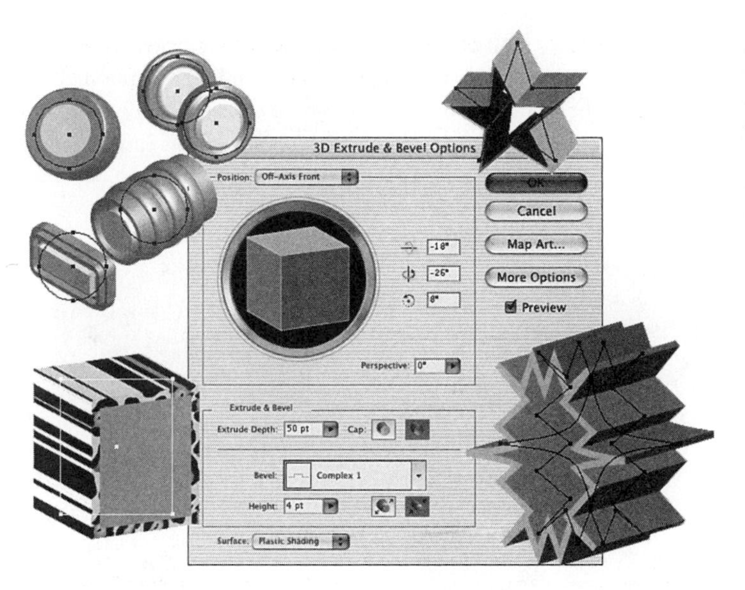


**Figure 35.11**
**Clicking the More Options button opens the advanced lighting section of the dialog box, shown in Figure 35.10. Advanced Lighting is discussed in the section "Illustrator at Work: Creating 3D Objects," later in this chapter.**

Here's what you're seeing in Figure 35.11's sample objects:

- **Upper left**—As you can see from the paths, each of these objects is a circle. There are several different bevel styles. One example shows that 3D Extrude & Bevel can be applied successfully to an object that already carries a Convert to Shape effect. Note from the longest round object that the bevel style is applied along the extruded stroke of the object. However, as the preceding button-shaped objects illustrate, the bevel style also has an effect on the fill of the object.
- **Upper right**—The star is extruded with the open Cap option (selected in the dialog box as shown). Consider the *cap* to be the end of the extruded object, whether it's solid (using the fill) or empty. This Cap option produces a hollow 3D object. The fill color "paints" the inside, and the stroke color is used outside. For a single-color object, use the same color for the stroke and fill.
- **Lower left**—This fun appearance comes from extruding an object that uses a pattern for the stroke. Note that the pattern is not applied to the sides of the 3D object, but rather it's stretched backward from the end of the object. Preview and screen redraw times are long when a pattern is extruded.
- **Lower right**—As can be confirmed by the visible path, the object itself is a compound shape, created from two separate paths using the Pathfinder palette. Compound shapes can also be extruded, although they may take some time to generate previews and for screen redraw.

> Although you can create compound shapes (using the Pathfinder palette) from two or more objects to which you've already applied 3D Extrude effects, they will not retain the lighting effects. Attempting to reapply a 3D effect will produce irregularities and long screen-redraw times.

- **3D Revolve (effect)**—This effect creates a 3D object by spinning a selected path or object around an axis. When the object is viewed from the top, you'll see a round or curved object, depending on the Angle setting. The Angle setting determines how far 3D Revolve will revolve the object around the designated axis. An angle of 360° completes the circle. Anything less leaves the 3D object open at one point. Figure 35.12 shows the 3D Revolve dialog box and some examples.

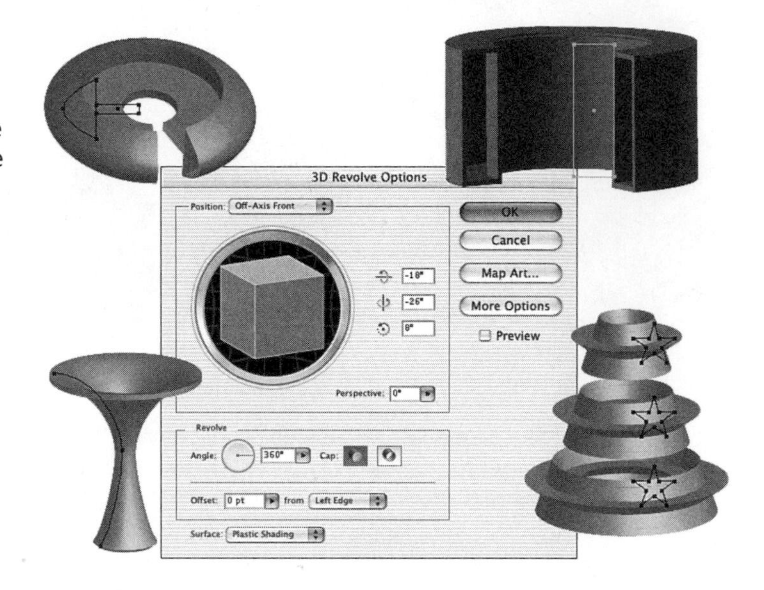


**Figure 35.12**
The upper area of the dialog box and the lighting effects shown with the More Options button are identical to what you'll find in the 3D Extrude & Bevel Options dialog box.

Here are descriptions of the examples shown in Figure 35.12:

- **Upper left**—A compound path is revolved less than 360° (the object is not closed), and the axis of revolution is offset several points from the right edge.
- **Upper right**—A rectangle is rotated, offset less than 360°. It uses the Cap option on the right, creating the appearance of a hollow 3D object.
- **Lower left**—An open path is revolved from the right edge. In addition to using the open Cap option, the object has no fill. If the object had a fill, the 3D appearance would include a solid appearance (of the fill color) between the path's endpoints.
- **Lower right**—The only difference among the three stars is the amount of offset in the 3D Revolve Options dialog box.

> Prior to using the Revolve effect on an open path to create a "solid" 3D object, select the endpoints and use the menu command Object, Path, Average, choosing Vertically. This aligns the points directly above each other, thus avoiding an unwanted gap at the top or bottom of the 3D object.



- **3D Rotate (effect)**—This 3D effect is intended for use with 2D objects. It simply rotates them in three-dimensional space. It uses the same controls seen in the dialog boxes for 3D Extrude & Bevel and 3D Revolve. 3D

Rotate has a simplified light scheme, offering only Diffuse Shading and No Shading. You can read about the lighting controls in the section "Illustrator at Work: Creating 3D Objects," later in this chapter. 3D Rotate does not offer the option Map Art, which is used to place artwork saved as symbols on the surfaces of a 3D object. (Remember that 3D Rotate doesn't create a 3D object; it simply manipulates a 2D object in three dimensions.)

**Caution**

Be aware that Illustrator files containing 3D effects get very large, very fast. The file containing just the four examples in Figure 35.12 is over 7MB (likewise for the single AI file containing the examples for Figure 35.11).

## Illustrator at Work: Creating 3D Objects

Although Illustrator's 3D effects may appear to be rather complex, a few minutes of practical hands-on experience will show how basic they really are. Follow these steps:

1. Open a new Illustrator document (800×600 pixels; RGB is fine).
2. Add a rectangle to the artboard, on the left side, that's 250 pixels wide by 300 pixels tall. A light gray fill and a dark gray stroke (5 pixels) are good choices for this project, but you can use any colors. Your artboard should look something like that shown in Figure 35.13.

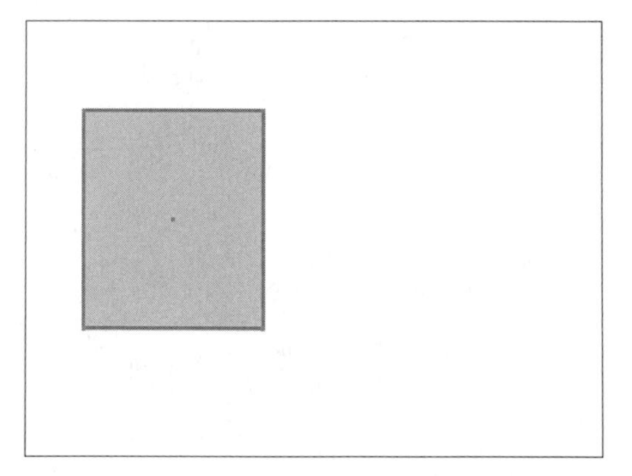

**Figure 35.13**
At this point, the project consists of a single rectangle.

3. Select the menu command Effect, 3D, Extrude & Bevel.
4. In the dialog box, set Position to Off-Axis Front, set Extrude Depth to 125 points, and select the solid Cap option (on the left). Leave the Bevel option set to None and—for now—ignore the lighting options. Your rectangle should now appear to be more of a box-shaped object (see Figure 35.14).
5. If you'd like, you can create your own artwork and define a symbol from it, or you can use one of the symbols supplied with Illustrator. In either case, when the symbol is ready, select your 3D object on the artboard, open the Appearance palette, and double-click the line 3D Extrude & Bevel. (For this example, type was added to the artboard, the New Symbol button was clicked in the Symbols palette, and the type was deleted.)

*For more information on creating and using symbols, see "Symbols and Symbolism for the Web" in Chapter 37, "Illustrator and the Web," p. 1098.*

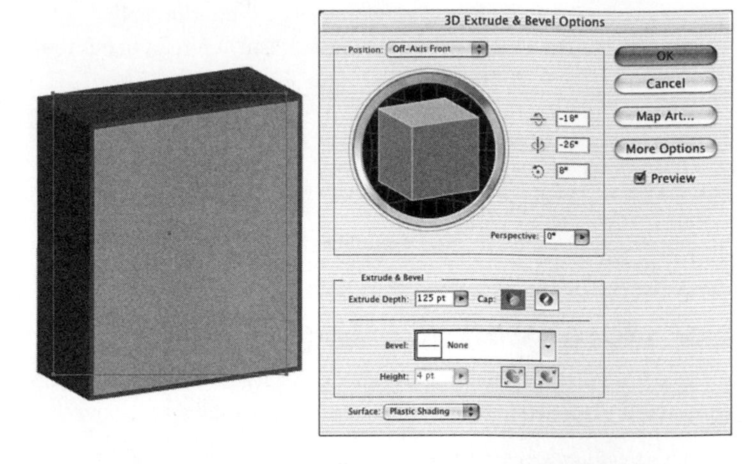


**Figure 35.14**
The settings in the dialog box should match those you used. You can double-click 3D Extrude & Bevel in the Appearance palette to reopen the dialog box to verify or make changes.

6. When the dialog box opens, click the Preview box and then click the button Map Art. The dialog box shown in Figure 35.15 will open. Assign a symbol to the cover of the "box" using the Symbol drop-down palette at the top of the dialog box. The front of the object will be Surface 1 in the dialog box.

7. Experiment with the Scale to Fit and Clear buttons. Take a look at what the Shade Artwork and Invisible Geometry options do to the preview on the artboard.

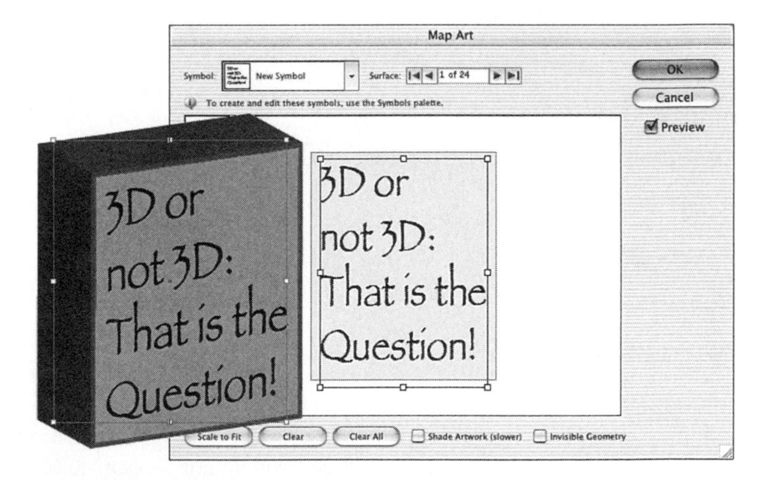


**Figure 35.15**
Even if not visible because of object rotation, the front surface of the 3D object is always Surface 1 in the Map Art dialog box.

8. The active surface of the 3D object will be outlined in red. Continue to click the arrow to the near-left of the Surface field until the left side of the box is active. Assign a symbol. If the symbol doesn't appear, the active surface may have been on the inside of the object. Reassign None to that surface and continue to click the Next Surface button until the correct surface is active (see Figure 35.16).

> The Shade Artwork option in the Map Art dialog box can add significantly to the amount of time it takes to redraw your 3D object, but with complex lighting adjustments, it can greatly improve the appearance of your project.

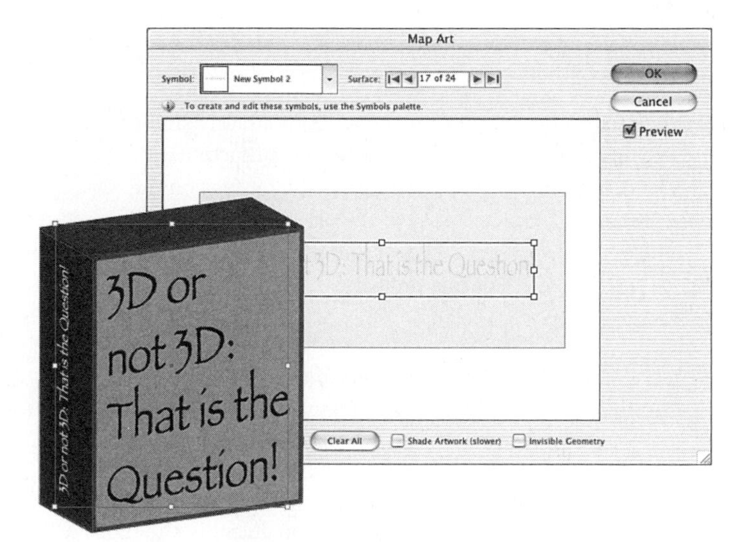


**Figure 35.16**
Of the 24 total (and three visible) surfaces, only two require artwork for this project.

9. Click OK in the Map Art dialog box and again in the 3D Extrude & Bevel Options dialog box to confirm your choices.

10. Reopen the 3D Extrude & Bevel Options dialog box by again double-clicking it in the Appearance palette. Note that the appearance characteristic is now called 3D Extrude & Bevel (Mapped). Click the Preview box so that you can see the changes as they're made.

11. Click the More Options button to expand the lighting controls area of the dialog box. The first thing to experiment with is the Surface pop-up menu. Switch from Plastic Shading to Wireframe. With this option, the individual surfaces and the paths of any mapped artwork are visible (see Figure 35.17, left). Note that no lighting options are available in Wireframe view because there are no surfaces on which to shine. (Likewise, the option No Shading hides the lighting controls.)

12. Switch from Wireframe to Diffuse Shading. Change the Shading Color pop-up menu from Black to Custom. Shading Color determines the color of the object away from the surface upon which your light source is directed. Click the color swatch to the right to open the Color Picker and select a bright yellow. When you close the Color Picker, you'll see how the color of the lighting affects the appearance of the object. Black is the default because Shading Color is most evident in shadow areas.

A rectangle with no stroke that's extruded has six sides on which you can map symbols. Add a stroke, and 3D Extrude & Bevel will find 10 or 18 more "sides," depending on the width of the stroke. Add a complex bevel, and the number of surfaces can soar to well over 100. If you'll be mapping artwork to a 3D object, consider adding the bevel *after* you've added the artwork.

If you're confounded by the number of surfaces 3D effects finds when trying to map artwork, switch to Wireframe and you'll see them all. This trick can also be used to locate mapped artwork on hidden surfaces, which you can then clear in the Map Art dialog box.

(Remember, too, that ambient light, even more than direct light, reduces the amount of shadow or shade on surfaces of your object.)

13. The Light Intensity slider determines the brightness of the "light" that is shining on the object. The higher the value, the less the shade color is apparent on the surface that the light is striking. The Ambient Light slider determines how much additional light falls on the object, including those surfaces away from the light source. Think of this as the light that's competing with your light source—and the higher the Ambient Light setting, the less shade there is on the object and, therefore, the less shade color. For this project, set Light Intensity to 80% and Ambient Light to 30%.

*Confused about the differences—or the slider values—among Light Intensity, Ambient Light, and Shade Color? See "Picking the Right Light," in the "Mastering Illustrator" section at the end of this chapter.*

14. To the left of the Light Intensity and Ambient Light sliders is a proxy area, showing the location of the light source and giving a small preview of the effects. (The object in the proxy is always a sphere.) There are three buttons below the preview. The left button moves the light source behind the object. This is of most value with curved surfaces. The middle button adds an additional light source. (You can add many light sources, but a practical limit is approximately six.) The button on the right deletes the active light source. Click the middle button to add a second light source. Move it to about the 10 o'clock position on the edge of the proxy's sphere and set it to Light Intensity 60%. Now click your first light source to make it the active light and drag it halfway between the center of the sphere and the 3 o'clock position. Your dialog box—and object—should look something like that shown to the right in Figure 35.17. Click OK to close the dialog box.

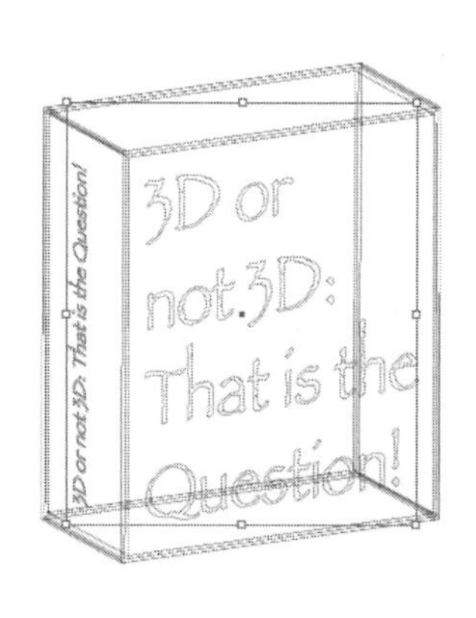


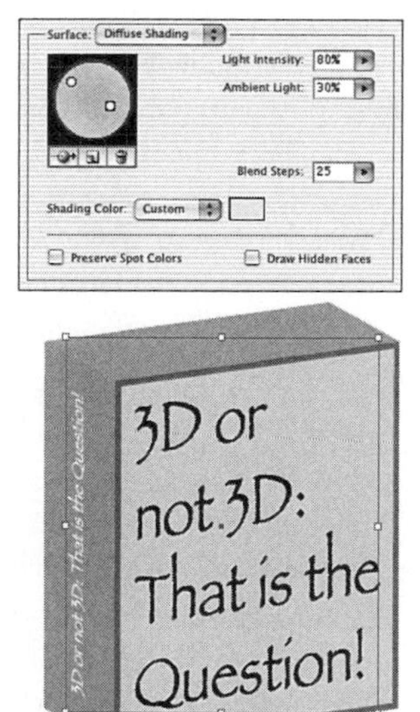


**Figure 35.17**
The Blend Steps value determines the smoothness of the light as it spreads across the object. Higher numbers can result in longer screen redraws and more complicated artwork.

15. Select the Arc tool from the Toolbox and click the artboard. In the Arc Segment Tool Options dialog box, enter 155 points for both Axis fields and click the upper-left box of the four-corner proxy next to the OK button. Use the options Type: Open and Base Along: X Axis, and make the Slope 50% Convex. Do not check the Fill Arc box. Click OK.

16. Set the stroke color to a dark gray and the stroke width to 5 points. Now open Effect, 3D, Revolve. Check the Preview box, set the Position pop-up menu to Off-Axis Front, and increase the Offset to 10 points.

17. Click the More Options button if the lighting controls are not visible in the dialog box. Leave the Surface pop-up menu set to Plastic Shading. (Think of the difference between Plastic Shading and Diffuse Shading as similar to the difference between glossy and matte.) Use the settings Light Intensity: 100%, Ambient Light: 10%, Highlight Intensity: 100%, and Highlight Size: 65%. Increase Blend Steps to 45 to reduce banding along the curved surface. Drag the lighting source to halfway between the sphere's center and the 2 o'clock position. The settings are shown in Figure 35.18 in the upper right.

18. Toward the left, under the lighting proxy, click the New Light button. Now click the button on the left to move the light source "behind" the object. Notice that the light's symbol in the proxy is now black rather than white. Change Light Intensity to 75%. Drag the light source to 10 o'clock and click OK to close the dialog box. These settings are shown in Figure 35.18 in the lower right.

19. In the Layers palette, move the stand below the box object, and use the Selection tool to position it under the box. Your final project should look something like that shown in Figure 35.18.

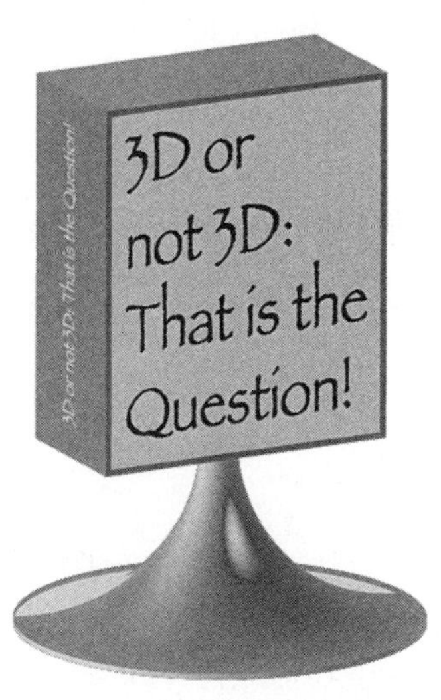


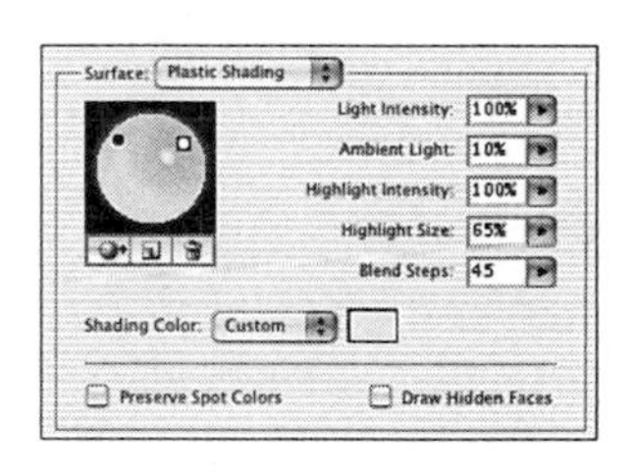


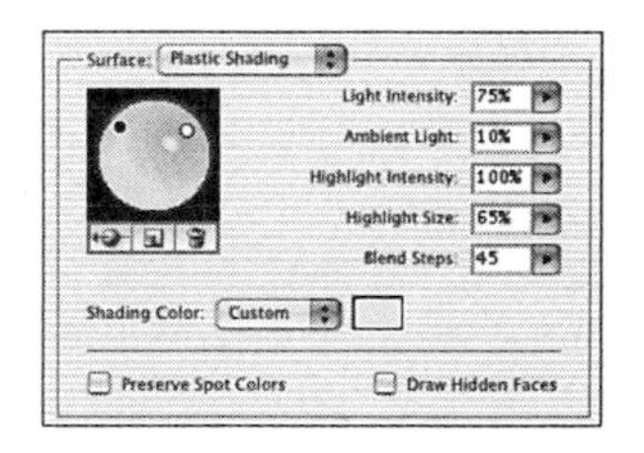


**Figure 35.18**
Normally, two 3D objects in close proximity use similar lighting sources. The difference between the positions of the lighting sources for the objects gives a visual cue to the location of each light relative to the objects.



## Convert to Shape (Effect Only)

The three Convert to Shape commands change a selected path into the selected object. The source path can be open or closed. The commands share a single dialog box with a pop-up menu to select the choice of object (see Figure 35.19).

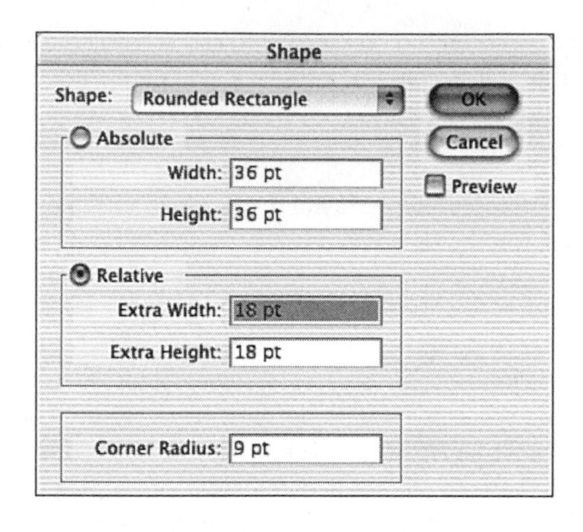


Figure 35.19
The Corner Radius option is available only for conversion to rounded rectangles; otherwise, the dialog box is identical for all three options.

Here are the three Convert to Shape commands:

- **Rectangle (effect)**—A selected path (open or closed) is converted to a rectangle, maintaining the stroke and fill of the original object. An absolute height and width can be assigned, or the resulting object's dimensions can be expressed relative to the source path's size.
- **Rounded Rectangle (effect)**—A selected path (open or closed) is converted to a rounded rectangle, maintaining the stroke and fill of the original object. An absolute height and width can be assigned, or the resulting object's dimensions can be expressed relative to the source path's size. The radius of the corners can be determined in the dialog box.
- **Ellipse (effect)**—A selected path (open or closed) is converted to an oval or circle, maintaining the stroke and fill of the original object. An absolute height and width can be assigned, or the resulting object's dimensions can be expressed relative to the source path's size.

When Convert to Shape is used, the object retains its original path and appearance characteristics, such as stroke and fill. If you use the Direct Selection tool to move any anchor point, the nearest edge of the effect-created object will move, but the object retains the assigned appearance.

## Create (Filter Only)

There are a pair of Create commands, one of which is production oriented and one of which is creative in nature:

- **Crop Marks (filter)**—The Crop Marks filter adds a set of crop marks around the selected object or objects. Like the Trim Marks filter in previous versions of Illustrator, you can use this command to create separate sets of marks around as many objects as you'd like on the artboard. Each set of marks is a group of eight short, straight path segments. This filter is nondestructive—the selected artwork remains undisturbed on the artboard. Contrast this behavior with that of the command

The 3D effect's lighting controls allow only one Highlight Intensity value and Highlight Size value per object, just as you can have only one Ambient Light value per object. Each light to the *front* of an object can have its own highlight. Highlights for lights *behind* an object are generally not seen.

Object, Crop Area, Make, which converts a selected rectangle to the crop marks, removing the rectangle unless the Crop Area, Release command is used. In addition, when you use the Object menu to create a crop area, you're restricted to a single set of uneditable marks.

- **Object Mosaic (filter)**—Working with placed raster images or rasterized vector art, this filter creates blocks of color that approximate the colors in the raster image. The blocks are vector objects. The Object Mosaic dialog box, shown in Figure 35.20, allows you to control the resulting size of the object, the number of tiles and the spacing between them, and whether the original object is deleted. The button Use Ratio works with the Constrain Ratio option to adjust the Number of Tiles fields to proper proportions.

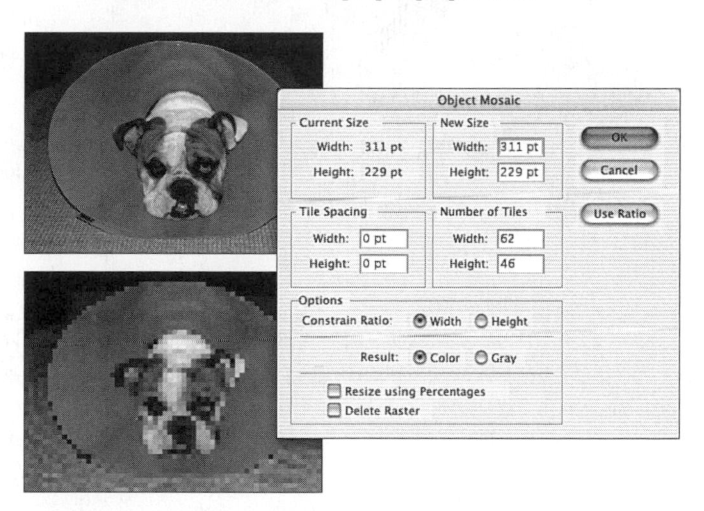


**Figure 35.20**
The upper figure is the original. The lower figure was created using the settings shown. It is a series of small vector rectangles, grouped together.

# Distort/Distort & Transform (Filter/Effect)

Under the Filter menu, these capabilities are listed under Distort. Under the Effect menu, you'll see Distort & Transform. The difference is that Transform is available only as an effect; the distortions are available as both filters and effects:

- **Free Distort (filter/effect)**—This command allows you to manipulate an object in two dimensions. The dialog box provides a preview and a Reset button for experimentation (see Figure 35.21).

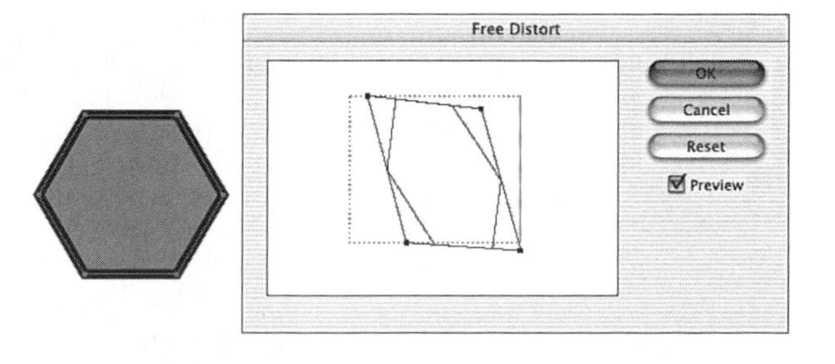


**Figure 35.21**
The Preview check box allows you to see an outline of the image in the dialog box rather than a live preview on the artboard. If the box is unchecked, only the bounding box is represented.

- **Pucker & Bloat (filter/effect)**—Puckering takes a vector object's existing anchor points and drags them outward, creating corner points and sharp extensions. Bloating, in contrast, drags existing anchor points inward, creating extensions from the original object that are smooth. In the Pucker & Bloat dialog box, shown in Figure 35.22, you can set a slider that ranges from extreme puckering (–200%) to extreme bloating (+200%). A Preview check box allows you to track your work.

Figure 35.22
The original object is in the center. To the left, it is shown after a Pucker distortion of –40%. To the right is a 40% Bloat.

- **Roughen (filter/effect)**—Points are added to a path according to a number of settings selected in the Roughen dialog box, shown in Figure 35.23. Size determines the amount of change (relative or absolute), Detail controls the number of anchor points added, and Points can be either smooth or corner points.

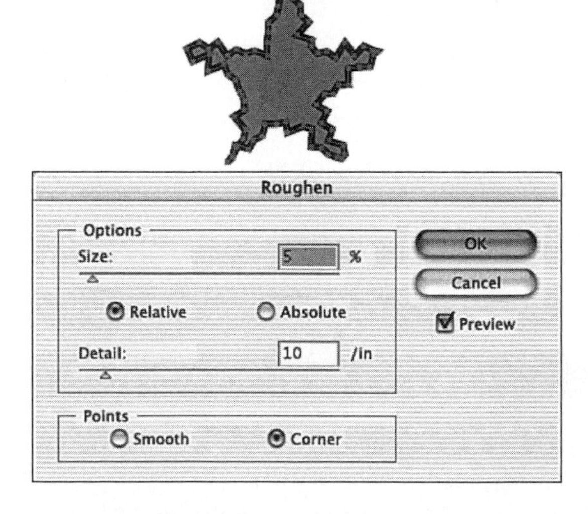


Figure 35.23
The original object was a star, with a total of 10 anchor points.

- **Transform (effect only)**—This command allows you to transform an object as an effect. The dialog box offers scaling, moving, reflecting, and rotating. In addition, you can make up to 360 copies of an object, each transformed by the amount and value you assign. The Transform

Effect dialog box, shown in Figure 35.24, is identical to the Transform Each dialog box, opened by the menu command Object, Transform, Transform Each. Consider Transform Each to be the filter version of this effect.

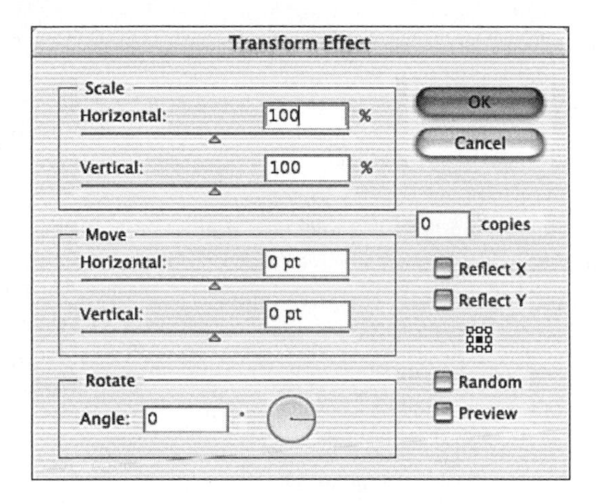


Figure 35.24
Transforming as an effect allows you to retain the object's original path.

- **Tweak (filter/effect)**—This dialog box allows you to distort existing anchor points in both the vertical and horizontal, either relative or absolute. The dialog box, shown in Figure 35.25, also allows you to apply the changes to anchor points, control points, or both.

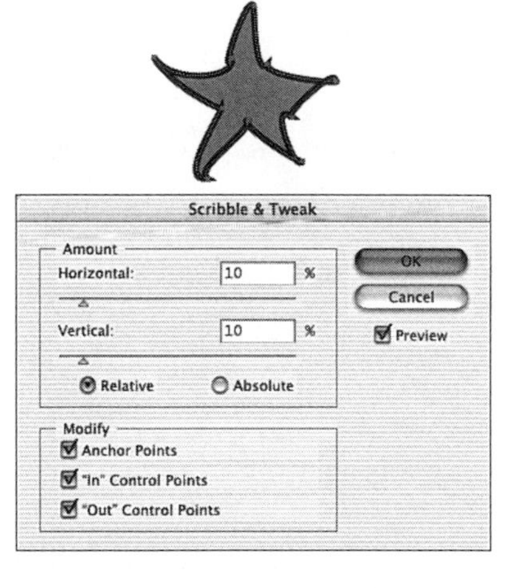


Figure 35.25
If Relative is selected, the amounts are measured in percents; for Absolute, they are listed in the unit of measure specified in the preferences.

- **Twist (filter/effect)**—This command distorts an object according to the angle (degrees) input. Additional anchor points are added as needed. The Twist command offers no preview. Consider using the Twist tool instead.
- **Zig Zag (filter/effect)**—Points are added to each segment of a path according to Ridges per Segment. The distance each point varies from the original path is governed by Size, which can be measured relatively or absolutely. The added points can be smooth or corner anchor points. This filter can turn a circle into a star (corner) and a star into a puddle (smooth). See Figure 35.26 for an example.

## Path (Effect Only)

You can often use the Path effects to avoid or cure printing problems. Here they are presented only as effects, because they are not found under the Filter menu. However, you'll also find these commands under the Object, Path menu (note that applying the command from that menu is equivalent to applying a filter):

- **Offset Path (effect)**—This command creates copies of paths, open or closed, filled or unfilled, and relocates the copy according to the distance specified in the Offset Path dialog box, shown in Figure 35.27. Negative numbers in the Offset field produce smaller copies; positive numbers produce enlarged copies. The original path remains unchanged.

  Because the copy is created to all sides of a path, copying an open path results in a closed-path copy. The copy retains the fill and stroke of the original, but not all filters or effects applied to the object are duplicated. When a filter or effect that alters the path (Pucker & Bloat, Roughen) has been applied, the altered shape is copied. Stylize effects (Drop Shadow, Inner Glow) are not copied.

The Tweak filter/effect (known as Scribble & Tweak in the previous version of Illustrator) varies the results every time you apply it. Check the Preview box and then check whichever of the three boxes at the bottom of the dialog box are appropriate. Drag the sliders until the approximate size you desire is shown. Then check and uncheck the Preview box until you see a shape you like. The shape changes every time you click a box. The results are sometimes subtle, sometimes drastic. Keep clicking until you see the perfect shape.

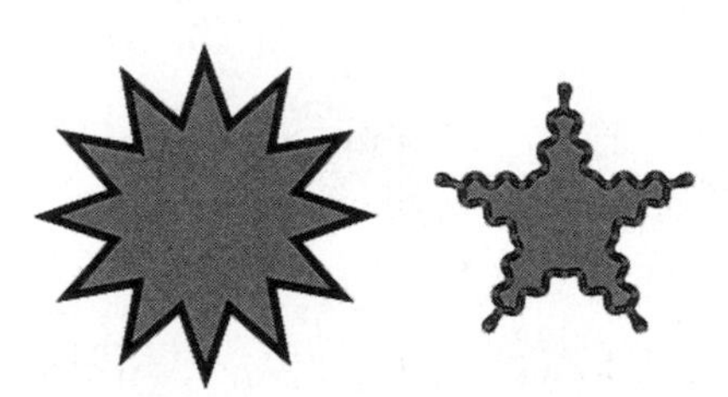

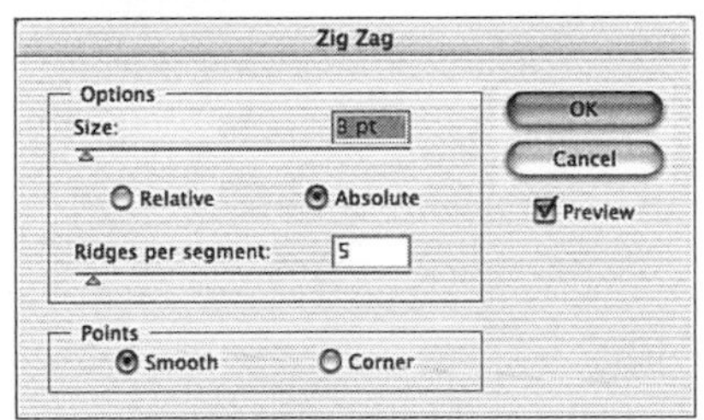


Figure 35.26
The effect of this filter is far more uniform than that of Roughen.

- **Outline Object (effect)**—This command generates a stroke with a value of None around an entire object.
- **Outline Stroke (Effect)**—This command creates a filled object in the shape and location of any selected path. In addition to adding a great deal of flexibility in the modification of shapes, Outline Stroke can be useful when you're preparing trapping. Figure 35.28 shows a compound path created when a heavy stroke is outlined.

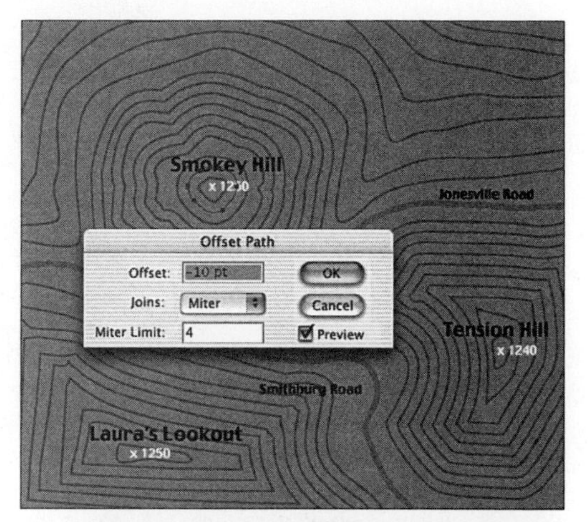


Figure 35.27
Negative numbers can be used to make smaller paths.

Figure 35.28
The Gradient fill becomes a separate, unstroked object. The former stroke is also now an unstroked fill.

## Pathfinder (Effect Only)

The Pathfinder effects work with multiple objects to create a single object. Like the compound shapes created with the Pathfinder palette, the shapes' original paths are retained. Objects should be grouped prior to using the Pathfinder commands. These commands can also be applied to layers and to type objects:

- **Add (effect)**—Simulates combining the selected objects, retaining the fill and stroke of the topmost object.
- **Intersect (effect)**—Retains the appearance of only areas of overlap in a stack of objects, again using the fill and stroke of the topmost object.
- **Exclude (effect)**—Hides areas of overlap where you have an even number of objects. Nonoverlapping areas and areas where an odd number of objects overlap are retained, and they assume the fill and stroke of the top object.

- **Subtract (effect)**—The upper paths ]are used as a "cookie cutter" to hide the lowest object. All parts of the bottom object that are below other objects in the group are hidden. The resulting object retains its original stroke and fill.
- **Minus Back (effect)**—The opposite of Subtract. The foremost object is retained, after hiding of any part overlapping any selected object behind it.
- **Divide (effect)**—Creates the appearance of multiple objects, with a new object created from the area where multiple paths overlap. Because this is an effect, no objects are actually created.
- **Trim (effect)**—Hides underlying parts of objects, removing strokes.
- **Merge (effect)**—Hides parts of objects that were not visible, removing strokes and seeming to merge objects of the same color.
- **Crop (effect)**—Uses the foremost object as the "cookie cutter," hiding anything outside it. It creates the appearance of individual objects of the faces remaining. Strokes are changed to None.
- **Outline (effect)**—Creates unfilled open paths from the objects' path segments. Every place that one path crosses another, the paths are both divided.
- **Hard Mix (effect)**—Blends the color by using the higher percentage for each of the CMYK values.
- **Soft Mix (effect)**—Allows the underlying color to show through, according to the percentage selected.
- **Trap (effect)**—Produces a slight overlap to compensate for misregistration of a printing press.

If text or an object with an effect or filter applied seems "clipped" on output, use Outline Object. When a drop shadow is clipped, for example, the fade isn't complete and may cut off abruptly at some point. Illustrator is not allowing enough of a cushion around the basic object to accommodate the shadow. Adding an invisible stroke with Outline Object forces Illustrator to recognize the true boundaries of the object with its effect.

This command is also a good safety net when stroked text is rasterized. Normally, Illustrator allows space for just the text—that is, the fill. When the text is stroked, the width of the stroke must be added to the space allocated for the text. Outline Object forces that to happen.

Selecting Soft Mix or Trap opens the dialog box shown in Figure 35.29. To change the advanced options for any of the other Pathfinder effects, double-click the effect's name in the Appearance palette.

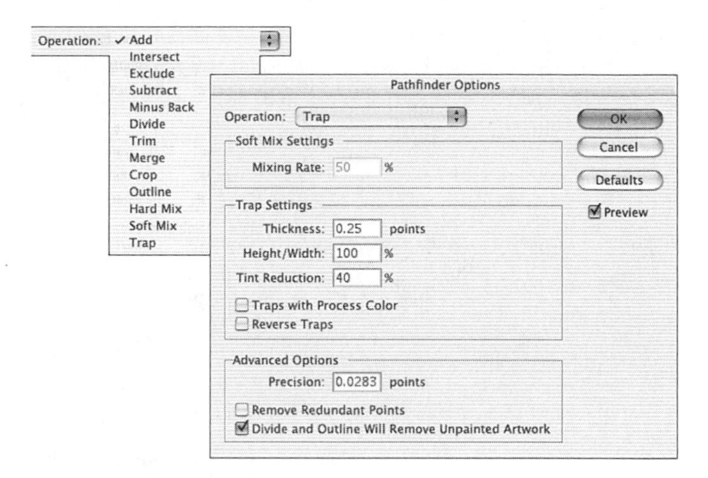


**Figure 35.29**
Precision and Remove Redundant Points are available for all the Pathfinder effects.

# Rasterize (Effect)

*Rasterization* is the process of converting a vector object to pixels. When this is used as an effect, Illustrator simulates a conversion to pixels. The original object is maintained, and the rasterization can be reversed later. In contrast, the menu command Object, Rasterize permanently changes the artwork, as if applying many of the filters. The settings in Effect, Document Raster Effects Settings can be used with this command, or you can specify other settings in the dialog box (see Figure 35.30).

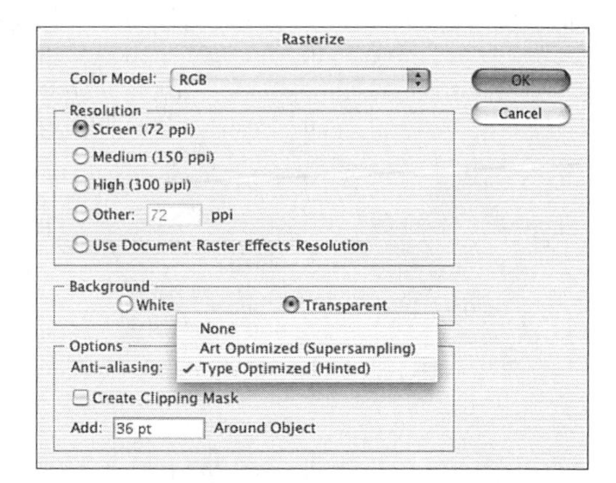


**Figure 35.30**
The settings in this dialog box are applied only to the current selection.

# Stylize (Filter and Effect)

Illustrator includes a number of effects and filters that add special artistic touches to objects. These are the Stylize commands:

- **Add Arrowheads (filter/effect)**—Illustrator has 27 different arrowheads that you can add to open paths. Using the dialog box, you can put an arrowhead on the path's beginning, end, or both. The size of the arrowhead can be scaled relative to the stroke of the path, from 1% to 1000%. Arrowheads assume the stroke and fill of the path, including None. After arrowheads have been applied, a path's stroke can be altered, which adjusts the size of the arrowhead's stroke without affecting its scale. There is no preview available for the Arrowhead filter, although that is an option for the Arrowhead effect. Figure 35.31 is provided as a handy reference, to save you dozens of clicks "auditioning" arrowheads.

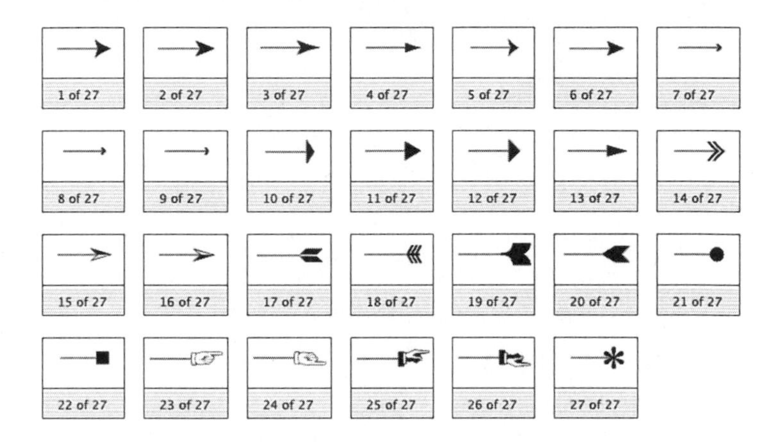


**Figure 35.31**
Reference chart of Illustrator's arrowheads.

- **Drop Shadow (filter/effect)**—A drop shadow is created as a separate object. (The option Create Separate Shadow is no longer available.) When you select Color, the original object's fill is treated as opaque. When you select Darkness, the fill is considered to be translucent. The difference is shown in the upper pair of objects in Figure 35.32. Shadows can also be applied to an object's stroke (as shown in the lower left of Figure 35.32) or to an object's fill. And, as you can see in the lower-right corner of Figure 35.32, multiple shadows can be applied as well. Theoretically, you can even apply a second drop shadow to the *first* drop shadow.

**Figure 35.32**
The object in the lower right has drop shadows applied to each of its three strokes, each shadow with different settings. Multiple shadows can also be applied to a single stroke or fill.



- **Feather (effect)**—This command, which is available only as an effect, fades a selected image over a specified distance.

- **Inner Glow (effect)**—Available only as an effect, this command applies a feathered effect to the selected object. In the dialog box, you can specify color, opacity, blur, and blending mode. In addition, you can determine whether the glow will start at the center of the object and fade outward, or start at the edge of the object and fade inward.

> You can simulate multiple light sources with multiple drop shadows. However, rather than applying more than one shadow to a single stroke, you duplicate the original stroke and give the copy the second shadow.

- **Outer Glow (effect)**—An outer glow, similar to an inner glow, is available only as an effect. The feathered appearance extends outward from the stroke of a selected object. You can specify color, opacity, blur, and blending mode.
- **Round Corners (filter/effect)**—Any corner anchor point on a path, open or closed, can be smoothed with this filter. You can apply it only to corner points; it allows adjustments from 1/100 of a point to 4,000 points (from 1/1,000 of an inch to more than 55 inches). The unit of measure is specified in the preferences.

- **Scribble (effect only)**—One of the new features in Illustrator CS, the Scribble effect is certain to appear in a wide variety of places in the coming years. This versatile effect has a number of customizable parameters, enabling you to produce effects ranging from subtle to overpowering.

## Illustrator at Work: Exploring the Scribble Effect

At first glance, Illustrator's new Scribble effect may produce a yawn and invoke comparisons to the previous release of Illustrator's one-trick pony, the Flare tool. But the incredible flexibility of this effect makes it a powerhouse that you may come to rely on. Follow these steps:

1. Open a new Illustrator document (RGB, 800×600 pixels).
2. Add a simple object to the artboard, such as a polygon with a 10-point black stroke and an orange fill.
3. Open the Scribble dialog box with Effect, Stylize, Scribble. Enter these values: Angle: 30° (150° if you're left-handed), Path Overlap: 1 pt, Variation: 1 pt, Stroke Width: 1 pt, Curviness: 3%, Variation: 4%, Spacing: 1.5 pt, and Variation 1.5 pt. Click OK. You should see a nicely controlled, very clean, stay-within-the-lines look (see Figure 35.33).
4. Press V on the keyboard to activate the Selection tool, hold down the (Option) [Alt] key, and drag your polygon to duplicate it.
5. Open the Appearance palette and double-click Scribble to reopen the dialog box.
6. Uncheck the Preview box. Not only does this speed things up for you, it may give you a great big "Wow!" in a moment. Change your settings as follows: Path Overlap: 10 pt, Variation: 16 pt, Stroke Width: 0.7 pt, Curviness: 30%, Variation: 10%, Spacing: 4 pt, and Variation: 2 pt. *Now* check the Preview box. Before you click OK, change the Path Overlap setting to –2. Click OK. You should have something along the lines of the polygon in Figure 35.34.

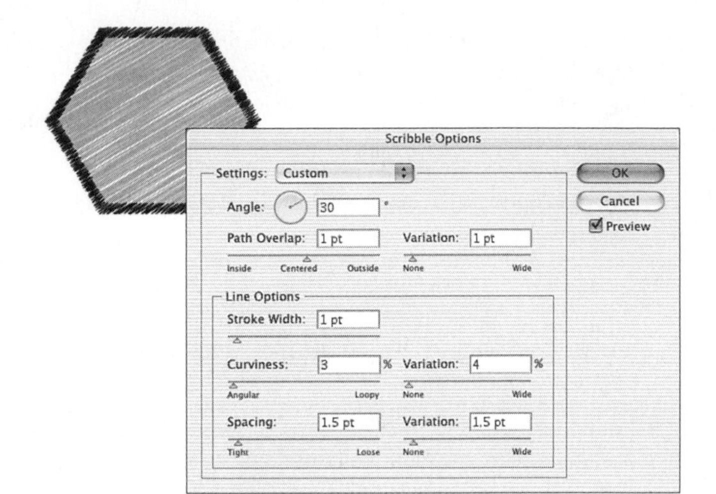


**Figure 35.33**
Nice orderly settings for a nice orderly sketch effect.

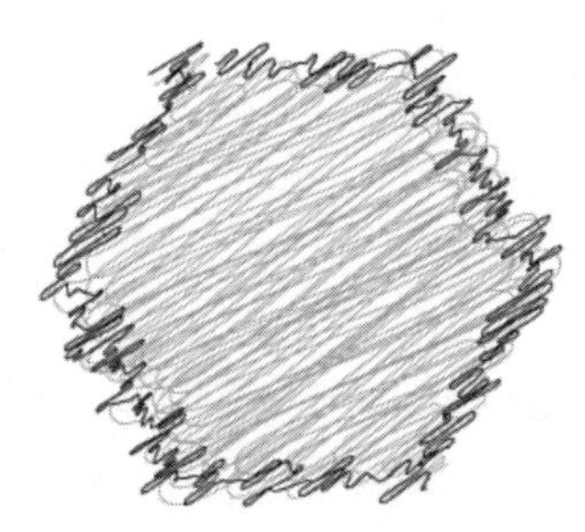

**Figure 35.34**
More extreme settings produce a more dramatic effect.

7. (Option)-drag [Alt]-drag to make another copy of the object.
8. In the Appearance palette, drag the Scribble effect to the trash icon to delete it. Now, from the palette's menu, select Add New Stroke. The new stroke should be identical to the first and, in the palette, it should be selected.
9. Open the Scribble dialog box again. Change only two settings—Path Overlap: 14 pt, Variation: 0 pt— and then click OK.
10. In the Appearance palette, click the original stroke to make it active and then reopen Scribble. Change only one setting: Angle: 150°. Click OK. Your new shape should look like the one on the left in Figure 35.35.

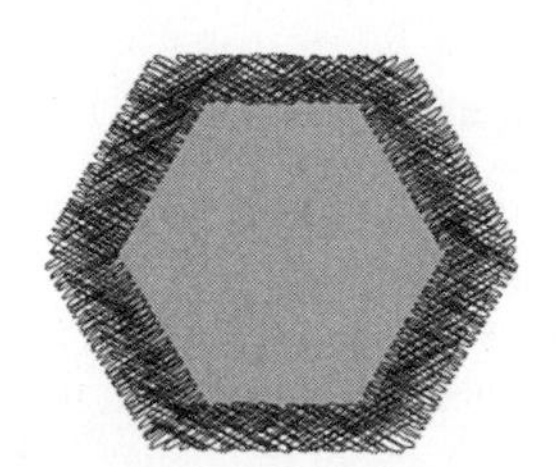

**Figure 35.35**
On the right, one more example of how you can use Scribble.

The best way to explore Scribble's power and versatility is to experiment with the settings. Open the dialog box and see how changes in one setting interact with changes to the others.

Immediately after applying multiple Scribble effects, use Object, Rasterize to prevent output problems and horrendous slowdowns.

In step 10, Scribble was applied to two different strokes. Applying Scribble twice to the *same* object can produce some incredibly good-looking effects and, with the right settings, can be a great way to produce a "grunge" or distressed look (see Figure 35.36). *However*, it takes a lot of horsepower—and time—to preview and redraw the screen with Scribble-on-Scribble.

Figure 35.36
With conservative settings, multiple applications of Scribble can produce interesting effects—but the result can be very slow to redraw onscreen and difficult to output unless rasterized.

## SVG Filters (Effect Only)

These effects are actually JavaScripts that are applied to Scalable Vector Graphics (SVG) files for use on the Web. *Scalable Vector Graphics* are vector artwork that can be rasterized when downloaded to a Web browser over the Internet. These effects are applied at the time of rasterization. This avoids scaling the effect to match the size of the vector artwork, and therefore avoids a degradation of the appearance.

## Warp (Effect Only)

The results of the Warp effect commands are comparable to those created with the Object, Envelope Distort, Make with Warp dialog box. However, rather than producing an envelope mesh that can be edited, the effects change only the appearance of the selection. Figure 35.37 shows a comparison of the envelope mesh (top), the Warp effect (middle), and how editing the path of an object affects the Warp effect (bottom).

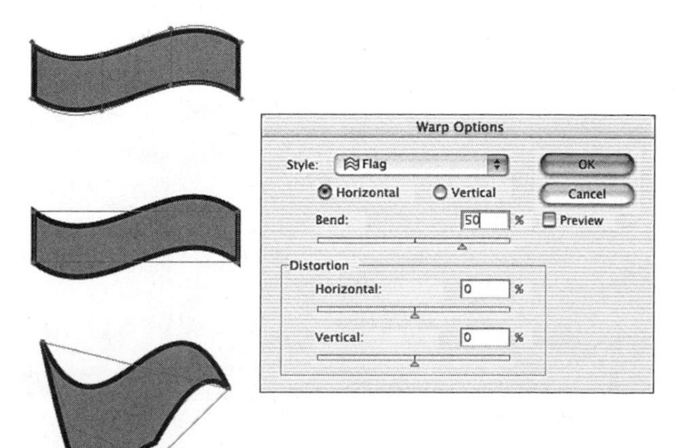


Figure 35.37
The settings shown were applied to three identical objects. The bottom object's path was changed with the Direct Selection tool, and the Warp effect automatically conformed to the new shape.

Both the Envelope Distort and Effects versions of Warp employ the Warp Options dialog box. They offer the same 15 variations.

*For more on the Envelope Distort capabilities, see "Envelope Distortions" in Chapter 28, "Transforming and Distorting Objects," p. 892.*

# THE BOTTOM OF THE MENUS—RASTER

Below the vector-related filters and effects in Illustrator's Filter and Effect menus is a blank line. Below the line, the lowest set of commands, are the filters and effects designed for use with raster artwork and rasterized objects.

## Artistic (Filter/Effect)

The Artistic filters and effects apply fine art looks to the selected artwork. They are meant to simulate natural or traditional art media. When an Artistic effect is applied, a vector selection is rasterized as an effect. The effect and filter versions can be applied to raster artwork that is opened or placed into an Illustrator document, or to rasterized objects. With filters, the objects must be rasterized using Object, Rasterize rather than Effect, Rasterize.

The Artistic filters and effects are some of the most demanding on your computer, requiring large amounts of memory. The amount of time required to preview and apply Artistic filters and effects depends on the size and resolution (pixels per inch) of the image and the speed of the computer's processor.

In Figure 35.38, you can see examples of the Artistic effects. Keep in mind that different settings can produce wildly different appearances. What you see here are examples of typical settings for each effect. The following list details these effects:

**Figure 35.38**
Remember that all the Artistic effects retain the basic color of an object or image.

- **Colored Pencil (filter/effect)**—This filter/effect simulates, as the name implies, the look of a colored sketch. It is not suitable for gradients, although it produces interesting effects on gradient mesh objects. Used subtly, it can greatly enhance many of Illustrator's patterns.

- **Cutout (filter/effect)**—Using the edges defined by changes in color, this filter/effect simulates a collage effect. The Number of Levels option defines color differences used to determine edges. Edge Simplicity and Edge Fidelity change the relationship of those edges to the shapes that will be created.

The resolution at which the artwork is rasterized has a tremendous impact on the settings for most of the Artistic effects and filters. If an effect seems too heavy-handed, you can rasterize the object at a higher resolution (using Object, Rasterize), use a filter or effect, and then rerasterize to the resolution you need.

- **Dry Brush (filter/effect)**—For this painterly filter/effect, the Brush Size and Brush Detail settings can produce gross effects or (when moderated) can have more subtle impact on an image. When Brush Size is minimized and Brush Detail is maximized, many computer-generated images can be softened just enough to look natural.

- **Film Grain (filter/effect)**—This filter/effect adds an even layer of noise to the midtones and shadows of an image. The noise, when applied minimally, can reproduce the grain of film and can be used with images from digital video. Grain controls the amount of noise, Highlight Area defines how much of the lighter areas of the image will have a smoother pattern of noise applied, and Intensity determines how much those highlight areas will be smoothed.

- **Fresco (filter/effect)**—Fresco uses short, round strokes to reproduce the image. It is intended to portray short, coarse strokes, as if the surface had been dabbed with a brush.

- **Neon Glow (filter/effect)**—Surrounding edges with a neon glow can do great things for flat or grayscale images. Depending on the settings, this filter/effect can also work to change a color image into a "colorized" image. High settings for Size and Brightness can produce a colorized effect. Using a negative number brings the glow "inside" the object.

- **Paint Daubs (filter/effect)**—This filter/effect simulates another painting technique. Brush sizes can range from 1 to 50, and several brush types are available in the dialog box. Variation in the Brush Type setting is of greater importance in detailed images than in simple objects.

- **Palette Knife (filter/effect)**—This filter/effect is designed to create the appearance that the texture of the canvas is showing through a thin layer of paint. Stroke Size has a significant impact on photographic images and gradient mesh objects.

- **Plastic Wrap (filter/effect)**—This filter/effect reproduces the effect of plastic wrap on wet paint. In the dialog box, Highlight Strength, Detail, and Smoothness all refer to the surface of the imaginary plastic. A low Detail setting on a photo can produce a smoothing effect.

- **Poster Edges (filter/effect)**—Posterizing reduces the number of colors in the image. This filter/effect also isolates areas of color with black lines along the edges. Edge Intensity determines the darkness of the black outlines. Posterization determines the reduction in the number of colors in the target object or image.

- **Rough Pastels (filter/effect)**—This filter/effect simulates chalk on rough surfaces. The textures available include canvas, burlap, brick, and sandstone, and custom textures can be loaded. This filter/effect can be applied very effectively to rasterized text.
- **Smudge Stick (filter/effect)**—As if the darker areas had been smudged, this filter/effect uses diagonal strokes to smear those areas. Lighter areas of an image become brighter and lose contrast.

When working with an effect that uses a texture, such as Rough Pastels or Underpainting, make sure you check the Lighting Direction setting. You won't see "Bricks" unless the light is coming from an angle—it's a totally different look with light from the top, bottom, left, or right.

- **Sponge (filter/effect)**—The Sponge filter/effect produces areas of contrast with high texture. The effect can be subtle or extreme, depending on the source image and the settings.
- **Underpainting (filter/effect)**—Another filter/effect that uses textures, Underpainting overlays the image on itself, with the bottom image appearing texturized.
- **Watercolor (filter/effect)**—As if painted with watercolors and a medium brush, images subject to this filter/effect lose detail and can experience high saturation at contrasting edges. It is ineffective on solid-color objects.

## Blur (Filter and Effect)

Blur filters and effects "unfocus" a raster image or a rasterized object. They soften edges and edge contrast. Figure 35.39 shows a comparison of Gaussian and radial blurs, and the following list details each:

Figure 35.39
The original is on the left. The center shows a Gaussian blur with a 1-pixel radius, and the right shows a radial zoom blur of 41.

- **Gaussian Blur (filter/effect)**—Among the most commonly applied raster filter/effect, the Gaussian blur is a workhorse. It is especially valuable for smoothing images and can be very effective in eliminating noise and pixelization in an image.
- **Radial Blur (filter/effect)**—As a special effect, the Radial Blur filter/effect has few equals. In either Zoom mode (refer to Figure 35.39) or Spin mode (see Figure 35.40), it is highly effective at what it does.

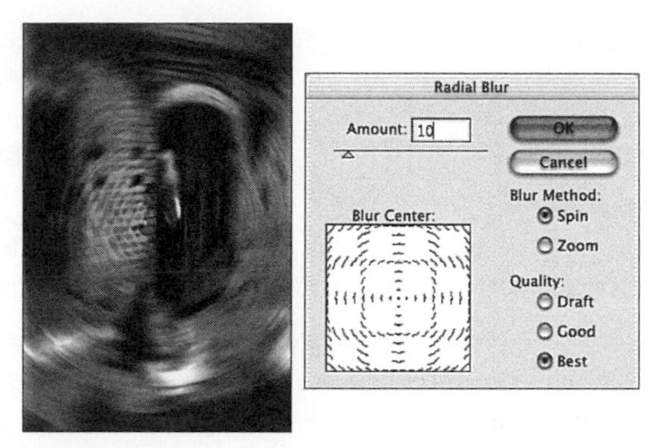


Figure 35.40
The dialog boxes for the Radial Blur filter and effect both offer settings for Amount, Blur Method, and Quality, but they do not offer a preview area.

## Brush Strokes (Filter and Effect)

The various Brush Stroke filters and effects are explored in Figure 35.41. Although each of the Brush Stroke effects has a wide variety of settings and a tremendous range, the sample images show some typical applications.

Figure 35.41
Like the other filters and effects in Illustrator, the impact of the Brush Stroke effects depends to a large degree on the Rasterize settings.

The various Brush Stroke filters and effects are detailed in the following list:

- **Accented Edges (filter/effect)**—Working with the edges of an image, this filter/effect can be set to accent the edges with white or black. Changing the Edge Brightness value from below 25 to above 25 changes the edge accent from black to white.
- **Angled Strokes (filter/effect)**—With light areas stroked in one direction and dark areas stroked in a perpendicular direction, this filter/effect produces interesting effects on images with fine detail and on text. In very dark or very light objects, you may see only one set of strokes.

- **Crosshatch (filter/effect)**—This filter/effect roughens edges and applies pencil strokes but preserves more of the image's detail than the two previous filters/effects. The Strength option determines the number of passes made by the filter/effect, from one to three. A larger Stroke Length setting substantially changes the effect of the Crosshatch filter/effect on gradient mesh objects and photos.
- **Dark Strokes (filter/effect)**—An image's shadow areas are painted by this filter/effect with short dark strokes, and highlight areas are treated with long white strokes.
- **Ink Outlines (filter/effect)**—This filter/effect overlays black lines, as if the image had been sketched in ink. It follows edges and allows for control of both light and dark areas. Non-edge areas of gradients and gradient mesh objects are ignored.
- **Spatter (filter/effect)**—The Spatter filter/effect is designed to replicate an airbrush. It is great for stylizing text.
- **Sprayed Strokes (filter/effect)**—Using the colors that appear most prominently in an image, this filter/effect repaints with angled strokes.
- **Sumi-e (filter/effect)**—Dark blacks and soft edges mark this command's attempt to replicate a Japanese painting technique that calls for a brush heavy with black ink applied to rice paper.

## Distort (Filter and Effect)

These Distort filters/effects should not be confused with those introduced earlier. Whereas the first set of distort capabilities (including Pucker & Bloat, Roughen, Twist, and Zig Zag) work with vector objects, these filters/effects are for use with raster and rasterized objects:

- **Diffuse Glow (filter/effect)**—Transparent white noise is added to the rasterized selection to create a glow. The glow fades along the edges. Figure 35.42 shows a preview in the filter's dialog box.

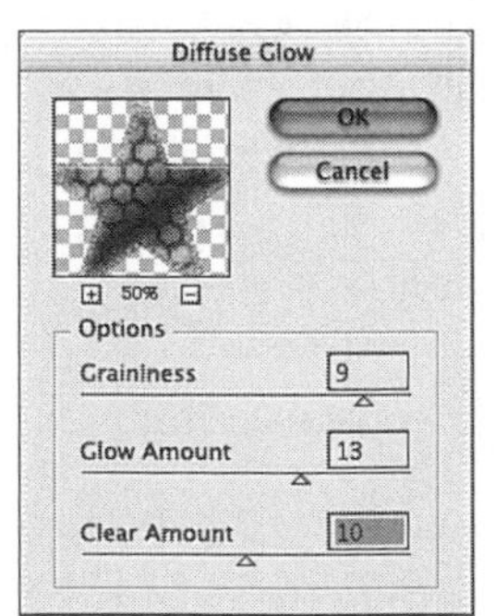


Figure 35.42
The Glow Amount and Clear Amount sliders are used in tandem to control the glow.

- **Glass (filter/effect)**—This filter/effect distorts shapes, as though you're looking through different kinds of glass windows and blocks, while leaving colors virtually unchanged (see Figure 35.43).

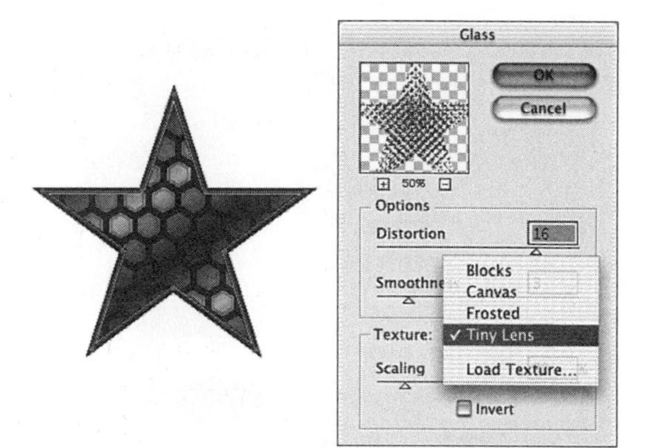


Figure 35.43
This filter/effect allows you to choose types of glass and other distortion patterns, including custom textures.

- **Ocean Ripple (filter/effect)**—Attempting to show an object as if under water, this filter/effect applies a pattern of random curved distortions. You can control the size and intensity of the ripples, as you can see in Figure 35.44.

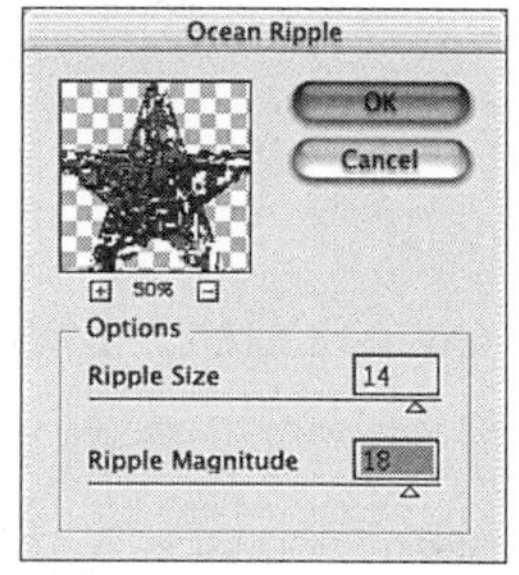


Figure 35.44
On the left, the Ripple Size and Ripple Magnitude settings applied were lower than those shown in the dialog box.

# Pixelate (Filter and Effect)

Pixelization can be a bad thing or a good thing in images. The visible appearance of individual pixels in, for example, a digital photograph taken at a wedding is unwelcome. On the other hand, the introduction of pixelization, when controlled, can produce artistic effects. In general, these filters and effects group pixels of similar colors into groups, called *cells*, that simulate a reduced resolution of the image:

- **Color Halftone (filter/effect)**—This filter/effect creates halftone-like circular cells by dividing the image into rectangular areas. The brighter an area, the larger the circle that's substituted for the pixels in that area. In the Color Halftone dialog box, shown in Figure 35.45, the dot size can range from 4 (as in the sample image) to 127.
- **Crystallize (filter/effect)**—Pixels are grouped into polygons and assigned one of the group's colors. Figure 35.46 shows that the only option is Cell Size.

If the Color Halftone filter's 4-pixel radius (the minimum) seems too dramatic for your purposes, you can rasterize an object to a higher resolution, apply the filter, and then rerasterize back to the original resolution.

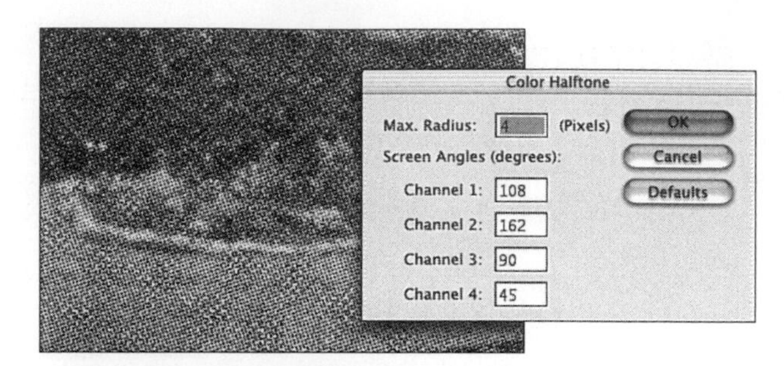


**Figure 35.45**
The Color Halftone filter/effect simulates a close-up of a four-color print.

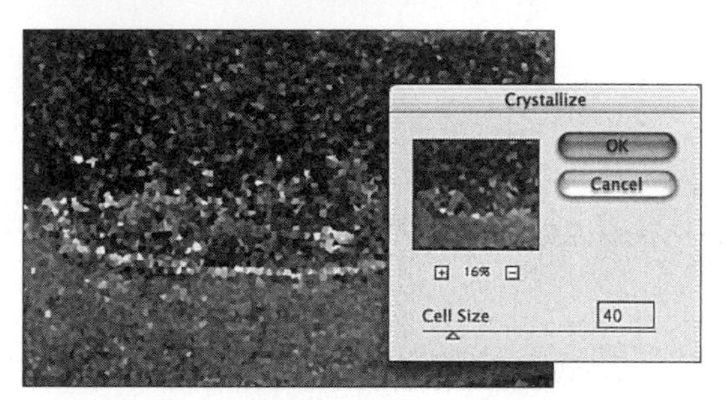


**Figure 35.46**
The preview area shows a cell size of 40, and the image behind the dialog box was created with a cell size of 10.

- **Mezzotint (filter/effect)**—A random pattern is created according to the option selected. For color images, each element of the pattern is a fully saturated color. Grayscale images are reduced to black and white. Figure 35.47 shows the filter's dialog box.

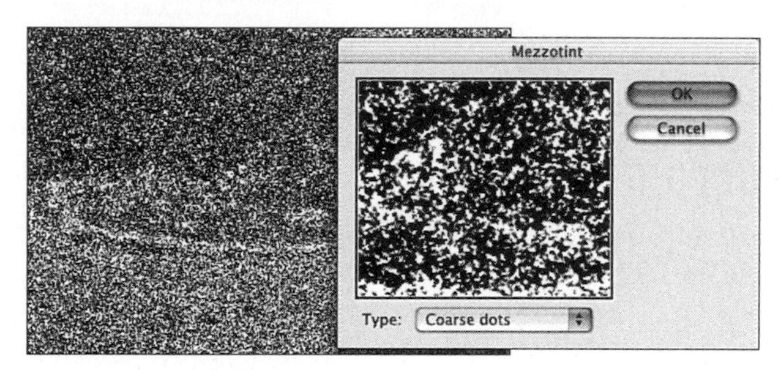


**Figure 35.47**
The image behind the dialog box shows the Fine Dots setting, in contrast to the Coarse Dots setting shown in the preview area.

- **Pointillize (filter/effect)**—A series of large dots are placed to represent the image (see Figure 35.48). The smallest dot size available is 3.

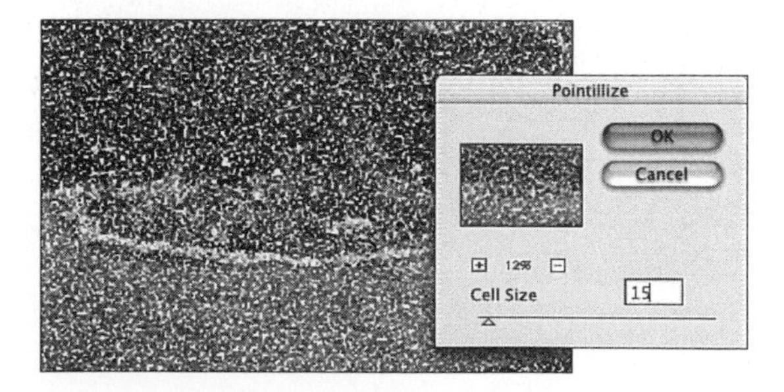


**Figure 35.48**
The difference between a setting of 6 (background image) and a setting of 15 (preview area) is substantial. Note that the preview area is showing the entire image, not just part of the image. The maximum value (300) creates fewer than a dozen cells for the entire image.

## Sharpen (Filter and Effect)

Illustrator's default installation includes only one Sharpen filter, but it is certainly the most valuable of those found in Adobe Photoshop:

- **Unsharp Mask (filter/effect)**—This filter/effect simulates a sharper focus on an image by increasing the contrast along edges. Where the filter/effect finds a significant difference between colors, it emphasizes the breaks. Figure 35.49 shows how Unsharp Mask can improve the detail of an image. Unsharp Mask is always worth considering when a raster image has been resized.

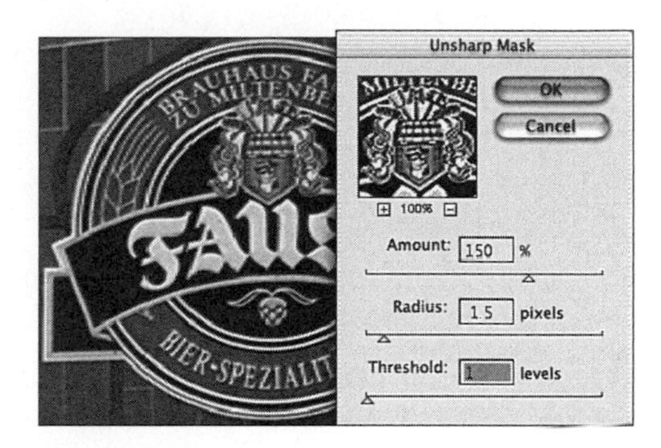


Figure 35.49
Compare the original image with the preview area to see the significant effect even a slight bit of sharpening can have on a detailed image.

## Sketch (Filter and Effect)

The Sketch commands include some that produce a fine-arts effect and some that attempt to portray 3D. Most of these filters and effects produce a grayscale image. Examples of each of the results are shown (in alphabetical/menu order) in Figure 35.50 and are detailed in the following list:

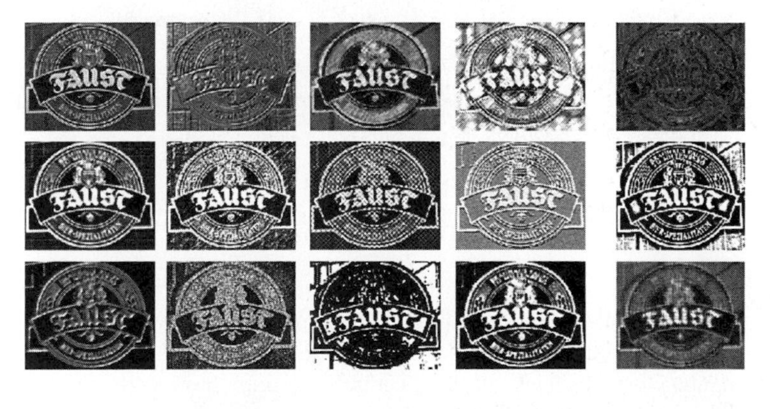

Figure 35.50
The original image is shown in the upper left. Each of the Sketch filters/effects has been applied with an appropriate setting to produce an image in this figure.

- **Bas Relief**—(Figure 35.50, top row, number 2.) The image looks as if it has been carved in stone. The dialog box allows you to control the amount of detail and smoothness, as well as the angle of lighting.
- **Chalk & Charcoal**—(Figure 35.50, top row, number 3.) This filter/effect works with a gray background and uses dark strokes (charcoal) for darker and shadow areas and light strokes (chalk) for highlights.

- **Charcoal**—(Figure 35.50, top row, number 4.) The Charcoal filter/effect is similar to Chalk & Charcoal, but the background is paper rather than chalk. Prominent edges are drawn; midtones are stroked.
- **Chrome**—(Figure 35.50, top row, number 5.) The image is prepared as if it were polished chrome, with highlights as elevations and shadows as recesses.
- **Conté Crayon**—(Figure 35.50, middle row, number 1.) This filter/effect offers several textures (including brick, as shown in this figure). The image can be incorporated into the background or placed above it.
- **Graphic Pen**—(Figure 35.50, middle row, number 2.) This filter/effect uses short diagonal lines to create a black-and-white version of the image.
- **Halftone Pattern**—(Figure 35.50, middle row, number 3.) You can reproduce a moiré pattern by using the Dots option with this filter/effect. In addition, you can use circles and lines to re-create the image.
- **Note Paper**—(Figure 35.50, middle row, number 4.) The image is reproduced as if made from layers of paper. Dark areas of the image are cut out of the top layer of paper.
- **Photocopy**—(Figure 35.50, middle row, number 5.) As if the image had been put on a photo-copier, midtones run to black or white, and areas of solid darkness are copied around the edges.
- **Plaster**—(Figure 35.50, bottom row, number 1.) Creating a 3D image, as if from plaster, this filter/effect has several lighting-direction options.
- **Reticulation**—(Figure 35.50, bottom row, number 2.) This filter/effect produces a grained effect, more pronounced in the highlights than in the shadows.
- **Stamp**—(Figure 35.50, bottom row, number 3.) High-contrast or bitmap (black-and-white) images are best for this filter/effect.
- **Torn Edges**—(Figure 35.50, bottom row, number 4.) This is another filter/effect that is best with high-contrast images. The subject is reproduced as if made from ripped paper.
- **Water Paper**—(Figure 35.50, bottom row, number 5.) As if painted with watercolors on a highly absorbent paper, the colors run and bleed with this filter/effect.

## Stylize (Filter and Effect)

The single Stylize filter/effect included with Illustrator is Glowing Edges. As you can see in Figure 35.51, the filter/effect finds and emphasizes edges, allowing control over brightness, width, and smoothness.

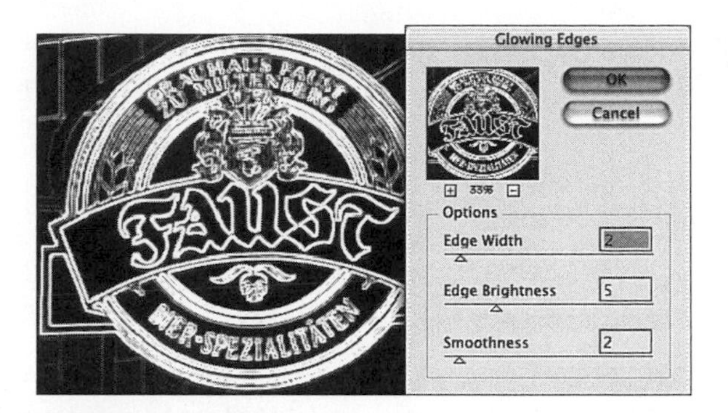


**Figure 35.51**
The settings shown in this dialog box produced the image shown.

## Texture (Filter and Effect)

The Texture filters/effects are designed not so much to add texture to an image as to portray the image as having been painted on a textured surface. Examples of the filters/effects are shown in Figure 35.52. These filters/effects are detailed in the following list:

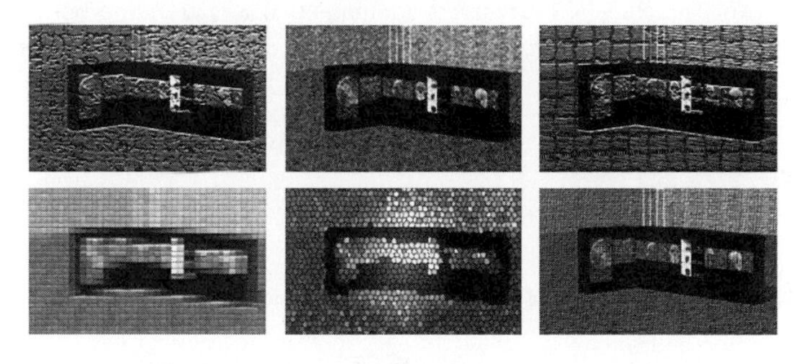

**Figure 35.52**
The effects of the six filters are shown here.

- **Craquelure (filter/effect)**—(Figure 35.52, top row, number 1.) The image is painted on a surface resembling a plaster wall, complete with cracks. The cracks follow the edges within the image. The dialog box offers control of crack spacing, depth, and brightness.
- **Grain (filter/effect)**—(Figure 35.52, top row, number 2.) This filter/effect offers 10 different varieties of grain to add to an image. In addition, intensity and contrast can be modified.
- **Mosaic Tiles (filter/effect)**—(Figure 35.52, top row, number 3.) The size of the tiles used to reconstruct the image can range from 2 to 100. The width and lightness of the grout between tiles can be optimized for each image.
- **Patchwork (filter/effect)**—(Figure 35.52, bottom row, number 1.) The image is divided into squares, and the dominant color of each is used for the entire segment. The "depth" of each tile is adjusted by the filter/effect to control highlights and shadows. The size of the squares and the relief are adjustable.
- **Stained Glass (filter/effect)**—(Figure 35.52, bottom row, number 2.) Individual cells are created and outlined in black to reproduce the image. The size of the cells, the thickness of border between them, and the back lighting intensity are all adjustable.

- **Texturizer (filter/effect)**—(Figure 35.52, bottom row, number 3.) This filter/effect offers a choice among brick, burlap, canvas, sandstone, and custom-made textures. The scaling, relief, and lighting direction are options.

## Video (Filter and Effect)

The two Video filters/effects approach an image from opposite directions. The first is designed to clean up images taken from video, whereas the second prepares images for video:

- **De-Interlace (filter/effect)**—Video images are broadcast one-half at a time. Every other line of an image is sent separately. Between these lines of the image are lines of black. When a video image is captured digitally, those black lines are prominent. De-Interlace replaces the black lines either by interpolation (calculating what color each pixel should be based on neighboring pixels) or by duplication (copying the neighboring line of the image). Odd or even scan lines can be selected.
- **NTSC Colors (filter/effect)**—This filter/effect restricts an image to colors with appropriate saturation for broadcast. The filter/effect desaturates highly saturated colors, which can bleed across scan lines.

# MASTERING ILLUSTRATOR

### Circumventing the Unavailable Filter

*Sometimes the filter I want to use is grayed out and unavailable. What can I do?*

Try the Effect menu. If the selection isn't rasterized, the effect may work when the filter won't. In other cases, you may be trying to apply an RGB filter in a CMYK document.

### Back to Normal

*If I apply an effect and want to remove it later, what do I do?*

Immediately after an effect is applied, you can use Undo. After that, select the object on the artboard and open the Appearance palette. Find the effect in the Appearance palette and drag it to the trash icon at the bottom of the palette. Remember that filters cannot be removed—they are permanent.

## Picking the Right Light

*What gives with the 3D effect light controls? The sliders seem backward and I really don't know what's going on with lowering the lights to make things brighter.*

Using the analogy of a book on a desk, think about the 3D lighting controls like this:

- Where there's little or no light, there's a lot of shade.
- Ambient light is that light that's native to the "place" where you've created your "object." Think about the sunlight coming through the windows of a room.
- Light Intensity controls the brightness of the light source you drag around in the little proxy area to the left of the sliders. Think of this as the lamp on the desk in the room with windows.
- The desk lamp and the sunshine both fall on a book on the desk, right? The brighter the sun outside, the more ambient light falls on the book. The lower the wattage of the desk lamp's bulb, the less "light intensity" there will be.
- On a cloudy day, with a high-wattage bulb in the lamp, you've got a low Ambient Light setting and a high Light Intensity setting. On a sunny day, with that same lamp, you've got both settings high—and the shading color virtually disappears because there's no shade on the book on the desk, right?
- You can add additional lights with the New Light button below the proxy. For example, you've already got some light coming through the window and from the desk lamp, but you can add a light in the ceiling, a floor lamp, and a flashlight, all falling on the book on the desk.
- Remember that the Ambient Light setting stays the same for all light sources. (Turning on a lamp in the room doesn't change the amount of sunshine coming through the window.) However, each of the light sources can have a different wattage bulb, the setting you select for that particular light source with Light Intensity.
- Shading Color is *not* the color of the ambient light. That is assumed to be white light. Think of the Shading Color setting as perhaps the color that lands on your object when the surface of the desk is reflected on it. If the desk is red and shiny, it will reflect some of that red onto the book on the desk. And, as in the real world, that reflected red will be much more noticeable on the surfaces of the book where there is less direct and ambient light.

To sum up, if there's no light, there's shade, and the shading color is prominent. Light Intensity increases on a specific spot on the object as the percentage is increased. The Ambient Light slider determines how much light falls on *all* of the object, thereby reducing the shadowy areas and, therefore, the shade color.

# LINKING AND EMBEDDING IMAGES AND FONTS

## IN THIS CHAPTER

When an illustration includes an image created outside Illustrator, that image is either linked or embedded. Linked images are not part of the Illustrator file, but embedded images are added to the document. Each method has its advantages. The choice often depends on your future plans for the artwork.

Vector file formats (CGM, WMF, EMF, SVG), AutoCAD files (DWG, DXF), and text files (TXT, DOC, RTF) must be embedded. Illustrator allows you to link only raster images.

When your illustration will spend its entire life on your computer, the difference between linking and embedding is not substantial. If you plan to send out the illustration for printing or place it in a page layout program, you must consider the difference between linking and embedding images in the file. If a linked file isn't included with the illustration, it can't be printed properly. However, embedding images may make the file too large, forcing you to link the placed images.

Illustrator allows you to link and embed a wide range of file types, as you can see in Figure 36.1. The list includes all file formats that Illustrator can open, with the exception of Illustrator's own AI format (which cannot be placed).

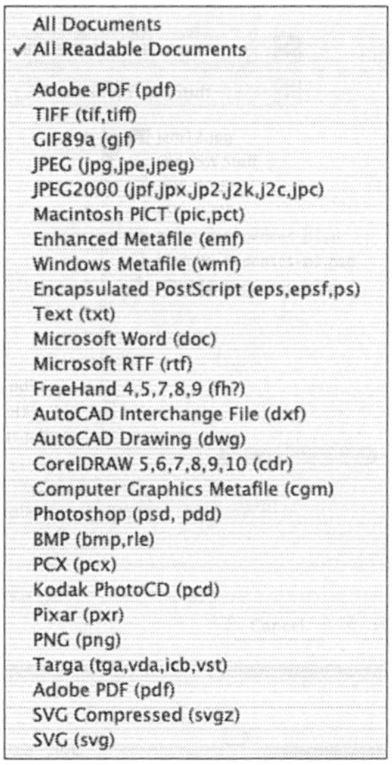

Figure 36.1
You are unlikely to ever work with files of some proprietary formats, such as Pixar and Targa.

All Documents
✓ All Readable Documents

Adobe PDF (pdf)
TIFF (tif,tiff)
GIF89a (gif)
JPEG (jpg,jpe,jpeg)
JPEG2000 (jpf,jpx,jp2,j2k,j2c,jpc)
Macintosh PICT (pic,pct)
Enhanced Metafile (emf)
Windows Metafile (wmf)
Encapsulated PostScript (eps,epsf,ps)
Text (txt)
Microsoft Word (doc)
Microsoft RTF (rtf)
FreeHand 4,5,7,8,9 (fh?)
AutoCAD Interchange File (dxf)
AutoCAD Drawing (dwg)
CorelDRAW 5,6,7,8,9,10 (cdr)
Computer Graphics Metafile (cgm)
Photoshop (psd, pdd)
BMP (bmp,rle)
PCX (pcx)
Kodak PhotoCD (pcd)
Pixar (pxr)
PNG (png)
Targa (tga,vda,icb,vst)
Adobe PDF (pdf)
SVG Compressed (svgz)
SVG (svg)

Fonts, too, can be embedded in an Illustrator file, but there are legal restrictions. If the file will be created, developed, and output from a single computer, you might not need to embed fonts. However, you may need to include fonts if the illustration will be placed into another file, such as a page layout program's document, or if it will be sent out for commercial printing.

# LINKING RASTER IMAGES

Images in raster file formats can be linked to an Illustrator file. (Files in vector formats supported by Illustrator must be embedded rather than linked.) As linked objects, they can be modified in their parent program and updated in your document. Illustrator does, if you choose, automatically update your document to the latest version of the linked file. Two palettes help you keep track of your linked images: Document Info and Links. Using the Links palette, you can also manage and update your linked images.

## The Basics of Image Linking

When you place an image in an Illustrator document (using the command File, Place), the default setting is Link. Figure 36.2 shows the Place dialog box.

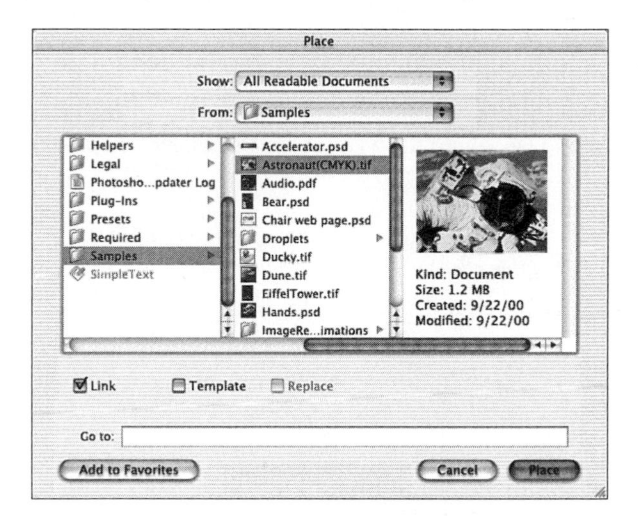


**Figure 36.2**
**The Link box is checked by default. Unchecking the box results in the image being embedded.**

Linking a file simply places a preview of the image (if one is available) in the Illustrator file, with a link to the original file. Just as a hyperlink on the World Wide Web leads you to a different page, so, too, does a linked image in Illustrator point to a different file.

The linked image appears in the center of the screen, regardless of the zoom factor or whether the artboard is off center. The image is selected on the artboard and added to the Links palette. Placed images are added to the top of the active layer.

> **Caution**
>
> If an Illustrator file containing linked images is to be placed into a page layout program's document or will be sent out to a service bureau or printer, you must ensure that copies of the linked files are sent along, too.

*Unsure of what to include with a document headed to the printer? See "Preflighting" in the "Mastering Illustrator" section at the end of this chapter.*

That linked file remains independent of the Illustrator document and can be modified in its parent program. If it is changed, Illustrator can warn you, automatically get the updated version, or ignore the change unless you want to update the image. Illustrator's behavior with linked files is set in the preferences. Figure 36.3 shows the File Handling & Clipboard panel of the Preferences dialog box.

36

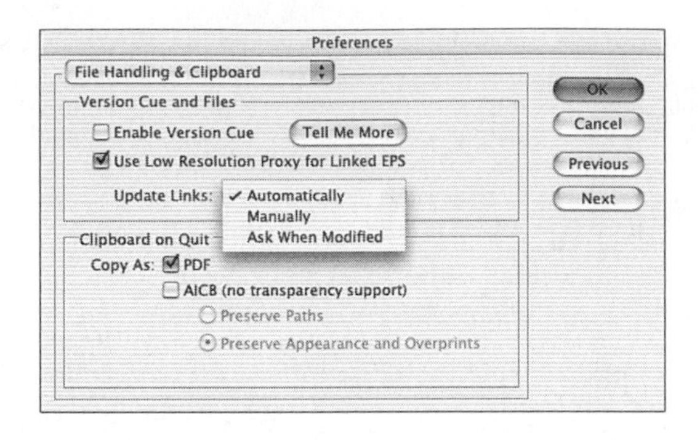


Figure 36.3
The Update Links option refers to linked files, not hyperlinks.

Illustrator offers a pair of palettes to help you manage your linked images. The Links palette gives you information and allows you to work with the images. The Document Info palette also tracks the linked images.

*Not able to see your placed images on the page? See "Preview Problems" in the "Mastering Illustrator" section at the end of this chapter.*

When you make edges visible (by using the command View, Show Edges), linked images in many formats are instantly recognizable. Most linked images have a pair of diagonal lines across the preview. Figure 36.4 shows the visual difference between linked and embedded images.

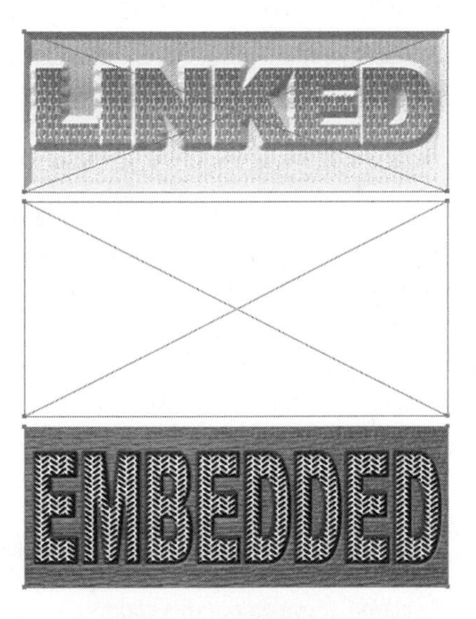


Figure 36.4
Both the top and center images are linked, but the center image has no preview available. The bottom image is embedded. All are selected on the artboard.

Not all file formats show the diagonal lines when linked. Figure 36.5 tells the tale. Note that the diagonal lines, as part of the edges, are not obscured by artwork higher in the stacking order. Like guides and bounding boxes, the edges are nonprinting.

Figure 36.5
The various images are, from the top, EPS, PDF, Photoshop native (PSD), JPEG, and TIFF. As you can see, the JPEG and TIFF previews do not have the crossed diagonal lines. The differences among the images are strictly for illustrative purposes.

*Do you find the diagonal lines across linked images annoying? See "Losing Link Lines" in the "Mastering Illustrator" section at the end of this chapter.*

Illustrator allows you to view linked (and embedded) images in two ways while you're working in Outline view. The Artboard panel of the Document Setup dialog box, shown in Figure 36.6, contains the option Show Images in Outline Mode.

If your Illustrator document takes advantage of Illustrator's transparency features, including blending modes, opacity, and certain effects, EPS files should be embedded rather than linked. Linked EPS files in documents with transparency may produce output irregularities.

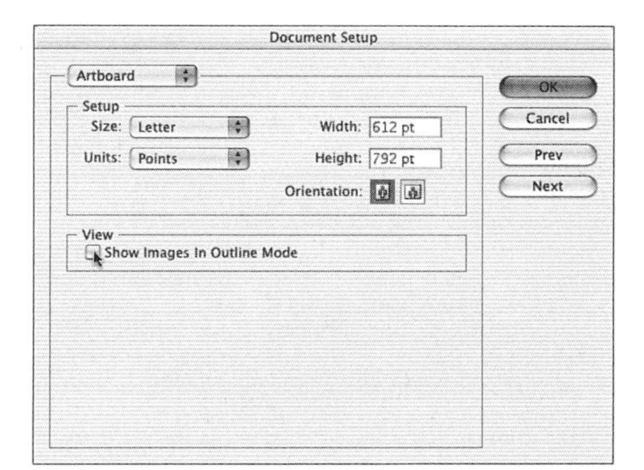


Figure 36.6
You open the Document Setup dialog box by choosing File, Document Setup.

When this option is selected, all linked and placed images are shown with black-and-white previews in Outline view. (Linked images that do not have previews are, of course, shown as empty boxes.) The difference in views is demonstrated in Figure 36.7.

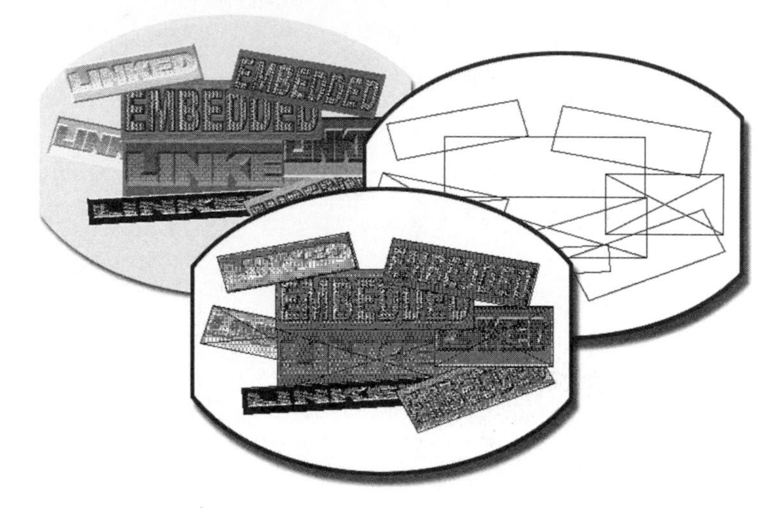

Figure 36.7
These sample views are, clockwise from the top, Preview, Outline, and Outline view with the Show Images in Outline option selected. You can switch between Preview and Outline views by using the View menu.

## Working with Linked Images

When linked images are raster images, they retain their specific file format qualities. Raster images are composed of pixels and can be manipulated as any rasterized object. When you place a linked image in an illustration, you can edit it in various ways. For example, you can apply transformations and effects.

Figure 36.8 shows several of the images that were placed in Figure 36.5. They have been transformed and had effects applied, just as any other rasterized artwork in Illustrator.

Figure 36.8
From the upper left, Rotate, Feather, Scale, Dry Brush, and Radial Blur are some of the transformations and effects that have been applied to these linked images.

If Illustrator cannot find a linked file or the linked file cannot be opened, you may see a dialog box like the one shown in Figure 36.9.

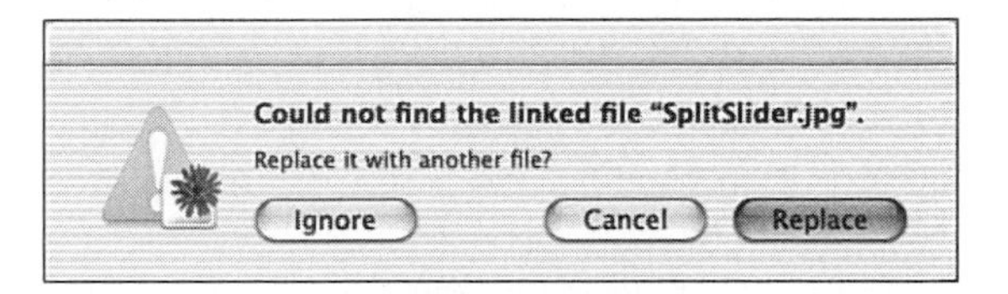


Figure 36.9
Missing or otherwise unavailable linked files generate this message.



If you get the error message shown in Figure 36.9 and click the Replace button, a dialog box called Replace appears (see Figure 36.10).

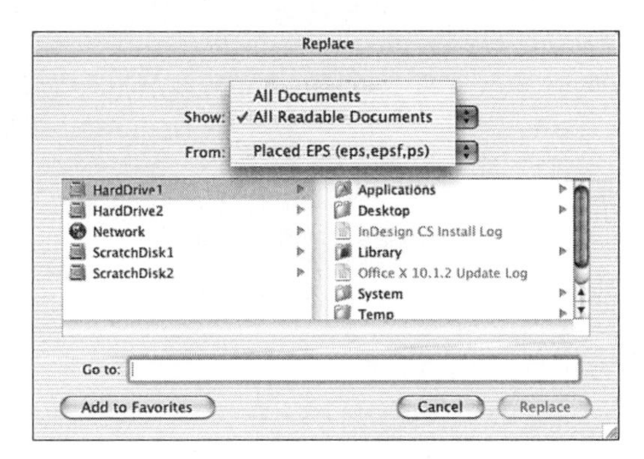


Figure 36.10
This dialog box is similar to both the Open and Place dialog boxes.

Use the Replace dialog box to locate the original image. However, if you must use a different file, the dialog box puts some restrictions on your choices. The choices are not as clear-cut as they may seem:

- If you select All Documents in the Show menu, you do, indeed, see a list of all documents. Illustrator even allows you to choose any of those documents. However, if the selected document is not appropriate, the file that you are opening continues to open, but the new image is not visible.
- The choice All Readable Documents shows only those files that can be used by the file being opened as a replacement for the missing image. This does not, however, guarantee that your decision will be correct. In Figure 36.11, you can see an example of how a file that *can* be used as a replacement image may not be a good choice for that use.

  Notice that the transformations and effects applied to the missing files remain in place for the replacements. Also notice, however, that the new images in the upper- and lower-left corners have different dimensions than

**Caution**

EPS files, if missing, should be replaced with like files. Illustrator handles EPS files somewhat differently from dedicated raster formats, such as TIFF and JPEG.

**Caution**

Although you are able to apply filters to linked TIFF and JPEG images, you lose the advantages of linking. After the image is filtered, it is embedded.

their predecessors. Their proportions have not been adjusted to those of the missing images.

- The third choice in the Replace dialog box shows you a list of acceptable file formats for substitution. In the case of a missing EPS file, as shown in Figure 36.11, only EPS, EPSF, and PostScript files are listed. If the missing file were, for example, a PDF image, Illustrator's Replace dialog box would show a list of all file formats that can be linked.

Trying to remember which linked file formats can have filters applied? Select the linked image on the artboard or in the Layers palette and then look for the crossed diagonal edge lines (refer to Figure 36.5). If the lines are there, you cannot apply filters to the linked image.

Figure 36.11
The content of the new image is different from the original file, as shown in Figure 36.8.

Filters should not be used with linked images. Filters, in fact, are available for only some of the linked file formats. Linked JPEG and TIFF images can have most filters applied. Photoshop (PSD), PDF, and EPS, on the other hand, cannot be filtered when placed as linked images. For these file formats, use effects rather than filters.

## The Links Palette

Using the Links palette is an excellent way to track and control images from external sources. It lists both linked and embedded images. In addition, the palette's menu offers the Information command, which displays details of the placed image. (See the section "Embedded Image Info," later in this chapter for details.) The palette and its menu are shown in Figure 36.12.

Icons to the right of an image indicate its status. A yellow warning triangle, like that next to the file 0010032_MED.TIF (highlighted in the Links palette), indicates that the linked file has been modified. The icon to the right of the image immediately above in the Links palette, 0120013_MED.TIF, indicates that the image is embedded rather than linked. A red stop sign with a white question mark (shown in Figure 36.12 next to 1.eps) indicates that a linked image's original file is missing. The first filename in Figure 36.12, ACE Example.jpg, has no icon to the right. The lack of an icon indicates that the file is linked and that there are no problems.

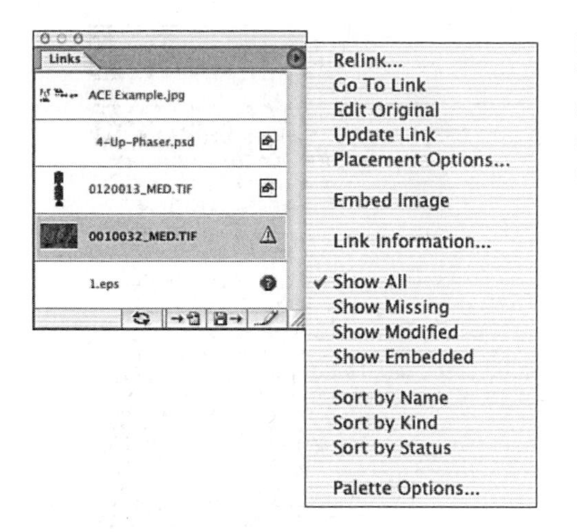


**Figure 36.12**
The Links palette can display subsets of all linked images, such as those missing, modified, or embedded.

The buttons at the bottom of the palette are as follows (from the left):

- **Relink**—Even if an image is not missing, this button allows you to put another image in its place on the artboard.
- **Go To Link**—When you select a file in the Links palette and click this button, the image is selected on the artboard and centered in the window. This feature is very convenient, especially when the illustration has numerous linked or embedded images.
- **Update Link**—When the preferences are set to Update Links: Manually, clicking this button is the way to update a link. When you select a linked image in the palette and click this button, the image is updated on the artboard and in the Illustrator file.
- **Edit Original**—If the linked image's originating program is available, it is launched and the image is opened for editing when you click this button.

The palette can display all linked or embedded images or display only those with potential problems. Individual problem images can be updated or replaced using the palette menu commands. If you've selected Ask When Modified in the Update Links menu of the Preferences dialog box, Illustrator may open the dialog box shown in Figure 36.13 when a linked file is missing or modified. When the preferences are set to update manually or automatically, the message will not appear.

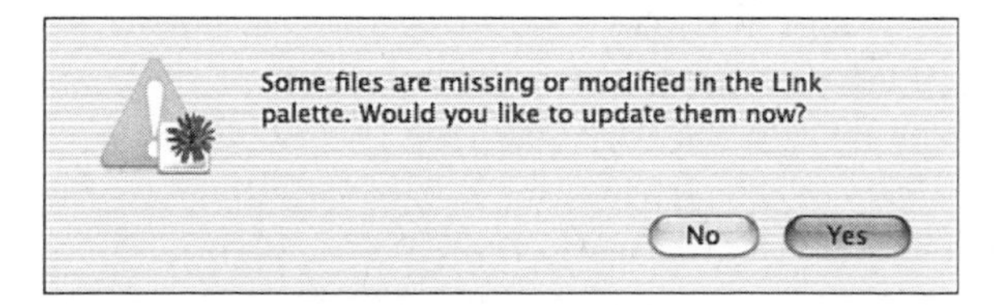


**Figure 36.13**
Clicking Yes updates all images as necessary.

Working within the Links palette, you can click a link and choose Information from the palette menu commands. Figure 36.14 shows the level of information available. You also can access a link's information window by double-clicking the link in the Links palette.

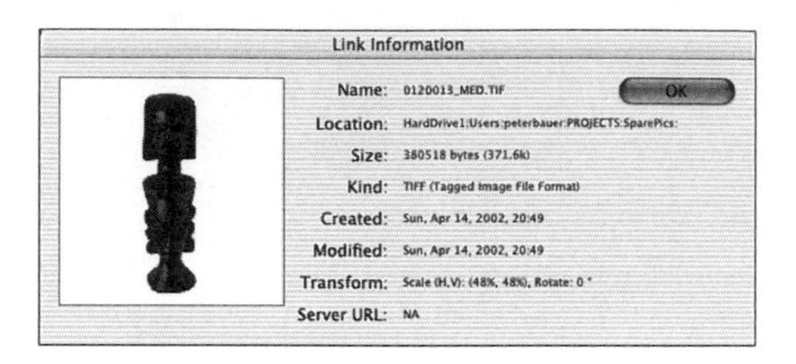


Figure 36.14
The Server URL field is used with images stored in a database.

You can select a group of contiguous links in the palette by clicking a link at one end of the list and Shift-clicking the farthest link. You can select noncontiguous links by (Command)-clicking [Ctrl]-clicking. When one or more links are selected, you can use the palette menu command Go To Link to select the image(s) in the document. The view automatically scrolls to show the images; however, it does not zoom out to accommodate the images.

In the Links palette, you also can choose to edit the original of a linked image. Click the link once in the palette to select it and then use the palette menu command Edit Original. If the program that created the image is available, it is launched and the image is opened for editing. When you return to Illustrator, the warning dialog box shown in Figure 36.13 is displayed, offering you an opportunity to update the linked image. Remember, however, that you see the warning message only if File Handling & Clipboard is set to Update Links: Ask When Modified.

# EMBEDDING RASTER AND VECTOR IMAGES

When the Link option is not selected in the Place dialog box, the selected image is embedded in the Illustrator document. Embedded images become part of the illustration, much like any other element on the artboard. Embedded images, because they become part of the Illustrator document, increase the file size.

Both raster and vector files can be embedded. Photoshop files offer the option of flattening or creating individual objects from the files' layers when embedded.

## Embedding Raster Images

Any raster image file format that can be linked can also be embedded. When a file is embedded, it loses its link to the original image and is not updated. Filters, effects, and transformations can be applied to any rasterized artwork. Embedded EPS and PDF files can be edited in Illustrator.

You embed raster images, like linked images, by using the Place command. To embed a raster image, simply deselect the Link option in the Place dialog box (see Figure 36.15).

Embedding images increases the size of your Illustrator document by the size of the placed file. Embedding numerous raster images in a document can result in a huge file.

## Embedded Image Info

Illustrator offers a wealth of information about embedded images. Between the Information command of the Links palette and the Document Info palette, there's little that you cannot learn about placed raster images (see Figure 36.16).

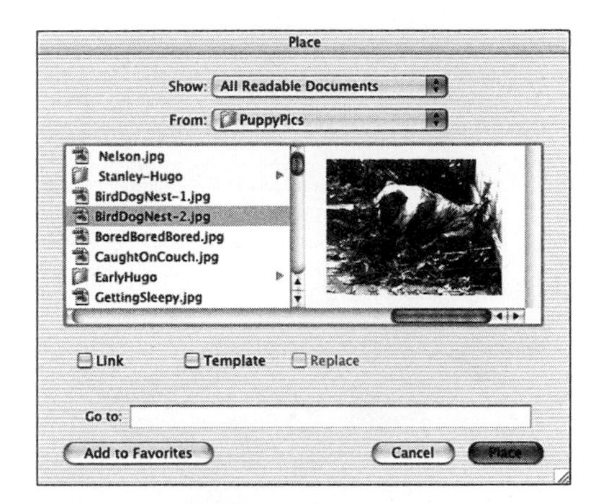


**Figure 36.15**
**When Link is not selected, the placed image is embedded.**

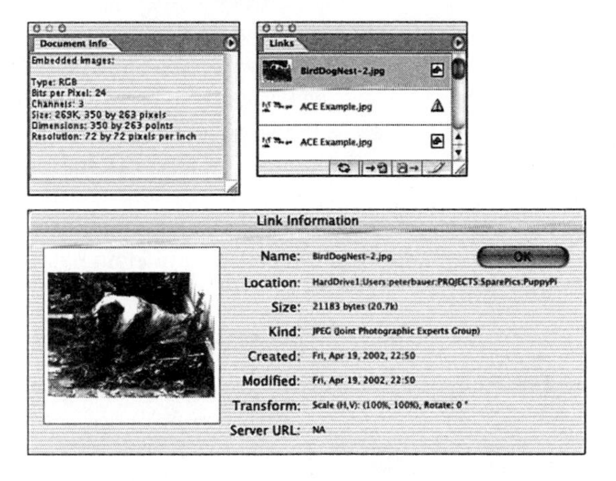


**Figure 36.16**
**The Document Info palette can show details of all linked or embedded images, or those of a selection. You access the Link Information window from the Links palette menu.**

Whether an image is linked or embedded, here's what the Document Info palette offers:

- **Type**—This line tells you the image's color mode. It is either the document's color mode (RGB or CMYK) or Grayscale. Remember that Illustrator 10 allows objects of either CMYK or RGB in a document, not both. Placing an image automatically converts it to the document's color mode. Illustrator also converts indexed color images but does not allow you to place images that use the Lab or multichannel color modes.
- **Bits per Pixel**—At 8 bits per channel, the number of bits can be 8, 24, 32, or 40. Illustrator allows a single alpha or spot channel in addition to the one (grayscale), three (RGB), or four (CMYK) 8-bit color channels.
- **Channels**—This line, like Bits per Pixel, tells you if the image has an alpha channel or spot channel. If there is not an extra channel, grayscale images have one channel, RGB images have three, and CMYK images have four channels.
- **Size**—The file size is followed by the image's pixel dimensions. They are the original width and height of the image, as placed into the Illustrator document.
- **Dimensions**—This line tells you the size of the placed image in points, measured horizontally and vertically as a rectangle (see Figure 36.17).

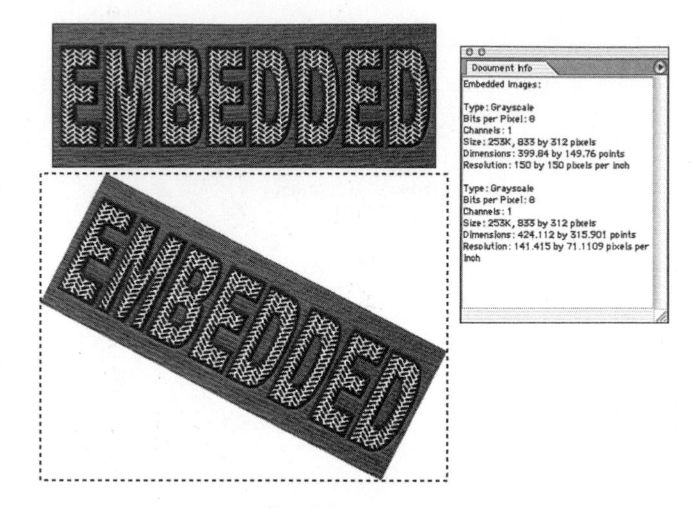


Figure 36.17
The upper image has not been transformed and is listed at the top of the Document Info palette. The lower copy's dimensions are indicated by the dashed rectangle.

- **Resolution**—If an image has not been transformed, this line tells you its original print resolution. If the image has been transformed, as has the lower image in Figure 36.17, the pixels are redistributed and the print resolution changes.

The Links palette offers additional data about placed objects, either linked or embedded. The palette menu command Information opens a separate window, as shown in Figure 36.18.

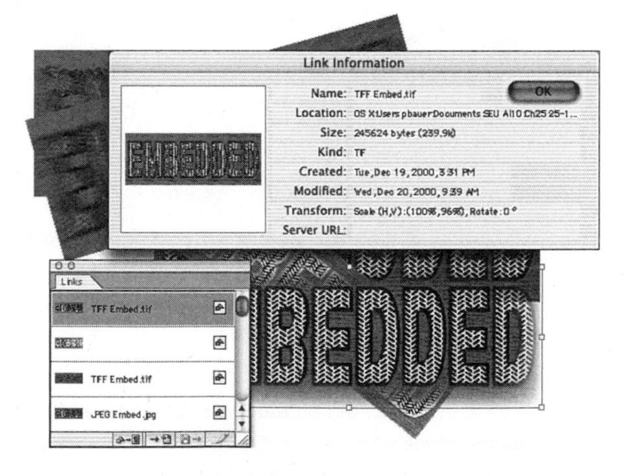


Figure 36.18
The Information command is available in the Links palette menu, which you can access by clicking the small triangle in the palette's upper-right corner.

The information displayed is that of the image selected in the Links palette, which may not be the same as the object selected on the artboard. Information is available for linked images and for embedded images of certain formats, including Photoshop, JPEG, and TIFF. For other embedded files, including EPS and PDF (and other formats when the original file is no longer available), the Link Information window shows only the transformation information.

The Link Information window shows you information related to the original file, including a thumbnail of what the image looked like before any transformations or effects were applied. In addition, you can see the following:

- **Name**—The placed file's name is listed as it appears in the file itself.
- **Location**—For both linked and embedded files, this is the location of the source file. If the original file of an embedded image is moved from this location, the window shows only transformation data.
- **Size**—The file size in bytes and kilobytes (K) is listed. (Remember that there are 1,024 bytes in a kilobyte.)
- **Kind**—For the Macintosh, the actual file format is shown rather than the filename extension. Macintosh users can open the File Exchange control panel to associate specific formats with the filename extensions used in downloaded files or files copied from a Windows computer. In Windows, the Link Information window shows the filename extension to indicate the file type.

You can easily predict whether the Link Information window will have more than just transformation data. If the file is listed by name in the Links palette, the information is complete. If the name of the embedded file is not listed, you see only transformation information. There's an exception, however. If an embedded image's original file has been moved or is otherwise not available, Illustrator does not display the additional information.

- **Created**—This line shows the creation date embedded in the file.
- **Modified**—This line shows the date and time of the latest changes to the original file.
- **Transform**—Present for all placed images, this entry relies on information stored in the Illustrator document rather than with the image's original file. It displays the horizontal and vertical scaling (in percent) and any rotation (in degrees).
- **Server URL**—When a linked image is drawn from a database using Illustrator's dynamic data-driven graphics, this entry will show the source location.

## Embedding Vector Images

Unlike linking, embedding allows you to add vector objects from other documents to your illustration. Like embedded raster artwork, these embedded files become part of the Illustrator document and have no ties to the original files. And, as embedded images, they increase the size of the Illustrator document.

The biggest difference between embedding vector artwork and embedding raster images, other than the actual nature of the files, is how the contents are handled. Vector objects embedded in an Illustrator object are converted into Illustrator paths. You can then edit them as you would objects created in Illustrator. This includes vector elements of PDF and EPS images.

## Embedding Photoshop Files

Embedding Photoshop files gives you some flexibility. You can convert each of the Photoshop file's layers to an object, or you can flatten the image and treat it as a single piece of raster artwork. If the file has slices or image maps, Illustrator can maintain them or ignore them. In addition, you'll get a warning if the Photoshop image's color mode does not match that of the Illustrator document (see Figure 36.19).

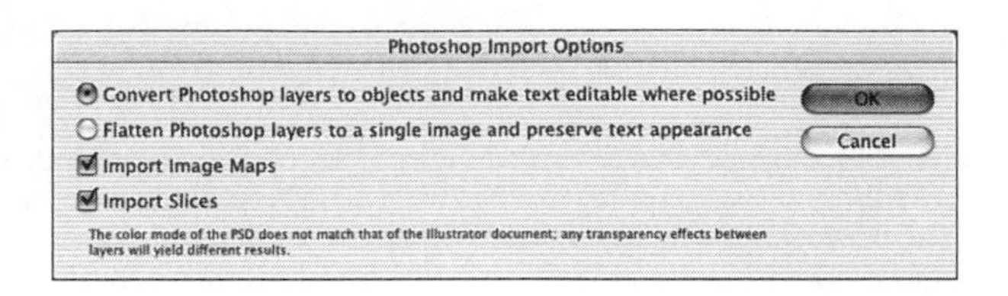


**Figure 36.19**

Converting layers to objects allows you to edit the embedded image.

Illustrator will maintain image data on Photoshop layers that can be used to re-create rollovers and animations (see Figure 36.20).

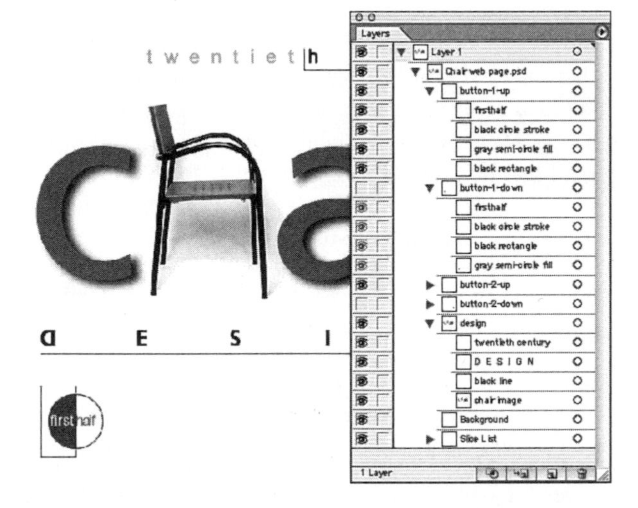


**Figure 36.20**

The original Photoshop image has Web features that can be re-created in Illustrator.

Note, however, that each Photoshop layer is not only a separate raster object in Illustrator's Layers palette, but also a separate unnamed file in Illustrator's Links palette (see Figure 36.21).

**Figure 36.21**

Each new object is embedded separately. It has no ties to the original file, and the Link Information window shows only transform information.

# EMBEDDING TEXT FILES AND FONTS

Text files can be embedded similarly to vector artwork. The contents of the file become part of the Illustrator document. Text can retain its formatting, including font attributes, when embedded. Unlike raster or vector artwork, however, embedded text files do not appear in the Links palette.

Fonts are not embedded on the artboard like text or artwork. Rather, they are included within the file's data on disk when you so choose. Including the fonts when an illustration is sent to a service bureau or printer ensures that the document will be output correctly—and will output at all. Missing fonts are a major source of problems at service bureaus and printers. There are, however, legal restrictions on font embedding (more about these restrictions in "Embedding Fonts," later in this chapter). In addition, fonts can be *subset*, which includes only part of the font. This can reduce file size.

## Embedding Text Files

You can embed text files, including Microsoft Word (DOC), Rich Text Format (RTF), and plain text (TXT) formats, in Illustrator documents by using the Place command. As you can see in Figure 36.22, Illustrator does not allow you to link text files; that option is not available.

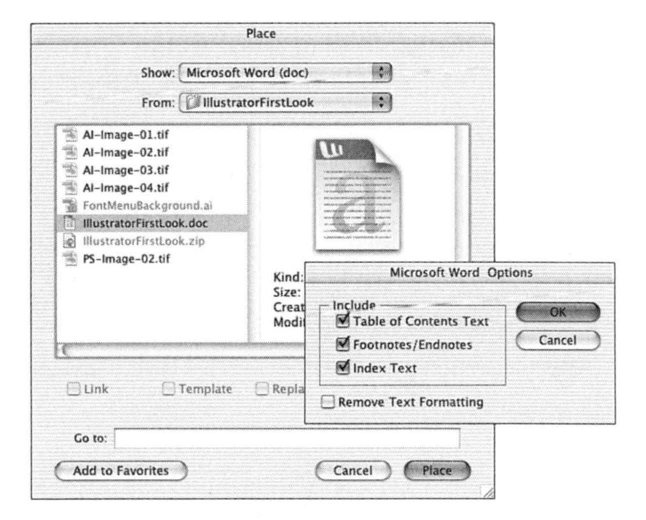


**Figure 36.22**
With the Link option grayed out, text files must be embedded rather than linked. The Microsoft Word Options dialog box opens after you select a file and click Place.

Text files embedded in an Illustrator document do not appear in the Links palette (see Figure 36.23). The text is placed in the center of the window in its own text box. It is fully editable, and the text container acts like any other.

You can wrap the newly placed text, use the spell checker, and even embed formatted text. In Figure 36.24, you can see that Illustrator accepted text of different font sizes, fonts, styles, and colors.

36

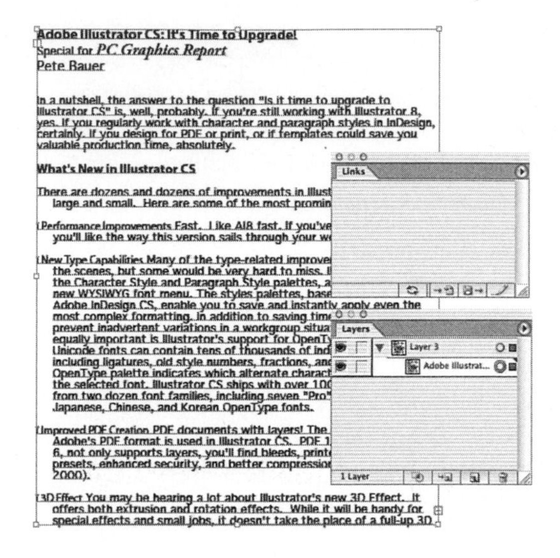


**Figure 36.23**
The Links palette ignores the embedded text file, regardless of file format.

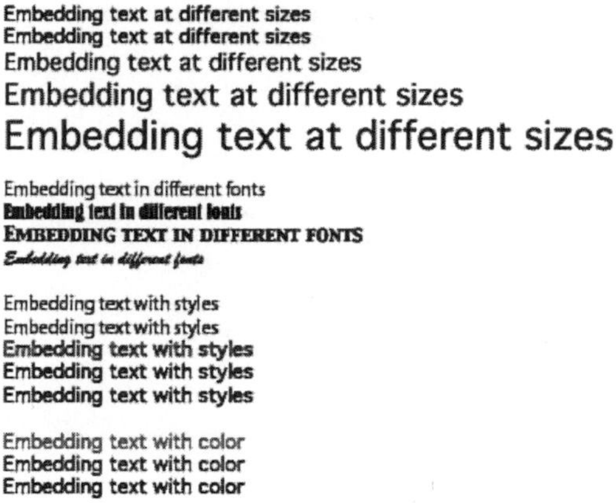

**Figure 36.24**
Illustrator substitutes a font if one isn't available.

Embedding text at different sizes
Embedding text at different sizes
Embedding text at different sizes
Embedding text at different sizes
Embedding text at different sizes

Embedding text in different fonts
Embedding text in different fonts
EMBEDDING TEXT IN DIFFERENT FONTS
Embedding text in different fonts

Embedding text with styles
Embedding text with styles
Embedding text with styles
Embedding text with styles
Embedding text with styles

Embedding text with color
Embedding text with color
Embedding text with color

## Embedding Fonts

Illustrator allows you to include the fonts that appear in the document when saving files in the Illustrator (AI), PDF, EPS, and SVG formats. Embedded fonts are available if the illustration is opened on a different computer or in a different program. When a font is not embedded and it is not installed on the computer opening the file, another font is substituted. However, that font may not have the same spacing, appearance, or size as the font originally used; therefore, the appearance of your image can be altered, sometimes drastically. Additionally, missing fonts can generate PostScript errors, preventing the document from outputting properly at a service bureau or print shop.

*Unsure about what fonts need to be embedded? See "Typefaces to Go" in the "Mastering Illustrator" section at the end of this chapter.*

Another aspect of font embedding deserves attention. Fonts are copyrighted. You may or may not have acquired the right to embed a font when you purchased or otherwise acquired the font itself. If you are sending a project to a print shop or service bureau that does not own copies of specific fonts, you must have permission from the copyright holders of these fonts to embed them. Fonts are commercial property, like any other software, and making unauthorized copies for others to use, even when you have paid for the fonts, is illegal. Adobe allows embedding of all its fonts (as long as you have acquired the fonts legally). Other foundries may not. For information on how to determine the ownership of a font, check the Adobe Web site at `www.adobe.com/type/embedding.html`.

Font subsetting is designed to reduce the size of your file by including only that part of the font necessary to reproduce your image. Subsetting is available for Illustrator (AI), SVG, and PDF formats, but not EPS.

When you're saving a file in Illustrator CS format, your choices (shown in Figure 36.25) include embedding all fonts and subsetting (if you're embedding). You can specify at what level of usage a font will be subset, but that is the extent of the option. When you're exporting as a Legacy Illustrator file, you have the options for that version of Illustrator (see Figure 36.25, rear).

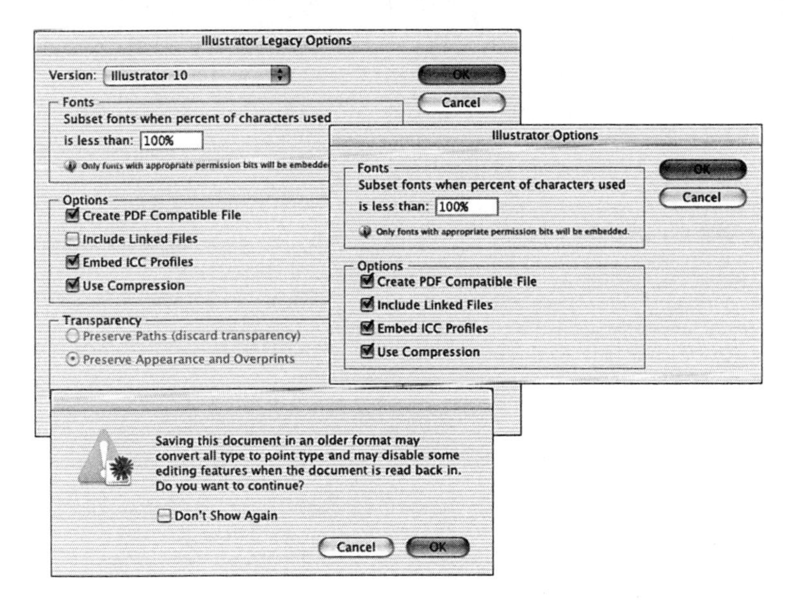


**Figure 36.25**

**Exporting as Illustrator 10 and Illustrator 9 allows you to embed fonts, just as when saving as Illustrator CS.**

# MASTERING ILLUSTRATOR

## Preflighting

*I'm sending a document with linked files to a printer. What do I have to do?*

The term *preflighting* actually refers to the quality-control process used in the prepress industry to ensure that a project can be printed successfully. Entire software programs have been designed to handle the job from top to bottom. A small part of that massive undertaking applies to this particular subject: You should gather together copies of all the linked files in a single folder, along with copies of the fonts used. Unsure of what you need in that folder? Use the command File, Document Info. The Document Info palette contains windows that list both fonts and linked images in the document. You can change the content of the palette through its menu.

## Preview Problems

*My linked image isn't showing up properly. It prints okay, but I want to be able to see it on the artboard. What's the problem?*

It's probable that the image was saved without a preview. Illustrator doesn't open the actual image to show you how it looks. Rather, the preview embedded in the original file is used. Open the file in an image-editing program and resave it with a preview. You can also open many raster image formats directly in Illustrator by choosing File, Open and then resaving them.

## Losing Link Lines

*I don't like seeing the diagonal lines across my linked images. Can I turn them off?*

Illustrator considers them to be part of the image's edges. You can make them disappear by choosing View, Hide Edges.

## Typefaces to Go

*I've heard that I don't need to include the "basic" fonts when I send out a file for printing. Is that true?*

As always, when you're sending a file to a service bureau or printer, call to confirm. It's usually better to include (with permission) all the fonts used in a document because fonts, like programs, come in different versions. Although you can easily see the difference between a program named Adobe Illustrator CS and one named Adobe Illustrator 8, it's not as easy to see the difference between font versions. Variations, however slight, can ruin your layout by changing character spacing.

37

# ILLUSTRATOR AND THE WEB

## IN THIS CHAPTER

When people discuss Illustrator and the Web, the conversation generally divides into two subjects: using Illustrator as a design tool and using Illustrator as a production tool. As a design tool, Illustrator excels in capturing the layout of each page and producing flow charts of the site links, and its nested layers enable you to plan an entire site in one document. As a production tool, Illustrator cannot be matched for creation of vector-based images.

> Although planning Web sites and creating components for the site's pages using Illustrator is great, remember that Illustrator is a vector graphics program, not a Web design tool. Use Adobe GoLive to actually put together your Web sites.



As you'll see in this chapter, transparency, Save for Web, Web-safe palette, Pixel Preview, file-optimization control, the Release to Layers command, and expanded file format import/export make Illustrator a virtual one-stop shop for graphic production. Illustrator also has support for Flash (SWF) and Scalable Vector Graphics (SVG) output, keeping it on the leading edge of Web technology.

# CREATING WEB GRAPHICS WITH ILLUSTRATOR

Here are a few concepts you should understand before you begin creating individual Web components:

- With the exception of SVG and Flash graphics, images on the Web consist of pixels. (See Chapter 4, "Pixels, Vectors, and Resolutions," for a discussion of the differences between raster and vector artwork.)
- All color on the Web is RGB, grayscale, or black and white.
- Web browsers, used to view Web sites and pages, can display only certain types of graphics images.
- You can place Illustrator's AI files into GoLive pages, but the images will be optimized and saved as pixels before being posted to the Web server.
- Each component of a Web page must be saved as a separate file for use in a Web design program, such as Adobe GoLive. Additional enhancements, such as GIF animation, button rollovers, and image slicing can be added in Adobe ImageReady (the Web production tool of Photoshop) or with Adobe LiveMotion.
- Images that are not square or rectangular require special preparation unless they are to appear on a plain white background. By default, raster images (including most Web graphics) are rectangular. With some file formats, transparency can be used to give the impression that an image is not rectangular.
- Special effects such as drop shadows must be handled with care. Despite Illustrator's transparency capabilities (see Chapter 34, "Using Masks, Transparency, and Blending Modes"), variable or graduated transparency is not generally supported on the Web.

The actual process of producing Web graphics relies on these principles: Create Web graphics at the actual pixel size, use appropriate colors, and save the graphics in an appropriate file format.

*See "Web Images Unavailable" in the "Mastering Illustrator" section at the end of this chapter if your graphics do not show up in a Web browser.*

> Web browsers ignore resolution when displaying JPEG, GIF, PNG, and other rasterized graphics. Rather than "72ppi" or "300ppi," the image is just seen as a certain number of pixels wide and a certain number of pixels high.



# Preparing for Web Graphic Creation

Establishing a Web-oriented work environment in Illustrator can save you a tremendous amount of time and effort. The time it takes to make changes to the color mode, document setup, and Illustrator interface is usually minimal.

## Units of Measure

When you're working with Web design, using pixels makes more sense than using points or inches. Virtually everything on the Web is pixel oriented. Working in pixels gives you a better perspective on the size of Web pages and graphics during the creation process.

Illustrator gives you the option of using pixels as your general unit of measure. The overall unit of measure can be changed in the Preferences (for all documents), in Document Setup (for the active document), or by (Control)-clicking right-clicking the ruler (for the active document). The Preferences dialog box's Units & Undo pane also enables you to change the unit of measure used for strokes and type.

## Setting Up the Other Preferences

In addition to the unit of measure, you may want to change several other Illustrator preferences when working with Web graphics. Here are a few:

- **General, Anti-Aliased Artwork**—Antialiasing smooths the appearance of artwork onscreen. When creating for the Web, many illustrators prefer to have this option unchecked.
- **General, Use Preview Bounds**—The bounding box can be expanded to include effects applied to a selection when this option is checked. When this option is unchecked, the bounding box uses the paths of selected objects. (A bounding box will always include the area of an applied filter.) Checking this option will help in properly aligning objects with applied effects.
- **Units & Display Performance, Identify Objects By**—When Web graphics are included as dynamic data-driven graphics, variables can be identified by an XML ID in the Variables palette. When you're not working with templates and variables, the XML ID is not required.

> Even though you have set your general unit of measure to pixels, Illustrator still does some things in inches. After changing your general unit of measure to pixels, show both the rulers and the grid to check this out. The grid is still divided into 1-inch squares. The ruler uses the nonintuitive 72 as a major unit. (It appears as 96 on monitors set for 96 pixels per inch.)
>
> Make the change in Edit, Preferences, Guides & Grid. There you can specify major gridline spacing and subdivisions.

- **Guides & Grid, Gridline Every**—By default, Illustrator is set to work with points as the general unit of measure. Switching to pixels does not change the default grid setup. Illustrator's default is one gridline every 72 points (one inch). Of more practical value for Web graphics is a gridline every 100 pixels, or for smaller work, every 10 pixels.
- **Guides & Grid, Subdivisions**—The default grid has a gridline every 72 points, with subdivisions every 8 points. Depending on the amount of precision required for the Web graphics, having subdivisions every 2, 5, or 10 pixels is perhaps more appropriate. When Snap to Grid is activated, Illustrator will align objects to the grid subdivision lines.
- **Smart Guides & Slices, Show Slice Numbers**—Slicing Web graphics allows increased control over optimization and hyperlink creation. In addition, sliced graphics appear in the browser window more quickly. Each slice is numbered consecutively, but the slice numbers are rarely needed unless you're editing an associated HTML file. However, having slice numbers visible makes it much more obvious when tiny alignment errors create unnecessary slices (see Figure 37.1).

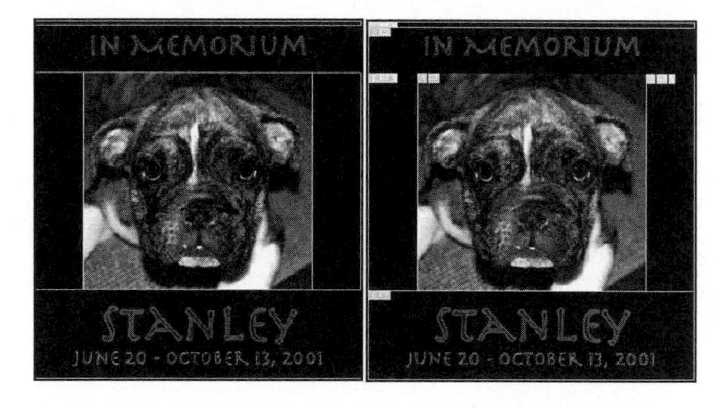


Figure 37.1
Look at the top-left corner of each of the examples. On the right, the partially hidden slice number at the top indicates that a slip of the Slice tool has resulted in a thin sliver of a slice that is totally unnecessary.

- **Smart Guides & Slices, Line Color**—Especially when slice numbers are hidden, it's a good idea to set your slice line color to a color other than that used for guides or the grid.

## Page Setup

In addition to the usual print size pages, Illustrator offers three default page sizes specifically for Web design (see Figure 37.2).

With pixels as the unit of measure, 640×480 and 800×600 are two standard monitor resolutions, whereas 468×60 is a standard size for a Web banner to be placed at the top of a Web page. When one of these page sizes is selected, Illustrator will automatically adjust the page orientation. Be aware that monitors set to 800×600 pixels will not display an 800×600 pixel page in a Web browser window. Make sure you allow room for the browser's interface items.

> Don't forget that Illustrator enables you to create templates. A template determines what Illustrator will look like when you begin work on a new document. There's no reason *not* to create a custom template that uses Web-centric settings, although one of Illustrator's predesigned templates may fit your needs.

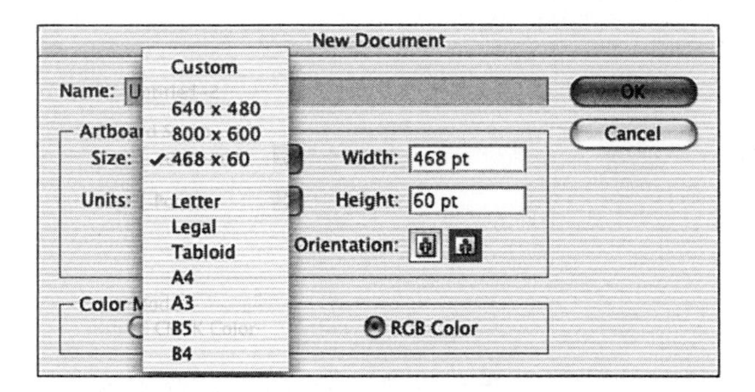


Figure 37.2
**The three default page sizes below Custom are measured in pixels.**



## View Options

Illustrator's View menu offers a couple commands that make it easier to create Web graphics. Pixel Preview simulates how your artwork will look when it has been rasterized. When Pixel Preview is selected, Illustrator changes the command Snap to Grid to the more-appropriate Snap to Pixel.

Snapping to pixels can help control how artwork rasterizes. When the edge of a vertical or horizontal line falls between two pixels, rasterization can result in a blurry or fuzzy line. Snapping to a pixel helps ensure that the artwork will rasterized cleanly.

Also in the View menu are the commands Show/Hide Page Tiling. Because Web graphics are not designed to be reproduced on paper, you can help keep your work area uncluttered by hiding the page tiling. (Of course, this does not prevent you from printing your graphics. As always, use Page Setup to select the page size and orientation. An 800×600 pixel document can usually be printed on a letter-sized, landscape-oriented page.)

# Color on the Web

Web graphics are designed and intended to be viewed via the Internet on a computer monitor. For that reason, software used to view Web pages works primarily with RGB images. The RGB color gamut can be subsetted, depending on file format and monitor color depth.

*For full information on RGB color, see Chapter 5, "Color, in Theory and in Practice," p. 159.*

The basic goal, of course, is to have the viewers of your Web pages and Web site see exactly what you intend for them to see. The epitome of this goal would be to have each and every visitor see precisely what is portrayed on your monitor.

That goal is not within reach of today's technology. Different visitors use different sizes and resolutions of monitors, set to various numbers of colors. And until such time when every monitor automatically self-calibrates and adjusts to ambient lighting changes, you cannot be assured that any given visitor to your site is seeing anything remotely close to the color scheme you spent hours devising. So why worry about this problem at all? Why spend time picking color schemes and worrying about file optimization? Because you *can* have an impact on what the viewer sees.

Although these document sizes are specifically for Web design, Illustrator does *not* automatically change the color mode. Make sure you click the button for RGB when starting a new file for the Web, even if you select a Web-specific page size.

By following certain conventions, you can limit the amount of variance from your design. You can even control exactly what your viewer sees and make a page look identical to every browser, regardless of version, platform, or color setting. Unfortunately, doing so requires using only black and white, and rather than text, each page would have to be rendered as a graphic. See Figure 37.3 for an example. Using color and modern Web technologies, such as animation, requires compromises. Limiting file size and reducing color palettes often restrict creativity, but these techniques help ensure that your message or vision is communicated accurately.



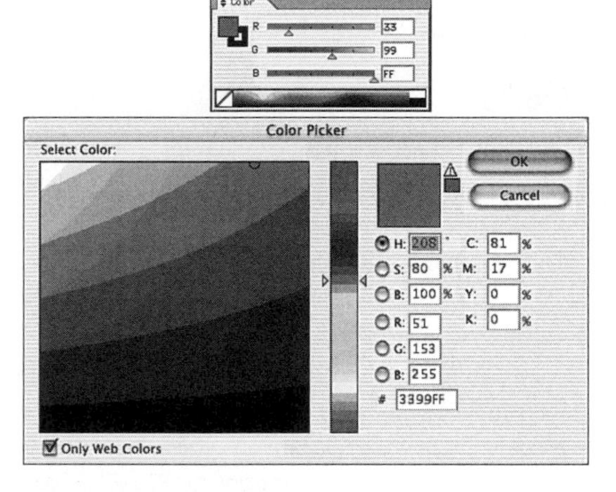


**Figure 37.3**
The appearance of a black-and-white GIF file is nearly universally consistent on the Web.

The image in Figure 37.3, saved in GIF format, is theoretically capable of appearing exactly the same with any browser capable of displaying graphics. (The original Web browsers were text-only.) The only colors used are black and white, which are common to all computer system palettes, and because the text is rendered as a graphic, you don't need to be concerned about installed fonts or the difference between Windows and Macintosh font display.

## Color Spaces for the Web

Basically, four types of color images are appropriate for the Web: black-and-white, grayscale, 8-bit RGB, and 24-bit RGB. The term *bit depth* refers to the amount of color information that can be stored for any pixel in an image.

Graphics in 8-bit RGB color can display up to 256 different colors due to the limited amount of file space available to store the color information. On the other hand, 24-bit images reserve three times as much space for each pixel's color information, allowing the recording of more than 16.7 million possible colors for each pixel. These files store 8 bits of information for each of the three color components: red, green, and blue. Of course, in each case only one of the 256

> Remember that we're discussing RGB color as 8-bit or 24-bit for the *image*, not *per channel*. Photoshop works with images that can have 8 bits of information for each color channel (24-bit RGB) or 16 bits per channel. Note that 16-bit images cannot be used on the Web.

or millions of colors is actually recorded for each pixel. Gradients or continuous-tone areas that are saved in 8-bit formats can experience severe distortion.

TROUBLESHOOTING

*If gradients are giving you problems, see "Correcting Banding in Images" in the "Mastering Illustrator" section at the end of this chapter.*

Grayscale images record as many as 256 levels of gray, including black and white. They use 8 bits of information per pixel. Black-and-white images use a single bit to record the appearance of each pixel, meaning the pixel can be white or it can be black.

Many PDAs and Internet-capable wireless devices and phones (as well as some older laptops still in use today) can display only 8-bit color. No matter the content of the image file, it is shown onscreen as 256 colors. To complicate matters a bit more, the Windows and Macintosh operating systems do not use the same 256 colors. They do, however, have 216 colors in common. These 216 colors are referred to as the *Web-safe palette.* Illustrator's Color palette and Color Picker can be set up to display (and allow you to choose) only Web-safe colors (see Figure 37.4).

If this page
appears,
your browser
is not capable
of displaying the
page you seek.
STOP

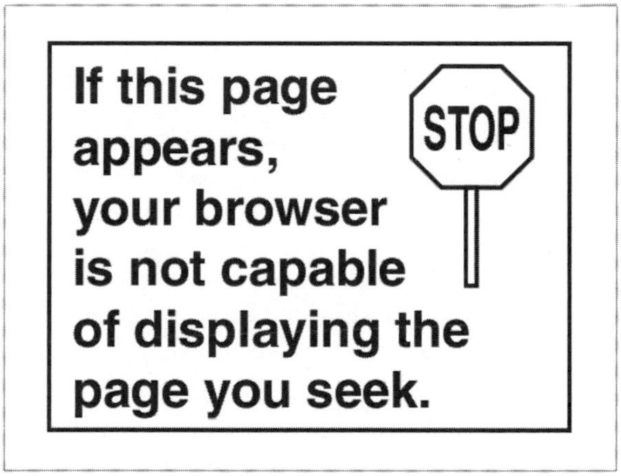

**Figure 37.4**
The Color palette menu and the check box at the bottom of the Color Picker can be used to restrict the palettes to Web-safe colors.

## HTML and Hexadecimal Notation

Web browsers use the language known as Hypertext Markup Language (HTML). This is a standardized computer language designed for use on the Internet. In HTML, each color is recorded as a series of three two-digit numbers. (Think in terms of ##, ##, and ## all run together.) If each of these two-digit numbers use our standard notation, each of them could range from 00 to 99, resulting in 100 unique numbers for each of the three pairs. That gives a total of 1,000,000 possible colors (100×100×100). However, HTML uses base-16 notation, where each of the digits can be any one of 16 different numbers (rather than 10 in our usual base-10 notation). Instead of one million possible combinations of three two-digit numbers, there are over 16.7 million possible combinations (16×16=256; 256×256=16,777,216).

Because we use only 10 numeric digits (0 through 9), HTML uses the letters A, B, C, D, E, and F to represent the additional digits. (A is equal to what we would normally consider 11, B is equal to 12, and so on.) HTML, therefore, can represent colors with such combinations as 112233, AABBCC, AA2244, and 1A2CFF. In all cases, there will be three pairs of characters (numbers or letters). Each digit in each pair will be a number from 0 to 9 *or* a letter from A through F. (Chapter 5 includes a complete explanation of how hexadecimal color nation works in HTML. See that chapter's sidebar "Hexadecimal Colors.")

In Figure 37.4, the hexadecimal notation for the selected color (a light blue, as you can tell from the RGB and CMYK components) is shown both in the Color palette and at the bottom of the Color Picker as 3399FF.



### The Return of the Web-Safe Palette

For several years now the vast majority of Web surfers have been using computers equipped with monitors and video cards that display more than 256 colors. For that reason, many leaders in the field of Web graphics (this author included) have downplayed the importance of the Web-safe palette. However, it may now be as important as ever for some Web sites. If your site is likely to be accessed regularly by visitors using PDAs or Internet-capable cell phones, then the Web-safe palette may be appropriate for your graphics. Some of these devices are already capable of displaying thousands of colors on their LCD screens, but models that are limited to 256 colors will be in use for years.

## File Format Considerations

Graphics produced for use on the Web must be saved in a file format that can be displayed by the Web browser. Only a half dozen or so graphics formats can be used on the Web successfully. Of them, only two are natively supported by all major Web browsers. The JPEG (Joint Photographic Experts Group) format is used for continuous-tone images, such as photographs and images with gradients or other gradual shifts in color. GIF (Graphic Interchange Format) is used for images with large areas of solid color and images whose colors have little or no variation. JPEG supports 24-bit color (millions of colors), whereas GIF files can contain a maximum of 256 colors (8-bit color).

Also growing in popularity for use on the Web, and supported by some later-generation browsers, are the 8-bit and 24-bit PNG file formats. PNG (Portable Network Graphics) is designed to supplement or replace JPEG and GIF. WBMP is a file format designed for use with wireless Internet devices, recording images as black-and-white for small file size and speedy download. Some other file formats can be viewed only with Web browser plug-ins, separate programs that work within the browser to interpret and display the images. These formats include Macromedia's Flash (SWF) format and the new Scalable Vector Graphics (SVG) format. JPEG, GIF, PNG, and WBMP are all raster image formats, whereas SWF and SVG support vector artwork.

Files in Adobe's PDF (Acrobat) format are often distributed over the Web and integrated into Web sites. When the appropriate plug-in is not installed for the Web browser, these documents and images are actually viewed in Adobe Acrobat Reader.

Illustrator's Save for Web capability is used to produce GIF, JPEG, PNG, and WBMP files and can also create SWF (Flash) and SVG graphics. You also can choose File, Export to create JPEG files (although this method is not recommended for Web-destined files), and you can use Export to create SWF (Flash) files and Save As for SVG files.

## Rasterization

The differences between vector art and raster art are explored in Chapter 4. In summary, vector art, such as that produced by Illustrator, is recorded as a series of mathematical descriptions of objects and paths and their strokes and fills. When the file is opened, the appearance of the objects and paths is uniform, no matter the size of the image. Each relationship among the various objects and paths is maintained, including the relative size and placement of strokes and fills. Vector-based art remains sharp and clear when displayed or printed at varying sizes, and it's therefore often called *resolution independent*.

Raster art, on the other hand, is recorded as a series of colored pixels. Each pixel's location and color are saved and then, when the file is opened, displayed on the screen. If a raster image is resized, the program displaying the image must recalculate the appearance of the image. Because pixels on a monitor are physically set by the monitor's resolution and cannot be resized by the program, this means simulating the appearance of each pixel by averaging its color with those of the surrounding pixels. Raster art can become blurred or distorted when enlarged or reduced.



When you use Save for Web or export to a raster format, Illustrator's vector artwork is automatically converted to pixels. You can manually covert to pixels using the Object, Rasterize command.

## File Size and the Web

Visitors to a Web site access the information remotely. The data is sent to their computers and forwarded to their monitors by means of wires and cables (and in some cases, wirelessly). Very often, the information travels, in part, along telephone cables. Such transmission of data has some limitations, not the least of which is speed. Only so much information can pass along the cables and wires during a specified period of time. The typical unit of measure is one second. The data-transfer rates are measured in kilobits per second (Kbps) or megabits per second (Mbps). Some internal networks can handle gigabits per second (Gbps), and one day soon that might be the norm for home Internet links. In the meantime, a massive number of Web surfers are surfing with download times measured at 53Kbps or slower.

To efficiently serve visitors who don't have access to DSL, cable modem, or other high-speed connections (those who still depend on dial-up Internet connections), you should keep file size to a minimum. The balance between size and speed can be hard to find. Keep in mind, however, that many Web surfers are not patient. They will not wait for a large image to download unless, perhaps, that particular image is the reason for their visit to your site. Art-related Web sites are one example of an exception. The connection speed is just one of many factors that affect how quickly a Web page downloads. A network server's traffic load, the route that the data must travel, and even how many people are surfing the Web at a particular time are just some of the other factors.

There are two types of file sizes for Web graphics. One is the actual pixel space occupied by the image on the computer screen, and the other is the file size as it is transmitted to the viewer's computer. A distinct relationship exists between the two, but you also can find ways to reduce the file size without changing the pixel size of an image.

The pixel dimensions of a graphic are typically determined by the Web page designer. Aesthetic and artistic considerations are often balanced with practicality. In some cases, a single image occupies an entire page. The image's dimensions in such a situation could depend on the expected monitor resolution of the typical visitor, with download times as an additional concern.

The file size and download time for individual images of given pixel dimensions depend on file format and compression. Compression reduces a file's size by using various types of "shorthand" to record the file's content. For example, rather than record a series of three pixels as

```
"pixel 1-blue; pixel 2-blue; pixel 3-blue."
```

compression could shorten the series to

```
"pixels 1-3-blue."
```

(This example is, of course, a simplification.)



### Animation on the Web

Illustrator can be used to create basic Flash animation for the Web, but it currently offers no support for animated GIF production. Although you can prepare layered images that can be used in such animations, the actual GIF file must be produced in another program, such as Adobe ImageReady. See Chapter 23, "Creating Rollovers and Adding Animation," for more information on creating animated GIFs.

### Cascading Style Sheets

Cascading Style Sheets (CSS) are an extension to HTML that allow for multiple layers on a Web page. The layers can be positioned absolutely, giving the designer more control over what a browser will display. In addition, layers can partially overlap with CSS. CSS also offers designers more control over the appearance of fonts, background images, and borders. Creating CSS is discussed later in this chapter, in the section "Save for Web and Image Optimizing."

## SYMBOLS AND SYMBOLISM FOR THE WEB

Symbols are artwork that can be included once in an image and used many times. Hundreds of instances of a single symbol can appear in a document, but the file need only contain the artwork itself once, along with a record of where the symbols should appear. Symbolism can substantially reduce the size of a graphics file.

### How Symbols Work in Illustrator

Artwork or text is saved as a symbol and stored in the Symbols palette (see Figure 37.5). The eight symbolism tools are used to add the artwork to the artboard and to manipulate it. Using the various symbolism tools, you can produce a wide variety of appearances among a set of symbol instances. This increased variation and randomness comes at a very low cost in terms of file size—the file actually contains only a single instance of each symbol that you use. Symbols can be saved in libraries, just like brushes, to be made available to any Illustrator document.

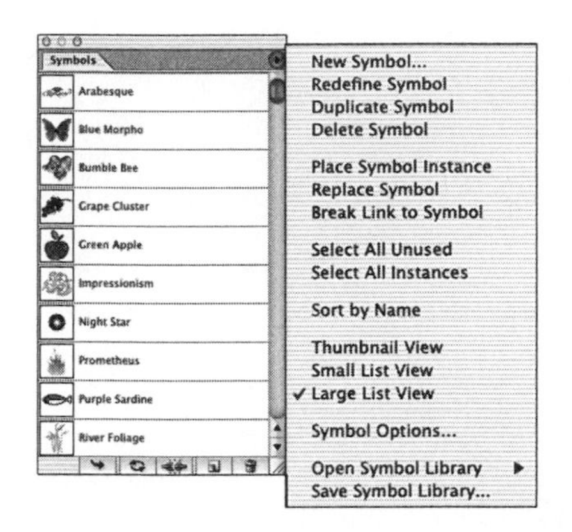


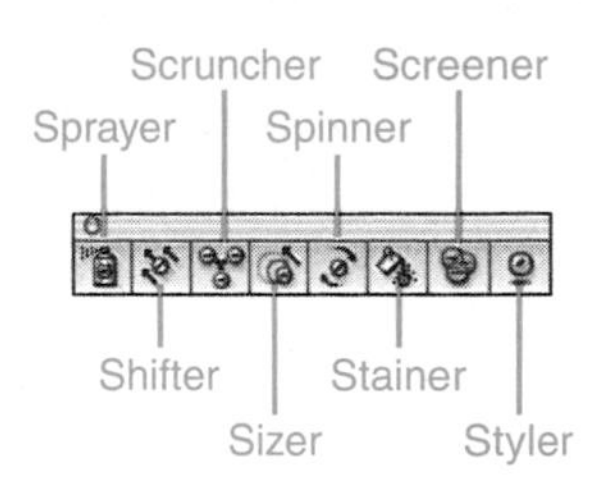


**Figure 37.5**
**The Symbols palette is shown with its menu open, along with the symbolism tools tearoff palette, detached from the Toolbox.**

Symbol *instances* can be automatically updated in a document to reflect changes to the symbol artwork. (The term *instance* is applied to each occurrence of the symbol artwork in a document.)

Symbol *sets* are groups of symbol instances that are treated as a single object. You can have multiple symbols (different artwork) in a single symbol set. A symbol set is created when the Symbol Sprayer tool is dragged on the artboard. If the set is selected on the artboard when the Symbol Sprayer is dragged again, additional instances will be added to the set, whether the same symbol or a different symbol is selected in the Symbols palette.

Symbols can be created from virtually any artwork or text in Illustrator, with the exception of linked images, graphs, and some groups (such as groups that include graphs).

## Illustrator at Work: Using the Symbolism Tools

The easiest way to get a feel for how symbols are created and manipulated is to work with the symbolism tools. Follow these steps:

1. Open a new Illustrator document (800×600m pixels, RGB).
2. In the Toolbox, click and hold on the Symbol Sprayer. With the mouse button still down, move to the tearoff arrow at the far right of the Symbols tools palette and then release the mouse button. Position this tools palette somewhere convenient onscreen. If you have a very large monitor, you can tear off multiple copies of the mini-palette and position them in a variety of spots.
3. Open the Symbols palette, position it in a convenient spot on the artboard, and select the symbol Blue Morpho. (You'll see it as a blue butterfly in thumbnail view. Refer to Figure 37.5, if necessary, to identify the symbol.)
4. Add some symbols instances to the artboard. Drag the mouse in a series of curves, from the upper left to the lower right. Drag at different speeds and pause the cursor in a spot or two. Watch how symbol instances are distributed according to the cursor movement and speed.

> Although symbols and symbolism have roots in Web design, they can be used with any illustration. In fact, Illustrator's 3D effect *requires* that artwork be defined as symbols before it can be mapped to an object.

37

5. Undo to remove those symbol instances from the artboard. Now that you've got some understanding of the Symbol Sprayer, add Blue Morpho symbols across the top of the artboard. Drag quickly at first, then more slowly for a greater density of symbols on the right half of the artboard.

6. With that set of symbols still active (selected on the artboard), go to the Symbols palette and switch to the Bumble Bee symbol. Click in a few places among the butterflies, and click and hold once to add a few symbols in the same place. Watch how the existing symbols shift to make room for the new symbols. Your work area might look something like that shown in Figure 37.6.

Symbols are applied to the artboard as collections of instances. Except when symbolism tools are in use, they are treated as a single entity. For example, the transform tools can be used, but the collection of symbol instances will be treated as if it were a group.



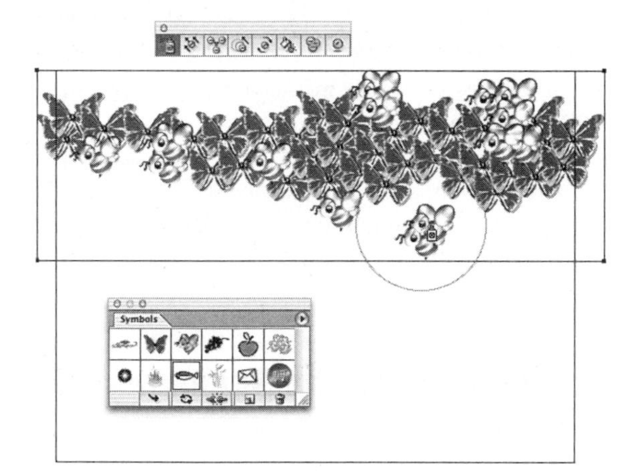


**Figure 37.6**
The only important aspect at this point is that you have a single set of symbols, with two different symbols included.

7. Switch from the Symbol Sprayer to the Symbol Shifter, the second tool in the tearoff palette. Click and drag some of the symbol instances around within the set. Observe how the change is concentrated within the circle that represents the tool's diameter, but also note how symbol instances that fall partially within the circle are also altered (to a lesser degree). If any instances are beyond the edges of the artboard, drag them in. With the Bumble Bee instance still selected in the Symbols palette, the effect will be greater on those symbols. In the palette, click the Blue Morpho symbol to move butterflies rather than bees.

8. Switch to the Symbol Scruncher tool. In areas of lower density of symbols, click and hold to bring them closer together. In areas where the butterflies are spread out, press the (Option) [Alt] key, then click and hold down the mouse button. This brings the artwork closer together. Switch to the Bumble Bee symbol in the Symbols palette to change those instances.

9. Use the Symbol Sizer tool to create variations and randomness in the size of both the bees and the butterflies. Click and hold to enlarge individual instances; add the (Option) [Alt] key to shrink them. The symbols on the artboard should show substantial variation, perhaps like that shown in Figure 37.7.

10. Change to the Symbol Spinner tool. In the Symbols palette, click the Bumble Bee symbol. The Symbol Spinner is best used by clicking and dragging left or right. Watch on the artboard as

arrows appear, indicating not only which symbol instances are being changed, but how they're being changed. Observe how symbol instances in the center of the tool's circle are changed much more dramatically than those near the edge of the circle. Vary the rotation of both bees and butterflies on the artboard, increasing the apparent randomness of the symbols.

Figure 37.7
Don't try to replicate this figure exactly—it's not important what size variations you show, just that some exist.



11. Select the Symbol Stainer tool. Set the fill color to yellow, make sure that the Blue Morpho symbol is selected in the Symbols palette, and click a couple times in different parts of the symbol set. Change to a different fill color and click a few more times. Watch what happens when you click and hold with the Symbol Stainer. (Undo, if the change was too extreme.) When you're working with the Symbol Stainer, the selected color gradually replaces the existing fill color.

12. Select the Symbol Screener tool. This tool varies the opacity of the symbol instances. A couple quick clicks here and there, especially in areas where the instances are densest, is all it should take to create variation.

13. Activate the Symbol Styler tool. In the Graphic Styles palette, click the style Tissue Paper Collage to activate it. Take a look at your symbol set. Look for a single symbol instance of the Blue Morpho somewhat off to itself. Click once, very quickly, on the most isolated instance of the butterfly symbol you see. (If none of the butterflies are isolated, use the Symbol Shifter and/or the Symbol Scruncher to move one aside.) Now click, again quickly, in the middle of a group of butterflies. Compare the time it takes to apply the style. If you'd like, click and hold for a half-second with the Symbol Styler. Be patient while Illustrator applies the style; then undo this change. Your symbol set may look something like the one at the bottom of Figure 37.8.

> You can click outside the symbol set, hold down the mouse button, and quickly drag across the symbols to produce a mild change with the Symbol Screener and related symbolism tools.

The capabilities of the symbolism tools can be summarized this way:

- **Symbol Sprayer**—This tool adds instances of a selected symbol to the artboard. Select a symbol from the Symbols palette and drag the Symbol Sprayer around. The longer the mouse button is held down in one place, the more instances of the selected symbol will be added. The same can be said about dragging: The slower the drag, the more dense the symbols.

> Create custom styles for use specifically with a symbol for a specific purpose—applying a style to a symbol can cause incredible slowdowns in screen redraw time. Also, once you've applied the style, consider putting the symbol set into Outline view in the Layers palette.

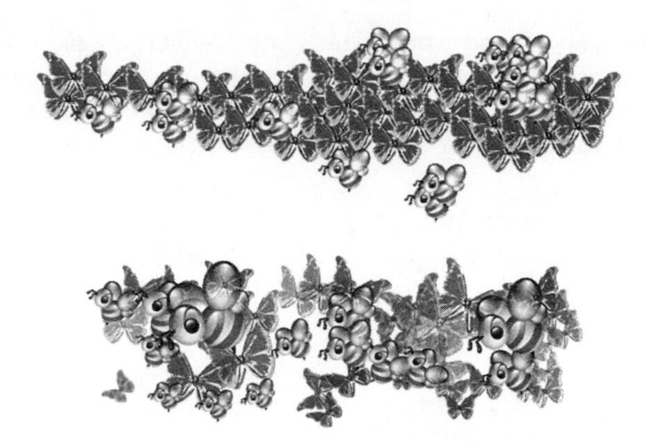

Figure 37.8

Compare the original set of symbols (top) with that created using the symbolism tools. Variety and randomness can be introduced—and precisely controlled—with these tools.



- **Symbol Shifter**—The Symbol Shifter is used to reposition symbol instances on the artboard. All instances that fall within the diameter of the brush can be dragged, and those nearby but outside the brush may also be shifted a bit. When using the Symbol Shifter on overlapping symbol instances, you can hold down the Shift key to bring the instances being shifted to the top of the stacking order. (Shift-Option) [Shift+Alt] sends the affected instances behind.
- **Symbol Scruncher**—This tool is best used by positioning the cursor and holding down the mouse button. Symbol instances within the diameter of the brush will be moved toward the center of the cursor. Those nearer the center will be affected more than those near the circumference of the brush. Holding down the (Option) [Alt] key while working with the Symbol Scruncher reverses the effect, moving symbol instances away from the center of the cursor.
- **Symbol Sizer**—Used to help randomize symbol instances, the Symbol Sizer creates various sizes of the symbol within the cursor. Like the Symbol Scruncher, the effect is more concentrated toward the center of the brush. The Symbol Sizer can also decrease the size of symbol instances—simply use it in conjunction with the (Option) [Alt] key. In addition, the Shift key can be used to maintain the symbol density.
- **Symbol Spinner**—The Symbol Spinner rotates symbol instances while it's dragged. The live previews on the artboard, rather than being outlines of the symbol, are arrows showing the direction of rotation. The modifier keys are not used with the Symbol Spinner tool.
- **Symbol Stainer**—This tool changes the color of symbol instances, using the fill color. The longer the mouse button is depressed and the cursor positioned over an area, the more of the fill color that will be applied, replacing the symbol instance's original color. A series of clicks or quick drags gives good control with this tool, providing a more random or mixed result. The (Option) [Alt] key works with the Symbol Stainer to reduce the amount of colorization. The Shift key will make the effect of the tool uniform while you work.
- **Symbol Screener**—The Symbol Screener reduces symbol opacity. The (Option) [Alt] key can be used with the Symbol Screener to restore opacity to symbol instances.

- **Symbol Styler**—To use the Symbol Styler, first select a style from Illustrator's Styles palette. Keep in mind that excellent results can be achieved with styles you create to be applied to a specific symbol. While working with the Symbol Styler tool, you can hold the effect constant by pressing the Shift key. The effect of the Symbol Styler can be reduced by holding down the (Option) [Alt] key and using the tool again on any instances that were "overstyled."

If complex symbols and styles are slowing your screen redraw, consider using the Layers palette to show that layer in Outline mode. (Command)-clicking [Ctrl]-clicking the eyeball icon will change the layer visibility to Outline mode. The symbols will be represented on the artboard by a single simple rectangle, and screen redraw time will be greatly improved.



## Symbolism Tool Options

The symbolism tools use a unified dialog box for the Symbolism Tool Options (see Figure 37.9). A single brush size is defined for all eight tools.

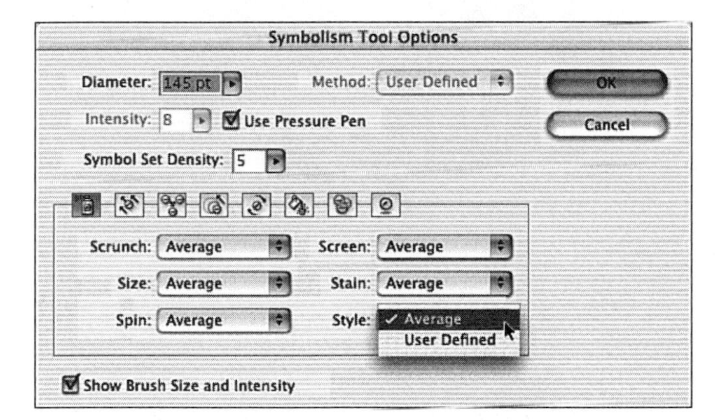


Figure 37.9
Shown are the Symbol Sprayer options.

To view and set the options for each symbolism tool, click the tool's icon in the dialog box. The top part of the dialog box is common to all these tools:

- The Diameter slider and numeric field determine the size of the active area for each tool, what can be referred to as the *brush size*. The value can range from 1 point to 999 points, or the equivalent in other units of measure.
- Intensity, which ranges from 1 to 10, determines the power of the tool. (It is grayed out in Figure 39.9 because Use Pressure Pen is checked.) In the case of the Symbol Sprayer, Intensity refers to the number of symbol instances placed on the artboard. For the other tools, Intensity governs how quickly the tool makes its changes to the selected symbol set. A low Intensity setting enables you to work more precisely, whereas a higher Intensity setting produces dramatic effects much more quickly.
- The Use Pressure Pen check box is available when a drawing tablet, such as a Wacom Intuos tablet, is connected to the computer. Pressure-sensitive tablets enable you to change the intensity as you draw by changing how hard you push on the tablet with the stylus. In Figure 37.10,

a Wacom tablet was used to create a symbol set with varying intensity. Using the mouse, the speed with which the cursor is moved could produce a similar change in the number of symbol instances added to the artboard. However, with the pressure-sensitive stylus, a smoother, more natural drawing movement can be used to change the intensity by changing the pressure on the tablet.



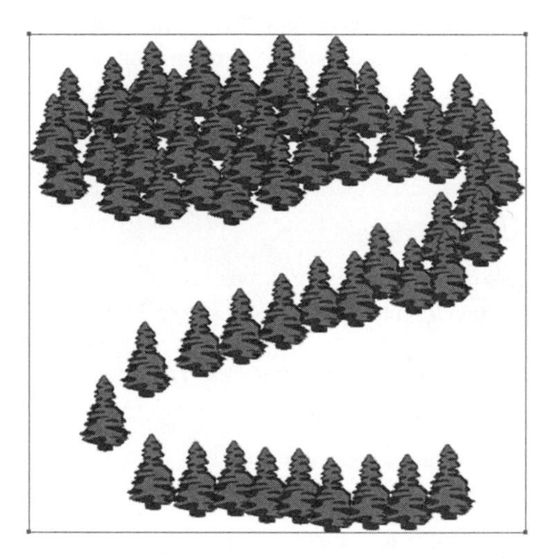

**Figure 37.10**
Using a pressure-sensitive pen provides an easy way to control the intensity of symbolism tools.

- Symbol Set Density can range from 1 to 10. This controls how tightly the individual symbol instances will be placed within the symbol set. In addition to setting this option before using the Symbol Sprayer, you should be aware that Symbol Set Density is "live" in Illustrator, so it can be adjusted at any time after the symbols are added to the artboard. To change the density of an existing set, select the set on the artboard, open the Symbolism Tool Options by double-clicking any symbolism tool icon in the Toolbox, and drag the slider. The change in density will be shown on the artboard as the slider is dragged. In Figure 37.11, a single set of symbols was copied twice, creating three identical symbol sets. The set on the left, the largest, has a density of 1. In the upper-right example, the density is set to 5. The lower-right symbol set has a density of 10.

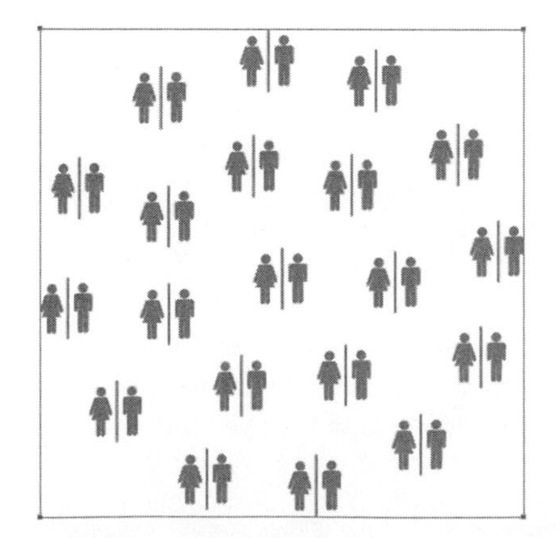

**Figure 37.11**
Each of the three symbol sets is identical except for density.

- To the upper-right of the Symbolism Tool Options dialog box, grayed out in Figure 37.9, is the Method pop-up menu. Although it is not used with the Symbol Sprayer and Shifter tools, it serves various functions with the other tools. For the other tools, the pop-up menu offers the choice of Average, User Defined, and Random. The default setting is User Defined, which enables you to control the tool's effect with the speed and direction of the cursor movement. Random produces variations in an effect. Average is designed to be used after you change a symbol set with a symbolism tool. By then switching that tool to the Average option, you can average the modifications of the symbol instances within the brush diameter, bringing their variations closer together.



In addition to the common options, the Symbol Sprayer and Symbol Sizer have tool-specific options. The Symbol Sprayer has the most complex options, each of which can be set to Average or User Defined. Average uses the values with which the symbol was originally designed when creating a symbol set. When you add symbols to an existing set whose instances have been modified, the Average option will create new instances based on the average of existing instances within the brush diameter. Here's the rundown on the options for the Symbol Sprayer and Symbol Sizer tools:

- Scrunch will space symbol instances according to the speed and direction of the mouse drag when set to User Defined.
- Setting Size to User Defined uses the symbol's default size. When you add instances to a symbol set that has been altered with the Symbol Sizer, the User Defined option allows the Symbol Sprayer to add default-sized symbol instances.
- When Spin is set to User Defined, the orientation of symbol instances is toward the direction of mouse movement.
- Screen uses the opacity of the Transparency palette when set to User Defined.
- When the User Defined option is selected, Stain adds the current background color.
- When Style is set to Average, the symbol is added as designed. When Style is changed to User Defined, any style selected in the Styles palette is added to the symbol instances.

# Replacing a Symbol in an Image

Symbols are "live" in Illustrator in a variety of ways. In addition to adjusting size, position, rotation, color, transparency, and applying a style, you can select a symbol set on the artboard and switch the symbol. Select a new symbol in the palette and then use either the Replace Symbol button at the bottom of the palette or the palette menu command Replace Symbol. All symbol instances within the selected set will be switched to the new symbol. They will also retain any changes made with the symbolism tools. For example, if the Symbol Stainer, Symbol Sizer, and Symbol Screener have all been used on a set of symbols prior to you replacing the

Illustrator also enables you to adjust the size of the symbolism tools' active area, the brush size, on the fly. With a symbolism tool active, use the left and right bracket keys (found to the right of the P key on the keyboard) to decrease and increase the brush diameter.

symbol, afterward the individual instances of the new symbol will retain the prior tint, size, and opacity changes.

## Updating a Symbol and Breaking Links



A symbol can be changed, even after it has been used on the artboard. Editing a symbol is simply a matter of adding it to the artboard, changing the artwork, and saving the symbol back to the Symbols palette.

In Figure 37.12, a symbol set was created and duplicated. The top symbol set was disassociated from the original symbol by clicking the Break Link button at the bottom of the Symbols palette. An instance of the symbol (dashed box to the left) was then placed on the artboard and expanded. Then the artwork was changed (dashed box on the right). When the symbol was *redefined* in the Symbols palette, the set whose link was maintained was updated automatically.

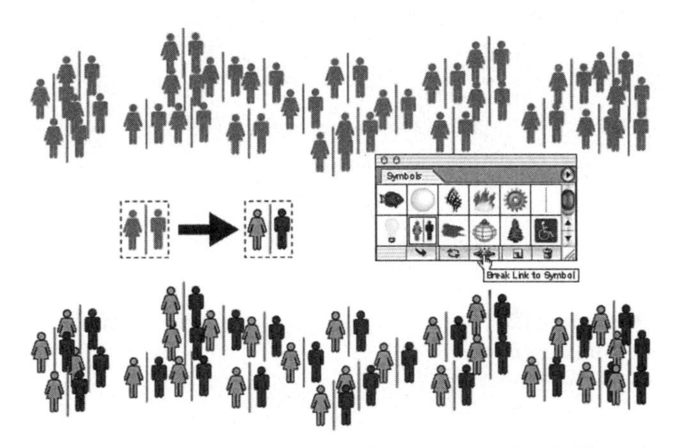


**Figure 37.12**
When the symbol was redefined, the lower set was updated. The link between the upper set and the symbol had been broken, so that set was not updated.

The concepts behind updating a symbol are similar to those that govern styles in Illustrator:

- Symbols on the artboard maintain their link to the original symbol in the Symbols palette, unless that link is broken.
- If a symbol in the Symbols palette is redefined, all artwork using that symbol will be updated, unless the link is broken.
- To redefine a symbol, add a single instance to the artboard, make changes, and then use the Symbols palette menu command Redefine Symbol. (The symbol to be redefined must be selected in the Symbols palette, and the new symbol artwork must be selected on the artboard.)
- After adding a symbol instance to the artboard, you can rotate, scale, and shear it; you can apply effects and styles; and you can make changes in the Appearance and Transparency palettes.
- You can also alter a symbol by using the menu command Object, Expand. You can ungroup and alter anything about the symbol's appearance.
- When multiple symbols occur in a symbol set, redefining a symbol affects only those instances that were originally that symbol.

- To break a link, select the symbol set on the artboard and click the Break Link to Symbol button (shown in Figure 37.12).
- Breaking a link severs the connection between a symbol set and the Symbols palette. If multiple symbols appear in a set, all links are broken.

Any artwork can be stored in the Symbols palette, even if you never use it with the symbolism tools. A company logo, for example, can be defined as a symbol and then added to any image, at any time, with the Place Symbol Instance button at the bottom of the Symbols palette.



## Creating a Custom Symbol

Virtually any Illustrator artwork (except linked files) can be used as a symbol. Select the artwork on the artboard and use the Symbols palette menu command New Symbol or click the New Symbol button (see Figure 37.13). The artwork is added to the Symbols palette, ready to go.

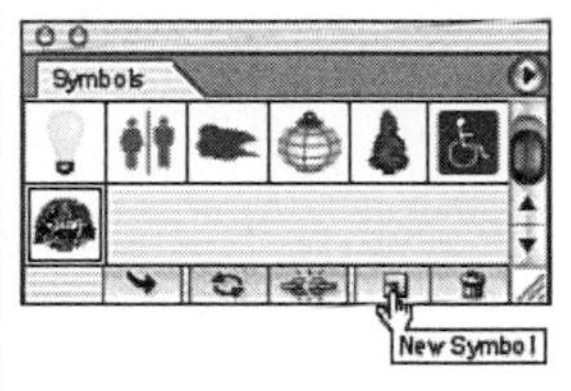


Figure 37.13
New symbols are added to the bottom of the Symbols palette.

As with other libraries in Illustrator, you can add the contents of another document's Symbols palette to the current document. Use the menu command Window, Symbol Library, Other Library. Navigate to the document whose symbols you want to add and select it. A separate palette will open, with the source document's name in the tab.

## Expanding Symbol Sets and Instances

The Expand menu command object works with both symbol sets and symbol instances. The difference between the two uses is shown in Figure 37.14. The top fish is an expanded instance, whereas the others in the school were expanded as a set.

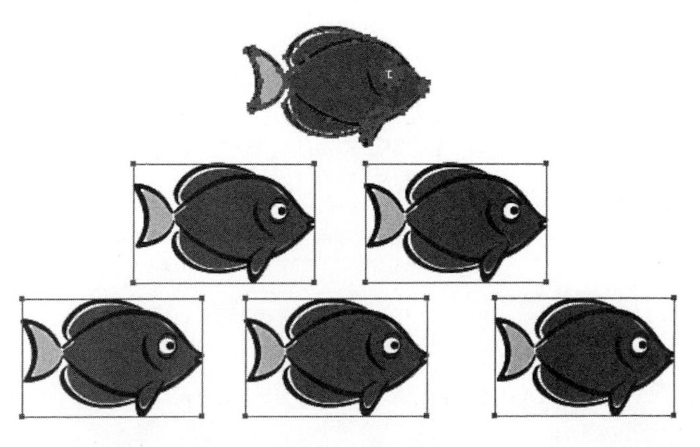

Figure 37.14
When a symbol set is expanded, the symbol instances become individual objects in a group. The instances can then be expanded to grouped paths.

# SAVE FOR WEB AND IMAGE OPTIMIZING

Save for Web is used with both Illustrator and Photoshop. Although there are a couple differences, generally speaking, the functions and options are the same. Illustrator's Save for Web feature offers SVG and SWF (Flash) output; Photoshop's version includes an Edit in ImageReady button. When it comes to creating GIF, JPEG, PNG, and WBMP files, the two versions have the same capabilities.

Save for Web is designed to do exactly that—save images for the Web. You use it to create an image that balances image quality with size (the smaller the file, the faster the download and the less the server storage requirement). It strips out most extraneous information, such as thumbnails and previews, although you can retain a file's EXIF information (metadata).



## Basic Image Optimization with Save for Web

At first glance, the Save for Web dialog box, shown in Figure 37.15, looks daunting. It almost seems to be a program in itself, with an entirely new interface to learn. However, it is not very imposing after the features are identified and explained. In fact, using Save for Web is far simpler than using the trial-and-error method often employed to optimize images for the Web.

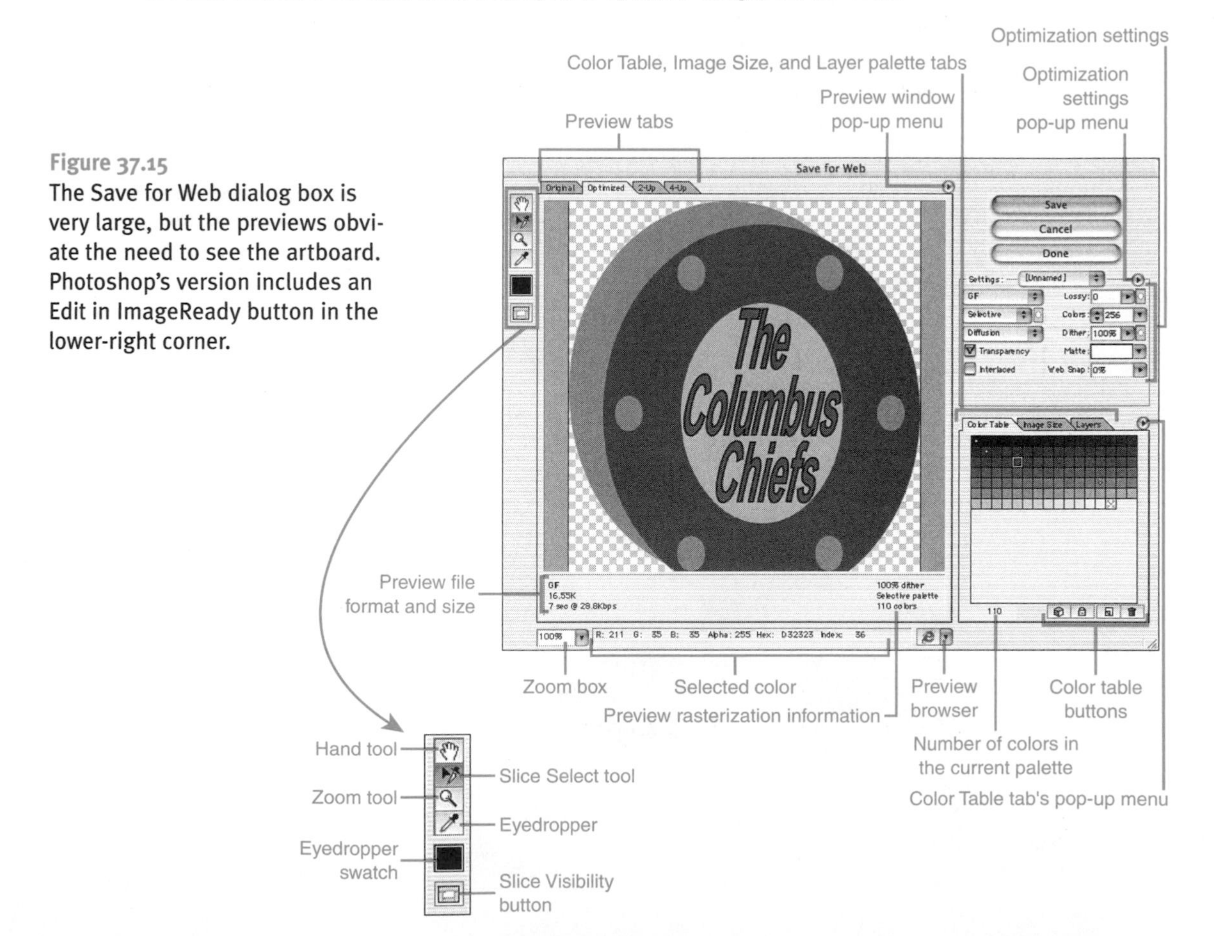


**Figure 37.15**
The Save for Web dialog box is very large, but the previews obviate the need to see the artboard. Photoshop's version includes an Edit in ImageReady button in the lower-right corner.

*Optimization* is the process of selecting the balance between file size (download time) and image quality (compression and number of colors in the image). Illustrator's Save for Web feature offers you choices and helps you make your decisions.

Figure 37.15 identifies the elements of the default Save for Web view. Here is further explanation:

- The four tabs in the preview window present the panels as labeled. Examples of the other panels and how they differ from the Optimized panel are shown in Figure 37.18 through Figure 37.20.
- The four tools available to you in Save for Web are the Hand tool, the Slice Select tool, the Zoom tool, and the Eyedropper. The swatch below the Eyedropper shows what color was most recently clicked with that tool. The button below the swatch allows you to toggle the visibility of slices.
- The information at the lower left of the preview window tells you what you are looking at in the preview window. Here, you can find the file format, the size of the file, and how long it will take to download from your Web site onto your visitor's screen (more or less). The connection speed shown is the default 28.8Kbps, but you can select a faster or slower modem speed from the preview window pop-up menu. The values are taken from the optimization settings.
- The Zoom box has a pop-up menu of nine levels, from 12.5% to 1600%, as well as a Fit in Window option. You can double-click in the box and type any value from 1 to 1600.
- The line at the bottom of the preview window tells you the color value under the cursor, either in the preview window or in the color table. When the cursor is over transparency or outside the preview area, the R, G, B, Alpha, and Hex values are empty. With the cursor over a color or over transparency, if there is any, the *index number* of the Save for Web window is shown. It refers to the specific swatch in the color palette that represents a particular color. The Alpha information refers to transparency. When a channel is used to store the information, it has 256 levels of transparency. The values in this item range from 0 to 255. Hex refers to the hexadecimal name of the Web-safe color. See the section "HTML and Hexadecimal Notation" earlier in this chapter for more information about this color numbering system.
- The information at the lower right tells you what you are seeing in the preview window. Whereas the information to the left of the window describes the file format and size, this section describes the number of colors and how they are handled. You can adjust the values by manipulating the optimization settings.

**Caution**

Despite the size and complexity of the Save for Web feature, remember that it is a dialog box. As such, when it is open, you have certain restrictions that you don't have in an Illustrator document window. For example, you cannot click to access Help; no Undo function is available, even with the keyboard shortcut (Command-Z) [Ctrl+Z]; there is no obvious way to save your work in the middle (you are offered OK and Cancel buttons); and you cannot collapse the window (Macintosh). Some tricks, however, are built in to Save for Web. You'll find them in the section "Taming the Save for Web Dialog Box," later in this chapter.

- The Preview Browser button allows you to preview your choices in an actual browser window. Your choices are the browsers installed on your computer. Illustrator starts the browser (if it is not already running) and opens a window with the image as it appears in the current window. (In 2-Up and 4-Up views, whichever preview is selected appears in the browser window.)
- The number in the lower left of the color table tells you how many colors actually are used in the image.
- The Color Table buttons in the lower right of the color table are as follows, starting from the left:
  - **Snap to Web Palette**—Changes any swatch selected in the color table to a Web-safe color.
  - **Lock Color**—Prevents a color swatch from being deleted or changed in the color table or in the image.
  - **Add Eyedropper Color**—Adds to the color table a color that has been sampled with the Eyedropper tool. This is useful in the 2-Up and 4-Up windows when a variation has altered a color.
  - **Delete Selected Color(s)**—Deletes from both the color table and the image itself any swatches selected in the table.
- The color table holds a swatch for each color currently in use in the image. This table, of course, is available only for the indexed color modes (GIF and PNG-8). Showing all 16.7 million possible colors of a continuous-tone image is not practical in table form. See the section "The Color Table," later in this chapter, for more details.
- The Color Table tab's pop-up menu will also be discussed in the section "The Color Table," later in the chapter.
- The optimization settings are the core of the Save for Web feature. Changes are made here during the optimization process. See the section "The Optimization Settings," later in this chapter, for more details.
- The Optimization Settings pop-up menu will be described later in detail in the section "The Optimization Settings."
- The Preview window pop-up menu offers the option of previewing how an image will look when dithered by a browser using 8-bit color. Browser dithering is not available for the original in 2-Up or 4-Up mode and can be turned on or off individually for each of the other three panes in 4-Up. You can also adjust the calculation of download time by selecting the target speed of the Internet connection. Save for Web calculates approximately how long it will take to download the image over a connection with a speed of 14.4Kbps, 28.8Kbps, or 56.6Kbps. Faster connections, such as cable modem, DSL, and T1, are not considered because of the minimal amount of time they require to download most graphics.

Optimizing a vector art illustration can be as simple as choosing the GIF format. With its built-in compression, the GIF format can produce very small files from images such as the one shown to the left in Figure 37.16. This image has large areas of solid color, with no areas where the color value changes gradually (such as a gradient). The Save for Web feature allows you to make simple decisions as well as fine-tune an image until you achieve the perfect balance between file size and image quality.

GIF, JPEG, and PNG all require a rasterized image—that is, an image turned into a series of pixels that can be displayed by a Web browser. This is best done in Illustrator by Save for Web. Figure 37.17 shows the results of choosing Effect, Rasterize.

When the two images in Figure 37.17 were rasterized, the resolution was set for Screen (72dpi), with Antialiasing checked. Note the degradation of the text and the slight banding in the gradated center of the image on the right.

Save for Web is much like a standalone application in more respects than one. In addition to having a complex interface, it has its own preferences file. If you start having problems with Save for Web, delete this file. You'll find it in the Settings folder for both Illustrator and Photoshop.

37

**Figure 37.16**
Before you explore the Save for Web options, take a look at the subject images. The image on the left is all vector art, with no gradients or rasterized objects. The logo on the right contains several gradients.

**Figure 37.17**
For reference, copies of the two pucks in Figure 37.16 were rasterized using the menu command Effect, Rasterize.

In addition to the Optimize panel of the Save for Web dialog box, Illustrator enables you to make a head-to-head comparison of your image with possible optimization configurations. The three additional tabs of the window allow you to visually see the effects of the various potential file format, color, and compression changes. The first of the other panels of Save for Web is Original (see Figure 37.18). It allows you to refer to a large version of the artwork as created. The third tab, after

Optimize, is 2-Up (see Figure 37.19). It gives you two panes in which to work. By default, the left pane is the original image, and the right pane is the place where you view your potential changes. However, you also can change the left pane as desired for comparison. Whichever pane is active (selected) at the time the OK button is clicked is the version saved. This is also true of the 4-Up version, which offers you three variations of optimization, as well as the original (see Figure 37.20).



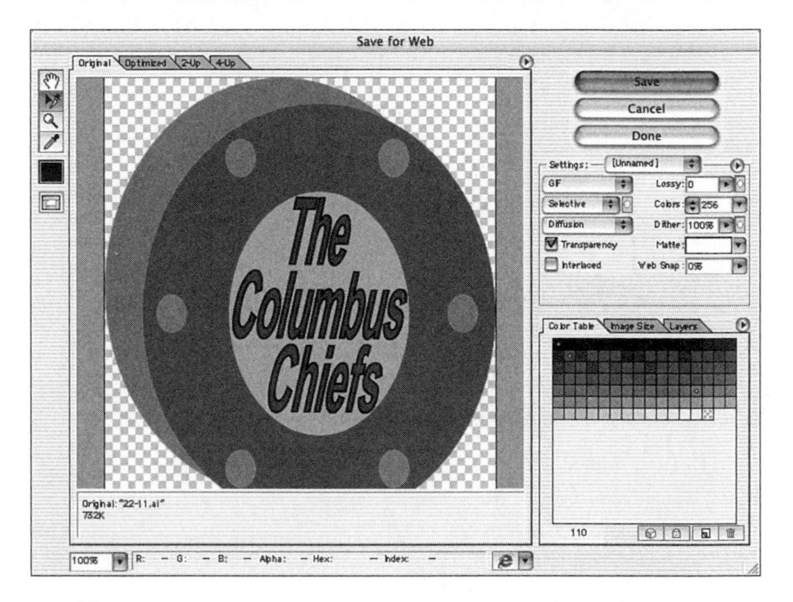


**Figure 37.18**

On the first tab in the Save for Web screen, you can easily view the original artwork with a single click.

In the lower-left corner of the Original tab in Figure 37.18, the zoom factor has been set to 100%. Note the other differences between this screen and that of the Optimized screen shown in Figure 37.15. In the lower-left corner, in addition to the zoom factor, the file size information lacks any reference to download speed, and rather than a file format, the filename is listed. The rasterization information to the lower right of the image is missing because there is no rasterization. Also note that, although you can change the optimization settings, the changes will not be reflected in the original. Any changes, however, are carried over to the Optimized panel, the 2-Up panel, and the top-right pane of the 4-Up panel.

Figures 37.19 and 37.20 show the other two panels of the Save for Web dialog box. These two panels allow comparisons between an original and one or three possible optimization schemes, or between two or four possible optimization settings.

In the 2-Up screen in Figure 37.19, the default is to have the original image on the left and to make changes to the image on the right. However, this isn't mandatory. You can click the original image once, use the Optimization Settings pop-up menu to make changes, and have two different optimized versions for comparison. At any time, you can switch back to the original image using the pop-up menu. Notice the several

> Always make your final selections in 100% zoom mode. Using zoom in conjunction with the Hand tool to check details of the artwork and zooming out to get an overall view are good working habits, but always base your decisions on the 100% view. Not only is it what your visitors will eventually see, it is a more accurate rendering of the rasterization.

differences between the Save for Web dialog box for this image, which uses 24-bit color, and the one in Figure 37.18, which shows the options for an 8-bit image. For example, no color table is available for 24-bit color, so the Image Size palette has been activated.

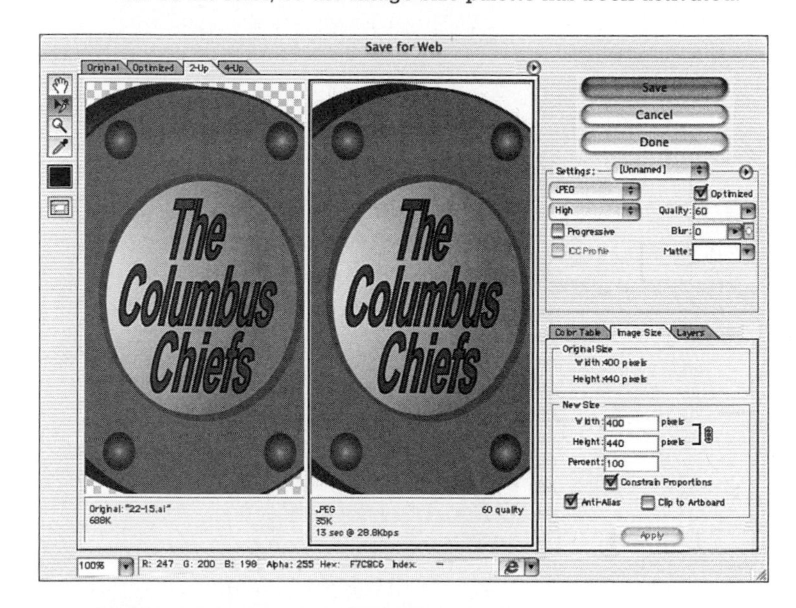


Figure 37.19

The 2-Up panel allows comparison between the original and the selected optimization settings. The zoom factor has been returned to 100%.



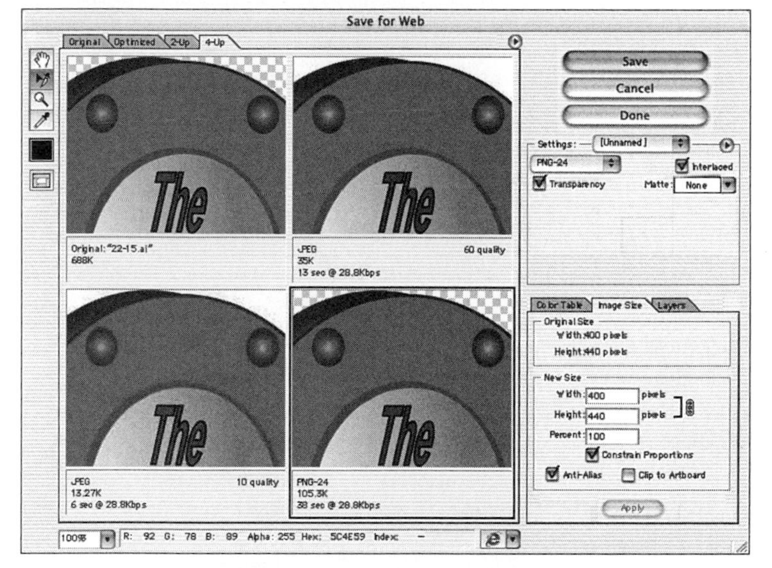


Figure 37.20

The 4-Up panel functions much like the 2-Up panel, except that you can experiment with three panes, along with the original image. As you can do in the 2-Up panel, click in an individual pane in the 4-Up panel to make it active.

As you can see in Figure 37.19 and Figure 37.20, Save for Web also works with continuous-tone images, such as those with gradients. Rather than GIF and PNG-8, the formats of choice are JPEG and PNG-24. The options and controls vary because of the nature of the images. For example, the Color Table tab is inactive. Figure 37.21 and Figure 37.22 illustrate some of the differences between the PNG-24 and JPEG file formats as employed by Save for Web.

In Figure 37.21, the order of figures is as follows (clockwise, from the top left): Interlaced PNG, non-Interlaced PNG, JPEG-Medium quality, JPEG-High quality. The JPEG-Medium file is less than one-fifth the size of the PNG-Interlaced file, yet the differences would not be apparent to a casual Web surfer.



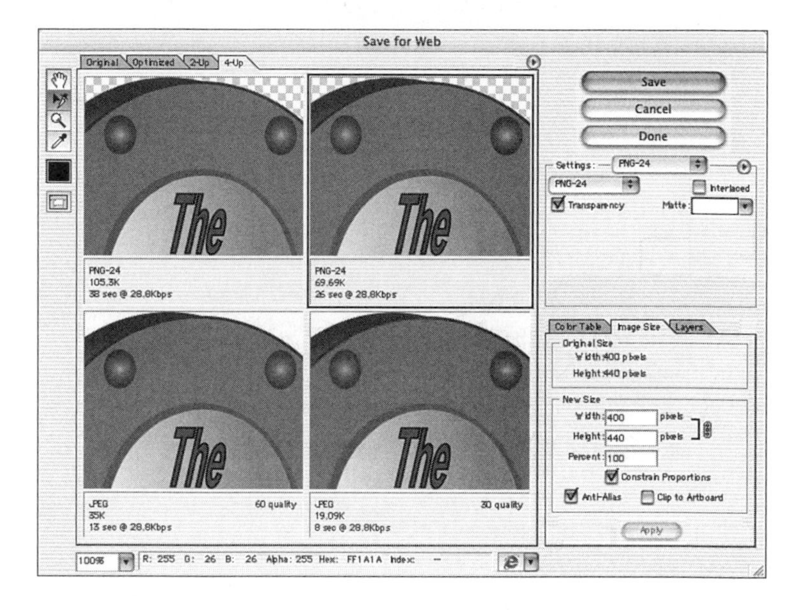


Figure 37.21
The Save for Web feature allows you to compare file formats, not just for quality, but for size and format options as well. Note that the Interlaced option for PNG has added about 50% to the image size.

The image in Figure 37.22 is reduced by PNG to 38% of its original size. In comparison, the hockey puck in Figure 37.20 was reduced to approximately 10% of its original size with the same PNG settings. The difference can be attributed to the fact that the previous image had a large area of transparency and more uniform colors. On the other hand, JPEG at 60% quality reduces either image to under 5% of its original size.

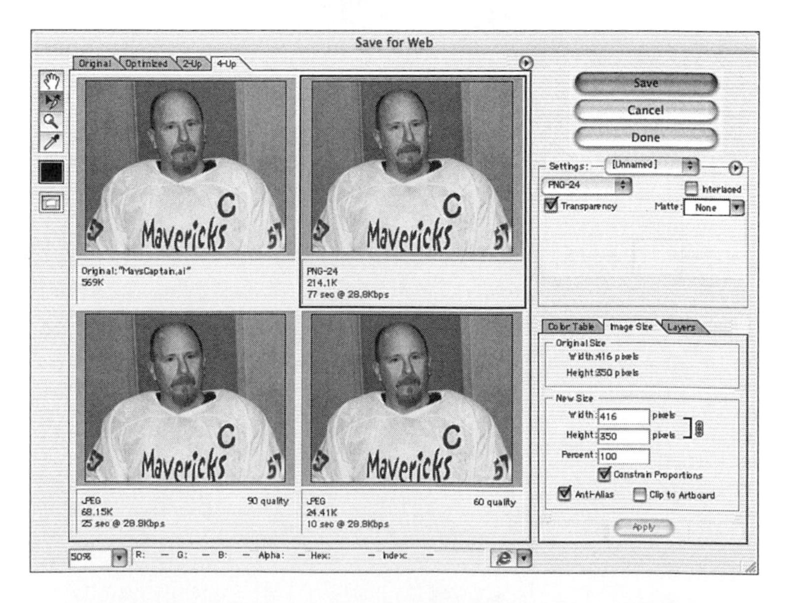


Figure 37.22
Because it doesn't have large areas of transparency, this image is less compressed by the PNG-24 format than that in the previous figure. (Figure 37.18 was originally 688KB.)

## Taming the Save for Web Dialog Box

The warning near the beginning of this discussion of Save for Web said that this feature's dialog box has no Undo function and no obvious way to save your work in the middle of an optimization. That is correct. However, a couple features can take the place of those capabilities. Rather than an option to save your work in the middle of an optimization, after you've made perhaps a dozen changes and still have a dozen to go, Illustrator offers you Remember. When you press (Option) [Alt], the OK button changes to Remember. It records the settings as they are at the time. For example, say you have edited several colors to make them Web-safe and adjusted the dithering, but you have not yet decided on GIF or PNG and are still considering lossiness. Then the phone rings, and an emergency project lands on your desk. Looking at the monitor, you decide that your only options are to optimize your image half-finished or cancel and lose the work you've done. By employing the Remember capability, you can store the settings as they are for the next time you open the image in the Save for Web dialog box. The changes are saved with that file and have no effect on other images being optimized. You cannot, however, use Remember and then return to the default Save for Web settings.



Also, when you press (Option) [Alt], the Cancel button changes to Reset. With the 2-Up and 4-Up panes, this works with the active pane only, allowing you to return that individual pane to its original values. Rather than removing the last operation, this removes all the settings since the last time the feature was started or the last time you used Remember. This capability can be a big help if you accidentally delete several key colors from the image while using the color table. Although it is not the same as Undo, it can salvage work that you would otherwise lose when you click Cancel.

You also can access Illustrator's Help files while working with Save for Web. Switch applications through your operating system and open your Web browser. Use the keyboard shortcut (Command-O) [Ctrl+O] to open the Open dialog box. Navigate to the Adobe Illustrator folder, inside of which you can find the folder Help. Open that folder and press H on the keyboard to jump to files starting with that letter. Select Help.html, and Illustrator Help starts right up. You can bookmark this page or add it to Favorites for easy access.

## The Color Table

The Color Table tab is available when you're working with GIF or PNG-8 file formats only. These formats use indexed color mode, whereas JPEG and PNG-24 use the full RGB gamut. The table displays all the colors currently in use in the 8-bit image. With the 2-Up and 4-Up tabs, it displays the colors of the currently selected version. Figure 37.23 shows the color table.

The color table in Figure 37.23 shows four Web-safe colors (indicated by the white diamond in the middle of the swatch), three colors that have been edited (with a black diamond in the middle), and some swatches that have been locked (a symbol in the lower-right corner of the swatch). Edited colors are automatically locked. Note that the last swatch in the color table represents transparency. In the bottom row, five colors have been selected, as indicated by the boxes around them.

To select a color (for deletion or to use a menu command, for example), click its swatch. To select two or more contiguous colors in the table, click the first swatch and Shift-click the last. You can select noncontiguous colors (those whose swatches are not consecutive in the color tables) by (Command)-clicking [Ctrl]-clicking.

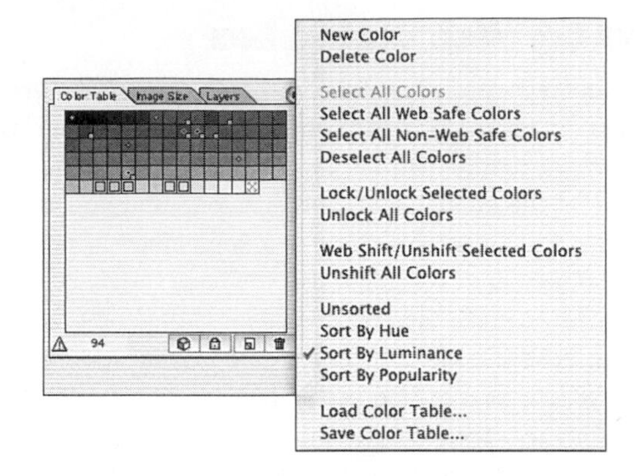


**Figure 37.23**
The color table is available only for GIF and PNG-8, the 8-bit file formats.



Colors can be deleted using the color table. Select a swatch and click the Delete Color button or choose the command from the table's pop-up menu. When a color is deleted from the table, it is also deleted from the image. In the image, the nearest remaining color is substituted. This is used not only to reduce the number of colors in the image but also to reduce the file size.

Editing colors by double-clicking a color table swatch opens the Color Picker. After you change colors, clicking the OK button does several things. The new color is added as a swatch to the color table, the color is updated throughout the particular pane (but not other panes, in the case of 2-Up and 4-Up modes), and the new color is locked.

In the event that a color is missing from the color table, you can add it by using the Eyedropper. This feature can sample a color in the original or an optimization pane. The color is added to the swatch below the Eyedropper tool on the left. To add it to a color table, click the image for which you've selected the color to make it active and then click the New Color button at the bottom of the color table.

The color table's pop-up menu, accessible through the arrow to the right of the tabs, is shown in Figure 37.23. In addition to the commands represented by the buttons on the bottom of the tab, it allows you to select colors based on a couple criteria and to rearrange the swatches.

The selection criteria of the color table's pop-up menu allow you to lock or shift the colors that fall into the two major categories—Web-safe and non-Web-safe—as well as to work with all colors in the table. The Select commands are most often used with the Lock and the Shift commands. Unshift All Colors returns colors forced to Web-safe values, as well as returns edited colors to their original values. Locked swatches remain locked.

The Unsorted command puts the colors into their original order in the color table. Sort by Hue works within the HSB color mode. Neutrals are placed with the reds. Sort by Luminance relies on the B (brightness) value of HSB. Sort by Popularity ranks the colors according to how many pixels contain each color. This command can be very useful for eliminating colors to reduce file size, but it can destroy antialiasing.

The final two commands in the color table's pop-up menu are Load Color Table and Save Color Table. Any collection of swatches from an optimization pane can be saved and accessed later on for a different image. Remember that only GIF and PNG-8 images can use color tables. This feature could be useful for producing uniformity in a series of images.

## The Optimization Settings

The choices for optimization vary according to the file format selected. The pop-up menu at the top of the Settings area allows you to choose a number of predetermined setting sets:

- PNG-8
- PNG-24
- JPEG, with settings for Low, Medium, and High compression
- GIF, with settings of 32, 64, and 128 colors. Also, each setting can be either dithered and undithered
- GIF with the Web-safe palette



Any change you make to a set of settings changes the pop-up menu to [Unnamed]. Like color tables, sets of settings can be saved and later exchanged between files. The Save Settings command is located in the Settings pop-up menu. Any sets saved appear with the Settings sets in the pop-up menu just below the Cancel button.

Also found in the Settings pop-up menu are the commands Delete Settings, Optimize to File Size, and Repopulate Views. Delete Settings removes the predetermined set of values currently active in the pop-up menu. Optimize to File Size allows you to determine the file format and the target size, leaving Illustrator to make decisions regarding the color table and compression. Repopulate Views, in the 2-Up and 4-Up modes, creates new compression options based on those of the active pane.

## GIF Optimization Choices

Figure 37.24 shows the Settings area that appears when any of the six sets of GIF settings are selected from the pop-up menu or when GIF is chosen as a file format.

The Settings pop-up menu is the same for all versions of the Settings area, giving a choice of the 12 predetermined sets described in Figure 37.24. The file format menu changes among the four possible formats, selecting by default the highest quality of each.

The Color palette pop-up menu allows a choice of Perceptual, Selective, Adaptive, Web, or Custom. Perceptual color palettes give priority to those colors that appear dominant to the human eye. Selective, the default, modifies the Perceptual palette to maintain priority for colors that appear in large areas of the image and for Web-safe colors. This option produces a palette closest to the image's original palette. Adaptive assigns the available number of colors in the color table to shades of the colors (hues) that are most common in an image. Choosing Web from the pop-up menu ensures that any color appearing in the color table is Web-safe. Custom is automatically selected if colors are deleted from the color table.

The Dithering pop-up menu allows you to choose among Diffusion, Pattern, Noise, and No Dither. Dithering is used to ease the transition between two adjacent colors. Figure 37.25 shows a comparison of the dithering styles.

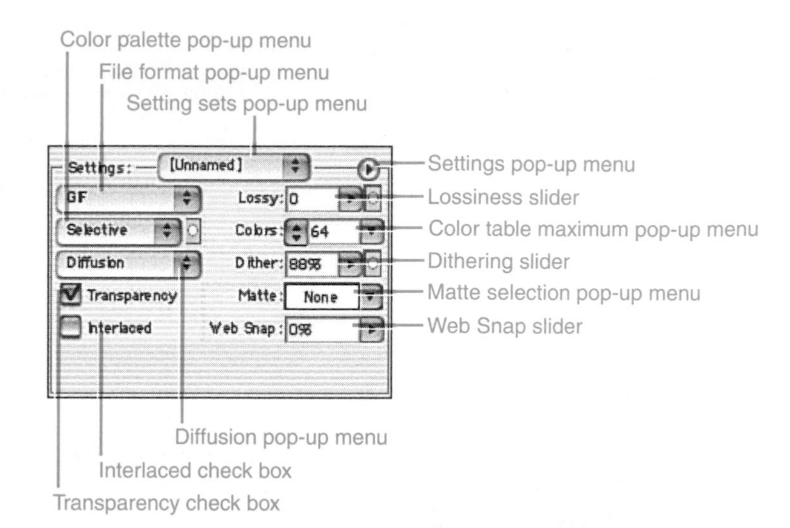


**Figure 37.24**
The fields do not vary among the predetermined GIF setting sets, but the values in the fields change.

**Figure 37.25**
The original and three dithering styles are compared at 100% zoom and 200% zoom.

These comparisons, which were easily generated in Save for Web, show in each set of four:

- **Upper left**—The original, a simple white-to-black radial gradient fill.
- **Upper right**—Diffusion dithering intermingles dots of the two adjacent colors. You control the amount, from 0% to 100% (shown).
- **Lower left**—Pattern dithering uses dots in a regular pattern. As you can see, it is very effective for radial gradients. There is no slider to control the amount of dithering.
- **Lower right**—Noise dithering uses a more random distribution of dots than Diffusion dithering. There is no amount control.

The Transparency check box toggles the appearance of any areas of the image that do not contain color. By default, it is checked. When the box is unchecked, any pixels that had been transparent become white or the color selected under Matte (see the following description). The transparent swatch is also removed from the color table.

*Interlacing* is the gradual appearance of an image in the browser's window as it downloads. Although interlacing adds somewhat to file size, it is becoming increasingly rare for any but the smallest images to be noninterlaced.

The Lossiness slider allows you to override GIF's default lossless compression. The amount of lossiness, from 0 to 100, does not directly correlate with a reduction in file size. Linear artifacts (lines of color) can start appearing at settings as low as 10 for many images. These lines give some indication of how the compression algorithm functions.

The maximum number of colors in the color table must be between 2 and 256 for GIF images. Reducing the number does not necessarily reduce file size. When you use dithering, the extra compensation can actually increase file size slightly when you remove a color from the table.



The Dithering slider is used only in conjunction with diffusion dithering.

The Matte selection pop-up menu offers choices of how the image interacts with its background. It works in conjunction with the Transparency check box. When the box is checked, transparency is maintained and Matte works with pixels that are semitransparent for antialiasing. When the box is unchecked, the entire range of transparency is used for matting. GIF supports transparency through the use of clipping paths. When the Web page on which the image will be placed has a solid color background, you can use this feature to help blend the image into its page. Areas that appear as transparent in the optimization window can be filled with the page's background color. The pop-up menu offers Black, White, Eyedropper Color, None, and Other. Selecting Other opens the Color Picker. Partially transparent pixels that are used to soften edges through antialiasing, when not matted, can produce a halo effect around the image. Selecting None from the Matte pop-up menu results in hard-edge transparency for GIF images. These hard edges can produce jagged lines on curves. In hard-edge transparency, any pixel more than 50% transparent becomes fully transparent; any pixel less than 50% transparent becomes fully opaque in its original color.

Web Snap refers to colors. The higher the value selected, the more colors of the color table that are automatically converted to Web-safe colors. By selecting individual colors in the color table and shifting them using the palette's button or pop-up menu command, you get much more control.

## PNG-8 Optimization Settings

Figure 37.26 shows the Settings area when PNG-8 is selected from the Format pop-up menu or from the Settings pop-up menu. The options and choices are virtually the same as for GIF. Note that PNG-8 does not offer the Lossiness slider because the format does not support lossy compression. For an explanation of the various settings, refer to the preceding section "GIF Optimization Choices."

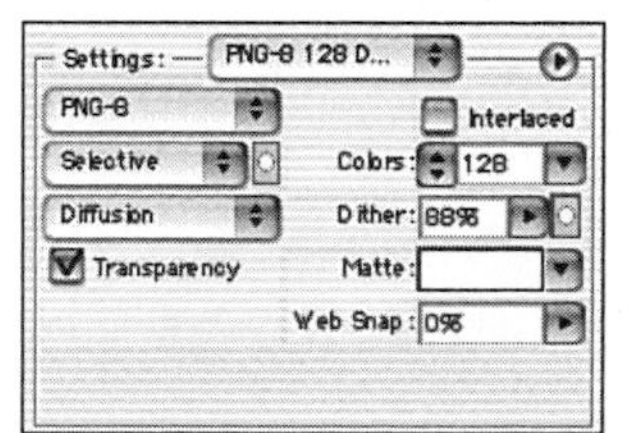


Figure 37.26
Other than the removal of the Lossiness slider and the subsequent relocation of the Interlaced box, the PNG options are identical to GIF.

## JPEG Optimization Settings

As a 24-bit format, JPEG has a different group of optimization settings. Because 24-bit images do not offer direct control over the color table, several settings seen for GIF and PNG-8 are missing. The Settings pop-up menu offers JPEG High, JPEG Low, and JPEG Medium. Figure 37.27 shows a view of the JPEG Settings area.



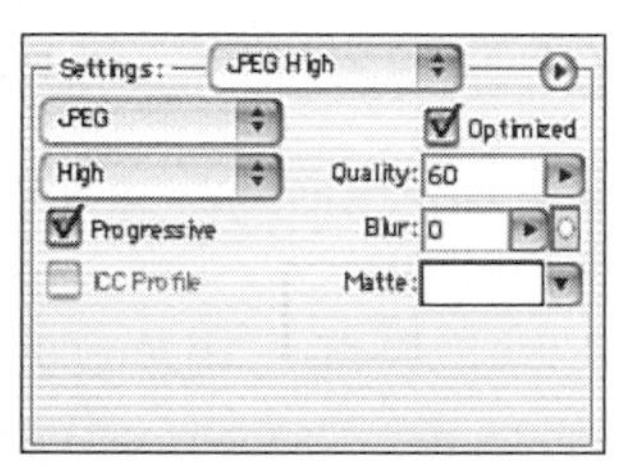


**Figure 37.27**
**The pop-up menus for settings, file format, and matte are the only items that the JPEG Settings area has in common with GIF or PNG-8.**

Beneath the file format pop-up menu (showing JPEG in Figure 37.27), you can see the pop-up menu for image quality. The choices are Low, Medium, High, and Maximum. This box automatically sets the value for the Quality slider to its right but does not override the slider. When the slider is moved to a value that is in a classification other than that shown in the pop-up menu, the menu automatically changes. The quality value is directly related to the number of colors saved with the file and, therefore, the file size.

The Progressive check box functions similarly to the Interlaced check box for GIF and PNG-8, allowing the image to appear gradually as it downloads.

The Optimized check box, when checked, produces a slightly different version of JPEG, known as *Optimized JPEG* or *Enhanced JPEG*. This version of the format results in slightly smaller file sizes but is not supported by all browsers.

Blur applies a Gaussian blur to the image, reducing artifacts but softening the overall appearance of the image. Named for the nineteenth-century German astronomer and mathematician Carl Friedrich Gauss, a Gaussian blur uses a mathematical formula to determine the relationship among adjoining pixels. Possible values range from 0 to 2.0 for this feature and represent the pixel radius of the blur. Save for Web actually calculates and redraws the screen for values as low as or lower than 0.000001 pixel, but this is a waste of time. No radius under approximately 0.1 pixel will have any effect on the image. Blurs can reduce file sizes by reducing the number of colors needed to display the image.

Because JPEG does not support transparency in any form, the Matte control takes on a larger role. A single circle in a JPEG image, unless modified, appears as a circle in a white square when placed into a Web page. When you're using JPEG, any pixel that does not have an assigned color value is, by default, white. To avoid a white rectangle or square around your image, use the Matte feature to match your image's background to that of the Web page. As noted previously, only solid colors can be matted.

## PNG-24 Optimization Settings

The simplest of all settings, PNG-24 offers the Settings pop-up menu, the file format pop-up menu, and only three options: Transparency, Interlaced, and Matte. These three options are virtually identical to those described in the preceding sections, with one exception. Although both PNG-8 and

PNG-24 support transparency, PNG-24 supports up to 256 levels of transparency. However, not all browsers support multilevel transparency. Figure 37.28 shows the PNG-24 Settings area.

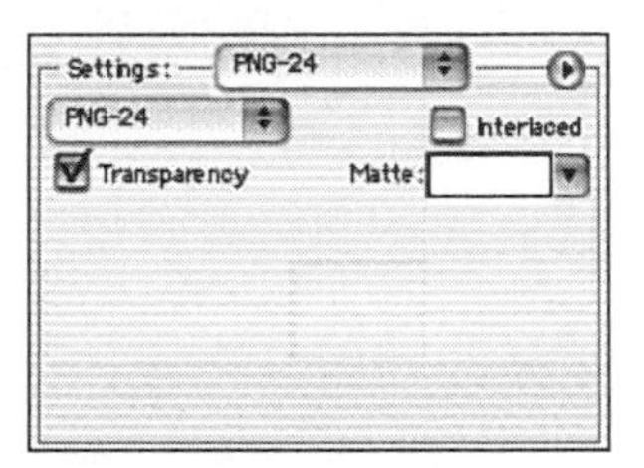


Figure 37.28
This set of options is both the simplest and most restrictive. As a 24-bit color mode, PNG-24 has no direct control over the color table. And unlike JPEG, PNG-24 offers no control over quality and cannot apply a Gaussian blur.

*Having trouble with PNG? See "Viewing PNG Files" in the "Mastering Illustrator" section at the end of this chapter.*

## SWF and SVG Optimization Settings

Illustrator allows you to use Save for Web to produce both Flash (SWF) and SVG images. The optimization setting options parallel the options for exporting to SWF or saving as SVG formats.

## WBMP Settings

The WBMP file format uses exactly two colors: black and white. The only option is dithering. Like GIF and PNG-8, you have the options of diffusion (0 to 100%), pattern, and noise dithering. Make the selection based strictly on appearance—there is no difference in file size.

# The Save Optimized As Dialog Box

Because Save for Web generates images for the World Wide Web, it offers you the opportunity to get a head start on creating a Web page. You can even generate the necessary HTML file to create a Web page itself from Save for Web.

## Saving Images, HTML, or Both

After clicking the Save button in the Save for Web dialog box, you're presented with the Save Optimized As dialog box (see Figure 37.29).

You have the option of saving just the image or images (when sliced), the HTML code, or both. When you're saving sliced images, typically both the HTML file and the images are required (see Figure 37.30). When you're optimizing a nonsliced image that will be placed into a Web page using a Web development tool such as GoLive, only the image is required.

The HTML file contains all the Web-ready code necessary to re-create a sliced image in a Web browser. In Figure 37.31, you can see that a table is generated.

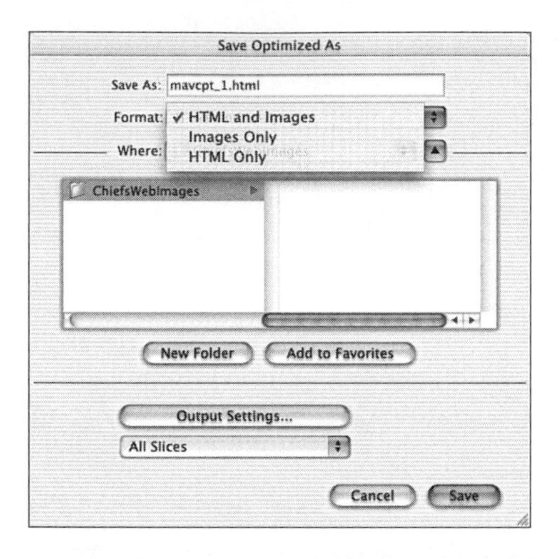


Figure 37.29
These options determine what files will be generated by Save for Web.

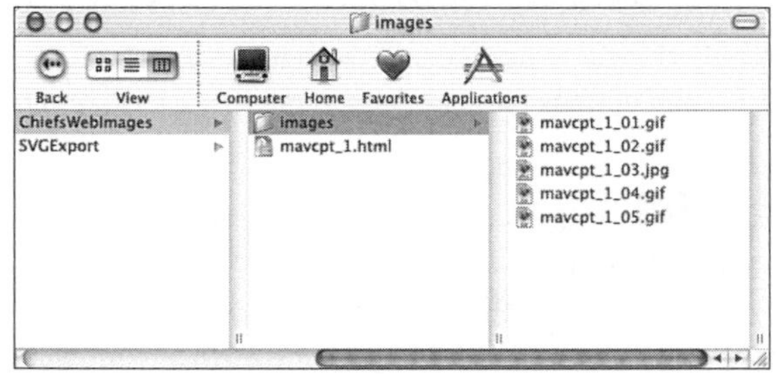


Figure 37.30
In this instance, both an HTML file and a folder of images have been generated.

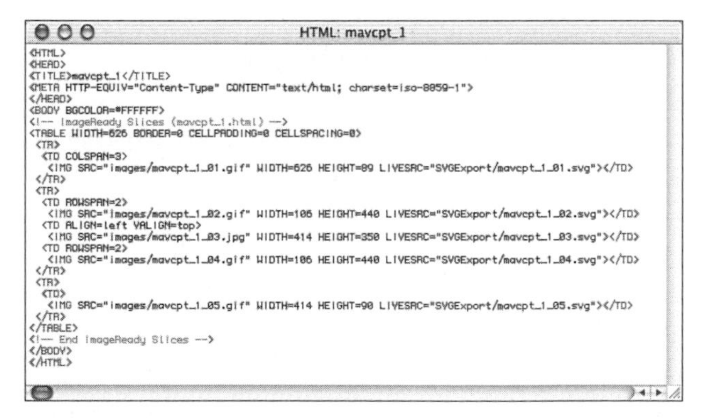


Figure 37.31
The HTML tags <TABLE> and </TABLE> indicate the beginning and end of the table.

In contrast, if an HTML file is generated for an unsliced image, the code references only a single slice, the image itself, and therefore is hardly necessary unless the image is to stand alone as a Web page in and of itself.

## Output Options

The Output Settings dialog box offers four panels of options. The pop-up menu directly below Settings changes the panel. In Figure 37.32, you can see the HTML options panel.

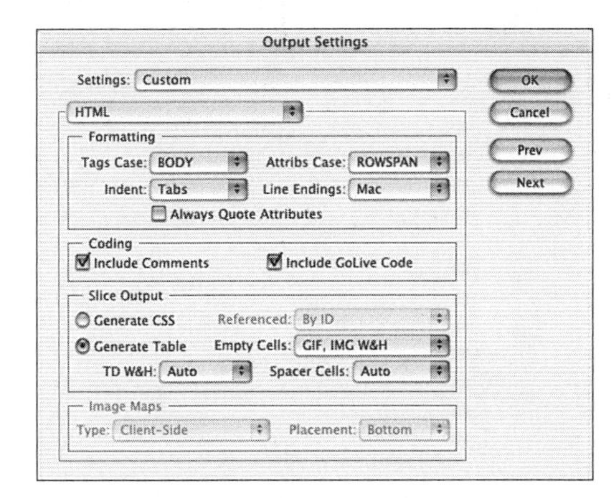


**Figure 37.32**
Those unfamiliar with HTML might find these options unintelligible.



Unless you work with HTML, the only option that needs to be addressed is Include GoLive Code. If you are saving an image with an HTML file and will be adding the HTML to an Adobe GoLive page, check this box. If not, leave the box unchecked.

In Figure 37.33, the Background panel allows you to create an image to be used as the background of a Web page.

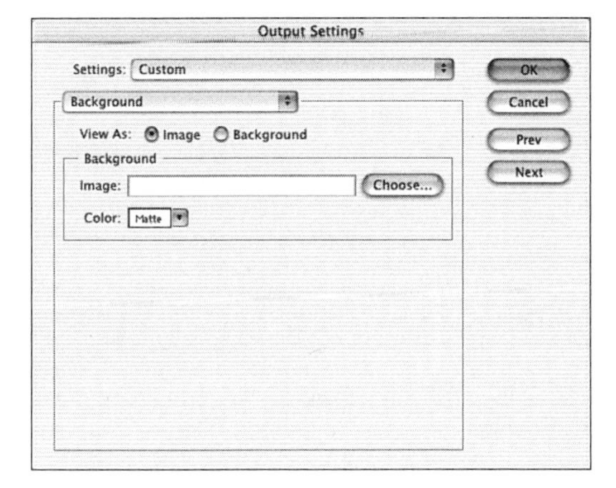


**Figure 37.33**
Unless you're actually generating a background to be added to a Web page, leave View As Image selected.

The Saving Files panel, shown in Figure 37.34, gives you some control over how Save for Web will name the files it generates.

The fourth panel of Output Settings options controls slice naming (see Figure 37.35).

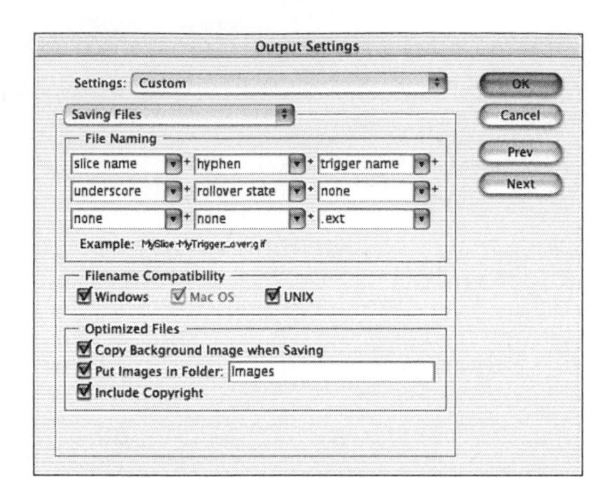


Figure 37.34
Each of the fields includes a pop-up list of options.

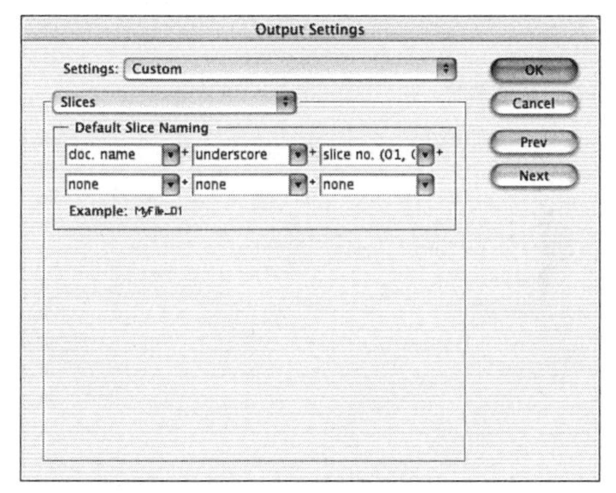


Figure 37.35
This panel is important when you're saving sliced images.

# ADVANCED WEB CAPABILITIES IN ILLUSTRATOR

In addition to generating HTML code with Save for Web, Illustrator can give you a head start on building your Web pages with a couple other sophisticated features. You can generate Cascading Style Sheets and subdivide your images into "slices" from Illustrator, and even create a link to another Web page or site as an image map.

## Creating and Saving CSS

Illustrator uses its layers and Save for Web to create Cascading Style Sheets. Objects are organized on the artboard and placed on appropriate layers. Each top layer can become a separate CSS layer when the file is optimized in Save for Web. (Only top layers can become CSS layers.)

One example of CSS in action is a multilingual Web site. Depending on the default language specified for use by the browser, a different CSS layer can be displayed. (Checking

Although most modern Web browsers can read CSS, there are some inconsistencies from browser to browser. It is important to check your work in all major browsers.

the browser's default language is not something that can be built in to a Web site using just Illustrator, but the pages themselves can be created.)

In Figure 37.36, a multilingual Web page is beginning to take shape. Each of the top layers is designated for a different language. Each layer has the first button created. As you can see in the Layers palette, each of the buttons is in the appropriate language.

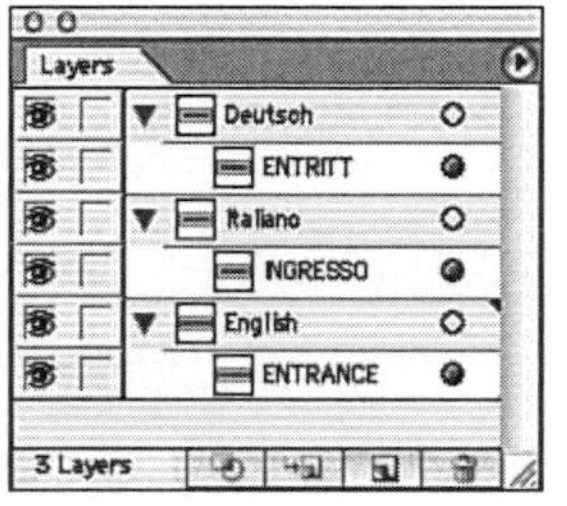


Figure 37.36
Each of the three layers can become a separate CSS layer.



In the Save for Web dialog box, the Layers tab in the lower-right corner offers the CSS layers capability (see Figure 37.37).

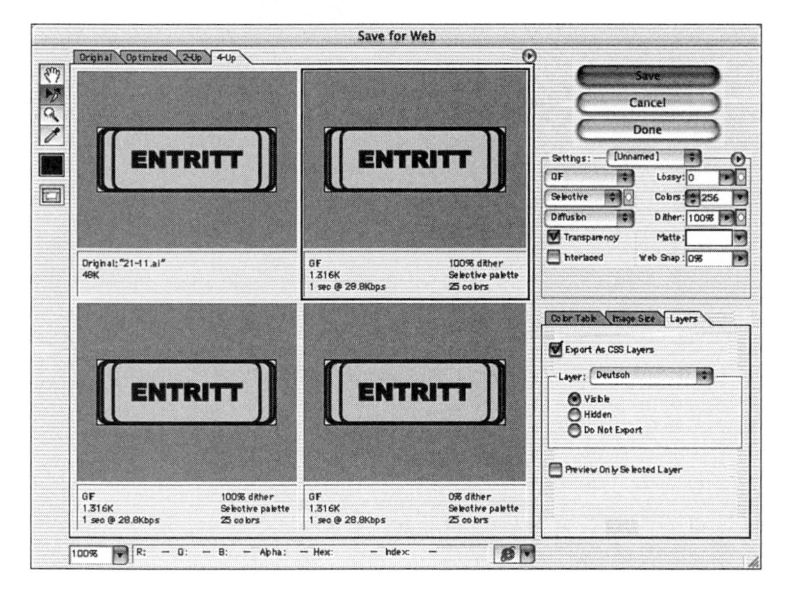


Figure 37.37
CSS layers are created in Save for Web's Layers tab.

With the Export as CSS Layers box checked, you can select each top layer from the pop-up menu. Each layer can be exported as a visible layer, exported as a hidden layer, or not exported.

After the layer options are determined, the optimization settings are selected, and the Save button is clicked, the Save Optimized As dialog box opens. From the Format pop-up menu, HTML and Images should be selected (see Figure 37.38).

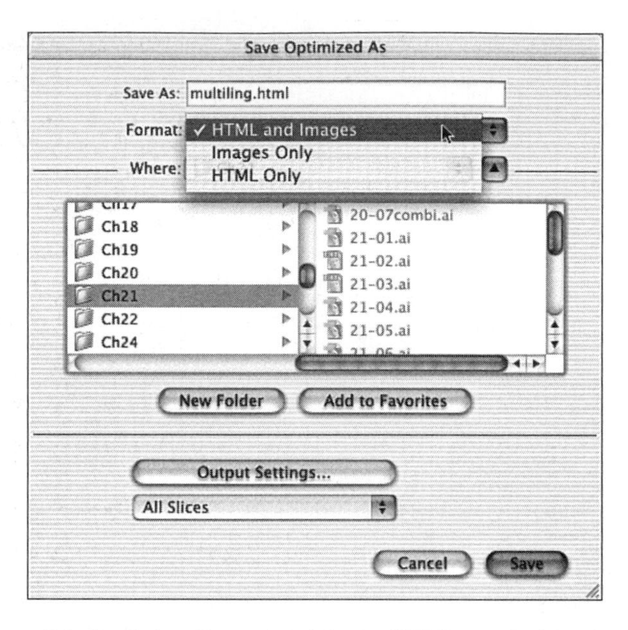


Figure 37.38
The HTML file must be included for CSS layers to work.

In addition, it's important to click the Output button and, in the HTML panel of the Output Settings dialog box, select Generate CSS under Slice Output (see Figure 37.39).

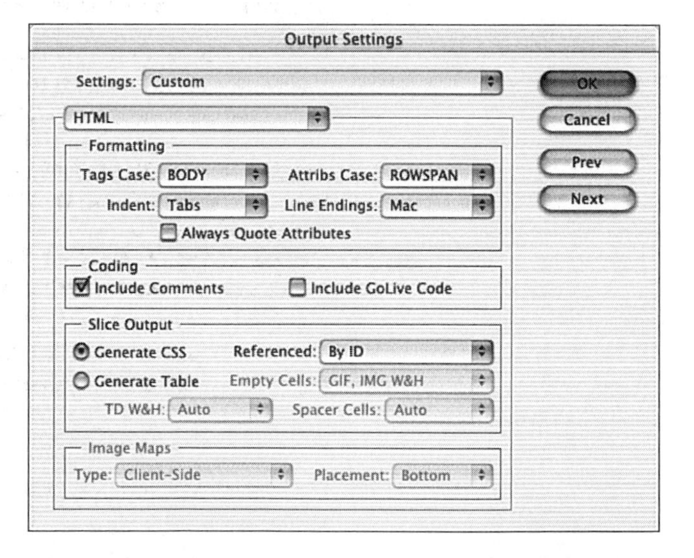


Figure 37.39
If Generate CSS is not selected, the CSS layers will not be produced.

## Slicing

Slicing an image for the Web identifies sections of a single file that can have some independent functions. For example, the slices of an image load into a Web browser's window individually. You can also assign specific optimizations

CSS can be very powerful. The documentation for your Web design program can assist you in determining how to create them.

settings for each slice of an image. Illustrator allows you to slice an image using a variety of techniques.

## The Two Types of Slices

When you designate a slice, using any of the techniques described in this section, you've created a user-defined slice, or a *user slice*. Illustrator automatically divides the rest of the image into appropriate rectangles so that the entire image is represented by slices. Those slices are called *automatic slices*, or *auto slices*. All slices are rectangular. If an image is not rectangular, surrounding parts of the artboard are included so that each slice is rectangular, as will be the image overall.



## The Slice Tool

You can drag the Slice tool to identify an area of an image as a slice. Illustrator automatically creates the other slices necessary to fill the HTML table in which the image will be displayed.

## Using a Selection for Slicing

After creating a selection, including one or more objects on the artboard, you can use the menu command Object, Slice, Create from Selection. A user-generated slice will be created, along with the required auto slices.

The user slice will be defined by the edge of the stroke (if any) or fill, not by an object's path. In addition, any effects (such as outer glows or drop shadows) will also be included.

## Using Guides for Selections

Illustrator enables you to create extremely precise slices by using the guides. Place each guide where you want the image to be sliced and then use the menu command Object, Slice, Create from Guides.

## Object-Based Slicing

The  command Object, Slice, Make creates a slice from the currently selected object. The slice is tied to the object; therefore, if the object is moved on the artboard, the slices are automatically redrawn to maintain the object-oriented slice.

In contrast, slices created with the command Create from Selection remain in place, even if that original selection is moved.

*Need to change the type of slice you're using from selection-based to object-based? See "Resetting Slices" in the "Mastering Illustrator" section at the end of this chapter.*

## Linking to a Slice in Illustrator

Another of the great advantages to using slices in a Web image is *hyperlinking*. Each slice can be used as a link to another Web page. A Web address, known as a *URL (uniform resource locator)*, is assigned in the Slice Options dialog box. You access the dialog box through the menu command Object, Slice, Slice Options.

## Creating Image Maps

An image map is similar to a linked slice in that a URL can be assigned to it, turning it into a hyperlink. When the image map is clicked in a Web browser, the viewer will be taken to the designated Web page.

Unlike slices, image maps do not have to be rectangular. Any object can be used. To assign a URL, open the Attributes palette, shown in Figure 37.40, and select either Rectangular or Polygon from the pop-up menu. Then enter the URL.

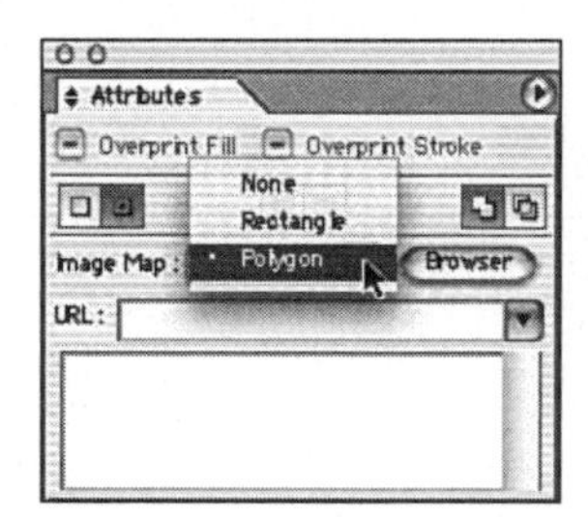


Figure 37.40
Assigning URLs to image maps is just one of the purposes of the Attributes palette.

## Optimizing Slices

It's not unusual to have an image that combines a variety of artwork. You might have, for example, an image that contains both a photograph and large areas of solid color, such as that shown in Figure 37.41.

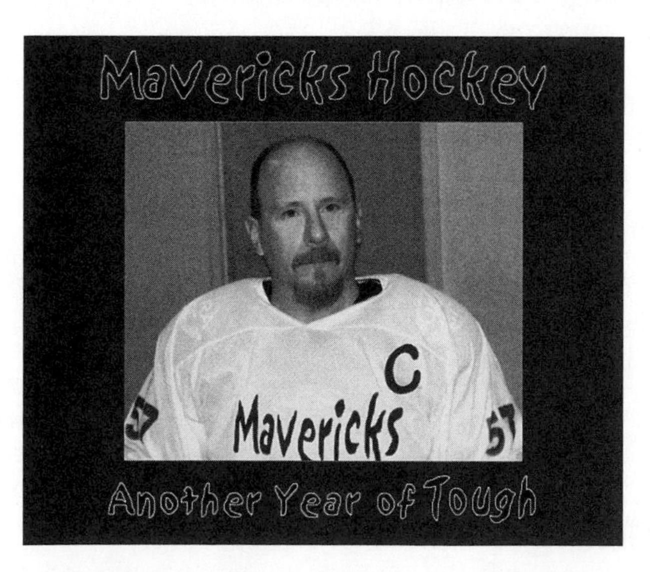


Figure 37.41
This image contains continuous-tone areas (the photo) and large blocks of solid color.

Such images used to pose problems for optimization. The photo would be best as a 24-bit image, such as JPEG or PNG-24. However, the areas of solid color are better optimized as GIF or PNG-8. If you optimize the entire image as JPEG, you run the risk of artifacts and other compression damage in the background areas. If you optimize the image as GIF, you lose quality in the foreground area. Illustrator's Save for Web feature includes the capability of optimizing different slices separately. In Figure 37.42 you can see that the image was sliced to create a separate area for the photographic image.

Figure 37.42

**The photo is a user-defined slice, whereas the rest of the image has been automatically sliced by Illustrator.**



In Save for Web, select a slice and assign the appropriate optimization settings. In Figure 37.43, the photo has been selected with the Slice Select tool, and JPEG settings have been determined.

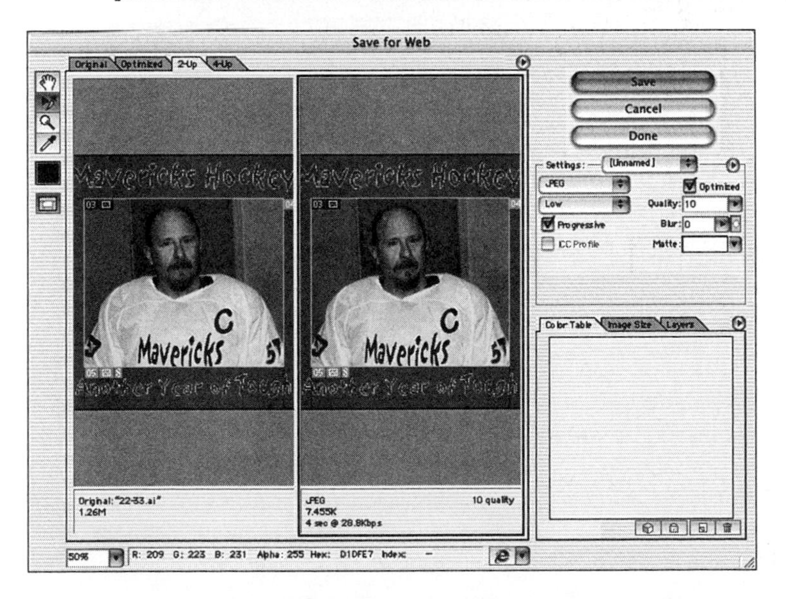


Figure 37.43

**The optimization settings shown will be applied only to the single selected slice.**

Again using the Slice Selection tool, you can Shift-click to select the remaining slices (or any combination thereof). Different settings can be assigned (see Figure 37.44).



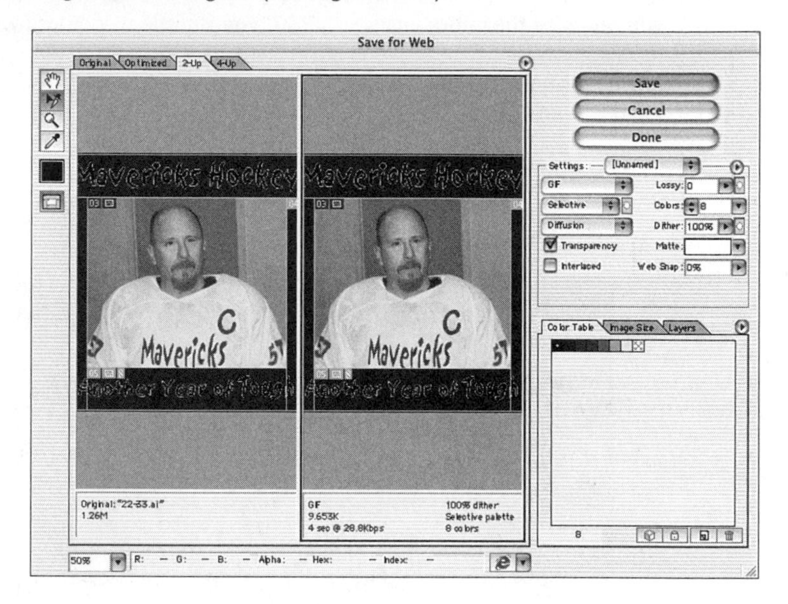


**Figure 37.44**
The four other slices will all be optimized as GIFs.

When Save for Web generates the optimized slices, one will be JPEG, and the others will be GIF.

# MASTERING ILLUSTRATOR

## Web Images Unavailable

*I worked very hard to optimize my images, choosing quality over size. However, now that I have them posted, I can't see them. Did I make them too big?*

No, the problem isn't likely to be size. Patience allows even the largest Web images to download. Perhaps your browser isn't the latest version and your images are in a format it doesn't support. Did you, by chance, save the images in PNG or Optimized JPEG format?

## Correcting Banding in Images

*My images are starting to look like targets at a bow-and-arrow convention. The concentric circles in areas that should be gradients are driving me crazy. What's wrong?*

You're experiencing banding. The reduction in the number of colors results in the grouping of several colors into one. For example, in a 24-bit image, a certain area might transition from light red to medium red to dark red. With a reduction of colors, it all becomes medium red. If the original transition were actually "dark purple—medium purple—light purple—light red—medium red—dark red," the result could be medium purple and medium red, side by side.

There are two solutions: Use a file format that supports 24-bit color (JPEG or PNG-24) or dither an 8-bit image. Dithering uses dots and/or patterns of the two colors in differing densities to simulate shades between the colors. Save for Web offers options and controls for dithering.

## Resetting Slices

*I thought my image was finished, so I sliced it up. Now, however, I have to shift one piece of artwork a little bit. Because I didn't use object-based slices, everything will be messed up. How do I handle it?*

You can use the Slice Select tool to adjust the boundaries of a slice. Click the slice and then use the handles in the corners of the box to resize, or you can simply drag to reposition. Illustrator updates the other auto slices automatically. (Be aware that it is possible to overlap user-defined slices. This can create problems for some Web browsers.)

The menu Object, Slice includes a handy command for situations that get out of hand. The Delete All command removes all slices and lets you start over.

## Viewing PNG Files

*I get an "image not available" icon when I try to view a PNG image in my browser. Any help?*

Check first to see that your browser supports PNG. Here's the status:

- **Microsoft Internet Explorer for Windows**—Versions 5 and higher support PNG with limited transparency. Version 4 can see inline (using an HTML IMG tag) PNG files but does not open a referenced file. IE4 has no support for transparency.
- **Microsoft Internet Explorer for Macintosh**—IE5 and higher for Macintosh have full support for PNG, including alpha channel transparency and support for gamma, sRGB, and ICC profiles.
- **Netscape Navigator/Communicator for Windows and Macintosh**—Versions 4.0 through 4.5 have limited PNG support, and numerous plug-ins are available as freeware to extend the capability. Version 4.7 has improved support, and Navigator 6 (and later) offers the same high-quality PNG support as Mozilla.

Next, check to see that PNG is properly associated with the browser application. (See your particular browser's Help for specific information.)

# MOVING ARTWORK BETWEEN ILLUSTRATOR AND PHOTOSHOP

## IN THIS CHAPTER

Adobe Illustrator CS is a state-of-the-art vector drawing program. Adobe Photoshop is the premier image-editing software and is, without question, the standard against which all other raster file editors are measured. No illustration or drawing program is better matched with Photoshop than Illustrator. And now the line between the programs has blurred even more.

In addition to sharing major interface components, Photoshop and Illustrator can exchange files with unprecedented ease, as you'll see in this chapter. Photoshop layers do not have to be flattened when placed in an Illustrator document. Illustrator's vector text—including type on a path—can be edited in Photoshop. The appearances of transparency, blending modes, and masks can be maintained as files go back and forth between the two programs.

# ILLUSTRATOR VERSUS PHOTOSHOP



Before learning how the two programs can work together, you need to understand how they differ. Although their capabilities have started to overlap, they remain two separate programs, with two different purposes.

## Illustrator's Vectors, Photoshop's Rasters

Illustrator is primarily a vector art program, whereas Photoshop is designed to work with raster images. (The difference between vector and raster was examined in depth in Chapter 4, "Pixels, Vectors, and Resolutions.")

Vector file formats record artwork as objects. Each object is described mathematically in relationship to the other objects in the file. Starting point, shape, stroke, fill, and effects are among the data recorded. Because these descriptions are independent of the size of the page, vector art can be scaled to any size and maintain its sharpness and appearance.

Photoshop simulates vector objects with shape layers. In reality, however, these shapes are not objects like those created by a vector-based program. Rather, they are pixel-filled layers combined with a vector mask to create a shape.

Raster images, also known as *bitmap images*, do not recognize objects. Each file is simply a record of a given number of squares, called *pixels*, each with its particular color. The squares are arranged in rows and columns, a raster. Every raster image is rectangular, although some file formats allow transparency that may make the outline of the image appear to be other than rectangular. Transparent pixels actually fill in the remainder of the rectangle.

You can increase the size of a raster image in two ways: by resampling and by scaling. When an image is resampled, the number of pixels is increased to fit the new dimensions. Each pixel remains the same size. When a raster image is scaled, the number of pixels remains the same, but their individual size is changed. (This can occur when you're printing a raster image at a size other than the size at which it was designed.)

Resampling is typically done in an image-editing program, such as Photoshop. Figure 38.1 shows an example.

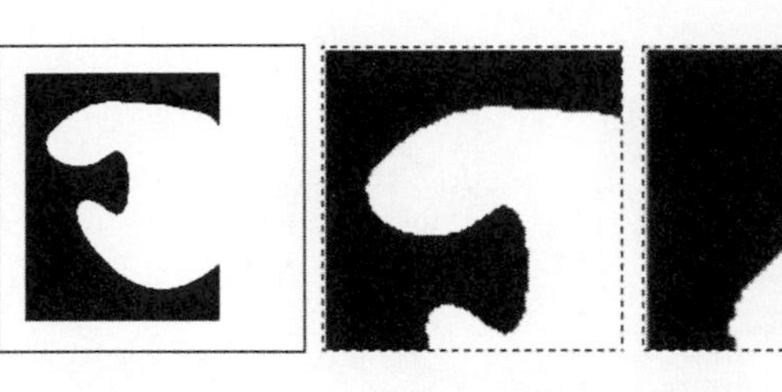

Figure 38.1

**On the left, the original image appears at 100% zoom. In the middle, the image has been scaled to 200%. On the right, the image has been scaled to 400%.**

The images in Figure 38.1 are not zoomed-in views. Rather, the image itself was resized in Photoshop. This process is comparable to using Illustrator's command Object, Transform, Scale. In the original object, the vertical and horizontal lines are perfectly straight and clean. The curves, however, are not as smooth as they would be in Illustrator. In the middle, after the object has been doubled in both width and height (and each pixel has been quadrupled), the straight lines are still sharp, but the curves show the corners of the individual pixels. This condition is known as the *jaggies*. In the third image, even the straight lines are starting to get blurry as new pixels are introduced. Photoshop has added gray pixels to help smooth the edges, a process known as *antialiasing*.

Note also in the right image of Figure 38.1 that the curves are now extremely blocky and jagged. Even antialiasing is ineffective. Keep in mind that antialiasing is available only in color and grayscale images. One-bit black-and-white images (also called *bitmap*) cannot be antialiased because each pixel can be only black or white, with no shades of gray. Figure 38.2 shows what happens when the design shown earlier is resampled as a 1-bit image.



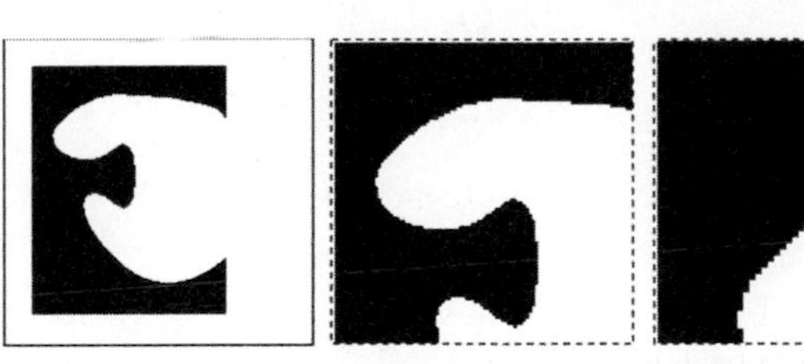

Figure 38.2

**Without antialiasing, the jagged edges are much more prominent.**

When a raster object is scaled in Illustrator, the number of pixels used to create the object remains constant. To fill a larger area, each pixel is increased in size. Figure 38.3 shows how this change can adversely affect an image.

The original object in Figure 38.3 was created in Photoshop at a size of 100 pixels by 25 pixels. When placed in Illustrator (using the command File, Place), it retained those original pixels. In Figure 38.4, the Document Info palette shows the details.

Figure 38.3
The original object is shown in the upper left. It has been scaled to 200%, 400%, 800%, and 1600%.



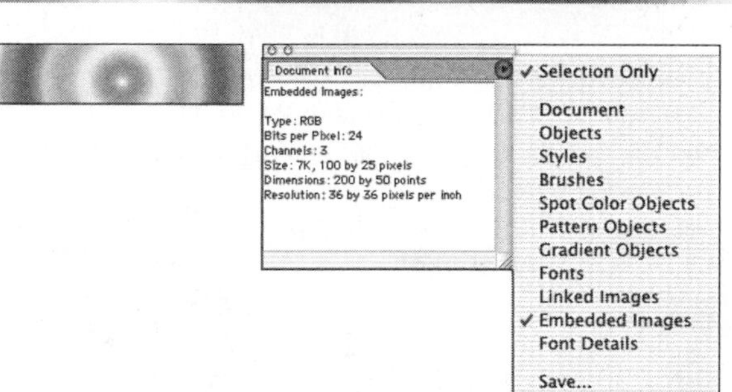


Figure 38.4
The Document Info palette is available through the Window menu.

In comparison, look at the information for the largest of the scaled copies, shown in Figure 38.5.

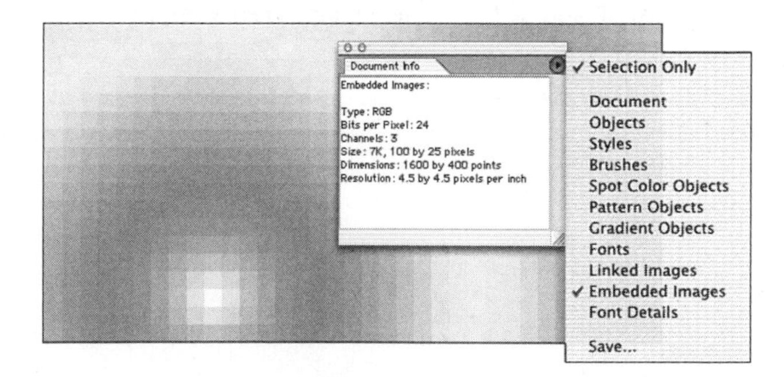


Figure 38.5
A copy of the object has been scaled to 1600% (not reproduced to scale).

Note that the only differences between the two Document Info listings are Dimensions and Resolution. The size remains 7KB, with dimensions of 100 pixels by 25 pixels. No pixels have been added to increase the object's size. The resolution, however, has dropped from 72 pixels per inch (ppi) to 4.5ppi. In effect, each pixel has jumped in size from 1/72 of an inch wide and tall to over 1/5 of an inch in each dimension.

## The Raster Advantage

Despite the potential problems of jaggies with raster images, in some areas, pixels have traditionally outshone vector art. In the past, creating such effects as drop shadows and glows was time consuming and difficult in vector artwork, and often resulted in output problems as numerous gradients and blends were introduced to simulate the interaction of semitransparent shadows and other effects. The image in Figure 38.6 would be extremely difficult to reconstruct in a program that does not support transparency.

Figure 38.6
The overlapping transparency is difficult to simulate with non-transparent vector objects.



If you wanted to create this image without transparency, the area of overlapping shadows (shown in Figure 38.7) alone would require some two dozen distinct objects.

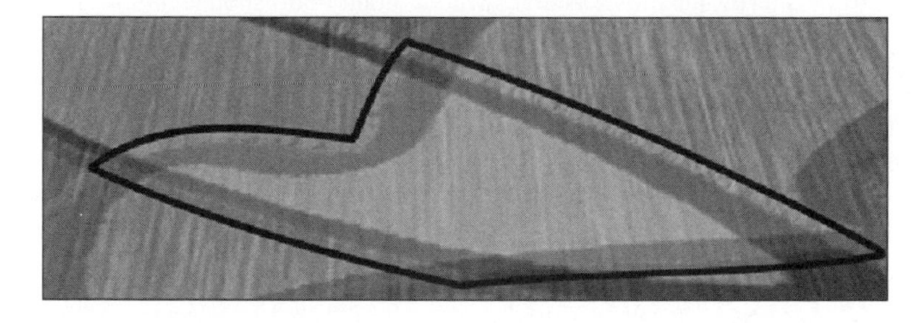

Figure 38.7
Each place where two colors overlap would become a separate object in a vector program that does not support transparency.

## The Vector Edge

Vector art's primary advantage over its raster cousin is sharpness. As mentioned earlier, vector art can be scaled to any size, and the edges remain sharp and clean, unlike raster art. In Figure 38.8, the same path used earlier has been imported into Illustrator and stroked and filled. Two additional copies were made and scaled to 200% and 400%. As you can see, they have suffered no degradation in the transformations.

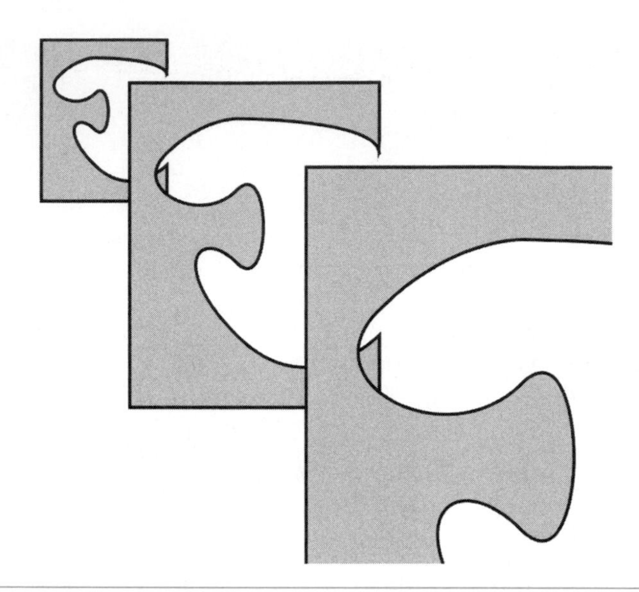

Figure 38.8

The curves are as sharp in the largest copy as they are in the original.



### Photoshop's Layers, Illustrator's Objects

As you know, Photoshop works with pixels instead of objects. However, that doesn't mean you can't manipulate parts of a Photoshop file independently in Illustrator. The key is understanding the relationship between Photoshop layers and Illustrator objects.

When creating an image in Photoshop, you have the option of working with multiple layers, just as you do in Illustrator. Each Photoshop layer can be treated as a separate entity in Illustrator. (Note the use of the word *entity* and not *object*.) As you'll see shortly, Illustrator enables you to retain Photoshop layers when placing a PSD file into an Illustrator document. You can then edit the contents of each layer as a separately placed raster image.

Conversely, you should keep layers in mind when exporting from Illustrator in Photoshop's PSD format. If each object is placed on a separate layer, later you can manipulate them individually in Photoshop. Don't overlook the power of Illustrator's Release to Layers (Sequence) command for this task!

## MOVING ARTWORK FROM ILLUSTRATOR TO PHOTOSHOP

You can move objects and images between programs in a number of different ways. Copy and paste, drag and drop, Save, Save As, and Export are some of the techniques and commands available. You can also insert Illustrator, EPS, and PDF files into a Photoshop document by using Photoshop's Place command. All three formats produce rasterized images with excellent fidelity to the original Illustrator file's appearance.

## Saving as Illustrator, Opening in Photoshop

At its core, the modern Illustrator file format is the Portable Document Format (PDF). Figure 38.9 shows a sample file created in Illustrator.

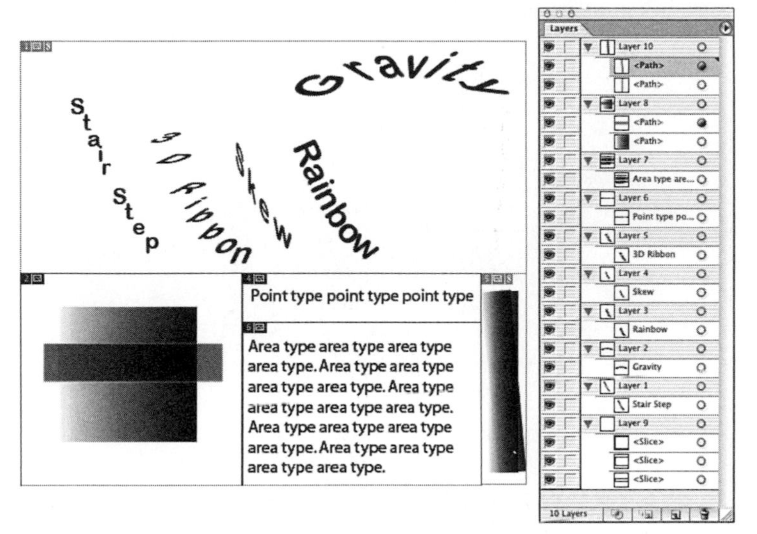


**Figure 38.9**
The image includes type on a path, point type, area type, gradients, reduced opacity, blending modes, and slices.



When opened in Photoshop, an Illustrator file is treated as a generic PDF document (see Figure 38.10).

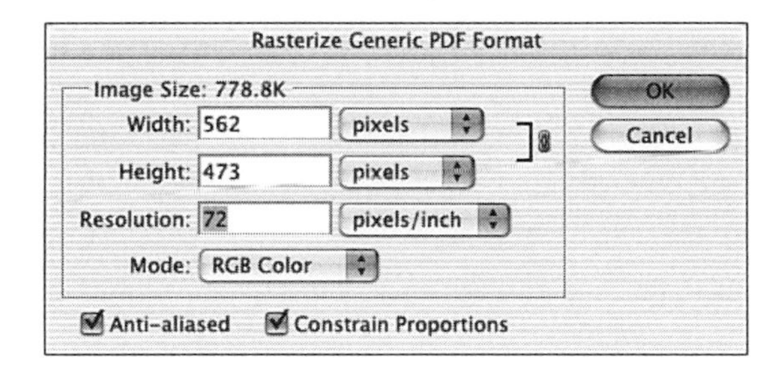


**Figure 38.10**
The dialog box will, by default, show you the actual size of the artwork. You can scale the image or change its resolution as you open it.

When the image is opened in Photoshop, it will consist of a single layer that contains all the artwork. As you can see in Figure 38.11, transparency is maintained, but the original slices are ignored.

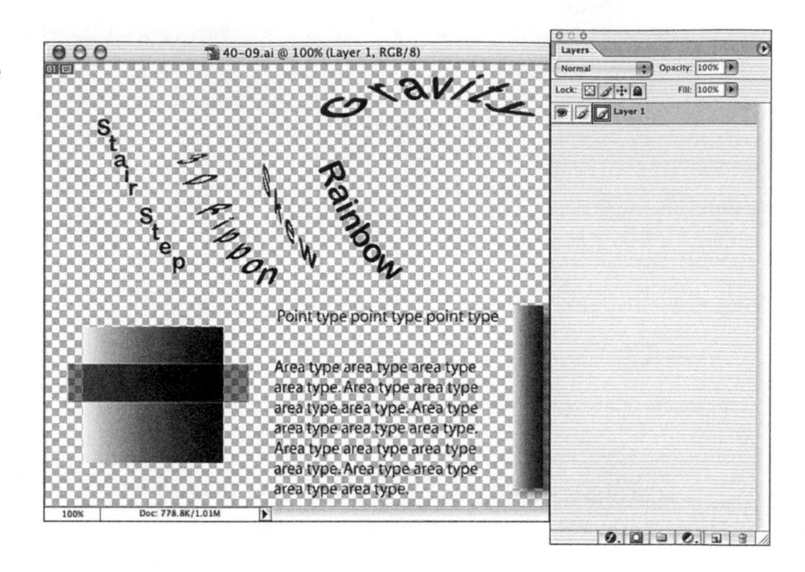


Figure 38.11
The rasterized image has a single layer.



Once in Photoshop, the file can be edited as a typical raster image.

# Exporting from Illustrator in Photoshop Format

Transferring artwork from Illustrator to its sister program using the Photoshop format requires two steps. First, you must export the file, and then you must open it.

When your artwork is ready, the first step in creating a Photoshop file from Illustrator is to choose the menu command File, Export. In the resulting dialog box, you specify the Photoshop format (see Figure 38.12).

After you've selected a name and location to go with the file format, Illustrator will present you with a series of export options (see Figure 38.13).

The options in this dialog box are as follows:

- **Color Model**—RGB, CMYK, and Grayscale are offered. You are not restricted to the document's original color mode.
- **Resolution**—Higher resolution is used for print, whereas Screen is appropriate for the Web. This choice determines how many pixels the Photoshop image will contain and how big the file will be.
- **Export As**—When you're working with Photoshop 6 or later, export as Photoshop CS. If you export as Photoshop 5.5, only point type will be editable.
- **Flat Image**—Clicking the Flat Image button produces a flattened version of the artwork. This option can be used to preserve the appearance of the artwork at the expense of editability. If you won't need to further edit

> The following discussion of Illustrator/Photoshop compatibility assumes that you are working with Illustrator CS and Photoshop 6 or later. Earlier versions of Photoshop do not support many of the compatibility features discussed here. Versions of Photoshop prior to 6 do not support, among other features, layer sets or vector type layers.

the artwork in Photoshop or if complex effects and transparency don't seem to export perfectly, select this option.

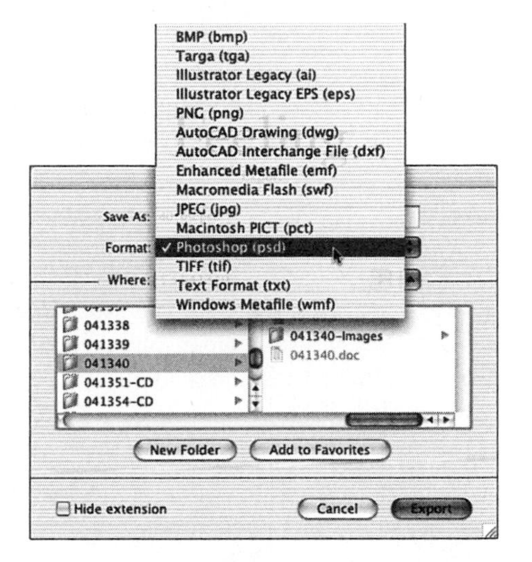


Figure 38.12
Photoshop's PSD is just one of many formats that can be exported from Illustrator.

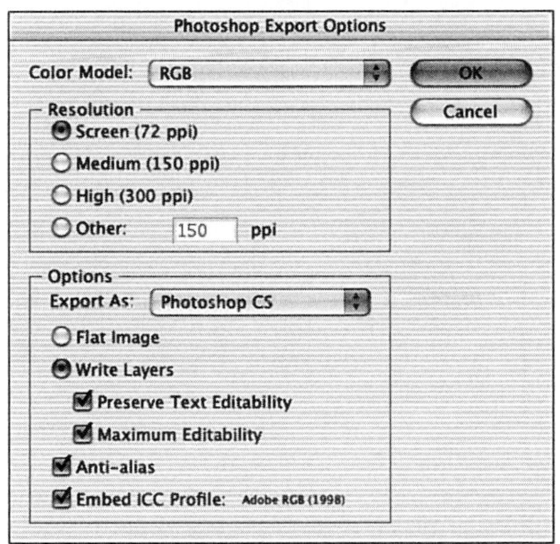


Figure 38.13
Options that are not available will be grayed out and may or may not show a check mark in the selection box. If objects have Illustrator's effects or filters applied, the artwork may have to be flattened.



- **Write Layers**—To maintain not only layers but also editable type, click the Write Layers button. Some of Illustrator's graphic styles and effects may prevent you from exporting with layers. Specifically, watch for shadows and glows.
- **Preserve Text Editability**—Type in top-level layers is exported as Photoshop-editable type. Type in sublayers is rasterized.
- **Maximum Editability**—As long as the appearance of the artwork won't change, this option forces top-level sublayers to Photoshop layers. Hidden layers in Illustrator become hidden layers in Photoshop (rather than being discarded). When possible (as long as the artwork's appearance doesn't change), Photoshop shape layers are created from Illustrator compound shapes.

- **Anti-alias**—The appearance of curves and diagonal lines is preserved by minimizing the appearance of pixel corners. If hard edges are required (such as for line art), you should deselect this option.
- **Embed ICC Profile**—An embedded color profile enables Photoshop to appropriately display the image's colors. A profile can only be embedded when one is selected in Illustrator's Edit, Assign Profile dialog box or when Illustrator's color settings automatically embed a profile.

*Write Layers grayed out in the Photoshop Export Options dialog box? See "Checking the Appearance" in the "Mastering Illustrator" section at the end of this chapter.*

The artwork shown in Figure 38.9 (which was opened in Photoshop as a PDF file in Figure 38.11) was exported to Photoshop's PSD format with all compatibility options selected. As you can see in Figure 38.14, Photoshop maintained all the relevant features.

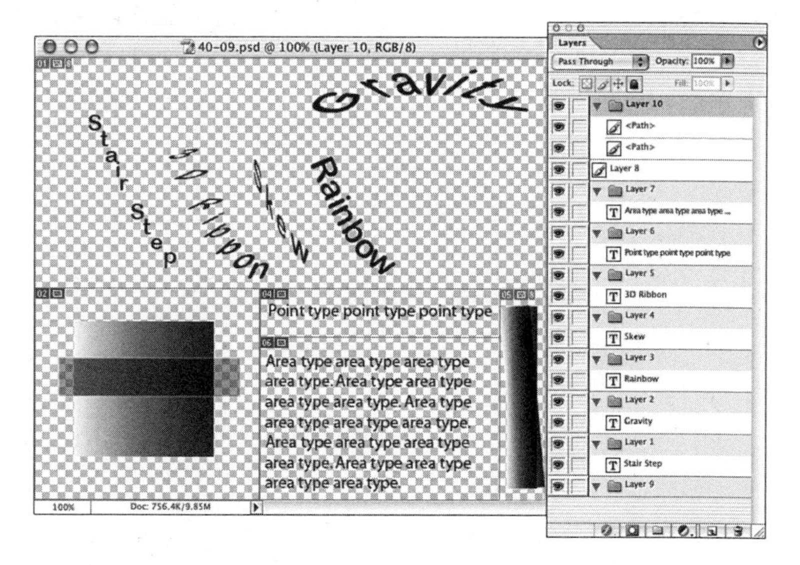


Figure 38.14
The file is shown opened in Photoshop CS.

As you can see, the opacity settings, gradients, blending modes, and editable type were maintained. Notice that the type layers are now parts of layer sets. New in the Illustrator CS/Photoshop CS relationship, type no longer needs to be on a separate layer. Type can share a layer with other objects and, after being exported as PSD, remains editable. For the first time, you can export type on a path and area type from Illustrator to Photoshop.

## Editable Text from Illustrator to Photoshop

Starting with version 6.0, Photoshop has been capable of handling vector type, such as that created in Illustrator. This is considered to be among the most important improvements in recent Photoshop upgrades.

Although you can now export type on a path, area type, and type that shares an Illustrator layer with paths or objects, there are still some restrictions. Applying an effect or a filter to type or adding a stroke keeps the type from being editable when exported.

*Illustrator text not editable in Photoshop? See "Checking Type Compatibility" in the "Mastering Illustrator" section at the end of this chapter.*

## Copy and Paste, Drag and Drop

When you copy a selection in Illustrator to paste into Photoshop, your actions are governed by one of the preferences. Choosing Preferences, File Handling & Clipboard opens the dialog box shown in Figure 38.15.

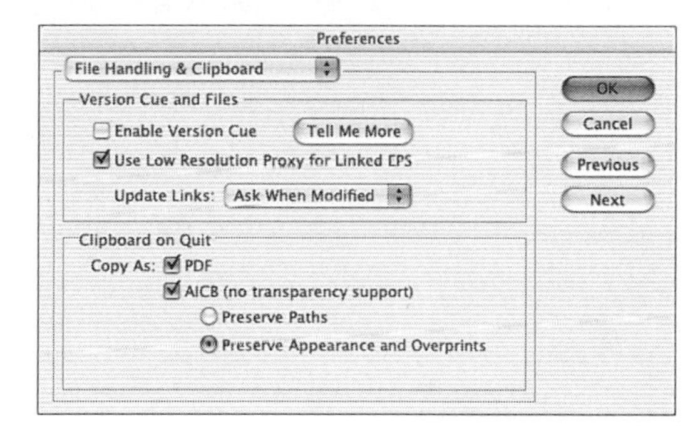


**Figure 38.15**
The lower half of the dialog box pertains to copying and pasting.



Illustrator copies selections to the Clipboard as PICT files and, if you so choose, PDF or AICB (Adobe Illustrator Clipboard). Here are descriptions of these file formats:

- **PICT**—On the Clipboard, this file format is raster only. The selection is converted to pixels and placed in memory. Most programs receive the PICT version of the selection. This version is added to the Clipboard automatically. The other options are in addition to the PICT data. When you're pasting into Photoshop, a new layer is created and the pixels are added to the layer.
- **PDF**—The PDF version, if available, copies a rasterized version of the selected object or objects to the Clipboard. When pasted into Photoshop, the artwork will be placed on a new layer and Free Transform will be active. As you can see in Figure 38.16, the pasted artwork has an active bounding box, which can be used to resize the artwork. Also, when the cursor is positioned just outside the bounding box, it will show as the curved double-arrow icon that indicates that the selection can be rotated.
- **AICB**—This format is best used with Photoshop. It offers you a choice of giving preference to the integrity of paths over the look of the illustration, or maintaining the appearance of the selection at the possible expense of editable paths.

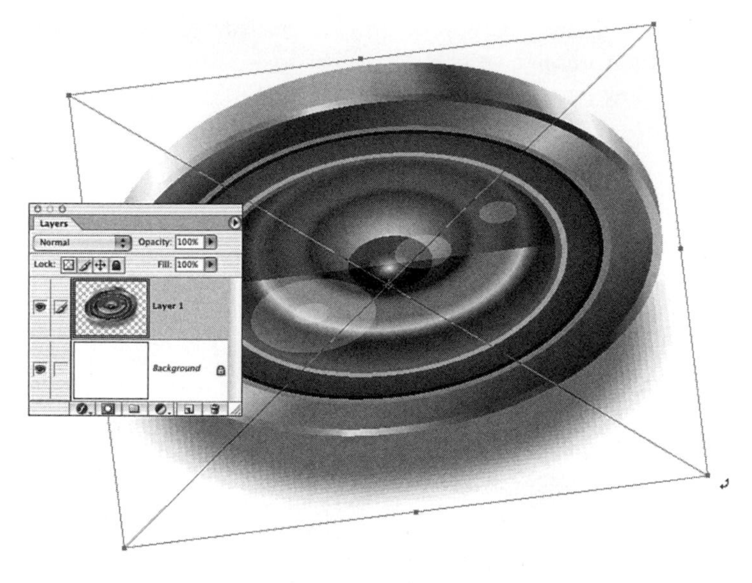


Figure 38.16

With Illustrator's PDF Clipboard option as the only active Clipboard choice, Photoshop pastes as pixels, ready to transform.



Regardless of whether Preserve Paths or Preserve Appearance is selected in the preferences, how Illustrator copies is less important than how Photoshop pastes. When you have AICB selected, Photoshop offers you a choice of how to handle the data on the Clipboard (see Figure 38.17).

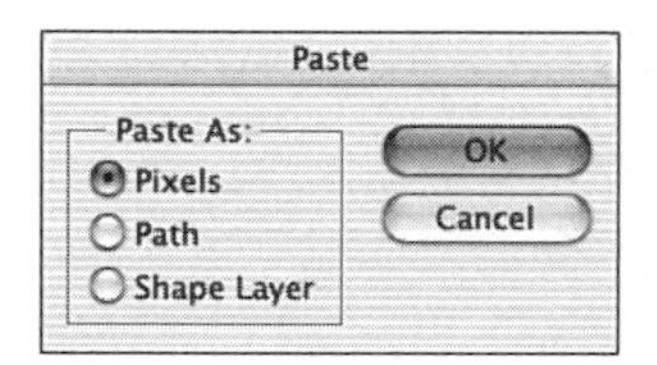


Figure 38.17

This dialog box appears when you're pasting into Photoshop with Illustrator's AICB option.

The results of the paste vary widely, depending on your selection:

- **Pixels**—Photoshop pastes a rasterized version of the artwork and activates Free Transform, just as it does when using Illustrator's PDF Clipboard option.
- **Path**—As you can see in Figure 38.18, a single work path is generated. The path loses any fill or stroke from Illustrator.
- **Shape Layer**—Photoshop creates a new layer, fills it, and creates a clipping path to expose the fill in the shape of the Illustrator object (see Figure 38.19). Although not equivalent to vector objects, Photoshop's shape layers can serve many of the same functions.

When you're using Illustrator's AICB Clipboard option with selections with appearances more complex than a simple object, expect to paste as pixels. Pasting as a path, of course, removes all appearance characteristics. Pasting as a shape layer results in a single color.

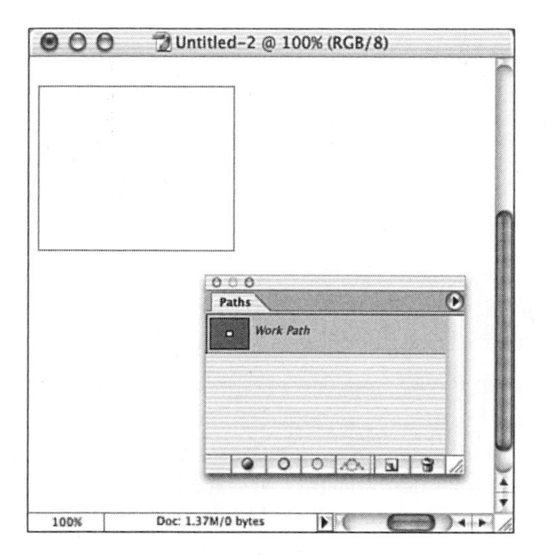


Figure 38.18
The Paths palette shows a single work path.



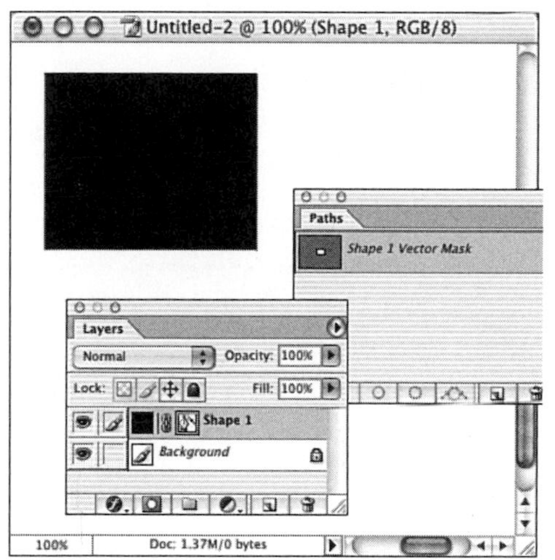


Figure 38.19
Because the shape layer is active in the Layers palette, the shape layer's vector clipping path is visible. Remember that Photoshop cannot stroke a layer clipping path.

If you press (Command) [Ctrl] while dragging from Illustrator to Photoshop, you create paths, much like pasting with the Path option selected.

Remember that you can paste as pixels *and* paste as a path. Simply paste twice, choosing each of the options. You can also preserve complex appearances by rasterizing the Illustrator object before copying. (And, of course, after copying, you can use Illustrator's Undo command to unrasterize the object, returning it to its vector state.)

## Alternative File Formats

Illustrator and Photoshop have a number of file formats in common, such as Tiff, EPS, PDF, BMP, and PICT. Most of them are raster formats. Exporting an Illustrator file in any such format rasterizes all data and flattens the image as well. Both TIFF and EPS do an excellent job of preserving the appearance of the Illustrator file. PDF also works well with the appearance of the file, but the entire image is rasterized, even if Preserve Illustrator Editing Capabilities is selected in the Adobe PDF Format Options dialog box.

# MOVING ARTWORK FROM PHOTOSHOP TO ILLUSTRATOR

Once upon a time, bringing a Photoshop image into Illustrator simply meant using an appropriate file format to get a rectangle full of pixels in place. Occasionally, you might have needed to export paths from Photoshop to Illustrator for the purposes of alignment or preparation of a trap.

Things changed, however, with the introduction of Photoshop 6. Vector type and shape layers make transferring images between the programs feasible, perhaps even attractive in a variety of situations. Illustrator's capability to maintain Photoshop layers and transparency also adds to the feasibility of moving Photoshop files into Illustrator. Type is still editable, blending modes are retained, and Photoshop's opacity masks are converted to layer masks when you open a Photoshop file in Illustrator.



## Opening Photoshop Files in Illustrator

When you choose Illustrator's menu command File, Open and select a sample file, you must decide whether to flatten the file or preserve layers, as shown in Figure 38.20.

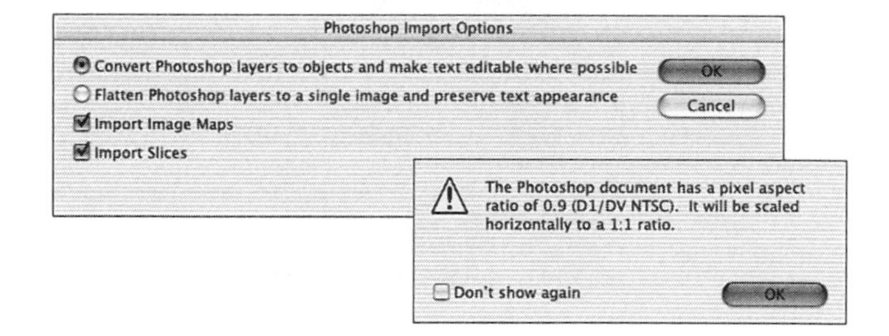


**Figure 38.20**
**If the Photoshop file contains image maps or slices, you also have the option of retaining them. Illustrator CS even recognizes—and compensates for—non-square pixels in Photoshop CS images.**

> **Caution**
>
> Illustrator has no 16-bit color capability. You can convert 16-bit images to 8-bit in Photoshop with the command Image, Mode, 8-Bits/Channel and save as a copy.

If you elect to flatten the layers of a Photoshop object, the file opens with one rasterized object on one layer, as shown in Figure 38.21.

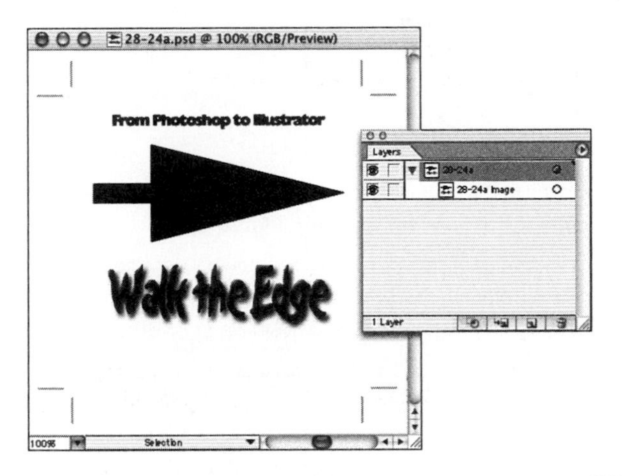


Figure 38.21
**The layer and object name are taken from the filename.**

When you elect to convert each Photoshop layer into an object, Illustrator creates a separate layer for each Photoshop layer and the content of each layer becomes a single rasterized object (see Figure 38.22).

In Figure 38.21, observe that Photoshop files are opened with crop marks visible. You can disable these crop marks like any others, by choosing Object, Crop Marks, Release.

## Copy and Paste, Drag and Drop

Using the Copy and Paste commands enables you to move image data from Photoshop CS to Illustrator CS, retaining the appearance of transparency and blending mode (unlike previous versions).

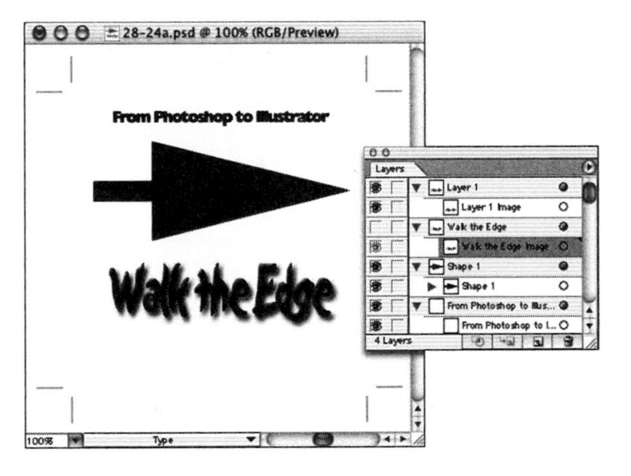


Figure 38.22
**Note that the hidden layer remains hidden in Illustrator.**

When dragging and dropping between a Photoshop window and an Illustrator window, you also lose transparency features, but you do gain some other capabilities. Dragging from Photoshop to Illustrator, for example, enables you to transfer linked layers as a set. (Copying and pasting requires that you put each layer on the Clipboard and transfer it individually.) Link the layers and then use the Move tool to drag the linked artwork from the Photoshop image window (not the Layers palette) to the Illustrator window.

## Exporting Paths to Illustrator

Photoshop enables you to transfer paths to Illustrator through an export process. Choosing File, Export, Paths to Illustrator opens the dialog box shown in Figure 38.23.

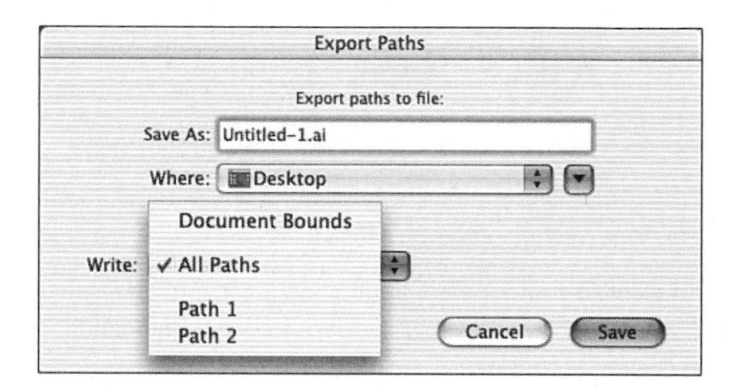


**Figure 38.23**
Notice that there is no file format choice; the file must be exported in Illustrator's format. If the image contains multiple paths, you have the option of which to export. Selecting Document Bounds creates crop marks in Illustrator using the Photoshop image's dimensions.



The file is exported as an Illustrator native file (add the file extension .ai to the name) and can be opened directly in Illustrator. The paths will appear in the Layers palette, but they will not be visible on the artboard unless selected because they are unstroked and unfilled (see Figure 38.24).

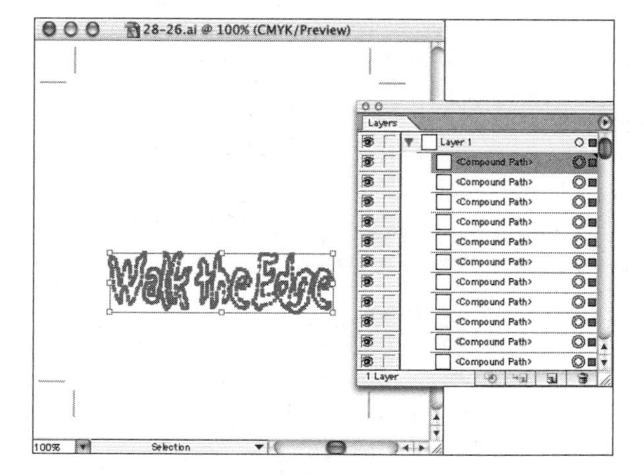


**Figure 38.24**
The file created when paths were exported from Photoshop can be opened in Illustrator using the File, Open command, just as any other Illustrator file.

## Round-Tripping

Sometimes an image must go from Photoshop to Illustrator and then back to Photoshop. (This so-called *round-tripping* is not as frequent as it was before Photoshop introduced its vector type and shapes tools.) Likewise, an Illustrator file may have to go into Photoshop and then back to Illustrator. (This, too, is far less common now that Illustrator has transparency capabilities.)

In Figure 38.25, a Photoshop file has been opened in Illustrator, and a group of Illustrator objects has been added.

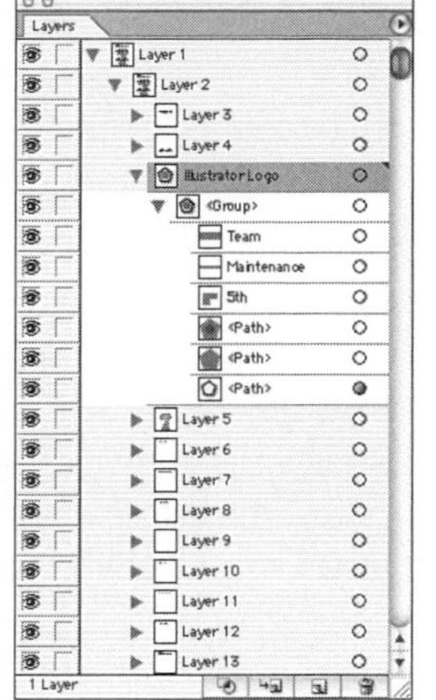


Figure 38.25
The insignia added in Illustrator is a group of vector objects and text, as seen in the Layers palette.



You can make several choices at this point:

- You can export the file back to Photoshop format. If you make this choice, the layers are rasterized.
- You can save the file as an Illustrator document. When you reopen it in Photoshop, it is opened as a generic PDF file and rasterized at the resolution and dimension you select.
- You can save the file as EPS or PDF. The results are identical to those for an Illustrator file.
- You can export the file in any of a variety of raster formats, including TIFF and JPEG. The image is rasterized and saved according to the capabilities of the individual file format. In all cases, a single layer is created, and the file is flattened.

Files going from Illustrator to Photoshop and back to Illustrator follow the same basic pattern: Images saved in the Illustrator, EPS, or PDF file format are rasterized and the layers are merged. When you export as Photoshop, the files retain their layers, but all objects are rasterized.

# MASTERING ILLUSTRATOR

## Checking the Appearance

*I want to export my Illustrator artwork to Photoshop with layers, but why I can't deselect Flat Image in the export options?*

Take a look at your artboard. Have graphic styles, effects, or filters been applied to one or more objects? Some effects and filters, such as Drop Shadow, prevent an export to Photoshop format with layers. Likewise, styles that use shadows require flattened images. Remove the offending appearance options and you'll be able to export with layers.

## Checking Type Compatibility

*I exported my Illustrator artwork in PSD format with layers, so how come I can't edit the text in Photoshop?*

First, check which version of Photoshop you're using. If it's not Photoshop CS, make sure there's nothing else on the layer with the type. That includes type on a path and area type—neither can be exported to pre-CS Photoshop.

Regardless of which version of Photoshop you're using, you'll also want to verify your type object in Illustrator. It shouldn't have a stroke applied, nor glows or shadows. Also, click in the type object with Illustrator's Type tool to make sure it's still a type object and hasn't been rasterized.

# INDEX

## Symbols



## A

## B

## C

## D



*How can we make this index more useful? Email us at indexes@quepublishing.com*

## F

*How can we make this index more useful? Email us at indexes@quepublishing.com*

## H



## I

## J

## N

## O

*How can we make this index more useful? Email us at indexes@quepublishing.com*

## P

## Q



## R

## S

## T

*How can we make this index more useful? Email us at indexes@quepublishing.com*

## U

## V

## W

## X-Y-Z